THE EXPERT'S
CROSSWORD PUZZLE
DICTIONARY

■ ■ ■

Also by Herbert M. Baus

MASTER CROSSWORD PUZZLE DICTIONARY

THE EXPERT'S CROSSWORD PUZZLE DICTIONARY

■ ■ ■

by Herbert M. Baus

DOUBLEDAY

NEW YORK LONDON TORONTO SYDNEY AUCKLAND

PUBLISHED BY DOUBLEDAY

A division of Bantam Doubleday Dell Publishing Group, Inc.
666 Fifth Avenue, New York, New York 10103

DOUBLEDAY and the portrayal of an anchor with a dolphin
are trademarks of Doubleday, a division of Bantam Doubleday
Dell Publishing Group, Inc.

ISBN 0-385-04788-6

Library of Congress Catalog Card Number 72–84960

To my wife

```
      H
      e
  Helene
  e   e
Helene
e   e
    n
    e
```

HOW TO USE THIS DICTIONARY

The *asterisk** means *see,* or *look up.* Thus, under ABATE we have

> ABATE: allay, **cool,* dilute, diminish,
> do away with, fall off, extinguish,
> mitigate, **quiet, *reduce, *temper*

All the words under ABATE are legitimate answer words. But **cool, *quiet, *reduce, *temper* are major answer words in this book—meaning that they have three lines or more of synonyms in the book which might apply to ABATE. Some of the other answer words to ABATE (allay, dilute, etc.) may or may not have several synonyms, but they will have fewer than three lines.

The asterisk* device is used to save space and still make available to the dictionary user the maximum possible number of useful synonyms out of the author's research file of more than 1,250,000 words.

Use of the asterisk* in combination words
"ABM MISSILE: **rocket: names*"

This means that to find names of ABM missiles, you should look up ROCKET, and under ROCKET look up the subtitle *names.* This is done because there are many combination clue words under ROCKET, but the information sought is under only one of them: ROCKET: *names*

Abbreviations
"COMB." means "combining form," which in turn means either "prefix" or "suffix."
"PREF." means "prefix."
"SUFF." means "suffix."

DOUBLE-WORD or MULTIPLE-WORD terms.

Extensive analysis shows that from one half to three fourths of crossword-puzzle clue words are double words, such as "ACHILLES' FATHER" or multiple words, such as "ACCORDING TO HOYLE." Multiple-word clues are hard to find in standard reference works such as regular dictionaries.

We feature a very large number of multiple words in this dictionary because of their importance in crossword-puzzle use.

Often we will not repeat a definition, and you should look up a multiple term *both ways* to find it. For example, LEG ARMOR will not appear as such, but you will find it under ARMOR: *leg.*

Sometimes we do repeat, hence you will find LEG: *bone* and BONE: *leg.*

"Of" is often eliminated, but the term will be contained in another usage.

For example TERM OF ENDEARMENT is not included as such but the clue word ENDEARMENT: *term* is included, with many answer words.

Word alternatives. For clue word subtitles we often use "child" for "son" or "daughter"; "kin" for any relationship; "parent" for father or mother.

Also, for example, if you don't find "cap" look up "hat" or "headdress"; if you don't find "dross" or "waste" look up "refuse"; if you don't find "garment" look up "robe" or "vestment" or "dress."

If you don't find the word given in your puzzle clue, look up other related words and you may find your answer.

Geographic Multiple Words

GEOGRAPHIC multiple words (continents, countries, states, cities) usually start with the name of the place:

"AFRICAN: *animal,*" not "ANIMAL: *african.*"

Indian Tribes

Indian tribes are almost all listed under INDIAN, as "INDIAN: New York" or "INDIAN: Nicaragua," *not* under state or nation as "NEW YORK: Indian" or "NICARAGUA: Indian."

Proper Names

Proper names in answer words are all given in lower case:

ACADEMY: annapolis, colorado springs, eton, grove of plato, lyceum, manege, sandhurst, school, st cyr, unsafa, usma, usna, west point, woolwich.

instead of

ACADEMY: Annapolis, Colorado Springs, Eton, Grove of Plato, lyceum, manege, Sandhurst, school, St. Cyr, UNSAFA, USMA, USNA, West Point, Woolwich.

Proper names (and initials) are treated this way because this is a crossword puzzle dictionary and in crossword puzzles it makes no difference whether an answer word is capitalized or lower cased, or whether the first letter is capitalized.

Thus in a crossword puzzle it can be USMA or usma; or it can be Eton or eton.

All accents are omitted, because they, too, make no difference in the spelling of a word.

By application you can accustom yourself to the use of this dictionary and its devices to equip you with the most comprehensive single array of references available anywhere in a single volume for crossword puzzle solution.

You have ahead of you many a verbal "gourmet feast" in the Wonderful World of Words.

Bon appétit!

ACKNOWLEDGMENTS

First and above all to my wife, Helene, for her patience and forbearance along with her encouragement and inspiration through the interminable hours of research and production; to my friend, consultant, and stanch supporter C. M. Vandeburg; to Frances Campbell and Sandra Blanchard for research help; to Dorothy D. Corey and Hal Bausell all for their painstaking and immaculate production of the manuscript; and to editors Ferris Mack and Tom Sloane for having the vision to undertake and the perseverance to sustain this work.

INTRODUCTION

The chain link of elements that build the world, tear it down, move empires, forge fortunes, determine dynasties, crystallize careers, and define destinies make up the Wonderful World of Words.

Words comprise the bridges between individuals, friends, enemies, lovers, groups, communities, and nations. Words serve us as the interstices of civilization, the catalysts of industry, the *sine qua non* of recreation, the sinews of war, the molders of peace, and the cement of populations.

How natural that in this Wonderful World of Words perhaps the most *universal* hobby-game-addiction has become the crossword puzzle. Millions of aficionados make a passion and pride of regularly engaging in this pastime of words and wits. On this matrix of word challenges and solutions the devotee finds a bouillabaisse of strategy, accomplishment, power, accommodation, construction, and triumph.

And when in his project he is blocked by a cluster of clues he cannot unglue, he finds frustration—the Hercules of hangups. Notwithstanding the determination of some in attacking a crossword puzzle to do or die without help of any kind, most true aficionados combat frustration by entering this periodic pitched battle of words armed with a marshaled array of references from encyclopedias to almanacs, from atlases to thesauri, from yearbooks to dictionaries. Above all, dictionaries.

Dictionaries there are of quality and in abundance, but they share an abysmal flaw for crossword-puzzle use. Being geared to different applications (for example, by writers or by technical workers), regular dictionaries tend to flow from single *clue words* into detailed definitions or *answer words*. For crossword-puzzle use, dictionaries need also to flow from detailed definitions to single words.

(Herein *clue words* are those numbered "questions" under a crossword puzzle to which the answers must be found to write in. The answers are *answer words*. Sometimes *one* answer word will unblock an impasse to start a chain reaction that will complete solution of an entire puzzle, or of a major pocket which prevents unraveling of the puzzle.)

Over a period of more than five years the author assembled a file of more than 100,000 index cards containing more than 1,250,000 words and terms from the following sources, among others:

Webster's New International Dictionary, 2nd edition
Random House Dictionary
Crossword Puzzle Dictionary, Andrew Swanfeldt
Unabridged Crossword Puzzle Dictionary, A. F. Sisson
New Practical Dictionary for Cross Word Puzzles,
    Frank Eaton
New American Crossword Puzzle Dictionary,
    Albert and Loy Morehead
Dell Crossword Dictionary, Kathleen Rafferty
Roget's International Thesaurus
The Holy Bible (analyzed cover-to-cover to extract names)
Goren's Hoyle Encyclopedia of Games
The American Thesaurus of Slang
Larousse Encyclopedia of Mythology
Encyclopaedia Britannica
The World Almanac and Book of Facts
The New York Times Encyclopedic Almanac
The Reader's Digest Almanac
Selected French, German, Spanish, and Latin dictionaries
Selected newspapers, magazines, and periodicals
Extracts from thousands of crossword puzzles

This all adds up to the most exhaustive *crossword-puzzle dictionary* ever undertaken—and it includes a combing of all major pre-existing crossword-puzzle dictionaries.

From this fertile research enterprise the author has selected approximately 60,000 *clue words* and terms supported by 150,000 *answer words* and terms.

Two features distinguish this work from other references as a remarkably versatile puzzle solver.

1. *Multiple-word clues.* This book contains a formidable array of such clues as

> ADJECTIVE: *jerker:* author
> AENEAS: *wife:* creusa, dido, lavinia
> AMERICAN: *buzzard:* buteo, condor, vulture
> CALIGULA: *steed:* incitatus

The most up-to-the-minute terms are included, as well as a liberal sprinkling of archaic and obsolete terms. Example of the latest:

> AMPHETAMINE: *pill:* benny, cartwheel,
> christmas tree, copilot, crystal, dexie,
> football, pep pill, speed, truck
> driver, upper, wake-up, water, white

And it includes one of the most important but also hardest-to-find fundamentals—an impressive marshaling of combining forms, prefixes, and suffixes; for example:

> BEAR: *comb.* arct(o), ursi
> ADJECTIVE: *suff.* ate, ant, ed, ent, est,
> ial, ian, ic(al), il, ile, ine, ish, ive,
> ous, ular

2. *Duplication control permitting maximum answers.* The problem was to compress more than 1,250,000 words into less than one-eighth that many to produce from the wealth of research material a handy-reference universal crossword-puzzle dictionary.

The solution was to screen out most duplications (although, of course, duplications are more comfortable and easy for the reader) and replace them with an effective cross-reference system to achieve maximum impact within the space limitations of an easily portable, economical paperback reference work.

Approximately 1,000 *key words* were selected and supported with from 10 to 50 or more synonyms each. Then, instead of repeating these synonyms after other *clue words* with a similar meaning, we refer you to the appropriate *key words* by a combination of asterisk and italics, for example, *accuse, *affair, *appropriate.

AAL: dye, morindin, mulberry

AARON: cuckoopint, levite
 brother: moses
 burial place: hor
 daughter: ithamar
 father: amram
 rod: mullein, plant, talisman
 sister: miriam
 son: abihu, eleazer, neadab

ABACA: canamo, hemp, linaga

ABACTOR: abigeus, cattle thief

ABACUS: box, panel, soroban, stone

ABAFT: astern, back, rearward

ABALONE: awabi, haliotis, ormer

ABANDON: abdicate, back out, cavalierness, cede, *discard, *escape, exuberance, flee, *quit, *refuse, *release, *yield

ABANDONED: *bad, *free, *wanton

ABASE: avale, denigrate, lower, mortify, *shame, throw down

ABASH: amaze, bully, cow, daunt, dismay, humiliate, nag, *shame

ABATE: allay, *cool, dilute, diminish, do away with, fall off, extinguish, mitigate, *quiet, *reduce, *temper

ABBEY: abadia, fly, *monastery

ABBREVIATE: abstract, capsulize, condense, cut, epitomize, *reduce, stunt, telescope

ABC's: basics, roots, rudiments

ABDICATE: *abandon

ABDOMEN: bulge, *stomach

ABDUCT: capture, shanghai

ABECEDARIAN: *beginner, fundamentalist, primer

ABELARD'S BELOVED: (h)eloise

ABERRATION: delirium, *error, hallucination, illusion, slip

ABET: advocate, aid, avail, contribute, egg on, endorse, favor, go for, instigate, *spell, *spur, *support, *urge

ABETTOR: bottleholder, partner

ABEYANCE: pause, suspense

ABHOR: agrise, execrate, *hate

ABHORRENCE: anathema, antipathy, aversion, odium, repugnance

ABI: *father:* zechariah
 husband: ahaz
 mother: hezekiah

ABIAH: *father:* samuel
 husband: herzon
 son: ashur

ABIDE: *accept, inhabit, *stand

ABIEL: *grandson:* abner, saul
 son: kish, ner

ABIES: abeto, acxoyatl, tree

ABIGAIL: brewing, maid, servant
 husband: david, ithra, nabal
 son: amasa

ABIHAIL'S HUSBAND: rehoboam

ABILITY: brainpower, caliber, energy, *force, *power, *skill, talent, what it takes, virtu(e)

ABIMELECH'S FRIEND: ahuzzath

ABITAL: *husband:* david
 son: shephatiah

ABJECT: contemptible, *low, *mean, obsequious, servile

ABJURE: *abandon, shun, spurn

ABLATION: aciurgy, surgery

ABLAZE: ardent, on fire, radiant

ABLE: *adept, *adroit, capable, expert, *fine, *good, *great, qualified, *ready, versatile

ABLUTION: bath, sidu, wuzu

ABM MISSILE: *rocket: names

ABNEGATE: deny, forego, renounce

ABNORMAL: aberrant, anomalous, *eccentric, *violent, *weird
 comb.: allotri, anomal, anomo

ABOARD: across, here, topside

ABODE: address, dar, *home, inn

ABOLISH: *discard, *end, finish, quash, *remove, stamp out

---

* Asterisk means to look up this word to find more answer words.

ABOMINABLE: *bad, goshawful
  snowman: yeti
ABOMINATION: *abhorrence
A BON MARCHE: bargain, cheap
ABORIGINAL: *ancient
ABORIGINE: indian, native, toda
ABORTION: failure, misfire
ABORTIVE: futile, sterile, vain
ABOUND: bristle, bustle, flow,
  luxuriate, swarm, teem
ABOUNDING: *abundant
  comb.: acity, poly
  suff.: acious, ful, ous, ulent
  with plants: braky
ABOUT: *adjacent, apropos, as
  to, current, *near, regarding
  comb.: amphi, ambi, peri
  face: change, pivot, reverse
  to: *ready
ABOVE: airborne, dorsal, *high,
  *paradise, past, super(ior)
  all: primarily
  board: candid, on the table
  comb.: hyper, super, supra
ABRACADABRA: *spell
ABRADE: excoriate, gall, rasp,
  scrape, scuff, *skin, wear off
ABRAHAM: *birthplace:* ur
  bosom: heaven, paradise
  brother: haran, nahor
  father: terah
  grandfather: nahor
  grandson: esau
  nephew: huz, lot
  son: isaac, ishbak, ishmael, jok-
  shan, medan, midian, shua(h),
  zimran
  wife: hagar, keturah, sara(h)
ABRASION: hurt, pulverization
ABRASIVE: attritive, galling,
  harsh, rasping, refractory
ABREAST: equal, even, parallel
  of the times: modern, popular
ABRI: cavity, refuge, shed
ABRIDGE: *abbreviate
ABROAD: away, far and wide,
  outdoors, overseas, remote

ABROGATE: *abolish
ABRUPT: blunt, *short, terse
ABSALOM: favorite son
  captain and cousin: amasa
  parent: david, maacah
  sister: tamar
ABSCOND: *escape, *hide, *quit
ABSENCE: awol, french leave,
  hooky, truancy, withdrawal
ABSENT: *abroad, lost, minus
  minded: distrait, oblivious
  oneself: be away, do a bunk
ABSINTH: genipi, wormwood
ABSOLUTE: categorical, dog-
  matic, imperious, *perfect,
  *pure, *supreme, *top
ABSOLUTION: acquittal, pardon
ABSORB: *arrest, assume, blot,
  engage, engross, grip, merge,
  soak, suck, swallow, understand
ABSORBED: monopolized, rapt
ABSORPTION: deep study, osmo-
  sis, preoccupation, submersion
ABSQUATULATE: elope, sit
ABSTAIN: avoid, forbear, *pass
  from buying: boycott
ABSTAINER: abstinent, *ascetic
ABSTEMIOUS: *ascetic
ABSTRACT: *abbreviate, blue
  print, precis, summary, *take
ABSTRUSE: acroamatic, arcane,
  obscure, recondite, *sage, *wise
ABSURD: *bizarre, crazy, *funny,
  *mad, outrageous, *weird, *wild
  question: car(ri)witchet
ABUNDANCE: *plenty, *quantity
ABUNDANT: *rich, *thick
ABUSE: *afflict, ballyrag, billings-
  gate, catachresis, chew out, con-
  tumely, cuss, ill-treat, objurgate,
  obloquy, *punish, *scold, *smear,
  *wrong
ABUT(TING): *adjacent, *adjoin
ABYSMAL: plumbless, yawning
ABYSS: apsu, *choas, chasm, gap,
  *opening, pit, pot, sheol, void
ABYSSINIA: *ethiopia

* Asterisk means to look up this word to find more answer words.

ACACIA: babul, boobyalla, boree, cooba(h), garad, gum mimosa, myall, saltbush, siris, tree
street: main street

ACADEMIC: classic, erudite, hypothetic, quodlibetic

ACADEMY: annapolis, colorado springs, eton, grove of plato, lyceum, manege, sandhurst, school, st cyr, unsafa, usma, usna, west point, woolwich

ACALEPH: jellyfish, sea nettle

ACCEDE: *accept, *accord

ACCELERATE: atomize, expedite, gun, railroad, rev, *speed, zip

ACCELERATOR: betatron, booster

ACCENT: arsis, emphasis, *mark, *meter, *stress, *time

ACCEPT: acknowledge, acquiesce, admit, adopt, agree, allow, consent, countenance, embrace, endure, fang, ratify, receive, reconcile, *understand, *yield

ACCEPTABLE: alright, authentic, bueno, correct, expedient, fine, good (enough), hunky-dory, ok, okay, okeh, safe

ACCESS: *approach, *opening

ACCESSIBLE: attainable, easy, handy, *open, public, reachable

ACCESSION: *adjunct

ACCESSORY: *additional

ACCIDENT: *catastrophe, case, contretemps, *error, event, luck, mishap, pile-up, slip

ACCIDENTAL: adventitious, by the way, casual, chance, episodic, fortuitous, freakish, lucky, occasional, secondary, sudden

ACCLAIM: applaud, approve, call, celebrate, clap, commend, *cry, compliment, encore, endorse, greet, hail, hand, huzza, laud, ole, plaudit, *praise, root, salute, salvo, vote, welcome

ACCLIVITY: ascent, climb, rise, slant, slope, talus, upgrade

ACCOLADE: award, ceremony, gree, laudation, notice, oscar, *praise, rite, salute, *token

ACCOMMODATE: *adapt, aid, apply, bed, billet, board, camp, do right by, favor, fit, help, lodge, orient, *settle, *supply

ACCOMPANY: associate, attend, chaperon, consort, couple, escort, follow, go with

ACCOMPLICE: accessory, ally, associate, buddy, confederate, conspirator, crony, louke, pal

ACCOMPLISH: achieve, *act, bring, complete, conclude, consummate, contrive, dispose, do, earn, effect(uate), encompass, *end, engineer, execute, fulfill, gain, *make, *perfect, *produce, realize, succeed, *win, *work

ACCORD: affinity, agree(ment), alliance, assent, blend, chime, community, *compact, concert, concur, empathy, fit, harmony, *settle, treaty, truce, *union

ACCORDING TO: after, a la, alla, aux, by, compared, pursuant
hoyle: *correct, *fair, *right
rule: conformably
the bill: a la carte

ACCOST: address, confront, hello, remark, solicit, waylay

ACCOUNT: advantage, anecdote, *answer, balance, basis, bill, calculate, check, *client, compute, credit, enumerate, esteem, estimate, importance, narrative, profit, *record, *report, *service, *story, tale, tally, *value

ACCOUNTANT: actuary, auditor, clerk, cpa, registrar, sircar

ACCRA: sapele, tree, wood

ACCREDIT: affirm, approve, attribute, authorize, clear, commission, license, ratify, sanction, send, *trust, vouch

* Asterisk means to look up this word to find more answer words.

ACCRUE: accumulate, acquire, ensue, fall due, happen, issue, mature, mesh, *result*, stitch

ACCUMULATE: *accrue*, amass, assemble, buy, cluster, fund, garner, grow, heap, hoard, *increase*, *save*, *store*

ACCURATE: acceptable, *correct*, exact, meticulous, nice, on the beam, precise, *perfect*, *right*, *straight*, *strict*, *true*

ACCUSE: arraign, *attack*, blame, call, censure, charge, file, frame, impugn, indict, *smear*

ACCUSTOM: *adapt*, addict, *break* (*in*), caseharden, drill, enure, *establish*, habit(uate), inure, *set*, *tame*, *train*, *use*

ACE: *acme*, adept, a-one, apex, aviator, bear, *best*, *bit*, brick, champ(ion), corker, crack, darb, dilly, dollar, expert, finest, first, flyer, *head*, hero, *high*, honey, humdinger, knockout, *leader*, lulu, *magnate*, *mark*, *one*(r), outstanding, peach, pilot, pip, plum, point, prodigy, score, single, spot, *supreme*, sweetheart, *top*, trump, whiz, *wonder*

ACERB: acid, acrid, acrimonious, astringent, austere, biting, harsh, rough, *severe*, *sharp*, *sour*, *stern*, *strict*, surly

ACHE: afflict, agonize, ail, anguish, crave, *desire*, *hurt*, long, *pain*, pine, *smart*, *sorrow*, *suffer*, wish, yearn

ACHELOUS: *wife:* melpomene
young: *sirens*

ACHEUS: *son:* telamon

ACHIEVE: *accomplish*

ACHILLES: *advisor:* nestor
charioteer: audomedon
friend: patroclus
heel: danger, vulnerability
horse: balius, xanthus
lover and captive: briseis

parent: peleus, thetis
slayer: paris
soldier: myrmidon
victim: hector

ACID: *acerb*, *drug*, *narcotic*
cashew nut: anacardic
cell: parietal
comb.: acer(o), oxy
crystalline: benzilic, berberon
drop: candy, tart
egg: blow, case
neutralizer: alkali
nitric: aquafortis
pert.: oleatic
protein: amino
radical: acetyl, acyl, anion
removing: edulcorant
shellac: aleuritic
test: showdown, *test*, *trial*
wood soot: asbolin

ACME: *ace*, apogee, climax, crest, ideal, ne plus ultra, paragon, peak, *prize*, *supreme*, tip, tittle, *top*, zenith

ACOLYTE: assistant, attendant, boy, candlelighter, learner, novice, satellite, tyro

ACONITE: bik(h), bish, remedy, sedative, wolfsbane, woodbane

ACORN: ballote, belote, camata
comb.: balan(o)

ACORUS: arum, herb

ACOUCHI: elemi, protium, resin

ACQUAINT: advise, inform, know, notify, school, teach, *tell*

ACQUIESCE: abide, *accept*

ACQUIRE: *accumulate*, annex, conquer, establish, gain, *get*, receive, *seize*, *steal*, *take*

ACQUISITIVE: *avaricious*

ACQUIT: absolve, amnesty, bear, behave, comport, conduct, exculpate, exonerate, forgive, free, let (go) (off), liberate, parole, purge, *release*, *settle*, vindicate

ACRE: arpent, piece, ptolemais
one-fourth: rood, snood

---

* Asterisk means to look up this word to find more answer words.

one-half: erven
one hundred: hectare
ten: decare
ACRID: *acerb*
ACRIMONIOUS: *acerb*
ACROAMATIC: abstruse, arcane
ACROBAT: cut up, schoenobatist, stuntsman, switcher, zany
garment: leotard
ACROPOLIS: cadmea, larissa
ACROSS: athwart, younder
pref.: dia, trans
the board: all, comprehensive
ACT: *accomplish*, ape, bill, decide, divertissement, do, fait accompli, feign, gest(e), *move*, *play*, portray, *show*, skit, strut
for: represent
like: imitate
suff.: ade, ado, age, ure
up: emote, grandstand, show off
ACTING: buffoonery, gag, hokum, make-believe, mummery, put on
ACTION: *affair*, *attack*, bout, case, cause, ceremony, combat, energy, enterprise, exercise, *play*, *rite*, *show*, *speed*
legal: gravamina, replevin, res
pert.: practical
suff.: ance, ancy, asia, asis, ence, ency, iasis
ACTIVE: assiduous, *enthusiast*, erupting, hearty, interest-bearing, in use, kinetic, mercurial, nimble, *quick*, *ready*, snappy, spry
ACTOR: aisteoir, barnstormer, extra, guisard, heavy, histrio, ingenue, mummer, protean, star, stooge, stripper, super
assignment: lead, part, role
cast: dramatis personae
cue: hint, prompt, word
group: afra, aftra, cast, retinue, troop, troupe
supporting: bit, ripieno, super
ACTUAL: carnal, esse, fleshly, in being, *present*, real, somatic,

sure-enough, *true*
ACTUATE: drive, egg, energize, *move*, *open*, operate, *start*
ACUMEN: acuity, *edge*, insight, perspicacity, *sense*, wit
ACUTE: astute, crucial, keen, *sage*, *sharp*, *smart*, *wise*
ADAGE: aphorism, apothegm, axiom, bromide, byword, *gnome*, homily, maxim, moral, mot(to), precept, proverb, saw, saying, slogan, sutra, theorem, truism
ADAH: *husband:* esau, lamech
offspring: jabal, jubal
ADAM: *ale:* water
apple: crape jasmine, larynx
rib: eve, wife
teacher: raisel
wife: eve, lilith
ADAMANT(INE): cast-iron, grim, refractory, *stern*
ADAPT: *amend*, apply, change, compare, dovetail, equalize, juxtapose, modify, orient, qualify, regulate, reconcile, *set(tle)*, *temper*, *turn*, vary
ADD: aggregate, annex, appose, augment, cast up, clap on, eke, encumber, figure, fortify, gain, hitch, postfix, reckon, saddle, supervene, tack on
ADDER: asp, krait, puff, viper
ADDICT: acidhead, buff, bummer, case, coky, dipsomaniac, dope (fiend), *drunk*, *enthusiast*, fiend, glue sniffer, hook, hop head, junkie, mainliner, pot head, pot lush, *slave*, speed freak, triad, tripper, user
ADDITION: appulse, augend, codicil, conjugation, paracoge, tab, tail, too, total, syzygy
pref.: ad, ap, ar, at, super
ADDLE: befuddle, bewilder, filth, mire, muddle, *spoil*
ADDRESS: *abode*, application, behight, buttonhole, call, dex-

terity, *ease, elocution, facility, halloo, ingenuity, *send, *skill, *talk, *title

ADEPT: *ace, consummate, handy, master(ful), *sharp, versed

ADEQUATE: *acceptable, broad, condign, roomy, wally, wide

ADHERE: affix, agglutinate, associate, cement, cleg, fuse, glue, grasp, gum, hug, *join, paste, persevere, stick, *unite

ADHERENCE: *allegiance
pref.: ac, ad, ap, ar, at

ADHERENT: devotee, ist, ite, partisan, rooter, satellite

ADHESIVE: bandaid, birdlime, epoxy, gluten, mucilage, putty, stickum, tape, tar, viscum, wax

ADIEU: adios, aloha, farewell, *good-by(e), vale(diction)

ADIPOSE: *fat, obese, squat

ADIT: *approach, entry, stulm

ADITYAS: mitra, varuna
mother: aditi

ADJACENT: abutting, contiguous, hard by, *near, next, nigh

ADJECTIVE: definer, modifier
demonstrative: that, these
jerker: author, writer
suff.: ate, ant, ed, ent, est, ial, ian, ic(al), il, ile, ine, ish, ive, ous
verbal: gerundive

ADJOIN: *add, border, butt, juxtapose, meet, trench, verge

ADJOURN: break, close, prorogue, put off, recess, shut

ADJUDGE: behight, decree, deem, *order, *pass, *rule, *value

ADJUNCT: access, add, aid(e), allonge, annex, appanage, appurtenance, *associate, ear, increment, lapel, *piece, pertain, plus, postscript, satellite, tab, tag, tuck

ADJUST: *accept, align, bow, *correct, dispose, fix, form, *pre-

pare, range, rectify, *remedy, *settle, temper

ADJUTANT: aide, argala, hurgila, marabou, officer, stork

ADMINISTER: aid, apply, chair, *control, deal, dispense, dose, *give, govern, impose, *pass, preside, *rule, *run, *spread

ADMIRABLE: *good, *great

ADMIRAL: atalanta, butterfly, commander, flagship, logwood, nymphalida, officer, sea leader

ADMIRE: adore, adulate, bubutsi, extol, *love, *prize, salute, *value, venerate, *worship

ADMISSION: comestication, *fee

ADMIT: avouch, ken, let in, own, *suffer, ticket, *trust

ADMONISH: *advise, censure, chide, job, *rebuke, *scold

ADMONITION: *alarm, caution, caveat, hint, indication, notice, *rebuke, warning

ADO: agitation, bearm, bother, bubble, bustle, confusion, effort, energy, flurry, fuss, howdedo, hubbub, hullaballoo, *noise, ruck, smuzz, *stir, to do, *trouble, *tumult, uproar

ADOBE: brick, clay, earth, gumbo, loamy, marly, mud, silt

ADOLESCENT: hebetic, nubile, prebetic, pubescent, subdeb

ADOPT: *accept, affiliate, arrogate, *copy, domesticate, espouse, foster, mock, *steal (one's stuff), *take, vote

ADORABLE: angelic, cuddlesome, exquisite, kissable, lovable, seraphic, winsome, worthy

ADORATION: devotion, dulia, obeisance, reverence, *worship

ADORE: *admire, be fond of, dote, *love, idolize, respect

ADORN: bedight, bedizen, bedub, bespangle, blazon, braid, caparison, dight, emblazon, garnish,

---

* Asterisk means to look up this word to find more answer words.

*ornament, *paint, rogue, set off, suborn, tassel

ADRIATIC: *queen:* venice

ADROIT: *able, deft, habile, *ready, resourceful, *right

ADULATE: blandish, butter, cajole, fawn, flatter, honey, *praise, softsoap, wheedle

ADULT: arrived, big, grown, imago, marriageable, mellow, nubile, ripe, seasoned, woman

ADULTERATE(D): alloy, alter, artificial, cut, corrupt, doctor, seduce, sophisticate

ADVANCE: *abet, aggrandize, anabasis, appreciate, *attack, breakthrough, develop, exalt, glorify, magnify, march, *move, prepay, *press, *push, spearhead, *start, *supply

ADVANTAGE: avail, bargain, boot, capital, exploit, handicap, inside track, leverage, odds, plus, privilege, sake, *service, *start, upper hand, *use

ADVENTURE: *venture

ADVENTURER: almogavar, beau sabreur, condottiere, gambler, entrepreneur, speculator

ADVERSARY: enemy, foe, rival

ADVERSE: against, calamitous, contrary, counter, diverse, *evil, loath, *opposite

ADVERTISE: blazon, blurb, bruit, exploit, parade, plug, post, promote, sky-write, spotlight

ADVISE: *admonish, alert, coach, consult, counsel, *direct, exhort, kibitz, *tell, *urge

ADVISOR: coach, egeria, nextor

ADVOCATE: abet, abogado, *agent, apologist, attorney, backer, champion, *enthusiast, lobbyist, paraclete, patron, *support, uphold, vindicate

AEGEAN ISLAND: amorgos, chios, cyclades, dodecanese, ios, ipsara, kariot, lemnos, naxos, nikaria, nio, paros, patmos, psara, rhodes, samos, santorin

AEGIS: *aid, *shield

AENEAS: *father:* anchises
friend: acamas, achates
grandfather: capys
grandson: brut
mother: aphrodite
rival: turnus
son: ascanius, iulus
wife: creusa, dido, lavinia

AERATE: *air

AERIAL: antenna, chimerical, imaginary, lofty

AESIR, VANIR: asynjur, balder, bragi, donar, eir, forseti, frey(a), frig(g), frija, gefjon, gerth, gullveig, heimdall(r), hel, hod, hoenir, idun, ithun, loki, mimir, nanna, nerthus, njord, njorth, odin, ran, sif, skathi, thincsus, things, thor, tiu, tiw, tyr, ull, vali, van, vidar, vili, ve, vitharr, woden, ziu

AESTHETIC: attic, cognoscente, connoisseur, dilettante, elegant, *epicure, *particular

AFFABLE: benign, bland, civil, complaisant, facile, polite, responsive, suave, urbane

AFFAIR: *action, duel, event, flirtation, intrigue, job, liaison, matinee, *party, rank, rendezvous, *rite, scandal, soiree, *thing, triangle, tryst

AFFECT: *act, assume, excite, feign, hypothecate, impel, mince, modify, play-act, pose, pretend, sham, *stir, *tell

AFFECTATION: cant, dandyism, gongorism, grimace, posture

AFFECTION: attachment, bosom, disease, emotion, front, heart, impulse, *love, loving, malady, mannerism, *passion, propensity, put-on, sham

AFFECTIONATE: *ardent
AFFIANCE: *promise, troth
AFFIDAVIT: *certificate
AFFILIATE: *adopt, *unite
AFFINITY: *accord
AFFIRM: *accept, *tell
AFFIRMATIVE: *absolute
AFFIX: *add, *unite
AFFLICT: ail, anguish, beset, grieve, gripe, harass, harm, *hurt, infect, injure, offend, *plague, rack, *scold, *torment
AFFLICTION: bane, burden, ennui, gall, millstone, pain, *plague, sore, thorn, *torment, trial
AFFLUENCE: *abundance
AFFORD: bear, cost, grant, manage, spare, *stand, *yield
AFFRONT: *abuse, offend
AFGHAN: carpet, durani, herat
AFICIONADO: *enthusiast
AFLOAT: asea, natant, volatile
AFOOT: *about
AFRAID: aghast, anxious, craven, fainthearted, gastfu, rade, scared, *shy, skeert, timid
AFRICAN: animal: aardvark, admi, aoudad, arui, ayeaye, genet, okapi, pangolin, potto, quagga, ratel, suricate, zebra
antelope: addax, bisa, blaubok, blesbok, bohor, bongo, bontebok, bosch(bok), buib, cervicapra, duikerbok, eland, etaac, gemsbok, gnu, grimme, grysbok, guevi, koba, kudu, leche, okapi, oribi, oryx, oterop, pallah, peele, poku, rhebok, saiga, sassaby, springbok, stembok, topi
arab tribe: battakhin
ass: quagga
base: tunts
beer: pombe
bird: adjutant, coly, kwe, taha
boat: almidia, dhow
bread: kisra
brown: chippendale

camp: boma, laager, lager
catfish: docmac, schal, shal
charm: grigri, obeah, saffi
cony: boomdas, daman, das(y)
dubeb: ashanti, cayenne
desert: elerg, igidi, sahara
dialect: akan, fanti, saho
dominoes: dice
dried meat: biltong
drink: omeires, skokiaan
eagle: bataleur, berghaan
fly: kivu(s), tsetse
food: cassava, paw-paw
fox: asse, caama, fennec
fruit: cubeb, pecego, terfa
god: mumbo jumbo
grass: cane, esparto, millet
greenhorn: ikona
gully: donga, nullah
hemp: ife, pangane, sisal
hornbill: tock
hottentot: nama
hut: kraal, tembe
jackal: dieb(s), thos
kingdom: abyssinia, ethiopia
language: *african people
lemur: anwantibo, galago
lynx: caracal, syagush
monkey: colobus, grivet, guenon, guereza, mona, nisnas, patas, potto, talapoin, tamarin, tee tee, vervet, waag
native: *african people
negro: *african people
palm: doom, doum, raffia
people: abo, afifi, akim, akka, asha(nti), bambuti, bantu, bapindi, bari, basuto, batonga, batwa, bechuana, boer, boni, damara, dinka, djerma, dorobo, efic, egbe, ekoi, ewe, fulani, golo, habe, hamite, hottentot, hutu, ibo, ijo, inkra, jur, kaffir, kikuyu, kindiga, kru, leda, lozi, luri, madi, majo, malinke, masai, mende, moor, nama, nilotic, nuba, pondo, pygmy, riff, san-

* Asterisk means to look up this word to find more answer words.

daww, sanye, somali, sonhai, sousou, suto, swahili, temni, tshi, tuareg, tutsi, ubani, vai, viti, voltaic, xosa, yao, zulu

pigeon: namaqua

plant: aloe, anthericum, argel, cacoon, calla, corn lily, ginger, ixia, okra, rue, uzara

pygmy: *african people*

ravine: donga

rug: kaross

secret society: mau-mau, poro

sheep: aoudad, arui, zenu

shrub: aalii, acocanthera, bocca, boxthorn, saffron

snake: bitis, boa, elaps, mamba

speak: assagai, assegai

stockade: boma, kraal, zareeba

stork: fe, marabou, simbil

title: saas, bwana, sidi

tree: abura, aegle, akee, almique, angola, artar, baku, balm of gilead, balsam, baobab, bito, bumbo, callitras, cola, copaiva, ekki, etui, bamdeboo, lilac, moli, njave, odum, olax, samandura, shea, siris, teak

tribe: *african people*

vine: bag-flower

war dance: calinda

wind: harmattan

yellowwood: podocarpus

AFRIKAAN: boer, taal

AFTER: abaft, ala, anon, behind, beyond, concerning, ensuing, infra, junior, nevertheless, out for, pursuing, resembling, sequel, tailing, then, there

a fashion: somehow

all: considering, therefore

awhile: anon, later, soon

birthweed: herb, pencil flower

death: the beyond

dinner drink: cognac, liqueur

glow: primrose, flower, shine

life: eden, paradise, tomorrow

one's own heart: desirable

pref.: meta, post

the manner of: ala, alla

this fashion: how

while: by and by, later

AGA: chief, commander, lord

wife: begum

AGAG SLAYER: samuel

AGAIN: anon, bis, de novo, eft, encore, newly, often, *over*, recently, twice, uber

AGAINST: *adverse*, *opposite*

pref.: ant, anth, anti, cat, cata, cath, con, contra, kat, kata, kath, ob, para

AGAL: cord, goat's hair, rope

AGALLOCH: agalwood, agar, aggur, agilawood, aloes, aquilaria, calambac, eaglewood, garoo, gelatin, incense, isinglass, lignaloes, perfume, tambac

AGAMA: iguana, lizard, tantra

AGAMEMNON: *avenger:* orestes

brother: menelaus

daughter: electra, iphigenia

father: atreus

rival: aegisthus

son: orestes

wife: clytemnestra

AGAPANTHUS: herb, lily, tulip

AGAPE: avid, *eager*, *love*

AGAR: *agalloch*, aloes, aquila

AGARIC: amanita, blewits, fungus

AGATE: achate, aggie, mig, onyx

AGAVE: aloe, amaryllis datil

AGE: autumn, century, day, *decline*, eon, era, fade, gray hairs, infirmity, maturity, olam

at the same: coeval

modern: atomic

moon on june first: epact

pert.: anile, eral, eval, geriatric, gerontic, senile

study: geriatrics, nostology

AGED: along, ancient, effete, gerontic, gothic, motheaten, *old*, passe, patriarchal, rusty

* **Asterisk means to look up this word to find more answer words.**

AGENCY: arm, department, *firm, means, *plant, *staff

AGENDA: calendar, call, docket, outline, *plan, schedule, slate

AGENOR: daughter: europe
father: antenor
son: cadmus
twin: belus

AGENT: *advocate, author, broker, comprador, contact, dealer, doer, expeditor, factor, henchman, liaison, proxy, *slave, *spy, *substitute
appoint: depute, deputize
narcotics: nark
native: aumildar
provocateur: instigator
secret: provocateur, *spy
servile: minion

AGGEUS: haggai

AGGLOMERATE: *accumulation

AGGLUTINATE: adhere, *unite

AGGRANDIZE: *advance

AGGRAVATE: amplify, annoy, burn up, disturb, gripe, irk, plague, *taunt, *torment

AGGREGATE: *accumulate

AGGRESSION: *attack, compulsion, encroachment, enterprise, *force, initiative, invasion, provocation, violation, war
anti, pill: estrogen

AGGRIEVE: *afflict

AGHAST: *afraid, agape

AGILE: *active, *quick

AGIO: batta, fee, percentage

AGITATE: alarm, bustle, canvass, churn, convulse, drive, *fire, foment, galvanize, incite, jar, *move, provoke, *riot, *upset

AGITATION: *ado, *trouble

AGLET: hawthorn, lace, stud, tab

AGNATE: akin, allied, relative

AGNI: parent: aditi, angiras, brahma, kasyapa
son: pavaka, pavamana, suci
tongue: kali

wife: svaha

AGNOSTIC: atheist, denier, iconoclast, minimifidia, pagan, skeptic, unbeliever

AGNUS: bell, dei, lamb, shrub

AGO: agone, back, past, since

AGOG: *agape, *upset

AGOGO: galore, *plenty

AGON: conflict, *contest, games

AGONY: emotion, *pain, throe

AGRA TOMB: taj mahal

AGREE: *accept, *accord, *yield

AGREEMENT: *accord, deal

AGRICULTURAL: campestral, farm, geoponic, rustic

AGRICULTURE: farming, *pastoral
area: breadbasket
building: barn, silo
chemical: fertilizer
college student: aggie
comb.: agro
establishment: farm, grove, orchard, ranch, spread
god, goddess: *vegetation god
machine: autoheaders, baler, binder, combine, cultivator, drill, harrow, mower, reaper, spreader, tedder, thresher
pert.: georgic, rural, rustic
worker: *peasant

AGRIMONY: bidens, borwort, hemp

AGRIPPINA'S: son: nero

AGRISE: *abhor

AGROSTIS: bent, grass

AGROUND: ashore, stuck

AGUAMAS: pinguin

AGUE: chill, cold, fever
bark: agrimony, wafer ash
drop: fowler's solution
grass: colicroot, herb
tree: sassafras
weed: boneset, comfrey, eupatorium, gentian

AGUJA: gar, marlin, spearfish

* Asterisk means to look up this word to find more answer words.

AHAB: *daughter:* athalia(h)
  wife: jezebel
AHASUERUS: artaxerxes, wanderer
  minister: aman, haman
  wife: esther, hadassah, vashti
AHAZ: offspring, helekia
  wife: abi
AHAZIAH: *sister:* jehosheba
AHEAD: adelante, beyond, first, leading, *supreme, *top
  of the game: successful
  of time: beforehand
  pref.: for, pre
AHIAM: *father:* sacar
AHIMSA: non-violence
AHINOAM: *husband:* david, saul
  offspring: amnon, jonathan, merab, michal
AHOLIBAMAH'S HUSBAND: esau
AHIRA'S: *son:* enan
AHRIMAN: evil spirit, lucifer
  angel: deev, deva, div
AHU: gazelle, memorial, waymark
AID: *abet, *spell, *support
AIDA: *lover:* radames
  rival: amneris
  role: amonasro
AIDE: *adjunct, henchman
AIGLET: *aglet
AIGUIERE: ewer, jug, pitcher
AIL: *ache
AILMENT: *affliction
AIM: aspire, big idea, course, design, ettle, level at, long, pant, *plan, *purpose, *try
AIMLESS: casual, idle, random
AIR: appear, aspect, aura, breath, breeze, bring out, cachet, cavatina, circulation, demeanor, deportment, ether, expose, fan, lay, manner, mien, *note, *open, oxygen, publicize, radio, *song, television, *tell, tube, tv, utter, vanity, ventilate, *way
  a grievance: complain

blow: water gas
-borne: aloft, flying, stirring
-built: chimerical
chill night: snelly
comb.: aer(o), atmo
component: argon, helium, krypton, neon, nitrogen, oxygen, xenon
-condition: cool, ventilate
containing: pneumatic
-cool: refrigerate
current: breeze, draft
drop: flight, parachuting
force units: anac, arf, atc, ats, casu, feaf, mats, nad, nats, raaf, raf, rcaf, sac, squadron, usaf, usnas
house: basha, hawaghar
mail: correspond, send
maneuver: buzz, chandelle, dive, nosedive, roll
measuring device: barometer
navigation terms: avigation, navar, omnidirectional
personification: amen, ammon
pump: antlia, constellation
raid: cover, mission, umbrella
  alarm: alert
  defense: blackout
  shelter: abri, cellar
spirit: ariel, genie, sylph
trip: flight, hop
upper: ether
warm: oam
wash: cool
waves: broadcasting, radio, television, the tube, tv
AIRCRAFT: bomber, fighter, plane
carrier: flattop
electronic gear: avionics
fleet formation: echelon
group: armada, echelon, fleet, flight, wing
inventors: wrights
keel: fin
lubricant: castor, ricimus

* **Asterisk means to look up this word to find more answer words.**

marker: pylon
motorless: glider
part: aileron, bay, blister, bubble, cabin, canopy, cowl, empennage, fin, flap, hatch, hood, monocoque, nacelle, pontoon, propeller, radome, stabilizer, stay, strut, tail
pilotless: drone
shelter: hangar
spotter: watch
takeoff: le decollage
throttle: gun, rev
turn: bank
vapor: contrail
vessel: carrier, flattop
AIRY: alfresco, animated, brisk, chimeric, debonair, delicate, empty, exposed, fluffy, gay, haughty, high, huffy, jaunty, merry, meteoric, *open, rare, speculative, vivacious, windy
AIT: eyot, holm, islet, oat
AJAJA: bird, jabiru, spoonbill
AJAX: hero, jakes, powder
butterfly: zebra swallowtail
father: oileus, telamon
AJUGA: bugleweed, bugloss, herb
AKIN: *agnate, germane, like
AKKADIAN: *goddess:* aruru
god of heaven: an, anu
sage: adapa, ziusudra
AKONGE: burbank, triumfetta
AKULE: fish, goggler
ALA: according, after, axil
bird: yellowhammer
ALABAMA: *flower:* camellia
nickname: yellowhammer
slider: terrapin, tortoise
state bird: yellowhammer
tree: yellow pine
ALABASTER: aragonite, gypsum
ALACRITY: celerity, haste, rapidity, speed, zeal
ALADDIN'S: *spirit:* genie, jinni
ALAISIAGES: beda, fimmilina
ALAMEDA: mall, path, *walk

ALAMO: battle, poplar, shrine
A LA MODE: chic, modish, stew
ALANGE: dismal, dreary, dull
ALARM: alert, appall, bell, bug, bear, buzzer, call, cow, din, dismay, dread, fear, foghorn, fright, hue, klaxon, *noise, outcry, *scare, siren, sos, *start, terror, tocsin, *upset
bird: lapwing, touraco
ALAS: ach, ah, eheu, helas, heu, och, ohone, oime, nebech, vae
ALASKA: *animal:* bear, kodiak
auk: arrie, murre
bird: auk, willow, ptarmigan
blizzard: purga
boat: angeyok, baidarka, kayak
capital: juneau, sitka
cod: wachna
cotton: eriphorum, grass
flower: blue forget-me-not
island: adak, aleut, amchitka, andreanof, atka, attu, kiska, pribilof, riska
liquor: hoochino
mountain: ada, blackburn, logan, mckinley, muir
native: ahtena, eskimo, tlingit
nickname: the great land
red-tail: hawk
river: atna, copper, innoko, koyukuk, kuskokwim, noatak, porcupine, susitana, tanana
sable: black skunk, fur
state bird: willow ptarmigan
tree: sitka spruce
ALBACORE: alalonga, maguro
ALBANIAN: gheg, gueb, tosk
city: avlona, berat, chimara, coritza, durazzo, elbasan, koritza, preyesa, scutari, tepelini, valona
coin: frank, lek, qintar
dialect: cham, geg, hish, tosk
foothills: maje jezerce
hero: king skanderbeg
lake: matia, ochrida, scutari
soldier: palikar

---

* Asterisk means to look up this word to find more answer words.

ALBARCO: cariniana, mahogany
ALBARDINE: error, esparto, grass
ALBATROSS: animal, bird, cape, fabric, gony, sheep, mallemuck
ALBEIT: altho(ugh), but, notwithstanding, tho(ugh)
ALBION: anglia, *england
ALBULA: chiro, elops, menhaden
ALCAEUS: *daughter:* anaxo
ALCATHOUS: *son:* callipolis
ALCESTIS: *father:* pelias
  husband: admetus
ALCHEMY: art, magic, sorcery
  god: hermes
  iron: mars
ALCHITRAN: bitumen, oil, pitch
ALCIDICE: *husband:* salmoneus
  son: tyro
ALCIMEDE: *son:* jason
ALCIMEDES: *father:* jason
  mother: medea
ALCIMEDON: *daughter:* philao
  father: laerces
ALCINOUS: *daughter:* nausicaa
  gardens: scheria
  son: laodamas
  wife: arete
ALCIPPE: *father:* area
ALCIS: dioscuri
  father: antipoenus
  sister: androclea
ALCITHOE: *father:* minyas
ALCMAEON: *brother:* amphilochus
  father: amphiaraus
  mother: eriphyle
  son: acarnan, amphoterus
  wife: arsinoe, callirrhoe
ALCMAON: *father:* thestor
  slayer: sarpedon
  victim: glaucus
ALCMENE: *husband:* amphitryon
  son: hercules
ALCOHOL: bug juice, ethanol, iditol, nerol, spirits, vinyl
  and amine compound: alcamine
  basis: ethyl

crystalline: guaiol, talitol
denaturer: brucia, brucin(e)
desire for: dipsomania
effect: intoxication, sludging
liquid: farnesol
radical: al, amyl, bornyl
secondary: benzohydrol
solid: cholesterol, sterol
standard: proof
suff.: ol
terpene: borneol, camphol
unsaturated: nerol
ALCOHOLIC: *addict, *drunk
  beverage: *drink: alcoholic content increase:* needle
  suff.: itol
  sugar: trosse
  treatment drug: doxepin
ALCOTT GIRL: amy, beth, jo, meg
ALCOVE: alhacena, apse, bower, cubicle, dinette, dormer, gable, gazebo, niche, oriel
ALDEHYDE: *colorless:* acrolein
  comb.: ald(o)
  derivative: acetal
  imino: aldime, aldimine
  sugar: aldose
ALDER: alnus, arn, fly, birch
  buckthorn: berry, bird cherry
  fly: sialidae
  flycatcher: bird, empidonax
  yellow: sage rose
ALDERMAN: archon, chief, head, magistrate, patriarch, ruler
ALE: beer, beverage, brew
  brewing: bummack, bummock
  and honey: bragget
  and stout: birch and tan
  conner: tester
  hoff: ground ivy, vine
  house: pub, saloon, tavern
  mug: black pot, stein, toby
  sour: alegar
  source: barley
  tester: conner
ALEA: athena, light

---

* Asterisk means to look up this word to find more answer words.

ALEMBIC: changer, distiller, furnace, retort, still, vessel
ALEPPO: berea, haleb
fabric: agabanee
stone: eye agate, gem
ALERT: **alarm, *prepare, *set*
ALETTE: abutment, jamb, wing
ALEUS: *daughter:* auge
ALEWIFE: bang, herring, shad
ALEXANDER: *birthplace:* pella
bodyguard: argyraspides
horse: bucephalus
kingdom: macedonia
mistress: campaspe
victory: arbela, issus
ALEXANDRIAN: *bishop:* athanasius
clover: berseem
laurel: poon tree, shrub
magistrate: alabarch
patriarch: papa
pleiad: apollonius, aratus, callimachus, homer, lycophron, nicander, theocritus
theologian: arius
ALFALFA: clover, fodder, hay
hopper: strictocephala
valve: pipe closer
weevil: insect, beetle
ALGA: ahnfeltia, anabaena, blue, green, botrydium, carrageen, cyanophyce, diatom, fucus, pondscum, sea moss, stonewort
envelope: ceramidium
flower: nostol
fresh-water: desmid
genus: alaria, capsa, dasya
node: chara, bulbil
pert.: algal
study: algology
ALGARROBA: calden, carob, tree
ALGEBRAIC: *function:* quintic
name, single: nominal
system: abelian
term: equation, nome
ALGERIAN: numidian, pomarian
capital: algiers

cavalryman: spahee, spahi
city: blida, bona, media, oran
commune: setif
grass: diss, esparto
measure: rebis, tarri, termin
medicinal earth: tfol
monastery: ribat
national anthem: kassaman
native quarters: casbah
roman name: pomaria
slums: bidonvilles
ships: xebec
tirailleur: turco
ALGONDONCILLO: majagua
ALGONQUIN: *dance:* cantico
friend: netop
god: manito(u)
indian: algic, ottawa
smoke: kinnikinnick
ALI: *descendant:* alides, fatimid
wife: fatima
ALI BABA: *brother:* cassim
word: sesame
ALIAS: anonym, else, epithet, name, otherwise, pseudonym, sobriquet, stage name, **title*
ALIBI: cop out, **excuse*
ALICE: *author:* carroll
character: cheshire cat, mad hatter, queen, rabbit, walrus
ALIEN: adverse, altud, auslander, exotic, foreign, fremd, ger, gringo, hostile, metic, other, remote, stranger
ALIENATE: **antagonize*
ALIGN: **adjust,* true
ALIKE: **agnate*
ALIMENT: allowance, broma, manna
ALIMONY: maintenance, subsidy
ALIVE: **active, *quick, *warm*
ALKALI: lye, reh, soda, usar
disease: milk sickness
flat: plain(s)
grass: puccinellia, zygadenus
-pegmatite: bowralite, mineral
-trachyte: beringite

* Asterisk means to look up this word to find more answer words.

volatile: ammonia
ALKALINE: lime, oxide
  remedy: antacid
  salt: borax
ALKALOID: *artificial:* apocodeine
  emetic: alangine
  hemlock: conine
  mustard: sinapine
  nux vomica: brucia, brucine
  poisonous: aconitin, anagyrin, anthorin, aristolachin
ALL: any, apiece, cosmos, each, entire, every, final, full, *general*, gross, only, *plenty*, *quantity*, *universal*, very
  -absorbing: paramount
  agog: eager, panting
  along: always, forever
  -American: *great*, *supreme*
  -around: *complete*
  bets off: ended
  but: almost, barely
  comb.: al, omni, pan
  ears: vigilant
  embracing: *complete*
  eyes: attentive, vigilant
  -fired: *extreme*, inordinate
  forty: maximum
  fours: game, smudge, snoozer
  get out: imaginable, maximum
  gone: dead
  heal: mistletoe, yarrow
  hollow: utterly
  hopped up: *anxious*
  hot and bothered: *anxious*
  in: exhausted, tired
  in all: generally, wholly
  in good time: opportunely
  in the wind: confused
  -knowing: almighty, omniscient
  nerves: shaky
  of a sudden: immediately, now
  of a twitter: agitated
  off: ended, erroneous
  one: equal, identical, same
  or nothing: everything, limit
  out: *complete*

  -overish: *anxious*
  over town: reported, rumored
  over with: dead, finished
  right: *acceptable*
  set: prepared, *ready*
  shook up: discombobulated
  spice: pimento, tree
  the rage: *popular*
  the more: a fortiori
  there: alert, sane, *smart*
  things being equal: possible
  through: finished, over
  thumbs: awkward
  to pieces: explosively
  up: dead, done for, ended
  washed up: exhausted, tired
  wet: mistaken
  wise: almighty, *supreme*
  wool: *supreme*
  wound up in: absorbed
ALLAH: *daughter:* al-lat, al-uzza
ALLATU: aralu, *hell*
  consort: nergal
  secretary: belit-seri
ALLAY: *abate*
  pref.: ant(i)
ALLEGE: affirm, aver, *state*
ALLEGIANCE: attachment, bond, devotion, fidelity, *tie*, truth
ALLEGORY: apologue, metaphor, parable, *symbol*, *story*
ALLERGY: antipathy, aversion
  remedy: antihistimine
ALLEVIATE: *abate*
ALLEY: *back:* slum
  cat: slattern
  -oops: excelsior, upward
ALLIANCE: *accord*, *union*
  anti-communist: nato, seato
ALLIGATOR: cayman, crocodile, jacare, lagarto, niger, yacare
  apple: pond apple
  bonnet: flower, pond lily
  fish: podothecus, sea poacher
  gar: fish, atractosteus
  head: button weed, dioda
  pear: aguacate, avocado

* Asterisk means to look up this word to find more answer words.

tree: sweet gum
wampee: pickerelweed
ALLOT: apply, assign, award, deal, designate, divide, dose, mete, **part, *split, *spread*
ALLOW: acknowledge, authorize, lend, permit, ratify, sanction
ALLOWANCE: agio, appenage, bot, burse, diet, **fee, *share*
commercial: tret
short: ration
traveling: mileage
weight: beamage, tare, tret
ALLOY: *aluminum:* dural
black copper: niello
chinese: paktong
copper: aich, brass, bronze, duralumin, oreide, oroide, paktong
fusible: solder
gold: asem, caracoli, oreide
lead: calin, pewter, terne
magnetic: bismanol
mercury: amalgam
nickel: alfenide, awaruite
non-ferrous: tula
pewter-like: bidri
principal: base metal
silver: billon
sulphuric: niello
tea-chest lining: calin
tin: ashberry, ashbury, britannia, pewter, terne
tungsten: carboloy
yellow: aich
ALLUDE: **attribute,* imply
ALLURE: agacerie, appeal, bait, bewitch, coax, **draw,* inveigle, seduce, sex appeal, tempt, **win*
ALLUVIAL: *clay:* adobe
deposit: delta, drift, geest, gravel, mud, placer, wash
fan: delta, geest
plain: bajada
ALLY: **associate, *friend,* unite
ALMANAC: emphemeris, ordo
ALMADINE: gem, ruby, spinel
ALMIGHTY: awesome, omnipo-

tent, **strong*
ALMIQUE: mahogany, manilkara, shorea, sapote, solenodon
ALMOND: amygdala, kanari, pili
emulsion: amarine, orgeat
-eyed: oriental
-flavored liqueur: ratafia
furnance: alman
kernels: tonsils
paste: marzipan
pert.: amygdaline
tumbler: bird, pigeon
willow: black hollander, salix
ALMOST: all but, feckly, nearly
pref.: pen(e)
ALMS: dole, maundy, passade
box: arca
deed: charity
dispenser: eleemosynar
fee: peter's pence
-giving: **altruistic*
house: **asylum*
man: beggar, bluecoat, pauper
ALOADAE: ephialtes, otus
ALOE: agave, lily, pita, tambac
compound: alicinic acid, aloin
creole: furcraea, plant
derivative: aloin
extract: orcin(ol)
malgache: furcraea, plant
root: colicroot, herb
substance: aloin, picra
ALOHA: farewell, good-bye, greetings, **hello,* salutation
ALONE: azygous, insular, lorn, singular, solitary, **unique*
pref.: soli
ALONG: advanced, ahead, forward, parallel, through, via, with
cry to: far away
in years: aged
pref.: para
these lines: how
the way: en route
towards: near
way off: far away
with: and, through, together

* Asterisk means to look up this word to find more answer words.

ALOOF: aback, cold, far, remote
ALPACA: coat, llama, paco
 fabric: rayon crepe, wool
 -like: guanaco, vicena
 -like fabric: brilliantine
ALPHA: chief, debut, first
 and omega: all, entire, whole
ALPHABET: abc's, brahmi
 -arian: novice, tryo
 character: ogham, rune, sarada
 pert.: abecedarian
 principle: acrology
ALPS: *austrian:* tirol, tyrol
 dance: gavot
 division: bernese, lepontine
 dock: beet, butter leaves
 dress: dirndl
 dwelling: chalet
 goat: bouquetin, ibex
 herdsman: senn
 italian: dolomites
 pass: brenner, cenis, simplon
 peak: bernina, blanc, jungfrau,
   matterhorn
 structure: fanfold
 tunnel: *tunnel: famous
 valley: moon gorge
 wind: bora, foehn
 yugoslav: dinaric, julian
ALREADY: before, een, now
ALRIGHT: *acceptable, *fair, ok
ALSATIAN: *clover:* alsike, herb
 coin: baetzner
 wine: gewurtztraminer, zwicker
ALSO-RAN: candidate, loser
ALTAR: ara, chantry, mensal
 area: apse
 boy: acolyte
 carpet: pedale
 cloth: antimenion, bisso, catsarka,
   cerement, chrismal, coster, dos-
   sal, haploma, palla
 decoration: antependium
 funeral pyre: acerra
 ledge: retable
 pert.: piscina, pyx
 piece: ancona, font

platform: predella
 screen: reredos
ALTER: *adapt, *change, edit
 ego: agent, friend, henchman
 garment: bushel
 one's course: deviate
ALTERCATION: *fight, *quarrel
ALTERNATE: *oscillate, *substitute
ALTERNATIVE: boot, option, or
ALTHAEA CONSORT♣ oeneus
ALTHOUGH: albeit, though
ALTITUDE: peak, *rank, *top
 measuring device: orometer
 parallel: almucantar
 sickness: soroche
ALTOGETHER: *all, au naturel
ALTRUISM: charity, do-goodism,
   good will, humanitarianism
ALUM: astringent, emetic
 bloom: geranium, herb
 schist: shale, slate, mineral
ALUMINUM: *discoverer:* davy
 family: gallium, indium
 nickel alloy: alumel
 nitrate: mordant
 phosphate: augelite, berlinite
 pistachio color: epidote
 silicate: andalusite, mineral
ALVAR: amba, beata, saint
ALWAYS: ever, forever, uniformly
 behind: slow
AMA: candlenut, cruet, vessel
AMADIS: *beloved:* oriana
AMAIN: bang, by force, speedily
AMALEK: *king:* agag
AMALGAMATE: fuse, *unite
AMALTHAEA: *horn:* cornucopia
AMARANTH: careless, coxcomb
AMARYLLIS: agave, datil, lily
AMASA: *father:* ithra
AMASS: *accumulate, *gather
AMATEUR: *enthusiast
AMAZE: awe, dumfound, stupefy
AMAZON: parrot, virago, warrior
 ant: polyergus

* Asterisk means to look up this word to find more answer words.

cetacean: inia
discoverer: orellawa
fish: candiru, catfish
headstream: maranon
hercules slew: aella
lily: eucharis, flower
mat: yapa
queen: calafia, hippolyta, penthesileia
rain forest: selva, silvas
rise: andes
stone: feldspar
tributary: apa, ica, napo
vs greeks: amazonomachia
AMBAGIOUS: devious, tortuous
AMBASSADOR: elchi, envoy, nuncio
representative: vakil
pert.: legatine
temp.: charge d'affaires
AMBER: *colored:* resinous
fish: medregal, runner
jack: gamefish, seriola
liquid: allethrin
mica: phlogopite
pear: ambrette
AMBIANCE: milieu, shteiger, tone
AMBIGUOUS: amphibolic, dubious, obscure, paradoxical, *vague
AMBITION: *desire, *fire, *spirit
AMBLE: gait, padnag, *walk
AMBOINA: *button:* the yaws
pine: agathis, galagala
pitch: kauri, resin
wood: andaman, lingoum
AMBROSIA: honey, manna, nectar
beetle: corthylus, scolytida
bidentata: blue curls, ragweed
elatior: carrotweed
trifida: asclepias, bloodweed
AMBSACE: bad luck, black ox
AMBUSH: artifice, attack, await, bushwhack, guerrilla, lurk, surprise, *trap, trojan horse
bug: phymatida

shooter: sniper
AMELIORATE: *amend, *perfect
AMEN: okay, so be it, yes
corner: pew
son: bast, khensu, khonsu
wife: mut
AMENABLE: docile, easy, *open, pliant, responsive, tractable
AMEND: adapt, chastise, convert, doctor, *remedy, revise, *right
AMENDS: *apology
AMENT: catkin, cjat, gosling, idiot, imbecile, jul, moron
AMERCE: *fine, forfeit, mulct, *punish, scone, treat
AMERICAN: *aborigine:* amerind
abscess root: blue bell
alkanet: hoary puccoon
allspice: strawberry
aloe: century plant
anteater: tamandua
apple: roxbury
aquatic plant: cabomba
balsam: tolu
bear: grizzly, musquaw
beauty: rose
buzzard: bueo, condor, vulture
canary: burion, chewink, junco, linnet, towhee
cat: angora, bob, jaguar, margay, ocelot
chinaroot: greenbriar
cudweed: pearly everlasting
date plum: persimmon
deer: caribou, moose, wapiti
discoverer: cabot, columbus, eric, leif, votan
ebony: granadilla
finch: chewink, junco, towhee
first child: virginia dare
grape: catawba
holly: assi
jade: californite
jasmine: quamoclit
leopard: jaguar
lion: cougar, puma
mandrake: may apple

* **Asterisk means to look up this word to find more answer words.**

ANNEAL: fuse, endurate, smelt
chamber: leer, lehr
oven: calcar
ANNELID: earthworm, leech
fresh-water: naid
marine: autolytus, lurg
ANNEX: *add(ition)*, *unite*
ANNIE OAKLEY: mozee, *pass*
ANNIHILATE: *defeat*, *end*,
ruin
ANNIVERSARY: birthday, jubilee
1st: paper
3rd: tricennial
5th: wooden
10th: decennial, tin
15th: crystal
20th: china, vigentennial
25th: silver
30th: pearl
35th: coral
40th: emerald, ruby
45th: ruby, sapphire
50th: golden
75th: diamond
100th: centenary, centennial
150th: sesquicentennial
1000th: millenial
ANNOUNCER: commentator,
disk jockey, emcee, gongman,
herald, nuncio, spieler, trumpeter
ANNOY: *aggravate*, *torment*
ANNUAL: booketesian, okra
bluegrass: meadow grass, poa
church service: encaenia
herb: primrose, trigonella
rent: canon
saga: chia, thistle
ANNUL: *abolish*
ANNWFN: elysium, utopia
ANODYNE: aspirin, balm, *drug*
necklace: hangman's noose
ANOINT: apply, balm, *bless*, oil,
prune, rub, *spread*
room: alipterion, ceroma
ANOMALOUS: *abnormal*
ANOMATHECA: lapeirousia
ANON: *again*, straightaway

ANONYM: incognito, nameless
ANOTHER: *alias*, *separate*
kind of being: anderssein
time: again
ANSEROUS: *dull*, *stupid*
ANSWER: avail, cable, come back,
conform, correspond, defense,
echo, flashback, rebut, reply, *result*, *report*, satisfy, suit
for: take responsibility
to: concern
ANT: emmet, formicid, pismire
acacia: myrmecophyte
bear: aardvark, myrmecophaga
bird: bush shrike, grallaria
bristle: ammochaeta
cattle: aphids, plant lice
comb.: myrmec(o)
kinds of: agricultural, amazon, argentine, army, carpenter
leaf-cutting: atta
lion: myrmekoleon
male: ergatandromorph
pipit: conopophagida, gnateater
queen: gyne, microgyne
-resisting wood: amuguis
rice: aristida, texas grass
shrike: batara
stinging: kelep
thrush: formicarius, pitta
worker: ergates, neuter
wren: microrhopias
ANTAGONIST: *adversary*
ANTARANGA: dharana, dhyana,
samadhi
ANTARCTIC: *explorer:* byrd,
cook, ross, scott, wilkins
icebreaker: atka
mountain: admiralty, siple
region: adelie coast, ross sea
seal: ross, sterrinck
ANTE: bet, cough up, hand over,
kick in, kitty, pot, *venture*
bellum: prewar
brachium: forearm
-date: accelerate, precede
-grade: progressive

* Asterisk means to look up this word to find more answer words.

lucan: before dawn
meridian: forenoon
-room: entrance, foyer, hall, lobby, lounge, vestibule
ANTELOPE: *ancient:* addax, pygarg
brown: ngor
brush: purshia, shrub
bubaline: blesbok, bontebok
chipmunk: ammospermophilus
forest: bongo
4-horned: chikara, chou, singha
gazelle-like: beira, gerenuk
goatlike: chamois, goral, serow
golden: impala
himalayan: chiru, goral
large: addak, aste, beisa, eland, defassa, gemsbok, hartebeest, koodoo, kudu, nilgai, nilgau, oryx, sassaby
mountain: chamois
mythic: yale
pronghorn: cabree, cabret
redbuck: palla(h)
reddish: grysbok
royal: ipete, kleeneboc
sheep-like: saiga
short-maned: gnu, nilagu
small: duiker, grimme, grysbok
state: nebraska
striped: bongo
tawny: oribi
tiger-like: agacella
young: kid
ANTENNA: arista, feeler, palp
end: clava
radar: directional, mattress, scanner, sontenna
ANTENOR: *father:* aesyetes
son: agenor, antheus, archelochus
ANTHEM: hymn, motet, psalm
ANTHER: *cell:* lobe, sac, theca
ozoid: cell
smut: fungus, ustilago
ANTHRACITE: *inferior:* culm
size: barley
ANTHROPOID: gibbon, lar, orang

ANTI: *adverse, *opposite*
ANTI-AIRCRAFT: a a, ack-ack, aerogun, archie, bofors, pom-pom, skysweeper
ANTIC: *clown, droll, *trick*
ANTICIPATE: devance, expect, hope, obviate, *predict, thwart*
ANTICLEA: camass, quamash
ANTIGONE: *mother:* jocasta
sister: ismene
ANTILLES: *god:* zeme
native: ineri
queen or pearl: cuba
ANTIMONY: *blende:* kermesite
bloom: valentinite
chloride: caustic, bronzer
glance: stibnite
hydride: stibine
lead sulphite: boulangerite
ocher: cervantite
oxide: bezoar, cervantite
oxychloride: algaroth
pert.: stibial
salt: algaroth
sulphate: explosive
sulphide: kermes, vulcanizer
ANTIQUE: bibelot, bric-a-brac, knickknack, *ornament, syrup*
bronze: cacao, cocoa, color
drab: color, fox
red: canna, color
ANTITHALIAN: killjoy
ANTLER: dag, *projection, spike*
bay: bezantler
branch: bay, bez, brow, prong
deer: bosset
knob: croche
mainstem: beam
moth: charaeas
point: prong, snag, tyne
unbranched: dag, pricket, spike
ANTWERP: *brown:* congo
native: anversois
ANVIL: ambos, incus, jaw, teest
bone: ambos, incudes, uncus
city: nome
end: bickiron

* Asterisk means to look up this word to find more answer words.

horn: beakiron, bickern
striker: smith
tinsmith's: teest
ANXIETY: **alarm,* anger, **desire,*
dread, fear, **sorrow,* **trouble*
ANXIOUS: **afraid,* **eager*
ANY: all, ary, each, **quantity*
body: no account, someone
day: imminently, soon
how: at all events, haphazard
minute: imminently, soon
more: additional, further
part: aught
thing: aught, no matter what
time: always, invariably
way: carelessly, haphazardly
APACHE: indian, killer, nomad
beverage: tiswin
chief: cochise, geronimo
jacket: bietle
plume: evergreen, fallugia
state: arizona
yma: tulkepaia
APART: abroad, alone, aside
pref.: dia, dis, se
APARTMENT: bachelor, pad
APATHETIC: calm, casual, **cool,*
comatose, insouciant, stoic
APE: boor, copy, gelada, gibbon,
kra, magot, maha, mime, mock,
pan, siamang, soko, wou-wou
dog-headed: aani, cynocephalus
largest: gorilla
-like animal: lemus
-long-tailed: kra
fissure: sulcus
man: alalus, pithecantropus
APER: boar, clown, mocker, snob
APERTURE: bore, chasm, crack
vignette: mask
APEX: **acme*
comb.: apic(o)
covering: epi
elbow: ancon
ornament: finial
pert.: apical(lary)
rounded: retuse

APHAREUS: *brother:* lynceus
son: idas
APHORISM: **adage*
APHRODITE: acraea, anady-
omene, androphonos, antheia,
astarte, cytherea, pandemos
consort: ares
father: zeus
lover: adonis, anchises
mother: dione
priestess: hero
son: aeneas, amor, cupid, eros
sweetheart: hephaestus, vulcan
temple: cerigo, kythera, paphos
APIECE: each, per, seriatim
APLOMB: **address,* balance, cool,
presence, restraint, **skill*
APOCRYPHAL: counterfeit,
*false, mythic, unorthodox
APOGEE: **acme,* **top*
APOLLO: acesius, **astronaut,* car-
neus, caster, **helios,* sun
abode: helicon
beloved: calliope, cyrene, daphne
birthplace: delos
father: jupiter, zeus
festival: carnea, delia
giant killed: ephialtes, otus
grandson: caphaurus
instrument: bow, lute, lyre
mother: latona, leto
pert.: delian
priest: abaris, calchas
seer of: carnus
sister: artemis, diana
son: amphissus, anius, apis, aris-
taeus, asclepius, garamis
vale: tempe
victims: niobe's young, **otus*
APOLOGUE: **allegory*
APOLOGY: **remorse,* **sorrow*
APOSTATE: backslider, convert,
*false, heretic, mugwump, rat,
recidivist, recreant, **traitor*
APOSTLE: **bit,* **enthusiast*
andrew's brother: peter
canaanite: simon

* **Asterisk means to look up this word to find more answer words.**

james' brother: john
john's brother: james
judas' successor: matthias
of indies: xavier
of rome: neri, scholar
of the franks: remi
of the goths: ulfilas
-ship: clergy
teaching of: didache
zealot: simon
APOTHECARY: gallipot, posologist
APOTHEGM: *adage*
APOTHEOSIZE: exalt, glorify
APPALL: *alarm, *repel, *shock*
APPANAGE: *adjunct*
APPAREL: array, *dress,* garment, livery, outfit, panoply
APPARENT: certain, *open, *plain*
pitch: screw thread
APPARITION: appearance, aspect, blue devil, eidolon, fantasy, hobgoblin, idol, *image, *spirit*
APPARATUS: *instrument*
APPEAL: *ask,* beg, call, pray
for judgment: anacoenosis
pert.: appellate
to prejudice: ad hominem
APPEAR: attend, be obvious, bob up, bow, crop out, emerge, fade in, manifest, *occur,* seem
APPEARANCE: advent, attire, countenance, *form,* front, hue, impact, manifestation, ostent, phenomenon, *show,* sight, state
APPEASE: *abate,* placate, *yield*
APPELLATION: *name, *title*
APPEND: *add, *join, *unite*
APPENZELL: embroidery
APPETITE: craving, cupidity, *desire,* edacity, greed, gusto, longing, lust, orexis, *passion,* polydipsia, propensity, relish, *urge,* void, want, *will,* zest
abnormal: bulimia, edacity, gulosity, pica, polyphagia

controller: amphetamine
deficiency: anepithymia, asitia
APPETIZER: canape, foretaste
APPLAUSE: *acclaim*
reaching after: esurience
sound: bravo, hurrah, ole, rah
APPLE: *acid:* malic
baked: biffin
bee: wasp
berry: billardiera
blight: apid, eriosoma
box: eucalyptus
brandy: applejack
butter: condiment, spread
canker: blight, blister, rot
cider-making: coccage
crushed: pomace
curculio: guadrigibbus, weevil
custard: anona
dried: beefin, biffin
genus: malus
grunt: dumpling, pie
immature: codlin(g)
juice: applejack, cider, sidar
kind: ambarella, astrachan, baldwin, ben davis, delicious, gravenstein, grimes, golden, jonathan, mcintosh, northern spy, ohia, oldenburg, pippin, queening, rome beauty, stayman, winesap, yellow newtown, york imperial
-like fruit: bel, pome, quince
love: tomato
moss: bartramia
of cain: arbutus, strawberry
of discord: issue
of hesperides: quince
of one's eye: darling
of peru: jimson weed, physalis
old: rennet
pastry: strudel
pert.: malic
pie order: neatness
polish: flatter
sauce: bunk, nonsense
seed: pip, putamen
-shaped: pomiform

* Asterisk means to look up this word to find more answer words.

thorn: datura, epigene, metel
tree: malus, pawpaw, shea, sorb
wild: crab, ducin
APPLIANCE: *instrument, *use
APPLICATION: *appeal, effort,
perseverance, practice, *use
APPLY: *administer, *spread, use
APPOINT: *allot, *name
APPOINTMENT: *accord, *meeting
APPORTION: *allot, *share
APPOSITE: *appropriate
APPRAISE: *assess, *value
APPRECIATE: *admire, *under-
stand
APPREHEND: *arrest, *under-
stand
APPRISE: *acquaint, *value
APPROACH: adit, *advance, begin, bribe, broach, close, court,
edge up, gain upon, loom, march,
method, offer, overture, sidle up,
solicit, stalk, woo
APPROPRIATE: annex, applica-
ble, apply, arrogate, assign, assume, claim, comely, *copy, *correct, due, felicitous, fit, germane,
pat, *right, *steal
APPROVE: *acclaim, *pass
APPROXIMATELY: *adjacent,
generally, nearly, roughly, say
APPROXIMATION: ballpark
APPURTENANCE: *instrument
APRICOT: *confection:* meebos
cordial: perisco(t)
disease: blight
palm: cocos
plum: amygdalus
scale: lecanium
vine: maypop
APRIORI: categorical, dialectic
knowledge: anticipation
principle: premise
APRON: bib, *cover, protection
APROPOS: *about, appropriate
APT: *able, pat, *ready, *smart
APTERYX: iao, kiwi, moa, oweni

APTITUDE: *disposition, *skill
AQUEDUCT: *waterway
ARABIAN: *abode:* dar
alphabet: alif, ayn, ba, dad, dal,
fa, gaf, kaf, jim, mim, qaf, ra,
sad, shin, tha, zay
banquet: diffa
bazaar: suq
boat: baggala, dhow
caliph: ali, sherif, shereef
caravan: cafila
chief: ameer, emir, ras, reis, sayid,
sayyid, shiek, sultan
city: aden, chafra, damar, hail,
irem, jidda, mareb, mecca
coat: aba, caban, ferijee
coffee: mocha
coin: kabik, peisa, riyal
commando: fatah, fedayeen
cosmetic: kohl
country: arabia, asir, egypt, iran,
iraq, jordan, lebanon, oman,
syria, yemen
date: khola
deity: allat, ankarih, atthar, chai-
al-kaum, el-makum, el-ozza,
haubas, hobal, isaf, itha, khol,
kozah, naila, nasr, raham, ruda,
sin, sowa, yaghut
demon: afreet, eblis, jinni
desert: ankaf, bedu, dahna, nefud,
nejd, nyd, petraea
division: el hasa, hedjax, mecca,
medina, nejd, oman, sinai, te-
hama, yemen
dish: couscous
doctrine: avicxennism
drink: bozah, leban
dromedary: belool, hejeem
drum: tara-booka
dynasty: aghlabid, aglabite
epic: moallakas
fabric: abas, haik
father: abba, abou, abu
flour: samh
flower: bela, jasmine
garment: burnoose, cabaan, haik

* Asterisk means to look up this word to find more answer words.

giraffe: xirapha
grammar: ajrumyia
greeting: effendi
gulf: aden, kutch, oman
gum: acacia, kafal
hand: neshki
head gear cord: agal
headpiece: kaffiyeh
hero: antara-el-absi
horse: anezeh, kadischi
jasmine: bela, sampaquita
land: feddan
leader: koleyb
measure: achir, ardeb, assbaa,
 barid, cabda, cafiz, caphite,
 covido, cuddy, farsakh, ferk,
 gariba, ghalva, kiladja, kist,
 makuk, nusfiah, qasab, woïbe
myrrh: commiphora
nights character: abu, aladdin, ali
 baba, alnaschar, badawi, barme-
 cide, bedreddin, fatima, ganem,
 haroun, hassanagib, houssain,
 judar, julnar, iram, kafur, morgi-
 ana, schacabac, schariah, sidi,
 sinbad, zobeide
panther: fahd
peasant: fellah
philosopher: averroes, farabi
poet: antara, kaab
puritan: wahhabi
scholar: ulema
script: neskhi, neski
shrine: kaaba
sultanate: mahra
tambourine: daire, taar
tribe: asir, aus, dedanite, diendel,
 hagarene, irad, kedar
weight: artaba, bahar, bokard,
 cheki, crat, danik, dirhem,
 farsalah, farzil, kella, nasch
ARACA: guava, terminalia
ARALIA: fatsia, hercules-club
ARAM: syria
 children: gether, hul, mash, uz
 deity: rimmon
 nomads: akhlame

ARAPUNGO: bellbird, campanero
ARBITER: conciliator, critic,
 judge, mediator, munsiff, referee,
 settler, umpire
ARBITRARY: *absolute*, *firm*
ARBITRATE: *decide*, *rule*
ARBOR: mandrel, pergola, recess
 shaft: cardan joint
 vine: morning glory, operculina
 vitae: cedar, libocedrus, thuja
ARC: bend, curve, halo, orbit
 chord: sine
 100th: centare
 horizon: azimuth
ARCADIA: eden, *paradise*, utopia
 deity: ladon
 god: pan
 huntress: atalanta
 king: lycaon
 nightingale: ass
 wicked widow: cecropia
ARCANE: *secret*
ARCAS: *mother:* callisto
 son: aphidas, azan
ARCH: *band:* masonry strip
 curve: extrados
 decorative: bonnet top
 filch: nim
 inner curve: intrados
 kind of: basket-handle, fixed, flat,
 horseshoe, lancet, ogee, ogive,
 rampant, rowlock, tudor
 memorial: pailo, pailou
 molding: accolade
 part: keystone, voussoir
 pointed: ogee, ogive
 solid: vossoir
ARCHAIC: *aged*, *old*
ARCHANGEL: angelica, gabriel,
 michael, raphael, satan, uriel
ARCHER: clim, cupid, robin hood,
 sagittarius, tell, toxophilite
 chief: ahiezer
 deity: apollo, artemis
 outlaw: adam, bell, hood
ARCHITECTURAL: tectonic
 base: dado, patten, plinch

* Asterisk means to look up this word to find more answer words.

convexity: entasis
design: epure, plan, print
feature: belvedere
figure: caryatid, telamones
pier: anta
term: aaron's rod, abatvent
ARCHITECTURE: **style*
ARCTIC: *base:* etah, thule
bird: auk, brant, fulmar, xema
canoe: kayak, oomiak, umiak
current: labrador
dog: husky, samoyed
explorer: amundsen, baffin, bering,
button, byrd, davis, eric, fro-
bisher, greely, hudson, kane, mc-
clure, nansen, peary, rae, ross,
stefanson
headland: odden
herb: arctotis, bartsia
jacket: anorak
musk ox: ovibos
native: alaskan, aleut, eskimo,
laplander, lapp
plain: tundra
rocket: parrya, plant
smoke: steam, fog
ARDENT: ablaze, adoring, afire,
affectionate, alow, amative, anacreontic, aphrodisiac, avid, biased,
boiling, burning, convivial, cordial, devoted, **eager,* enamored,
fervent, fierce, hot, impetuous,
intent, on fire, passionate, **violent,* **warm,* **wild,* zealous
AREA: environs, superficies
measure: acre, are, arpent, cen-
tiare, hectare, parish, perch, pole,
radius, rood
pert.: spatial
ARENA: amphitheatre, area, bear
garden, bowl, bullring, campus,
circus, coliseum, colosseum,
course, court, drome, ground,
gym, lists, oval, palaestra, pit,
platform, ring, rink, sand, scene,
*sphere, stadium, stage, theatre
ARES: *nurse:* thero

parent: enyo, hera, zeus
sister: eris
son: cycnus
ARETE: **ridge,* **top*
ARGENTINA: *arcade:* galeria
armadillo: peludo
barge: chalana
cloth: tarlatan
cocktail: clarito
cowboy: gaucho
dance: cuando, tango
dish: chivitos, criollo, luna, par-
rillada, puchero
garment: chiripa
measure: cuadra, fanega, legua,
manzana, sino, vara
mountain: aconcagua
native: porteno
plant: bromelia, caraguata
ranch: estancia
tree: ambay, cecropia, palo
ARGOLIS: *valley:* nemea
ARGONAUT: acastus, admetus,
aethalides, amphidamas, ascala-
phus, asterion, butes, caeneus,
canthus, jason
ARGOS: *hero:* amphiaraos
king: abas, acrisius, adrastus,
danaus, lynceus
ARGOT: cant, dialect, idiom, jargon, lingo, patois, slang
ARGUE: advocate, affirm, assert,
*attack, bicker, cavil, debate, ex-
postulate, **fight,* hassle, **protest,* **prove,* **quarrel*
ARGUMENT: abstract, agon, angle, case, combat, **fight,* fuss,
litigation, polemics, rhubarb,
set-to, **talk,* theme, words
conclusive: clincher, corker,
crusher, knockdown, sockdolager
fallacious: sophism
negative: con
positive: pro
specious: claptrap, moonshine,
*nonsense, paralogism, rot,
solecism, sophistry

* Asterisk means to look up this word to find more answer words.

ARGUS: -*eyed:* keen, vigilant
fish: india fish, scatophagus
pheasant: peacock, tragopan
shell: cyraea, gastropod
ARIANRHOD: *mother:* don
consort: gwydion
ARID: barren, dessicated, dry, jejune, meager, sec, sere, vapid, withered, xeric
ARIEL: *petrel:* prion
toucan: bird, rhamphastos
ARISE: **appear, *occur, *stand*
ARISTOCRACY: **society, *top*
ARISTOTLE: greek, philosopher
birthplace: stagira, thrace
category: action, passivity, place, position, possession, quality, quantity, relation, substance, time
causes: efficient, final, formal, material
disciple: peripatetic
father: amyntas, nicomachus
school: lyceum
teacher: plato
work: ethica, nimomachea, organon, poetics
ARITHMETIC: algorism
ineptitude: acalculia
rules: allegations
ARIZONA: *buckthorn:* bumelia
bird: cactus wren
desert: painted
flower: saguaro cactus
gourd: calabazilla
motto: ditat deus
nickname: apache, grand canyon
palm: fanleaf
river: colorado, gila
ruby: cape, garnet, pyrope
shellac: sonora gum
tree: paloverde
walnut: juglans major
ARK: chest, receptacle, wanigan
builder: noah, noe
landing place: ararat
porter: ben

shell: arca, arcida
ARKANSAS: cabbage, quapaw
bird: mockingbird
city: booneville, little rock
flower: apple blossom
motto: regnat populus
nickname: bear state, bowie state, land of opportunity
stone: novaculite, whetstone
tree: pine
ARM: alidade, authority, bras, cove(r), equip, fit, flipper, force, fortify, jib, outfit, power, **prepare, *ready*, sleeve
badge: brassard
band: brassard, maniple
bone: humerus, ulna, radius
chair: cacqueteuse, caquetoire
comb.: brachi(o)
eight, having: ocotopod
-ful: **quantity, *plenty*
-guard: bracer, protection
hole: mail, scye
hollow at bend: chelidon
in arm: together
lack: abrachia
-like: brachial
muscle: biceps, triceps
of flesh: aid, strength
of the law: police(man)
part: ares, elbow, wrist
pert.: brachial
vein: basilic, cephalic
walk: oxter
ARMADA: fleet, flotilla, navy
ARMADILLO: *giant:* peludo, tatu
-like extinct animal: glyptodon
small: peba, quirquincho
three-banded: apara, mataco
ARMENIA: anatolia, minni
angel worshipper: yezedi
apostle: gregory
cap: calpac
city: erivan, erzurum
cumin: caraway, plant
extinct volcano: aragats
lake: urumiyah, van

* Asterisk means to look up this word to find more answer words.

mountain: rarat, taurus
people: gomer
river: ara, cyrus, euphrates, halys, kizil-trmak, tigris
ARMOR: *arm:* brazzard, gardebras, rerebrace
bearer: armiger, custrel, squire
body: action, braguet, broigne, byrnie, crevisse, corium, cuirass, culet, dossiere, gambeson, harbergeon, hauberk, lamboys, lorica, mameliere, pansiere, plastron, surcoat, tace, tasse(t), tonlet
cap: cerveliere
chain: mail
elbow guard: cutitiere
face: (a)ventail, beaver
head and neck: armet, aventail, basonet, beaver, burgonet, cabasset, camail, casque, cerveliere, coif(fette), galera, gorge(rin), heaume, helmet, mentoniere, morion, sallet, secret, ventail, visor
horse: barde, poitrel, testiere
jacket: action, gipon
knee: genouillere
lance rest: faucre
leg: boot, braconniere, cuisse, greave, jamb(eau), tuille
-less: baresark
plate: besague, moton
shoulder to hand: ailette, armlet, brassard, cubitiere, epauliere, gardebras, gauntlet, passegarde, pauldron, rerebrace
skirt: braconniere, taslet
suit, full: barde, brigandine, cataphract, cuirass, jazerant, mail, panoply, placcate, weed
thigh to foot: chausse, cuisse, geouillere, gorget, greave, jamb(eau), sabbaton, tuille
throat: gorget
undergarment: action

wrist: brace(let) brassart, vambrace
ARMPIT: *pert.:* axillar
ARMS: *depository:* arsenal
limitation talks: salt
ARMY: *ant:* driver, legionary
brown color: rosario
camp: barracks, *fort
camp neighbor: cannaba
car: carroccio, jeep
chaplain: padre
clothes: fatigues, gis, khaki, monkey suit, ods, uniform
coat: blouse, capote, sagum
color: o d, olive drab, tan
commission: brevet, *officer
core: cadre
engineer: pioneer, sapper
follower: sutler
food: chow, mess
horse: cavalry, hussar, uhlan
installation: base, camp, *fort, post, station
man: *soldier
nco: corporal, sergeant
officer: aide, brass, captain, colonel, general, lieutenant, major, marshal, *nco, warrant
pert.: martial, military
postal address: apo
quarters: casern, *fort
school: *academy, ocs, ots
special forces: green berets
storehouse: armory, arsenal
supplies: materiel, ordnance
uniform: *army: clothes
unit: battalion, brigade, cadre, cohort, command, company, corps, division, legion, maniple, phalanx, platoon, regiment, squad, troop
women: waac, wac, wraf, wren
-worm: caterpillar
AROMA: *scent
AROUET: voltaire
AROUND: about, circa, through
comb.: amph(i), circum, peri

* Asterisk means to look up this word to find more answer words.

the clock: all the time
AROUSE: *animate,* *stir*
ARRAIGN: *accuse*
ARRANGE: *adapt,* *adjust*
ARRANGEMENT: *comb.:* taxeo, taxo
pert.: tactical
ARRANGER: composer
ARRANT: *bad*
ARRAY: *adorn,* *dress,* *order*
ARREST: absorb, apprehend, balk, check, collar, confine, curb, dwarf, *end,* halt, intercept, lag, pinch, pull in, put down, restrain, *run in,* *secure,* *seize,* *slow,* *stop,* *take*
ARRIERE-PENSEE: sequel
ARRIVE: *accomplish,* appear
ARROGANT: audacious, brazen, contumelious, hoity-toity, imperious, insolent, officious, overbearing, *vain,* *wanton*
ARROGATE: *adopt,* *seize,* *take*
ARROW: dart, missile, shaft
  adjunct: penna
  arum: peltandra, plant
  barbless: butt shaft
  body: stele
  bush: weed
  cane: uva, grass
  case: quiver
  comb.: belo
  end: nock
  feathered: vire
  fit to string: nock
  handle: stele
  maker: bowyer, fletcher
  part: barb, butt, feather, head
  pert.: sagittal
  point: barb, neb
  poison: antiar, curare, echugin, haya, inee, sumpitan, upas, urali, wagogo, woorali
  root: ararao, arum, canna, curcuma, maranta, mehl, tacca
  -shaped: beloid, caggitate
  short: sprite

stone: belemnite, mineral
thrower: anisocycle
weed: pluchea
wood: alder, sericotheca, wahoo
ARROYO: canyon, *waterway*
ARS ARTIUM: logic
ARSENIC: medicine, poison
  antimony: allemontite
  bloom: arsenolite
  compound: alloclasite, arsenide
  copper: erinite
  mirror: marsh test
  mixture: erinite, speiss
  sulphide: realgar
ART: *ability,* beauty, cheesecake, *skill,* *style,* *system,* *trade*
  black: alchemy, necromancy
  brown: argentina, mirador
  cheap work: buckeye
  fancier: aesthete, connoisseur, dilettante, esthere, votary
  gallery: museum, salon
  glass: agata, amberina
  gray: blue red, quaker
  gum: cleaner, eraser
  manual: craft, sloid, sloyd
  schools: american, barbizon, blue rider, bolognese, british, dutch, eclectic, flemish, florentine, french, honfleur, italian, lombard, milanese, modernese, neapolitan, paduan, plein-air, raphaelite, roman, scottish, sienese, tuscan, umbrian, venetian
  style: abstractionism, baroque, classic, cloisonnism, cubism, dada, existentialism, fauvism, futurism, genre, gothicism, idealism, impressionism, intimism, modernism, mystic, natural, objectivism, pop, primitivism, purism, realism, romanticism, surrealism, symbolism, votricism
ARTAGUS: *country:* spain
ARTAXERXES: *ahasuerus*
ARTEMIS: agrotera, apollousa, brauronia, *diana,* hymnia,

* Asterisk means to look up this word to find more answer words.

iocheaira, *phoebe
brother: apollo
companion: aura
festival: brauronia
parent: demeter, dionysus, isis,
leto, persephone, zeus
priestess: iphigenia
victim: admetus, callisto, chione,
*niobe's children, oeneus, orion
ARTERIAL: aorta, *road, *route
ARTHUR: *king arthur
ARTICHOKE: drink: cynar
leafstalk: chard
relative: cardoon
ARTICLE: *piece, *study
ARTIFICE: *deception, *trick
ARTIFICIAL: affected, assumed,
campy, contrived, counterfeit,
crafty, ersatz, factitious, *false,
fictitious, histrionic, imaginary,
insincere, overdone, *sly, *superficial, *theatrical
ARTILLERY: emplacement: battery
fire: barrage, rafale, salvo
man: bombardier, cannoneer, gun-
ner, lascar, topechee
plant: adicea, dittany, gas plant,
mock cypress, wahoo
saint: barbara
ARTIST: equipment: brush, canvas, easel, palette
paint: oil, tempera, watercolor
primitive: moses
signature word: fecit
workshop: atelier, studio
ARTISTIC: production: facture
strewing: seme
ARTLESS: *candid, naive
ARUM: acorus, arad, calla, taro
ARYAN: deity: ormuzd
fire god: agni
indian: hindu
language: sanskrit
sage: agastya
ASA: healer, king, physician
dulcis: benzoin, plant, shrub

kin: abia, jehoshaphat
ASCEND: escalate, *tower, zoom
ASCENDANCY: *authority
ASCENT: *acclivity
ASCERTAIN: *assure, *prove
ASCETIC: abstemious, abstinent,
austere, avadhuta, banyan, beggar, cathar, cynic, diorite, dy-
dropot, *enthusiast, eremite, flag-
ellant, frugal, hermit, moderate,
moral, *monk, *plain, recluse,
*severe, *stern, stoic, stylite, yoga
mendicant: bairagi
moslem: dervish
ASCRIBE: *attribute
ASEXUAL: comb.: agam(o)
ASGARD: bridge: bifrost
goddesses: *aesir, asynjur
gods: *aesir
12 mansions: bilskirnir, breithablik, folkvang, glitner, himinb-
jorg, hlithskjalf, jotunnheim,
noatun, sessyrmnir, sokkvabekk,
thrymheim, valaskjalf, valhalla,
vanaheim, vingolf, ydalir
ASH: artar, *dregs, *refuse, rone,
rowan, sorb, tree
ASHANTI: pepper: cubeb
religion: obia
ASHER: daughter: beriah, serah
father: jacob
son: isui, jimnah, usui
ASIAN: eastern, oriental
antelope: dzerin, goral, serow
ass: onager, loulan
bean: gram, mungo
bird: brambling, dotterel
christian: uniat
conjuror: shaman
cow: zobo
crowfoot: buttercup, ranunculus
deer: axis, kakar, roe, sambar
dog, wild: dhole
eskimo: innuit, tuski, yuit
falcon: laggar, lanneret
fox: adive, corsac
goat: jagla, serow, tahr

* Asterisk means to look up this word to find more answer words.

grass: coix, munj
horse: tarpan
jay: sirgang
lemur: loris, macaco
mammal: chevrotain, panda
mink: kolinsky
mountains: altai, himalayas, hindu-kush, kalka, sayan, ural
nomad: kipchak, tatar
palm: areca, assai, calami
peninsula: anatolia, arabia, kamchatka, korea, malay
pheasant: tragopan
plain: chol, maidan, steppe
religion: brahman, buddhist, hinayana, hindu, islam, mahayana, shinto, tao
salmon: taimen
sandstorm: simoon, tebbad
sheep: argali, bharal, nahoor, oorial, rasse, sha, sna, urial
snake: bongar, daboia, jessur
storm: buran, monsoon, typhoon
tableland: pamir, tibet
tree: acle, asak, bito, medlar
ASININE: *absurd, *stupid
ASK: appeal, apply, beseech, inquire, *need, plead, query, question, quiz, request, sue
ASKEW: *awry, *eccentric, odd
ASPARAGUS: *bean:* vigna
beetle: crioceris
broccoli: calabrese
lettuce: lactuca
plumosis: fern
stone: apatite, mineral
ASPECT: *particular, *state
ASPERSE, ASPERSION: *abuse
ASPIC: cannon, gelatin, jelly
ASPIRATION, ASPIRE: *aim
ASS: asinego, blockhead, burro, cuddy, dolt, duff, imbecile, janny, kiang, kulan, moke, neddy, onager, putz, quagga
comb.: ono
in lion skin: *impostor
pert.: *asinine

ASSAIL: *abuse, *attack
ASSAM: *capital:* shillong
city: ledo, shillangle
dialect: aka, ao, khami, lhota
mongoloid: garo
native: ahom, aka, garo
rubber: rambong
silkworm: eri, eria
ASSAULT: *abuse, *attack
ASSAY: *analyze
ASSEMBLE: *accumulate, *unite
ASSEMBLY: *group, *meeting
circuits: breadboard
eccles: coetus, sederunt
full: plena
line: factory, plant, process
place: agora, auditorium, bouleuterion, estufa, kiva
threads: capillitium
ASSENT: *accept, *accord, *yield
ASSES' BRIDGE: *dilemma
ASSESS: adjudge, *analyze, estimate, evaluate, inventory, judge, measure, *test, *value
ASSET: capital, bond, bonus, cash, credit, estate, *goods, means, *money, note, *property, security, *supply, *value
ASSIDUOUS: *active, *quick
ASSIGN: *allot, *name
ASSIMILATE: *absorb
ASSISTANT: aide, adjutant
ASSIZES: court, drum, oyer, writ
ASSOCIATE: *accomplice, adjunct, blend, buddy, chum, clique, concomitant, consort, crony, *friend, hobnob, merge, mix, partner, spouse, *unite
ASSUAGE: *abate, *reduce
ASSUME: *accept, *venture
ASSUMED: *artificial
ASSURE: avail, back, certify, *cinch, *clinch, convince, guarantee, *promise, *secure
ASSUREDLY: amen, truly, verily
ASSYRIA: *city:* akkad, antioch,

---

* Asterisk means to look up this word to find more answer words.

arbella, calah, hara, kalakh, nineveh, obis
god: adad, assur, hadad, nebo, nergal, niniby, nusky, shamas
goddess: allatu, ishtar, nana
king: asenapper, ashurbanipal, belus, osnapper, phul, sargon, sennacherib, shalmaneser, tiglathpileser
measure: artaba, gariba, gasab, ghalva, makuk, mansion
mountain: zagros
queen: semiramis
river: adhian, zab
ASTER: daisy, fleabane, oxeye
ASTERISK: bug, emphasis, star
ASTERIUS: argonaut, minotaur
father: anax, hyperasius
mother: pasiphae
wife: europa
ASTONISH, ASTOUND: **shock,* upset
ASTRINGENT: acid
ASTRONAUT: **rocket, *space*
american: aldrin, anders, armstrong, bassett, bean, carpenter, cernan, collins, conrad, cooper, cunningham, eisele, enos, glenn, gordon, grissom, lovell, mcdivitt, schirra, schweickert, scott, stafford, white, young
apollo 7: cunningham, eisele, schirra
apollo 8: anders, borman, lovell
apollo 9: mcdivitt, schweickert, scott
apollo 10: cernan, stafford, young
apollo 11: aldrin, armstrong, collins
apollo 14: mitchell, roosa, shepard
ballast: junk
boss: phillips, slayton
killed in action: chaffee, grissom, white
lunar module: columbia, eagle, intrepid

mercury: glenn, shepard
rockets: **rocket: names*
russian: gagarin, komarof, rukavishnikov, shatalov, yeliseyev
satellites and spaceships: alouette, apollo, ariel, cosmos, courier, echo, essa, explorer, gemini, greb, idscp, injun, intelsat, lanibird, lofti, luna, mariner, mars, mercury, midas, molniya, oao, ogo, orbiter, oso, pageos, pioneer, polyot, proton, ranger, relay, samos, snap, sputnik, surveyor, syncom, telstar, tiros, topsi, traac, transit, vanguard, vela, voskhod, yantar, zond
ASTRONOMIC: celestial, colossal
calendar: almanac
cloud: nebula
cycle: saros
instrument: aba, armil, orrery, sector, sextant, telescope
measure: apsis, azimuth
muse: urania
terms: apogee, colures, ecliptic, equino, galactic, geocentric, heliocentric, meridian, orbit, perigee, trajectory, zodiac, zone
ASTUTE: **acute, *sly, *smart*
ASYLUM: ark, bedlam, harbor, haven, **home,* hospice, jail, recourse, refuge, **retreat,* sanctuary, shelter, xenodochium
ATALANTA: *consort: *melanion*
ATHAMAS: *daughter:* helle
son: learchus, phrixos
wife: ino
ATHENA: *aegis head:* medusa
arma: aegis
bird: owl
festival: arrhephoria
pert.: alea, palladian
temple: parthenon
victim: pallas
ATHENIAN: attic, metic
architect: ictinus
assembly: boule, pnyx

* **Asterisk means to look up this word to find more answer words.**

astronomer: meton
bee: plato
cemetery: ceramicus
clan: obe
coin: chalcus, obolus
colonies: cleruchies
courtesan: aspasia, thais
festival: amphidromia, anthesteria, apaturia
founder: cecrops
fountain: callirrhoe
general: alcibiades, nicias, phocion, zenophon
harbor: piraeus
hill: acropolis, areopagus, lycabettus, pnyx
historian: thucydides, xenophon
intellectual: anaxagoras, damon, protagoras, sophocles, zeno
judge: dicast
lawgiver: draco, solon
leader: cleomenes, clisthenes, pericles
market place: agora
of america: boston
of ireland: belfast, cork
of switzerland: zurich
of the north: copenhagen, edinburgh
of the west: cordoba
pert.: attic
philosopher: aristotle, plato, socrates
platform: bema, bemata
rival: corinth, sparta
room: adytum, atrium, cella
sculptor: phidias
seaport: piraeus
spring: callirrhoe
tribunal: aeropagus
tyrant: cleon, hippias
ATLANTIC: ocean
flier: corrigan, lindbergh
sisters: pleiades
ATLANTIDES: **hesperides*, **pleiades*
ATLAS: folio, map, titan, volume

comb.: atlanto, atlo(iodo)
daughters: alcyone, asterope, calypso, electra, kelaine, maiia, merope, pleiade, tayget
-like: atlantean, toros
moth: attacus
mother: clymene
powder: dynamite, explosive
ATLI: *wife:* gudrun
ATMOSPHERE: *disturbance: *storm*
gas: argon, nitron, oxygen
phenomenon: aurora, meteor
pressure: baric, barometric
ATOM: ace, **bit*, body, ion, jot, mite, molecule, monad, mote, **part*, shade, speck, tracer, **trifle*, whim, whit
component: electron, neutron, nucleus, proton
element: dyad, heptad, hexad, monad, octad, pentad, tetrad
machine: betatron, rheotron
particles: alpha, beta, meson, photon, pion, teutron
ATOMIC: bantom, dibasic, homocyclic, infinitesimal, minute, molecular, nuclear, tiny, tribasic
bomb types: a, fission, fusion, hydrogen, megaton, nuclear, plutonium, super, thermonuclear
energy: a-blast, fission, mach
machine: betatron, rheotron
order: ring
pile: reactor
submarine: nautilus, skate
terms: deuteride, heavy water, pleiad, protium, tritium
theory: bohr, octet, quantum, rutherford, schroedinger
ATONE: **accord*, **adjust*
ATREUS: *brother:* thyestes
daughter: anaxibia
half-brother: chrysippus
parent: hippodamia, pelops
slayer: aegisthus
son: agamemnon, atridae, mene-

* Asterisk means to look up this word to find more answer words.

laus, pleisthenes
wife: aerope
ATROCIOUS: *bad,* *evil*
ATROPHY: *decline*
ATTA: ant, flour, native, soul
ATTACH: *add,* *seize,* *take*
  importance to: esteem
  little importance: under rate
  oneself to: follow
  some weight to: believe
ATTACHE: aide, diplomat
  case: *bag,* etui, etwee, tashie
ATTACHMENT: *love,* *passion*
ATTACK: *advance,* abuse, ambush, *argue,* belt, blame, blast, breakthrough, camisado, catch, coup, *fight,* fire, hit, lay into, light into, open fire, *press,* *push,* *rebuke,* run at, sortie, stab, *start,* *strike*
  false: feint
  of illness: bout
  sudden: blitz
  suicidal: kamikaze
ATTAIN: *accomplish,* *get,* *win*
ATTEMPT: *attack,* *trial,* *try*
ATTEND: *accompany,* *join*
ATTENDANT: *agent,* *servant*
ATTIC: *athenian,* esthetic
  salt: wit
ATTIRE: *apparel,* *dress*
ATTITUDE: *disposition*
ATTRACT: *allure,* *draw*
ATTRIBUTE: *symbol,* *token*
ATTRITION: *decline,* erosion
AUDACIOUS: *bold,* brave
AUDIT: examine, hear, probe
AUGEAN: *gulf:* argolis
  stable: slum
  task: chore
AUGEAS: *daughter:* agamede
AUGMENT: *add,* *grow,* *increase*
AUGUR: *predict,* *prophet*
AUGUST: *great,* majestic, *wise*
  first: lammas
  meteors: perseids

  24: bartholomewtide
AUK: alca, alle, arrie, dovekie, elorios, falk, guillemot, murre, puffin, razorbill, rotch, uria
  pert.: alcine
AULD: *clootie:* devil
  lang syne: past, solitaire
  reekie: edinburgh
  sod: homeland
  wives'-tongue: american aspen
AURA: *air,* emanation, *scent*
  consort: dionysus
  friend: artemis
AUSPICES: *aid,* omen, *sign*
AUSPICIOUS: *bright,* *good*
AUSTERE: *acerb,* *severe,* *stern*
AUSTRALIAN: *acacia:* myall
  animal: bandicoot, bunyip, carbora, cuscus, dasyure, kangaroo, koala, panda, wombat
  beach grass: marram
  bear: koala, panda, wombat
  boomerang: kiley
  bustard: bebilya
  cake: brownie, damper
  catfish: tandan
  clover: nardoo
  club: waddy
  cockatoo: galah
  colonist: sterling
  cranberry: astroloma, lissanthe
  dog: merle
  eucalyptus: bimbil, carbeen
  falcon: berigora
  flower: waratah
  grass tree: kingia, richea
  horse: brumbee, prad, warragal
  ironbark: eucalyptus
  kangaroo: bettong, joey, tungo
  lifeguard: beltman
  mahogany: gunnung, jarrah
  mountain: blue, bongong, bruce, cradle, garnet, ise, magnet
  plant: alstonia, calomba, lakea
  pond: billabong
  ranch hand: boundary rider
  rustler: duffer

* Asterisk means to look up this word to find more answer words.

shamrock: menindie clover
sorcerer: boolya, boyla
thicket: mallee
tree: boree, eucalyptus, gmelina, marara, myall, todart
weapon: boomerang, waddy, womal
workman: billjim
AUSTRIAN: *alps:* tirol, tyrol
composer: berg, bruckner, liszt, mahler, strauss
grass: marram
psychologist: adler, freud
vermillion: cinnabar
AUTHENTIC: *correct*, *true*
AUTHOR: begetter, creator, designer, father, free lance, ghost write, inventor, knock off, originator, progenitor, *spark*, *start*
AUTHORITY: certificate, court, credit, dynasty, expert, franchise, government, hegemony, *order*, *power*, *right*, *rule(r)*
symbol: mace, scepter
woman's: distaff
AUTHORIZE: license, *suffer*
AUTO: car, coach, crate, motor
part: bonnet, carburetor, chassis, choke, distributor, engine, ignition, magneto
race: derby, drag, 500
court: inn, motel
AVAIL: *abet*, *advantage*, *use*
AVALON, AVALLON: *paradise*
queen: argante, morgaine le fay
AVANT: *-courier:* forerunner
-garde: experimental, vanguard
-propos: prelude
AVENUE: *road*, *walk*, *way*
AVER: *state*, *talk*, *tell*
AVERAGE: common, equaling, fair, *general*, mean, middle, normal, par, ratio, so-so, *usual*
man: babbitt, proletarian
AVESTA: *demigod:* yima
division: gathas, ventidad
vispered: yashts, hasna

translation: zend
AVID: agape, *ardent*, *eager*
AVIDITY: *desire*, *passion*
AVOCADO: alligator pear, palto
AVOID: avert, balk, elude, *escape*, evade, evitate, flee, fly, keep away, *quit*, shun
AWARD: *accolade*, oscar, tony
AWARE: *active*, *smart*, *wise*
AWAY: *abroad*, distant, far
pref.: abs, aph, cat, de, di
from its place: anachronism
from right: astray
AWE: daunt, *shock*, *wonder*
AWKWARD: *clumsy*
AWL: *bird:* woodpecker
sailmaker's: stabber
-shaped: subulate
-wort: plant, subularia
AWN: avel, barb, bristle, pile
A W O L: absence, bug out
be: play hookey
AWRY: *askew*, *bad*, *evil*, *wrong*
AXE: *blade:* bit
butt: poll
double-edged: besague
handle: boondoggle, helve
AXIOM: *adage*
AXIS: alliance, center, hinge
comb.: atlo, axi, axo
power: italy, japan, germany
AZORES: *district:* horta
island: fayal, flores, pico
port: angra de heroismo, horta
volcano: pico
AZTEC: *conquests:* huastecs, otomi, toltecs
deity: camaxtli, centeotle, chalchiuhtlicue, coatlicue, huitzilopochtli, meztli, nagual, quetzalcoatl, tezcatlipoca, tlaloc, tonatiuti, tzinteotl, xipe
epic: nana, natl
language: anhuatl
marigold: tagetes
ritual ballgame: tlachtli

* Asterisk means to look up this word to find more answer words.

sib: calpulli
spear: atlatl
stone: chalcihihuitl
temple: teocalli, teopan
AZURE: bice, blue, celeste, co-balt, gem, lapis, smalt
AZYGOUS: along, odd, single

BAAL: asherah, baltis, idol, mas-sebah, melkarth, moloch
BABA: baby, cake, child, dessert
BABASSU: oil, palm, soap
BABBITT: *average,* mediocre
BABBLE: betray, blab, blather, confusion, gab(ble), *gossip,* *noise,* prate, rave, *talk*
BABEL: din, *mixture,* *noise*
site: shinar
BABICHE: lacing, thong, thread
BABILLARD: bird, whitethroat
BABOON: ape, chacma, drill, papa
BABU: clerk, gent, man, title
BABY: doll, *forte,* indulge, proj-ect, *spoil,* sweetheart
BABYLONIAN: luxurious, sinful
adam: adapa
epic hero: gilgamesh
god: adad, anu, bel, dagan, enki, enzu, nabu, nebu, sin
goddess: ai, aya, astarte, nina
hero: adepa, etana, gilgamesh
priest, king: patesi
BACALAO: bird, fish, grouper
BACCATE: berried, pulpy
BACCHANAL: *drunk(ard),* *tear*
BACHELOR: agamist, apartment, celibate, free, graduate
button: bluebottle, milkwort
BACK: *aid,* *stern,* *support*
alley: *dirty,* *secret*
and fill: alternate, *oscillate*
-bite: *abuse,* sass, *scold*
-bone: *force,* *power,* *spirit*
country: bush, brush, sticks
down: *quit,* *retreat,* *yield*

-ground: facts, history, rear
-log: *store,* *supply*
pref.: ana, cat(a), cath, kat, kata, kath, re(tro)
scratcher: apple-polisher
-slide: *decline,* *quit*
-stairs: *secret,* *sly*
-ward: *dull,* *shy,* *stupid*
BACKER: angel, *enthusiast*
BACON: bowrp, lard, prize, pork
BACTERIA: germ, microbe, virus
BAD: atrocious, base, black, bunk, corrupt, counterfeit, *criminal,* *evil,* *dirty,* *false,* flagrant, ill, immoral, *low,* *mean,* *poor,* *rotten,* *sick,* *sinister,* *sorry,* *ugly*
comb.: caco, dys, kako, mal
blood: anger, hate, hostility
debt: default
dream: hallucination
egg: *hoodlum,* rogue, villain
habit: vice
legislation: asynomy, dysnomy
luck: adversity, ambsace, black ox, ill wind, misfortune
name: caconym, dishonor
scent, comb.: brom(o)
-tempered: atrabilious, cross
BADGE: emblem, insigne, *honor,* *mark,* plaque, *sign,* *symbol*
honor: blue ribbon, decoration
infamy: stigma
rayed: star
slavery: bondage
BADGER: *afflict,* bandicoot, *scold,* *torment,* wombat
cape: cony, daman, hyrax
game: extortion
group: cete
state: wisconsin
weed: pasqueflower
BADIGEON: cement, composi-tion
BADINAGE: banter, raillery
BAFFLE: *addle,* *puzzle,* *upset*
gab: *argot,* gobbledegook

* **Asterisk means to look up this word to find more answer words.**

BAG: *acquire, alforja, bouge, case, dorine, en tout cas, etui, etwee, *forte, *get, gladstone, grip, luggage, makeup kit, *pack, portmanteau, pouch, purse, *quantity, reticule, satchel, *seize, *stomach, suitcase, *take, *thing, *trap, valise, vanity case
and baggage: *all, *complete
comb.: sacc, sacci, sacco
-ful: *plenty, *quantity
BAGATELLE: *bit, game, verse
BAGGAGE: impedimenta, *prostitute, *wanton
man: bellhop, porter, redcap
BAGGY: *fat, flabby, puffy
BAGMAN: henchman, swagman
BAGNIO: bathhouse, brothel
BAGS: *lots, *plenty, *pants
BAH: fiddledee, pshaw, *nonsense
BAHAMA: bay rush: coontie
candy: benni cake
capital: nassau
grass: devil, scutch
island: abaco, andros, bimini, eleuthera
redwood: colubrina
tea: lantana
whitewood: canella
BAHIA: arrowroot: cassava
grass: paspalum, pasture
powder: goa
BAIL: bond, custody, *throw
out: *escape, *release, *save
BAILE: father: buan
BAILIWICK: area, *forte, *skill
BAIN: direct, lithe, ready
-marie: double boiler, vessel
BAIT: *afflict, lure, *trap
BAKER: bird, cook, fly, oast
dish: cocotte, ramekin
dozen: thirteen
itch: psoriasis, rash
kneading trough: brake
knee: knockknee
shovel: peel
workshop: imu, umu, yale

BALANCE: *accord, harmony, keep step, poise, sanity, *settle
lose: *fall, stagger, trip
of power: *peace, policy
of sails: atry
of sentence: parison
part: scale pan
sheet: bilan, statement
BALCONY: gallery, porch, stoop
BALD: bare, meager, stark, *ugly
berry: orchis maculata
brant: goose
buzzard: bird, osprey
coot: bell kite, gallinule
crown: widgeon
cypress: swamp tree
head: crow, goose, pigeon
locust: attacus
money: gentian, spicknel
BALDER: herb: amaranthus
home: breithablik
murder weapon: mistletoe
parent: frigg, odin
slayer: hod, hoth, loke, loki
son: forsete, forseti
wife: nanna
BALDERDASH: bombast, *nonsense
BALDNESS: acomia, alopecia
BALDRIC: band, belt, girdle
BALE: *bad, fire, *pack, *sorrow
BALEARIC: island: cabrera, formentera, majorca, minorca
language: catalan
measure: barcella, misura
weight: artal, cargo, corta, libra, mayor, ratel, quartano
BALEFUL: *bad, deadly, *sad
BALI: *demon, *dwarf, oblation
capital: den pasar
dance: ardja, baris, djanger, ketjak, kriss, sanghyang
dish: riasi goring, sate
masked players: darma an djaja
musical instrument: gamelang
rice field: sawaii
temple: batur, samantiga

* Asterisk means to look up this word to find more answer words.

volcano: agung
winged creature: garuda
BALK: **avoid, *refuse, *stop*
BALKAN: *bandit:* haiduk, hey-
  duke
 coin: novcic
 instrument: gusla, gusle
 ridged area: bilo
BALKY: mulish, **obstinate*
BALL: casaba, dance, **sphere*
 and chain: burden, wife
 club: eleven, nine, team
 of fire: genius, whiz
 of snow: sneezewort
 of wax: **package*, situation
 player: athlete
 rose: cranberry
 thistle: artichoke
 up: complicate, mix up, **upset*
BALLET: *artist:* danseuse
 term: allonge, arabesque, aterre,
  ballonne, barre, battlement, bat-
  terie, bourree, brise, broadleap,
  brush, cabriole, chaine, chasse,
  coupe, developpe, fouette, glissade, jete, leap, pas de bourree,
  passe, pirouette, pile, pointe,
  sissone, tutu
BALLOON: **bag*, puff, swell, toy
 basket: car, gondola, nacelle
 fish: porcupine fish
 flower: platycodon grandiflorum
 sail: spinnaker
 vine: cardiospermum halicacabum
BALLY: bloody, **good*
 gum: litsea, tree
 hack: destruction, perdition
 -hoo: **noise*, outcry, uproar
 -rag: **abuse*, bully, **plague*
BALM: anodyne, ointment, salve,
  solace, spikenard, **remedy*
BALMY: aromatic, **silly, *soft*
BALONEY: humbug, **nonsense*
BALSAM: amyris, balm, bikkia,
  copaiba, liard, tolu, torchwood,
  tree, wilga
 apple: amargoso, ampalaya

bog: azorella, sphagnous
-copaiba: wilga, tree
extract: toluene
fig: clusia, scotch attorney
fir: amyris, balm of gilead
groundsel: senecia
herb: costmary
hickory: carya ovalis, tree
resin: benzoin, plant
of mecca: perfume
of peru: myroxylon
of umiri: humiria, resin
root: ageratum, boltonia
pear: momordica charantia
poplar: amyris, tacahamac
shrub: torchroot
weed: celandine, everlasting
BALTEUS: band, belt, **walk*
BALTIC: *barge:* praam
 finn: vod
 gulf: riga
 island: alsen, ahvenanmaa, dago,
  oesel, oland, osel, ossel
BALUCHISTAN: *capital:* kelat
 grain: jowar
 mountain: hala, kohistan
 race: brahoes, mari, marri
 river: bolan, dashi, gaj, moola
 state: kalat, khelat, lus
BAMBOO: cane, nandin, spinosa
 brier: smilax
 curtain: barrier, border, china
 fern: coniogramme
 fish: box salpa, sparida
 hut: basha
 pickled shoots: achar
 sugar: tabasheer
BAN: **banish*, curse, taboo
BANA: *conqueror:* krishna
 daughter: usha
BANAL: **dull, *stupid*
BANANA: *-bird:* oriole, icterus
 bunch: hand, stem
 disease: big foot, blackhead
 fish: albula, ladyfish
 land: queensland
 -leaf: frond

* **Asterisk means to look up this word to find more answer words.**

-like: plantain
moth: pisang
oil: *nonsense, rot, softsoap
-quit: coereba, creeper
plant: musa, penang
root borer: snout beetle
water lily: nymphaea mexicana
BAND: *group, cummerbund, *staff
-aid: adhesive, dressing
armed: askari, host, posse
brain: ligula
dance: combo, orchestra
-decorative: cornice
framing: architrave, archivolt
-garment-fastening: patte
leader: conductor, maestro
narrow: stria, tape
ornamental: bracelet
plant: periwinkle, vinca
small: bandelette
together: *gather, *unite
trousers, about: boyang
wheel: rigger
BANDAGE: *dress, swathe, wrap
fastener: ligator
nose: accipiter
surgical: fascia, spica
BANDIT: *criminal, *thief
BANE: *affliction, *plague
BANEFUL: *bad, *evil, *ugly
BANG: *beat, blow, bust, crump, detonation, explosion, *force, *hit, kick, *narcotic, *power
beggar: beadle
into: collide, crash, *hit
-off: at once
on: apropos, pertinent
tail: geegee, racehorse
up: blighty, crack, excellent
BANGER: lie, specie, whopper
BANGING: *big, *great, huge
BANISH: *discharge, *dismiss, exile, ostracize, *punish, rusticate, send to coventry
BANI: *son:* amram, amzi, uel
BANK: berm, buttress, depend,

deposit, fortify, heap, pile, reckon, rely, *save, *store
acceptance: certificate
account: capital, funds
beaver: otter
bird: phlarope
book: log, *record
credit: cash account
cress: barbarea, hedge mustard
dominoes: boneyard
examiner: accountant
fish: cod
jug: bird, willow warbler
martin: swallow
note: bill, paper money
on: count on, expect, rely
pert.: riparian
piggy: knippel, pishke, pushkeh
rider: bogier
robber: burglar
-roll: cash, *support, wad
-rupt: broke, failure
thistle: bull thistle, musk
weed: hedge mustard
BANKER: backer, guarantor, dealer, saraf, seth, teller
BANNER: *badge, *flag, *symbol
cloth: bunting
cloud: cloudcap, pileus
fish: istiophorus, sailfish
man: publicist, standard bearer
plant: anthurium
pompano: trachinotus palometa
BANQUET: carousal, dine, feast, festival, repast, spread
BANTAM: feisty, *small, tiny
BANTER: borak, chaff, guy, *joke, josh, persiflage, rag, rib, ridicule, *taunt, twit
BANTU: bashilange, baya, ejam, ekoi, gogo, goma, guha, jaga, kaffir, luba, rua, soga, swazi, tswana, xhosa, yaka, zulu
BANZAI: *attack, *cry, *reckless
BAOBAB: sourgourd, tree
BAPTISM: aspergation, immersion

font: basin, spring
opponent: catabaptist
vessel: font, laver, piscina
BAR: ban, bolt, grill, jimmy, lock, saloon, *stop,* *tavern
door: lock, risp, stang
fly: carouser, *drunk,* stiff
legally: estop
goose: sheldrake
gown: lawyer
millstone: rynd
pressure-resisting: strut
screen: grizzly
sinister: stigma
soap frame: sess
steel: bull point, bull prick
supporting: fid, rod, stanchion
tamping: stemmer
window: forcing, jemmy, jimmy
BARB: awn, bristle, dart, mot
anchor: flue
feather: harl, pinnula, ramus
the dart: pain
BARBADOS: *capital:* bridgetown
gooseberry: blade apple, cactus
lily: amaryllis, hippeastrum
liquor: rum
native: bim
pride: bear tree, flower fence, peacock flower, red sandalwood
BARBARIAN: alien, brute, goth, hun, primitive, vandal, *wild
troops: caterva
BARBARISM: caconym, solecism
BARBARY: *ape:* magot, simian
buttons: snail clover
fig: opuntia, prickly pear
sheep: aoudad
states: algiers, morocco, tripoli, tunis
thorn: cat's-claw
BARBECUE: bake, broil, grill
rod: skewer, spit
BARBER: cut, dress, figaro, frost, smoke, shaver, tonsor
bug: barbeiro, conenose
fifth brother: alnaschar

fish: anthias, surgeon fish
itch: ringworm
shop: beauty parlor, quartet
BARBET: puffbird, poodle
BARBICAN: *fortification,* *tower
BARBITURATE: *drug:* addictive
BARD: bhat, minstrel, troubadour
BARDY: audacious, *bold,* defiant
BARE: blank, bleak, divulge, nude, *open,* ordinary, *plain,* *poor, *simple,* stark, *strip
back: saddleless
-faced: impudent, shameless
-fisted: brawly, *brutal,* rough
poles: spars
skin: buff
BARELY: all but, faint, hardly, jimp, merely, only, scarcely
BARGAIN: a bon marche, agree, beat down, bid, buy, chaffer, deal, dicker, haggle, money's worth, negotiate, steal, *trade
and sale: barter
-basement: cheap, tawdry
for: bring on, expect
penny: arles, earnest
BARGE: collide, *scold,* scow
BARK: abrade, advertise, *alarm, clamor, command, cough, crut, *protest,* *skin,* *snarl,* *yelp
aromatic: canella, sassafras
at: *rebuke,* *scold
beetle: borer, dendroctonus
bitter: angostura, cinchona, niepa, niota, quinine
-bound: prudish
canoe: cascara
cloth: brachystegia, tapa, tree
exterior: ross
fiber: olona
having: corticated
inner: bast, cortex, liber
medical: casca, cinchona, coto, mudar, quinine, sassafras
outer: periderm
pert.: cortical
remove: ross, scale, spud

* Asterisk means to look up this word to find more answer words.

up the wrong tree: err, stray
BARKER: dog, gun, speiler, tout
BARKING: latrant, loud, noisy
deer: muntjac
frog: robber frog
iron: spud
squirrel: prairie dog
BARLEY: *cry*, grain, ptisan
beer: chang
-bird: siskin, nightingale, wagtail, wryneck
4-rowed: big(g)
disease: scale, stripe
-gree: liquor
ground: tsamba
island: alehouse, pub, saloon
malt globulin: byndestin
meal divination: alphitomancy
parched: tsamba
pert.: hordeaceous
-sick: intoxicated, stiff
6-rowed: bere
steep: malt
water: ptisan, tisane
BARLOW: jackknife
plate: flinders bar
BARMY: scatterbrained, silly
BARN: cowshed, mew, stable
dance: hoedown, *party*, social
grass: ankee, cockspur, millet
owl: lulu, tyto
part: bag, hayloft, mow, stall
BARNACLE: incumbent, parasite
back: mariner, veteran
body: capitulum
BARNACLES: glasses, spectacles
BARNEY: brawl, free-for-all, hoax, put-up-job, row, rumpus
-clapper: lily-of-the-valley
BARNSTORM: campaign, stump
BARNYARD: bucolic, corny
golf: horseshoes
BARONG: cleaver, knife, *sword*
BAROQUE: gauche, outre, rococo
BARRACK: billet, camp, canaba
BARRACKS: bullpen, *camp*
bag: equipment, luggage

lawyer: unqualified authority
BARRANCA: arroyo, gorge, gully
BARRACUDA: pelon, sennet, spet
BARREL: *quantity*, *receptacle*
herring: cade
-house: dive, jazz, saloon, pub
maker: cooper, tubber, tubman
-organ: autophon
palm: hyophorbe
part: gantry, hoop, side, stave
raising device: parbuckle
BARREN: *arid*, sterile, *stupid*
oak: blackjack, cerris
privet: alatern, houseleek
shoot: apoblast
-wort: bishop's-hat, epimedium
BARRICADE: abatis, *fort*, *stop*
BARRIER: alp, buffer, obstacle
BARRING: except, save, without
BARRIO: ghetto, slum, village
BARROW: *memorial*, swine
boy: costermonger
BARTENDER: mixer, tapster
BARTER: *bargain*, *trade*
BASE: *bad*, *foundation*
arch: dado, plinth, socle
attached by: sessil
-ball founder: abner doubleday
boom: woadwaxen
born: *low*, *mean*, plebeian
coin: counterfeit
fellow: carl, churl
-hearted: mean-spirited
hit: bingle, double, homer, looper, single, triple
marker: bag
metal: alloy, black metal
military: camp, depot, station
on balls: pass, walk
tree: laburnum
vervain: germander speedwell
wallah: soldier
BASELESS: *false*, idle, *vain*
BASH: blow, party, swat, wham
BASHEMATH: *husband:* esau
BASHFUL: coy, modest, *shy*
billy: animal, slow loris

* Asterisk means to look up this word to find more answer words.

BASIC: elemental, essential
 basalt: araphite
 facts: alphabet, abc's
 lead carbonate: ceruse
 magenta: fuchsin
 material: body
 military unit: cadre
 protein: arbacin
BASIL: crown, mint, ocimum
 balm: clinopodium, thyme
 mint: penny royal, pycanthemum
 thyme: bed's-fot, clinopodium
 weed: clinopodium vulgare
BASIN: bowl, tub, *waterway
BASIS: base, anlage, premise
BASK: apricate, revel, *warm
BASKET: *quantity, *receptacle
 -ball: casaba, pelota, sphere
 -ball founder: dr james naismith
 ball player: cager, hoopman
 ball team: five, cagemen
 balloon: car, nacelle
 bearer: canephora, canephoros
 boat: coracle
 coal: corb, corf
 eel: buck
 fern: nephrolepsis
 fig: caba, frail, tapnet
 fish: astrophyton, caul, cawl, corf,
    crail, crate, creel, gabion, ham-
    per, hask, maund, pannier, sea
    spider, wicker
 fruit: caba, frail, molly, pottle,
    punnet
 grass: turkey beard
 material: osier, otate
 palm: talipot
 rummy: canasta, game
 star: echinoderm, wattle
 strip: rand
 twig: wattle
 water-tight: wattape
 wicker: bassinet, cobb, coop, ham-
    per, hanaper, willy
 willow: osier, prickle
 withe: heliotropium, vine
 work: cabas, slarth, tee, wale

BASQUE: scoter, iberian, waist
 cap: beret
 dance: aurrescu, zortizico
 game: pelota
 hello: alo nola zera
 language: euskara, uskara
 petticoat: basquine
 province: alava
 shirt: pullover, knitted
BASS: brasse, iyo, perch, shale
 fiber: pissava, raphia
 group: shoal
 killy: may fish
 -wood: bast, lin, linden, tilia
BAST: catena, flax, hemp, jute,
    phloem, piassava, ramie
 father: amen, amon
BASTARD: adulterate, artificial,
    fake, *false, illicit, odd
BAT: blow, club, spree, vampire
 around: debate, ponder, roam
 european: barbastel(le)
 fruit: peca
 fish: diablo, ray, stingray
 -minded: blind, obtuse
 of an eye: instant
 the breeze: *gossip, *talk
 tree: evergreen magnolia
BATAVIA: djakarta
BATCH: bunch, *group, *quantity
BATEAU: boat, dhow, pontoon
BATH: dip, ruin, soak, swim
 comb.: balneo
 asparagus: star-of-bethlehem
 attendant: aleiptes, aliptes
 flower: trillium
 house: bagnio, cabana, lavatory
 king: beau nash
 luxurious: bubble bath
 metal: brass
 pert.: balneal, balneatory
 sponge: loofah, luffa
 treatment: balneotherapy
 tub: bassinet, tosh
 -wort: birthroot, plant
BATHOS: comedown, mawkish-
    ness

* Asterisk means to look up this word to find more answer words.

BATHSHEBA: *husband:* uriah, david
father: eliam
son: solomon
BATON: cudgel, *staff, *symbol
BATTER: *beat, *mixture, pelt
dock: butter bur, pond weed
cake: waffle
BATTERY: artillery, beating
floating: cell, parapet, praam
metal: lead
part: cable, cell, charger, grid, plate, post, terminal
BATTLE: *action, *fight
area: arena, front, sector
array: acies, herse, *order
ax: oldster, shrew, wife
cry: abu, alala, banzai, slogan
frogs vs mice: batrachomyomachy
last: armageddon
quoit: chakra
trophy: medal, ribbon, scalp
BATTUE: massacre, slaughter
BATTY: crazy, *insane, *silly
BAUBLE: gewgaw, gimcrack, toy
BAWD: dirty, madam, pander
BAWL: *cry, boohoo, glaster
BAY: *-bay:* byrsonima, locust
bean: canavalia lineata
berry: cinnamon, wild clove
bark: candleberry, tonic
oil: laurel butter
bird: curlew, godwit, plover
bush: sweet gale
camphor: laurin
cedar: tassel plant
coot: surf scoter
gall: marsh, swampland
hops: seabeach morning glory
lambs: scotch pine flowers
laurel: oleander
michel de: baius
plum: guava
poplar: nyssa, tupelo gum
state: massachusetts
sweet: brewster
window: belly, oriel, paunch

-winged bunting: vesper sparrow
BAYONET: agave, dagger, datil, *kill, palm, *pierce, yucca
BAYOU: *waterway
BEACH: *apple:* fir marigold
aster: erigeron, seaside daisy
bird: knot, plover, snipe
comber: vagabond, vagrant, wave
flea: amphipod, crustacean
goldenrod: solidago
grass: ammophila, arenaria, bent star, marram
-head: foothold, landing, van
-la-mar: jargon
master: bull seal
-sap: sea-rocket
wormwood: dusty miller
BEACON: *light:* cresset, lantern
BEACONSFIELD: d'israeli
BEAD: ball, drop, *sphere, *tear
glass: bugle
roll: list, novena, roster
string: chaplet, rosary
BEADLE: bang beggar, bumble
harriett: tattycoram
BEADY: bulbous, glittery, *small
BEAGLE: copy, dog, shark, *spy
BEAKER: cup, glass, goblet, jug
BEAMY: bright, radiant, *thick
BEAN: *eye:* hilum
fly: midas
gregoire: cockeye, damselfish
kind: castor, goa, navy, soy
lima: haba
locust: carob
mexican: frijole
plant: licorice, locust, senna
poisonous: calabar, eserine
shooter: catapult, slingshot
shrub: broom, ilex, ulex
town: boston
tree: agati, carob, catalpa, sapan
weed: butterwort
weevil: haria, obtectus
BEANY: *crazy, high-fed, tam
BEAR: *accept, *enthusiast, pessimist, *stand, *yield

* Asterisk means to look up this word to find more answer words.

comb.: arct(o), ursi
down: exert, **press*, stress
fruit: deliver, prosper, thrive
garden: arena, **noise*, tumult
group: sloth
mat: mountain misery
off: attain, deviate, flee
out: authenticate, confirm
teddy: koala
the brunt: endure, suffer
upon: affect, concern, **urge*
with: condone, endure, **suffer*
BEARD: awn, hair, oppose, tease
BEARER: carrier, servant, sirdar
BEARING: demeanor, position
BEARISH: blunt, grump, negative
BEAST: **animal*, brute, savage
of burden: ass, dromedary, elephant, hathi, horse, mule, onager, oont, ox, percheron
BEAT: **bang*, **circle*, **defeat*, **hit*, **meter*, **punish*, **sphere*
it: scram, skiddoo, vamoose
BEATIFY: bless, canonize, gladde, glorify, delight
BEAU: flame, **love*, **spark*
brummel: coxcomb, dandy, fop
geste: good turn, favor
gregory: damselfish
ideal: beauty, model, paradigm
monde: fashion, society
sabreur: adventurer, murat
BEAUTIFUL: comely, **fine*, **good*, gorgeous, **pretty*, **pure*
comb.: bel, calli, calo
BEAVER: animal, armor, beard, cloth, rodent, top hat
BECKON: entice, nod, summon
BECOMING: apt, flair, seemly
BED: base, **rest*, **waterway*
BEE: insect, notion, social, wax
bread: ambrosia, cerago
colony: bike, hive, swarm
comb.: api
female: queen
house: alveary, apiary, hive
male: drone

pert.: apian, apiarian
tree: basswood, linden
BEECH: buck, fagus, flindosa, hornbeam, myrtle, roble, tree
drops: orobancha, squawroot
BEEF: **fight*, gripe, **power*
cut: baron, brisket, chuck, loin, miroton, rib, round
dried: bucan, charqui, jerky
made with: bouillon
pickled: bully
salted: junk, salt horse
spiced: pastrami
tinned: bullamacow
-wood: belah, belar, tree
BEEFY: **heavy*, **strong*, **thick*
BEEK: bask, harden, shine, **warm*
BEEP: signal, sound, tone, toot
BEER: brew, grog, kvas, suds
and skittles: fun, **play*
barley: chang
cask: butt
ingredient: hops, malt
king: gambrinus
money: allowance
mug: **vessel: drinking*
parlor: **drinking: place*
BEETLE: amara, dor, gogo, stag
-browed: morose, scowling
click: dor, elater, tora
fire: cucuyo
gaudy: ladybug
grain: cadelle
grapevine: thrip
ground: amara, fidia
head: goldeneye duck, plover
headed god: khepri
horny substance: chitin
larva: birch borer
mustard: blackjack
oil: meloe
pepper: itmorhinoceros, uang
sacred: scarab
slender: agrilus
snout: curculo
BEFORE: front, prior, rather

* Asterisk means to look up this word to find more answer words.

comb.: ac, ad, an, ante, at, avant, ob, prae, pre
long: by and by, soon
BEG: **appeal,* bone, cadge, evade, panhandle, pass the hat
BEGET: **author,* sire, **yield*
BEGGAR: arnaeus, bacach, dog, fakir, hobo, idler, lazar, mendicant, pariah, sannyasi
all description: bloom
king: carew
lice: achene, bidens, marigold
licensed: beadsman, bluegown
saint: alexius, giles
BEGGAR'S: *blanket:* mullein
needle: lady's-comb
BEGIN: break, fang, **fire,* **get,* **issue,* kick off, **open,* pioneer, **start,* take off
BEGINNER: abecedarian, boot, candidate, deb, neophyte, novice, novitiate, postulate, pupil, student, trainee, tyro
BEGINNING: **opening,* **start*
BEGONE: avaunt, away, cheese it, get, git, off, out, scat, shoo, skiddoo, vamoose, va-t'en, wag
BEGUILE: **amuse,* charm, dupe, gull, hoax, lure, **trick,* vamp
BEGUM: clog, empress, soil, widow
BEHALF: advantage, affair, stead
BEHAVE: **act,* **bear,* work
BEHAVIOR: gestalt, **walk,* way
BEHEN: bladder campion, centaury
BEHEST: bid, command, law, **will*
BEHIND: **after,* derriere, tot
the eightball: endangered, sunk
the scenes: hidden, invisible
the times: old-fashioned
BEHOLD: **look,* **see,* vise, viola
BEHOOF: **advantage,* profit, **use*
BEH'S SON: iri
BEIGE: ecru, grege, hopi, tan
BEING: brahma, creature, life
abstract: ens, entia

actual: esse
as how: since
done: conventional, popular
in front: anteal, leading, van
on hand: here, present
physiological: bion
science of: ontology
simple: amoeba, monad
spirit of: ens, entia
suff.: ure
three signs: anatman, anatia
BEJA: bishari, hamite, hanendoa
son: iri
BEL: golden apple, **lord,* owner
child: ninurta
-esprit: wit
wife: belit, beltis
BELA SON: ard, ezbon, iri, uzzi
BELAIT: europe
BELAY: invest, **quit,* **secure*
BELDAM: fury, **hag,* **witch*
BELEAGUER: **attack,* siege
BELGIAN: fleming, walloon
ancient tribe: bellevaci
anthem: brabanconne
commune: ans, ath, tamies
endive: witloof
gaul tribe: remi, nervii
horse: brabancon
lowland: polder
marble: rance, ranse
BELIAL: **demon,* **devil,* satan
BELIEF: credo, **doctrine,* doxy
BELIEVE: **accept,* **think,* **trust*
BELL: carillon, signal, tocsin
axle-bearing: cod
bird: arapunga, campanero, cotinga, mako, procnias, shrike
book and candle: excommunication
bottoms: trousers
boy: page, porter, redcap
clapper: tongue
cow: leader
ear: cannon
kind of: cow, church, door, gong
maker: yaktayvian

* Asterisk means to look up this word to find more answer words.

metal: stannite
ring the: score, succeed, *win*
pert.: campanular, campanulate
shaped: campaniform
sound: bong, ding, dong, knell
the cat: attempt, brave, *try*
tongue: clapper
tower: belfry, campanile
tree: snowdrop
weed: knapweed
wort: campanula, daffodil
BELLADONNA: manicon, nightshade
poisoning: atropism
BELLIGERENT: choleric, hostile
BELLINI OPERA: norma, puritani
  sonnambula
sleepwalker: amina
BELLOW: bawl, roar, wail, yawp
BELLY: bouk, gut, pot, *stomach*
-*ache:* *complain,* *cry*
-*ful:* *plenty,* *quantity*
pert.: alvine, visceral
wash: beer, coffee, slop, soda
BELONG: apply, bear, go, inhere
BELONGING: *asset,* natural
suff.: aceous, al, an, ar, ary
BELOW: down, *hell,* sotto, under
par: mediocre, off, sick
standard: *bad,* inferior, worse
the belt: *dirty,* foul
the mark: inferior, substandard
the salt: plebeian
zero: cold, freezing, gelid
BELT: band, *beat,* *drink,* *whip*
conveyor: apron
ecclesiastical: balteus
line: waist
man: lifeguard
of calms: the doldrums
sword: baldric, bawdric
BELUGA: caviar, huso, whale
BELUS: *child:* aegyptus, cepheus,
  danaus, dido, ninus, phineus
parent: libya
twin: agenor
BEMUSE: addle, confuse, distract

BEN: hill, hog, peak, seed, son
BENCH: pull out, subs, zygon
chervil: parsley
church: pew, pue, sedile
hook: cramp
made: custom-made
plane handle: tote
warmer: idler, scrub, sub
BEND: *accept,* flex, *yield*
an ear: listen, prate, *talk*
backward: retort
one's steps: pursue, travel
over backward: go all out, *try*
rope: bight
sinister: stigma
the knee: salaam
the elbow: drink
timber: sny
to one's will: dominate
-*wise:* diagonal
BENDER: guzzler, *party,* *tear*
BENEATH: *below,* unworthy
contempt: offensive, paltry
the sod: buried, dead, gone
BENEDICTION: grace, prayer
BENEFICE: cure, fief, income
BENEFIT: *abet,* event, *interest,*
  profit, *service,* *use,* *value*
BENEVOLENCE: *good,* *love*
BENGAL: *ant thrush:* nurang
bison: gaur
boat: batel, bateau, dhow
capital: dacca
caste member: baidya
cotton: adati, adaty
cultivation: joom, jum
district: dacca, nadia
gentlemen: baboo
gram: chick pea
grass: millet
groom: saice, syce
hemp: sunn
measure: cottah, chattack
mendicant: baul
native: banian, eboe, kol
quince: bael, bel, bhel
root: cassumunar

* Asterisk means to look up this word to find more answer words.

sectist or singer: baul
soldier: sepoy
thrush: nurang
tree: bola
BENIGN: **good,* suave, tender
BENJAMIN: balsam, trillium
  clan head: iri
  descendant: aher
  mess: plurality, share
  son: bela, ehi, gera, rosh
  tree: ficus, spice bush, styrax
  tribe: belaites
BENNY: amphetamine, benzedrine, hat, overcoat, pill, tablet
BENT: **disposition, *gift, *turn*
  grass: agrostis
  like a bow: arcuate
  star: beach grass
  upward: antrose
BEQUEATH: commit, endow
BERATE: **abuse, *rebuke, *scold*
BERBER: hamite, haratin, moor
  chief: caid, qaid
  tribe: daza, riff, tibu, tuareg
BEREFT: barren, destitute, lost
BERGAMOT: essence, mint,
  orange, pear, perfume, rug, snuff
  camphor: bergaptene
  mint: mentha citrata
BERI BERI: dropsy, kakki
BERM: bank, brim, **edge,* ledge
BERMUDA: *arrowroot:* ararao,
  araru, maranta arundinacea
  barracuda: spet
  berry: soap berry
  buttercup: oxalis cernua
  catfish: coelho
  ceremony: gombay
  flag: iris, blue-eyed grass
  grass: devil grass, doob, doub
  lily: easter lily, trumpet
  shilling: hog money
  snowberry: chiococca
BERRY: *comb.:* bacci
  bearing: bacciferous
  fish: coccosteus, fossil fish
  disease: blue stem

medicinal: cubeb
oil: olive
pert.: baccaceous, baccate
shrub: elder, holly, salal
BERSERK: amok, **mad, *violent*
BERTH: billet, dock, job, post
BERYX: alfonsin
BESEECH: **ask,* obsecrate, sue
BESET: **attack,* harry, worry
BESIDES: and, except, then, too
BESIEGE: **attack, *plague*
BESOM: broom, mop, strigil
BESOT: **dull,* infatuate, stupefy
BESPANGLE: **adorn, *ornament*
BESPEAK: **address, *ask,* imply
BEST: **acme,* a-one, champion,
  *defeat, gem, nonpareil, pick,
  *prize, *supreme, *top, *win
  comb.: arist, aristo
BESTEAD: **abet,* assist, help
BESTIAL: **brutal,* feral, savage
BESTOW: **add,* aid, **give, *use*
BET: **ante,* back, contribute, fade,
  hedge, kick in, make book, raise,
  play, plunge, pot, risk, shot,
  *venture, vie
  broker: bookmaker
  fail to pay: renege, welch
  faro: sleeper
  roulette: bas, carre, dernier
BETAKE: boun, grant, repair
BETCHERI: **fine, *good*
BETE: atone, beast, improve, repair, repent, silly, **stupid*
  noire: bugbear, hate, terror
  rouge: chigger, bed bug
BETEL: areca, bonga, buyo, catechu, ikmo, itmo, pan, paun, pepper, penang, puan, seri, siri(h)
BETHEL: chapel, hostel, refuge
BETIDE: chance, occur, presage
BETISE: folly, stupidity
BETOKEN: augur, evince, portend
BETRAY: **blab,* cross up, inform,
  quisle, seduce, **show,* squeal,
  stab, **tell, *trick,* two-time
BETROTH: affy, **promise, *token*

* Asterisk means to look up this word to find more answer words.

BETTER: aid, rectify, more, *top
 half: mate, spouse, wife
BETTING: adviser: tout
 figures: odds, price
 machine: pari-mutuel
 system: parlay
BETTY: dessert, solitaire
BETULA: beat, birch, samara
 camphor: beulin, beulinol
 glandulosa: dwarf bush
 oil: methyl salicylate
BETWEEN: amid, entre
 law: mesne
 pref.: dia, inter, meta
 scylla and charybdis: *dilemma
 -the lines: latent, *secret
 times: occasionally
 us: bosom, confidentially
BEVEL: angle, cant, *edge, fleam,
 miter, oblique, slant, snape
 corners: splay
 out: ream
BEVERAGE: apple: bunnell
 alcoholic: *drink: alcoholic
BEVIS: victim: ascopart
 immortality: ambrosia, amrita,
 haoma, rasa, sama, soma
BEVY: *group, muster, suite
BEWAIL: *complain, *cry, regret
BEWARE: *avoid, caveat, shun
BEWILDER: addle, buffalo, bush,
 muddle, nonplus, *puzzle, *stop
BEWITCH: charm, ensorcel, hex
BEWITH: makeshift, substitute
BEWRAY: *betray, malign, reveal
BEYOND: above, *after
 all expectation: successfully
 all praise: *perfect
 a shadow of doubt: certain
 belief: amazing, incredible
 compare: peerless
 control: impossible, refractory
 doubt: all right, certainly
 help: done for, finished
 him: over his head
 limits: excess, out of bounds
 one: excess, too much

 pref.: sur, meta, ultra
 price: dear, valuable, worthy
 question: absolute, certain
 reach: inaccessible
 recall: hopeless
 seas: abroad, travelling
 the ability: too much
 the bounds of reason: absurd
 the pale: too far, too much
 understanding: unintelligible
BEZEL: *edge, face, template
BEZOAR: calculus, coprolite
 goat: pasang
 mineral: antimony oxide
BEZZLE: plunder, *steal, *tear
BHAGAVAT: blessed, hindu
BHANG: hashish, hemp, narcotic
BHANGI: scavenger, untouchable
BHIKKU: *church man, *monk
BHOOT: *demon, ghost, goblin
B'HOY: *criminal, *hoodlum
BHUTAN: disease: dha
 pine: kail
 recruit: jawan
 robe: bakkhu
 religion: bon, shamanism
BIAS: bigotry, cant, deviate
 son: areus
BIB: apron, cloth, *cover, *drink
BIBELOT: *ornament, *token
BIBLE: book, gospel, scripture
 animal: ass, behemoth, daman,
 hydrax, shapan, reem
 apocrypha: baruch, bel, daniel,
 esdras, esther, jeremiah, judith,
 maccabees, manasseh, sirach,
 snake, solomon, song of the
 three, susanna, syriac, tobit, wisdom
 battle: armageddon, jericho
 chamberlain: carcas
 charioteer: jehu
 christian: bryanite
 clan: shelah
 class organization: baraca
 coin: daric, mite, shekel
 desert: paran

* Asterisk means to look up this word to find more answer words.

disease: leprosy, plague
eagle: gier
field: ager, aner
fortress: dathema
garden: eden, uzza
garment: beged, cesuth, pethigi
giant: anakim, behemoth, emim,
goliath, leviathan, samson, zam-
zummim, zuzim
gold source: ophir
liar: ananias
peaks: ararat, carmel, eba, ezem,
ezra, gadi, horeb, nebo, olivet,
peor, pisgah, seir, shigionoth,
sinai, thanach
ornament: thummin, urim
pause: selah
plains: jericho, mamre, pilar
plenty, land of: goshen, ophir
plotter: haman
pool: siloah, siloam
priest: *ecclesiastic:* hebrew
prophet: *prophet: famous*
queen: abi, esther, jezebel
reading substitute: kere, qeri
scholar: biblicist, elohist
society: gideon
spice: frankincense, myrrh
transgression: averah
weed: tare
witch: endor
BIBLIA REGIA: polyglot
BICKER: *argue,* fuss, quibble
BID: *ask,* *offer,* *order,* say
ale: benefit, commorth
defiance: resist, withstand
fair: bargain, court, volunteer
farewell: depart, take leave
BIDDY: fuss budget, hen, servant
-biddy: piripiri
BIELD: dwell, refuge, shelter
BIEN: *good,* prosperous
BIER: catafalque, pyre, tabut
BIFF: blow, *hit,* punch, *strike*
BIFURCATE: branch, fork, split
BIG: bouncing, chief, *fat,* grand,
great, *heavy,* huge, loud, *lib-*

eral, magnanimous, powerful, rotund, *thick,* vast
baby: coward, weakling
bed bug: cone nose
beef: powerhouse, stalwart
bend state: tennessee
cottonwood: necklace poplar
drink: ocean, sea
eye: catalufa, priacanthus
-eyed: astonished, impressed
game: decisive, *prize,* quarry
head: conceit, goby, sculpin
-hearted: *kind,* magnanimous
house: penitentiary, *jail*
idea: *plan,* *purpose*
-league: *important,* major
lie: propaganda
muddy: mississippi river
one: *lie,* *story,* whopper
push: *attack,* drive, offensive
shot: *head,* *lord,* *magnate*
stick: *force,* *power,* terror
talk: bluster, bragging, *noise*
time: broadway, majors, *party*
top: circus, tent, theatre
BIGENER: hybrid, mule
BIGHORN: aoudad, argali, sheep
BIGHT: angle, bay, loop, noose
BILBO: bolt, footlock, rapier
BILE: choler, spleen, venom
deficiency: acholia
cyst: gall bladder
pigment: bilirubin, biliverdin
BILK: *cheat,* *deceive,* *trick*
BILL: beak, card, dun, law, menu
and coo: court, kiss, make love
board: ad, announce, outdoor
-bug: grass-eater, weevil
fish: gar, saury, spearfish
five-dollar: fin, vee
-fold: pocketbook, purse, wallet
head: *address,* *title*
hook: dhaw, knife, snagger
of fare: carte, list, menu
one-dollar: buck, frogskin
stroke: masse, pick
ten-dollar: sawbuck

* Asterisk means to look up this word to find more answer words.

BILLABONG: *waterway
BILLET: allot, berth, stay
-doux: capon, love letter
BILLIARD: rod: cue, mace
shot: bricole, carom, masse
BILLINGSGATE: *abuse, fish-market, vituperation
BILLIONTH: comb.: bicro
BILLOW: bore, eagre, roller, sea
BILLY: baton, club, goat, male
blind: *demon, game, *spirit
boy: barge
brighteye: germander speedwell
button: burdock, daisy, geranium, red campion
clipper: bindweed
cock: bowler, derby, wide-awake
the kid: bonney
white's buttons: stitchwort
wix: tawny owl
BILSH: brat, luster, *monster
BIMBO: loose woman, man, tramp
BIN: ark, box, crib, *store
-burn: discolored, heated, poor
coal: bunker
fish: canch, kench
BIND: *adhere, *dress, *fetter, gyve, manacle, *tie, truss
comb.: desmo
over: indenture
to secrecy: tile, tyle
up in: *absorb
weed: billy clipper, senecio
wood: english ivy
BINDER: contract, girdle, ring
BINDING: fabric, selvage
limp: yapp
machine: baler
BINDLE STIFF: hobo, tramp
BING: bedroll, heap, pile, sound
boy: *soldier
BINGE: *drunk, *party, *tear
BINGO: bang, brandy, lotto, ring
BINT: daughter, girl, woman
BIOLOGICAL: class: genus
decadence: paracme
factor: gene, id, idant

fissure: rima
division: genera
weapon: armature
BIOLOGIST: *life: scientist
BIOLOGY: *dna, *life: science
BIOTA: flora and fauna
BIRCH: alder, ansu, betula, whip
borer: beetle
camphor: betulin(ol)
-leaf mahogany: hardtack
man: schoolmaster
of jamaica: gumbo limbo
partridge: ruffed grouse
BIRD: boo, chap, fellow, gink, girl, guy, oddity, saucer
apteryx: iao, kiwi, moa, oweni
aquatic: avocet, coot, crane, dabshick, godwit, hern, heron, ibis, jacana, rail, snipe, sora, stilt, stork, tern
black: amsel, ani, daw, darr, merl(e), jackdaw, ouzel, pie
bob-white: colin, quail
brain: dunce, dolt, *fool
crying: limpkin, ramage
extinct: auk, dodo, moa, roc
-eye: cuckooflower
gallinaceous: peacock, rasores
group: bank, bevy, brood, covey
house: aviary, cote, nest, nid
in hand: possession
in the bush: prickly poppy
jay-like: magpie, piet
lamellirostral: duck, flamingo
-like: agile, light, quick
limicoline: avocet
male: chanticleer, cob, cock, drake, gander, tom, rooster
myth: hansa, phoenix, roc, rook, rukh, simurg(h)
non-passerine: hoopoe, hornbill, kingfisher, motmot, tody
of freedom; of love: eagle
of juno: peacock
of paradise: apodis, cardinal, manucode, regent, strelitzia
of passage: transient, wanderer

* Asterisk means to look up this word to find more answer words.

of peace: dove
of prey: accipiter, buzzard, eagle, elanet, falcon, goshawk, kestrel, kite, owl, vulture
  pert.: accipital, accipitrine
of wonder: phenix, phoenix
oscine: bunyah, *titmouse
passerine: finch, pita, sparrow
  pert.: avian, avicular, ornithic
raptores: eagle, hawk, owl
ratite: emu, moa, ostrich
sea: auk, cahow, ern, fulmar, gannet, gull, kestrel, murre, petrel, puffin, scaup, skua
song: *song: bird
talking: magg, mina, parrot
tropical: barbet, jacamar, jacana, koae, mankin, toco, tody, toucan, trogon
unfledged: eyas, gor(lin), quab
web-footed: duck, goose, swan
witted: flighty, shallow
young: chick, eya, flapper, fledgling, nestling, piper
BIRL: gamble, rotate, *turn
BIRN: brand, burden, stem
BIRR: blow, *force, *storm
BIRSE: beard, *storm, *temper
BIRSLE: broil, scorch, toast
BIRTH: blood, race, *start
 by: nee
 child: blessed event
 day: anniversary, borning
  poem: genethliac
  suit: altogether, skin
  goddess: lucina, parca, taweret
 mark: blain, mole, nevus
 pert.: natal, primogenitive
 place: brooder, hatchery, hotbed, incubator, nest, nidus, nursery, rookery
 rate: natality
 right: bequest, heritage, patrimony, primogeniture
BIS: again, encore, replica
BISCUIT: almond, bun, doe, rusk
 leaves: greenbrier, smilax

root: camass, cogswellia
ship: bonne bouche, crackerhash
BISHOP: angel, beverage, *drink, pope, prelate, primate
 apron: gremial
 assistant: coadjutor, verger
 buskin: caliga
 cap: biretta, mitre(lla)
 chess: alfin
 coptic: anba
 office: dataria, lawn
 private room: accubitus
 revenue: annate, benefice
 robe: alb, chimar, dalmatic, gremial, omophorion, rochet
 seven: ken, lake, lloyd, sancroft, trelawney, turner, white
 staff: cambuca, crook, crosier
 stocking: buskin, caliga
 title: abba, excellency
 weed: ammi, ammeos, bolewort, bullwort, goutweed, mint
BISHOPRIC: apse, bema, diocese, lawn, see
BISMER: reproach, scorn, *shame
BISON: aurochs, gaur, wisent
BISQUE: ceramics, point, soup
BISTORT: adderwort, blueweed, buckwheat, polygonum
BISTRO: *restaurant, *saloon
BIT: ace, atom, beans, canch, cantle(t), cast, chip, coin, crumb, curb, cut, dab(let), dash, detail, dight, doit, dole, dose, dot, drab, dram, dribble, drop, fico, fig, fleck, flyspeck, fraction, fragment, fritter, gobbet, grain, granule, hair, handful, hang, hoot, iota, item, jot, minim, minutiae, mite, modicum, molecule, morceau, morsel, mote, nip, nutshell, ort, *part, patch, *piece, pittance, point, *quantity, rag, rap, scrap, screed, scrimption, shadow, *share, shive(r), shred, slip, sliver, smatter, smidge(n), smitch, smither, smithereen,

---

* Asterisk means to look up this word to find more answer words.

snack, snaffle, snatch, snick,
snip, soupcon, spark, speck,
splinter, spoonful, spot, sprinkling, stitch, suspicion, tag, tate,
tatter, thimbleful, tittle, touch,
trace, *trifle, whit
by bit: by degrees, gradually
least: fico
part: walk-on
-wise: responsive, tractable
BITE: acrimony, *cheat, crunch,
*eat, gnash, *hurt, macerate, nip,
*pierce, *take, *tear
one's nails: fret, stew, worry
one's tongue: regret
the dust: *die, go down, lose
the hand that feeds: *betray
BITING: *clematis:* traveler's-joy
dragon: tarragon
gnat: midge, punkie
knotweed: water pepper
stonecrop: sedum acre
the nails: anxious, phaneromania
BITO: balm, hajilij, oil, poison
BITT: apostle, bollard, post
BITTER: *acerb, cruel, irate
almond: badam, benzaldehyde
apple: colocynth
ash: aeschrion, quassia, wahoo
bark: alstonia, cascara
blain: vandellia diffusa
bloom: american centaury
bur: sweet coltsfoot
bush: blackjack, snakeroot
cress: cardamine
cup: affliction, woe
dogbane: apocynum
earth: magnesia
ender: diehard, extremist
gentian: baldmoney, spicknel
grass: colicroot
head: calico bass, gold shiner
herb: astrofel, horseradish
nut: hickory, pignut
oak: cerris, blackjack
orange: bigarade, marmalade
osier: purple willow

pecan: water hickory
pill: defeat, disaster, drop
pit: baldwin spot
principle: absinthin
spar: dolomite
sweet: bindweed, chocolate, dulca-
mara, nightshade
trefoil: bog myrtle, buck bean
vetch: black pea, ers, vicia
weed: helenium, sneezeweed
wintergreen: chimaphila
wort: dandelion, gentiana
BITTERN: boon, heron, kakkak
cry: bill
BITTERS: aigre, amer, angostura
BITUMEN: alkitran, asphalt,
elaterite, gilsonite, maltha
BIVALVE: anomia, brachiopod,
clam, cockle, diatom, mussel,
oyster, pandora, scallop, spat
hinge: articulus, cardo
mollusk: anisomyarian
BIVOUAC: camp, etape, *gather
BIZARRE: *absurd, antic, daedal,
*eccentric, exotic, *extreme, fan-
tastic, garish, gauche, grotesque,
odd, outre, quaint, rococo, unusual, *weird, *wild
BLAB: *betray, chat, fink, nark,
snitch, *talk, tattle, *tell
BLACK: *bad, dhu, *dirty, ebon,
funky, murky, sombre, tragic
alloy: niello
amber: jet, labdanum
and blue spot: bruise, shiner
and white: chiaroscuro, print
antimony: stibnite
art: evil, magic, witchcraft
ash: eucalyptus, mulberry
ball: deny, ostracize, veto
bead: cat's-claw
beech: ironwood, leather jacket
bellied sandpiper: dunlin
belly: summer herring
bent: foxtail, switch grass
berry: agawam, dewberry, bramble, dog rose, pennacook

* Asterisk means to look up this word to find more answer words.

bindweed: bearbine, convolvulus
birch: nothofagus, river birch
bird: ani, ara, cuckoo, kanaka
birder: kidnapper, slave trader
blooded: atrabilious, moody
browed: gloomy, morose, scowling
buck: sasin
bully: sapodilla, tree
bunch grass: galleta
cabbage tree: melanodendron
calla: solomon's-lily
cap: cattail, chickadee, stonechat, titmouse, typha
cat: fisher, omen, superstition
centaury: knapweed
ceramic: bucchero
coat: clergyman, ecclesiastic
cod: beshow, bishowk, sablefish
cohosh: baneberry, bugbane
columbite: annerodite
comb.: ater, atro, mela(n)
copper: melaconite, mineral
coral: fish, gorgonian
corn: cowwheat
crappier: calico bass
current: cassis, fruit
cushion: zafu
dammar: canarium, resin
damp: chokedamp, miasma, vapor
diamond: carbonado, coal, oil
dog: despondency, melancholy
dogwood: alder buckthorn
draft: ilex, senna, yaupon
drongo: king crow
durgon: trigger fish
earth: ampelite, chernozem
elder: hackberry
eye: bruise, scandal, shame
-eyed susan: coneflower, ketmia
fever: kala azar, typhus
fish: bottlehead, girella, salmon, swart, tautog, whale
gang: crewmen, stokers
gold: maldonite, oil, petroleum
gram: pea, pulse, urd
grass: hop clover, shamrock
grouper: bonaci, jewfish, garrupa

grunt: tripletail
-guard: rascal, rogue, *smear*
guativere: niggerfish
gum: nyssa, pepperidge, tupelo
hag: sooty shearwater
hand: camorra, la mano nera
haw: alisier, honeysuckle, sheep-berry, sloe, stag bush
hazel: hop hornbeam
hematite: psilomelane
hickory: mockernut, pignut
hole: cell, dungeon, solitary
hollander: almond willow
jack: *hit*, hearts, pershing, twenty-one
lady: poplar, queen of spades
lead: graphite, plumbago
leg: *betray*, *deceive*, scab
letter: gothic, out-of-date
list: ban, thumbs down, veto
magic: sorcery, witchcraft
-mail: bribe, extort, *force*
margate: grunt, pompon
maria: coal box, patrol car, shell, queen of spades
market: racket, underground
mercury: poison ivy
mustard: brassica, cadlock
myrobalan: chebule, fruit
nightshade: blueberry, duscle, morel, solanum, wonderberry
oldwife: triggerfish
-out: amnesia, anoxia, *hide*
pan: hoddle, manavelins
partridge: francolin
pert.: ebon(y), negrine
pilot: cockeye, rudder fish
pine: loblolly, podocarpus
pot: ale mug, beer mug, sausage
rock cod: priest fish
root: colicroot, comfrey
sap: melaxuma
scale: lecanium, saissetia
seaweed: alaria, badderlocks, hen-ware, honeyware, murlin
seed: hop clover, medic, sham-rock, smut grass

* Asterisk means to look up this word to find more answer words.

sheep: deviate, reprobate
silver: stephanite
-smith: farrier, shoer
snake: racer, whip, zemenis
snakeweed: bugbane, sanicle
soap: knapweed, scabious
stick: clarinet, quinoiodine
storm: karaburan
-strap: knotgrass
sunfish: warmouth
-tail: dassie, godwit, ruffe
-thorn: sloe
tie: dinner jacket, tuxedo
tin: cassiterite
toner: aspergillin, lampblack
top: asphalt, pave, wave, weed
turnip: lion's leaf
vomit: yellow fever
vulture: urubu
wash: calumny, lotion, nigra
widow: spider, pokomoo
wort: bilberry, comfrey
BLACKEN: defame, malign
BLADDER: bubble, sac, vesicle
  comb.: asco
  wrack: bottle ore, seaweed
BLADE: beau, dandy, *spark
BLAME: *accuse, odium, *sin
BLAND: balmy, *smooth, *soft
BLANDISH: flatter, soothe, *urge
BLANK: absolute, bare, obscure,
  schneider, vacant, vapid, void
  cartridge: impotent
  check: discretion, go-ahead
  determination: experiment
BLANKET: *cover, stifle, *wrap
  coarse: cotta, cumbly
  cowboy: soogan, sougan, sugan
  deposit: mango
  drill: nap
  flower: firewheel, gaillardia
  horse: manta
  indian: stroud
  roll: sleeping bag, tarpaulin
  wool: barraclade
BLARE: *blast, tantarara
BLARNEY: butter, cajolery

BLASE: calm, insouciant, sated
BLASPHEMY: anathema, *curse
BLAST: *attack, bang, *blow,
  damn, dynamite, *noise, *rebuke
  furnace: smelter
  part: bod, bosh, bott, tymp
BLATANT: garish, gross, vulgar
BLAZE: *fire, *shine, *sparkle
BLAZON: celebrate, *describe,
  *ornament, promulgate, shield
BLEACH: chlore, etiolate, purify
BLEAK: *bare, bley, sprat
BLEAR: *deceive, *vague
BLEB: blister, bubble, pimple
BLEED: agonize, exploit, ooze
BLEMISH: *flaw, *hurt, *smear
BLENCH: *avoid, quail, whiten
BLEND: amalgamate, fuse, merge
BLENNY: brotula, bully, shanny
BLESS: approve, dedicate, exalt,
  extol, *praise, saint
BLESSED: bhagavat, divine, sacred
  bread: eulogia
  event: birth
  herb: bennet, hemlock, valerian
BLIGHT: *afflict, *plague, *spoil
  bird: white-eye, zosterops
BLIGHTER: beast, guy, rascal
BLIGHTY: england, furlough,
  home
BLIND: *obscure, *stupid, *vague
  alley: cul-de-sac, impasse
  as a hawk: seel
  bargain: chance
  dolphin: fish, susu
  flower girl: nydia
  -fold: hoodwink, *reckless
  gladiator: andabata
  eel: congo snake
  eyes: corn poppy, papaver
  fish: brotulid, cyprinid, goby
  goby: pinkfish
  god: hoth
  language: braille
  pig: saloon, speakeasy
  set: *ambush, *trap

* Asterisk means to look up this word to find more answer words.

shaft: winze
simon: johnny darter
spot: bigotry, hang-up
staggers: barleyhood, vertigo
weed: shepherd's-purse
BLINDNESS: ablepsia, amaurosis,
 anopsia, cecity, ignorance
color: achromatopsia
day: hemeralopia
partial: cecutiency, meropia
BLINK: nictate, *shine, *sparkle
BLINKER: bluff, mackerel
BLIP: echo, nickel, radar warning
BLISS: *joy, *paradise, *utopia
BLISTER: bleg, bulge, dome, whip
BLITHE: buoyant, jocular, merry
BLITZ: *attack, *hit, surprise
BLOAT: distend, expand, swell
BLOATED: *fat, pompous
BLOATER: *herring, mooneye
BLOB: pimple, smere, splash, wen
BLOC: *group, *part(y), *union
BLOCK: *arrest, *fool, *stop
 architectural: dentil, mutule
 -buster: bomb, knockout
 falconry: perch
 flat: mutule, tile
 hawser: bitt
 -head: *fool, moke
 -house: cottage, *fort
 ice: cube, serac
 mechanical: pulley
 metal: quad, quod
 nautical: deadeye
 out: excavate, outline, screen
 paving: sett
 pedestal plinth: die, socle
 perforated: nut
 rope: bull's-eye
 small: tessera
 topmast: bollock
 wood: beset, bust, cube, loon
BLOCKADE: *arrest, *stop
BLOKE: chap, fellow, man, toff
BLOOD: blade, *force, heritage,
 *passion, *spark, *spirit
and thunder: uproar, *violence

bad: anger, enmity, hate
bath: abattoir, massacre
-boiling: agitation, rage
boltered: clotted, cruor
brother: friend, intimate
clot: ball thrombus
comb.: haem(o), hema, hemo
cup: peziza, sac fungus
-curdling: horrible, terrifying
defective: anhematosis
deficiency: anaemia, anemia
drops: the wind poppy
dust: hemoconia
feud: vendetta, vengeance
field of: aceldama, akeldama
fine: bloodwite, wergild
flower: ambrosia, asclepias
fluid: opsonin, plasma, serum
fluke: bilharzia, schistosome
god's: ichor
leaf: aerva, amaranth, iresine
-letting: carnage, phlebotomy
-like: burke, gory, hematoid
money: breaghe, cro, galanas
parasite: tryp
pert.: haemal, haemic, hemal,
 hemic, xanthine
plasma chemical: fibrinogen,
 gamma globulin
poisoning: pyaemia, pyemia, septicemia, toxemia
pudding: sausage
purge: mass execution, massacre
root: bolo, indian paint, puccoon,
 tetterwort, tormentil
-shed: gore, murder, *violence
stagnation: clot, cruor, gore,
 grume, stasis
stanch: horseweed
stone: chalcedony, heliotrope
strain: family, race, stock
sucker: bed bug, blackmailer,
 leech, parasite, tick, vampire
-sucking: rapacious
thirsty: carnal, feral, fierce, gory,
 sanguinary, savage, wile
tree: croton draco, eucalyptus

* Asterisk means to look up this word to find more answer words.

vessel: aorta, artery, vein
  comb.: angio, vaso
  rupture: rhexis
  ulcer: angionoma
wood: ajhar, baloghia, lingoum
worm: chironomous, midge, poly-
  cirrus, terebellida
wort: burnet, dock, yarrow
BLOODED: pedigreed, thoroughbred
BLOODLESS: anemic, atony, pale
BLOODY: *brutal,* cruel, *violent*
  one's hands: *kill,* murder, slay
BLOOM: beauty, *shine,* *yield*
BLOOMER: *err,* *error,* pants
BLOOPER: *err,* error, radio
BLOSSOM: bud, produce, *yield*
BLOT(CH): *error,* *hurt,* *mark,*
  obscure, *spoil,* stain, sully
BLOTTER: pad, police log, soaker
BLOUSE: casaque, jacket, shirt,
  skivvy, smock, tunic, uniform
  front: japot
  medieval: bleaunt
BLOUSY: coarse, dowdy, unkempt
BLOW: *attack,* burst, calamity,
  pant, scram, *throw,* wheeze
  ball: dandelion, pappus
  by blow: detailed, first hand
  down: disparage, fell, raze
  fish: puffer, wall-eyed pike
  fly: blue bottle, calliphorid
  hard: braggart, plosher, shvitz
  hole: nostril, spiracle
  hot and cold: vacillate, waver
  in: enter, arrive, squander
  off: boaster, climax, explosion
  oneself to: purchase, splurge
  one's top: break down, go mad
  out: erupt, extinguish, flat, fete,
  gala, revel, spree, tantrum
  over: *end,* *pass,* subside
  sky-high: disprove, *upset*
  the whistle: expose, reveal, sing,
  spill the beans, *tell*
  the duke: drop the ball, *err*
  to: treat

up: berate, collapse, *destroy,* in-
  flate, promote, vesuvius
valve: *release,* safeguard
BLOWER: braggart, fumarole, machine, sacheverell, swellfish
BLOWZE: slattern, trull, *wanton*
BLUBBER: *cry,* *thick*
  cut: flensed, lipper
  grass: soft chess
BLUDGEON: billy, coerce, *hit*
BLUE: *asbestos:* crocidolite
  -back: herring, salmon, trout
  bass: green sunfish
  bead: yellow quintonia
  -beard: chevalier raoul, perrault,
  wife killer
  -beard wife: fatima
  beech: carpinus, hornbeam
  bell: blawort, campanula, columbine, hyacinth, veronica
  berry: cockatoo, dianella, papooseroot, squaw root
  bill: scaup duck, widgeon
  bird: irena, jay
  blazing star: gay feather
  blood: aristocrat, *lord,* noble
  boneset: agrimony, mistflower
  bonnet: cornflower, parrot
  book: atlas, *society*
  bottle: campanula, policeman
  brick university: cambridge
  bug: argas, chicken tick
  bull: nilgai
  bush: acacia, wattle
  button: periwinkle, titmouse
  camomile: sea starwort
  catalpa: paulownia
  chip: exemplary, prestigious
  collar worker: unionist
  coral: heliopora
  curls: ragweed, selfheal
  daisy: chicory, marguerite
  dandelion: chicory
  dark: perse, woad
  devils: amytal, apparitions, chasseur alpin, delirium tremens, de-

* Asterisk means to look up this word to find more answer words.

mons, doldrums, spanish legion, viper's bugloss
dogwood: pigeonberry
earth: kimberlite
eye: germander speedwell, herb
eyed mary: collinsia, innocence
false indigo: rattlebush
fig: brisbane quandong, tree
fin: bass, herring, saury, tuna
fish: sea bass, squeteague, saury, tailer, tuna, weakfish
funk: depression, fear
gill: bream, pondfish, sunfish
ginseng: cohosh, papooseroot
grass: andropogon, agropyron
gray: azurine, cesious, merle, pearl, perse, slate
green: beryl, bice, calamine, cyan, email, saxe, teal
grotto: capri cave
gum: eucalyptus, tree
handkerchief: belcher
hen state: delaware
herring: alewife, pomolobus
huckleberry: tangleberry
indigo: rattlebush
in the face: exhausted, frantic
iron earth: vivianite
jacket: gob, *sailor, tar
jay: cyanocitta, road monkey
jeans: chinos, denims, levis
johnny: fish, rainbow darter
joint: western wheat grass
lavender: ontario violet
law state: connecticut
lead: galena
legs: bird, hudsonian curlew
lettuce: lactuca
lucy: herb, selfheal
magnolia: cucumber tree
men's cup: columbine, flower
mold: fungus, penicillium
moon: eternity, never, rarely
mountain tea: goldenrod, plant
mud: clay, sediment, silt
nose: nova scotian, prude, snob
oxalis: herb, shamrock pea

pencil: alter, edit, revise
peter: coot, flag, gallinule
pigeon: cuckoo shrike
pimpernel: mad-dog skullcap
point: oyster, siamese cat
pointer: isurus, mako, shark
print: diagram, draft, map outline, plan, plot, schedule
red: ageratum, amethyst, campanula, gridelin, mallow, mazarine, quaker, sea mist
ribbon: *best, *supreme, *top
rocket: delphinium, monkshood
rockfish: priestfish, sebastode
runner: caranx, fish, jurel
sailors: chicory
shade: russian
sky: impractical, theoretical
spar: lazulite
starry: aquilegia, columbine
stem: andropogon, palmetto
stocking: avocet, bas bleu
streak: lightning
succory: cupid's-dart, plant
tongue: heartwater, thickhead
top: knapweed, solanum
wood: chaparral, condalia
BLUES: boogie woogie, doldrums
BLUET: bright eyes, cornflower, farkleberry, innocence
BLUEY: bundle, blanket, swag
BLUFF: *cliff, *short, *trick
BLUNDER: *err, *error, solecism
BLUNDERBUSS: espingole, musket
BLUNGE: amalgamate, blend, mix
BLUNT: *dull, *short, *thick
 arrow: butt shaft
 comb.: ambly
BLUR: cloud, fog, *obscure
BLURB: ad, build-up, plug, puff
BLURT: bolt, divulge, ejaculate
BLUSTER: *anger, bravura, fuss, hot air, swagger, swashbucklery
BO: chief, hobo, captain, man
BOA: aboma, scarf, snake, stole
BOANN'S COUSIN: dagda

* **Asterisk means to look up this word to find more answer words.**

BOARD: embark, feed, group, slab
BOAST: bombast, brag, vaunt
BOASTER: braggadocio, cacafuego
BOASTING: fanfaronade, gasconade, rodomontade
BOAT: *basket:* coracle
 cabin: baulea(h)
 coal cargo: collier
 comb.: scapo
 deck: orlop, poop
 dispatch: aviso, oolak
 duck shooting: skag
 engine-driven: sampan
 15th century: balinger
 fishing: bank(er), barcolongo, bracozzo, baris, bawley, buss, cog(gle), coracle, dogger
 flag officer's: barge
 flat-bottomed: bac, barge, baris, bateau, bun, coble, dory, punt, scow
 freight: lighter
 front: bow, prow, stem
 garbage: hopper
 group: armada, fleet, navy
 half-decked: wherry
 harbor: barge, bumboat, tug
 heavy: ballatoon, canaler
 jason's: argo
 jolly: yawl
 landing: lci, lst
 lateen-rigged: dhow, mistic
 load: burden, cargo
 man: boat bug, ferrier, gondolier, oarsman, phaon
 man-of-war: brig, pinnace
 merchant: argosy, holcad
 moorage: harbor, roadstead
 one-master: balandra, catboat
 ornamental: navicella
 part: deck, keel, prow, rail, scupper, skeg, stern, thwart
 passenger: bilalo
 pin: thole
 pirate: brigantine
 post: biff, bollard, capstan

river: baidak, bateau, bauleah, billyboy, ferry, packet, wheeler
 round: goofa, gufa, kufa
 sailing: *vessel: sailing
 sealskin: baidarka, bidarka
 shaped: cymbiform, navicular, naviform, scaphoid
 clock: nef
 small: canoe, dory, punt, scull, shallop, skiff
 song: barcarole
 steerer: coxswain, helmsman
BOAZ: *father:* salmon
 son: obed
 wife: ruth
BOBOLINK: bird, ortolan, reed
BOBWHITE: bird, colin, quail
BODACIOUS: insolent, *reckless
BODAI: enlightenment, salvation
BODKIN: dagger, needle, poniard
BODY: *form, *group, *society
 comb.: soma, somatic, somato
 politic: electorate, *state
BODYGUARD: burkundaz, *staff
BOEOTIAN: *fool, obtuse, *stupid
 capital: thebes
 prophet: bacis
 region: ionia
BOG: marsh, mire, sink, syrt
 manganese: wad
 peat: cess, moss
 plant: abama, butterbur, narthecium
BOGEY: bugaboo, *demon, ogre
BOGGLE: *alarm, *shock, *shy
BOGUS: fake, *false, phony, sham
BOHEMIAN: arty, gypsy, informal
 dance: redowa
 glass: schmelze
BOIL: agitate, cyst, foam, stew
BOILER: caldron, cook, retort
BOISTEROUS: *violent, *wild
BOLD: bossy, brazen, defiant, epilose, heroic, impudent, rash
BOLE: clay, dose, stem, trunk
BOLERO: dance, jacket, music
BOLL: bulb, capsule, knob, pod

* **Asterisk means to look up this word to find more answer words.**

BOLLARD: apostle, bitt, post
BOLSTER: add, aid, pad, repair
BOLT: arrow, dart, dash, elope, *escape*, missile, *strike*
BOLUS: ball, bite, cud, pill
BOMB: blockbuster, dud, explode, pineapple, sensation, strafe
BOMBAST: ampollosity, bunk, rage
BONANZA: eureka, jackpot, mint
BONBON: confection, sugar plum
BOND: chains, debenture, debt, *fetter*, guarantee, security, *tie*
BONDAGE: servitude, thralldom
BONDSMAN: *servant*, *slave*
BONE: *ankle:* astragalus, talus
arm: humerus, radius, ulna
box: bier, casket, coffin
breast: ratite, sterna, xiphoid
cell: osteoblast
comb.: os, osseo, osteo
cheek: malar, zygoma
ear: ambos, anvil, incus, stape
house: body, ossuary, tomb
face: malar, mandible, maxilla
finger: digit, phalange
leg: femur, fibula, patella, shin, tibia
manipulator: osteopath
pert.: osseous, osteal, ulnar
scraper: xyster
-set: agueweed, common, comfrey, sage, teasel, thoroughwort
skull: sphenoid, vomer
yard: scrapheap, *store*, supply
BONER: blunder, brodie, *error*
BONES: dice, *money*, *refuse*
BONGO: antelope, beetle, drum
BONIFACE: innkeeper, landlord
BONITO: aku, atu, fish, robalo, sarda, skipjack
BONNET: *cover*, *top*
string: bride
BONNEY: billy the kid, outlaw
BONNY: braw, fair, plump, sweet
clabber: clot, curd, milk, skyr
-vis: bonavist, hyacinth bean

BONUS: award, cash, *gift*, *income*, *money*, *yield*
BONZER: a-one, first-rate, *top*
BOO: bird, catcall, hoot, razz
BOOB(Y): *error*, *fool*, *trap*
stunt: blunder, folly, gaffe
tube: television, tv
BOODLE: graft, *money*, *spoil*
BOO HOO: *cry*, sailfish, sob, weep
BOOK: annual, diary, *engage*, indict, list, log, opus, mo, *place*, primer, *record*, *schedule*, script, text, tome
of account: journal, ledger
of apocrypha: bel and the dragon
of books: the bible
of feasts: ordo
of hours: hora, nones
of kings: shah namah
of life: beadroll
of maps: atlas
of masses: missal
of moses: pentateuch
of nobility: peerage
of songs: hymnal, psalter
BOOKKEEPING TERM: carryover, charge, credit, debit, docket, enter, log, post, statement
BOOKLET: brochure, literature
BOOM: campaign for, cannonade, prosperity, reverberation, roll
BOOMERANG: kiley, recoil, resile
BOON: blessing, *good*, windfall
companion: bullyrock, chum, pal
BOONDOCKS: sticks, tulies
BOONDOGGLE: goldbrick, *trifle*
BOOR: *clown*, *fool*, *peasant*
BOOST: *abet*, promote, *raise*
BOOSTER: *enthusiast*
BOOT: *error*, help, shoe, *use*
bird's: ocrea
eskimo: kamik
hill: cemetery
half: blucher, bottine, buskin, cocker, cothurnus, pac, pack
heavy: balmoral, brogan, stogy
hose: spatterdashes, stockings

* **Asterisk means to look up this word to find more answer words.**

jack: molding, notch
lace: lacet, string
-leg: hooch, moonshine, mountain dew, rotgut, smuggle
-lick: fawn, sycophant, toady
loose-topped: wellington
out: eject, evict, expel, fire
riding: jemmy, gambado
small: bottekin, bottine
winged: talaria
BOOTY: haul, pork, *spoil, *take
BORRACHO: *drunk(ard)
BORAX: flux, junk, tincal
BORDER: abut, *edge, flank, *limit, periphery, rim, verge
baseboard: dado
fluted: frill
minstrel: scott
BORE: *afflict, drill, droop, eagre, ennui, pest, *pierce
BOREAS: aquilo, norther, wind
son: butes, calais
BORER: beetle, hagfish, termite
BORN: *days:* lifetime, long-time
dead: stillborn
fool: simpleton
tired: indolent, lazy
to the purple: highborn, regal, royal, thoroughbred
under lucky star: fortunate
well: eugenic, *free, *noble
with silver spoon: wealthy
yesterday: inexperienced, naive
BORNEO: *ape:* orang(utan)
island near: alor, bali, java
mountain: kini-balu
native: dayak, dyak, iban
pepper plant: ara
pirates: bajau
river: baram, bruni, kajan
serpent: boiga
squirrel stew: pentail
timber tree: billian
tribe: bakatan, bukat, dusuns
BORROW: *adopt, *take, *use
chief: borsholder
money: break shins

trouble: fret, stew, worry
BOSCAGE: grove, thicket, wood
BOSH: bushwa, humbug, nonsense, pooh, rot, spoil, trash, trivia
BOSKY: *drunk, tipsy, sylvan
BOSOM: bust, embrace, heart, intimate, root, *secret, waist
friend: alter ego
BOSS: chief, dean, *head, knop
circular: bur, burr
eyed: out of true, squint-eyed
political: cacique, sachem
shield: umbo
BOSSY: cow, imperious, nagging
BOSTON: beantown, game, waltz
culture symbol: beacon street
district: back bay, hub
iris: narrow blue flag
leader: brahmin
pink: soapwort
ridge: shingles, slates
BOTCH: bobble, gum up, hash
BOTCHER: cobbler, grilse, salmon
BOTH: *comb.:* ambi, amphi, bi
BOTHER: *torment, *trouble
BOTTLE: *bird:* bittern, boonk
cod: capparis, jamaica
gourd: calabash, lagenaria
grass: fox tail, rabbit-foot
holder: backer, rack, supporter
neck: barrier, blockade, *stop
nose: dipsomania, dolphin
size: baby, balthazar, barrique, feuillette, fifth, jeroboam, liter, magnum, methuselah, nebuchadnezzar, nip, pint, pipe, quart, queue, rehoboam, salmanazar, tappit, tonneau, tregnum
small: ampul, costrel, cruet, decanter, flagon, vial
tree: kurrajong, sourgourd
up: censor, confine, suppress
BOTTOM: base, duff, foot, rump
BOUFFANT: coiffure, full, puffed
BOULEVARDIER: dandy, idler, roue
BOUNCE: bang, energy, fire, sack

* **Asterisk means to look up this word to find more answer words.**

BOUNCING: exuberant, hale, lusty

BOUND: *border, *move, *speed

BOUNDER: *boor, cad, cub, lout

BOUNTEOUS: *ample, *good

BOUNTY: boon, *prize, subsidy

BOUQUET: posy, *scent, spray

BOURGEOIS: common, merchant

BOURGEON: bud, breed, develop

BOURN: *limit, *waterway

BOUSE: *drink, *drunk(ard)

BOUT: *contest, *tear, *turn

BOVARY, MADAME: emma, delphine delamare

BOVINE: cow, *slow, *stupid

BOW: defend, salaam, *yield

BOWDLERIZE: censor, expurgate

BOWED: arcuate, bent, stooped

BOWELS: belly, viscera, *stomach

BOWER: boudoir, recess, shelter

BOWFIN: amia, grindle, mudfish

BOWL: *arena, dish, speed
  over: astonish, *start, *upset

BOWMAN: archer, cupid

BOX: *fight, *hit, *quantity
  alms: arca
  ammunition: caisson, bandolier
  bow and arrows: ascham
  car: carrier, gondola, six
  cars: dice, sixes
  cigar: boite nature, humidor
  coot: surf scoter
  crab: calappa
  head: sawfish
  in: confine, contain, trap
  office: gate, income, receipts
  opener: pandora
  papers: cartonnier, hanaper
  salpa: bamboo fish, sparida
  small: inro
  tea: canister
  thorn: matrimony vine
  wood: seron, tree

BOXER: chinese, dog, hat, pug

BOXING: blow: feint, jab, punch
  match: bout, go, setto
  pert.: fistic, pugilistic

  term: cestus, kayo, mitt, spar

BOY: mafu, *servant, tad, *trick
  bishop: st nicholas
  friend: beau, escort, *spark
  pope: benedict ix, john xii
  scout founder: baden-powell
  scout gathering: jamboree
  scout motto: be prepared

BOYCOTT: blackball, ostracize

BRABBLE: *argue, *quarrel

BRACER: pick-me-up, shot, tonic

BRACHYURE: cajaco, crab, pitta

BRACING: cold, stimulating

BRACK: brine, crack, crag, *flaw

BRACKEN: fern pteris, tartan

BRACKET: cantilever, category

BRACT: leaf, palea, spadix

BRAD: nail, pin, rivet, sprig

BRAG: bukh, crow, gasconade, prate, strut, vapor, vaunt

BRAGGART: blowhard, gasbag, know-it-all, jive, windbag

BRAGI: wife: idun, ithun(n)

BRAHMA: atman, bull, chicken, cow, creator, essence, steer
  child: daksha, manu, svayambhuva, vedas, viraj
  consort: sarasvati, shakti
  egg: hiranyagarbha, world
  first woman: ahalya
  four faces: caturanana
  reunion with: nirvana
  three traits: ananda, chit, sat
  wife: brahmani, gayatri, sarasvati, satarupa, savitri

BRAHMAN: aryan, *india references, hindu
  bliss: sat
  bull: zebu
  deity: *india: god, goddess
  learned: pundit
  precept: netineti, sutra, sutta
  temple vestibule: antarala
  title: aya

BRAHMIN: bostonian, *brahman

BRAID: adorn, knit, tress, weave

---

* Asterisk means to look up this word to find more answer words.

BRAIN: kill, psyche, sense, wits
 box: cranium, pan, skull
 cavity: coelia
 child: manuscript, opus, work
 canal: iter
 comb.: cereb, cerebri, cebrebro
 energy: cerebricity
 fever bird: hawk cuckoo
 fissures: zyga
 groove: sulcus
 layer: cortex, obex
 matter: alba, dura, obex, pia
 membrane: meninges, tela
 opening: lura, pyla
 operate on: trepan
 part: aula, cerebellum, cerebrum,
  encephalon, lobe pons, medulla,
  pericranium
 pert.: cerebral, encephalic
 ridge: carina fornicis, gyrus
 storm: confusion, good idea
 trust: advisers, council, panel
 wash: build up, snow job
BRAINLESS: nutty, silly, *stupid
BRAINS: grey matter, *sense, wit
BRAKE: *slow, *stop, *trap
BRAN: boil, chaff, powder, seed
 brother: branwen, manawyddan
 father: llyr
 sister: branwen
BRANCH: limb, *part, spur, twig
 pert.: comal, ramal, remeal
BRAND: burn, *kind, *smear
BRANDISH: flaunt, flourish, wave
BRANDY: armagnac, cognac
 and soda: peg
 and water: mahogany
 -based liqueur: angelica
 cocktail: alexander, rosolio, sidecar, stinger
 indian: pinga
 mastic: rakee, raki
 mazzard: cherry
 plum: slivovitz
BRANK: pillory, prance, strut
BRANNIGAN: brawl, carouse
BRANT: bold, erect, goose, proud

BRASS: cheek, *magnate, nerve,
  ormolu, *prostitute, tablet
 band: orchestra
 bound: inflexible, rigid, set
 buttons: swine's-cress
 farthing: trifle
 hat: general, officer
 man: talos, talus
 tacks: essentials, facts
 -visaged: bold, impudent
BRASSICA: cabbage, kale, turnip
BRAVE: dare, *soldier, valiant
BRAVO: assassin, cheer, ole, rah
BRAW: good, fair, fine, sporty
BRAWL: *fight, *riot, *tear
BRAY: *cry, heehaw, outburst
BRAZEN: bold, callous, vulgar
BRAZIL: antilia, hardwood, dye
 aborigine: carib
 animal: apa, epurua, wallaba
 ant: tucandera
 arrowroot: cassava
 bird: agami, ara, arvara, cariama,
  chaja, darter, iva, jacamar, ma-
  racan, soco, tiriba
 clover: alfalfa, lucerne
 club moss: pilligan
 coffee plantation: fazenda
 crane: cariama, seriama
 dance: batuque, maxixe, samba
 discoverer: cabral
 drink: assai
 fish: arapaima
 flycatcher: yetapas
 forest: caatinga, matta
 herb: arachis, bertolonia, manihot,
  nolana
 indian: acroa, anta, araquaju,
  arara, arawak, bravo, bororo,
  botocudo, baboculo, caingang,
  caraja, coroado, guana, katukina,
  mura, tapuya, tariana
 mahogany: carapa, plathymenia
 monkey: macaco, miriki, sai
 mountains: organ, serra do mar,
  serra dos orgaos, maritime
 music: bossa nova

* Asterisk means to look up this word to find more answer words.

palm: assai, bacaba, babassu, inaja, jara, tucum, urucuri

parrot: ara, arara, tiriba

plant: aveloz, ayapana, caroa, chica, imbe, jaborandi, seringa

rubber: caucho, hule, para, ule

tree: anda, araca, araroba, ava-remotemo, babassu, bakupari, becuba, caraipa, caucho, hevea, seringa, tingi, uhle, wallaba

BREACH: *error,* *opening,* *split

of contract: assumpsit

BREAD: fare, *money,* pan, staple

and butter: practical, thank-you

and cheese: sorrel

and wine: eucharist

basket: artophorion, *stomach

boiled: cush, panada

broth-soaked: brewis

browned: crouton, sippet, toast

communion: azyme

comb.: arto

crumb dish: panada

leavened: cocket, kisra

line: charity, queue, relief

plant: babkery, samh

pudding: randa

root: cinnamon fern, pomme blanche

spread: butter, oleomargarine

unleavened: afikomen, azyme, bannock, matzos, matzoth

wafer: abret, kisra

winner: earner, father, husband

BREADTH: atma, expanse, extent, girth, scope, size, space

and depth: thickness

riders: strengthening timbers

BREAK: *advantage,* bankrupt, burst, *discharge,* *dismiss,* domesticate, faux pas, *flaw,* gap, *give,* lapse, *occur,* *open(ing),* opportunity, *reduce,* *rent,* *ruin,* *split,* *spoil,* *start,* *stop,* *tame,* *tear,* *train,* *yield

a lance: joust

a leg: exert, strive, *try

away: bolt, *escape,* stampede

bone fever: dengue

bones: ossifrage

bread: eat with

down: analysis, cataclasm, cry, debacle, decompose, fail, raze, reduce, sob, subdue, torture

even: knot, split, *tie

in: domesticate, interrupt, *start,* stave, *tame,* *train

it to: divulge, inform, *tell

it up: cease, *separate,* *stop

-neck: dangerous, *reckless

of day: dawn, morning, sunup

one's heart: agonize, grieve

one's neck: exert, hurry, *try

out: analyze, erupt, *escape,* rash, *spread,* upsurgence

-over: continuation, jump

stone: burnet, calculus

the ice: begin, cultivate

the news: broadcast, release

-through: advance, *attack,* intrude, open, triumph, victory

up: debacle, *disintegrate,* divide, double up, laugh, revolution, sever, thaw, *upset

-water: cob, dam, pile, quay

BREAKABLE: brittle, delicate, frail, friable, shelly

BREAKER: comber, fabric, wave

BREAM: fish, porgy, scup, shad

BREAST: bosom, crop, *meet

-beating: emotionalism, remorse

bone: gladiolus, sterna, xiphoid

feed: nourish, nurse, suckle

plate: aegis, ephod, lorica, plastron, poitrel, shield, thummin, urim

weed: lizard's-tail

-work: fort, redan, rampart

BREATH: air, gulp, huff, life

BREATHE: aspirate, blow, pause, puff, respire, sniff, snort, tip

comb.: pneo, pneuma

hard: gasp, pant, try

one's last: *die, expire, *pass

* Asterisk means to look up this word to find more answer words.

BREATHER: break, recess, truce
BREATHING: *disease:* asthma
 hard: dyspnea, dyspnoea
 harsh: rale, stridor
 place: caesura, pause, vent
 smooth: lene
 spell: armistice, *rest, truce
BREATHLESS: aghast, anxious,
 *eager, mute, spent, winded
BREDE: boil, embroidery, plait
BREECH: blemish, butt, posterior
 cloth: clout, dhoti, dydee, malo,
 moocha, pagne, string
BREECHES: denims, jeans, pants
BREED: beget, cause, family,
 *kind, pedigree, race, strain
BREEDING: behavior, gentility,
 main, *polish, savoir faire
BREEZE: aura, cinch, easy, rumor
BREEZY: airy, *fresh, vivacious
BREVE: bird, compose, mark, tell
BREVET: appoint, commission
BREVIARY: abstract, compend,
 epitome, ordo, portas, psalter
BREVITY: conciseness, terseness
BREW: ale, beer, drink, *make
BREWER'S: *grain:* barley, corn,
 hops, malt, rye
 refuse: draff, dregs
 vat: kive
BREWING: afoot, gail, imminent
BRIAR: plant, thorn, zarzuela
BRIBE: bait, buy, dash, fix, hire
BRIBERY: bite, graft, payola
BRIC-A-BRAC: bibelot, curio,
 knickknack, trinket, virtu
BRICK: block, ideal, paragon
 bat: affront, criticism
 best class: stock
 carrier: hod
 clay: malm
 dried: adobe, bat
 fielder: buster, wind
 group: stack
 handler: hacker
 layer: cantling, mason
 mix clay for: pug

 molder: bumper
 part burned: bat, bur(r), clinker
 red: lateritious, saravan
 refuse: samel, sandal
 rounded: bull header, bull nose
 timber: mountain holly, plant
 vitrified: burr, clinker
 wood: dook, nog, scutch
BRIDE: bar, kallah, loop, *tie
 bed: marriage
 groom: benedict, newlywed
 gift to bride: handsel
 laces: dodder, ribbon grass
 of the sea: aphrodite, venus
 wain: carved chest, wedding
 weed: meadowsweet, toadflax
 -well: gaol, jail, prison
BRIDGE: arch, cross, ford, game,
 *pass, pont, prop, span, *way
 bird: peewee, phoebe
 bow instrument: ponticello
 combination: tenace
 coup: slam
 five-handed: quintract
 forerunner: whist
 head: breach, foothold, opening
 lever: bascule
 part: arch, cable, caisson, crown,
 deck, hangar, pier, pylon, shoe,
 spandrel, tressel
 plank: chess
 player: east, north, south, west
 term: blackwood, block, book,
 bye, cash, contract, double, cue
 bid, defender, end play, false-
 card, finesse, force, game, honor,
 no trump, pass, raise, renege, revoke, set, slam, squeeze, takeout,
 trick, trump
 type: bascule, bateau, draw, foot,
 over, suspension
BRIDLE: bristle, check, curb, restrain, shackle, snaffle
 goose: bridoie
 iron: stirrup
 noseband: cavesson, musrol
 -wise: obedient, responsive

* Asterisk means to look up this word to find more answer words.

BRIEF: abrupt, argument, case, catalog, curt, outline, *plan, *short, *small, syllabus
BRIER: *briar, pipe
BRIGAND: bandit, cateran, picaroon, pirate, *thief
BRIGHT: alert, apt, auspicious, brilliant, cute, gay, glorious, *smart, *splendid, *wise
clouds: good times
colored: serrano
BRIGHTEN: cheer, *polish, shine
BRIGIT'S: father: dagda
spouse: bres
BRILLIANT: *bright, *smart
BRIM: bluff, *border, *edge, *limit, skirt, strumpet, verge
BRIMSTONE: shrew, sulphur
pref.: thio
BRINDISI: drinking song, toast
BRINDLEE: spotted, tawny
gnu: blaaw, wildebeest
BRINE: brack, ocean, pickle, sea
fly: ephydra
pit: salt well, wych
preserve in: corn, cure, salt
BRING: attract, cause, convey, entail, *get, *lead, *yield
about: achieve, complete, tack
around: convince, persuade
back: effect, instigate, revive
down: capture, fell, raze
forth: *bear, elicit, *produce
forward: introduce, present
home the bacon: earn, triumph
in: gather, reap, score, *yield
into court: accuse, sist, sue
off: achieve, complete, succeed
on: attract, create, incur
out: announce, display, invent
over: convert, persuade, *win
pressure: compel, influence
to: convert, halt, revive
to bay: engage, *trap, tree
to bear: apply, focus
together: assemble, compile
to terms: compel, *defeat

to the hammer: auction
up: halt, mention, rear, *train
up to date: brief, inform, post
BRINK: *brim, *edge, margin, rim
BRIOCHE: bun, roll, savarin
BRISEIS: lover: achilles
BRISK: *active, *quick, *smart
BRISTLE: acicula, arista, awn, plume, ruffle, seta, swagger
comb.: seti
grass: setaria
tail: campodea, duck, lepisma
BRISTLES: beard
BRISTLY: barbellate, hairy, hirsute, scopate, strigal
crowfoot: buttercup, ranunculus
flowered plant: teasel
locust: rose acacia, tree
oxtongue: aralia, picris, weed
BRIT: crustacean, herring, sprat
BRITAIN: albion, *england
BRITISH: *english references
personification: brittania
empire exclusively: all red
guiana timber tree: bethabara
gum: dextrin
tobacco: coltsfoot, plant
BRITOMARTIS: aphaia, artemis, chastity, dyctynna, lady knight
mother: carme
BRITON: celt, pict, scot
BRITTANY: armorica
canvas: vandelas
island: ushant
magic forest: broceliande
poetry: soniou
saint: anne
BRITTLE: brash, candy, crisp, delicate, *hard, *weak
bush: encelia, plant
silver oar: stephanite
star: echinoderm, fish
stem: aralia, sarsaparilla
wood: yellow buckthorn
BROACH: air, drill, finish, gimlet, *pierce, pin, *start

* Asterisk means to look up this word to find more answer words.

BROAD: ample, beamy, *big, candid, *fat, *free, girl, generous, *obvious, *open, *thick, tolerant, *vague, woman
arrow: stigma
-beamed: *fat, stout, *thick
belt: bandolier
bill: bird, duck, gaper, scaup
brim: friend, quaker
-cast: air, divulge, sow, say, sponsor, *spread, *tell
-casting: radio, television
comb.: lati
elevation: bank
-gauged: *broad-minded
-horn: flatboat, wanigan
-leaved ginger: zerumbet
-minded: catholic, generous, lenient, liberal, tolerant
-shouldered: athletic, *strong
side: bill, circular, salvo
sole: flatfish, hogchoker
-way: big time, great white way
BROADEN: *amplify, widen
BROBDINGNAGIAN: *big
BROCADE: balachin, baudekin, cloth, kincob, powder
BROCARD: barb, gibe, sarcasm
BROCHURE: leaflet, pamphlet
BROCKET: coassus, deer, pita
BRODIE: blooper, boner, *error
BROGAN: boot, shoe, stogy
BROGUE: accent, shoe, *trick
BROIL: bake, brawl, brouhaha, cook, *fight, heat, *riot
BROILER: chicken, mushroom
BROKE: bankrupt, *poor, ragged
BROKEN: crushed, tamed, torn
-backed: chined
bellied: ruptured
color: impressionism
down: out-of-order, shattered
glass: calx
heart: anguish, despair, sorrow
mirror: omen, superstition
number: fraction
pieces: catastrophe

pottery: sherd
stone: rubble
BROKER: agent, dealer, factor, go-between, merchant, salesman
BROKERAGE: agio, *fee
BROLLY: parachute, umbrella
BROMELIA: ananas
BROMIAN DRINK: catawba, wine
BROMIDE: cliche, platitude
BRONCO: broomtail, buckjumper, cayuse, estrapade, mustang
buster: buckaroo, cowboy
BRONX CHEER: bird, boo, raspberry
BRONZE: alloy, pigment, statue
age man: aborigine
backer: black bass
film: patina
-gilded: ormolu
nude: olive brown
pert.: aeneous
variety: latten, patina
BROOCH: adorn, cameo, clasp, ouch, *ornament, pedant, tiara
BROOD: agonize, cherish, covey, family, hatch, incubate, *think
bud: bulbil, gemma, soredium
cell: gonidium
BROODER: birdhouse, kill-joy
BROOK: *stand, *water course
celandine: jewelweed
flower: waterleaf
lime: gratiola, speedwell veronica, water cress
sunflower: bur marigold
tongue: cicuta, water hemlock
BROOKIE: char(r), fish, trout
BROOM: besom, brush, cow, fray, heather, mop, spart, swab
brush: st john's-wort
bush: bastard fever-few, weed
corn: kaoliant, shallu, sorghum
corn millet: hirse
cypress: goosefoot, toadflax
hickory: pignut

* Asterisk means to look up this word to find more answer words.

plant: cyticus, deerweed, genista, heather, hirse, spart
rape: indian pipe, orobanche
sage: rabbit brush
sedge: andropogon, arrow grass
squire: gypsy squatter
tea tree: manuka
weed: scoparia, triumfetta
wort: orobanch, water betony
BROSIMUM: breadnut, capomo, cow tree, leopardwood, mulberry
BROTH: bree, brewis, broo, caldera, imrich, jussel, pottage, skillagalee, soup
clear: bouillon, consomme
BROTHEL: bagnio, bath, bordel, cat house, crib, dive, joint, shinjuku, stew, whorehouse
BROTHER: associate, brer, bub, comrade, fellow, friar, *monk*, member, oblate, pal, peer, sib
comb.: adelpho, frat(r)
pert.: fraternal
BROTHERHOOD: bratstro, guild, fraternity, profession, society
BROTHERWORT: pennyroyal, thyme
BROUGHAM: cab, carriage
BROUHAHA: *brawl*, *broil*
BROW: crest, edge, mien, snab
beat: abash, bully, domineer, harass, hector, intimidate, nag
BROWN: cook, dark, dun, dusky, gloomy, saute, sear, sepia
and white: roan
back: bird, dowitcher, snipe
bay: chestnut, color
bess: gun, prairie wake robin
betty: coneflower, daisy, pudding
bullhead: catfish, ictalurus
clover: trifolium badium
coal: bovey, lignite
cocoa: sahara, teak
dark: bistre, burnet, puce
dark reddish: bay, henna, khaki
ebony: coffeewood, wamara
hyena: strandwolf

iron ore: limonite, ocher
jolly: brinjal, eggplant
light: beige, ecru, fawn, tan, tenna, toasted
lily: mission bells
mica: phlogopite
-nose: apple-polish, fawn
off: aggravate, *anger*
pigment: bister, umber
print: roto(gravure), sepia
shirt: nazi, storm trooper
spar: dolomite, magnesite
stone: ascot tan, chestnut, coconut, kermanshah
study: absorption, dream, funk
sugar: caraibe, panela
-wort: selfheal, scrophularia
BROWNIE: cake, camera, cookie, fay, kobold, pixie, sprite
BROWSE: brut, crop, dip, *eat*, feed, glance, graze, nibble
BRUISE: *beat*, *break*, buffet, bung up, dent, *good*, humble, ictus, maul, mouse, shiner
BRUISED: ecchymotic, froisse
BRUISER: boxer, bully, *hoodlum*
BRUIT: clamor, *report*, *tell*
BRUMAL: cold, hiemal, wintry
BRUME: fog, haze, smog, vapor
BRUMMAGEM: counterfeit
BRUNET: black, brown, dark, melanous, olive, swarthy
BRUNT: *force*, impact, jar
BRUSH: *action*, beard, bramble, brosse, clean, *contest*, dry, *fight*, groom, *move*, paint, *polish*, *remove*, skim, *speed*
aside: dismiss, ignore, skip
box: tristiania, shrub
breaker: moldboard plow
-footed butterfly: comma, fritillary, nymphalida
kangaroo: wallaby
-like: aspergilliform
popper: cowboy
up: cram, groom, review, study
wolf: coyote

* Asterisk means to look up this word to find more answer words.

wood: boscage, coppice, copse, scrog, slack, teenet, thicket

BRUSQUE: abrupt, bluff, blunt, candid, cavalier, rude, **short*

BRUSTLE: crackle, dry, parch

BRUTAL: bestial, carnal, coarse, cruel, feral, gothic, gross, **mad,* savage, **violent,* **wild*

BRUTE: animal, barbarian, **hoodlum,* **ogre,* scoundrel

BRYTHON: cambrian, celt, **welsh*

BUB: blast, boy, buddy, gust

BUBAL: antelope, hartebeest, topi

BUBBLE: **air,* ball, bead, bleb, blister, blob, boil, bulge, **cheat,* delusion, dream, foam, glob, hiss, nil, mirage, pop

over: effervesce, overflow

snail: bulimus, bulla, physa

up: boil, intumesce

BUBBLER: drumfish, promoter

BUBBY: breast, boy, bush, shrub

BUBO: bird, eagle, owl, swelling

BUCCA: **dwarf,* **spirit*

BUCCANEER: corsair, freebooter, picaroon, pirate, rifler, vike

BUCEPHALUS: charger, steed

BUCEROS: bromvogel, hornbill

BUCK: balk, bouk, brag, bukh, bull, butt, dandy, dollar, fop, frame, jig, male, nob, **pass,* **play,* **spark,* stag, **throw*

and wing: tap dance

bean: bog myrtle, sweet gale

blue: etaac

board: carriage, four-wheeler

brush: coralberry, wolfberry

eye: bold, butterfly, loud, ohioan, precis lavinia, shrill

fat: goat lard

fever: jitters, nerves

off: unhorse, unseat

passer: dodger, evader, shifter

red: pallah

-skin: backwoodsman, breeches, color, horse, leather, purse

slip: memo

stall: deertrap, net, toil

-thorn: alatern, bearberry, cascara, ceanothus, chaparral, chittamwood, lotebush, rhamn

-thorn brown: sumac

up: brace, cheer, **dress,* encourage, **rally,* **stir*

-wheat: teetee, titi, tree

-wheat sage: shad scale, shrub

BUCKAROO: cowboy, horseman

BUCKET: basket, carrier, cup, dipper, draw, hod, lift, pail, pour, scuttle, socket, soe, tub

handle: bail

in a mill: awe

molten glass: cuvette

orchid: coryanthes

shop: boiler room, speculation

BUCKLANDITE: allanite, epidote

BUCKLE: bend, bow, close, **yield*

down: concentrate, exert, focus

BUCKLER: aegis, roundel, shield

BUCKO: bully, **fellow,* **spark*

BUCKRAM: bag, cuckoopint, formal

fabric: bocasine

BUCOLIC: agrestic, barnyard, georgic, naive, rural, simple

BUD: acrospire, blossom, bulb, child, develop, **fellow,* **grow,* **imp,* **source,* spirit, sprout

arrangement: aestivation

brush: artemisia

BUDDHA: amida, amitabha, arhat, ashuku, bodhisattva, butsu, dhrtarastra, fo, gautama, maitreya, miroku, myoo, nyorai, sakyamuni, shakyamuni, siddhartha, tathagata, vaisravana, virudhaka, virupaksa, yakushi

cousin: devadatta

disciple: ananda

enlightenment: bodhi

father-in-law: mahanama

footprints: sripada

image: daibutsu

mother: maya

* **Asterisk means to look up this word to find more answer words.**

patron: bimbisara
son: rahula
squire: chandaka
statue: bodhisattva
steed: kantaka
story: barlaam and josaphat
titles: blessed one, teacher
wife: yasodhara devi
BUDDHI: intellect, soul
BUDDHIST: *angel:* diva
 city, sacred: lassa, lhasa
 diety: bodhisat, deva, maitreya
 delusion: moha
 doctrine: anatman, anatta, sutta
 dialect: pali, sutta
 dialogues: sutra
 dryad: yaksha
 eightfold path: (right) action,
  concentration, effort, intention,
  livelihood, mindfulness, speech,
  views
 evil spirit: mara
 existence cause: nidana
 fate: karma
 festival: bon
 final beatitude: raga, nirvana
 form: rupa
 gateway: toran(a), torii
 greater: hinavana
 hatred: dosa
 heaven: chingtu, gokaruku, jodo
 hell: naraka
 japanese image: amita, daibutsu
 justice: dharna, dhurna
 king of india: asoka
 knowledge, supreme: bodhi
 language, sacred: pali
 lesser: mahayana
 life cycle: anicca
 mendicant: bhikku, gelong
 monastery: bonzery, gompas, tera,
  vihara
 mongol: eleut
 monk: *ecclesiastic: buddhist
 monument: amaravati, stupa
 mountain, holy: omei
 nexus: karma

novice: goim
passion: raga
pillar: lat
prayer: mani
priest: *ecclesiastic: buddhist
relic mound: amaravati, stupa
ruins: anuradhapura
saint: arahat, arhat, lohan
scripture: sutra
shrine: ajanta, chorten, dagoba
stories: avadana
temple: boro, budur, pagoda,
 ratha, tera, tope, vihara
temple gateway: toran(a)
throne: asana
title: mahatma
tree, sacred: botree, pipal
truths, 4: cessation, craving,
 eightfold path (*above*), pain
virtue: dharma
BUDDING: development, emerg-
 ing
BUDDLE: corn marigold, wash
BUDDY: crony, *friend, *pal
BUDDY-BUDDY: chummy, fa-
 miliar
BUDGE: austere, booze, brisk,
 *move, *stern, *stir, *thief
BUDGET: *allowance, batch, cost,
 estimate, funds, *plan, *press
 wire, program, ration, *share
BUFF: beat, clean, *enthusiast,
 *fellow, *firm, *hit, *shine
BUFFALO: aurochs, baffle, bluff,
 cajole, harass, intimidate
apple: ground plum
back: white fish
bird: starling
butter: ghee, ghi
chips: bodewash, bois de vache
clover: bluebonnet, trifolium
disease: barbone, cholera
fish: rooter, sucker
gnat: horn fly, similium
gourd: calabazilla
hybrid: catalo
jack: caranx, jurel

* Asterisk means to look up this word to find more answer words.

large: arna, arnee
meat: biltong
nut: oil nut, rabbitwood
pea: bluebonnet, vetch
tree: rabbitwood
water: carabao
wild: anoa, arna, seladang
BUFFER: cushion, pad, protector
BUFFET: *abuse,* bar, cabinet, credenza, cupboard, food, *hit
BUFFLEHEAD: *clown,* duck, *fool
BUFFOON: andrew, *fool,* jester
BUG: *enthusiast,* germ, insect, *plague, *scold, *spy, *symbol
aquatic: belostoma
juice: coffee, liquor, whiskey
june: dor
lightning: firefly
needle: ranatra
out: awol, desert, play hooky
under the chip: ambush
BUGABOO and BUGBEAR: *alarm,* bete-noire, bogy, goblin, *ogre
BUGGER: *fellow,* rogue, *spoil
BUGGY: auto, infested, *insane
BUGLE: clarion, horn, ox, sound
blare: tantara
call: retreat, reveille, tantara, taps, tatoo
note: blare, mot, tiralee
weed: indigo, mint
yellow: iva
BUILD: create, develop, *make,* proportions, *raise,* stature
*up: *quantity: accumulation, *praise
BUILDER: maker, tectonic
BUILDING: edifice, structure
addition: annex, apse, ell
farm: barn, crib, shed, silo
BUILT-IN: incorporate, natural
BULB: ampul, lamp, root, *sphere
edible: garlic, onion, sego
BULBUL: bird, kala, nightingale
BULGARIAN: slav, tatar

assembly: sobranje
capital: sofia
commission: sistoua
commune: slivno, sistova
finns: cheremiss, chuvash
liquor: slivova
measure: krine, lekha, oka
milk: yoghurt
moslem: pomak
mountain: rhodope
race, mongrel: gagaous
river: danube, marica, mesta
sect: bogomile
BULGE: *advantage,* jut, *stomach
BULK: *plenty, *quantity
-head: barrier, fence, portal
modulus: elasticity
store: warehouse
BULKY: *big, *policeman, *thick
BULL: *cop, *error, *nonsense
bat: nighthawk
bay: evergreen magnolia
buttercup: marsh marigold
castrated: bullock, steer, stot
chain: jack ladder
comber: beetle, scarab
*dog: *attack, *obstinate,* throw
*doze: *force, *press, *push
eye: decisive, target
fice: fungus, giant puffball
fight: corrida
fight attendant: bandillero, capeador, picador, toreador
fight cape: rebolero, veronica
fight cell: toril
fight seat: barrera, sol, sombara
fight weapon: estoque, muleta
fighter: capeador, matador, spontano, toreador, torero
finch: blood alp, nope, olph
flower: marsh marigold
fur seal: beachmaster
grape: muscadine
grip: plant, smilax
half and half man: minotaur
head: catfish, goby, plover, sculpin, tadpole, widemouth

* Asterisk means to look up this word to find more answer words.

head kelp: sea otter's cabbage
headed: *hard, *obstinate
heart: custard apple
hoof: jamaica, passionflower
hornless: doddie, doddy
in a china shop: bungler, uproar
lily: spatterdock
moose: progessive party
noon: midnight
nose: quahog, round clam
oak: beefwood, casuarina
of bashan: oppressor
papal: document, edict, letter
peep: sanderling, sandpiper
pen: barracks, prison, subs
pout: ameirus, catfish
rattle: bladder campion, herb
roarer: buzz, thunderstick, toy
seal: beachmaster
session: brainstorming, talk
sacred: apis
tongue: plow
wort: betony, bishop's-weed
young: bullock, stirk, stot
BULLA: bleb, bulge, vesicle
BULLACE: damson, grape, plum
BULLET: ace, ball, missile, shot
diameter: calibre
expanding: dumdum
fake: dud, pellet
group: canister
-proof shelter: abri, pillbox
BULLETIN: flash, news, notice
BULLION: bar, billot, ingot
BULLISH: headstrong, optimistic
BULLY: *abuse, bravo, bucko,
  cow, *great, *plague, ruffian
BULRUSH: cattail, papyrus, sedge
BULWARK: *fort, *support,
  *tower
BUM: *bad, *drunk, mooch, *tear
BUMBLE: bee, *err, idler, muffle
BUMP: bulge, *cry, *discard, *dis-
  miss, fire, *hit, *raise
BUMPER: *drink, *fine, *edge
BUMPKIN: *clown, *fool
BUMPY: corduroy, rough, uneven

BUMPTIOUS: insolent, *obstinate
BUN: *drunk, roll, wig
BUNCH: *group, *quantity, *unite
hits: boast, concentrate, score
pert.: comal
BUNCOMBE: *nonsense
BUND: band, dam, league, quay
BUNDLE: *group, *pack, *quan-
  tity
BUNG: *bag, *hurt, plum, *thief
BUNGALOW: cottage, *house
BUNGLE: boggle, bollix, *err
BUNK: bluster, *nonsense, sleep
BUNKER: abri, *fort, menhaden
BUNKO: *deceive, *deception
BUNT: bat, butt, *hit, tap
BUNTING: etamine, ortolan, sham
BUNYIP: counterfeit, phony, sham
BUOYANCY: cheer, *spirit
BUR: *burr
BURBLE: boil, bubble, confuse
BURBOT: cod, ell pout, ling, lot
BURDEN: onus, *pack, *trouble
BURDENSOME: *heavy, onerous
BURDOCK: clite, daisy, geranium,
  gobo, hurr-bur, lappa
BUREAU: agency, chest, office
BURGEON: bud, *grow, *increase
BURGESS: citizen, magistrate
BURGLAR: gopher, *thief, yegg
BURGONET: *helmet, morion
BURGOO: gruel, *mixture, stew
BURIAL: *case:* casket, coffin
ceremony: funeral
chamber: catacomb, tomb
comb.: taphe
pile: pyre
place: ahu, barrow, cemetery, gol-
  gotha, grave, mausoleum, necrop-
  olis, pyramid, tumulus
preparation: cere, pollincture
BURKE: get rid of, *kill, murder
BURL: bulge, knot, pimple, roe
BURLAP: *bag, gunny, hemp, jute
BURLESQUE: caricature, *copy,
  lampoon, satire, slapstick, wit
serenade: charivari

---

* Asterisk means to look up this word to find more answer words.

BURLY: *big, lusty, *thick
BURMESE: canopy, tazaung
 chief: bo, boh, woon, wun
 dagger: dah, dout, dow
 deer: thamin, thameng
 dice: anzamia
 district: toungoo
 division: arakam, pegu, yeu
 garment: tamein
 gate: toran
 headhunter: naga
 hill: chin, kachin
 knife: dah, dhao, dow
 measure: byee, dain, dha, lan,
 palgat, seit, taim, tha, teng
 mountains: arakan
 people: akha, chin, kachin, lai,
 mon, pequan, shan, shaw, vu
 plateau: shan
 river: irrawadi, salwin, sutang
 robber: dacoit
 ruby: peony
 sash: tubbeck
 shelter: zayat
 shrimp: balachan, napee
 weight: candy, kait, kyat, mat,
 moo, ruay, tical, ticul, viss
BURN: *anger, *desire, *fire,
 *hurt, *pain, *waterway
 balm: carron oil
 midnight oil: cram, study
 out: debilitate, exhaust, overdo
 -the-wind: blacksmith
 up: *aggravate, enrage, *speed
BURNING: *ardent, *eager, torrid
 bush: gas plant, dittany, wahoo
 for heresy: bonnering
 ghat: incinerator
 mountain: volcano
 of a heretic: auto-da-fe
 pain: *smart
 taste: *acerb, acrid
BURNISH: buff, *shine, *turn
BURNSIDES: beard, mustache
BURNT: baked, seared, spent
 almond: coconut brown
 brass: copper vitriol

 cork: blackface, makeup
 offering: sacrifice
 out: bushed, exhausted, spent
 roman ochre: color, tangier
 rose: color, pompeii
 sugar: blackjack, caramel
 weed: hart tongue, willow herb
 work: pyrography
BURR: accent, banyan, circle,
 excavate, halo, knot, nut, pad,
 reamer, ridge, ring, saw, whirr
BURRO: ass, fish, grunt, mule
BURROW: dig, hole, liar, tube
BURSA: pouch, sac, vesicle
BURSE: *bag, case, fund, *pack
BURST: *blast, *split, *spread
 forth: erupt, flare, pop, sally
 into flame: burn, ignite, light
 into tears: blurt, cry, sob
 inward: implode
 out: *laugh, roar, yell
 the bubble: disillusion
 upon: *meet, *startle, surprise
BURSTING: abuzz, lavish, loaded
 comb.: rrhage, rrhagia
 of the bubble: collapse
BURY: cache, cover, *hide, lose
BUSH: crude, foliage, jungle, mediocre, small time, rural
 beater: ivory hunter, scout
 forest: chaparral
 hair: mop, shag
 -league: mediocre, two-bit
 man: nomad, pioneer, rustic
 master: lachesis, snake, viper
 pepper: capsicum, chili
 ranger: footpad, hoodlum
 telegraph: grapevine, rumor
BUSHED: exhausted, spent, worn
BUSHWA: bosh, bull, *nonsense
BUSHWHACKER: guerrilla,
 scythe
BUSINESS: *interest, *trade, way
 big: cartel, *trust
 place: *plant, *shop, *store
BUSK: array, fix, hie, seek, stir
BUSKIN: boot, shoe, tragedy

* Asterisk means to look up this word to find more answer words.

BUST: *fail, *tame, *tear, *train
  in: enter, intrude, open
  up: divorce, failure, party
BUSTARD: crane, kori, otide
BUSTLE: *ado, cushion, *spirit
BUSY: *active, fussy, rococo
  body: gossip, pry, snoop, tabby
BUTCHER: botch, *kill, *spoil
  hook: cammock, gambrel
  rabbi: shochtim
BUTLER: sommelier, steward
BUTT: *adjoin, duff, goat, scag
BUTTE: hill, picacho, ridge
BUTTER: cajole, flatter, spread
  artificial: anatto, oleo
  comb.: butyro
  cup: achene, ranunculus
  fish: blenny, gunnel
  fly: idalia, morpho, satyr
    expert: lepidopterist
    fish: angel fish, blenny, paru
    larva: caterpillar, proteus
  lily: mariposa, sego
  secretion: acrelin
BUTTERY: pantry, *soft, spence
BUTTON: *badge, *bit, *symbol
  ball: plane tree, sycamore
  down: nail, *secure, *tie
  hole: boutonniere, detain, sew
  up: *bag, capture, *complete, *se-
    cure, *settle, *take
BUTTRESS: bulwark, *support
BUTTY: *friend, partner, worker
BUXOM: bouncing, jolly, plump
BUZZ: *ado, annoy, greet, hiss
  along: depart, leave, *speed
BUZZARD: condor, vulture
BYBLOS: king: malcandre
BYE: *good-by(e), *pass, sleep
BYSTANDER: doppess, innocent
  spectator, tsitser, witness
BYWORD: *adage, motto, shame
BYZANTINE: complex, labyrin-
  thine
  art form: anastasis
  capital: nicaea
  chapel: antiparabema

ornament: bezant, solidus
scepter: ferula
BYZANTIUM: *istanbul

C MARK: cedilla
CAAM: heddles, loom
CAAMA: asse, fox, hartebeest
CAB: hansom, shelter, taxi
  driver: cabby, cocher(o), hack
  four-wheeled: bouquet
CABAL: block, clique, junto, plot
  pert.: factional
CAB(B)ALA: mystery, occultism
  author: moses de leon
CABALLERO: gentleman, *lord
CABANA: bathhouse, cabin
CABARET: bar, boit, cafe, casino
CABBAGE: kale, *money, *steal
  bark: angelin
  bug: calico back, harlequin
  broth: borecole, borscht, schee
  daisy: globeflower
  disease: blackleg, yellows
  family: brassicaceae
  gum: eucalyptus
  head: *fool, numskull, screwball
  palm: area, assai, sabal
  plant: rape, wahoo
  salad: coleslaw, kraut, slaw
  stalk: castock, custock
  tree: andira, angelin, yaba
  type: cale, colewort, colza, kale,
    kohlrabi, kraut, savoy
  warmed over: cloyer, platitude
  white: butterfly, colewort
  wood: lingustrum, privet
  worm: caterpillar, herb, looper
CABER: beam, pole, rafter, spar
CABIN: berth, cottage, den, *hut
  boat: baulea(h)
CABINET: almirah, bahut, buhl,
  case, chest, council, cupboard,
  ministry, private, whatnot
  d'aisance: toilet
  open-shelved: etagere

* Asterisk means to look up this word to find more answer words.

-*work wood:* calamander
CABLE: boom, chain, line, wire
 fake: tier
 lifter: wildcat
 pert.: coaxal, coaxial
 post: bitt
 railway: ascenseur, funicular
 vault: chamber
CABLING: molding, rudenture
CABOCHON: gem, ornament
CABOODLE: *bag, calabash, lot
CABOOSE: cab, car, galley, tail
CABRILLA: bass, grouper, ser-
 ranus
CACAO: arriba, broma, cocker
 disease: black pod
 extract: butter, fat, martol
 seed powder: broma
CACHE: *hide, *store, *supply
CACHET: design, pill, prestige,
 seal, slogan, standing, wafer
CACHEXIC: morbid, *sick
CACHOU: auburn, dye, pastil
CACK: discharge, muck, saddle
CACKLE: gabble, *laugh, *noise
CACOETHES: desire, itch, mania
CACOGRAPHY: error, inelegance
CACOPHONOUS: harsh, raucous
CACTUS: bisnaga, bleo, cacapana,
 cereus, chaute, cholla, dildo,
 mescal, saguaro, xerophyte
 aborescent: barbados gooseberry
 climbing: queen of the night
 drug: peyote
 fruit: cochal
 plantation: nopalry
CAD: gyp, heel, *peasant, rascal
CADAVER: body, corpse, stiff
CADDIE: boy, cadet, teamwarmer
CADDIS: crewel, fly, lint, rags
CADDLE: fuss, *gossip, tease
CADE: keg, lamb, pet, rebel
CADENCE: beat, lilt, *meter
CADET: plebe, son, *student
CADGE: beg, frame, mooch, *tie
CADGER: beggar, dealer, vendor
CADMUS: *cousin:* harmonia

 daughter: agave, autonoe, ino,
 semele
 parent: agenor, argiope
 sister: europa
 wife: harmonia
CADOR: *son:* constantyne
CADRE: frame, list, *source
CADUCEUS: insigne, *staff, wand
CAECUM: cavity, cell, pit, pore
CAESALPINIA: brea, cassia,
 senna
CAESAR: emperor, salad, tyrant
 assassin: casca, brutus, marcus
 colleague: bibulus, pompey
 conquest: gaul
 death place: nola
 fatal day: ides
 friend: antony, marc
 message site: zela
 mother: aurelia
 river of decision: rubicon
 sister: atia
 weed fiber: aramina, urena
 wife: calpurnia, cornelia, uxor
CAESURA: *break, *meter, pause
CAFE: *restaurant
 au lait: alesan
 creme: color, suede
 noir: color, musk
CAGE: box, basket, *jail, *trap
CAHOOTS: collusion, league
CAIMAN: alligator, jacare
CAIMITILLO: satinleaf
CAIN: crops, fine, killer, rent
 and abel: table
 brother: abel, pur, seth
 descendant: enoch, enos, lamech
 land: nod
 parent: adam, eve
 wife: adah
CAIRO: *old:* al-fustat, el-fostat
CAISSON: camel, case, chest
 disease: bends, seizure
CAITIFF: *bad, base, *mean, vile
CAJOLE: coax, *cheat, kid, *trick
CAKE: harden, lump, scone, tart
 almond: macaroon

---

* Asterisk means to look up this word to find more answer words.

coffee: blueberry buckle
corn: fritter, pone
custard: creampuff, eclair
dough: batter
filled: flan
fried: cruller, doughnut
funeral: arthel, arval, averil
griddle: bannock, crumpet, hotcake, pancake
mango juice: amsath
part: farl, icing, layer
plum: baba
rich: madeleine, torte
round: charlotte, nut, torte
sacrificial: hallah
seed: wiff, wig(g)
small: batty, bun, cupcake, jumble, ladyfinger
tea: scone
thin: farl, jumble, placent, scone, tortilla, wafer
unleavened: damper, matzo, wafer
walk: march, promenade, strut
CAKEEATER: dilettante, sissy
CALABA: balsam, birma, fir, tree
bean: esere, isere, ordeal bean
ebony: diospyros dendo
CALABASH: basket, gourd, kettle
tree: baobab, crescentia
CALAISE: *father:* boreas
CALAMITY: *catastrophe, *evil
howler: pessimist
CALAMUS: palm, pen, sweetflag
CALANGAY: abacay, cockatoo
CALASH: bonnet, carriage
CALCIMINE: paint, whitewash
CALCITE: amygdaloid, argentine, spar, stalacite, stalagmite
CALCIUM: *aluminum silicate:* bavenite, cebolite
antimonite: atopite
borate: borocalcite
borosilicate: bakerite
carbide: acetylenogen
carbonate: aragonite, tufa
-iron garnet: andradite, aplome
oxide: quicklime

phosphate: apatite, baking powder, brushite, fertilizer
soda zeolite: arduinite
sulphate: anhydrite, annaline, bassanite, gypsum, hepar
CALC-SINTER: travertine
CALCULATE: *add, *think
CALCULATING: cautious, shrewd
CALCUTTA: *hemp:* jute
measure: dhan, jaob, kunk, raik
police station: thana
river: hooghly
weight: hubba, pally, pank
CALDRON: alfet, boiler, pot
CALEB: *daughter:* achsah
descendants: eshtaulites, ithrites, mishraites, shobal, shumathites, zareathites
son: ardon, elah, gazez, haran, hur, iru, jesher, mareshah, mesha, moza, naam, shaaph, shebar, sheva, shobab, tirhana
wife: azubah, ephah, eprath, jerioth, maacah
CALEFACTION: heat, stove
CALENDAR: *agenda, list, *schedule
deficiency: epact
CALENDURE: ardor, fever, *fire, infect, *passion, sunstroke
CALF: bobby, dogie, *fool, moggy
atrophy: acnemia
cry: baa, blat, bleat
days: salad days, youth
flesh: bob veal, veal, veau
jelly: fisnoga
love: infatuation
-kill: calico, kalmia, sheep laurel, velvet grass
motherless: dogie, maverick
pert.: sural
skin: kip, suede
CALF'S: *-foot:* cuckoopint, plant, wake-robin
-jelly: gelatin
-mouth: snapdragon

* Asterisk means to look up this word to find more answer words.

CALIBAN: beast, monster, slave
  adversary of: prospero
  deity of: setebos
  witch mother: sycorax
CALIBER: *ability, bore, degree,
  mettle, *quality, rank, talent
CALICO: goldfish, salloo, woman
  back: harlequin bug
  bass: bachelor, bitterhead, black
  crappie, golden shiner
  bush: calfkill, flower, kalmia
  calm: macrocallista
  horse: piebald, pinto
  indian: sallo(o)
  mix colors for: teer
  pigment: canarin(e)
  printing: fondu, lapis, teer
CALIFORNIA: el dorado, golden
  christmasberry: holly, toyon
  coffee: bearberry, cascara
  buckthorn: coffeeberry, rhamnus
  bulrush: marsh sedge, tule
  calycanth: spicebush
  condor: gymnogyp, vulture
  cress: hedge mustard
  dandelion: cat's-ear, weed
  desert: mohave, mojave
  fan palm: erythea
  first capital: molina del ray, mol-
  ley del ray, monterey
  fish: chi, reina, sprat, sur
  gold-mining town: bodie, columbia, igo, jackson, ono
  hare bell: campanula
  herb: amole, bird's-beak
  holly: christmasberry, toyon
  indian deity: acaragui, amayi-
  coyondi, cucumunic, niparaya,
  purutabui, quaayayp
  indigo bush: mock locust
  jack: seven up
  lake: buena, eagle, goose, honey,
  mono, owens, tahoe
  laurel: cajeput, oleander, sassafras, umbellularia
  motto: eureka
  oak: encina, roble

  observatory: lick, palomar
  onyx: aragonite
  pass: donner, sonora
  plant: brodia, elderberry, hookera,
  tarweed, thimbleberry
  rockfish: bocaccio, rena, viuva
  shrub: bush poppy, chamiso, chaparral, manzanita, salal
  state flower: golden poppy
  state symbol: grizzly bear
  tree: alder, madrone, redwood,
  sequoia, sycamore, torrey
  wine area: cucamonga, lodi, napa,
  paicenes, sonoma, st helena
CALIGULA: *steed:* incitatus
CALL: *alarm, *name, summon
  all bets off: end, terminate
  a spade a spade: be frank
  attention to: remind
  away: extricate, *remove, send
  back: recant, revoke, retrieve
  bird: decoy
  distress: sos
  down: chide, rebuke, *scold
  for: ask, demand, escort, oblige,
  request, summon, visit
  forth: appeal, arouse, avail, evoke,
  excite, *order, prompt
  girl: *prostitute, *wanton
  hogs: sook
  in: admit, gather, invite
  into play: create, effectuate
  it a day: close, *quit, *stop
  it square: agree, *settle
  money: loan
  names: *abuse, *smear
  of the wild: wanderlust
  off: cancel, *end, *stop
  on: ask, *order, *meet
  on the carpet: *call down (*above*)
  one's bluff: challenge, see
  out: *cry, elicit, invoke
  signals: *direct, *order, *run
  the turn: augur, command, run
  to account: blame, book, indict
  to arms: mobilize, recruit
  to attention: hop, remind

* Asterisk means to look up this word to find more answer words.

to mind: cite, recall, remember
together: *gather,* muster
up: advocate, phone, recruit
upon: appeal, petition, *urge*
CALLING: *forte, *trade, *work
CALLIOPE'S: *son:* orpheus
CALLISTO'S: *son:* arcas
CALLITHUMP: burlesque, chari-
vari, parade, serenade, uproar
CALLOUS: *hard, *obstinate
CALLOW: green, immature
CALM: *abate, *cool, *smooth
CALOPHYLLUM: balsam, calaba
CALOTTE: coif, glacier, summit
CALUMNIATE: *abuse, libel, slur
CALVARY: cemetery, golgotha
CALX: ashes, cullet, residue
CALYX: covering, cup, husk, leaf
division: sepal
flower's: perianth
helmet-shaped: galea
CAM: awry, *form, lobe, *move
CAMAIL: aventail, guard, tippet
CAMARADERIE: cheer, convi-
viality, friendship
CAMARILLA: cabal, council,
junto
CAMAS: lobelia, *plain, prairie
rat: pocket gopher, thomomys
CAMBIUM: exchange, juice,
*trade
CAMBODIA: khmer empire
ancient capital: angkor
CAMBRAI: *swan:* fenelon
CAMBRIA: *wales
CAMBRIC: batiste, percale, ramie
leaf: pond lily
CAMBRIDGE: *boat races:* lent
college official: bedell
council: caput
examination: tripos
man: by-fellow, tab
ruling body: caput
student: optime, sizar, spoon
CAME: band, bar, ribbon, rod
CAMEL: caisson, cont, deloul,
dromedary, float, mehari, oont

-back: deformed, deformity
bird: ostrich, struthio
corps: infantry
driver: sarwan
female: naga
fermented milk: koumyss, kumys
hair: aba, camlet, fabric
hay: cymbopogon
horse: mantis
insect: mantis
keeper: obil
thorn: alhagi
pert.: bactrian
two-humped: bactrian
CAMELINA: gold-of-pleasure
CAMEO: anaglyph, camaieu, onyx
conch: cassis, mollusk, shell
cutting tool: spade
encrustation: sulphide
glass: portland vase
material: gem, onyx, sardonyx
ware: jasper
CAMERA: box, gobo, *secret
dark: obscura
eye: retention
light: lucida
part: finder, lens, shutter
platform: dolly, tripod
revolving: panoram
shot: flash, snap, still
small: brownie
CAMERATED: arched, vascular
CAMION: bus, cart, dray, truck
CAMLET: angora, *mark, poncho
CAMMOCK: crook, hockey, stick,
st john's-wort, tansy, yarrow
CAMORRA: blouse, extort, mafia
CAMP: bivouac, faction, shelter
flux: dysentery
follower: bildar, girl, gudget,
prostitute, sympathizer, tramp
guard: askar(i)
it up: *display, *show
master: colonel
on the trail of: *follow
pert.: castral, castrensian
pot: dixy

* Asterisk means to look up this word to find more answer words.

provisioner: sutler
recruit's: boot, training
root: yellow avens
royal: army, host
CAMPAIGN: crusade, drive, jihad, politick, stump, whistlestop
CAMPANERO: arapunga, bellbird, shrike, wood thrush
CAMPEADOR: cid, guy de bivar
CAMPER: *ape, *gossip
CAMPHOR: alant, apiol, asarone, borneol, racemic, remedy
ball: moth ball, naphthalene
tree: laurel, cinnamomum, kapur
weed: ambrosia, blue curls, ragweed, vinegar weed
wood: black pine, callitris
CAMPY: affected, *artificial, banal, *bizarre, *eccentric, mannered, off-color, *weird
CAMSHACH: crooked, distorted
CANAAN: israel, *paradise
city: ai, hazor
descendant: amorite, arkite, arvadite, girgasite, hamathite
son: heth, sidon
CANADA: balm of gilead, brook, elecampane, herb, jerusalem artichoke, populus, valley, tree, *waterway
airport: gander
asphalt: albertite
balsam: turpentine
bay: griper, hecla
cabin berth: baulk
canal: soo, welland
cape: canso
first settlement: annapolis royal, port royal
fleabane: horseweed
free grant district: muskoka
fur company man: voyageur
gannet: margot
goose: blackie, brant, bustard, honker, outarde
grape: isabella
grouse: spruce partridge

half-breed: bois brule
indian game: bagataway
jay: moose bird, whisky jack
judas tree: cercis, red bud
lake: athabaska, cree, gras, louise, seul, teslin
land measure: arpent, roture
lark: alouette
lyme grass: wild rye
lynx: carcajou, pishu
mayfair: bead ruby, lily
measure: chainon, minot, perch
peak, highest: logan
peninsula: gaspe
physician: osler
policeman: mountie
pondweed: waterweed
poplar: liard
porcupine: cawquaw, urson
potato: jerusalem artichoke
robin: cedar waxwing
rockrose: frostweed
root: butterfly weed
sleigh: cariole, carriole
small reed: bluejoint
snakeroot: herb, wild ginger
squaw: mahala
tea: herb, wintergreen
thistle: cocklebur, xanthium
yew: ground hemlock
CANADIAN: canuck, jean baptiste
CANAILLE: canaglia, *rabble
CANAL: *waterway
alimentary, part: anus
bank: berm(e)
broad: shat
dredging machine: couloir
slack water: lode
zone city: ancon, balboa, colon
CANARD: duck, hoax, *lie
CANARY: dance, informer, singer
balm: dragon's-herb, cedronella
bellflower: canarina campanula
bird: convict, dendroica, finch
broom: cytisus, genista
grass: birdseed, lepidium

* Asterisk means to look up this word to find more answer words.

island: allegranza, clara, ferro, fuerteventura, gomero, graciosa, grand hierro, inferno, lobos, palma, roca
island commune: icod
island measure: fanegada
island peak: el cumbre, gran canaria, la cruz, tenerife
tea: queensland hemp
moss: archil, parmelia
stone: carnelian
vine: climbing fumitory
wine: aristippus, vidonia
wood: mulberry, persea
yellow: capucine, meline
CANAVALIA: jack beans, herbs
galeata: awikiwiki
lineata: bay bean
CANCEL: clear, *remove,* void
CANCER: crab, *evil,* tumor
-*blood:* leukemia
cause: nucleic acid, virus
chicken: sarcoma
comb.: carcino
drug: amygdalin, laetrile
jalap: pokeberry
-*like:* cancroid, crabby
-*producer:* carcinogen
root: beechdrop, orobancha
stick: cigarette
study of: oncology
weed: premanthes, sage, salvia
wort: kickia, squawroot
CANDELABRA: stonewort
CANDESCENT: dazzling, luminous
CANDID: *direct, *honest, *open
CANDLE: cierge, chandelle, dip serge, tallow, taper, test, wax
base: abilla, cetin
berry: wax myrtle
cactus: ocotillo, plant
fish: beshow, eulachon, skil
holder: bracket, lampad, sconce
larkspur: delphinium, flower
light: dusk, nightfall, twilite
lighter: acolyte, spill

melt: sweal
nut: ama, bankul, kekuna, kukui
plant: kleinia, mullein
shaped: bougie
stick: chandelier, dicerion, cruisie, girandole, jesse, lampad, lustre, pricket
tree: catalpa, parmentiea
wax catcher: bobeche
wick: cattail, mullein
wood: coachwhip, ocotillo, tree
CANDY: confection, *sweet
base: fondant
container: bonbonniere
mixture: fourre
nut: praline
peppermint: bull's-eye
pulled sugar: penide, taffy
-*stick:* coral snake
stuffs: iberis
sugar: caramel, sucrose
-*weed:* orange milkwort
CANE: *beat, liana, pipe, *staff, rattan, sorghum, warp, *whip
apple: arbutus, strawberry tree
-*bearing:* arundiferous
borer: beetle, oberea
brake: thicket
brimstone: roll sulphur
cactus: opuntia
disease: black knot, sereh
grass: bamboo, glyceria, herb
killer: melasma
knife: machete
osier: salix viminalis, willow
part: ferrule
-*pin:* leather
rat: ground pig, hutia
sugar: sucrose
withy: golden willow
CANFIELD: china, fascination, klondike, pounce, solitaire
CANGLE: *fight, *quarrel
CANIDIA: *wanton, *witch
CANISTER: box, case, solitaire
CANKER: *cancer, *eat, *sore
berry: corn poppy, dog rose

* Asterisk means to look up this word to find more answer words.

bird: cedar waxwing
-fret: corroded, diseased
lettuce: consumption weed
rash: scarlet fever
root: gold thread, sorrel
weed: ragwort, senecio
worm: paleacrita, rucel
wort: dandelion
CANNABIS: *drug, *hemp
cousins: fig, hop, nettle
drugs: bhang, charas, marijuana
CANNIBAL: anthropophagite, killer, maneater, savage
secret society: bachichi
CANNON: bagatelle, bomb, carom, pickpocket, quill, *thief
ball: ammunition, bufflehead, duck, missile, pellet, train
basket: gabion
breech end knob: cascabel
early: aspic, robinet, saker
firing pin: linstock
fodder: infantry, soldiers
group: artillery, battery
merchant ship: bow-chaser
mop for: merkin, swab
part: bore, breech, cascabel, chamber, chase, frette, muzzle
shot: grape
16th cent.: bastarc, culverin
support: trunnion
CANNONADE: artillery, barrage, bombardment, booming, enfilade, salvo, volley
CANOE: *bark:* cascara
cedar: arborvitae, thuja
dugout: banca, baroto, corial, pambanmanche, pirogue, piroque
large: bungo, pah
oystering: buckeye
skin-covered: baidara, kayak
CANON: *adage, code, *rule
CANONICAL: orthodox, religious
hours: compline, lauds, matins, nones, sext, tierce, vespers
punishment: excommunication
sins: heresy, idolatry, murder

CANOPY: baldaquin, hood, sky
CANT: *argot, *throw, *turn
CANTERBURY: *bell:* campanula
first archbishop: augustine
gallop: aubin, canter
palm: umbrella palm
story: fable, legend, yarn
tales inn: tabard
CANTICO: *dance, *party, social
CANTILEVER: beam, cartouch, truss
CANTLE: *bit, cheer, *join
CANTON: *allot, *part, *separate
CANTOR: chaver, *leader, soloist
CANTRIP: *magic, *spell, *trick
CANUTE: *consort:* emma
CANVAS: ada, burlap, duck, tewk
-back: aythya, duck, nyroca
climber: *sailor, salt, tar
cover: awning, tent, tilt
-like fabric: wigan
waterproof: tarp(aulin)
CANVASS: *beat, comb, inquire
CANYON: *opening, *waterway
box: cajon
live oak: encina
mouth: abra
wall: dalle
wren: catherpes mexicanus
CAOUTCHOUC: *rubber tree, ule
CAP: *acme, lid, *seize, *stop
a-pie: throughout, utterly
and bells: costume, marotte
basque: beret
child's: biggin, bonnet, mutch, toque
close: calotte, cloche, coif
covering: havelock
ecclesiastic: *vestment: religious
flat: balmoral, barret
helmet-like: alopeke
heraldic: chapeau
hunter's: montero
ignition: fuse, fuze
in hand: humble, sycophantic
knitted: thrum
military: busby, kepi, shako

* Asterisk means to look up this word to find more answer words.

night: biggin, mutch
part: bill, peak, visor
round: balmoral
seaman's: blackball cheeser
shaped: pileate
sheepskin: calpac(k)
16th cent.: bycocket
skull: beame, beanie, callot, chechia, coif, pileus, yarmulka
steel: cerveliere
woman's: biggonet, *ladies hat*
wool: balaclava, boina, bonnet
CAPABLE: *able*, equal, fit, up
CAPACIOUS: *able*, ample, full
CAPACITATE: *prepare*, *train*
CAPARISON: *adorn*, *dress*, equip
CAPE: cloak, headland, *wrap*
acute or angled: point
anteater: aardvark
armadillo: pangolin, smutsia
cart: carriage
chestnut: calodendrum
clerical: cope, fanon, orale
crocheted: sontag
dutch: afrikaans
elk: eland
florida: sable
fur: palatine, stole
gaullish: sagum
gooseberry: ground cherry, poha
gum: acacia, karroo bush
hen: catharacta, petrel, skua
hooded: almuce, amice, tippet
horn: cape stiff
horn fever: malingering
horn native: ona
jasmine: gardenia
lace: bertha, collaret, fichu, mantilla
lancewood: assagai, *spear*
land: head, ness, promontory
large: pelerine, talma
may warbler: dendroica tigrina
of goodhope: cape colony
pigeon: petrel, pintado
polecat: muishond, zoril

pondweed: water hawthorn
province people: pondo xosa
ruby: garnet, pyrope
seal: arctocephalus
sheep: albatross
-skin: goatskin, leather
tulip: blood lily
verde island: fago, sal
verde capital: praia
verde native: brava, serer
verde volcano: fogo
weed: cat's-ear, roccella
CAPER: *antic*, shrub, *trick*
CAPITAL: *asset*, basic, *best*, *principal*, *supply*, *supreme*
bonus: dividend
impairment: deficit, depletion
letter: majuscule
levy: property tax
provide: angel, back, finance
punishment: death penalty
CAPITALIST: banker, baron, moneybags, nabob, plutocrat
CAPRI CAVE: blue grotto
CAPRICE: fad, idea, notion, whim
CAPRICIOUS: frivolous, *wanton*
CAPSIZE: go down, sink, *upset*
CAPSULE: *bit*, pill, *short*
CAPTAIN: *leader*, *principal*
to the host: joab
CAPTION: *describe*, *title*
CAPTIOUS: irascible, *severe*
CAPTURE: *arrest*, *take*, *trap*
CAPUT: fallen, *head*, paragraph
mortuum: death's-head, skull
mundi: rome
CAR: *armored:* tank
barn: depot, station
cable: telpher
group: train
old: reo, stutz
price list: blue book
CARACAL: *cat: wild*, fur, *skin*
CARACOLE: *antic*, snailflower
CARAFE: bottle, croft, decanter
CARAPACE: case, shell, shield
CARAT: estimate, *value*, worth

* Asterisk means to look up this word to find more answer words.

CARBINE: escopet, musket, rifle
CARBON: black, dupe, fuel, soot
  allotrope: charcoal, diamond
  comb.: but
  copy: ditto, dupe, replica
  dioxide: choke damp, dry ice
  -like: anthracoid
  oxychloride: phosgene
  process: auto type
  sulphochloride: thiophosgene
CARCAJOU: badger, *cat: wild
CARD: agenda, list, ticket, wag
  best: command, soda
  card game, bid: misere, slam
  card game, old: brag, comet, gilet,
    hoc, hombre, loo, ombre, pam,
    primero, ruff, whist
  dominoes: fan tan
  group: deck, hand, pack
  hand, poor: bust
  holding: tenace
  number, suff.: spot
  player right of dealer: pone
  ranking: ace, face card, trump
  rules author: goren, hoyle
  sharp: *cheat, swindler
  sharping: fraud
  slam: vole
  spare hand: cat, pot, widow
  spot: pip
  suit: actor, bastos, braun, carreau,
    clubs, coeur, crowns, diamonds,
    eagles, eckstein, espadas, farbe,
    hearts, palo, pip, royals, spades
  thistle: plant, teasel
  up sleeve: reserve, surprise
  wild: bug, comet, freak, joker
  wool: comb, tease, tum
CARDINAL: bird, chief, fish, red
  assembly at rome: college
  blue herb: lobelia
  cap: berrettino
  chairman: camerlengo
  fish: agonida, apogon, mullet
  flower: bird of paradise, lobelia,
    scarlet lobelia
  notification: biglietto

  number: centillion, potency
  office: dataria, hat
  points: four directions, zenith
  rank: hat
  sauce: veloute
  smallest transfinite: alephnull
  symbol: red hat
  vestment: charity, faith, fortitude,
    hope, justice, prudence, temper-
    ance
  woolsey: little boy blue
CARE: *anxiety, *desire, *think
  cloth: bridal veil
  for: chaperon, esteem, foster, like,
    nurse, relish, tend
  for children: baby-sit
  -free: blase, blithe, debonair
  nothing for: scorn
  requiring: fragile, ticklish
  under another's: apprentice,
    charge, protege, ward
CAREEN: cant, heel, sway, *turn
CAREER: *speed, *trade, *work
CARESS: coddle, *love, *pet
CARGO: *pack, *quantity
  discard: flotsam, jetsam
  loader: stevedore
  space: bottom, hold
  stabilizer: ballast
CARIBBEAN: *bird:* tody
  garment: jupee
  gulf: darien
CARIBE: iranha, pirana
CARICA: jacaratia, papaya, tree
CARICATURE: burlesque, lam-
    poon
  plant: acanthaca, graptophyllum
CARILLON: glockenspiel, peal
CARK: harass, *plague, *trouble
CARL: miser, *peasant, *servant
CARNAL: gross, lewd, *wanton
CARNATION: flake, flesh, pink
CARNIVAL: apokeros, festival
  lace: reticella
  wild man: geek
CAROL: chant, *dance, *song

* **Asterisk means to look up this word to find more answer words.**

CAROLINA: *beechdrops:* pinesap
  catchfly: wild pink
  chinaroot: greenbrier, smilax
  poplar: balsam, cottonwood
  water shield: fanwort, plant
  wild woodbine: jasmine
CAROM: billiard, glance, *strike
CAROUSE: *drink, *party, *tear
CAROUSEL: *inspiration:* lilliom
CARP: chub, dace, ide, loach, orf,
  roud, rud(d), *scold
  comb.: endo, fruit
CARPEL: leaf, pistil, sorema
  mass: sorema
CARPENTER: ant, idler, joiner
  bee: xylocopa
  bird: woodpecker
  grass: yarrow
  herb: prunella, selfheal
  machine: lathe, planer, shaper
  moth: goat moth, prinoxysus
  pin: dowel
  square: figwort, scrophularia
  tool: adz, auger, awl, axe, gimlet,
    hammer, hatchet, plane, plumb
    level, square
CARPINUS: beech, betula, birch
  caroliniana: hornbeam
CARRIAGE: *vehicle references
  dog: dalmatian
  entrance: portal
  forward: cod
  trade: *society
CARRIER: freighter, hod, plane,
  railroad, truck, ship, *vehicle
CARROT: ammiace, anethum,
  carom, daucus, enticement,
  plant, root
  beetle: ligyrus
  deadly: drias
  genus: carum
  plant: anise
  ridges: juga
  top: red-head
  tree: madeira, melanoselinum
  weed: ambrosia elatior, ragweed
  wild: hilltrot, laceflower

  wood: cupania anacardioides
CARRY: bear, *pack, *win, *yield
  -all: *bag, case, etui, *pack
  arms: *fight, serve
  away: charm, eloin, *seize
  off: *kill, *seize, *take, *win
  on: continue, emote, endure, man-
    age, misbehave, operate, pursue,
    *storm, *work
  one's point: convince, score
  out: achieve, *complete
  over: extend, postpone, table
  -tale: gossip
  the ball: *direct, *run
  the banner: campaign, *lead
  the day: triumph, *win
  through: persevere, persist
  too far: exaggerate, overdo
  weight: bear, influence, matter
CART: *end of:* gate, tib
  freight: carreton
  horse: cartaver
  ladder: rack, zave
  license: caroome, carroon
  milkman's: pram
  racing: sulky
  rope: wanty
  rough: tumbril
  strong: dray
  -track plant: plantago, plantain
  two-wheeled: butt, dandy, shay
  -wheel: dollar, handspring
  -whip: lash, *punish
CARTEL: defy, pool, *trust
CARTER: fish, marysole, teamster
CARTHAGE: *apple:* pomegranate
  capital: caralis
  citadel: bozra, bursa, byrsa
  district: mara
  division: taenia
  family: barca
  foe: cato, rome, scipio
  fort: goletta
  founder: aeneas, dido
  general: hannibal, hanno
  god: moloch, vaal
  goddess: tanit(h)

* Asterisk means to look up this word to find more answer words.

government head: suffete
inhabitants: poeni
language: punic
lion: hannibal
magistrate: suffete
pert.: punic
queen: dido
ruler: dido, hannibal, hasdrubal
subjects: libyans, nomads
suburb: megara
warrior: mago
zama defeater: scipio
CARTHUSIAN: eremite, *monk
chronicler: ferrari
monastery: certosa, pavia
noted: hugh
order founder: st bruno
superior: prior
CARTOUCHE: cantilever, case, corbel, modillion, roll, shield
CARTRIDGE: cassette, missile
belt: bandoleer, bandolier
box: cartouch(e)
buff: color, putty
holder: clip
without bullet: blank, dud
CARVING: *art:* anaglyphy
ornamental: cameo, sculpture
pert.: glyphic, glyptic
relief: cameo
stone: incision, intaglio
technique: bori
CARYA: bitternut, hickory, pecan, pignut, shagbark, shellbark
CASE: *quantity, *test, *try
book-holding: forel, forrel
cigar: humidor
cosmetic: compact
divinity: casuistry
explosive: firecracker, shell
grammatical: ablative, accusative, dative, genitive, nominative, objective
harden: accustom, callous
hardened: *strong, tough, vet
history: *record, *story
in point: example

liquor: cellaret
mate: bombshelter, *fort
-ment: cavetto, scotia, window
shot: canister, cartouche
small: bulla, etui, etwee, tye
weed: shepherd's-purse
CASH: *asset, *money, specie
account: bank credit
book: log
box: caisse, coffer, till
in: convert, take profit
keeper: bursar, cashier, steller
on delivery: cod
note: melt
CASHEW: cushaw, mesquite
bird: curassow, tanager
fruit: anacardium
lake: auburn, color
nut: color, sedge
CASHIER: bursar, *dismiss
CASK: barrel, firkin, hogshead
bulge: bilge
42-gallon: tierce
headpiece: cant
oil: rier
orifice: bunghole
part: bulge, chime, lag
rim: chimb, chime
stave: lag
tap: canel, cannel
wine: butt, fust, pipe, tierce
CASS: *dismiss, quash, void
CASSANDRA: *prophet, shrub
father: priam
CASSAVA: aipi, manioc, tapioca
juice: casiri
starch: brazilian arrowroot
CASSIA: herb, drug, senna, shrub
alata: acapulco, ringworm bush
bark: cinnamon, lignea
fistula: drumstick tree
occidentalis: mogdad coffee
CASSIOPEIA: *daughter:* andromeda
CAST: *allot, *throw, *yield
about: *consider, *try, *turn
a glance: *look, peer, *see

* Asterisk means to look up this word to find more answer words.

anchor: moor, **stop*
aside, away: **discard,* **dismiss,* maroon, reject, squander
aspersions: malign, **smear*
ballot: vote
down: **abase,* **low,* **sad*
eye: strabismus
forth: disgorge, emit, vomit
iron: adamant, **hard,* **solid*
loose: let go, **release,* unlash
lots: gamble, **venture*
off: **abandon,* **discard,* spew
out: **banish,* **dismiss*
out nines: check, **test,* verify
shadow over: **obscure*
spell: bewitch, **trap*
the die: **decide,* **settle*
the first stone: **open,* **start*
theatrical: actors, players
up: appeal, compute, reckon
CASTE: *agricultural:* meo
cowherds: ahir
gardener: mali
group: varna
high: amelu, babhan
hindu: sudra, varna
labor: sudra
low: bhil, koli, kuli, pariah
mercantile: agarwal, banyan
member: balija
minor, hindu: gati, kula
priestly: brahman, magus
tamil merchant: chetty
top: cream, elite, four hundred
trader: balija
vaisya: aroras
warrior: kshatriya
CASTIGATE: **beat,* **whip*
CASTING: *horoscope:* apotelesm
-line: leader
mold: die, matrix
rough: pig
vote: decider
CASTLE: *build:* dream
builder: visionary
gilliflower: brompton stock
in the air in spain: daydream

part: bawn, donjon, drawbridge, keep, moat, portcullis, tower
CASTOR: **dioscuri*
bean meal: fertilizer
bean poison: ricin
brother: pollux
eater: eri(a)
gray: yellow-green
horse: cyllaros
parent: leda, zeus
plant: kiki, palma christi
silk: eri, eria, sums
slayer: idas
CASUALS: loafers, slacks
CAT: *-and-dog:* quarrelsome, vicious
bed: red valerian
berry: gooseberry, holly
bird: bowerbird, mimidae
breed: angora, burmese, cheshire, chincilla, coon, maltese, manul, manx, margay, persian, russian, siamese, tabby, tortoise-shell, turkish
brier: carrion flower, smilax
call: assail, boo, hoot, deride
-chop: fig marigold
civetlike: genet
-clover: bird's-foot trefoil
comb.: aleuro
cry: meow, mew, miaou, miaow, miau, purr, waul, yelp, yow
fancier: aelurophile
female: grimalkin
fever: distemper
fish: aspredo, bagre, bullhead, candiru, channel fish, cusk, cuttlefish, docmac, elod, hassar, mudfish, raad, raash, sheatfish, tandau, threadfin
fish row lovers: porgy and bess
fit: tantrum
-footed: stealthy
group: clowder
-gut: cord, goat's-rue, rope string, tharm, wild sweet pea
-headed goddess: bast, pacht

* **Asterisk means to look up this word to find more answer words.**

house: bagnio, brothel, mouser
like: feline, noiseless, sly
-locks: cotton grass
-o-nine-tails: flogger, lash
pea: cow vetch, vicia cracca
shark: dogfish, scylliorhinus
silver: mica
skinner: engineer
squirrel: cacomistle
-tail: ament, black cap, candle-
wick, carbungi, dod, matreed,
murray down, musk, raupo,
reree, totra, tule
thyme: germander, teucrium
-walk: footway
-whistles: horsetail, plant
wild: balu, bobcat, chaus, civet,
cougar, eyra, jaguar, lion, lynx,
manul, ocelot, panther, puma,
serval, tiger
-witted: conceited
CATS: *and dogs:* securities
-claw: acacia, black bead, vetch
-concert: noise, uproar
-cradle: ribwort
-ear: capeweed, cudweed, gosmore
-eye: chatoyant, gem, speedwell
-faces: pansy, flower
-foot: thistle, wild ginger
-grass: sun spurge
-paw: agent, amarantha, cully,
dupe, gull, hitch, stooge
-tail: blueweed, corn god, reed
mace, timothy, viper's bugloss
-tongue: velvet bur, verbena
-whiskers: smeller, vibrissa
CATACLYSM: **catastrophe*
CATALOG: file, list, **schedule*
CATAPULT: onager, **throw*
CATASTROPHE: **accident,* debacle, disaster, **plague, *trouble*
CATCH: **take, *trap, *trick,* win
CATCHING: infectious, taking
CATERPILLAR: aweto, eruca,
woubit
eater: beetle, calosoma

fern: hart's-tongue
hunter: carabida, crow shrike
CATHEDRAL: church, official
chapter house: cabildo
endowment: prebend
-like: ecclesiastical
passage: slype
CATKIN: ament, rag, spike
CATOISM: austerity, harshness
CATREUS: *daughter:* apemosyne
CATTLE: beeves, bulls, cow
black: angus, kerry
brand: buist, duff
breed: aberdeen, afrikander, angus, brahma, charolais, devon,
durham, galloway, guernsey,
hereford, holstein, jersey, santa
gertrudis, zebu
bush: atalaya, sapinda
call: sook
comb.: bovi
damara: herero
dealer: drover, herder, rancher
dehorned: muley, mulley
disease: anthrax, blackleg
dung: casson
dwarf: devon, nata, niata
feed for hire: agist
food: bhoosa, chaff, soilage
goddess: bubona
group: creaght, drove, herd
grub: warble fly
intestine: casing
leader: nose ring
long-haired: dishley
man: byreman, cowboy, stockman
mange: texas itch
pen: barn, barth, bawn, byre, corral, hovel, kraal, reeve
plague: murie, rinderpest
raik: pasture, range
stealing: abigeat
thief: abactor, abigeus, rustler
tick: carapato, garrapata
yard: cancha
CAUCASIAN: *carpet:* kuba
goat: bharal, tehr, tur, zac

* Asterisk means to look up this word to find more answer words.

language: adigne, andi, avar, itranican, laz, semitic, udic
moslem: laz(zi)
peak: elbruz, kazbek
race: aryan, iran, lolo, nosu, osset(e), semite
rug: baku, chila, derbend, kazak, kuba, sumak
tribe: budukha, imer, kubachi, kurd, lazi, pshav, svan
CAUSE: *account,* reason, *work*
comb.: aetio, aitio, etio
science of: etiology
CAUSING: *suff.:* able
CAUSTIC: *acerb,* keen, lye, tart
creeper: euporbia, milk plant
vine: sacrostemma, australe
CAUTELOUS: crafty, *smart*
CAUTERIZE: singe, sterilize
CAUTION: *advise,* *care,* tip off
money: deposit
CAUTIOUS: chary, fabian, wary
CAVALIER: brave, debonair, *fellow,* proud, *soldier,* *spark*
servente: follower
CAVALRY: horses, knighthood
horse: lancer
man: carabinero, dragoon, hussar, sowar, spahi, uhlan
twill: tricotine
weapon: lance, saber
CAVE: beware, *opening,* *retreat*
comb.: antr, antro
cricket: ceuthophilus
dweller: taurus, troglodyte
fish: amblyopsis, blindfish
in: debacle, fall, *yield*
man: aborigine, ancient
of trophonius: despair
researcher: spelunker
science of: speleology
CAVIAR: ova, ikra, relish, roe
source: shad, sterlet, sturgeon
CAVIL: carp, censure, *scold*
CAVITY: abri, cup, *opening*
body: antrum aula, coelum, fossa, sinus

comb.: antro, coele, sunu
filler: bone plombe, cement, silver, gold
gun: bore
heart: atrium, ventricle
lode: voog, vugg, vugh
pert.: atrial, geodic, sinal
rock: geode, lode
sac-like: bursa, vesicle
skull: aula, fossa, sinus
CAW(K): *cry,* mineral, quark
CAXI: fish, snapper
CAY: island, islet, key
CAYENNE: copepod, pepper, whist
cherry: surinam
incense: elemi
lin-aloe oil: bois de rose
pepper extract: capsicin
rose: pottery-bark tree, sassafras
CEASE: break, *end,* *pass,* *stop*
fire: armistice, truce
CECROPIA: bast fiber, mulberry
adenopus: ambay, timber tree
moth: samia, silkworm
CECROPS: *daughter:* herse
wife: agraulos
CEDE: *allot,* give up, *yield*
CEILING: *cover,* roof, *top*
covering: calcimine, kalsomine
division: trave
mine: astel
paneled: artesonado, lacunaria
wooden: plancher
zero: atmosphere
CELEBES: *bovine:* anoa
island: muna
people: alfuro, bugi, toraja
sea: banda
wind: barat
CELEBRATE: *honor,* *praise*
CELEBRATED: famed, *great*
CELEBRITY: lion, *magnate,* star
CELERITY: dispatch, *speed,* zip
CELESTIAL: empyrean, *holy*
being: angel, cherub, seraph

* Asterisk means to look up this word to find more answer words.

body: ball, comet, meteor, nebual, planet, **star*
city: jerusalem, zion
elevation of mind: anagoge
matter: nebula
mechanics: astronomy
space: blue, infinity
sphere: planet, **star*
teacher: master of heaven
CELEUS: *daughter:* andromeda
CELIBATE: **ascetic*, **monk*
CELL: *-alga:* autospore
bull: toril
coloring: endochrome
colorless: achroacyte, lymphocyte
connecting: heterocyst
-degeneration: cataplasia, lyse
division: amitosis, linin, spirem(e)
family: coenobium
generative: gamete
granule: blepharoplast
group: blastema, cascade, ceptor
kernel: nucleus
layer: blastoderm, blastula
migratory: leucocyte
part: energid, linin, nucleus, plastid, protoplast, vacuole
pert.: cytoid
plant: meristem
process: axon
reproductive: agamete, gamete
star-shaped: astroblast
suff.: ont
-transfer: metastasize
unit: biogen
wall constituent: callose
white: leucocyte, macrophage
CELT: erse, gael, **irish*, ith, manx, **scotch*, **welsh*
abbot: coarb
book of: ballymote, conquests, dun cow, hergest, lecan, leinster, rhydderch
chariot: essed
chieftain: tanist
church: iona
clan: sept

dart: colp
feast: beltane, imbolc, lugnas(ad), samain
giant: domnu, fionn, fomors
giant land: ysbaddaden
giantess: domnu
god: aengus, amaethon, angus og, arawn, artor, beal, belinus, bran, camulus, dagda, dea, dylan, eochaid ollathair, esus, gobniu, govannan, gwydion, gwyn, hafgan, lamfhada, ler, ller, lludd, llyr, lug(h), mannan, midir, nuada, nudd, oengus, pwyll, ruad rofhessa, taranis, teutates, the dagda
goddess: ana, anu, arianrhod, badb, bodb, brigid, brigit, bridget, dana, danu, don, macha, rhiannon, tailtiu, the badb, the morrigan
god's abode: brugh na boinne
harp: clairschach, telyn
hero: cu chulainn, finn mac cumal, goll, ossian, setanta
hero's sword: calad-bolg
land-holding system: rundale
language: brythonic, cymric, gaelic, irish, manx, welsh
literature, myths: **celt: book*, duan, lebor gabala, mabinogion
otherworld: mag mel, tir fothuinn, tir nanoc
paradise: avalon
pasture: collop, colp
priest: druid
shrine: avebury, stonehenge
spirit: banshee, kelpie
sword: sax, seax
warrior: dagda, fenian, kern
CEMENT: **join*, **stick*, **unite*
and stone: bumicky
hydraulic: paar, roman
infusible: lute
plaster: stucco
plastic: albolite, albolith
quick-drying: mastic

* Asterisk means to look up this word to find more answer words.

well-lining: steen
window glass: putty
work: covering
CEMETERY: calvary, **dead:*
home
CENSURE: **abuse,* **criticize*
CENTIMANES: **hecatoncheires*
CENTURY: age, eon, eternity
plant: agave, maguey, pita
ten: chiliad, millennium
CEPANEUS COUSIN: evadne
CEPHALUS COUSIN: eos, procris
CEPHAS: peter, simon, **stone*
CEPHEUS: *daughter:* andromeda
CERCYON: *daughter:* alope
CEREMONY: **rite*
CERTAIN: **absolute,* **true*
CERTIFICATE: authorize, bond,
credential, diploma, ticket
cargo: navicert
debt: bond, debenture, iou
illness: aegrotat
invention: patent
land: amparo, deed
CERTIFY: **assure,* endorse, okay
CETO: *young:* **gorgons,* **graeae*
CEYLON: lanka, serendip, sinhala
aborigine: toda, vedda(h)
ancient capital: anuradhapura,
polonnaruwa, sigiriya
animal: buffalo, elephant, sambar,
spotted deer
ape: maha, langur
athens: kandy
bird: peacock, wanderoo
boat: balsa, dhoni, warkamoowee
capitals: colombo, kandy
dravidian: tamil
food: curry, egg hopper
footsoldier: peon
fortress city: sigiriya
garment: sarong
gooseberry: ketembilla
governor: disawa
hemp: ifa, murva, pangane
language: pali, tamil
lemur: lori(s)

lion race: sinhalese
litter: tonjon
lotus: nelumbo
measure: para(h), seer
monkey: langur, maha, rilawa
moss: agar, alga, gracilaria, gula-
man, jaffna
national park: ruhuna, wilpattu
native: veddah, weddah
nelumbo: lotus
oak: kusam, schleichera
pageant: esala perahera
palm: talipat, talipot
port: batticaloa, galle
prince, patricide: kasyapa
resort: bentota, hikkaduwa,
ruhuna, trincomalee, wilpattu
rest house: abalam, tissamaharama
rose: oleander, shrub
ruins: **ancient capital*
sedan: tomjon, tonjon
shrine: dagoba
skirt: reddha
snake: adjiger
temple: asokharamaya, kelaniya,
lankatilaka
tree: bo, doon, sri maha bodhi
CHAFE: **anger,* **annoy,* fret, vex
CHAFF: **banter,* refuse, riffraff
finch: robinet, shelly, spink
CHAGRIN: **abash,* **trouble*
CHAIN: **bind,* **fetter,* **tie*
collar: tore, torque
grab: wildcat
key: chatelaine
-like: catenulate
logs: bull chain, jack ladder
-mail: byrnie
pert.: catenarian, catenary
rocks: reef
steps: cascade
ten square: acre
CHAINS: bondage, irons, shackles
lady in: andromeda
CHAMPION: **abet,* **ace*
CHANCE: **accident,* **venture*
comb.: tycho

* Asterisk means to look up this word to find more answer words.

favorable: odds
goddess: tyche
medley: haphazard, potluck
upon: encounter, *meet
CHANGE: *amend, *oscillate,
  *remedy, *remove, *trade, *turn
back: *return, revert
character: denature
color: blush, dye, flush
comb.: ac, ad, ap, ar, at, tropo
course: bear away, cant, tack
for: *substitute
into: become
life: climacteric, menopause
maker: boxman
over: *convert
radical: revolution
resistance to: inertia
CHANNEL: *route, *waterway,
  *way
CHAOS: *abyss, *noise, snafu
babylonian: apsu
daughter: nox, nyx
maori: kore
personification: anarch
son: aether, erebus
utter: tophet(h)
CHARACTER: *actor, *form,
  *disposition, *kind, *symbol
CHARGE: *accuse, *attack, *trust
CHARIOT: auto, seven, vehicle
ancient: curre, essed, rath
four-wheeled: quadriga
god-carrying: rath(a)
poetic: wain
three-wheeled: troga
top: calash
two-wheeled: biga, essed, gig
CHARISMA: impact, oomph,
  power
CHARLEMAGNE: *adviser:* alcuin
brother: carloman
conquest: avars
enemy: baligant, marsile
father: pepin
horse: tencendur
nephew: orlando, roland

paladin: acelin, anseis, astor,
  berengier, engeber, gaifer, geof-
  frey, gerard, gerier, gerin, ivoiere,
  ivon, ogier, oliver, otes, richard,
  roland, samson, turpin
pert.: caroline, carolinian
shield: biterne
sword: joyeuse
traitor: ganelon
war cry: montjoie
CHARM: *allure, *fetish, *symbol
CHARON: *father:* erebus
CHASE: court, *search, woo
along: depart, scat, scram
away: drive, repulse, rout
deity: apollo, artemis, diana
CHASM: *abyss, *opening
CHASTEN, CHASTISE: *punish
CHATTER: *babble, *gossip, *talk
box: blue jay, magpie, piet
CHEAP: *low, *mean, *small
-jack: huckster, pedlar, vendor
-skate: miser, piker, skinflint
CHEAT: bamboozle, bunko, con,
  *deceive, *impostor, *lie, *sharp,
  *skin, *take, *trick
cards: blackleg, crimp, greek, mechanic, milk, philosopher, shark,
  shill, snow, stack
CHECK: *analyze, *stop, *token
mate: *defeat, *stop, thwart
out: depart, die, leave, vanish
over: examine, inspect, verify
rein: curb, harness, saccade
up on: bomb, *test, *try
CHECKERS: draughts, giveaway
opening: defiance, dyke, fife
term: block, bridge, crown, king,
  man off, squeeze, stroke
CHEEK: audacity, gall, temerity
bone: malar, zygoma
comb.: bucco
pert.: buccal, genal, malar
CHEER: *acclaim, *support
CHEESE: *blue:* gorgonzola, **my**-
  cella, pipcreme
box: quadrangle

* Asterisk means to look up this word to find more answer words.

cake: gam, leg, photo(graph)
cement: glue
cloth: butter muslin
dish: fondue, rarebit, souffle
green: sapsago
hard: asiago, fontinella, jack, kasseri, parmesian, romano
inferior: dick
it: begone, don't, *stop
knife: spatula
maggot: skipper
-pairing: parsimonious
pert.: caseic, caseous
soft: babybel, bonbel, brie, camembert, sanglier, tybo
CHEESY: *cheap, paltry, punk
CHEMICAL: *agent:* catalyst
cleansant: krypton
compound: amide, amine, azine,
azo, boride, ceria, elaterin, ester,
imide, imine, iodide, inosite,
isomer, leucine, metamer, tou-
lene, ytterbia
container: aludel, retort
pref.: aci, amid, amino, oxa
process: catalysis, titration
salt: borate, ester, niter, sal
suff.: ac, amid, ane, ein, enol, ile,
ine, ion, ite, ole, ose
test: assay
variability: allomerism
CHERISH: *love, *prize, *value
CHERRY: amerelle, bigarreau,
bing, cerasus, cordia, cornel,
duke, egriot, gean, lambert, mascara, mazzard, morel(lo), padus
bird: cedar waxwing
color: cerise, red, scarlet
extract: cerasein
orange: kumquat
CHERUB: *angel, child, eudemon
CHESS: *ancestor:* chaturanga
board: solitaire
draw game: stalemate
goddess: caissa
man: bishop, king, knight, man,
pawn, rook, queen, springer

move: castle, check, fianchetto
term: en passant, fork, gambit
variant: kriegspiel, pachisi
CHEST: bin, bureau, casket, case
alms: almoin, almoign
animal: brisket
bone: costa
human: breast, thorax
maker: arkwright
meal: girnal, girnel
-nut: chinquapin, *joke, tan
-nut and gray: roan
-nut blight: bark disease
-nut clam: astarte
-nut dwarf: chinquapin
-nut, pert.: castanean, esculic
-nut, water: ling, stripe, tapa
pert.: pectoral, thoracic
sacred: arca, ark, cist, kist
sound: rale, rhoncus, wheeze
supply: wangan, wanigan
CHEVALIER: *lord, *noble
d'industrie: *sharp(er)
raoul: bluebeard, murderer
CHEW: *bite, *eat, *rally, *rebuke
inability to: amasesis
the rag: *chatter, *gossip
up the scenery: emote, overact
CHIC: dapper, natty, *smart
CHICANERY: *deception, *trick
CHICK: babe, child, fowl, girl
CHICKEN: *group:* brood, poultry
heart: cold feet, *coward(ice)
out: *quit, renege
raising device: brooder
snake: boba
soup: caldo tlalpeno
tick: argas, blue bug
young: broiler, chick, fryer, poult,
pullet
CHICORY: bunk, plant, succory
CHIDE: *abuse, *chew, rate
CHIEF: *buffoon:* archimime
comb.: arch, archi, archy
executive: boss, chairman, *leader,
president, *ruler
magistrate: avoyer, syndic

* Asterisk means to look up this word to find more answer words.

CHILD: *birth:* accouchement
birth feast food: blithemeat
chubby: butterball, rolypoly
comb.: paedo, ped(o)
dainty: elf, fairy
foster: dalt, norry, nurry
game: bob cherry, hide-and-seek
homeless: waif
illegitimate: bastard, by-blow
killer: infanticide
-like: artless, innocent, naive
mixed blood: mustee, octoroon
-naming festival: amphidromia
parentless: orphan
patron saint: claus, nicholas
pert.: filial
play: trifle
protector: adeona
roguish: hellion, imp, smatche, scamp, urchin
spoiled: brat, cockney, mardy
street: arab, gamin
tiny: babe, peewee, tot
CHILE: *aborigine:* inca
arborvitae: alerce, cedar
coastal wind: sures
coin: condor, escudo, libra
deer: pudu
desert: atacama
indian: araucanian, atacameno
marxist: alleudl
measure: cuadra, fanega, vara
mineral bath: colina, toro
palm: coquito
peak: juncal, maipu, pular
rodent: chinchilla
shrub: boldo, lithi, pepino
tree: alerce, brea, coigue, coleu, muermo, pelu, rauli, roble, ulmo
weight: grano, libra, quintal
workman: roto
CHIMERA: *killer:* bellerophon
CHIMNEY: *cap:* abatvent, cowl
corner: hearth, residence
deposit: soot
lining: parget
piece: ingle, mantle, parel

pipe: flue
post: speer
CHIN: chat, converse, jaw, *talk*
comb.: genio
CHINA: *abacus:* suan-pan
aborigine: mans, miao, yao-min
alloy: packtong, paktong
ancient: cathay, seres, tsao
animals, magic: dragon, lung, phoenix, tortoise, unicorn
anise: badian, illicium verum
annals: bamboo books
antelope: dzeren
arch: pailoo, pailou, pailow
aromatic root: ginseng
artichoke: chorogi
assembly: hui
aster: callistephus
backgammon: double sixes, sheung luk
bamboo: whangee
banker: schroff
bean: cowpea, soy
berry: azedarach, soapberry
bird, mythological: shang yang
black tea: oolong
blue: nikko
boat: bark, junk, sampan
brick bed: k'ang
brigand: hunghutzu
cabbage: pakchoi
calculator: suan-pan
canton: fu, hsein
caucasian: lolo, nosu
chestnut: ling
chopsticks: fie jie
christian god: shen
clay: kaolin
cloth: moxa, nankin, pulo, sha
club: tong
comb.: sinic, sinico, sino
commissioner: lin
communist leader: chen pota, chou-en-lai, kang sheng, lin piao, mao tse-tung
concubine: tsip
condiment: balachong, napee

* Asterisk means to look up this word to find more answer words.

cooking: cantonese, fukien, honan, mandarin, peking, shantung, szechuen, yangchow

cosmic order: tao

court: uemen

cult: amidism, joss

customs collector: hoppo

date: jujube

deer: elaphure

desert: gobi, shamo

dialect: amoy, canton, foochow, hakka, ningpo, swaton, wenchow

dice: shik tsz

dignitary: celestiality

dish: bao, bean curd, bird's-nest soup, buddha's feast, bum bum, cha chiang mein, chiang poa, chop suey, chow mein, dim sum, egg roll, eight jewel, fun-ga, fun see, gai bao, gingko nut, hsiang-su-ya-tze, hung-shao-yee, kung poa, lichee, lion's-head, moo-shi, moo-shu pork, paper-wrapped chicken, peking duck, pickled cabbage, pig's-stomach, rice, sa-kwa-ya, seaweed, shark's-fin, shrimp toast, sizzling rice, snow peas, sour-hot soup, suan-la-tang, sub gum, sui mai, sweet and sour, szechwan pepper, thousand-year eggs, water chestnut, whole fish, wo choy, woh won ton, yang chao

dog: chow, peke(ingese)

domino: kwat pai, nga, tim tsz

dragon: chilin, lung

drink: bean wine, samshu

duck: mandarin

duck eggs: pidan

dulcimer: yang-kin

dynasty: chin, chou, chow, fo, ghos, han, hao, heh, hsia, kin, liao, ming, shang, sui, sung, tang, tsin, wei, yuan

dynasty, first: hsia

early race: khitans

empire, pert.: celestial

exchange medium: sycee

extra tax: squeeze

factory: hong

fan palm: bourbon, latania

festival: ching ming

feudal state: wei

figure puzzle: tangram

figurine: magot

fish: trepang

flute: tche

frontier: heavenly mountains, tien shan

fruit: lichee, litchi

game: hoi tap, kap tai shap, kong poh, mah jongg, pat cha sheung luk, shing ku to, tiuu

gateway: pailou

gelatin: agalloch, haitsai

ginger: galingale

god: cheng-huang, *dragon king*, fan kuei, feng-po, ghos, *happiness: gods*, *immortals: eight*, jos, juant, ksitigarbha, kuan-ti, kuei-hsing, lei-kung, lu-pan, men-shen, shen, sun-pin, tai-yueh, tatior, ti-tsang, tsao-shen, tsao-wang, tung-yueh-tati, tuti, wen chang, yun-tung, yu-tzu

goddess: chango, chih-nii, feng-popo, hengo, mei-chou, tien-hou, tien-mu

gong: tamtam

gooseberry: averrhoa, carambola

grand secretariat: neiko

grape: wampee

grass: bon, ramie, rhia

grass linen: barandos

group: guild, hui, tong

gruel: congee, conjee

heaven: kun-lun mountain

herb: ginseng, nandina, tea

hero: hai jui

houseboat: tanka

idol: joss, pagoda

immigrant: hakka

indigo: isatis

isinglass: agalloch, agar

* Asterisk means to look up this word to find more answer words.

island: amoy, formosa, hainan, macao, quemoy, taiwan
jute: chingma
kingdom: shu, wei, wu
knockhead: cotow
laborer: coolie, cooly
language: cantonese, mandarin
language, pert.: sinological
lantern plant: alkekengi
lawn grass: eremochloa
lemon: citron
letter: mana
licentiate"s degree: siutsai
limestone: sinian
magistrate: mandarin
magnolia: yulan
mandarin's residence: oyamen
merchant's corporation: hong
measure: chang, chih, ching, cho, fang, kung, quei, sheng, shing, tchung, teke, tsan, tsun
mongol dynasty: yuan
monkey: douc
mountain: alashan, funiu-shan, kuen-lun, kuliang, omei, omi, pu-ling, sung, ta-yu-ling
musical instrument: cheng, kin, samisen, sang, sheng
name, first: ming
name, last: hsing
noodles: mein
numbers: (1) yi(h), (2) er, urh, (3) san, shan, (4) sze, (5) woo, wu, (6) liu, luh, (7) tsi(eh), (8) pa, (9) chiu, kew, (10) shih tsu, (100) pih, (1,000) tseen
nurse: amah
nut: litchi
official: ahoug, amban, kuan, kwan, mandarin, taoyan
oil: tung
orange: kumquat, mandarin
ounce: tael
ox: zebu
pagoda: ta, taa, taag
parasol tree: aogiri
pea tree: caragana

peony: moutan
pert.: cataian, seric, sinic
philosopher: confucius, laotzu
plant: ginseng, ramie, rice
poet: li po, li tai-po
pony: griffin
porcelain: blanc de chine, celadon, eelskin, ju, ko
porgy: tai
pottery: boccaro, chien, chun, kuan, ming, ting, tzuchou
pound: catty
principle: li, tao, yin, yang
provincial chief: taoyin
public: kung
puzzle: enigma, tangram
red: bittersweet, chrome
religion: caodaism, confucianism, shinto, taoism
roller: sirgant
root, dried: galangal, ginseng
ruler: yao(u), yau
sage: lao-tzu, sun wa
salutation: bow, kowtow
sand pear: pyrus
sauce: soy
sect: taoism, taou
sedge: kali, mati
shop: toko
shrub: che, fatsia, kerria, rea
sidestreet: hutung
silkworm: ailanthus, tussur
skiff: sampan
sky: tien
society: boxer, hoey, huey, hui, hung, tong, triad
sovereign: kee, kublai, yaou
squash: cushaw
spirit: kuei, kwei
stocks: cangue
street: hutung
student: sinologue
sugar cane: sorgo
supply line: burma road
taa: pagoda
tartar tribe: toda
tax: likin

* Asterisk means to look up this word to find more answer words.

tea: bohea, cha, congo, congu, emesa, hyson, oolong, padra
temple: pagoda, taa(g)
tourist attraction: forbidden city, great wall, hall of the people, ming tombs, shanghai bund, summer palace, sun yat-sen memorial, temple of heaven, trade fair
toy: tangram
travel service: luxingshe
treaty port: amoy, ichang
tree: apricot plum, azedarach, bandoline, bead, gingko, kaya, kinkan, kumquat, matsu, nikko, yulan
tribe: heh, hei, hu, miao, shan
truth: tao
vegetable: udo
vine: kudzu, yangtao
walking stick: whangee
ware: ceramic, cinchona, crockery, delft, dishes, dresden, eggshell, enamel, faience, limoges, porcelain, sevres, spode, wedgewood
wax: cere, pela
weight: catty, chien, fen, hao, kin, picul, tael, tan
wife: tsai
wind instrument: cheng, sheng
wine: shao hsing
wormwood: moxa
CHINGACHGOOK: *son:* uncas
CHINOOK: *chief:* tyee
god: tamanoas
people: tilikum, tillicum
powwow: wawa
salmon: quinnat
state: washington
woman: klootchman
CHIP: **bit,* nig, **part,* **token*
in: ante, interrupt, **settle*
off the old block: offspring
CHIPPER: **active,* cocky, **quick*
CHISEL: **cheat,* engrave, gouge
broad: drove
corner: bruzz
edge: basil, bezel, face

engraving: scooper, scorper
in: intrude
-like tool: ade, adze
mason's: pommel
mine: gad, peeker
paring: skew, slick
sculpture: ebauchoir, gradine
-shaped: scalpiform
stone: broach, celt
stonemason's: drove
toothed: jagger
triangular: bur, burr
wheelwright's: bruzz (iron)
CHISION SON: elidad
CHIVALRY: *saint:* george
CHIVY: chase, **cry,* nag, **scold*
CHOCOLATE: assonia, candy
family: sterculiaceae
flower: alpine bloom, geranium
machine: conche
mixer: molinet
powder: cocoa, pinole
seed: cacao
tree: cacao, cola
CHOICE: **best,* **unique,* **will*
CHOKE: *berries:* aronia
coil: reactor
damp: carbon dioxide, miasma
off: gag, stifle, suppress
CHOLER: **anger,* fury, ire, wrath
CHOOSE: **adopt,* opt, pick, **will*
CHOP: *down:* fell
eye of: noisette
fallen: downcast, sullen
house: cafe, restaurant
logic: argue, contend, vie
off: amputate, drib, lop, prune
sticks: fie jie, hashie, tools
CHORUS: **accord,* sing, speak
girl: beauty, dancer, rockette
leader: cantor, coryphaeus
CHOW: dog, eats, grub, mess
chow: cuckoo, olio, slaw
CHRISTIAN: *early:* alogi
eastern: uniate
egyptian: copt
feast: agape, eucharist

* **Asterisk means to look up this word to find more answer words.**

persecuted: martyr
scientist: mind healer
symbol: cross, ichthus, orant
CHRISTMAS: *carol:* noel, nowel
  crib: creche
  decoration: holly, mistletoe
  drink: eggnog, nog, nogg
  entertainment: bummack
  hymn: adeste fidelis
  mass supper: reveillon
  rose: bearfoot, hellebore
  symbol: santa claus, stars, tree
CHRONICLE: *account,* diary, life
CHRYSAOR: *wife:* callirrhoe
CHUCK: *discard, *quit, *throw
  -full: replete
  -luck: bird cage, hazard, sweat
  wagon: cafe, restaurant
CHURCH: *and state:* erastian
  balcony: cantoria
  calendar: ordo
  chapel: oratory
  council: synod
  court: rota
  deputy: curate, vicat
  dissenter: sectary
  doorkeeper: ostiary
  doxology: gloria
  early christian: basilica
  episcopacy: prelacy
  goer: communicant, devotee
  government: archiepiscopacy
  house: parsonage
  judicatory: classis
  jurisdiction: deanery, diocese,
    parish, see
  man: abbe, archbishop, beadle,
    bishop, cardinal, cleric, cure,
    deacon, dean, devotee, ecclesias-
    tic, elder, father, layman, lector,
    minister, origen, papas, pope,
    preacher, prelate, priest, primate,
    prophet, rector, reverend, sex-
    ton, verger, vicar
  men, group: clergy
  offering: altarage
  part: aisle, altar, ambry, apse,

  chancel, cloister, crypt, font,
    nave, sacristy
  prayer: kyrie eleison
  reader: lector
  recess: apse, apsidiole, apsis
  retreat: *monastery
  revenue: annat, benefice, tithe
  room: galilee, sacristy, vestry
  seat: bench, pew, pue, sedile
  seaman's: bethel
  service: matin, mass, rite
  side, pert.: cantoris
  stand: ambo
  stipend: prebend
  traffic in: simony
  vault: crypt
  vessel: ama, amula, columba,
    colymbion, monstrance, piscina
  wall: cashel
  warden: ecclesiastic, sexton
  warden's aide: hoggler, sideman
  wash basin: lavabo
  yard: cemetery
CHURL: *peasant, *servant
CHURN: *agitate, beat, *whip
CHUTE: *waterway
CICADA: cagale, jarfly, locust
  noise: chirr
CICERO TARGET: catiline
CID: bivar, campeador, chief
  sword: colada, tizona
CIGAR: *black:* maduro, toscani
  crude: cheroot, culebra
  dark: colorado, maduro
  cheap: broom, cabbage, el ropo,
    stogie, stinker, toby, twofer
  factory: buckeye
  fish: quiaquia, scad
  grader: escojedore
  group: box, bundle, humidor
  maker: tabaquero
  maker, first: pela, demetrio
  mild: claro
  pioneer: ignacio haya
  process: curing, fermentation
  salesman: drummer
  shape: belvedere, bonanza, bonita,

---

* **Asterisk means to look up this word to find more answer words.**

breva, monte carlo, palma,
panatela, swagger
size: barcelona, cheroot, churchill,
cigarillo, kohinorr
tobacco: broad leaf, havana
tree: catalpa
wrapper: candela
CINCH: assure, breeze, pipe
up: fasten, grip, harness, *set
CINCHONA: quinidine, quinine
CINNAMON: cassia, ishipingo
apple: sweetsop
fern: bread root, buckhorn
oak: bluejack
stone: essonite, garnet
tree: canela, cannella
tree extract: camphor
CIRCE: *brother:* aeetes
father: helios
island: aeaea
niece: medea
son: comus
CIRCLE: *group, *party, *sphere
altitude: almucantar
celestial: colure
geographic: tropic
light: aura, halo, nimbus
longest chord: diameter
parquet: orchestra
part: arc, chord, radius, secant,
segment, tangent
squared: ring
squaring: cyclometry, cyclotomy
CIRCUIT: *auxiliary:* relay
heterodyne: autodyne
inductance: henry
rider: *church man
CIRCUMSTANCE: *affair, detail,
item, *particular, strait
CIRCUS: *arena, big top, *show
column: meta
cyaneus: blue glede
employee: clown, flea, tamer
geat: rings, tent, trapeze
post: meta
rider: desultor
ring: arena

wall: spina
CITE: *accuse, *name, quote
CITRUS: *aurantium:* bigarade
belt: california, florida
black fly: bean aphis, similium
disease: buckskin
drink: ade
fruit: citron, grapefruit, lemon,
lime, orange, shaddock, tangelo,
tangerine
mitis: calamansi, calamondin
CITY: *administrator:* amphodarch
block: square
cathedral: ely, paris, york
celestial: zion
court: municipal
district: barrio, business, central,
chinatown, downtown, east side,
ghetto, redlight, residential, shopping, skid row, slums, suburbs,
uptown
eternal: roma, rome
hall: capitol, ag* untamiento
heavenly: jerusalem
holy: mecca, medina, jerusalem
leaning tower: pisa
man: sophisticate, urbanite
official: aedile, alderman, council-
man, mayor, ward boss
of angels: los angeles
of bells: strasbourg
of bridges: bruges
of brotherly love: philadelphia
of churches: brooklyn
of david: jerusalem
of god: heaven, paradise, zion
of gods: asgard
of golden gate: san francisco
of hundred towers: pavia
of kings: lima
of lilies: florence
of luxury: sybaris
of lights: paris
of masts: london
of palm trees: jericho
of rams: canton
of refuge: medina

* Asterisk means to look up this word to find more answer words.

of roses: pasadena, portland
of saints: montreal
of seven hills: rome
of the prophet: medina
of the straits: detroit
of the sun: balbec
of the violet crown: athens
of victory: cairo
pert.: civic, metropolitan, municipal, oppidan, urban
petrified: ishmonie
problem: crime, ghettos, riots, slums, smog, traffic, zoning
section: block, square, ward
slicker: busker, townsman
white: helsinki
windy: chicago
CIVET: *cat:* dandy, fop
-like: genet
palm: musang, paguma
tree-climbing: rasse
CLACK: *babble, *nonsense, *talk
CLAIM: *ask, *right, *title
CLAMBER: *fight, *noise
CLAMOR: *appeal, *ask, *noise
CLAMOROUS: *bold, turbulent
CLANDESTINE: *secret, *sly
CLAP: *acclaim, *strike, *throw
trap: *buncombe, *nonsense
CLARENCE: *cousin:* landau
CLASH: *contest, collide, *meet
CLASP: *adhere, buckle, ouch
CLASS: bracket, brand, breed, category, estimate, family, *form, genus, *group, *kind, *order, *range, *state, *style
consciousness: discrimination
member, comb.: ander
names, comb.: ander, aet(o), ale, ane
CLASSICAL: *aesthetic, greek
CLATTER: *babble, *noise, *talk
CLAUDIA: *husband:* pilate
CLAUDIUS: *wife:* messalina
CLAY: *and magma:* buchite
articles: ceramics
-baked: adobe, brick, tile

bed: galt, gault
box: sagger
brained: *dull, *stupid
-burned piece: testa
-casting: slip
calcium carbonate: marl
comb.: argillaceo, argillo, pel
composition: lute
constituent: alumina
covered with: lutose
deposit: loess, marl
fine tryable: pryan
fragment: bat
iron: bull
lacustrine: berg till
layer: lias, sloam, sloom
lump: clag, clod
made of: fictile
manure: malm, marl
melting pot: tasco
mineral: attapulgite, nacrite
mold: dod
molded: brick, pug
-more: broadsword
nodule: bob
pert.: argillaceous, bolar
pack with: tamp
piece: brick, tile
pigeon: cinch, dupe, easy mark
pipe: td
plastic: pug
plug: bott
polishing: rabat
potter's: argil
pottery: kaolin(e)
poultice: cataplasm of kaolin
slab of: bat
stone: argillite
tropical: laterite
CLEAR: *acclaim, *acquit, *open
as crystal: evident, manifest
away: clean, feigh, eliminate, evacuate, fay, fey, wash out
coast: clean slate, facility
-cut: apparent, exact, open
decks: prepare, set up, tidy
for action: prepare

* **Asterisk means to look up this word to find more answer words.**

hurdle: break through, go ahead
off: distant, evacuate
out: begone, *escape,* utterly
skirts: *acquit
stage: opportunity
-story: floor, top
up: explain, police, solve
way: advance, facilitate
-wing moth: aegerida, sesiida
CLEAVE: *adhere, *split, *stick
CLEFT: *break, *flaw, *waterway
CLEOME: bee plant, figwort
CLEOPATRA: *attendant:* iras
downfall: asp
lover: caesar, marc antony
needle: obelisk
nurse: ftatateeta
river: nile
sister: arsinoe
CLERGYMAN: *church man
CLERIC: *church man
non: laic
pert.: ministerial, secretarial
office: canonry, priorship
vestment: *vestment: religious
vestment cloth: bissonata
CLEVER: *able, *adroit, *bright
CLIENT: account, charge, patient,
  patron, retainer
CLIFF: arete, col, crag, klip, palisade, precipice, scarp
dwelling: house
hanger: melodrama
CLIMAX: *acme, catastasis, *top
CLIMB: acclivity, ascend, soar
down: dismount, *fall, *retreat
on: mount, scale
one's frame: *punish, *rebuke
on bandwagon: *accept, *follow
CLINCH: *assure, *seize, *take
CLING: *adhere, be wont, rely on
-fish: testar
CLINK: *jail, rap, slap, ting
CLIP: *abbreviate, *blow, mow
CLIQUE: bloc, *group, junto, set
CLOAK: *-and-dagger:* conspira-
  tional

armor-covering: tabard
baptismal: chrisom
bishop's: mantelleta
clerical: analabos, cope, habit
hooded: burnoose, byrrus, camail,
  capote, mozzetta
large-sleeved: witzchoura
loose: *overcoat
monk's: analabos
military: paludament
sleeveless: dolman, paenula
12th century: balandrana
woman's: dolman
CLOBBER: *beat, *defeat, *whip
CLOCK: *arrangement:* caliper
astronomical: sidereal
electro-magnetic: buhl, bulle
maker: horologer
part: bundy, detent, dial, foliot,
  pendulum, recorder
self-winding: atmos
ship-shaped: nef
watcher: goldbrick, idler
water: clepsydra
weight: peise
-wise: right, round
works: time piece
CLOD: blockhead, *fool, *peasant
CLOG: *arrest, *balk, jam, shoe
dance: black bottom
CLOSE: *near, *settle, *thick
CLOTH: *fabric references
altar: bis, bisso
ancient: byssus
baptismal: chrisom
bark: tapa
beam: breast roll
blemish: amper, snag, tear, yaw
camel's-hair: aba, camlet
chalice: burse
checkered: plaid, tartan
coarse: *fabric: coarse
coat: bath, bombazette, cheviot
cord insertion: shirr
cotton: *cotton cloth
crinkled: crepe, seersucker
dealer: draper, mercer, ragman

* **Asterisk means to look up this word to find more answer words.**

dressing: stupe
dye method: batik, tie
fine: mull, percale, pima, silk
finisher: beetler
goat's-hair: camlet, mohair
hemp: baline, burlap, canamo
homespun: kelt
hood: bashlyk
instrument: ringhead
knitted: jersey, tricot
light: challis, etamine, tissue
linen: *fabric: linen
lining: sarcenet, serge
measure: ell, nail, yard
measuring officer: alnager
mesh: cheesecloth, net, tulle
metallic: acca, lame, tash
mourning: crape, crepe
mulberry bark: tapa
muslin: adati
narrow: braid, edging, ribbon
old: acca, cheyney, samite, tewke,
tuke
ornamental: lace, lampas, gimp,
riband, tapestry
piece: capot
poplin: tabbinet
print: calico, percale
printer: candroy
raised design: brocade
remnant: fent
roll: bolt, carding, slub
rug: mat, matting
selvage: listing, roon
sheets: batting
shop: mercery
silk: *fabric: silk
sitting: boultel
soft: fleece, montagnac, panne,
plush, rugene, surah
stiff: crinoline, taffeta
stout: brin
straining: cheese, tamis, tammy
stretcher: tenter
synthetic: *fabric: synthetic
towelling: terry
triangular piece: gore

twill: denim, jean, rep, serge
velvet: panne
weatherproof: canvas, tarp
winding: ceres
woolen: *fabric: wool
wrapping: burlap, tillot
wreath: bourrelet
-yard shaft: arrow
CLOTHE: *dress, *ornament,
*wrap
CLOTHES, CLOTHING: *dress
civilian: mufti
dryer: tenter
horse: testle
moth: larentiida, tinea
press: armoire
spy: keek
CLOUD: *berry:* averin, molka
born: chimerical, ethereal
broken: rack
burst: rainstorm
capped: *high, lofty
cirriform: capillatus
comb.: nepho
filmy: cirrus, nubia
gaseous: nebula
god: *sky god
-land: utopia
-less: azure, clear, light
-like: nebular
luminous: nebula, nimbus
masses: cumuli, racks, strati
morning: velo
pert.: nebular, nephological
study: nephology
wind-driven: scud
CLOUT: *force, *hit, *power
CLOVER: alsike, burnet, comfrey,
ease, luxury, nardoo, trefoil
disease: black patch
dodder: ailweed
leaf: crossway, fan, freeway
CLOWN: acrobat, aper, boor,
bounder, bum(pkin), card, churl,
club, cutup, dotterel, drawlatch,
dromedary, drone, *fellow, *fool,
footer, galoot, goff, hob, hodge,

* **Asterisk means to look up this word to find more answer words.**

jester, joker, jokester, larrikin, lavache, lout, merry andrew, mime, mountebank, *peasant, punchinello, ragamuffin, roarer, scaramouch, sop, stocah, tatterdemalion, wag, wit, yahoo

CLOY: glut, gorge, gut, *surfeit

CLUB: *associate, *beat, *group, *hit, *staff, team, *unite
ace: pussyfoot
foot: deformity, taliped
four: devil's bed posts
jack: mistigri, pam
law: anarchy, despotism
moss: bunch evergreen, buckhorn
police: billy, truncheon
queen: spadilla
root: ambury
-shaped: clavate
start: stoat
suit: bastos, braun, eckern, eicheln, kreuz, pussyfoot

CLUE: *sign, *token

CLUMP: bunch, heap, *hit, mass, patch, thud, tuft, *walk

CLUMSY: awkward, *big, bulky, cumbrous, gauche, inapt, jumbo, maladroit, massive, ponderous, rigid, slipshod, tense, uncouth

CLUSTER: *accumulate, cyme
bean: guar
fern spore: sorus
flower: ament, anthemia, cyme, panicle, raceme, umbel
flower-like: rosette
grape: raceme
grown in: acervate
pine: bordeaux pine, pinaster
seven stars: pleiad

CLUTCH: brood, catch, crisis, control, grab, hatch, nest, *power, *seize, *take, talon
lifting device: grampon

CLYMENE: kin: atlas, iapetus

CLYTEMNESTRA: daughter: electra
half-sister: helen

husband: agamemnon
lover: aegisthus
mother: leda
son: aletes, orestes

COACH: *lead, *train, *vessel
and four: rig
dog: dalmatian
hackney: jarvey
man: driver, jehu, pilot
railway: car, pullman, sleeper
whip: flag

COAL: agent: fitter
bad: smut, swad
bed: seam, blossom
bin: bunker
black: atrous, anthraconite
block: jud
box: black maria, dan, hod, jack johnson, scuttle, shell
brown: lignite
car part: hopper
comb.: anthrac(o)
constituent: benzene, carbon, creosote, ethene, goaf, naphthalene, phenol, pyrene
dust: coom(b), culm, slack, smut, soot, sut
fish: baddock, beshow, billet, blue fish, cuddy, glashan, parr, podler, pollack, sarthe, sey
from off the altar: genius
gas: miasma
heat-treated: coke
immature: lignite
kind: anthracite, bituminous, cannel, dant, hard, lignite, soft, tasmanite
-like: anthracoid, jet
live: ember
lump: cob
mine explosive: bobbinite
miner: collier
miner's TB: anthracosis
mining implement: breaker
oil: kerosene, photogen
producing: barbonigenous
refuse: ash, backing, cinder,

---

* Asterisk means to look up this word to find more answer words.

clinker, coom(b), culm, slag, smut, soot, thurst
scuttle: bucket, hod
size: broken, buckwheat, chestnut, cob, egg, ett, lump, pea, slack, stove
tar base: aniline
tar derivative: pitch
tar distillage: toluene
tar, paraffine: decane
tar product: lysol
wagon: carf, corb, tram
worker: chaffman, geordie
COALESCE: *gather, *unite
COARSE: *bad, *brutal, *thick
-*grained:* uneven
COAST: glide, *run, *slide
area: seaside, shore
bird: gull, tern
dweller: orarian
guarder: navy man, spar
pert.: orarian, riparian
COAT: *a metal:* anodize
alloy: terne
animal: hair, *skin, wool
coarse: capot(e)
double-breasted: edwardian, redingote, reefer
fastener: button, frog
hair: melote
hunter's: pink
long: redingote
long-sleeved: caftan
loose: *overcoat
mail: armor, hauberk, cataphract
man's: surtout
metal with aluminum: calorize
monk's: paletot
neck: george
of arms: blazonry, crest
of arms, pert.: heraldic
outer: *overcoat, ulster
part: collar, cuff, george, lapel, pocket, skirt, sleeve
rack: valet
seaman's: grego, monkey jacket
soldier's: blouse, tunic

woman's: brunswick
COAX: blandish, tempt, *urge
COB: *hit, horse, *leader
black-backed: gull
-*nut:* hazelnut
COBIA: bonito, coal, sergeant
COBRA: asp, haje, mamba, naga, ringhals, snake, uraeus, viper
COCAINE: anesthetic, candy, *drug, *narcotic, snow
addict: cokey, dope fiend
source: coca, cuca
substitute: butyn
taking: snuffing up
COCHIN CHINA: mekong delta, vietnam
COCK: capon, mass, prime, tap
-*a-hoop:* awry, boastful, elated, exultant, lively
-*and-bull-story:* canard, *lie
-*boat:* cog
-*chafer:* buzzard, dorbeetle
chaparral: road runner
-*crow:* dawn
-*eyed:* alop, askew, awry
-*eye pilot:* bean gregoire, fish
-*eyes:* three dice
fight: *contest, game, match
fighting: alectryomachy
-*horse:* astride, exultant, lofty, proud, upstart
-*light:* dawn, twilight
-*loft:* attic
-*pit:* arena, cabin, field, ring
-*pit of Europe:* belgium
of the walk: chief
of the wood: capercaillie
-*roach:* black beetle
-*shut:* evening
-*spur:* acacia, thorn, tree
sure: *confident
the ears: listen
the eye: squint
up: arise, protrude
COCKAIGNE: *paradise, utopia
COCKER: *caress, pamper, pet

* Asterisk means to look up this word to find more answer words.

COCKLE: compress, oast, shell
-*brained:* scatterbrained
bur: burdock, plant, xanthium
of the heart: essence
COCKTAIL: *drink:* mixed
COCO(A): apache, head, palm, taro
-*nut:* coquito, nargil
-*nut brown:* burnt almond
-*nut fiber:* coir, koir, kyar
-*nut husk:* cascara, coir
-*nut meat:* calapit(t)e, copra
nut palm: niog
-*palm leaves:* cadjan
-*plum:* icaco
COD: bacalao, *bag,* bank, beardie, bib, burbot, cabeliau, cor, cultus, cusk, gadus, glashan, hake, ling, pollack, pout, scrod, torsk
bait: capelin, mallotus
pert.: gadoid
young: codling, scrod, sprag
CODDLE: indulge, *love,* *spoil*
CODE: canon, equity, key, *rule*
filler: null
inventor: morse
message: cipher, cryptogram
CODGER: *churl,* oddity, oldster
CODIFY: *analyze,* organize
COERCE: *force,* *press,* *push*
COEUS: *daughter:* leto
COFFEE: bellywash, bugjuice
after dinner: demitasse
alkaloid: caffeine
bean: nib
berry: buckthorn, cascara, chaparral, jojoba, soybean
beverage: arabica, brazil, java, maracaibo, medellin, milds, rio, santos, sumatra
break: respite
cake: blueberry buckle
-*chocolate flavor:* mocha
cup: finjan
cup holder: zarf
extract: caffeine
house: cafe, inn

housing: *gossip,* *talk*
maker: urn, silex
plantation: cafetal
pot: biggin, cafetiere
refuse: triage
root used with: chicory
senna: cassia, stinking weed
tree: chicot
wood: brown ebony, wamara
COFFER: caisson, chest, treasury
-*dam:* batardeau
COFFIN: ossuary, sarcophagus
cloth: cloak, pall
display: catafalque
nail: cigarette
prehistoric: chest, cist
varnish: liquor
COHERE: *adhere,* fit, make sense
COIF: cerveliere, calotte, *top*
COIL: curl, kink, screw, worm
electric: teaser
COIN: *agola:* macuta
base: black money
box: register, meter, pyx, till
collector: numismatist
copper: batz, bodle, brown, cent
counterfeit: brummagem, slug
defect: brockage, fault
difference: seigniorage, value
edging: knurling, milling, nig
front: head, obverse
hole: slot
medieval: banco
metallic: specie
mill: nurl
money: get rich, profit, wax
pert.: numismatic(al)
reverse: tail, verso
ringer: sharp(er)
roll: rouleau
science: numismatics
silver: batz, bezzo, dime, dump, pina, sceat, tara
stamper: mill
tester: saraf, shroff
tin: tra
toss: birl

* Asterisk means to look up this word to find more answer words.

trifling: doit, rap
trim: nig
weight: shekel
words: neologize
COINCIDE: **agree,* concur, tally
COLD: *and damp:* bleak, dank, raw
biting: algid
blooded: callous, heterothermic
chap: kibe
cock: deaden, flatten
comb.: cryo, gel
cream: balm, salve
creeps: trepidation
deck: ice
feet: chicken heart, fear
hearted: flinty, **hard*
pert.: frigid, gelid, icy
producing: algific
preventative: ascorbic acid
remedy: antihistamine
shivers: shakes, trepidation
shoulder: snub
steel: bayonet, dagger, sword
storage: ice plant, frigidaire
sweat: trepidation
-water flat: apartment
COLLAPSE: **fall, *yield*
COLLAR: **arrest, *seize, *trap*
bone: clavicle, iwilei
cell: choanocyte
clerical: rabat(o)
convict: caran(et)
deep: bertha, rebato
frilled: ruff
furniture: bracelet
jewelled: carcanet
papal: fanon, orale
plaited: ruche
starched: buster brown
turned down: rabat, rebato
twisted: torque
wheel-shaped: ruff
COLLATERAL: **accidental, *credit*
COLLECT: **accumulate, *acquire*
COLLEGE: *absence license:* exeat

accounts: battel
barracks: dorm, fraternity
building: gym, lab, library
campus: quad(rangle)
course: major, minor, seminar
exam form: blue book
girl: coed
grad: alum, bachelor, master
grounds: campus, lawn, quad
group: fraternity, sorority
official: beadle, bursar, dean, proctor, rector, regent
pert.: academic
professor: docent, doctor, don
servant: gyp
term: semester
training mode: dressure
treasurer: bursar
tree: elm
COLLIDE: **hit, *meet,* smash
COLLOQUIAL: common, everyday, familiar, idiom, informal
COLLOQUY: chat, confab, **talk*
COLLUSION: cahoots, chicanery
law: covin
COLLYWOBBLES: jitters, nerves
COLOMBIA: *coin:* centavo, condor, peseta, peso, real
deity: bachuo, chaquen, chibchacum, cuchavira, fomagata, guesa, thomagata
indian: andaqui, betoya, boros, chitas, guacicos, morcotes, pedrazas, quimbaya, sinsabas, tahami, tunebos, yahuna
mahogany: albarco, cariniana
measure: celemin, vara
plant: yocco
tree: arboloco
volcano: huila, pasto, purace
weight: bag, carga, libra, saco
COLON: planter, viscera, vitals
COLOR: *achromatic:* black, white
bar: discrimination
blind: achromate, daltonist
change: iridesce, opalesce
dull: drab, dun, terne

* Asterisk means to look up this word to find more answer words.

expert: artist, dyer, painter
full of: chromatic
graduation: shade
light: pastel, tint
line: bigotry, prejudice, streak
malachite: bice
mark: nebulation, rivulation
mat white: alabaster
mulberry: morello
neutral: beige, black, ecru, gray, white
organ: clavilux
color photography inventor: ives
pert.: chrom(o)
play: kaleidoscope, opalescence
primary: blue, red, yellow
print: picture
quality: keeping, key, note, tone, value
second: green, orange, purple
set: palette
shade of difference: nuance
shift: bezold-brucke effect
spectrum: vibgyor
streak: fleck
stripe: plaga
vehicle: megilp
without: achroma, pale, plain
COLORADO: cigar, solitaire
bird: lark bunting
flower: mountain columbine
indian: arapahoe, ute
mountain pass: alpine, argentine, cottonwood
nickname: centennial state
park: estes, mesa verde
peak: arapahoe, audubon, baldy, castle, elbert, ethel, grays, harvard, longs, maroon, pikes, princeton, rosalie, snowmass
tree: blue spruce
COLOSSAL: *great, *supreme
COLUMBUS: *birthplace:* genoa
banner: green cross
burial place: seville
embarkation place: palos
funeral place: valladolid

patron: ferdinand, isabella
school: university of pavia
ship: nina, pinta, santa maria
son: diego
supporter: juan perez
wife: felipa moniz perestrello
COLUMN: *memorial, *tower
annulated ring: bague
arrange in: tabulate, marshal
base: dado, patten, plinth
both ends: amphistylar
figure: atlantes, caryatid, telamon
outward form: entasis, galbe
part: anta, entasis, fust, galbe, pilaster, plinth, scape
ring: bague
series: colonnade
set in: tabular
shaft: fust, scale, scape, tige
small: stele
square: anta, pilaster
sub-base: stylobate
support: socle
top: capital
twisted: torse, torso
type: corinthian, doric, ionic
without: astylar
COMB: *comb.:* cten(o), pect(i)
cotton: card, tease
flax: hacle
jelly: ctenophore
-like: pectinal, pectinate
rat: gundi
teeth filer: burrgrailer
COMBAT: *action, *attack, *fight
branch: arm
code: duello
COMBINE: *add, *group, *join, *party, *set, *trust, *unite
against: boycott
COME: *accrue, *advance, *approach, ensue, *near, reach
about: occur, pivot, tack
a cropper: fall
across: ante, confess, *meet
across with: cough up, deliver
after: ensue, *follow, *succeed

* Asterisk means to look up this word to find more answer words.

again: *ante, bye-bye, *return
along: fare, improve, progress
and go: alternate, commute, fluctuate, *oscillate, recur
apart: *break
around: *accept, *quit, *yield
at: *attack
back: *answer, *rally
before: *appear, face, present
between: alienate, interpose
by: *accrue, *accumulate, *get
clean: confess
down: land, rain, sink
down on: *punish, *rebuke
down with: catch, contract
face to face with: *meet
first: *lead, *open, *start
forth: *appear, *begin, emerge
forward: *appear, *volunteer
from: ensue, *result
-hither: alluring
-hither look: coquetry, ogle
home to: *affect, realize
in: *appear, *enter
in for: *acquire, *get, inherit
into: *acquire, *appear, *join
into being: *appear, *start
into money: flourish, go over, prosper, *succeed, *win
it: manage, reveal, *speed
it over: *deceive
it strong: exaggerate
near: *approach, approximate
of age: mature
off: *escape, *occur, *succeed
off it: *stop
on: *approach, decoy, impend, *meet, *near, prosper, *succeed
out: *appear, *issue, *result
out of it: cheer up, *rally
out on top: *hit, *succeed, *win
out with it: *admit, spill
over: *acquiesce, effect, visit
round: *accept, *acquiesce, buy
through: *give, *succeed, *show
to: *acquiesce, *equal, *rally
to a head: climax, suppurate

to grief: *fail, *fall, *suffer
to man's estate: *grow, mature
to nothing: cease, *end, *stop
to one's senses: cool it, sober
to pass: befall, eventuate, hap
to terms: *acquiesce, make up
to the fore: *succeed, *win
to the point: be brief, speak
together: *accord, *gather, *meet
true: *occur, realize
under: *follow, list, subvene
unstuck: *break
up: *appear, *occur
up against: engage, *meet
up to: equal, match, total
what may: certainly, earnestly
COMEDY: burlesque, drama, exode, *farce, harlequinade, slapstick
character: pantaloon
muse: thalia
pert.: thalian
symbol: cap and bells, coxcomb, motley, sock
COMET: *finder:* biela, donati, encke, halley, holmes, olber
head: coma
tail: streamer
COMEUPPANCE: deserts, revenge
COMFORT: *abet, *assure, soothe
producing: eudemonic
symbol: old shoe
COMMAND: *order, *unit, military
COMMANDMENTS: *ten:* decalog(ue)
COMMENCE: *open, *start
COMMEND: *advocate, *praise
COMMENSURATE: *adequate, *equal
COMMENT: aside, criticism, exegesis, explain, gloss, memo, *note, reference, postil, remark, rubric, review, *state
COMMENTARY: *account, *analysis

* Asterisk means to look up this word to find more answer words.

COMMERCE: *barter, business, conversation, exchange, market, merchandising, *trade, traffic
COMMERCIAL: ad, break, spot
COMMISSION: *accredit, *allot, *authority, *income, *trust
COMMIT: *accomplish, *allot, *arrest, *assign, *give, *trust
COMMON: *universal, *usual
  comb.: ceno, coen, homo, hyo, pre
  comfrey: agueweed, ass-ear, boneset, hempweed, thoroughwort
  effort: teamwork
  fellow: bourgeois, carl, ruck
  fund: pool, pot, purse
  gazelle: ahu
  gennet: solan
  law: tradition
  lilac: blue ash, green ash
  mullein: beggar's-blanket
  man, ruck: bourgeoisie, *rabble
  place: *average, *dull
  sense: judgment
  sorrel: canker root, rumex
  stock: blue chip, security
  talk: *gossip, rumor
  vetch: okra
  wood rush: blackhead grass
COMMOTION: *ado, *noise, *stir
COMMUNICATE: *report, *tell
COMMUNICATION: *address, *note
  stoppage: blackout
COMMUNIST: *socialist
COMORO ISLAND: moheli
COMPACT: *accord, bargain, bind, bond, capsule, close, compress, *contract, deal, entente, hard, *promise, *short, *solid
COMPANION: *associate, *friend
COMPANY: *agency, battery, business, cast, comrade, concern, enterprise, *firm, *group, guest, *party, *society
COMPARE: *apply, *balance
COMPASS: *accomplish, *bearing, *caliber, *range, *sphere

  about: protect, surround
  brick: adobe
  card: rose
  direction: bearing, course
  dummy: pelorus
  housing: binnacle
  kind of: gyro, solar, sun
  mind: intelligence
  part: airt, gimbal, needle, pen, rhumb, trammel, vane
  pocket: diacle
  point: airt, azimuth, rhumb
  sight: vane
  stand: binnacle
COMPASSION: charity, heart
COMPEL: *bring, coerce, drive, *make, *order, *press, *urge
  accounting: bring to book
  by threat: blackjack, menace
COMPENDIUM: *brief, digest
COMPENSATE: *adjust, pay, tally
COMPETENCE: *ability, *plenty
COMPETENT: *able, *smart
COMPETITOR: athlete, enemy, rival
COMPILE: *accumulate, *adapt
COMPLACENT: *kind, polite
COMPLAIN: ail, beef, bellyache, bitch, carp, charge, clamor, crab, criticize, croak, *cry, fret, fume, fuss, gripe, *grouch, grouse, growl, grumble, holler, *howl, kick, lament, mutter, *protest, rage, scream, squawk, whine, yammer, yell
COMPLAINT: burden: gravamen
COMPLAISANT: *affable, *good
COMPLETE: absolute, *accomplish, all-out, button up, clean up, conclude, consummate, do up brown, *end, execute, infinite, make good, mature, *perfect, quite, replenish, round out, siker, sole, stark, top off, total, unqualified, utter, versatile, well rounded, wind up
  pref.: hol, tele

* Asterisk means to look up this word to find more answer words.

COMPLETELY: bag and baggage, from a to z, thoroughly
pref.: cata, cath, kata, kath
COMPLEX: balled up, daedal, involute, mania, maze, whole
of communities: biome
progressively: anamorphic
COMPLEXION: blee, cast, hue
COMPLIANT: *soft, *weak
COMPLICATE: foul up, tangle
COMPLICATED: *abstruse, *obscure
COMPLIMENT: *acclaim, *praise
COMPLINE: apodeipnon, *service
COMPLY: *accept, *adapt, obey
COMPONENT: *bit, *part, *piece
COMPORT: *accord, *act, involve
COMPOSE: *abate, *accord, *adapt, score, *set(tle), write
COMPOSITION: *art:* rhetoric
choral: motet
for two: duetino, duetto
literary: article, cento, drama, essay, ms, novel, satire, theme, tragedy, treatise
metrical: poem, poesy, rhyme
mournful: dirge
nine instruments: nonet
pert.: synthesis, synthetic
sacred: hymn, motet
select works: cento
COMPOSURE: *aplomb, *balance, nonchalance, repose, sangfroid
COMPOUND: *alkaline:* soda
amorphous: phenose
assarabacca: asarone, root
bitter crystalline: alion
chemical: amid(e), amin(e), azin(e), azola, borid, ceria, chloride, diazo, ester, imid(e), imin(e), inosite, leucine, metamer, osone, oxide
crystalline: *crystalline: compound
dual bonded: triene
for: *substitute

hypnotic: trional
interest: anatocism
organic: amid(e), amin(e), enol, ester, ketole, ketone
word: bahuvrihi
COMPREHEND: be aware of, *get, grasp, *sense, *understand
inability to: asemia
COMPREHENSIVE: *complete
COMPRESS: *compact, *press
COMPRISE: embody, hold, involve
COMPROMISE: *adjust, medium
COMPULSION: *force, *urge
COMPULSORY: binding, peremptory
labor: begar
military: conscription, draft
service: angaria, slavery
COMPULSION: *conscience, *urge
COMPUTE: *account, *add, *assess, calculate, estimate
COMPUTER: abacus, univac
algebraic language: algol
billionth of second: nanosecond
correct: debug
data holder: memory, storage
information: data, input, output
inventor: babbage
plan for action: program
program symbol: block
solving mathematics: analog
symbol system: code
term: access time
work basis: binary
COMRADE: *associate, *friend
CON: anti, *cheat, *deceive
CONCEAL: *hide, *obscure
CONCEALED: *abstruse, *secret
comb.: adelo
CONCEALMENT: *ambush, *secret
CONCEDE: *accept, *accord, *yield
CONCEIT: big head, caprice, whim
CONCEIVE: *think, *understand

* **Asterisk means to look up this word to find more answer words.**

CONCENTRATE: essence, *think
CONCENTRATION: *absorption, *application, build-up, extract
camp: prison, stalag
of desire: cathexis
of wealth: capital(ism)
CONCEPT: idea, *image, *picture
CONCERN: *affair, *affect, *agitate, *anxiety, *interest
oneself with: attend, care
unselfish: altruism, charity
CONCERT: harmony, *unity
hall: academe, lyceum, odeon
CONCHOBOR: wife: medb
CONCILIATE: *abate, atone, *ease
CONCILATRIX: bawd, trollop
CONCINNITY: elegance, harmony
CONCISE: *compact, *short, terse
CONCLUDE: *decide, *end
CONCLUSION: *end, *result
CONCLUSIVE: *correct, decisive
answer: sockdologer
evidence: demonstration
CONCOCT: brew, *form, *make
CONCOMITANT: *associate, escort
CONCORD: *accord, rapport
CONCOURSE: assembly, resort
CONCRETE: *actual, *hard, *solid
depositor: tremie
structure: blockhouse, pillbox
CONCRETION: clot, pearl, stone
stony: calculus
CONCUBINE: adalisk, dasi, wife
CONCUR: *accept, *accord, echo
CONCUSSION: *hurt, *pain
CONDEMN: *accuse, damn, doom
CONDALIA: capulin, chaparral
CONDENSE: *abbreviate, decoct
CONDESCEND: deign, patronize
CONDIGN: deserved, fitting, just
CONDIMENT: achar, appetizer, asafoetida, balachan, capsicin, cardamon, catchup, chili, chive,

chutney, curry, dill, ginger, mustard, pepper, sage
CONDITION: *adapt, *accustom, case, *prepare, *state, *train
comb.: ance, ancy, ate, blasty, ence, ency
critical: emergency
favorable: odds
CONDITIONAL: *accidental, iffy
CONDOLENCE: consolation, pity
CONDONE: *accept, *allow, bear
CONDOR: buzzard, vulture
CONDUCE: *abet, *administer, *advance, effect, *lead, tend
CONDUCT: *action, *administer, *affair, *accompany, *walk, *way
scandalous: esclandre
suff.: ery
CONDUCTANCE: unit: abmho, mho
CONDUCTOR: aqueduct, bond, cad, carrier, cicerone, guide, karajan, leader, maestro, operator, trainman
stick: baton, wand
CONDUIT: *opening, *waterway
CONE: flower: black-eyed susan, brown betty, yellow daisy
-noise: barbeiro, bedbug
retorting and silver: pina
section: parabola
shaped: conic(al), pineal
tree: fir, larch, pine, spruce
CONEY: chervil, daman, hare, hyracid, parsley, rabbit
CONFEDERATE: *accomplice, *associate, butternut, rebel
general: beauregard, bragg, jackson, lee, morgan, price
guerrilla: bushwhacker
note: blueback
president: davis
vice-president: stephens
CONFEDERATION: *bloc
CONFER: *advise, *give, *talk
CONFERENCE: *meeting
technique: brainstorming

* Asterisk means to look up this word to find more answer words.

CONFESS: *admit, *allow, grant, own, sing, squawk, *talk

CONFETTI: bonbons, streamers
carrier: cascaron

CONFIDANT: eminence grise

CONFIDE: hope, repose, *trust

CONFIDENCE: poise, *spirit
game: bunko, *deception, fraud
man: *sharp(er)

CONFIDENT: *bold, sanguine, *sure

CONFIDENTIAL: privy, *secret

CONFINE: *arrest, *edge, *limit

CONFIRM: *assure, *support

CONFISCATE: *arrest, *seize

CONFLICT: *attack, *fight

CONFLUENCE: *group, joining

CONFORM: *accept, *accommodate, *adapt, *adjust, *settle

CONFORMING: groovy, hep, kosher, observant, with it

CONFORMIST: babbitt, bromidite, pedant, philistine, precisian

CONFOUND: *shock, *trap

CONFRATERNITY: *group

CONFRERE: *associate, *friend

CONFRONT: brave, dare, oppose

CONFUSE: *abash, *addle, *upset

CONFUSED: lost, *upset, *vague

CONFUSION: *ado, *noise

CONGEAL: gel, glot, knot, lump

CONGERIES: *group, heap, mass

CONGESTION: bottleneck, *mass

CONGLOMERATE: *trust

CONGO: asphaltum, bitumen, brown, eel, salamander, susu
beer: garapa
capital: boma, brazzaville, kinshasa
common tongue: fiote
councillor: macota
discoverer: cam
lake: tumba
language: bangala, susu
mist: cacimbo
plant: manioc
premiere: adoula

pygmy: achuas, akka
river: aruwimi, zaire, zahir
ruminant: okapi
season: balanga, cacimbo, kundey
shrub: bocca
snake: amphiuma, blind eel
tribe: ababua, bacongo, bafyot, bangala, fiot, susa, wabuma, zambi

CONGRATULATE: *bless, *praise

CONGREGATE: herd, mass, teem

CONGREGATION: *group, herd

CONGRESS: *meeting, parliament

CONGRUITY: *accord, symmetry

CONJECTURE: *aim, *think

CONJUGATE: dwell upon, yoked

CONJUNCTION: combination, *union
omission: asyndeton

CONJURE: *ask, *beg, exorcise

CONJUROR: *magician, shaman

CONK: bean, *head, *hit, nose
out: *die, *spoil, stall

CONLAECH: father: cuchulainn
mother: aoife

CONNACHT: king: ailill

CONNECT: *add, *adjoin, affix, *associate, *join, *succeed

CONNECTED: suff.: arious, ary
with a purpose: met, telic

CONNECTIVE: syndetic
tissue: band web, fascia

CONNIPTION FIT: tantrum

CONNIVE: *abet, *plan, *plot

CONNOISSEUR: *epicure, *esthetic

CONNOTE: imply, *mean

CONOR: consort: deirdre medb

CONQUER: *defeat, master, *win

CONQUEST: sweetheart, triumph

CONSANGUINE: *akin, carnal

CONSCIENCE: casuistry, cricket, compunction, erinys, grace, inwit, monitor, probity, psyche, punctilio, qualm, scruple, sense, thought, virtue

* Asterisk means to look up this word to find more answer words.

money: tax
personification: aidos
-stricken: rueful, sorry
CONSCIOUS: **active, *quick,* shy
CONSCIOUSNESS: aniruddha, limen
-altering: psychedelic
loss: apoplexy, apsychid, coma
CONSECRATE: **anoint, *bless*
CONSECRATED: *for deity:* anathema
cloth: antimension
host: blessed sacrament
oil: chrism
thing: sacrum
CONSENT: **accept, *accord*
CONSEQUENCE: apodosis, effect, **end,* influence, **issue,* outcome, **result,* sequel
CONSEQUENTLY: hence, **therefore*
CONSERVATIVE: bourbon, diehard, reactionary, right, tory
CONSERVATORY: **academy,* college
CONSERVE: **save,* shield, **secure*
CONSIDER: **account, *admit, *advise, *aim,* call, **think*
the source: discount
CONSIDERABLE: **important*
CONSIDERATE: delicate, **gentle*
CONSIDERATION: esteem, fee
CONSIDERING: after all, since
everything: all told
CONSIGN: **allot, *commit, *give*
to a place: locate
to oblivion: bury, forget
CONSIST: **comprise,* hold, inhere
CONSISTENCY: **group,* symmetry
CONSOLE: cabinet, grieve, weep
CONSOLIDATE: **add, *bloc, *unite*
CONSONANT: atonal, spirant
aspirate: sonant, surd
hard: fortis, fricative
hissing: sibilant

pert.: fricative, palatal
smooth: lene, lenis
sound: surd
voiceless: atonic, lene, spirate, surd
CONSORT: date, mate, mingle
CONSORTIUM: alliance, **group*
CONSPECTUS: **analysis,* apercu
CONSPICUOUS: **apparent, *bright*
CONSPIRACY: **cabal, *group*
CONSPIRATOR: **accomplice*
CONSPIRE: **plan, *plot,* scheme
CONSTANCY: fidelity, homeostasis
symbol: diamond, garnet
CONSTANT: **fast, *permanent, *true*
CONSTANTINE: *birthplace:* nish
CONSTANTINOPLE: **istanbul*
CONSTANTLY: **always,* forever
CONSTELLATIONS: **group, *star*
argo division: vela
altar: ara
archer: sagittarius
arrow: sagitta
atlantides: pleiades
balance: libra
bear: ursa (major) (minor)
berenice's hair: coma berenice
bull: taurus
champion: perseus
charioteer: auriga
charles's wain: dipper
clock: horologium
compasses: circinus, pyxis
crab: cancer
crane: grus
cross: crux, cruz
crow: corvus
crown: corona
cup: crater
dipper: charles's wain
dog: canis
dogs, hunting: canes venatici
dolphin: delphinus

* Asterisk means to look up this word to find more answer words.

dove: columba
dragon: draco
eagle: aquila
easel, painter's: pictor
fish, flying: piscis volans
fly: musca
foal: equuleus
fox, little: vulpecula
furnace: fornax
giraffe: camelopardalis
goat: capricorn
goblet: crater
goldfish: dorado
hare: lepus
hevelius: antinous, cerberus, lacerta, lynx
harp: lyra, lyre
herdsman: bootes
horse, little: equuleus
horse, winged: pegasus
hunter: orion
keel: carina
lady, chained: andromeda
lady in the chair: cassiopeia
lion: leo
lizard: lacerta
long-winding: eridanus
maiden: virgo
mariner's compass: pyxis
mast: malus
milky way: argo
monarch: cepheus
mountain, table: mensa
nautical box: pyxis
net: reticulum
noah's dove: columba
northern: andromeda, aquila, aries, auriga, bootes, cancer, canes, cassiopeia, cepheus, coma, cygnus, delphinus, draco, gemini, hercules, lacerta, leo, lynx, lyra, pegasus, perseus, sagitta, taurus, ursa, vulpecula
orion's hound: canis major
paradise bird: apus
pleiades: atlantides
pump, air: antlia

rabbit: leporis
ram: aries
rescuer: perseus
river: eridanus
rule: norma
sails: vela
sculptor's tool: caelum
sea monster: cetus, hydra
sea serpent: hydra
serpent bearer: ophiuchus
shield of sobieski: scutum
ship: argo
southern: antilia, apus, aquarius, ara, argo, caelum, capricornus, canis, carina, centaurus, cetus, chameleon, circinus, columba, corvus, crater, crux, dorado, fornax, grus, horologium, hydra, indus, lepus, libra, mensa, microscopium, monoceros, musca, norma, pavo, phoenix, pictor, pisces, puppis, reticulum, sagittarius, sculptor, scorpius, sextans, tucana, vela, virgo, volans
square: norma
stern: puppis
swan: cygnus
swordfish: dorado
toucan: tucana
twins: gemini
unicorn: monoceros
ursa: bear, dipper
wagoner: auriga
wain, charles's: dipper
water bearer: aquarius
water snake: hydrus
whale: cetus
winged horse: pegasus
wolf: lupus
wreath: corona australis
CONSTERNATION: *alarm*
CONSTITUTE: *allow,* comprise
CONSTITUTION: canon, charter, code, composition, ingredients, law, make-up, nature, structure
opponents: anti-federalists
ship: old ironsides

* Asterisk means to look up this word to find more answer words.

supporter: cartist
CONSTRAIN: *force, *tie, *urge
CONSTRICT: choke, compress
CONSTRICTOR: anaconda, boa, python, snake, sphincter
CONSTRUCT: *build, *produce
CONSTRUCTION: *meaning
CONSTRUE: explain, infer, parse
CONSULT: *advise, *ask, confer
one's pillow: delay
CONSUME: *absorb, *eat, *use
CONSUMMATE: *accomplish, *acme, *best, *supreme
CONSUMMATION: *acme, *end, *top
CONSUMPTION: phthisis, *use
weed: canker lettuce, false wintergreen
CONTACT: *adjoin, *agent, impact, impinge, *spy, syzygy
mine: magnetic mine, sonic mine
CONTAGION: epidemic, plague
preventive: antidote, shot
CONTAIN: *abstain, *accept, *carry
CONTAINER: ampule, artophorion, *bag, barrel, bath, blunger, boat, bomb, bottle, box, bushel, cage, capsule, carboy, caster, compact, cruet, cup, drum, jar, jug, *pack, pail, pyx, *receptacle, *tank, tub, tube, urn, vat, *vessel
comb.: angio
CONTAMINATE: corrupt, defile, *hurt, poison, pollute, *spoil
CONTAMINATION: radioactivity
CONTEMN: despise, flout, scorn
CONTEMPLATE: *consider, focus, *look, *see, *study, *think
CONTEMPORARY: *current
comb.: neo
CONTEMPT: affront, *scorn, slight
exclamation: bah, foh, fico
CONTEMPTIBLE: *abject, *bad, *low, *mean, *sorry, terrible
CONTEMPTUOUS: *arrogant,

*bold, contumelious, scornful
CONTEND: *argue, claim, compete, *fight, *mean, struggle, vie
CONTENT: at ease, capacity, gratified, replete, sans souci
oneself with: *accept
CONTENTIOUS: *angry, argumental, belligerent, cantankerous, controversial, litigious
CONTERMINOUS: *adjacent
CONTEST: *action, *affair, agon, *argue, barney, *break, buck, *campaign, clash, combat, cope, duel, *fight, free-for-all, game, joust, mix-up, oppose, *quarrel, race, regatta, runoff, scramble, scrap, scrimmage, set to, skirmish, sport, strife, suit, tournament, *trial
CONTIGUOUS: *adjacent, *near
CONTINENCE: chastity, virtue
CONTINENT: *good, *pure
covering all: epeiric
legendary: atlantis, cascadia, lemuria, mu
CONTINENTAL: *bit, *trifle
CONTINGENCY: case, chance, liability, prospect, *venture
dependent on: aleatory
CONTINGENT: *accidental, *part
on discretion: arbitrary
CONTINUAL: *endless, *universal
CONTINUALLY: at a stretch, aye, on and on, without a break
CONTINUANCE: deferment, sequel
CONTINUE: *abide, endure, go along, keep on, persevere
CONTINUED: chronic, protracted
CONTINUOUS: around-the-clock, *continual, never-ending
CONTINUITY: cohesion, script
CONTORT: distort, gnarl, twist
CONTORTED: *bad, wound, wry
CONTORTIONIST: acrobat
CONTOUR: galbe, graph, isobase, outline, periphery, profile, shape,

* Asterisk means to look up this word to find more answer words.

silhouette, tournure
outline: configuration
CONTRA: **adverse,* offset
CONTRABAND: illegal, taboo
CONTRACEPTIVE: preventive, pill
CONTRACT: **abbreviate, *acquire,* bag, **bargain, *bond, *book, *compact,* deal, engage, incur, **promise,* shrink, shrivel, stipulate, take, **yield*
addition: codicil, rider
furnishing slaves: assiento
matrimony: marry, wed, unite
part: clause, proviso
unlawful: chevisance
CONTRACTION: coup, fist, spasm
common: arent, een, eer, oer, oft, shant, tis
heart: systolic
pert.: systonlic, typist
CONTRACTOR: builder, declarer
CONTRADICT: belie, counteract, cross, deny, gainsay, impugn, negate, oppose, oppugn, rebut
CONTRARY: **adverse,* antagonism, antipathetic, balky, hostile, **obstinate,* perverse, reverse
to fact: false
to law: criminal, illegal
to reason: **absurd*
CONTRAST: antithesis, **compare*
pert.: against
CONTRAVENE: **break, *contradict,* defy, deny, oppose, thwart
CONTRETEMPS: **accident*
CONTRIBUTE: **abet, *administer, *advance, *ante,* chip in, **give,* kick in, participate, subscribe, sweeten the kitty
CONTRITE: humble, rued, **sorry*
CONTRITION: penance, **remorse*
CONTRIVANCE: **deception,* device, **expedient,* intrigue, plan
CONTRIVE: **accomplish,* devise, **make, *plan, *plot, *start*

CONTRIVED: **artificial,* pat
CONTROL: **administer, *arrest,* command, discipline, dominate, influence, master, **power, *range, *rule, *run, *temper*
symbol: apron string, baton
CONTROVERSIAL: **contentious*
CONTROVERSY: **contest, *issue*
CONTROVERT: **contradict*
CONTUMACIOUS: **contrary, *sharp*
CONTUMELIOUS: **arrogant*
CONTUMELY: **abuse, *contempt*
CONTUSION: blow, **bruise, *bump*
CONUNDRUM: **enigma, *puzzle*
CONVALESCE: heal, **rally*
CONVALESCENCE: anastasis
CONVENE: assemble, call, **meet*
CONVENIENCES: benefits, cakes and ale, comforts, good things of life, leisure, luxury
CONVENIENT: **expedient,* handy
CONVENT: **abbey, *monastery*
dweller: friar, monk, nun
CONVENTION: babbittry, **compact, *contract, *custom,* decorum, grundyism, **meeting,* main street, mores, propriety, **rule*
CONVENTIONAL: **artificial,* being done, groovy, orthodox, popular, **right,* traditional, **usual*
expressions: cant
CONVERGE: focus, **meet, *unite*
CONVERGING: centripetal, focal
at both ends: amphicentric
jaws: aristotle's lantern
to center: centrolinear
CONVERSANT: at home, skilled
CONVERSATION: **affair, *chat*
water: liquor
CONVERSE: chat, **gossip, *talk*
CONVERSION: *factor:* value
into coal: carbonification
into flesh: carnification
into stocks: capitalization

---

* Asterisk means to look up this word to find more answer words.

into steel: acieration
into sugar: amylolysis
CONVERT: alter, become, blend, cash in, catechumen, change, convict, convince, disciple, persuade, proselyte, redeem
CONVERTIBLE: bond, cabriolet, coupe, debenture, security
CONVEX: arched, biggose, bowed, excurvated, gibbous, humped
CONVEXITY: entasis
CONVEY: *allot, *bring, cede, deed, grant, eloign, pass, sell
CONVEYANCE: demise, piracy, theft, van, *vehicle, waftage
CONVICT: *accuse, *approve, cast, *criminal, felon, lifer, trusty
collar: carcan(et)
CONVICTION: *authority, *belief
demonstration: act of faith
CONVINCE: *assure, *convert
CONVIVIAL: amatory, gay, genial
CONVOCATION: assembly, *meeting
CONVOKE: call, *gather, summon
CONVOLUTION: coil, crinkle, wave
brain: gyrus
CONVOLVULUS: bearbine, bindweed
CONVOY: bodyguard, escort
CONVULSE: *agitate, *amuse, *laugh, *pain, *torment
CONVULSIONS: chorea, jerks, tics
CONY: asakoko, badger, daman, das, ganam, lapin, pika, rabbit
catcher: *cheat, *sharp
COO: chirr, chough, curr, murmur
COOK: alter, bake, barbecue, baste, boil, braise, brew, broil, brown, chef, coddle, concoct, devil, do, escallop, fire, fricassee, fry, griddle, grill, heat, jipper, magirist, pan-broil, perspire,

poach, prepare, roast, saute, scallop, scorch, sear, shirr, simmer, steam, stew, toast
male native: bawarchi
one's goose: defeat, spoil
up: fabricate, *plot, *start
COOKING: *art:* cuisine, magirics
device: brazier, etna, griddle, oven, range, rotisserie, stove
odor: nidor
pert.: culinary
room: cuddy, galley, kitchen
vessel: autoclave, broiler, cassolette, caster, etna, fleshpot, griddle, olla, pan, pot, roaster, skillet, spider, steamer, tureen
COOL: aloof, *aplomb, calm, frosty, gelid, icy, insolent, sensible, *slow, *smooth
one's heels: mark time, wait
COOLER: can, fan, icer, jail, lockup, prison, refrigerator
COOM(B): cirque, corrie, cwm, *refuse, slack, valley
COON: cat, climb, mapach, rascal
age: eternity, long time
oyster: bunch oyster
-tie: arrowroot, bay rush
COOP: case, cote, jail, pen
COOPERATE: *accept, *accord, go along, play ball, pull together, *share, string along
COOPERATIVE: guild, market
workers: artel, union
COOPERATOR: *accomplice
COORDINATE: *adapt, *adjust
COORDINATION: *inability:* abasia
lack: asynergy
loss: locomotor ataxia
COOT: baltie, dolt, oddity, rail, scoter, smyth
COP: *policeman, *steal, *throw
out: defection, *retreat
COPACETIC: capital, dandy, fine
COPE: *contend, *cover, get by

* **Asterisk means to look up this word to find more answer words.**

COPENHAGEN: *park:* tivoli
 shopping district: stroget
COPIER: secretary, stat, xerox
COPIOUS: ample, profuse, replete
COPPER: **cop,* caldron, cent
 alloy: barberite, brass, bronze, oroide, rheotan
 aluminum arsenate: ceruleite
 and zinc alloy: brass
 arsenate: bayldonite
 arsenic sulphide: enargite
 arsenide: algodonite, domeykite
 brass: chalco
 brown: armenian red, color
 carbonate: azurite, bice, gem
 chloride: atacamite
 cobalt sulphide: carrollite
 coin: brown, cent, penny
 comb.: chalco, cupro
 cup: dop
 engraving: mezzotint
 green phosphate: ehlite
 head: beech leaf snake
 iron sulphide: bornite
 lead sulphate: caledonite
 nickel: niccolite
 red: carnelian
 rust: canker
 selenide: berzelianite
 silicate: bisbeeite
 strap: branch bar
 sulphate: antlerite, arzrunite, blue jack, blue stone, boothite, brochantite, burnt brass, sandstone, vitriol
 -zinc alloy: beta brass
 zinc carbonate: aurichalcite
 zinc phosphate: arakawaite
COPPICE, COPSE: thicket
COPT: egyptian, christian
 dialect: bohairic
 title: amba, anba
COPY: **adopt,* article, draft, dupe, edition, **image,* **model,* **plan,* print, replica, stat
COPYRIGHT: patent
 infringe: pirate, plagiarize

COQUETTE: dally, flirt, humming bird, philander, toy, **trifle*
COQUILA: attalea, cohune, palm
CORAL: aporosa, millepore, pearl
 berry: buck bush, purshia
 branch: ramicle
 cavity: calyculus
 division: aporosa
 formation: paar, palus
 group: caratophyta
 growth zooid: polypite
 island: atoll, key, reef
 part: palus, septum
 pea: bleeding heart
 porous walled: porite
 reef: island, lagoon, shoal
 septa: pali
 snake: bead snake, candy stick
 tree: dapdap, gabgab
CORBEL: ancon, bracket, cartouche, projection, strut
 pert.: pannier
CORBIE: chough, crow, raven
 -step: catstep
CORD: boom, braid, **tie,* twist
 drapery: torsade
 goat's hair: agal
 -like structure: funicule
 parachute: ripcord
 strong: catgut
 twisted: torsade
 -wood: lumber
CORDAGE: gear, rope, sennit
 fiber: ambari, anodendron, anonang, coir, eruc, feru, hemp, imbe, jute, kenaf, pita
 fiber source: anilau, grewia
 length: catenary
 tree: sida
CORDAY: *victim:* marat
CORDELIA: *father:* lear
CORDIAL: **affable,* **ardent*
CORDON: **badge,* **group,* guard
 bleu: decoration
 sanitaire: quarantine
CORE: ame, burden, center, crux, essence, **foundation,* heart

---

* Asterisk means to look up this word to find more answer words.

earth material: nife
mold: matrix, nowel
CORF: basket, cage, creel, skip
CORINTH: *citadel:* acrocorinth
king: polybus
CORK: balsa, float, shive, stop
extract: cerin
flat: shive
helmet: topee, topi
jacket: life preserver
noise: cloop
pert.: suberic
screw: coil, opener, spiral
source: suberin
wax: serin
wood: balsa, blolly
CORKER: stopper, top-notcher
CORKING: *fine, *great, whit
CORMORANT: glutton, norie, urile
CORN: callous, chestnut, clavus, *money, preserve, shmaltz
belt: country
bread: pone, tortilla
bunting: lark
cake: pone, hoecake
cob: ear
cockle: agrostemma
cracker state: kentucky
crake: bird, crex, rail
crib: bin
disease: black bundle, smut
dodger: bread, dumpling, pone
ear: cob, mealie, nubbin
earworm: pink bollworm
flag: gladiolus, iris
flower: bachelor's button, blue bonnet, blue bottle, ixia
gromwell: bastard alkanet
ground: grist, meal
house: corncrib, granary
hulled: hominy, samp
indian: maize, samp, zea
juice: whiskey
knife: machete
leaf: blade
lily: ixia

marigold: buddle, herb
meal: atole, hoecake, johnny cake, masa, samp, sofki
meal bread: anadama
poppy: blaver, blind eyes, canker berry
shock: stook
spike: cob, ear
stalk: stem
weevil: calandra
whiskey: bourbon
CORNER: *retreat, *trap, *trust
piece: cantle
stone: basis, coyn, coign, diatonus, foundation, quoin
CORNICE: *basket:* caul
diamond: quartz
part: stagline
support: ancon
CORNUCOPIA: amalthaea, *plenty
CORNWALL: *castle:* tintagil
crow: aylet
diamond: quartz
mine: bal, ball, wheal
name pref.: lan, ros, tre
ore: whits
prince: constantine
CORNWALLIS: dance, general
surrender site: yorktown
CORNY: *dull, stale, trite
COROLLA: bell, perianth
part: galea, petal, unie
COROLLARY: *adjunct, concomitant
CORONA: bur, cigar, circle, crown, syphus, solitaire
lucis: chandelier
sun: aureole, bishop's ring
type lighting: andes glow
CORONATION: abhiseka, inaugural
gulf tribe: blond eskimo
robe: armil, armilla
stone: scone
CORONIS: *son:* asclepius

* Asterisk means to look up this word to find more answer words.

CORPORAL: fano, hitler, nco
  little: napoleon
  punishment: death, whipping
CORPORATION: *company,
  *stomach
CORPOREAL: *actual, somatic
CORPSE: *fat:* adipocere
  pert.: cadaverous, deathly
CORPULENT: *fat, obese, *thick
CORRAL: atajo, herd, pen, sty
CORRECT: *accurate, *adjust,
  *amend, *appropriate, chasten,
  *conventional, due, inform,
  meticulous, ok, orthodox, *pun-
  ish, *rebuke, *right, *true
CORRESPOND: *accord, *answer
CORRIDA: bullfight
CORROBORATE: *assure, confirm
CORRODE: *abrade, rust, *spoil
CORRUGATE: furrow, wrinkle
CORRUPT: *bad, *deceive, *evil,
  *rotten, *ruin, *spoil
CORSAIR: caper, picaroon, pirate
CORSET: *bone:* busk
  cover: camisole
  stay source: bowhead whale
  strip: bone, busk, stay
CORTEX: *cover, rind, shell
CORUSCATE: brandish, *sparkle
COSA NOSTRA: mafia, syndicate
COSMETIC: *bismuth:* blanc de
  fard
  medicated: lotion
  paste: pack
  white lead: ceruse
COSMIC: *infinite, *universal
  cycle: eon
  dust: meteor
  opposed to: acronycal
  order: rita, tao
COSMOGRAPHIC: *cosmic
COSSACK: *captain:* sotnik
  chief: ataman, hetman
  district: voisko
  mount: charger, steed
  post: guard, warden

regiment: polk, pulk
squadron: sotnia, sotnya
unit: stanitsa
whip: knout
COSSET: *caress, darling, pet
COST: *afford, *value, *yield
COSTA RICA: *coin:* centimo,
  colon
  measure: caballeria, cajuela,
  fanega, manzana, tercia
  people: guaymie
  volcano: barba, poas
  weight: bag, caja
COSTUME: apparel, *dress
COT: bothy, charpoy, coop, *hut
COTE: cottage, *house, *hut, wine
  d'azur: riviera
COTERIE: clique, *group, *set
COTTAGE: bower, cabin, *house
  cheese: smearcase
  partition: hallan, speer
  tulip: bouton d'or
COTTON: *agree, *beat, *succeed
  and linen: fustian
  ball: bolly, lint
  belt: country
  blight: black arm, weevil
  cleaner: willow, willy
  clearer: gin
  cloth: *fabric: cotton
  cloth blemish: nit
  coarse: bagging, baline, buckskin,
  bunting, hemp, jute
  disease: black arm, boll rot
  fabric: *fabric: cotton
  fiber: lint, stapel
  fiber knot: nep
  filament: thread
  flowered: chintz
  gauze: leno
  gin attachment: moter
  gin inventor: eli whitney
  grass: bog down, cannach, cat-
  locks, eriophorum
  handkerchief: malabar
  knot in: nep, slub
  lawn: batiste

* Asterisk means to look up this word to find more answer words.

light: etamine, pima
long-staple: maco
machine: bale breaker, gin
material: jaconet, malabar
measure: hank, lea
mercerized: silkaline
moth: alabama
pest: boll weevil, snout beetle
printed: calico, indienne
printing dye: alizarin
refuse: grabbots
seed kernel: meat
seed oil test: becchi test
seed pod: boll, bolly
seed remover: gin
sheet: batting, drilling, manta, muslin, percale
striped: bezan, express
strong: denim, duck, scrim
tail: cony, hare, leveret
thread: lisle
to: like, love, take to
tree: simal
twilled: jean, silesia
variety: maco, pima
warp cloth: satinet
waste: blowings, card strip
wilt: black rot
wood: alamo, poplar, tree
wool: caddice, caddis
worker: baler
COUCH: **bed,* divan, recline
grass: quack, quitch, scutch
in terms: phrase, word
pert.: sofane
COUCI-COUCI: mediocre, **poor*
COUGAR: **cat: wild*
COUGH: **bark,* hack, tussis, yex
drop: lozenge, pastil, troche
medicine: horehound
pert.: bechic, tussive
up: **ante,* **contribute,* **yield*
COULEE: **bed,* gap, gorge, gulch
COUNCIL: **group,* **meeting*
chamber: bouleterion, camarilla
church: synod
man: alderman, legislator

national: congress, dail, diet, parliament
political: cabal, junto
pert.: cameral
table cover: tapis
COUNSEL: **advise,* coach, lawyer
COUNT: **add,* **compute,* canvass, score, tally, **tell,* **value*
down: launch time, start
of monte cristo: dantes
on: expect, lean on, rely
pert.: comital
COUNTENANCE: **abet,* **accept,* **encourage,* **face,* look, **suffer*
COUNTER: **adverse,* **combat,* man, **piece,* react, **shelf,* **token*
comb.: ant, anti
-attack: **answer,* charge
earth: antichthon
march: reverse
COUNTERACT: balance, cancel, defend, react, resist, thwart
COUNTERFEIT: **act,* **affect,* **artificial,* **bad,* phony, queer
apparatus for: bogus
COUNTERMAND: **abolish,* **cancel*
COUNTERPART: **copy,* **image*
COUNTRY: **bush,* **power,* **state*
dance: barn dance, blue grass
gallant: swain
gentleman: allworthy, bob acres
gentlewoman: lady bountiful
girl: amaryllis
group of: **nations*
house: bastide, casino, cassine
man: **peasant*
open: heath, moot, weald, wold
pert.: agrestic, pastoral, predial, rural, rustic
place: farm, peat, ranch, villa
reside in: rusticate
road: byway, lane, path
tract: basin
COUNTY: bute, domain, fylke, lan, parish, seat, shire
seat: capital

* Asterisk means to look up this word to find more answer words.

COUP: *act, *blow, feat, ploy
  d'etat: master stroke, revolution, stratagem
  de grace: *end
  de main: *attack, stratagem
  d'oeil: glance
COUPLE: gemini, *pair, *unite
COUPON: *certificate, *token
  clipper: bondholder, retired
COURAGE: *symbol:* bloodstone
COURAGEOUS: *bold, *brave
COURIER: dragoman, estafet
  horse: bidet
  relay system: angaria
COURLAN: bird, jacamar, tinamon
COURSE: *policy, procedure, progress, *route, *set, *way
  alter: detour, veer
  easy: cinch, pipe, sinecure
  habitual: regimen, routine, rut
  meal: dessert, entree, salad
  of action: career, demarche
  of sprouts: training
  of study: curriculum, seminar
  part: lap, leg
  suff.: agog, agogue
COURT: *address, *area, *arena, flatter, forum, *spark, *staff
  action: case, suit, trial
  assistant: amala, amlah, clerk, crier, elisor, eyre, juror
  belonging to public: forensic
  body: jury
  bring to: *arrest, sist, sue
  call: arraignment, oyez
  church: classis, rota
  circuit: eyre, iter
  crier: bailiff, beadle
  criminal: assizes
  cry: oyes, oyez
  decision: arret, verdict
  ecclesiastical: consistory
  exemption: essoin
  hearing: action, oyer, suit, trial
  house: capital
  inner: patio

  ladies: bedoyo
  local: gemote
  martial: drumhead, try
  mikado's: dairo, dari
  minutes: acta
  of equity: chancery
  of one hundred: centumvir
  old: arret, gemot, leet, mote
  order: decree, nisi, rule, writ
  panel: jury
  pert.: aulic, fornaneous, rotal
  plaster: dressing
  rule: authority
  session: oyer, sederunt, trial
  writ: capias, subpoena, summons
COURTEOUS: debonair, gallant, gracious, polite, suave, urbane
COURTESAN: *prostitute
COURTIER: cavalier, sycophant
COVE: *retreat, *waterway
COVENANT: *contract
COVER: *aim, armor, bet, blanket, *bury, *cap, crust, *disguise, *dress, *hat, *hide, mask, *obscure, *ornament, pave, protect, *secret, *shell, shield, *spread, *stop, *top
  a bet: fade
  a fire: bank
  a hatch: batten
  dark: umbra
  charge: fee
  eyes: blindfold
  ground: *advance, speed
  protective: apron, armor, big camouflage, helmet, shell
  thin: film, veneer
  up: conceal, put on
  up for: be the goat, protect
  with bacon strips: lard
  with mud: belute
  with straw: thatch
COVERLET: blanket, caddow, robe
COVERT: furtive, latent, *secret
COVET: *desire, envy, pine, want

* Asterisk means to look up this word to find more answer words.

COVETOUS: *greedy, mean, miserly
COVEY: brood, flock ,*group
COW: *awe, cattle, ox
barn: byre, shed
barren: drape
bird: blackbird, bunting
boy: broncobuster, brushpopper, buckaroo, gaucho, herder, horseman, jackaroo, llanero, rider, roper, vaquero, waddi
boy garment: chaps, levis, jodhpurs
boy contest: rodeo, round-up
boy strap: latigo
catcher: bumper, front, guard, pilot, protector, safeguard
cud: rumen
dung: upla
fish: manatee, ray, sirenia
foot, ulcer: foul
group: cattle, herd, kine
headed goddess: isis
hide: beat, buff
hornless: doddie, doddy, moil, muley, mulley, pollard
hybrid: cattabu, cattalo
kind of: sacred
like: bovine, cous
nourishing ymir: audhumla
oak: basket tree
parsnip: bear's breech, cadweed, knapweed, ragwort, scabious
pea: sitao
pen: vachery
protectress: bubona
pert.: bovine, cous
puncher: *cowboy
sea: *cowfish
slip: auricula, marigold
sound: low, moo
vetch: canada pea, cat pea
young: calf, heifer, stirk
COWARD: baby, chicken, craven, jellyfish, milksop, poltroon
COWARDLY: *afraid, caitiff
adventurer: captain bobadil

COWER: crouch, fawn, quail
COWL: bonnet, *cap, *hat, hood
COXCOMB: amaranth, dandy, fop
COY: *bashful, demure, *shy
COZE: converse, *gossip, *talk
COZEN: *cheat, *deceive
COZY: intimate, safe, snug
CRAB: beef, cancer, gripe, *ruin
abdomen: apron
apple: malus, scrog, solitaire
claw: chela, nipper
comb.: carcin(o)
eating: cancrivorous
fiddler: uca
front: metope
genus: birgus, maia, squilla
grass: button grass, digitaria
king: horseshoe, limulus
like: cancroid
mantis: squilla
middle: metope
pert.: carcinomorphic
petrified: cancerite
shaped: cancriform, cancroid
split-shelled: buster
stick: cane, crank, cudgel
suborder: brachyura
the deal: queer, spoil, wreck
wood: andiroba, mahogany
CRACK: *joke, *opening, *try
brain: lunatic, screwball
brained: crazy, insane, nutty
down on: *attack, discipline
of doom: fate, tomorrow
on: *accelerate, *speed
pert.: alutaceous, coriaceous
pot: *eccentric, lunatic, nut
shot: *ace, expert, *marksman
the whip: discipline, *punish
up: *break up, *crash, go mad
willow: brittle willow
CRACKED: harsh, *insane, *mad
CRACKER: biscuit, georgian
berry: dwarf cornel
jack: *ace, *great
CRACKLE: *break, crink, snap
CRACKSMAN: burglar, *thief

* Asterisk means to look up this word to find more answer words.

CRADLE: *bed, foster, *source
  song: berceuse, lullaby
  wicker: bassinet
CRAFT: *deceit, *skill, *trade
CRAFTY: cunning, *smart, *wise
CRAG: arete, cliff, scarp, tor
  above glacier: nunatak
CRAKE: crow, rail, raven, sora
CRAM: *press, *study, *surfeit
  down the throat: convince
  -full: replete, satiated
CRAMBO CLINK: doggerel, poem
CRAMP: compress, confine, spasm
  iron: agrafe, agraffe
  one's style: frustrate, queer
CRANBERRY: cascara, holly
  habitat: bog
  scald: blast
  small: bogwort, herb
  tree: ball rose, pembina
CRANE: balaerica, bird, davit
  arm: gib, jib
  charges: cranage
  clip: caliper, calliper
  fly: tipula
  genus: grus
  ichabod rival: brom bones
  -like bird: chunga, seriema
  ship's: davit
  small: demoiselle
  the neck: gaze, stare
  traveling: jenny titan
CRANIUM: brainpan, head, *skull
  nerve root: radix
  part: calotte, calvaria
  -metrical point: inion, pterion, stenion
CRANK: angle, buzzard, caprice, *eccentric, *enthusiast, fanatic, fireeater, fussbudget, hothead, nut, sorehead, wind up
CRANKLE: *oscillate, turn
CRANKY: *short, *sullen, *ugly
CRAP: *dregs, *money, *refuse
  out: *die, *fail, *quit, *yield
CRAPE: crimp, curl, shroud

  hanger: killjoy, spoilsport
  jasmine: adam's apple
  myrtle: blood wood
CRAPS: *term:* back line, box cars, buck it, drag, fade, field, hard way, lay the odds, line, lumber, manna from heaven, miss, nick, pass, phoebe, point
CRASH: *bang, burst, collapse, collide, debacle, *defeat, failure, fiasco, misfortune, smash, splinter, thunder
CRASS: *bad, crude, *thick
CRATE: auto, *package, *quantity
CRATER: caldera, cavity, cup
CRAVAT: ascot, stock, teck, tie
CRAVE: *ask, *desire, *need
CRAVEN: *afraid, *coward
CRAW: *stomach, viscera
  -dad: *retreat
  fish: *apostate, crustacean, lobster, recede, sidle, yabby
CRAWL: creep, cringe, drag, fawn, grovel, inch, *retreat
  in: retire
  out of: *quit, *retreat
  with: *abound, infest, teem
CRAYFISH: cambarus, *crawfish
CRAZE: *break, bug, fad, mod
CRAZY: *absurd, *eccentric, *insane, *mad, *weird, *wild
  about: enthusiastic, in love
  idea: bee (in one's bonnet)
  like a fox: *cunning, *sly
  quilt: japanese rug, solitaire
  water: liquor
CREAK: groan, screech, scroop
CREAM: *balm, *best, *top, *whip
  mixed with wine: sillabub
  of tartar: adansonia, argol
  puff: effeminate, weakling
CREASE: crimp, fold, ruck, seam
CREATE: *form, *make, *set up
  a disturbance: rampage, *riot
  for one's self: carve out
CREATION: cosmos, universe

* Asterisk means to look up this word to find more answer words.

CREATIVE: ideaed, inventive
effort: origination
imagination: muse
thought: conception, genius
CREATOR: *author*, *god*
CREATURE: *agent*, animal, minion
comforts: conveniences
CREDENTIAL: *certificate*, *form*
carrier: breviger, mendicant
CREDIBLE: *correct*, logical
CREDIT: *accommodate*, *account*, charge, esteem, *praise*, *trust*
instrument: *certificate*, *form*
transfer: giro
term: interest, time
CREDO: belief, *doctrine*
suff.: doxy
CREED: *doctrine*, *symbol*
CREEK: *indian*, *waterway*
indian festival: busk
sedge: branch grass
CREEL: basket, caul, cawl, *trap*
CREEP: *crawl*, gumshoe, lurk, pussyfoot, skulk, tarry, worm
into good graces of: flatter
upon: *surprise*
with: *abound*, infest, teem
CREEPER: ivy, snake, vine, worm
CREEPS: all-overs, jimjams, shivers, trepidation, willies
CREMATE: burn, incinerate
CREMONA: amati, violin
CRENATE: notched, scalloped
CREOLE: mestizo, patois
state: louisiana
CREPE: *crape*, pancake, wrinkled
material: aerophane
myrtle: astromeda, tree
CREPITATE: crackle, roll, snap
CREPUSCULE: twilight
CRESCENDO: increasing
CRESCENT: horn, lunar, moon, semicircle, solitaire
point: cusp
-shaped: bicorn, corniform, horny,

lunar, menisciform, meniscoid, sigmoid, two-horned
CRESPIE: whale
CRESS: eker, kers, leaf
CRESSET: flambeau, torch
CREST: *acme*, *ridge*, *top*
fallen: downcast, embarrassed
CRESTED: coronate, cristate, muffed, pileate(d), tufted
CRETE: *cape:* krio(s)
earth spirit: curete
goddess: aphaia, britomartis, dictynna
king: cateus, idomeneus, minos
king, purified apollo: carmanor
man of brass: talos
monster: minotaur
mount: ida, psiloriti
people: caphtorim, philistines
princess: ariadne
seaport: canea, candia, khania
spikenard: phu
CRETHEUS: *son:* amythaon
wife: biadice
CRETIN: idiot, myxedema
CRETISM: falsehood, lie
CREUS: *offspring:* pallas
CREUSA: *consort:* aeneas, apollo
offspring: ion
CREVASSE: bergshrund, *opening*
CREVICE: cleft, cranny, rime
CREW: band, gang, *group*, *staff*
CREWEL: caddice, worsted
CREX: bird, corn crake
CRIB: bin, bunker, cab, *cheat*, *deceive*, manger, rack, *steal*
CRICK: *creek*, hitch, pang, spasm
CRICKET: equity, *fair*, *right*
ball: edger
genus: achetida, gryllus
position in: leg, mid-off, slip
run: bye
score: blob, duck egg, zero
side: offs, ons
sound: stridulate
team: eleven
term: over, smick, snick, tice

* **Asterisk means to look up this word to find more answer words.**

yorker in: tye
CRICKSAND: marsh
CRIER: announcer, beadle, herald
CRIME: *abuse, felony, *wrong
 ecclesiastical: simony
 goddess: ate
 organized: *underworld
 scene of: venue
CRIMEA: krym
 city: kerch, sevastopal, yalta
 people: tauri
 river: alma
 sea: azof, azov
 seaport: balaklava
 tribe: inkerman
CRIMINAL: *bad, convict, crook,
 culprit, desperado, felon, fugitive,
 gangster, *guilty, *hoodlum, jail-
 bird, malefactor, outlaw, proscrit,
 public enemy, racketeer, scoff-
 law, swindler, *thief, thug,
 wrongdoer, yegg
 act: caper
 court: bureo
 group: black hand, la cosa nostra,
 mafia, mob, syndicate
 habitual: recidivist, repeater
 identification: bertillonnage
 intent: dole, dolose
 refuge: alsatia, whitefriars
CRIMP: *abduct, *cheat, coil
CRIMSON: blushing, *red, scarlet
CRINE: hair, shrink, shrivel
CRINGE: fawn, flinch, submit
CRINGLE: disk, eyelet, grommet,
 orb, rope, terret, withe
CRINKLED: contortuplicate
CRINOID: batocrinus
 order: camerata
CRIPPLE: bacach, halt, hobble,
 scotch, spavine, *spoil, wing
 saint: giles
CRISIS: eleventh hour, epitasis,
 exigency, *pass, panic, *push,
 squeeze, strait, *state
CRISP: aphoristic, brittle, cheep,
 clear, concise, *short

CRISPIN: coat, shoemaker
CRITERION: *model, *rule, *test
CRITIC: *authority, exegete,
 judge, scold, slater, zoilus
CRITICAL: abusive, crucial, cynical, dangerous, edgy, *important,
 meticulous, precarious, *severe
 mark: obelisk, obelus
CRITICISM: *blame, nagging, rap
CRITICIZE: *accuse, *attack,
 *blame, cavil, *flaw, kibbitz, *re-
 buke, *scold, slam, *taunt
CROAK: complain, *cry, die, kill
CROATIAN: hrvati, sclav, serb,
 slav, sloven, sorb, wend
 capital: zagreb
 city: agram, fiume
 mountain: kapela
 river: bednya
 territory: banat
CROCK: dud, ewe, failure, flop,
 intoxicate, smut, soil, soot
CROCODILE: aetosaurus, gavial,
 goa, jacare, reptile
 bird: plover, sicsac, trochilus
 common: mugger, nilotic
 headed god: sobk
 -like: gavial, nako(o)
 marsh: goa
 nile: vulgaris
 tears: hypocrisy
CROCUS: irid, irus
 bulb: corm
CROFT: bottle, cottage, farm
CROMLECH: dolmen, cyclolith
CRONE: beldam, *hag, *witch
CRONUS: *daughter:* demeter, hera,
 hestia
 parent: gaea, uranus
 son: hades, poseidon, zeus
 wife: rhea
CRONY: comrade, *friend, pal
CROOK: *bias, *criminal, *staff
CROOKED: *corrupt, *rotten
 comb.: ankyl(o), cam
 stick: crank
 symbol: dogleg

* **Asterisk means to look up this word to find more answer words.**

CROP: *stomach, *whip, *yield
 destroyer: army-worm
 fowl's: craw, gebbie, ingluvies
 hunting: quirt, whip
 out: *appear, basset
 second-growth: rowen
 up: *begin, *occur, turn up
CROPPER: collapse, disaster
CROQUET(TE): cecil, roque
CROSS: *affliction, *against, ankh,
  bridge, counteract, cranky, crucifix, disappoint, *memorial, mix,
  oppose, *short, *staff, *sullen,
  *symbol, *ugly
 bar: axle, rung, transverse
 barred: trabeculate
 beam: bar, grill, trave, treve
 bill, genus: loxia
 -bombard: atomize
 bow: arbalest, ballista, rodd
 bowman: balistarius
 breed: cape boy, generate, hybrid-
  (ize), husky, *mixture
 current: opposition
 cut: beeline, economize
 cut saw: briar, tool
 examine: grille, question
 fertilization: allogamy, pollination
 fiery: crantara, crostarie
 fire: interchange
 grained: cantankerous, *coarse
 guard: chape
 hatch: engrave
 oneself: sain
 one's heart: depose, swear
 one's mind: occur to, think of
 out: blank, *cancel, deduct,
  dele(te), eliminate, erase
 patch: crab, crank, grouch
 piece: bar, cleat, buck, doubletree,
  evener, grill, rung, spar, transverse, yoke
 piece, on wicket: bail
 purposes: difference
 question: backspear, examine
 roads: carfax, carrefour, intersec-
  tion, village

 roads goddess: hecate, trivia
 roads of the world: lisbon
 row: alphabet
 rubicon: burn bridges, *decide
 -ruff: *oscillate, seesaw, trump
 section: *part, representation
 shaped: cleche, crucial
 spar: bougar
 staff: stiff
 stroke: beard, ceriph, serif
 swords: combat, duel, *fight
 tau: ankh, crux, tace
 the path of: encounter, *meet
 threads: weft, woof
 timber: spale
 type: celtic, egyptian, greek, latin,
  maltese, papal
 up: *betray, *deceive
 way: carrefour, cloverleaf, inter-
  section, rotary
 ways: athwart, contrawise
 wires: confuse, reticle
 wise: acrostic, diagonal
 word puzzle: acrostic, anagram
CROTCH: fork, pole, notch, prong
CROTCHET: *angle, *caprice
CROTCHETY: *eccentric, grumpy
CROTON: bug: cockroach
 cascarilla: cascalote
 draco: blood tree
 eluteria: cascarilla
 lucidus: basket hoop
CROUCH: bend, bow, cower, fawn
CROUCHING: deferential
CROUSE: *bold, *brisk, cocky
CROW: aga, aylet, *brag, crone,
  *cry, daw, hag, *laugh, vapor
 bait: corpse
 bar: gablock, gavelock, jimmy
 berry: baby heathberry
 carrion: black neb
 comb.: corvus
 cry: caw
 foot: batrachium, butter cress,
  gold cup, ranunculus, wrinkle
 -like: corvine
 nest: bird nest, eyrie, outlook

* Asterisk means to look up this word to find more answer words.

to pluck: *issue
CROWD: audience, cramp, *group
around: *besiege
builder: barker
comb.: ochlo
in: enter, intrude
out: supplant
sail: *accelerate, *speed
CROWN: atef, capital, *complete,
crest, diadem, glorify, *head
dress, *honor, tiara, *top
and anchor: chuck-a-luck
glass source: aluminum borate
northern: corona borealis
of thorns: *affliction, curse
pert.: coronal
piece: bull
post: upright
prince: atheling, heir
southern: corona australia
vetch: axseed, coronilla varia
wheel: contrate
CRU: growth, vineyard
CRUCIAL: *acute, *critical
CRUCIBLE: etna, pot, retort
lining: brasque
CRUCIFIX: *cross, pax, rood
CRUCIFY: *torment, *torture
CRUCIFIXION: site: calvary
CRUD: curd, *nonsense, *refuse
CRUDE: *brutal, *bad, raw, *wild
CRUEL: *brutal, feral, violent
CRUELTY: ferocity, *violence
CRUET: ama, buret, cruse, vial
CRUISE: coast, fly, ride, sail
CRUMB: *bit, oaf, *peasant
CRUMBLE: *break, *decay
CRUMP: *bang, deviate, thud
CRUMPLE: *contract, *yield
CRUNCH: *bite, gnash, grind
CRUSADE: campaign, cause, jihad
CRUSADER: pilgrim, templar
foe: infidel, saladin, saracen
headquarters: acre
CRUSH: *break, *defeat, *group
room: foyer
CRUST: *armor, *brass, *cover

CRUSTACEAN: arthropod, crab
antenna, suff.: cerite
antenna, joint: carpocerite
appendage: exite
aquatic: anostraca
claw: chela
extinct: archaeocyathid
feeler: antenna
fifth segment: carpos
footless: apus
fossil: trilobite
genus: cancer, copepoda, eryon,
hippa, triops
group: caridea
larva: alima
limb: podite
limb segment: carpos
malacostracan: amphipoda
marine: callianassa
phyllopod: artemia, branchipus
shrimplike: anaspida
small: barnacle, copepod, fiddler
crab, isopod
ten-footed: crab
CRUSTY: *hard, *obstinate, *short
CRUTCH: *staff, *stick, *support
CRUX: *core, *crisis, *cross
CRY: *acclaim, *bark, barley,
bawl, caterwaul, *complain, *desire, *howl, *lament, moan, *protest, rage, *sorrow, *style
about: *issue, *report, *spread
back: revert
cattle: hoy
child: mewl, pule
court: hear, oyes, oyez
derisive: bah, boo, catcall, hiss,
hoot, phooey, rats
down: censure
for: demand, *desire, *need
for truce: barla, barley, barly
havoc: mobilize
hawking: auvol
hunting: tantivy, yoick(s)
of approval: bravo, ole, rah
of attention: hey, holla
of pain: ouch

* Asterisk means to look up this word to find more answer words.

of relief: phew, whew
of sorrow: alack, alas, ay, woe
of triumph: aha, hurrah
off: *abandon
out: *accuse, blat, blazon, call, clamor, *complain, crake, denounce, scream, shout, yell
out against: censure, dissuade, incriminate, protest
political: shibboleth, slogan
quits: surrender, *yield
up: extol, laud, *praise
urging on: tantivy, yoick(s)
wild: evoe
CRYPT: cavity, tomb, treasury
CRYPTIC: *secret, *vague
CRYPTOGRAM: cipher, code
CRYSTAL: *bit, diamond, ice
clear: *open, *plain
form: bisphenoid, disphenoid
-gaze: foresee, predict, scry
-gazer: *prophet
-gazing: catoptromancy
ice: frazil
studded: druse
twin: baveno, macle
vision: esp
CRYSTALLINE: *acid:* alanine, aspartic, atrolactic
alkaloid: amarine, apoatropine, apomorphine, aporphine, aspidospermine, atropine, berbamine, daturine, jervine
base: alanine, anserine
colorless: acacetin
compound: aciculite, aconite, aikinite, alban, aloin, amarin(e), anisil, asarite, asarin, asparagine, atropine, azoxybenzenebenzaldoxime, benzil, benzimidazole, biuret, bixin, camphor, haemin, indol, oscine, serine
diacid: azelaic
ether: apiol(e)
flavone derivative: apigenin
globuline: avenalin, vitellin
glucoside: acacin, androsin, anti-

arin, apiin, asperuloside, baptisin, calycanthine, camelin
hollow nodule: geode
hydrocarbon: acenapthene, anthemene, anthracene
ketone: anthraquinone, anthrone
lactone: bergaptene
locust leaves: acacetin
monoacid: atropic
phenol: ammoresinol, apionol, orcin(e), orsinol
pine tar: retene
powder: acetobromanilide, anthracene, barbital, barbitone
rock: diorite, greisen
salt: analgene, borax, racemate
schists: caledonian, calloway
sterol: anthesterin
structure: siderite, sparry
substance: alban, amarine, dulcin, orcine, urea
tannin: acertannin
vanadosilicate: ardennite
CRYSTALLITE: bacillite, belonite, whinstone
aggregation: acrulite
CRYSTALLIZE: candy, solidify
CTENOPHORE: beroe, cestida, jellyfish, nuda
CUB: baby, bear, fry, pup, whelp
scout leader: akela
CUBA: *asphalt:* chapapote
ballerina: alicia alonso
bird: tocororo, trogon
carriage: volante
castle: morro
cigar: havana
city: bayamo, camaguay, cienfuego, guines, havana, matanzas, palmira, puerto principe, santa clara
dance: conga, danzon, rhumba, rumba, samba, tango
dictator: batista, castro
disaster: bay of pigs
document: ostend manifesto
dollar: gourde

* Asterisk means to look up this word to find more answer words.

fish: bacalao, diablo, escolar, palu, viajaca

fortification: morro, trocha

hutia: pilori

island: de pinos, pines

measure: bocoy, caballeria, cordel, fanega, tarea, vara

peak: copper, guaniguanico, pico turquinos, pinar del rio

port: baracoa, cardenas, duabi

revolutionary: castro, guevara

rodent: hutia, pilori

root: malanga

rum: bacardi

secret police: porra

snake: juba

solenodon: alamaqui, almique

storm: bayamo

tobacco: capa, havana, vuelta

tree: almendro, culla, cuya

ward: barrio

weapon: machete

weight: libra, tercio

CUBBYHOLE: corner, *retreat

CUBE: *angle, block, die, tessera

spar: anhydrite

CUBIC: *contents:* capacity

decimeter: liter, litre

measure: cord, kilo, stere

shape: cuboid

CUBICLE: *alcove, cell, niche

CUBISM: *founder:* picasso

CUCHULAINN: *wife:* eimer, emer

CUCKOO: ani, bird, coel, clock, crazy, *insane, koel, *mad

bee genus: nomada

family: cuculidae

flower: bird-eye, bog pink, canterbury bell, quaking grass

mate: wryneck

pint: aaron, adder's-meat, arum bobbins, wake-robin

shrike: blue pigeon

spits: cercopis

vulgate: larus

word: platitude

CUCUMBER: conger, gherkin,

gourd, pedata, pepino, pepo

tree: black linn, magnolia

CUCURBIT: cassabanana, gourd

CUD: bite, chew, quid, rumen

CUDDLE: curl up, hug, nestle

CUDGEL: *beat, sandbag, *staff

CUE: clew, hint, mood, prompt

shot: masse

word: presto

CUFF: blow, glove, manacle, slap

fastener: link, tab

off the: ad lib, impromptu

CUIRASS: armor, lorica, mail

CUL-DE-SAC: deadend, impasse

CULLY: *cheat, deceive, *trick

CULMEN: *acme, *ridge, *top

CULMINATION: *end, *stop, *top

CULPABLE: *bad, guilty, laches

CULPRIT: *criminal, malefactor

CULT: *doctrine, fad, ism, sect

CULTIVATE: *acquire, *affect, *approach, *prepare, *train

CULTIVATION: *art:* geoponics

method: goom, jhum, joom, jum

CULTURE: art, breeding, *polish

medium: agar, gelatin, pectin

CUMBERSOME: *clumsy, *great

CUMMERBUND: band, belt, obi

CUMSHAW: bonus, gratuity, tip

CUNEIFORM: hieroglyphics, bone

inscription: behistun, isitun

CUNNER: blue fish, perch, wrasse

CUNNING: *acute, *deception, *skill, *smart, wily, *wise

CUP: *assay:* breaker, cupel, *test

bearer: ganymede, hebe, saki

diamond-cutting: dop

drinking: bowl, godet, tass

eared: quaich, quaigh

earthenware: mug

-feast (pl): anthesteria

flower: calyx

fungus: aecium

handle: ear, lug

holder: zarf

horn-shaped: holmos

* **Asterisk means to look up this word to find more answer words.**

large: grail, jorium
-like: calicular, poculiform
looped handle: cantharus, kylix
loving: award, *prize, tyg
metals-assaying: beaker, cupel
of tea: *forte, metier, thing
olympus: depas
pastry: dariole
resembling: calicular
seed: calycocarpum, moonseed
-shaped: calithiform, concave, cyathiform
small: calicular, cannikin, chark, cruse, demitasse, nipperkin, noggin, shot
stand: zarf
two-handled: depas, tig, tyg
CUPBOARD: *ambry, *cabinet
CUPEL: burn, refine, *test
CUPID: amor, dan, *eros, *love
beloved: psyche
dart: catananche, succory
mother: aphrodite, venus
CUPIDITY: *desire, greed, lust
demon: mammon
CUPOLA: *cap, *dome, *tower
CUR: *mixture, mongrel, mutt
group: cowardice
CURARE: oorali, poison, urari
CURATE: *church man
CURATOR: guardian, steward
CURB: *arrest, *bit, drag, *slow
CURE: *church man, *remedy
-all: elixir, panacea
in smoke: bloat
CURIO: souvenir, *token
CURIOUS: *agape, *eccentric
one: *gossip, quidnunc
CURLED: coiled, savoyed, spiry
dock: bitter bur, petasites
wood: amboina, lingoum
CURLEW: bankera, bustard, fute, godwit, kioea, marlin, snipe
CURLING: *term:* besom, button, hack, hog, house, patlid, port, soop, tee, wick
CURLY: crispy, frizzly, kinky

clematis: blue jessamine
locks: charles ii
top: beet blight
CURMUDGEON: miser, tightwad
CURRENT: *actual, *course, eddy, *popular, rife, trend, *usual
air: thermal
generator: electromotor
event: *activity, *affair
ocean: agulhas, benguela, brazil
CURRY: comb, cook, *prepare
favor: apple polish, brown nose
CURSE: *abuse, *afflict, *blast, malison, marantha, oath, *spell
CURVE: *arch:* extrados
convex side up: anticlinal
cusp: spinode
couble point: acnode
diocles invention: cissoid
ellipse parallel: toroid
kind: memniscate, parabolic
part: arc, arch
quartic: limacon
quick descent: brachistochrone
rise: camber
top: apophyge
CURVED: *comb.:* campyl(o)
in: adunc, concave, hooked
out: bombe, convex
CUSH: *father:* ham
son: havilah, nimrod, raamah, sabtah, sabtechah, seba
CUSTARD: *apple:* sweetsop
tree: annoa, ates, atta
CUSTOM: *convention, *use, *way
comb.: nomo
house: aduana
house goods list: bill of entry
-made: bespoke, tailored
CUSTOMER: *group:* clientele
CUT: *dismiss, *reduce, *remove
across: economize, slice
a figure: flaunt, *show
along: *speed
a melon: *allot, dispense

* Asterisk means to look up this word to find more answer words.

and come again: *repeat
and dried: trite
and run: depart, flee, vanish
and thrust: *attack
apart: *criticize, *separate
a rug: dance
a shine: rampage
a swath: *succeed
back: economize, *save
capers: *play
corners: *cut back
dead: slight, snub
down: *cut back, fell, *kill
in: dance, interrupt, intrude
it out: don't, *stop
loose: play, rampage, release
off: *abridge, *clip, elide, mow
of one's jib: *appearance, look
out: clip, *speed, *stop, *win
purse: pickpocket, *thief
short: abbreviate, *end, trim
the mustard: manage, *succeed
throat: bitter, butcher, rascal
to pieces: *defeat, *destroy
up: *caper, *play, rogue, wag
CUTTING: *acerb, *refuse, *sharp
CUTTLEFISH: octopus, squid
CYBELE: berecyntia, rhea
consort: attis, attys, atys
CYCLADES: ios, kea, milos, naxos
CYCLOPES: arges, brontes, steropes
CYCNUS: *father:* ares
CYDIPPE: *son:* biton, cleobis
CYLINDER: *armored:* barbette
central: stele
CYMBALS: becken, castinets, piatti, tal, zel
CYMBELINE: *daughter:* imogen
CYMOSE: *inflorescence:* anthela
CYMRIC: *welsh
CYNIC: *ascetic, ironic, sardonic
school founder: antisthenes
CYNICAL: *acerb, *critical
CYPRESS: *mock:* belvedere
pine relative: cape cedar

spurge: balsam, bonaparte's crown
vine: jasmine, quamoclit
CYPRINUS: carp, fish, sea bream
CYPRUS: *city:* famagusta, limasol, nicosia, paphos
coin: para, piaster
measure: cass, donum, gomari, kartos, kouza, medimno, oka
mountain: troodos
CYRENAIC: hedonic
CYRUS: *daughter:* atossa
treasurer: mithradates
CYST: *bag, pouch, sac, wen
without head: acephalocyst
CYTHEREA: anadyomene, aphrodite, astarte, calypso, orchid, venus
CZAR: caesar, dictator, emperor, ruler, tsar, tyrant, tzar
CZECH: slav, slovak, zips
city: asch, bratislava, brno, budweis, carlsbad, eger, opava, praha, prague, teplitz
coin: ducat, heller, koruna
dance: furiant, polka, redowa
gypsy: bohemian
measure: lan, liket, merice, mira, sah, stopa
mountain: tatra
munition plant: skoda
national saint: wenceslas
playwright: capek
reformer: huss
region: bohemia
river: eger, elbe, gran, hron, isar, iser, moldau, nitra, oder, ohre, waag, vag, vah
statesman: benes

DAB: *bit, blotch, *paint, *try
DABBLE: dally, meddle, *trifle
DABBLER: amateur, dilettante
DABCHICK: gallinule, grebe
DACE: chub, fish, two

* **Asterisk means to look up this word to find more answer words.**

DACTYL: finger, *meter*, piddock
DACTYLOLOGY: gesture
DADO: base, grove, wainscot
DAEDAL: *complex*, *cunning*
DAEDALUS: *son:* icarus
  victim and nephew: talos
DAFFODIL: asphodel, campanula
DAFFY, DAFT: *insane*, *wild*
DAG: *horse:* hrimfaxi, skinfaxi
  parent: delling, nott
DAGDA: *cousin:* boann
  daughter: brigit
  son: aengus, angus
DAGGER: *sword: short*
  stroke: stab, stoccado
DAILY: constantly, newspaper
  bread: *support*, sustenance
  dozen: exercise, routine
  grind: habit, routine, *work*
  meals: board
DAINTY: cute, *pretty*, *small*
DAIRY: *food:* butter, yogurt
  house: larder
  maid: dey, milkmaid
  man: farmer, milkman, stockman
  tool: separator
DAIS: estrade, pulpit, rostrum
  synagogue: alemar, bema, bimah
DAISY: aster, bowwort, burdock,
  gerbera, gowan, morgan, oxeye
DAKSHA: *father:* brahma
DALAI LAMA: incarnation, *ruler*
DALLY: loiter, *play*, *wanton*
DALMATIA: *yugoslavia*, serbia
DAM: *close*, dike, lady, *stop*
DAMAGE: bill, *evil*, *hurt*, *tear*,
  price, *spoil*, strafe, wreck
  pert.: noxal, noxious
DAMAGES: *award*, payment
DAMAN: ashkoko, cony, hyrax
DAMASCUS: *king:* aretas, ben-
  hadad
  river: abana, barada, pharpar
DAMASK: cloth, linen, pin, rose
DAMN: *abuse*, *blast*, curse
DAMP: deter, humid, *wet*
DAMSEL: donzella, girl, maiden

fish: blacksmith, pintano
DAN: buoy, river, title
  sister: una
  town: elon
  tribe head: ahiezer
DANAE: *kin:* acrisius, perseus
DANAUS: asclepias, butterfly
  daughter: amymone
  father: belus
  slayer: lynceus
DANCE: *party*, *play*, trip
  art of: choreography, orchesis
  attendance: *praise*, *serve*
  ballroom: bunnyhug, czardas, fox-
    trot, mazurka, polka, waltz
  basket-carrying: calathiscus
  bolero-like: cachucha
  ceremonial: areito, basse, bat
  chorus: cancan, cordax, strut
  clumsily: balter
  college: hop, prom, trot
  country: adson saraband, alther,
    argeers, aurrescu, baile, barn,
    bergamask, haymaker, reel, tar-
    antella, villanella
  designer: choreographer
  18th century: cassation, diverti-
    mento, serenade
  exhibition: ballet, tap
  formal: farandola, pavan, prom
  gay: galliard, reel, rigadoon
  gesture: siva
  girl: alma, artiste, ballerina, baya-
    dere, chorine, coryphere, dan-
    seuse, devadasi, gaisha, nautch,
    terpsichorienne
  hall: ballroom, casino
  lively: allemande, bolero, branle,
    canary, coranto, corybantic, fling,
    galliard, galop, gavot, jib, polka,
    reel, rigadoon, rhumba, rumba,
    shakedown, schottish, trot
  masked: ridotto
  mirthful: caper, conga, galop
  modern: chacha, charleston, frug,
    mashed potato, monkey, pony,

* Asterisk means to look up this word to find more answer words.

rock, shag, tango, twist, two-step, watusi
morris: bobby, joe
movement: brisse, chasse(d), coule, coupe, entrechat, fouette, gambado, glissade, grapevine, heel-and-toe, jete, pas, pigeon-wing, pirouette, quickstep, shuffle, step
muse: terpsichore
music: bebop, boogie-woogie, bop, gymnopedie, jazz, jive, rag, rock-and-roll, swing
nimbly: canary
19th century: redowa, tempete
1920s: big apple, black bottom, castle walk
nude: bubble dance, fan dance
old: allemande, bource, branle, canary, carole, cebell, chaccon, chacona, coranto, courant, farandola, furlana, galop, gavotte, hore, jig, jog, lavolta, minuet, morris, pavan, reel, rondo, tarantella
partner: gigolo
pert.: bijestic, gestic, nautch, saltant, terpsichorean
round: branle, polka, schottish
rustic: *country dance
17th century: allemande
shoes: pumps, slippers, taps
16th century: bergerette
slow: adagio, minuet, waltz
square: argeers, caledonian, lanciers, quadrille
step: *dance movement
sword: flamborough, matachin
the back step: reverse
voluptuous: belly, habanera
weird: macabre
DANDELION: bitterwort, cat's ear, chicory, gosmore, taraxacum, yellow gentian
stalk: scape
DANDIFY: *dress, *ornament
DANDLE: caress, dally, *pet, toy

DANDY: bantam, *great, *spark
DANGER: hazard, peril, *venture
DANGEROUS: *bad, *ugly
DANIEL: belteshazzar
colleagues: azariah, hananiah
companion: abednego, mishael
dancer: miser
dream animals: bear, dragon, leopard, lion, ram
prince: michael
DANISH: *denmark
DANITE: *band:* avenging angels
DANTE: *beloved:* beatrice
demon: alichino, cagnazzo
hell circle: caina
illustrator: dore
patron: scala
verse form: sestina
work: divine comedy, inferno, vita nuova
DANUBE: *fish:* huch, hucho
gorge: irongate
people: dacian
town: linz, ulm, vienna
tributary: arges, drau, drava, iller, inn, ipel, ipoly, isar, jui, naab, olt, prut, raab, raba, schyl, siret, traun
DAPHNE: laurel, mezereon
father: ladon, peneus
DAPHNIS: *lover:* chloe
DARBIES: handcuffs, manacles
DARE: *taunt, *venture
devil: fireeater, hellcat
say: remark, suppose, *think
DARING: *bold, bravura, intrepid
DARIUS: *concubine:* apame
father: ahasuerus, artaxerxes
prince: daniel
prize-winner: zerubbabel
DARK: *bad, *black, *obscure
colored: carbonous
comb.: nyct(i), nycto
complexioned: swarthy
depths: hole, dungeon, lock-up
earth: chernozen
horse: candidate

* Asterisk means to look up this word to find more answer words.

in the: blind
DARLING: acushla, aroon, *pet
DART: *bolt, *run, *start, *throw
like: dartling, spicular
shaped: belemnoid
snake: arrow snake
thrower: anisocycle, bow
D'ARTAGNAN: *companion:* aramis, athos, porthos
creator: dumas
DARWIN: *boat:* beagle
doctrine: evolution
tulip: admiral togo
DASH: *bit, *beat, *speed
board: safeguard
into: collide, *meet
off: *author, flee, improvise
DASHING: *bold, gay, *smart
DATE: *meeting, *spark, *time
clause: teste
juice: dibs
plum: sapote
strangers: blind date
DAUB: *administer, *paint, soil
DAUGHTER: *in law:* shnir, shnur
of joy: *prostitute, *wanton
of moon: nokomis
pert.: filial
DAUNT: *alarm, *awe, faze, *stop
DAUPHIN: delphinium, guigo, heir
pert.: delphine
DAVID: *armor bearer:* naharai
brother: ozem
cave: adullam
chief: abiel, abiezer, abishai, adina, ahiam, ahijah, amasai, asahel, azmoth, benaiah, dodaian, eleazar, elhanan, eliab, eliphal, elzabad, ezer, gareb, hanan, heldai, helez, ilai, ira, ittai, joel, maharai, obadiah, shammoth, sibbecai, uriah, zabad, zelek
chief rulers: amasai, ira
companion: hushai
consorts: abigail, abisha, abital, ahinoam, bathsheba, eglah, hag-

gith, maacah, michal
counsellor: ahitophel, jonathan
daughter: maacah, tamar
employer: nabal
father: jesse
favorite son: absalom
friend: barzillai, ittai, rei
general: abner, amasa, igal, ira, joab, rei, shammah
goliath's valley: elam
grandfathers: amminadab, boaz, hezron, nashon, obed, pharez, ram, salmon
herdsman: jaziz, jehdeiah, obil, shaphat, shitrai
minister: ira
musician: asaph
nephew: amasa
olive master: baalhanan, joash
priest: zadoc
princes: azareel, eliezer, elihu, hoshea, iddo, ishmaiah, jeri, moth, omri, shepatiah
prophet: nathan
recorder: jehoshaphat
scribe: shavsha
sons: absalom, adonijah, ammon, beeliada, daniel, eliada, eliphelet, elishua, hattush, ibhar, ishar, japhia, nathan, nepheg, nogah, shammua, shepatiah, shimea, solomon
supporter: achimaas, ahimaaz
traitor to: ahithophel
vintner: shimei, zabdi
DAWDLE: *dally, tarry, toy, wait
DAWKINS, JOHN: artful dodger
DAWN: *opening, *start
goddess: aurora, eos, usas
gods: asvins, dyaus
on: occur to, penetrate
pert.: auroral, eoan
symbol: dew
toward the: eastward
DAY: *after day:* *always
and night: *always, constantly
bed: baigneuse

* Asterisk means to look up this word to find more answer words.

before: eve, yesterday
blind: hemeralopia, nyctalopia
book: diary, journal, log
break: dawn, morning, sunup
by day: repeatedly
comb.: hemer(o)
dream: fancy, reverie, vision
every other: tertian
father of: erebus
god: horus, janus
hot: scorcher
in and day out: *always
joyful: festival
judgment: doomsday
light: dawn, enlightenment, hope,
  information, publicity
longest: barnaby bright, d-day
nursery: creche
of atonement: alhet, ashamnu
of rest: sabbath
-peep: dawn
scholar: extern
shape: anchor ball
-sight: hemeralopia
spring: dawn, morning
star: sphere, sun
DAYS: *fateful:* ides
fifty: quinquagesima
fourteen: fortnight
gone by: past
man: arbiter, mediator, umpire
march: diet(a), etape
of yore: ago, has-been, past
work: darg(ue), diet(a)
DAZE: astonish, astound, awe
DEACON: *prayers:* ectene
stole: orarion
DEAD: *ahead:* directly
alive: spent
beat: bum, parasite, sponger
body: carcass, carrion
city of: necropolis
deity: *underworld god(dess)
duck: goner
end: blind alley, cul de sac
end channel: billabong
fall: *trap

from the neck up: *stupid
hand: freehold
head: bobber, empty, pass
heat: draw, impasse, tie
home of: boneyard, catacomb, cin-
  erarium, crematory, golgotha,
  grave, lichhouse, morgue, mortu-
  ary, ossuarium, tomb
language: archaism, latin
lift: chore, exertion
-line: boundary, *limit
-lock: draw, impasse, stalemate
of night: midnight, silence
pan: impassive, vacant
pledge: mortgage
rap: likeness, similarity
region: amenti, erebus, *hell
right: accurate
ringer: identical, likeness
service: black mass
sea city: sodom
sea mountain: pisgah
sea pass: akrabbin
sea plateau: seir
sea territory: moab
set: determined, *stop
set at: *attack
shot: marksman, sniper
spirits: akh, amanes
spit: likeness
-still: likeness
sure: *absolute, *actual
tired: spent
to the world: asleep, oblivious
trees: driki
weight: impediment
-wood: weight
-wood character: calamity jane
DEAF AND DUMB: surdomute
DEAL: *dispense, *quantity, *turn
a blow: strike
a deathblow: *defeat, *destroy
directly: make no bones about
illegally: bootleg
harshly: discipline
in: include, purvey, *trade
out: *administer, scatter

* **Asterisk means to look up this word to find more answer words.**

with: *accomplish*, concern, discuss, perform, *punish*

DEALER: *agent*, banker, broker house, monger, retailer, vendor
crooked: mechanic

DEAN: chief, *church man*, vale
pert.: decanal

DEATH: *after:* posthumous
angel: azrael, danite, sanuel
aware of portending: fey
black: plague
blow: coup de grace, *defeat*
bringing: funest
-dealing planet: anareta
-defying: audacious, *bold*
deity: *underworld deity*
eternal: perdition
house: *jail*
light: candle
march: cortege, dirge, funeral
mercy: euthanasia
note: mort
notice: obit(uary)
personification: ankou, azrael, charos, grim reaper, mors
portent: barghest
put to: *kill*
rate: mortality, statistic
rattle: rale
register: necrology
song: dirge, elegy, threnody
stroke: coup de grace, *end*
struggle: *agony*, *contest*
sword: morglay
warrant: condemnation, verdict

DEBACLE: *catastrophe*, *ruin*

DEBASE: *abase*, *spoil*, taint

DEBATE: *agitate*, *argue*, rebut
pert.: cloture, forensic, polemical, quodlibet
place: forum, senate

DEBILITATE: *afflict*, *sap*

DE BIVAR: campeador, cid

DEBORAH: *husband:* lapidoth

DEBRIEFING: followup, postmortem

DEBUT: *opening*, *start*

DECAY: blet, blight, *break up*, caries, conk, corrode, corrupt, crumble, decompose, defile, disintegrate, druxiness, erode, *fail*, fester, gangrene, go bad, impair, mildew, mold, mortify, exidation, putrefy, rankle, rot, *ruin*, rust, sphacelate, spile, *spoil*, wear
comb.: sapr(o)

DECEIT: *deception*

DECEIVE: *abuse*, bamboozle, bedote, beflum, befool, beguile, betray, bilk, bite, blackleg, bluff, cajole, camouflage, catch, *cheat*, circumvent, come over, con, conjure, *corrupt*, cozen, daddle, delude, desert, diddle, do in, dupe, *fail*, falsify, flam, fob, *fool*, forsake, fub, gammon, get around, gudgeon, gull, gum, have, hoax, hocus, honeyfogle, hornswoggle, humbug, illude, jape, jockey, juggle, let down, *lie*, mask, mislead, mock, mump, pigeon, seduce, slicker, *take*, *trap*, *trick*

DECENT: decorous, *good*, *right*

DECEPTION: *abuse*, *artifice*, blaflum, chicanery, covin, fake, flimflam, guile, hoax, ruse, spoofery, *trick*, wile

DECIDE: *act*, *adopt*, arbitrate, *call*, cast the die, cern, commit, conclude, cross the rubicon, determine, elect, find, fix, govern, hold, rate, *rule*, *settle*, *will*

DECIDED: *emphatic*, unqualified

DECISION: *act*, aplomb, *award*, call, canon, choice, doom, finding, judgment, mettle, nerve, *report*, *result*, *will*

DECK: *hand:* crewman
head: trump, turn-up
lower: orlop
out: *adorn*, *array*, *attire*
part: scupper
post: bitt

* Asterisk means to look up this word to find more answer words.

ship: berth, bridge, fore castle, lower, orlop, poop, promenade, spar, upper

space: bay

DECLARE: *acclaim, *argue, bid, *issue, *protest, *show, *state

one's opinion: allow

war: challenge, dare

DECLINE: *abate, *break, bust, catabasis, cataplasis, dip, droop, ebb, *end, fad, *fail, *fall (*short*), flag, go down, lapse, pine, recede, *refuse, reject, run down, shortcoming, sink, slide, slip, slump, *spoil, spurn, tabes

DECOMPOSE: *analyze, *break down

DECORATE, DECORATION: *ornament

DECORATED: nielled, sigilate

coat: brandenburg

pert.: medallic

waist: jabot

wall: dado

DECOROUS: *good, nice, prim

DECORUM: *convention, gravity

DECREE: *act, *law, *order, writ

authoritative: arret, canon

imperial: fiat, irade

papal: bull

DECRY: *abase, *complain, croak

DEDAN: *son:* asshurim, letushim

DEDICATE: *allot, *anoint, *apply

DEDUCE: *argue, *conclude

DEED: *act, *action, *adventure, coup, document, escrow, *title

evil: malefaction, *sin

good: benefice, boon, favor

DEEM: *account, opine, *think

DEEP: *acute, *broad, *great, *obscure, *sage, *wise

bosomed: bathycolpian

comb.: abysso, bathy

-dye: color, fix

-dyed: established, fast, indelible, thorough, unfading

freezing: refrigeration

in: involved, slow

-rooted: established

-sea: abyssal, bassalian

-seated: established, intrinsic

sense: *passion

-set: cavernous

six: tomb

study: absorption

well: artesian

-worn: ragged

DEER: *axis:* chital

barking: muntjac, muntjak

berry: gaylussacia, huckleberry

big: caribou, elk, moose, wapiti

coat, winter: blue

comb.: cervi

fallow: dama

female: doe, hind, roe

genus: cervus, dama, pudu, rusa

grass: rhexia

hog: atlas, para

horn: balcon, bez, buckhorn, croche, dag, mussel, testine

hound: buckhound

-let: chevrotain, napu

-like giraffe: okapi

male: buck, hart, olen, stag

marsh: suacupucu

meat: charqui, jerky, venison

muntjac: kakar, kakur

path: run, slot, trail

pert.: cervine, damine

red: axis, hart, olen, roe

small: fawn, muntjac, ratwa

tail: scut

trap: buckstall

three-year-old: sorel, sorrel

two-year-old: brocket

young: brocket, fawn, spay, spitter

DEFAME: *abuse, *brand, mar

DEFEAT: annihilate, balk, bar, bath, beat, bug-out, collapse, confuse, confute, conquer, crash, *destroy, disappoint, do in, downfall, euchre, facer, failure, fall, fell, fix, foil, frustrate, *kill,

---

* **Asterisk means to look up this word to find more answer words.**

lick, master, mate, nose out, outdo, overcome, quietus, *reduce, rout, *ruin, *skin, smash, subdue, subjugate, thwart, *throw, top, *upset, vanquish, waterloo, wax, *whip
DEFECT: *abandon, bug-out, *fail
DEFECTIVE: comb.: atel
DEFEND: *advocate, *back
DEFENSE: *answer, *fort, *tower
armor: caparison
castle: matchecold
colored for: aposematic
dike: estacade
garment: broigne
mechanism: autism, dereism, dynamism, escapism, fantasy, negativism, projection, sublimation, withdrawal
outpost: barbacan, barbican
position: bridgehead, rampart
slope: glacis
wall: bailey, ballium
work: base, *fort, redan
DEFER: *bow, respect, *yield
DEFILE: *abuse, *smear, *spoil
DEFINE: *allot, *limit, *name
DEFINITE: *absolute, *actual, *open, *plain, *special, *set
DEFRAUD: *cheat, *fool, *trick
DEFT: *able, *adroit, expert
DEFY: beard, dare, flout, spurn
DEGRADE: *abase, *corrupt
DEGREE: *amount, *range, *rank
conferral: laureation
elevation: ascent
excellence: caliber
highest: cum laude, nth, sum
seeker: candidate
slight: *ace, hair, inch, nth
taken: inceptor
without honors: pol
DEIGN: *accept, consent, stoop
DEIRDRE: consort: conor, noise
DEJECTED: blue, doleful, *sad
DELATE: *accuse, denounce
DELAY: *abide, *arrest, *slow

DELAWARE: indian: lenape
nickname: blue hen state
DELEGATE: *agent, envoy, man
group: convention
DELETE: *blank, *cancel, erase
DELIBERATE: *advise, *cool, *think
DELIBERATELY: in cold blood
DELICATE: elegant, *fine, *soft
DELICIOUS: *good, sapid, tasty
DELIGHT: *amuse, *please, feast
in: *acclaim, *admire, relish
DELILAH: courtesan
paramour: samson, sampson
DELIRIOUS: *ardent, *mad
DELIVER: bring, *release, *yield
DELLING: daughter: dag
DELPHI: kastri
priestess: pythia
DELUDE: *cheat, *deceive, *trick
DELUGE: *catastrophe, *flood
DELUSION: *cheat, *deceit, *deception, fake, fraud, mirage
of grandeur: megalomania
DEMAND: *ask, *call for, *need
bill: certificate
DEMARIUS: 1/12: assarion, assary
DEMEAN: *abase, *corrupt
oneself: condescend, *fall
DEMEANOR: *address, *air, mien
DEMENTED: *insane, *mad
DEMENTIA: cataphrenia
praecox: catatonia, paranoia
DEMETER: antaea, brimo, ceres
daughter: cora, despoina, kore, persephone, proserpina
headdress: polos
mother: rhea
shrine: anaktoron
DEMETRIUS: general: apollonius, nicanor
friends: alcimus, bacchides
DEMI-REP: *prostitute, *wanton
DEMOCRAT: barnburner, hunker
DEMOCRITUS JUNIOR: burton
DEMOLISH: *destroy, *ruin

* Asterisk means to look up this word to find more answer words.

DEMON: abigor, aitu, alukah, angra, anito, apepi, apoplus, arioch, ashmodai, asura, atua, babajaga, badb, baka, bali, barghest, bhoot, bhut, bodb, boko, bug, caco, daeva, deuce, deva, *devil, dook, genie, goblin, gyre, harpy, hellion, hyle, incubus, jann, jinni, ketu, lamia, mainyu, mara, *monster, nat, rahu, shedu, sobk, succubus, troll, *underworld god, vampire, *werewolf
assembly of: sabbat
cunning: daedal, imp, ogre
female: ataensic, *witch
friendly: billy blind
king: asmodeus
kur: asag
patience: klondike, solitaire
pert.: demoniacal, exorcist
possessed by: energumen
prince: beelzebub, pasupati, rudra, siva
rum: liquor
vanity: asmodeus
vengeance: arioch
DEMONSTRATE: *argue, *establish, *show
DEMORALIZE: *abash, *addle, *corrupt, *ruin, *upset
DEMOTE: *abase, *break, *dismiss
DEMOTION: irish promotion
DEMUR: *balk, boggle, *stop
DEMURE: coy, nice, prim, *shy
DEN: lair, *retreat, *studio
of iniquity: sin
of thieves: alsatia, whitefriar
of vice: brothel
DENIGRATE: slur, *smear
DENMARK: *anatomist:* steno
ancient name: thule
animal: aurochs
astronomer: brahe
author: andersen, bajer
ballet dancer: bruhn
borough: borg

cheese: blue, camembert, mycella, samsoe, tybo
chief: jarl, yarl
city: aalborg, aarhuus, alborg, copenhagen, elsinore, helsingor, morsens, randers, odense
coin: fyrk, horse, krone, ore
composer: gade, weyse
council: rigsraad
county: aabenraa, aalborg, amt
dependency: faroes
division: alt, amt, ribe
downs: klitten
drink: glogg
embroidery: hedebo
explorer: bering, vitus
first king: gorm
fjord: ise
flag: dannebrog
freeholder: junster
goblin: nis
historian: brandes
inlet: fjord, ise
island: aero, als, bornholm, falster, faroe, fyn, oe, romo, rum, samso, seeland
king: canute, christian, cnut, ethelred, gorm, knut, olaf
knighthood order: dannebrog
legislature: folketing, landsting, risdag
measure: achtel, album, alen, ell, favn, fjerding, fod, kande, korntonde, landmil, linje, mil, oltonde, ottingkar, paegl, pot, rode, skeppe
musical instrument: lure
organist: buxtehude
peninsula: jutland
physicist: bohr, niels
possession: faroe, greenland, iceland, st john, st thomas
prince: hamlet, havelok, ogier
river: asa, guden, holm, stor
sand ridge: skagen, scaw
seaport: aarhus, korsor
settlers: ostmen

* Asterisk means to look up this word to find more answer words.

speech sound: stod
trading post: thule
tribunal: rigsret
weight: bismerpund, carat, centner, eser, kvint, last, lispund, lod, ort, pound, quint, skibslast, skippund
DENOUEMENT: anagnorisis, *end, *finish
DENOUNCE: *accuse, *rebuke
DENSE: *solid, *stupid, *thick
rock: adinole
DENT: *blow, *effect, *hit
DENY: *abjure, *abstain, *refuse
DEPART: *abandon, check out, *die, get away, *escape, hike, leg it, march, *move, perish, *retreat, scat, scamper, scoot, scram, tear off, vamoose
rapidly: bug out
DEPARTMENT: agency, bureau
part: arrondissement
store: au bon marche, market
DEPENDENT: beggar, collateral, contingent, liable, minion, retainer, satellite, subject
DEPICT: *describe, limn, outline
DEPLETE: evacuate, *reduce, *sap
DEPLORE: *complain, *cry
DEPLORABLE: *bad, *sad
DEPORT: *act, *banish, *dismiss
DEPORTMENT: *action, *address
DEPOSE: *affirm, *break, *throw
DEPOSIT: *aeolian:* loess
alluvial: delta, geest
black: soot
black tissue: melanosis
box: meter, pyx
clay: marl
earthy: alluvium, asar, delta, eskar, geest, gobi, lode, loess, manto, marl, moraine, ore, placer, silt, sludge
geological: bone breccia
geyser: sinter
gold-containing: placer
gravel: apron

loam: loess
mineral: lode
ore: gulf lode, vug
river: alluvium, delta, silt
roric: dew
teeth: calculus, tartar
wine: beeswing, tartar
DEPOT: cache, gare, station
DEPRAVED: *bad, *corrupt, *evil
DEPRECIATE: *abase, *break, *fall
DEPRESS: *abase, *abate, ail
DEPRIVE: bereave, cashier, *take
DEPTH: *abyss, *acumen, expanse
charge: ash can, mine
interview: psychoanalysis
pert.: bathic
DEPUTY: *advocate, *agent
DERIDE: *banter, *laugh, *taunt
DERIVATION: etymology, *source
DERIVE: *acquire, *appear, issue
DERNIER: final, last, ultimate
cri: fashion, novelty
ressort: expedient, recourse
DEROGATE: disparage, repeal
DERRICK: crane, davit, *tower
part: boom, gin, leg
DERRING-DO: audacity, gest
DERVISH: *ascetic, *monk, yogi
arabian nights: agib
cap: taj
moslem: sadite
DESCANT: *air, expatiate, tune
DESCEND: avale, gravitate, sink
DESCENT: *attack, *decline, line
lines: phyla
water: cascade, *flood, rain
DESCRIBE: *analyze, blazon, caption, characterize, circuit, delineate, depict, *draw, explain, express, *form, image, limn, *name, outline, *paint, *picture, point, portray, relate, *report
DESDEMONA: *husband:* othello
traducer: iago
DESECRATE: *abuse, profane

* Asterisk means to look up this word to find more answer words.

DESERT: *abandon, bug out, *quit
  beast: camel
  candle: ocotillo, plant
  driver: cameleer, camelteer
  dweller: arab, eremite, nomad
  group: caravan
  hallucination: mirage
  herb: bluebell, phacelia
  pert.: arid, dry, eremic, sere
  plant: afernan, agave, alhagi,
    black brush, *cactus, encelia,
    euphorbia, ocotillo, retem, tar-
    bush, yucca
  rat: miner, prospector
  science: eremology
  ship: camel
  valley: bolson
  watering spot: *oasis
DESERVE: earn, merit, rate
DESIGN: *art, *make, *plan, *purpose, *system, *way
DESIGNATE: *allot, *name
DESIPIENCE: conceit, folly
DESIRE: *ache, *aim, ambition,
  anxiety, aphrodisia, appetite,
  *ask, avarice, avidity, beg, bias,
  burn, care, choose, clamor for,
  covet, crave, *cry, entreat, *fire,
  goal, greed, heart, hope, hunger,
  idol, impulse, itch, libido, like,
  long, *love, lust, mind, *need,
  nostalgia, objective, *passion,
  pine, psyche, pursue, request,
  sign for, spoil for, starve, take
  to, target, thirst, *urge, want,
  *will, wish, yearn, yen
  affective basis: appet
  concentration: cathexis
  good, to do: benevolence
  inborn: conatus
  removal: catharsis, sublimation
  want of: inappetence
DESIROUS: *ardent, *eager, fain
DESIST: *abandon, don't, *stop
DESK: ambo, bureau, escritoire,
  lectern, pulpit, secretary
DESMODIUM: canadense: trefoil

rensoni: barajillo
tortuosum: beggar-weed
DESOLATE: *alone, *destroy,
  *wild
DESOLATION: desert, despair
DESPERADO: *criminal, hood
DESPERATE: *mad, *reckless
DESPICABLE: *bad, caitiff, *sad
DESPISE: abhor, *hate, *scorn
DESPITE: notwithstanding
DESPOIL: *spoil, *steal, *take
DESPONDENT: downcast, *sad
DESPOT: autocrat, caesar, czar,
  dictator, kaiser, tyrant
DESSERT: *sweet, *sweetmeat
DESTINATION: *aim, cause, *end
DESTINY: *end, *fate, kismet
DESTITUTE: *bare, *poor, void
DESTROY: *abolish, annihilate,
  atomize, *blast, blot out, *blow,
  *break, burn, decimate, *defeat,
  demolish, desolate, devastate, de-
  vour, do in, *end, erase, extermi-
  nate, extinguish, finish, fix, gut,
  *kill, k o, knock out, lay waste,
  nip, obliterate, overthrow, rav-
  age, raze, *reduce, *ruin, sack,
  *settle, shipwreck, *split, *spoil,
  swallow, *tear, wreck
DESTROYING ANGEL: amanita,
  fungus
DESTRUCTION: *end, *fate
  deity: ara, kali(ka), siva
DETACH: *discard, *dismiss, part
DETACHED: *alone, *aloof, *cool
DETACHMENT: *group, *part,
  *piece
DETAIL: *account, *allot, *bit,
  *part(icular), *thing, *trifle
DETAILED: blow by blow, prolix
DETAIN: *arrest, *slow, *stop
DETECT: *see, *smell, *spy, *trap
  device: dowser, sonar, radar
DETECTIVE: *agent, gumshoe
  famous: charlie chan, ellery queen,
    hercule poirot, james bond, miss
    marple, nero wolfe, nick carter,

philip marlowe, philo vance, sam
spade, shayne, sherlock holmes
writer: christie, doyle, queen
DETENT: catch, dog, *stop*, stud
DETENTION: *arrest*, delay
DETER: *arrest*, *cool*, *stop*
DETERIORATE: *corrupt*, *decay*, go to pot, impair, *spoil*
DETERMINATION: resolve, *will*
DETERMINE: *adjust*, *analyze*, *assess*, *decide*, *end*, *prove*, *test*, *think*, *will*
DETEST: abhor, *hate*, scorn
DETONATE: *burst*, explode
DETRACT: libel, malign, *smear*
DETRIMENT: *evil*, *hurt*, injury
DETRITUS: *dregs*, *refuse*, waste
DETROIT: *founder:* cadillac
DEUCALION: consort, pyrrha
son: amphictyon, hellen
DEUTEROCANONICAL: antilegomena
DEVAKI: *son:* krishna
DEVAS: *king:* indra
DEVASTATE: *destroy*, *spoil*
DEVASTATING: gorgeous, ravishing
DEVELOP: *advance*, *grow*, *open*
DEVELOPMENT: *arrested:* aplasia
full: maturity, ripeness
going back: retrogression
pert.: genetic
total: eosere
DEVI: annapurna, chandi, durga, gauri, haimavati, kali, lady, madam, mrs, parvati, shakti, uma
consort: siva
DEVIATE: *err*, go astray, *turn*
DEVICE: *instrument*, *trick*
DEVIL: afreet, ahriman, amaimon, amayon, amamon, anhanga, apollyon, auld clootie, azazel, bang, beelpeor, beelzebub, belial, beng, blackguard, bother, bwana, cagnazzo, deil, *demon*, dule,

deuce, *dwarf*, eblis, enemy, fiend, goblin, hellcat, hellion, hugon, imp, lucifer, *monster*, ogre, roarer, satan, shaitan, *spirit*, *torment*, wat, wretch
bottomless pit: apollyon
dante's: cagnazzo
dodger: ecclesiastic
-dog: marine
fish: manta, octopus, ray
grass: bahama, bermuda, scutch
-lore: sorcery
-may-care: blase, cavalier
nickname: old bendy, old goose berry, old harry, old horny, old ned, old nick, old poker
pert.: diabolical, satanic
printer's: apprentice
ruler: diabolarch
the: black man, bogey, bogie
tree: dita
wood: american olive
worship: black mass, sorcery
DEVIL'S: *advocate:* *church: man*
bones: dice
box: dice box
dung: asafoetida, condiment
godmother: baba
DEVILISH: *bad*, *brutal*, *evil*
DEVIOUS: crooked, oblique, *sly*
DEVISE: *form*, *make*, *will*
DEVOID: *bare*, barren, without
DEVOTE: *addict*, *administer*
oneself: practice, undertake
DEVOTED: *active*, *ardent*, *true*
DEVOTEE: *enthusiast*, hound
DEVOTION: ardor, *worship*, zeal
object: *fetish*, idol, totem
others: altruism, philanthropy
DEVOUR: *eat*, gobble, imbibe
DEVOURING: edacious, voracious
DEVOUT: *ardent*, *holy*, pious
DEXTERITY: *magic*, *skill*
DEXTEROUS: *adept*, *adroit*, *apt*, *smart*
comb.: ambi

* Asterisk means to look up this word to find more answer words.

D'HERBLAY: amadis, aramis
DIABETES: *remedy:* antimellin, insulin, orinase
DIALECT: **argot*, **talk*
DIAMETER: caliber, chord, width
  half: radius
  inside: bore
DIAMOND: gem, ice, lozenge, ring
  back moth: cabbage moth, mamestra, noctuida
  blue: hope
  coarse: bort
  corner: base
  crystal: ballas, glassie
  cup: cop, dopp, facet
  cut: facet
  cutter: brilliandeer
  cutting process: bruting
  face: bezel, crown, culet, girdle, pavilion, table
  famous: cullinan, hope, jubilee, kohinoor, mogul, orloff, pitt, regency, sancy
  feature: base
  flaw: carbon spot
  geometrical: lozenge, rhomb
  hard: adamant
  imitation: paste, schlenter
  imperfect: bort, bywater
  jack: **fool*, gimbarde
  -like: naif
  native: carbon
  necklace: riviere
  nine: bragger, curse of scotland, pope
  oval: briolette
  perfect: paragon
  queen: guinguette, nazarene
  rough: brait
  seven: peneech
  -shaped pattern: argyle
  six: brilliant
  snake: carpet, python spilotes
  splinterlike: rose
  suit: carreau, coin, cuadros, eckstein, gelb, gold, oro, ruthen, schellen
  surface: **diamond face*, facet
  ten: big casino
  wheel: skive
DIANA: artemis, cynthia, delia
  cult, pert.: arician
  grove: nemus
  monkey: roloway
  parent: jupiter, latona, zeus
  twin: apollo
DIANTHUS: carnation, pink
DIAPER: breechcloth, hippin
DIAPHANOUS: lucid, sheer, **thin*
DIAPHRAGM: middle, partition
  pert.: phrenic
DIARMET: *consort:* brianne
DIARIST: evelyn, pepys
DIARY: blotter, chronicle, journal, log, **record*, register
DIASKEUAST: critic, editor
DIASPORA: galuth, golah
DIATOM: animalcule, brittlewort
  reproductive scale: auxospore
DIATONIC: chord, scale
  opposed to: chromatic
  run: tirade
  scale: gamut
DIATRIBE: harangue, jeremiad, philippic, screed, tirade
DIB(BLE): **bit*, bob, dap, dip, money, rupee, token, **trifle*
DIBDIN: *song:* black-eyed susan
DIBLAIM: *daughter:* gomer
DIBS: claim, **money*, syrup
DICE: bones, chop, craps, cubes, flats, goads, ivories, kabat, mince, pase, rice, shik tsz
  box: bird cage
  cheater: cogger, topper
  game naturals: sevens
  game: backgammon, barbooth, barbudi, baseball, bingo, cameroon, canoga, centennial, chicago, chuck-luck, cootie, craps, destroyers, drop dead, esperance, everest, fourteen, grand hazard, hamburgen, hazard, hooligan,

* Asterisk means to look up this word to find more answer words.

klondike, newmark, pat cha, qualify, sing luk, yacht
number six: boxcars, sice
six throw: boxcars, sice
term: baseball bum, bones, carolina, cog, come, cup, dispatchers, doublet, fade, flat, float, joe, miss, nick, phoebe, point, raffle, roll
DICEY: *dangerous*
DICK: *agent*, detective, *whip*
DICKENS: *character:* bill sikes, cuttle, dora, dorritt, fagin, gamp, nell, pip, podsnap, sydney parton, tim, uriah heep
DICKER: *bargain*, *barter*
DICKEY: bird, collar, donkey, make, petticoat, seat, waist
DICTATE: *adage*, *advise*, *order*
DICTATOR: boss, *despot*, ruler
DICTIONARY: calepin, thesaurus
compiler: lexicographer
geographical: atlas, gazetteer
poet's: gradus
sanskrit: amara-kosha
DICTUM: *adage*, maxim, saying
DIDACTIC: *academic*, preceptive
DIDDLE: *cheat*, *deceive*, liquor
DIDO: antic, caper, *trick*
father: belus
lover: acerbas, aeneas
sister: anna
DIE: *at one's post:* persevere
away: decrease, *end*, persevere
fledermaus girl: adele
for: *desire*
gambling: tat, tessera
hard: conservative, resist
loaded: fulham, fullam
on the vine: languish, weaken
out: disappear, *stop*
DIFFERENCE: *disagree*
comb.: ant, anti
DIFFERENT: *fresh*, new, *wild*
pref.: ap, aph, apo
in nature: allogeneous

DIFFICULT: *clumsy*, *obstinate*
pref.: dys
DIFFICULTY: *ado*, *affliction*, dilemma, *pass*, rub, *trouble*
DIFFIDENT: anxious, coy, *shy*
DIFFUSE: copious, sned, *spread*
DIG: *absorb*, excavate, mine, relish, *scold*, *spade*, *speed*, *study*, *taunt*, *understand*
fitted to: fodient, fossorial
in: fortify, intrench, *start*
into: investigate
out: depart, go, extract, mine, research, scoop, shove, spade
up: collect, find, disclose
DIGEST: *absorb*, brief, *study*, *system*, *think*, *understand*
DIGESTION: *agent:* maltase, pepsin, rennin
ailments: acidosis, cardialgia, colic, constipation, dyspepsia, gripes, pyrosis, tormina
having good: eupeptic
pert.: cyle, chyme
product: amphopeptone
sac: archenteron, gastrula
units: alimentary canal, bile, gastric glands, liver, pancreas, saliva
DIGIT: *dog's:* dewclaw
human: finger, thumb, toe
shield for: cot, stall, thimble
DIGNIFIED: *august*, decorous
DIGNITY: *glory*, *honor*, merit
DIKE: bank, *waterway*
DILAPIDATE: *decay*, *destroy*
DILATE: bulge, *grow*, *spread*
DILATORY: fabian, *late*, *slow*
DILEMMA: *problem*, *puzzle*
DILETTANTE: aesthete, amateur, sciolist, *superficial*, tyro
DILIGENCE: care, effort, vehicle
DILIGENT: *active*, *ardent*
DILL: *seed:* anet, anise, fennel
DILLY: *ace*, pip, *top*(-notcher)
-dally: dawdle, idle, *slow*
DILOGY: redundancy
DILUTE: *qualify*, *reduce*, *thin*

* Asterisk means to look up this word to find more answer words.

DIM: dark, hazy, *vague, *weak
-sighted: cecil, purblind
view: objection
-wit: simpleton
DIME: coin, disme, hog, ten cent
-a-dozen: *cheap, paltry
-store: *cheap, market
DIMINISH: *abate, ebb, *reduce
DIMINUTIVE: *bit, *little, pony
suff.: cle, cule, culus, el, et, ette,
ie, in, ita, kin, let, ling, ock, ule
DIMORPHOTHECA: cape mari-
gold
DIN: clamor, hubbub, *noise
DINAR: twenty: bisti
DINDLE: hawkweed
DINE: *eat, fare, feed, regale
DING: *beat, *noise, *urge, veto
-aling: *eccentric, weird(o)
-dong: *active, busy, tedious
DINGY: *cold, *dirty, *small
DINING: room: cafe, cenacle, eatery, mess, oecus, refectory,
spence, restaurant, salon
DINNER: course: appetizer, dessert, entree, fruit, hors d'oeuvre,
salad, soup
jacket: black-tie, formal, tux
pert.: cenatory, prandial
DINT: *blow, *force, *power
DIOMEDES: companion: acmon
DIONE: brother: titan
consort: zeus
daughter: aphrodite, venus
DIONYSUS: bacchus, zagreus
attendant: maenad
consort: aura
festival: agrania, agrionia
mother: semele
pert.: bromian
DIOSCURI: anaces, anax, castor,
gemini, pollux, twins
parents: leda, tyndareus, zeus
sister: clytemnestra, helen
DIP: *bail, *immerse, *thief
DIPHTHONG: ae, ia, oe, uo
DIPLOMA: *certificate, sheepskin

DIPLOMATIC: *cunning, tactful
DIPPER: baptist, car, grebe, ladle,
piet, scoop, pickpocket
big: charles's wain
DIPSOMANIAC: *drunk
DIPTERA: alula, flies, gnats
DIRCE: husband: lycus
slayer: farnese bull
DIRE: *bad, *evil, *ugly
DIRECT: *address, *administer,
*advise, blunt, cast, *control, de-
termine, *honest, *lead, *open,
*order, regulate, *rule, *set,
*short, *straight, *train
descent lines: phyla
hit: bomb, bull's-eye, score
DIRECTION: biblical: selah
court: order, verdict
finder: compass
in chorus: soli
line of: *range
musical: *musical direction
pole to pole: axial
pref.: ac, ad, ap, ar, at
printer's: stet
without: astatic
DIRECTIONS: *address, formula,
pattern, program, specification
of compass: cardinal points
DIRECTLY: anon, bang, blankly,
expressly, flat, forthright, forthwith, instantly, promptly, quickly,
right, soon, spang
DIRECTOR: boss, *head, *leader
group: administration, board
DIRECTORY: reference, register
DIRGE: elegy, grief, requiem
DIRK: *sword: short
DIRT: *earth, *gossip, grapevine
comb.: myso, ryo
DIRTY: back-alley, *bad, bemire,
black, cabby, dingy, dust up,
filthy, foul, grimy, grubby,
muddy, nasty, obscene, profane,
rank, *rotten, *smear, sordid,
spatter, squalid, *ugly, vile
dig: *taunt

* Asterisk means to look up this word to find more answer words.

look: frown
politics: *smear
story: *joke
weather: *storm
DISABLE: *afflict, *break, *hurt
DISADVANTAGE: handicap,
*trouble
DISAFFECTION: *break, *decep-
tion
DISAGREE: *argue, *fight, *hate
DISAGREEABLE: *bad, *ugly
DISAPPEAR: *depart, drop dead,
fade, get lost, go away, flee, pass,
scram, sink, vanish
DISAPPOINT: balk, *defeat, foil,
*spoil, *stop, *throw, thwart
DISAPPROVAL: bird, boo, catcall, censure, condemnation, hiss,
razz, thumbs down, veto
DISARRAY: *disturb, *upset
DISASTER: *blow, *catastrophe
DISBELIEVER: *agnostic, atheist
DISBURSE: *dispense, *distribute
DISC: *disk
DISCARD: *abandon, desert, *dismiss, divorce, drop, dump, eliminate, flotsam, jetsam, jettison,
oust, molt, *part, *refuse, reject,
*release, relegate, *remove, re-
pudiate, shed, slough, sluff,
*throw out
pile: boneyard, heap, trash
DISCERN: *see, *understand
DISCERNING: *acute, *wise
DISCERNMENT: *acumen
DISCHARGE: *accomplish, *acquit, *air, *annul, *answer,
*blast, bounce, *break, cancel,
catapult, catharsis, detonate,
*discard, *dismiss, eject, emerge,
emit, erupt, evict, excrete, expel,
explode, exude, fire, *free, fulfil,
fusillade, launch, lay off, liberate,
license, pay, perform, purge,
sack, salvo, *settle, shot, *speed,
unburden, volley
DISCIPLE: devotee, *enthusiast

DISCIPLINE: *aplomb, *control,
*lead, *order, *punish, *train
DISCLOSE: *air, bare, *blow,
*break, divulge, expose, *open,
show, spill the beans, *tell
DISCOMFIT: chagrin, *upset
DISCOMFORT: *ache, *bore,
*trial
DISCONCERT: *abash, *alarm
DISCONSOLATE: *alone, *sad
DISCONTENT: *anger, ill-humor
DISCONTINUE: *abandon,
*break, *end, *stop
DISCORD: *brawl, *fight, *noise
deity: ate, eris, loki
DISCOTHEQUE: agogo, cabaret
DISCOUNT: *abate, agio, batta,
charge-off, contango, cut, draw-
back, ignore, percentage, *re-
duce, rebate, set off
DISCOURAGE: *alarm, *daunt
DISCOURSE: *argue, article, con-
fer, discuss, *piece, *talk
DISCOVER: *hit, *see, *think
DISCREDIT: *shame, *smear
DISCRETION: option, *will
DISCRIMINATE: critical, fine,
nice, *particular, sift, subtle
DISCRIMINATION: *acumen,
bias, choice, elegance, perception
DISCUSS: *air, *analyze, *talk
DISDAIN: contempt, repudiate
DISEASE: *affliction, blemish,
blight, bunt, cause, collapse, epidemic, fever, infection, malady,
malaise, *plague
animal: amoeba, anthrax, braxy,
coath, coe, colic, dartars, distemper, farcy, garget, glanders,
hammer, hoose, mange, myxoma-
tosis, nagana, pip, psittacosis,
rout, sacbrood, spavins, takosis,
tularemia
brain: paranoia, schizophrenia
brain, comb.: agra, noso
contagious: measles, mumps, pox

* Asterisk means to look up this word to find more answer words.

crippling: arthritis, polio, rheumatism, sclerosis
declining stage: catabasis
deficiency: pellagra, scurvy
divers: bends, caisson
eye: conjunctivitis, glaucoma, pterygium, trachoma
fatal: lyssa, malignancy, pest
favorable termination: lysis
first period: anabasis
fly-caused: trachoma
fowl: perosis, pip, roup
fungus: ergot, tinea
grape: coleur, erinose
hair: plica, psilosis, xerasia
heart: aneurysm, angina pectoris, arrhythmia, cardialgia, cardiodynia, carditis, coarctation, coronary thrombosis, endocarditis, myocarditis
hereditary: anemia, poprhyria
horse: azotemia, bots, bursattee, caloris, canker, carney, distemper, farcy, heaves, lampas, lampers, nagana, pinkeye, quitter, spavin(s), surra, thickhead
investigator: etiologist
jumping: xatah, tic
liver: cirrhosis, hepatitis, jaundice
local: endemic
lung: consumption, emphysema, phthisis, pneumonia, tb
malignant: cancer, plague
nervous: pellagra, tic
plant: blister, brindle, calico, coleur, ergot, erinose, fen, fungus, gall, kermes, melanose, mildew, rot, rust, scab, scale, smut, viruela, wallon
pert.: clinic, endemic, loimic
prediction about: prognosis
recognition: diagnosis
science: etiology, nosology
science, children's: pediatrics
skin: acne, argyria, boil, brash, caloris, canker, courap, dartre, dermatitis, eczema, erytheme,

exanthema, frambesia, herpes, hives, impetigo, itch, lepra, lichen, mange, pemphigus, pian, prickly heat, psoriasis, ringworm, rupia, scabies, scleroderma, serpigo, shingles, tetter, tinea, uredo, xeroderma
spreader: bacteria, carrier, fly, germ, microbe, mosquito, vector, virus
suff.: algia, itis, oma
tropical: sprue
wasting: cancer, phthisic
DISEASED: *comb.:* cac(e), caco
DISENCUMBER: *ease, *free
DISENTANGLE: *part, *solve
DISGORGE: *discharge, spew
DISGRACE: *blot, *shame, stigma
DISGUISE: *affect, *ambush, camouflage, cloak, color, *cover, domino, false front, feign, *hide, incognito, mask, masquerade, misrepresent, sham
DISGUSTING: hateful, nauseous
DISH: beauty, boat, boil, bowl, course, entree, food, girl, grill, ladle, pan, patina, piece de resistance, plate
cooking: blazer
gravy: boat
out: *administer, *give, mete
pyramid-style: buisson
spiced: cloves, salmi, sausage
the dirt: *gossip, rumor
washer: domestic, machine
water: *dregs, *refuse
DISHABILLE: bathrobe, disarray, housecoat, kimono, negligee, peignoir, robe, undress, wrap
DISHAN: *son:* aran, uz
DISHEARTEN: *daunt, *deter
DISHON: *son:* amram, cheran, eshban, ithran
DISHONEST, DISHONORABLE: *bad, *corrupt, *evil
DISHONOR: *abase, *abuse, fraud, infamy, obloquy, *shame

* **Asterisk means to look up this word to find more answer words.**

DISILLUSION: *disappoint

DISINTEGRATE: atomize, *break, calcine, corrode, *decay, *decline, dissolve, *fall, powder, pulverize, rot, *spoil

DISK: aten, button, cam, circle, dial, exterior, harrow, medal, orb, *ornament, paten, plate, platter, pook, quoit, *record
admitting light: bull's-eye
hockey: puck
-like: discal, discoid
metal: flan, ghurry, gong, sequin, tag, zecchino
solar: aten
symbol: feroher

DISLIKE: antipathy, *hate, odium
comb.: mis, miso
object of: anathema

DISLODGE: *discard, *dismiss

DISMAL: *bad, dark, *sorry

DISMAY: *abash, *alarm, *awe, *shock, *stop, *throw, *wonder

DISMISS: *abandon, *banish, *break, brush off, bump, bust, can, cashier, cast off or out, *discard, *discharge, *fire, forget, gate, give the ax, let go, quash, *punish, refute, *release, *remove, sack, *throw

DISOBEDIENT: *bad, insubordinate

DISOBEY: *break, *defy, violate

DISORDER: *abyss, *afflict(ion), *anarchy, mess, *mixture, *snarl
place of: mare's nest

DISORDERLY: awry, *bad, messy

DISORDERED: brainsick, frowsy

DISORGANIZED: *spoil, *upset

DISPARAGE: *abase, *abuse, *smear

DISPATCH: *address, *end, *kill, *note, send, slay, *speed
case: *bag

DISPEL: *discard, *dismiss
suff.: agogue

DISPENSE: *acquit, *administer, *allot, deal, *issue, mete, ration, sell, *spread, vend

DISPERSE: *break, face, *spread

DISPLACE: *dismiss, *start

DISPLACEMENT: cavity, change, draft, sinkage, transformation

DISPLAY: *air, array, aspect, bare, betray, *blow, boast, brandish, bring out, camp it up, ceremony, etalage, evince, flaunt, flourish, grandstand, *open, ostentation, pageantry, *present, pomp, pose, *show

DISPLEASE: *anger, *upset

DISPOSE: *accomplish, *discard, *dispense, *eat, *give

DISPOSED: *apt, prone, *ready

DISPOSITION: adjustment, affect, animus, aptitude, attitude, bent, bequest, bias, cast, character, custom, habit, idiosyncrasy, inclination, leaning, mood, morale, nature, organization, placement, *plan, predilection, proclivity, sale, *set, slant, *spirit, *temper, tendency, *turn, *use, *will

DISPOSSESS: *dismiss, *take

DISPUTE: *agitate, *argue, carp, *contest, *fight, *quarrel, spat

DISQUIET: *agitate, *alarm

DISQUISITION: *piece, *study

DISREGARD: defy, forget, ignore

DISREPUTABLE: *bad, notorious

DISRESPECT: *affront, insolence

DISRUPT: *break, *spoil, *tear

DISSECT: analyze, *break down

DISSEMBLE: cloak, feign, *hide

DISSEMINATE: *spread

DISSENSION: *discord, *fight

DISSENT: *balk, *demur, *fight

DISSENTER: apostate, heretic
pert.: pantile

DISSEPIMENT: *part(ition)

DISSERTATION: *piece, *study

DISSIMILAR: pref.: allo

DISSIMULATE: *act, *deceive

DISSIPATE: carouse, debauch, indulge, rake, scatter, sow wild oats, *wanton, waste

DISSOLUTE: *bad, *wanton, *weak, *wild

DISSOLVE: *abolish, *break, melt

DISSONANT: *absurd, cacophonous

DISSUADE: *admonish, bluff

DISTAFF: axis, female, woman

DISTANCE: afar, background, carry, cast, chance, compass, day, extent, far cry, good ways, horizon, interval, length, long ways, mileage, offing, perspective, *piece, *range, reach, reserve, space, span, spell, stretch, *way
map: latitude, longitude
-measuring device: odograph, odometer, pedometer, stadia, telemeter, viameter
pref.: tel
side to side: breadth

DISTASTEFUL: *bitter, brackish

DISTEMPER: *aggravate, *anger

DISTEND: bloat, *grow, *spread

DISTICH: couplet, two

DISTIL: extract, purify, render

DISTILLING: device: alembic, matrass, retort, still
product: dew, liquor, spirits

DISTINCT: *definite, *open, *plain, *sharp, *unique
comb.: idio

DISTINCTION: *glory, *honor

DISTINGUISH: *analyze, *honor

DISTINGUISHED: *great, different, *important, storied

DISTORT: bend, pervert, *turn

DISTORTED: *bad, crooked, *evil

DISTRACT: *addle, *puzzle

DISTRACTED: *crazy, *mad

DISTRAINT: fine, naam, poind

DISTRAUGHT: *insane, *mad

DISTRESS: *pain, *sorrow, *upset
call: mayday, sos

DISTRESSING: *heavy, *sad

DISTRIBUTE: *dispense, *spread

DISTRICT: area, barrio, belt, border, borough, burg, canton, circuit, community, demesne, department, division, field, gau, ghetto, locale, miao, pale, precinct, province, realm, region, section, site, slum, soc, soke, *sphere, zone

DISTRUST: doubt, envy, fear

DISTURB: *aggravate, *agitate, *distress, *start(le), *stir

DISTURBANCE: *alarm, *fight

DITCH: *hide, *quit, *waterway
millet: hureek
part: graffage, scarp
reed: bennel, grass
slope: scarp
stonecrop: nightshade, pokeweed

DITHER: *ado, flap, jitters

DITHYRAMB: hymn, ode, poem

DITHYRAMBIC: *wild

DITTANY: artillery plant, burning-bush, fraxinella, gas plant, mock cypress, wahoo

DITTO: *accord, *copy, *repeat

DIURNAL: butterfly, daily

DIVAGATE: *range, wander

DIVAN: canape, couch, council, court, davenport, saloon, *sofa

DIVE: bar, brothel, den, dump
bomber: stuka
into: *begin, *start, *test, *try

DIVERGE: *adapt, deviate, *err

DIVERS: *cruel, *evil, many
colored: variegated

DIVER: plunger, *thief

DIVERSE: *different, several
pref.: vari

DIVERSIFY: *change, modify
with colors: bespatter

DIVERSION: *move, *play, sport

DIVERT: *amuse, change, *deceive

DIVEST: *bare, doff, *remove

DIVI-DIVI: brazilwood, sumac

DIVIDE: *break, *share, *split

DIVIDEND: *income, *part, *yield

DIVINE: almighty, *anticipate, celestial, *church man, *holy, *predict, *sacred, *supreme
artificer: tvashtar, tvashtri
being: deity, deva, god
comedy author: dante
communication: oracle
favor: grace
messenger: apostle, hermes
render: deify
right: *authority
spirit: numen
vocation: call
word: grace, logos
work: theurgy

DIVING: *bird:* alcid, auk, grebe, loon, pelican
equipment: aqualung, aquascope, bathysphere, bell, benthoscope, nautilus, periscope, snorkel
hazard: bends
rod: dowser, wand

DIVINING: *rod:* doodlebug, wand

DIVISION: age, branch, *part
line: boundary
many: eogaea

DIVORCE: *part, *separate
law: get(t), talak

DIVOT: clod, sod, turf

DIVULGE: *break, *release, *tell

DIVVY: *allot, *share, *split

DIXIE: *paradise, south, *utopia

DIZEN: *dress, *ornament

DIZZARD: *fool, nut, *sap

DIZZY: farchadat, *insane, *mad

DJAKARTA: batavia, jakarta

DNA: deoxyribonucleic acid, double helix, mitochondria
bases: adenine, amino, antigen, cytosine, guanine, thymine
decoder: *life: scientist
helper: ribonucleic acid, rna

DO: *accomplish, *act, *affair, *cheat, commit, *trick, *try
a daring deed: bell the cat

a fadeout: disappear
again: repeat
a land-office business: thrive
-all: factotum
all one can: shoot one's bolt
all right: get rich, *succeed
away: *abate, *abolish, *stop
for: *defeat, *kill, *punish
-gooder: give-away, *liberal
in: *defeat, *destroy, *kill
justice: be fair, perform
nothing: indolent, lazy
oneself proud: *succeed, *win
one's worst: *abuse
out of: *cheat, *deceive
-re-mi: *money, sing
right by: *accommodate, behave
some good: *aid, assist, help
something: *act
to a turn: *complete
up brown: *complete, *deceive
well: prosper, *succeed, *win

DOCILE: *amenable, *soft

DOCIMASY: *analysis, experiment, *test, *trial, *try

DOCK: *cut (off), harbor, pier
part: bollard, camber, pile
ship's: basin, berth, slip
worker: longshoreman, stevedore
yard: arsenal

DOCKET: *agenda, *certificate

DOCTOR: *medical, *medicine, *surgeon
assistant: interne, nurse

DOCTRINE: *canon, catechism, confirm, credo, creed, cult, dogma, esotery, faith, ism, logic, lore, maxim, monism, opinion, *philosophy, precept, principle, religion, rite, *rule, *system, tenet, theory
comb.: doxy, ism, osophy
good, all tends to: agathism
inferiority: adlerian
origins: archology
pert.: dogmatic, teleological
psychological: behaviorism

* **Asterisk means to look up this word to find more answer words.**

DOCUMENT: *act, *certificate
add: amendment, codicil, rider
file: dossier
original record: protocol
provisional: draft, rough, scrip
receptacle: hanaper
signed by all: syngraph
true copy: estreat
DOD(D): clip, die, fit, huff
DODAVAH: son: eliezer
DODDER: acotyledon, amil, cuscata, knotweed, ribbon grass, shake, spurry, tickseed
DODDERING: anile, inane, senile
DODECANESE ISLAND: astropalia, calchi, calino, caso, coo, cos, karpathos, kos, lero, lipso, nisyros, scarpanto, simi, stampalia, syme, tilos
DODGE: *avoid, deception, *trick
DODGER: buck passer, folder, leaflet, pamphlet, rascal
artful: dawkins, john
DODO: has-been, oldster
son: eleazar, elhanan
DOE: deer, girl, rabbit, woman
DOER: *actor, *agent, *author
suff.: ast, ator, eer, er, euse, ier, ist, or, ster
DOFF: *headdress, *remove
DOG: bane: acocanthera, alstonia, apocynum, beaumontia, big root, bitter root, dita
bark: *alarm, alert, bow wow, braggadocio, clamor, snarl
bird: pointer, retriever, setter
buster brown's: tige
cart: bounder, gadabout, tum tum
chops: flews
close-haired: boxer, pug
coach: dalmatian
comb.: can(i), cyn(o)
command: come, hyke, sit, stand
days: canicule, summer
disease: black tongue, rabies
ear: acroterium, bracket, fold
extinct: talbot

-face: gi, private, soldier
-faced: cynocephalous
-faced ape: aani
famous: argus, asta, checkers, cleo, devil, fala, feller, king, lassie, rab, rin-tin-tin
female: bitch, brach(et)
fennel: hogweed
fierce: bandog, kolsun
fish: bone dog, bowfin, burbot, cat shark, hoe, huss, roussette, shark, scyllium, tope, wrasse
fisher: otter
fox-like: colpeo
group: kennel, leash
hauling: dalmatian, husky, malemute, samoyed
house: kennel, lair, limbo
howling: arr, grr, ululation
hunting: alan(d), basset, beagle, bloodhound, borzoi, courser, elkhound, griffon, pointer, rache, ratch, retriever, saluki, setter, talbot, treer, wolfhound
hyena-like: simir
in the manger: spoilsport
it: idle, laze
john brown's: rab
large: alan, bawty, boxer, briard, collie, mastiff, newfoundland, police, shepherd
latin: gibberish
-like animal: coyote, fox, hyena, jackal, wolf
-like goblin: barghest
long-hair: alco, chow, spaniel
lost: estray, stray
mercury: bristol weed
multi-headed: cerberus, garm
on the job: goldbrick, shirk
nondescript: cur, malemute, pooch, mut, mutt
pack: canaglia, canaille
pert.: canicular, canine
punch and judy: toby
rose: bedegar, bird brier, black-

* Asterisk means to look up this word to find more answer words.

berry, bramble, bucky, canker, eglantine, hip, rubus

salmon: calico, holia, keta

short-eared: alan

short-legged: beagle, dachshund

small: alco, ascob, chihuahua, feist, fist, messan, messin, peke, pekingese, pomeranian, pug, pup, purp, schipperke, spaniel, tike, toy

snapper: jocu

star: sept, sirius, sopt, veps

swift: greyhound, whippet

thin man's: asta

three-headed: cerberus

trio: leash

tropical: alco

trot: dance, *run, *walk

upper lip: flews

underworld: cerberus

wild: aboli, adjag, agouara, bushdog, coyote, cuon, cyon, dhole, dingo, jackal, tanate

wood: aucuba, boxwood, cormel, nyssa, osier, sumac, tupelo

DOGE: *venice references

DOGGEREL: *absurd, burlesque

DOGIE: calf, derelict, maverick

DOGMA: *doctrine, ism, tenet

DOGMATIC: *absolute

DOINGS: *action, *ado, *affair

DOLDRUMS: blue devils, blues, boredom, calm, ennui, misery

DOLE: *bit, *disperse, *distress

DOLEFUL: dismal, gloomy, *sad

DOLL: *dress, girl, moppet, toy

 -like: infantile

up: *adorn, *dress

DOLLAR: bean, berry, bill, boffo, bone, buck, cartwheel, coin, iron man, money, one, smacker, peso, simoleon, wheel

fish: gunnel, kelp fish

gap: arrears

group: bundle, fortune, pile

to doughnuts (*pl*): probably

DOLLY: carrier, *sweetheart

DOLOR: grief, *pain, *sorrow

DOLPHIN: bouto, cowfish, dorado, inia, mahi mahi, porpoise, susu

comb.: delphinus

DOLT: *fool, niais, *peasant

DOMAIN: area, *sphere, *state

DOME: blister, bubble, cupola, *head, pate, roof, *top, *tower

DOMESTIC: *servant, *tame

animal: ass, cat, cow, dog, hog, mule, pig, ram, sow

DOMESTICATE: *adopt, *break, *gentle, *settle, *tame

DOMICILE: *home, mansion

DOMINANT: *principal, *supreme, *top

DOMINATE: *lead, *order, *rule

DOMINEER: *control, *scold

DOMINEERING: *arrogant

DOMINION: *authority, *sphere

church: sacerdotium, see

joint: condominium

DOMINOES: amice, bones, cards, cloaks, costumes, dice, hoods, ivories, kol-hpai, kwat-pai, nga pai, rocks, tiles

games: all-fives, bergen, bingo, doublet, fortress, forty-two, hoi tap, matador, sebastopol, sniff, tiddly-winks

DON: *array, *dress, teacher

juan: libertine, love

juan's mother: inez

quixote: visionary

quixote doctor: pedro

squire: sancho panza

steed: rosinante

DONAR: *thor

DONATE: *contribute, *give

DONE: ended, enough said

for: all over, all up, dead

in: exhausted, spent

unconsciously: automatic, robot

up brown: invalid, with class

with: by hand, ended, through

---

* Asterisk means to look up this word to find more answer words.

DONKEY: ass, burro, bussock, *fool, engine, moke, neddy
comb.: ono
cry: bray, hee-haw
engine: auxiliary, yarder
DON'T: can it, desist, enough, forbear, hands off, ixnay, lay off, leave off, nix, *stop
DOODLE: dally, *draw, *fool
bug: divining rod
sack: bagpipe
DOOHICKEY: *instrument, *thing
DOOM: *condemn, *fate, future
palm: dum, gingerbread tree
spirit: ker
DOOMED: dead, fey, goner, kaput
DOOMSDAY: future, ragnarok
DOOR: *approach, *opening, outlet, *pass(age)
back: postern
bar: risp, stang
central: amphithyron
cross piece: lintel
fixer: bar, bolt, catch, hasp
frame: buck, casing, jamb
hinge goddess: cardea
holy: amphithyron
jamb: alette, post
keep: concierge, hasp, janitor, ostiary, porter, tiler, tyler
knocker: hammer, rapper, risp
latch: haggaday
lock keeper: nab, rasp, stang
man: attendant, *servant
mat: bearskin, weakling
part: ansel, butt, jamb, knob, lintel, mullion, panel, rail, risp, sash, sill, stile
post: alette, jamb, upright
storm: dingle
trap: drop
way: entrance, exit, *opening
DOPE: *deceive, *drug, *fool, information, news, solution
fiend: addict
out: calculate, solve
up: adulterate, debase

DOPESTER: tipster, tout(er)
DOPPELGANGER: apparition, counterpart, *spirit, wraith
DOR: *deceive, *deception, *joke
DORBEETLE: bumclock, buzzard
DORCAS: gazelle, tabitha
DOREMA: bombay sumbul, root
DORIAN: rustic, simple
festival: carnea, carneia
DORIC: capital part: abacus
frieze part: metope, taenia
DORIS: offspring: nereids
DORMANT: *idle, inert, lethargic
DORMITORY: apartment, *home
monastery: dorter, dortour
DORMOUSE: glis, lerot, loir, moy
pert.: myoxine
words: feed your head
DORP: city, hamlet, village
DORSAL: back, neural, posterial
opposed to: ventral
DORUS: son: aegimius
DORYMENES: son: ptolemaeus
DOSE: *bit, *drug, *part, *quantity, *remedy
DOSITHEUS: son: ptolemaeus
DOSS: bed(room), sleep, tuft
house: hotel, inn
DOSSERET: abacus, pulvino
DOSSIER: black book, compendium
DOT: *bit, dowry, period, whit
DOTARD: *fool, henhussy, senile
DOTE: *adore, drivel, *love, rot
DOTS: costume
cover with: stipple
game: quadrangles
DOTTED: piebald, pinto, seme
DOTTEREL: dupe, *fool, gull
DOTTY: *insane, *mad, unsteady
DOUAY BIBLE: aree, naara
DOUBLE: ambiguous, apartment, appreciate, binary, breve, dual, duplex, duplicate, evade, fold, gemel, *grow, paired
a point: tack
back: return, reverse

* Asterisk means to look up this word to find more answer words.

-*barrelled:* *important
boiler: bain-marie
check: verify
chin: buccula
cocoon: dupion
comb.: bini
cross: *cheat, *deceive
crosser: rat, traitor
curse: anathema marantha
dagger: diesis
dare: challenge
dealing: *deception, perfidy
dutch: enigma, jargon
-*edged:* *acerb, keen, *sharp
-*entendre:* ambiguity, *joke
-*faced:* ancipital, *false
-*ganger:* *doppelganger
in brass: *act, represent
life: amphibiety
meaning: ambiguity
-*o:* scrutiny
pedro: cinch, game
point of curve: acnode
quick: *fast, march, speedy
reed: bassanello
ring: gemel
ripper: bobsled, sled
salt: alum, selenium, soda
talk: gobbledegook, *nonsense
thread: bave
tree: evener, transverse
truck: ad, layout, *spread
DOUBLET: gipon, pourpoint, two
DOUBT: challenge, *wonder
DOUBTFUL: *ambiguous, skeptical
DOUCEUR: bribe, sop, tip
DOUGH: batter, *money, paste
boy: soldier
-*faced:* irresolute, pliant
-*head:* clodpoll, *fool
-*nut:* bagel, cruller, sinker
DOUGHTY: *bold, *strong
DOUGLAS: *song:* annie laurie
DOUR: *obstinate, *sour, *sullen
DOUSE: immerse, *remove, *strike
DOVE: columba, coo, inca, inno-

cent, peace-nik, tumbler
cote: aviary, columbarium
home: columbary, cote
-*like:* *gentle, lovable, *pure
pert.: columbine
ring: cushat, pigeon
sound: coo, curr
-*tail:* *adapt, *fit, insert, join, suit, tenon, tongue
-*tailed:* angular
DOVEKIE: alle, auk, guillemot
DOWDY: *bad, coarse, *fat, ruddy
DOWEL: coak, peg, pin, skittle
DOWER: *dress, *gift, *give
DOWN: fell, fuzz, lint, *sick
-*and-out:* destitute, needy
-*and-outer:* pauper, wretch
at the heels: seedy, shabby
-*cast:* blue, low, unhappy
comb.: bas, cata, cath, de, kat
-*facing:* prostrate
fall: *defeat, rain, *ruin
feather: plume, plumule
feathery: dowl
grade: bust, demote, declivity
hearted: melancholy, *sad
hill: declining, falling
hill rush: schuss
in the mouth: *low, *sad, *sick
market: bear, depression
payment: advance, binder
pour: cataract, deluge, rain
quilt: duvet
-*right:* *absolute, candid, frank, *great, plumb, rank
-*side:* bottom, rear
stage or stairs: below
the alley: *straight
the drain: gone, lost
to earth: realistic
to the ground: utterly
town: center, city
-*trodden:* abused, under
turn: *decline, dip, *fall
under: antipodes, australia
ward: below, netherwards

---

* **Asterisk means to look up this word to find more answer words.**

curve: deflex
slope: declivity, quaquaverse
with: abas
DOWNY: *cunning*, feathery, flocculent, lanate, pubescent
mildews: bremia
DOWRY: *gift*, *money*, talent
DOXOLOGIZE: *praise*
DOXOLOGY: acoteleutic, hymn
DOXY: *doctrine*, mistress
DOZEN: *long:* baer's, thirteen
short: eleven
DP: outcast, pariah
DRAB: *bit*, *dull*, *sad*, *wanton*
DRACHMA, 1/20th: obol
DRACONIAN: *brutal*, *severe*
DRACUL(A): *demon*, *devil*
home: bran, hunedoara, risnov
DRAFF: *dregs*, *refuse*
DRAFT: *certificate*, conscript, *draw*, *drink*, *plan*, version
DRAG: bother, dawdle, *draw*, escort, hang, influence, poke, race, *slow*, toddle, tow, worm
behind chariot: *defeat*
deer: toll, tump
into: involve
one's freight: beat it, flee
out: elicit, extend, protract
reducer, missile: boattail
stone mill: arrastra, arrastre
through mud: bemire, stain
DRAGNET: seizure, *trap*, trawl
DRAGOMAN: *agent*, guide
DRAGON: continue, crank, drake, duenna, ladon, lizard, monster, musket, ogre, pigeon, tractor
biblical: rahab
biting: tarragon
cloud: ahi
darkness: rahab
fly: adder bolt, odonata
head: anabibazon, rahu
king: ao chin, ao jun, ao kuang, ao shun, lung wang
-like: dracontine
tail: catabibazon, ketu

teeth sower: cadmus
two-legged: wivern, wyvern
DRAGOON: *force*, *soldier*
DRAIN: *draw*, *dregs*, *waterway*
arched: culvert
blood: exsanguinate
DRAM· *bit*, *drink*, shot, slug
DRAMA: *play*
climax: catastasis
court: trial
dance: ballet
18th century: burletta
expression system: delsarte
god: dionysus
group: cast, company, troupe
introduction: prelude, protasis
main action: epitasis
muse: melpomene, thalia
part: *play:* part
pert.: histrionic
representation: impersonation
scene: cameo, *play:* place
short: saynete, skit
sudden reverse in: peripetia
DRAMATIC: emotional, spectacular
DRAPE: *dress*, hang, pendant
DRASTIC: *severe*, stern, violent
DRAUGHT: *draft*, outline, wind
DRAVIDIAN: *india:* dravidian
DRAW: abduce, *acquire*, *allure*, attract, *bring*, broach, catch, charisma, choose, delineate, *describe*, draft, *drag*, entice, etch, evoke, *get*, hale, haul, influence, inhale, limn, lottery, lure, magnetism, *paint*, *picture*, *plan*, pull, *remove*, select, siphon, *show*, sketch, *tie*, tow, trace
a bead on: *aim*, *attack*
a blank: black out, forget
and quarter: torture
an inference: interpret
a parallel: compare, relate
away: divert, shrink, *speed*
back: blench, cringe, defect, disadvantage, discount, fault, flaw,

* Asterisk means to look up this word to find more answer words.

hindrance, obstacle, recoil, *re-treat*, wince
close: *approach, *near
down: be paid, *get, *receive
forth: derive, elicit, tug
from: bottle, decant, derive
in: compress, retreat, taper
in horns: *quit, *yield
iron: *attack
it fine: be accurate
latch: *thief
lots: gamble, *venture
near: *approach, impend
off: bleed, distract, drain
on: *approach, *receive, *use
out: *continue, elicit, prolong
play: fake, feint
rein: *control, *slow, *stop
the line: challenge, select
the long bow: exaggerate, *lie
the sword: *attack
the teeth: disarm, paralyze
tight: bind, *secure, *tie
to a close: *end, *stop
to a head: suppurate
together: *gather, *meet
up: *array, *prepare, *stop
water: influence, matter

DRAWING: card: attraction, lure
back: retrahent
room: parlor, salon, *society

DREAD: *alarm, *anxiety, fear

DREADFUL: *bad, dire, *great

DREAM: muse, *think, *wonder
comb.: oneir
god: morpheus, oniros, serapis
interpretation: oneirocritics
land: sleep, *utopia
pert.: oneirotic, somnial
symbolism: psychoanalysis
time: alcheringa
up: conceive, create, originate

DREAR: *dull, *sad, *sorry

DRECK: *dregs, *refuse, trash

DREDGE: dig, drag, *raise, sift

DREGS: bottoms, crap, dirt, draff, dross, faex, grounds, lees, magma, marc, *refuse, remainder, residue, salin, scum, sediment, silt, slag, sludge, sordes, trash, vinasse

DRENCH: *drink, sog, *wet

DRESS: accouter, *adorn, adz, apparel, *array, attire, bandage, bedeck, bedizen, bind, bonnet, broach, buck up, burl, busk, buss, caparison, card, clothe(s), costume, dab, deck, decorate, dight, doll up, don, duds, enclothe, envelop, equip, fancy, fig up, finish up, fit, fix, frock, garb, garment, garnish, gear, get up, gown, habiliment, habit, invest, jupon, knot, lubricate, lump, muffle, nig, *ornament, outfit, prank, preen, *prepare, pretty, primp, prink, rags, raiment, *rebuke, rig, robe, *scold, sheathe, shroud, skirt, smooth, spiff up, slick up, smarten, spruce, swaddle, suit, swathe, tan, taw, togs, vestment, *wrap
civilian: mufti
feathers: preen
feature: gore, waist
formal: tails, tux(edo)
in full armor: panoply
leather: curry, tan, taw, tew
looped part: pouf
maker: couturier, modiste
term: godet, gore, gusset
mean: rags, tatters
ornament: chequeen, embroidery, frog, jabot, lace, ruche, sequin, zecchino, zequin
padding: bustle
parade: promenade, solitaire
riding: breeches, jodhpurs
stone: nidge, nig, ray, spall
suit: formal, tails, tux(edo)
up: *array, bedizen, deck out, decorate, falsify, *ornament, prank, preen, primp, prink
warmly: bundle up

---

* Asterisk means to look up this word to find more answer words.

wound: panse, **remedy*, treat
DRESSED: all gussied up
DRESSER: bureau, chest, vanity
DRESSING: bandage, cast, cravat
jacket: camisole
room: apothesis, toilet
roomer: johnnie
top: mulch
DRESSY: modish, **smart*, sporty
DRIBBLE: **bit*, **nonsense*, saliva
DRIFT: coast, **idle*, **range*
along: current, float, tide
anchor: curb
away: recede
off to sleep: bye-low
plug: bobbin
sandy: dene, esker
wood: lumber, spars
DRIFTER: nogoodnik, vagrant
DRILL: auger, bore, **discipline*,
exercise, **pierce*, **train*
DRINK: **absorb*, ade, aperitif,
bellywash, belt, bend the elbow,
beverage, bezzle, bibble, bouse,
bum, carouse, casu, chaser,
cheer, coffee, cola, draft, drain,
dram, draught, drench, drop, eye-
opener, fog-chaser, fizz, flip,
grog, gulp, hocus, imbibe, jigger,
jolt, lap up, libation, liquor, lush,
milk, morat, nectar, negus, night-
cap, nip, ocean, peg, pony, pop,
posset, punch, quaff, refresh,
shot, sip, slake, sling, slug, smile,
snort, soak, soda, sot, souse,
suck, swallow, swig, swill, swizzle, tipple, toast, toddy, tope,
waucht, waught, **wet*
alcoholic: akvavit, ale, aquavit, arrack, balche, beer, bombo, bootleg, booze, bourbon, brandy, bugjuice, cider, cocktail, cognac, gin,
grog, highball, hooch, intoxicant,
lager, liquor, mead, mescal, negus, porter, posset, rum,
schnapps, tequila, vodka, whiskey, wine

ancient: morat
beer after whiskey: boilermaker
bitters: americano, angostura,
campari, cardinale, fernet
branca, negroni, spritzer
brewed: ale, beer, bock, lager,
porter, stout
carbonated: fizz, pop, soda
christmas: nog, nogg, wassail
comb.: dipso
farinaceous: ptisan
fermented: mead, ptisan
frozen: frappe
fruit: ade, assai, bland, julep, morat, ratafia, rickey
gods: ambrosia, nectar
gruel-like: caudle
honey: mead, morat, oenomel
hot: caudle, cocoa, coffee, copus,
negus, posset, tea, toddy
magic: nepenthe, potion
mixed: alexander, bloody mary,
cocktail, collins, cooler, cuba
libre, daiquiri, egg nog, grass-
hopper, highball, hot toddy, irish
coffee, julep, manhattan, mar-
garita, martini, mint julep, moscow mule, old-fashioned, pink
lady, side car, stinger, tom and
jerry, tom collins, whiskey smash
mixer: bartender, mixologist
money for: bonamano, pourboire
plant juice: nipa, soma
portion: dollop, jigger, ounce,
shot, two fingers
rum: bombo, bumbo, grog
sassafras: saloop
small: bull, diluent, dram, hum,
nip, peg, shot, sniff, snifter,
snort, tabor, tot
soft: ade, pop, soda
stimulating: bracer
sweet: julep, nectar, orgeat
wine, sugar and water: negus
DRINKING: bibulous, poculation
bout: bacchanalia, binge, bouse,
bum, bust, carousal, fuddle, go-

---

* **Asterisk means to look up this word to find more answer words.**

down, orgy, potation, rat, revel, shindig, soiree, spree, wassail

cup: *drinking: vessel*

fountain: bubbler

glass: *drinking: vessel*

god: bacchus, dionysus, siris

horn: rhyton

pert.: bibitory, bibulous

place: barrelhouse, bar, bierstube, bistro, faro, pub, saloon, taproom, tavern

song: brindisi

toast: *toasts*

vessel: aleyard, ama, ampulla, beaker, blackjack, black pot, bowl, bratina, bugle, can, cannikin, cappie, chalice, cup, cylix, dipper, facer, fifth, flagon, flask, glass, goblet, gourd, hanaper, holmos, horn, jollyboys, jorum, jug, keg, kylix, magnum, mazer, mug, noggin, patera, pony, pourie, rhyton, rumkin, schooner, seidel, stein, stoop, stoup, tankard, tass, teacup, toby, tumbler, tyg

DRIP: bore, creep, ooze, seep

DRIVE: attack, campaign, crusade, *force,* *power,* *push,* *urge*

at: *aim,* hint, intend

away: banish, chase, dispel, exile, reject, repulse, shoo

back: repel, repulse, rout

down: nail, tamp

dull care away: cheer, play

fast: barrel, bucket, *speed*

home: convince, prove

frantic: bedevil

in: cafe, dint, *enter,* hammer, market, nail, tamp, theater

out: *discharge,* *dismiss*

public: esplanade, mall

stakes: build, camp, *settle*

DRIVEL: *nonsense,* slobber

DROLL: funny, waggish, zany

DRONE: bee, boom, buzz, sloth

DROOL: exult, *nonsense,* *talk*

DROOP: bore, *fail,* hang, lag

DROP: *abandon,* *agent,* *break*

a line: correspond, write

anchor: moor, *settle,* *stop*

bait: chum, dab, dib, lure

by drop: degree, guttatim

dead: *don't,* get lost, *stop*

-dry: impervious, seaworthy

everything: cease, *stop*

in: *arrive,* *enter,* surprise

it: *discard,* relinquish, *stop*

-like: guttate

off: decrease, doze, nap, sleep

out: cop out, *quit(ter)*

serene: amaurosis

sudden: hance, plop, thud

syllable: elide, elision

DROPSY: anasarca, edema, tumor

remedy: broom tails

DROSS: *dregs,* *refuse,* scobs

DROVE: *group,* multitude, *pack*

DROWSE: doze, nap, nod, *rest*

DRUB: *beat,* *defeat,* *whip*

DRUDGE: dig, grind, hack, *work*

DRUG: anodyne, aromatic, atropia, commodity, dope, dose, hypnotic, medicate, narcotic, nepenthe, opiate, *remedy,* sedative, tranquilizer

active principle: aloin

addict: *addict*

addictive: acid, amphetamine, barbiturate, benj, bennie, benzedrine, bethesda gold, blue heaven, bromide, candy, cannabis, christmas tree, cocaine, codeia, codeine, crank, dexedrine, dexy, dope, double trouble, down(er), ether, freaky, ghow, glue, goofball, goofer, gow, green dragon, greenie, *hallucinogen,* *heroin,* hops, hyoscyamus, junk, laudanum, lotus, lsd, mandrake, *marijuana,* meth, methedrine, mickey finn, morphine, munchie, nimby, opium,

---

* Asterisk means to look up this word to find more answer words.

pheenie, pot, rainbow, red bird, red devil, reefer, rizla, roach clip, scag, seccy, sleep-eze, smack, snappers, snow, sominex, speed, stramonium, stuff, suckie, synthetic, tooie, white, zig-zag, yellowjacket
and ship: shanghai
anti-cancer: camptothecin
anti-heroin: methadone
bitter: aloe
container: capsule, gallipot
convulsion causing: tetanic
crocus: saffron
dealer: mule, pusher
effect: crash, goose up, kaif, kef, kick, kiff, rush
forgetfulness: nepenthe
habit: monkey
hippocratic: mecon
hypnotic: trional, verenol
injector: hypo, needle
jar: albarello
nux vomica: tetanic
painkilling: darvon
purgative: aloe, laxative
shot: fix
sleeping: sedative, somnifacient
social: pot party
synthesizer: aniline
take: cop out, get high, pop pills, smoke grass, smoke pot
taking: acid-rap, chemical vacation, hype, injection, lighting up, mainlining, popping, skin popping, snorting, trip, turning on
withdrawal: come down, crash
wonder: acth
DRUGGED: acid-rapped, freaked out, hyped, lit up, pot-high, spaced out, turned on, zonked
DRUM: *beat:* *alarm, berloque, flam, tattoo
call to arms: rappel
codes: bush telegraph
fire: volley
fish: bubbler

kettle: atabal, naker, timpano
-like: barrel, naker, tabret
out: *discharge, *dismiss
roll: dian, reveille, roulade
small: bongo, tabor, tabret
stick: tampon
stick tree: canafistulo, cassia
DRUNK(ARD): alcoholic, *ardent, bacchanal, binge, blah, blasted, blotto, borracho, bouse, bout, brawl, bum, canned, carouser, dipsomaniac, gooned, high, intoxicated, juiced, lit, loaded, oiled, out, *party, polluted, potted, rummy, smashed, soak(ed), sot, souse(d), splifiticated, stewed, stoned, swillbelly, tank, *tear, tiddly, tippler, toper, tosspot, zapped, zorched
DRY: *arid, brut, *dull, vapid
comb.: ser, xer, xero
goods: linens, napery, wear
goods dealer: draper, mercer
ice: carbon dioxide
out: rizzar, siccate, toast
run: maneuver, rehearsal, try
stone diker: cowan
up: abstain, parch, shrink
wit: attic salt
DUBLIN: baile atha cliath
DUCK: *avoid, *bow, *retreat
bill: platypus
black-headed: naloonga
bluebill: scaup
cooking: caneton
egg: nothing, pidan, zero
eider: colk, wamp
footless: cannet, merlette
fresh water: aix, anas, mandarin
gen: aex, aix, anas, anseres, aythya, clangula, nettion, nyroca
golden-eye: gowdnie
group: skein, sord, team
hooked bill: merganser
-like: anatine, coot, decoy
long-tailed: hareld
male: drake

* **Asterisk means to look up this word to find more answer words.**

old squaw: quandy
out: escape, flee, vanish
pintail: piketail, querquedule, smee, smew, widgeon
ring-necked: bunty
river: dogy, eider, greenwing, pike, pintail, shoveler, teal
scaup: bluebill, widgeon
sea: coot, eider, harlequin, scaup, scoter
sitting: decoy
soup: cinch, facility, set-up
tree: yaguaza
weed: lemna
wild: gadwall, mallard, teal
wood: branchier, canard
yellow-billed: geelbec(k)
young: caneton

DUDGEON: *anger*, malice, stew

DULL: anesthetic, *apathetic*, *arid*, backward, bald, barren, blah, bland, blate, blunt, boeotian, boring, bovine, bromidic, callous, cold, *cool*, dead, dim, dense, drab, drear, dry, dun, elephantine, flat, *heavy*, *idle*, impassive, inert, insensible, insipid, jejune, lackluster, languid, logy, numb, obtuse, ox-like, passive, patient, pedestrian, philistine, *sad*, *simple*, slow, *stupid*, *thick*, *vain*
become: hebetate, pall
comb.: ambly

DUMB: *dull*, *stupid*, taciturn
DUMFOUND: *astound*, *upset*
DUMMY: *fool*, *substitute*
DUN: *ask*, bill, *dull*, *urge*
DUNCE: *fool*, golem, goon
DUNGEON: cave, hole, *jail*, pit
DUPLICITY: *cunning*, *deception*
DURABLE: *firm*, *strong*
DUTCH: *aborigine:* celt
assembly: iraad
badger: das
bailiff: baljew, schout

bargain: koop, toast
boat: hooker, koff, praam, schuyt, treckshuy, yanky
breakfast: balkenbrij, brey
capital: amsterdam, the hague
coin: cent, crown, daalder, doit, dubbeltje, ducatoon, escalan, florin, guilder, gulden, raps, ryder, stiver
colonist: boer
colony, past: borneo, celebes, java, new guinea, sumatra
commune: amsterdam, assen, baarn, breda, delft, dongen, doniawestal, doorn, ede, hague, leyden, oss, rotterdam, voorst, vught, zeist, zuilen, zwolle
concert: noise, uproar
courage: intoxication, liquor
cupboard: kas
dialect: frankish, frisian, saxon, taal
fish boat: dogger, hooker, tode
gipsy: aptal, bazigar, heidenen
harlot: kippetje
inlet: zuider zee
island: ameland, arroe, aru, schelling, texel, vlieland
lake: haarlem
leave: absence
legislature: raad
liquor: advocaat, schnapps
man: blanda, butterbox, hogen
man's-breeches: bleeding heart
man's-pipe: big sarsaparilla
meadow: betaw
measure: aam, ahm, anker, aum, bunder, carat, duim, ell, kan, kop(pen), leaguer, legger, lood, maatje, mijl, mud(dle), mutsje, okshoofd, roede, rood, rope, schepel, steekkan, stoop, streep, vingerhoed, voet, wigt, wisse
merchant vessel: galliot
metal: arsedine
militia: schuttery
mister: heer, van

* **Asterisk means to look up this word to find more answer words.**

news agency: aneta
painter: bosch, dou, eyck, hals, helst, hobbema, kalf, kroninck, lely, leyden, lis, mostaert, neer, rembrandt, seghers, steen, ter borch
pancake: poffertje
pile worm: navalis, teredo
poet: dacosta, decker
political party: cod, hoek, hook, geuzen
printer: elzevir
reclaimed land: polder
redlight dist.: gezellig, zeedijk
river: eem, ijssel, leck, maas, meuse, rhine, waal, ysel
river gravel: heibanen
scholar: erasmus
sheriff: schout
town hall: stadhouse
turf: plaggen
uncle: eme, oom
weight: bahar, esterlin, last, lood, ons, pond, wichtje
DUTY: *service,* tax, *tie*
DWARF: ablach, alberich, alviss, andvari, atomy, bali, bantam, blastie, brokk, crownie, crile, *decline,* droich, durgan, elf, fairy, gnome, grib, homunculus, ivaldir, lilliputian, *little,* midget, negrillo, negrito, nibelung, nix, peewee, pig wiggen, pixy, puck, pygmy, regin, runt, scraggy, scrubby, shee, shrimp, sindri, sprite, tom thumb, troll, wart
animal: runt
archaic: dandiprat
cornel: bunchberry, shrub
fabled: pigmy, pygmy
fifth avatar: vaman
fish-shaped: andvare
king: alberich
palmetto: andropogon, blue stem
plant: cumin, cummin
poinciana: barbados pride
race: nibelung

tribe: abongo, babongo, obongo
DWELL: *abide,* *live,* *stop*
DYE: *base:* aniline
blue: anil, cyanine, wad, woad
blue-red: orchal, orselle
brown: sumac
coaltar: azarin, eosin, magenta
component: azo, diazine
cosmetic: henna, red
crimson: relbun
delicate: tinge
early: alizarin(e)
flavin: quercitron
gum: kino
hair: henna, rastik
indigo: aal, al, anil
lichen: archil, litmus, orchal
plant: alhenna, alkanet, anil, annatto, chay, henna, kamala, madder, orselle, sumac, woad
purple: murex
quercitron: flavin
red: aal, al, alkannin, annatto, cerise, eosin, morindin, orseilline, rhodamin
root pigment: madder
silk: luteolin
soot: kohl
stuff: carajura, chica, isatin, madder, orpiment
treatment: bottom chrome
violet: archil, orselle
weed: woadwaxen
wood: brazil, sapan, tua, tuwi
yellow: arusa, weld, woald
DYERS: *apparatus:* ager, vat
chamber: oast, oven
grape: pokeweed
weed: ash of jerusalem, woad
DYNAMIC: *active,* *live,* *strong*
DYNAMITE: *blast,* dangerous
inventor: nobel
projectile: dualin
DYNAMO: *enthusiast,* livewire
inventor: faraday
part: limb, stator, yoke
DYNASTY: *rule(r),* sovereign

* Asterisk means to look up this word to find more answer words.

DYSENTERY: *treatment:* acetar-
sone
DYSPEPTIC: **bitter, *sick*
DZHUGASHVILI: stalin

EA: *daughter:* nina
EAGER: **agape, *apt, *ardent,*
fervid, keen, **ready,* willing
beaver: dynamo, **enthusiast*
EAGLE: aquila, bateleur, etana
beaked: aquiline
constellation: aquila
group: convocation, eyrie
-like: accipital, aquiline
male: tercel
nest: aerie, eyrie, eyry
owl: bubo, horned owl
ray: aetobatid, obispo
sea: ern(e)
stone: etite, ironstone
wing: solitaire
-winged: fast
-wood: agalloch, agar, aloes
EAGRE: bore, flood, flow, wave
EAR: *absence:* anotia
ache: otalgia, otalgy
affecting: diotic
anvil: ambos, incus
attachment: corn
auricle: pinna
bone: ambos, incus, malleus,
stapes, stirrup, tegmen
canal: scala
canal part: ampullula
cartilage elevation: antihelix
cave: cochlea, meatus, utricle
cleaning device: aurilave
cockle: purples
comb.: auri, ot, oto
corn: cob, spike
covering: earcap, muff
deformity: cauliflower ear
depression: scapha
doctor: aurist, otologist
drop: earring, pendant

drum: membrane, tympanum
hammer: malleus
inflammation: otitis
lobe: lap, lug, pendant, pinna
lock: tress
mark: **badge, *bit,* character,
designate, identify, label, **name,*
*sign, *symbol, *token
-minded: audile
muscle: auricularis
opening: bur, burr
part: auricle, burr, cauda, cavum,
cochlea, concha, **drum,* helix,
lobe, lug, pinna, tragus
passage: auditory meatus
pert.: aural, auric(ular), binotic,
binural, lobar, entotic, otic
pick: auriscalp
-piercing: shrill
ring: band, girandole, pendle
ringing: syrigmus
science: otology
shell: abalone, omer, snail
shot: hearing, nearness, range
splitting: loud, uproarious
stone: otolite, otolith, sagitta
trumpet: auriphone, topophone
wax: cerumen
wheat: cape, spica
wig: golach, goloch
EARLY: ancient, before, first,
matutional, prehistoric, soon
EARN: **acquire, *get,* merit, **win*
EARNEST: **ardent,* sober, **token*
comb.: serio
EARTH: *air cover:* biosphere
axis: hinge, pole
bob: grub, maggot
born: autochthonous, human, low,
mortal, plebeian, temporal, ter-
rigenous, worldly
center: barysphere, centrosphere,
core
clayey: bion, byon
comb.: geo, telluro, terra
compound: tierras
core: nife

* Asterisk means to look up this word to find more answer words.

cover: air, sial
crust: epigene, horst, silica
deposit: loam, marl, mold, soil
drake: dragon
fall: avalanche, landslide
flax: amianthus, asbestos
god: bel, cabeiri, dagan, geb, kabeiri, keb, seb, tellus
goddess: auxesia, ceres, damia, demeter, erda, gaea, herta, lua, mannu, semele, tari, terra
hog: aardvark
interior: *earth: center
kin: terella
layer: sloam
lump: clod, sod
metal: erbium, ore, protore
nut: arnot, chufa, goober, peanut, pod, root, truffle
pert.: clayey, geal, planetary, seismic, telluric, temporal, terra, terrene, terrestrial
pigment: ochre, umber
prepare for seeding: cultivate, harrow, plow, shovel, spade
-quake: lindol, seism, temblor, tremor, upheaval
-quake measurer: seismograph
-quake, pert.: seismic
-quake, point above: epicenter
-quake, protectress: st agatha
-quake science: seismology
sample: boring
satellite: moon
-shaking: *important, loud
science: geology, geography
spirits: annunaki, igigi
star: fungus, geaster
surface: *crust, sial, sima
  gravel: eratum, erratice
vitriol-infused: sory
volcanic: lava, trass, tuff
work: dike, *font, *ridge, tump
worm: angle-twitch, annelid, bramble, brandling, easse, ersenia, ess, ipomoea
EARTHLY: carnal, coarse, *low

EASE: *abate, buffer, calm, comfort, content, euphoria, facilitate, fluency, leisure, prosperity, *quiet, *slow
at: degage, otiose, relaxed
of: deprive
off: retard, slack, slow
the rudder: tack
EAST: asia, dawn, levant, orient
pert.: asian, eoan, oriental
queen: zenobia
EAST AFRICA: *cedar:* deodar
dialect: kiswahili
discoverer: da gama
house: tembe
native: somli
slave vessel: dhow
spiritual power: ngai
sultanate: zanzibar
tool: panga
tree: moli
tribe: asha, bari
EAST INDIES: *animal:* babirusa, tana, tapaia, tarsier, tupaia
arrowroot: tikor
bark: lodh, niepa
bead tree: margosa, neemba, nim
bison: bauteug, tsine
broad-bill: raya
carpet: amritsar
cashmere: ulwan
cedar: mahogany, toon(a)
chamois: sarau
cheroot: lunkah
civet: dedes, musang, rasse
cotton tree: simal
cypress: bhutan
decoration: ardish, tracery
disease: lanas
dodder: amil
dye tree: dhak, toon
fabric: sallo(o)
fiber plant: badaga, hibiscus, oadal, nilgiri, sana, sunn
fig tree: banian, banyan
fish: darter, dorab, gourami
flower: hibiscus, jasmine

* Asterisk means to look up this word to find more answer words.

food: sago
freight boat: oolak
fruit: bel(leric), bilimbing, carda-
mom, cubeb, durian, myrobalan,
papaw, zanonia
gum tree: kino
harbor master: shabandar
hemp: pangane
herb: chay, choy, eggplant, pia,
roselle, sesame, sola
hog: babiroussa, pigmy
insectivore: banx ring, tupaia
island: adi, arroe, aru, bali, borneo, celebes, java, leti, muna,
nias, sumatra, timor
liquor: arrack
mangrove: ceriops, tagal
measure: bamboo, bouw, coyang,
depa, depoh, gantang, kilan, kit,
kos, parah, rood, rope, takar,
tjenkal, toenbak
mint: java tea
money changer: shroff
monkey: entellus
muskmelon: wungee
muslin: ban, beteela, jamdanee
nose flute: upanga
nut: ben
palm: book, corypha, gebang, jaggery, nipa, palmyra, tala, talipot,
tokopat
panda: wah
pine: chir
plant: ambary, amil, benne, chay,
creat, dal, jute, madar, rea,
sesame, sola, sunn
post: dak, dawk
road: praya
ruler: akbar, rajah
ruminant: zebu
shrub: ak, ancistrocladus, bastard
indigo, carandas, caraunda, ca-
rissa, cubeb, mudar, odal, sola,
soma, upas
snake: bokadam, kupper
squirrel: taguan
starch: sago, tikor

sugar: glaga(h), raab, talthib
swine: babirusa
tree: abroma, acana, ach, ailanthus, asoka, antiar(is), averrhoa,
bahera, banyan, bastard manchineel, ben-teak, bloodwood,
butea, cadamba, cajeput, cannonball, carajura, caramba, chica,
coromandel, couroupita, deodar,
dhak, eng, engelg, fig, kajeput,
margosa, mee, neem, niepa,
oodal, poon, press, punk, rohan,
roman, saj, sal(ai), sapan, simal,
siris, sissu, teak, tikur, toon, upas
vessel: balloon, gallivat
vine: amil, anamirta, gilo, jasmine, moonseed, odal, soma
weight: catty, ratti, ser, toen, tola
wild honeybee: dingar
wood: eng, kokra, sal, satin
xylophone: saron
EASTER: eed, eostre, paas, pasch
EASTERN CHURCH: *choir platform:* solea
convent head: hegumene
doxology: doxa
festival day: apodosis
monk: caloyer
prayer: ectene, ektene
priest: catholicos, katholikos
saint: anargyros
EASY: **gentle, *soft, *wanton*
going: blase, calm, relaxed
job: breeze, cinch, pipe, snap
mark: chump, **fool*, sucker
street: bed of roses, comfort, luxury, prosperity, wealth
thing: duck soup, gravy, picnic,
pushover, sinecure
EAT: board, **bite*, browse, burn,
canker, chew, chop, consume,
corrode, devour, dine, down,
erode, fall to, fare, feast, feed,
fret, glut, gnaw, gobble, gorge,
gulp, ingest, nourish, partake,
picnic, piece, pitch in, raven,
rust, sate, scoff, snack, stuff, sup

---

* Asterisk means to look up this word to find more answer words.

between meals: bever
crow: bow, condescend, recant
grass: forage, graze
humble pie: crawl, *eat crow
loving to:* esurient
one's heart out: agonize
out of one's hand: *yield
pert.:* dietary, edacious
sparingly: diet
sumptuously: regale, stuff
up: *accept, believe, go for
with: break bread
EATING: *comb.:* phag, vore
place: *dining room
EAVESDROP: *listen, stillicide
EAVESDROPPER: lot's wife, peeper
EBB: *decline, *reduce, *wane
and flow: alternate, estus, tide
tide: low water, neap
EBED: *son:* gaal
EBER: *father:* shem
son: joktan, peleg
EBONY: black, diospyros, tree
EBULLATE: boil, bubble, stew
EBULLIENT: *hot, passionate
ECCENTRIC: abnormal, *awry, balmy, buggy, card, character, crackpot, crank(y), crotchety, curious, deviative, divergent, erratic, freak(ish), *funny, gink, idiosyncratic, *insane, kinky, *mad, maggoty, misfit, nut(ty), odd, oddball, oddity, outre, peculiar, queer, screw ball, screwy, strange, uncommon, *unique, *weird(o), *wild
ECCLESIASTIC: *church: man
assistant: acolyte
banner: labarum
buddhist: arhat, bhikku, bo, bonze, dalai lama, grand lama, mahatma, panchen, poongee, poonghie, talapoin, yaham
cap: *vestment: religious
chapter, pert.:* capitular(y)
council: synod

court: classis, rota
curse: anathema
garment: *vestment: religious
hindu: atharvan, bairagi, bashara, bhikhari, bhikku, bhikkshu, brahman, guru, hotar, mobed, mulla(h), pujari, pundit, purohit, ramanandi, ramwat, sannyasi, vairagi, yogi(n)
income: benefice, glebe
jewish: cohen, darshan, levite, maggid, *prophet, rabbi, scribe
jurisdiction: deanery, diocese, parish, see
law: canon
muslim: abdal, dervish, fakir, hadji, imam, imaum, kahin, kasis, muezzin, mufti, mullah, murshid, santon, sheik, wahabi
officer: bishop, deacon, rector
order: cassinese
pagan: daduchus, druid, epopt, flamen, hierodule, hierophant, hieros, mystes
prince: cardinal, hierarch
punishment: censure
seat: deanery, sedile, sedilia
service: matin
statute: capitular
surplice: cotta
vestment: *vestment: religious
widow's office: viduate
ECDYSIAST: stripteaser
ECHETUS: *daughter:* amphissa
ECHXINOCLOA: camalote
ECHINODERM: amphiuroide, annuloid, asteroid, basket star, gorgonocephalus, starfish
devonian: agelacrinite
extinct: blastoid
radial area: ambulacrum
ECHO: *answer, *repeat, sympathy
ECLAT: *glory, *honor, *praise
ECLIPSE: *beat, *blot, *hide
demon: ketu, rahu
predictor: basselian elements
shadow: umbra, penumbra

* Asterisk means **to** look up this word to find more answer words.

ECOLOGY: bionomics, environment
pioneer: commoner, barry
ECONOMICS: finance, plutology
element: commodity
practitioner: moneybug
ECONOMIZE: *save,* scrimp, stint
ECSTASY: *joy,* rapture, trance
ECUADOR: *coin:* condor, sucre
god: umina
island: galapagos
measure: cuadra, fanega, libra
mountain: antisana, cayambe, chimborazo, cotacachi, cotopaxi, pichincha
volcano: sangay
ECUMENIC: catholic, *universal*
council: lyon, trent
ECZEMA: dermatitis, malanders
EDACITY: *appetite,* avarice
EDAM: *relative:* gouda
EDDISH: arrish, eegrass, sequel
EDDY: *turn,* twirl, vortex
EDEN: *paradise,* *utopia*
river: euphrates, gihon, hiddekel, pishon, tigris
EDESSA: *king:* abgar
EDGE: *advantage,* *back,* basil, bench, berm, bezel, blade, board, *border,* bound, brim, brink, brow, cusp, *end,* gal, hem, hone, labrum, *limit,* lip, margin, nerves, odds, picot, pien, rand, selvage, sharpen, shelf, shoulder, sidle, sill, skirt, *top*
bone: aitch, meat cut, rump
in: *enter,* intrude
metal: bur, buhr, burr
stone: pavement
up to: *approach,* *near*
EDGY: anxious, *critical,* *sharp*
EDICT: *act,* *law,* *order*
EDINBURG: auld reekie, edina
EDIT: *adapt,* bluepencil, *issue*
EDOM: esau, idumaea, seir, tema
city: dedan, pau, teman
duke: aholibamah, aliah, aran,

elah, iram, jetheth, kenaz, magdiel, mibzar, pinon, teman, timnah, uz
king: baalhanan, bela, hadad, husham, jobab, samlah, shaul
mountain: hor
EEL: conger, cuchia, elver, lamprey, link, moray, olm, opah
basket: buck
boat: schuit
cut and cooked: spitchcock
fish for: sniggle
-like salamander: amphiuma
-pout: blenny, burbot, tuffer, ling, muttonfish, weasel, yowler
sand: crig, launce
-shape: anguilliform, anguilloid
spear: elger
ware: crowfoot
worm: nema(tode)
EERIE: *eccentric,* *weird*
EFFECT: *accomplish,* *action,* bearing, compass, consequence, corollary, derivative, development, drift, *end,* *force,* fruit, gain, impact, influence, *issue,* offshot, *power,* *result,* upshot
EFFECTS: goods, *property,* wares
EFFICIENT: *active,* *adept*
EGG: *bake:* shirr
beater: helicopter, mixer
case: outheca, ovisac, shell
collector: oologist
comb.: oario, oo, ovi
fertilized: oosperm, zoon
fish: berry, caviar, roe
group: clutch
-head: intellectual
holder: nest
insect: larva, nit
measuring device: oometer
on: *abet,* *drive,* spur, *urge*
part: albumen, archiblast, glair, latebra, shell, white, helk, yellow, yolk
plant: aubergine, berengena, brinjal, brown jolly, solanum

---

* **Asterisk means to look up this word to find more answer words.**

-shaped: obovoid, ooidal, oval, ovaloid, ovate, oviform, ovoid

shell: cascaron, ecru, shard

small: nit, ovule, pea

strand: chalaza, treadle

tester: candler

unfertilized: oosphere

white: albumen, glair

EGIL: *brother:* volund

EGLAH: *husband:* david

son: ithream

EGLON: *king:* debir

EGYPTIAN: ababdeh, arab, gipsy, kem, misr, mizraim, nilot, wafd

adam: atum, tum

air god: shu

alloy: asem

animal: adda, fox, gazelle, genet, ichneumon, jerboa

antelope: bubal

ape sacred to thoth: aani

artist god: ptah

beer: zythum

beetle: scarab

bird: ba-bird, bennu, benu, ibis, sicsac, wryneck

boat: baris, cangia, dahabeah, felucca, nuggar, sandal

body: ka, khet, sahu

bottle: doruck

bull: apis, bacis, mont

burial jar: canopus

calendar: ahet, apap, choik, hathor, mechir, mesore, pachons, paophi, payni, phamenoth, pharmuthi, shemu, thoth

cap: fez

capacity unit: ardeb

cape: sudr

capital: akhetaton, alexandria, asyoot, cairo, memphis

captain: rais, reis

cat: bast, mut, pakht, sekhet

catfish: bagre, docmac

childbirth goddess: apet, hathor, meskhent, nekhebet, opet, renenet, taueret

christian: copt

city: abydox, alexandria, argo, aswan, asyut, aven, cairo, canopus, esna, gizeh, idfu, isna, karnak, luxor, memphis, qina, qus, rejaf, rosetta, sais, tanis, tanta, thebes

clover: berseem

coin: bedidlik, foddah, gersh, girsh, kees, millieme, para, piaster, purse, tallard

commander: sirdar

concubine: hagar

conquerors: amru, hyksos

cosmetic: kohl

cotton: pima, sak

cow-headed goddess: isis, nut

crocodile: amemait, sebek, sobk

cross: ankh

crown: atef

dam: aswan, sadd, sudd

dancer: alma, alme, ghawazi

dead, deities: amemait, amenti, anubis, horus, maat, ophois, osiris, serapis, sekhet, upuaut

dead, servants: shawabti

dead, statue: shabtis

desert: libyan, nubian, sahara, scete, skete, tih

dog: saluki

dog-headed ape: hapi, thoth

drink: bosa, boza, bozah

drug: nepenthe

dye plant: henna, hinna

early era: amratian

earth god: geb, keb, seb

elf: ouphe

elysium: aalu

embalming booth: good house

emblem: aten, lotus

eternity god: neheh(heh)

evil, god of: set(h)

falcon-headed god: horus, mont, khons hor, ra-harakhte

farmers: fellahin

fertility symbol: serapis

festival: isis

* Asterisk means to look up this word to find more answer words.

fish: bagre, bouri, bichir, docmac, lates, mormyrid, saide

gate: pylon

genie: amset, hapi

god: (*egyptian: dead, deities; god, animal-headed; sun god*) aah, apet, apuat, atum, bes, chnemu, djed, djehuti, geb, imhotep, iphtimis, keb, khem, khepera, khnemu, khnum, min, mnevis, neph, nun, onnophris, onuphis, opet, pasht, ptah, seb, seker, sutekh, zehuti

god, animal-headed: aani, amemait, amon, anubis, apis, arsaphes, duamutef, hapi, harakhte-ra, hershef, knenti, khepri, khons-hor, khnum, mont, nefertum, osorapis, pakht, qebhsnuf, sebek, set(h), sobk, thoth, upuaut

god, man-deified: amenhotep, imhotep, pharaoh

goddess: (*egyptian: childbirth goddess; dead, deities; goddess, animal-headed*) amenti, anta, anuket, athor, athyr, dor, ensos, iusaas, mehit, min, nehmauit, neit(h), nephthys, rat, sati, seshat, shait, uert-hekeu

goddess, animal-headed: bast, buto, hathor, heket, isis, metseger, mut, nekhebet, nut, renenet, sekhet, sekhmet, selkit, selquet, taueret, tefnut

governor: bey, pasha

grass: halfeh, sadd, sudd

gunde: dragoman

harelike mammal: hyrax

hawk-headed god: horus

headdress: uraeus

healer: arabi

heaven: aalu, aaru, ialu, yaru

heavenly region: field of reeds

hebrew name: mizraim

herb: anise

hippo: amemait, apet, taueret

holy bird: bennu, benu

immortal heart: ab, hati

insignia: uraeus

instrument: arghoul, sistrum

jackal-headed god: anubis, apuat, ophois, upuaut, wepwawet

khedive's estate: daira

king: amenhotep, busiris, euergetes, farok, farouk, faud, fuad, hophra, necho, pharaoh, philometor, proteus, ptolemy, rameses, shishak, zoser

laborer: aperu

lake: birket-el-kurun, bitter lakes, menzaleh, moeris

land: feddan, goshen, sennar

language: arabic, coptic

lighthouse: pharos

lily: calla, lotos, lotus

lion-headed goddess: mut, renenet, sekhmet, tefnut

lizard: adda, scink, skink

lotus: nymphaea, water lily

measure: abdat, apt, ardeb, aurure, baladi, cubit, daribah, farde, keleh, kharouba, malouah, nief keddah, ocha, robhah, theb

men deified: amenhotep, imhotep

month: *calendar

monument: obelisk, sphinx

moon god: aah, khons, thoth

mountain: horeb, sinai, uekia

mouse: jerboa

mullet: bouri

nature god: osiris

new kingdom founder: ahmose

oasis: bahriyeh, dakhel, farafra, kharga, khargeh, siwa

ocean god: chaos, nu(n)

official: mudir

opium: thebain

party: wafd

peasant: fellah

pebble: jasper

period: amarna, amratian, badarian, tasian

petrified city: ishmonie

* **Asterisk means to look up this word to find more answer words.**

pharaoh headdress: pschent
pharaoh's hen: vulture
physician: imhotep
plain: asaseff
plant: cumin, cummin, lentil
pleasure goddess: bast, hathor
policeman: ghaffir, ghafir
pound: rotl
president: nasser, sadat
priest: psammetichus
privet: henna, hinna
predynamic culture: badarian
queen: cleopatra, khazneh, nefer-
  titi, nofretete, sati
rain goddess: tefnut
ram-headed god: amon, arsaphes,
  harsphes, hershef, khnum
rattle: sistrum
reed: byblus, papyrus
relic: mummy
romance reciter: anteri
religion book: book of the dead
ruler: khedive, pharaoh
sacred bird: bennu, benu, ibis
sacred bull: apis, buchis, hapi,
  menuis, merwer, mneris, onuphis
sacred crocodile: lutembi, pete-
  suchos
sacred flower: lotos, lotus
sacred ram: banaded, baneb,
  djedet, mendes
sage: imhotep
sanctuary: secos, sekos
scarab god: khepera, khepri
scorpion: selkit, selquet
seal: scarab
season: ahet, pert, shemu
serpent: asp, apepi, apeti, buto
shrub: kat
sky goddess: hathor, nut
snake goddess: mertseger
solar disk: aten
spirit: akh, ba, chu, ka, sahu
stone: rosetta
sun god: amen, amon, amun,
  anhur-shu, aten, atmu, atum,
  behdety, chepera, haroeris, horus,

khepri, osiris, phra, ra-harakhte,
  rhe, shu, tem, tum
symbol: ankh, asp, maat, scarab,
  uraeus, uta
talisman: angle
tambourine: rikk
temple: abydos, dendera, edoon,
  idfu, karnak, luxor, osiris
thorn: babul, gonakie, kikar
title: atef, caliph, pasha
tomb: mastaba, pyramid, serdab
tree: ambatch, herminiera, sudd
underworld: aaru, amenti, duat
union: sam-taui
vase: canopic
vegetable: lentil, lupin, vetch
vegetation god: seker
viper: asp, cerates, cobra, haje
vulture: nekhebet
war god: anhur(-shu), mont,
  montmenthu, sutekh
war goddess: neith, sekhmet
weight: artal, deben, dera,
  drachma, hamlah, kantar, kerat,
  ocha, oke, quintal, rotel, uckia
wind: kamsin, khamsin
EHUD: *son:* ahiah, gera, naaman
EIGHTEEN: *benedictions:* aboth
 carat: genuine
 inches: cubit
ELABORATE: **great, *make*
ELAM: *capital:* susa
 king: arioch, chedorlaomer
 son: abdi, eliah, jehiel, jeremoth,
  mattaniah, zechariah
ELAN: morale, **spirit*
ELATHA: *son:* bres
ELATUS: *daughter:* caenis
ELBOW: *pert.:* anconeal, ulnar
ELDER: bour, **church:* man,
  trammon
ELEASAH: *son:* sisamai
ELEAZAR: *son:* jason, matthan,
  phineas, phinehas
ELECTRA: *brother:* orestes
 daughter: harpies, iris
 father: agamemnon

* Asterisk means to look up this word to find more answer words.

husband: thaumas
mother: clytemnestra
son: dardanus
ELECTRIC: *amplifier:* maser
atom: anion, cation, electron, ion, kation
capacity: *electric: unit
catfish: raad, torpedo
circuit regulator: booster
current, pert.: audio
current meter: attenuator, coder, rheometer, voltmeter
device: amplifier, capacitator, condenser, dynamo, rheostat
force: elod, od
measure: *electric: unit
part: *electric: atom
pole: anode, cathode
property: capacitance
unit: abhenry, abohm, abwatt, amp(ere), barad, begohm, bel, coulomb, farad, henry, hertz, mho, oerstad, ohm, perm, proton, rel, tesla, volt, watt, weber
ELECTRONIC: *control:* automation
detector: radar, sonar
stream: beta ray
tube: klystron, magnetron, pentode, tetrode, thyratron, triode, vaccum
ELEEMOSYNARY: altruistic, *free, philanthropic
ELEGANT: *aesthetic, *artificial
ELEMENT: *agent, *air, essence
combining power: valence
decomposed: anion
devouring: fire, flame
even valence: artiad
form of: allotrope
rare: cerium, erbium, yttrium
ELEPHANT: *apple tree:* feronia
boy: sabu
carrying bird: roc
cry: barr, trumpet
dentin: ivory
ear: fern, taro

extinct: mastodon
goad: ankus
group: herd
keeper: mahout
male: bull
pen: kraal
pert.: pachydermic
saddle or seat: howdah
trappings: jhool
trunk: proboscis
tusk: ivory, scrivello
young: calf
ELEPHANTINE: *big, *dull
ELEVATE: *advance, *boost, lift
ELEVATED: *great, *high, *noble
ELF: *dwarf, goblin, oaf, shee
ELI: *son:* hophni, phinehas
ELIAB: *son:* chelkias
ELIAKIM: *son:* azor, melea
ELIAM: *daughter:* bathsheba
ELIAS: *son:* helkias
ELIASAPH: *father:* lael
ELIASHIB: *son:* johanan, joiada
ELIEZER: *son:* joshua
ELIHU: *son:* jeroham
ELIMELECH: *wife:* naomi
ELIOENAI: *son:* akkub, anani, dalaiah, eliashib, hodaiah, johanan, pelaiah
ELIPHAZ: *son:* amalek, gatam, kenaz, omar, teman, timna
ELISHA: *father:* shaphat
home: abelmeholah
servant: genazi
ELISHEBA: *husband:* aaron
ELISSA: *dido
ELITE: *society, *top, *unique
corps: green berets, marines
ELIUD: *son:* eleazar
ELIXIR: amrita, panacea, *spirit
ELIZABETH: bess, lizzie, oriana
enemy: erin
jingle: cat and fiddle
mother: boleyn
ELIZAPHAN: *son:* jeiel, shimri
ELK: *bark:* bay, big bloom, magnolia

* Asterisk means to look up this word to find more answer words.

group: gang
nut: buffalo tree, rabbit wood
ELKANAH: *son:* samuel
wife: hannah
ELLASAR: *king:* arioch
ELM: *borer:* lamiid
fruit: samara
genus: celtis, planera, trema, ulmus
rock or *wing:* wahoo
ELON: *offspring:* adah, bashemath
ELOTH: *builder:* uzziah
ELMADAM: *son:* cosam
ELPAAL: *son:* beriah, eber, heber, hezeki, ismerai, jezliah, jobab, meshullam, misham, shamed, shema, zebadiah
ELUDE: *avoid, *escape, shun
ELYSIUM: *paradise, *utopia
EMACIATION: *decline, marasmus, reducing, thinning
EMANATE: *arise, *occur, *result
EMANCIPATE: *free, *release
EMBARRASS: *abash, *upset
EMBELLISH: *dress, *ornament
EMBEZZLE: *cheat, *steal
EMBLAZON: *adorn, *embellish
EMBLEM: *badge, *fetish, *sign
EMBRACE: *accept, include, *love
EMBROCATION: arnica, balm
EMBROIDER: *adorn, *embellish
fabric: bolting cloth
figure: etoile, tabouret
frame: hoop, ring, tabouret
hole: eyelet
machine-made: bonnaz
material: arrasene
stitch: breadstitch
thread: floss
type: appenzell
EMBRYO: *comb.:* amnio, blasto
young: blastema
EMEND: *adapt, *amend, edit
EMERGE: *appear, *issue, *occur
EMERGENCY: *crisis, exigency
EMINENT: *great, *splendid

EMISSARY: *agent, scout, *spy
EMOLLIENT: *balm, lotion, salve
EMOLUMENT: *fee, *income
EMOTE: *act, feel, ham, spout
EMOTION: *anger, *love, *passion
EMPATHY: *accord, *passion
EMPHATIC: *absolute, energetic, forcible, *important, *sure
EMPLOY: engage, *use, *work
EMPTY: *arid, *dull, *vain
headed: scatterbrained, *stupid
pref.: keno
EMPYREAN: blue, celestial, sky
EMULATE: ape, compete, *equal
ENABLE: *adapt, *allow, let
ENACT: *accomplish, authorize
ENCHANT: *allure, attract
ENCOMIUM: eulogy, *praise
ENCOMPASS: *accomplish, belt
ENCORE: *again, echo, *repeat
ENCOUNTER: *action, *attack, *contest, *fight, *meet(ing)
ENCOURAGE: *abet, *support
ENCYCLICAL: *piece, *study
END: abolish, *aim, armageddon, *arrest, *bit, boundary, butt, call off, *catastrophe, cause, check, clapper, close, coda, *complete, consequence, consummation, coup de grace, death, decline, define, demise, denouement, design, destiny, *destroy, die, doom, expire, *extreme, fate, finale, finish, fragment, goal, halt, intent, *issue, kayo, kibosh, *kill, lapse, *limit, *mark, nib, object, omega, over, *part, *pass, period, *purpose, quietus, *quit, *result, stem, *stop, stub, tail, telic, thirty, term(inal), tip, toe, upshot, wash up, wear, windup
at: *abut
comb.: acro, telo
having: acockbill, autotelic
loose: tag
-most: farthest, remotest

* Asterisk means to look up this word to find more answer words.

of the line: blank wall
of the world: gotterdammerung
on: afoul
plea: abater
remove: clip, tip
result: *product
seat hog: egotist
to end: *adjacent
upper: *acme, apex, *head, *top

ENDEARMENT: *term:* achree, acushla, agrah, alannah, aroon, aruin, asthor, ashthore, astor, avourneen, bobeleh, bonito, bubby, bubeleh, bunting, darling, dear, honey, sweetie

ENDEAVOR: *aim, *affair, *try

ENDLESS: *infinite, *universal

ENDLESSLY: *forever

ENDORSE: *abet, *acclaim, back, *join, *praise, *sign, *support

ENDOW: *award, *give

ENDUE: clothe, *dress, *supply

ENDURE: *abide, *accept, *stand

ENDURING: *permanent

ENDYMION: *mother:* calyce
son: aetolus
wife: seene

ENEMY: *devil, foe, rival

ENERGETIC: *active, *fresh

ENERGY: *force, *power, *spirit
lack: anemia, aneuria, atony, debility, inertia, neurasthenia
multiplied by time: *action
pert.: actinic
potential: edar, ergal, latency
unit: atomerg, dinamode, dyne, erg(on), energid, foot-pound, horsepower, joule, megajoule, megerg, quantum

ENERVATE: drain, sap, tire

ENFILADE: barrage, bomb, rake

ENFORCE: compel, oblige, *urge

ENGAGE: *absorb, *allure, *book, *enter, *fight, *use

ENGENDER: *form, *make, *start

ENGINE: *instrument, *machine

kind: corvy, diesel, dollbeer, gin, helper, locomotive, mallet, mogul, pusher, turbine
part: bearings, boiler, cam, carburetor, crankcase, cylinder, differential, gear, piston, stator, transmission
rotary: turbine
war: abatis, arbalest, artillery, ballista, battering ram, boar, cannon, catapult, espringal, halftrack, helepole, jeep, mangonel, missile, onager, ordnance, robinet, rocket, ribaudequin, scorpion, tank, terebra

ENGINEER: *accomplish, operator
term: arc of action

ENGLAND: albion, anglia, beretania, blighty, britain, britannia, egbert, john bull, limeyland, united kingdom, punch
pert.: anglican, britannic, british, silurian

ENGLISH: *anglo-saxon references*
abbot: aelfric
actor: arliss, burbage, donat, evans, guinness, gwenn, maude
actress: ashcroft, gwyn, neagle, terry
admiral: benbow, blake, drake, nelson, rodney, vernon
ancient: angle, brython, celt, iceni, jute, pict, scot, silure
apartment: flat
apostle: augustine, austin
apple: beefin, biffin, beaufin, coccagee, coling, costard, guarenden, rennet
apron: barmskin
architect: abercrombie, adam, bodley, scott, wren
art gallery: tate
astronomer: herschel
autopart: wind screen
badger: hawker

---

* **Asterisk means to look up this word to find more answer words.**

bailiff: reeve
ballet dancer: beriosova
bard: beowulf, scop
barilla: black ash, kelp
basket: caul, ped
battle, early: agned, badon, camlan, cat coit, celidon, dubglass, glein, guinnion
battle wager: ornest
bean: mazagan
bed: doss
bird: godwit
biologist: huxley
biscuit: bath bun, oliver
boat: coracle
bread slice: canch
buttercup: crowtoe
canal worker: navvy
capers: capuchin, seed pods
carriage: fly, growler
cascade: ladore
cassandra: adversity hume
castle site: arundel, windsor
cathedral: coventry, ely, york
cattle: devon, sussex
cattle tender: byreman
cavalry: yeomenry
channel: solent
channel island: jersey, sark
cheese: cheshire, stilton, truckle
chemist: abel, cavendish
chief: caractacus, caradoc, cassibelan, cassivelaunus, pendragon
china: bone, spode, wedgwood
chronicles: harleian
church caretaker: verger
civil wars: bishops', roses
class: form
clergyman: becket, donne, inge, latimer, neale, newman, oates, wesley
cloth: tweed
coin: ackey, angel(et), bawbee, bob, carolus, crown, farthing, fiver, florin, fourpence, groat, guinea, half crown, ha'penny, mag, marigold, meg, mite, monkey, pence, penny, plum, pound, quid, shilling, sixpence, tanner, teston, thrippence, tuppence
college: baliol, eton, harrow
comb.: anglo
comedian: chaplin, gingold
comic weekly: ally sloper
composer: arne, balfe, britten, delius, elgar, gay, gilbert, handel, leginska, neale, purcel, sullivan, williams
communist group: agapemone
conductor: barbirolli, beecham
conservative: tory
conspirator: fawkes
converter: augustine
conveyance: tram, waggon
corporal: lance jack
county division: wapentake
county hundreds: lathes, rapes
court: eyre, gemote, hustling, leet, old bailey, sake soc
crown tax: geld
daisy: avens, bennet, bruise wort, burnet, hemlock, herb bennet, saxifrage, soap wort, wild valerian
dance: anglaise, althea, bobbing joan, brawle, cebell, morris
dandy: toff
dessert: sillibub, syllabub
diarist: pepys
diplomat: bryce, bulwer, eden
dish: kidney pie, trifle
domain: manor
dramatist: beaumont, besier, betterton, coward, dryden, peele, pinero, reade, shakespeare, shaw, tobin, wilde
duck: aylesbury
economist: bagehot, gresham, keynes, ricardo
editor: addison, mee, steele
elevator: lift
elm: campestris
emblem: lion, rose
enclosure: barton, croft, hoard

* Asterisk means to look up this word to find more answer words.

entertainment: busk, ridotto
epic: beowulf
essayist: addison, beerbohm, belloc, elia, lamb, lang, raleigh, sala, steele
etcher: haden
exclamation: by george
executioner: ketch
explorer: cabot, cook, drake, hudson, ross, scott
falcon: hobby, peregrine
festival: ale
financier: gresham, rothschild
fish: allice, allis, dragonet, sewen, sewin, shad
flower: lupine, rose
food dealer: costermonger
forest: arden
fortified town: berg
franchise: soc
freeman: churl, thane, thegn
free tenant: dreng
gaiters: galligaskins
gallon: imperial
game: cricket, darts, fives, rugby, soccer
gift to bride: dos, dot, dower
gun: armstrong, bren, brown bess, enfield, snider, sten
half penny: bawbee
hamlet: dorp
hat: billycock, fantail
headland: bolerium, naze
hero: beowulf, offa
hills: clee, wolds
historian: bede, ensebius, gibbon, gildas, grote, jerome, layamon, nennius, wells
hog: essex
honor exam: tripos
horse: prad
horse dealer: coper
houseworker: char
humorist: lear
hymnist: neale, wesley
idealist: cambridge platonist
idiom: anglicism, briticism

inspector: exciseman
invader: angel, caesar, dane, hengist, horsa, norman, roman, saxon, william
inventor: bessemer, bramah
island: alderney, anglesey, ascension, farne, holy(head), ireland, lundy, man, scilly, sheppey, thanet, walney, wight
ivy: bindwood
jail: bocardo, gaol, old bailey
jurist: blackstone
king: alfred, artegal, arthur, beli, belinus, bladud, bran, brennius, brut, canute, charles, cole, edred, edward, edwin, egbert, elidure, george, gorboduc, hal, harold, henry, ine, james, john, knut, lear, ludd, nudd, offa, phillip, richard, stephen, sweyn, william
kingdom, early: deira
laborer: navvy
lake: coniston, derwent, ullswater, windermere
land proprietor: squire
law: danelaw, esnecy, soke
lawbook: fleta
lawn billiards: troco
lawyer: barrister, solicitor
legislature: parliament
liberal: whig
limestone: oolite
logician: boole
lunch: tiffin
magistrate: beak
marshes: the broads
mathematician: briggs, cayley
man: atkins, bono, britisher, briton, cockney, goddam, john bull, limey, sassenach, tommy
measure: acre, alnage, barrel, bind, bodge, bovate, carat, carucate, chain, chaldron, coomb, cran, cubit, digit, ell, fathom, firkin, float, furlong, gallon, goad, hand, hide, hobbet, hogshead, hutch, inch, jugrum, kilder-

* Asterisk means to look up this word to find more answer words.

skin, landyard, last, league, line,
manent, mile, mimim, once, ox-
gang, palm, peek, perch, pint,
pipe, pole, pottle, puncheon,
quart(er), rood, sack, skein,
span, spindle, stack, standard,
ton, trug, truss, tun, vat, wist,
yoke

midlands: black country

military cap: busby

mine wagon: rolley

missionary: asbury, boniface, win-
frid

molasses: treacle

monk: bede, baeda, boniface

monument: cromlech

mountain: cheviot, cumbrian,
pennine, scawfell, wyddva

murderer: aram

musician: *composer

naturalist: banks, darwin, seton

news agency: reuters

orator: disraeli, pitt

organist: biggs, burney

painter: bonington, burne-jones,
hogarth, opie, orpen, poynter,
romney, ryland

pamphleteer: defoe, paine, swift

parliament: commons, lords

parliament record: hansard

party: conservative, labor, labour,
liberal, tory, whig

peasant: churl, esne, serf

pert.: anglican, british

philanthropist: angell

philosopher: ayer, bacon, ben-
tham, berkeley, bradley, broad,
burke, hobbes, hume, locke, oc-
cam, russell, spencer

physicist: appleton, barkla

pirate: drake, hawkins, kidd, morgan

poet: aldington, auden, binyon,
blake, brooke, browning, butler,
byron, caedmon, carew, donne,
eliot, gray, keats, marlowe, mase-
field, pope, shelley

policeman: bobby, cop, peeler

porcelain: celadon, spode

political satire: mother goose

potherb: clary

prairie: heath, moor

printer: caxton

protection right: mund

public school: eton, harrow,
rugby, sandhurst

queen: anne, bess, bloody mary,
elizabeth, mab, victoria

race course: ascot, epsom downs

radio: wireless

ready money: prest

rebel: cade, essex, cromwell, washington, wat tyler

regiment: black watch

region: weald

resort: bath, brighton

revolution song: lillibul-lero

river: avon, boyne, cam, eden, esk,
exe, nen, ouse, tees, thames,
trent, tyne

royal officer: equerry, exon

royal house: blois, hanover, lan-
caster, plantagenet, stuart, tudor,
windsor

royal residence: buckingham palace, windsor

saint: alban, anne, george

sand dune: dene, medano

scholar: alcuin, blue coat

school: cambridge, eton, oxford

schoolboy: etonian

schoolmaster: aram

scientist: aston, connel, darwin,
fleming, haldane

sculptor: armitage, epstein

seaport: deal, dover, liverpool

sea: atlantic, english channel,
north sea, norwegian sea

serf: esne, thrall

settler: angle, jute, norman, pict,
saxon

sheep: cheviot, costwold, dishley,
lonk, wensleydale

ship money: prest

---

* Asterisk means to look up this word to find more answer words.

shoemaker: snob
shrub: heath
signal flag: blue peter
socialist: fabian
soldier: atkins, bloody-back, carabinier, redcoat, tommy
song: ben bolt
spa: bath, margate
spy: andre, cavell, major john
statesman: addington, asquith, attlee, balfour, baring, bevan, bolingbroke, cecil, chamberlain, churchill, disraeli, eden, grey, hoare, lloyd george, macdonald, macmillan, peel, pitt, simon, walsingham
stock exchange member: orchid
stole: armil, armill, armilla
streetcar: tram
surgeon: haden, hunter, lister, paget, pott
symbol: john bull, lion, rose
tavern: pub
tax: excise, geld, prest, rate
tea muffin: crumpet
teacher's fee: minerval
tenant: laet
textile: flax, hemp, jute
thicket: spinney
thrush: mavis
title: baron(et), count, dame, duke, earl, king, knight, lady, lord, marquess, marquis, peer, prince, queen, viscount
tourist: tripper
traveler: borrow, cook, ligon
treasury note: bradbury
truck: lorry
tutor: don
typographer: baskerville
uplands: downs
valley: coomb, coquet, dean, dene, eden, tees, tyne
vessel, coal: cat
veterans organization: legion
violin maker: hill
wager of battle: ornest

walnut: akhrot, bannut
ware: albert, albertine, albion
weight: keel, mast, stone, tod
weight system: avoirdupois
west point: rma, sandhurst
woolen cloth: shoddy
writer: allen, amis, angell, arlen, austen, bacon, baxter, beaton, belloc, beddoes, blackmore, bronte, defoe, eliot, fox, gray, hardy, hente, huxley, lamb, landor, monumetensis, moore, more, paget, reade, shakespeare, sterne, shaw, tennent, waugh, wells, wren
ENGRAVING: carving, *plan*, print, stamp
chemical: copperas, vitriol
pert.: glyphic, glyptic
stone: cameo, intaglio
tool: burin, steel rod, stylet
wood: xylograph
ENIGMA: cryptic, *puzzle*, riddle
ENJOY: delight, *possess*, *use*
ENLIGHTENMENT: aufklarung, bodai, bodhi, knowledge, prajna
ENNEAD: *egyptian god(dess)*
ENOCH: *father:* cain, jared
son: irad, methuselah
ENORMOUS: *big*, *bad*, *evil*
ENOS: *father:* seth
grandparents: adam and eve
son: cainan
uncle: abel, cain
ENOUGH: adequate, *plenty*
said: done, silence
ENRAGE: *anger*, ire, irk, *stir*
ENSIGN: *flag*, officer, *symbol*
bearer: oriflamme
ENTENTE: *accord*, *compact*
ENTER: *admit*, *begin*, blow in, board, book, bore, *break in*, breeze in, burst in, bust in, card, catalog, come in, compose, creep, drop in, *eat*, *edge*, embark, enlist, enroll, file, get in, go in, hop in, incur, insert, invade, *join*,

* Asterisk means to look up this word to find more answer words.

jump in, list, *pass (in)*, penetrate, *pierce*, pop in, *press*, *push*, put in(to), *record*, slip in, squeeze, *start*, step in, trespass, *venture*, worm
into: compose, participate
one's mind: occur to
upon: *approach*
ENTERPRISE: *action*, *venture*
pert.: capitalistic
ENTERTAIN: *accommodate*, *amuse*, *delight*, *please*
ENTERTAINER: *actor*, dancer, geisha, hetaera, *prostitute*
ENTERTAINMENT: *affair*, *party*, *show*
ENTHUSIASM: ardor, estro, *fire*, *interest*, mania, *spirit*, zest
ENTHUSIAST: *active*, *addict*, *advocate*, aficionado, amateur, angel, apostle, *ascetic*, backer, bear, bigot, booster, buff, bug, crank, devotee, dilettante, disciple, dynamo, energumen, exponent, faddist, fan, fanatic, fancier, follower, highflier, hobbyist, hound, ist, ite, nik, nut, patron, rhapsodist, rooter, supporter, visionary, votary, zealot
ENTICE: *allure*, bait, seduce
ENTIRE: *all*, sound, *universal*
comb.: al, all
ENTRANCE: *amuse*, *opening*, *start*, *way*
ENTREAT: *ask*, *beg*, *desire*
ENVELOPE: *cover*, *hide*, *dress*
fruit: bur, burr
nebulous: chevelure, coma
ENVIRONMENT: *district*, *sphere*
comb.: eco
science: ecology
ENVISAGE, ENVISION: face, *see*
ENVY: *desire*, jealousy, spite
ENYO: *son:* ares

ENZU: *sin*
ENZYME: amidase, aminopeptidase, arginase, ase, carbohydrase, esterase, ficin, glutaminase, insulase, kinase, laccase, lotase, maltase, mutase, olease, papain, pepsin, rennin, saccharase, trypsin, zymase
leather-making: tannase
opposed to: azym
pineapple: bromelin
suff.: ase
EON: *age*, cycle, olam, period
EOS: *consort:* ares, astraeus, atlas, cephalus, cleitus, orion, procris, tithonus
father: hyperion
mother: euryphaessa, theia
son: boreas, emathion, eurus, four winds, hesperus, memnon, notus, phaeton, phosphorus, zephyrus
EPEAN: *chief:* amphimachus
EPHAH: *husband:* caleb
1/10th: omer
ten: homer
EPHEMERAL: *brief*, evanescent, *quick*, *short*, volatile
EPHESUS: *deity:* diana
EPHIALTES: *slayer:* apollo
EPHLAL: *son:* obed
EPHRAIM: *grandson:* eran
son: beriah, elead, ezer, rephah, shuthelah
EPIC: aeneid, beowulf, cid, edda, eneid, epopee, epyllion, grand, *great*, heroic, homeric, iliad, kalevala, mahabharata, narrative, noble, odyssey, poem, ramayana, saga, *story*
EPICURE: apician, authority, bon vivant, connoisseur, friand, glutton, gourmand, gourmet, hedonist, luxurious, sybarite
EPIGRAM: *adage*, *joke*, poem
EPIMETHEUS: *daughter:* pyrrha
wife: pandora
EPITHET: *curse*, *name*, *oath*

* Asterisk means to look up this word to find more answer words.

EPITOME: *brief, digest, precis

EPOCH: *age, *eon, series, time

EPONYMOUS: ancestor: eber

EQUAL: all one, alike, amount, call, come to, compeer, drawn, even, free, fifty-fifty, iso, level with, like, mat, match, measure, *meet, par(allel), peer, pari, quits, pro rata, rival, run abreast, same, *tie
  angled figure: isogon
  comb.: iso, equi, pari
  distribution: balance
  quantity: ana, identical
  sides: isosceles
  to: *able, *adequate, *ready

EQUILIBRIUM: *aplomb, sanity
  lack: astasia

EQUIP: *accomplish, *dress, fit, gear, *prepare, *supply

EQUITABLE: *fair, *right, *wise

EQUIVOCATE: fib, hedge, *lie

ER: son: elmadam

ERA: *age, *eon, period, time

ERADICATE, ERASE: *abolish, *end, extirpate, *kill, *remove

ERATO: son: thamyris

EREBUS: brother: nox, nyx
  father: chaos
  odora: black witch
  offspring: aether, day, chaos, charon, erebus
  sister: night, nox

ERECTHEID: *theseus

ERECT: *address, *build, *make, ramrod, *straight, upright

EREMITE: *ascetic, *monk

EREWHON: *paradise, *utopia

ERGINUS: son: agamedes

ERICA: besom, broom, heath

ERIDU: god: ea, hea

ERIN: eire, hibernia, *ireland

ERINYES: *furies

ERIS: brother: eres
  daughter: ate
  missile: apple

ERITREA: *ethiopia

ERODE: *eat, decay, *decline

EROS: amor, *cupid, *love
  brother: anteros
  parents: ares, erebus, hermes, ilithyia, night, zeus
  opponent: anteros

ERR: blow, boot, deviate, diverge, go off, lapse, lose, *mess, miscalculate, mistake, offend, *sin, slip, stray, stumble, trespass, *wrong

ERROR: albardine, blunder, blooper, bobble, bone, booboo, boot, brodie, bulba, bumble, bungle, clanger, *evil, fallacy, falsity, *flaw, gaffe, heresy, illusion, indiscretion, lapse, miscue, *mess, mistake, *sin, smear, trip, typo, wogh, *wrong

ERSATZ: *artificial, *substitute

ERSE: *celt, gaelic, *irish

ERUDITE: *sage, *smart, *wise

ERUPT: burst, eject, eruct

ERYTHRA THALASSA: red sea

ESAU: brother: jacob
  country: edom
  descendant: edomite
  father-in-law: elon
  grandson: amalek, omar
  home: edom, seir
  parent: isaac, rebecca, rebekah
  son: eliphaz, jaalam, jeush, korah, reuel
  wife: adah, aholibamah, anah, bashemath, judith

ESAY: *isaiah

ESCAPADE: caprice, dido, prank

ESCAPE: abscond, *avoid, bail out, bilk, blow, *break, close call, come-off, cut loose, decamp, elope, elude, evade, evaporate, flee, flight, fly, *free, get away, *issue, jailbreak, jump, lam, leak, loophole, ooze, outlet, *quit, *release, *retreat, *run, shun, skip, slip, squeek, squeeze, take refuge, throw off

ESCHEW: *abstain, *avoid, shun

* Asterisk means to look up this word to find more answer words.

ESCORT: *company, *spark, *staff

ESDRAS: apocrypha
angel: uriel

ESKIMO: *asiatic:* innuit, yuit
bird: curlew, fute
boat: baidar(ka), bidar, kayak, oomiak, umiak
boot: kamik
coat: netcha, parka, temiak
descent: turanian
dish: muk tuk, reindeer stew, seal liver
dog: husky, malemute
game: amazualat
god: ataksak, aumanil, crepitus
goddess: sedna, tootega
hood: amowt
house: barrabora, igloo, iglu, topek, tupek, tupik
knife: ulu
male attire, pert.: labret
medicine man: angakok, angekut
memorial post: xat
mountain: nunatak
pantheon: innua
settlement: etah
sledge: komatik
spirit: torngak, torngarsak
tribe: aleut, atka, unalaska

ESOTERIC: *abstruse, *secret
doctrine: cabala
knowledge: gnosis
one: epopt
reality: mysticism

E S P: clairvoyance, intuition

ESPIEGLERIE: *deception, mischief

ESPOUSE: *adopt, *advocate

ESPRIT: morale, *spirit, wit
fort: freethinker

ESROM: *son:* aram

ESSAY: *piece, *test, *try

ESSENCE: *form, *foundation
of life: archeus
of the universe: brahma
pert.: basic

ESSENTIAL: *great, *important
being: bhutatatha, suchness
oil: anemonol, nerol

ESTABLISH: accustom, *acquire, authorize, base, *bring out, *build, constitute, create, decree, erect, fix, *form, *foundation, ground, install, institute, *make, ordain, organize, originate, pitch, plant, *prove, put up, root, *secure, *settle, *set, *start

ESTABLISHMENT: city hall, ins, *power, *society, *state

ESTATE: assets, *class, *rank
fourth: press, newspapers
manager: administrator, executor, guardian, steward
owner: hacendero
partition: boedelscheiding
pert.: demesne, press
purchaser: acquereur
rent deduction: reprise
three: clergy, commons, nobles
to hold: tenancy

ESTEEM: *account, *admire, *bless, *glory, *love, *value

ESTHER: hadassah, vashti
cousin: mardochaeus, mordecai
eunuch: hachrathaeus
father: aminadab
festival: purim
foster father: *cousin (above)
husband: ahasuerus, artaxerxes

ESTHETIC: *aesthetic, particular

ESTIMABLE: *good, *great

ESTIMATE: *add, *adjudge, *aim, *analyze, audit, bid, *value

ESTONIA: *city:* reval, tallinn
coin: estmark, kroon, sent
island: dago, muhu, oesel, saare, sarema
measure: elle, faden, kulimet, liin, lofstelle, pang, sagene, sund, tool, toop, verchok
weight: lood, nael, puud

ETAM: *son:* ezer, idbash, ishma, jezreel, penuel

---

* Asterisk means to look up this word to find more answer words.

ETERNAL: *permanent
city: rome
home: *paradise
sleep: death
verities: *truth
ETERNITY: *age, *paradise
ETHAN: son: azariah
ETHICAL: *good, kosher, moral
ETHIOPIA: abyssinia, afrogaea,
   eritrea, kafa, kaffa, seba
ancient capital: meroe
ape: gelada
banana: ensete
battleground: adowa
bible version: geez
bishop: abuna
capital: addis ababa, aksum, as-
   mara, meroe
catholic: cush, geez, uniate
cattle: sanga
cereal: teff
city: ankober, antalo, assab,
   axum, gambela, gondar, harrar
coin: amole, ashrafi, besa, harf,
   kharaf, levant, maria theresa,
   piaster, talari
dialect: geez, giz, grese, tigre
district: amhara, bana, harer,
   shoa, tigre
game: shum-shir
hamite: afar, blemmyes, bogo
ibex: saol, walie
jews: emigrants, falashas
king: memnon, merops, negus,
   ras, tirhakah, zerah
lake: dembel, stefanie, tana,
   tanna, tzana, zeway
language: afar, agow, amharic,
   galla, geez, harari, saho
lyre: kissar
measure: cabaho, cubi, derah, en-
   telam, farsakh, farsang, ghebeta,
   kuba, messe, sinjer
mountain: ras dashan
native: assamite, beja, doko, hamite, harari, kala, negro
oxen: galla, sanga, sangu

plant: teff
princess: aida, andromeda
province: arusi, bagemder, gama-
   gofa, gojam, harage, ilubabor,
   jima, shawa, wallo
pygmy: doko
queen: candace, kandake
river: abbai, albai, baro, gash
   gash, gibe, giubo, juba, mareb,
   mofer, rahad, tacazze
title: abuna, negus, ras
torah: tetel
tree: cusso, koho, koso
tribe: afar, agows, donakus, galas,
   somalis, shoa, tigres
violin: masinko
weight: alada, artal, farasula,
   kasm, mocha, mutagalla, natr,
   pek, rotl, wakea, wogiet
ETIQUETTE: ceremony, custom,
   decorum, good form, manners
breach of: solecism
required by: de rigueur
ETON: townsman: oppidan
ETOURDERIE: *error
ETRUSCAN: chieftain: astur
deity: lar, menfra, tinia, uni
king: lars porsena
pottery: bucchero
wine god: fufluns
EUCALYPTUS: gum: kino
leaf deposit: cerf
secretion: laap, larp, lerp
tree: bloodwood, carbeen, mallee,
   yate
EUCHARIST: box: pix, pyx
cloth: fano(n), fanum
container: artophorion
cup: calix, chalice
elements: bread, host, loaf, wafer,
   wine
plate: paten, patina
spoon: labis
vessel: ama, amula, ciborium
wafer: host
wine: krama

* Asterisk means to look up this word to find more answer words.

EUCLID: *origin:* megara
 proposition: asses' bridge
EUMENIDES: **furies*
EUNICE: *son:* timothy
EUNUCH: *bible:* bukhayt, kafur
 one of seven: bazatha, biztha
 pert.: spadonic
EUPHORIA: fog, haze, **joy*
 didyma: alupag
EURASIAN: *grass:* arrhenatherum
 herb: berteroa, betonica, buphthalmum, speedwell, veronica
 plant: parelle
 range: urals
 region: tatary
 shrub: lonicera, honeysuckle
EUROPA: *father:* agenor, phoenix
 husband: asterius
 lover: zeus
 mother: telephassa
 son: minos, rhadamanthys, sarpedon
EUROPEAN: *annual:* snod
 antelope: chamois
 ape: baboon
 arum: bobby and joan, cuckoopint
 ash: sorb
 aspen: black poplar
 badger: brock
 barracuda: spet
 bass: brasse
 bat: noctule, sertine
 bellflower: rampion
 berry tree: arbutus
 birthwort: clematite
 bittern: bog bull, bog bumper
 blackbird: amsel, merle, ousel
 boar: aper, sus
 boxing: savate
 broadcloth: suclat
 buckthorn: alatern(us)
 buffalo: aurochs, bison
 bulrush: akaakai
 bunting: ortolan
 burbot: lote
 canary: serin, tarin
 cavalryman: hussar, uhlan

cherry: gean
clover: alsike, trifolium
coal basin: saar
columbine: aquilegia
dance: kolo, polka, tarantella
deer: fallow
dormouse: loir
duck: bar goose, sheldrake
elder: bour tree, danewort
elk: alces
falcon: kestrel, merlin, saker
finch: serin, tarln, terin
fish: allice, allis, alose, barbel, barrel, barse, boces, brasse, bream,
 chad, doree, lavaret, lyrie, maigre, marena, picarel, rudd, sprat
flatfish: bret, brill, turbot
food fish: atherine, silverside
flycatcher: bee bird, kingbird
fruit: azarole
germander: bastard hyssop
grape: muscat
grass: anthoxanthum, poa
ground squirrel: suslik
gulf: aegina, riga
gull: mew, pewee, pewit
hawk: falcon, faller, glede, kestrel,
 puttock
herb: alfilaria, anthriscus, apium,
 astrantia, atropa, baby's-breath,
 base horehound, bassia, bear's-
 foot, black sanicle, borage, cat-
 bed, dill, elecampane, eryngo,
 gosmore, henbane, iva, lovage,
 mandrake, meum, pin grass,
 spicknel, tarragon, yarrow
holly: acebo, aunt mary's tree
honeysuckle: gold and silver
hyssop: mint
hundredweight: zentner
hunting dog: griffon
industrial region: ruhr, saar
invaders: alani, arabs, huns, mon-
 gols, turks
iris: orris
juniper: cade
kite: gled(e)

* **Asterisk means to look up this word to find more answer words.**

lake: enare, geneva, lagoda
larkspur: stavesacre
laurel: bay, sweet bay
lavender: aspic
lime: teil
madder: garance
maple: bird's-tongue
mint: ballata, bastard dittany, clare, clarry, hyssop, iva
mountain: alps, apennines
oak: durmast, holm
ox: urus
owl: cue
peninsula: balkan, iberian, italian, scandinavian
perch: barse
plain: steppe
plant: alkanet, alyssum, azarole, bevy, borage, burstwort, capon's-tail, eelware, elderwort, escobilla, lavender, orpine, sneezewort, ulex, valeriana
plover: dotterel
polecat: ferret, fitchet
porgy: besugo, pargo
rabbit: coney, cony
ragwort: cankerweed, senecio
rail: bilcock, ortolan, runner
redstart: brantail
resort: baden, ems, riviera
roach: braise, sea bream
rodent: erd, hamster
sea: adriatic, aegean, aral, azov, baltic, mediterranean
sea bream: braise, pagrus
sedge: chufa
shad: allice, alosa, alose
shark: acrodus, tope
shrew: erd
shrub: alder, azarole, bastard quince, cade, caper, cistus, furze, olea, ruta, savin, sorb
siskin: aberdevire, barleybird, nightingale, wagtail, wryneck
squirrel: polatouche, sisel, souslik, suslik
swallow: martlet

swift: black martin
thrush: ousel, throstle
tree: medlar, sorb, terebrinth
vetchlike herb: axseed
water crowfoot: eelware
weasel: stote, whitrack
weed: alfilaria, black top
whortleberry: black heart
wheat: einkorn, emmer, whizen
wild boar: aper
willow: sallow
willow warbler: bank jug
wood anemone: bow bells
wood sage: ambrose, teucrium
wool: calamanco
worm: sao
wrasse: ballan
wryneck: barleybird, **siskin*
EURYBIA: *husband:* creus, crius
  offspring: astraeus, pallas, perses
EURYDICE: *husband:* agriope
EURYSTHEUS: *daughter:* admete
EURYTUS: *daughter:* iole
EUTERPE: *lover:* strymon
  son: rhesus
EVADE: **avoid, *cheat, *escape*
EVADNE: *consort:* apollo, cepaneus, poseidon
  father: iphis, pitane
  guardian: aepytus
  son: iamus
EVE: *serpent's tree:* amanita
EVENING: *dress:* formal
  party: soiree
  pert.: crepuscular, vesper
  primrose: afterglow, anogra
  star: hesper, mercury, moon, venus
EVENT: **act, *action, *affair, *meeting, *particular, *result*
  blessed: birth
  first: opener, premiere
  ghostly: seance
  happy: godsend, hit, marriage
  heroic: epic, saga
EVERGREEN: **shrub, *tree*
EVERLASTING: **permanent*

* Asterisk means to look up this word to find more answer words.

EVICT: *dismiss, expel, sack

EVIDENCE: clew, *show, *token

EVIL: abominable, atrocious, *bad, bale, bane, base, black, calamity, cancer, corrupt, dark, detriment, enormous, *error, execrable, foul, harm, havoc, heinous, *hurt, ill, inauspicious, infamous, *low, malign, monstrous, naughty, nefarious, *rank, *rotten, *sick, *sin, *ugly, *wrong

averter: *fetish, *symbol
child: deev, imp, nis, nixie
comb.: mal, mis
day: hard times
deity: girru, loki, sobk, varuna
disposition: the old adam
doer: *cheat, *criminal, felon
eye: malevolence, *spell
father of: *devil, satan
omen: knell, *sign
personification: apepi, belial
spirit: *demon, *devil, oki

EVINCE: *argue, *display, *show

EVOKE: bring, elicit, prompt

EVOLVE: create, develop, *make

EXACERBATE: *aggravate, *agitate

EXACT: *absolute, *ask, *call, *force, *particular, *severe

EXAGGERATE: blow up, *brag

EXALT: *advance, *bless, *praise

EXAMINE: *analyze, *study, *test

EXAMPLE: case, ideal, *model

EXASPERATE: *agitate, *anger

EXCEL: *beat, *shine, *top

EXCESS: nimiety, plus, *surfeit

EXCHANGE: *bargain, *barter, *store, *substitute, *trade
rate: agio, batta

EXCISE: *eradicate, tax, tithe

EXCITE: *agitate, *alarm, *anger, *fire, *interest, *start, *stir

EXCITED: *ardent, *eager, *wild

EXCLUDE: *banish, blackball

EXCLUSIVE: elite, *special, sole

EXCORIATE: *abuse, *attack

EXCUSE: *acquit, *free, *release

EXECRABLE: *bad, *evil, vile

EXECRATE: damn, *hate, *smear

EXECUTE: *accomplish, *force, *kill, *make, *rule, *sign

EXEGETE: *advisor, *authority

EXEMPLARY: banner, blue-chip

EXEMPT: *excuse, immune, relieve

EXERCISE: *action, *train, *use
book: cahier
skill: *excel
system: aerobics

EXERT: *act, *try, *use, *work

EXERTION: *action, *trouble

EXHAUST: *eat, spend, *use

EXHIBIT: *act, *display, *show

EXHILARATE: *amuse, elate, *fire

EXHORT: preach, *urge, warn

EXHORTATION: *son:* barnabas

EXIGENCY: *crisis, *speed, *urge

EXIGUOUS: meager, *small

EXIST: *live, *occur, *stand

EXISTENCE: *self-originated:* aseity

EXIT: death, *end, *escape

EXODUS: *exit, flight, hegira

EXONERATE: *acquit, *free

EXORBITANT: *great, *high, outre

EXORCISM: charm, *fetish, *spell

EXOTIC: alien, foreign, peregrine

EXPAND: *add, *amplify, *spread

EXPATIATE: *amplify, rant, *tell

EXPECT: *accept, *aim, *think

EXPECTANT: *ardent, *eager

EXPEDIENT: *appropriate, *good, *instrument, stopgap, *wise

EXPEDITE: *ease, send, *speed

EXPEL: *banish, *dismiss

EXPERIENCE: *address, *event, *skill, *test, *trial, *try

EXPERIMENT: *test, *trial, *try

* Asterisk means to look up this word to find more answer words.

EXPERT: *ace, bear, *smart, whiz
 group: brain trust, board, cabinet, panel, seminar
EXPIRE: die, *end, *fall
EXPLAIN: *analyze, *talk, *tell
EXPLETIVE: curse, *oath, voila
EXPLICATE: amplify, *analyze
EXPLICIT: clear, *open, specific
EXPLODE: *anger, *blast, *spread
EXPLOIT: *act, *use, *venture
EXPLORE: *examine, scout, seek
EXPLOSIVE: device: cap, detonator, initiator, petard
 coal mine: bobbinite
 high: cordite, powder, tnt
 igniter: fuse
 isometric: thorite
 lightning-produced: fulgurite
 picric acid: lyddite
 power: brissance
 sound: bang, bark, boom, chug, oomph, pluff, vroom
EXPONENT: *devotee, *enthusiast
EXPOSE: *air, *betray, *open
EXPOSITION: *display, *piece, market, pageant, *show
EXPOUND: *analyze, *state, *tell
EXPRESS: *accurate, *mean, *tell
 appreciation: thank
 approval: applaud, *praise
 excitedly: bubble, gush
 man: carrier, messenger
 pity: bemoan
 regret: apologize
 train: cannonball
 volubly: blatter, chat, *gossip
 way: freeway, *road, thoroughfare
EXPRESSION: *symbol, *token
 algebraic: binomial
 approval: clap, ovation, smile
 assent: placet
 contempt: bah, fie, geck, hiss, pshaw, sneer
 disapproval: fie

 elegant: atticism
 facial: grimace, grin, laugh, scowl, smile
 incredulity: indeed
 opinion: vote
 pet: cant, catchword, slogan
 sorrow: alas, ay, lamentation
 weariness: sigh
EXPURGATE: bowdlerize, censor
EXQUISITE: *beautiful, *fine, *perfect, *pure, *special
EXTEMPORANEOUS: ad-lib, impromptu, spontaneous
EXTEND: *add, *amplify, *spread
 credit: advance, carry, finance
EXTENSIVE: *big, *broad, *great
EXTENT: area, *quantity, *range
EXTERIOR: alien, extrinsic, out
 toward: ectad
EXTERMINATE, EXTINGUISH, EXTIRPATE: *destroy, *erase, *kill, *remove, *stop
EXTOL: *bless, *praise
EXTORT: blackmail, *steal
EXTRA: additional, bonus, more, occasional, odd, over, plus, premium, *special, *substitute
EXTRACT: *ask, *draw, elicit
EXTRADITE: *banish, exile
EXTRANEOUS: alien, exotic
EXTRAORDINARY: *great, *special, *unique
EXTRAVAGANCE: overage, *plenty, *surfeit
EXTRAVAGANT: *wanton, *weird, *wild
EXTREME: all-fired, black, blue, butt, dire, drastic, *end, excess, exorbitant, fanatic, far out, *great, *last, outrageous, radical, *severe, *supreme, *top, ultra, *violent
 comb.: arch, acro
EXTREMITY: *end, *need, limb
EXTRICATE: *free, *save, release
EXUBERANCE: *enthusiasm, *plenty, *spirit

* Asterisk means to look up this word to find more answer words.

EXUDE: bleed, discharge, flow
EXULT: boast, elate, *joy
EYE: blinker, circle, detective, glimpse, goggle, inspect, lamp, *look, ogle, *opening, optic, orb, outlook, *see, *spy, stare
agate: aleppo stone
angle: canthus
askance: fear
ball: glene, globe, orb
ball covering: cornea
black: hypopyon, mouse, shiner
brow: bree, supercilium
cast: strabismus
cavity: orbit
color: daw
colored portion: iris
comb.: opto, video
corner: canthus
cosmetic: kohl, kuhl, mascara
defect or disease: amaurosis, amblyopia, aniridia, anopia, anopsia, astigmatism, axanthopsia, cataract, conjunctivitis, glaucoma, gutta serena, iritis, myopia pin and web, pinkeye, strabismus, trachoma, uveitis
dropper: pipette
enlargement: buphthalmia
examiner: ophthalmoscope, otoscope
-filling: *beautiful
film: nebula
flap: blinder, lid, patch, visor
glass: lens, lorgnette, lorgnon, monocle, nippers, pince-nez, spectacles
inner coat: retina
hollow: orbit, socket
lashes: blinkers, brees, brows, cilia, eyewinkers, winkers
-less: blind
-lessness: anophthalmia
-let: agraffe, circlet, grommet
-lid: bree
-lid comb.: blephar(o), canth(o)
-lid darkener: kohl, ourma

-lid droop: ptosis
-lid hair: brills
-lid incision: tarsotomy
-lid-like: ocellated
-lid pert.: palpebral
loss: madarosis
magic: radar
measurer: campimeter
membrane: conjunctiva, retina
of a storm: bull's-eye
of the master: supervision
opener: *drink, surprise
opening: apocalyptic(al)
parasite: loa
part: areola, cornea, disc, iris, pupil, retina, sclera, strale, uvea
pert.: irian, ocellated
protection or shade: *flap
shot: range, reach
sight: vision
sore: blemish, defect, sight
symbol: uta
to eye: unanimous
wash: alibi, *nonsense, rubbish
water: boric acid, liquor
witness: spectator
EYELETEER: bodkin, stiletto
EYOT: ait, ile, island
EYRA: jaguarundi, wildcat
EZEKIAL: father: buzi, jeremiah
four beasts: aniel, azriel, haniel, kafziel
EZEKIAS: son: manasses
EZER: son: bilhan, jakan, zavan
EZERIAS: son: saraeas
EZIAS: son: amariah, amarias
EZRA: salathiel
dragons: carmanians
field: ardat
son: epher, jalon, jether, mered
woman mourner: zion
writer: asiel, dibri, ethan, seraiah, shelemiah

FABIAN: cautious, shaw
policy: delay, inertia

* Asterisk means to look up this word to find more answer words.

FABLE: *lie, *story, tale, yarn
collection: bestiary
man: aesop, andersen, bilpai, grimm, parabolist, pilpay
FABRIC: *cloth references
canvas-like: wigan
coarse: baize, baline, bocking, buffin, bure, burlap, caddis, crash, denim, duck, gunny, linsey, putto, ratine
corded: pique, rep(p)
cotton: bafta, baline, bluet, bourette, buckram, burrah, cambaye, cangan, cantoon, canvas, denim, doria, galatea, hickory, humhum, jaconet, jean, khaki, lawn, leno, lisle, madras, manta, mull, nankeen, percale, scrim, silesia, surat, susi, wigan, vichy
cotton and worsted: paramatta
cotton knit: balbriggan
cotton, light: jaconet, leno, organza, silka line
cotton mixture: bombasine, delaine, grusaille, mashru, zanella
cotton print: calico, cretonne
cotton, silk touched: agabanee
cotton twilled: denim, sallco, sallo, fustian, silesia
crinkled: crape, crepe
curtain: leno, moreen, net, scrim, silesia, velvet
damask-like: caffoy, cafoy
dealer: draper, mercer
defect: scob
design: pencil stripe
drape: cretonne
figured: damask, moreen, paisley
fine: byssus
finisher: beetle
flag: buntine, bunting
gauze-like: barege
glazed: cire
heavy: brocade, canvas, denim
knapped: ras
knitted: barre, tricot
light: etamine

linen: barras, bewpers, bocasine, brin, buckram, carde, crash, crea, dowlas, drabbet, ecru, huckaback, lawn, scrim, sinelon, taffeta
lustrous: poplin, sateen
medieval: acca, samite
metallic: lame
mourning: alma
net: maline, tulle
nubby: ratine, rep
old: ciclatoun
open: mesh
ornamental: lame
printed: batik, battik, calico, challis, percale
remnants: lint, mung
rib: wale
ribbed: cord, pique, rep, twill
sheer: gauze, lawn, voile
silk: alamode, alma, armure, barathea, blatta, bourette, caffa, camaca, canton, cendal, charmeuse, chiffon, china, crepe, faille, foulard, gimp, gros, ikat, levantine, mantua, marabou, matelasse, moff, moire, ninon, pang, patola, pekin, pongee, rumal, samite, sarcenet, sarsnet, satin, sendal, soie, surah, tabby, taffeta, tash, tiraz, tsatlee, tulle, tussah, tusser, tussore
silk mixture: acca, balda, baldachin, bombazine, brocatelle, challie, crepon, eolienne, farandine, gloria, grogram, kin, mashru
silk-ribbed: epingle, faille, marocain, rep(p)
silk yarn: schappe
stiff: wigan
straw: mat(ting)
striped: aba, doria, galatea, madras, susi
suiting: acrilan, dacron
synthetic: acetate, dacron, nylon, orlon, rayon, satinet

* Asterisk means to look up this word to find more answer words.

textile: delaine, etamine, moire, rep(p)
texture: woof
thick: drab, gros
thin: gauze, gossamer, grenadine, tarlatan, toile
towel: huck, terry
twilled: alma, bombazine, coburg, corduroy, gabardine, kerseymere, levantine, messaline, rep, sallo(o), serge, shalloon, surah, tricotine, whipcord
unbleached: beige
uncolored: blunk
upholstery: brocatel, frieze, rep(p), tabaret
velvet-like: duvetine, panne, plush, velure, velveteen
voile-like: etamine
waste material: lint, mungo
watered silk: moire
water-proof: burberry, loden
white: coteline
wool: afghan, albatross, alpaca, angora, armure, baize, baline, balzarine, barragan, batiste, bearskin, beaver, beige, bissonata, bocking, bolivia, bombazet(te), broadcloth, buckskin, buffin, bunting, burnet, casha, cashmere, cassimere, cataloon, cotta, debeige, delaine, djersa, doeskin, dreadnaught, droguet, duffel, duroy, estamin, etamine, fearnought, felt, flannel, frieze, frisado, frisca, frizado, gabardine, grenadine, harrateen, hauberget, hernani, hodden, kelt, kersey, loden, melton, merino, mohair, montagnac, moreen, prunella, ratine, ratteen, rattinet, sarcilis, satara, serge, stammel, tabinet, tamin(e), tamis, tartan, tricot, tweed, vicuna, wildbore, witney, yerga, zibellin
wool mix: grisaille, zanella
wool-ribbed: marocain, repp

worsted: balzarine, etamine
woven: blanket, broadcloth, broigne, damasse, lame, pique, sarsanet, textile, tissue, tricot, tweed, twill
FABRICATE: **lie,* **make,* mint
FABRICATION: **art,* **deception*
FABULOUS: **artificial,* legendary
FACE: *artery:* maxillary
card: cavalier, figure, king, konig, paintskin, picture, redskin, roi, royal, tete
cardless hand: beggar, carte blanche, yarborough
covering: mask, veil, yashmak
cream: balm
defect: harelip
down: outstare, prone, resist
eastward: orientate
guard: beaver, mask
-less card: spot, whiteskin
-lessness: aprosopia
-making: gurning
masonry, with: revet
ornament: cosmetic, jewel, patch
paint: fard, parget, rouge
part: brow, cheek, chin, eye, jaw, lid, lip, nose
the music: brave, **suffer*
to face: openly, vis a vis
12-planed: dodecahedral
upon: overlook
wall: revetment
white-streaked: brock-faced
FACER: **drink,* **puzzle,* tankard
FACETIOUS: **funny,* waggish
FACILE: apt, easy, **quick*
FACILITATE: **accommodate*
FACT: *collection:* analecta
suff.: ance, ancy, ence
FACTOR: **agent,* **part,* **thing*
FAD: fancy, **style,* vogue
FAERIE QUEEN: *author:* spenser
character: acrasis, alma, amoret, ate, britomartis, calidore, gloriana, guyon, una

* Asterisk means to look up this word to find more answer words.

FAFNIR: *brother:* regin
slayer: siegfried, sigurd
FAIL: **blow, *break,* bust, collapse, conk, crap out, crash, **deceive,* decline, defect, desert, die, droop, dwindle, **err,* explode, fade, fan, fizzle, flop, freak out, flunk, fold, founder, lose, miscarry, misfire, neglect, **pass,* pine, renege, sicken, sink, stall, strike, zap out
FAINT: **obscure, *vague, *weak*
comb.: ambly
heart: cold feet, fear
hearted: **afraid*
FAIR: affair, balmy, **beautiful,* becoming, braw, calm, comely, equal, even, **fine, *good,* just, kermis, kosher, market, mediocre, **open,* pastel, **right,* shapely, **show,* soso, sunny
ball: base hit, hit
-complexioned: blond(e)
field: opportunity
game: butt, dupe, victim
lady: belle dame
-lead: wapp
maid of perth: catherine glover
mindedness: equity
penitent: rowe
shake: good chance, shot
-spoken: bland, **soft,* soothing
trade: commerce, smuggling
weather: good times
winds: formal
words: suavity
FAIRY: **dwarf, *spirit*
abode: shee, sidhe
chief: puck
fort: lis, liss
ghost: sprite
king: oberon
land: eden, **paradise, *utopia*
-like: elfin, sylphish
-lore: mythology
martin: bottle swallow
queen: argante, mab, morgaine le

fay, titania, una
shoemaker: leprechaun
spirit of death: banshee
tale: allegory, fabrication, fiction, **lie,* narrative
tricky: puck
FAITH: **doctrine, *trust*
article: credenda, tenet
deity: clotho, sanctus, set
healing: christian science
pert.: pistic
steadfast: conviction
FAITOUR: **cheat, *imposter*
FAKE: **cheat, *deceive, *false*
article: schlag, shlock
comb.: pseud(o)
up: fabricate, **lie*
FAKIR: **ascetic, *monk,* yogi
FALCON: lanner, raptores
-headed god: ment(u)
-like: accipital, raptorial
male: tercel
small: besra, merlin
term: bewit, hood, jess, seel
young: eyas
FALL: autumn, bolt, **break,* calve, cascade, cataract, cave in, crumble, death, **defeat, *decline,* descend, dive, drop, expire, **fail,* flop, hang, lose, **occur,* rain, **ruin, *sin(k),* stumble, topple
all over oneself: hurry
apart: deteriorate
at one's feet: fawn, salaam
back: **follow,* lag, **retreat*
before: bow, salaam
behind: **follow,* lag, lose
down: **die, *err, *fail*
fish: chub
flat: **err, *fail*
for: bite at, **love*
from grace: **err, *sin*
headlong: come a cropper
in: **accept, *gather, *yield*
in price: depreciate
in with: **accept,* concur, **meet*
into: find, incur, undertake

off: lose, relapse, slump
of the cards: chance
on: *attack, *meet
out: *argue, radioactivity
short: *fail, *need, *stop
through: collapse, *fail
to: *fight, *meet, *start
to pieces: *break, disintegrate
upon: ambush, *attack, surprise
FALSE: absurd, *artificial, *bad, crooked, fake, feigned, erroneous, hypocritical, luke, mendacious, perfidious, pious sham, spurious, *superficial, *wrong
alarm: failure, sham, wolf
colors: *disguise
comb.: pseudo
doctrine: heresy
friend: iago, judas, traitor
front: *deception, *disguise
goat's-beard: astilbe
pennyroyal: blue gentian, herb
pretense: *lie, sham
wing: alula
wintergreen: canker lettuce
witness: liar
FALSTAFF: *follower:* nym, pistol
meeting place: boar's head
FAMILY: *pert.:* lineal, nepotic
FAN: *cool, *enthusiast, *spread
alluvial: delta
dancer: ecdysiast, stripper
form: plicate
light: transom, window
-like: spread
oriental: ogi, punkah
out: *fail, go hitless, *spread
palm: inodes
plate: brin
stick: blade, brin, panache
tan: game, parliament, sevens
the flame: *agitate, *stir
-wort: cabomba, water shield
FANATIC, FANCIER: *enthusiast
FANION: *flag, *symbol
FANTASTIC: *absurd, *extreme

FAR: *and wide:* extensively
comb.: tel, tele
-gone: enamored, intoxicated
out: campy, *extreme, *wild
FARCE: *comedy, parody, satire
FARM: *building:* barn, crib, silo
fee: manor
grazing: ranch
house: caserio, onstead, villa
implement: disk, harrow, plow
laborer: bywoner, hand, hind, orraman, sharecropper
land: acreage
machine: *agriculture: machine
stead: byre
yard: barton, werf
FARMER: *peasant
FARO: *bet:* sleeper
card: hock, soda
card combination: cathop, split
dealer: gut-puller
-like game: bingo, florentini, garbage, haufeln, monte, pharaoh, put and take, red and black, schnitt, skinball, stuss, swy, two-up, ziginette
player: punter
symbol: tiger
FAROE: *colonizer:* kamban
duck: eider, puffin
fish: char(r)
island: bordo, ostero, sando, stromo, vaag(o)
judge: foud
sheep: faar
FASCINATE: *absorb, *interest
FASHION: *make, *style, *way
comb.: guise, timber, ton
world: *society
FAST: *active, *cheap, close, devoted, dharna, diet, ember, expeditious, express, fleet, hasty, hypersonic, lent, lock, loose, *near, *quick, *reckless, reliable, *secure, *strong
day: banyan, ember, fish day, jour

* **Asterisk means to look up this word to find more answer words.**

maigre, lent, quadragesima, ramadan, sabbath

FASTEN: *comb.:* desmo

FASTIDIOUS: **aesthetic,* **fine*

FAT: adipose, aliphatic, axunge, **big,* blowzy, blubber, coarse, dowdy, frowzy, grease, gross, **heavy,* lard, lipid, lucrative, oil, pinguid, **plenty,* **rich,* **solid,* stout, suet, **thick*
city: good life
comb.: adipo, lipo, pio, sebo, steato
-frying: corruption, graft
-headed: **stupid*
liquid: elain, oleine
man: blimp, grampus, humpty-dumpty, lump, man mountain, porpoise, potbelly, pudge, roly-poly, squab, tubby
natural: ester
of the land: **plenty*
pert.: adipic, obese, sebacic
pig: axunge
render: lard, **try*
wool: lanolin(e)

FATAL: dire, **heavy,* lethal

FATE: atropos, cavel, **chance,* cup, destiny, disaster, **end,* fortune, handwriting, heaven, issue, karma, ker, kismet, lot, **luck,* outcome, **paradise,* providence, **result,* **ruin*
buddhist: karma
goddess: adrastea, ananke, atropos, clotho, decuma, lachesis, moerae, moirai, morta, nona, norns, skuld, tyche, ur, urth, verthandi
mohammedan: kismet
personification: ananke

FATHER: *brother:* eme, uncle
pert.: agnate, paternal
time: methuselah, solitaire

FATIMA: *husband:* ali, bluebeard
descendant: fatimid, said, seid
sister: anne

step-brother: ali

FATUOUS: **silly,* **stupid*

FAULT: **error,* **flaw,* **sin*

FAUNUS: *grandfather:* saturn
son: acis

FAUSTULUS: *wife:* acca larentia

FAUX PAS: **break,* **error,* slip

FAVOR: **abet,* aid, esteem, **turn*

FAVORITE: **pet,* **popular*
son: absalom, candidate

FAY: **dwarf,* fairy, **spirit*

FAZE: **abash,* **disturb,* **upset*

FEAR: **alarm,* anxiety, terror

FEAST: agape, anthesteria, arthel, arval, banquet, bon, chanukah, christmas, dirgie, eucharist, festival, fiesta, hanukkah, meal, purim, seder, shabuoth, **spread,* succoth
comb.: mas

FEAT: **act,* **adventure,* **trick*

FEATHER: *alum:* alunogen, hair salt, halotrichite
barb: harl, pinnula, ramus
-brained: shallow, **stupid*
comb.: ptero, ptile
-crowned goddess: anukit
down: dowl, plumule
edge: **sharp*
fringe: barbicel
group: beard, mustache
-headed: **silly,* **stupid*
in one's cap: trophy, **token*
key: spline
-less: callow
mature: teleoptile
neckpiece: boa
nest: **accumulate,* **prepare*
palm: ejoo, irok
quill: calamus, remex
shaft: barrel, scape
shank: boot
shoulder: cape
star: comatula, comatulid
tuft: hulu
weight: diminutive, **small*

---

* Asterisk means to look up this word to find more answer words.

FEATHERS: clothes, finery, duds
 provide with: fletch
 shed: molt, moult
FEATURE: *form, *story, *token
FECUNDITY: *god:* khnemu, khnum, min, priapus
FEDERATION: body, *group, *union
FEE: admission, advance, agio, allowance, anchorage, assessment, blackmail, *blood: money*, bribe, brokerage, car fare, charge, commission, cost, demand, dues, emolument, exaction, fare, feu, fief, gratuity, honorarium, hire, mileage, pay, portage, price, reckoning, remuneration, rent, retainer, *return, *reward*, settlement, stipend, tax, tip, toll, tribute, *value*, wage
 -faw-fum: bugbear, ogre
 delivery delay: backwardation
 hauling: boatage
 suff.: -age
 welsh manor lord: amobyr
FEEBLE: *soft, *vague, *weak
FEEL: *sense, *think, *understand
 ashamed: atone, regret
 around: grope
 better: be relieved
 confident: hope
 fine: flourish
 for: grope, pity, sympathize
 shame: blush, *suffer
 the pulse: examiner, *test
FEELING: *love, *passion, *sense
 capable of: sentient
 insensibility: numbness
 lack: anaesthesia, analgesia
 show: emote
FEIGN, FEINT: *act, *trick
FELL: *bad, *brutal, *kill
FELLOW: academician, associate, baby, bean, bezonian, birkie, boke, bon homme, boy friend, bozo, brick, brother, bub, buddy, buff, bugger, bully, cad(dy), cat(so), cavil, chap, *clown, companion, comrad(e), coward, dalteen, dandiprat, dick, dodo, dring, drip, duck, fogey, *fool, *friend, gazebo, geezer, glayde, glutton, guy, knave, libertine, lover, man, mate, *peasant, peer, rake, rascal, roue, scamp, schlemiel, sir(rah), *spark, squirt, trusty, vaurien, wat, worthy
 -feeling: sympathy
 members: brethren, comrads
 traveler: communist, fifth columnist, subversive
FELT: *cap:* calpac(k)
 fabric: baize, batswing, beaver
 -like: pannose
 -work: nettle, neuropile
 -wort: herb, mullein, plant
FEMALE: *comb.:* gyne, enne, ette
FENCE: *crossing:* stile
 fish: net, weir
 heavy log: bunk
 interwoven: raddle
 lifter: rainstorm
 movable: glance, hurdle, stile
 picket: pale, paling
 slang: rasper
 steps over: stile
 sunken: aha, haha, hawhaw
FENCING: *attack:* assalto
 breastplate: plastrom
 cry: en garde, hai, hay, sasa, touche
 feint: appel
 hit: punto
 leap: gait, volt
 move: appel, balestra, butt, jump, lunge, punto, remise, reprise, tripost(e)
 position: carte, guard, octave, prime, pronation, quarte, quinte, seconde, septime, supination, tierce
 sword: epee, foil, forte, rapier, spathoe, tucke
FENRIS: *father:* loki

FERAL: *brutal*, fierce, *wild*

FERMENT: *agitate*, barm, boil, brew, bubble, buzz, change, disorder, dudgeon, *enzyme*, *excite*, fever, fret, leaven, moil, must, seethe, sour, stum, *tumult*, *turn*, *work*

FERN: *aquatic:* ceratopteris
climbing: alice's, nito
cluster: bracken, sorus
edible: roi, tara
flowering: osmund
fossil: caulopteris
kind: adiantum, anemia, bracken, brake, maidenhair, nito, onoclea, osmunda, polypody, psilotum, pteris, todea
leaf: frond
-like: pteroid, pteridophytic
-like plant: acrogen, pteroid
male: osmund
owl: nightjar
part: sorus, spore
patches: sori
polynesian: tara
primitive: botyropterid
royal: osmund
scales: chaff, ramentum
seed: spore, talisman

FEROCIOUS: *brutal*, *violent*

FERTILITY: *deity:* annona, apet, aphrodite, ashtoreth, astarte, atargatis, baal, ceres, cybele, damia, dagan, danu, demeter, fauna, freya, isis, istarte, mama, osiris, venus

FERVENT, FERVID: *ardent*, *eager*

FESCENNINE: obscene

FESTIVAL: *comb.:* mas
day, last: apodosis
procession: corso

FETCH: bear, fette, *get*, *trick*

FETID: *bad*, fulsome, miasmic

FETISH: abracadabra, amulet, anito, avatar, grigri, idol, juju, karma, mojo, *magic*, obeah, obi, periapt, *spell*, *symbol*, totem, voodoo, zeme

FETTER: band, *bind*, bond, chafe, chain, check, cuff, curb, hobble, iron, strain, *tie*

FEUD: *fight*, spat, vendetta

FEUDAL: *benefice:* feu(d)
chief: capite
domain: feod, feud, fief
jurisdiction: feoff, soc, soke
land free from feudal service: allod(ium), alod, alodial
lord: liege, suzerain, vavasor
penalty: sursise
pert.: banal
service: avera(ge), bedrip
tenant: bordar, cottier, homager, leud(e), socager, socman, vassal
tax: tailage, tallage
tenure: socage
tribute: brennage, heriot

FEVER: ardor, *desire*, *fire*
affected with: pyretic
chills and: ague
comb.: pyr, pyro
in the south: five
kind: ague, brucellosis, calentural, hay, helodes, malarial, malta, marsh, milk, octan, quartan, rose, sextan, sodoku, spotted, tap, texas, trench, undulant, yellow
reducer: antipyretic
root: bastard ipecac
spots: petechiae
without: afebrile, apyretic

FEVERISH: *ardent*, *eager*

FEW: *comb.:* oligo, pauci

FEY: dead, timid, visionary

FIASCO: bottle, *catastrophe*

FIAT: *law*, *order*, permit, writ

FIBER: *artificial:* aralac
band: fillet
bark: olona, tapa, terap
basket: datil
board: beaverboard, celotex
century plant: clusters, pita

coarse: adad, bassine
cordage: abaca, ambargy, anong, bass, coir, da, eruc, feru, hemp, imbe, jute, rhea, sisal
group: rope, spindle
hat: datil
istle: pita, pito
-like: byssoid, cottony, towy
knot: nep, noyl
matting: coir
palm: agave, coquito, raffia
pineapple: pita, pito
plant: ambary, caroa, ehuawa, flax, istle, ixle, ixtle, pita, ramie, rossele, sana, sisal, sunn
pressed: felt
ramie: amiray
source: arusha, callicarpa
synthetic: acetate, acrilan, dacron, nylon, orlon, rayon
tree: hau, majagua
tropical: istle, ixle, ixtle
wood: aralac, bast(e)
wool: gare, kemp, nep, pile
yarn: strand
FIDDLE: *cheat, *trifle, violin
FIELD: *athletic: *play: place
biblical: ager, aner
common share: dale
comb.: agro
day: festival, tournament
duck: bustard
dwelling: arvicoline
extensive: *plain, savannah
glass: binocle, telescope
god: pellervoinen
gun: amusette, artillery
hospital: ambulance
madder: rubiacin
mouse: vole
of blood: aceldama, akeldama
of mars: arena, campus martius
of vision: *range
pert.: agrarian, campestral
scabious: billy button, blue bottle, burdock, daisy, geranium, periwinkle, vinca

stubble: rowen
vocational: calling, forte, metier, profession, vocation
work: *fort(ification)
worker: *agent
FIEND: *demon, *devil, monster
FIERCE: *ardent, *brutal, *wild
FIERY: *cross:* crantara
FIG: *bale:* seron, seroon
basket: caba(s)
black: ficus laurifolia
cured by: hezekiah
first crop: breba
leaf: covering, garment
-like: caricous
marigold: cat-chop, samh
out or up: *dress, *ornament
sacred: pipal
shaped: ficiform
smyrna: eleme, elemi
tree: gondang, pipal, upas
FIGHT: *action, affray, *argue, *attack, bandy, barney, battle, bear arms, beef, bicker, blood feud, bout, box, brabble, brangle, brawl, break, cample, cangle, compete, conflict, contend, *contest, controversy, cross swords, demele, differ, discord, dispute, dissent, duel, encounter, engage, fence, feud, fracas, fray, grapple, hassle, jangle, jostle, joust, lock horns, make war, melee, miff, mill, *quarrel, rassle, resist, rhubarb, *riot, rumpus, run-in, set-to, snarl, spar, spat, squabble, stickle, struggle, tilt, vie, wage war, words
FIGHTING: *fish:* betta
street: bovver, brawl, riot
FIGURE: *form, *image, *mark, *ornament, *symbol, *token
architecture: atlantes, atlas, caryatid, telamon(es)
clay: bodhisattva
covered: seme
earth: geoid

equiangular: isagon, isogon
geometrical: *geometry: figure
-*head:* charlie mccarthy, dummy,
 front, insignia, puppet
out: calculate, solve
praying: orant
third: ferison
winged: eidolon, idolon, idolum
FIJI: *chestnut:* rata
 drug: tonga
 feudal service: lala
 gesture dance: siva
 island: koro, lau, ono, vita
 tree: buri, parinarium
FILAMENT: *cotton:* thread
 dermal: hair
 feather: dowl(e)
 flax: harl(e)
 having: capillaceous, capillary
 lamp: incandescent
 silky: byssus, byssine
FILCH: *cheat, *steal, *take
FILE: *circular:* bull's-foot
 comb-maker's: carlet
 document: dossier
 fish: triggerfish
 flat: quannet
 half-round: grail(le)
 rough: rasp
 six soldiers: rot
 thirteen: scrap
FILL: *pack(age)
FILLET: *architectural:* cimbia,
 lintel, listel, regular, taenia
 frieze: regula taenia
 hair: band, snood
 jeweled: diadem, tiara
 narrow: anaden, listel, orle, reglet, stria
FILM: *cover, *hide, *obscure
FINE: *able, amerce, *beautiful,
 braw, bully, bumper, cain, cro,
 damages, delicate, distress, elegant, escheat, exact, exquisite,
 fancy, filmy, *good, *great, handsome, healthy, jake, levy, meticulous, minute, mulct, nice, *no-

ble, penalty, *pretty, *punish,
 rare, *small, *smooth, *splendid,
 subtle, sweet, tax, *thin, wergild
arts: aesthetics, beaux-arts
letter line: serif
record of: estreat
-*spoken:* adulatory, bland
FINESSE: *aplomb, *skill, *trick
FINGER: *comb.:* dactyl(o),
 digit(i)
FINISH: *accomplish, *defeat,
 *end, *perfect, *shine, *top
FINN: suomi, vod, vot
 air divinity: ilma
 architect: aalto
 bath: sauna
 city: helsingfors, helsinki
 coin: markka, penni
 composer: sibelius
 death goddess: kalma
 dialect: karel
 division: ijore, villipuri
 earth goddess: mother of mannu,
 mother of metsola
 epic: *kalevala
 evil spirit: hiisi, lempo, paha
 field god: pellervoinen
 forest god: tapio
 fortress: suomenlinna
 gods and heroes: *kalevala
 illness goddess: kipu-tytto
 island: aaland, aland, skar
 isthmus: karelia
 ingria name: vot(e)
 lake: enare, saima(a)
 language: *finn people
 legislature: eduskunta
 measure: fathom, kannu, ottinger,
 sjomil, skalpund, tunna, tunn-
 land, verst
 moon god: kuu
 monster: surma
 musical instrument: kantele
 pain goddess: kivutar, loviatar,
 vammatar
 people: avar, cheremis, estonian,
 karelian, lapp, livonian, magyar,

* Asterisk means to look up this word to find more answer words.

mordvin, ostyak, permian, samoyed, tarast, ugric, uralian, votyak, zyrian
pert.: suomic, suomish
resilience: sisu
sacred stone: saivo, sejda
scholar: lonnrot
son: ossian
soul: halt, ija
sun god: paiva
supreme god: jumala, ukko
talisman: sampo
tribe: chud, ugrian, veps, voth
underworld: manala, tuonela
 deities: tuonetar, tuoni
water genii: tursas, vetehinen
water god: ahti, ahto
water sprite: jelpin-tur, nakki,
 passe-jokka, pyhaj-oki
woods divinity: mielikki, nyyrikki,
 tapio, tuulikki
FINNO-UGRIC: **finn*
FIONN: *son:* oisin
FIRE: **anger,* ardor, arouse, bake,
 bale, blaze, bonner, bounce,
 burn, calenture, char, combustion, conflagration, cook, **discharge, *dismiss,* flame, heat, ignite, incite, inspire, **love,* mania,
 oust, **passion,* rapture, scorch,
 *shine, signal, **smart, *spark,
 *sparkle, *spirit, *throw,* vehemence, **violence,* war
-arm: **gun*
-back: pheasant, reredos
-ball: bolide, meteor, pistol
basket: cresset, grate
boat: palander
brand: agitator, extremist, mili-
 tant, revolutionary, torch
bug: arsonist
bullet: tracer
ceremonial: bonfire
comb.: igni, pyr(o)
cracker: banger, petard
damp: gas, methane
deity: agni, dyaus, girru, hephaes-

tus, hestia, loki, nusku, pele,
 vesta, vulcan
dog: andiron, **support*
drill: chark
eater: crank, daredevil
fear of: pyrophobia
fly: glowworm, lightning bug
guard: hearth, watch
man: stoker, tizeur, vamp
 gear: axe, hook, hose, ladder
military: artillery, barrage, broad-
 side, enfilade, flak, rafale
opal: girasol
pert.: igneous, fiery
place: fogon, grate, hearth
 accessory: andiron
 ledge: hobb, mantel, shelf
proof: **secure*
proofing: amianthus, asbestos,
 earth flax, mountain flax
sacrificial: agni
side: hearthstone, ingleside
up: **agitate, *drink*
upon: **attack*
wood: bavin, billot, clog, fagot,
 kindling, lena, log, lumber, stove-
 wood, yule log
works: bomb, cap, cascade,
 cracker, fizgig, flare, flowerport,
 gerbe, girandole, petard, pin-
 wheel, rip-rap, rocket, roman
 candle, salute, serpent, skyrocket,
 snake, sparkler, squib, torpedo,
 tourbillion, whiz-bang
works case: cartouch(e)
worshipper: gheber, idolator, igni-
 colist, parsi, pyrolator, zoroas-
 trian
FIRM: adamant, business, close,
 compact, company, concern,
 corporation, dauntless, dense,
 determined, devoted, **fast,
 hard, inexorable, iron, moor,
 *obstinate, *plant, rigid, safe,
 *secure, *set, *solid, stanch,
 *stern, stiff, **strict, *strong,
 thick, tight, **true*

---

* Asterisk means to look up this word to find more answer words.

FIRST: *head, *opening
FISH: *amber:* medregal
 backbone: grate
 bag net: fyke
 bait: chum, fly, killy, worms
 barbed tail: stingaree, stingray
 basket: caul, cawl, corf, creel
 bathypelagic: barrel eye
 berycoid: barbudo, catfish
 bivalve: calm, diatom, mollusk
 bony: carp, teleost
 bright-colored: opah
 broken-bellied: thoke
 carangid: amberfish, big-eye,
  bumper, cavalla, goggle-eye, jack,
  jurel, pilot, pompano, runner,
  saurel, scad, seriola
 catch: shack, string
 cephaloptera: manta
 characin: bloodfin, piranha
 climbing: anabas, skipper
 colorful: boce, opah, wrasse
 condiment: paste
 cutlass: savola
 cuttle: octopus, sepia, squid
 cyprinoid: barbel, bitterling, blay,
  bleak, bley, blindfish, carp, chi,
  chub, dace, id, lulu, orfe, pap,
  rudd, sentoree, spot, sundoree,
  tench, uit
 deep sea: argyropelecus, blenny,
  brotula
 dish: bloater, mousseline
 elasmobranch: chimera, ray, sawfish, shark
 fabled: ihi, mah
 female: henfish, raun
 flat: bream, butt, dad, dace,
  flounder, fluke, halibut, plaice,
  ray, sand dab, skate, sole, sunfish,
  torpedo, turbot
 flying: gurnard, saury
 food: aimara, akule, alewife, ant-
  egg, baleen, barracuda, barramunda, bass, baya, beshow,
  bichir, big-eye, blue catfish, boga,
  bolti, cabrilla, carp, catalufa,

cero, cisco, cod, escolar, eel,
flounder, gar, garlopa, grouper,
guasa, haak, haik, hake, halibut,
hilsa, ictalurus, ide, iki, jurel,
ling, loach, mackerel, meagre,
mullet, pentado, plaice, red fish,
sablefish, salmon, sand dab, sardine, scup, sesele, shad, siera,
smelt, snapper, swordfish, tautog,
trout, tuna
 fresh water: anabas, arapaima,
  barbel, bass, bream, carp, crappie, dace, darter, durbot, esox,
  gar, ide, loach, mooneye, pike,
  redeye, roach, rudd, tench
 game: bass, cero, grayling, grilse,
  marlin, salmon, sword, tarpon,
  trout, tuna
 ganoid: bowfin, dipnoi, sturgeon
 gig: spear
 globe: diodon
 gobioid: loter
 gobylike: dragonet
 gold-colored: aurata
 hadoid: hake
 half-beak: ihi
 haul off: catch, drave, mess
 hook: angle, barb, carlisle, drail,
  fly, gaff, gange, gig, hackle,
  sedge, sproat, *trap
 horned: pout
 jugular: batrachid
 land-traveling: anabas
 large: arapaima, blanquillo, bichir,
  chiro, cusk, escolar, gourami,
  maskalonge, muskellunge, sen-
  nett, sturgeon, swordfish, tarpon,
  whale
 line: cord, snell, trot
 long: eel, gar, lamprey, pike
 mammal: manatee, whale
 marine: apogon, blenny, bonito,
  chopa, cusk, grunt, ling, menhaden, robalo, scup, tarpon
 nesting: acara, stickleback
 net: bunt, fyke, sagene, seine
 net line: meter

* **Asterisk means to look up this word to find more answer words.**

net mender: beatster
ornamental: paradise
parasitic: remora, pega(dor)
permian: acanthode
pert.: piscatory, ichthyic
pimelopteroid: bream
poisonous: fugu
preserve: warren
prong: gaff, pew
raw: ceviche, sashimi
rice dish: kedgeree
river-ascending: anadrom, salmon, shad
salmonoid: char, gwyniad, nelma, pollan, powan, trout
sauce: alec, anchovy, botargo, garum, soy, tartar
scale: ganoid
scaleless: alepidote
scombroid: bonito, cero, tuna
sea: cod, hake, ling, mero, opah, pollack, tomcod, tuna
serranoid: aguavina, bonaci, diplectrum, guapena, lates
small: blenny, brit, cunner, darter, goby, halfbeak, ide, killifish, limpet, minnow, riggle, seahorse, sennet, shiner, smelt, sprat
sparoid: napa, porgy, salema
spiny-finned: blanquillo, goby, perch, tilefish
sucking: remora, pega(dor)
synodontoid: tiru
teleost: abdominale, ammodyte, anacarthin, apoda, bony fish, catfish, eel, iniomi
trap: coop, ellpot, fyke, net, sagene, seine, spiller, weir
voracious: barracuda, caribe, pike, piranha, piraya, shark
young: alevin, brit, fry, minnow, parr, smelt, sprod
FIT: **able, *accommodate, *adapt, *appropriate, *attack, *meet, *ready, *pet, *supply*
FIX: **allot, *arrange, *defeat, *dress, *establish, *kill, *orna-*

ment, **pack, *repair, *set*
FIXER: **agent,* lobbyist
FLAG: alem, banderol, banner, blackjack, blue peter, brattach, bunting, burgee, championship, colors, **decline,* ensign, jolly roger, gonfalon, guidon, iris, jack, old glory, oriflamme, pennant, pennon, roger, **sign,* sink, standard, stars and stripes, **stop,* streamer, **symbol, *title,* tricolor, union jack, whip
waving: chauvinism, patriotism
FLAGRANT: **bad, *evil, *wanton*
FLAME: **fire, *interest, *love*
FLARE: **flame, *sparkle, *spread*
FLASH: **flame, *flare,* news
FLAT: **dull, *low, *weak*
  comb.: plani
FLATTER: please, **praise,* toady
FLAUNT: dare, challenge, **taunt*
FLAW: blast, blemish, brack, breach, **break,* crack, defect, **error,* fault, gale, hangup, **hurt,* mar, **opening, *problem, *smear, *split, *tear,* wind
FLEE: bolt, desert, **escape,* fly
FLEECE: **cheat, *deceive,* rob
FLEER: **scold, *taunt*
FLEET: **active,* armada, **quick*
FLESH: body, man, pulp, stock
  comb.: kreato
  -eat: carnivorous, sarcophagy
  pert.: carnic, carnose, carnous
  -shearing: carnassial
  -resembling: carniform, sarcoid
FLESHY: **big,* burly, **fat*
FLEXIBLE: *comb.:* campto
FLIGHT: **course, *escape,* hop
  of fancy: imagination, sally
  of steps: perron, stairs
  operation: mission
  pert.: volar
FLIGHTY: **mad, *silly, *stupid*
FLIMSY: **superficial, *vain*
FLING: **taunt, *throw, *venture*

* **Asterisk means to look up this word to find more answer words.**

FLIP: crack, sassy, *throw
FLIT: *escape, *speed, vanish
FLOAT: *aid, loan, *start, waft
FLOCK: *company, *gather, *group
 pert.: gregal
FLOG: *defeat, tan, *urge, *whip
FLOOD: bore, *catastrophe, deluge, eagre, engulf, float, freshet, inundate, *plenty, pour, *quantity, rain, spate, *storm, *surfeit, surplus, tide, torrent, washout, water, whelm
FLOOR: base, bed, bottom, fell
 covering: carpet, linoleum, mat, planks, rug, tapis, tile
 show: *act, cabaret, feature
FLOP: dud, *fail, *fall, slump
FLORIDA: bird: mockingbird
 feature: everglades
 fish: snook, tarpon, tetard
 fishing boat: smackee
 flower: orange blossom
 Indian farmer: calusa
 nickname: flower, sunshine state
 plain: savannah
 song: swanee river
 tree: gomart, palmetto, royal palm, sabel palm
FLOTILLA: fleet, *group
FLOURISH: develop, *grow, sweep
FLOUT: *abuse, *attack, *insult
FLOW: *flood, *harmony, *issue
 comb.: rheo
FLOWER: apetalus: cactus, trema
 appendage: bract
 aromatic: camomile
 artificial: gloxinia, rosette
 axis prolongation: carpophore
 band: garland, lei, wreath
 bearing: anthophorous
 bed pattern: parterre
 beetle: cetonia
 bell-shaped: lily, tulip
 blue: harebell, lupine
 border: floroon

bud: ament, caper, knot, spadix
cardinal: lobelia
cluster: ament, anadem, anthemia, bract, cime, corymb, cyme, glomerule, panicle, paniculate, raceme, umbel
comb.: anth(o), anthus
compound: anthodium
cormus: crocus
cotula: brass button, weed
-cup fern: woodsia alpinia
death, of: asphodel
description: anthography
dry: azalea, cactus, oleander
envelope: perianth
expansion: anthesis, full bloom
extract: atar, attar, ottar, otto, perfume
fall: aster, cosmos, salvia
feeding on: anthophilious
felwort: gentian
fence: adenanthera, barbados pride, bear tree, peacock flower, red sandalwood
field: gowan
forgetfulness: lotus
fragrant: jasmine, rose
full bloom: anthesis
garden: asalia, aster, bletilla, buttercup, campella, canna, carnation, daffodil, dahlia, daisy, freesia, gladiolus, gloxinia, greenery, heliotrope, honeysuckle, hyacinth, iris, ixia, lilac, lily, narcissus, olivia, orchid, pansy, peony, petunia, phlox, pink, primrose, ranunculus, rose, solitaire, tulip, verbena, violet, zinnia
girl: bouquetiere
goddess: chloris, flora, nanna
group: bed, bouquet, *flower: cluster, posy
having affinity for: anthophilous
head: anthodium, bloom, capitulum, *cluster
holder: lapel, pot, vase
imaginary: amarant(h)

* Asterisk means to look up this word to find more answer words.

large: canna, peony
late-blooming: aster
leaf: bract, petal, sepal
leaves: perianth
sets of four: quadrifoliate
sets of three: trillium
-like: anthoid, beautiful
literature, of: anthology
lily: aloe, arum, ixia, lotus, mariposa, sego, ti, toi
meadow: bluets, pratal
medicinal: aloe, rue
ornament: anthemion, bouquet
part: ament, androecium, anther, bract, calyx, carpel, corolla, corona, epicalyx, filament, gynoecium, microsporophyll, ovary, ovule, peduncle, perianth, pericarp, petal, pistil, pollen, sepal, spadix, stamen, stem, stigma
pert.: anthine
pink: rhodora, rose, silence
pistil part: carpel
poet's: chaucer
pot: bough, cachepot, jardiniere
producing: cauliflorous
purple: lilac, pense
receptacle: pot, torus, vase
seed: ovule
shape: bell, fleuron
sheath: spathe
showy: azalea, bird of paradise, calla, camellia, orchid
sifter: bolter
speech, of: rhetoric
spicule, star-shaped: aster
spike: ament, spadix
spring: arbutus, crocus, hepatica, hyacinth, iris, lilac, peony, tulip
stalk: peduncle, petiole, scape, stem
stamen: androecium, anther
stand for: epergne
state: florida
stipe: anthophore
study: anthoecology
unfading: amarant(h)

unknown kind: belamour
white: barton, daisy, gowan
wild: anemone, arbutus, baby blue-eyes, bluebell, bluet, buttercup, ceanothus, chamise, cyclamen, daisy, hepatica, innocence, sage
wind: anemone
yellow: buttercup, daffodil, daisy, gowan, jonquil, marigold, pense, rue
FLUCTUATE: *change,* *oscillate
FLUENT: *apt,* *free,* *ready
FLUFF: *dress,* *err,* girl, shiv
FLUID: *blood:* plasma, serum
collection: blister, bottle
inky: melena
liver: bile
milk: plasma
medical: serum
mythological, blood: ichor
pert.: humoral
portion: boundary layer
spiders, of: aranein
stratification: baroclivity
without: aneroid
FLUKE: *advantage,* flounder, worm
FLURRY: *agitate,* *ado,* *blast,* fuss, *speed,* *stir,* wind
FLUSH: enema, *plenty,* *smooth
FLUSHED: *ardent,* *eager,* *hot
FLUTE: bin, crimp, chamfer, channel, fife, flageolet, flauto, fold, furrow, gauffer, groove, hemiope, magadis, matalan, nei, piccolo, pipe, shuttle, tche, zuffolo
ancient: tibia
bagpipe: chanter
comb.: aulo
hindu: bin, pungi
mouth: aulostomi, shrimp, snipe
player: auletris, flautist, flutist, piper, tootler
stop: ventage
wood for: kokra

* Asterisk means to look up this word to find more answer words.

FLUTTER: *agitate, *oscillate

FLY: *escape, soar, *speed
agaric: amanita muscaria
artificial: abbey, alder alexandra, ashy hackle, babcock, baker, bass bug, beaver kill, black ant, blue dun, brown may, butcher, buzz, caddice, cahill, coachman, grannom, hare's-ear, buzzard, lure, nymph, sassy cat, sedge
at: *attack
ball: blooper, *hit, out
bane: cinnamonroot, silenus
block: pulley
bull: detective
case: elytra
catcher: alder, fielder, grignet, grinder, kingbird, peewee, phoebe, redstart, tody, vireo, web, yetapa
chalcid: anastatus, aphelinus
clouds: scud
constellation: musca
eggs: ahuatle
enemy: spider
genus: dacus, musca, psila
golden-eyed: lacewing
green-tail: grannom
honeysuckle: black twinberry
ichneumon: apanteles, aphidiina
in the ointment: catch, *evil
larva: blood worm, bot, bott
life stages: adult, larval, maggot, pupal, puparium
press: bower, operator
small: gnat, midge
speck: *bit, *trifle
two-winged: asilus, athericera, dipteron
wheel: whorl
white: asterochiton
wings: alytra, elytron

FLYER: *ace, *piece, *venture

FLYING: adder: dragonfly
boat: amphibian, seaplane
body: meteor
buttress: arc-boutant

condition: yarak
dutchman: mariner, wanderer
dutchman heroine: senta
fish: butterfly, gurnard, saury
fox: kalong
lemur: colugo
phalanger: ariel
saucer: ufo

FOAM: comb.: aphr, aphro

FOIL: *cheat, *defeat, *frustrate

FOLD: dog-ear, *quit, *wrap

FOLDEROL: *bit, *nonsense

FOLLOW: accompany, *act, ape, attend, bedog, chase, come, conform, copy, court, dangle, dog, emanate, ensue, fall back, hang, heed, heel, hound, hunt, imitate, *issue, *move, next, obey, observe, practice, pursue, *result, seek, shadow, succeed, tag, tail, trace, trail, tread, *understand

FOLLOWER: *enthusiast
body: claque, clique, crowd, gate, *group, *staff
comb.: ist, ite, nik

FOMORIANS, FOMORS: king: balot

FOOD: additive: coumarin, cyclamate, monochloracetic acid, monosodium glutamate, nitrogen trichloride
animal: feed, fodder, forage, grain, grass, provender
choice: cates, pastry
comb.: sito, troph(o)
container: bowl, box, crock, dish, jar, olla, plate, saucer
daily: tucker
desire for: bulimia, pica
diet: regimen
dislike: asitia, cibophobia, sitomania
dressing: sauce
element: gluten, protein, vitamin
eton: batel
farinaceous: sago
garnish: sauce, socle

* Asterisk means to look up this word to find more answer words.

fish: *fish: *food*
gods: ambrosia, amrita, manna
health: brewer's yeast, fruits, grits,
 liver, middlings, milk, nuts, peanut flower, rice polish, soybeans,
 wheat germ, whole wheat, yoghurt, yogurt
invalid: broth, pap
lack, suff.: atrophia
list: carte, diet, menu
pert.: cibarial, nourishing
plant: soia, taro
protein: eggs, fish, meat
provide: cater, mess, ration
room: spence
seller: grocer, viander
semi-digested: chyme
storage pit: cist
starchy: macaroni, paste
unclean: tref
FOOL: antic, asinego, ass, badaud,
 bayard, block(head), blunder-
 head, boeotian, fluff, boob(y),
 boor, buffle(head), buffo(on),
 bum, bungler, butt, cake, calf,
 *cheat, chump, clod, *clown,
 club, codshead, comic, cozen,
 cretin, daff, *deceive, dimwit,
 dolt, dope, dotard, dumbell,
 dunce, dupe, *enthusiast, foozle,
 gabby, gobbin, golem, goose,
 gowk, gull, gump, hash, heavy-
 head, hoodwink, idiot, ignora-
 mus, imbecile, jerk, jester, *joke,
 jokester, kid, lubber, looby, mislead, moron, naar, narr, nincompoop, ninny, nizy, noddy, nonny,
 nut, oaf, *peasant, putz, raca,
 ridicule, *sap, scatterbrain, simon, simp, simpleton, softy, sop,
 sot, stooge, stumblebum, stupe,
 *trick, *trifle, wiseacre, witling,
 yold, zany
around: experiment, kibitz, interfere, *play, *trifle
sage: jester
FOOL'S: *bauble:* cap and bells,

 gewgaw, marotte
gold: pyrites
paradise: chimera, illusion, gol-
 deneh medina
parsley: wild chervil
stitch: tricot
FOOLISH: *insane, *stupid, *vain
FOOT: *and mouth disease:* murrain
animal: fetlock, hoof, paw
comb.: pedi, pod, podo
cushion: brioche
deformity: planus, talipes
doctor: chiropodist, podiatrist
having: pedate
hold: *advantage, purchase
-less: apod, *clumsy, *stupid
lights: drama, broadway, stage
like: pedate
lock: bilbo
loose: ambulatory, *free, no-
 madic, untrammeled
man: flunkey, menial, servant
note: explanation, memorandum
pad: *outlaw, *thief, thug
pain: talalgia
part: ankle, arsis, astragal, calcis,
 instep, metatarsus, scaphoid,
 tarsus, thenar
path: lane, senda, trail
pert.: pedal, pedary, podal
pick: caschrom
poetic: *meter
print: ichnolite, *mark, prick, pug,
 trace, track, slot, spore
race: dash, diaulos, sprint
soldier: *soldier
step: pace, vestige
stone: base, *memorial
stool: buffet, cricket, hassock,
 mora, ottoman
study of: podiatry
the bill: pay, *settle, treat
traveler: pedestrian
way: banquette, path, catwalk
wear: *shoe
worked by: lever, pedal, treadle
FOP: *fellow, *spark

* Asterisk means to look up this word to find more answer words.

FORBES: four bits, half dollar

FORCE: activity, *advance, *agent, amain, *attack, bear down, biod, birr, blackmail, blood and iron, body, brawn, *break, brunt, bull, cause, coerce, cogency, compel, crew, dint, *discharge, *dismiss, drive, duress, effort, emphasis, employees, exact, *group, have, impact, impel, impetus, influence, *make, might, *move, oblige, oust, *pack, police, *power, *press, *push, *shock, soup, *sparkle, *spirit, *staff, steamroller, *strength, *stress, *throw, *urge, vehemence, *violence
alleged: biod, elod, odic, odyl
air upon: *blow
armed: army, navy, posse
down: cramp, stuff, tamp
electromotive: becquerel effect
from: grab, seize, wrest
god of: ment, ptah, shu
hypothetical: *force: alleged
passage: bore
rotation: torque
uniting: bond, *tie
unit: dyne, kinit, tonal, volt

FORCES: *opposing:* yang, yin

FORE: *comb.:* anter, antero

FOREARM: antebrachium, get ready, insure, prepare
bone: radius, ulna
pert.: cubital, ulnar

FORECAST: anticipate, *predict

FORECASTER: *prophet, tipster

FOREHEAD: *pert.:* metopic
projection: antinion

FOREIGN: adventitious, *alien
comb.: xeno
geology: epigene
laborers: aperu
office: embassy, legation
quarter: barrio, enclave, ghetto

FOREMOST: *ace, *acme, *best

FORESEE, FORESHADOW:
*forecast

FOREST: *antelope:* banded duiker
deity: aegipan, faun, pan, saturn, silenus, sylvanus, tane
destroyed by fire: brule
fire locator: alidade
flooded seasonally: gapo
glade: camass, cammas, quamash
keeper: ranger
love of: hemophily
pert.: nemoral, sylvan
road: ride, trail
subarctic: taiga
tillage, land for: thwaite

FORETELL: *forecast

FOREVER: ad infinitum, ake, always, aye, ceaselessly, constantly, continually, endlessly, eternally, everlastingly, for all time, incessantly, interminably, invariably, perennially, *permanent(ly), perpetually, semper, unceasingly

FORGE: *form, *make, *press
nozzle: tew(el)
waste: dross, sprue

FORGET: ignore, neglect, omit

FORGIVE: *acquit, pardon, remit

FORM: *address, ame, apparition, appearance, blank, block, body, brew, *build, carve, cast, caul, ceremony, chic, chisel, *class, conceive, concoct, contour, *describe, devise, document, eidos, fashion, figure, fix, forge, frame, gestalt, ghost, hammer, *image, impress, invent, *kind, knead, *law, *make, *mark, *model, *mold, organize, outline, *plan, plot, *produce, *rite, *rule, *set(tle), shape, *shell, stamp, *start, *style, *train, *turn, *use, *way, *work, write
bend: cope
carved: bust, statuary
display: manikin, rack
literary: novel, ode, poetry, romance, saga, satire, sonnet
liturgical: service

* Asterisk means to look up this word to find more answer words.

lyrical: rondel, sestina
pert.: modal
printed: acknowledgement, bill, blank, discharge, receipt, voucher, warrant
FORMLESS: *comb.:* amorph(o)
FORMORIAN: *giant:* balor
FORMULATE: build, *form, *make
FORSAKE: *abandon, leave, *quit
FORSETTI: *father:* balder
FORT: abatis, acropolis, agger, akazava, alcazar, balistraria, bank, banquette, barbed wire, barbican, barricade, bartizan, bastille, bastion, battery, bawn, blockhouse, breastwork, brattice, bretese, bulwark, bunker, buttress, casemate, castillo, castle, citadel, contravallation, cota, curtain, defense, depot, donjon, dun, garrison, glacis, half-moon, hornwork, kame, keep, kota, lis(s), loophole, lunette, machicolation, mantlet, merlon, mole, mound, muniment, outwork, pah, palisade, parados, portcullis, post, rampart, ravelin, redan, redoubt, scarp, stockade, stronghold, tenaille, *tower, wall, vallation, vallum
FORTE: bag, bailiwick, calling, cup of tea, loud, metier, specialty, *skill, *thing, *work
FORTHWITH: away, instantly, now
FORTIFICATION: *fort
FORTIFY: *add, *arm, defend, lace, man, strengthen, spike
FORTITUDE: *power, *strength
FORTRESS: *fort
FORTUITOUS: *accidental
FORTUNE: *accident, *fate, luck, millions, pile, *riches, wad
goddess: tyche
hunter: adventurer, opportunist
teller: *prophet

FORTY: *day's fast:* carene, lent
five degree angle: octant
inches: ell
niners: argonauts, goldseekers
points in piquet: capot
thieves: napoleon at st helena
43,560 square feet: acre
two gallon cask: tierce
ways: in all directions
winks: nap
FORWARD: *active, *advance, *ardent, *eager, *support
looking: modern
moving: proal
pass: throw
FOSS(E): *opening, *waterway
FOSSIL: *bone:* ivory, odontolite
cambrian: archaeocyathus
coral: alveolite
egg: ovulite
eurypteroid: king crab
fish: berrybone, coccosteus
flower: antholite
footprint: ichnite
fruit: carpolite
lemur: adapis
mollusk: dolite
plant: asterophyllite, calamite
resin: amber, retinite
scene: matrix, shale
science: paleontology
shell: ammonite, balante, dolite
toothlike: conodont
track: amphibichnite
tree: amber, pinites
trunk: caulopteris
tubular: sciolite
turquoise: ivory, odontolite
worm track: nereite
FOSTER: *aid, *cultivate, *train
child: dalt, nurry, stepohild
FOUL: *bad, *evil, *rotten
fiend: *demon, *devil
in marbles: fulk
-mouthed: obscene
play: murder, perfidy
-smelling: fetid, olid, reeky

* Asterisk means to look up this word to find more answer words.

speaker: blackmouth
up: *confuse, crab, *spoil
weather: storm
FOUNDATION: anlage, base, bed, bottom, *build, *establish, footing, ground, installation, organization, premise, slab, *start, support
pert.: basic
FOUNTAIN: *changed into:* byblis
near helicon: aganippe
nymph: albunea, egeria, naiad
of hippocrene: caballine
of youth: bimini
sacred: aganippe
FOUR: *bagger:* home run, homer
bits: half dollar
books: analects, learning, mean, mencius
books authors: chung yung, lun yu, meng tzu, ta hsueh
comb.: tessar, tetra, vier
-five-six: acey-out, see-low
-flush: *deception, sham
-flusher: *impostor, trombenik
-footed: quadruped, tetrapod
genii of amenti: amseti, duamutef, hapi, kebhsenuf
gills: pint
group: quartet, tetrad
horsemen: conquest, death, famine, war, notre dame
hundred: aristocracy, *society
hundred years: baktun
-in-hand: ascot, rig, scarf, tie
inches: hand
kreutzers: batz
metonic cycles: cappipic
o'clock: boerhavia, herb
of a kind: clock, mournival, quatorze, solitaire, virlicque
pecks: bushel
pence: flag, groat, joey
sided: quadrilateral
-some: bridge, quartet, tetrad
square: honest, quadrangular
-syllable foot: antispast

-wheeler: barge, berlin, buckboard, calash, carriage
FOX: *brown:* corsac
female: vixen
fire: luminescence
flying: kalong
foot: pad
glove: blob, bloody fingers, figwort, orchis, popdock
glove leaves: digitalis
group: skulk
hold: entrenchment
hunter's coat: pink
hunter's cry: all on
hunter's hazard: oxer
-like: alopecoid, vulpine
little: vulpecula
male: stag
tail: alopeourus, brush, grass
trot: dance, run
FRACAS: *fight, *noise, *riot
FRACTION: *bit, *piece, *share
FRAGMENT: *fraction, excerpt
FRAGRANCE: *scent, smell, spice
FRAIL: girl, *thin, *weak
FRAME: *bar of soap:* cess
circular: cadge
cloth-stretch: counter, tenter
coffin: bier
counting: abacus
fish line: cadar, cader
glass-making: drosser
mind, of: bent, humor, mood
reference: outlook
ship's table: fiddle
skin-drying: herse
supporting: horse, trestle
torch: cresset
work: bail, bracketing, cadre, case, outline, shell, skeleton, structure, *support
work, skeletal: armature
work, bleaching: stillage
work, pods: peoplum
FRANCE: blefuscu, gaul, *french
FRANCHISE: license, *right

* Asterisk means to look up this word to find more answer words.

FRANK: candid, *free, *sign
FRANKISH: *dynasty:* merovingian
  hero: oliver, roland
  judge: centenar
  king: charlemagne, clovis, gontran, pepin, pippin
  kingdom: austrasia
  law: capitulary, salic
  peasant: litus
  pert.: salic
  vassal: leud
FRANTIC: *avid, *frenetic, *upset
FRAUD: *cheat, *quack, *trick
FRAXINUS: ash, evergreen, tree
FRAY: *contest, *fight, wear
FREAK: *eccentric, *weird
  of nature: monster
  out: bad trip
FREDERICK: alaric, alte fritz
FREE: abandoned, *absolute, abundant, absolve, *acquit, blank, bondless, broad, candid, clear, discharge, emancipate, *escape, except, excuse, exempt, extricate, foot-loose, frank, generous, gift, gratis, *idle, immune, *independent, lax, leisure, let off, *liberal, loosen, manumit, *open, pass, prodigal, ransom, *release, remise, remit, rescue, rid, spare, spontaneous, unbound
  admission: annie oakley, *pass
  -and-easy: blase, bohemian, convivial, debonair, *open
  -booter: cateran, corsair, filibusterer, pirate, *thief
  enterprise: capitalism
  -for-all: *contest, *fight
  hand: carte blanche, latitude
  -hold: alod(ium), property
  -holder: bonder, yeoman
  lance: paparazzo, writer
  living: dissipation
  loader: guest, parasite
  -love institution: agapemone
  man: bonder, burgess, ceorl, churl, citizen, laet, latin, thane,

thegn, tiro, villein
  mason: templar
  of charge: buckshee
  oneself: *break, *escape
  quartering: bonaught
  scope: carte blanche
  silver: bryanism
  stone: bathstone, color
  stone state: connecticut
  thinker: *agnostic, aladinist, esprit, fort, infidel, skeptic
  time: leisure, recess
  trade: commerce, policy
  will: discretion
FREEZE: awe, *scare, *shock
FRENCH: *airplane:* avion, spad
  alb: aube
  art cult: dada, impressionism
  art group: fauves
  article: des, las, les, une
  artist: bonnard, bonheur, boucher, bouguereau, braque, breton, carrier, cezanne, chagall, chardin, chirico, cormon, corot, daubigny, degas, derain, dore, doyen, dufy, gros, legros, lemoyne, lorrain, manet, millet, matisse, rapin, renoir, steinlen, vernet, watteau
  astrologer: nostradamus
  author: apollinaire, aragon, aubanel, ayme, baif, balzac, barres, baudelaire, bazin, beauvoir, bellay, beranger, bernardin, bernanos, boileau, bossuet, bourget, breton, brillat-savarin, camus, collette, d'alembert, daudet, deportes, deschamps, dumas, flaubert, gide, halevy, hugo, labe, loti, marot, merimee, ohnet, proust, racine, renan, rimbaud, rostand, sagan, sartre, stael, verne, villon, voltaire, zola
  baby: bebe, enfant, poupee
  bachelor: garcon
  bacteriologist: pasteur
  ballad: virelai
  beach: plage, rivage, rive

bean: fauve, haricot, phasel
beast: bete
beauty: ninon
bed: couche, lit
beef: boeuf
beef country: charolais
bicycle: velo
billiards: bouchon
bitters: amer(tume)
blessed: beni, sacre
boat: caravelle, chaloupe
bond: rente
botanist: audibert
bottle: clavelin
boxing: savate
brandy: armagnac, cognac
brewery: brasserie
brush: brosse
bullet: mitraille
butcher shop: charcuterie
cafe: coffee, estaminet
cake: dariole, gateau
canadian: baptiste, canuck
cannon: aspic
cape: talma
capital: paris
card game: baccarat, ecarte
cardinal: mazarin, richelieu
carriage: caleche, dormeuse
cathedral: nantes, reims, rouen
cavalryman: argolet(ier)
chalk: talc
chanteuse: piaf
chaperon: gouvernante
chasseurs: blue devils
cheese: babybel, bonbel, brie, camembert, fromage, marsigny, pipocreme, roquefort, sanglier
chemist: curie, holbach, pasteur
chestnut: maroon, marone
cleric: abbe
cloth: blancard, drap, toile
cloud: nuage, nue
coffee house: estaminet
coin: agnel, blanc, cavalier, centime, denier, dizain, ecu, franc, gros, livre, obole, louis d'or, napoleon, sol, sou
comedie: sotie
commerce: agen
commune: albi, ancre, cenon, croix, dole, laon, laval, nerac, pau, pessac, reze, rodez, stains, terare, ussel, vichy
company: cie
composer: auber, bizet, charpentier, debussey, gluck, gounod, gretry, ibert, indy, lalo, lully, massanet, rameau, ravel, spontini, thome
conqueror: caesar, clovis
cooking mode: saute
cordial: absinthe, anisette, pernod
corn, mixed: meslin
cotton: jasmine
cowboy: baille, gardian
critic: brunetiere, taine
cupboard: etagere, secretaire
curate: abbe
currency: assignat
custom: gallicism
daffodil: polyanthus
daisy: marguerite
dance: allemande, apache, bal, basse, bourree, boutade, branle, can can, canary, courante, gavot, tarantelle
dash: elan
dean: doyen
dear: cher, chere, cheri
decree: arret
deed: fait
degree: agrege
delicatessen: charcuterie
designer: balenciaga, chanel, courreges, dior, givenchy, gres, patou, st laurent
dessert: ambrette
dialect: argot, patois
diplomat: cambon, genet, ronsard, segur, senet
division: arrondissement, brie, canton, cercle, commune, department

---

* Asterisk means to look up this word to find more answer words.

doorkeeper: concierge
dramatist: anouilh, angier, banville, beaumarchais, dumas, halevy, moliere, piron, racine, sardou
dream: reve(rie), songe(r)
dressmaker: couturiere
drink: pastis, petanque
dry: brut, sec
dungeon: cachot
dye: garanceux
dynasty: bourbon, capet, valois
edict: arret
empress: eugenie, josephine
enamelware: limoges
engraver: callot, pastre
equality: egalite
exclamation: hein, sacre bleu
explorer: cartier
fabric: etoffe, lame, ras, tissu
festival: bargemon, les trois
fighting method: savate
gambling game: brelan
game: brelan, petits chevaux
general: boulanger, foch, gamelin, hoche, marechal
german: bal
gipsy: bohemian
good-bye: adieu, au revoir
gourmet: lyonnais
government center: quai d'orsay
government grant: octroi
greeting: bienvenu, bon soir
guerillas: maquis
hackney coach: fiacre
hairdresser: friseur
half-mask: loup
handwriting: batarde
helmet: heaume
hero: foch, roland
historian: aulard, blanc, guizot, renan, segur, thiers
home: chez, logis, maison, soi
honeysuckle: sulla
illustrator: dore
impressionist: monet
income: rente

island: comoro, corsica, elba, if, ile, lerin, loos, oceania
journalist: barbusse
lace: alencon, cluny, colberteen, valenciennes
lake: annecy, bourget
lamp: veilleuse
language: catalan, provencal
laundry: blanchisserie
lavender: cassidony, plant
leather: cuir
leave: absence, conge
lenten season: careme
light standard: carcel
linen cloth: blancard
literary society: academie goncourt
litter: cacolet
lord: seigneur
lyric: descort
magistrate: echevin
maidservant: bonne, lisette
man: frog, jean, picard, poilu
market town: bourg
marshal: bazaine, bernadotte, canrobert, foch, joffre, murat, ney, petain, saxe
mask: loups
mathematician: borel, cauchy
measure: arpent, aune, boisseau, carat, chopine, decillion, hemine, lieue, ligne, line, mile, mine, muid, perch, pied, point, poisson, pouce, quartaut, quarteron, roquille, sack, setier, stere, toise, tonneau de mer, volte
medal: croix de guerre
metaphysician: descartes
mount: alps, auvergne, blanc, cenis, cevennes, cote d'or, puy de dome, puy de sancy, pyrenees, vignemale, vosges
mountain troops: blue devils
mulberry: beauty berry
mushroom: chanterelle, grisatre, morille
music form: allemande, aubade,

* Asterisk means to look up this word to find more answer words.

bourree, chaconne, forlane, morceau, valse
national anthem: marseillaise
national flower: lily
national holiday: bastille day
naturalist: buffon
naval base: brest, lorient
navigator: freycinet
novelist: *french: author
nursemaid: bonne
officer: prefect
ornament: conge, fleuron
painter: *french: artist
palace: elysee
pancake: crepe
pastry shop: patisserie
philosopher: abelard, bayle, bend, bergson, caro, compte, descartes, pascal, rousseau
physician: bichat, celine
physicist: ampere, arago, becquerel, broglie, curie
poem: dit, lai, rondeau, vers
poet: *french: author
police: gendarme, surete
political club: jacobin
porcelain: limoges, sevres, vendee
port: brest, caen, havre, sete
priest: abbe, cure, pere
promissory note: assignat
pronoun: ces, elle, ils, mes, moi, nous, une, votre, vous
psychologist: binet
racecourse: auteuil
railroad: tortillard
republic calendar: brumaire, fervidor, floreal, frimaire, fructior, germinal, messidor, nivose, pluviose, prairial, thermidore, vendemaiaire, ventose
recruit: bleu, recrue
resort: cannes, cote d'azur, juan-les-pins, menton, midi, nice, pau, riviera, st tropez, vichy
restaurant: boite, bistro, cafe
restaurant guide: michelin
revolution costume: carmagnole

revolutionist: blanqui, bourgeoisie, communard, danton, jacobin, marat, reign of terrorist, robespierre, sans-culottes
rifle: chassepot
saint: bernadette, denis, martin
school: academie, ecole, lycee
sculptor: anguier, bartholdi, bouchard, figuriste, rodin
shield: bouclier, egide, targe
sect: albigenses, cathari
shopgirl: midinette
silk center: arles, lyons
singer: calve, piaf, pons
soldier: assis, chasseur, poilu, soldat, zouave
song: aubade, caira, chanson, madelon, virelai
stock exchange: bourse
store: boutique
sutler: vivandier
symbol: cock, fleur-de-lis, lily
thank you: merci (beaucoup)
waiter: garcon
weight: carat, esterlin, gros, livre, marc, once, tonne
war cry: montjoie
welcome: bienvenu
wine: bois, sauterne, vin
FRENETIC: *insane, mad, *violent, *wild
FRENZIED: *frenetic, *violent
FREQUENT: often, *use, *usual
FRESH: additional, airy, another, blooming, brand-new, brassy, breezy, brisk, chilly, clear, *cool, different, energetic, facy, first-hand, flip, flush, green, *hot, impudent, keen, late-model, lively, lush, neopteric, new, novel, original, other, *pure, raw, recent, sassy, sprightly, strange, *sweet, uncommon, *unique, untried, vernal, vigorous, virgin, vivacious, vivid, windy, young
FRET: abrade, *agitate, *anger, chafe, fidget, grate, kvetch

* Asterisk means to look up this word to find more answer words.

FREY: *friend:* skirnir
parent: njord, skadi
sister: freya, freyja
slayer: surt(r)
wife: gerd(a), gerth
FREYA: *husband:* oder
necklace: brisingamen
FRIAR: *ascetic, *monk
bird: pimlico
black: dominican
cowl: arum
gray: franciscan
lantern: luminescence
mendicant: servite
robin hood's: tuck
white: carmelite
FRIEND: achates, acquaintance,
advocate, ally, alter ego,
ami(go), *associate,* companion,
comrade, confidant, confrere,
dog, *fellow,* intimate, kith,
neighbor, pal, patron, pickup,
quaker, sympathizer
at court: influence, supporter
false: brutus, judas
group: band, chevra, circle, clique,
club, company, flock
of the court: amicus curiae
FRIENDLY: *island:* tonga
FRIEZE: *fillet:* taenia
space: metope
FRIGG: *husband:* odin, woden
maid: fulla
messenger: gnas
son: balder, baldr
FRIGHT: *alarm, anxiety, *start
FRIGHTFUL: *bad, *great, *hideous, *terrible, *ugly
FRILL: *bit, *ornament, spinach
FRINGE: *border, *edge, zizith
FRISK: caper, frolic, *play
FROCK: *dress, ordain, tunic
FROG: *comb.:* batracho, rani
genus: anura, hyla, rana, salientia
fish: antennariid
hopper: cercopid, insect
man: diver, scavenger, swimmer

mouth: bird, caprimulgus
pert.: batrachian, ranine
FROLIC: *frisk, fun, *wanton
FROM: *comb.:* ab, abs, ap, aph,
apho, de, ec, fro
FRONT: *comb.:* anter, antero
FRONTIER: border, *edge, *limit
boundary: limtrophe
cemetery: boothill
post: *fort
FROST: *bite:* chilblains, kibe
-covered: iced, rimed
fish: kokopu, para, tomcod, scabbard, smelt, whitefish
giant: hrym
smoke: barber
weed: canada rockrose
FRUIT: *income, *yield
aggregate: etaerio, magnolia, raspberry
astringent: sloe
baccate: berry
basket: pottel, pottle
bat: peca
-bearing: productive
beverage: ade, wine
blackthorn: sloe
buttercup: achene, akene
carminative: anise, badian
collective: syncarpium
comb.: carp, carpo, carpous
compound: pectin
decay: blet, rot, spot
dish: compote
dried: currant, prune, raisin
drupaceous: cherry, olive, plum
dry: achene, legume, regma
early maturing: rareripe
eater: bananaquit, coereba honey
creeper
eating: carpophagous
envelope: burr, rind
fleshy: apple, berry, cherry, drupe,
melon, orange, pear, pepo, plum,
pome, tomato
fungus: apothecium, ascocarp
goddess: pomona

* Asterisk means to look up this word to find more answer words.

gourd: cucumber, melon, pepo, pumpkin, seton, squash
hard-shelled: gourd, nut
husk: lemma
hybrid: pomato, tangelo
imperfect: button, nubbin
indehiscent: amphisarca, gourd
jar ring: gasket, lute, rubber
juicy: apricot, grape, lemon, lime, peach, pear, pineapple
layer: epicarp
lichen: apothecium
of jove: persimmon
of paradise: grapefruit, pomelo
of rose: cynorr hodon
of strawberry: etaerio
one-seeded: achene, samara
part: pulp, rind, seed, skin
pear-shaped: avocado, fig
peddler: coster, greengrocer
pert.: pomonal, pomonic
plum-like: sloe
pomegranate-like: balausta
preserve: compote, jam, jelly
producing: carpogenous
prune-like: myrobalan
pulpy: berry, drupe, fig, grape, pear, pome, uva
refuse: marc
science of: carpology
seed: achene, drupe, pip, pit
skin: epicarp, peel, rind
spore: aecium
squeezer: reamer
stalk: peduncle
stone: apricot, cherry, drupe, nectarine, paip, peach, plum
tree: *tree: fruit
tropical: anana, banana, *citrus, date, gourd, guava, inca, mango, papaya, sapodilla
winged: samara
FRUSTRATE: anient, balk, *beat, blight, block, check, confuse, cross, dash, *defeat, disappoint, foil, nullify, outwit, scotch, thwart, *trick

FUGITIVE: *criminal, renegade
FUGUE: *anser:* comes
 exponent: bach, handel
 special passage: stretta
FULFILL: *accomplish, *acquit, *act, *answer, execute, *meet
FULL: *comb.:* ose, itous, ulent
FULLER'S: *earth:* bole
 earth ingredient: attapulgite
 grass: soapwort
 herb: teasel, teazel
FULSOME: *bad, *terrible
FULTON: *folly:* clermont, ship
FUMBLE: *error, turnover
FUME: *anger, *scent, *smoke
FUNCTION: *use, *value, *work
FUNERAL: *bell:* knell, mortbell
 feast: arthel, arvel, averil
 march: cortege, crawl, dirge
 oration: eloge, encomium, eulogy, panegyric
 pyre: balefire, pile, suttee
 song: dirge, elegy, elogium, epicedium, nenia, requiem, threnody
 structure: catafalque
 urn: bone pot, ossuarium
FUNGUS: *black:* ergot
 cells: asci
 disease: framboesia, mycosis
 dots: telia
 edible: blewits, cepe, morel, mushroom, truffle
 -like: agaric
 parasitic: aweto, ergot, tinea
 poisonous: amanita, mushroom
 primitive: archimycetes
FUNK: *hole:* cellar, refuge
FUNNY: *absurd, amusing, antic, brilliant, clever, eomic, curious, droll, *eccentric, facetious, humorous, jocose, keen, ludicrous, nimble, pungent, quizzical, *rich, ridiculous, risible, salty, scintillating, *sharp, *smart, sprightly, whimsical, witty
 man: buffoon, clown, comic, wit

* Asterisk means to look up this word to find more answer words.

FUR: *coat:* pelage, pelisse
 hat: busby
 lamb: astrakhan
 pattern: agouti, agouty
 refuse: kemp
FURIES: alecto, dirae, erinyes, erinys, eumenides, megaera, semnae, tisiphone
FURNACE: *comb.:* fornax
 electric: arsem
 fiery, three thrown into: ananias, shadrach, sidrach
 front: breast
 man: bustler, stoker
 mouth: bocca
 opening: glory hole
 ore: aludel, bustamente
 part: bosh
F U R N I S H : *accommodate, *adapt,* afford, *supply, *yield
 battlements: crenelate
 meals: board, cater, feed
 money: bank, capitalize
FURNITURE: *foot:* ball-and-claw
 leg: baluster
 ornamentation: bottle-turning
 part: shook
 style: adam, arkwright, biedermeir, bombay, break front, chippendale, colonial, hepplewhite, renaissance
 wood: avodire, calamander, cedar, mahogany
FURROW: *opening, *waterway
 comb.: aulaco
 having: gluted, grooved, guttery
 mark: feer(e), scratch
 minute: stria
 notch: score
 plank: rabbet
 rod: burin
FURY: *anger,* passion, *violence
FUSE: *join,* merge, mix, *unite
FUSS: *ado, *bluster, *confuse
 -budget: biddy, granny, old maid, perfectionist
 ceremonial: panjandrum

FUSSY: *exact,* finical, prissy
FUTILE: *arid, *dull, *vague
FYKE: *trap
FYLFOT: *fetish,* swastika

GAAL: *father:* ebel
GAB: *gabble, *lie,* persimmon
GABAEL: *son:* aduel
GABBLE: *nonsense, *talk
GABLE: aileron, pinion, wall
GABRI: *son:* gabael
GABRIEL: *instrument:* trumpet
GAD: roam, sting, *urge, *walk
 chieftain: ahi
 descendant: zia
 father: jacob
 fly: breeze, brims, cleg, spur
 mother: zilpah
 son: areli, arod, eri, ezbon
 tribe: erites
GADDIEL: *father:* sodi
GADGET: gimmick, gismo, *thing
GADHELIC: erse, *irish,* manx
GAEA: *children:* anteus, ceto, cybele, *cyclopes,* echidna, erechtheus, eurybia, *hecatoncheires,* nereus, phorcys, pontus, thaumas, *titans,* typoeus, uranus
 consort: pontus, tartarus, uranus
GAELIC: *celt, *irish, *scotch
GAFF: *spear, *talk, *trick
GAFFE: blunder, *error
GAG: *act, *joke, *stop, *trick
GAGA: *insane, *mad,* nutty
GAGE: challenge, *gauge,* measure
GAIN: booty, *get, *grow, *make,* net, profit, *return, *take
GAINSAY: deny, oppose, refute
GALA: *affair,* fiesta, *party
GALAL: *son:* shammua
GALAHAD: *father:* lancelot
 mother: elaine
 quest: holy grail
GALAPAGOS ISLANDS: tortoise

* Asterisk means to look up this word to find more answer words.

GALATEA: *lover:* acis, polyphemus

GALAXY: *group, *quantity

GALE: blast, bog shrub, *storm

GALILEE: holy land, mare tyberiadis, porch, portico, stoa, tiberias
prince: herod
town: capernaum, nazareth

GALL: abrade, *anger, chutzpa, effrontery, *hurt, spite, vex

GALLANT: *cavalier, *spark

GALLEON: argosy, carack, ship

GALLERY: arcade, museum, *walk
protecting troops: ecoute

GALLEY: *armed:* aesc, dromond
chieftain's: birling, birlinn
norse: aesc
slave: drudge
west: crooked

GALLOP: lope, *speed, tantivy

GALLOWS: braces, gibbet, *good
bird: *criminal
pert.: patibulary

GALORE: *plenty, *quantity

GAMBLE: bet, *fate, *venture

GAMBLING: *device:* crap table, dice, pinball, roulette wheel, slot machine, wheel of fortune
house man: croupier, dealer, gutpuller, stickman, tab
pert.: aleatory
place: domdaniel, bucket shop, casino, crib, flat, hell, joint, las vegas, nevada, pool room, reno, tripot
pool: calcutta
stake: ante, bet, kitty, layout, mise, pool, pot

GAMBOGE: calaba, garcina, resin

GAMBOL: *caper, *play, sport

GAME: brave, fun, hobby, quarry
ball: baseball, billiards, cat, cricket, croquet, fives, football, golf, handball, hockey, pelota, polo, pool, rugby, soccer, squash
bird: duck, grouse, quail

board: bingo, checkers, chess, cribbage, parcheesi, scrabble
carnival: darts, hoopla
child's: hide-and-seek, tag
cock: fighter, stag
confidence: bunco, bunko
fish: blanquillo, marlin, shark
follow: dog, hunt, stalk
gambling: baccarat, backgammon, craps, fantan, faro, poker
lumberjack: birling
parlor: bingo, cards, charades, dibs, dominoes, jacks, matador
piece: man, domino, tile
pin: bowling, kegling, skittles
war: kriegspiel
word: acrostic, anagram, crambo

GAMESTER: bettor, cardsharp, crapshooter, dicer, gambler, oraler, player, plunger, sport

GAMMON: bacon, foot, *nonsense

GAMUT: *range, scale, sweep

GANDHI: *name:* aba, abba, abou, bapu, bu, mahatma
ism: non-violence, satyagraha
prison: poona
publication: harijan

GANELON: *friend:* pinabel
son: baldwin
steed: tachebrun
sword: murgleis

GANESHA: *father:* siva
moth: parvati

GANG: band, crew, *group, *staff

GANGES: *barge:* budgero(w)
boat: putelee, puteli
city: benares
dolphin: susu
efflorescence: reh
goddess: gangadevi
landing place: ghat

GANGSTER: *criminal, *hoodlum
girl: moll

GANYMEDE: catamitus
consort: hebe
mother: callirrhoe

* Asterisk means to look up this word to find more answer words.

sire: assaracus, erichthonius, ilus, laomedon, tros

GAOL: **jail,* imprison, prison

GAP: **flaw, *split, *waterway*

GAPE: glare, stare, yawn

seen: sight, starer

GARAGE: body shop, car house

GARB: apparel, **dress,* guise

GARBAGE: **nonsense, *refuse*

GARDEN: *aster:* callistephus

balm: monarda, oswego tea

bower: alcove

city: chicago, kent

eden: **paradise, *utopia*

house: casino, gazebo

huckleberry: morel, nightshade

orach: alpine dock, beet

pest: aphid(is)

phlox: beacon, flower

produced in: olitory

tool: dibber, hoe, mower, rake, scythe, sickle, trowel, weeder

variety: **average,* ordinary

warbler: beam bird, beccafico

GARGANTUA: *son:* pantagruel

wife: badebec

GARGANTUAN: **big,* brobdingnagian, **great,* huge

GARLAND: anadem, fillet, lei

GARLIC: *oil radical:* allyl

pert.: alliaceous

root: bulb, moly, ramson

segment: clove

GARMENT: **dress,* tog, vestment

alterer: bushman

ancient: chiton, chlamys, ephod, himation, paenula, palla, stola, synthesis, toga

bishop's: **vestment: religious*

cloak: caputium

close-fitting: coatee

fitted: reefer

infant's: bunting, woolly

loose: camise, cloak, cymar, mantle, robe, simar

making: cobbling, haberdashery, millinery, sewing, tailoring

medieval: chausses, kirtle, rochet, simar, tabard

men's: belt, cap, coat, drawers, hat, jacket, pants, shirt, shorts, slacks, suspenders, trousers

mourning: black, crepe, cypress, sackcloth, weeds, weepers

outer: aba, capote, cloak, coat, dress, haori, jacket, paletot, parka, polonaise, robe, shawl, skirt, sweater

part: arm, bosom, collar, cuff, fly, lapel, leg, neck, pocket, seat, sleeve, waist

protective: apron, armor, brat, broigne, chaps, coveralls, cuculla, gaberdine, pinafore

priest: **vestment: religious*

rain: oilskin, poncho, slicker

rehearsal: leotard

repairer: bushelman

scarflike: tippet

skins: parka

sleeveless: aba, cape, mantle, slipover, sweater, vest

tuniclike: tabard

under: bra, bvds, shift, slip

upper: blouse, coat, guernsey, jersey, jupon, peplus, shirt, sweater, tunic, vest, waist

women's: bodice, blouse, bra, bourkha, burga, burkha, **dress,* mantua, shift, simar

GARNER: **accumulate, *gather*

GARNET: *berry:* currant

black: melanite

clew: rope

green: olivine, uvarovite

red: almandine, almandite

GARNISH: **adorn, *ornament*

GARRISON: **fort, *fortify*

GAS: **nonsense, *talk*

apparatus: aerator

bag: ballonet, braggart

balloon: helium, nitrogen

blue: ozone

charcoal: oxane

* **Asterisk means to look up this word to find more answer words.**

colorless: ammonia, arsine, ethane, keten, oxane, ozone
comb.: aer(o)
container: cell
inert: argon, helium, nitrogen, xenon
inflammable: butane, ethane, methane
intestinal: borborygamus
light burner: batswing
marsh: methane
military: adamsite
mustard: yperite
oxygen: ozone
pipe: tube
plant: artillery plant, burning-bush, dittany, fraxinella, mock cypress, wahoo
poison: arsine, chlorine, mustard, stribine
radioactive: niton, radon
rating: octane
-separating: atmolysis
stoker: blockman
GASCONADE: bluster, boasting
GASTROPOD: *ear-shaped:* abalone, haliotis, ormer
extinct: bellerophon
marine: acera, aplysia, buccinida, cowry, limpet, murex, tethys
GATE: audience, *opening, *take
comb.: pyle
crasher: guest, intruder
house: bar, lodge
keeper: porter, warden
post: durn, upright
rear: postern
tower: barbican
way: arch, dar, pylon, toril
GATH: *king:* achish, maoch
GATHER: *accumulate, *acquire, assemble, blow, brew, bulk, bunch, collect, compile, conclude, congregate, convene, cull, deduce, derive, develop, fold, *get, garner, glean, harvest, herd, huddle, impend, infer, judge,

mass, *meet, mobilize, muster, pick, plait, pluck, *raise, rally, reap, sheave, *store, *take, *think
GAUCHE: absurd, *bizarre, *weird
GAUCHO: *knife:* bolo, machete
lariat: bolas
tree: use
GAUGE: *estimate, *fee, *model
GAUL: *ancient people:* celt, remi
apostle: irenaeus
chariot: esseda, essede
city: alesia
god: belenus, esus, taranis
magistrate: vergobret
nation: aedui
priest: druid
river god: belisama
seer: vates
GAUTAMA: *buddha, siddhartha
wife: ahalya
GAWAIN: *brother:* gaheris, gareth
father: lot
son: florence, gyngalyn, lovel
GAWK, GAWP: *fool, *look
GAY: *bright, *happy, *wanton
GAZE: *look, ogle, *see, watch
GAZELLE: *clark's:* dibatag
four-horned: chikara
hound: saluki
GE: *child:* titan, uranus
GEAR: *baggage, *dress, rig
parts: manavelins
tooth: cog
transmission: speed
wheel: pinion
GEATA: *prince:* beowulf
GEB: *bird form:* goose
daughter: isis, nephthys
father: shu
names: cronus, keb, seb
son: osiris, set
wife: nut
GEDALIAH: *son:* cushi
GEE: *accord, agree, *right
-gee: bangtail, horse, nag

* Asterisk means to look up this word to find more answer words.

GEHENNA: *hell
GEM: *stone
  artificial: paste, strass
  -bearing earth: byon
  blue: aquamarine, sapphire, turquoise
  carnelian: sard
  carved: cameo
  cutter: geniostat
  face: bezel, culet, facet
  friendship: topaz
  good luck: moonstone
  green: chrysolite, emerald, peridot
  health: agate
  immortality: emerald
  imperfect: glass, loupe
  inlaying: crusta
  iridescent: cat's-eye, moonstone, opal, pearl
  law: ruby
  love: amethyst
  modern: jacinth, ligure, zircon
  peace: diamond
  pert.: lapidary, lapideous
  purity: pearl
  purple: amethyst
  rectangular: baguet(te)
  red: avena, carnelian, garnet, pyrope, ruby, sard
  relief: cameo
  rose spinel: balas
  ruby-colored: spinel
  setting: chaton, ouch, pave
  state: idaho
  truth: sapphire
  weight: carat, karat
  youth: beryl
GEMARA: baraithas, talmud
  contents: haggada, halakah
GEMARIAH: *son:* michaiah
GEMINI: *castor, pollux, twins
GENERAL: *all, *average, *broad, catholic, commander, common, epidemic, officer, ordinary, overall, *popular, *regular, total, *universal, *usual, *vague, whole, widespread

GENERATE: *get, *make, *start
GENEROUS: *big, *good, *great
GENII: *demon, *devil
GENIP honeyberry, lana, madder
GENIUS: *gift, *power, *skill
GENOA: *city:* cuneo
  coin: genovino, jane
  family: doria
  magistrate: abbot of the people
GENRE: art, category, *kind
  painting: bambacciata
GENTILE: goy, heathen, infidel
  apostle: st paul
  boy: shaygets
GENTLE: affable, amiable, balmy, bland, *break, broken, calm, chastened, chivalrous, clement, dainty, delicate, docile, easy, faint, humane, *kind, lamblike, lenient, *light, meek, mild, moderate, noble, *quiet, *slow, *smooth, *soft, *sweet, *tame
GENUINE: *good, *pure, *right
GEOLOGICAL: *age:* archeozoic, azoic, cambrian, carboniferous, cenozoic, comanchean, cretaceous, devonian, eocene, jurassic, mesozoic, miocene, mississippian, oligocene, ordovician, paleozoic, permian, pleistocene, proterozoic, silurian, triassic
  pert.: arenig
  remains: fossils
  suff.: cene, ian, oic
  vein angle: hade
GEOMETRY: *coordinate:* abscissas
  father: euclid
  figure: circle, cone, crescent, cube, cuboid, cusp, cylinder, decagon, ellipse, gnomon, heptagon, hexagon, hexahedron, icosahedron, isagon, lozenge, lune, nonagon, oblong, octagon, octahedron, oxygon, parallelepipedon, parallelogram, pelcoid, pentacle, pentagon, pentahedron, polygon,

---

* Asterisk means to look up this word to find more answer words.

prism, quadrant, quadrilateral, rectangle, rhombus, solid, sphere, square, tetragon, trapezium, triangle, versor
line: locus, secant
point relating to curve: acnode
premise: postulate
proponent: euclid, pascal
proposition: theorem
ratio: pi, sine
surface: nappe, torus
GEORGIA: *bark:* cascara buckthorn
bird: brown thrasher
flower: cherokee rose
island: sapelo
nickname: empire, peach state
queen: tamara, thamara
tree: live oak
GERA: *son:* ehud, shimei
GERAHS: *twenty:* shekel
GERAINT: *wife:* enid
GERAR: *king:* abimelech
GERD: *father:* gymer
GERM: *cell:* egg, gamete, ovum
comb.: blasto
fermenting: zyme
-free: antiseptic, aseptic
plasm: genes
seed: chit
GERMAN: aleman, almain, boche, dutchman, fritz(ie), heinie, hun, kraut, jerry, related, saxon, teuton, yekke
antiaircraft gun: archie
admiral: raeder, spee, tirpitz
air force: luftwaffe
apostle: st boniface
architect: behrens, bohm, mies van der rohe
aristocracy: junker(s)
armament works: krupp
army unit: panzer, taxis
article: das, der, die, ein
artist group: blaue reiter
bomber: stuka

cake: kuchel, lebkuchen, pfeffernuss, torte
camp: stalag
canal: kiel
castle: schloss
cathedral: cologne, essen
chemist: bosch, buchner, bunsen
coal region: aachen, krefeld, ruhr, saar, sarre
coin: achtethaler, albus, batz, blaffert, groschen, kronen, mark, pfennig, plappert, thaler
commune: marl
communist: spartacist
composer: abt, bach, beethoven, blacher, brahms, bruch, handel, hasse, wagner, weber
conductor: busch, mengelberg
cutlass: dusack, tesack
-czech region: sudeten
dam: eder
dance: allemande
demon: alp, kobold
district: gau
elite flyers: jagdstaffel
emperor: frederick, wilhelm
engraver: durer
exclamation: ach, himmel, hoch
first man: mannus
game: quodlibet, radmuhle, schafkopf, tapp-tarok, tippen, vierzig vom konig, wendish, wurfelspiel, zwicken
geologist: heyne
glass city: jena
forester: waldgrave
gipsy: zigeuner
goblin: kobold
gods: *aesir, *norse references
gun: bertha, big bertha
hall: aula, bursa, diele, saal
hero: arminius, siegfried
high command: okh
highway: autobahn
historian: agricola, dahn, georgius, moser, neander
inventor: bunsen, diesel

* Asterisk means to look up this word to find more answer words.

island: alsen, fohr, insel
jew: ashkenazi
knight: ritter
lake: chiem, see, wurm
lancer: uhlan, ulan
legislature: bundesrat, herrenhaus, landtag, reichstag
lias: black jura
liquor: schnapps
lyric poems: lieder
mathematician: liebnitz
measles: masern, rubella
measure: aam, anker, carat, eimer, imi, kanne, kette, klafter, last, mass, masskanne, sack, scheffel, schoppen, strich, stubchen
metaphysician: kant
military medal: iron cross
mister: herr
mountain: alps, berg, harz
music form: abendmusik, nachtmusik, zigeunerlied
naturalist: hugel
naval base: emden, kiel
nobleman: adlig, billung, edel, graf, junker, ritter
numbers 1–10: eins, zwei, drei, vier, funf, sechs, sieben, acht, neun, zehn
occupation zone: bizonia
overture: vorspiel
painter: begas, ernst, roos
people: jute, quadi, ubii, volk
philologist: beneke, grimm
philosopher: hegel, kant, nietzsche, schopenhauer, weiss
physicist: born, bothe, braun, doppler, erman, ohm, weber
pietist: francke, spener
port: bremen, emden, hamburg
postwar boom: wirtschaftswunder
president, first: ebert
prison: stalag
pronoun: du, ich, sie, uns
pubs: kneipen
resort: ems, baden, weisbaden
rifleman: jager, yager

rocket: buzz bomb
rocket engineer: braun
school: gymnasium, volkschule
seeress: alruna
society: bund, gesellschaft, turnverein, verein
soldier: boche, jerry, kraut
song: lied(er)
spirit: geist
student: abiturient
student cap: cerevis
sub: u-boot, unterseeboot
teacher: docent, dozent
theologian: arnd, bauer, eck
title: graf, herr, prinz, von
toast: prosit
tobacco: schwarzer krauser
town: stadt
tribal leader: ariovistus
vowel change: umlaut
wheat: emmer, speltz
wine: hock, mosel, rhine, wein
woman: frau(lein), frow

GERMANE: akin, *appropriate
GERRYMANDER: *adjust, jigsaw
GERSHONITE: *father:* lael
GEST: *deed, romance, tale
GESTALT: *form, pattern, shape
GESTURE: *gest, motion, posture
GET: *accomplish, *acquire, *begone, catch, delve, dig, discover, gain, *gather, hear, incur, *kill, *make, obtain, receive, *run, *secure, *seize, *steal, *take, *trap, *understand, *win
aboard: catch, embark, *join
across: penetrate, sell
ahead: *speed, *succeed, *win
along: agree, fare, *get ahead
around: *evade, mingle, travel
at: *acquire, bribe, *reach
away: *escape, fly, lam, shoo
back: redeem, *return
behind: back, boost, *support
by: cope with, make it, *pass
even: retaliate, *settle, square
hitched: marry

* Asterisk means to look up this word to find more answer words.

hot under the collar: *anger
in: *accumulate, *enter, reap
in there: begin, *start
into line: conform, obey
in with: cultivate, *join
it: comprehend, *understand
lost: *begone, *escape
next to: convince, seduce
off: begin, *speed, *start
on: age, depart, *succeed
out: *begone, *escape, *issue
out of: *avoid, evade, shirk
over: move, recover, *succeed
plastered: *drink
results: *accomplish, *succeed
rid of: *destroy, *discard, *kill,
  liquidate, purge
satisfaction: duel, *settle
set: *prepare, *ready, *set
the best of: *defeat, *skin
the drop on: *aim, *attack
the hang of: *understand
the message: *understand
the show on the road: *start
there: *enter, *succeed
together: *accumulate, *affair
up: arise, *dress, *make, *set
up and go: energy, enterprise
GEZER: *king:* horam
GHASTLY: *bad, dismal, *ugly
GHETTO: barrio, confine, slum
GHOST: author, *demon, *spirit
belief in: eidolism, superstition
comb.: scio
crab: sprite
deity: enlil, hecate
fish: chiro
noise-making: poltergeist
plant: tumbleweed
-ridden: possessed
spectre: revenant
spiritualism: guide, control
story: *lie
town: dead city
write: compose, *substitute
GHOUL: *demon, *devil, *thief
GIANT: *demon, *devil, *norse

giant, *titan
comb.: giganto, titano
deformed: fomors
100-eyed: argus
100-handed: aegaeon, briareus,
  cottus, gyges
land of: bashan, utgarthar
man-eating: cacus
oison's father: fionn
primeval: ymir
progenitor of: ymir
stride: distance, league
thousand-armed: bana
GIBBER(ISH): *gossip, *nonsense
GIBRALTAR: pillars of hercules
GIDEON: jerubbaal
father and victim: oreb
servant: phurah
son: abimelech, jotham
GIFT: alms, *aptitude, benefit,
  blessing, bonus, boon, bribe,
  cadeau, charity, dole, dow, endowment, faculty, flair, foy,
  *free, genius, grant, gratuity,
  handsel, honorarium, knack,
  largesse, offering, *present,
  *prize, *skill, subsidy, *token
GIGANTES: *parent:* gaea, uranus
subduer: hercules
GIGANTIC: *big, *great, *large
GILD: falsify, *ornament, tempt
the lily: lay it on, overdo
GILDA: *father:* rigoletto
GILEAD: *descendant:* ulam
father: machir
judge: jair
towns: bezer, casphor, maked
GILGAMESH: *friend:* engudi
GILL: brook, collar, girl, lung
comb.: branchi(a), branchio
four: pint
GILT: *money, *show, *thief
-edged: *good, superior
GIMCRACK: gewgaw, *plot, toy
GIMMICK: device, *thing, *trick
GINGER: *fire, *force, *spirit
-bread: parkin, trimming, wealth

* **Asterisk means to look up this word to find more answer words.**

-bread girl: gretel
-bread tree: doom, dum
cookie: snap
genus: aralia, mioga, zingiber
pine: cedar
root: coltsfoot
wild: asarum, bugbane, cohosh,
  sanicle, snakeroot
GIRL: *adolescent:* bobby soxer
chasing: kadritsa
cover: *model
friday: assistant, secretary
friend: *sweet: heart
graceful: nymph, sylph
lively: filly, giglet, *wanton
play: bunny, chorine, showgirl
GIST: chat, heart, kernel, nub
GIVE: *accord, *administer, afford, *allot, allow, apply, attribute, award, bear, be pliant,
  bequeath, bestow, cast, cede,
  commit, confer, contribute, deal,
  deliver, devise, dish out, dispense,
  dole, donate, elasticity, endow,
  extend, fork, furnish, grant, help,
  import, *issue, *present, proffer,
  provide, remise, *return, sacrifice, *send, serve, slip, spare, subsidize, *supply, tender, tip, *yield
a bum steer: *deceive, mislead
a hand: *abet, *aid
a lift: boost, encourage
and take: equity, trade
away: *betray, *discard, *divulge,
  relinquish, *yield
back: remit, restore, *return
forth: afford, emit, proclaim
ground, in: *quit, *stop, *yield
it to: *rebuke, *punish, *scold
off: emit, *issue, exude
out: *administer, *quit, *spoil
over: deliver, relinquish, *stop
rise: engender, *make, *start
satisfaction: atone, duel
the air: *discharge, *dismiss
the business: do in, *kill
the nod: assent, signal

up: *abandon, *discard, *fail,
  *quit, *stop, resign, *yield
way: *break, despond, relent,
  *quit, *stop, weaken, *yield
GIVEN: *suff.:* able, acious
GLACIER: *chasm:* crevasse
deposit: asar, eskar, kame, moraine, osar, paha, placer
erosion: cirque, corrie
facing: stoss
fragment: serac
hill: drumlin, paha
ice: firn, neve, serac
mill: moulin
period: boulder, wurm
pinnacle: serac
ridge: *glacier deposit
snow: *glacier ice
structure: cipollino
waste: diluvium, drift
GLACIS: *fort
GLAD: *happy, satisfied, willing
GLADE: *comb.:* nemo
GLADIATOR: athlete, spartacus
competitions: ludi
trainer: lanista
GLAND: *absence:* anadenia
comb.: aden(o)
dissection: adenotomy
ductless: pineal, thyroid
edible: liver, noix, ris
hardening: adenosclerosis
inflammation: adenia, adenitis
-like: adenoid
salivary: parotid, racemose
secretion: adrenalin, autapoid,
  bile, chalone, gall, hormone, insulin, saliva, sebum
swelling: adenoma, bubo
GLASS: *art:* amberina
artificial gems: strass
atomizer: autospray
beads: aggri, aggry, bugles
blowpipe: matrass
blue: smalt
bubble: bleb, boil, candleball,
  candlebomb, ream, seed

* Asterisk means to look up this word to find more answer words.

colored: aventurine, opaline
-coloring metal: selenium
container: bottle, matrass, jar
defect: tear
design: etch
drinking: *drinking: vessel
furnace: alee, glory hole, lehr
furnace mouth: bocca
fused: frit
gall: anatron
handling rod: punty
jar: bocal, mason, tallboy
layer: casing
-like: hyaline, sanidine, vitric
magnifying: loupe
-maker: glazier, teaser
-making receptacle: boot
material: potash, sand, silica
molten: metal, parison
mosaic: tessera
piece: pane
pox: alastrim, smallpox
refuse: calx, cullet, gull
sheeted: platten
showcase: vitrine
small: pony, shot, vial
transparent: uviol
volcanic: obsidian
ware: crystal
wort: hyaline, jume, kali, kelp
GLASSES: cheaters, spectacles
GLAUCUS: *brother:* learchus
  daughter: deiphobe
  epithets: melicertes, palaemon
  parent: athamas, ino, sisyphus
  son: bellerophon
  wife: ione, syme
GLEAM: burst, *shine, *sparkle
GLEE: delight, gayety, *joy
GLIDE: coast, *slide
GLORY: aureola, blaze, boast, brilliance, celebrity, eclat, esteem, exult, fame, figure, grandeur, halo, *honor, importance, kudos, luster, memory, *name, *note, notoriety, *paradise, popularity, prestige, recognition, rejoice, re-

nown, *report, reputation, *spell, splendor, tir, *title
GLOVE: *material:* cabretta
  castor: cotton, kid, lisle, mocha, napa, nylon, silk, suede
  shape: trank
GLOW: fervor, *light, *shine
GLUT: *eat, satiate, *surfeit
GLUTTON: *epicure, gourmand
GNASH, GNAW: *bite, crunch
GNOME: *adage, *dwarf, *spirit
  race: cercopes
GNOSTIC: *god:* abrasax, abraxas
  sect: bardesanist
GO: *aboard:* embark, mount
  about: pivot, tack, *turn
  after: *follow, *succeed
  against: *attack, oppose
  ahead: aggressive, blank check, dynamo, hustle, progress, *speed, surpass
  all out: compete, *speed, *try
  along: *accept, *support
  astray: deviate, *err, *sin
  at: *attack, *start, *venture
  away: *begone, jump, scat, scram
  back: *retreat, *return, *quit
  berserk: *anger, foam, rave
  -between: *agent, mouthpiece
  down: *decline, *fail, sink
  far: endure, rise, *succeed
  for: *accept, *attack, *love
  great guns: *advance, *succeed
  in for: *start, *try, *venture
  into: *analyze, *enter, *start
  mad: *anger, erupt, rage, roar
  off: *decline, explode, *occur
  on: *anger, continue, *storm
  out: *begone, die, *end, *play
  over: *analyze, *look, *succeed
  places: *accomplish, *succeed
  through: *act, *eat, spend, *use
  to canossa: apologize, *yield
  together: accompany, date
  to glory: *die, perish, vanish
  to pieces: blow up, *fail
  to pot: *decline, die, *fail

---

* Asterisk means to look up this word to find more answer words.

to town: *accomplish, *succeed
to work on: *attack, *start
up: burn, ignite, vanish
with: *accompany, date, escort
GOAL: *desire, *end, *fate, home
GOAT: *and fish:* capricorn
angora: chamal
antelope: chamois, goral, serow
bezoar: pasan(g)
bush bark: amargoso
comb.: aego, capri
cry: bleat
disease: takosis
female: capra, nanny
fish: upeneus
flesh: chevon
god of: aegipan, pan
group: herd, trip
hair: agal, camlet, mohair
jaal: beden, ibex
male: billy, buck
moth: auger worm
pert.: capric, caprine, hircine
rue: catgut, wild sweet pea
skin: capeskin, leather, suede
sucker: antrostomus, caprimulgus, dorhawk, potoo
wild: aegragrus, bezoar, ibex, kras, markhor, pasang, tahr, tair, tehr, thar, tur
GOB: *navy: man, *quantity
GOBI: *lake:* hara
part: alashan
GOBLIN: *demon, *dwarf, *spirit
GODS, GODDESSES (*listed under place, religion or function*)
comb.: dei, theo
father: amen, amon, anshar, apsu, ashur, odin, wotan, zeus
mother: allat, amman, ana, anu, brigantia, brigit, cybele, frigga, madonna, mary, rhea
queen: hera, juno, sati
sons: angiras, rishis
sword: khaled
GOLAN HEIGHTS: *capital:* kuneitra

GOLD: *alloy:* asem, auryl
bar: ingot
bird: canna, plant
black: oil
braid: orris
brick: *cheat, *deceive, shirk
-colored metal: gilt, ormolu
comb.: auri, auro
compound: auride
cup: crowfoot, ranunculus
deposit: placer
digger: flirt, hussy, *wanton
discoverer: sutter
embroider: auriphrygia, orphrey
field: ophir, rand
finch: redcap, yellow bird
fish: calico, dorado
fool's: pyrite(s)
imitation: ormolu, oroide
lace: filigree, orris
magic hoard: rheingold
measure: carat
mine: cornucopia, *plenty
mosaic: ormolu
miner: black sander, prospector
-of-ophir: flower, rose
-of-pleasure: camelina, mustard
pagoda: hoon
pert.: aureate, auric, dore
plate: gild, gilt
property of: aureity
producing: aurific
seeker: argonaut, forty niner, jason, miner, prospector
-silver: calaverite, caracoli
smith: artificer, aurifex
smith crucible: crevet, cruset
-stone: aventurin(e)
telluride: calaverite
thin sheet: foil, latten
thread: canker root, plant
uncoined: bullion
vein: lode
vessel: cupel
washing: lavadero
washing pan: batea

* Asterisk means to look up this word to find more answer words.

GOLDEN: *age:* siecle d'or
apple claimants: aphrodite, athene, hera
apple giver: paris
apple keeper: ithun
bough: mistletoe
calf: idol
chain: laburnum
club: bog torch, orontium
dream: chimera, optimism
eye: beetlehead, bullhead, cur, duck, merrywing, plover
fleece keeper: aeetes
fleece home: colchis
fleece seeker: argonauts, jason
-haired: auricomous
horde leader: batu khan
hours: halcyon days, overtime
king: midas
mean: moderation, medium
oriole: loriot, pirol
robin: baltimore oriole
rod: blue mountain tea, bone wort, daisy, solidago
shiner: bitterhead, bream, calico bass
willow: cane-withy, shrub, tree
GOLF: *attendant:* caddy
ball cover: balata
club: baffy, brassie, bulger, cleek, driver, iron, mashie, midiron, niblick, putter, spoon, wedge, wood
club part: hosel, toe
course: fairway, green, links
cry: fore
error: chop, slice
hazard: bunker, stymy, trap
mound: cup, tee
score: ace, birdie, bogey, bogy, eagle, nassau, par, putt
target: cup, flag, green
tournament: open
GOLGOTHA: calvary, the skull
thief: dismas
GOLIATH: *brother:* lahmi
home town: gath

place of death: elah
slayer: david
GOMER: *husband:* hosea
sire: diblaim, japheth
son: ashkenaz, riphath, togarma
GOMORRAH: *king:* birshaking
GONDOLIER: *song:* barcarolle
GONERIL: *sister:* cordelia, regan
GOOD: *able, *advantage, agatha, all right, auspicious, avail, bally, beau, behalf, bene, benefaction, beneficial, benefit, betcherie, bien, blessing, bonny, bonzer, boon, bravo, brawlie, buckra, bueno, bully, capital, clever, edible, excellent, expedient, facile, *fair, famous, favorable, *fine, first rate, gain, gallows, genuine, gracious, grand, *great, gustatory, gut, handsome, *holy, *honest, *interest, *kind, *meet, moral, nice, *noble, palatable, *popular, *pretty, *pure, *right, ripe, *sacred, sincere, solvent, *splendid, spur, *straight, *supreme, *sweet, tolerable, *top, *true, valid, valuable, virtuous, welfare, well-being, worthy
bye: *adieu, auf wiedersehen, au revoir, bon voyage, buenas tardes, cheerio, ciaou, sayonara, shalom, tata, vale
comb.: agath(o), bene, eu
form: cricket
for nothing: *bad, lazy, mean, otiose, *worthless, wretch
king henry: blite, goosefoot
-looking: *beautiful, *fair
luck: *good-bye, fortune
luck god: bonus eventus
natured: gemutlich, outgoing
news: evangel, gospel
one: gag, *joke, mot, quip, pun
terms: *accord, rapport
time: bash, ball, fete, *party
working order: kilter
GOODLY: *big, *fair, *great

* Asterisk means to look up this word to find more answer words.

GOODS: belongings, bona, bulk, chattels, cloth, commodities, effects, fee, freight, impedimenta, merchandise, *property, *supply, wares
admission of taking: avowry
animal hides: ceroon, seroon
movable: chattels
stolen: booty, graft, loot, pelf, *spoil
shipwrecked: flotsam, jetsam, jettison, lagan, ligan
GOON: *criminal, *hoodlum
GOOSE: brant, *fool, fowl, solan
barnacle: anatifa, crustacean
beakless: gannet
berry: chaperon, obstacle, thape
cry: cackle, cronk, honk, yang
egg: blank, nought, zero, zilch
fat: axunge
fen: graylag, grayling
fish: angler
flesh: cold, pimples
flesh producer: arrector
foot: allseed, atriplex, bassia, blite, plant, shrub
foot seed: allabuta, allseed
genus: anser, brant, chen
group: flock, gaggle, raft
haw: nene, neni
male: gander
pert.: anserine, answerous
sea: gannet, phalarope, solan
snow: brant, chen, wavey
wild: barnacle, brant, ganza, greylag, jacobite
young: gosling
GOPHER: burglar, tucan, tuza
berry: huckleberry, gaylussacia
snake: bull, namer, pituophis
state: minnesota
tortoise: mungofa
GORGEOUS: *beautiful, *splendid
gorge: *opening, *waterway
GORGON: eurale, jezebel, medusa, pephredo, stheno, terror
father: phorcys

mother: ceto
watcher: *graeae
GOSSIP: *babble, *blab, busybody, caddle, callet, camper, cant, cat, cause, chat, chitchat, clat(ter), claver, gup, *noise, on-dit, plosher, quidnunc, *report, scandal, shmooz, slander, *spread, *story, talebearer, *talk, *tell, yachna, yak(ker), yente
GOTH: *apostle:* ulfilas
hero: wudga
last: roderick
GOURD: cucumber, *melon, pepo, pumpkin, seton, squash
GOVERNMENT: politics, *state
by best: aristocracy
by church: hierarchy
by few: oligarchy
by people: democracy
by rich: plutocracy
official: bureaucrat, syndic
GRAB: *seize, *steal, *take
GRACE: *adorn, aglaia, charis, euphrosyne, *ornament, thalia
mother: aegle
GRADE: *class, *rank, *value
GRAEAE: deino, enyo, pephredo
parent: ceto, phorcys
GRAIL: ama, cup, sangreal
knight: bors, galahad, percival
GRAIN: *beard:* arista, awn
beetle: cadelle, tenebroides
brewing: malt
bundle: gravel, sheaf
chaff: bran, grit
coarse: samp
comb.: sito
disease: ergot, smut, thistle
dried: groats, rissom, straw
ear: epi, ressum, spike
food: cereal
fruit: caryopsis
funnel: hopper
gather: glean, harvest, reap
goddess: annona, ceres, demeter
ground: flour, grist, meal

* Asterisk means to look up this word to find more answer words.

husk: bran, glume
line: swath
measure: bushel, grist, mite, moy, peck, thrave
mixture: bullimong, farrage
outer membrane: exine, extine
parched: graddan
pit: exchange, silo
processor: mill
pulpy fruit: drupelet
receptacle: bin, elevator, silo
refuse: chaff, pug
sacrificial: ador
scoop: shaul
sorghum: dari, durr, kafir
spike: chob, ear
stack: rick
stalks: haulm
tool: flail
wood: bate
GRAND: **big, *great, *important*
comb.: bel
GRANT: **accord, *gift, *give*
GRAPE: *acid:* acemic
comb.: botry(o), oen(o)
conserve: jelly, uvate
cure: ampelotherapy
deposit: tartar
disease: anaheim, anthracnose, coleur, esca, erinose
drink: brandy, dibs, sapa, wine
dried: raisin
fermentation: cuvage
fern: botrychium, moonwort
gatherer: vintager
genus: muscadinia, vitis
group: bob, bunch, cluster, racemation
hyacinth: baby's breath, blue bell
jelly: sapa
juice: dibs, must, sapa, stum
parasite: procris
pert.: botryoidal, uval, uvic
product: enin, oenin, wine
pulp: pomace, rape
refuse: bagasse, mark, murk
seed: acinus

sugar: dextrose, fructose, maltose
-vine: bush telegraph, **rumor*
-vine pest: phylloxera
GRAPPLE: **attack,* hook, **seize*
GRASP: **seize, *understand,* take
GRASS: *arrow:* esparto
bamboo-like: reed
barn: ankee
beach: mat
beard: awn
bermuda: devil grass, doob
blade: leaf, spike, traneen
blue: poa
bull: gama, slough
bunch: stipa
burden's: redtop
cantlike: sorghum
carpet: louisiana, smut
cattail: timothy
cereal: barley, millet, oat, rice, rye, wheat
ceremonial: kusa
cloth-plant: ramie
clump: lawn, sward
coarse: bent, gama, reed, sedge
corn: kafir, sedge
couch: brome, devil's, foxtail, quitch, redtop
creeping beard: fescue
darnel: tare, rye
disease: black ring
ditch: enalid
dog's tail: bent, traneen
dried: fodder, hay
esparto: alfa
feather: stipa
fiber: bhabar, flax, istle
fodder: alfalfa, bouteloua, clover, corn, dura, gama, millet, redtop, timothy
fringed brome: chess
fruit: caryopsis
gama: sesame
genus: aira, alopeouruii, arundinaria, arundo, avena, briza, clover, coix, lygeum, poa, setaria, stipa

* **Asterisk means to look up this word to find more answer words.**

goose: loveman, spear

hay: alfalfa, clover, fescue, millet, redtop, timothy

hopper: acridium, ceresa, ceutho-philus, cub, grig, katydid, locust, schistocerca

hunger: foxtail

husk: glume

job's-tears: croix

johnson: sorghum

jointed stem: culm

land: campo, greensward, lea, pampa, pasture, prairie, range, savanna, sward, veldt

leaf: blade, spike, traneen

lemon: cockspur

lyme: hassock

marsh: cane, reed, sedge, spart

mat: nard

meadow: alfalfa, clover, fescue, poa, timothy

mesquite: grama, needle

millet: bengal, panic

oat: avena

pasture: *meadow grass*

plot: lawn, meadow

poison rye: darnel

purple beard: needle

quaking: briza, rattlesnake

quitch: couch

roots: country, *source*

rope: mung, munj, soga

salt: alkali, spart

scale: glume, palea

sedge: broom

seneca: vanilla

silt: knot

stem: culm, reed

stiff: bent, reed

swamp: *marsh grass*

thatch: alang, cogon

trampled: abature

treatise on: agrostography

tree: black boy

trembling: amourette

tuft: tussock

weed: eelgrass

wiry: bent, poa, reed

GRAVE: *dead: home*

cloth: cerement, shroud

comb.: cerio

digger: burier, fossor

flower: frangipani, plumeria

mound: barrow, tumulus

pert.: sepulchral

robber: ghoul

stone: *memorial*, *monument*, sarcophagus, stela, tombstone

wax: adipocere

GRAY: *beard:* bellarmine, oldster

blue: azurine, cesious, perse

brown: dun, taupe

comb.: polio

dark: charcoal, oxford, taupe

haired: aged, badgerly

light: ashy, pearl

-ling: fish, herring, pink, umber

matter: brains, cortex, obex

metal: manganese, steel

mole: taupe

out: blackout, faint, swoon

parrot: jako, psittacus

plaid: maud

quaker: acier

rock: andesite

snapper: cabellerote, lutianus

whale: ripsack

yellow: pongee

GREASE: *coating:* camouis

rack: lubritorium

spot: bird's-eye

the palm: ante, bribe, pay

the wheels: expedite, lubricate

wood: chamiso, chico, orache

GREAT: *able*, *absolute*, *ace*, *acme*, almighty, astronomical, august, awful, behemothic, *big*, brobdingnagian, bulky, bully, burra, but good, celebrated, co-lossal, consequential, consider-able, consummate, cosmic, crack-erjack, dandy, deadly, distin-guished, downright, dreadful, elevated, eminent, enormous, es-

* **Asterisk means to look up this word to find more answer words.**

timable, exalted, expansive, *extreme*, fearful, *fine*, frightful, generous, *good*, grave, *heavy*, herculean, *high*, hot, huge, hunkydory, illustrious, immense, *important*, intense, jake, keen, *large*, lofty, majestic, mammoth, marked, mighty, mogul, monumental, *noble*, noted, notorious, okay, out of sight, outstanding, *perfect*, plenary, ponderous, precious, *principal*, prodigious, profound, prominent, *rich*, rum, *solid*, *special*, *splendid*, *strong*, stupendous, *supreme*, swell, terrible, titanic, *top*, tremendous, *unique*, vast, *violent*, vip, whacking

albacore: bluefin, tunny
barrier island: otea, shea
blue heron: arsnicker, crane
britain: *england*
bulrush: boulder bast, piassava
coat: cothamore, grego, jimmy
comb.: arch, macro, magni, megal
commoner: pitt
dane: boarhound
divide: rockies
grandchild: ieroe
gun: *lord*, *magnate*, *ruler*
hearted: brave, generous, *good*
lake: erie, huron, michigan, ontario, superior
lake fish: bowback, rooter
lavender: aspic
man: *lord*, *magnate*, *ruler*
mother: agdistis
number: *plenty*, *quantity*
sea: black, mediterranean
serpent: apepi
skua: bird, bonxie
white brother: mahatma
white throne: *paradise*
white way: broadway
GREECE: attica, hellas
GREEK: argive, attic, babel, hellene, jargon, mixup, *sharp*

abbess: amma
admiral: navarch
allies: abantes
alphabet: alpha, beta, chi, delta, eta, epsilon, gamma, iota, kappa, lambda, omega, omicron, phi, pi, psi, rho, sigma, theta, upsilon, zeta
altar: eschara
army arm: axis, evzone, phalanx
assembly: agora, boulet
astronomer: anaximander, aristarchus, calippus
author: aesop, anacreon, hesiod, homer, pindar, plato, plutarch, sappho, thales, zeno
avenging spirit: ate, *erinyes*
beauty: lais
cape: araxos, malea, matapan
castanet: crotalum
catholic: uniat(e)
chariot: biga
charioteer: helios, phaeton
cheese: kasseri
church: orthodox
church leader: arius, origen
church monk: caloyer
citadel: acropolis
cloak: chlamys
commonality: demos
community: deme
conscience: aidos
contest: agon
counsellor: mentor, nestor
courtesan: aspasia, lais
coward: epeus
cup: cotyle, depas, holmos
dance: hormos, pyrrhic, strophe
dance, antiquity: calathiscus
dialect: aeolic, doric, ionic
dirge: linos
district: achaea, arcadia, argolis, arta, attica, boeotia, chios, corfu, elis, euboea, evros, florina, ilia, imathia, ionnania, kazala, kilkis, laconia, laris, lasith, lesbos, leukas, magnisia, messinia, pella,

---

* Asterisk means to look up this word to find more answer words.

phocis, pieria, rhodophe, samos
dragon: basilisk, ladon
dramatist: aeschylus, agathon, aristophanes, euripides, sophocles, thespis
entertainers: hetaera
eparchy: doris
epic: iliad, odyssey
essence: ousia
eve: pandora
evil spirit: momus, python
fabulist: aesop
fate: atropos, clotho, lachesis
festival: agon, delia, haloa
first man: alalcomeneus, deucalion, phanes
flask: aryballos, olpe
flute: hemiope
flyer: icarus
fury: *erinyes
fountain nymph: abarbarea
garment: abolla, chiton, chlamys, peplos, tunic
geographer: strabo
giant: alcyoneus, aloadae, atlas, clytius, cyclops, enceladus, ephialtes, gyges, mimas, pallas, pelorus, polybutes, porphyrion
guerrilla: andart
helmet: alopeke
hero: achilles, ajax, alcinous, diomede, hercules, jason, meleager, perseus, theseus
historian: ctesias, polybius, thucydides, xenophon
history stones: arundel, ian
hobgoblin: empusa
house: andron, thalamos
hunter: orion
huntress: atalanta
image: agalma
immigrant: metic
initiate: epopt(a)
island: chios, cos, crete, delos, elis, ionia, rhodes, samos, santorin, sifnos, syros
january: gamelion

javelin: acontium
judge: dikast, heliast
jug: ascos
ladel: cyathus
lawgiver: draco, minos, solon
legislation goddess: eunomia
legislature: boule, vouli
letter: *greek alphabet
lyre: cithara
magistrate: archon, boeotarch, eparch, ephor, nomarch
market place: agora
mask: onkos
mathematician: euclid, archimedes
mercenaries: armatoles
monster: gorgon, hydra, sphinx
mountain: actium, athos, cambunian, cithaeron, helicon, hymettus, ida, lycabettus, oeta, olympus, ossa, parnassus, parus, pelion, pindus, psiloriti, taygetus
mysteries site: eleusis
noah: deucalion
official: alytarch, amphodarch, archon, boeotarch, eparch, ephor, nomarch
orthodox code: nomocanon
painter: apelles, el greco
paradise: elysium
philosopher: *greek sage
poet: arion, homer, ion, pindar
poetess: corinna, erinna, sapho
portico: stoa, xyst
priest: hierophant, myst, papa
priestess: auge, caryatid
resistance army: elas
river god: achelous, alpheius, asopus, cephissus, inachus, ladon, maeander, peneius, scamander, xanthus
rose: campion, glaieul
sacred city: argos
sacred grove: altis
sacred shield: ancile
sage: abaris, anaxagoras, anaximander, antisthenes, arius, aristotle, carneades, diogenes, galen,

* Asterisk means to look up this word to find more answer words.

mentor, nestor, plato, pythagoras, socrates, zeno
sages, seven: bias, chilon, cleobulus, epimenides, periander, pittacus, solon, thales
sculptor: myron, phidias
seer: calchas, cassandra, melampus, sybil, tiresias
shrine: abatom, heiron, temenos
slave: baube, helot, penest
soldier: acamas, hoplite, palik
sorceress: circe, medea, siren
spirit: ker, pneuma
sun god: apollo, helios, hyperion, ment, phoebus
temple: cella, naos, theseus
theatre: odeon
truth personification: alethia
valley: nemea, tempe
vase: deinos, dinos, pelike
vessel: amphora, cadus, diota, holcad, olpe
voting place: pnyx
war cry: alala
warrior's belt: zouave
warship: cataphract
witch: aganice
wooden statue: xoanon
GREEN: *alga:* blanket-weed
arrow: yarrow
ash: common lilac
backs: bills, dollars, money
bag: lawyer
berets: elite, special forces
blue: aqua, brittany, ceruleum, cyan, saxe, sistine, turquoise
briar: chinaroot, bamboo, smilax, toadflax
chalcedony: jasper
cheese: moon, sapsago
chrysolite: peridot
comb.: praseo, verdi, vern
copper arsenate: erinite
dragon: arum, wake robin
-eyed: envious, jealous
famous: gretna
feldspar: amazonite

fish: girella
gage: plum
goods: counterfeit
gray: olive, reseda
heart: bebeeru, bibiri, tree
horn: amateur, dupe, gull, novice, rookie, tyro, yahoo
house: nursery
light: go ahead, signal
liqueur: angelica
mountain hero: allen
mountain state: vermont
pail: clair de lune
pale: celadon
parrot: amazon, cagit
sand: marl
serpentine: bowenite
sickness: chlorosis
shade: apple, bottle, emerald, kelly, nile, paris, parrot
-tail: fly, grannom
tea: hyson
woodbine: peridot
yellow: artichoke, celadine, citrin, olive, opalie, reseda
GREETING: *hello, *toast
GREMLIN: *dwarf, fairy, imp
GREY: *gray
GREYA: *husband:* oder
GRIP: *absorb, *power, *seize
GROOVE: *opening, *waterway
GROOVY: conventional, in tune, modern, on the beam, with it
make: elate, enthuse, please
GROSS: *all, *brutal, *stupid
GROTESQUE: *bizarre, *weird
GROUND: *bait:* berley, trap
beetle: amara, carabid
cherry: alkekengi, capulin
hog: digger, marmot, woodchuck
hog day: candlemas
inhabiting: terricole
ivy: alehoof, hove
nut: chufa, gobbe, goober
piece: acre, lot, plat, tract
rise: hill, hummock, hurst
shark: carcharhinus, carcharias

* **Asterisk means to look up this word to find more answer words.**

squirrel: chipmunk, hackee
water: vadose
work: basis, *foundation*
GROUP: alliance, armada, army, arrange, assemblage, association, assort, audience, axis, band, bank, batch, bevy, bloc(k), body, board, boodle, breadline, breed, brigade, brood, brotherhood, bunch, bund, bureau, cabal, cabinet, caboodle, cadre, camarilla, camp, cell, chain, chamber, circle, clan, class, clique, club, clump, cluster, clutch, coalition, cohort, collection, colony, community, *company*, congress, cordon, corps, cortege, coterie, covey, crew, crop, crowd, deck, detachment, detail, drift, drove, entente, family, federation, file, fleet, flight, flock, *force*, gang, genus, grange, grove, herd, hive, junta, kennel, *kind*, league, legion, lot, mass, *meet*(ing), mob, mop, mulada, multitude, muster, network, nye, *order*, organization, outfit, *pack*, panel, *party*, *people*, phalanx, platoon, posse, *press*, pride, *push*, *quantity*, queue, ring, sect, *set*, shoal, school, *society*, sort, squad, *staff*, string, swarm, team, thicket, *train*, tribe, troop, troupe, *union*
GROUPER: guasa, hind, mero
GROW: *accrue*, *advance*, boom, bourgeon, branch, breed, bud, burgeon, develop, enhance, flourish, germinate, *increase*, luxuriate, mature, produce, pullulate, *raise*, *spread*, sprout, thrive, *tower*, wax
GRUMBLE, GRUMP: *complain*
GRUNT: croaker, ronco
GUACHONCHO: pelon
GUAM: *capital:* agana

idol: anito
native: chamorro
port: apra
tree: ipil, nangka
GUATEMALA: *ant:* kelep
coin: centavo, peso, quetzal
fruit: anay, banana
grass: teosinte
lake: amatitland, atitlan, dulce, peten
measure: caballeria, cajuela, cuarta, fanega, manzana, vara
novelist: arevalo
volcano: agua, atitlan, fuego
GUDRUN: *brother:* gunnar
consort: atli, sigurd
GUIDO: *notes:* alt, ela, elami, fa, la, re, mi, sol, ut
GUINEA: *bight:* benin
corn: durra, millet
fowl: galeeny, guttera, keel, keet, pintado
hut: benab
pepper: capsicum annum
pig: capybara, cavy
rush: adrue
tree: akee, camara, dalli, genip, icica, lana, mora
tribesman: boni, boschneger
turtle: matamata
weight: aguirage, akey, benda, piso, quinto, seron, uzan
GUITAR: bandore, banjo, bina, pandora, rote, samise(n), sitar, uke, ukulele, vina
fish: batoides
pitch raise: dital
GULCH, GULLY: *gap*, *waterway*
GULF: *pert.:* vortical
weed: sargasso
GULL: *deceive*, *gyp*, skua
pert.: larine
GUM: *animal:* galago
artificial: dextrine
-like: thick, viscid
-like compound: adonin

* Asterisk means to look up this word to find more answer words.

resin: albetad, bdellium, bisabol, cava, commiphora, elemi, frankincense, myrrh
tree: *tree: gum
up: botch, queer, *spoil
GUMS: *comb.:* ulo
pain: ulalgia
pert.: gingival, uletic
GUN: *carriage:* barbette, lunet
catch: sear
cleaner: ramrod
cock: nab
cotton: pyroxylin
fire: fusillade, rafale, salvo
hunting: roer
kinds: ack ack, amusette, *anti-aircraft, archie, armstrong, baril, bazooka, bofors, bore, bren, colt, enfield, gatling, lewis, luger, marlin, *machine: gun, mauser, maxim, remington
-man: *criminal, hoodlum
park: arsenal
part: barrel, bolt, bore, breech, butt, chamber, cock, cylinder, gomer, hammer, lock, magazine, sight, stock, trigger
powder: explosive, green tea
GUNNAR, GUNTHER: *parent:* givki, grimhild
sister: gudrun
uncle: hagen
wife: brunhild(e), brynhild
GURKHA: *sword:* kukri
GUTTER: *opening, *waterway
GWYDION: *consort:* arianrhod
son: dylan
GWYNN: *father:* lludd
GYP: *deceive, *fool, *trick
GYPSY: *boy:* chal
camp: tan
dance: farruca, zingaresca
devil: bang, beng
dialect: rommany, romany
fortune: bahi
girl: chai, chi
great: baro

horse: gras, gri, gry
lady: rani
language: chib, romany
man: calo, rom, rye
mare: grasni
married woman: romi
non: gahjee, gajo
pocketbook: lil
thief: chor
tongue: chib
tribe: aptal, selung
village: gav
winch: crab
GYRATE: spin, *turn

H: *shaped:* zygal
sound: aitch, aspirate
HABAZINIAH: *son:* jeremiah
HABERDASHERY: menswear, *shop, *store
HABILE: *able, *fit, *quick
HABILIMENT, HABILITATE: *dress
HABINGTON: *wife:* castara
HABIT: *disposition, *dress, *rule, *use, *way
pert.: usitative
HABITAT: *home, *range, station
comb.: eco, oeco, oiko
plant form: ecad
HABITUAL: *regular, *usual
HABITUATE: *train, *use
HACATAN: *son:* joannes
HACHALIAH: *son:* nemehiah
HACK: cab, cough, cut, mercenary
berry: beaver, elder, sweet bay
HADASSAH: *esther
HADAREZER: *captain:* shopach
HADES: *hell, pluto, tartarus
assessor: aecus, minos, rhadamanthys
entrance: aornum, erebus
god: *underworld god(dess)
herdsman: menoetes
inhabitant: hellion

* **Asterisk means to look up this word to find more answer words.**

lake: avernus
love: kore, minthe, persephone, proserpina
messenger: namtaru
mother: rhea
pert.: infernal, sheolic
prison: tartarus
river: acheron, cocytus, lethe, phlegethon, styx
HADITH: *compilation:* alsahih
HADJI: ecclesiastic, pilgrim
goal: caaba
HADLAI: *son:* amasa
HADRIAN: *favorite:* antinotis
HAEMOSTATIC: adrenaline
HAFT: *fix, *handle, *settle
HAG: beldam, cailleach, crone, fright, fury, harpy, harridan, jezebel, oldster, shrew, vecke, virago, vixen, *witch
fish: agnatha, borer, myxine
-*ridden:* spellbound
-*ride:* bewitch, harass, *scold
HAGAR: *husband:* abraham
son: ishmael
HAGEN: *slayer:* kriemhild
HAGGARD: *poor, *thin, *wild
HAGGITH: *husband:* david
HAGGLE: *bargain, cavil, palter
HAHA: fence, *laugh, trench
HAIL: *acclaim, *address
-*storm preventative:* paragrele
HAILI, CLARA: hilo hattie
HAIR: *bit, bristle, down, iota
accessory: barrette
braid: coif, cue, pigtail, plait, queue
brained: giddy, shallow
breadth: ace, close, margin
brush: shag
cloth: aba, cilice
coarse: bristle, cerda, chaeta, kemp, seta, setula, shag
coat: fur, hide, melote, pelt
comb.: pil, pili, pilo
covering: snood, toment
curl: buckle, ringlet, tress

cut: bob, butch, crew, tonsure
cutter: barber
disease: dandruff, psilosis
do: chignon, coiffure, marcel
dresser: barber, coiffeur, coiffeuse, beautician, friseur
falling out: dandruff, psilosis
false: peruke, rat, toupee, wig
feeler: palpus
fillet: snood
fix: permanent, set, wave
fringe: bangs, frizette
group: arbuscle, crine, mop
growing: capilliculture
horse: fetlock, mane, seton
intestinal: villus
knot: bun, chignon
-*less:* depilous, glabrous
-*lessness:* acomia, alopecia
lock: burger, cowlick, curl, feak, flock, harigalds, tate
loss: baldness, alopecia
molting: ecdysis
neck: mane
-*net:* lint, snood
-*of-the-dog:* bracer
ornament: bow, comb, coronet
pert.: crinal, linus, pilar
piece: fall, rat, switch
plant: pulus, rubes, villus
raising: terrifying
remover: bob, epilate, depilate
roll: chignon, pompadour, puff
rope: cabestro
salt: alum, alunogen
shirt: burden, cilice, penance
-*splitting:* *critical, picky
unguent: pomade
unruly: cowlick, mop, tousle
worm: gordius
HAIRY: barbate, barbigerous, capillose, ciliate, comate, crinite, floccose, fuzzy, hirsute, hirtellous, pubigerous
HAITI: *bandit:* caco
coin: gourde
deity: atabei, coatrischie, guaban-

---

* Asterisk means to look up this word to find more answer words.

cex, guantuava, joca-huva, opita, zemis
demon: baka, boko
island: gonave, mona
liberator: toussaint
magic: obeah, obi
ruler: dessalines, duvalier
solenodon: agouta
sweet potato: batata
HALAKOTH: *collection:* mishnah
HALBERD: ax, bill, glaive, pike
-shaped: gisarme, hastate
HALCYON: **happy,* kingfisher
days: good times
father: aeolus
husband: ceyx
HALF: *baked:* green, premature
beak: balao, ballyhoo, ihi
breed: griff, ladino, mestizo, mulatto, mule, octoroon
comb.: demi, hemi, semi
gable: aileron
man: centaur, garuda, minotaur
mask: domino, loup
moon: arc, crescent, scimitar
note: minim
turn: caracol(e)
-wit: *fool, simpleton
HALITUS: **air,* aura, fog, vapor
HALL: *athlete:* gym, xystus
justice: basilica
music: gaff, odeon, odeum
odin: valhalla
reception: parlor, salon
student: bursa, dormitory
HALLOW: bless, *honor, revere
HALLUCINOGEN: acetone, benzene, det, dmt, dpt, ether, glue, jimsonweed, lsd, mescal, peyote
HALO: aura, *glory, nimbus
HALT: **arrest, *end, *stop*
HAM: *brother:* shem
father: noah, noe
smoked: serrano
son: canaan, cush, kush, mizraim, phut, put
HAMADAN: achmetha, ectabana

HAMAN: *father:* hamadathus
successor: mardochaeus
wife: zeresh, zosara
HAMATH: *king:* toi, tou
HAMATHITE: *deity:* ashima
HAMBURG: *part:* altona
HAMILTON: *birthplace:* nevis
HAMITE: *father:* abel
language: afar, agao, agau, beja, belin, berber, bilin, bogo, cushitic, ethiopian, gaetulian, gallas, kabyle, masai, mauretanian, numidian, shilha, somali, tamashek
religion: coptic, moslem
HAMLET: *character:* gertrude, laertes, ophelia, polonius
castle: elsinore
country: denmark
friend: horatio
HAMMELECH: *son:* jerahmeel, malchiah
HAMMER: *blacksmith:* fuller, oliver
blow: martel, pound
bricklayer: scutch
face: trip
firearm: cock, doghead
hatter's: beater
head: peen, pein, poll, shark
heavy: bully, butt, kevel, mallet, maul, sledge
lead: madge
medical: plessor, plexor
out: anvil, *form, *make
paver's: reel, tup
pneumatic: buster
presiding officer: gavel
slate: sax
stone: kevel, mash, spall
stonebreaking: bull set
tilt: oliver
toastmaster: gavel
wooden: beetle, gavel, maul
HAMPER: **arrest,* bar, *stop
HAMUTAL: *father:* jeremiah
husband: josiah
son: zedekiah

* Asterisk means to look up this word to find more answer words.

HANANIAH: shadrach
 father: azun, azur
 son: isaiah, pelatiah, shelemiah, zedekiah
HAND: *acclaim, *agent, *aid, deal, *give, man, *part, skill
 ax: boucher
 back: opisthenar
 bag: *bag, etui, purse, valise
 ball: jai alai, pelota
 barrow: bier
 bill: ad, dodger, pamphlet
 book: enchiridion, manual
 breadth: shaftmon, *spread
 cart: go-devil, wheelbarrow
 clenched: fist
 cloth: napkin, towel
 comb.: cheir, chiro, mani, manu
 covering: cestus, glove, mitt
 cuff: bind, bracelet, manacle
 deformity: apehand, talipomanus
 disease: acrodynia
 down: bequeath, endow, *give
 exposed: dummy
 -ful: *bit, *problem, *quantity
 gun: caliver
 hollow: gowpen, gowpin
 in: deliver, *quit, *yield
 -jar: dagger, khanjar, knife
 left: *sinister
 maid: *agent, *instrument
 -me-down: cheap, second-hand
 mill: grinder, quern
 on hip: akimbo, obliquely
 -out: *aid, dole, *gift, *give
 over: ante, cough up, *yield
 palm: loof, thenar, vola
 part: digit, finger, goupen, knuckle, *palm, thumb
 pert.: chiral, manual
 rail: banister, bar, safeguard
 reading: palmistry
 right: dexter
 shaker: candidate, sycophant
 spring: cartwheel
 stone: mano
 -to-mouth: improvident

 without: amanous
HANDICAP: *bet, disadvantage
HANDKERCHIEF: bandanna, barcelona, malabar, scarf
HANDLE: *name, *title, *use
 auto: wheel
 bars: mustache
 bucket: bail, bale
 cross: hilt, potent
 curved: bool
 end: butt
 having: ansate
 -making: ansation
 plane: toat, tote
 printing press: rounce
 scythe: snath, snead, thole
 ship: helm
 spade: tiller
 sword: haft, hilt
 vase: ansa
 whip: crop
HANDSEL: *gift, *money, *use
HANDWRITING: autograph, calligraphy, chirography, griffonage, john hancock, ronde, script, signature
 analysis: bibliotiks
 on the wall: doom, *fate
 words: mene, tekel, upharsin
HANDY: *able, *near, *ready
HANG: *around:* *associate, cling
 back: delay, lag, *retreat
 bird: baltimore oriole, robin
 dog: *bad, furtive, *mean
 down: dangle, suspend
 fire: pend, *stop, suspend
 in there: pursue, resist, *stick
 man: carnifex, executioner
 man's noose: anodyne necklace
 man's rope: caudle of hempseed
 nail: backfriend, whitlow
 on: *adhere, depend, *stick
 one's head: atone, regret
 out: den, joint, resort, spa
 over: impend, morning after
 together: cohere, *unite

---

* Asterisk means to look up this word to find more answer words.

up: dead end, **flaw,* hitch, obsession, obstacle, **thing*
HANKY-PANKY: **play, *trick*
HANNAH: *husband:* elkanah
son: samuel
HANNIBAL: *battle:* cannae, zama
father: barca, hamilcar
HANUMAN: *father:* vayu
HAP(PEN): **occur, *venture*
HAPPINESS: **joy, *paradise*
ethics: eudomonics
god: benzaiten, bishamonten,
comus, daikoku, ebisu, fu hsing,
fukurokuju, hotei osho, jurojin,
lu hsing, pusa, shichi fukujin,
shou hsing
incapacity: anhedonia
HAPPY: appropriate, apt, beata,
blessed, **bright,* cheerful, con-
tented, cosh, delighted, fitting,
fortunate, gay, glad, joyful,
lucky, proper, **quiet*
-go-lucky: easy, improvident
hunting grounds: **paradise*
landings: **good bye*
valley: **paradise, *utopia*
HAPU: *son:* amenhotep
HARAN: *brother:* abraham
father: terah
offspring: ischa, lot, milcah
HARANGUE: **address, *talk*
HARASS: **abuse, *harry, *torment*
HARBINGER: herald, **sign,* usher
HARBOR: **asylum,* cherish, port
protection: breakwater
HARD: adamant, arduous, austere,
bony, brawny, brazen, brittle,
callous, chondric, close, compact, concrete, dense, difficult,
dour, dry, **firm,* flinty, granitic,
harsh, horny, impenetrable, inflexible, knotty, laboriously,
lapideous, **near, *obscure, *obstinate,* onerous, osseous, per-
plexing, rocky, **severe, *solid,*
sound, steely, **stern,* stony,
*strict, stringent, **strong,* stub-

born, **thick,* tough, unyielding
comb.: dys
nut to crack: dilemma, enigma
-pressed: hurried, straitened
-shell: conservative, extremist
-ship: **need, *trial,* want
times: depression, recession
-wood: **tree: hardwood*
HARDIHOOD: endurance,
*strength
HARDY: **solid,* spartan, **strong*
heroine: tess
HARE: *bell:* bluebell, campanula
brained: **foolish*
comb.: lag, lago
pert.: leporine
ragout: hassenpfeffer
young: leveret
HAREM: anderun, gynaeceum,
odah, purdah, seraglio, serai,
zenana
male attendant: eunuch
pert.: odalisk
room: ada, ida, oda
slave: odalisque
HARICOT: **hash,* stew
HARIM: *son:* benjamin, eliezer,
elijach, ishijan, jehiel, maaseiah,
malchijah, malluch, melchiah,
shemaiah, uzziah
HARLEQUIN: **clown,* scaramouch
bug: cabbage bug, calico
duck: canne-de-roche, lady
HARLOT: **prostitute, *wanton*
HARM: **bad, *evil, *hurt, *spoil*
HARMONIA: *father:* ares
husband: cadmus
mother: aphrodite
HARMONIOUS: euphonious,
tuneful
HARMONIZE: **accord, *adapt,*
*set
HARMONY: **accord,* amity, balance, chime, consonance, diapason, empathy, euphony, flow,
monochord, music, **order,*

peace, proportion, rapport, rhythm, symmetry, symphony, tone, tune, tranquility, *union
lack: discord
of the gospels: diatessaron
of the spheres: stars
HARNESS: *bull:* policeman
ornamental: caparison
part: backstrap, billet, blind, bridle, button, collar, crupper, girth, hame, martingale, rein, saddle, terret, trace, tug
HARP: koto, lyre, nag, plectrum, *repeat, *scold, *talk
ancient: trigon
guitar key: dital
seal: blue sides
string: chord
HARPOON: *pierce, *spear, *strike
explosive headed: bomblance
HARPY: aello, bat, celaeno, *demon, eagle, extortionist, had, ocypete, monster, podarge
attacker: argonauts, boreads, calais, zetes
parent: electra, thaumas
HARRIDAN: *hag, *prostitute
HARRIER: dog, hawk, pest
marsh: harpy, puttock
pert.: accipital, accipitrine
HARRIETT BEADLE: tattycoram
HARROW, HARRY: *break, *pain, *spoil, *steal, *tear, *torment, *torture
HARSH: *acerb, *brutal, *severe
HARUM-SCARUM: *reckless, *wild
HARUSPEX: *prophet, soothsayer
HARVEST: *acquire, *get, *yield
deity: *agriculture god, goddess
festival: kirn, opalia
home: hockey, kirn
machine: binder, reaper
man: carter, farmer
tick: acarid

time: autumn, fall, october
HAS-BEEN: candidate, vestige
HASADIAH: *father:* hilkiah
son: zedekiah
HASH: *error, gallimaufry, goulash, haricot, *mark, medley, *mess, mince, *mixture, olio, ollapodrida, potpourri, ragout, ramekin, rechauffe, salmagundi, slumgillion, stew
HASHISH: *drug, *hemp, narcotic
HASHUM: *son:* eliphelet, jeremai, manasseh, shimei, zabad
HASSLE: *argue, *fight, *quarrel
HASTE: dash, dispatch, *speed
HASTY: abrupt, *fast, *short
impression: apercu
pudding: mush, sepon, supawn
retreat: bug out, *defeat, rout
HAT: *broad-rimmed:* shovel
cocked: chapeau bras, tricorne
covering: havelock
crown: poll
ecclesiastic: *vestment: religious
felt: billycock
fiber: felt, soda, straw
fur: beaver, coney, coonskin, ermine, mink
hanger: hall tree
hunter's: deer stalker, terai
ladies: breton, caddy, cooie, duckbill, gainsborough, harlequin, leghorn, slouch
medieval: abacot, bycoket
oilskin: souwester, squam
opera: beaver, caroline, claque, crush, gibus, stovepipe, tile, topper
palmleaf: salacot
pert.: castorial
pith: topee, topi
plant: sola
quaker: broadbrim
silk: catskin, *hat: opera
slang for: dicer
slouch: caddie, caddy
soft: fedora

---

* Asterisk means to look up this word to find more answer words.

soldier: helmet, **cap: military*
stovepipe: caroline, **hat: opera*
straw: baku, ballibuntl, bangkok,
   boater, brazilian, milan, panama
ten-gallon: sombrero
top: beaver, **hat: opera*
trimming: cache-peigne
HATCHET: *-faced:* dour, lean
   man: henchman, stooge, tool
   stone: hache, mogo, tomahawk
HATE: abhor, abominate, animus,
   aversion, bete noir, despise,
   detest, disdain, dislike, dosa,
   enmity, execrate, loathe, malice,
   odium, poison, rancor, revile,
   *scorn, venom
   comb.: mis, miso
HATHAWAY: *home:* shottery
HATHOR: *emblem:* sistrum
   husband: horus
   son: ahi, harsomtus, ihi, shu
HAUL: **drag, *draw,* loot, tug
HAUNT: **home, *spirit, *walk*
HAVE: capitalist, **deceive, *get*
HAVEN: **harbor, *home,* refuge
HAVOC: **evil,* ravage, **ruin*
HAWAII: *apple:* maile
   baking pit: imu
   ballad: mele
   beverage: kava-kava
   bird: alala, apapani, drepanis,
      iiwi, io, ioa, iwa, kioea, koae,
      mamo, omao, ooaa, palila,
      pikake
   blueberry: ohelo
   breech cloth: malo
   bulrush: aka
   bush: olona
   canoe: waapa
   canoe paddle: iakus
   capital: honolulu, lahaina
   channel: auau
   chant: mele
   chief: alii nui
   cliff: pali
   climber: akala, rubus macraei
   cloak: ahuula, mamo

cloth: kapa, olong, tapa, tappa
coffee: kona
cord: aea
crater: kilauea
cudweed: enaena
dance: hula
dancer: hilo hattie
deity: kane(loa), lono, pele
discoverer: cook, gaetano
drink: kava, mai tai
farewell: aloha
feast: ahaaina, luau
fern: amaumau, ekaha, heii,
   iwaiwa, pulu, uluhi
fiber: ehuawa, pulu, wauke
fire goddess: pele
first governor: dole
fish: ahi, akule, alaihi, awa,
   humuhumunukunukuapuaa,
   kaaawa, kahala, lania, palani,
   ulua
fish bait: hola
fish poison: auhuhu, hola
floral emblem: lehua, lei
flower: emoloa, ilima, hibiscus
food: apii, kalo, poi, taro
founder: captain cook
fruit: poha
garland: lei
goose: nene, neni
gooseberry: poha
grass: emoloa, hilo, anounou
greeting: aloha
harbor: pearl
herb: ape, auhuhu, awiwi, hola
house of sun: haleakala
island: hawaii, kahoolawe, kauai,
   kure, lanai, maui, molokai, ni-
   ihau, oahu
king: kamehameha
lava: aa, pahoehoe
liquor: awa, kawa
loin cloth: malo, maro
lomilomi: massage, rub, shampoo
love: aloha
massage: lomilomi
morning glory: koali

* Asterisk means to look up this word to find more answer words.

mountain: kea, koolau, mauna loa
mulberry bark: kapa, tapa
music instrument: uke, ukulele
native: kanaka
newcomer: malihini
nickname: aloha state
octopus: hee
old name: sandwich islands
parrot fish: lauia
partnership: hoey, hui
peacock: pikake
pepper: ava
pit, baking: imu
plant: hala, kalo, olona, pandanus, pia, taro
plant wool: pulu
poem: mele
porch: lanai
precipice: pali
pygmy: menehune
raven: alala
rose: akala, flower, shrub
royalty: alii
salutation: aloha
seaweed: limu
shaman: kahuna
shampoo: lomilomi
shrub: akala, akia, anapanapa, aupaka, colubrina, olona, poha
song: mele
squirrel fish: alaihi
starch: apii, pia, poi, taro
storm: kona
taboo: kapu
temple: heiau
tern: noi(o)
thrush: amao, olomao, omao
tree: aalii, aiea, alani, amaumau, aulu, hau, hauula, iliahi, india, kino, koa, kou, kukui, lehua, majagua, mokihana, ohia, pulu, walahee
tree fern: amamau, amau, pulu
valley: manoa
veranda: lanai
vine: awikiwiki, ie, io, kaiwi
volcano: kilauea, mauna kea, mauna loa
white man: haole
wind: kona
woman: wahini
worsted: tapa
wreath: lei
yam: hoi
HAWK: *bill:* pawl
bit: dandelion
blind: seel
cage: mew
cuckoo: brain-fever bird
falconry: bater
fish: osprey
fly: asilus
frame: cadge
-headed god: horus
genus: accipiter, buteo
group: cast
leash: jess, lune
male: tercel
moth: phalus achemon
nest: aerie
parrot: hia
pert.: accipital, accipitrine
pinion feather: sarcel
sparrow: nisus
stomach: pannel
thong: brail
trainer: astringer
weed: cat's-ear, dindle
young: brancher, eyas, kite
HAWKSHAW: *detective,* dick, sleuth
HAWSER: *hole:* cathole
iron: calking
post: bitt, bollard, capstan
HAY: *bird:* blackcap
bundle: bale, gavel, mow, rick, stack, truss, wisp
cock: cob, coil, goaf, pike
fever: rose, sneezing
fodder plant: sainfoin
fork: pickle, pikel
loft: granary
line: swath, windrow
second growth: rowen

* Asterisk means to look up this word to find more answer words.

seed: rube, rustic, yokel
spread(er): ted(der)
storage: loft, mow
sweep: buck
-wire: *insane,* *mad,* *wrong
HEAD: attic, bead, bean, *bear,*
  begin, belfry, block, bun, brain,
  cabeza, cape, capita, capernoite,
  capital, captain, caput, cephalon,
  chief, chump, cid, cocoa, conk,
  control, cranium, crown, crumpet, direct(or), dominant, dome,
  duce, first, foam, front, froth,
  fuhrer, hand, intellect, jefe,
  knob, *lead(er),* loft, *magnate,*
  noggin, noodle, nut, pate, point,
  poll, *power,* principal, *skull,*
  source, *start,* tete, *title,*
  thrust, toilet, *top,* topic, van
ache: annoyance, caphalgia,
  hemialgia, megrim, migraine,
  misery, *trial,* *trouble*
and shoulders: utterly
back: crown, occiput, poll
bald: pilgarlic
band: agal, carcanet, circlet, coronet, diadem, fillet, frontlet, in-
  fula, mitre, sphendone, vitta
bandage: gaka, galfa
boar: hure
bone: *skull*
chute: drain
comb.: cephal(ous), cephalus
covering or dress: *cap,* *hat*
crown: cantle, pate, vertex
distortion: loxia
first: impulsive(ly), *reckless*
gear: bridle, *cap,* *hat*
having: cephalophorus
house: breadwinner, sire
hunter: italone, killer
into: *attack,* *meet,* *start*
-land: bill, bluff, cape, ness
-less: acephal, etete, *stupid*
-line: banner, caption, *title*
liner: *leader,* star
-long: bellyflaught, *reckless*

man: boss, chief, executioner
master: archididascalos, gymnasiarch, principal
membrane: caul, omentum
-most: before
muscle: occipitalis
off: blanch, divert, turn back
over heels: engrossed, obsessed
penny: tax
pert.: capital, capitate, cephalic,
  encephalic, cranial
-quarters: base, central, seat
race: channel
science: phrenology
sculpture: bust
shave: tonsure
ship: *authority*
shrunken: tsantsa
side: ear, lorum, temple
spring: *source,* *start*
stall: harness
start: *advantage,* priority
stone: memorial
-strong: *obstinate,* *stupid*
to foot: cap-a-pie
top: coxcomb, pate, scalp
toward: cephalad
waiter: captain
water: *source,* *start*
way: progress, room, space
work: *study,* thought
HEALING: *agent:* balsam, spa
art, pert.: aesculapian, medical
god: apollo, asclepius, belenus,
  beli, osiris, paeon
goddess: bau, eir, damia, gula,
  hygea, minerva, salus
pert.: medical, medicinal
plant: bonewort, daisy
science: iatrology, medicine
HEALTH: *comb.:* sani
resort: spa
station: hospital
symbol: pansy
HEALTHY: *fine,* *fit,* *good*
HEAP: *plenty,* *quantity*

* Asterisk means to look up this word to find more answer words.

HEARING: *comb.:* acou(sia), oto
pert.: acoustic, audio, auditory, auricular, otic
HEART: *ache:* *sorrow, *trouble
and soul: *hard, utterly
beat: pulse, systole, throb
bleeding: dicentra
break: *sorrow, *trouble
breaker: philanderer, tress
broken: overcome, *sad
burn: cardialgia, envy, enmity
cavity or chamber: atrium, auricle, camera, ventricle
comb.: cardi, cardio, cardium
contraction: systole
covering: pericardium
dilation: diastole
felt: deep, real, *true
in hand: readily, willingly
incision: cardiotomy
interest: *love, melodrama
lack: acardia
leaf: medic
-less: *brutal, *hard, tough
measurer: electrocardiograph
medicine: cardin, nitroglycerin
pert.: cardiac, cardial
queen: elizabeth, guimbarde
-shaped: cardioid, cordate
-sick: desolate, sore
sound: murmur
stimulant: adrenaline, amyl nitrite, cardiant, digitalis, epinephrin, quinidine
throb: dunt, *love
valve, pert.: aortic, mitral
water: blue tongue, fever
water transmitter: bont tick
wood: alburnum, brazilette, catechu, duramen, notelaea
HEARTH: *accessory:* andiron
gods: lares, penates
goddess: hestia, vestia
HEAT: *comb.:* calori, therm(o)
disease: calenture, stroke
gentle: calor, tepor, warmth
imperviousness: adiathermancy

pert.: caloric, thermal
resistant: amosite, anthophyll
unit: btu, calorie, therme
HEATH: azalia, briar, erica, poverty plant, savin, tamarisk
HEAVEN: *joy, *paradise, *utopia
comb.: urano
deities: *sky: god, goddess
myth: elysium, olympus
object: quasar
personified: anu
pert.: celestial, empyrean, uranic, orrery
queen: astarte, mary, moon
tree: ailanthus
HEAVY: afflictive, *big, burly, complicated, cumbersome, *deep, dense, distressing, *dull, expecting, *fat, firm, gloomy, *great, *hard, hefty, *idle, languid, large, leaden, massy, obese, obtuse, onerous, oppressive, ponderous, profound, role, *sad, serious, *slow, sluggish, *solid, steep, *sullen, *thick, villain, *violent
comb.: bary
-eyed: sleepy
HEBER: *daughter:* shua(h)
son: hotham, japhlet, shomer
wife: jael
HEBREW: *acrostic:* agla
agnostic: apikoros, epicoris
alien: ger, goy
allies: habiri
alphabet: aleph, ayin, beth, caph, cheth, daleth, gimel, he, koph, lamed, mem, nun, resh, samekh, shin, sin, taf, tet(h), tsade, vav, yod, yud, zayin
anagrammatic system: atbash
ancestor: eber
anecdotal history: elohist
apostate: meshumad
ascetic: essene
assembly: sanhedrin
automation: golem
atonement: kapora, kaporeh

* Asterisk means to look up this word to find more answer words.

avenger: goel
belt: zonar
benediction: mizpah, motzi, shema
bible analysis: midrash
bible books: nebiim
bible notes: masorah
bible pronunciation aid: gri, kere, keri, qere, queri
bible prophets: haftarah
blessing: bensh, broche, motzi
bread: challa, halla, matzo(h)
bride: kallah
brotherhood: essene
bushel: emer
calendar: ab, adar, elul, heshvan, iyar, kislev, nisan, sebat, shebat, sivan, tammuz, tebet, tishri, veadar
candelabrum: menorah
canonical book: talmud
cantor's garment: kittel
cap: mitre
ceremony: bar mitzva, bath mitzvah, chan(n)ukah, habdala, hanukka(h), kiddush, lag baomer, maariv, mincha, minhan, pesach, purim, rosh hoshanah, seder, sefirah, shabuot, shevuoth, shivah, simchath, torah, succoth, yom kippur
christian minister: gallah
clean: kosher
coin: gerah, mite, shekel
cloak: gaberdine, kittel
collective: kibbutz(im)
commandment: mitzva(h)
compassion: rachmones
confection: alhet, halava(h)
confession: yom kippur
congregation official: parnas
cooperative: kibbutz(im)
court: beth din, sanhedrin
curse: choleria
day: yom
demon: asmodeus, dybbuk, golem
devil: teivel, teufel, teuvel
dialect: ladino

doctrine: anamism, karaism
dowry: nadan
drum: toph
dumpling: knaydl, knish
education: haskala, maskilin
eternity: olam
evening: ereb
excommunication: cherem, herem
exile: diaspora, galus, galut
fast day: asarah betevet
father: abba, abraham, eber
feast: *hebrew ceremony*
flute: nehiloth
folklore: agada, haggadah
food inspector: shomer
general: josephus, joshua
gentile: goi, goy(im)
god: adonai, adoshem, bore olam, el, eloah, elohim, en sof, hamakom, hashem, ihvh, jehovah, jhvh, jhwh, kedosh yisrael, kiddush hashem, melech hamlochim, shaddai, shechinah, yah, yahveh, yaveh, yhvh, yhwh
greeting: aleichem shalom
group: kabbala
harp: guimbard
hell: gehenna, sheol
high priest: aaron, caiaphas
historian: josephus
holiday: *hebrew ceremony*
homeland: eretz israel
horn: shofar, shophar
hymn: adon olam
infinity: adolam
instrument: asor, timbrel
judge: dayan, dayen, dayyan
juniper: ezel
last stand symbol: masada
law: halakha, talmud, torah
lawbreaking: averah
learned man: hakam, hakim
lesson: haphtarah
liturgical poems: azharoth
liturgical prayer: amidah
lots: purim, thummin, urim
lyre: asor

* Asterisk means to look up this word to find more answer words.

magistrate: alabarch
man: bahur, bakam, neshuma, rab
margin note: kere, kri, queri
marriage contract: ketuba
marriage custom: levirate
meadow: abel
measure: bath, cab, caph, chomer,
  choros, digit, epa(h), epha(h),
  kab, kor, hin, homer, kanch,
  letch, log, omer, reed, seah,
  zareth
moses, books of: teitch-chumesh
mourning: lag baomer, shivah
mysticism: cabala, kabbalah
numerology: gematria
offering: corban
order: bnai brith, ito, essene
organization: agudath yisrael
parchment: mezuza(h)
passover: abib, nisan, seder
passover story: agada, haggadah
penitence days: yom kippur
pentecost: shabuot, shevuoth
philosopher: avicebron, buber
pious man: chasid, hassid
pity: rachmones
poet: avicebron, bialik
prayer: abinu, alenu, amidah,
  broche, kaddish, kol nidre,
  mairev, minchah, shachris
prayer book: mahzor, siddur
precept: sutra, torah
priest: *ecclesiastic: jewish
priest's mark: abnet, ephod, thummim, urim
prophet: *prophet: famous
psalms: hallel
rabbi's wife: rebbetsen
ram's horn: shofar
reclaimer: goel
reincarnation: gilgul
religious law: halakha
revolt: masada
revolt chief: eleazar ben yair
robot: golem
roman foe: silva, titus
roll: bagel, bialy

sabbath food: cholent, gefulte fish,
  knaydel, kugel, matzo
sacred book: cabala, cabbala, talmud, torah, zohar
saintly men: baal shem
scholar: amora, sabora, tanna
school: heder, schul, yeshiva
secret: marrano
straps: tefillin, t'fillin
shawl: abnet, talith, tallit
sect: essene
skullcap: yarmulkah, yarmulke
son: ben, kaddishel
song: eli eli
soul: neshamah, neshuma
splendor, book of: zohar
sun god: baal
tabernacle feast: succoth
talmud parts: gemara, mishnah
talmud scholar: chachem
teacher: rab, rabbi, reb, rov
thanksgiving: succoth
thief: ganef, gonoph
title: abba, adoni, gaon, rabbi
vestment: breastplate
toast: l'chayim
universe: olam
vowel point: sego, tsere
warrior: ehud
wedding: chasseneh, khasseneh
weight: bekah, gerah, maneh,
  shekel, talent
wisdom: chachma, khaukhma
wise man: chacham, kaham
zionist organization: hadassah
HEBRIDES: *breeze:* caver
  island: barra, harris, iona, islay,
  jura, rum, scarba, skye, staffa,
  uist, uisy
HECATE: brimo, moon, prytania
  father: perses, zeus
  mother: asteria, hera
HECATONCHEIRES: briareus,
  centimanes, cottus, gyges
  parents: gaea, uranus
HECTOR: *charioteer:* cebriones
  cousin: caletor

* Asterisk means to look up this word to find more answer words.

parent: hecuba, priam
rescuer: agenor
slayer: achilles
son: astyanax, scamandrius
wife: andromache
HECUBA: *husband:* priam
children: cassandra, deiphobus, hector, helenus, paris, polydorus, polyxena, troilus
HEDGE: **adjust,* **border,* **limit*
HEEL: *comb.:* calcaneo
HEFTY: **big,* **heavy,* **strong*
HEIGHT: **fort,* **top,* **tower*
comb.: acro, aero, alt, batho
HEINOUS: **bad,* **evil,* terrible
HEL: *dog:* garm
parent: angerbotha, loki, sigyn
river: gjoll
HELEN: *abductor:* paris, theseus
brother: **dioscuri*
daughter: hermione
executioner: queen polyxo
father: tyndareus
husband: menelaus
lover: deiphobus, paris
mother: leda
sister: clytemnestra
son: aganus, dorus
suitor: ajax, theseus
HELICOPTER: autogiro, chopper, eggbeater, puddlejumper, rotor, whirlybird, windmill
HELIOS: hyperion, sol, sun
consort: anaxibia, clymene, clytie, gaea, iphiboe, iphinoe, leucothea, naupiadame
offspring: achelous, aeetes, augeias, circe, electryone, heliads, lampetia, pasiphae, perses, phaethon, tenagis
parent: hyperion, thia
winged horses: **horses: winged*
HELL: abaddon, **abyss,* acheron, allatu, amenti, avernus, avichi, barathron, below, caina, crater, duat, erebus, **evil,* fire, gehenna, hades, hole, heat, inferno, jahan-

nan, **jail,* jigoku, limbo, misery, naraka, nastrond, nifelheim, orcus, **pain,* pandemonium, perdition, purgatory, sheol, tartarus, **torment,* **trouble,* underworld, xibalba
god(dess): **underworld: god(dess)*
HELLEN: *father:* deucalion
son: aeolus, dorus, xuthus
HELLES: *mother:* nephele
HELLO: addio, allo, alo nola zera, aloha, bonjour, buen giorno, buena sera, evviva, guten tag, hola, pronto, shalom
HELMET: armet, barbut, basinet, cabasset, casque, galea, heaume, morion, sallet, topi
part: aventail, beaver, bell, coif, crest, nasal, visor, vue
pert.: cassideous, galeate
shell: cameo, cassis, conch
HELOISE: *lover:* abelard
HELP: **abet,* **accommodate,* sos
HEMP: abaca, alpargata, baline, bast, bung, burlap, cannabis, flax, henbit, jute, phloem, pita, pooa, sida, sunn, tow
drug: **marijuana*
weed: boneset, thoroughwort
HENGIST: *brother:* horsa
daughter: rowena
HENRY VIII: *wives:*
1st: catherine, katherine
2nd: ann boleyn
3rd: jane seymour
4th: anne of cleves
5th: catherine howard
6th: catherine parr
HEPHAESTUS: *aides:* cabeiri, cedalion, cyclopes, polyphemus, satyrs, sileni, telchines
daughter: pandora
epithet: mulciber, vulcan
love: aetna, aglaia, aphrodite, cabeiro, charis, gaea, maia
product: malos
son: ardalus, cabeiri, cacus, ce-

---

* **Asterisk means to look up this word to find more answer words.**

dalion, erichthonous, paleamon, palici, periphetes
victim: clytius
workshop: etna
HERA: anthea, bunaea, juno
husband: zeus
mother: rhea
rival: io, leto
son: ares
victim: antigone, iphianassa, lysippe, trojans
H E R B : *acquatic:* aponogaton, featherfoil, hornwort, ranale
aromatic: anet, anise, basil, catnip, chervil, clary, dill, fennel, hemp, hyssop, mint, mustard, nard, okra, sage, spearmint, tansy, wormseed
bennet: avens, daisy, hemlock
bitter: aletris, aloe, boneset, centaury, gentian, rue, tansy, turtlehead, woad
bog: calla, steepwort
climbing: basellace, faba, lens
coarse: eryngo, iva, leafcup
flowering: anemone, celandine, dittane, hepatica, stapelia
genus: abfa, acuan, aletris, arum, canna, cassia, cicer, cruca, dondia, ervum, galax, grindelia, hedeoma, inula, iva, lemna, loasa, mentha, meum, nerine, psoralea, rheum, rulac, sesseli, tacca, torenia, tovaria, urena
medicinal: aconite, aloe, arnica, boneset, coriander, lovage, rue, senna, sumac
perennial: balm, bugbane, digitalis, fennel, geum, irid, madder, pia, sainfoin, sedum, sego, soapwort, talis, yarrow
poisonous: conium, hellebore, hemlock, henbane, mandrake
HERCULES: alcides, buphagus
ancestor: alcaeus, perseus
captive: iole
father: amphityron, zeus

friend: alcon, hylas, iolaus, lichas, telamon
giant killed: antaeus
labor affiliations: augean, cerberus, ceryneian, cretan, diomedes, erymanthus, geryon, hesperides, hippolyte, lernaean, nemean, stymphalian
lion killed: nemean
loves: auge, deianeira, hebe, iole, megara, omphale
mother: alcmene
nurse: abia
pillars: abila, calpe, gibraltar
son: aechmagoras, agathyrsus, agelaus, albion, alexiares, anicetus, antiochus, telephus
victim: amazons, boar, busiris, calais, charybdis, emathon, eunomus, eurypylus, eurytus, hydra, iphitus, laomedon, linus, lion, megara, nessus, periclymenus, syleus, zetes
HERD: *group,* people, public
god: pales, pan
HERMES: *birthplace:* cyllene
cap: petasos, petasus
footgear: talaria
love: akakallis, aphrodite, chione, hecate, penelope, persephone, phene, polymele
parent: maia, zeus
personification: wind
son: abderus, aethalides, autolycus, cydon, daphnis, evander, pan, polydorus, saon
slew: argus, hippolytus, pelops
staff: caduceus
HERMIT: *ascetic,* *monk*
HERNIA: *comb.:* cele, coele
HEROD: *brother:* philip
chamberlain: blastus
courtier: manaean
father-in-law: aretas
sister-in-law: herodias
son: antipas
steward: chuza

---

* Asterisk means to look up this word to find more answer words.

HERODIA: *daughter:* salome
HEROIN: acetomorphine, big h, diamorphine, dope, horse, junk, nepenthe, opiate, scag, smack, snow, stuff, the big h
antidote: methadone
place: shooting gallery, skag bar
source: opium poppy, papaver
take: inject, mainline, shotgun, skin-pop, snort
HERRING: alewife, alosa, anchovy, cisco, clupea, pilchard, shad, sprat, sprot
HESPERIDES: *father:* erebus, hesperus, phorcys, zeus
names: aegle, arethusa, erytheis, hespera, hestia
mother: ceto, night, themis
HESPERUS: *daughter:* erythea
father: astraeus, atlas
mother: aurora, eos
offspring: ceyx, daedalion, *hesperides
HESTIA: *parent:* cronus, rhea
HETHIN: *foe:* hild, hogni
HIBISCUS: flower, roseble
HICKORY: carya, nut, pecan, tree
HIDDEN: adelo, *obscure
HIDE: *beat, burrow, cache, casate, cloak, coat, conceal, *cover, *disguise, fell, *hit, *lie, *obscure, plew, refuge, screen, secrete, shelter, *skin, skulk, suppress, *wrap
HIDEOUS: *bad, *evil, *ugly
HIE: accelerate, *speed
HIGGLE: *bargain, delay, peddle
HIGH: *acme, aerial, aloft, alpine, alto, apex, arrogant, aspiring, *best, dear, *drunk, ela, exorbitant, expensive, fetid, first, gamy, *great, master, mountainous, *noble, proud, raised, rancid, serene, shrill, soaring, spiralling, *splendid, *supreme, *top, supernal, towery, trump, winner
comb.: acro, aero, alti, alto

muck-a-muck: *big shot, *magnate
HIMALAYAN: *animal:* bearcat, goral, ibex, kail, marmot, ounce, panda, seron
bear: bhalu
bearcat: panda
bird: chough
broadmouth: raya
cedar: deodar
cypress: bhutan
dweller: nepalese
forest: bhabar
goat: goral, jemlah, kras, tahr, tair, thar
guide: sherpa
monkshood: api, atis
peak: annapurna, dhaulagiri, everest, kanchenjunga, lamna la chooyu, lhotse, makalu, mansalu
sheep: bharal, nahoor
sub-ranges: siwaliks
swamp: terai
tableland: tibet
tea plant: aucuba
territory: sikkim
tree: deodar, sal, toon
tribe: lepchas, pamir
valley: dun, mari
walnut: corylus
HIMAVAT: *children:* devi, diva, parvati, shakti
HINDER: hamper, *slow, *stop
HINDU: babhan, babu, gentoo, *india references, jain(a), kolarian, koli, seik, ser, sikh, tamil
HINDUISM: animism, brahmanism
HINDUSTAN: *dravidian:* toda
hemp: sabzi, siddhi
language: hindi, urdu
magic: jadoo, jadu
poet: siraj, wali
rice crop: aghanee
HINNOM VALLEY: gehenna
HIP: *pert.:* iliac, sciatic

* **Asterisk means to look up this word to find more answer words.**

HIPPIE: acidhead, anti, copout, escapist, horse-tamer, mod, rebel, runaway, unconventional
japanese: *japan: hippies
predecessor: beatnik
term: grass, groovy, junk
HIPPOCRATES: *birthplace:* kos
drug: mecon, opium
sleeve: refiner
HIPPOMENES: *melanion
HIRE: bribe, *rent, *use
HIT: ace, *arrive, bat, *beat, biff, blooper, blow, bludgeon, bop, box, buff(et), bull's-eye, bump, bunt, bust, butt, catch, clout, collide, contact, conk, crash, criticize, cuff, discover, el dorado, favorite, find, fly, *fortune, foul, *get, homer, impact, impress, knock, lambaste, larrup, *meet, occur, pink, polt, punch, *punish, rap, score, sensation, single, slam, slog, slug, smash, smite, sock, *strike, *success, swat, thrash, thwack, triple, *whip
HITCH: *connect, hang-up, *unite
HITLER: *aerie:* berchtesgaden
dog: blondi
follower: nazi
second man: goering
HITTITE: *ancestor:* heth, hett
capital: charchemish, pterir
kingdom: ahhiyawa
language: arzava, pala
storm god: teshub, teshup
HOARD: *gather, *group, *save
HOAX: *cheat, *deceive, *trick
HOBGOBLIN: *dwarf, *spirit
HOCKEY: *ball:* nur, orr, puck
cup: stanley
goal: cage
schoolboy: shinney
stick: bulger, caman
term: bully, cage, cammock, face-off, goalie, icing, puck
HOCUS: *drink, *hoax, *nonsense
HODGEPODGE: *hash, *mixture

HOG: monopolize, *swine
back: *ridge
call: sook
choker: broad sole, flatfish
cholera: rouget
deer: axis
fish: capitan, scorpine, wrasse
food: acorn, mast, slops, swill
ground: marmot, woodchuck
innards: haslet
like: peccary
money: bermuda shilling
-nose snake: adder, viper
nut: earthnut, ouabe, pignut
peanut: earth pea
plum: ambaree, amra, jobo
side: flitch
sucker: fish, stone roller
thigh: ham
-tie: *secure, *stop, *tie
-wash: *nonsense, *refuse
weed: dog-fennel
-wild: frantic, *mad
HOI POLLOI: canaille, *group
HOIST: cannon, drop, *raise
anchor: trip
sail: hoise, swig
the blue peter: sail
the white flag: *quit, *yield
HOITY-TOITY: *arrogant, snooty
HOKUM: bunk, *nonsense
HOLD: *argue, *arrest, possess, *seize, *stick, *stop, *think
back: *absorb, *hamper, *slow
dear: cherish, *love
out: deny, endure, offer
up: *arrest, *steal, *support
with: agree, approve, consent
HOLE: abyss, *jail, *opening
in one: eagle
HOLLAND: *dutch
HOLLOW: abyss, *false, *weak
HOLLY: holm, ilex, tree, yaupon
comb.: ililic
HOLOPHERNES: *eunuch:* bagoas
slayer: judith

HOLY: angelic, blessed, chaste, christlike, consecrated, devout, divine, godlike, *good, hallowed, heavenly, *perfect, *pure, *right, *sacred, saintly, sanctified, seraphic, spiritual, sri, vestal
bottle: bacbuc
bread: antidoron
breathing: prayer
city: allahabad, benares, jerusalem, kiev, lhasa, mecca, medina, moscow, rome, zion
cross star: beta crucis
father: *church: man
field: campo santo, cemetery
grail: sangraal, sangreal
grail castle: monsalvat
grail knight: bors, galahad, percival
hill: athos
joe: *church: man
land: palestine
man: *church: man, fakir, sadhu
of holies: sanctuary, toilet
oil: chrism
one: *church: man, christ, deity, god, jehovah, saint
place: altar, shrine, temple
scriptures: bible, canon
statue: icon, ikon(o)
stone: specie, wash
terror: *demon, *devil
text: zend avesta
thursday: ascension day
war: crusade, jihad
water vessel: aspergillum, aspersorium, benitier, brechites, brush, cantharus, cruet, font, paten, stoup
words lord: thoth
writ: bible, scripture
HOME: abode, address, astre, *asylum, biggin, domestic, domicile, fatherland, fireside, habitat, hearth, hospital, *house, *hut, ingleside, kern, nest, locale, *place, quarters, range, residence, seat, shelter
base: plate
-like: cheerful, cozy, *warm
maker: mistress, wife, woman
rule: independence
run: coup, *hit, score, swat
stretch: *end, finish
HOMER: birthplace: chios, smyrna
character: achilles, ajax, diomede, hector, odysseus, paris
epic: iliad, odyssey
HOMINY: bran, cereal, corn, grits, poi, posole, samp
HONEST: aboveboard, bluff, *fair, forthright, guileless, *good, *open, *plain, *pure, *simple, square, *straight, *true
man: abe, diogenes, lincoln
HONEY: badger: ratel
bear: kinkajou, melursus
bee: angelito, deseret, melipona
-berry: genip(ap), tree
buzzard: chalcedony, hawk, pern
comb.: melli
-comb cell: alveola
-combed: alveolar, favose, pitted, riddled
creeper: bananaquit, coereba
dew: melon, mildew, orange
drink: mead, morat, oenomel
eater: iao, manuao, moho
-eyed: mellifluous, *sweet
-fogle: flatter, sweettalk
mesquite: algarroba
pert.: melissic
plant: cleome, figwort, hoya
source: bee, bimbil, nectar
-suckle: azalea, black horn, elder, hawthorn, sheepberry, sambuccus, widbin
ware: badderlocks
HONOR: *accept, accolade, admire, adore, *adorn, athel, award, brevet, celebrate, cite, civility, credit, crown, decorate, deference, dignify, distinction, eminence, eulogize, faith, fame,

* Asterisk means to look up this word to find more answer words.

fealty, *glory, grace, gree, homage, integrity, *mark, medal, nobility, *ornament, point, *praise, *prize, recognition, respect, *revere, *reward, tip, *title, *token, trophy, trust, venerate, virtue
hungering for: esurient
HOOD: *cap, *hat, *hoodlum, *top
HOODLUM: apache, bandit, bravo, bully, *criminal, cutthroat, *devil, goombah, goon, gorilla, gunman, hatchetman, highbinder, hooligan, larrikin, monster, mug, muscle man, plug-ugly, rodman, roisterer, roughneck, rowdy, ruffian, savage, *thief, torpedo, tough, trigger
teen age: cheery red, hairie, hell's angel, hippie, mod, rocker, skinhead, teddy boy
HOODOO: jinx, oppress, *spell
HOOK: agraffe, *seize, *trap
comb.: anchylo, ankylo, ham(i)
dagger: chape
fireplace: hangle, poker
fish: barb, fly, gaff, gig, kirby, spoon, sproat
large: cleek, gaff, hangle
money: lari(n), larree
pert.: falcate, sarp, uncinal
pruning: calabozo
-shaped: ancistroid, hamulate
stretcher: tenter
worm: ancylostoma
up: association, chain, network
HOOKER: *prostitute, *thief
HOOLIGAN: *criminal, *hoodlum
HOOSEGOW: *jail
HOPE: *desire, *trust, yearn
goddess: spes
HOPHNI: *brother:* phineas
father: eli
HORAE: carpo, dike, eirene, eunomia, thallo
HORDE: *gather, *group
HORMONE: aldosterone, estrogen, cortisol, cortisone

HORN: *alarm, prong, *sign
-beam: beech, carpinus, ostrya
-bill: bromvogel, homrai, tock
bird beak: epithema
blast: beep, fanfare, tantara
-blende: amphibole, buchonite
book: battledore
comb.: cera(to), cornu, kera(to)
crescent: cusp
drinking: rhyton
fly: buffalo gnat, simulium
in: intrude
insect: antenna, feeler, palp
-less: acerous, poley, polled
mouthpiece: bocal
painter's: amassette
pert.: ceres, cornu, kera
pipe: dance, matelote, tune
point: broach
quicksilver: calomel
-shaped: ceratoid, cornu
silver: cerargyrite
sounded for kill: mort
stag: antler
stunted: button
-swoggle: *cheat, *deceive
tissue: keratin, scur
without: acerous, doddy, mulley
work: *fort
wort: ceratophyllum, ranale
HORRIBLE: *bad, *evil, *ugly
HORSE: *ankle:* hock
around: caper, *fool, *play
autobiography: black beauty
back: ridge
bit: cannon, pelham
blanket: apishamore, caparison, manta, manda, tilpah
breastplate: poitrel, peytrel
breed: albino, appaloosa, arab, barb, bronco, cayuse, hackney, houyhnhnm, jennet, lippizaner, morgan, mustang, palomino, percheron, punch, quarter, saddle, shetland, shire, spanish, suffolk, tarpan, turk
brown: bay, roan, sorrel

* Asterisk means to look up this word to find more answer words.

buyer: coper, knacker, trader
calico: pinto
chestnut: aesculus, buckeye
collar: bargham
color: bay(ard), calico, chestnut, gray, grizzle, palomino, piebald, pied, pinto, roan, schimmel, sorrel
command: gee, giddap, haw, hup, hupp, proo, whoa
cry: neigh, nie, whinny
dappled: piebald, pinto, roan
dealer: *horse: buyer
disease: *disease: horse
draft: aiver, hairy, shire
driver: coachman, *horseman
eyelid hair: brill
eyelid inflammation: haw
famous: alborak, bayard, black bess, bucephalus, copenhagen, grani, houyhnhnm, incitatus, marengo, pegasus, rosinante, sleipnir, vegliantino, xanthus
farm: dobbin
feathers: *nonsense
feeding box: manger
female: filly, mare, yaud
fennel: seseli
flesh ore: bornite, erubescite
fly: botfly, brachycerus, bulldog, cleg, gadfly, stut
foot: coronet, fetlock, frog, hoof, pastern
forehead: chanfrin
gait: amble, canter, gallop, lope, pace, prance, rack, run, step, trot, vott, walk
genus: equus
giant: goldfax
goddess: epona
golden: palomino
gray: schimmel
group: atajo, caviya, drove, herd, randem, remuda, span, stable, string, team
guide: longe, rein
hair: mane, seton, snell

half-man: centaur
harness: pacer, trotter
-hide: baseball
hired: hack(ney)
hock: gambrel
horned: monoceros, unicorn
inferior: balker, crock, crow bait, dog, goat, hatrack, jade, ladino, outlaw, plug, rackabones, rip, roarer, rosinante, scalawag, scrag, screw, skate, stiff, weed
jump: ballotade, curvet
keeper: groom, hostler
last: also ran, thill(er)
leech: alukah
leg part: cannon, coronet, fetlock, gaskin, hock, hoof, instep, pastern, shank, stifle
mackerel: akule, atule, bonito, fish, saurel, scad, tunny
male: entire, gelding, stallion, steed
man: broncobuster, buckaroo, caballero, cavalier, cavalry man, centaur, courier, cowboy, dragoon, equestrian, gaucho, jockey, postboy, postilion, puncher, sumpter, vaquero
-manship: equitation, manage
measure: hand
men: cavalry
manege: academy, school
mint: monarda
mottled: pinto
muscle: cephalohumeralis
noseband: cavesson
old: aver, garran, jade, plug, rosinante, skate
opera: oater, western
pace: *horse: gait
pack: bidet, sumpter
pair: span, team
pert.: caballine, equine, hippic
piebald: pinto
play: antics, pranks
power: energy
prehistoric: eohippus

* **Asterisk means to look up this word to find more answer words.**

racing: bangtail, entry, gee-gee, mudder, pacer, plater, pony, speeder, staker

radish: angel tree, behen, behn, ben, *nonsense*, tree

rearing: pesade

relay: remuda

sacrifice: ashvamedha

saddle: cob, mount, palfrey

sense: intelligence, judgment

shoe: bearpaw, ringer

shoe part: caltrop, web

shoe frame or stall: trave

shoer: blacksmith, farrier

shoes: barnyard golf

show: dressage

small: bidet, cayuse, cob, colt, galloway, genet(te), jennet, nag, pony, shetland

sorrel: chestnut, roan

spirited: arab, barb, charger, courser, stallion, steed

sun: alsvinn, alsvith, arvak

swelling: capellet

swift: arab, courser, pacolet

tail: bob, cat-whistles

tail standard: toug, utug

tail tree: balata, beefwood, blolly

talking: arion

track slope: calade

trade: *bargain*

trader: *sharp(er)*

trainer: valet

trapping: harness, tackle

tread: volt

trotting: cob, morgan

tumor: anbury

turn: passade

war: charger, courser, destrier

weed: bloodstanch, fleabane

western range: broomtail

wheel: poler

-whip: *beat*, *punish*, quirt

white-streak: blaze, reach, shim

wild: bronco, brumby, mustang, tarpan, warragal, warrigal

winged: aethon, astrope, bronte, chronos, eous, lampon, pegasus, phaethon, phlegon, pyroesis

wooden: trestle

work: aver, garran, percheron

worthless: *inferior horse*

HORUS: behdety, harwer, ra, re

brother: anubis

parent: isis, osiris

son: duamutef, hapi, imsety, qebhsnuf

HOSEA: *daughter:* loruhamah

son: jezreel, loammi

wife: gomer

HOST: emcee, *group*, *quantity*

HOT: *angry*, calid, candent, close, *eager*, ebullient, excellent, fashionable, fiery, flaming, fresh, *great*, heated, impetuous, lustful, *near*, parching, scalding, stolen, torrid, *violent*, *warm*

air: *chatter*, *nonsense*

spur: madcap, *reckless*

water: geyser, *trouble*

HOTTENTOT: *cloak:* kaross

encampment: kraal

instrument: gorah, ramkee

tobacco: daccha

tribe: damara, gona, griqua kora, goura, namaqua, sandawi

war club: knobkerrie

HOUND: *dog*, *enthusiast*, *follow*, *press*, *urge*

fish: gar(fish)

HOUSE: audience, bahay, board, bungalow, cabin, casa, castle, chamber, cote, cottage, *cover*, dwelling, edifice, enterprise, family, firm, gazebo, grange, *home*, igloo, kiosk, hotel, inn, line(age), lodge, maison, mansion, pad, protect, temple, theatre, villa

comb.: eco

hold: family, menage, *usual*

hold god: lares, penates, steraph

leek: alatern, foose, privet

man: butler, croupier, dealer

many-doored: baradari

---

* Asterisk means to look up this word to find more answer words.

organ: magazine, periodical
part: cellar, estre, room
public: hotel, inn, tavern
servant: atriensis, domestic
summer: baradari, belvedere, bower, cabin, gazebo, kiosk, paudal, pergola, villa
take: vigorish
twelfth mundane: cacodaemon
warming: infare, party, tea
HOVEL: *hut
HOWL: *complain, *cry, *protest, ululate, wail, yipe, yowl
HOWLING: *extreme, *great, *wild
HUBBUB: *ado, chatter, *noise
HUDDLE: *gather, *group
HUE: *alarm, color, *cry, shade
HUGE: *big, *great, *large, vast
HUMAN: *people
comb.: anthrop(o)
HUMANITY: *father:* adam, irpetus
HUMBUG: *impostor, *nonsense
HUMOR: *joke, *pet, *please
HUNDRED: *comb.:* centi, hecto
division into: centuriation
HUNGARIAN: *army:* honvedseg
cavalryman: hussar
coin: balas, gara, filler, gulden, pengo, korona
composer: bartok, lehar
dance: czardas, varsoviana
dog: kuvasz, puli
game: alsos, felsos, kalabrias
hero: arpad, navy
legislature: felsohaz
mountain: alp, tatra, vertes
HUNT: chase, *search
HUR: *son:* ephrathah, rephaiah
wife: miriam
HURRY: *ado, *speed, *urge
HURT: *abuse, *ache, *afflict, bark, bloody, bruise, burn(ing), chafe, concussion, crush, cut, damage, deface, detriment, *evil, *flaw, fracture, gall, gash, harry,

impair, incision, lacerate, lesion, maim, mangle, mutilate, oppress, *pierce, puncture, *ruin, rupture, scar, scrape, scratch, scuff, *skin, *sorrow, *spoil, *strain, *suffer, *tear, *trouble, *whip, *wrong
HUT: balagan, barabara, bohawn, bothy, bourock, camalig, canaba, cote, crib, dugout, dump, hogan, hole, hovel, humpy, isba, jacal, kral, lean to, linter, miam, pagliaio, pigpen, shack, shanty, shed, slum, stack, sty, *tent, tepee, toldo, wickiup, wigwam
HYACINTH: bonavist, lablab, gallinule, sapphire
HYADES: *father:* atlas
mother: aethra, pleione
names: ambrosia, coronis, endora
pert.: aldebaran
HYBRID: *hash, *mixture
animal: catalo, hinny, mule
dog: cur, mongrel
equine: zebec, zebrass, zebrule
fruit: agawam, tangelo
growth: meterosis
HYMEN: *father:* apollo
mother: urania
HYMN: *book:* psalter
funeral: dirge
ode-like: epinicion
praise: anthem, paean
praising god: hallelujah
psalm, after: sticheron
ritual: encomium
sacred: anthem, ode, trisagion
tune: chorale
victory: epinikion
HYPERION: *children:* aurora, eos, helios, helius, selene, mene
love: euryphaessa, theia
HYPOTHALAMUS: acth

I: ego, iota, self
excessive use: iotacism

have found it: eureka
love you: amo
told you so: so there
understand: roger
IAGO: *wife:* emelia
IAPETUS: *consort:* asia, clymene, gaea, ge, themis
son: atlas, epimetheus, menoetius, prometheus
IASION: *son:* plutus
IBSEN: *character:* ase, gynt, hedda, nora
play: brand, rosmersholm
ICARIAN: daring, rash, *reckless*
ICARUS: *child:* erigone, penelope
ICBM: atlas, missile, weapon
ICE: *age man:* aborigine
berg, small: bergy bit, growler
block: serac
box: cooler, refrigerator
cap: calotte
cream dish: bisque, frappe, malt, parfait, soda, sundae
crystal: frost, sleet, snow
floe: berg, calf, hummock, pack, pan, quern, sconce
fragment: brash
glacial: neve, serac, sish
mass: *ice:* floe
patch: rone
pendant: icicle
sea: sludge
slushy: lolly, sish
thin: grue
ICELAND: *bay:* faxa
bishopric: holar, skalholt
coin: aurer, ehrir, krona
deities: *aesir,* tivi
epic: edda, saga
giant: *norse: giant*
golden falls: gullfoss
hero: audun, bele, eilif
legislature: althing
measure: alin, almenn, almude, angjateigur, fathmur, feralin, fermila, ferthumlungur, korn-

tunna, lina, oltunna, pottur, sjomila, turma
mountain: jokul, orafajokul
newspaper: morgunbladid
poet: skald
town pond: tjornin
volcano: askja, hekla, laki
weight: pund, tunna, smjors
ICENI: *queen:* boadicea
ICON: *figure:* *image,* *symbol*
ICTUS: *accent,* *attack,* spasm
IDAHO: *bird:* mountain bluebird
flower: syringa
nickname: gem state
tree: western pine
IDAS: *consort:* marpessa
IDEA: design, *image,* *model*
IDEAL: *acme,* *image,* *model*
life: asrama
remote: thule
state: *paradise,* *utopia*
universal ruler: chakravartin
IDIOM: *argot*
IDIOT: cretin, *fool,* imbecile
IDLE: asleep, at leisure, bum, dally, dog it, do nothing, drone, *dull,* empty, fallow, *free,* futile, goof off, haze, *heavy,* inactive, inert, jobless, languid, lazy, leisurely, loaf, loiter, loll, lounge, mooch, moon, otiose, petty, sit, squander, tiffle, *trifle,* trivial, unemployed, *vain,* vegetate
talk: *gossip,* *nonsense*
IDOL: *desire,* *image,* *symbol*
IDOLIZE: *adore,* *love,* *worship*
IGLOO: *hut,* *house,* *home*
IGNOBLE: *bad,* *evil,* *low*
IGNORANT: *dull,* *stupid,* *vain*
IGNORE: *avoid,* duck, slight
ILIAD: *homer*
ILK: *class,* *group,* *kind*
ILL: *bad,* *evil,* *sick,* *wrong*
-*blood:* animosity, enmity
-*considered:* *reckless*
counsel: abulia
-*favored:* unprepossessing

* **Asterisk means to look up this word to find more answer words.**

-gotten: *bad, corrupt, *evil
-humored: *cross, *mad, *short
-repute: dishonor
pref.: mal
-tempered: *cross, *mad, *short
will: enmity, malice, venom
wind: bad luck, jinx
ILLINOIS: bird: cardinal
flower: native violet
native: sucker
nickname: prairie or tall state
river: big muddy, spoon
tree: burl oak
ILLNESS: feign: goldbrick, malinger
ILLUMINATION: *light
ILLUSION: *error, *image, *trick
ILLUSTRIOUS: *bright, *great
IMAGE: allegory, apparition, appearance, archetype, aspect, association, cast, concept, copy, counterpart, description, effigy, efod, eidolon, fancy, *fetish, figure, *form, *god, *icon, idea(1), likeness, map, miniature, miracle, mirage, *model, *name, percent, photo, *picture, pieta, *plan, reflection, replica, shadow, statue, *symbol, teraph, vision
breaker: iconoclast
distorted: anamorphism
good luck: alraun
graven: idol, ikon
maker: iconoplast
mental: concept, eidolon, idea, phantasm, recept
pert.: iconic, simulacral
rainbowlike: spectrum
religious: icon, idol, ikon, orant, pieta
stone: herma
wooden: tiki, xoanon
worship: ararati, idolatry
IMAGINE: *picture, *sense, *think
IMAM: *church: man
last: mahdi

IMBECILE: *fool, moron, *weak
IMBIBE: *absorb, *drink, gulp
IMBROGLIO: *fight, *plot
IMITATE: *adopt, ape, *copy, mime, mock, *model, *repeat
IMMENSE: *big, *fine, *great
IMMER: son: magormissabib, pashur, zadok, zebadiah
IMMERSE: *absorb, baptize, bathe, bury, deluge, dip, douse, drown, duck, dunk, engage, engross, engulf, infuse, inundate, involve, merge, overwhelm, plunge, souse, submerge, *wet
IMMORAL: *evil, *wanton, *wrong
woman: baggage, *prostitute
IMMORTAL: *divine, *god
eight: chang-kuo lao, hanchung li, han hsiang-tzu, hohsienku, lantsaiho, lu tung pin, tieh kuai, tsaokuochiu
IMP: *demon, *devil, *dwarf
IMPACT: *fix, *force, *shock
IMPAIR: *hurt, *ruin, *spoil
IMPASSE: cul de sac, *stop
IMPASSIVE: *dull, *hard, *solid
IMPATIENT: *angry, *eager
IMPEL: *force, *start, *spur
IMPENDING: close, *near
IMPERFECT: comb.: atelo, mal
fish: thoke
goods: fent
hand: ateles
IMPERIAL: *great, *supreme
woodpecker: ivorybill
IMPERSONAL: *fair, *general
IMPERSONATE: *imitate
IMPETUOUS: *ardent, *eager, *reckless, *violent, *wild
IMPETUS: *body, *impact, vigor
IMPLEMENT: *accomplish, *agent, *instrument, *thing
IMPLICATE: *join, *unite
IMPLORE: *ask, *beg, pray
IMPLY: *argue, *mean, suggest

* Asterisk means to look up this word to find more answer words.

IMPORTANT: august, *big, conspicuous, *critical, egregious,
emphatic, essential, extraordinary, front-page, *great,
heavy(weight), high-powered,
influential, major-league, mo-
mentous, *name, necessary, *noble, outstanding, paramount, salient, significant, *splendid, *top,
*unique, urgent, vital
person: big shot, *magnate
IMPORTANCE: *range, *rank,
*value
IMPORTUNE: *implore, *press
IMPOSE: *abuse, *administer,
*force, *press, *set
IMPOSTOR: ass in lion's skin,
blagueur, bluff, bunyip, charlatan, *cheat, con man, counterfeit, deceiver, empiric, fake(r),
fourflusher, fraud, gammoner,
humbug, hypocrite, mountebank,
pharisee, phony, *quack, sham,
*sharp, swindler
famous: cagliostro, macpherson,
psalmanazar, romanoff
IMPRESA: *adage, *sign, *symbol
IMPRESS: *affect, *hit, *press
IMPRESSION: *image, *mark
IMPROPER: *bad, *evil, *poor
IMPROVE: *grow, *perfect
IMPULSE: *force, *press(ure)
IMPURE: *dirty, obscene, *rotten
IN: chic, elected, faddish, *home,
powerful, regime
a bad way: *sick, tired
a straight line: eregione
a whisper: sotto voce
abeyance: pending
abundance: galore, *plenty
addition: also, besides, more
any case: ever, regardless
any event: notwithstanding
arms: infantile, *ready
being: *active, actual, alive
camera: privately
case: lest, provided, supposing
circulation: about, around

common: alike, jointly, public
concert: accordant, together
condition: healthy, ok, robust
due course: opportunely, soon
dutch: disgraced, troubled
effect: actually, really
every respect: exactly, utterly
excess: beyond, over, too
fact: certainly, to be sure
few cases: seldom
force: active, operating
front: ahead, before, leading
full: *all, altogether, entire
general: by and large, mutual
good order: bristol fashion
good shape: healthy, neat
good taste: *aesthetic
good time: early, opportunely
harness: busy, *ready
heat: blissom
heaven: *happy, rapturous
hell: below, troubled
high: *ready, rolling
higher degree: nothing else but
high feather: debonair, healthy
hysterics: frantic, *mad
juxtaposition: beside, ferninst
kind: similar, thus
large part: almost
lieu: instead
loco parentis: instead
love: devoted, enamored, taken
mint condition: fit, healthy
name only: nominal, supposedly
plain english: candidly
place of: instead, *substitute
proportion: according, equal
re: about, anent, pertaining
reserve: *ready, *substitute
round numbers: *average
same place: ibid
shape: *fit, neat, *ready, trim
so far as: qua, since
spite: maugre, notwithstanding
step: agreeable, harmonious
stitches: amused, laughing
store: destined, imminent

* Asterisk means to look up this word to find more answer words.

style: modish, popular
substance: basically
that: because
the air: aloft, rumored
the altogether: bare, nude
the background: behind, *obscure
the bag: certain, cinch, *sure
the balance: at issue
the cards: likely, probable
the clear: *free, protected, safe
the gazette: bankrupt
the groove: hep, *straight
the interim: meanwhile
the know: aware, hep, on to
the least: aughtlins
the limelight: *important
the main: chiefly, generally
the matter of: about, anent
the meantime: ad interim
the mood: willing
the name of allah: bismillah
the name of another: benamee
the near future: anon
the open: al fresco, outdoors
the past: ago, over
the pink: *fit, healthy
the presence of: coram
the process of: during
the raw: dishabille, nude
the rear: atergo, behind
the red: bankrupt, broke, out
the shade: also ran, secondary
the shadow of god: bezaleel
the style of: ala, alla
the swim: popular, with it
the time of: during
the way: between, obstructing
the works: coming, looming
there: on the ball, with it
thing: *style
toto: *all, completely
trouble: hurting, in a bind
truth: certes, indeed, verily
tune: groovy
vogue: groovy, popular, with it
what way: how, quo modo
with: belonging, influential

words of one syllable: plainly
INACTIVE: *dull, *idle, *quiet
INADEQUATE: *bad, *poor, *short
INAMORATA: beloved, lover
INANE: *dull, *idle, *stupid
INASMUCH AS: because, since
INAUGURATE: celebrate, *start
INAUSPICIOUS: *bad, *evil, *sad
INC: cie, ltd, sa
INCA: *empire:* peru
clan: ayllu
deity: apu-punchau, chasca, choun, inti, iraya, mama-cuna, mama-quilla, manco-capac, pachacamac, urcaguay, viracocha
king: atabalipa, atahualpa
last: atahualpa
priest: amauta
queen: ccoya
solar feast: ccapac cocha, ccapac raymi, ccapac situa
INCANTATION: abracadabra, charm, *fetish, *magic, *nonsense
INCARNATION: avatar, balarama
blessed: dalai lama, rinpoche
INCENSE: *anger, myrrh, *scent
bowl: acerra, censer, thurible
burn: thurify
ingredient: gum, spice, stacte
tree: boswellia, bursara, icica
INCENTIVE: carrot, *force, *urge
INCH: *45:* ell
four: hand
meal: gradually
nine: span
-1/12th: line
pin: sweetbread
39.37: meter
two and one-fourth: nail
12 seconds: prime
INCITE: *abet, *spur, *urge
INCLINATION: *disposition
INCLUDED: among, *present

* Asterisk means to look up this word to find more answer words.

INCOME: annuity, box office, dividends, earnings, emolument, entrance, *fee*, gain, gate, gross, honorarium, intake, *make*, net, port, proceeds, *produce*, profits, receipts, *rent*, *return*, revenue, royalty, salary, stipend, *take*, usance, wages, wealth, *yield*
pert.: rental, tontine
property: apanage, appanage
tax term: carryback, deduction
INCOMPLETE: *comb.:* atelo
INCONSISTENT: absurd, different, illogical
INCORPORATE: *absorb*, *unite*
INCORRECT: *bad*, *wrong*
naming: paranomia
INCREASE: accelerate, access, *accumulate*, *add*, *advance*, aggravate, amplify, ascent, balloon, biggen, blow up, boom, boost, broaden, build up, bulge, bump, dilate, double, enhance, enlarge, expand, get ahead, greaten, *grow*, heighten, heist, hike, hop up, increment, intensify, jack up, jazz up, jump, key up, leap, lengthen, mount, multiply, parlay, pick up, produce, proliferate, pyramid, *raise*, redouble, return, rise, sharpen, shoot up, *spread*, step up, swell, thicken, triple
comb.: auxo
possessions: amass, enrich
price: appreciate
salary: *raise*
sound: crescendo
INCREDIBLE: baroque, *weird*
INCREMENT: *income*, *increase*
INCRIMINATE: *accuse*, *attack*
INCUBUS: *demon*, *devil*, *spirit*
son: cambion
wife: succuba
INCUR: *acquire*, *get*
INCUS: ambos, anvil, bone
INDECENT: *bad*, *evil*, *wanton*

INDECISION: *problem*, *puzzle*
INDEED: aroo, aru, iwis, really
INDEFINITE: *obscure*, *vague*
INDEPENDENT: *absolute*, autonomous, *free*, individual, neutral, proud, *rich*
INDETERMINATE: apeiron, *vague*
botany: racemose
INDEX: file, list, *sign*, *token*
card: pip, table
finger: pointer
mark: fist
sundial: gnomon
INDIA: bharat, hindustan, tamil
aborigine: dasyus, dravidian
absolute: tat
abuse: galee, gali
acrobat: nat
age cycle: kalpa, yuga
agricultural caste: meo, vaisya
air conditioner: tatty
air house: hawaghar
alphabet: devanagari, sarada
ancestor: manu, pitri
ancestor's rite: sraddha
ancestral race: ayran
anglicized: babu
animal: arctonyx, balisaur, dhole, elephant, tiger, zebu, zibet
antelope: bezoar, cervicapra, chicara, chikara, chiru, goral, nilgai, nilgau, sasin
apartment: mahal, zenana
army officer: jemadar, naigue, naik, tanadar, thanadar
artisan caste: sudra
ascetic: avadhuta, bhiksu, fakir, jogi, sadh, sadhu, sannyasi, yati, yogi
astrologer: joshi
atheist: nastika
awning: shamianah
ayran: *hindu*, swat
bandit: dacoit
banker: saraf, schroff, seth
bard: bhat

* Asterisk means to look up this word to find more answer words.

bathing place: ghat, ghaut

bazaar: chawk, chowk

bean: urd

bear: baloo, balu, bhalu

bearer: sirdar

bed: charpai, charpoy

bed cover: palampore

beer: apong

beverage, immortality: amrita

bible: *india: scripture

bill of exchange: hundi

bird: amadavit, amaduvade, argala, baya, bulbul, kala, koel, lowa, mina, myna, munia, raya, sarus, shama

bison: arna, gaur, gayal, tsine

blacksmith: lohar

black wood: biti

blight: soka

boar: varaha

boat: almadia, budgerow, dhoni, dingey, dinghy, dingy, donga, dunga, masula, puteli, shibar

boat skipper: serang

bodice: choli

bodyguard: burkundaz

bond: andi

bread root: pomme blanche

buck: sasin

bull: zebu

bush: kanher

butter: ghee, ghi

buzzard: tesa

cabinet: almirah, almura

calendar: *india: month

cannabis: *india: hemp

canoe: tanee

canvas enclosure: canaut

cape: divi

capital: delhi, simla

carpet: agra, asan, azan

carriage: bandy, ekka, gharri, gharry, hackery, rath, tonga

cashmere: ulwan

caste: agarwal, ahir, arora, ambastha, babhan, bania, banyan, bhil, brahmin, caddi, dacoit, dasi, dhangar, dhanuk, dhobie, dhoby, dom, goala, gola, jain, jat, koli, kori, kshatriya, lohana, madi, mal(i), meo, palli, pasi, rajpoot, rajput, sansi, sudra, tai, teli, toty, vaisya, vakkaliga, varna

caste mark: tilka

cattle: gaekwar, gaur, gayal, nilgai, tsine, zebu

cavalry: ressala, risala, sowar

celestial light gods: aditya

chamber: kiva, tahkhana

chamois: sarau

charm: mantra

chess: chaturanga, shatranj

church: arya, samaj

cigarette: beedi, bidi, biri

city: agra, ajanta, ajmer, akola, arcot, arrah, ava, bally, baroda, benares, calcutta, calicut, cawnpore, delhi, dhar, gaur, gaya, hansi, mahe, mau, mhow, mohenjo-daro, nasik, patna, puri, simla, surat, unao

civet: rasse, zibet(h)

clan: gotra

class: *india: caste

clerk: baboo, babu, gomashta(h)

cloth: dhurrie, pata, salloo, saloo, salu, surat, tat, ulwan

coast: malabar

coast range: ghat

coat: achkan, choga, chuddar

coconut: nargil

cognate: bandhava

coin: abidi, adha, ahmed, akhter, ana, anna, cronin, crore, dam, faloo, fanam, fels, gunda, kano, lakh, mohur, paisa, pice, pie, rupee, tara

concubine: dasi

congregation: samaj, somaj

consciousness: aniruddha

continent: ashrama, brahmachari

convent: math

cook: bawarchi

coronation: abhiseka

---

* Asterisk means to look up this word to find more answer words.

cosmic order: rita
court: adawlut, sudder
cowherd caste: ahir(a)
cowrie: zimbi
crane: saras, sarus
cremation: sati, suttee
crocodile: gavial, muggar
crop: rabi
cuisine: chapatis, dhal, gajar, halwa, haleem, lentil, moglai biryani, pappadums, raita
custom: dastur, suttee
cymbal: tal
dagger: katar
dais: chabutra
dance: cantico, nautch
dancer: bayadeer, devadasi, nat(araja), tandava
dawn gods: asvins
deer: atlas, axis, barasingha, cervus, cheetal, chitra, gerau, kakar, rusa, sambar
dead, god of: yama
demon: *india: spirit
dependency: taluk
deposit: adhi
desert: thar
devil tree: dita
devotee: yati
dialect: *india: language
dice: kabat
dictionary: amara-kosha
dill: soya
disciple: chela, sikh
discount: batta
disease: agrom
distiller: abkar
district: agra, daya, faizabad, gya, malabar, mofussil, nasik, nellore, oudh, patna, sibi, simla, zillah
divine artificer: tvashtar
divorce law: talak
doctrine: anatta, dharma, karma
dog: buansu, kolsun, pariah
dragon: ahi, ketu, rahu, vritra
drama: nataka
dramatist: bhavabhuti

dravidian: andhra, arava, brahui, gond, kanarese, khond, kodagu, kota, kurukh, malayalam, male, malto, nair, oraon, tamil, telugu, toda, tulu
drink: arrack, nipa, soma
drinking pot: lotah
drought: soka
drug: charas, *india: hemp, sina
drum: nagara
due: hak
dust storm: shaitan, sheitan
duty: dharma
dye: aal, al, awl, morindin
dynasty: gupta
earth: regur
elephant: airavata, hathi
elephant driver: mahout
elephant-headed god: ganesha
elixir: amreeta, amrita
elk: sambar
english founder: clive
epic: mahabharata, ramayana
essence: amrita, atman, rata
estate: taluk
exchange rate: batta
existence tenet: prana, tattva
fabled people: astomoi
fabled mountain: meru
fables: bidpal, book of good counsel
fabric: baft(ah), dewali, mela, romal, tanjib, tats, zenana
fair: mela
falcon: besara, besra, dhoti, laggar, lugger, shaheen
family: gotra
fan: punka(h)
farmer: hamal, meo, ryot
fate: dharma
father: baboo, babu, manu
female energy: sakati, shakti
festival: burra khana, dashara, dewali, holi, mela, phag, puja
fiber: ambary, bhabar, jute, kumbi, oadal
fig tree: botree, peepul, pipal

* Asterisk means to look up this word to find more answer words.

fine: abwab
fire god: agni, akal, civa, deva, kama, siva
fire priests: atharvans
first man: yama
fish: argus, chenas, dorab, hilsa, lile, scatophagus
flour: ata, atta
flower: laria, larigot, lotus
fluid: rasi
flute: bin, matalan, pungi
flying being: garuda
foot dye: alta
foot print: pug
foot stool: mora
forage plant: guar
*friar: *ecclesiastic: hindu*
frontier bulwark: nefa
frost: hemanta
fruit: amchoor, amhar, bel, bhel, lansa, mango
game: bagataway
gardener caste: mali
garment: banyan, burqa, dhoti, jama(h), saree, sari
gatehouse: cerami
gateway: dar, toran(a)
gazelle: chikara, shri, sri
gentleman: baboo, babu, sahib
giant: bana, sesha, shesha
gift: enam, khilat, killut, lepa
goat: markhor, tahr
god: agni, akal, antaka, apa, asvins, bhaga, bhrama, bhrigus, brihaspati, *buddha,* civa, daksha, dandadhara, deva(ta), dewa(ta), dharmaraja, dyaus, ganesa, ganesha, haoma, *indra,* jagannath, juggernaut, kala, kama, karttikeya, khuda, krishna, kritantapasupati, kubera, kuvera, manu, matarisvan, maya, mitra, narasimha, nasatyas, parjanya, pasupati, pitripati, prajapati, prithivi, puchan, rama(chandra), rudra, samana, samavurti, savitar, savitri, simia,

shiva, *siva,* skanda, soma, sraddhadeva, surya, tryambaka, tvashtar, *varuna,* vata, vayu, vishnu, vivasvat, yama
god's abode: meru
god's artisan: ribhus
god's messenger: bhrugi
god's sons: angiras, rishis
goddess: aditi, ambika, amma(n), annapurna, bhairavi, bhumi, cnandi, devi, durga, gauri, haimavati, kali, lakshmi, matris, parvati, sakti, sarasvati, sati, shakti, shree, shri, sri, uma, ushas, vac, vach
golden triangle cities: agra, delhi, jaipur
goldsmith: sonar
gorge: nullah
government: sircar
government lands: amani
granary: gola, gunge, gunj
grant: enam, inam, sasan
grass: bhabar, darbha, doorba, glaga, kasa, kusha, man, ragee, raggee, ragi, roosa, usar
greeting: sri
griddlecake: chapatty
grinding stone: mano, metate
groom: oboli, sais, sice, syce
group: sang, varna
grove: sarna
guard: daloyet
guide: shikaree, shikari
guitar: bina, sitar, vina
gum: amra(d)
gypsy: bazigar, karachee
hall: durbar, kiva
handkerchief: malabar
hardwood: calamander, poon, teak
harem: serai, zenana
harvest: rabbi, rabi
hawk: badius, shikra
headdress: puggree, rumal, sola
heaven: ananta, devachan, dyaus,

---

* Asterisk means to look up this word to find more answer words.

kamaloka, kamavachara, nirvana, svarga
heiress: begum
helmet: topee, topi
hemp: bang, bhang, carl, chirata, dagga, ganja, hashish, keef, kef, keif, kief, pooa(h), pua, ramie
hemp oil: cannabene
herb: curcuma, **india: hemp,* sesame, sola, zeodary
heresies: buddhism, jainism
hermitage: ashrama, asrama
hero: nala, rama, sita
high caste: babhan, bibar man
hill dweller: bhil, dogra
hills: garo
holly: assi
holy book: **india: literature*
holy center: ajodhya
holy city: benares, nasik
holy grove: sarna
holy man: alvar, fakeer, fakir, rishi, sadh(u)
holy river: ganga, ganges
holy plant: banyan, bo tree, creeper, ephedra, kusa, milk weed, millet, periploca, pipal, sarcostemma, soma, valli
house: baradari, bari, basha, bungalow, hawaghar, mahal
hunting expedition: shikar
hymn: mantra
idol: pagoda, swami
idol worship: arati
ignorance: tamas
incarnation: avatar, rama
infinity: ananta
invader: sacae, saka
invalid resort: abu, simla
irrigation ditch: annicut
islam convert: shaikh
isle: agatti, andaman, nicobar
jackal: kola
juggernaut: krishna
jungle: shola
kala: bulbul
king: **india: prince*

kinsman: bandhava
knife: dah, kukri
laborer: palli, sudra
lady: begum, bibi, devi, ranee, rani, sahibah
lake: chilka, jheel, kolair
lancer: sowar
land grant: enam, inam, sasan
landing place: gaut, ghat
language: arua, awadhi, hindi, hindustani, marathi, oriya, pali, pamir, pashto, prakrit, pushtu, sanskrit, tamil, telugu, urdu, vedic
law term: futwa, hak(h), manu
lawyer: muktar, vakeel, vakil
leader: gandhi, nehru, sirdar
lease: patta, pottah
lease holder: ijaradar
leopard: cheetah
library: bhandar
life: atman, jiva, prana
life stage: ashrama, asrama
liquor: shrab, soma, sura
literature: agama, akhyana, atharva, aranyaka, ayurveda, brahmana, gayatri, gita, purana, sakha, sama, samhita, sastra, shaka, shastra, shruti, smitri, sruti, tantra, upanishad, veda(nga), vedanta, yajnavalka, yajur
litter: doly, doolee, jampan, kajawah, polki
loam: regur
loin cloth: dhoti, pata
lord: isvara, mian, swami
love god: kama
low caste: dom, kori, kuli
macaque: rhesus
magic: jadoo, jadu, maya
magician: fakeer, fakir
mahogany: toon(a)
mail: dak, dauk, dawk
male principle: purusha
man-horses: gandharvas
mangrove: goran

---

* Asterisk means to look up this word to find more answer words.

mantras: atharva-veda
mark: bottu, tilaka
market: pasar
marriage: arsharite
master: mian, sahib, swami
matting: tatta
meal: ata, atta
measure: adhaka, adoulie, ady, amunam, angula, bigha, byee, cahar, coss, covido, cudava, cumbha, dain, danda, denda, depa, doph, dha(nush), drona, garce, gavyuti, gaz, gez, gireh, guz, hath, jaob, jow, khahoon, kos(s), krosa, kunk, lamany, lan, moolum, moot, mushti, niranga, okthabah, palgat, pally, para, parran, prasha, raik, rati, ropani, salay, seit, ser, taun, teng, tipree, tola, unglee, vitasti, yojana
medical caste: ambastha, baidya
medical man: shaman
medical nut: malabar
medicine: ayurveda
melody: raga
mendicant: bairagi, naga, sannyasi, vairagi
mental discipline: yoga
merchant: banian, brinjaree, seth, soudagar, teli
merchant caste: agarwal, vaisya
mercenary: sepoy
midwife: dhai
millet: dhoor, durra, koda
mine laborer: mita
minstrel: bhat
missionary: bodhidharma
mistress: annapurna
mogul emperor: akbar, baber
monastery: math
moneylender: mahajan
monkey: rhesus
monkey god: hanuman
month: aghan, asarh, asin, baisakh, bhadon, chait, jeth, kartik, katik, kuar, magn, phagun, phal-gun, pus, sawan
moslem: swat
mother goddess: amma(n), matris
mountain: abil, abu, ghat, himalayas, hindu-kush, meru, neilgherries, siwalik, suleiman, trisul, vindhya
mountain pass: ghat(s), ghaut
mountaineer: bhil
mouse: metad
mrs: devi
mulberry: aal, ach, al
musical instrument: been, bina, ruana, sarod, sitar, vina
musical composition: raga, rasa
musket ball: goli
muslin: adat, charkhana, dorea, doria, gurrah, madras
mystic: bhave, yogi
myth: adi-shesha, purana
narcotic: *india: hemp
nature principle: guna
nco: havildar, naik
negro: hubshi
nilgiri tribesman: badaga
noble: ashraf, rajah
non violence: ahimsa
number: lakh
nurse: amah, ayah, dhai
nymphs: apsaras
ocher: almagra
offering: bali, lepa, pinda
officer's son: akhundzada
official: amalah, ameen, amin, aumildar, daroga(h), dedan, jemadar, nabob, naib, nawab, nazim, nazir, ressaldar, subahdar, tenet
ornament: amalaka, bottu
package: robbin
pageant: tamasha
palace: baradari
palanquin: palkee
palm: nipa
paradise: nirvana
partridge: kyah
patriarch: pitri

* **Asterisk means to look up this word to find more answer words.**

peasant: ryot
peddler: boxwallah
perfect bliss: ananda, nirvana
pheasant: moonal, monal, monaul
philosopher: shankara, yoga
philosophy: advaita, kosha, mimansa, tamas, vedanta, yoga
pigeon: treron
pipe: hookah
plains: usar
plant stalk: amsu
plum: amra
poem: bhagavad-gita, *india:* epic, raghuvansa, sloka
poet: tagore
poison: abrin, bikh, bisk
police chief: daroga(h), darogha
police man: peon, sepoy
police station: thana
porter: chokidar, durwaun
pot: chatty
powder: abir
power: sakti
prayer call: azan
prayer carpet: asan(a), asani
*priest: *ecclesiastic: hindu*
priest caste: brahman
prince: ahlualia, asoka, bana, bharata, maharaja(h), nala, nawab, nizam, raja(h), rana, sesha, shesha, sirdar
princess: begum, kumari, kunwari, maharani, malikzadi, raj-kumari, ranee, shahzadi
*principles: *principles: seven*
property: dhan
pundit: swami
punjabi people: sansi, sikh
*queen: *india: princess*
race: dravidian, hindu, jat, swat, tamil, varna
rainy season: monsoon, varsha
rat: bandicoot
reception: durbar
reign: nawab, raj
religion: brahmanism, buddhism, hinduism, islam, jainism, parsee,

parsi, sivaism
retreat: ashram
revenue sources: amani
revenue collector: aumil(dar)
rice: boro
rifle pit: sangar
rite: achar(a), satyagraha
robber: dacoit
room: kiva
root: atees, atis
rubber: caoutchouc
*ruler: *india: prince, princess*
*sacred: *holy designations*
sacrificial fire: agni
sacrificial victim: traga
safari: shikar
sage: agastya, amanda, bharata, bhat, gautama, katha, kishi, mahatma, pandit, pundit
sailor: lascar
saint: alvar
salesman: brinjaree, brinjary
salvation: moksha
scarf: saree, sari
scavenger: bungi(ni), bungy
school, vedanta: advaita
schoolmaster: akoond, akhund
science book: ayur-veda
score: corge
script: brahmi
*scripture: *india: literature*
seaport: bombay, bhaunagar, calcutta, cannanore, madras
sect: aghori, ahmadiya, ajivika, jain(a), meda, sadh, samaj, seik, sikh, siva
serpent: adjiger, ahi, bongar, bungarus, cobra, daboya, katuka, krait, naga
serpent king: sesha, vasuki
servant: amah, ayah, bearer, bildar, dasi, ferash, hamal, maty, mussalchee, sirdar, syce
shade: purdah
shed: pandal
*sheep: *asia: sheep, barwal*
shirt: banian

* Asterisk means to look up this word to find more answer words.

shrine: dagaba, dagoba, dewal

shrub: adhatoda, callicarpa, arusa, madar, mudar, odal

silk: cabeca, corah, muga, romal, rumal

silversmith: sonar

sloth: aswail, melursus

snake: *india: serpent

social division: *india: caste

soil, rich: segur

soldier: gurkha, peon, sepoy, sikh

sorceress: usha

sorghum: chena, cush, dari, darra, darso, dhurra, dora, dourah, durr, hegari, milo

spinning wheel: charka, charkha

spirit: asura, atman, bali, bhoot, bhudapati, bhut, daitya, dasyus, dust devil, hiranyakasipu, jiva, jalandhara, kalika, mara, muktama, naga, pisachee, pisachi, prana, rahu, rakshasa, ravana, sura, tamas, vibhishana, yaksha

spirit, absolute: purusha

spirit prince: pasupati, rudra, shiva, siva

split pea: dal, pigeon pea

state ceremony: durbar

state lands: amani

steward: bhandari

stone: lingham

stool: mora

storehouse: bhandar, gola

storm: peesash, tufan

streambed: nullah

sugar: goor, gur, raab

suicide: suttee

sun god: *aditya, agni, mitra, savitar, surya, varuna

sun worshipper: parsee, parsi

surety: andi

swamp belt: terai

swan: hansa

sword: pata

tableland: balaghat, balaghaut

tablets: bogaz-keui, pteria

tapir: saladang

tariff: zabeta

tax: abkari, abwab, chaukidari

tax district: tahsil

taxi: tonga

teacher: akhoond, akhun(d), alfaqui, guru, mulla(h), pundit

temple: deul, vimana

temple tower: sikhora, sikhra

tenant: ryot

tent: pawl

thrush: sama, shama

title: ahluwalia, akhundzada, aya, baboo, babu, bahadur, begum, bibi, burra, gaekwad, gaekwar, gaikwar, guicowar, huzoor, mian, mir, naic, nawab, raja(h), ranee, rani, sahib(ah), shree, shri, sidi, singh, sirdar, sri, swami

tower: minar, *sikhara, stupa

tracker: puggi

trader: banian, banyan

tree: aal, ach, al, alus, amboina, amli, amra, angili, anjan, banyan, bel, beyr, black dammar, canarium, dar, deodar, dhak, dita, eng, goran, kokra, lin, majagua, mahwa, mangrove, morus, neem, nim, oadal, pipal, poon, salai, sain, sal, shoq, simal, sissoo, tala, teak, toon

tribe: ao, badaga, bhil, colleri, gor, jat, kadu, sherani, shirani

trimurti: brahma, shiva, vishnu

troop: ressala, risala(h)

truck: tonga

turban: puggree, seerband

turks: afridi

umbrella: chatta

underworld: patala

universe: loka

unorthodox: jaina

upanishad: isha, veda, vedanta

valley: dhoon

vedas, introducer to: agastya

vegetable: dal, sabzi

vessel: lota, patamar, shibar

viceroy: nabob, nawab

* Asterisk means to look up this word to find more answer words.

village: abati, mouzah
village chief: patel
village lands: bhaiyachara, pattidari, zamindari
village meeting place: ambalam
violin: ruana, sarinda, saroh
waistband: cummerbund
ware: biddery, bidri
warrior caste: kshatriya
warrior god: indra
watchman: mina
water carrier: bheestie
water god: varuna
water nymph: apas
wayside stop: parao
weaver: tanti
weight: abucco, adpao, bahar,
bhar(a), candy, catty, chittak,
dhan, dhurra, drum, hoen,
hubba, karsha, kona, mangelin,
masha, maund, myat, pai, pala,
pally, pank, peiktha, pice, pouah,
raik, rati, ratti, retti, ruay, ruttee,
seer, ser, tael, tali, ticul, tola, vis,
wang, yava
whaler: hoh
wheat: sujee, suji
widow: sati, suttee
wild dog: dhole
wild sheep: nahoor, oorial, sha
wine: shrab
wine seller: abkar
wind god: marut
window screen: tatty
wisdom god: ganesha
wood: biti, eng, kokra, sal, sissoo,
toon
world: loka
world age: yuga
world guardian: lokapala
world lord: jagannath(a)
worship: pooja, puja
worshipper: jain(a), saiva
writer: sircar
xylophone: saron
INDIAN: aborigine, amerind, native, ocean, red, savage

abanic: siouan
abnaki: arosaguntacook, malecite,
norridgewock, passamaquoddy,
penobscot
agricultural: pawnee
agriculturalist: campesino
aht confederacy: nootka
alabama: creek
alaska: akkhas, aleut, sitka, tlingit
algonquian: abnaki, algic, arap-
aho, armouchiquois, arosaguntacook, bersiamite, blackfoot,
blood, brotherton, cahokia, can-
arsee, cheyenne, cree, delaware,
fox, illinois, massachuset, miami,
micmac, mohican, montagnais,
niantic, ojibway, ottawa, piegan,
sac, sauk, shawnee, sihasapa, siksika, sokoki, wea, weitspekan,
wishoskan
amazon: tapajo, tupy, xingu
and white: griffe, ladino, mestizo
andes: antisi, antisians
antilles: carib
apache: arivaipa
araucanian: aucanian, auca, huil-
liche, mapuche, moluche, pam-
pean, pehuenche, picunche, pu-
relche, ranquel
arawakan: apolistan, araua, arawak, atorai, baniva, baniwa,
bare, baure, campa, caquetio,
changoan, ciboney, goajiro,
guana, ineri, island carib, javi-
tero, jucuna, jumana, lorenzan,
lucayo, maipure, moxo, piro,
puquinan, puru, tacanan, taino,
tariana, ticunan, uran, waura,
wapisiana, ypurinan
arikara: caddo, rees
arizona: apache, hano, hopi, moki,
moqui, name, navaho, papago,
pima, tewa, yuma
arkansas: wichita
athabascan: babine, beaver
athapascan: ahtena, dene, hoopa,

---

* Asterisk means to look up this word to find more answer words.

hupa, lipan, hahani, navaho, tin-neh, taku, wahane

aueto: tupian

aymaran: cana, canchi, caranga, cauqui

barbacoan: cayapa

basket: bokaak

bean: bignonia, catalpa, trumpet creeper

blackfoot: algonquian, blood, pie-gan, sihasapa, siksika

blanket: stroud

boat: bull boat

bolivian: aymara, charca, chiri-guano, ite(n), leca, maropa, mojo, moxo, otuke, uro

boro: *indian: miranhan

brazil: acroa, araua, bororo, boto-cudo, bravo, caraja, carib, carira, diau, ge, guana, guarani, inca, maku(a), manao, mura, puru, siusi, tapuya, tariana, *tupian, yao, zaparo

british columbia: gitksan, nass

buzzard: tesa

caddo: adai, andarko, arikara, eyeish, hainai, ioni, nachitoch, pawnee, rees, waco

cahita: mayo, piman, tehueco, yaqui

calchaqui: diaguite

calgary: sarsi

california: hupa, koso, maidu, mono, nozi, pericui, pomo, sa-lina, seri, wintun, yana, yuki, yuman, yunan, yurok

canada: abnaki, aht, athabasca, cree, dene, haida, micmac, moka, nahane, nootka, oneida, sanetch, sioux, slave, taku, tinne, tinneh

canoeiro: *tupian

cape province: amafingo, amakosa

cariban: akawai, aparai, apiaca, arara, arecuna, bakairi, carib-(isi), chayma, cumanagoto, ma-cusi, maquiritare, mayana, ta-manaco, trio, woyaway, yao, yauapery

caribbean: carib, tao, trio

cashibo: buninahua, carapache, puchanahua

cayapo: caraho, caraja chambioa, javahai

central america: maya, ulva

ceremonial dance: cantico

ceremonial pipe: calumet

ceremony: potlatch

chaddo: ioni, hainai

chibchan: aruac, betoya, curetus, duit, muso, nuzo, pioxe, rama, tama, tucano, tunebo, yahuna

chickpea: gram

chief: cacique, cazique, inca, lo-gan, sachem, sagamore, sannup, tyee

chief, famous: black hawk, geron-imo, joseph, osceola, pontiac, sitting bull, tecumseh

child: papoose

chile: auca, *arauca(nian)

chipewyan: *indian: athabascan

chitchan: tunebo

choctaw: apalachee

cigar tree: catalpa

colombia: choco, colima, duit, mocoa, muzo, paeze, tama, tapa

colonist's friend: netop

colorado: arapaho(e)

copehan: wintun

corn: kanga, maize, samp, tara, zea

corn disease: boilsmut

costa rica: bribri, guatuso, voto

council: powwow

cowichanan: nanaimo

craft: canoe, dugout, kayak

creek: alabama

cuckoo: bird, koel

dakota: arikara, caddo, mandan, ree, santee, sioux, teton

dance: buffalo dance

delaware: lenape

duit: *chibchan

---

* **Asterisk means to look up this word to find more answer words.**

ecuadorian: ardan, barbacoa, canelo, cixo, maina
eskimo: *indian:* alaska
farmer: calusa
female: mahala, mahaly, squaw
festival: busk, potlatch
fighter: boone, custer, miles
file: procession, single line
flathead: chinook
florida: calusa, seminole
food: camas(s), cammas, *indian:* corn, pemmican
fuegian: ona
game: canute
georgia: creek, uchean
ges or ghes: tapuyan
give: *deceive,* renege
god: atira, gahonga, gandayak, manitou, ohdowa, poia, sesondowah, shakuru, soatsaki, tirawa, wakan
great lake: cayuga, erie, huron
greeting: how, netop
grindstone: mano
guana: arawakan
guarani: cain-gua
guatemala: chol, chorti, chube, itza, ixil, kerchi, kiche, lenca, mam, maya, pipil, quiche, ulva, voto, xinca
hatchet: tomahawk
headdress: feathers, topknot
hippo: ipecac, spurge
honduras: carib, chorti, lenca, maya, moreno, paya
hopi: moki, moqui
hupa: *athapascan
hut: hogan, tepee, toldo, wickiup, wigwam, wikiup
indiana: miami, wea
iowa: fox, sac, sauk
iroquois: caughnawaga, cayuga, erie, hochelaga, huron, mingo, mohawk, oneida, seneca
jalisco: cora
jova: piman
kansas: kaw, pani, pawnee

keresan: acoma, pueblo, sia
kwakiutl: awaitlala
leader: *indian:* chief, *famous*
lesser antilles: ineri
liquor: firewater
lodge: *indian:* hut
louisiana: *caddo
madder: bengal madder
mallow: buttonweed, canapina, hemp, jute
mam: mayan
man: buck, brave, chief, sannup
manitoba: cree
marauder: gaucho
matacan: ashluslay
maya: cakchiquel, itza, ixil, mam, quiche
meal bread: corncake
memorial post: totem, xat, xyst
mestizo: griffe, ladino
mexican: apache, aztec, chol, cora, eudeve, huave, huichoi, jonaz, jova, mam, maya, meco, mie, opata, otomi, pame, pinto, pueblo, ser, toboso, trike, yakui, yaqui, zoque
miami: wea
miranhan: boro, mariana, mirana
mississippi: biloxi, mandan, natchez, tiou, tonikan
missouri: osage
moccasin: pac
money: beads, ioqua, peag, seawan, sewan, *shell,* wampum
montana: bannock, crow, hohe
moon daughter: nakomis, nokomis
moxo: *arawakan
mulberry: aal, ach, al, awl, canary wood, rubra
muskhogean or muskogee: creek, seminole, yamasi
muso: chibchan
nebraska: kiowa, omaha, ote, otoe, ponca
nevada: digger
new mexico: acoma, apache, isleta, keres, laguna, navajo,

---

* Asterisk means to look up this word to find more answer words.

pecos, piro, pueblo, sia, tano, taos, tigua, tonoa, zuni

new york: erie, **iriquois,* mohawk, oneida, seneca, tuscarora

nicaragua: cukra, diria, lenca, mangue, mico, mixe, rama, sambo, smoo, toaca, ulva

north carolina: buffalo, coree

northwest: cree

nuzo: chibchan

ocean arm: arabian sea

ocean island: amindivi, ceylon, laccadive, maldive, mauritius, minicoy

oklahoma: arapahoe, caddo, cherokee, choctaw, creek, kansa, kaw, kiowa, loup, osage, otoe, pawnee, ponca, quapaw

opata: piman

oregon: chinook, coos, kusan, modoc, yanan, yunca

orinoco: guahiribo

ornament: runtee

ova: piman

pacific: chinook, nootka

paint: bloodwort, puccoon, red root, sanguinaria, tormentil

panama: carien, cueva, cuna, guaymi(e)

panamint: koso

panoan: amahuaca, cashibo

paraguay: guayaqui

para river: araquaju

pawnee: loup

payagna: agaz

peban: yagua

peace pipe: calumet

people: pomos

peru: andes, aymara, boro, campa, cana, carib, chanka, changos, inca, inka, jibaro, jiyaro, kechua, pano, peba, piro, quechau, quiche, yagua, ynka, yunca, yutu

physic: *indian: hippo

pipe: anoplanthus, bird's-nest, broom rape, calumet, orobanche

pillar: lat, totem, xat, xyst

piman: cahita, cora, eudeve, jova, mayo, opata, ova, pima, yaqui, xova

piro: tanoan

plains: arapahoe, cree, sioux

platte: pawnee

plum: casearia, flacourtiace

pole: *indian: memorial post

pony: cayuse, tinder

porridge: samp

potato: breadroot, yamp

prayer stick: baho, paho, pajo

prehistoric: basketweaver

pre-inca: canari

pueblo: hopi, moki, piro, tana, taos, zuni

puru: *indian: arawakan

quapaw: arkansas, ozark

quechuan: aymara, calchaquian, cholo, cuzceno, inca, nasca, quiteno, runa-simi, yunca

reservation: preserve

rio grande: tao

salishan: atnah, bella-coola, tulalip, twana

seowan: oto, otoe, sioux

shell money: allocochick

shot: aliipoe

shoshone: banak, bannock, cahuilla, comanche, hopi, moki, mono, moqui, otoe, paiute, piute, utah, ute

sioux: abanic, assiniboin, biloxi, catawba, crow, dakota, hidata, iowa, hohe, kansa, kaw, mandan, omaha, osage, otoe, pinca, santee, saponi, teton, tutelo

skidi: loup

snake dancer: hopi

sonora: seri

sorcery: obe, obeah, obi

south american: aneto, **arawak,* aymara, aztec, carib, ges, inca, ineri, ite(n), lule, moxo, ona, ota, piro, tapuyan, toba, tupi, uro, yao

south carolina: yamasi

* Asterisk means to look up this word to find more answer words.

south dakota: brule
southwest: apache, hopi, navajo, pima, yuma, zuni
spirit: manitou, totem
summer: st augustine's, st luke's, st martin's
tacana: cavina
tanoan: isleta, piro, *pueblo
tapuyan: bugre, cain-gang, camaca, capayo, caraho, cayapo, coroado, ghes, ser
tea holly: yapon
tent or tepee: *indian: hut
texas: adai, lipan
tierra del fuego: agni, ona
tinne: caribou-eater, chipewyan
tlingit: auk
tobacco: asthma weed, bladder pod, wundtkraut
tonickan: tiou
tribal symbol: totem
trophy: scalp
tupian: aneto, anta, araquaju, aveto, canoeiro, tapajo, xingo
uchean: yuchi
uintah: ute
uruguay: yaro
utah: paiute, piute, ute
vancouver: ehatisaht, sooke
venezuela: carib, guarauno, timote(x)
vera cruz: totonac
village: campoody, pueblo
virginia: powhatan, tutelo
waiilatpuan: cayuse
wakashan: aht, nootka
war prize: scalp
warrior: brave, sannup
washington: aht, callam, hoh, lummi, makah
wea: *algonquin
weapon: bow and arrow, club, macana, rock, tomahawk
western: hopi, haw, otoe, ree, seri, ute
wigwam: *indian: hut
wisconsin: oneida, sac

woman: *indian: female
wundtkraut: tobacco
wyoming: crow, kiowa
xingu: aneto
yellow: puri
yes: how
yucatan: maya
yukia: huchnom, wappo
zuni land: cibola
INDIANA: *bird:* cardinal
flower: peony
nickname: hoosier state
tree: tulip
INDICATE: *argue, *mark, *show
INDICT: *accuse, blame, charge
INDIFFERENT: *dull, *idle
INDIGENCE: *need, want
INDIGNANT: *angry, *hot, *mad
INDIGO: *pert.:* anilic
INDISTINCT: *obscure, *vague
INDITE: write
INDIVIDUAL: *particular, *special, *unique
comb.: idio
compound: zoon
development: ontogeny
essence: atman
particle: bion
selfish: egoist, egotist
smug: prig
thing: article
INDO-ARABIC SYSTEM: *pert.:* abacus
INDO-ARYAN: jat, khatri, rajput
INDO-CHINA: annam, cambodia, laos, siam, thailand, *vietnam
aborigine: ho, kha, yao
agriculture caste: meo
city: hanoi, pakse, saigon
coin: piaster, sapek
language: ahom, aka, akha, amoy, anu, ao, bama, bodo, burmese, garo, kami, lai, lao, mro, mru(s), naga, pwo, rong, sac, sai, sak, sgau, shan, tai, thai, wa, yao
military command: arvn, cosvn
tree: eng, mee, teak

* Asterisk means to look up this word to find more answer words.

INDONESIAN: ata, batavian, battak, dyak, igorot, lampong
aborigine: alfur
administrators: priyayi, satyra
behavior principles: musjawarah
coin: rupiah
communist party: pki
congress: mprs
dagger: kri(s)
dance: horse trance dance
fruit: mangosteen, salak
herb: aglaonema
hindu empire: madjapahit
island: arru, bali, bangka, belitoeng, biliton, borneo, celebes, ceram, flores, java, lombok, madoera, moluccas, new guinea, nias, obi, pagai, roti, sawu, soembowa, spice islands, sulawesi, sumatra, tidore, timor, weh, wetar
lake: toba
law: adat
leader: suharto, sukarno
national airline: djakarta
orchestra: gamelan
palace: kraton
party: masjumi
people: alfurata, atta, bagobo, batak, batta(k), bontok, bukidnon, dyak, ifugao, igorot, lampong, manobo
priest caste: brahmana
pyramid: stupa
sea gypsy: selung
shop: toko
soothsayers: dukun
teacher: abangan, kijai, santri, ulama
temple: mendut, prambanan
villager: abangan
volcano: agung, awoe, raung
weight: soekoe
wind: broeboe, brubu
INDOOR: *golf:* dice
INDORSE: *back, *support, visa
INDRA: mahendra, meghavahana, sakka, sakra, svargapati, vajri, visvakarma
dragon: vritra
elephant: airvata
enemy: durvasas, tvashtri, vritra
heaven: amaravati, svarga
home: mount meru
son: arjuna, sitragupta
steed: airavata
thunderbolt: vajra
wife: indrani
INDUCE: actuate, impel, *urge
INDUCING: *suff.:* agogue
INDUCTANCE: *unit:* henry
INDULGE: favor, *pet, *spoil
INDUS: *city:* mohenjo-daro
tribesman: gor
INDUSTRY: *plant, *work
INEPT: absurd, *clumsy, *stupid
INFER: *argue, *mean, *think
INFERIOR: *bad, *mean, *poor
INFERIORITY: *comb.:* aster
INFERNAL: *bad, *cruel, *evil
machine: bomb
region: *hell
INFINITE: *big, boundless, endless, everlasting, *great, olamic, ubiquitous, *universal
INFLUENCE: *control, *effect
peddling: intrigue, lobbying
planet: atazir, hyleg
region: orbit, *sphere
reward. bribe
using: wire-pulling
INFORM: acquaint, *betray, *tell
INHERITANCE: *pert.:* salic
INHIBITION: *comb.:* ant(i)
INHUMAN: *bad, *brutal, *weird
INIQUITOUS: *criminal, *evil
INJUNCTION: *advice, *order
INJURE: abuse, *hurt, *spoil
causing to: malefic, traumatic
INJURY: *civil:* tort
pert.: noxal, noxious
pressure: barotrauma
sense of: umbrage

* **Asterisk means to look up this word to find more answer words.**

INK: *bag:* sac
 berry: brier, holly, indigo, pokeweed, randia, wild box
 pad: dabber, tompion
 pert.: atramental
 slinger: *author, writer
INNER: *comb.:* ent, ental, ento
 bay: ensenada
 circle: cabal, clique, coterie, elite,
  establishment, ins
 directed: autotelic
 horde: bukeyet, kazak, kirghiz
 man: essence, self, *spirit
 meaning: core, heart
 nature: essence
 sole: rand
INNISFAIL: eire, erin, *ireland
INNOCENCE: *saint:* agnes
 symbol: diamond
INNOCENT: *good, *holy, *pure
INO: *consort:* athamas
 grandfather: agenor
 sons: melicertes, palaemon
INOPPORTUNE: *clumsy
INPUT: data, facts, entrance
INSANE: balmy, bats, batty,
  beany, bereft, brainsick, bugs,
  cracked, crazy, cuckoo, daffy,
  daft, demented, deranged, dippy,
  dotty, foolish, frantic, goofy,
  gaga, haywire, incompetent, loco,
  loony, loopy, luny, *mad, ma-
  niacal, moonstruck, morbid, mo-
  ronic, nuts, off, potty, psychotic,
  rabid, senseless, teched, touched,
  *violent, whacky, *wild
 asylum: bedlam, booby hatch,
  bughouse, college, home, institution, loonybin, mad house,
  mental institution, nuthouse,
  padded cell
 delusion: appersonation
INSCRIPTION: *adage, *title
 coins: sigla
 explanatory: titulus
 publisher's: colophon
INSECT: *adult:* imago

 annoying: bicho
 antenna: feeler, palp(us)
 antenna end: clava
 aquatic: ranatra
 armored scale: aspidiotus
 back: notum
 body: thorax
 chalcidoid: blastophaga
 chirping: cricket
 deadly: holotrichious, reduvid
 destructive: locust, predator, scale,
  termite
 dipterous: beef fly, bombyliida,
  mosquito
 ears: *antenna
 edible: attacus
 eyes: ocelli, stemma
 feeler: antenna, cercus, palpus
 female: gyne, queen
 front: acron
 genus: acarus, cicada, cicala,
  emesa, mantis, nepa, termes,
  thripidae
 group: flight, swarm
 hard covering: chitine
 hemipterous: assassin bug, backswimmer, boat bug, calico back,
  harlequin cabbage bug, murgan-
  tia, notonectida
 homopterous: aleyrode, aphid,
  cicada, locust
 hymenopterous: ant, bee, gall fly,
  ichneumon, sawfly, wasp
 joint: cardo
 larva: grub, maggot
 lepidopterous: butterfly, moth
 linguae: glossae
 molting: ecdysis
 noisy: cicada, cricket
 order: acarina, aptera, coleoptera,
  diptera, hempiptera, homoptera,
  hymenoptera, palaeodictyoptera
 parasitic: chigger, chigoe, flea,
  louse, pediculus, tick, turcata
 part: acron, antenna, chirr, clava,
  coxa, labium, media, notium,
  ocellus, palpus, plantula, pro-

* Asterisk means to look up this word to find more answer words.

notum, scutella, stemma, tentacle
pert.: entomic, entomologic
plant: aphid, beetle, borer, thrips
plate: scutum
powder: pyrethrum
praying: mantis
primitive: apterygote
science: entomology
secretion: lac
six-legged: chigger, chigoe
slender: emesa, mantis
small: aphid, bug, bullhead, chigger, chigoe, flea, garfly, gnat, mico, midge, mite
social: ant, bee, emmet
sound: chirk, creak, crick, stridor, stridulation
stage: chrysalis, cocoon, egg, imago, instar, larva, nymph, prepupa, pupa, redio
sting: ictus
stinging: ant, bee, gadfly, hornet, sciniph, yellowjacket, wasp
tail forceps, having: earwig
wing: alula
wing margin: termen
wing spot: isle
winged: bee, diptera, fly, hornet, yellowjacket, wasp
wingless: anoplura, aphorurid, aptera, atropid, centipede, spider
young: callow, larva, pupa
INSIDE: back room, confidential
and out: everywhere, utterly
dope: lowdown
man: *spy
toward: entad
track: *advantage, favor
INSIDES: *abdomen
INSIGNIA: *mark, *symbol
INSIPID: *dull, jejune, *weak
INSOMNIA: agrypnia, ahypnia
INSTEAD: *comb.:* ant, anti
INSTRUCTION: *art:* didactics, paideutics, pedagogy
INSTRUMENT: *agency, *agent, agreement, apparatus, appliance, appurtenance, armamentarium, bond, brake, capitulation, cat's-paw, channel, complex, compose, contract, contrivance, creation, creature, deed, device, dingus, document, dupe, engine, equipment, gadget, gear, handmaid, implement, indenture, lease, *machine, means, mechanism, medium, organ, outfit, paper, pawn, puppet, rig, *sign, *slave, stooge, *system, *thing, tool, utensil, *vehicle, *way
collection: armamentarium, set, trousse
comb.: arium, orium
INSULT: abase, *abuse, affront, cag, cheek, fig, flout, *hurt, indignity, injure, insolence, knock, offend, outrage, potch, slap, slur, snub, *smear, *taunt, *wrong
INSURANCE: *applicant:* risk
computer: actuary, adjuster
payee: beneficiary
system: tontine
INTACT: *all, *perfect, *solid
INTAGLIO: design, *ornament
INTANGIBLE: *obscure, *vague
INTEGRAL: *complete, *intact
INTELLECTUAL: *group:* bloomsbury, think tank
knowledge: aparavidya
INTELLIGENCE: *agent:* *spy
center: brain, gray matter
military: data, information
only: noesis
test deviser: binet, simon
without: *dull, *stupid
INTEND: *aim, *mean, *plan, *try
INTENSE: *ardent, *eager, *great
INTENT: *aim, *end, *set, *will
INTERCEPT: arrest, *seize, *stop
INTEREST: *absorb, *advantage, *affair, *affect, allure, attachment, attention, attract, behalf, behoof, benefit, business, cause, claim, concern, discount,

ego(tism), entertain, excite, fascinate, favor, *forte, *good, hold, incentive, induce, involve, *love, motive, *part(y), *passion, payment, percentage, pique, portion, premium, profit, regard, *right, savor, *service, *share, *spark, *spirit, titillate, *title, touch, *use, usury, weal, *work

INTESTINE: comb.: entero, ileo
 pert.: alvine, enteric, visceral
INTIMATE: *friend, cater-cousin
INTRIGUE: *affair, *deception, *interest, *plan, *plot, *trick
INTRINSIC: *absolute, *good, *pure, real, *right, *true
INTRUDER: buttinsky, carpet bagger, outsider, scalawag
INVALID: *sick, *vain, *weak
INVENT: *form, *make, *start
INVENTORY: method: fifo, lifo
INVERSE: relation: antistrophe
INVESTIGATION: *analysis, *test, *trial
 pert.: heuristic, zetetic
IO: father: inachus
 guard: argus
 son: epaphus
IOLCUS: king: pelias
IOLE: father: eurytus
ION: mother: creusa
 negative: anion
 pert.: caton
 positive: cation, kation
 son: aegicores, argades
 surface: adion
IONIAN: city: myus, teos
 coin: obol(o)
 gulf: arta
 island: cephalonia, cerigo, corfu, ithaca, kai, kei, kythera, laut, leti, letti, paxos, zante
IOTA: *ace, *bit, *part, *trifle
IOWA: bird: eastern goldfinch
 flower: wild rose
 nickname: hawkeye state
 tree: oak

IPHITUS: son: archeptolemus
IRAN: *persia
IRAQ: *mesopotamia
 ancient: kish
IRATE: *angry, *hot, *mad
IRELAND: banba, bogland, cathleen ni houlahan, eire, erin, erse, hibernia, iern(e), innisfail, irena, ivernia, old sod, roisin dubh, scotia
IRENIC: calm, henotic, peaceful
IRIS: comb.: irid(o)
 husband: zephyrus
 inflammation: *eye: defect
 -like plant: avendbloem
 parent: electra, thaumas
 part: argola, uvea
 pert.: irian, uveal
 plant: flag, orris, tileroot
 son: eros
IRISH: *celt, erse, temper
 abbess: bride, brigid
 accent: blas, brogue
 acre: colp
 adam: partholon
 ancestors: fir bolg, fir domnann, ith, miledh, milesius, tuatha de danaan
 assembly: aenach, aonach, dail
 bard: ecna, fergus
 basket: skeough
 battle cry: aboo, abu
 battle goddess: badb, bodb
 battle, myth: mag tuireadh
 bit: traneen
 boat: boston hooker, pookhaun
 bootleg: poteen
 borrowed stock: daer
 british force: black and tan
 cabstand: hazard
 cap: barrad
 cape: clear
 capital: balleathacliath, belfast, dublin, tara
 carriage: shandrydan, sidecar
 cattle: kerry
 castle: tara

* Asterisk means to look up this word to find more answer words.

chisel: celt
clan: cinel, sept, siol
clansman: aire
club: alpeen, oah, shillelagh
cobbler: potato
coin: rap, real, turney
confetti: bricks
cordial: usquebaugh
coronation stone: lia fail
crowning stone: lia fail
dagger: dhu, skean, skene
dance: rinkafadda, rinncefada
dane: ostman
demon: amadan, badb, bodb
demon race: fomorians
dialect: agam, ogham, ogum
dirge: keen
disrict: birr
dividend: assessment
dramatist: shaw, synge, keats
early kingdom: munster
ecclesiastic: erenaches, herenach, patric(k)
endearment term: acushla, alannah, aroon, aruin, asthor(e), astor, avourneen
epic: tain, tana
exclamation: adad, ahey, arar, arra(h), aroo, aru, begorra, och(one), orra, whist, wurra
fair: aenach, aonach
fairy: amadan, banshee, leprechaun, shee, sidhe
festival: feis
fort: lis, rath
free thinker: blaster
freebooter: rapparee
freeman: aire
garment: inar, lenn
general: shea
giant: fionn, fomors
girdle: criss
girl: colleen
goblin: leprechaun
god(dess): *celt: god(dess)
good-for-nothing: spalpeen
groggery: shebeen

harvester: spalpeen
herring: scud-dawn
holiday: whitmonday
hurricane: calm
independence: sinn fein
infantryman: kern(e)
island: achill, alan, aran, bear, clear, holy, man
king: angwyshaunce, aed, ardri, bres, brian boru, enna, eochaid mac eire, nuada, ri(g)
king's home: tara
lake: conn, corrib, derg, erne, lough, mask, neagh, ree
landholding system: rundale
lawyer: brehon
legislature: dail, eireann, oireachtas
limestone: calp
linen center: belfast
liquor: poteen, potheen
lord: aire, tanist
luck: cess
man: aire, bogtrotter, celt, eamon, eireannach, gael, greek, harp, hibernian, kern, kerne, manxman, mick, milesian, paddy(whack), pat, shoneen, spalpeen
measure: bandle, mile
meet: feis
melody: planxty
militia: fenian
mineral springs: chalybeate
moccasin: pampootee, pampootie
monk: culdee
monk cell: kil, kill
moss: carrageen, sloke
mountain: carrantual, errigal, lugnaquilla, macgillicuddy, ox, wicklow
music instrument: crut, timpano
name: moira, sean, shamus
national emblem: shamrock
national theatre: abbey
negative: sorra
nobleman: aire
oath: bedad, begorra

* Asterisk means to look up this word to find more answer words.

patriot: emmet, pearse
peasant: kern(e)
pennant: raveling, thread
people: daoine
personified: irena
pert.: celtic, gaelic
pig: bonav
poem: amhran
poetic name: banba, innisfail
porcelain: belleek
princess: iseult
proprietor: tanist
protestant: sassenagh
rebel group: ira
refugee: saer
republicanism: fenianism
robber: woodkern
saint: aidan, patric(k)
salutation: achara
shield: sciath
society: sinn fein(n), siol
soldier: ashe, galloglass, kern
song: rann
speech mode: ogam, ogham, ogum
steward: erenach, herenach
surgeon: colles
sweetheart: colleen, gra
tenant: fuidhir, saer
verse: rann
white: bawn
writer: ae, ashe, colum, fili, joyce,
  moore, ossian, pearse, russell,
  shaw, tighe, yeats
IRON: adamant, gat, gun, *hard,
  *piece, press, shackle, *strong
bar: bilbo
boot: despotism, tyranny
-clad: *firm, monitor
city: cleveland, pittsburgh
collar: carcan(et), joug
coated: terne
comb.: ferr(o), sider(o)
curtain: border, cold war
deficiency: anemia, chlorosis
dross: sinter, slag
hand: despotism, discipline
hook-shaped: croc, kilp

horse: locomotive, steam engine
magnet: armature
man: dollar, *money, strongman
mass: bloom
meteorite: catarinite, siderite
mongery: hardware, store
ore: hematite, turgite
rations: ammo, ammunition
sheet: acicul, plate, terne
stone nodule: cathead
sulphide: bravoite
weed: vernonia
wood: acle, colima, hornebeam,
  ixora, mesquite, tree
IROQUOIS: *demon:* oki, otkon
moon: ataensic, ataentsic
IRRATIONAL: *insane, *mad,
  odd
number: surd
IRREGULAR: *eccentric, unusual
comb.: anom, anomali, anomo
ISAAC: *kin:* abraham, edom, esau,
  israel, jacob, kedar
home: beersheba, gerar, lahairoi,
  rehoboth, sitnah
well: esek, lahairoi
ISAIAH: *father:* amox
son: mahershalalhashbaz, shear-
  jashub
ISENLAND: *queen:* brunnehilde
ISEULT: *consort:* mark, tristram
ISHMAEL: outcast, pariah, rover
kin: abraham, adbeel, dumah,
  hadad, hadar, hagar, jetur,
  kedar, kedemah, massa, mibsam,
  mishma, naphish, nebajoth, tema,
  zebadiah
ISHTAR: *kin:* sin, tammuz
ISIS: *kin:* anubis, geb, horus,
  nephthys, nut, osiris, tat
hiding place: swamps of buto
priest: apuleius
shrine: iseium, iseum
ISLAM: *mohammed(an)
ISLAND: ait, archipelago, atoll,
  bute, calf, cat, cay(o), eyot,
  holm(e), ile, ilot, inch, insula(te),

* Asterisk means to look up this word to find more answer words.

isla, isle(t), isolate, key, oe, ree, runway
born: kamaaina
inhabiting: nesiote
universe: galaxy
ISLES: *queen:* albion
ISM: **doctrine, *style, *system*
IST: **enthusiast*
ISOLDE: *maid:* brangwaine
ISRAEL: **jacob,* tziyon, zion
ISRAEL(I): **bible, *hebrew,* jew
airport: lydda
anthem: hatikva, hattikvah
army: haganah
born: sabra
camp: etham
capital: samaria, tel aviv
civil defense corps: haga
coin: agora, agura
coop: kibbutz, moshav
dance: hora
desert: negeb, negev
dish: ajuj, humus, pitta
doctrine: zionism
drink: sabra
dust storm: khamseen
exclamation: tov, yihye beseder
farmer: kibbutznik
fish: ajuj
forbidden food: terefa
general: abner, dayan, joshua
governor: nehemiah
immigration wave: aliyah
king: ahab, ahaziah, baasha, david, elah, hosea, hoshea, ishbosheth, jehoahaz, jehoash, jehoram, jehoshaphat, jehu, jeroboam, jonathan maccabaeus, joash, josiah, judas, menahem, nadab, omri, pekah(iah), rehoboam, remaliah, saul, shallum, solomon, zachariah
labor federation: histradrut
labor party: mapai
law giver: moses
measure: bath, cab, cor, cubit, epha(h), ezba, handbreadth, hin, homer, kab, kaneh, kor, log, omer, qaneh, reed, seah
missiles: tilim
national anthem: hatikva(h)
native: sabra
parliament: knesset, sanhedrin
people: yisrael, yisroel
plain: sharon
port: acre, haifa, jaffa
priest: abiathor, eli
roads: goldene wegen
rule of judges: kritarchy
scribe: ezra
senate: sanhedrin
statesman: ben-gurion, maier
youth corps: nahal, noar halutzi lohen
ISSUE: apple of discord, appear, arise, battleground, become public, begin, blow, blue chip, bone of contention, **break,* broach, burst (forth), casus belli, cause, circulate, coin, come, controversy, deliver, **dispense,* distribute, dole, edition, **effect,* egress, emanate, emerge, emit, **end,* eristic, event, float, flow, flux, **follow,* get out, **give,* mete, monetize, offer, offspring, outcome, point, posterity, **present,* print, **problem,* proceed, **product,* progeny, publish, put out, question, **release, *result,* rise, **run,* scatter, security, **send, *share,* solution, spout, **spread,* spring, **start,* stem, stock, **tell,* term, topic, upshot, utter, vent
ISTANBUL: byzantium, constantinople
bridge: eurasia bridge
caravansary: imaret, serai
foreign quarter: pera
greek quarter: fanar
schools: mahaleh
valley: lycus
IT: **big shot,* (the) **thing*
ITALIAN: *actress:* duse

* **Asterisk means to look up this word to find more answer words.**

adventurer: cagliostro, casanova, cellini

airplane: caproni

alps: dolomites

ancient: ausonian, etruscan, oscan, picene, roman, sabine, samnite, tuscan, volsci

art center: siena

article: il, la, le, egli, ella

artist: amigoni, angelico, arcimboldi, balla, bassano, bartolomo, bellotto, bernardo, bernini, boccioni, bodoni, boticelli, bramante, bronzino, cagliari, canaletto, caracciolo, caravaggio, carpaccio, carracci, cellini, colle, corregio, crespi, da vinci, del piombo, di credi, di paolo, guardi, lippi, lotto, mainardi, raphael, reni, robusti, sacci, sassetta, tiepolo, tintoretto, tisi, titian

astronomer: amici, galileo

author: ariosto, bandello, dante, petrarch, silone

bandit: brigante, caco

boat: gondola

bowl: tazza

bowling game: bocce, bocci

breeze: breva

cafe: osteria, trattoria

car: fiat

carriage: vettura

cathedral: duomo, milan

cattle: modica, padolian

cheese: asiago, caciocavallo, gorgonzola, grana, gruyere, parmesan, provolone, romano

chest: cassone

cigar: toscani

coin: aquilino, augustal, centisimo, chequeen, deni, doppia, ducato, grano, lira, marengo, paoli, ruspone, scudo, sildo, soldo, tari, teston(e), zecchini, zequin

commune: alba, asola, asti, atessa, aversa, bra, dego, eboli, este, massa, meda, nola, paola, rivoli, siena, urbino

composer: bellini, boccherini, boito, bononcini, cesti, donizetti, leoncavallo, mascagni, monteverde, puccini, rinuccini, rossini, scarlatti, verdi

condiment: tamara

culture, 14th century: trecento

dance: calata, courante, furlana, passamezzo, rigoletto, tarantella, volta

day breeze: ora

deity: consus, faunus, flora

dictator: mussolini

drink: grappa, vino

dramatist: alfieri, aretino

engraver: bartolozzi, raimondi

entertainment: ridoto

estate: latifundium

explorer: abruzzi, belzoni

family: amati, asti, borghese, colonna, donati, este, medici

festival: festa, ridoto

flask: fiaschi, fiasco

food: gnocchi, lasagna, pasta, pizza, ravioli, spaghetti, spumoni, zabaglione

game: mora, tarot, trappola

general: badoglio, cadorna

gentleman: ser, signor

grape: verdea

gun: lupara

gypsy: zingabi

hamlet: borgo, casal(e)

hello: addio, buen giorno, buena sera, evviva, pronto

house: casa, casino, pagliaio

inn: locanda

innkeeper: padrone

instrument: arpa, colascione

island: capri, corsica, elba, ischia, leros, lido, linosa, lipari, sardinia, sicily

lace: buratto

lady: dona, donna, signora

lake: albano, averno, bolsena,

* Asterisk means to look up this word to find more answer words.

como, garda, lugano, maggiore, nemi, trasimene, vico
land: maremma
landlord: padrone
leader: duce
limestone: scaglia
lover: amoroso
magistrate: podesta
marble: bardiglio, carrara
measure: barile, boccale, braccio, canna, carat, giornata, miglio, moggio, palma, piede, polonick, punto, quadrato, rubbio, salma, secchio, staio, stero, tavola
millet: buda, moha(r), tenai
mother goose: pentamerone
mountain: alp, amaro, apennine, cavo, cenis, dolomite, somma
music form: furlana, passacaglia
needlework: trapunto
noblewoman: contessa, marchesa
omelet: frittata
opera house: la scala
pasta: cannelloni, fettuccini, macaroni, ravioli, rigatoni, spaghetti, vermicelli
patriot: aleardi, cavour, garibaldi
peasant: contadini
philosopher: aquinas, bruno, dion, rosmini, vera
physicist: galileo, rossi
policeman: carabinieri, sbirri
political party: bianchi, blue shirts, calderai, neri
porridge: polenta
port: anzio, avola, bari, fiume, gaeta, genoa, naples, ostia, pesaro, pola, salerno, savona, trani, venice, zara
pottery: faenza, majolica
prima donna: diva
queen: elena
resort: agnone, baiae, capri, como, lido
sacred thing: bambino, pieta
saint: philip neri
salad: cat-bed, red, valerian

sausage: salami
scientist: fermi
sculptor: bandinelli, bernini, bologna, borromini, canonica, canova, cellini, dupre, egenesean, leoni, rosso
sharpshooter: bersagliere
sheep: merino
ship: nave, polacca
singer: caruso, gigli, pinza
society: camorra, carbonari, cosa nostra, mafia, mano nera
song: canzone, villanella
street: strada, via
university: bari, bologna, pisa
verse form: ballata
violin maker: amati
volcano: etna, somma, stromboli, vesuvius
water, bottled: fuiggi
weight: carat, chilogrammo, denaro, libra, oncia, ottava
wind: andar, ora, sirocco
wine: asti, barolo, chianti
ITE: *enthusiast
ITEM: ana, *bit, factor, *particular, *thing, *trifle
ITHACA: *head:* odysseus, penelope, ulysses
ITHAMAR: *son:* daniel, gamael
ITHRA: *son:* amasa
IVAN: *wife:* anastasia
IVANHOE: *author:* scott
  character: beowulf, cedric, rowena, ulrica, wamba
IVORIES: dice, keys, teeth
IVORY: *carving:* toreutics
  black: carbo animalis
  bill: cempephilus
  coast city: abidjan, bouake
  dust: eburin, eburite
  nut: anta, tagua
  pert.: dentine, eburnean
  source: tusk
  synthetic: ivoride
  tower: dream, retreat
IVY: *crowned with:* hederated

* **Asterisk means to look up this word to find more answer words.**

ground: alehoof, hovea
pert.: hederal, hederic
poison: rhus, sumac(h)
thicket: tod
IXION: *descendants:* centaurs
stone: rotator
IZZARD: *end*

JAAL: beden, goat, ibex
JABAL: *father:* lamech
JABBER: *gossip*, *nonsense*
JACK: *-anapes:* *fellow*, *spark*
-aroo: tyro
around: kid, rib, tease
-ass: dolt, dunce, *fool*
-ass clover: alkali mustard
-at-a-pinch: friend, helper
bean globulin: canavalin
cards: bower, knave
clubs: bragger, pam
-daw: caddow, coe, crow
-full-of-money: capitalist
group: quatorze
-in-office: incumbent, official
-in-the-pulpit: arad, arum, bog
  union, brown dragon, figwort,
  snakeroot, wake robin
johnson: black maria, coal box
-ketch: hangman
-knife: barlow, dive, mumble the
  peg
ladder: bull chain
leg: *sharp(er)*
milieu: beanstalk, steeple
nasty: bounder, cad
pine: loblolly, lodgepole
pot: *all*, award, windfall
pudding: buffoon, *fool*, zany
saw: goosander
snipe: sandpiper
spratt: charles I
stay: horse, rope, *staff*
stones: dibs
straw: figure, nonentity
up: *add*, *increase*, rebuke

JACKAL: *god:* anubis, apuat
JACKET: *arctic:* anorak
army: blouse, tunic
dust: book cover
hooded: anorak, parka, temiak
knitted: cardigan, gansey, penelope, sontag, sweater
light: blouse, jump
-like: camisole
short: eton, jerkin, spencer
short-flapped: coatee
sleeveless: bolero, vest
steel-plated: action, aketoun
woman's: jupe, jupon, spencer
JACOB: *israel*
brother: edom, esau
daughter: dinah
descendant: israelite, levite
father-in-law: laban
ladder: flower, phlox
mountain: gilead
parent: isaac, rebekah
son: aser, asher, benjamin, benoni,
  dan, gad, gershon, issachar, joseph, judah, judas, levi, naphtali,
  reuben, sarasadae, simeon, zebu-
  lun
wife: bilhah, leah, rachel, zilpah
JADU: *jinx*, *magic*
JAEL: *kin:* heber, shua(h)
JAGANNATH: *home:* puri
JAHDAI: *son:* ephah, geshan,
  jotham, pelet, regem, shaaph
JAI ALAI: *term:* cancha, cesta,
  fronton, pelota, quante, rebote
JAIL: asylum, bagne, bagnio,
  bailey, barracoon, bars, bastille,
  big house, black hole, bocardo,
  booby hatch, bridewell, brig, bull
  pen, cage, calaboose, can, carcel,
  carcer, cell, chauki, choky, clink,
  college, cooler, coop, concentration camp, death house, donjon,
  dump, dungeon, enclosure, farm,
  gaol, gehenna, gib, grate, guard-
  house, hell, hold, hole, honor,
  hoosegow, imprison, incarcerate,

* Asterisk means to look up this word to find more answer words.

intern, jug, keep, kidcote, limbo, lock-up, mure, oubliette, pandopticon, pen(itentiary), poky, pound, prison, rattle, reformatory, rock, stalag, stir, thana, tolbooth, *tower

bird: *criminal, *hoodlum

-break: *escape

fever: typhus

term: rap, sentence, verdict

JAKE: *fine, *great, *peasant

JAM: *arrest, *group, *stop

JAMAICA: bitter wood: quassi

cobnut: quabe

dogwood: barbasco, cinnamon

liquor: tia maria, jake

rosewood: amyris

sugar cane: caledonian queen

tree: black guava

JAPAN: cipango, nippon, zipangu

abacus: soroban

abalone: awabi

aborigine: aino, ainu

ada, eve: izanagi, izanami

admiral: ito

air base: chitose

alloy: mokum

allspice: chimonanthus

american: ainoko, issei, kibei, nisei, sansei

amusement hall: pachinko parlor

apricot: ansu, ume

army reserve: hoju, kobi

badge: kirimon, mon

banjo: samisen

barbecue: naga hibachi

baron: daimio, daimyo, han

battle cry: banzai

bay: amort, ise, miku, osaka, toso, tokyo, yedo

bean: adzuki

beer: biiru

boxes, set of: inro

brake: warabi

bream: tai

brocade: nishiki

broth: osumono

brothel: shinjuku

buddha: amida, amita, apis, ashuku, maitreya, miroku, myoo, nyorai, yakushi

buddhism: amidism, len, zen

bush clover: hagi

button: netsuke

cake: koji

calculator: abacus, soroban

cape: daio, iro, jizo, mela, mino, nomo, oki, oma, sada, sawa, se, su, suzu, toi, ya

capital: edo, kyoto, nara, saikio, tokio, tokyo

carp: koi

carriage: kago, sados

case: inro

cedar: sugi

cherry: fuji

ceremony: chanoyu, tea

chant: nam myoho renge kyo

chess: shogi

chevrotain: napu

chopsticks: hashi

circle: maru

clan: gen, hei, satsuma

class: eta, heimin, kwazoku, roi, samurai, shizoku

clogs: geta

clover: hagi

coat: mino

coin: bu, cobang, ichebu, itzebu, itziboo, koban(g), nibu, nishu, oban(g), rin, rio, sen, shu, temp, yen

commoner: heimin

composition: haikai

confection: ame

costume: netsuke

court: dairo, dari

courtier: kuge

crepe: chirimen

crest: kikumon, mon

cult: zen

current: black stream

cushion: zabaton

dancing girl: geisha

* Asterisk means to look up this word to find more answer words.

deer: sika
deity: amaterasu, amatsukami, amatsumikaboshi, benten, funado, hachiman, hariti, hayaji, hiruko, homasubi, inari, *japan: buddha, *japan: happiness god, kaguzuchi, kami, kishimojin, kompira, kunado, kunitsukami, kuvera, myoken, nigihaya-hi, ninigi, okuninushi, sengensama, shinatobe, shiozuchi, sukunabikona, susanoo, takamimusubi, takemikazuchi, tatsutahime, tsukiyomi, wakahiru-me
dish: sukiyaki, tempura
dog: tanate
door: fusuma, sika
drama: kabuki, nogaku, noh
drink: mate, sake, uisukki
drum: tarko
dye process: yuzen
earthenware: banko, raku
emperor: hirohito, mikado
empress: nagako
ethics: bushido
evergreen: akeki
explosive: shimose
fabric: birodi, chirimen, habutai, habutaye, nishiki
fan: ogi
feast: bon, matsuir, tanabata, utas
fern: ball fern, bamboo, coniogramme, davallia
fetish: obe
fish: ayu, fugu, funa, koi, masu, porgie, tai, tho
flower: nelumbium, udo
flute: fuye
food: kobu, kombu, miso
footwear: geta, tabi
game: gimmi, go, goban(g), ken, igo, sugoruku, wei-chi-i
garment: haori, inro, kimono, mino, mompei, obi
gateway: toran, torii
gentry: shizoku
giant: daidarabotchi

girl: geisha, mousme(e)
god(dess): *japan: deity
greeting: banzai, irasshaimase, konban wa, konnichi wa, mokari makka, ohayo gozaimasu
happiness god: *happiness god
harp: koto
healer: binzuru
herb: udo
hippies: bozuoku, futen, gaijin
honor code: bushido
industrial drive: meiji miracle
instrument: aoi tsuba, biwa, koto, samisen
island: bonin, cipango, hokkaido, hondo, honshu, izu, kiushu, kuril(e), kyushu, loochoo, oita, okinawa, riu-kiu, sado, shikoko, sikok
kelp: kome
knife: aikuchi
lacquer: urushi
lake: biwa, suwa
lily: auratum
litter: cango, kago, norimon
lyric: haiku, hokku
magnolia: yulan
mats: tatami
measure: boo, bu, carat, catty, cho, fun, go(go), hiro, hiyakhiro, inc, isse, issho, ittan, kati, ken, koku, komma-ichida, kon, kujira-shaku, kwamme, momme, niyo, picul, rin, shaku, sho(o), sun, tan, tsubo
metal work: bori, zogan
mikado: dairi
military service: yobi
monastery: tera
monopoly: zaibatsu
mountain: asama, asosan, fuji, fujisan, fujiyama, hondo kiusiu, usu, yesso
mulberry: kozo
news agency: domei
noble: daimyo, kuge, samurai
number one: ichiban

* **Asterisk means to look up this word to find more answer words.**

numbers, 1 to 9: ichi(ban), ni, san, shi, go, roku, shichi, hachi, ku

outcast: eta, yeta

outlaw: ronin

overcoat: mino

pagoda: taa

painter: hokusai

painting style: kano, ukiyoye

paper-folding art: origami

pearl: mikimoto

persimmon: hyakume, kaki

plane: zero

plant: aucuba, cydonia, kudzu, sugamo, tea, udo

plum: kelsey

poet: basho

porcelain: hirado, hizen, imari, nabeshima

porgy: tai

port: akita, aomori, hakodate, hiogo, kobe, nagasaki, niigata, oita, osaka, otaru, sakata, tokio, tokyo, tsu, ube, wakatama, yokohama

porter: akabo

potato: imo

pottery: awaji, bizen, mimpei

prayers: norito

prefecture: ehime, fu, ken, kin, kori, mino, oita, owari

province: suff.: shiu

radish: daikon

railroad: new tokaido line, shinkansen

raincoat: mino

religion: buddhism, shinto, shintoism, *sokagakki*

rice product: ame, sake, saki

robe: kimono

rose: aino

rug: crazy quilt, solitaire

ruler: shogun, taikun, tenno

salmon: masu

sash: obi

sauce: udo

screen: shoji

scriptures: engishiki, fudoki, jindaiki, kogoshui, kojiki, nihongi, nihonshoki, shojiroku

scroll: gohonzon

seaweed: nori

sect: ryobu, *sokagakkai*

self-defense: judo, jujitsu, jujutsu, karate, sumo

ship name: maro, maru

shoe: geta, zori

shogun family: askikaga

shrub: aburachan, aucuba, cydonia, fuji, goumi, kerria, japonica, quince

sock: tabi, tabo

song: uta

statesman: genro, hara, mori

stockmarket: kabutocho

storm: taifu, tsunami, typhoon

straw hat: ballibuntl

suicide: hara-kiri, hari-kari, kamikaze, seppuku

sword: catan, cattan, wacadash

sword guard: tsuba

temple: jinja, jinsha, yashiro

thanks: arigato gozaimasu, domo arigato

throne: shinza

tidal wave: tsunami

title: kami, mikado, shogun

tortoise shell: bekko

tower: pagoda, tope

trade organization: jetro

train: the bullet

tree: akamatsu, akeki, camphor, castoralia, cycas, ginkgo, hinoki, kiaki, shirakashi, sugi, urushi, yeddo

union federation: sohyo

vegetable: gobo, udo

vehicle: jinrikisha, ricksha(w)

velvet: birodo

verse: hokku, tanka

vine: bibnonia, kudzu

volcano: asama(yama), aso(san), fuji(yama), mihara

wall: shoji

* Asterisk means to look up this word to find more answer words.

war cry: banzai, tora
warrior class: samurai
winged being: tengu
yeast: koji
yeoman: goshi
zither: koto
JAPE: *insult, *taunt
JAPHETH: *kin:* noah, javan, tubal
JAR: *coarse:* crock, terrine
  earthen: olla, terrine
  fly: cicada
  fruit: mason
  large: cadus, dolium, situal
  long-necked: goglet, gurglet
  majolica: albarello
  opening: anthesteria
  ring: lute, rubber
  water: goglet, gurglet
  wide-mouthed: ewer
JARGON: *argot, *talk
JASMINE: matrimony vine, papaw
JASON: *men:* argonauts
  parent: aeson, alcimede
  son: alcimedes, antipater
  uncle: pelias
  wife: creusa, medea
JAVA: coffee, *east indies, tji
  almond: canarium, pili, talisay
  arrow poison: upas
  badger: ratel, teledu
  berry: cubeb
  canvas: ada
  carriage: sado(o)
  commune: dessa
  cotton: kapok
  dancers: bedoyo
  drama: topeng
  dutchman: blanda
  fabric: ikat
  fruit: gondang, lomboy
  grackle: beo
  instrument: bonang, gambang, gamelan(g), gender, saron
  language: kavi, kawi
  measure: kan, paal, palen, rand
  mountain: amat, gede, lawoe,

prahu, raoeng, semeroe, slameta, soembing
ox: batens
pepper: cubeb
port: batavia, surabaya, tegal
puppet show: wajang, wayang
rice field: sawah
seed: ajava, ajowan
skunk: teledu
speech: krama, ngoko
squirrel: jelerang
straw: peanit
sumac: fuyang
temple: borobudur, candi, chandi, tjandi
tree: antiar, gondang, upas
village: dessa
volcanic plateau: ijen
volcano: bromo, gede, kelut, merapi, raung, semeru, slamet
weight: amat, pond, pound, soekel, tali
wild dog: adjag
JAVELIN: *spear
JAW: *gossip, mouth, *talk
  comb.: gnatho
  -less: agnathic, agnathous
  lower: chin, mandible
  lumpy: actinomycosis
  muscle: masseter
  pert.: gnathic, malar
  smith: dentist, orator
  upper: maxilla
JAZZ: bebop, boogie woogie, bossa nova, megillah, rag
  fan: cat, hepcat, syncopator
  loud: barrelhouse
  up: *increase, *speed
JEDIDAH: *kin:* adaiah, amon, josiah
JEER: *insult, *laugh, *taunt
JEHOAHAZ: *kin:* hamutal, joash
JEHORAM: *son:* ahaziah, jehoahaz
JEHOSHAPHAT: *captain:* amasiah, eliada, jehohanan, jehozabad
  chief: adnah

* Asterisk means to look up this word to find more answer words.

mother: azubah
son: azariah, jehiel, michael
wife: athaliah
JEHOVAH: *hebrew: god
JEHU: driver, speeder
son: azariah, jehoahaz
JEJUNE: arid, *dull
JELLYFISH: acaleph, medusa, nettle, quarl
comb.: cetene
group: acrespeda, discophora
part: (ex)umbrella, pileus
JEREMIAH: *friend:* baruch
kin: hamutal, jaazaniah
JERICHO: *despoiler:* achan
publican: zacchaeus
rebuilder: hiel
woman: rahab
JERUBBAAL: *servant:* phurah
son: abimelech, jotham
JERUSALEM: city of david, zion
captor: omar
corn: durra, kafir
garden: gethsemane
haddock: opah
hill: moriah, olivet, zion
king: adonizedec
mosque: omar
oak: ambrose, chenopidium
pert.: hierosolymitan
poetic: ariel, jebus
pool: bethesda, gihon, siloam
prophetess: anna, anne
region: perea
temple: solomon's cloister
thorn or tree: retama
JESSE: *daughter:* abigail, zeruia
father: obed
son: abinadab, david, eliab, nethaneel, ozem, raddai, shammah, shimma
JEST: *insult, *joke, *taunt
JESUIT: *bark:* cinchona
founder: loyola
head: black pope
saint: regis
JESUS: emmanuel, messiah, rabbi, resurrection, savior, shepherd
agony: gesthemane
cross-carrier: simon
crucifixion: golgotha
gift: frankincense, gold, myrrh
home: capernaum, nazareth
image: angel, bambino, bata
jericho host: zacchaeus
miracle words: talitha cum
resurrection observer: cleopas
sayings: agrapha
surname: boanerges
symbol: ihc, ihs, inri, jhs
thief crucified near: desmas, dismas, dysmas
words on cross: eli, eli, lem sabach-tania
JEW, JEWISH: *hebrew
fish: grouper, mero, tarpon
JEWEL: gem, *prize, *stone
JEWELER: *eyepiece:* loupe
JEWELRY: *mock:* glass, logie, paste, strass
JEZEBEL: *prostitute, *wanton
father: ethbaal
husband: ahab
son: athaliah, johoram
victim: elijah, naboth
JIBE: *insult, *taunt
JINX: *magic, *sign, *spell
JOB: *daughter:* jemima, kezia
friend: bildad, eliphaz, zophar
tears: adlai, coix lacryma
JOCASTA: *children:* antigone, eteocles, ismene, polynices
consort: laius, oedipus
JOIN: abut, *add, adject, affiliate, append, *associate, attach, belong, *bind, bond, cement, coalesce, combine, connect, dovetail, *enter, incorporate, league, link, *meet, merge, pair, *sign, splice, *tie, *unite, weld
JOKE: *banter, butt, crack, fun, gag, hoax, humor, jest, kid, mot, *play, point, prank, pun, quip, sally, *sparkle, *story, *taunt,

---

* Asterisk means to look up this word to find more answer words.

*trick, *trifle, yarn
JONAH: *jinx
 kin: amittai, andrew, cephas
JONATHAN: friend: david
 son: jadua, obeth, peleth, zaza
JONSON, BEN: tavern: mermaid
JOSEPH: barnabas, barsabbas
 brother: *jacob: sons
 buyer: popiphar
 -coat: amaranth
 parent: jacob, rachel
 nephew: tola
 son: ephraim, igal, jannai, jesus,
  joseph, jude, manasseh
 surface: hypocrite
 wife: asenath, mary
JOSHUA: associate: caleb
 burial: ephraim, timnath-serah
 camp: gilgal
 conquest: adullam, aphek, arad,
  bethel, debir, eglon, gezer, hebron, hormah, jarmuth, jericho,
  jerusalem, lachish
 father: nun
 tree: cactus, redbud, yucca
JOSIAH: father: amon
 courtier: asaph, zacharias
 governor: maaseiah
 messenger: achbor, asahiah
 officer: jahath, mechonias, joram,
  obadiah, ozielus, sabias, zechariah
 son: joconiah, johanan, shallum
JOT: *ace, *bit, *mark, *trifle
JOY: bliss, delight, ecstasy, elation,
  enchantment, euphoria, felicity,
  gayety, gladness, glee, happiness,
  heaven, hilarity, intoxication,
  mirth, *paradise, pleasure, rapture, serendipity, *utopia
JUBILANT: *happy
JUDAH: king: ahaz, amon, asa,
  david, hezekiah, josiah, uzziah
 queen: athaliah
 son: carmi, hezron, hur, onan,
  perez, shelah, zara, zerah
JUDAISM: *hebrew

JUDITH: father: beeri, merari
 husband: manasses
 victim: holophernes
JUGGERNAUT: krishna, *vishnu
JUGOSLAV: *yugoslav
JUNEBERRY: service berry, tree
JUNIPER: cade, cedar, retem
JUNK: *drug, *refuse, stuff
JUPITER: *zeus
 angel: zadkiel
 moon: callisto, europa, io, ganymede
 pluvius: rain
JURGENS: adventure: poictesme
JUSTICE: deity: astraea, dice,
  fides, fidius, forseti, maat, nemesis, ramman, rhadamanthus

KABBALA: sefer yecirah, zohar
KAFFIR: beer: home brew
 corn: grain, millet, sorghum
 servant: umfaan
 tribe: xosa, zulu
 warriors: impi
KALEIDOSCOPIC: psychedelic
KALEVALA: hero: aino, ilma-
  rinen, joukahainen, kullervo,
  lemminkainen, louhi, pohja
 deities: ahti, ahto, akka, ilma,
  jumala, kuu, luonnotar, mielikki,
  nyyrikki, paiva, pellervoinen,
  rauni, tapio, tuulikki, ukko, vel-
  lamo
KANGAROO: boongary, dendro-
  lagus, gin, jeroba, nacrioiduab,
  paddymelon, roo, wallaby
 female: doe, gin, roo
 male: bilbi, boomer
 rat: potoroo
 young: joey
KANSAS: bird: western meadowlark
 nickname: sunflower state
 tree: cottonwood
KANT: categories: modality, quality, quantity, relation

* Asterisk means to look up this word to find more answer words.

KARMA: destiny, duty, *fate
 stories: avadana
KASHMIR: alphabet: sarada
 capital: srinagar
 deer: hangul
 language: burushaski, shina
 official: pundit
KATUN: twenty: baktun
KEEL: -bill: ani, ano, bird
 block: templet
 -haul: torture
 -less: ecarinate, ratite
 -like: carinal, carinated
 over: capsize, swoon
 part: skag, skeg
 right angle to: abeam
 -shaped: carinate
KEEN: *acute, *great, *sharp
KEEP: *hide, *save, *support
 back: *arrest, *slow, *stop
 the faith: *good bye
KEEPERS: finders
KEEPSAKE: souvenir, *token
KELP: bellware, *seaweed
 edible: badderlocks, henware
 fish: dollar fish, rock gunnel
KENAZ: kin: caleb, elah, othneil
KENT: borough: erith, penge
 founder: hengist, horsa
 freedman: laet
 -ledge: ballast, metal
 sheep: romney
KENTUCKY: bird: cardinal
 bluegrass: poa
 coffee tree: bonduc, chicot
 flower: goldenrod
 honoree: colonel
 nickname: bluegrass state
 tree: tulip poplar
KENYA: game area: amboselli,
 arusha, manyara, nakuru, nyeri,
 rift valley, samburu
 native: masa
 reserve: masai
 tree: ayieke
KERNEL: comb.: caryo, karyo
KETTLE: covered: canner

drum: atabal, *party, tabor
fish: *mess
nose: spout
KEY: art: alembroth
 board: clavier, pedalier
 crib: pony
 false: glut
 filler: uller
 fruit: samara
 instrument: dital, manual
 keeper: steward
 locksmithing: ward
 man: boss, chief, *leader
 music: tasto
 -note: ison, theme, topic
 noter: boss, orator
 part: bit, bow, collar, loop, pin,
 stem, web
 pert.: tonal
 position: anchor
 pounder: pianist, steno
 -shaped: cleche, urde, urdy
 skeleton: gilt, screw, twirler
 -stone: arch, basic, *important,
 sagitta, *support, voussoir
 -stone state: pennsylvania
 telegraph: bug, tapper
KHEPERA: symbol: scarab
KHNEMU, KHNUM: wife: an-
 quet, anukit, satet, sati
KHONSU: father: amen
KIBBITZ: comment, *joke, *look
KIBOSH: *end, *nonsense, *stop
KICK: *dismiss, *force, thrill
KICKSHAW: *bit, gadget, *thing
KID: child, *joke, tease, twit
KIDNAP: *seize, *steal, *take
KIDNEY: comb.: nephr, reni
 disease: bright's, uremia
 part: nephron, glomerulus
 pert.: (ad)renal, suprarenal
 shaped: reniform
 -stone: jade, nephrite
 vetch: cat's-claw
KILL: achieve, asphyxiate, assas-
 sinate, astonish, *bag, bayonet,
 brain, bump off, burke, butcher,

* Asterisk means to look up this word to find more answer words.

cancel, chloroform, choke, creek, cut, *defeat, *destroy, dispose of, drown, *end, eliminate, execute, garrot(te), *get, *hurt, jugulate, lapidate, liquidate, massacre, muffle, murder, overwhelm, poison, *punish, purge, put away, quarry, *remove, send west, shoot, silence, slaughter, slay, smother, stifle, stone, *stop, strangle, *strike, stymy, throttle, veto, *waterway

KILT: *pouch:* sporran

KIMONO: *cotton:* yukata
sash: obi

KIND: affectionate, benign, breed, cast, character, *class, compassionate, denomination, description, designation, division, genial, genre, *gentle, grain, *group, kidney, kosher, ilk, indulgent, *make, manner, mold, nature, number, persuasion, *quality, species, *strain, *style, *sweet

KING: *kings, *king arthur, etc.
ass-eared: midas
beasts: lion
bird: bee eater, pipiri
crab: aglaspis, limulus
crab's body: cephaletron
cup: crowfoot, ranunculus
fish: bagara, barb(el), cero, haku, opah, pintado, sierra
fisher: alcedo, ceyx, halcyon
-geld: escuage
pert.: regal, regnal, royal
pin: chief, *lead(er), *top
petty: regulus
snake: ophibolus
tyrant: kingbird
vulture: catharta, falconiformis
wealthy: croesus, midas
wheel-bound: ixion

KING'S: *beadsman:* beggar
bodyguard: thane
chamber: camarilla
clover: melilot

evil: scrofula
family: dynasty, line
garment: armil(la)
letter: brief
personnel: avener, bailiff, dapifer, palatine, viceroy
ransom: fortune
symbol: mace, scepter
title: basileus, highness, majesty, sir(e)
topper: ace
yellow: orpiment, pigment

KING ALFRED: *city:* lon

KING ARTHUR: *abode:* avalon
battle: badon, camlan
brother: kay
brother-in-law: loth
butler: bedivere, lucas
capital: astolat, camelot
chamberlain: ulphius
chaplain: pyramus
constable: badouin
crowner: dubric
dagger: carnwenhau
enemy: mordred, morgan le fay
father: uther
father-in-law: leogadan
fool: dagonet
forest: calydon
half sister: bellicent
hall: ehangwen
hound: cavall
knight: arrok, ascamour, balan, balin, bedivere, bellengerus, bellyaunce, bleheris, boarte, brandiles, brastias, brewnor, bryan, cador, caradoc, clegis, darras, degrave, dynas, edyrn, eglamore, epynogres, fergus, galahad, gareth, gawain, geraint, *lancelot: friends, mordred, ozanna, parsifal, percival, pelleas, pertolope, sagramore, severause, tristram
lampoonist: dynadan
lance: ron, rone
magician: merlin

---

* Asterisk means to look up this word to find more answer words.

mare: llamrei
mistress: garwen, gwyl, indec
mother: igerne, igraine, ygerne
nephew: gareth, gawain, mordred
queen: guinevere
seneschal: kay, ken, lreux
shield: pridwin
sister: morgain, morgan le fay
spear: rhongomyant
sword: caledvwlch, caliburn, excalibur
KING AUGEAS: *brother:* actor
KING CANUTE: *consort:* emma
KING CYMBELINE: *son:* arviragus
KING LEAR: *daughter:* cordelia, goneril, regan
follower: kent
dog: tray
KING MARSILE: *wife:* bramimonde
KINGDOM: *come:* *paradise, *utopia
three: shu, wei, wu
KINO: bija, butea, cinema, gum
KISH: *kin:* ner, saul, shimei
KISMET: doom, *fate, lot
KISS: *-me-quick:* bonnet
science: philematology
KITCHEN: *pert.:* culinary
KNACK: ability, *skill, *trick
KNEE: *bend:* genuflect, kneel
bends: ballet, plies
bone: cap, dib, patella, rotula
comb.: genu
-deep: shallow
drill: prayer
gout: gonagra, gonitis
-high: low
hole: desk
joint: hock
ornament: canion
part: hock, hough-bone
slapper: *joke, whopper
KNICKKNACK: *kickshaw
KNIFE: *case:* sheath
comb.: dori

handle: bolster
large: bolo, snee
one-bladed: barlow
painter's: spatula
surgical: *surgeon: instrument
KNIGHT: *alde:* page, squire
banner: gonfalon, gonfanon
carpet: lover
champion: paladin
cloak: tabard
elbow: gamester, toper
errantry: chivalry
famous: *king arthur: knight
fight: joust, tilt, tournament
head: apostle
hood: cavalry, chivalry
lady: bradamante, britomartis
make: accolade, dub
rank above: baronet
road: hobo, tramp, vagabond
round table: *king arthur: knight
templar: mason, shriner
templar standard: beauseant
young: bachelor
wife: dame, lady
without fear: chevalier bayard
wreathe: orle
KNOCK: *beat, *hit, *smear
KNOW: *see, *sense, *understand
KNOWLEDGE: aparavidya, capacity, cunning, erudition, experience, fact, familiarity, information, intelligence, learning, lore, ology, science, *sense, *skill
instrument: organon
object of: cognitum, scibile
pert.: gnostic
profound: omniscience, pansophy
pure: noesis
seeker: philonoist
summary: encyclopaedia
universal: pantology
KORAN: *angel:* israfil
chapter: al-fatiha, sura
pert.: alcoranic
teacher: alfaqui, ulema
tree: zaggum

* Asterisk means to look up this word to find more answer words.

verse: ayah, iya
wall: alaraf
watchdog: al rakim
KOREA: *leader:* rhee
  port: gensan, inchon, pusan
  soldier: rok
KOSHER: **fair,* proper, **pure*
KRISHNA: juggernaut, **vishnu*
KYMRIC: **welsh*

LABAN: *daughter:* leah, rachel
LABEL: **mark, *name, *title*
LABOR: birth, **service, *work*
  symbol: blue shirt, hard hat
  union: afl, cio, ilgwu, umw
LABORATORY: *gear:* beaker,
  bunsen burner, pipet, retort
LABORER: **peasant, *servant*
LABYRINTH: maze, **puzzle*
  builder: daedalus, minos
  fish: anabantid
LACE: *bark:* akaroa, kurrajong,
  lagetta, ribbon wood, tree
  edge: picot
  front: jabot
  kind: alencon, argentan, arras,
  aurillac, bobbin(et), bruges,
  brussels, burano, buratto, cannetille, chantilly, clunis crepine,
  duchesse, filigree, grill(e), jabot,
  macrame, mechlin, milan, orris,
  ruche, val, valenciennes
  make: tat
  net: breton
  opening: eyelet
  pattern: cascade, larme
  square hole: filet
  string: thong
  tag or tip: aglet, aiglette
  trimming: gard, jabot
LACEDAEMON: *descendants:*
  *clytaemnestra, *dioscuri, helen,
  hippocoon, icarius, penelope,
  tyndareus
  wife: sparta

LACERATE: **break, *hurt, *tear*
LACK: absence, dearth, **need*
LAD: **fellow,* lover, youth
LADAKH: *animal:* ammon, antelope, ibex, markhor, ovis, ox
  language: oldi
  mountains: himalaya, karakoram
  stove: bukhari
LADDER: *fort scaling:* escalade
  part: hook, ratline, rung
  pert.: scalar, scalose
LADRONE ISLAND: guajan,
  guam, marianas, saipan
LADY: belle, bibi, begum, burd,
  dame, devi, domina, dona,
  donna, female, frau, gentlewoman, madam, matron, mistress, noblewoman, peeress,
  ranee, senora, signora, spouse,
  *title, toast, wife, woman
  bird or bug: beetle, burnie bee,
  cardinalis, coccinellid, epilachna,
  hippodamia, insect, novius, ve-
  dalia
  chained: andromeda
  crab: calico crab
  curious: pandora
  day: annunciation
  fern: backache brake
  finger: effeminate, weakling
  fish: chiro, elops, grubber, menhaden, oio, pudano, wrasse
  in waiting: **lady's:* maid
  killer: carpetmonger, casanova,
  don juan, gallant, sheik, wolf
  knight: bradamante, britomartis
  -like: chic, genteel, refined
  -love: amour, delia, **sweetheart*
  of lake: ellen, nimue, vivian
  quality symbol: white stockings
LADY'S: *boot:* bottekin, bottine
  comb: beggar's needle, herb
  maid: abigail, bower may, cam-
  eriera, tirewoman
  silk habit: pelisse
  slipper: orchid, valerian
  thumb: peachwort, persicary

* Asterisk means to look up this word to find more answer words.

LAERTES: *son:* odysseus, ulysses
LAGAN: *pert.:* flotsam, jetsam
LAGNIAPPE: *bit, *gift, *trifle
LAGOON: *islands:* ellice
LAIS: burmese, *prostitute
LAIUS: *kin:* jocasta, oedipus
LAKE: *deposit:* trona
  constance: bodensee
  deepest: baikal
  geneva breeze: bornan, rebat
  george: horicon
  herring: blueback, sockeye
  highest: titicaca
  island: ait
  man-made: mead
  marshy: liman
  mother: naal
  mountain: tarn
  of the cat: erie
  outlet: bayou
  pert.: lacustral, lacustrine
  shallow: lagun
  state: michigan
  third largest: aral
  trout: waha
  whitefish: pollan
LAKH: *iod:* crore
LAKSHMI: *consort:* vishnu
LAM: *escape, *hit, *strike
LAMAISM: *dignitary:* hutukhtu
  priest: getsul
  stupa: chorten
LAMB: *breast of:* carre
  bring forth: ean, yean
  female: ewe
  fur: broadtail
  hand-raised: hob
  holy: agnus
  leg of: gigot
  -like: *gentle
  male: ram
  of god: agnus dei
  pen name: elia
  pet: cade, cosset
  quarters: baconweed
  skin: baghdad, krimme, suede
  swayback: warfa

LAMECH: *children:* jabal, jubal, naamah, noah, tubalcain
  father: methuselah
  wife: adah
LAMENT: *complain, *cry, pine
LAMIA: *demon, *hag, *witch
LAMPOON: *abuse, satirize, skit
LANCE: *pierce, *spear, stab
LANCELOT: *castle:* joyous gard
  father: ban
  friends: blamoure, bleobris, bors, clarrus, clegis, dynas, ector, gahalantyne, galyhoden, harry, hebes, lavayne, lyonel, melyas, menaduke, neroveus, palomides, plenoryus, sadoke, safere, selyses, urry, valyaunte, vyllyars
  love: elaine, guinevere
  nephew: bohort, bort
  son: galahad, gawain
  sword: aroundight, aroundite
  uncle: bors
LAND: *alluvial:* bottoms, delta
  ancestral: ethel
  arid or barren: desert, waste
  body: continent, *state
  breeze: terral
  church: abadengo, glebe
  clear: acre, assart, allody, alod-(ium), field, sart
  connection: neck, nek, reach
  cultivated: arada, arado, farm, orchard, ranch, tillage, tilth
  dealer: realtor
  depressed: graben
  diked: polder
  division: agrarianism, area
  east of eden: nod
  elevated: alp, hill, mesa, mound, mountain, plateau
  end, guardian: bellerus
  extension: cape
  fallow: arder, lea
  feudal: benefice
  grant: enam(dar)
  held in fee simple: *clear land
  heritable: alodium, allod, fief

* Asterisk means to look up this word to find more answer words.

holder: coscet, laird, thane, thegn, yeoman, zamindar
householder's: barton, demesne
law: solum
living on: terrestrial
-lord: *land: holder, lessor
louper: nomad, vagabond
low: carse, polder, vale
low stream: holm
mark: cairn, copa, dole, dool, meith, mere, milestone, senal
marshy: swale
measure: acre, are, bovate, carucate, decare, hide, meter, perch, plowland, rod, rood
meadow: lea
mythical: *paradise, *utopia
narrow: isthmus, neck, peninsula, strake
native: blighty
north, farthest: ultima thule
of: beulah: *paradise
 cakes: scotland
 midnight sun: finland, norway, sweden
 milk and honey: israel
 nod: sleep
 philosophers: balnibarbi
 plenty: *paradise, *utopia
 prester john: *paradise
 promise: canaan, palestine
 rising sun: japan, nippon
 steady habits: connecticut
 the leal: *heaven, *paradise
 the rose: england
 the shamrock: *ireland
 the thistle: scotland
 the thousand lakes: finland
 the white elephant: siam, thai
on: *punish, *rebuke
open: heath, moor, vega, wold
owned clear: *land: clear
owner: cacique, landlord
ownership; pert.: odal, udal
parcel: clearing, erf, estate, field, *land: cultivated, laine, patch, piece, plat, plot, ranch, range, spong

pert.: agrarian, geoponic, real
pirate: claim jumper, squatter
plowed: fallow, furrow, *land: cultivated, thwaite
point: cape, ness, ras, spit
prepare for seed: plow, till
profit: crop, esplees, rent(e)
reclaimed: novalia, polder
reeve: steward
river-drained: basin
rock-covered: brule
sandy: dene, dune
-scape: *ornament, painting, paysage, *picture, scene(ry)
scurvey: purpura
service, return for: feoff
share: dher
slide: avalanche, eboulement
snail: bubble shell, bulimus, bulla, cerion, physa
spring: lavant
state, reverting to: escheat
tag: diet, legislature
taxes, valued for: cadastre
tenure: feu, fief, leasehold
tilled: *land: plowed
tongue: doab
treeless: *plain
triangular: delta, gore
uncultivated: brush, bush
waste: desert, heath, moor
waterlocked: ile, island, isle
watery: bog, flow, maremma, marsh, moor, morass, swamp
LANDING: arrival, splashdown
place: airfield, dock, harbor, pier, quay, tarmac, wharf
LANGUAGE: *artificial:* esperanto, *language: international
classical: attic, greek, latin
figurative: imagery, trope
inflection-lacking: aptotic
informal: slang
international: antido, arulo, blaia, esperanto, ido, monario, novial, od, optez, ro, romanal, solresol, volapuk

* Asterisk means to look up this word to find more answer words.

know all: pantoglot, polyglot
letters: alphabet
loss: aphasia, aphemia
pert.: lingual, semantical
pompous: bombast, bull, **nonsense,* oratory, rhetoric
rules: grammar, syntax
spoken: diction, pronunciation
synthetic or universal: *language:
international
LANGUISH: die, **fail, *spoil*
LANTERN: *feast:* bon
LAOCOON: *son:* antiphas, persis
LAODAMIA: *father:* acastus
husband: protesilaus
LAOMEDON: *father:* ilus, tithonus
servant: apollo, poseidon
son: bucolion, priam
LAPIDOTH: *wife:* deborah
LAPITH: *king:* ixion, phlegyas
LAPLAND: *city:* kola
god: rot
magic drum: quodba
sled: pulk(a)
LAPSE: **break, *end, *error, *sin*
LARGE: **big, *fat, *great*
comb.: macro
LARRUP: **beat, *hit, *whip*
LASCAR: *boatswain:* serang
LASCIVIOUS: **bad, *evil, *wanton*
LASH: **larrup, *tie, *urge, *whip*
LAST: **end, *extreme, *stand*
but one: penult(imate)
supper: communion, eucharist
supper room: cenacle
LASTING: **permanent, *solid*
LATE: arrears, backward, behind,
dead, deep, delayed, detained,
dilatory, dillydallying, easy going, held up, in abeyance, lacka-
daisical, lagging, lax, micaw-
berish, moratory, new, overdue,
past, recent(ly), remiss, sero,
slack, **slow,* sluggish, tardy
comb.: neo

LATEST: fad, rage, **style*
LATHE: *copying:* blanchard
holder: monitor
operator: turner
part: mandrel, setover
primitive: pole
LATIN: **roman*
LATITUDE: extent, **play, *way*
LATTER DAY SAINT: mormon
LAUD: **acclaim, *praise,* sing
LAUGH: boffo, burst out, cachin-
nate, cackle, chortle, chuckle,
convulsion, crow, deride, fleer,
giggle, guffaw, haha, hawhaw,
heehee, jeer, jubilate, mirth, rejoice, risibility, roar, scoff, shake,
shout, shriek, smile, snicker,
snigger, snort, split, teehee
comb.: gelo(to)
pert.: gelastic, gelogemic
LAUNCHING: blast off, count
down, **opening, *start*
LAUREL: bay, kalmia, oleander,
pittosporum, **reward,* tarairi
LAVA: *cinder:* scoria
field: pedregal
fragment: ash, lapillos
mass: bomb, coulee
LAVISH: **free, *give, *wild*
LAW: act, **adage, *authority,* bill,
canon, code, command, decree,
dictate, droit, edict, **form(ula),*
institution, jure, litigation, no-
mology, **order,* ordinance, pre-
scription, regulation, **rule,*
statute
-abiding: obedient
action: replevin, **law: suit*
and order: enforcement, **order*
body: code, constitution
breaker: *criminal, *hoodlum
case, postponed: remanet
claim: lien
court official: amala(h)
decree: edict, fiat, nisi
degree: llb, lld
delay: mora

* Asterisk means to look up this word to find more answer words.

divine: fas
document: deed, elegit, writ
enforcers: police, sheriffs
-lessness: anarchy, insurrection, license, mutiny, *rioting, vice
magnetic induction: biot-savart
maker: legislator, solon
man: attorney, barrister, counsel, jurist, lawyer
mosaic: pentateuch, tora(h)
offense: crime, delict, *error, malum, *sin, tort
opposer: anarchist, *criminal
opposing: antinomy
oral: noncupative, parol
pert.: canonic, forensic, judicial, legal, legislative
philosophy: jurisprudence
points: gonia, lis, res
religious: halakha
students: stagiary
suit: action, case, lege, lis, litigation, prosecution
term: constat, detinue, ivisi, nisi, res, trover
volume: codex
warning: caveat
within the: canonic, due, ennomic, just, lawful, legal, legitimate, licit, *right
LAWYER: *bad:* ambulance chaser, pettifogger, shyster
saint: ives
woman: portia
LAX: *free, *late, *slow, *weak
LAY: *place, *rest, *set, *song
about: *attack, *try
an egg: bomb, *fail, flop
aside, away: *abandon, *dismiss, *prepare, *save, *store
bare: disclose, *open, *show
by: *lay: aside
down: *rest, *store, *yield
for: *ambush
hands on: *attack, *get, *seize
hold of: *arrest, *get, *seize
in: *accumulate, *save, *store

low: *beat, *defeat, *kill
off: *discharge, *dismiss, *stop
out: *kill, *plan, *spread
to: *attack, *blame, *try
up: *afflict, *save, *store
waste: *destroy, *ruin
LEAD: *actor, *advance, allure, bear, beckon, blaze, captain, carry, clew, clue, conduct, *control, counsel, *direct, dominate, escort, excel, fix, graphite, *head, induce, metal, *open, *order, persuade, pilot, plumb, point, precede, role, *run, *set, sinker, solder, spend, star, *start, steer, surpass, *top, van, wad, weight
and tin: calin, terne
antimonate: bindheimite
astray: *betray, inveigle, lure
black: graphite, plumbago, wad
carbonate: cerussite
chromo-arsenate: bellite
color: *dull, gray, livid
copper arsenate: bayldonite
-copper-bismuth: aikinite
glass for gem-making: strass
manganite: cesarolite
mock: blende, sphalerite
monoxide: litharge
ore: galena
pellet: bb, bullet, shot
pencil: graphite
silicate: barysilite
sounding: plummet
sulphate: anglesite, caracolite
telluride: altaite
thioarsenite: baumhauerite
white: ceruse
LEADER: article, bell cow, *best, boss, cantor, captain, caudillo, chairman, chieftain, cid, cock, commander, conductor, coryphaeus, cox, *despot, director, duce, dux, editorial, ethnarch, first, foreman, fuhrer, governor, guide, *head, king, *magnate, master, officer, pacer, pilot,

* Asterisk means to look up this word to find more answer words.

predecessor, prophet, quarterback, *ruler, sinew, standardbearer, tendon, titan, viceroy
comb.: agog, agogue
ecclesiastic: *church: man
LEADERSHIP: authority, balbatim, charisma, establishment, management, power structure
LEAF: *bud:* gemma
curvature: epinasty
cutting ant: atta
disease: erinea
eater: koala
grass: blade
heddles: gear
hinged: flap
hopper: dikrella
large: frond
manna: lerp
miner: hispa
part: areola, angle, axil, blade, bract, corolla, costa, crenation, lenticel, ligule, lobe, midrib, nervure, pagina, pen, petal, petiole, pores, rib, sepal, stem, stipel, stipule, stoma(ta), vein, yapa
pert.: foliar, peltate, sinuate
set: calyx, corolla
stemmed: caulescent
LEAGUE: bund, *combine, *union
greek: amphictyony
pert.: federal
LEAH: *kin:* dinah, jacob, levi
LEAK: *betray, *escape, ooze
LEANDER: *love:* hero
LEAP YEAR: bissextile
LEAR: *king lear
LEARN: discover, *get, *see
LEATHER: *alum-dressed:* aluta
apron: barmskin
artificial: keratol
bag: alforja, cheek pouch
band: armguard
bottle: borachio, matara, olpe
convert into: tan, taw
drinking mug: jack
dry(ing): sam, samm, sammy

fine: kid, suede, vellum
finish: buff
fish: lija
flask: *leather: bottle
flexible: kid, roan, suede
glove: capeskin, napa, suede
hamper: buffalo
inspector: sealer
jacket: black beech
machine: edgekey, edger
-neck: marine
pare: skive
piece: clout, latigo, thong, welt
sheepskin: cabretta, skiver
sheet: buffing
slice: skive
soft: aluta, chamois, napa
strong: buckskin
tool: skiver
waste: tanite
whip: blacksnake
worker: chamar, chuckler, saddler, tanner
LEAVE: *escape, *quit, *yield
LEAVEN: alloy, permeate, yeast
LEBANON: *castle:* beaufort, saida, sidon, toron
city: arca, beirut, ehden, tyre
dance: dabkey
mountain: kadischa, kenisseh
LECTURE: *rebuke, scold, *talk
LEDA: *kin:* *dioscuri, helen
wooer: swan, zeus
LEECH: *comb.:* bdella, bdello
LEES: draff, *refuse, slag
LEEWARD: *island:* anguilla, antigua, barbuda, dominica, montserrat, nevis, st kitts
LEFT: *comb.:* levo
handed: sinister, southpaw
over: *hash, *refuse, surplus
page: levo, verso, vo
toward: haw, herring, levo
LEG: *bail:* *escape, flight
bone: femur, fibula, ilium, shin, tibia
covering: pedule

---

* Asterisk means to look up this word to find more answer words.

it: depart, *escape, *walk
part: ankle, anticnemion, calf, crus, drumstick, femur, fibula, gambrel, gigot, ham, hock, knee, peronaeus, shank, shin, tibia, thigh
pert.: crural, sural
LEGAL: *law
LEGEND: *adage, *story, *title
LEGERDEMAIN: *magic, *trick
LEGION: *group, *quantity
LELEGES: *king:* altes
LEMON: *disease:* black pit
grass: roosa, rusa, siri
seed: pip, putamen
sole: carter, marysole
verbena: aloysia
vine: barbados gooseberry
LEMUR: *flying:* colugo
fossil: adapis
pref.: vari
ring-tailed: macaco
LENS: *combination:* barlow
flat: plano
hand: reader
inflammation: glenitis
measurement: ligne
tele-photic: adon
type: meniscus, toric, unar
LENT: careme, fast, quadragesima
first day: ash wednesday
LENTIL: *comb.:* phac(o)
LEONTES: *wife:* hermione
LEOPARD: *group:* leap
pert.: pardine
LEPER: cagot, lazar, pariah
king: uzziah
quarter: lazar cote, lazareet
LEPRECHAUN: *dwarf, *spirit
LEPROSY: *form:* alphos
remedy: chaulmooga oil
LER: *consort:* aoife
LESBOS: *boatman:* phaon
poet: alcaeus, arion, sappho
LET: *allow, charter, franchise, hire, lease, license, obstacle, *release, *rent, *suffer, *will

alone: and, *avoid, miss, *pass
down: *deceive, *fail, *slow
drop or fall: *release, *tell
fly: *attack, *throw
go: *dismiss, *free, *yield
have it: *beat, *punish, *whip
in: *admit, *enter, receive
in on: *release, *tell
know: *advise, *tell
loose: *play, relax, *release
off: *acquit, *free, *release
on: *act, *play, sham
oneself go: deteriorate, *play
out: *dismiss, *release, *tell
the buyer beware: caveat emptor
up: *abate, *quit, *slow, *stop
LETHE: abyss, *hell, oblivion
LETITIA: paris
LETO: *parent:* leto, phoebe
sister: asteria
twins: apollo, artemis, diana
LETTER: *note, *record, *report
according to: literal
authoritative: breve, writ
challenge: cartel
cross stroke: serif
cut off last: apocope
decorated: fac, paraph
first: alpha
formal: brief
harmony: eutony
-head: *address, *title
illuminate with: miniate
last: omega, zed, zee
marque: piracy
opener: censor, salutation
pope's: bull
seal: cachet
LEVANT: *bet, mideast, renig
dollar: marie theresa dollar
fabric: barracan, camlet
garment: caftan
jacket: grego
madder: alizari
pastry: baklava
room, cool: serdab
ship: bum, caique, jerm, saic, settee, xebec

* **Asterisk means to look up this word to find more answer words.**

sponge: turkey cup (sponge)
valley: wadi, wady
warrant: berat
wind: chamsin, etesian, shamal
worm seed: aleppo, artemisia
LEVEE: **party, *waterway*
LEVEL: *at: *aim, *attack*
  comb.: plani
  common: average, par
  headed: balanced, calm
  headedness: aplomb
  plot: parterre, terrace
  social: caste, class
  with: **equal,* make good, **tell*
LEVI: *father:* jacob
  son: elizaphan, gershon, hebron,
    jochebed, kohath, matthat, me-
    rari, mooli, uzziel
  tribe: amramites
LEVITE: *chief:* chenaniah
  composer: asaph
  patriarch: lael
LEWD: **bad, *evil, *wanton*
LIAR: ananias, **cheat,* pinto
LIBERAL: **abundant,* accessible,
    advanced, **big,* bounteous,
    bountiful, **broad,* catholic, cor-
    dial, cosmopolitan, **free, *great,*
    handsome, lenient, munificent,
    *noble, *open, plentiful, profuse,
    progressive, tolerant, unselfish,
    *wanton, wide
LIBERATE: **escape, *free*
LIBERIAN: bassa, gi, gibbi, greba,
    kra, kroo, krooboy, krooman,
    kruman, toma, vai, vei
LIBYA: *city:* tripoli
  gulf: sidra
  measure: barile, bozze, donam,
    dra, gorraf, jabia, kele, kharouba,
    mattaro, pik, teman, termino,
    uckie
  moon-goddess: neith
  oasis: sebha
  port: bengazi, derna, tobruk
  queen loved by zeus: lamia
  son: belus

wind: sirocco
LICENSE: allow, **let, *right*
LICORICE: *derivative:* abrin
  flavored drinks: absinthe, arak,
    creme de menthe, ouzo, pastis,
    perroquet, tomate
  pill: cachou
  seed: goonch, jequirity
LID: **cap, *cover, *hat, *top*
LIE: abide, banger, be present, big
    one, blague, bouncer, canard,
    *cheat, cram, **deceive, *decep-
    tion,* deviate, direction, equivo-
    cate, exaggerate, exist, fable,
    fabricate, fairy tale, falsehood,
    fish story, fishify, ghost story,
    half-truth, hoax, howler, inhere,
    large order, **lay,* lodge, mendac-
    ity, palter, prevaricate, **range,*
    *reach, *rest, sleep, **smear,*
    *story, stretcher, subsist, tale, tall
    one, tarradiddle, twister, un-
    truth, yarn, whopper
  down: **rest, *yield*
  in wait: **ambush,* skulk
LIFE: **action, *spirit, *story*
  airless: anaerobiosis
  animal: bios, biota, fauna
  after death: future, tomorrow
  belt filling: kapok
  buoy: float
  car: ark
  chemical: **dna references*
  comb.: bi, bia, bio
  cycle: anicca
  deity: balder, baldr, faunus lub,
    lucina, mitra, osiris, shu
  destroyer: antibiotic
  force: anima mundi, atman,
    bathmism, biod, breath, elan
    vital, heartblood, jiva(tma),
    ousia, pneuma, pranavis, vitalis
  giver: apheta
  insurance: tontine
  -like: realistic
  of ease: comfort, prosperity
  pert.: biotic, mortal, vital

---

* **Asterisk means to look up this word to find more answer words.**

plant: bios, biota, flora
preserver: breeches buoy, mae west, safety belt
principle: *life: force
prolonger: elixir
raft: balsa, collapsible, float
science: anatomy, biology, genetic, paleontology, zoology
science term: central dogma, codon, *dna references, *enzyme, inducer, nucleotide, peptide, protovirus, psi, represser, rho, scotophobin, shope papilloma, sigma, template
scientist: agranoff, allfrey, avery, burger, chase, crick, gallo, gamow, haldane, hershey, huebner, kornberg, matthaei, mendel, nirenberg, petrucci, shettles, temin, watson, wilkins, zamecnik
sea: benthos, coral, plankton
staff of: bread
story: biography, chronicle, history, memoir, vita
symbol: ankh, cross, tau
time: aeon, age, being, born days, duration, eon, eternity
unit: amoeba, cell, embryo
without: *arid, azoic, *dead
without, comb.: abio
LIFT: *abet, *raise, *steal
LIGHT: aerial, agile, airy, arc, attitude, blond, *bright, bude, candle, carefree, clear, dawn, daybreak, debonair, dismount, emanation, ethereal, facile, *fair, fire, flare, flash, fluffy, foamy, fragile, frivolous, frothy, gay, *gentle, glim, ignite, illume, impalpable, kindle, klieg, *knowledge, lamp, lantern, leger, *little, lucid, lumen, match, moon, opinion, outlook, pastel, pellucid, perch, *puny, *quick, radiant, roost, serene, shallow, *short, *simple, sleazy, *small, *soft, *sparkle, star, sunny, *superficial, taper,

torch, trivial, *truth, *vague, *wanton, white, yang
act of making: levitation
beacon: fanal
bulb filler: argon
burning: cresset, torch
celestial: moon, star, sun
circle: aureole, corona, halo, nimb, nimbus
comb.: luce, luci, phot(o)
feast: channukah, hanukka(h)
-fingered: larcenous
flux: hefner, lumen
globe: bulb
god: apollo, balder, heimdall
headed: dizzy, *silly, *simple
hearted: gay, glad, *happy
house: beacon, pharos, warning
image: spectra
into: *attack, *punish, *start
on: *enter, *meet
science: optics
spirit: ormazd, ormuzd
unit: carcel, flux, hefner, lumen, lux, phot(on), quantum
weight: diminutive, nonentity
without: aphotic, blind, dark
LIGHTNING: *bug:* firefly
cyclops: steropes
god: agni, jupiter, thor, zeus
pert.: fulgural
protector: arrester, rod
war: blitz, blitzkrieg
LIKE: *love, similar
suff.: ar, ic, ine, oid, ose
LIKENESS: *image, *picture
LILITH: *successor:* eve
LILLIPUTIAN: *dwarf, *small
LILY: *african corn:* ixia
butterfly: mariposa, sego
daffodil: narcissus
encrinite: paleon
family: aloe, arum, bessera, camass, ixia, lotus, mariposa, plantain, sego, squill, toi
gold-banded: auratum
iron: harpoon

* **Asterisk means to look up this word to find more answer words.**

leaf: pad
maid of astolat: elaine
of france: fleur-de-lis
of the valley: asparagus, aspidistra, barney-clapper, bead ruby, canada mayfair, convallily, fetterbush, mugget, pepperbush, sourwood
plant: camas, camass, cammas
pond: kelp
sand: soaproot
-shaped: crinoid
turk's cap: martagon
water: castalia, lotus, nelumbo, nymphaea, wokas
LIMB: *flexion:* anaclasis
without: acolous, amelia, anarthrous, apterygial
LIMBO: al araf, **hell,* **jail*
LIME: *bush:* snare, **trap*
dark: raupenlein
derivative: apatite, calcic
hound: lyam
juicer: mariner
light: oxycalcium, publicity
liniment: carron oil
pert.: calcareous, oolitic
phosphate: apatite
powder: conite, konite
-stone: anthraconite, caen, caliche, calcrete, camstane, chalk, dolomite, leith, lias, malm, marble, oolite, silica
tree: linden, teyl, tupelo
uranite: autunite
wild fruit: colima
-wort: dianthus
LIMIT: abstain, ambit, assign, barrier, **border,* boundary, **brim,* capacity, circumscribe, condition, confine, deadline, define, demarcation, determine, **edge,* **end,* fix, frontier, hinder, line, **mark,* narrow, number, ori, pale, point, prescribe, qualify, **range,* regulate, restrain, restrict, scant, span, specialize,

stent, straiten, stunt, **top*
comb.: ori
LIMP: **soft,* **walk,* **weak*
LINCOLN: *assassin:* booth
friend: speed
nickname: honest abe
secretaries: seward, stanton
son: tad
wife: mary todd
LINDEN: lime, shield, tilicetum
LINE: *barometric:* isobar
color: streak, stripe
comb.: lino, sticho
converting: balun
curved: arc, bowl, brace
fishing: boulter, cord, snell
geographic: equator, latitude, longitude, meridian, tropic
geometric: cant, ess, parallel, secant, sine, tangent
imaginary: axis, capital
measurer: campylometer
nautical: earing, hawser, marline, painter, ratline
pert.: filar, linear
scant: stud
soldiers: column, file, rank
thin: stria
up: **gather,* **join,* **plan*
waiting: cue, queue
with bricks: revet
with stone: stean, steen(e)
LINEN: *coarse:* barras, dowlas, galipot, lockram
closet: ewery
fabric: **fabric: linen*
fiber: flax
fine: cambric, damask, nacarat
flowered: damasse
household: bedding, napery
sail: canvas, duck
tape: inkle
vestment: alb, amice, amit
window shades: holland
yarn: lea
LINES: harness, network, reticle, role, script, **style*

* **Asterisk means to look up this word to find more answer words.**

marked by: ruled, striate(d)
LINN: **waterway*
LINOTYPE: *trigger:* verge
LION: *group:* pride
headed goddess: mut
leaf: black turnip
mountain: catamount, cougar, painter, panther, puma
movie: elsa, lahr
mythical: griffin, sphinx
pert.: leonine
toothless: morne
winged: achech, sphinx
young: cub, lionet, whelp
LIP: *comb.:* cheil(o), chil(o)
LIQUID: **drink*
alkaloid: anabasine, anatabine
ambar: bilsted, sweet gum
colorless: acetol, alcohol
comb.: elaio
container: **drinking vessel*
dialectric: askarel
gaseous: steam, vapor
hydrocarbon: aplotaxene
measure: aam, ahm, dram, gallon, pint, ounce, tierce
oily: aniline, cresol, picamar
volatile: acetone, alcohol, benzine, butane, ether, gasoline, ligroine
LIQUIDATE: **kill*, melt, **settle*
LIQUOR: **drink: alcoholic*
bad: balderdash, rotgut, smoke
cabinet: cellaret
-drinking: bibulous
fruit: applejack, brandy, wine
maker: abkari, distiller
malt: ale, beer, bock, bub
residue: dregs, heeltaps, must
sacred: ambrosia, haomi, nectar
shop: bar, saloon, tavern
vessel: **drinking: vessel*
LISTEN: attend, ear, hark, hear, heed, hist, lest, list, look, obey, oyez, pay attention, tend
LITTLE: base, bitsy, brief, contemptible, cramped, dapper, darling, diminutive, dinky, exiguous,

feeble, **light*, **mean*, minute, miniscule, one-horse, paltry, petite, pindling, pint-sized, poco, punty, scanty, selfish, **short*, **small*, **thin*, tiny, **weak*, wee
comb.: micr(o), steno
women: amy, beth, jo, meg
LIVE: abide, **active*, **ardent*, animated, be somebody, breathe, continue, dwell, eager, endure, energetic, exist, glowing, inhabit, last, lodge, remain, reside, stay, **settle*, vital
LIVER: *brown:* autumn oaf
extract: acanthine
pert.: hepatic, visceral
secretion: bile
tester: bromsulfalein
-wort: acrogen, anthocerote, archegoniate, agrimony, blasum, bryophyte, fern, hepatica, moss, pyrola, riccia
LIVING: *again:* redivivus
dead: phantom, **spirit*, zombi
different depths: allopelagic
off others: entozoic, parasitic
LIZARD: *agamoid:* dabb, hardim
beaded: gila
climbing: iguana
comb.: sauro
fabulous: basilisk, dragon
fish: bummalo, saury
genus: agama, ameiva, lacerta
mammal similar to: salamander
monitor: anoli, uran, varan(us)
pert.: iguanoid, saurian
poisonous: gila monster
sand: adda, skink
spiny: dabb
star red: agama, hardim
veranoid: waran
wall: gecko, tarente
winged: basilisk, dragon
LLUDD, LLYR: *son:* bran(wen), gwyn(n), manawyddan
LOAD: **quantity*, **surfeit*
LOB: box, fire, **strike*, **throw*

* Asterisk means to look up this word to find more answer words.

LOBBY: *agent*, influence, press
LOBSTER: *female:* hen
  part: chela, claw, nipper, pincer, telson, thorax
  roe: coral
  trap: bownet, corf, creel, pot
LOCK: *-jaw:* amasesis, ankylostoma, tetanus, trismus
  part: bolt, cylinder, stump
  stepper: convict
  stock and barrel: *all*, utterly
  -up: *jail*
LOCO: crazy, *insane*, *mad*
  weed: marijuana
LOCOMOTIVE: bigboy, diesel, engine, mallet, mikado, mogul
  front: cowcatcher, pilot
  service car: coalcar, tender
LOCRINE: *kin:* brut, sabrina
LOCUST: *eater:* acridophagus
  group: plague
  insect: cicada, mantis
  noise: stridulation
  tree: acacia, carob, clammy, courbaril, honey, kowhai
LODGE: *live*, *settle*, *store*
LOFTY: *arrogant*, *great*, *high*
LOG: *collection:* drive, raft
  contest: roleo
  gin: jammer
  haul: sloop
  kind: puncheon, slab, spalt
  manipulator: cattyman
  measure: scalage
  noser: sniper
  revolve, roll: birl, logroll
  roller: birler, canter, decker
  skid: tode
  split: puncheon
  splitter: wedge
  tool: cant, hook, peavey, tode
  truck: bummer
  wood: admiral, campeche
LOGGER: *boot:* pac, pack
  boss: bully
  device: bucking board
  -head: *fool*, turtle

  -heads: odds, outs
  sled: tode, travois(e)
  wheels: pair, katydid
LOGIC: *affirm in:* ponent
  aristotelian: organon
  assumption: premise
  baconian: inductive
  branch: alethiology
  fallacy: idol, odolum
  inductive: epagoge
  omission: saltus
  premise: idolum, lemma
  specious: sophism
LOGION: *adage*, *truth*
LOHENGRIN: *role:* elsa, parsifal
LOINCLOTH: cache, dhooti, dhoti, girdle, izar, lungi, malo, maro, pagne, parue
LOIS: *daughter:* eunice
LOKI: *consort:* angerboda, sigyn
  child: fenris, hel, midgard
  parent: farbauti, laufey, naal
LOLIGO: calamary, octopus, squid
LOMBARDY: *governor:* catapan
  king: alboin
  lake: como, garda
  poplar: black lady
LONDON: *ancient:* agusta
  airport: heathrow
  art gallery: tate
  bohemian sector: chelsea, soho
  brown: carbuncle
  bus conductor: clippy
  club: almack, carlton, kitcat
  fishmarket: billingsgate
  founder: brut
  hawker: coster, mun
  landmark: big ben, st paul's
  monument: cenotaph, gog, magog
  novel: call of the wild
  police court: bow street
  porter: georgina
  prison: fleta, newgate
  quarter: acton, adelphi, alsatia, bankside, battersea, belgravia, bethnal green, black friars, bloomsbury, camberwell, chel-

* **Asterisk means to look up this word to find more answer words.**

sea, holborn, lambeth, mayfair, soho
society: mayfair
square: leicester
stables: mews
street: bond, cheapside, haymarket, savile, wardour
tavern: boar's head, pub
theatre: adelphi
LONG: *ago:* eld, yore
beard: bellarmine
bench: banquette
comb.: macro
hair: conservative, dryball, hippie, intellectual, oldster
headed: shrewd, *wise
-nosed: nasute
prayer: cathisma
-shoreman: docker, stevedore
shot: improbability, odds
-suffering: forbearing, patient
suit: *skill, specialty, talent
-winded: tedious, verbose
LOOK: *air, *appear, await, bearing, blush, bode, browse, cast, con, *eye, examine, expect, face, gaze, glance, hist, hope, inspect, ken, leer, manner, mien, observe, ogle, peek, peep, peer, pore, pose, preview, pry, regard, scan, *search, *see, seek, seem, sight, skew, *spy, view, watch
after: *attend, serve
ahead: *prepare, *ready
back: recall, retrospect
into: investigate
out: atalaya, bantayan, cockatoo, conner, watchtower
sharp: beware, *dress, primp
sullen: frown, glare, scowl
to: avail, *prepare, tend
up: call, improve, *meet, visit
upon: contemplate, *think
up to: *honor
LOOM: *inventor:* cartwright
part: batten, beam, caam, easer, griff, heald, heddles, lam, leaf,

lingoe, shed, sley, temple, treadle, warp
LOON: *fool, grebe, *hoodlum
LOONEY: *insane, *mad
LOOP: *fabric:* terry
forming: brochidodromous
-hole: aperture, *escape, meuse, oilet, plea, pretext, slit
lace: picot
lariat: honda, hondoo
rope: bight
running: noose
-shaped: fundiform
LOOSENING: *comb.:* lys
LOOT: booty, *spoil, *steal
receipt: theftbote
LOQUAT: biwa, eriobotrya
LORD: baron, bel, chan, count, duke, earl, governor, grandee, kaan, khan, knight, liege, *magnate, marquis, *noble, paladin, peer, *ruler, seid, viscount
day: sabbath, sunday
group: *society, *top
have mercy: kyrie eleison
jim's ship: patna
messenger: malachi
of the dance: balmarcodes
prayer: paternoster
-ship: *authority
supper: eucharist, last
table: altar
wife: *lady
LORDLY: *lofty
LORE: *knowledge, science, *skill
LORETTE: *prostitute, *wanton
LOSE: *bury, *fail, *yield
LOSER: also-ran, prey, shlemiel
LOSS: *defeat, *hurt, *ruin
LOT: *fate, *group, *quantity
kin: abraham, benammi, haran, milcah, moab
ordeal: sodom
wife: bellicent, eavesdropper
LOTAN: *kin:* homam, hori, seir, timna
LOTH: *son:* gawain, mordred

---

* Asterisk means to look up this word to find more answer words.

divination by: sortilege
feast: purim
LOTTERY: bingo, chance, draw, lotto, raffle, sweepstakes, tern, tombola, turkey draw
LOTUS: *bird:* jacana
eater: utopian, visionary
grass: bird's-foot trefoil, melilot, nelumbo
lily: water chinquapin
tree: jubube, persimmon, sadr
LOUD: **big,* forte, noisy, showy
-mouthed: blatant, thersitical
speaker: bullhorn, megaphone
LOUISE DE LA RAMEE: ouida
LOUISIANA: *account book:* bilan
bayou: teche
county: parish
flower: magnolia
grass: bena, carpet, vetiver
man: cajun, creole, pelican
nickname: pelican state
tree: bald cypress
LOUT: **boor, *clown,* oaf, yahoo
LOVE: **admire, *affection,* agape, amor, ardency, care for, charity, clemency, compassion, comprehension, cupid, darling, dear, **desire,* devotion, dote, enamor, enjoy, eros, fervor, **fire,* fondness, go for, gra, have a crush on, idolatry, infatuation, **interest,* like, **passion, *pet, *prize, *spark, *sweetheart, *worship,* zero
affair: amour
apple: tomato
bird: parrot, turtle dove
comb.: amat, phil, philo
feast: agape
gift: amatorio
god: aengus, amor, angus og, apollo, baal, bhaga, cupid, dagda, eros, frey, kama, oengus, pothos
goddess: aphrodite, ashtarte, athor, freya, hathor, ishtar, urania, venus

-in-a-mist: bishop's-wort
knot: amoret, memento
letter: billet-doux
lock: cadenette, curl, tress
muse: erato
nest: rendezvous, tryst
of beauty: aesthetics
of country: patriotism
of god for mankind: agape
of wisdom: philosophy
parental: storge
poem: amoretto
potion: aphrodisiac, charm, philter
sacrificer: amintor
science: erotology
sick: enamored, fond, stricken
song: canso, canzo
story: fiction, romance
LOW: abject, **bad,* beggarly, bestial, blore, blue, cheap, coarse, common, debased, deep, depressed, down(cast), **evil,* faint, feeble, gross, humble, ignoble, inferior, knee-high, **mean,* menial, moo, neap, off, orra, **popular, *sad, *short, *sick, *soft, *sorry, *small,* vulgar, **weak*
comb.: tapin(o)
country: belgium, holland, luxemburg, netherlands
-down: confidential, inside
-necked: decollete
tide: ebb, neap
LOZENGE: figure, **mark,* pill
LSD: acid, cubes, pearly gates
effect: backlash, hallucination
experience: bad trip, freakout
source: ergot, rye fungus
LUCIFER: **demon, *devil*
LUCK: **accident, *break,* cess, chance, **fate,* lot, prosperity, success, **venture*
bad: ace, cess, deuce, doom
charm: clover, horseshoe, jonah, mascot, rabbit-foot, shamrock, swastika

* Asterisk means to look up this word to find more answer words.

god: happiness god
goddess: lakshmi, shree, sri
pert.: aleatory
stroke of: fluke
LUCKY: *appropriate, *happy
stone: alectorian
stroke: fluke, fortune
LUDICROUS: *absurd, *funny,
*mad
LULL: *abate, *break, silence
LUMBER(MAN): *log, *logger,
*walk
decay: red heart
LUNAR: *moon references
LUNATIC: *mad, maniac, *insane
LUNG: *comb.:* pulmo
fish: barramunda, ceratodus
having: pulmonate
part: alveolus, pleura
sound: bruit, rale, rattle
wort: bluebell, cowslip
LURE: *draw, tempt, *trap
LURK: *ambush, *hide, *steal
LUSH: *drunk, *rich, *splendid
LUST: argante, avarice, *desire
LUSTY: athletic, *solid, *strong
LUTETIA: asteroid, paris
LUXURY: *ease, *joy, shmaltz
lover: sybarite, voluptuary
LUZON: *philippine islands
LYCAON: *daughter:* callisto
LYDIA: *capital:* sardis
king: alyattes, croesus, gyges
lover: captain anthony absolute
river: pactolus
LYDIAN: *gentle, *soft
LYNCEUS: *kin:* arene, idas
foe: danaus
LYNETTE: *knight:* gareth
LYNX: *eyed:* oxyopia
rufus: bobcat, wildcat
LYRIC: *muse:* erato, polymnia
pert.: catullian
poem: canzone, epode, lay, melic,
song
poet: odist
13 lines: rondeau

MAACAH: *father:* talmai
husband: david, rehoboam
son: abijah, absalom, asa
MACAW: ara(ra), aracanga, parrot
pert.: arine
MACBETH: *part:* angus, banquo,
hecate, lennox, macduff, ross
victim: duncan
MACCABEE: john, jonathan, josephus, judas, simon
MACE: *bearer:* bailiff, beadle
nutmeg: aril(lode)
reed: dod
royal: scepter, sceptre, *staff
MACEDONIA: *city:* berea, be-
roea, edessa, pella, pydna
general: antipater
king: abgar, alexander, cassander,
pierus, phillip
peak: athos
royal line founder: archelaus
statesman: antipater
MACHINE: association, automation, barker, breaker, car, caster,
*instrument, *make, motor, or-
ganization, *tool, *vehicle
gun: bren, chatterbox, gatling,
hotchkiss, maxim, sten
political: *party, *system
war: *engine: war
MACKEREL: bluefish, bonito,
cero, chub, coelho, escolar, jurel,
peto, pintado, saurel, scomber,
tinker, tunny, wahoo
net: spiller
shark: carcharias
young: blinker, spike, tinker
MAD: *absurd, *anger, *angry,
*ardent, brainsick, distracted,
doting, *eager, enraged, excited,
frenetic, frenzied, furious, gay,
hilarious, *hot, infatuated, *insane, *reckless, *violent, *wild
about: *ardent, *eager
-cap: daredevil, *reckless
-dog skullcap: blue pimpernel

* Asterisk means to look up this word to find more answer words.

get: *boil, *burn, erupt
house: *asylum, babel, *chaos
MADAGASCAR: malagasy republic
animal: aye-aye, indri, lemur, tanrec, tendrac, tenrec
city: antananarivo, mojanga
civet: fossa(ne), foussa
island group: aldabra
lemur: avahi, aye-aye, babacoote, indri
measure: gantang
mountains: ankaratra
periwinkle: vinca rosea
tree: antankarana, rafia
tribe: ambahakoana, antaiva, antanandro, avaradrano, bara, betsileo, betsimasaraka, merina, sakalava, tsirinana
MADAM BUTTERFLY: chocho(san)
MADDER: *genus:* rubia
root pigment: mull
tree: bangcal, chincona
MADEIRA: *capital:* funchal
shrub: carrot tree
vine: maiden's-wreath
wind: leste
wine: bual, canary, gomera, malmsey, marsala, tinta, tinto, verdelho
wine-making: estufado, stoving
MAFIA: beauty, la cosa nostra, lcn, pride, refuge, swank, syndicate, underworld
code: maranzano, omerta
members: button men
official: capo, commission, consigliori, sottocapo
MAFURRA: elcaja, tree
MAGE: magician, thaumaturge
MAGI: balthazar, gaspar, melchior, sages, wise men
gift: frankincense, gold, myrrh
MAGIC: apotropaism, art, brujeria, cantrip, conjury, divination, enchantment, *fetish, hoo-

doo, hypnotism, jadoo, jadu, juju, mana, maya, necromancy, obeah, phylacteric, *power: supernatural, *rite, rune, *show, *sign, sorcery, *spell, talisman, thaumaturgy, theurgy, *trick, voodoo, *weird, witchcraft
belt: talisman
bullets: miracle drug
city: miami
cube: nasik
forest: broceliande
goddess: circe, hecate
lantern: epidiascope, megascope
pert.: bewitching, circean, goetic, necromantic, occult, thaumaturgic, theurgic
ring king: gyges
seals: sigilla
stone: agate, alectoria
symbol: caract, charm, pentacle
word: abracadabra, incantation, om, presto, selah, sesame, um
MAGICAL: *magic: pert.
MAGICIAN: archimage, charlatan, circe, conjuror, houdini, mage, mandrake, merlin, necromancer, prestidigitator, shaman, sorcerer, thaumaturge, voodooist, witch, wizard
assistant: famulus
MAGNANIMOUS: *big, *free, *great, *liberal, *noble, unselfish
MAGNATE: bashaw, big cheese, big name, big shot, bigwig, brass, celebrity, cob, fat cat, grandee, *head, *leader, lion, *lord, important person, millionaire, mogul, nabob, nawab, personage, *power, *ruler, somebody, star, titan, *top, tycoon, vip, wheel
MAGNETIC: *unit:* gauss, gilber, kapp, maxwell, oersted, weber
MAGNETISM: biod, charisma, *draw
MAGNIFICENT: *big, *great, *noble, *splendid, *supreme

* Asterisk means to look up this word to find more answer words.

MAGNIFY: *increase, *praise

MAGNITUDE: *quantity, *range

MAGNOLIA: cucumber tree, umbrella tree, yulan

MAGNUS: son: cnut, knut

MAGPIE: babbler, bird, chatterer, daw, haggister, madge, magg, ninut, pianet, piat, pica, piet, piot, pyat, pyet, *scold, shrike, smew, talker, tanager

MAGSMAN: *sharp(er), swindler

MAGYAR: *hungarian
water spirits: viz-anya, vizi-ember, vizi-leany

MAHOGANY: acajou, toon

MAHU: *demon, *devil, *eccentric

MAIA: son: hermes

MAIDENHAIR: ginkgo, tree

MAIM: *hurt, *spoil

MAIN: *force, *principal, sea
action: epitasis
course: blue plate, entree
drag: artery, boulevard, heart
spring: *source, *start

MAINE: bird: chickadee
flower: white pine cone
nickname: pine tree, wonderland

MAINTAIN: *argue, keep, *support

MAJESTIC: *big, *great, *noble

MAJESTY: *power, sovereignty

MAKE: *accomplish, *acquire, arrive, beat, brand, *build, cause, compose, construct, create, fabricate, finish, *force, *form, generate, *get, *income, induce, *kind, *model, *prepare, *produce, recognize, *settle, *sign, *style, *win
believe: drama, *magic, sham
bold: challenge, dare, venture
book: *bet, wager
clear: *argue, emphasize
do: eke, get by, manage
eyes: flirt, *love
fast: fasten, *secure, *tie

fun: *joke, quip, ridicule

good, it: *accomplish, *complete, *succeed, *win

love: bundle, ricky-chow

mincemeat of: *destroy, *hurt

off: depart, *escape, leave

one's mark: *make good

out: know, *see, *succeed

over: convert, *praise

peace: bury hatchet, *settle

-shift: expedient, stopgap

short work: *destroy, triumph

tracks: *escape, *run, *speed

up: *form, *kind, layout, *prepare, *range, *ready

MAL: *bad, *evil, *rotten
de mer: seasickness
du pays: homesickness

MALABAR: almond: almendron
bark: ochna
canoe: ballam, tonee
monkey: wanderoo
nutmeg: bombay mace
palm: talipot

MALAGASY: madagascar

MALARIA: cause: anopheles
cure: quinine, verbena

MALARKEY: *nonsense

MALAY: malacca, maori, polynesia
adam: tiki
almond: kanari
apple: kawika, ohia
archipelago: *malay: island
backgammon: tabal
banana: fei
beefwood: belah, toa, tooa
beverage: ava, kava, kawa
bird: poe, tue, tui, weka
boat: ballam, caracora, catamaran, cougnar, moguey, moki, praam, prah(am), prahu, prao, prau, proa, toup, waka
buffalo: carabao, seladang
burial place: ahu
camphor: borneol
canoe: *malay: boat

* Asterisk means to look up this word to find more answer words.

charm: heitiki
chestnut: rata
chief: ariki, dato, datto, datu
christian: ilokano
city: malacca, singapore
clan: ati, hapu, ringatu
cloth: batik, malo, pareu
club: marree, mere, patu, rata
coin: tampang, tapa, taro, tra
condiment: sambal, semball
creator: maui, tiki
crane: saras, sarus
dagger: barong, crees(e), cris, krees(e), kris, parang, patu
dance: haka
deer: plandok
demon: akua, atua
dragon: ati
dress or garment: cabaya, kabaya, malo, pareu, sarong
fish: isda, kai, moki, tagalog
food: kai, poi, taro
gibbon: lar
god: ateo, atua, mana, maui, oro, pele, tane, tiki
headhunter: italone
herb: entada, pia, taro
hero: maui
homeland: havaiki
house: whare(wananga)
image: ahu, tiki, zogo
isthmus: kra
jacket: baju
king: baginda
knife: *malay: dagger*
language: *malay: native*
law: adat
loria: tiria
lugger: toup
magic: mana
malady: amok, lata
marriage: ambilanak, ambilian
measure: chupak, gantang, para, parah, parrah, pau, pipe, tun
memorial: *malay: statue*
mountain: gunong, gunung, tahan
mulberry bark: tapa

musical instrument: anklong
myth: avaiki, kore
native: abongo, aripas, ata, babongo, bajau, bicol, bikol, bilaan, bisayan, bugi, hapu, hawaiian, ita, kanaka, marquesan, obongo, samoan, semang, tagal-(og), tahitian, tongan, vicol, visayan
nerve ailment: lata
orangutan: mias
oven: imu, umu
ox: banteng, ox
palm: areng(a), atap, ejoo, gebang, gomuti, nibong, nibung, sago, talipot, tara
parrot: lories, lory, tui
pepper: avas, siri(h)
pigeon: lupe
pine: ara, hala
plant: kanaka, taro, ube, uvi
priest: tuhunga
public square: alun-alun
rice field: sawah
ruler: faipule
saying: auwe
shrine: ahurewa
sky: langi
spirit: atua
state: kedah, johore, negri sembilan, pahang, perak, selangor, sungei ujong
statue: ahu, tiki, zogo
store: pataka
sword: parang
tattooing: moko
tic: lata(h)
title: tuan
tree: akaroa, akia, benkulen, canangium, duku, durian, ilang ilang, ipil, kapur, lanseh, *malay: palm*, manuka, mapau, niepa, ohia, rata, tanehakas, terap, upas
tribe: *malay: native*
ungulate: tapir
verse form: pantum

* Asterisk means to look up this word to find more answer words.

village: kaika, kainga, pah
wages: utu
weapon: *malay:* club
MALE: *animal:* *animal: male
comb.: andr(o), androus, andry
MALEDICTION: anathema, curse
MALEFACTOR: *criminal,
*hoodlum
MALEVOLENCE: *bad, *evil,
*hate
MALFEASANCE: *error, *sin
MALICE: *malevolence, *sin
MALIGN: *abuse, *bad, *smear
MALIGNANT: *bad, *evil
MALLET, MALLEUS: *hammer
MALPRAMIS: *father:* baligant
slayer: duke naimes
MALT: *drink:* ale, beer, bock,
brew, lager, porter, stout
froth: barm, suds
ground: grist
infusion: wort
mixture: maltate, zythum
pert.: aly
-tasting: corny
vinegar: alegar, wort
worm: tippler, toper
MALTA: *capital:* valetta
coin: grain, grano
fever: brucellosis
hamlet: casal(e)
measure: artal, caffiso, canna,
parto, ratel, rotl, salma
wind: gregale
MAMMAL: *aquatic:* beaver,
coypu, desman, dolphin, dugong,
hippo, hippopotamus, manatee,
otter, porpoise, rytina, sea(lion),
sirenian, walrus, whale
arboreal: banxring, fisher, glutton,
kinkajou, lemur, monkey, orangutan, raccoon, sloth, tarsier
armored: apara, armadillo
badgerlike: balisaur, ratel
bovine: bison, bos, bull, calf, cow,
longhorn, taurine, zebu
burrowing: armadillo, badger,

gopher, mole, squirrel, wombat
camellike: guanaco
canine: coyote, dog, fox, wolf
caprine: goat
cetacean: dolphin, porpoise, whale
civetlike: genet
coat: hide, nutria, pelt, skin
deerlike: chevrotain
domestic: cat(tle), cow, dog,
horse, sheep
edentate: ant bear, anteater, pangolin, tamandua
equine: ass, colt, filly, foal, horse,
mare, stallion, zebra
extinct: amblypod, brontops, mastodon, pantodonta, rytina, titan-
otherium
feline: cat, cheetah, cougar, jaguar, leopard, lion, lynx, ocelot,
panther, polecat, puma, serval,
tiger, wildcat
flying: bat
giraffelike: okapi
gnawing: mole, mouse, rat, rodent, vole
herbivorous: *bovine, daman,
*equine, hippo, rhinoceros
insectivorous: banxring, bat, des-
mani, hedgehog, tenrec
llama-like: vicuna
marsupial: kangaroo, kaola, opossum, phalanger, tapoa
musteline: otter, ratel
nocturnal: bat, coon, hyena, kinkajou, lemur, macaco, platypus,
possum, raccoon, ratel, tapir,
tarsier
omniverous: hog, pig, swine
plantigrade: bear, coon, panda
porcine: boar, hog, peccary, pig,
swine
ringtailed: coon, lemur
ruminant: alpaca, antelope, bison,
buffalo, camel, cattle, chewer,
deer, giraffe, goat, llama, moose,
sheep, yak
scaled: pangolin

* Asterisk means to look up this word to find more answer words.

shelled: armadillo
ursine: bear, panda
viverrine: falanaka
vulpine: fox, wolf
web-footed: otter, platypus
MAMMOTH: **big, *giant, *great*
MAN: *-bird:* garuda
brass: talos, talus
-bull: bucentaur, minotaur
comb.: andro, anthropo, homo
dressed as woman: berdache
effeminate: androgyne
first: adam, askr, bure, buri,
  iapetus, izanagi, tiki, yama
handsome: adonis, apollo, **fellow*, fop, **sharp*
hater: misanthrope
-horse: apsara, centaur, gandharva
important: **lord, *magnate*
-machine: cyborg
married, newly: benedict, groom
of action: dynamo
of all work: factotum, joey
of god: bethuel
of letters: litterateur, savant
of straw: figure, nonentity
of war: andrew, ship, **soldier*
of world: cosmopolite, layman,
  secularist, sophisticate
old: alte(r kocker), back number,
  boss, centenarian, codger, cuff,
  dodo, dotard, duffer, fogram,
  fogrum, fogy, fuddy-duddy, gaffer, geezer, general, grandsire,
  graybeard, husband, longbeard,
  methuselah, mossback, nestor,
  nonagenarian, octogenarian, patriarch, senex, senior, square,
  superior, warhorse
one-hundred-eyed: argus
pert.: anthropoid, human, mortal
primitive: aborigine, savage
rich: capitalist, croesus, have,
  midas, nabob, nawab, plutocrat,
  rockefeller, tycoon
serpent: king erichthonius
single: bachelor, celibate

spirit of: akh
strong: **power: house*
without a country: nolan
MANAGE: **control, *direct, *use*
MANAGEMENT: *good:* eutaxie
poor: cacoeconomy
MANAGER: **agent, *head, *ruler*
MANASSEH: *city:* aner
son: amon, jair
MANCIPLE: **servant, *slave*
MANDATE: **law, *order*
MANEUVER: **action, *trick,
  work
MANGLE: **break, *hurt, *press,
  *ruin, *spoil, *tear (apart)*
MANGO: amchoor, amhar, amini,
  anacardium, bauno, carabao,
  drupe, fruit, oriole, pepper
MANGROVE: catechu, goran
pole: bority
MANIA: bug, delirium, **passion*
comb.: itis, opio
MANIAC: **insane, *mad, *violent*
MANIFEST: **definite,* list, **open,
  *present, *show, *token*
MANIFESTO: edict, **law, *order*
MANIKIN: **dwarf, *model*
MANILA: *airfield:* clark
bay boat: bilalo
creek: estero
elemi: amyrin
hemp: abaca, cebu, linaga
hero: dewey
river: pasig
MANIPULATE: **maneuver, *use*
MANNA: ambrosia, gazangabin,
  godsend, nectar, **support*
MANNER: **air, *form, *kind,
  way
MANNERED: artificial, campy
MANTLE: **cover, *form, *spread*
MANTRA: **charm, *fetish, *spell*
hindu: atharva-veda
MANUFACTURE: **form, *make*
MANUSCRIPT: **copy, *piece,
  work
ancient: relic

* **Asterisk means to look up this word to find more answer words.**

mark: dorso, obelus
preservative: cedrium
unpublished: inedita
MANY: hoi polloi, *lots,* various
  comb.: multi, poly, vari
MAO TSE-TUNG: *wife:* chiang
  ching
MAORI: arawa, ati, *malay,* utu
MAP: atlas, chart, face, *plan
  copier:* pantograph
  maker: cartographer, mercator
  weather line: isobar
MAPLE: *cup:* mazer
  flowering: abutilon
  grove: camp
  sap: humbo
  seed: key, samara, wing
  spout or tap: spile
  tree: acer, box elder, mapau
MAQUEREAU: *prostitute, *wanton
MAR: *flaw, *hurt, *ruin, *spoil
MARAUD: invade, raid, *steal
MARBLE: *game:* agate, aggie, alley, dobie, doby, glassy, mib, mig(g), shooter, taw
  head: fulmar
  mosaic: tessera
  term: fulk
  slab: dalle, stele
  toning: genosis
  tool: boucharde
MARCH: *cyrus:* anabasis
  dates: ides, nones
  day's: etape
  horsemen: cavalcade
  king: sousa
  -land: frontier
  sisters: amy, beth, jo, meg
MARDUK: *enemy:* kingu
  love: erua, sarpanitu, zirbanit
MARE'S: *-nest:* hoax, *trick
  -tail: arks, cirrus, clouds
MARGIN: *edge, *end, *limit
  narrow: hair
  notched: erose
  note: apostil, scholium

purchaser: bull
reading: kere, kri
slope: cess
up: speculate
MARIJUANA: acapulco gold, bang, bhang, bleu de hue, broccoli, charas, churrus, dope, *drug,* ganja, gigglesmoke, grass, green (dragon), greenies, griffo, hashish, hay, hemp, joy smoke, kaif, keef, kef, kif(f), locoweed, narcotic, panama red, park lane number two, pleiku pink, pot
  cigarette: bambalacha, goof butt, gigglesmoke, greefa, griffo, indian hay, joint, mary jane, mary warner, mary weaver, mohasky, moocah, mooter, muggle, reefer, stick
  cigarette holder: crutch
  exporter: coyote, martha, painter, possum
  user: mugglehead, pothead
MARGOSA: melia, neem, nim
MARINER: *navy: man,* sailor
  ancient, cry: asail
  compass card: rose
  compass points: rhumbs
MARK: *aim, *badge,* band, bar, blaze, blot, brand, buist, bush, cairn, cancel, catstone, celebrate, chalk, character, check, cicatrix, coda, coin, cut, dapple, dent, designate, die, discolor, distinguish, dupe, *end,* emboss, engrave, evidence, express, figure, *flaw,* fleck, flick, freckle, gash, hack, hash, hatch, heed, *hurt,* importance, label, lentigo, letter, lighthouse, line, lozenge, *memorial,* menhir, *meter,* milepost, mole, *monument,* mottle, *name,* nevus, notch, note, notice, objective, observe, patch, pharos, *pierce,* pimple, point, price, print, proof, *record,* scar, score, scotch, scratch, scrive,

seal, *shame, *smear, speck, splash, *spoil, spoor, spot, stain, stamp, stigma, *strain, streak, striate, stripe, stroke, sully, *symbol, tally, target, tick, tilaka, *title, *token, trace, write
comb.: lineo
printing, punctuation, or reference: accent, apostrophe, asper, asterisk, bracket, breve, caret, caesura, cedilla, colon, comma, dagger, dash, dele, diaresis, diesis, dot, ellipse, erotema, finger, fist, guillemet, hand, hyphen, leader, letter, line, macron, obelisk, obelus, parallel, paren-(thesis), period, point, prime, question, quotation, semicolon, serif, slant, solidus, space, star, stet, tilde, tr, virgule
question: erotema, eroteme
quotation: guillemet
sectarian: bottu, tilaka
surveyor's: bench
twain: samuel langhorne clemens
MARKED: *big, *great, *open
MARKER: *memorial, *monument
MARMELADE: *quince:* codiniac
tree: achras, chico, mamey, mammee, sapodilla, sapote
MARPESSA: *abductor:* idas
MARRAKECH: gueliz, medina
park place: l'hivernage
MARRIAGE: *absence:* agamy
agreement: betrothal
broker: matchmaker, schatchen
comb.: gamo, hymen(o)
forswearer: bachelor, celibate
deity: frigg, hera, hymen, juno, pronuba, teleia, vor
hater: misogamist
husband, multiple: polyandry
lower class woman: anuloma
notice: banns
pert.: connubial, endogamic, hymeneal, marital, spousal

settlement: dot, dowry, mahr
symbol: sardonyx
wife, multiple: polyandry
MARS: *ares
band or belt: libya
comb.: areo
discoverer: hall
marking: canal, mare, oasis
moon: deimos, phobos
pert.: arean, martian
priests: deimos, salii
red: colcothat, totem
twin sons: remus, romulus
MARSH: *swale, *swamp
bird: auk, auklet, alca, alle, arrie, bittern, halycon, murre, snipe, sora, stilt
chickweed: bog stitchwort
comb.: helo, limno
crocodile: goa
elder: iva
fever: helodes, traidenum
gas: firedamp, methane, miasma
grass: *marsh: plant
hawk: bob glede, harpy, harrier
hen: rail
land: fen, maremma, muskeg, pontine, slew, sough, swale
marigold: boots, buttercup, bullflower, bull's-eye, caltha, caper, cowslip
pert.: miasmic, paludal, paludine, uliginous, uvid
plant: bulrush, caltha, catch fly, cattail, elatine, fescue, iva, reed, sedge, spart, tule
rosemary: cankerroot, moorwort
salt: corcass, salina
trefoil: bitter worm, bog bean
-wort: cranberry, sium
MARSHAL: *gather, *lead, *order
MARSILE: *followers:* blancandrin, clarin, estamarin, eudropin, guarlan, jouner, machiner, malbein, priamun
MARSUPIAL: *feature:* pouch
MARTINIQUE: *cigar:* bout

---

* Asterisk means to look up this word to find more answer words.

garment: jupee
volcano: pelee
MARTYR: saint, *torture
 first christian: stephen
 child: agnes
 4th century: blaise
 royal: charles
MARVELOUS: *great, *splendid
MARX BIBLE: communist manifesto
MARY: *brother:* lazarus
 husband: cleophas, clopas, joseph
 hymn: ave regina coelorum
 mother: anna, anne
 sister: martha
 son: jesus, john, mark
 queen of scots: bloody mary, bo
 peep, miss muffet, moppet
   disease: chlorosis, porphyria
   husband: darnley, stuart
   mother: mary of guise
   secretary: riccio
MARYLAND: *bird:* baltimore
 oriole
 flower: black-eyed susan, daisy
 founder: calvert
 nickname: old line state
 tree: white oak
MASADA: *builder:* king herod
 commander: eliezer ben yair
 defenders: zealots
 enemy: roma, silva, titus
 historian: josephus flavius
MASK: *cover, *disguise, *hide
 crest: onkos
 half: domino, loup
MASKANONGE: fish, longe
MASON: *door keeper:* tiler, tyler
 gear: hod
 order: templars
 tool: gurlet, hawk, rab, shim
MASS: *gather, *group, *meet,
 *quantity, *solid, *store, *unit
 basin: aquamanale, aquamanile
 dead: black mass, requiem
 directory: ordo
 music: agnus dei, credo, dona no-

bis, gloria, kyrie eleison
 pert.: missal, missatical, molar
MASSACHUSETTS: *bird:* chickadee
 flower: arbutus, mayflower
 mountains: berkshires, taconic
 nickname: old bay state
 oyster: cotuit
 port: boston, salem
 tree: american elm
MASSIVE: *great, *heavy, *solid
MASTER: artist, *defeat, *head,
 *lead(er), *lord, *principal
 card: ace, king, trump
 ceremonies: chairman, emcee
 comb.: arch, archi
 house: paterfamilias
 -mind: *make, *plan, *plot
 pert.: herile
 piece: coup, triumph, trump
MASTODON: *big, *demon,
 *great, monster
MATADOR: *bull fight or fighter
MATCH: *accord, *equal, *fit
MATE: *associate, *cap, *equal,
 *friend, spouse, twin, wife
MATERIAL: *cloth, *fabric, *important, *substance, vital
MATHEMATICS: *term:* aliquant,
 aliquot, analysis, apothem, arbalest, constant, cosh, cosine, digit,
 equal, faciend, figure, minus,
 multiplicand, nabla, nappe, number, operand, parameter, plus,
 quadrant, quaternion, radix, rep-
 tary, scalar, sech, sine, speck,
 surd, tanh, tensor, variable, vector, vernier, vessor
MATINEE IDOL: actor, darling,
 lion, star
MATTER: *affair, *problem, *tell
 law: res
 pert.: hylic
MATTING: bump, tatty
MATTOCK: adze, ax, hoe, twibil
MATURE: age, *grow, *old, ripen
MAUD: *hag, mule, plaid, rug

* **Asterisk means to look up this word to find more answer words.**

MAUDLIN: foolish, mushy, *silly
MAUL: *abuse, *beat, *hit, *hurt
MAUSOLEUM: *memorial
MAUVE: lilac, purple, violet
MAVERICK: calf, stray, tyro
MAWKISH: nasty, stale, vapid
MAXIM: *adage, *rule, *truth
MAXIMUM: *all, *limit, *top
MAY: apple: barberry, mandrake
  bird: thrush
  cock: maypop, melon, plover
  curlew: whimbrel
  day: beltane, signal, *sos
  festival: ambarvalia, beltane
  first 11 days: borrowed days
  fish: bass killy, killifish
  flower: arbutus, cuckoo, haw-
    thorn, marigold, stitchwort
  flower sister ship: speedwell
  fly: dun, ephemerid
  fowl: whimbrel
  gowan: daisy
  haw: applehaw
  magic: weaverbird
  pear: shadbush
  pop: apricot, passion flower
  weed: anthemis, balder, balderis-
    brae, feverfew
MAYA: aguacatec, cho, pokonchi,
    yucatan, yucatec
  day: uayeb
  deity: acat, akanchob, akna,
    bacabs, backlum-chaam, chin,
    cukulcan, echua, hapikern,
    hunab-ku, itzamna, ixazaluoh,
    kinebahan, kisin, nohochacyum,
    usukun, uyitzin, xamaniquinqu,
    yantho, yuncemil
  history: chilam balam
  month: uninal
  period: baktun, haab, katun
  ruined city: calakmul
MAYENCE: count, ganelon
MEAD: hydromel, metheglin
MEADOW: bog, field, swale
  brook: bottle green
  flower: bluets, harebell

grass: poa
heroes, dead: asphodel fields
lark: medlar
mouse: arvicole, vole
parsnip: alexander
pea: angleberry
pippit: butty lark
saffron: colchicum, crocus
saxifrage: seseli
sweet: brideweed, bridewort,
    spirea, toadflax
MEAGER: *poor, *small, *thin
MEAL: ata, atta, bever, bite, bran,
    breakfast, bub, buffet, cena,
    chow, collation, cribble, dinner,
    eats, farina, feast, feed, flour,
    graddan, grain, grout, gurgeons,
    lunch(eon), masa, mess, mush,
    pinole, powder, ration, repast,
    sago, salep, supper, tea, tiffin
  ticket: breadwinner, *forte, job,
    patron, patsy, *skill
MEALY-MOUTHED: *false,
    *mean
MEAN: *abject, *argue, *average,
    *bad, betoken, breathe, caitiff,
    churlish, connote, contemplate,
    convey, denote, design, express,
    grudging, illiberal, imply, im-
    port, indicate, intend, intermedi-
    ate, irascible, *little, *low, ma-
    licious, measly, medial, medium,
    mercenary, miserly, parsimoni-
    ous, penurious, petty, *poor,
    *purpose, sense, shabby, signifi-
    cance, signify, *small, sordid,
    *sorry, spell, stingy, suggest,
    *value, venal, vile
  line: bisectrix
MEANDER: roam, stray, *turn
MEANING: *force, *purpose,
    *sense, *sign, *spirit, *value
  comb.: iatro, iatry
  pert.: literal, semantical
  science: semantics
MEANS: *agency, *agent, *asset,
    *instrument, *power, *supply

* Asterisk means to look up this word to find more answer words.

MEASURE: (*country involved)
*account, *estimate, *law,
*means, *model, *part, *quan-
tity, *share, *test, *trial, *try,
*value

MEASURING: *instrument:* alidade, caliper, container, chain,
gage, gauge, meter, ruler, scales,
tape, *value, yardstick

MEAT: *ball:* croquette, dumpling,
fricandel(le), ravioli, rissole
barbecued: kebab, sate
bony: scrag, spareribs
-cabbage fry: bubble and squeak
cured: bacon, biltong(ue), flitch,
ham, pastrami, pemmican, salami, sausage
cut: aiguillette, aitchbone, breast,
brisket, chop, chuck, clod, cold,
cutlet, filet, fillet, flank, ham, ice-
bone, knuckle, leg, loin, rasher,
rib, roast, round, rump, saddle,
shank, shoulder, sirloin, steak,
tenderloin
dealer: butcher
dish: fricandeau, goulash, haricot,
hash, lobscouse, mulligan, pasty,
potpie, pelmeni, ravioli, salmi,
stew
dried: *meat: cured
eater: carnivore
fat: speck, suet
ground: hamburger, rissole, sausage
inspection: bedikah
jelly: aspic
-less: fasting, lenten, maigre
outdoor cooked: barbecued
pie: bakemeat, pasty, pate pirozhki, rissole
potted: rillett(e)
raw: steak tartar(e)
raw-eating: omophagia
roasted: brede, cabob, kebob
sauce: a-one, caper, gravy, worces-
tershire
slice: collop

smoking place: bucan
stewed: haricot, ragout
unwholesome: cagmag
works: abattoir, slaughterhouse

MECCA: *deity:* hobal, hubal
first caliph: abu-bekr
governor: shereef, sherif
pilgrim garb: ihram
pilgrimage: hadj, hegira
shrine: caaba, kaaba, mosque

MECHAIEH: *joy, pleasure

MECHANICAL: ad-lib, automatic, banausic, extemporaneous, impromptu, involuntary,
pavlovian, perfunctory, spontaneous, stereotyped
man: automaton, golem, robot

MECHANISM: *machine,
*means, *instrument, *system,
*thing

MEDAL: *badge, *honor, *mark

MEDB: *consort:* ailill, conor

MEDE: aryan, mesne, *persian
city: ecbatana, rages
caste: magi
king: ahasuerus, arphaxad, cyax-
ares, deioces, evi, reba

MEDEA: *kin:* absyrtus, aeetes,
apsyrtus
lover: jason

MEDIAL: *mean

MEDIATOR: agent, referee, umpire

MEDICAGO: alfalfa, bur clover,
burgundy trefoil, butter jags,
calvary, caterpillars lucerne,
spanish trefoil

MEDICAL, MEDICINAL: aesculapian, curative, healing, iatric,
remedial, salutary, *surgeon
bark: cartex
berry: cubeb
capsule: cachet
comb.: algia, itis, oma
compound: hepar, iodine, pill,
serum, turpeth
discharge, comb.: cenosis

* **Asterisk means to look up this word to find more answer words.**

file: case, chart, history
fluid: serum
fruit: *medical: plant
group: ama
herb: *medical: plant
history: catamnesis, *file
institution: clinic, hospital
instrument: *surgeon: instrument
insurance: blue cross or shield
mint: bengal sage
officer: coroner
pioneer: aristotle, bernard, descartes, galen, harvey, hippocrates, imhotep, lister, pare, pasteur, vesalius
plant: agar, ajava, ajowa, alem, aloe, arabic, arnica, artar, boneset, chirata, cohosh, cola, cubeb, ergot, herb, ipecac, jalap, jena, kino, licorice, orris, rue, seneca, senega, senna, spurge, tansy, tisane, valerian
powder: catapasm
remedy: antidote, elixir, shot
solution: tincture
student: interne, resident
tablet: lozenge, pellet, pill, pilula, troche
water: bristol water
wax: cerate
MEDICINE: antidote, *balm, cure, dose, *drug, heal(er), liquor, profession, punishment, *remedy, *surgeon
comb.: iatric, iatro
god: aesculapius, asklepios, hippocrates, ningishzida, okuninushi
man: angekok, basir, curandero, doctor, intern, kahuna, lutern, magician, peay, physician, piache, piay, priest, resident, shaman, surgeon, voodoo, wizard
symbol: caduceus
MEDIEVAL: *coin:* bracteate
court costume: hawbuck harness

dagger: anlace
dandelion mix: taraxacum
drama: auto sacramental
ewer: aquamanale, aquamanile
fabric: acca, baldacchino, baudekin, brocade, samite
fiddle: giga
fort: carcassonne
galley: aesc, bireme, galiot
gown: chiton, cyclas
guild: hanse(atic league)
helmet: armet, heaume
lyric: alba
monster: werewolf
officer: bailli, vogt
prayer book: portass
receptacle: bahut
shield: ecu
shirt: bleaunt
tribunal: vehm
vessel: dromon
weapon: crossbow, gisarme, lance, oncin, *sword
MEDIOCRE: *bad, *poor
MEDIOCRITY: also-ran, loser, nobody, nonentity, so-so
MEDITATE: *plan, *study, *think
MEDITERRANEAN: della robia
boat: accon, felucca, galliot, mistico, nef, polacre, saic, settee, tartan, xebec, zebec
chicken: ancona
coast: riviera
dish: octopus, squid
falcon: lanner
fever: brucellosis
fish: aco, remora, sargo(n)
fruit fly: ceratitis
grass: diss
herb: acanthus, ammi, asphodel, aubrietia, bessera, borago, catananche, chicory, satureia
island: antikythera, candia, capri, crete, cyprus, ebusus, elba, gozo, ibiza, iviza, lesbos, lipari, majorca, malta, panaria, rhodes, sardinia, sicily, stromboli

---

* Asterisk means to look up this word to find more answer words.

liqueur: alkermes
pert.: levantine
plant: **herb,* arbutus, eucalyptus, euphorbia, lentisc, medlar, mimosa
shrub: caper
tree: azarole, carob, ceratonia, olea
wind: etesian, euroclyden, gregale, levanter, mistral, siroc(co), solano, tramontana
MEDIUM: **mean,* **mediocre,* middle
communication: bulletin, cable, magazine, mail, newspaper, periodical, phone, press, radio, telegraph, television
MEDLEY: air, bariolage, **melange*
MEDULLA: center, marrow, spine
MEDUSA: gorgon, jellyfish
child: chrysaor, pegasus
sister: euryale, stheno
slain by: perseus
MEED: **praise, *reward, *share*
MEERSCHAUM: seafoam, sepiolite
MEET: **answer,* approach, appropriate, butt, chance upon, combat, come across, conform, confront, converge, **cross,* encounter, **equal,* event, face, fall upon, **fit,* fulfill, game, **gather, *good,* greet, **hit,* intersect, light on, observe, pay, pop upon, proper, **rally,* rendezvous, **right,* satisfy, (**see*)*mly,* sit, stumble on, suffice, suitable
MEETING: **adjacent,* audience, assembly, body, cabal, confab, conference, conflux, congress, connection, consultation, convention, council, counsel, discussion, **fight,* gathering, **group,* hearing, huddle, indaba, interview, joining, junction, **near,* palaver, **rally,* parliament, reception, recontre, rendezvous, seance, session, synod, tribunal, tryst, **union*
site: amphitheatre, auditorium, hall, hotel, resort, room
MEGILLAH: jazz, **nonsense*
MEGRIM: ache, caprice, fad, hypochondria, migraine, vertigo
MEHUJAEL: *kin:* irad, methuselah
MEKONG: lantsang, **vietnam*
MELAMPUS: *son:* antiphates
MELANCHOLY: drear, **sad, *sorry*
MELANESIA: *deity:* adaro, qat
native: fiji, papuan, santo
MELANGE: **hash, *mixture*
MELANION: hippomenes
wife: atalanta
MELANODENDRON: black cabbage tree
MELCHI: *son:* levi, neri
MELD: announce, **show, *unite*
MELEAGER: *accomplice:* atalanta
half-brother: tydeus
parent: althaea, oeneus
wife: cleopatra
MELEE: **contest, *fight, *riot*
MELISSEUS: *consort:* amaltheia
daughter: adrasteia, ida
MELLOW: **aged, *old, *rich, *soft, *sweet, *warm*
MELODIOUS: **happy, *mellow*
MELODY: **air, *harmony,* theme
pert.: ariose, plagal
sequence: melos, rosalia, round
unaccompanied: monody, solo
MELON: fruit, **gourd, *profit*
foot: ballfoot
-like ornament: amalaka
pear: pepino
rock: cantaloup(e), muskmelon
tree: papaya
MELPOMENE: *lover:* achelous
offspring: **sirens*
MELT: **affect, *escape, *move*

---

* **Asterisk means to look up this word to find more answer words.**

MEMBER: *part, *piece, *unit

MEMBRANE: caul, film, layer, sac
 comb.: amnio
 diffusion: osmosis
 fold: plica
 fringe: loma
 spore: intine

MEMENTO: curio, *token, trophy

MEMNON: *father*: tithonus
 founder: babylon walls, susa
 grandfather: hyperion
 mother: aurora, eos
 slayer: achilles
 victim: antilochus

MEMO: *note, *record, *report

MEMORIAL: arch, bauta, cairn, cenotaph, chronicle, column, cromlech, *cross, cyclolith, dolmen, gravestone, *letter, *mark(er), megalith, monolith, *monument, needle, obelisk, pillar, pyramid, *record, relic, reliquary, *ruin, shaft, shrine, slab, stele, stone, stupa, *symbol, tablet, testimonial, *token, tomb, tope, *tower, *work

MEMORY: fame, *glory, *honor
 aid: acetycholine, anemnestic, petite madeleine, rna
 book: album, diary, scrapbook
 goddess: mnemosyne
 loss: amnesia, aphasia, blackout, blank, lethe
 pattern: engram
 pert.: con, mnemonic, mnesic
 unit, computer: buffer
 vivid: eidetic

MEMPHIS: *deities*: dor, imhotep, nefertum, ptah, ra, sekhmet
 dominoes: dice

MEN: *group, *party, *people, soldiers, sons, *staff
 dread of: androphobia
 wise: *magi

MEND: better, fix, heal, *remedy

MENDACITY: *deception, *lie

MENDICANT: *ascetic, *monk

MENELAUS: *brother*: agamemnon
 daughter: hermione
 father: atreus
 steersman: canopus
 wife: helen

MENESTHEUS: *sire*: areithous
 son: apollonius

MENIAL: *mean, *servant, *slave

MENTAL: *disorder*: amentia, anoesia, anoia, aphasia, ataxia, brainstorm, hypochondria, idiocy, insanity, megalomania, melomania, neuritis, paranoia, paranomia, psychosis, schizophrenia
 discipline: yoga
 force: afflatus
 hygiene: psychiatry
 picture: *image
 suffering: calvary

MEPHISTO(PHELES): *demon, *devil

MEPHITIC: *bad, *evil, *rotten

MERARI: *kin*: judith, mahli, mushi

MERCENARY: abject, brabanter, condottieri, greedy, hack, hessian, hireling, janizary, *mean, myrmidon, sordid, venal

MERCHANDISE: goods, sell, *trade
 cheap: borax, camelot
 pert.: emporeutic

MERCHANT: *caste*: banyan, teli
 group: cartel, guild, hansa
 of venice: antonio
 role: jessica, lorenzo, nerissa, portia, shylock
 vessel: argosy, bilander

MERCILESS: *brutal, *hard

MERCURIAL: active, *fast, *quick

MERCURY: azoth, god, guide, hermes, hydrargyrum, messenger, newspaper, planet, quicksilver

---

* Asterisk means to look up this word to find more answer words.

alloy: ammiolite, calomel
son: cupid, eleusis
staff: caduceus
surface: artificial horizon
winged hat: petasos, petasus
winged shoes: talaria
MERCY: grace, *passion*, pity
goddess: kwannon
seat: bench
sword: curteen
MERE: lake, ocean, only, *small*
MERGANSER: *duck*, herald, nun
MERGE: *join*, *unite*, wed
MERIDIAN: *acme*, *top*, zone
MERIT: *mark*, *reward*, *value*
MEROPS: *son:* adrestus
MERRIMENT: gaiety, glee, *joy*
MERRY: *andrew:* *clown*, *fool*
dancers: aurora borealis
-go-round: carousel, carrousel
make: carnival, revel, wassail
thought: talisman, wishbone
trotter: seesaw, swing
wing: bufflehead, goldeneye
MESH: gear, net, *seize*, *trap*
MESMERIZE: hypnotize, spellbind
MESOGASTER: viscera, vitals
MESOLITHIC: *pert.:* azilian
MESOPOTAMIA: irak, iraq
boat: gufa, kufa
captives' place: halah
city: babylon, bagdad, basra, edessa, kerbela, mosul, urfa
diviner: balaam
king: chushanrishathaim
people: aramean, babylonian, chaldean, iraki, iraqi
river: euphrates, tigris
wind: shamal
MESS: befoul, blunder, botch, cauch, confusion, chow, clat, clutter, defile, disorder, err, farrago, feed, fiasco, fright, *hash*, higgledy-piggledy, hodgepodge, jumble, litter, meal, *mixture*, muddle, muss, predicament, *problem*, putter, *quantity*, scramble, *spoil*, tumble, untidiness, variety
MESSAGE: *note*, *report*, word
MESSALINA: *prostitute*, *wanton*
MESSENE: *king:* amarynceus
MESSENGER: *gods:* bhrugi, hermes, malachi, mercury, valkyrie
magazine: pacolet
mounted: cossid, courier, estafet(te), paul revere
MESSIAH: christ, prophet, savior
MESSINA: *evil:* charybdis, scylla
MESSY: every which way
MESTIZO: *cross*, *mixture*
METABOLISM: anabolism, catabolism, change, process
test: bmr
METAL: *mineral*
alloy: brass, bronze, matte, monel, niello, steel
arch: bow iron
band: bail
bar: gad, i-beam, ingot, risp
base: dross, matte, sprue
box: canister
capping: calotte
casting: pig
clippings: scissel
coat: armature, patina
cross: asteriscus
crude: ore
cutter: acetylene
decorate: damaskeen, emboss
decorating: etching, niello
decorative: tole
deposit: lode
disc: badge, medal, paten, tag
fastener: bolt, brad, cotter, nail, pin, rivet, screw
filings: lemel
film: patina
fissure: lode
hardness tester: brinnell
heavy: lead, osmium, uranium

* Asterisk means to look up this word to find more answer words.

impure: alloy, matte, regulus
layer: seam, stope
leaf: foil
lightest: lithium
lining: bush
mass: pig, nugget, ore, regulus
nonexpanding: invar
oblong piece: sow
patch: solder
plate: *metal: sheet
rare: cerium, erbium, gold, iridium, lutecium, platinum, terbium, uranium, yttrium
refuse: dross, scoria, slag
scrap: filing
shaper: swage
sheet: ampyx, apron, armor, foil, gib, lames, lamina, latten, plate, shim
sleeve: bushing
spike: gad
suit: armor, mail
tag: aglet, aiglet
unrefined: ore
ware: revere, tole
waste: recrement, *refuse
white: calcium, silver
work god: hephaestus, vulcan
worker: barman, riveter, smith, vulcan, welder
METAMORPHOSIS: change, mutation
suff.: ody
METAPHOR: analogy, *image
faulty: catachresis
prolonged: allegory
METASTASIS: anastrophe, change, chiasmus, hysteron, metathesis, palindrome, parenthesis, pypallage, synchysis, tmesis, transfer
METE: *allot, *dispense, *give
METEOR: aerolite, andromede, antlid, bielid, bolide, bolis, bottid, comet, cosmic dust, falling star, fireball, leonid
METEORITE: aerosiderite, argid,

asiderite, aurigid, baetulus
stony: achondrite
METER: accent, anapest, amphimacer, antibacchius, arsis, bacchius, beat, cadence, dactyl, epitrite, iambus, ictus, lilt, measure, molossus, pace, paeon, pulse, rhyme, rhythm, spondee, *stress, swing, *time, triseme, trochee
cubic: liter, litre, stere
millionth: micron
square: centare
unit: mora(e)
METHOD: *order, *plan, *plot, *rule, *style, *system, *way
METHUSELAH: *father:* enoch
grandson: noah
son: lamech
METHYL: *compounds:* acetol, acetonitrile, anisole, anserine, butanone, carbinyl, carbonium, cresol, cressol, nitrile, toluene
METICULOUS: *fine, *particular
METIER: *forte, *sphere, *work
METRIC: *meter
foot: anapest, arsis, choriamb, dipody, iamb(us), ionic, spondee, syzygy, trochee
METTLE: nerve, pluck, *spirit
MEW: cage, *cry, den, gull, molt
MEXICAN-AMERICAN: chicano, gringo, pachuco, pinto
battle: alamo, buena vista
defector: agringada, malinchista, tio taco, vendido
district: barrio
MEXICO: *agave:* datil, zapupe
annuity: censo
antelope: pronghorn
basket: otate
bean: frejol, frijole
bedbug: conenose
beetle: bookworm
beverage: chia, mescal, octli, pulque, tepache, tequila
bird: jacamar, jacana, tinamou, towhee, zopilote

* Asterisk means to look up this word to find more answer words.

blanket: serape
bread: pan
brigand: ladrone, villa
bull: toro
cactus: alfilerillo, alicoche, ba-
voso, chaute, chende, chichipe,
echinocereus, mescal
candlewood: ocotillo
carriage: arana
cat: eyra, margay
chaps, leather: chaparajos
cloak: manta, narica, serape
clover: coca
coin: adobe, azteca, centavo, peso,
piaster, tlaco
colonial city: guanajuato
conqueror: cortes, cortez
coral drops: bessera
cottonwood: alamo
dance: hat dance
dish: ahuatle, albondigas, atole,
burrito, camerone, chilaquilles,
chili verde, enchilada, menudo,
quesadilla, relleno, taco, tamale,
taquito, tortilla, tostada
dollar: peso
dove: inca
drug: damiana, jalap
early dweller: aztec, maya
farm laborer: bracero, peon
fern: bird's-nest moss
fiber: catena, datil, istle, ixtle,
pita, sisal
fish: bobo, lisita, salema, totuava
fox: zorro
garment: chirapa, manga, serape
god: *aztec: deity
gopher: quachil, tucan, tuza
grapefruit: toronja
grass: broomroot, deer, hanequin,
otate, zacaton
groundsel: geranium, senecio
gruel: atole
herb: gillyflower, marigold
hero: diaz, juarez
hog: peccary
house or hut: jacal

independence city: queretaro
indian: *mexico: people
ivy: cobaea
lake: chapala
landmark: senal
landowner: ranchero
laurel: madrona
lava field: pedregal
lizard: basilisk
masonry: adobe
mat: petate
measure: adarme, alma, almude,
arroba, baril, caballeria, carega,
carga, cuarteron, cuartillo, fanega, jarra, labor, legua, libra,
linea, marco, ochava, onza, pie,
pulgada, quintal, tercio, vara
medicine man: curandero
mixed blood: mestizo
mountain: citlaltepetl, ixtacci-
huatl, orizaba, popocatepetl
mullet: bobo, lisita
mush: atole
musical instrument: cabacas,
chiapanecas, clarin, guiros, ma-
racas
musician: mariachi
noble: tzin
novelist: azuela
octaroon: albino
onyx: tecali
orange: choisya
pack saddle: aparejo
painter: castellanos, rivera
palmetto: big thatch
pancake: arepa
peasant: peon
peninsula: yucatan
people: aztec, campesino, cora,
cuitlateca, haustec, huave, ixe,
lipan, mam, maya, mixtec,
nahau, opata, otomi, otonia, seri,
tarascan, tehuana, tepanec, toltec, totonaco, xova, yaqui, zaca-
tec, zapotec, zoque
persimmon: chapote
pine: ayacahuite, ocote, pinon

* Asterisk means to look up this word to find more answer words.

plant: acapulco, agave, agrito, amole, amolilla, cassia, chaute, chia, datil, jalap, maguey, sabadilla, salvia, sotol, tequila
plantation: hacienda
poet: balbuena
policeman: mordito, rurale
poppy: argemone
porridge: atole
president: aleman, arista, avila, calles, cardenas, carranza, diaz, echeverria, gil, herta, juarez, lopez-mateos, madero, ordaz
resin tree: drago
river: panuco, rio grande, tabasco
salamander: axolotl
saloon: cantina
sandal: guaracho, huarache
sauce: jalapena, tabasco
scarf: rebozo, serape, tapalo
seaport: acapulco, campeche, tampico, vera cruz
seed: jumping bean
shawl: rebozo, serape, tapalo
shrub: agarita, agrito, algerita, allthorn, amoreuxia, anagua, anama, anaqua, apache plume, azafran, ceiba, choisya, colima, escobeda
skunk: conepate
slums: barrios, vecindades
stirrup: tajoader
stirrup cover: tapadera
sugar: panocha
tea: alpasotes, apasote, basote, chenopodium
temple: teocalli
thong: romal
throwing stick: atlatl
tree: abeto, acxoyatl, ahuehuete, aliso, alnus, amapa, anacahuite, archipin, ayacahuite, canadulce, capulin, cascalote, chacte, colima, colorin, condalia, ebano, fustic, mezcal, ocote, parahancornia, sabino, sero
volcano: colima, jorullo, popocatepetl, tuxtla
worker: bracero, peon, wetback
yucca: isote
MIASMA: effluvium, malaria
MICA: alurgite, anomite, biotite, cat silver, damourite, diorite, glist, isinglass, lepidolite, muscovite, nacrite, silicate, talc
compound: astite, aviolite, lepidolite, ripidolite
son: ozias
trap: minette
MICAH: *son:* abdon, ahaz, melech, pithon, tahrea
MICHIGAN: *bird:* robin
flower: apple blossom
nickname: wolverine state
tree: white pine
MICKLE: *big, *great, many
MICRONESIA: *island:* bikini, ellice, gilbert, guam, kwajalein, majuro, palau, ponape, saipan, truk, wake
MIDAS: *benefactor:* dionysus
misfortune: ass's-ears
parent: cybele, gordius
river: pactolus
touch: philosopher's stone
MIDDLE: *core, *mean, *medium
ages, pert.: medieval
class: bourgeoisie
class man: babbitt, bourgeois
comb.: medi, mes(o)
ear: tympanum
east: *levant
man: *agent, broker, dealer
principles: axiomata media
toward: mesad, mesiad
MIDGE: *bit, *dwarf, fish, fly
MIDIAN: *king:* evi, hur, reba, zalmunna, zebah, zur
son: abida, eldaah, ephah, epher, hanoch, henoch
MIDSUMMER NIGHT'S DREAM: *role:* egeus, hermia, oberon, puck, quince, snout, snug, theseus

* Asterisk means to look up this word to find more answer words.

MIEN: *air, *look, *way
MIFF: aggravate, *anger, *fight
MIGHT: force, *power, *strength
MIGHTY: *big, *great, *impor-
  tant, *strong, *violent
MIGRAINE: *ache, cephalgia
MIKADO: *ruler, sovereign
  court: dairi, dairo
  role: koko, nankipoo, poohbah
MIKE: gobo, loaf, speaker
MILCAH: kin: haran, huz, nahor,
  rebekah
MILD: *gentle, *kind, *warm
MILETUS: kin: aria, byblis
MILFOIL: ahartalav, yarrow
MILIEU: purlieu, *sphere
MILITARISTIC: belligerent, jingo
MILITARY: *army
  command: achtung, at ease, attention, halt
  drive: advance, anabasis, big
  push, breakthrough, penetration
  engine: *engine: war
MILK: and honey: prosperity
  coagulator: rennet, rennin
  coagulated: curd
  comb.: lacti, lacto
  curd: casein, tayir, zeiga
  curdled: clabber, yogurt
  fat: butter, spread
  fat measurer: butyrometer
  fermented: kefir, koumis, kumiss,
  lacto, matzoon
  fever: cerebral anemia
  first: beestings, colostrum
  fish: awa, chanos, savola
  float: bungey
  food: lacticinia
  -less: barren, eild, yeld
  mouse: spurge
  pail: bowie, eshin, soa, soe
  part: casein, lactose, plasma,
  serum, whey
  pert.: *milky
  plant: creeper, euphorbia
  sap: latex
  separator: creamer

shop: creamery, dairy, lactarium
sickness: alkali disease
skimmed: lanital
sop: cockney, coward, drip, effeminate, milquetoast, mollycod-
  dle, sissy, weakling
sour: blinky, bonnyclabber, curd,
  whey, whig
sugar: lactose
test: babcock
vetch: bird-egg pea
weed: acerates, araujia, asclepias,
  butterfly family, hoya, swallow-
  wort
weed fluid: latex
weed tuft: coma
whey: serum
wood: paperbark
MILKY: adularescent, chalky,
  filmy, galactic, *gentle, lactic,
  opaline, pearly, *soft
  way: galaxy, heavens, nebula
MILL: *beat, *fight, *machine,
  *plant, *press, typewriter
  beetle: cockroach
  bill: adz
  clapper: chatterbox
  end: remnant
  -foil: ahartalav
  pond: binnacle, dam, dike, sea
  race: binnacle, flow, lade
  rind: moline
  run: flow, *average, ordinary
  sail: vane
  stone: *affliction, albatross, burden, burr, grinder, rynd
  stream: fleam
  -town: sedative, tranquilizer
  wheel part: awe, ladle
  work: backband
  worker: batterman
MILLENNIUM: good times,
  *paradise, *utopia
MILLET: arzun, buda, emu, joar,
  juar, koda, proso, zaburro
  broom-corn: hirse, kadikane
  painting: the angelus

---

* Asterisk means to look up this word to find more answer words.

pearl: bajra, bajree, bajri
pert.: miliary
seed drink: bosa, boza(h)
MILLIMETER: *1/1000th:* micron
MILLION: fortune, many, pile
elephants, land of: laos
millions: trega, trillion
thousand: milliard
MILTON: *speech:* areopagitica
MIME, MIMIC: *act, *copy,
*play
MINAEAN: *sun god:* athtar
MINCE: *hash, smirk, *walk
MIND: animus, attend, beware,
brain, care, chit, *complain, *desire, faculty, hear, heed, inclination, intellect, intelligence, intend, intent, memory, mood,
*note, notice, nous, obey, object,
observe, opinion, psyche, *reason, reck, *sense, soul, *spirit,
tend, *think, *will, wish, wits
comb.: menti, noo
cure: psychotherapy
elevation: anagogue
peace of: ataraxia
reading: esp, telepathy
MINDANAO: *philippine
MINE: *air passage:* brattice
basket: corf
car: buggy, tram
ceiling: astel, nog
coal: rob
deposit: lode, placer, vein
engine: barney
entrance: adit, portal, stulm
excavation: stope
floor: sill
guardian: *gnome
partition: sollar, soller
prop: nog, sprag, stull
railroad: coal road
refuse: attle, goaf, gob, slag
reservoir: standage, sump
rich: bonanza, golconda, lode
roof (support): astel, nog
shaft drain: sump

shaft support: sollar, soller
shaft step: stempel, stemple
sifter: lue
surface: placer
sweeper: paravane
tender: trapper
thrower: minenwerfer, minnie
tub: corf
unsystematically: gopher
vehicle or wagon: tram
vein: roke
worker: cager, canary, onsetter
MINER: argonaut, butty, collier,
digger, driller, forty-niner, pan-
ner, prospector, sourdough
anemia: ancylostomiasis
consumption: phthisis
lamp: davy
pickaxe: bede, flang, mandrel
surveying instrument: dial
worm: hookworm
MINERAL: *metal
adamantine: diamond
alkaline: trona
amorphous: pinite
black: cerine, coal, graphite,
hematite, irite, knopite, minguet-
ite, niobite, yenite
blue: beryl, iolite
brittle: euclase
brown: cerine, egeran, elaterite,
lederite, rutile
comb.: ite, lite
crystalline: apatite, boracite, diamond, dolomite, elaterin, feldspar, galena, garnet, mica, pyrites, quartz, spar, topaz
deposit cavity: voog, vugg
fibrous: asbestos, oakenite
flaky: mica
gray: chromium, edenite, trona
green: alalite, apatite, demantoid,
epidote, erinite, prasine, uralite
hard: adamant, corundum, diamond, ruby, spinel(le)
jelly: vaseline
lustrous: blendes, smaltine, smal-
tite, spar

* Asterisk means to look up this word to find more answer words.

magnetic: lodestone
mixture: magma
non-combustible: asbestos, mica
non-metallic: boron, gangue, iodine, spar
oil: colza, *oil: mineral*
organic: asphalt, coal, tar
rare: *metal: rare*
red: balas, garnet, rutile
salt: alum
soft: gypsum, salt, talc
spot: macle
spring: aqua, bath, spa, well
tallow: hatchettine
tar: asphalt, brea, maltha
transparent: fluor, mica
vitreous: apatite, quartz, spar
water: pullna, selzer, vichy
wax: baikerite, ozocerite
yellow: epidote, pyrite, sulfur
MING: *dynasty hero:* hai jui
MINGLE: *join, *stir, *unite
MINIATURE: *copy, *dwarf, elzevir, *image, *little, puppet, *small
MINISTER: aid, officer, serve
MINNESOTA: *bird:* common loon
flower: lady's-slipper
iron range: cuyuna, mesabi, vermilion
nickname: gopher, north star
tree: norway pine
MINOS: *brother:* rhadamanthys, sarpedon
children: androgeus, ariadne, catreus, phaedra
consort: pasiphae, scylla
parent: europa, zeus
slayer: cocalus
stepfather: asterius
MINOTAUR: asterius
parent: bull, pasiphae
slayer: theseus
MINSTREL: bard, troubadour
show term: bones, olio
society: areoi, arioi
13th century: goliard

MINT: *form, *make, *source
genus: melissa, mentha, moluccella, nepeta
levy: brassage, seigniorage
MINUSCULE: *little, *small
MINUTE: *fine, *little, *small
MINUTEMAN: missile, pioneer
air base: malmstrom, whiteman
MINYAE: *king:* athamas
MINYAS: *daughter:* alcithoe, arsippe, leucippe
MIRACLE: cana, fatima, lourdes
worker: balshem, *magician
MIRANDA: *father:* prospero
MIRE: addle, mud, swamp, *wet
MIRIAM: *kin:* aaron, hur
MIRROR: glass, *image, *model
pert.: catoptric(al)
MIRTH: *fun, *joy, *laugh
god: comus, komos
MISANTHROPE: cynic, hater, miser
MISCELLANY: *hash, *mixture
MISCHIEF: *bad, *evil, *trouble
deities: ate, eris, loke, loki
MISCREANT: *criminal, *hoodlum
MISCUE: *error, *flaw, *sin
MISDEED: *error, *sin, *wrong
MISDEMEANOR: *error, *sin
MISER: churl, codger, muckworm, shylock, skinflint, uriah heep
MISERABLE: *bad, *mean, *poor, *sick, *worthless
MISERY: *hurt, *pain, *sorrow
valley: baca
MISFEASANCE: *error, *sin
MISFIT: chotchke, schlemiel
MISFORTUNE: *accident, blow
MISGIVING: *alarm, *anxiety
MISH-MASH: *hash, *mess, *mixture
MISHAP: *accident, *catastrophe
MISHNAH: scripture, talmud
complement: baraithas, gemara
pert.: mishnaic, tannaic
section: aboth, halakoth, koda-

* **Asterisk means to look up this word to find more answer words.**

shim, massekhtoth, moed, na-
shim, nezikin, perakim, pirke
aboth, sedarim, tohoroth, zeraim
supplement: tosephta
MISINTERPRET: *err, garble
MISLEAD: *betray, *fool
MISMANAGE: *err, fumble
MISPRONUNCIATION: cacol-
ogy
MISS: *avoid, *error, girl, lose,
*need, oversight, skip
MISSILE: ammunition, arrow, assegai, ball, bola, bolt, bomb,
bullet, cartridge, dart, grenade,
knobkerrie, outcast, projectile,
*rocket, sinker, *spear, sprint,
weapon
ball-rope: bola
guided: *rocket: names, terms
pert.: ballistic
satellite launch: blue scout
spotter: dew, msr, par
tapered base: boattail
target, striking: bull's-eye
MISSING: awol, lost, truant
MISSION: *end, *fate, objective
MISSISSIPPI: big muddy, father
of waters
bird: mockingbird
fish: crapet, crappie, deerhorn
flatboat: ark
flower: magnolia
marbles: dice
nickname: bayou, magnolia, mud-
cat state
source: itasca
MISSIVE: *note, *record, *report
MISSOURI: *bird:* bluebird
flower: hawthorn
gourd: calabazilla
grape: catbird
hummingbird: ass
nickname: bullion, show me
skylark: pipit
tree: flowering dogwood
MIST: cloud, dim, fog, haze
flower: blue boneset

goddess: nephele
MISTAKE: *error, *mess, *sin
date: anachronism
printing: errata
sport: foul
syntax: solecism
MISTER: baboo, babu, don, good-
man, herr, man, messieur, mian,
monsieur, pan, sahib, senor, signor, sir(e), *title
MISTREAT: *abuse, violate
MISTRESS: beebe, bibi, dame,
dulcinea, first lady, frau, frau-
lein, goodwife, governess, housewife, madame, mademoiselle,
matron, mother, mrs, senora,
senorita, signora
MISUNDERSTANDING: *error,
*fight, *quarrel
MISUSE: *abuse, pervert
MITE: *bit, coin, *trifle
comb.: acaro
MITER: *cap, *hat, *symbol
MITIGATE: *ease, *temper
MIX: *associate, *fight, *join,
*mess, *stir, *temper, *unite
MIXTURE: adulteration, amalgam, assortment, babel, baluga,
blend, cacophony, cafuso, cattalo, chowchow, citrange, coales-
cence, combination, combo, composite, composition, compound,
conglomeration, crossbreed, cur,
dustee, eurasian, farrago,
fusion, fustee, griffe, griqua,
halfbreed, *hash, heterogeneous,
high yellow, *hybrid, jumble,
kelt, ladino, magma, marabou,
mash, melange, merger, *mess,
mestee, mestizo, metis(se), mis-
cegenation, miscellany, mongrel,
mulatto, mustee, mux, octoroon,
odds and ends, paste, pasticcio,
patchwork, plumcot, pomato,
quadroon, quintroon, sacatra,
salad, sambo, scramble, tangelo
MIZPAH: *ruler:* colhozeh, jeshua

* Asterisk means to look up this word to find more answer words.

MNEMOSYNE: *children:* *muses

MOAB: *city:* arnon, aroer, baal-meon, bethjeshimoth, bethmeon, bozrah, elealeh, heshbon, holon, horonaim, kerioth, kir, kirheres, kiriathaim, jahaz(ah), luhith, mephaath, misgab, nebo, sihon, ur, zoar
giant: emim, etym, zuzim
god: chemosh
king: balak, eglon, malak
mountain: nebo
woman, famous: ruth

MOAN: **complain, *cry, *suffer*

MOAT: defense, **waterway*

MOB: **group, *press, *set*
impersonation: blatant beast
law or rule: anarchy, violence

MOBILIZE: **gather, *start*

MOBSTER: **criminal, *hoodlum*

MOCK: **copy, *deceive, *false, *insult, *taunt*
blow: feint
cypress: fraxinella, wahoo
orange: seringa, syringe

MOD: craze, fad, garish, gauche, neo, offbeat, outre, **weird*

MODE: **style, *system, *way*

MODEL: anatomy, ancestry, archetype, **copy,* drawing, example, **form, *make,* manikin, mockup, paradigm, paragon, pattern, **perfect, *plan,* pose, prototype, **rule,* sit(ter), standard, subject, type

MODERATE: **abate, *cool, *dull, *slow, *small, *temper*

MODERATOR: judge, referee

MODERN: **fresh,* groovy
movement: hippie, pop-drug

MODEST: **good, *shy, *small*

MODIFY: **adapt,* increase, **limit*

MODULATE: **modify, *temper*

MOGUL: **lord, *magnate, *ruler*
capital: agra
ruler: akbar, aurungzeb, babar
tent: yurt

MOHAMMED: mahomet, mahoud, mahound, mahund, mohomet, muhammad
associates: ashab
birthplace: mecca
child: ali, fatima
descendant: ali, hasan, hosein, husain, ibrahim, said, sayid, seid, shereef, sherif
father: abdallah
flight: hegira, hejira
follower: wahabi, wahhabi
horse: alborak
successor: calif, caliph
supporters: ansar
title: ali, imam
tomb: medina
uncle: abbas, abu-talib
wife: aisha, ayesha(h), khadija

MOHAMMEDAN: abdal, aga, agha, dervish, islamite, **moor-(ish)*, moslem, motazilite, muslim, mussulman, saracen, shiah, shiite, sufi, sunnite, wahabi
ablution: widu, wudu, wuzu
alexandria sect: senussi
angel: azrael, israfil, isrefel
ascetic: fakeer, fakir, **sufi*
bazaar: sook
belt: zonar, zonnar
berber dynasty: hafsid, hafsite
bible: alcoran, coran, **koran*
bier: tabut
blacksmith: lohar
blood relationship: nasab
calendar: jumada, mulharram, rabia, rajab, ramadan, safar, shaban, shawwal, zulhijah, zulkadah
caravansary: imaret
caste: mopla(h)
city, sacred: mecca, medina
cloak: albornoz, jubbah
coin: altun, dinar
college or council: ulema
convert: ansar, mured
covenant ark: tabut

---

* **Asterisk means to look up this word to find more answer words.**

creed: sunna
crusade: jehad, jihad
decree: irade
demon: afreet, afrit, eblis, genie, jann, jinnee, jinni, shaitan, sheitan
dervish: sadite, santon
diadem: taj
divorce: ahsan, hasan, mubarat, talak
drinking cup: lotah
dynasty, first: bahmani(d)
easter: eed
fast: ashura, ramadan
festival: bairam, eed
finance minister: dewan
free thinker: aladinist
garment: bourkha, burga, burka, burkha, ihram, isar, izar, jama(h), jubbah, jupon, kamis
god: allah
guide: pir
headdress: fez, kulah, kullah, taj, tarbush, turban
heaven: alfardaws, assama, falak al aflak
heaven and hell boundary: alaraf
holy man: imam, imaum
infidel: kaffir, kafir, rayan
interpreters, body: ulema
jerusalem captor: omar
judge: cadi, caid, cazi, cazy, hakim, imam, imaum, kadi, kazy, qaid
kartvelian tribe: laz
kinship: nasab
lady: begum, tola
law: adat, halal, sheriat, sunna
lawyer: mufti
malay: sassak
market: souk
marriage: mahr, mota, muta
mendicant: fakeer, fakir
men's quarters: selamlik
messiah: mahdi
minaret crier: muezzin
monastery: tekke

mosque: masjid
musical instrument: rebab
mystic: sufi
nymph: houri
orthodox: hanif, sunnite
people: bazigar, dehgan, egyptian, hanif, isawa, laz(i), moro, salar, samal, senusite, sufi, swat(i), turk
physician: hakeem, hakin
pilgrim: hadji, haji, hajji
prayer: namaz, salat
prayer call: adan, azan
prayer place: idgah, mosque
priest: *ecclesiastic: muslim
priests body: ulema
principle: ijma
property grant: wakf, waqf, wukf
purification: abdest, wudu
reformer: wahabi
relationship, blood: nasab
religion: islam
ruler: aga, agha, ameer, amir, begum, calif, caliph, datto, emir, hakeem, hakim, imam, kalif, kaliph, khan, mian, mir(za), mufti, nawab, nizam, rais, reis, sayid, sheik, shereef, sherif, sidi, sultan, syed, tola, vali, vizier, vizir, wali
sacred book, scripture: *koran
saint: pir
sect: abadite, ahmadi(ya), almohades, almoravides, ibadite, wahabi
seminary: madras(a), ulema
shrine: kaaba, kaabeh, *mosque
slave: mameluke
student: softa, ulema
teacher: alfaqui, alim, imam, molla(h), mujtahid, mullah, pir
title: *judge, *ruler, *teacher
tomb: pir, taboot, tabut
uncle: abbas, abu, talib
weight: rotl
women's quarters: harem
MOHICANS: *last of:* uncas

* **Asterisk means to look up this word to find more answer words.**

MOHURI: *gold:* ahmadi, ahmedi
MOIETY: middle, *part*, *share*
MOIL: soil, spot, wet, *work*
MOISTEN: *moil*, *temper*, *wet*
MOLASSES: melada, sugar
MOLD: *form*, *kind*, *make*, *mixture*, *model*, stamp
MOLDAVIA: balta, iasi, *rumania*
MOLDING: *box:* babbitting jig
  concave: cavetto, coving, gula, oxeye, scotia
  combination: ledgement
  convex: astragal, baguet(te), boltel, boutel(l), bowtel(l), ovolo, ovulo, reeding, torus
  curved: cyma, nebule, ogee
  disk-ornamented: bezantee
  edge: aris, arris
  egg-shaped: ovolo, ovulo
  flat: fillet
  hollow: scotia
  narrow: fillet, listel, reglet
  ogee: cyma, gola, gula, talon
  pedestal: surbase
  projection: coving
  rounded: billet, ovolo, torus
  rule: screed
  s-shaped: ogee
  square: listel
  wavelike: cyme, nebule, ogee
MOLDY: fusty, musty, *old*
MOLE: fault, *mark*, quay, *tower*
  cricket: churrworm, talpa
  -like mammal: desman, tape
  rat: nesokia
MOLECULE: *bit*, *part*, *trifle*
  component: anion, atom, ion
MOLEST: *attack*, *trouble*
MOLLIFY: *abate*, *temper*
MOLLUSK: *bivalve:* chama, clam, cockle, conch, leda, mussel, oyster, scallop, spat, venerid
  double-shelled: limpet
  edible: abalone, asi, clam, mussel, oyster, snail
  eight-armed: octopus
  extinct: ammonoid

  fresh water: chiton, etheria, mussel
  gastropod: abalone, slug, snail, taenioglossa, whelk
  genus: arca, astarte, buccinum, eolis, ledum, murex, nerita, oliva
  gills: cerata
  group: pteropod
  heteropod: atlanta
  highest class: argonaut
  hinge: articulus
  large part: mantle
  largest: chama
  larval: veliger
  marine: abalone, amphineura, asi, murex, nautilus, scallop
  one shell: snail
  rasp organ: radula
  shell: cowrie, cowry, testa
  shell concretion: pearl
  shell-less: slug
  teeth: radula
  ten-armed: squid
  univalve shell: cowrie, cowry
  wrinkled shell: cockle
  young: spat
MOLUCCA: balm, bells of ireland, shellflower
  island: amboina, banda, ceram, maluku
MOMENT: breathing, gravity, influence, instant, period
  of truth: anagnorisis, *crisis*, denouement, epiphany
MOMZER: impudent, scalawag
MONAD: *bit*, *part*, *unit*
MONARCH: despot, *leader*, *ruler*
MONASTERY: abbey, badia, bonzery, cell, cenoby, certosa, church, cloister, convent, friary, gompas, hospice, lamasery, mandra, math, minster, nunnery, priory, ribat, sanctuary, tekke, tekya, tera, vihara
  apartment: calefactory
  haircut: tonsure

* Asterisk means to look up this word to find more answer words.

head: abbott, archimandrite, hegumen, prior
layman: oblate
librarian: armarian
pert.: celibate, cenobitic
republic: athos
room: cell
visitor: definitor
MONEY: actual, ante, ballast, bankroll, beans, bees and honey, berries, bills, blunt, bones, bonus, boodle, booty, brass, bread, bucks, bullets, bunce, cabbage, capital, cash, certificate, chink, chips, clinkers, coin(age), crap, cush, dibs, dinero, dollars, dough, dust, filthy lucre, finance, folding stuff, gate, gelt, gilt, gingerbread, glue, grease, green stuff, grig(s), ichor, jack, jake, juice, kale, lar(n), legal tender, lettuce, loot, lucre, marbles, mazuma, mint(sauce), mopus, moss, muck, notes, ochre, oil, ointment, oof, pelf, plunks, potatoes, property, remedy, rhino, rocks, root of evil, salt, sap, sauce, scrip, *shell: money*, specie, spondulics, stakes, sugar, *supply*, talent, tender, tin, *value*, wampum, wealth
bag: purse
bags: capitalist, follicle
blood: breaghe, cro, wergild
box: arca, drawer, safe, till
bribe: boodle, payola
bronze: aes
bug: economist
certificate: bond, check, scrip
changer: argentarium, banker, broker, cambist, seraf, shroff
changing: agio
chest for: brazier
coined: minted, specie
counterfeit: boodle, queer
cowrie: shells
down: cash, cod, deposit

earnest: arles, arrha, deposit, handgeld, handsel, *token*
exchange fee: agio
found: treasure, trove
gamblers: barato
gift: alms, bequest, charity, endowment
grubber: miser
hearth: fumage
hook: larin, larree
lender: banker, creditor, loanshark, lumberer, mahajan, pawnbroker, shylock, uriah heep, usurer
manual: cambist
much: *quantity*
oversupply: inflation
paper: flimsy, kale, lettuce
power: almighty dollar
premium: agio
ready: alcontado, *asset*, cash, darby
receiver: cash register, safe
roll: rouleau, wad
small amount: chicken feed, mite, peanuts
standard: banco, gold, specie
without: bankrupt, broke, flat, hungry, hurting, impecunious, impoverished, pinched, *poor*, poverty-struck
MONGER: dealer, mercer, trader
MONGOL: *ass:* chigetai
buddhist leader: bodgo gegen
capital: urga
caravan leader: bashi
city: kobdo, ulan bator, urga
coin: mungo, tugrik
conjuror: shaman
conqueror: genghis kahn, tamerlane, timour guragen
desert: gobi, ordos
dynasty: yuan
fuel: argal, argol, argul
liquor: chi
people: aimak, annamese, aymak, buriat, buryat, chud, eleut(h),

* Asterisk means to look up this word to find more answer words.

garo, kalmuck, khalkha, lai,
lapp, rai, shan, sharra, tartar,
tatar, yacoot
priest: shaman
religion: confucianism, shamanism, shintoism
river: onon, pei(ho)
ruler: dua
tent: yurt
MONGREL: *cross, *mixture
MONIKER: *name, *title
MONITOR: advise, mentor, warn
lizard: anoli, uran, varan(us)
MONK: abbacomes, abbate, abbe,
ajivika, anchorite, ar(a)hat, *ascetic,* bairagi, baldicoot, beadsman, bhikk(sh)u, bonze, breviger, brother, caloyer, celibate,
cenobite, conventual, dandy, dervish, fakir, friar, hieromonach,
lama, lohan, *mendicant,* monas-
tic, padre, palmer, pilgrim, pillarist, pongyi, prior, religieux, santon, stylite, sufi, talapoin
cap: kulah, kullah
cell: kil
fish: angel shark, butterfly fish,
spade fish, squatinid
franciscan: capuchin
greek church: caloyer, starets
hair cut: tonsure
habit: analabos
hood: amice, atis, cowl
librarian: armarian
parrot: loro
settlement: scete, skete
MONKEY: *arboreal:* grivet, titi
bear: koala
bearded: entellus
beautiful: guereza, mona
bonnet: toque, zati
bread: baobab tree
business: *monkeyshines
callicebus: yapock, yapok
capuchin: sai, sapajou
cebine: sai
diana: roloway

entellus: hanuman, hoonoomaun
flower: mimulus, toadflax
genus: alouatta, cebus
god: hanuman
grivet: tota, waag
guenon: mona, nisnas, vervet
hand: ass's-foot, coltsfoot
howling: alouatta, araba, araguato, gauriba, stentor
king: bali, ramayana
large: sajou
long-tailed: entellus, guenon,
langur, maha, patas, sai, tela-
poin, wanderoo
macaque: rhesus
nut: peanut
pot: fruit
proboscis: kaha, noseape
purple-faced: wanderoo
puzzle: pinon
rhesus: bandar
rigged: trimmed
saki: couxia, couxio
sapajou: sai
shines: antics, buffoonery, horse-
play, pranks, tricks
small: apelet, apeling, lemur, marmoset, teetee, titi
spider: ateles, belzebuth, coaita
squirrel: marmoset, saimiri
tailless: ape
with: interfere, meddle
MONK'S-HEAD: dandelion
MONKSHOOD: aconite, atees,
atis, bearbane, wolfsbane, woodbane
MONOGRAM: *letter, *name,
*sign
MONOPOLIZE: *absorb, *control
MONOPOLY: *trust
MONOTONOUS: *dull, uniform
MONSTER: *big, *demon, *devil,
*giant references, *hoodlum
comb.: terat(o)
famed: argus, bagwyn, basilisk,
bucentaur, *centaur, charybdis,
chimera, dragon, echidna, ger-

* Asterisk means to look up this word to find more answer words.

yon, *giant, griffin, hydra, kraken, lamassu, lamia, manticore,
minotaur, ogre, pegasus, pistrix,
sagittary, satyr, scylla, silenus,
sphinx, *titan, typhon, unicorn
female: *gorgon, *harpy, medusa
fire-breathing: chimera, dragon
green-eyed: envy, jealousy
handless: acheirus
headless: acephalus
independent: autosite
legless: api, apus
lion's head: chimera
man-bull: bucentaur, minotaur
man-horse: centaur, ghandharva
medical: teras
nine-headed: hydra
pert.: taratoid
serpent: dragon, ellops
short-limbed: nanomelus
single: autosite
two-bodied: disomus
two-headed: dicephalus
winged: harpy
woman-bird: siren
woman-serpent: echidna
MONSTROUS: *bad, *big, *evil,
*great, *large, *ugly
MONTANA: *bird:* meadowlark
flower: bitterroot
nickname: big sky country, bonanza state, treasure state
tree: ponderosa pine
MONTH: *calendar excess:* epact
comb.: meno
first day: calends, kalends
following: proximo
half: fortnight
preceding: ultimo
present: instant
MONUMENT: bilithon, figure,
lech, *memorial, menhir, plaque,
*record, statue, stele, tabut,
*tower, *work
MONUMENTAL: *big, *great,
*large
MOOCH: beg, *idle, *steal

MOOD: *sense, *spirit, *state,
*style, *temper
MOON: *idle, languish, *look
-ack: woodchuck
age: epact
angel: mah(i)
area: barrow, mare
basin: mare
beam: ray
bill: duck
calf: dolt, dunce, *fool, monster
crater: euler, linne, plana
creeper: *moonflower, *moonseed
crescent: cusp, horn, isis
descending node: catabibazon
distance: apsis
dog: halo
down or fall: moonset
-eye cisco: bloater
fern: *moon: wort
festival: neomenia
first quarter: crescent
fish: opah, spadefish, sunfish
flight: *moon: shot
flower: achete, calonyction, daisy,
oxeye
geographer: selenographer
god: aah, ensu, khensu, khons,
kuu, nannar, sin, thoth, toth
goddess: artemis, astarte, bendid,
chango, cynthia, diana, hecate,
hekate, hengo, io, isis, lucina,
luna, men, neith, ngame, orthia,
phoebe, salena, selene, sin,
tanit(h)
gorge: alpine valley
halo: bur(r)
horn: cusp
inhabitant: selenite
january first: epact
jellyfish: aurelia, chrysalis
-landing vehicle: eagle
lighting: bootlegging, job, racket,
raid
lily: moonflower
mad: *insane, lunatic
man: gipsy, robber

* **Asterisk means to look up this word to find more answer words.**

mansion: alnath, cancer
mock: paraselene
module: columbia, eagle, intrepid
mountains: altai, altay, apennine, haemus, jura
new: phasis
new year's age: epact
observing instrument: senoscope
orbit phase: anabibazon
perigee: apsis
pert.: lunar, selenic
phase: full, gibbous, horning
picture: selenograph
point: cusp, horn
  farthest from earth: apogee
  nearest earth: perigee
position: octant
raking: woolgathering
rocks: grapefruits
seed: anamirta, arbuta, calycocarpum, cupseed, vine
-shaped: cynthian, lunate
shine: liquor, *nonsense
shot: *astronaut
shot term: alsep, aristarchus, ascent, boot hill, censorinus, copernicus, diamondback, fra munro, impact, lrl, manetometer, mount marilyn, ocean of storms, sea of storms, sea of tranquility, seismometer, serenity, spectometer, surveyor, tycho, vulcanism
sick: *insane, *mad
spots: baily's beads
station: botein
stone of commerce: adularia, albite, feldspar, hecatolite, orthoclase
struck: *insane, *mad
valley: rille, sonoma
walking: eva, extra-vehicular activity
wort: botrychium, grape fern
MOOR: bedouin, berber, *mohammedan, moroccan, othello, riff, saracen, *tie
-age: anchorage, fee

bird: grouse
blackbird: ouzel
-burn: *anger, *fight
buzzard: harpy, harrier
cock: blackcock, grouse
evil: dysentery
fowl or game: grouse
grass: nard
hawk: harpy, harrier
hen: coot, gallinule, gorhen
land: fen, moose
wort: andromeda, bog rosemary
MOORING: *space:* berth, dock, harbor, marina, port, slip
MOORISH: *mohammedan references
drum: atabal, attabal, kettledrum, tabor
fabric: tiraz
garment: albornoz, burnoose, burnous, jupon
god: tervagant
horse: barb
king of granada: boabdil
opiate: kief
palace: alcazar, alhambra
ship: caramoussal, sapit
MOOSE: alces, eland, elk
berry: hobblebush
bird: canada jay
pouch: bel
MOOT: *argue, debatable
MOPE: brood, *idle, *walk
MOPSY: *prostitute, *wanton
MORAL: *adage, *good, *pure, *right, *story, tag, *true
fable: apologue
lapse: *sin, venality, vice
rearmament founder: buchman
MORALE: *mood, *spirit
MORASS: *marsh: land
MORAY: eel, hamlet, muraena
MORBID: *bad, *evil, *ugly
MORDANT: *acerb, *acute
MORDECAI: *daughter:* *esther
benefactor: ahasuerus, artaxerxes, xerxes

* Asterisk means to look up this word to find more answer words.

enemy: haman
father: jair
uncle: abihail
MORE: better, encore, *extra
island: *utopia
MORGAIN LE FAY: argante
MORMON: josephite, laman, latter-day saint, mandrill
destroying angel: danite
emblem: bee
founder: smith
heaven: celestial *or* telestial *or* terrestrial glory
officer: elder
priesthood: aaronic, melchizedek
prophet: moroni
sacred instrument: urim
state: utah
weed: flower, mallow
MORNING: ack emma, ante meridiem, aurora, dawn, daybreak, eos, forenoon, matin, sunrise, umaga, underne
coat: cutaway
concert: aubade
drink: antifogmatic, coffee
glory: aguinaldo, alamovine, convolvulus, gaybine, impomoea, merganser, nil, vine
line: odds
prayer: aubade, matins
reception: levee
song: aubade, prayer
star: daystar, jupiter, lucifer, mars, mercury, phosphor, saturn, venus
MOROCCO: berber: *moor, shlu
chief: abd-el krim
coin: floos, flue, mouzouna, okia, okieh, ounce, rial
district: riff, sus
dynasty: almoravide
emperor: miramolin, miramomolin
general: kaid
government: maghzen, makhzan
gown: djellaba, jelab, jellaba
hat: fez

imitation: roan
measure: artal, cadee, covado, dirhem, fanega, gerbe, kintar, muhd, quintal, ratel, rotl, sahh, tangin, tomini, ueba
military expedition: harka
official: calapha
people: berber, glaoua, kabyle, maghzen, makhzan, *moor, riff, shlu
port: agadir, casablanca, ceuta, el araish, ifni, laraiche, mogador, rabat, rabbat, saffi, safi, sali, sla, tangier, tetuan
public land: gish
red: caldron, cauldron
ruler: shereef, sherif, sultan
ruler's wife: sherifa
soldier: askar
tree: alerse, arar, argan, sandarac
MORON: *fool, idiot, olive
MOROSE: *acerb, *mad, *sullen
MORSEL: *bit, ort, *part, *piece
MORTAL: *bad, *great, *severe
MORTAR: *instrument:* bray, cap, hawk, hod, pestle, rab
MORTGAGE: antichresis, bottomry, hypothecation, monkey, *promise, security, trust deed, vadium, vivum, wad-set
giver: lienee, moneylender
receiver: debtor, lienor
MORTIFICATION: *shame
MORTIFY: *punish, *shame
MORTISE: *fit, *join, *tool
and tenon: joint
complement: tenon
machine: slotter
MOSAIC: *apply:* incrust, inlay
formed like a: tesselated
gold: ormolu
inlay: certosina, certosino
pavement: asarotum
tile: abaciscus, abaculus
MOSCOW: *cathedral:* arkhangelsky
feature: arsenal, kremlin, oruzheinaya, soborny square

* **Asterisk means to look up this word to find more answer words.**

MOSES: *brother:* aaron
 conspirators against: abiram,
  dathan, korah
 father-in-law: jethro
 general: caleb, joshua
 law: pentateuch, tora(h)
 mountain: ebal, gerizim, horeb,
  nebo, sina(i)
 parent: amram, jochebed
 sister: miriam
 son: eliezer, gershon
 spy: caleb, gaddiel, igal, nahbi
 successor: joshua
 wife: zipporah
MOSLEM: **mohammedan*
MOSQUE: caaba, durgah, kaabeh,
  kiblah, masjid, shrine, temple
 official: ahong, imam, nazir
 part: mihrab, mimbah, minaret
 student: softa, ulema
MOSQUITO: aedes, anopheles,
  culucid, gallinipper, imago
 bee: angelito, karbi
 fish: gambusia
 hawk: dragonfly
 killer: culicide, spray
 larvae: wigglers
 order: diptera
 plant: mint, pennyroyal
 state: jersey
MOSS: acrocarpus, acrogen, agar,
  barbula, bryace, buxbaumia, carrageen, fern, fungus, lichen
 animalcule: bryozoan
 back: conservative, fogy
 basal lobe: ala
 bunker: menhaden
 cheeper: bunting, pipit
 club: lycoped
 comb.: bry(o)
 coral: bryozoan
 corn: silverweed
 duck: mallard
 edible: agar(agar)
 fruit: sporogonium
 grown: antiquated, stale
 hammer: bittern

 life: bryology
 like plant: baby tears
 mat: bear's bed
 pert.: aploperistomatous, hepatic,
  mnioid
 polyp: bryozoan
 tooth: blephara
 trooper: bogtrotter, freebooter
 wort: bryophyte
MOT: chachma, gag, **joke,* **piece*
MOTE: atomy, **bit,* fleck, **part*
MOTH: *aloeus:* canace
 buff-tipped: phalera bucephala
 cabbage: mamestra, noctuida
 carpenter: prinoxysus
 carpet: larentiid, trichophaga
 cecropia: silkworm
 clearwing: sesia
 clothes: larentiid, tinea
 codling: carpocapsa, tortricida
 diamondback: mamestra, noctuida
 -eaten: blighted, decrepit, stale,
  trite
 genus: sesia, tinea, urania
 goat: prinoxystus
 green: luna
 gypsy: liparian
 hawk: goatsucker, phalus
 larva: bagworm, bean cutworm,
  caterpillar, ogodonta cinereola
 mullein: verbascum blattaria
 noctuid: agrotis
 pearl: botys
 proofer: ammonium selenate
 silkworm: anthera, eria, muga
 spots: chloasma, fenestra
 spotted: forester
 suborder: heterocera
 tapestry: trichophaga
 tiger: apantesis
 wingspot: fenestra
MOTHER: *carey's chickens:*
  omens, stormy petrel(s)
 carey's goose: giant fulmar
 comb.: ina, matri
 country: homeland

---

* **Asterisk means to look up this word to find more answer words.**

gate: bord, tramway
goose author: perrault
goose characters: betty spider, big bad wolf, bobby shaftoe, cross patch, curly locks, daffy down dilly, georgey porgey, goosey gander, handy spandy, jack-a-dandy, jack spratt, jennie wren, little miss muffet, lucy locket, mistress mary, peter piper, polly flinders, pumpkin eater, pussy, simple simon, taffy, tommy trot, wee willie winkie, willie wanbeard
goose publisher: newbery
government by: matriarchy
heart: shepherd's-purse
hubbard: *dress, nursery rhymes
-in-law: back-seat driver, belle mere, eldmother, ersatz mother, shviger
MOTHER OF: *believers:* aisha, ayeshah
millions: kenilworth ivy
months: moon
parliaments: england
pearl: abalone, nacre, oyster, river mussel
presidents: virginia
revolutions: paris
sorrows: virgin mary
the gods: brigantia, cybele
thousands: beefsteak saxifrage, daisy, kenilworth ivy
MOTHER: *pert.:* maternal, spindle
related: enate, enatic
superior: abbess, mistress
three deliveries: tripara
-wort: feverfew, joe-pye weed
MOTION: *action, *move, pace, *sign, *speed, step, *stir
circular: gyre, revolution
comb.: ac, ad, ap, at
convulsive: twitch, vellication
energetic: appulse
imparting: kinetic
impetuous: bensail, bensel

jerky: bob, lipe
-less: fixed, inert, still
pert.: kinematic, kinetic
picture: celluloid, cinema, film, flick(er), movie, trailer
-picture award: emmy, oscar
picture, pert.: cinematographic
picture term: boom shot, kleig, klieg, oscar, pan, reel, retake, reverse, scenario, script, shot, take, trucking
producing: motile
quality: momentum
rate: rpm, speed, tempo
reverse: backrun
science: ballistics, kinematics
suspended particles: pedesis
transmitter: belt, cog, gear
viewing device: strobe
MOTIVATE: *force, *forward, *spur, *start, *stir
MOTIVE: *end, *force, *press
force: id, psyche
MOTLEY: *fool, *mixture
MOTOR: *instrument, *machine, *power, *system, transport
agraphia: anorthography
aphasia: alalia
boat: palander
court: inn, motel
electric: dynamo
hand-powered: baromotor
man: engineer, mechanic
part: cam, capacitor, carburetor, coil, piston, rotor, stator
rotary: turbine
speed control: rheocrat
speed up: gun, rev
MOTTO: *adage, thought, *title
MOULD(Y): *mold(y)
MOUND: bulwark, dune, hill(ock)
bird: leipoa, megapod(e)
city: st louis
light: kohinoor
pert.: tumular
pitcher's: box, slab
prehistoric: terp

* Asterisk means to look up this word to find more answer words.

MOUNT: *ascend, *increase, *set
helicon fountain: aganippe
ida nymph: oenone
parnassus fountain: castalia
MOUNTAIN: *quantity, *ridge,
  *top
andromeda: fetterbush
ash: ron, rowan, rowen
badger: marmot
banana: fei
base: foothill, piedmont
beaver: sewellel
beyond: tramontine, transalpine
bluet: centaury
burning: volcano
canary: ass
climber: alpestrian
climbing: alpinism
climbing peg: piton
cock: capercaillie
comb.: ore(o), oro
crest: arete, peak, tor
curassow: oreophasis
depression: col
devil: moloch
dew: bootleg
duck: harlequin, sheldrake
finch: brambling
flax: centaury
formation: orogenesis, orogeny
fringe: fumitory, wormwood
gap: corrie, defile, *pass
goat: ibex
god: atlas, olympus, tmolus
herb: brook saxifrage
highest: everest, mckinley
holly: brick timber, catberry,
  gooseberry, nempanthus
ivy: laurel
lake: tarn
laurel: calfkill, calico bush, kalmia latifolia
laurel root: briarroot
leather: palygorskite
lion: *lion: mountain
low: butte
magpie: butcherbird, woodpecker

maple: acer spicatum
mint: basil, ocimum, pycanthemum, sheepskin
misery: bear mat
muses: helicon
mythical: candy, glass, helicon,
  kaf, meru, olympus, parnassus,
  pelion, qaf
nymph: dryad, oread
panther: cougar, leopard, ounce
parrot: kea
partridge: dove, quail
pass: brenner, cenis, col, cove, cut,
  defile, donner, duar, gap, gate,
  gaut, ghat, gorge, kotal
pasture: alp, saeter, seter
peak: alp, cima, cone
peg: piton
pert.: *mountainous
pheasant: grouse
pool: tarn
range: alaska, allegheny, alp, altai,
  andes, appalachian, blue ridge,
  brooks, byrranga, cascade, catskill, cherskogo, chukotskoye,
  coast, himalaya, kolymskiy, kor-
  yakskiy, kunlun shan, pamir,
  putorana, pyrenees, rocky, sa-
  yany, sierra, sikhote alin, teton,
  tien shan, ural, verkhoyanskiy
range summit: divide
raspberry: cloudberry
ridge: arete, crest, peak, sawbuck,
  serra, sierra, summit
road: ess
rose: laurel
science: orology
shelter: gite
sickness: puna, soroche, veta
side, sunny: adret
snow: jokul
spinach: orach(e)
state: arizona, colorado, idaho,
  montana, nevada, new mexico,
  utah, wyoming
study: orography
sunset reflection: alpenglow

* Asterisk means to look up this word to find more answer words.

tea: wintergreen
top: cone, peak, summit
MOUNTAINEER: aaron, climber
song: yodel
MOUNTAINOUS: alpen, alpestrine, alpigene, alpine, elevated, etiolin, monticuline, montigeneous, orological
MOUNTEBANK: *cheat*, fraud
MOURN: *cry*, keen, sigh, wail
MOURNFUL: *sad*, threnodic
MOURNING: *bride:* plant, scabious
cloak: butterfly, camberwell
dress: black, crepe, weeds
fabric: bombasine, bombazeen
group: cortege
MOUSE: *bird:* coly, shrike
comb.: mys
deer: chevrotain
ear: chickweed, hawkweed
field: harvest, metad, vole
gray: boulevard
hare: pika
leaping: jerboa
-like: drab, murine, nugale, quiet, retiring, shy, timid
male: buck
milk: spurge
shrew: hyrax, migale, sorex
tiny: harvest
trap: tipe
web: cobweb, gossamer
MOUTH: entrance, *opening*, *trap*
away from: aborad, aboral
comb.: bucco, ori, stom(o)
deformity: harelip
disease: canker, noma, stomatitis
-ful: bite, sup
furnace: bocca
-less: astomatous, astomous
muscle: caninus
off: blahblah, chatter, *talk*
open: agape
organ: crembalum, harmonica
part: palate, pharynx, uvula

pert.: oral, orificial, oscular, palatal, rictal, stomatic
-piece: *agent*, attorney, bocal, interlocutrix, lawyer, mike
projecting: spout
river: delta, firth, lade
roof: palate
through: peroral
tissue: gum
-ward: orad
wash: collutory, prophylactic
-watering: alluring, appetite
MOVE: *act(uate)*, *advance*, *advantage*, *affect*, *agitate*, *animate*, arouse, attempt, barge, bear, birl, blow, bob, boom, bound, brush, budge, cam, canter, career, carry, cater, cause, change, dislodge, enjoin, excite, *force*, gee, goad, impress, induce, influence, introduce, kelter, kindle, make hay, market, melt, *pass*, *play*, *power*, proceed, propose, *push*, rouse, *send*, shift, slink, sneak, soften, *speed*, *start*, *stir*, *strike*, *urge*, *work*
along: depart, mosey, progress
away: depart, ebb, recede
back: *retreat*
behind: *follow*
camera: pan
false: balk, feint, misstep
fast: scat, *speed*
first: advantage, initiative
forward: *advance*, *progress*
heaven and earth: *try*
quickly: dart, flit, *speed*
to: greet, salaam
together: *join*, *unite*
MOVEMENT: *action*, *stir*, *style*
biological: taxis
brownian: pedesis
capable of: mobile, motile
cure: motorpathy
fluid, through: cataphoresis
surface: seiche

* Asterisk means to look up this word to find more answer words.

MOVIE: *motion: picture
MOWGLI: friend: akela, baloo
 elephant: hathi
MUCH: *great, *plenty, *quantity
 ado about nothing role: antonio,
  claudio, hero, leonato, ursula
 comb.: eri, multi, poly
MUCUS: comb.: blenn(o)
MUD: *dregs, ooze, slander
 bass: sunfish
 bath: illulation
 cat: catfish
 cat state: mississippi
 comb.: pel
 dab: flounder
 dabbler: killifish
 dauber: wasp
 deposit: silt
 devil: hellbender
 eel: siren
 enclosure: bawn
 fish: amia, bowfin, grindle
 hole: *mudpuddle, slew, slough
 lark: gamin, magpie, vagabond
 living in: limicolous
 mark: mudflow
 peep: sandpiper
 pert.: luteous
 puddle: chuckhole, loblolly, quagmire, slop, wallow
 puppy: hellbender, salamander
 rake: claut
 sling: slander, smear
 snipe: woodcock
 sunfish: bass, warmouth
 volcano: salse
 worm: earthworm, ipo
 wort: mudweed
MUDDLE: *err, *mess, *puzzle
MUFFLE: *dress, *dull, *stop
M U G : *attack, emote, *fool,
  *hoodlum, shot, stein, toby
 house: saloon, tavern
 shot: photo, *picture
 wump: apostate, personage
MULBERRY: aal, ach, blackberry,
  castillo, caucho, dodder, morel-

lol, murrey, whitebeam
 bark: atap, tapa
 beverage: morat
 bird: starling
 cloth: tapa
 fig: sycamore
MULCT: *fine, *punish, *steal
MULE: ass, hybrid, *mixture
 deer: blacktail, dassie, ruffe
 driver: almocrebe, arriero
 group: atajo, drove
 killer: mantis
 male: jack
 pack train leader: cencerro
 skinner: *mule: driver, peon
 untrained: shavetail
MULL: *err, spice, *think
MULLET: bobo, bouri, lisita
 hawk: osprey
 king: apogon, bass, cardinal
MULTITUDE: *group, *rabble
MUMBO JUMBO: *demon, *fe-
 tish
MUMMU: father: apsu
MUNRO, H. H.: saki
MURAD IV: amurath
MURDER: *destroy, *kill, *ruin
 fine: cro, wergild
MURDEROUS: *brutal, cruel
MUSCLE: column: sarcostyle
 contracting: agonist
 curve: myogram
 derived from: inosic
 expansion: dilator
 flexor: brachialis
 ill: abasia, ataxia, crick
 lifting: levator
 limb-straightening: extensor
 man: bully, *hoodlum
 pert.: myoid, scalene
 poison: albopannin
 round: teres
 segment: myocomma
 spasm: tonus
 straight: rectus
 stretching: tensor
 sugar: inosite, inositol

* Asterisk means to look up this word to find more answer words.

trapezius: cucularris
triangular: deltoid
turning: evertor, rotator
MUSCULAR: **big,* **strong*
  deficiency: abasia, amyotaxia
  rigidity: catalepsy
MUSE: **study,* **think,* **wonder*
  astronomy: urania
  attic: xenophon
  birthplace: piera
  chief: calliope
  comedy: thalia
  dancing: terpsichore
  eloquence: calliope
  fountain: aganippe
  history: clio
  home: aonia, helicon, parnassus
  music: euterpe, polymnia
  pert.: pierian
  poetry: calliope, erato
  sacred lyric: polyhymnia
  sacred spring: castalia
  shrine: aolea, aonia, piera
  tragedy: melpomene
MUSHROOM: *cap:* pileus
  disease: flock
  edible: chanterelle, morel
  fairy-ring: champignon
  hallucinogenic: amanita
  part: annulus, basidiospore, gill, hymenium, pileus, sterigma, stipe, trama
  poisoning: mycetism
  poisonous: amanita, toadstool
MUSIC: *angel:* israfil
  entertainment: ceilidh
  god: apollo, bes
  group: arioso, band, cantata, chorus, duet, duo, madrigal, nonet, octet, orchestra, quartet, quintet, septet, septuor, sestole(t), sextet, solo, terzet(to), trio
  hall: alhambra, bijou, carnegie, gaff, hippodrome, la scala, odeon, odeum, palladium, theatre, windmill

  ignorance: amusia
  lover: cat, hepcat, jitterbug, music monger, philharmonic
  muse: euterpe, polyhymnia
  note: **note: music*
  patron saint: cecilia
  3 b's: bach, beethoven, brahms
MUSICAL COMPOSITION: accentus, accompaniment, adaptation, air(varie), alba, anthem, arabesque, arrangement, ars nova, art song, aubade, background, bagatelle, ballad(e), ballata, berceuse, blues, boat song, boutade, brautlied, brindisi, cabaletta, calypso, canon, canticle, cantus, canzone(tta), carol, cassation, cavatina, cento, chant(y), chaser, concerto, contrapunto, ditty, etude, exercise, fantasia, faux-bourdon, fugue, harmonization, hymeneal, intermezzo, lay, lied, lullaby, march, medley, monody, nocturne, noel, opera, operetta, opus, overture, piece, prelude, raga, rasa, rondo-(letto), round(elay), scherzo, serenade, song, suite, tema, troll, virelai, work
MUSICAL DIRECTION: *above:* sopra
  accented: sforzando, sforzato
  actively: allegretto, allegro
  again: bis, da capo, dal segno
  all: tutto
  alone: arioso, scena
  alternate: ossia
  always: sempre
  ardent: appassionato, ardente
  as written: alloco, sta
  augmentation: accrescimento
  backwards: cancrizans
  begin now: attacca
  below: sotto
  bitter: amarevole
  bold: audace
  bowed: arco

* Asterisk means to look up this word to find more answer words.

bright: anime
brilliant: bravura, chiaro
cold: fredo
contrary: a rovescio
dignified: maestoso
diminishing: calando
disconnected: staccato
discordant: charivari, scordato
distorted: rubato
duple measure: alla breve
dying: calando, perd(endosi)
embellishment: agremens, appog-
  giatura
emotional: appassionato
emphatic: marcato
energetic: animato, animoso
enough: basta
evenly: egualmente
excited: agitato, spiritoso
fantastic: capriccioso
fast: accelerando, affrettando, allegretto, allegro, animato, desto,
  prestissimo, presto, stretto, tos-
  tamente, tosto, veloce, vivace,
  vivacissimo
faster: accelerando, affrettando
flat: bemol, molle
flourish: roulade
florid: bravura
flowing: andante, legato
follow: segue
freely: ad libitum
gay: brillante, giocoso
gentle: amabile, dolce
graceful: allegretto
gravely: serioso
half: mezzo
harsh: apre
heavy: pesante
held: tenuto
high: alt(issimo)
hurried: agitato
in time: a tempo
irregular: rubato
jump or leap: salto
keynote: ison
less: meno

let it stand: sta
light: allegretto
little by little: poco a poco
lively: *fast
loud: forte
louder: crescendo, fortissimo
lovingly: amabile, amoroso
majestic: maestoso
march-like: alla marcia
melodious: arioso
moderate: andante, moderato
more: piu
much: molto
muted: sorda
natural voice: dipetto
one voice: asoluto, solo
otherwise: ossia
performed, being: arpeggiando
performer pleasure: a capriccio
plaintive: dolente, lacrimando
playful: giocoso, scherzando
plucked: pizzicato
poignant: amarevole
quadruple measure: alla breve
quick: *fast, con moto, snell
quickening: affrettando
quiet: tacet
rapid succession: arpeggiando
repeat: ancoro, bis, represa
restless: agitato
retarding: lentando
return, recommence: alsegno
revert: antistrophe
robbed: rubato
run: rolle
sad: dolente, doloroso, mesto
sentimental: affettuoso
sharp: sforzando, staccato
singing: cantabile
slackening: allentato, rit(ardando)
sliding: glissando
slow: adagio, andante, grave,
  larghetto, largo, lento, tardo
slower: rit(ard)(ando)
slower, louder: allargando
slowing: (r)allentando
smooth: legato, piacevole

* Asterisk means to look up this word to find more answer words.

so much: tanto
soft: dolce, dulce, piano
soft pedal, with: a una corda
softer: decrescendo, diminuendo
solemn: grave
solo: a cappella, arioso
speed up: accelerando
spirited: animato, spiritoso
stop: basta
strong: forte, fortissimo
sustained: sostenuto, tenuto
sweet: dolce, dulce
tender: affettuoso, amabile, amoroso
then: poi
thrice: ter
throughout: sempre
together: adue, ensemble
to the end: al fine
too much: tanto, troppo
tranquil: calmato
turn: gruppetto, volti
turn over: verti
very: assai, dimolto, tres
very much: molto
vibrate: tremolo
well marked: vibrato
whole: tutto
MUSICAL EVENT: ballet, chorale, comedy, concert, dance, drama, eisteddfod, grand opera, minstrelsy, musicale, opera, opus, oratorio, prom, recital, revue, sonata, symphony
MUSICAL INSTRUMENT: *aid:* diapason, metronome, pitch pipe, sonometer, tuning bar
brass: althorn, altohorn, baroxyton, bombardon, bugle, cornet, helicon, samisen, saxhorn, trombone, trumpet
guitar-like: balalaia, bandore, bandurria, banjo(rine), lute, rote, samisen, uke(lele)
keyboard: accordion, adiaphon, aelodicon, aeolina, celesta, cembalo, choraleon, clavichord, con-

certina, harmonichord, klavier, melodeon, organ, piano
lute-like: angelote, bandore, bandurria, cithern, colascione
lyre-like: asor, barbiton, kinnar, kissar, zither
old: bandore, barbiton, celesta, dulcimer, gittern, marimba, nabla, pandura, rebec
percussion: atabal, bells, block, castanets, cymbals, drum, glockenspiel, gong, maraca, marimba, naker, tabor, tambourine, timpano, xylophone
reed: aulos, bagpipe, bassoon, clarinet, gora, oboe, saxophone
stringed: asor, balalaika, bandore, banjo, baryton, bass, cello, cittern, cythara, dulcimer, fiddle, guitar, harp(sichord), lute, lyre, mandolin, nabla, pandura, polychord, rebec(k), rocta, ruana, samisen, sarad, sitar, theorbo, uke(lele), vina, viol(a), violin, zither
wind: althorn, alto, bagpipe, baroxyton, bassoon, bombardon, brass, buccina, bugle, cervelat, clarinet, clarion, cornet, flageolet, flute, harmonica, horn, jug, oboe, ocarina, organ, panpipe, piccolo, ranket, reed, sarusphone, sax, trombone, trumpet, tuba, zampogna
MUSK: *beaver:* muskrat
cat: civet
cavy: hutia
cucumber: cassabanana
deer: chevrotain
hog: peccary
lorikeet: parakeet
mallow: abelmosk
melon: atimon, cantaloupe, casaba, rock melon
rat: desman, shrew
seed: amber
shrew: desman

thistle: cirsium lanceolatum
wood: caoba, guarea
MUSKETEER: aramis, athos, porthos
author: dumas
friend: d'artagnan
MUSLIM: *mohammedan*
MUSLIN: *bag:* tillot
fine: shela
lace: carrickmacross
striped: dorea, doria
MUSS: *fight, *mess, row
MUSSEL: *fresh water:* naiad, unio
genus: modiolus, mytilus, unio
large: horse
part: byssus
sea: nerita
MUSSULMAN: *mohammedan*
MUST: essential, *need*
MUSTARD: *beetle:* blackjack
black: nigra
chemical: allyl
genus: brassica, sinapis
pert.: brassic, sinapic
plant: aethionema, alyssum, anastatica, arabidopsis, arabis, camelina, cole, cress
plaster: capsicum, sinapism
pod: silicle
wild: charlock
MUSTER: *gather, *order, *show
MUSTY: *bad, *dull, *sour
MUT: *father:* chons
husband: amen, amon
offspring: chunsu, khonsu
MUTILATE: *hurt, *ruin, *spoil
MUTTON: *bird:* petrel, shearwater
chop: beard, burnside, whisker
dried: vifda, vivda
fish: eelpot, mojarra, porgy
leg: cabob, gigot, wobbler
head: dunce, *fool, screwball
MUX: *mess, *mixture
MYCANAE KING: atreus, eurystheus
vase: bugelkanne

MYGALE: bird spider
MYRIAD: *plenty, *quantity
MYRMIDON: *mercenary, *slave
king: agabus
MYSTERIOUS, MYSTERY: *doctrine, *obscure, *puzzle, *secret
MYSTIC: *magic, *obscure
pert.: bourignian
MYTH: fable, legend, *story

NAAR, NARR: *clown, *fool
NAB: *ambush, *arrest, *seize
NABAL: *home:* maon
wife: abigail
NABOB: *lord, *magnate
deputy: nawab
NABONIDUS: *son:* belshazzar
NAG: *plague, *scold, *torment
NAHOR: *father:* serug
offspring: huz, maacah, terah
wife: milcah
NAHUATLAN: *aztec*
NAIL: *get, *set(tle), *trap
comb.: helo
headless: sprig
holder: nog
hooked: tenter
ingrowing: acronyx
marking: lunule
mining: spad
set: brad punch
shoemaker's: brad, sparable
size: penny, tenpenny
thin: brad
without: anonychia
wooden: fid, peg
NAIVE: *open, *simple, *stupid
NAKED: barren, *open, *plain
NAMAYCUSH: cree, togue, trout
NAMBY-PAMBY: *dull, *silly
NAME: adduce, agnomen, alias, announce, antonym, appellation, appoint, assign, baptize, caconym, call, category, celebrity,

---

christen, cite, clepe, cognomen, define, denominate, *describe, dub, entitle, enumerate, epithet, eponym, fay, fix, *glory, handle, hypocorism, identify, *image, *important, indicate, mention, monicker, nemel, nomen(clature), nominate, *note, noun, onym, patronym, personage, pseudonym, select, *set, sobriquet, specify, *symbol, tag, term, *title

assumed: alias, anonym, incognito, nom de plume, pen, pseudonym, sobriquet

backwards: ananym

bad: caconym

call: berascall, clepe

city, from a: eponym

collection: onomasticon

consisting of: onomastic

family: cognomen, eponymy, sirname, surname

father-derived: patronym

first: forename, praenomen

last: cognomen, surname

-less: anonymous

maiden: nee

mother-derived: matronym

pet: nickname, sobriquet

plate: facia, plaque

sake: eponym, homonym, junior

tablet: *plate

thing: noun

two terms: dionym

unknown: anonymous

without: anomia

NAMELY: icet, videlicet, viz

NANNA: *husband:* baldr, baldur

NAOMI: *daughter-in-law:* ruth

husband: elimelech

place settled in: moab

name claimed by: mara

son: chilion, mahlon

NAP: *coarse:* gig, pile, ras, shag, teasel, teazle

-like cloth: duffel

machine: gig, gog

NAPHTALI: *mother:* bilhah

prince: enan

son: guni, jahziel, jezer, shallum

NAPLES: *biscuit:* ladyfinger

coin: carlin(e)

king: murat

secret society: camorra

NAPOLEON: *battle:* acre, auerstadt, austerlitz, bautzen, beresina, borodino, dresden, eckmulh, elchingen, eylau, friedland, jena, leipzig, ligny, lutzen, marengo, pultusk, ulm, wagram, waterloo

birthplace: ajaccio, corsica

brother: jerome, joseph, louis, lucien

isle: corsica, elba, st helena

marshal: augereau, bernadotte, davout, lannes, marmont, murat, ney, soult, vandamme

nickname: boney

sister: elisa

vanquisher: blucher, nelson, russians, wellington

wife: josephine, marie louise

wine favorite: chambertin

NAPOLEON III: boustrapa, louis

friend: fialin

grandmother: letitia

mother: hortense

NARCOTIC: *drug: addictive

NARK: annoy, *note, *spy, *tell

NARRATIVE: *account, *report

NARROW: *limit, *little, *near, *poor, *small, *thin

blue flag: boston iris

comb.: angusti, sten(o)

-minded: biased, bigoted

NASH, RICHARD: beau ideal

NASTY: *bad, *evil, *ugly

NATION: country, *power, *state

NATIVITY: *feast:* christmas

NATTY: *smart, spruce, trim

NATURAL: *home, *open, *plain, *simple, *usual, *wild

NATURE: *disposition, *form,

*kind, *quality, *range, *sort, *universal, *way
daughter: luonnotar
deity: artemis, cybele, indra
pert.: cosmic, natural, real
preservation science: ecology
spirit: nat
worship: physiolatry
NAUGHTY: *bad, *evil, impish
NAURU: pleasant island
NAUSEATED: *sick, squeamish
NAUSEATING, NAUSEOUS: *nasty, sickening
NAUTICAL: equipment: becket, binnacle, bobstay, capstan, compass, earing, grapnel, helm, marline, marling, pelorus, sextant, sonar, toggle, wapp
measure: fathom, knot, seam
signal: bell, flag, light
term: abaft, abeam, abox, afore, ahoy, alow, atrip, atry, avast, batten, haul off, heave to, ohoy, uphelm
NAUTILUS: argonauta, mollusk
NAVIGATION: *nautical
NAVIGATOR'S ISLAND: samoa
NAVY: man: blue(jacket), cadet, devil dog, galiongee, gob, gyrene, jack, jolly, leatherneck, marine, middy, midshipman, sailor, salt, seabee, sea dog, swab, tar, toty
officer: admiral, bosun, captain, commander, commodore, ensign, lieutenant, mate
vessel: battleship, carrier, cruiser, destroyer, dreadnaught, flattop, frigate, galleon, gunboat, lst, submarine, tender, u-boat
NAZI: fascist, hitlerite, rightist
concentration camp: auschwitz, bergen-belsen, buchenwald, dachau, mauthausen, oswiecim, schirmeck, theresienstadt
police: gestapo, ss
symbol: flyfot, swastika
NEAR: about, adjacent, against, akin, almost, anigh, *approach, approximate, around, aside, beside, bordering, burning, close, dear, familiar, fast by, hard by, *hot, imminent, intimate, like, match, narrow, neighboring, next, nigh, parsimonious, proximal, *short, similar, stingy, touch, *warm
comb.: juxto, par(a)
east: *levant
NEARIAH: son: azrikam, elioenai
NEAT: *fine, *good, *smart
NEBRASKA: bird: meadowlark
flower: goldenrod
nickname: cornhusker state
tree: american elm
NEBUCHADNEZZAR: god destroyed by: bethshemesh
general: holophernes
guard: arioch, nebuzaradan
jewish governors: abednego, azariah, hananiah, meshach, mishal, shadrach
magician: belteshazzar, daniel
servant: ashpenaz, melzar
son: belshazzer
NEBULOUS: *obscure, *vague
NECESSARY, NECESSITY: *need, *use
NECK: channel, hang, pet, woo
and neck: close, even, tie
armor: gorget
artery: carotid
back: nape, nuque, scruff
cloth: *neck: piece
coat: george
comb.: cervic(o), der(a)
frill: jabot, ruff
guard: camail, mozzetta
hair: mane
horse: withers
-lace: baldric(k), band, beads, carcanet, chain, chaplet, choker, collar, cravat, esclavage, grivna, haltern, hiaqua, lavalier(e), locket, noose, pearls, riviere, rope, sautoir, tie, tore, torque

* Asterisk means to look up this word to find more answer words.

-lace poplar: big cottonwood
land: strake
line: boat, crew, vee
part: gula, throat
pert.: cervical, nuchal, wattled
piece: amice, ascot, bandanna,
   barcelona, bib, boa, burdash,
   choker, collar, cravat, dickey,
   fichu, jabot, neckerchief, pan-
   nelo, rabat, ruche, ruff, scarf,
   stole, tie
-tie: *neck: piece
-tie party: hanging, lynching
NECROMANCER: *magician
NECROMANCY: *magic, *spell
NECTAR: *drink, *manna
NEED: *ask, call for, claim, compulsion, defect, demand, *desire,
   destitution, essential, exact, exigency, extremity, imperative, indigence, indispensible, lack,
   must, necessary, necessity, obligation, penury, poverty, prere-
   quisite, privation, require(ment),
   requisite, strait(s), urgency,
   *use, want
NEEDLE: *scold, *taunt, *urge
 bath: sprinkler
 bug: nepa, ranatra
 case: etui, etwee
 coarse: baby threader
 comb.: acu
 finisher: eyer
 fish: agujon, belone, earl, gar,
   pipefish, sailfish, saury, spearfish,
   strongylura
 grass: beard grass
 gun: dreyse, rifle
 hole: eye, seton
 man: tailor
 medical: hypo(dermic)
 pert.: acerate, acerose, acicular,
   aciform, belonoid, pointed, spicular, styloid
 -point: angleterre, argentan, ar-
   gentella, point d'argentan
 short: blunt

 work: basting, binding, crochet,
   embroidery, hemming, knitting,
   picot, purling, quilting, sampler,
   seam, sewing, tacking, tatting
 work piece: petit point
NEEDY: indigent, *poor
NEFARIOUS: *bad, *evil, *rotten
NEGATE: deny, *refuse, veto
NEGATIVE: comb.: dis, il, im, in,
   ir, non, un
NEGLECT: failure, ignore, omit
NEGLIGEE: dishabille, kimono
NEGOTIATE: *bargain, *trade
NEIGHBOR: *friend
NEIGHBORHOOD: *district,
   *near
NEITHER: comb.: neutro
NELEUS: son: nestor
NEOTERIC: *fresh, late, modern
NEPAL: city: bhatgaon, katmandu,
   khatmandu, palan
 cloth: changa, khadi
 coin: anna, mohar
 district: terai
 dynasty: malla kings
 fighter: gurkha
 peak: *himalaya: peak
 people: aoul, bhotia, bokra, gork-
   hali, gurkha, hindu, kha, kiranti,
   lepcha, limbu, murmi, newar,
   tharu
 river: babai, gandak, karnali,
   sarda, tamur
 ruler: rana
 scimitar: khukri
 sheep: bharal, nahoor, nayaur
 shrine: bodhnath, stupa, sway-
   ambhunath
 title: mukhtiyar, rana
 tree: sal, sisoo, toon
NEPHELE: consort: athamus
 daughter: helle
NEPHEW: nepote, neve, vasu
NEPHTHYS: aphrodite, nike
 husband: set
 kin: isis, osiris, set
 son: anubis

* Asterisk means to look up this word to find more answer words.

NEPTUNE: miron, *poseidon, sea
  discoverer: galle
NEREIDS: arethusa, galatea,
  psamathe, thetis
  parent: doris, nereus
NEREUS: consort: doris
  child: amphitrite, *nereids
NERIAH: father: mahseiah
  son: baruch, seraiah
NERO: mother: agrippina
  successor: galba
  victim: lucan, seneca
  wife: octavia, poppaea
NERVE: *force, *power, *spirit
  ailment: aneuria, aphasia, apraxia,
    beri-beri, brachialgia, chorea,
    epilepsy, floccillation, ischialgia,
    lata, neuralgia, parenthesia,
    sciatica, st vitus dance, subsultus,
    tic
  band: taenis
  cell: anaxon, neuron
  center: brain, cortex, plexus
  comb.: neur(o)
  ingredient: lecithin
  layer: alveus
  network: plexus, rete, retia
  pert.: neural, neurotic
  science: neurology
  sedative: celery seed
  sensory: afferent
NERVES: buck fever, butterflies,
  collywobbles, fidgets, shakes
NERVOUS: *critical, edgy, *upset
NEST: aerie, nide, *retreat
  boxes: inro
  build: nidificate, nidify
  builder: ant, bee, bird, wasp
  pert.: cubilose, nidic
  science of: caliology
NESTLE: cherish, *lie, *pet
NESTOR: kin: anaxibia, antilochus
NET: bait, profit, *trap, *value
  fishing: flue, fyke, sagene, seine,
    stent, trawl
  fly-catching: jabb

hair: snood
pert.: cancellate, reticulated
silk: malines, reticle
-works: abc, cbs, *group, nbc,
  rete, reticulum, *system
NETHERLANDS: *dutch
NETTLE: *anger, *taunt, *trouble
  rash: hives, uredo, urticaria
NEVADA: bird: mountain bluebird
  flower: sagebrush
  nickname: sagebrush, silver
  tree: single-leaf pinon
NEW: *fresh, *late, novel, young
  comb.: ceno, neo
NEW BRUNSWICK: isle: campo-
  bello
  river: miramashee, miramichi
NEW CALEDONIA: bird: kagu
  port: numea
NEW DEAL: agency: ccc, nra, tva
NEW ENGLAND: aristocrat:
  brahmin
  chair: brewster, carver
  clock: acorn clock
  flower: bluets, rue
  native: down-easter, yankee
  settler: pilgrim, puritan
  ship: down-easter
NEW GUINEA: bay: oro
  city: daru, kitbadi, lae, soron
  export: copra
  hog: bene
  island: aru, ceram, jobie, papua,
    solomons
  kingfisher: torotoro
  mountain: albert, carstensz, vic-
    toria, wilhelmina
  parrot: lorikeet, lory
  people: arau, karon, kebar, kuku-
    kuku, papuan
  port: buna, duan, lae
  river: amberno, degul, fly, kai-
    serin augusta, sepik
  section: bunagona
  shrub: bitter king
  victory: gona

* Asterisk means to look up this word to find more answer words.

NEW HAMPSHIRE: *academy:* exeter
bird: purple finch
flower: purple lilac
lake: sunapee
mountain: flume
nickname: granite state
tree: white birch

NEW HEBRIDES: *island:* api, efate, epi, tana, tanna, vate
port: vila
volcano: lopevi

NEW JERSEY: *bird:* goldfinch
flower: purple violet
nickname: garden state
tree: red oak

NEW JERUSALEM: utopia, zion
foundation: jasper

NEW MEXICO: *art colony:* taos
bird: road runner
capital: santa fe
ceremony: corn dances
flower: yucca
indian: acoma, anasazi, sia
music instrument: ollabumba
nickname: land of enchantment
old name: cibola
pueblo: nambe, picuris, pojoaque, san ildefonso, taos
river: gila, pecos, rio grande
tree: nut pine, pinon
turpentine tree: taranta(h)

NEW RICH: belgravia

NEW YORK: *bohemian section:* bowery, chelsea, coenties slip, greenwich village
borough: bronx, brooklyn, manhattan, queens, richmond, staten island
fern: bear's-paw
flower: rose
harbor island: ellis, staten
lake: cayuga, croton, finger, oneida, onondaga, placid, saranac, seneca, skaneateles
law: baumes
monastery: new skete

mountain: adirondack, catskill
nickname: empire state
prison: sing sing, tombs
river: ausable, canisteo, cohocton, genessee, harlem, hudson, niagara, tioga
stock exchange: big board
symbol: eustace tilley, gotham, knickerbocker
tree: sugar maple

NEW ZEALAND: antipodes, aotearoa
anteater: echidna
army man: anzac
bird: apteryx, bellbird, huia, kaka(po), kea, kiwi, koko, kulu, lowan, mako, moa, morepark, notornis, oii, poe, roa, ruru, weka, wrybill
bramble: bush lawyer
caterpillar: aweto, weri
cattail: raupo
clay: papa
dance: haka
fern: pitau, poi, pteris, tara, weki, wheki
fiord: isse
fish: hiku(s), ihi, mako
flax: harakeke
food: kai
fort: pa, pah, pau
fruit pigeon: kuku
grass: toetoe
gun: tupara
herb: alpine eyebright
heron: kotuku
holly: olearia
hut: whare
indian corn: kanga
island: niue, otea, stewart
laburnum: goani
lake: ada, brunner, diamond, gunn, hawea, kanieri, manapouri, okareka, okataina, paradise, pukaki, rerewhakaitu, rotoaira, rotokawau, rotoma(hana), rotoroa, tarawera, taupo, teanau, tekapo, waikaremoana

* Asterisk means to look up this word to find more answer words.

locust: weta
mollusk: pipi
morepark: ruru
myrtle: ramarama
national bird: apteryx, kiwi
owl: ruru
palm: nikau
parrot: kakapo, kara, kea, lorikeet, lory, tarapo
parson bird: koko
peak: aorangi, aspiring, blackburn, cook, egmont, messenger, ngauruhoe, ngongotaha, ohope, pihanga, raupehu, ruapehu, tapuaenuka, tarawera, tauhera, tauranga, tongariro
people: arawa, ati, kiwi, maori, mori, ringatu, totara, tutu
pine: kahikatea, rima, totara
port: aukland, dunedin, lae, otago, wellington
raft: moti
reptile: tuatara, tuatera
river: rangitikei, taramarkau, tongariro, waimakariri, wanganui, whakapapa
shark: mako
shrub: goai, grama, karo, kowhai, ramarama, ti, tutu
song: waiata
spa: aroha, rotorua, tearoha
storehouse: whata
tree: ake(ake), akepiro, dodonaea, hinau, hiropito, hopbush, kaikawaka, karaka, kauri, kio, kopi, kowhai, libocedrus, maho, maire, mako, manuka, mapau, miro, ngaio, nikau, pelo, pelu, pohutukawa, puka, puriri, ramarama, rata, rimu, tarata(h), tawa, titoki, toatoa, toro, totara, wahahen
vine: aka
volcano: ruapehu
wages: utu
weapon: mere, meri, patu
welcome: haeremai

wineberry: mako
wren: xenicus
NEWS: *agency:* aneta, ap, dnb, domei, ins, reuters, tass, upi
beat: scoop
carrier: camelot, newsboy
media: journal, magazine, newspaper, periodical, press, radio, television, tv
-*paperman:* columnist, commentator, copyreader, correspondent, editor(ialist), gazetter, journalist, legman, paragrapher, photographer, redactor, reporter
-*paper part:* business, comics, editorial, family, financial, magazine, news, obit, opinion, real estate, society, sports, travel, weather, women
-*stand:* booth, canterbury, kiosk, stall
NEXT: adjacent, *near
NIB: beak, bill, *end, point
NIBELUNG: *chief:* alberich
goddess: erda
smith: mime
NICARAGUA: *lake:* managua
measure: cabelleria, cahiz, cajuela, estadel, manzana, milla, suerte, tercia, vara
volcano: leon, managua, telica
NICE: *acute, *fine, *good, *kind, *pure, *right, *sweet
NICHE: aedicule, cant, *retreat
NIDAUAS: *chief:* avidya
NIFTY: *fine, *great, *smart
NIGERIA: *people:* abo, angas, aro, benin, bini, djo, ebo(e), edo, efik, ejam, ekoi, hausa, ibibio, ibo, ijaw, ijo, nupe, vai, yoruba
province: bornu, isa, nupe, ondo, warri
spirit: juju
town: aba, abeokuta, benin, bida, calabar, ede, ibadan, isa, iwo, jos, kano, lagos, offa, ogbomosho, oyo, yola
tree: afara, terminalia

---

* Asterisk means to look up this word to find more answer words.

NIGGARD: *mean, miser, stingy
NIGH: *near
NIGHT: air: snelly
attack: camisado
bird: *nightingale, shearwater
blind: hemeralopia, nyctalopia
cap: biggin, *drink
churr: goatsucker
club: bistro, boit, cabaret, cafe, dive, restaurant, spot
comb.: noct(i), nyct(i)
fall: candlelight, dusk, eve, evening, twilight
fall, pert.: acronical
god: somnus
goddess: artemis, hecate, leda, leto, natt, nott, nox, nyx
hawk: bullbat, pisk, vehicle
-jar: caprimulgus, goatsucker, potoo
-mare: alp, cauchemar, *demon, elf, ephialtes, fiend, incubus, terror, *torment, vision
-mare preventive: antephialtic
offspring: death, doom, dreams, eris, *fates, fraud, gaiety, *hesperides, ker, misery, moera, momus, moros, nemesis, oizus, old age, sleep
owl: dissipater, roue
pert.: nocturnal
queen: moon
-shade: belladonna, datura, henbane, morelle, pokeweed
sight: nyctalopia
soil: fertilizer
-walking: noctambulism, noctivigation, somnambulation
watchman: guard, sentry, sereno
wear: gown, pjs, pajamas
NIGHTINGALE: attic bird, barley, bulbul, florence, philomel, progne, wagtail, wryneck
NIK: *enthusiast
NIKE: parent: pallas, styx
NILE: *egyptian references
falls: ripon

island: philae, roda
native: bari, beja, golo, jur, luoh, madi, nilot, nuo, suk
pert.: nilotic
plant: lotus, sadd, sudd
reptile: croc(odile)
source: lake albert, tsana
tributary: atbara, kagera
waste matter: sadd, sudd
NILUS: daughter: anchinoe
NIMBLE: *alert, *funny, *light, *quick, *smart
kate: bur cucumber
will: grass muhlenbergia
NIMIETY: excess, *surfeit
NIMROD: *despot, orion, *ruler
city: accad, achad, akkad
kingdom: babel
NINCOMPOOP: *fool, *peasant
NINE: comb.: enne(a), nona
day's devotion: novena
day's wonder: ephemerid
-eyes: lamprey
group of: ennead, nonet
holes: bumble puppy
hundred: sampi
inches: span
-killer: shrike
pert.: enneatic, nonary
pins: kayles, keels, skittles
points of the law: possession
NINNY: *fool, goose, *peasant
NINURTA: consort: gula
father: bel
NINUS: consort: semiramis
NIOBE: brother: pelops
enemy: apollo, artemis
father: tantalus
husband: amphion
pert.: columbic
sister-in-law: aedon
son: amyclas, argus
NIP: *bit(e), *pain, *steal
NIPPON: *japan
NIRVANA: maga, *paradise
triple fire: dosa, moha, raga
NISSE: *dwarf, *spirit

* Asterisk means to look up this word to find more answer words.

NISUS: *power, *try
daughter: scylla
NITROGEN: comb.: azo, azoto
compound: ammonia, betainogen
NITROGLYCERINE: dynamite,
tnt
finder: nobel, sobrero
NITROHYDROCHLORIC: aqua
regia
NITWIT: boob, *fool, *peasant
NIVAL, NIVEOUS: snowy, white
NIX: *dwarf, *spirit, *stop
NJORTH: child: frey(a), freyja
father-in-law: thjazi
home: noatun
wife: skadi, skathi
NOAH: ark: mixture
dove: columba
father: lamech
grandson: aram
mountain: ararat
pert.: noachian, noetic
raven: corvus
son: ham, japheth, sem, shem
wine cup: crater
NOBBY: *fine, *great, *smart
NOBLE: archducal, aristocratic,
amigerous, ashraf, athel, bashaw,
blue blood, brahman, burly,
chivalrous, dignified, doge, don,
ducal, edel, epic, fidalgo, *fine,
genteel, gentle(man), *good,
graf, grandee, *great, heroic, hidalgo, *important, just, kami,
khas, kingly, knightly, kuge,
ladylike, laird, *liberal, magnificent, pasha, patrician, princely,
*pure, queenly, renowned, ritter,
seigneur, seignior, senor, signor,
*splendid, *supreme, swell,
thane, thoroughbred, titled, upright, worthy
personification: almaviva
NOISE: *ado, air, *alarm, babel,
ballyhoo, bedlam, bellow, blare,
*blast, bluster, boom, brawl,
bruit, cackle, call, charivari,

chortle, clamor, clang(or), clatter, confusion, din, discord, fracas, *gossip, hell, jangle, pandemonium, racket, rattle, *riot,
roar, row, rowdy, ruckus, ruction, rumor, rumpus, sass, scandal, shivaree, sound, strepor,
stridor, talk, thunder, tumult
-maker: bell, calliope, clacker,
clapper, cracker, horn, klaxon,
rattle, siren, snapper, ticktack
-making ghost: poltergeist
NONCONFORMIST: beatnik, bohemian, deviationist, dissenter,
heretic, hippie, maverick, rebel,
revisionist, square, sulphite
NONENTITY: cipher, nothing,
zero
NONESUCH: *nonpareil, supreme
NONPAREIL: *acme, *best, *top
NONPLUS: bewilder, *puzzle
NONSENSE: amphigory, apple-
sauce, balderdash, baloney, banana oil, baragouin, bavardage,
bilge, blah-blah, bletheration,
bosh, buff, bull, buncombe, bun-
kum, claptrap, crud, double
talk, dribble, drivel, drool, eye-
wash, falderal, farrago, fiddle-
deedee, fiddle-faddle, flapdoodle,
flummery, folderol, folly, frivol-
ity, fudge, fustian, gabble, gag,
gammon, gibberish, gobbledegook, *gossip, guff, hocus pocus,
hogwash, hokum, hooey, horse-
feathers, hot air, humbug, jab-
ber(wocky), jargon, jazz, kibosh,
malarkey, megillah, moonshine,
mumbo jumbo, pah, parody, patter, phooey, piffle, pish, poof,
pooh, poppycock, prate, prattle, pshaw, *refuse, rigamarole,
rot, rubbish, shtuss, slipslop,
stuff, *talk, tommyrot, trash,
*trifle, tripe, trumpery, twaddle,
whoopla, wish-wash
creature: gaboon, gazook, golly-

wog, goluk, goof, goop, gyas-
cutus, hoofenpoofer, oink, prock,
smoo, snark, splintercat, wam-
pus, whangdoodle, whifflebird
verse: doggerel
NONVIOLENCE PRINCIPLE:
ahimsa
NOODLE: *fool, *head, loksh
NOODLES: ferfel, pasta, ravioli
NOOSE: hang, loop, *trap
armed with: laquearian
NORM: *model, *rule, *test
NORMAL: *mean, *regular,
*usual
NORMANDY: *bagpipe:* loure
beach: omaha, utah
capital: caen, rouen
cheese: angelot
conqueror: eisenhower, rollo
department: calvados, eure, orne,
manche
NORN: fate, skuld, urd, urth,
verthandi, weird sister, wyrd
NORSE: *norwegian
adam: askr, bure, buri
bard: sagaman, scald, skald
bridge, myth: bifrost, rainbow
chief: jarl, rollo, yarl
demon: fylgja, hatto, nidhogg,
surt(r), wode
dragon: fafner, fafnir
drink, sacred: hydromel, odrerir
fate: *norn
fount: hvergelmir, mimir, urd
giant: aegir, atli, baugi, eggther,
fafnir, geirrod, groa, gymir,
hrungnir, hrym, jotun(n), mimir,
mymir, natt, nott, skrymir, surt,
suttung, thjazi, thrym, urth,
utgardaloki, utgartha, ymir
giant's ship: naglfar
giantess: gerda, grid, gunnlod,
skadi
goat, myth: heidrun
god, goddess: *aesir
heaven: asgard, bilskirnir, folkvang, glathsheim, glitnir, himinb-

jorg, hlithskjalf, sessrymnir, sokkvabekk, thruthheim, valaskjalf,
valhalla, vingolf, ydalir
heaven guardian: heimdall(r)
hero: egil, siegfried, sigurd
horse: alsvinn, arvak, goldfax
king: atli, nibelung, schilbung
liquor: akvavit, aquavit
monster: fenrir, garm, kraken,
midgard, serpent
poem: edda, rune, saga
rainbow bridge: bifrost
ring: draupnir
ring guardian: andvari
river, myth: gjoll
serpent: midgard, nidhogg
ship: naglfar, skidbladnir
spear: gungnir
tree, ash or world: yggdrasil
underworld: niflheim, niflhel
violent one, warrior: berserker
wolf, myth: fenrir
youth apple custodian: ithun
NORTH AFRICAN: berber,
*moor
antelope: addax
bread: abret, kisra
coast: barbary
country: algeria, egypt, morocco,
sudan, tripoli, tunis
dialect: sabir
dynasty: aghlabid, aglabite
fruit: date, fig
garment: haik
gnome: owl
jackal: dieb(s)
lyre: kissar
olive: barouni
sheep: aoudad, arui, udad
NORTH AMERICAN: *american
bat: corynorhinus
bird: baird's-sandpiper, bufflehead, cardinal, fulmar, grackle,
killdeer, kingrail, pisobia
cactus: cacanapa, opuntia
cedar: red, savine, waxwing
constrictor: bullsnake, gopher

* Asterisk means to look up this word to find more answer words.

snake, pituophis
duck: bufflehead, charitonetta
fern: flower-cup, woodsia
herb: abronia, alkanet, anise, arbutus, chickweed, verbena
maple: box elder
marmoset: tamarin
orchid: arethusa
owl: wapacut
shrub: arrowwood, chokeberry
tree: arbor vitae, balsam, basswood, bladdernut, catalpa, hemlock, hickory, hornbeam, mabi, oneberry, pawpaw, redbud, sassafras, sweetsop, tamarack, titi, tupelo
NORTH CAROLINA: *bird:* cardinal
cape: fear, hatteras
flower: flowering dogwood
native: buffalo, tarheel
nickname: tarheel state
river: neuse, pee dee, tar
tree: pine
NORTH DAKOTA: *bird:* meadowlark
flower: wild prairie rose
nickname: flickertail state
tree: american elm
NORTHEAST WIND: bise, bora, burga, euryclydon, gregale
NORTH PACIFIC: *fish:* beshow
island: bonin, kuril, ogasawara
NORTH POLE DISCOVERER: peary
NORTH SEA: *duck:* scoter
port: bergen, bremen, emden, hamburg, hull
river to: aller dee, eider, elbe, ems, maas, meuse, rhine, tees, tyne, weser
NORTH STAR: cynosure, lodestar, polaris, polestar
NORTH VIETNAM: *forces:* communsi, cosvn, viet cong, viet minh
NORTH WIND: aquillo, badisa-

dobistroz, boreas, kabibonokka, mistral, seistan
NORTHERN: arctic, boreal, polar septentrional
bear: russia
constellation: andromeda, aquila, camelopardalis, cancer, cynosure, eagle, ursa
lights: aurora borealis
-most land: thule, ultima thule
-most north america: boothia
rhodesia: zambia
seas: arctalia
spy: apple
sucker: stone roller
NORTHUMBERLAND KING: clarivaunce
NORTHWEST: *highway:* alcan
wind: barat, belat, boreas, caurus, chocolate gale
NORWEGIAN: *norse references
author: bjornson, hamsun, ibsen
bird: ptarmigan, rype
boat: praam, praham, pram
cart: stolkjaerre
coin: krone, ora, ore
converter: olaf tryggvason
counties: amter
county: amt, finmark, fylke
dance: halling
embroidery: hardanger
explorer: amundsen, eric, leif, mohn, nansen, sars
goblin: kobold, nisse
governor: amtman(d)
haddock: rosefish
inlet: fiord, fjord
island: seiland
measure: alen, fathom, fot, kande, korntonde, mal, pot, skieppe
mesa: dovre, fjeld, hardanger
mythology: *norse references
parliament: lagthing, storthing
peak: blodfjell, galdhoepig, glitretind, hallingskarvet, hardangerjokul, harteigen, kjolen,

---

* **Asterisk means to look up this word to find more answer words.**

myrdalfjell, numedal, ramnanosi, skagastolstind, telemark, ustetind, vibmesnosi

port: alesund, bodo, mo, moss, narvik, tromso

river: ena, glomma, klar, lougen, namsen, rana, tana

ruler: hakon, hersir, olaf

saint: olaf, olaus

toast: skal, skoal

NOSE: *ailment:* catarrh, cold, coryza, ozena, rhinitis

bees: lor

bleed: bloody butchers, herb, orchis, red trillium

bleeding: epistaxis

cartilage: septum

comb.: nasi

dive: collapse, *end

elongated: proboscis

finish: *draw, *tie

flat: pug, simous, snub

flute: bin, pungi, vina

gay: bouquet, corsage, scent

gay tree: frangipani

having large: nasute

-lessness: arrhinia

long: snout

medicine: errhine

muscle: nasalio

opening: nares, nostril

paint: liquor

part: bridge, septum, vomer

pert.: narial, nasal, rhinal

pincher: barnacle

ring: band, cattle-leader, pirn

snub: pug, simous

NOSTALGIC: homesick, sentimental

NOSTOLOGY: geriatrics

NOSTRADAMUS: astrologer, seer

NOT: *comb.:* an, il, im, ir, un

NOTABLE: *magnate, *noted

NOTATION: *note, *record

phonetic: romic

NOTE: *air, apostil(le), asset, attend, attention, billet, certificate, chit, *comment, correspond, dispatch, eminence, entry, explain, *glory, heed, indicate, iou, item, jot, letter, line, loan, *mark, memo(randum), minute, postil, *promise, *record, remark, *see, *sign, song, statement, strain, token, tone, tune

bank: finnip, flimsy, frogskin

book: adversaria, *record

bugle: mot

case: pocketbook

circular: credit

double: breve

eighth: mora, unca

endorsement: aval

explain by: gloss

explanatory: scholium

guido: ela(mi), gamut, ut

half: minim

highest: ela

marginal: apostil(le)

middle: mese

music: di, do, fa, fi, la, le, li, me, mi, ra, re, ri, se, si, so, sol, te, ti

promissory: bon, good

sequence: cadence, *meter

sharpening: ecbole

short: chit(ty), memo

succession: gamut, strain, tiralee

tail: filum

whole: semibreve

writer: annotator

NOTED: *big, *great, *important

NOTHING: nihil, trifle, void, zero

but: mere, only

else but: de facto, ipso facto

NOTICE: *mark, *order, *see, *sign, *spy

NOTICEABLE: *open, salient

NOTIFY: *advise, *tell, warn

NOTION: idea, *image, *model

NOTORIETY: *glory, *honor

NOTT: *son:* dag

horse: hrimfaxi

NOTWITHSTANDING: but, despite

* Asterisk means to look up this word to find more answer words.

NOUN: *form:* case, gender
  gender: epicene
  indeclinable: aptote
  kind: common, proper
  suff.: ac, ana, ance, anse, eer,
    ence, ent, ery, et, fer, ia, ial, ier,
    ing, ion, ior, ise, ist, orium
  to cases: dipote
  verbal: gerund
NOURISH: *aid, feed, *support
NOUS: intellect, *mind, reason
NOVA SCOTIA: acadia, acadie
  bay: fundy
  cape: breton, canso, george
  lake: bras d'or
  mountain ash: dogberry
  people: acadians, blue noses
NOVELTY: dernier cri, *style
NOVICE: abecedarian, rookie
NOX: *nyx
NOXIOUS: *bad, *evil, *ugly
NUBIAN: *harp:* nanga, sistrum
  palm: doom, doum, dum
NUCLEAR: *carrier:* cvan
  chemistry: atomics
  cross section: barn
  element: proton
  fission term: atom smasher, bom-
    bardment, breeding, bullet, chain
    reaction, cleavage, critical mass,
    disintegration
  fuel: uranium
  fusion: ionization, neutron, pro-
    ton, splitting the atom
  machine: betatron
  network fiber: linin
  physics: atomics
  reactor: breeder
  moderator: boron carbide
NUCLEIC ACID MOLECULE:
  dna, enzyme, rna
NUCLEUS: cadre, core, *source
  diploid: amphikaryon
NUDD: *consort:* morrigu
NUDIST: adamite
NUISANCE: *evil, *pain, *trial
NUMB: *dull, *funny, *stupid

NUMBER: *act, *bit, *kind,
  *quantity, *symbol, *unit
  cardinal: four, one, three, two
  comb.: arithmo, by, deci, eth,
    numero, penta, quadro, st, th, tri
  corpuscles: blood count
  describable by: scalar
  dice: sise
  extra: encore
  indefinite: lac, several, steen
  indeterminate: umpteen, zillion
  one: ego, me, self
  ordinal: first, second, third
  prime: eleven, five, one, seven,
    thirteen, three, two
  pure: scalar
  suff.: eth, st, th
  ten, under: digit
  to which another added: augend
  two: second fiddle
  whole: integer
NUMBERS: *group, *quantity
NUMEROUS: *big, *large, *plenty
NUMIDIA: *bird:* crane, demoiselle
  city: hippo
NUMSKULL: *fool, *stupid
NUN: *bird:* monasa, titmouse
  chief: abbess, amma, mother
  dress: faille, habit, wimple
  habit part: analav, kerchief
  roman: vesta
  order: dominican, lorettine, mar-
    ist, trappist
  son: joshua
NUPSON: *fool, *peasant
NURSE: *bottle:* biberon
  headgear: wimples
  shark: gata
NURTURE: feed, nourish, *support
NUT: *eccentric, *enthusiast
  almond-like: pili
  bearing: nuciferous
  beverage: cola, kola
  brother: geb
  brown: chestnut, hazel, walnut
  cake: doughnut

* Asterisk means to look up this word to find more answer words.

coal: anthracite
collective: mast, shack
comb.: caryo, karyo, nuci
companion: bolt
confection: marchpane, marzipan
cracker: pillory, xenops
father: shu
grass: sedge
hatch: sitta, titmouse, xenops
hickory: pecan
hook: beadle, constable
husband: geb, keb
ivory: anta
kola: bichy, gourou
-let: pyrene
-like drupe: tryma
medicinal: cola, kola
-meg: calabash, seed, spice
-meg husk: mace
-meg-like fruit: camara(n)
-meg state: connecticut
offspring: aah, horoeris, horus, isis, khons, nephthys, osiris, ra, set, thoth
-pecker: *nuthatch
NUTS, NUTTY: *insane, *mad
NYMPH: cave: oread
flower: limoniad
fountain: abarbarea, albunea, camena, egeria
glen: napaea
grove: alseides
hills: oread
lake: limniad, naiad
meadow: limoniad
moslem: houri
mountain: oread
sea: callirrhoe, galatea, mermaid, nereid, oceanid
tree: dryad, hamadryad, nereid
water: apsaras, arethusa, hydriad, kelpie, limniad, lorelei, naiad, nais, nix, nixie, undine
woods: alsaeids, auloniads, hylaeorae, napaeae, *tree
NYX: brother: erebus
daughter: day, eris, hesperides

father: chaos
husband: chaos, erebus
personified: night
son: charon, thanatos

OAF: *clown, *fool, *peasant
OAK: ambrose, casuarina, cerris, chaparro, encina, holly, holm, ilex, quercitron, roble
bark: crut, emory, mill
beauty: moth
blight: louse
comb.: querci
fern: polypody
fruit: acorn, bellote, camata
fungus: armillaria
gall: oak apple
moss: evernia
tannin: quercinic, queric
thicket: chaparral
web: cockchafer
wood: cartouch(e), mesa
young: flittern
OAKEN: *hard, *strong
OAR: blade: palm, peel, wash
boss: button
comb.: remi
fulcrum: axis, oarlock, thole
part: blade, loom, palm, peel
shaped: remiform, remiped
short: scull
steering: swape, swipe
OARSMAN: bostanji, remex, rower, sculler, stroke
OASIS: aguada, dakhla, gafsa, merv, spa, spring, *waterway
OAT: cake: caper
ear: wagtail
genus, grass: avena
head: panicle
husks: shude
meal: brewis, brochan, browis
meal cake: pone, scone
paid in lieu of rent: avenage
pert.: avenaceous
wile: cheat

* Asterisk means to look up this word to find more answer words.

OATH: affirmation, attestation, blasphemy, bond, curse, dirty name, epithet, execration, expletive, imprecation, invective, malediction, pledge, *promise, serment, vow, word
mild: ahem, all-fired, beans, begad, begorra, bejabbers, blamed, blasted, blessed, blimy, bloody, by cracky, by jove, confounded, consarn, creeps, dadblamed, dadblasted, dadburn, dagnab, dang, darn, dash, dern, deuced, dingbust, doggone, drat, egad, gad, gee, goldang, golly, gosh, great scott, heck, hell-fired, infernal, lud, ods, oons, mackins, parbleu, plagued

OBDURATE: *firm, *hard, *obstinate, *severe

OBEAH: *fetish, sorcery, voodoo
doctor: magician

OBED: parent: boaz, ruth
son: azariah, jehu, jesse

OBEDIENT: compliant, *tame

OBELISK: mark, *memorial, *tower

OBERON: fairy king, *spirit
wife: titania

OBESE: *big, *fat, great, *heavy

OBEY: heed, *mind, *yield

OBI: *fetish, girdle, inro

OBJECT: *complain, *design, *desire, *end, gadget, *image, *protest, *purpose, *thing
biblical: thummim, urim
d'art: curio, *token, vase
lesson: example
man-made: artifact
tilted at: quintain

OBJECTIVE: *fair, *object

OBJURGATE: *abuse, *criticize

OBLIGATE, OBLIGE: *force, *press, *urge

OBLITERATE: abolish, *destroy

OBLIVION: lethe, limbo, silence
producer: *drug, narcotic

OBLOQUY: *abuse, *shame, *smear

OBNOXIOUS: *bad, *evil, *ugly

OBOE: reed, shawn, szopelka
comb.: aulo

OBSCENE: *dirty, *evil, *wanton

OBSCURE: *abstruse, adumbrate, ambiguous, becloud, bewilder, blacken, blot(ch), blur(ry), caliginous, cloud(y), *cover, cryptic, dark(en), deep, delude, dewy, dim, disguise, doubtful, dubious, dull, dusky, envelop, esoteric, film, fog, gloomy, *hard, *hide, humble, indefinite, indistinct, inky, involve, latent, lowly, murky, nameless, nubilate, obfuscate, occulate, occult, opaque, overcast, remote, *sage, *secret, *smear, *vague
comb.: adelo, aphano

OBSEQUIOUS: menial, servile

OBSERVATION: *image, *note

OBSERVE: *look, *mark, *meet, *note, regard, remark, *see

OBSESS: *press, *push, *seize

OBSESSION: hang-up, *passion

OBSOLETE: *old, passe, past

OBSTACLE: bar, drag, rub, snag

OBSTINATE: assish, balky, bull dogged, camelish, dogged, dour, entete, fixed, *hard, heady, intractable, mulish, obdurate, opinionated, pertinacious, perverse, pigheaded, refractory, renitent, resolute, self-willed, *set, sot, *stern, stiff, *strict, *sullen, tenacious, *wild, willful

OBSTREPEROUS: *obstinate

OBSTRUCT: *arrest, *slow, *stop

OBTAIN: *acquire, *get, *mean

OBTRUDE: *dismiss, *give, *press

OBTUSE: *dull, *slow, *stupid
comb.: ambly

OBVERSE: face, front, *opposite

OBVIOUS: broad, clear, *open

OCCASION: *affair, *need, *time

* Asterisk means to look up this word to find more answer words.

OCCASIONAL: extra, odd, off
OCCULT: *magic, *obscure
OCCUPATION: *trade, *use, *work
OCCUPY: *arrest, *interest, possess, *seize, *take, *use
OCCUR: *appear, arise, arrive, befall, be present, break, chance, come off, ensue, eventuate, exist, fall, go off, hap(pen), *light, *pass, rise
OCCURRENCE: episode, event
OCEAN: *sea
OCEANIA: *malaya, pacific island, polynesia
OCEANIC: bonito: sarda sarda, skipjack
 tunicate: salp
OCEANID: aethra, clymene, pluto
OCEANUS: child: argia, caanthus, dione, doris, eurynome, metis, *oceanid, styx, tyche
 parent: gaea, uranus
 sister, wife: tethys
OCELOT: juagatirica, leopard
OCHER: almagra, kiel, tiver
OCTAVE: key, organ, *stop, utas
OCTAVIA: kin: anthony, augustus
ODD: *eccentric, *funny, *weird
ODDS: *advantage, *bet
 and ends: *bit, *hash, *mixture
ODE: birthday: genethliacon
 part: epode
 pert.: odic, pindaric
 victory: epinicion, epinikion
ODIN: alfadir, woden, wotan
 crow: hugin, mugin
 daughter-in-law: nanna
 descendant: scyld
 favorite family: volsungs
 hall: valhalla
 horse: sleipner
 maiden: valkyrie
 olympus: asgard
 nephew: ve, vile, vili
 palace: syn
 pantheon: *aesir

 parents: bestla, bor
 protege: hadding
 ring: draupnir
 skald: bragi
 son: balder, donar, hermod, thor, *tyr, vali, vidar, vithar
 spear: gungnir
 steed: sleipnir
 sword: gram
 wife: frea, freya, freyja, fria, frigg, jord, rind(r)
 wolf: freki, gere, geri
ODIOUS: *bad, *dirty, *ugly
ODOR: *aroma, breath, *scent
 cooking: fumet, nidor
 foul: fetor, stench
ODYSSEUS: beggar: irus
 captor: calypso
 chronicler: homer.
 dog: argos
 enemy: poseidon, irus
 friend: elpenor, mentor
 home: ithaca
 parents: anticlea, laertes
 plant: moly
 son: telegonus, telemachus
 swineherd: eumaeus
 temptress: circe
 voyage: odyssey
 wife: penelope
OEDIPUS: brother-in-law: creon
 daughter: antigone, ismene
 father, adopted: polybus
 parents: jocasta, laius
 refuge: colonus
 son: eteocles, polynices
 victim: laius, sphinx
 wife: jocasta
OENEUS: wife: althaea
OENOMAUS: charioteer: myrtilus
 daughter: hippodameia
OENONE: husband: paris
OFF: *insane, *mad, *weird, *wet
 beat: mod, old-fashioned
 color: campy, risque
 comb.: ap, aph, apo
 -hand: abrupt, impromptu

* Asterisk means to look up this word to find more answer words.

one's feed: *bad, *low, *sick
-*scourings:* *dregs, *refuse
-*set:* *adjust, cancel, print
-*shoot:* *issue, *result
OFFAL: *refuse, slough, swill
OFFEND: *anger, *err, *hurt
OFFENSE: *attack, *evil, *sin
  civil: stellionate, tort
  law: crime, delict, felony
OFFENSIVE: *attack, *bad, *evil
OFFER: *advance, *issue, *present, *promise, *supply
  last: ultimatum
OFFERING: *gift, *present
OFFICE: *plant, *service, *studio
  chief: boss, manager
  comb.: ate
  divine: akoluthia
  ecclesiastic: matins
  help: clerk, secretary, staff, stenographer, typist
  holder: in, incumbent, winner
  machine: calculator, computer, mimeograph, stenotype, xerox
  purchase or sale: barratry
  seeker: candidate, nominee
OFFICER: *assistant:* aide, deputy
  church: *church: man
  college: beadle, bursar, dean
  military: *army: officer
  presiding: archon, chairman, emcee, moderator, president
  stable: avener
OFFICIAL: *agent, *lord, *magnate, *title, *true
OGEE: *molding
OGLE: eye, flirt, *look, *see
OGRE: *demon, *devil, *dwarf, *hag, spectre, *spirit, *witch
OHIO: *bird:* cardinal
  flower: scarlet carnation
  nickname: buckeye state
OHM: *millionth:* microhm
OIL: *almond-odored:* benzonitrile
  animal: adipose, blubber, butter, castor, cod, dripping, fat, ghee, haliver, lanolin, lard, mutton tallow

  bird: guacharo
  bone: olanin
  butter: ghee, oleo
  can: bomb
  cedar: alchitran, alkitran
  cloth: linoleum
  coating: cambouis
  colorless: cetane
  comb.: ole(o)
  consecrated: chrism
  edible: aceite
  fish: escolar
  flax: linseed
  fragrant: attar, cedar, irone
  gas: blaugas
  juniper: alchitran, alkitran
  lamp: argand, lantern, lucigen
  linseed: carron
  liquid: olein
  market: teli
  mineral: anthracene, benzine, carbolic, coal, creosote, cresol, gasoline, kerosene, naphtha, paraffin, petrolatum
  myrcia: bay oil, perfume
  nut: pyrularia, rabbitwood
  odoriferous: ericinol
  painting: canvas
  palms: bribery, money, tip
  pert.: elaic, oleic
  plant: sesame
  poisonous: anemonol
  producing: olifiant
  rock: limestone, shale
  rub with: anoint
  salt: bittern
  seed: castor bean, cottonseed, linseed, rapeseed, sesame, teel
  skin: sebum
  stone: hone, shale, whetstone
  torch: lucigen
  vegetable: absinthe, almond, anise(ed), avocado, bay, beechnut, cacao, carapa, castor, citronella, cocoa, colaz, copaiba, copra, corn, cottonseed, croton, eucalyptus, flaxseed, fusel, ke-

kuna, kokum, laurel, lemon, linseed, macassar, maize, oleoresin, olive, peanut, resin, rosin, sesame, spikenard, turpentine
vessel: alabastos, alabastron, ampulla, aryballos, askos, cruce, cruet, cruize, lekythos, olpe, rier
water fennel: androl
well, dry: duster, gasser
OILEUS: *son:* ajax, medon
OILY: bland, servile, *smooth
OINTMENT: balm, nard, salve
application: embrocation
biblical: spikenard
dry: xeromyron, xeromyrum
hair: pomade, pomatum
oil: carron, cerate, oleamen
veterinary: remolade, remoulade
wax: cerate
OISIN: *father:* fionn
OJIBWAY: *group:* meda, mide
OJO: oasis, spring
OK: *accept, *great, groovy, ratify, *right, roger, yes
OKINAWA: *city:* naha, shuri
OKLAHOMA: *bird:* flycatcher
flower: mistletoe
lake: atoka, hulah, tenkiller
nickname: boomer, sooner
reservoir: eufaula, oologah
tree: redbud
OLD: *aged, anile, antediluvian, antiquated, antique, archaic, auld, back number, blighted, dated, decaying, earthy, eld, erst, experienced, feeble, former, fusty, gone to seed, gray, hasbeen, hoary, mature, medieval, model-t, moldering, moldy, mosy, mucid, musty, obsolete, ogygian, quondam, senescent, senile, shabby, stale, tintype, worn
adam: *evil, *sin, wickedness
age: *age references
bailey: gaol, *jail, prison
bay state: massachusetts
blood and guts: patton

boy: alumnus, *fellow, man
campaigner: politician, veteran
cedar: brown madder, tanagra
dominion state: virginia
english: black letter
fashioned: fogram, horse-and-buggy, offbeat, outmoded, out of date, quaint, tintype
fogy: dotard, stodgy
franklin state: tennessee
gooseberry: *demon, *devil
hand: vet(eran)
hat: platitudinous, trite
hickory: andrew jackson
joke: chestnut
king cole preceder: asclepoid
line: conservative, established
line state: maryland
maid: celibate, prude, spinster
man: *man: old
-man cactus: cephalocereus
noll: oliver cromwell
refrain: fa la
rough and ready: taylor
serpent: adi-sesha, adi-shesha
sledge: all fours, high-low jack, pitch, seven-up
sod: eire, erin, ireland
soldier: butt, veteran
song: platitude, *trifle
squaw: duck
stager: actor, veteran
story: platitude
testament: apocrypha, *bible, hexateuch, ketubim, nebiim, octateuch, pentateuch, torah
timer: kamaaina, native
times: ago, eld, former, late, past, quondam, yore
wife: dotard, effeminate
wives tale: superstition
woman: *woman: old
OLD WORLD: *ape:* baboon, catarrhina
carnivore: genet
curlew: bustard, marlin
dish: tansy

falcon: saker
finch: brambling
goat: ibex
grass: alang, imperata
herb: anchusa, anthemis, aponogeton, arctium, armoracia
lizard: agama, sepa
orchid: arachnite
partridge: alectoris
plant: anthyllis, axseed, coronilla
varia, crown vetch
shrub: alangium, genista
swift: apus
tree: balanite
vine: balsam apple
OLEAGINOUS: **smooth*
OLIO: **hash, *mixture*
OLIVE: *brown:* bronze nude
enzyme: olease
fly genus: dacus
fruit: drupe
inferior: moron
oil, comb.: elaio
oil, lees: amurca
oil substitute: argan
pert.: oleaceous
stuffed: pimola
tree: ash, olea
wild: oleaster
wood: brun dore
OLIVER: *bark:* black sassafras
sword: hauteclaire
OLIVINE: chrysolite, peridot
OLLA-PODRIDA: **mixture*
OLYMPIA: *husband:* bireno
OLYMPIC: *game site:* elis
god: **greek god, *goddess*
police chief: alytarch
sacred grove: altis
sled: luge
statue: zan
OLYMPUS: *hindu:* meru
OMASUM: belly, **stomach*
OMEN: **mark, *promise, *sign*
OMERS: *ten:* epha(h)
OMINOUS: **bad, *evil, *sinister*
OMISSION: **error, *need, *sin*

pretended: paralepsis
tacit: silence
OMIT: **abandon, *pass*
OMNIPOTENCE: **power*
OMNIPOTENT: **strong*
OMNISCIENT: **smart, *wise*
OMRI: *daughter:* athaliah
successor: ahab
ON: *account of:* because, for
all sides: about, around
and on: forever, tedious
board: here, **present*
-dit: **gossip, *report,* rumor
edge: **critical, *upset*
fire: **ardent, *eager, *hot*
ice: **absolute, *actual*
ON THE: *ball:* **active, *quick,*
ready, **smart,* with it
beam: groovy, **straight*
double: **fast, *quick*
fence: neutral
go: **active, *fast, *quick*
house: **free,* gratis
level: **fair, *honest, *true*
march: aggressive, attacking
nose: accurate, punctual
other hand: again, contrary
road: abroad, **active*
run: **active, *frantic*
side: moonlighting, **secret*
spot: dangerous, here, trapped
square or up-and-up: **fair, *honest, *open, *true*
verge: imminent, **near*
ONAGER: ass, catapult, kiang
ONAM: *son:* jada, shammai
ONCE: ago, erst, former, past
around: cycle
more: **again*
-over: scrutiny
ONE: **ace,* eins, ichi, monad, only,
person, sole, **unit,* uno
after other: serially, seriatim
and half, comb.: sesqui
behind other: tandem
berry: hackberry
-chambered: unicameral

* **Asterisk means to look up this word to find more answer words.**

character: byte, eight bit
colored: monochromatic
comb.: heno, idio, mono, uni
dyne: barad
eighth troy ounce: dram
fold: *simple, sincere
footed: uniped
for the book: marvel, wonder
-horse: petty, *small
knowing: insider
master: sloop
-sided: askew, biased, bigoted, partial, prejudiced, unjust
spot: *ace
tenth: tithe
thousand: mil
twenty-fourth: carat, karat
year old: annatinous, annotine
ONE HUNDRED: *and 44:* gross
percent: *all, *pure, total
twenty: long hundred
ONER: *ace, best, lalapaloosa
ONEROUS: *dull, *hard, *heavy
ONIAS: *kin:* jason, simon
ONION: *bulb:* set
disease: bulb rot
genus: allium
-like: chive, leek, shallot
set: button
small: eschalot, scallion, shallot
ONLY: *best, mere, save, *unique
ONOMATOPOEIC: echoic, imitative
ONSET, ONSLAUGHT: *attack
ONUS: load, *trouble, *work
ONYX: chalcedony, nicolo, tecali
marble: alabaster
OODLES: *plenty, *quantity
OOZE: *escape, mire, seep, sop
OPAL: cacholong, gem, girasol, hyalite, menilite, noble, stone
OPAQUE: *dirty, *dull, *thick
OPEN: activate, agape, ajar, alert, amenable, apparent, artless, available, bald, *bare, begin, blossom, bluff, *break, broach, cave in, chink, commence, cor-

dial, crack, cut, develop, disclose, *display, divaricate, divide, enlarge, evident, exhibit, expand, expose, exterior, fissure, frank, *honest, ingenuous, initiate, liable, *liberal, make room, manifest, naked, obvious, on the table, overt, *part, passageway, patent, *plain, *present, *produce, rend, responsive, reveal, rip, rive, separate, *show, *simple, sincere, slit, *split, *spread, *start, *straight, tear, vacant
air: alfresco, out of doors
bill: anastomus, bird
country: champaign, great outdoors, plains, weald
-eyed: alert, curious, *sharp
fire: *attack, invade, *start
gape: dehiscence
sesame: incantation, password
space, dread of: agoraphobia
the door: *admit, *prepare
up: *attack, *speed, *start
work: a jour, bratticing
OPENING: *abyss, access, adit, aperture, appearance, *approach, arch, bay, beginning, brack, breach, bull's-eye, burr, canal, cave, cavity, chance, cleft, commencement, dawn, development, door, entrance, eye(let), fenestra, first, fissure, flaw, fontanel, foramen, fusuma, gambit, gap, gape, gate, *head, hiatus, hole, initiation, interstice, introduction, jauna, job, loophole, meatus, opportunity, orifice, outlet, *pass(age), perforation, *place, pore, rent, rift, rima, sinus, slit, slot, *start, stomata, *tear, *trap, vacancy, *waterway, window, yat, yawn
enlarge: ream
escape: meuse, muse
having: fenestrate
sponge: apopyle
two, having: biporose, biporous

* **Asterisk means to look up this word to find more answer words.**

OPERA: africaine, aida, barber of seville, bartered bride, boheme, carmen, cid, coq d'or, dead city, demon, dinorah, don quixote, ernani, euranthe, falstaff, faust, fidelio, fra diavolo, gioconda, hamlet, herodiade, lakme, lohengrin, lucia di lammermoor, madam butterfly, manon, mignon, mikado, norma, othello, pagliacci, parsifal, pinafore, rienzi, rigoletto, romeo and juliet, rosenkavalier, sadko, thasis, tosca, traviata
comic: buffa, buffo
composer: alfano, auber, balfe, beethoven, bellini, berlioz, bizet, borodin, charpentier, debussy, donizetti, flotow, gay, giordano, glinka, gluck, halevy, handel, leoncavallo, massenet, puccini
daytime: soap
division: scena
glass: binocle, lorgnette
hat: *hat:* opera
house: met, scala, theatre
part: aria, recitative
singer: alda, bori, callas, caruso, diva, eames, farrar, gigli, melba, patti, pons, raisa, rise, steber
OPERATE: *run, *use, *work
OPERATION: *action, *plant
suff.: ectomy
OPERATOR: *actor, *agent, doer, pilot, player, swinger
OPIATE: *drug: addictive
OPINE: suppose, *think
OPINION: *doctrine, *mind, value
OPIUM: *drug, narcotic
alkaloid: codein, morphine, narcotin, papaverine
camphorate: paregoric
concentrate: heroin
derivative: meconic
extract: chandoo, chandu
seed: maw
source: poppy

OPOSSUM: quica, sarigue
water: yapock, yapok
OPPORTUNE: apt, *fit, *ready
OPPORTUNITY: *advantage, occasion, *opening, *show
OPPOSE: *fight, *meet, *protest
OPPOSITE: abreast, *adverse, antagonistic, anti(thetic), antipodal, confronting, contra(dictory), converse, facing, fronting, hostile, incompatible, inimical, obverse, other, polaric, repugnant, reverse, toward, versus, vis-a-vis
comb.: ant(i)
extremities: antipodes, poles
OPPRESS: *abuse, *afflict, wrong
OPPRESSOR: bull of bashan, *despot, *ruler
OPPROBRIUM: infamy, *shame
OPS: *associate:* consus
child: ceres, demeter, hades, hera, hestia, poseidon, zeus
consort: cronus, saturn
father: saturn, uranus
festival: opalia
OPT: *decide, select, *will
OPTIMISTIC: *happy, sanguine
OPTION: preference, privilege
OPULENCE: *plenty, wealth
OPULENT: *rich
OPUS: *study, *work
ORACLE: *adage, *prophet
pert.: erudite, pythonic, vatic
seat: dodona
ORAL: buccal, parol, vocal
instruction: catechesis
ORANGE: *berry:* cranberry
bird: tanager
blight: quick decline
city: bloemfontein
flower oil: neroli
grass: bastard gentian
heraldry: tenne
leaf: karamu
-like fruit: bel, tangerine
membrane: zest
milkweed: asclepias, butterfly

* **Asterisk means to look up this word to find more answer words.**

milkwort: candy-weed
mock: seringa, syringe
oil: neroli
peel: aurautiicortex, zest
pert.: aurantiaceous
red: alga, coral, saffron, sard
seed: pip
seedless: navel
-shaped: oblate
spring: styrax
sulphur: alfalfa butterfly
tree: osage, troyer citrange
variety: blood, hedge, mock, navel, osage, seville
virus: tristeza
wood: osage
ORANGUTAN: bimi, mias, pongo
ORATION: philippic, **talk*
ORATORIO: *coda:* stretto
 handel's: semele
 haydn's: seasons
ORBIT: **range,* route, **sphere*
 point: aphelion, apogee, apsis, nadir, node, perigee
ORCHESTRA: band, ensemble
 bells: glockenspiel
 circle: parquet, parterre, pit
ORCHID: *appendage:* caudicle
 egg: oosphere
 food: salep, vanilla
 genus: arethusa, gymnadenia, laelia, listera, vanda
 leaves: faam, faham
 male: cullion, purple
 part: anther, labellum
ORCUS: hades, **hell*
ORDAIN: **allot,* **order,* **will*
ORDEAL: **test,* **torment,* **trial*
 bean: calabar bean, poison
 tree: bushman's poison
ORDER: aline, appoint(ment), array, assign, bid, call, case, caste, ceremonial, charge, choose, decree, direct, dispose, fiat, govern, **group,* guide, injunction, **kind,* **law,* line, lodge, mandate, method, peace, precept, pro-

nounce, **quiet,* **rank,* requisition, select, **society,* **system,* verdict, **way,* **will*
 back: recommit, remand
 connected: seriatim
 cosmic: rita, tao
 garter, symbol: blue ribbon
 goddess: dice, dike, irene
 good: eutaxie, eutaxy
 grammar: taxis
 legal: subpoena, summons, writ
 merit: albert, aviz, bath, christ, crown, leopold, st louis, stolaf, sword, vasa
 official: billet
 parliamentary: procedure
 prayers: book of hours
 religious: augustinian, austin, benedictine, bernardine, black friar, bonhomme, capuchin, carmelite, carthusian, cistercian, cluniac, dominican, franciscan, friar, gilbertine, hospitaler, jesuit, lorettine, loyolite, maturine, minorite, recollet, templar, trappist
 repetition: antimetabole, antistrophe
 separately: a la carte
 suff.: ales, an, ini
 writ: precipe
ORDERLY: aide, tidy, trim
ORDINAL: book, number, regular
 suff.: eth
ORDINANCE: **law,* **order,* **rule*
ORDINARY: **plain,* **regular,* **ugly,* **usual*
ORDNANCE: ammunition, **supply*
 17th century: rabinet
ORDURE: dirt, filth, **refuse*
ORE: **metal,* **mineral*
OREAD: fairy, nymph, peri
OREGON: *bird:* western meadowlark
 crabapple: powitch
 first explorer: feno

flower: mahonia, oregon grape
nickname: beaver state
peak: hood
range: blue, cascade, coast
tree: douglas fir
wind: chinook
ORESTES: *father:* agamemnon
friend: pylades
mother: clytemnestra
nurse: arsinoe
sister: electra
wife: hermione
ORGAN: **agent, *part, *unit*
adjust: registrate
algaic: procarp
auricular: ear
barrel: autophon
bristle-like: seta
cactus: saguaro
deficiency: aplasia
desk: console
elongated: tentacle
examining instrument: autoscope
fish: drumfish
flutter device: tremolo
gallery: loft
interlude: verset
inventor: st cecilia
lymphoid: tonsil
motion: muscle
note: tremolent
olfactory: nares, nose
opening: ora, os
optical: eye
original: syrinx
part: action, altar, antiphonal,
box, chancel, choir, console,
coupler, drawknob, echo, gallery, pallet, pedal, pipe, piston,
roller, shutter, slider, solo, swell,
tracker, wind
pert.: afferent
prehensile: chela, claw, clutch,
digit, duke, finger, fist, hand,
hook, manus, nail, nipper, palm,
paw, pincer, pounce, talon, tentacle, ungula

prelude: verset
saw-like: serra
seed-bearing: pistil
sense: sensilla
sensory: ear, eye, nose
speech: lip, throat, tongue
stop: aeoline, bassoon, bombarde,
bourdon, carillon, celesta, celes-
tina, diapason, dolcan, dolce,
dolcian, dulciana, gadekt,
gamba, gemshorn, harmonica,
larigot, melodia, montre, nacht-
horn, nasard, nasat, oboe,
orage, posaune, prestant, quint,
rankett, reed, regale, scharf,
sext, subbass, tertian, terz, tierce,
tremolo, undamaris, viola, wald-
flote
toner: voicer
ORGANIC: *body:* zooid
compound: amine, ketol
nature: bios
principle: cardaissin
radical: ethyl
remains, without: azoic
ORGANISM: amoeba, anaerobe,
animal, bacterium, being, benthos, bion, biota, body, ecad,
fauna, flora, germ, idorgan, monad, monas, morphon, nekton,
person, plankton, plant, spore,
system, zooid
ORGANIZATION: **firm, *group,*
setup, **society, *system, *unit*
ORGANIZE: **establish, *form,*
*make, *plan, *play, *start
ORGY: binge, revel, **tear*
ORIENTAL: almond-eyed, **asian,*
bright, **chinese,* eastern, **jap-*
anese, levantine, ortive
ORIFICE: **opening*
ORIGIN: **source, *start*
ORIGINAL: native, **unique*
comb.: arch, archi
ORIGINATE: **form, *make,*
*start
ORIOLE: banana bird, icterus,
loriot, pirol, tan

* **Asterisk means to look up this word to find more answer words.**

ORION: nimrod, rigel, samson
 dog: aratus, canis, sirius
 father: hyrieus, poseidon
 guide: cedalion
 lover: merope, side
 mother: earth, euryale
 slayer: artemis
ORKNEY: *bay:* voe
 capital: kirkwall
 fishing bank: haaf
 freehold: odal, udal
 hut: skeo, skio
 island: hoy, pomona, sanday
 promontory: noup
 queen: bellicent
 tower: broch
ORLANDO: *steed:* vegliantino, veillantif
ORMENIUM: *king:* amyntor
ORNAMENT: **adorn,* amalaka, amulet, anaglyph, armlet, bangle, **badge,* beautify, bibelot, boss, bracelet, bracket, braid, brooch, buckle, bucrane, bulla, cameo, canion, carcanet, cartouche, color, decorate, **dress,* embellish, emboss, embroider, enthemion, epi, etch, **fetish,* finial, fob, fret, gem, gild, jewel, knob, ouch, **paint,* pin, schmuck, scroll, seme, sequin, spangle, stud, **symbol,* **token,* **trifle,* **trim(ming),* trinket
 architectural: acanthus, apophyge, astragal, beading, beak, billet, boss, cartouche, cinquefoil, conge, cornice, cusp, fascia, foil, frieze, **molding,* patera, quatrefoil, reed, scotia, splay, terminal, trefoil, volute
 ball: balloon
 band: bracelet
 bell-shaped: clochette
 biblical: urim
 boat-shaped: nef
 border: dado
 braid: aiguillette

 buckthorn: alatern
 building: alcove
 button: stud
 carving: arcade
 chain: carcanet
 cheap: bauble
 circlet: anklet
 circular: rosette
 clawlike: griff
 covering: bedspread
 crescent: lunette, lunula
 curly: scroll
 dart: banderilla
 delicate: tracery
 diamond: epigonation
 dress: bar pin, chequeen, embroidery, frog, jabot, lace, sequin, spangle, zecchino
 floral: anthemion, honeysuckle
 foot: cabriole
 grass: eulalia
 hanging: anadem, bangle, lavaliere, pendant, tassel
 human figure: anthropomorph
 jewelled: biliment
 lace edge: picot
 magical: amulet, **fetish*
 mantel: bibelot
 marble: bori, brocatel(le)
 mark: botiu
 neck: chain, choker, gorget
 pagoda: tee
 plant: aguinaldo, morningglory
 protuberant: boss
 roof: antefix
 scroll-like: volute
 sculptured: bucrane, bucranium
 set of: parure
 ship: acrostolium, acroterium, aphlaston, aplustre
 shrub: acanthus
 silver: tinsel
 spiral: helix
 strip: border
 terminal: finial
 tufted: pompon, rosette, tassel
 type: aglet, aiglet, aigrette, ap-

plique, arabesque, arras, batik,
bouquet, boutonniere, bow, bugle, chaplet, corsage, damask,
drapery, egret, epaulet, festoon,
filigree, fleuron, foliage, graffito,
niello, panache, pompom, ruffle,
snood, tracery, wreath
window: balcone
woody vine: asiatic creeper
ORNATE: elegant, *rich
ORNERY: *low, *mean, *obstinate
ORPAH: *husband:* chilion
ORPHEUS: *birthplace:* pieria
 destination: hades
 instrument: lyre
 parent: apollo, calliope
 wife: eurydice
ORT: *bit, morsel, scrap
ORTHODOX: *right, *true, *usual
ORTOLAN: bobolink, bunting,
sora
OSCILLATE: bob(ble), change,
coggle, dangle, *fluctuate, flutter,
librate, lurch, pendulate, *quiver,
reel, rock, roll, shake, sway,
swing, toss, *turn, waver, wobble
OSCITANT: *dull, *stupid
OSIER: rod, twig, wand, willow
OSIRIS: *brother:* set, seth
 crown: atef, hershef
 father: geb, keb, seb
 grand vizier: thoth
 lieutenant: anubis, upuaut
 mother: nut
 names: amenti, bennu, djed,
 khenti, mendes, onnophris,
 onuphis
 sister: isis
 son: anubis, horus
 wife: isis
OSSEOUS: bony, *hard, *solid
OSSIAN: *father:* finn
OSSUARY: *dead: home, tomb
OSTENSIBLE: *open, *specious
OSTENTATION: *display, *show
OSTENTATIOUS: *splendid

OSTIOLE: *opening
OSTRACIZE: *banish, *dismiss
OSTRICH: nandu, rhea, struthio
 extinct: moa
 feather: boa, boo, plume
 -like bird: emeu, emu, ratite
OTAHEITE: *tahiti
OTHELLO: jealous, moor
 friend: cassio, iago, michael
 wife: desdemona
OTHER: alia, else, *fresh, *rest
 comb.: all(o), heter(o)
OTHNIEL: *father:* kenaz
 son: hathath, meonothai
 wife: achsah
OTIC: auditory, auricular
OTIOSE: *dull, *heavy, *idle
OTTER: annotto, lutra, paravane
 sea: kalan
 sheep: ancon
 track: spur
OTTOMAN: couch, seat, *turkish
OUCH: *adorn, *ornament
OUNCE: *eighth:* dram
 times 16: pound
OUST: *banish, *dismiss, *remove
OUT: away, *bad, *eccentric,
 *end, *evil, passe, scram
 and out: *complete, *great
 comb.: ecto, egt, exo
 of date: *old, passe
 of line: askew, awry, *bad
 of order: broken-down, infirm
 of pocket: expenses, *poor
 of sight: *extreme, *great
 of sorts: cranky, *cross
 the ordinary: *unique
 the way: distant, remote
 this world: *great, superb
OUTBACK: country, sticks
OUTBREAK: *fight, *violence
OUTBURST: *anger, blast
OUTCAST: cagot, castaway, cast-
off, chandala, declasse, derelict,
dp, eta, exile, expatriate, for-
saken, ishmael, leper, outlaw,
oysvorf, pariah, proscript, reprobate, ronin, untouchable, yeta

---

* Asterisk means to look up this word to find more answer words.

OUTCOME: *end, *issue, *result
OUTCRY: *cry, *noise, roar
OUTDO: *defeat, *pass, *top
OUTFIT: *dress, *group, *unit
OUTGROWTH: *effect, *result
OUTLANDISH: *brutal, campy, *eccentric, strange, *weird
OUTLAW: *criminal, *hoodlum, *stop, taboo, tabu, *thief
OUTLET: *escape, *issue, *way
OUTLINE: *form, *model, *plan
OUTLOOK: *angle, *range, scope
OUTPUT: *produce, *result, yield
OUTRAGE: *abuse, *evil, *shame
OUTRAGEOUS: *bad, *evil
OUTRE: *eccentric, *weird
OUTSET: *opening, *start
OUTSPOKEN: *free, *plain
OUTSTANDING: *big, *great, *important, *splendid, *supreme
OUTSTRIP: *best, *defeat, *lead, *pass, *top, *win
OUTWIT: *cheat, *outstrip
OUTWORK: *fort, *outstrip
OVAL: ellipse, ovule, stadium
OVEN: calcar, hibachi, imu, kiln, lehr, oast, stove, umu
  goddess: fornax
  mop: scovel
OVER: above, dead, ended, more, past, plus, superior, twice
  comb.: epi, hyper, super, sur
OVERBEARING: *arrogant
OVERCHARGE: bleed, fleece
OVERCOAT: abolla, aquascutum, balmacan, benny, burberry, burnoose, bursattee, byrrus, camail, capote, chesterfield, duster, greatcoat, inverness, joseph, loden, mackintosh, mantle, mino, mozzetta, oilskin, paletot, parka, pelisse, poncho, raglan, raincoat, robe, sack, slicker, surtout, tabard, tarpaulin, topcoat, trench coat, tunic, ulster, wraparound
OVERCOME: *overwhelm
OVERDUE: *late, *slow, tardy

OVERFLOW: *outlet, *plenty
OVERHEAD: *above, cost
OVERLAY: *cover, *hide, lap
OVERLOOK: *free, *pass, *tower
OVERPOWER: *overwhelm
OVERRIDE: *defeat, repeal, veto
OVERRUN: *flood, *spread
OVERSEE: *administer, *control
OVERSEER: *head, *lead, *magnate
OVERSHADOW: *beat, *pass
OVERSIGHT: *control, *error
OVERT: *open
OVERTAKE: *pass, *seize
OVERTURE: *approach, offer
OVERTURN: *best, refute, *upset
OVERWEENING: *overbearing, *vain
OVERWEIGHT: *fat, *heavy
OVERWHELM: *beat, *best, *defeat, *destroy, *top, *upset
OVID: burial: tomi
  work: amores, medea, tristia
OWL: lulu, madbe, pouie, tyto
  call: hoot, screech, ululation
  clover: butter-and-eggs
  eagle: bubo, katogle
  genus: ninox, strix, syrnium
  hawk: surn
  horned: bubo
  parrot: kakapo, tarapo
  pert.: strigine
  plumed eye area: disk
  short-eared: momo
  small: aziola, howlet, utum
OWN: *admit, *possess, *tell
  comb.: idio
OX: cattle, cow, stot
  driver: bullwhacker
  extinct: urus
  harness: span, yoke
  pert.: bovid, bovine, taurine
  skull: bucrane, bucranium
  son: merari
  stall: boose
  stomach: tripe
  wild: gaur, seladang, urus

* Asterisk means to look up this word to find more answer words.

OXFORD: *alumnus:* aunt
 earl: asquith, harley
 examination: great (go)
 library: bodleian
 museum, pert.: ashmolean
 officer: beadle, bedel, don
 principles: buchmanism
 scholar: demy
 scholarship: rhodes
OXIDE: *aluminum:* alumina
 barium: baryta
 calcium: lime
 hydrocarbon radical: ether
 iron: rust
OXYGIAN: **old*
OYSTER: *bed:* bank, claire, layer,
 oysterage, park, stew
 material: culch, cutch, spat
 catcher: bird, olive, tirma
 cut: tidbit
 drill: borer
 eggs: spawn
 farm: **oyster: bed,* parc, park
 fish: tautog, toad(fish)
 fossil: ostracite
 gatherer: tongman
 genus: ostrea
 grass: kelp
 loit: bistort
 pest: boring sponge, cliona
 plant: salsify
 rake: tongs
 shell: husk, shuck, test
 small: blister
 spawn: cultch
 tree: mangrove
 young: set, spat
OZARK STATE: arkansas, missouri
OZONE: air, atmosphere, ether

PABULUM: food, fuel, **support*
PACE: **run, *speed, *walk*
PACHYDERM: elephant, mam-
 moth

PACIFIC: ocean, **quiet*
PACIFIC COAST: *bird:* turnstone
 herb: campanula, pink, silene
 shrub: bayberry, myrica
 state: california, oregon, washington
PACIFIC ISLAND: aru, atoll,
 bali, carolines, ducie, ellice, fiji,
 guam, hawaiian, komodo, lifu,
 marianas, munga, okinawa,
 philippines, rapa, saipan, samoa,
 tahiti, truk, uap, uvea, wake, yap
 aborigine: amphinesian
 bird: kagu
 cloth: tapa
 grass: neti
 plant: neti, salal
 region: oceania, polynesia
 tree: dasheen, eddyroot, ipil, kou,
 madrona, taro
PACIFY: **abate,* soothe, **temper*
PACK(AGE): all-expense, arrange, **bag,* bale, ball of wax,
 begone, bindle, bolt, book, bottle, bundle, carton, cartridge,
 case, cask, ceroon, compress,
 *container, cram, crate, deck,
 embale, encase, enclose, fadge,
 fagot, fardel, fascine, fill, fix,
 freight, **group,* hamper, heap,
 impediment, lade, line, load,
 parcel, pile, pocket, pot, **pre-*
 pare, *press, *quantity, *recep-
 tacle, sack, seroon, **set,* sheaf,
 ship, shook, stevedore, stive,
 *store, stow, **surfeit,* tamp, tin,
 transport, **vessel,* wad, **wrap*
PACT: **accord, *bargain*
PAD: **home, *pack, *place, *walk*
 collar: housing
 harness: terret
PADDLE: **beat,* oar, **punish,* row
PADISHAH: **ruler, *title*
PADRE: **church: man,* father
PAEON: *son:* agastrophus
PAGE: **record, *servant*
 beginning: flyleaf, leaf

* **Asterisk means to look up this word to find more answer words.**

book: cahier, folio
lady: escudero
left: verso, vo
number: folio, paginate
paper: sheet
right: recto
section: box
title: rubric, unwan
PAGEANT: *display, *show
PAGODA: hoon, kryailteyo, pon,
taa, temple, *tower
ornament: epi, finial, tee
PAHLAVI: *country:* iran
text: bundahish, scripture
PAIL: bucket, can, sou, vessel
PAIN: *ache, *afflict(ion), aggravate, agony, anxiety, appal(l),
bite, blow, bore, bother, *disease,
distress, dolor, grief, grieve,
grate, gripe, harrow, *hurt,
malaise, misery, pang, *passion,
penalty, prick, rack, *shock,
*smart, *sorrow, sting, strain,
stroke, throb, throe, *torment,
*torture, *trouble, wound
comb.: agra, algia, algio, algy
fear of: algophobia
killer: analgesic, anodyne, aspirin,
*drug, *narcotic, opiate, pare-
goric, sedative
measurer: algometer
relayer: nerve
sensitivity: algesia
PAINS: *trouble, *work
PAINT: *adorn, beautify, bedaub,
besmear, *blot, brush, calcimine,
coat, color, *cover, dab, daub,
enamel, face, fard, figure, flat,
fresco, gild, glaze, gloss, japan,
lacquer, miniate, *ornament,
parget, *picture, pigment, portray, prime, represent, rouge,
shellac, sketch, slapdash, slick
on, *smear, stain, stipple, turpentine, varnish
comb.: picto
PAINTING: *equipment:* brush,

canvas, easel, paint, palette
medium: casein, fresco, gouache,
grisaille, oil, secco, tempera, watercolor
mixture: megilp
one-color: monochrome, monotint
sacred: pieta
style: abstract, bolognese, classic,
cubist, dadaist, fauvism, futurist,
genre, idealistic, realistic
three panels: triptych
wall: fresco, mural, panel
PAIR: brace, case, combine, couple, diad, duad, duet, duo, dyad,
marry, mate, rig, span, team,
twins, two, *unite
having two: bigeminate
PAKISTAN: *city:* dacca, dir, kalat,
lahore, multan, quetta, sidi
delta: char manpura, ganges
part: bahawalpur, baluchistan,
kalat, peshawar, sindh, swat
pass: bolan
PAL: *associate, *friend
PALACE: alcazar, belvedere, castle, court, edifice, kraton, mansion, palais, palazzo, praetorium,
serai, stead
PALADIN: champion, hero, *lord
PALAEMON: *mother:* ino
rival: arcite
wife: emelye
PALANQUIN: chair, dooley, juan,
kago, litter, palkee, sedan
bearer: halal, sirdar
PALATE: relish, taste, velum
pert.: uranic, uvular, velar
PALATIAL: *big, *noble, *splendid
PALATINE: *paladin, *palatial
PALAVER: *gossip, *talk
PALE: *fair, *light, *limit, *pastel,
*sphere, *weak, *white
PALEOZOIC ERA: *periods:* cambrian, carboniferous, devonian,
ordovician, permian, silurian
land mass: cascadia

* Asterisk means to look up this word to find more answer words.

plant: bothrodendron, calamarian, calamite, lepidodendron, lycopodium sigillaria

PALESTINE: **hebrew, *israeli*
city: acrew, akir, arimathaea, bire, cana, dan, endor, gath, gaza, ghazze, haifa, hebron, jaffa, jerusalem, samaria, tob
conqueror: assyrians, turks
country: canaan, edom, erets, moab, philistia, yisroel
lake: galilee, merom, tiberias
peak: carmel, ebal, gerizim, gilead, hermon, jebel tur, moriah, nebo, olives, pisgah, ramon, zion

PALIMPSEST: parchment, tablet
PALISADE: cliff, **fort,* rimer
PALL: **cover, *dull, *surfeit*
PALLAS: asteroid, athena
kin: creus, eurybia, nike
sand grouse: attagen
PALLIATE: **abate, *ease, *hide*
PALLID: **pale, *thin,* wan, **weak*
PALLION: **bit, *part, *piece*
PALLU: *father:* reuben
PALM: **hide, *prize, *steal*
betel: areca, bonga
book: taliera, tara
bussu: troolie
cabbage: palmetto, saw
civet: bondar, musang
climbing: calamus, rattan
cockatoo: arara
coconut: coco, niog
drink: assai, beno, bino, milk, nipa, sura, taree, toddy
dwarf: sabal
fabric: bassine
fanleaf: earthea, palmetto, sabal, talipot, taliput
feather: gomuti, howea, urucuri
fiber: buri, datil, dok, iyo, raffia, tal, tucum(a)
food: date, nut, sago
fruit: coconut, date, nipa
gingerbread: doom, doum, dum
hand: thenar, vola

kind: acrocomia, acuyari, arak, areca, arenga, assai, atap, attalea, babassu, bacaba, baytop, betel, bombaje, brab, buriti, bussu, cachou, calamus, caranda, carnauba, caryota, cashcuttee, cashoo, cayota, coquilla, coquito, erythea, fanleaf, fishtail, gambier, gomuti, jaggery, koko, niog, nipa, olay, piaussaua, raphia, ratan, sabal, sago, tala, talipot, tokopot, tucuma
leaf: frond, olay, ole, olla
leaf mat: petate, yapa
lily: ti, toi
low: trooly, trouie, ubussu
palmyra: brab, ola, ole, olla, ronier, tal(a), talipot
pert.: frondous, palmar, pinnate
pith: sago
product: copra, date
reader: palmist
sago: areng, gomuti, irok
spiny: grigri, grugru
starch: sago, talipot
stem: cane, ratan, rattan
stemless: curua
sugar: gur, jaggery
thatch: barriguda, nipa
wax: ceroxyle
wing-leaved: cohune

PALMERSTON: fanny, lord cupid
PALMYRA: *queen:* zenobia
PALP: antenna, **praise,* touch
PALPABLE: **open, *plain*
PALTER: **cheat, *lie, *oscillate*
PALTRY: **low, *mean, *poor, *sad, *small, *sorry*
PAMPER: **pet, *spoil*
PAN: *beloved:* autonoe, eurydice, pitys, syrinx
instrument: pipe, reed, syrinx
kin: faunus
parent: hermes, penelope
son: seilenos, silenus
worship place: arcadia

* **Asterisk means to look up this word to find more answer words.**

PANACEA: elixir, *remedy
PANAMA: *city:* aspinwall, colon, cristobal
coin: balboa
disease: banana wilt
engineer: de lesseps
fish: berrugate, verrugato
gulf: darien
hat: carludovica, cylanthus
lake and locks: gatun
measure: celemin
river: chagres, sambu, tuira
rubber: castilla
tree: alfaje, cativo, copa, fabace, trichilia, yaya
PANAY: *philippine
PANCAKE: arepa, blintz, crepe, flapjack, fritter, froise, latke
PANDAREUS: *daughter:* aedon
PANDEMONIUM: *ado, *hell, *noise
PANDION: *ally:* tereus
enemy: labdacus
kin: butes, erichthonius, philomela, procne, procris
PANDORA: *box:* *evil, *trouble
brother-in-law: prometheus
husband: epimetheus
PANEGYRIC: eulogy, *praise
PANEL: *group, *part
ceiling: artesonado
framing: stile
sculptured: boiserie
PANG: *ache, *hurt, *pain
PANIC: *alarm, *crisis, *hit
PANJANDRUM: *magnate
PANSY: orchid, pensee, violet
PANT: *desire, *need, throb
PANTAGRUEL: *companion:* panurge
parent: badebec, gargantua
PANTHEUS: *mother:* agave
PANTRY: ambry, larder, spence
PANTS: bags, bloomers, breeches, britches, cords, denims, ducks, duffs, galligaskins, jeans, jodhpurs, kicks, knickers, levis, over-

alls, pajamas, rompers, shalwar, shintiyan, shorts, tights, trunks
hangers: galluses, hips, suspenders
leather: calzoneras, chaparajos, chapareras, chaps, lederhosen
opening: fly
strap: bowyang
PAPAL: *pope references
PAPAYA: *enzyme:* papain
extract: carpaine
juice: caroid, vegetable pepsin
PAPER: *certificate, *instrument, *piece, tapa
absorbent: blotter, towelling
back: book, cahier, reprint
bark: cajeput, melaleuca, punk
box: carton(nier)
bush: *paper: bark
case: binder, file, folio
cloth-like: tapa
crisp, thin: pelure
cutlets: papilote
cutter: scissors, slitter
damaged: casse, retree, salle
design: watermark
detachable: coupon, stub, tab
fabric: bark cloth
fine: bond, linen, vellum
folded: folio
group: corpus, dossier, file
gummed: label, stamp, sticker
hard: pelure
large-size: atlas
legal: binder, contract, writ
lighter: spill
measure: bundle, quire, ream
medicinal powders: charta
money: assignat, bill, cash, certificate, dollar, fiat, folding stuff, frogskin, greenback, lettuce, note, rags, scrip, shinplaster
mulberry: aute, kozo, tapa
nautilus: argonaut
official: targe, white
pad: tablet
piece: leaf, page, scrip, sheet
postage stamp: pelure

* Asterisk means to look up this word to find more answer words.

pulp: ulla
scroll: gohonzon, parchment
size: antiquarian, atlas, bastard, cap, casing, colombier, copy, crown, demy, elephant, emperor, folio, foolscap, imperial, octavo, post, pott, royal
source: acaroid, gum, resin
thin: bible, india, onionskin, pelure, tissue
untrimmed edge: deckle
watermarked: batonne
web: ply
PAPYRUS: *paper,* *piece,* scroll
PAR: *average,* *equal,* *value
one over: bogey, bogie
under: birdie, eagle
value: face, nominal, price
PARABLE: *adage,* *story,* *tale
objective: moral, proverb
PARACHUTE: *goods:* nylon, silk
part: brollyhop, canopy, harness, pack, rip cord, safety loop, shroud lines
PARACLETE: *advocate,* *servant
PARADE: *display,* *show,* *walk
PARADIGM: *example,* *model
PARADISE: aalu, aaru, *above, *abraham's bosom,* afterlife, aidenn, ananda, arcadia, avalon, beulah, canaan, ciel, eden, elysium, empyrean, eternal home, eternity, ether, *fate,* firmament, garden, *glory,* gokuraku, great white throne, happy hunting grounds, hereafter, ialu, jenna, jodo, *joy,* kingdom come, nirvana, *norse: heaven,* olympus, promised land, seventh heaven, sky, urano, *utopia,* valhalla, welkin, wonderland, yaru, zion
bird: apus, con, emerald
lost angel: ariel, uriel
river: geon
tree: aceituna, bitter wood, china tree, quassia amara
PARADOX: dilemma, *puzzle

PARAGON: *ace,* *acme,* *model
PARAGUAY: *city:* asuncion, belen, ita, luque, villa rica, yuty
indian: guarani
measure: cordel, cuadra, fanega
money: guarani, peso
tea: mate, yerba
PARALLEL: *equal,* same, similar
PARALYZE: *alarm,* *shock
PARAMOUNT: *above,* *great, *important,* *supreme,* *top
PARAPET: *fort,* *support,* wall
PARASITE: cadge, leech, sponge
animal: cowbird, cuckoo, flea, mite, tick
blood: fluke, tryp
plant: agaric, aphid, dodder, entophyte, lichen, moss, thrips
PARCEL: *allot,* *bit,* *group, *pack,* *part,* *piece,* *share
PARCHMENT: *book:* forel, forrel
constituent: amyloid
fine: vel(lum)
manuscript: palimpsest
piece: membrane
roll: pell, scroll
PARDON: *acquit,* *free,* *release
PARE: *abate,* *reduce,* *skin
PARIAH: *outcast
PARIS: lutetia
airport: le bounget, orly, roissy
bishop, first: denis
consort: helen, oenone
dress: souffle pompadour skirt
green: acetoarsenite
hat: belltopper
palace: elysee, louvre, tuileries
parent: hecuba, priam
park: bois de boulogne
police: flics, surete
revolutionaries: communards
river: seine
stock exchange: bourse
suburb: anteuil, aubervilliers, billancourt, boulogne, passy
subway: metro
thug: apache

* Asterisk means to look up this word to find more answer words.

PARITY: *par
PARKINSON'S DISEASE
  CURE: l-dopa
PARLEY: *argue, *gossip, *talk
PARODY: caricature, satire
PAROXYSM: *anger, *attack, *fit
PARROT: abacay, agapornis, ama-
  zona, ara, arara, ararauna, bor-
  beta, broadtail, budgerigar, cagit,
  caracanga, cockatoo, corella,
  echo, jako, kaka, kea, loro, lory,
  polly, *repeat, tiriba, touraco
fish: labroidea, lania, loro, scarid
hawk: hia
PARRY: *avoid, dodge, refute
PARSI: *prayer:* ahuna vairya
priest: dastur, mobed
scripture: avesta, bundahish,
  pahlavi
PARSIMONIOUS: *mean, *poor
PARSLEY: cilantro, coriander,
  cumin, dill, eltrot, selinum
derivative: apiin, apiol, ether
pert.: bowel-hive, breakstone,
  pearl wort, saxifrage
relative: anise, celery
PARSON: *church: man
bird: fey, koko, poe, rook, tui
-in-the-pulpit: cuckoopint
PART: allot, area, arm, article,
  *bit, bough, branch, *break,
  butt, canch, cantlet, chapter,
  clause, cleave, clip, collop, column, component, constituent,
  contingent, detachment, detail,
  distribute, district, diverge, divide, dole, element, *end, faction, fascicle, flinder, fraction,
  function, hunk, installment, *interest, item, joint, leg, length,
  limb, link, livraison, lobe, lobule,
  lot, lump, member, moiety,
  *number, offshoot, *opening, or-
  gan, paragraph, parcel, paring,
  *particular, *pass, phrase,
  *piece, pinion, portion, *projec-
  tion, quarter, region, remnant,

role, scale, section, segment,
  *separate, serial, sever, *share,
  shaving, shiver, shred, slice,
  smithereen, snack, snatch, snip,
  some, *spear, *split, spray, sprig,
  stitch, stump, subdivision, sunder, switch, tatter, *tear, tendril,
  *thing, tithe, twig, verse, volume,
  ward, wing
comb.: demi, hemi, meri, semi
with: *abandon, *give, *trade
PARTHIAN: *emperor:* arsaces I
shot: taunt
PARTICIPANT: *actor, *party
PARTICIPATE: *join, *share
PARTICLE: *bit, *part, *piece
cosmic: meson
electric: anion, ion, proton
elementary: boson
small: amicron, granule
unstable: pion
PARTICULAR: *accurate, article,
  aspect, atom, *bit, certain,
  character(istic), circumstance,
  conscientious, detail(ed), discriminate, especial, event, fastidious, feature, fussy, individual,
  instance, item, *part, peculiar,
  personal, *quality, regard, singular, sole, *special, specific,
  *thing, *unique
PARTISAN: *enthusiast, *friend
PARTITION: *part, panel, screen
PARTNER: *associate, *friend
PARTRIDGE: bobwhite, chukar,
  grouse, kyah, perdix, quail, seesee, tinamou, titar, yutu
berry: boxberry, snowberry
call: juck, juke
group: covey
young: cheeper, squealer
PARTY: *affair, ball, bash, blowout, bust-up, carouse, cantico,
  ceilidh, dance, drum, division,
  entertainment, faction, *fellow,
  festivity, fete, gala, gathering,
  *group, hop, masquerade, *part,

---

* **Asterisk means to look up this word to find more answer words.**

*play, scrum, shindig, shower, smoker, social, soiree, stag, *tear
PARVATI: son: ganesha
PASIPHAE: husband: minos
 offspring: ariadne, phaedra
PASS: annie oakley, approve, avenue, bandy, beallach, bet, bomb, bridge, bygo, call, clearance, col, convey, *crisis, deadhead, defile, deliver, difficulty, disappear, duar, elapse, *end, exceed, excrete, fade, flit, gap, gaut, ghat, go by, graduate, hand, happen, hold up, legislate, license, *move, narrows, neglect, omit, *opening, perish, permit, predicament, proceed, promote, ratify, reeve, relay, *road, *route, *send, skip, slip, *state, *succeed, *throw, thrust, ticket, transcend, transfer, travel, *trick, *walk, warrant, *waterway, *way
 out: *administer, *dispense
 the time: *idle, relax
 -word: grip, sesame, tessera
PASSAGE: *open(ing), *pass, *road, *route, *walk, *way
PASSE: *old, out, past
PASSION: *anger, blood, choler, cordiality, emotion, enthusiasm, experience, feeling, fervidity, *fire, furor, gusto, impression, *interest, *love, mania, melodrama, *pain, rage, rapture, sensation, sentiment, *spirit, suffering, *tear, transport, *urge, *violence, warmth, yen
 flower: bull hoof, jamaica, maracock, maypop, tacsonia
PASSIVE: *dull, *quiet, stoic
PASSOVER: pascha, pesach, seder
 bread: afikomen, matzo(th)
 commencement: nisan
 pert.: paschal
 songs: hallel
 story: haggada(h)
PAST: *after, *old, over, prior

PASTE: *adhere, *mixture, stick
 aromatic: pastil(le)
 clay: barbotine
 dried: guarana
 hearth-lining: brasque
 hole-filling: badigeon
 plastic-repair: slurry
 rice: ame
 -up: collage, layout
 weaver's: buckety
PASTEL: crayon, *fair, *light
PASTORAL: arcadian, agriculture
 cantata: serenata
 crook: crosier, pedum
 pert.: agrestic, agricultural, bucolic, geoponic
 pipe: oat, reed
 poem: eclogue, georgic, idyll
 staff: cane, crosier, pedum
PASTRY: garnish: cream, meringue
 shell: barquette, bouchee, dariole, incrustation, timbale
PASTY: *pastel, *soft, *thick
PAT: *fit, *happy, *piece
PATAGONIA: cattle: niatas
 deity: setebos
 people: onas
 rodent: capybara, cavy, mara
 plant: balsam bog
 tree: alerce, alerse
PATCH: *piece, *remedy, *repair
 -head: surfer
 -work: *hash, *mixture
PATE: *head
PATENT: grant, *open, *plain, *medicine: nostrum, *remedy
PATH: *opening, *route, *way
PATHAN: people: bangash, turi
PATIENT: *dull, *quiet, *slow
PATOIS: *argot, *gossip, speech
PATRICIAN: *lord, *magnate
PATRON: *advocate, *enthusiast
PATRONAGE: aid, help, *support
PATTER: *argot, *nonsense, *talk
PATTERN: *form, *model
PATULOUS: *open, spreading

* Asterisk means to look up this word to find more answer words.

PAUCITY: *need, scarcity
PAUL: saint, saul, tentmaker
  aide: apollos, archippus, aristarchus, artemas, demas, epaphras, erastus, gaius, luke, mark, mnason, onesimus, secundus, sopater, sylvanus, timothy, trophimus, tychicus
  birthplace: tarsus
  companion: barnabas, silas
  convert: apollos, crispus, damaris, dionysius, gaius, stephanas, titius justus
  correspondents: apphia, archippus, colossians, corinthians, demas, epaphras, ephesians, galatians, hebrews, philemon, philippians, romans, thessalonians, timothy, titus
  crown: tiara
  enemies: alexander, hymenaeus
  friend: andronicus, apelles, aquila, asyncritus, epaenetus, hermas, herodion, jason, julia, junias, nereus, patrobas, persis, philologus, phlegon, phoebe, priscilla, rufus, stachys, urban, zenas
PAUNCH: *fat, *stomach
PAUSE: *break, *slow, *stop
PAVE: *cover, *ease, *prepare
PAWN: *agent, *promise, stake
PAY: *fee, *money, *produce, *punish, *return, *reward, *settle, *use, *yield
  extra: batta, bonus, tip
  homage: adore, *honor, *worship
  load: *pack(age)
  off: *acquit, *end, *free, *result, *settle
PEA: bird: oriole, wryneck
  chick: cicer, gram
  disease: black pit
  dove: zenaida
  family: fabaceae
  finch: chaffinch
  flour: erbswurst
  heath: carmele

  herb: aeschynomene, amorpha, baptisia, cajanus
  pigeon: dal
  pod: quash
  sausage: erbswurst
  seeds: pulse
  shaped: pisiform
  shoe, in the: bane
  shrub: anagyris
  soup: fog, smaze, smog
  split: dal, dhal
  tree: agati, baphia, bowdichia, butea
  vine: earthpea
PEACE: *accord, *order, *quiet
  god: balder, eir, forseti, frey
  goddess: dice, eir, irene, pax
  king: jesus, melchizedek
  mind: ataraxia, satisfaction
  monger: pacifist
  passionate: nirvana
  pipe: calumet, overture
  symbol: calumet, dove, olive, pax, pipe, toga
  to you: aleichem shalom
PEACEFUL: *gentle, *happy, *kind, *shy, *smooth
PEACH: *ace, *betray, *top
  brandy: boof
  family: amygdalaceae
  kind: carman, cling, crawford, crosby, elberta, freestone, nectarine, pavo, quandong
  origin: almond, china, persia
  stone: pit, putamen
  wort: lady's thumb, persicary
PEACHY: *fine, *great, *splendid
PEACOCK: bird of juno, mao, pawn
  bittern: sun
  blue: paon, pigment
  butterfly: io, kiho
  fan: flabellum
  feather fiber: marl
  female: hen, peahen
  fish: wrasse
  flower: adenanthera, barbados, poinciana, pride, sandalwood

* Asterisk means to look up this word to find more answer words.

group: muster
heron: bittern
ore: bornite, chalcopyrite, erubescite
pert.: pavonine, vain
tail spot: eye
PEAK: **acme, *mountain, *top*
comb.: acr(o), apic(o)
ice: serac
needle-shaped: aiguille
ornament: epi, finial
rocky: alp, arete, crag, tor
snow-capped: calotte
PEAKED: **pale, *poor, *sick*
PEANUT: **bit,* bur, **drug,* goober, katchung, mani, pinda
oil: arachis oil
PEAR: anjou, bartlett, bergamot, bosc, brandywine, burrel, nopal, perry, pyrus, seckel
autumn: bosc
cider: perry
disease: black end, brown blotch, bull's-eye rot
haw: blackthorn, crataegus, prunus spinosa, sloe
prickly: nopal
-shaped: obconic, pyriform
-shaped figure: apioid
-shaped gem: briolette
squash: chayote, perry
PEARL: bouton, nacre, onion
artificial: alburnus, blay, bleak, olivet, seed
bird: barbet
blue: metal
blush: rosetan
fish: carapus, fierasfer
flat: bouton, butter pearl
imitation: argentine, olivet
millet: bajri, buzzard grass, cattail, pennisetum glaucum
moss: carrageen
of great luster: orient
opal: cacholong
oyster: black lip
seed: aliofar

source: argenteum, blanc d'ablette
weed: sagina, sealwort
wort: breakstone, burnet saxifrage, parsley piert
PEARLY: clear, limpid, milky, nacreous, opalescent, pellucid
everlasting: american cudweed
PEASANT: agricole, arkie, billjim, bonhomme, boor, bumpkin, campesino, carl, ceorl, churl, clod, cocker, coistrel, coolie, cottar, countryman, cullion, **farmer, *fellow,* fouter, hayseed, hind, jacques, jake, kern, kulak, laborer, liti, moujik, muxhik, okie, paisano, peon, plebeian, proletarian, rascal, rayat, rustic, ryot, **servant, *slave,* smatchet, swain, tiller, tyke, yahoo, yokel, wetback
crop-sharing: metayer
freeholder: bonder
painters: barbizon school
rebellion leader: wat tyler
stone, turned to: battus
PEAT: *bog:* cess, moss
cutter: piner
shovel: slade, slane, spade
wood: loosestrife
PEBBLE: **bit, *stone*
shaped: calciform, calculiform
PECCADILLO: **error, *flaw, *sin*
PECCANT: **bad, *evil, *rotten*
PECULIAR: **eccentric,* odd, off, **particular, *special, *unique*
comb.: idio
PECUNIOUS: **rich*
PEDAGOGUE, PEDANT: teacher
PEDDLE: cadge, dally, **trade*
PEDESTAL: **foundation, *support*
part: base, dado, die, orlo, plinch, quadra, socle, surbase
PEDESTRIAN: **dull,* hiker
PEDIGREE: **breed, *kind, *model*

* Asterisk means to look up this word to find more answer words.

PEEK: *look, *see, *spy
PEEL: *fort, *reduce, *tower
PEEP: *appear, *peek, view
  hole: judas window, *opening
  show: raree, spectacle
PEER: *equal, *lord, *peek
PEER GYNT: author: ibsen
  composer: grieg
  mother: ase
  role: anitra, king
PEERLESS: *best, *supreme, *top
PEEVISH: *acerb, *sour, *sullen
  one: attercop, schlag, shlock
PEG: *drink, *pierce, *run, *see,
  *support, *throw, *walk
PEGA: fish, remora
PEGASUS: rider: bellerophon
  son: aquarius
  source: medusa, perseus
PEIPING, PEKING: cambaluc,
  tatu
PELAGIC: aquatic, marine, ocean
PELEUS: brother: telamon
  father: aeacus
  father-in-law: eurytion
  half brother: phocus
  purifier: acastus
  son: achilles, pelides
  wife: antigone, thetis
PELF: *money, *spoil, wealth
PELIAS: offspring: acastus, alcestis, ampyx, evadne
PELLET: *missile, sphere, *stone
PELOPS: kin: atreus, chrysippus,
  tantalus, thyestes
  wife: hippodamia
PELORUS: slayer: ares
PELOTA: *jai alai
PELT: *prize, *skin, *stone
PEN: *jail, *limit, *record
  pert.: styloid
  point: neb, nib, stub
PENALIZE: *abuse, *punish
PENCIL: pert.: desmic
  point: apicula
  pusher: writer
PENDANT: hanging, *ornament

PENDING: during, *open, until
PENELOPE: father: icarius
  father-in-law: laertes
  husband: odysseus, ulysses
  suitor: agelaus, amphinomus, antinous
PENETRABLE: accessible, *open
PENETRATE: *break, *enter,
  *pierce, *reach, *understand
PENETRATING: *acute, *sharp
PENEUS: child: atrax, daphne
PENGUIN: adelie, auk, johny
  home: penguinery, pole, rookery
PENITENCE: *remorse, *shame
PENITENT: magdalen, *sorry
PENITENTIARY: *church: man,
  *jail
PENMANSHIP: cacography, calligraphy, chirography
PENNANT: *flag, *prize, *title
PENNSYLVANIA: bird: ruffed
  grouse
  borough: media
  flower: mountain laurel
  nickname: keystone state
  sect: amish
  tree: hemlock
PENNY: cent, copper, *money
  cress: boor's-mustard
  1/16th: cee
  pinching: *mean, *poor
  royal: brotherwort, thyme
  worth: *bargain, *value
PENSION: *aid, *income, inn
PENTACLE: medal, star, *symbol
PENTATEUCH: bible, law, torah
PENTHEUS: grandfather: cadmus
  mother: agave
PENURIOUS: *mean, *poor
PENURY: *need
PEON: *peasant, *slave, *soldier
PEOPLE: family: clan, folk, gente,
  kin, tribe, volk
  group: convention, culture, demos, fold, *group, host, humanity, knot, laity, *society, they,
  throng

* Asterisk means to look up this word to find more answer words.

masses: *rabble
pert.: demotic, ethnic
politics: citizenry, community, country, nation, party, populace, public, race, state, subjects, voters
PEP: *force, *spirit, vigor
pills: *drugs, narcotics
PEPPER: *attack, rain, *stone
  -and-salt: gray, mottled
  betel: ikmo, itmo
  beverage: kava, kavakava
  corn: trifle
  cress: boor's-mustard
  grass: canary, cress, lepidium
  grass extract: benzyl cyanide
  kind: ara, ava, betel, capsicum, cayenne, chili, cubeb, ikmo, itmo, paprika, pimiento, siri(h), topepo
  -mint: black mitchum
    camphor: menthol
    colored liquid: alantol
    synthetic: anisyl
  package: robbin
  picker: piper
  pot basis: cassareep
  -ridge: nyssa, tupelo
PEPPERY: *angry, *hot, *sharp
PER: each, for, through, via
PERAMBULATE: *walk
PERCEIVABLE: *open
PERCEIVE: *sense, *understand
PERCENTAGE: *advantage, *part
PERCEPTIBLE: *open, patent
PERCEPTION: *knowledge, *sense
PERCH: fish, *rest, *settle
  -like fish· anabas, darter
PERCOLATE: *absorb, *run, *stir
PERDITION: *fall, *hell, *ruin
PEREMPTORY: *absolute
PERENNIAL: *permanent
PERFECT: *absolute, *accomplish, *accurate, blameless, blank, develop, entire, faultless,

finished, flawless, *great, ideal, immaculate, impeccable, improve, intact, inviolate, *model, praiseworthy, *pure, *right, spotless, stainless, thorough, *train, *true, whole
  comb.: teleo
PERFIDIOUS: *bad, *evil, *false
PERFORATE: cancel, *pierce, tap
PERFORATION: *opening
PERFORM: *accomplish, *act, *complete, *end, *reach, *work
PERFORMANCE: *act(ion), *play, *work
PERFORMER: *actor, *agent
PERFUME: attar, balm, *scent
  source: acaroid, acetaldol, acetophenone, acetylbenzene, aldol, allyl, ambergris, ambrain, amyl, anethole, anise, anisol, anisyl, aubepine, bay rum, ben, benzalacetone, benzoin, benzyl, benzylidene, bergamiol, borneol, bornyl, hypnone, neroli, orris, whale
PERFUMER: atomizer, censer, fumigator, incensory, odorizer, pomander, potpourri, sachet, scent bag, thurible, vinaigrette
PERFUNCTORY: *superficial
PERGAMUM: *king:* attalid, attalus
PERI: *dwarf, fairy, *spirit
  king: jamshid, jamshyd, yima
PERIAPT: charm, *fetish
PERICLES: *mistress:* aspasia
  ward: alcibiades
PERIDOT: chrysolite, olivine
PERIMETER: *periphery
PERIOD: *age, *bit, *end, *say, *spell, *time, *trick, *turn
PERIODICAL: communication, *medium
PERIPHERY: *end, *rim, *space
PERISH: *end, *fall, *pass
PERIWINKLE: mussel, myrtle
PERJURE: *cheat, *lie

* Asterisk means to look up this word to find more answer words.

PERMANENT: abiding, changeless, coiffure, constant, continuing, durable, enduring, everlasting, *forever, hairdo, immutable, intact, invariable, lasting, perpetual, persistent, remaining, *solid, stable, steadfast, unfading

PERMEATE: soak, *spread, steep

PERMIT: *accord, *let, *suffer

PERNICIOUS: *bad, *evil, fatal

PERPETUAL: *permanent

PERPETUITY: *forever, olam

PERPLEX: *fool, *puzzle, *upset

PERPLEXITY: *problem, *puzzle

PERQUISITE: *fee, *income

PERSECUTE: *abuse, *torment

PERSEPHONE: brimo, cora, despoina, kore, proserpina
  daughter: cora, kore
  father: zeus
  husband: hades, pluto
  mother: ceres, demeter

PERSEUS: *grandfather:* acrisius
  grandson: aphareus
  parent: danae, zeus
  star: algol, atik
  victim: acrisius, medusa, polydectes
  wife: andromeda

PERSEVERANCE: *strength

PERSEVERE: *stand, *stick

PERSEVERING: *solid, *strong

PERSIAN: irani, lur, kurd, tudah
  almond: badam
  ancient: elamite, mede, tat
  angel: mah
  apple: peach
  assembly: majlis, meklis
  bed: divan, sofa
  berry: avignon, buckthorn
  bird: bulbul
  books: avesta, gathas, koran, *vendidad, vispered, yashts
  bug: miana
  builder: shah abbas
  capital: isfahan, persepolis, shiraz, teheran, tehran

  carpet: ardebil, bakshaish, hamadan, isfahan, ispahan, kali, nammad, sarouk, saruk, senna, serabend, teheran
  cat: angora
  chess: chaturanga, shatranj
  chief: dewan, diwan, mir
  city: abadan, ahwaz, amol, babul, balfroosh, bandar abbas, bushire, fao, hamadan, hilla, jask, kasvin, kerman, knoi, kom, kum, meshed, mosul, niriz, qum, resht, susa, tabriz, tauris, yezd
  coin: abbasi, asar, ashrafi, bisti, cran, daric, dinar, flouch, kasbeke, kran, lari, pahlavi, pul, rial, rupee, shahi, siglos, stater, toman
  comb.: rano
  comedy: temacha
  courier relay system: angaria
  deer: fallow, maral
  deity: ahriman, ahura, anahita, angra mainyu, assara mazaas, asura, deva, hvare-khshaeta, mah, mazda, mithra, mitra, ormazd, tishtriya, vivanhvat, yima
  demon: aeshma, ahriman, apaosha, azidahaka, daeva, druj, ized, karapan, kavi, naonhaithya, nasatya, nasu, pairaka, sauru, taurvi, velidi, yatu, yezidi, zairhi(sha), zohak
  drink: haoma, soma
  dynasty: achmaemenidae, buyid, parthian, safavi, sassanid
  epic: shah namah
  fabric: ardassine
  fairy: elf, fay, peri
  fire-maker: fratakara
  fire-worshiper: ateshperest, mazdaian, parsee, parsi
  first man: gayomart, mashya
  founder: cyrus
  garment: candys, chedar
  gate: bar, dar
  goat: bezoar, pasang

---

* Asterisk means to look up this word to find more answer words.

governor: khan, satrap
grass: millet
gulf islands: bahrain
gulf wind: shamal, sharki
gum: tragacanth
gypsy: sisech
hall: apadana
headdress: fez, tiara, turban
hero: feridun, rustem, rustum, thraetona, yima, zal
javelin: jereed, jerid
king: achmaemenes, ahasuerus, arsakes, artaxerxes, cambyses, cyrus, darius, feisal, feridun, giamschid, hoshang, husheng, jam(shyd), jemshid, *mede: king, minucher, rustem, sha(h), tahmuras, xerxes, yima, zal
koran student: hafix
lake: niriz, sahweh, urumiyeh
language: aryan, avestan, pahlavi, pahlevi, zend
lord: kaan, kaun, kawn, khan
lynx: caracal
measure: arasni, artaba, cane, capicha, charac, chebel, chenica, farsakh, farsang, gareh, gariba, gaz, gez, ghalva, gireh, guz, jerib, kafix, makuk, mansion, mishara, mou, ourub, parasang, piamaneh, qasab, sabbitha, stathmos, yava, zar, zer
monk: dervish
monster: azhidahaka
moon: mahi
mystic: sufi
new year's day: nowroze
nightingale: bulbul
oil center: abadan
palace hall: apadana
pantheist: babist
parliament: majlis, mejlis
people: bactrian, bakhtiari, beluchi, farsi, hadnemi, kajar, kurd, lur, mede, mukri, nomad, parsi, persian, sart, susian, tadjik, tajik
pipe: calean, hookah, narghile

plant: opium, poppy
poet: jami, omar, saadi, sadi
port: bandar abbas, basra, bushire
priest: archimage, atharvan, magi, nadab
prince, bible: admatha, carshena, marsena, memucan, meres, shethar, tarshish
queen: astin
religion: ateshperest, babism, bahaism, fire-worshipers, manichaeism, mazda(ian), zendavesta, zoroastrianism
religion founder: baha ullah, zarathustra, zoroaster
river: euphrates, karun, kizil uzen, mand, mund, safid rud, tab, tigris, zab, zuhreh
rose: gul
ruler: ameer, atabeg, ismail, mir(za), satrap, shah, sultan
sacred cord: kusti
saint: safavi(d), safawi(d)
salt swamp: kavir
sect: babi, ithnasheri, shiah, shiite, sunnee, sunni(te)
shah: mohammed riza pahlevi
spirit, good: *amshapends, fravashis, yazatas
sword: acinaces
tapestry: susanee
tax collector: tahsildar
tentmaker: omar
throne room: aiwan
tiara: cidaris
tick: miana bug
tiger: shek, sher, shir
tile: kashi, kasi
title: azam, khan, mir, sophy
tobacco: tumbaki, tumbeki
utopia: bashdi, ghaon, haroju, muru, nissa
water vessel: aftaba
weight: abbas(si), artal, batman, danar, dang, dirhem, dram, dung, gandum, karwar, maund, miscal, miskal, nakhod, pinar,

* Asterisk means to look up this word to find more answer words.

rik, saddingham, sang, seer, ser, sir, tcheirek, una
wheel: noria, tympana, tympanum
wine: red hermitage, shiraz
PERSIFLAGE: badinage, **banter*
PERSISTENT: **obstinate*
PERSON: **fellow*, individual, one
 comb.: ego, idio
PERSONAGE, PERSONALITY:
 *magnate
PERSONNEL: **group*, **staff*
PERSPECTIVE: **distance*, **range*
PERSPICACIOUS: **acute*, **smart*
PERSPICUOUS: clear, **open*
PERSUADE: **lead*, **move*, **urge*
PERSUASION: **doctrine*, **kind*
PERUSE: read, **study*
PERT: **bright*, **quick*, **smart*
PERTAIN: **belong*, **fit*
PERTAINING: **about*, in re
 comb.: aceous, al, an, ar, arious,
 ary, ese, ic
PERTINENT: **about*, **fit*, **right*
PERTURB: **agitate*, **alarm*, **upset*
PERU: *altitude sickness:* soroche
 animal: alpaca, llama, paco
 bird: guanay, yeni, yutu
 city: arequipa, ayacucho, callao,
 cuzco, ica, iquitos, lima, paita,
 pisco, piura
 coin: centavo, dinero, libra,
 peseta, sol
 dance: cueca
 deer: alpaca, taruco
 deity: huaca, mama
 fog: garua
 fox: atoc
 hill: loma, medano
 indian: atalan, aymaran, inca,
 quechua, tiahuanacan
 inn: tambo
 king: cacique, montezuma
 lake: titicaca
 liquor: pisco
 llama: alpaca, paco
 measure: celemin, fanegada, ga-
 lon, topo, vara

nobility emblem: llautu
party, political: apra
people: ande, aymara, boros,
 campa, cana, carib, inca, jibaro,
 jiyaro, kechua, lamano, panos,
 peba, quechau
plant: learco, massua, oca, pito,
 rhatany, tola, ulluco
plateau: tablazo
port: callao, ilo, pisco, ylo
rain: garua
relic: huaco
river: acara, apurimac, ene, hual-
 laga, ica, ilo, maranon, oroton,
 paucartambo, piura, rimac, sama,
 santa, ucayale, urubamba
rodent: chinchilla
shrub: chilca, matico, ratanhia,
 rhatany, shansa
tableland: puna
tanager: lindo, yeni
tavern: tambo
tinamou: yutu
tobacco: sana
tree: algarrobo, bucare, cinchona,
 erythrina, vichaya
tuber: oca
volcano: el misti
weight: libra, quintal
wind: puna, sures
PERVADE: fill, **penetrate*
PERVERSE: **obstinate*, **sinister*
PERVERSION: **error*, **passion*
PERVERT: abuse, **deceive*, **spoil*
PERVERTED: **bad*, **eccentric*
 comb.: allotri(o)
PESCADORES: boko gunto, bo-
 koto
 part: hoko, mako
PESHKOV: gorki, gorky
PESSIMISTIC: black, dark,
 gloomy
PEST: **plague*, **trouble*
 household: ant, fly, mosquito,
 mouse, rat, rodent, termite
PESTER: afflict, **plague*, **scold*
PESTILENCE: **plague*

---

* Asterisk means to look up this word to find more answer words.

PESTLE: grind, masher, pound

PET: *anger, animal, baby(sit), beastie, cade, canoodle, cant, caress, cat, coddle, cosset, dandle, dither, dog, dudgeon, favor(ite), fit, fondle, huff, indulge, *love, miff, neck, peeve, pique, *popular, rage, snit, *spark, *spoil, *special, *temper, tizzy

PETAIN: exile: ile d'yeu

PETAL: leaf, *part, plate, sepal
  pert.: ala, corolla, whorl

PETASUS: *cap, *hat

PETER: *end, *fail, simon, wane
  brother: andrew
  centurion follower: cornelius
  maid announcer: rhoda
  miracle: aeneas, dorcas, tabith
  pan role: hook, nana, smee, wendy

PETIOLE: stalk, *stem, stipe
  base shield: ocrea

PETITE: *little, *small

PETITION: *ask, *beg, pray, sue

PETRARCH: love: laura

PETREL: allamoth, assilag, cahow, mallemuck, mitty, titi

PETRIFY: *alarm, *scare, *shock

PETTICOAT: balmoral, basquine, benjy, farthingale, fustanella, half-slip, jupon, kilt, kirtle, pagne, vasquine, weskit

PETTIFOGGER: lawyer, shyster

PETTISH: fretful, *obstinate

PETTY: *little, *mean, *vain

PETULANT: *angry, *sullen, testy

PEW: bench, seat, sedilia, stall

PHANTASM, PHANTASY, PHANTOM: *demon, *devil, *image, *spirit

PHAON: consort: sappho

PHARAOH: *king, necho, rameses

PHASE: *form, *look, *part

PHEASANT: argusianus, kallege, leipoa, monal, pukras, tragopan
  breeding place: stew
  brood: nid(e), nye

eye: adonis annua, buttercup

PHENOMENAL: *big, *great, *large, *splendid

PHILIPPINES: animal: civet, lemur
ant: anai, anay
archipelago: sulu
attendant: alila
aunt: caca
banana: saguing
barracks: cuartel
bird: abacay
boat: balangay, balsa, banca, banka, barangay, casco
breadfruit: camansi
brigand: ladrone
buffalo: carabao, timarau
capital: cabecera
carriage: calash, calesa, carretela, carromata
cedar: calantas
century plant: maguey
chief: cato, dato, datto, datu, ilocano, iloco, ilokano
child: anac, bata
cigar: bunco
city: agoa, albay, aparri, bago, baguio, cabanatuan, cavite, cebu, dagupan, davao, ilagan, iriga, lanao, manila, naga, palo, vigan
coin: centavo, conant, peso
cyclone: bagio, baguio
deity: batala, bathala
dialect: bamboo english
discoverer: magellan
drink: beno, bubud, pangasi
duck egg: balut
dwarf: aeta, negrito
fabric: bandala, pina
fern: nito
fetish: anito
fiber: baroi, buntal, camansi, castuli, eruc, grewia, husi, jusi, pandanus, pineapple, pterospermum, saba
fig: agamid, balete
fish: dalag, langaray

* Asterisk means to look up this word to find more answer words.

food: baha, balut, poi, saba, taro
forest: dita, gubat
fort: corregidor, cota, cotta, gota, kota
game: panguingui
garment: saya
grass: boho, bojo, cogon
guerrilla: huk
gulf: davao, ragay
gun: baril
hardwood: acle, aranga, ipil
hat: salacon
hemp: abaca, manila
herb: bamban, donax canna formis
house: bahay, camalig
idol: anito
island: babuyan, batan, bohol, cebu, cuyo, jolo, leyte, luzon, masbate, mindanao, mindora, negros, palawan, panay, paragua, samar, sulu, ticao
jar: banga
kitchen: calan
knife: balarao, barong, bolo, campit, itac, itak, machet(te)
lake: lanao, taal
language: *philippines: people
liquor: *philippines: drink
litter: talabon
lizard: ibid, ibit
mahogany: almon, shorea eximia
malayan: italone
mammal: tarsier
mango: bauno, carabao, pahutan
market-day: tiangue
measure: apatan, balita, braza, caban, catty, cavan, chinanta, chupa, fardo, ganta, lachsa, loan, picul, punto, quilate, quinon
monkey: douc, langur, macaque, machin
mountaineer: mentesco
mother: ina
muskmelon: atimon
muslim: moro
native: *philippines: people

nut: pili
outlaw: babaylan
pagan: italone
palm: niog
parrot: cagit
peak: apo, iba, mayon, pagsan
peasant: tao
peninsula: bataan
people: abaca, aeta, ati, atta, bagobo, baluga, batak, bicol, etas, ibanag, ifil, ifugao, igorot, illano, ilocano, ita(nega), lutao, lutayo, moro, sulu, tagala, tagalog, timaua, timawa, tinguiane, vicol, visayan
pigeon: bleeding-heart
plant: abaca, aga(mid), alasas, alem, baroi, batad, ficus, pandanus
plum: duhat, lansa, lanseh, mabolo, sapote
port: aparri, bacolod, cavite, cebu, iloilo
priest: babaylan, pandita, pandito, sarip
prince: cachil
reptile: python
rice: aga, barit, bigas, canin, macan, paga
river: abra, agno, cagayan, mindanao, pampanga, pasig
road: daan
rope: anabo, nabo
sack: bayon
sapodilla: chico
sarong: padadion
sash: tapis
sea: sulu
sentinel: bantay
servant: alila, alipin, bata
shirt: baro
shrub: abroma, alem, anabo, anilao, columbia, nabo
silk: alcaiceria
skirt: saya
slipper: chinela
soldier: gugu, ladrone, moro

* Asterisk means to look up this word to find more answer words.

spirit: anito
springs: tibi
stream: ilog
sumac: anam, anan
summer capital: baguio
sweetsop: ates
sword: barong, campilan
termite: anai, anay
textile: pina, saba, sina-may
thatch: nipa
tree: aclang-parang, acle, agoho, alagao, alibangbang, almaciga, alupag, amaga, amboina, amuguis, amuyon, anabo, anagap, anonang, apalit, apitong, aranga, balao, balau, balibago, banaba, bancal, banilad, bansalague, banuyo, batino, bayok, binukau, botong, bulak, cabo, calantas, camagon, camuning, cebur, dao, dita, iba, ipil, lanete, lebur, ligas, macaasim, malapaho, mambong, marang, molave, supa, tanguile, tindalo, tua, tui, tuwi, vitex, yate
vine: amlong, gogo, iyo
volcano: albay, apo, askja, hibok, mayo, taal
watchtower: atalaya, bantayan
water jar: bango
white man: cachil(a)
wine: alac
wood: ebony, narra, sandal
yam: ubi, uve
PHILISTINE: barbarian, hypocrite
city: gath, gaza, ekron
foe: david, samson
giant: goliath
god: baal, dagan, dagon
king: abimelech
original home: caphtor
PHILOMELA: nightingale
kin: pandion, procne
PHILOSOPHER: *land:* balnibarbi
stone: carmot, elixir, panacea
stone substance: carmot
PHILOSOPHICAL: **cool,* **ra-*

tional, serene, tranquil, **wise*
pleiad: **greece: sages, seven*
PHILOSOPHY: agnosticism, animalism, animism, atomism, averroism, casuistry, comtism, cosmology, cynicism, cyrenaicism, deism, **doctrine,* eclecticism, eleaticism, elian, empiricism, epicureanism, esoterics, esthetics, ethics, existentialism, gnosticism, hedonism, humanism, hylism, idealism, individualism, leibnitzianism, manichaeism, materialism, megarianism, mimamsa, monism, mysticism, naturalism, noxumenalism, nyaya, ontologism, panlogism, pantheism, patristicism, physicalism, pluralism, positivism, pragmatism, realism, sankhya, schellingism, sensationalism, skepticism, somatism, sophism, stoicism, syncretism, theism, thomism
first: metaphysics
pert.: eleatic
PHINEAS: *son:* abishua, ahijah, eleazar, gershom, ichabod
victim: zimri
PHLEGMATIC: **dull,* **slow*
PHOBOS: *father:* ares
PHOEBE: **artemis,* diana, selene
daughter: asteria, leto
husband: coeus
PHOEBUS: **apollo,* **light,* sol
PHOENICIA: *capital:* tyre
city: acre, byblos, gebal, sidon, tyre
colony: carthage
god: baal, balmarcodes, melkart
goddess: astarte, baltis, tanit
governor, bible: sisinnes
king: agenor
pert.: punic
princess: europa
PHOENIX: beauty, bennu, benu, bird of wonder, hero
PHONETIC: oral, vocal

---

* Asterisk means to look up this word to find more answer words.

notation: romic
sound: palatal
PHONY: *false, *impostor
PHORCYS: *children:* *gorgons,
*graeae, *hesperides, ladon,
scylla, thoosa
lover: hecate
parent: gaea, pontus
wife: ceto, crataeis
PHORONEUS: *kin:* car, io, niobe
wife: cerdo, laodice
PHOSPHATE: apatite, arrojadite,
attacolite, palaite, wavellite
center: nauru, pleasant island
PHOTO(GRAPH): cheesecake,
daguerreotype, film, *image,
montage, mug, *pic(ture), print,
shot, snap, still, tintype
bath: developer, fixer, toner
book: album
chemistry: actino
color process: pinachromy
color tool: blimp
copy: contact, print, stat
description: caption
developer: adurol, amidol, aminophenol, hypo, metol, ortol, para-
aminophenol, rodinal, soup,
toner
development place: darkroom
finish: nose
inventor: daguerre, niepce, talbot
powder: amidol, metol, selenium
solution: hypo
tools: diaphragm, dryer, easel, en-
larger, filter, finder, flash, lens,
meter, range finder, reflector,
shutter, timer, tripod, viewer
PHOTOMETRIC UNIT: lumen,
lux, pyr, rad
PHOTOSTAT: copy, dupe
PHRASE: *adage, *part, *style
PHRATRY: clan, *part, tribe
PHRENETIC: avid, *insane, *mad
PHRIXOS, PHRIXUS: *parent:*
athamas, nephele
sacrifice: golden fleece

sister: helle
stepmother: ino
PHRYGIA: *converter:* montanist
god: attis, atys, cabeiri, kabeiri,
kabiri, men, sabazios
king: gordius, midas, otreus
river: meander
sect: cataphrygian, montanist
town: ipsus
PHRYNE: *prostitute, *wanton
PHYLACTERIC: *magic
PHYLACTERY: *fetish, *spell
PHYSICIAN: *medical, *medicine
PHYSICIST: abbe, ampere, boyle,
bunsen, curie, erman, faraday,
galvani, hahn, hylozoist, mach,
marconi, materialist, naturalist,
ohm, rossi, volta
atomic: bohr, compton, einstein,
fermi, meitner, millikan, pauli,
rabi, urey
PHYSIOGNOMY: face, *image
study: phrenology
PIANIST: *famous:* anda, arrau,
busoni, cliburn, curzon, gould,
hofmann, horowitz, iturbi,
kempf, levant, lhevinne, pach-
mann, richter, rosen, serkin
PIANO: anemochord, grand,
spinet
dumb: digitoria
key: digital
keyboard: clavier
pedal: celestex
PIASTER: *1/20th:* asper
PICAROON: *criminal, *hoodlum
PICAYUNE: *little, *mean, *small
PICK: *best, *gather, *pierce,
*scold, *seize, *steal, *take
-up: *arrest, call, *friend, *increase, *prostitute, tonic
PICKET: fence, squad, *torture
PICKLE: cure, *mess, *problem
PICKPOCKET: *criminal, *thief
helper: bulker
PICNIC: *eat, party
spot: bois, country, woods

---

* Asterisk means to look up this word to find more answer words.

PICTURE: abstract(ion), ancona, batik, canvas, cartoon, chalk, charcoal, collage, *copy, crayon, cyclorama, dash off, decal, *describe, design, diagram, doodle, draught, *draw, engraving, envisage, envision, epitome, etching, fresco, illumination, illustration, *image, mosaic, movie, mural, nude, *paint, pastel, pastoral, pattern, pencil, *photo, pinup, profile, representation, reproduction, scene, scratch, *study, tableau, tapestry, view
border: frame, mat
group: album, ancona
puzzle: jigsaw, rebus
section: gravure
viewer: alethoscope, projector
PIEBALD: calico, dapple, *mixture
PIECE: *adjunct, *bit, block, bone, chunk, coin, composition, *distance, drama, *eat, gun, *join, manuscript, mend, *move, *part, *prostitute, *range, *repair, *share, stone, *study, *thing, tune, *unit, *work
de resistance: *acme, *best
out: *complete, eke
together: *form, *make, *unite
PIED: *piebald, pintado, pinto
PIER: moor, post, quay, *support
architectural: anta
base: socle
part: alette, pile, piling
shaft: convex, *molding
PIERCE: *bore, broach, brob, brod, chill, discern, *enter, gore, gouge, gride, *hurt, lance, *pain, perforate, pike, prick, punch, *spear, *stick, *strike, *tear
PIERCING: *acerb, *high, *sharp
PIERUS: consort: clio
son: hyacinthus
PIFFLE: *nonsense
PIG: hog, *swine

bed: pen, reeve, sand, sty
boat: submarine, u-boat
deer: babiroussa
dialect: elt
fat: axunge
feet: pettitoes, souse
female: elt, gilt, shoat, sow
-fish: sailor's-choice
flesh: bacon, pork
group: swine
-headed: *obstinate
iron ballast: kentledge
latin: *argot, *chatter
-like animal: aardvark, peccary
male: boar, hog
metal: bar, ingot
nut: broom hickory, carya
pen: mess, slum, sty
pert.: porcine
potato: cowbane
rat: bandicoot
sconce: pighead
skin: football, glove, saddle
sound: oink, wee
sticker: knife, sled, sword
tail: braid, cue, queue
-tailed macaque: bruh, macaca
tender: swineherd
wash: hogwash, swill
weed: amaranthus, beet root, careless, chenopodium, goatfoot
young: bonav, bonham, elt, far(row), gilt, grice, shoat, shote, snork, teatman
wiggen: *dwarf
wild: boar, javelina, peccary
PIGEON: berry: dogwood, pokeweed
blood: garnet, red
carrier: homer, horseman, scandaroon
clay: skeet, target
domestic: barb, nun, ruff, runt, satinette, trumpeter
extinct: dodo
food: saltcat
fruit: kuku, lupe

* Asterisk means to look up this word to find more answer words.

genus: columba, goura
grass: crabgrass, foxtail
hawk: falcon, merlin
-hole: *analyze, ignore, *store
house: aviary, columbary, cote, dovecote, rook(ery)
-livered: *gentle, meek, mild
pea: angola, arhar, cajanus, catjang, dal, gandul, tur
pert.: columboid, peristeronic
shooting: skeet
short-beaked: barb(ed)
tooth-billed: dodlet
wood: kuku
woodpecker: flicker
young: piper, squealer
PIGMENT: color, dye, paint
black: almond, aspergillin, bone charcoal, melanin, sepia, tar
blood: hemoglobin
blue: alkali, azurite, bice, iolite, smalt, verditer, zinc
board: palette
brown: bilifuscin, bister, bistre, burnt ochre, melanin, sepia, sienna, umber
calico printing: canarin(e)
carotinoid: arumin
coal tar: aniline
copper borate: bolley's green
crinoid: antedonin
cuttle fish: sepia
green: bice, biliprasin, biliverdin, verditer
hollyhock: althaein, althein
lack: achroma, albino, alphosis
lake: madder
lead: cerussite, massicot
orange: realgar
pepper: capsumin
red: actiniochrome, alizarin, amatito, bilirubin, cappagh, carmine, carotenoid, chica, realgar, russian calf, turacin
soluble: anthocyanidin, pelargoni-din
white: baryta, blanc fixe, lead

yellow: anthochlor, anthoxanthin, carotenoid, etiolin, lead oxychloride, ochre, orpiment, retinene
PIKE: *road, *spear, *staff
fish: arapaima, blenny, brasse, dore, esox, gedd, luce, robalo, sauger
PIKER: *coward, gambler, *thief
PILASTER: ailette, anta, *tower
PILATE: *prisoner:* barabbas
tribunal: gabbatha, pavement
wife: claudia
PILCHAR: fumado, sardine
PILE: *gather, *quantity, *store
body: barrel
driver: beetle, fistuca, gin, oliver, ram, tup
it on: exaggerate
up: accident, *increase, *save
-wort: adad, celandine, ficary, fireweed
PILFER: filch, *steal, theft
PILGRIM: hadji, *monk, pioneer
bottle: ampulla, costrel
garb: ihram
holy land: palmer
saint: alexius
ship: mayflower, speedwell
PILL: bore, jer, *remedy
birth control: chlormadinone, enovid, ethynerone, neonovum
box: *cap, *fort, *hat
bug: armadillid, louse
pep: *drug, *narcotic
PILLAGE: *spoil, *steal
PILLAR: *memorial, *pier, *tower
capital: chapter
figured: osiride
ore: jam
pert.: stelar
stone: *memorial, *monument
top: chapiter pommel, wreath
PILLARIST: *monk, stylite
PILLORY: *punish, *torture, yoke
PILLOW: bolster, *support
cover: sham
PILON: *bonus, *gift, *present

* **Asterisk means to look up this word to find more answer words.**

PILOT: *head, *lead(er), *run
 bird: plover
 fish: mackerel, remora, romero, seriola, whitefish
 grounded: kiwi
 snake: bull, copperhead
 speaking tube: gosport
 weed: compass, rosinweed
 whale: blackfish
PIMPLE: *bit, boil, sty, tumor
PIN: *badge, *bit, *secure
 ball: bagatelle, flipper
 blocks: dowell, nog
 dial: style
 feather: pen, plume
 fold: *jail
 grass: alfilaria, erodiom
 head: *clown, *fool
 jackstraw: spilikin
 machine: cotter
 meat-fastening: skewer
 money: allowance, cash
 oar: thole
 on: attach, attribute, charge
 pivot: pintle
 plant: tacca
 point: *aim, *exact, *fix
 rifle: tige
 tail: duck, smee, smew
 wheel: catherine wheel
 worm: ascarid, nematode
PINCERS: caliper, chela, forceps
PINCH: *arrest, *crisis, *limit, *pain, *press, *steal
 -bar: lever, pry
 -beck: cheap, *false
 -fist: *miser, tightwad
 -hitter: *substitute
 -penny: carl, *miser
PINE: *ache, *cry, *desire
 -apple: anana, bomb, nana, *ornament, pinguin, pip, puya
 -apple island: lanai
 -apple weed: marigold
 bark aphid: phylloxera
 cone: clog, strobile
 disease: blister rust

grove: pinetum
gum: sandarac
knot: dovekie
marten: american sable
plant: bromeliaci
resin: carpathian balsam
sap: bino
siskin: finch
snake: bull, constrictor, gopher snake, pituophis
tar: retene
textile screw: ara, pandan
tree: *tree: evergreen
tree state: idaho, maine, montana, new mexico
tulip: pipsissewa
wood: candlewood
PINGUID: *bland, *fat, *rich
PINION: *flag, *part, *tie, wing
PINK: *acme, *pierce, *smart
 bollworm: corn earworm
 eye: conjunctivitis
 fish: blind goby
 needle: alfilaria
 pill: cure-all
PINKS: seconal, silene
PINNACLE: *acme, *top, *tower
 glacial: serac
 rocky: scar, tor
PINOCHLE: term: bete, dux, flush, kitty, meld, open, widow
PINTADO: cero, guinea, pigeon
PIOUS: *false, *good, *holy
PIP: *ace, *bit, *hit, *speed
PIPAL: bo tree, fig, sacred
PIPE: smoke, *waterway
 angle: tee
 ashes: dottle
 bend: elbow
 body: barrel
 clay: camstone, churchwarden, straw, td, tile
 closer: alfalfa valve
 dream: chimera, illusion
 end: hub, nozzle, taft
 fish: earl, snacot
 joint: calepin, coupling, cross, elbow, ell, nipple, tee, wye

* Asterisk means to look up this word to find more answer words.

furnace: tuyere
layer: politician, schemer
line: channel, grapevine
part: bowl, stem
pastoral: larigot, oat, reed
pert.: tubate
player: fifer, flautist, pan
short: dudeen
small: tubule
smoke: tewel
source: briar, brier
spiral: coil
steam: riser
stone: catlinite
stove: chimney, flue, tewel
terra cotta: bleeder
water: calean, hookah, narghile
wrench: stillson
PIPER: *son:* tom
PIPIT: anthus, teetan, wekeen
PIQUANCY: spice, *spirit
PIQUANT: *acerb, *sharp
PIQUE: *anger, *interest, *pain
PIRATE: hijack, *steal, *thief
flag: blackjack, jolly roger
PIT: *hell, *jail, *opening
baking: imu, oven
bottomless: abaddon, *hell
fall: *ambush, *trap
medical: fossa
mouth: bank head
peach: putamen, seed
sacrificial: bothros
small: alveola, foveola, lacuna
viper: agkistrodon, bothrops, bushmaster, habu, lachesis
PITCH: *accept, *range, slope, spiel, sway, *tell, *throw
above: sharp
apple: copei, cupay
below: flat
blende: radium, uranium
cobbler's: code
fork: *evil, sheppick, *throw
hole: cahot, recess
instrument: tonometer
into: *attack, *eat, *start

pine: loblolly, lodgepole
pipe: epitonion, tuner
system of symbols: neume
PITCHER: *left-handed:* southpaw
mound: box, hill, slab
plant: adam's-cup, biscuit, cephalotus, chrysamphora, darlingtonia, huntsman's cup, nepenthe, sarracenia
-shaped: ascidiform, urceolate
warm-up area: bull pen
PITH: core, *force, *strength
PITHY: *short, *solid
PITIFUL: *bad, *paltry, *sorry
PITILESS: *brutal, *hard, *mean
PITTANCE: *bit, *gift, *share
PITUITARY: *product:* acth
PITY: mercy, *passion, *shame
PIVOT: rotate, swing, *turn
PIXIE: *dwarf, *spirit
PLACATE: *please, *smooth
PLACE: area, arrange, assort, attribute, base, bestow, book, cast, cater, cell, city, deposit, district, dive, duty, fix, *fort, function, hangout, haunt, haven, *home, house, impose, insert, inset, install, invest, lair, lay, lieu, location, lodge, office, *opening, *order, pad, park, *part, patio, period, point, pose, posit(ion), post(ure), premises, put, *rank, recognition, region, repose, rest, *road, role, room, scene, schedule, seat, *set(up), site, situation, spa, spot, spread, *stand, station, status, stead, stick, *stop, street, *throw, town, tract, venue
apart: enisle, separate
before: appose, confront, prefix
beneath: infrapose
between: insert, interpose
business: *plant, *store
camping: etape
comb.: age, arium, ery, gaea, gea, orium, topo
end for end: reverse

* Asterisk means to look up this word to find more answer words.

hiding: cave, mew
holy: shrine
in the sun: *glory, recognition
last: also-ran, booby prize
meeting: rendezvous, tryst
one inside another: nest
poetic: clime
side by side: appose, juxtapose
trial: venue
PLACID: *gentle, *quiet, *smooth
PLAGIARIZE: crib, pirate, *steal
PLAGUE: *afflict(ion), annoy,
badger, bane, bother, calamity,
*catastrophe, chafe, *curse, *dis-
ease, fret, gall, harass, hector,
*hurt, importune, infest, *pain,
pest(er), pestilence, tease, *torment, *trouble, twit, worry
carrier: germ, rat, virus
pert.: loimic
PLAID: maud, tartan
PLAIN: *ascetic, attic, audible,
basin, blair, blunt, *broad, bush,
campagna, campaign, campestral, campo, certain, champaign,
chaste, chol, clean, clear, desert,
distinct, down, downright, dry,
elemental, even, expanse, flat(s),
flush, forthright, heath, homely,
informal, ingenuous, level, llano,
*low(land), lucid, mere, mesa,
mesilla, moor(land), *open, ordinary, outspoken, pampa(s),
plateau, playa, plot, *popular,
prairie, *pure, *regular, salada,
savanna(h), sebkha, simon-pure,
*simple, *smooth, spartan,
steppe(s), stretch, tableland,
thorough, tundra, *ugly, vega,
veld(t), weald, wide-open space
-clothes man: detective, *spy
depression: swale
dweller: llanero
stone: flagstone, paving
PLAINT: *cry
PLAINTIVE: *sad, *short, *sullen
PLAIT: braid, fold, mesh, ply

PLAN: agenda, aim, architecture,
arrange(ment), blueprint, brief,
brouillon, budget, cabal, card,
chart, conspire, *copy, *design,
device, diagram, draught, *draw,
epure, ettle, *form, *image, intend, itinerary, layout, line-up,
method, *model, pattern, *plot,
*prepare, profile, project, *pur-
pose, ready, rough, scheme, *set,
sketch, strategy, *system, *think,
*way, *work
PLANE: *aircraft, even, flat,
grade, jet, level, surface
block: stock
boundary: perimeter
chart: mercator
handle: toat, tote
inclined: chute, shute
iron: bit, blade
kind: block, grooving, iron, jack,
router, tounging
median: meson
point: cone
tree: buttonbush, buttonwood,
chinar, platanus, sycamore
PLANET: *aspect:* biquintile, cusp,
trine
brightest: venus
cone: strobile
influence: almuten, atazir
nativity influencing: almuten
newest: pluto
orbit: ellipse
orbit point: apogee, apsis, nadir,
parigree, zenith
period: alfridary
position: alichel, alictisal
red: mars
relation: conjunction, sextile
relative position: aspect
representation: orrery
ruling: dominator
satellite: moon
PLANK: *breadth:* strake
curved: sny
down: *advance, ante, pay

* Asterisk means to look up this word to find more answer words.

end: butt
facing: campshedding, campshot
lengthwise: stringer
surface, increasing: shole
PLANKTON: *collector:* d-net
PLANT: **agency,* arsenal, assembly line, bindery, bios, broadcast, bury, cannery, company, concern, corporation, equipment, factory, firm, fix, flower, fruit, herb, market, mill, mint, office, packer, **place,* pottery, **put,* refinery, seed, seminate, **set, *settle, *shop,* shrub, sow, stock, **store,* tannery, tree, vegetable, vine, **work*
abnormal: ecad
aconite: bikh
ammoniac: oshac
ancestor: ortet
apiaceous: ache, anise, cumin
appendage: ascidium, stipule
araceous: arum, cabbage, lily
aromatic: anise, carum, clary, dill, lavender, nard, nondo, nutmeg, sage, tansy, tarragon
association: bush swamp
axis: stalk
base: alkaloid, caudex
benthonic: enalid
bignoniaceous: catalpa
bitter: colicroot, ers, rue
body: cormus
boraginaceous: bugloss, forget-me-not, heliotrope
bramble: briar, furze, gorse
brassica: cale, cole, rape
breathing organ: stoma(ta)
bromeliaceous: pineapple
bruise-healing: soapwort
bud: cion
bulb: camass, nerine, quamash
capsule: pod
caustic: moxa
cell: gamete
climbing: bine, byrony, creeper, ivy, liana, philodendron, smilax

color: chlorophyll, endochrome
comb.: botano, phyto
coniferous: brachyphyllum
cruciferous: alga, alyssum, awlwort, cabbage, cress, fern
cryptogamous: alga, fern, moss
cutting: phyton, slip
cyperaceous: sedge
decorative: bush, fern, flower
dicotyledonous: apetala
dipsacus: teasel
ericaceous: azalea, cardinal, kurume, minerva, rhododendron
everlasting: orpine
exudate: gum, latex, milk, resin, rosin, sap
fabaceous: axseed, baby's-slippers, butter jags, ers, pea
floating: frogbit, lotus
flowerless: acrogen, fern, lichen, moss, thalogen
form: ecad
fossil: annularia, aptiana
group: batch, cluster, family, order, thicket
growing from inside: endogenic
growing from outside: exogenic
growing in another: aulophyte
growth layer: cambium
growth measurer: auxanometer
habitat: ecad, form
habitat adjustment: ecesis
head: bud, burr, flower, fruit
honey secreter: nectary
hybridization: xenia
imprint: autophytograph
joined to another: graft
juice: **plant:* exudate
labiate: calamint, satureja
leguminous: alfalfa, bean, pea
life: bios, flora, vegetation
lilaceous: aloe, asphodel, camas(s), cammas, leek, lotus, onion, sabadilla, sotol, squill, tulip, yucca
louse: aphid, aphis
malvaceous: abelmosk, algalia,

* Asterisk means to look up this word to find more answer words.

altea, cotton, escoba, hibiscus, mallow, okra
menthaceous: catmint, catnip
multicellular: metaphyte
oil-yielding: odal, sesame
part: leaf, petal, pistil, raphe, stamen, stipel, stomata, tendril
perennial: carex, sedum
pert.: agamic, botanic, floral, phytic, vegetal, vegetative
poisonous: amanita, banewort, belladonna, black nightshade, calfkill, castor oil, datura, death cup, foxglove, gastrolobium, greyana, hellebore, hemp, henbane, loco(weed), mescal, monkshood, oleander, opium poppy, pokeweed, sheep laurel, swainsona, upas, water hemlock
pore: lenticel
provisional name: adelaster
reproducer: archegonium, spore
round-leaved: pennywort
salad: celery, cress, endive, lettuce, purslane, romaine
science: botany
sea: alga, alimon, enalid
seedless: fern
shoot: cion, rod, runner, scion, sprig, stolon
skin-irritating: ivy, smartweed
solanaceous: tobacco
starch-yielding: pia, taro
stem: bine, birn, caulis, shaft
stemless: acaulescent, thallus
trifoliate: clover, shamrock
urticaceous: nettle
verbenaceous: lantana
winter-flowering: epacris
xyloid: tree
PLANTAIN: banana, pala, tree
PLANTER: *decorative:* lavabo
PLASTER: adobe, cement, cerate, clay, compo, gatch, gesso, grout, gypsum, intoxicate, mortar, parget, roughcast, scagliola, *smooth,* stucco

coat: arriciato, arricio, cat
glue: size
tool: spatula
PLAT: *plain, *plan, *plot
PLATAEA: *founder:* androcrates
PLATE: *cover, *piece
battery: grid
boiler: sput
bone: scapula
communion: paten
cooking: grid
holder: cassette
horny: scute
iron: latten
-like vessel: latten
metal: dod
perforated: dog, grid, stencil
reptile's: scute
thin: lamella, lamina, paten
throwing: discus
PLATFORM: *church:* solea
mining: sollar, soller
raised: dais, podium, solea, stand, tribune
sleeping: kang
temple: dukan
theatre: logeion
PLATO: *grove:* academe
idea: eide, eidos
knowledge: noesis
PLATTER: *shaped:* scutellate
PLAY: accompany, *act(ion), affect, amuse(ment), antic, *bet, blow, caper, carouse, carry on, cavort, celebrate, contend, cut up, dally, dance, debauch, disport, *drama, farce, feign, frisk, frolic, fun, gamble, gambol, game, have fun, hell around, horse around, jest, *joke, jolly, kill time, let on, make merry, masque(rade), melodrama, miracle, *move, mystery, opera(te), pageant, perform, prank, pretend, recreation, revel, roister, rollick, romp, *run, scenario, *show, speculate, sport, spree,

* Asterisk means to look up this word to find more answer words.

step out, swing, symphonize, tragedy, *trifle, trip, tune, *use, *wanton, *work
ball: cooperate, *open, *start
for: accompany, court, *try
hooky: awol, be absent, bug out
-mate: *fellow, *friend
part: act, aside, *bit, curtain, epilogue, epitasis, finale, prelude, prologue, prop, role, scene
place: arena, bowl, casino, coliseum, colosseum, commons, course, court, diamond, fairway, field, forum, gridiron, links, oval, park, ring, rink, stadium, stage, stand(s), theater, track
possum: *ambush, *deceive, *trap
room: bar, den, gym. studio
thing: *agent, hobby, *toy
words, on: acronym, carriwitchet, *joke, pun
PLAYER: actor, athlete, card, competitor, contractor, gambler, hand, idler, *man, speculator, sport, star, thespian
band: cast, squad, team, troupe
fundless: lumber
PLEA(D): *argue, *press, *urge
PLEASANT: *gentle, *good
island: nauru
trip: bon voyage, *good bye
PLEASE: agree, amuse, arride, bewitch, bitte, choose, elate, exalt, fancy, gladden, go over, gratify, *hit, humor, indulge, prefer, regale, satisfy, *send
PLEASING: *fair, *pleasant
PLEASURE: *joy, *paradise, *will
god: bes(a), comus
lack: anhedonia, unhappiness
pert.: apolaustic, epicurean, hedonistic, sybaritic
PLEBEIAN: *low, *mean, *plain
PLEDGE: *promise, *tie, *token
PLEIADES: alcyone, asterope, atlantides, celaeno, electra, maia, merope, sterope, taygeta

constellation: *hesperides, taurus
lover: ares, poseidon, sisyphus
parent: aethra, atlas, pleione
PLEIONE: *offspring:* *pleiades
PLENARY: *absolute, *all, *great
PLENTY: abundance, affluence, agogo, *all, ample, amplitude, bags, barrels, bounteous, cheap, competence, copious, easy street, effuse, enough, extravagance, exuberance, *fat (of the land), *flood, fortune, full(ness), galore, generosity, generous, greatly, lavish, liberal, luxury, opulence, overflow, plethora, prodigal, *quantity, replete, *rich, satisfaction, *store, *surfeit, sufficiency, uberty, wealth
father: abiathar
goddess: annapurna, ops, rhea
horn: amalthaea, cornucopia
personification: abundantia
PLETHORA: *plenty, *surfeit
PLIABLE, PLIANT: *gentle, *soft
PLIGHT: *promise, *state
PLINTH: block, orlo, socle
PLOD: *try, *walk, *work
PLOT: acre, area, artifice, block, brew, cabal, casate, cast, clique, close, collude, concoct, connive, conspire, cook up, *design, diagram, draft, enclave, engineer, fainague, field, finagle, graph, hatch, intrigue, lot, machinate, map, maneuver, node, outline, *pack, *part, patch, *plan, *purpose, ruse, scenario, scheme, site, square, tract, *trick, wangle
PLOUGH, PLOW: *dig, furrow
blade: colter, coulter, share
cotton: bull tongue, scooter
land: carucate
man: farmer, tiller
part: beam, clevis, hale, sheath, slade, sole, stilt
PLOY: *move, *plan, *play
PLUCK: *nerve, *seize, *will

* Asterisk means to look up this word to find more answer words.

PLUG: *nag, shoot, *stop, *try
  cannon: tampion
  clay: bod, bott
  fishing: bug
  medicine: clot, embolus, tampon
  -ugly: *criminal, *hoodlum
PLUM: fruit, *prize, treasure
  cake: baba, barmbrack
  colored: puce
  curculio: weevil
  kind: amatungula, amra, bullace,
    cheston, damson, drupe, duhat,
    greengage, icaco, islay, jambul,
    lomboy, prunus, sapote, sloe
  sapodilla: chico, lanzon
PLUMB: solve, sound, thorough
PLUMP: *fat, *support, *throw
PLUNDER: prey, *spoil, *steal
PLUNDERER: *hoodlum, *thief
PLUNGE: *absorb, *fall, *run
PLUNK: deposit, *strike
PLUS: *add, *extra, *over
PLUTO: dis, *hades, *hell, orcus
  discoverer: tombaugh
PLUTUS: *parent:* demeter, iasion
PLY: *urge, *use, *work, *yield
PNEUMA: breath, soul, *spirit
PNEUMONIA: *pert.:* croupous,
  lobar
POACH: boil, *mix, *steal
POCAHONTAS: *spouse:* rolfe
POCKET: *bit, *get, *pack, *small,
  *steal, swallow, *take
  billiards: pool
  book: bag, fob, *money, purse
  gopher: camass rat, thomomys
  ore: bonanza, lode
  water: alberca, tinaja
POD: aril, bag, belly, group, pipi,
  pouch, sac, school, sunt
  frame: replum
  -snappery: output
POE: *bird:* raven
  poem: annabel lee, bells, gold
  bug, lenore, raven, ulalume
POEM: alba, amhran, amphigory,
  anacreontic, azharoth, ballad,

bucolic, cantara, cantic(le), carmen, cento, decastich, dit,
dithyramb, ditty, dizain(e), doggerel, duan, eclogue, edda, elegy
epic, epigram, epode, epopee
gazel, georgic, haiku, heptastich
hexastich, iambic, idyl, jingle,
lay, limerick, lyric, macaronics,
madrigal, monody, ode, pali-
node, parody, pastoral, quatrain,
rhapsody, rhyme, romance, rondeau, rondel(et), roundel(ay),
rune, saga, sestina, *song, sonnet, *story, triolet, verse
  collection: anthology, cancionero,
  divan, sylva
  part: anacrusis, antistrophe, arsis,
  canto, chorus, envoy, foot, line,
  measure, stanza, stave, stich,
  strain, strophe, syllable, verse
POETRY: *god:* apollo, bragi, odin
  muse: calliope, erato, thalia
POIGNANT: *severe, *sharp
POINT: *ace, *aim, *bit, *issue,
  *joke, *particular, *top(ic)
  curve: acnode, crunode
  d'appui: fulcrum
  highest: apex, apogee, zenith
  lowest: nadir
  main: gist, jet, kernel, pith
  pert.: apical, cacuminal, focal
  turning: *crisis
POINTED: *sharp, significant
  upward: acockbill
POINTLESS: *dull, *idle, *stupid
POISON: corrupt, infect, *kill
  arrow: haya, inee, sumpit, upas,
  urali, urare, wagogo
  ash: sumac, torchwood
  auto: carbon monoxide, pan
  berry tree: butterbush, pittosporum phillyraeoides
  comb.: arseno
  dogwood: sumac, sumach
  fear of: toxiphobia
  fish: fugu, toadfish, weever
  flag: iris

* Asterisk means to look up this word to find more answer words.

flower: bittersweet
fungus: amanita
hemlock: bunk, cash, chicory, conine, conium, wild chervil
herb: aconitum
hexapod: insecticide
ivy: black mercury, laurel
lizard: gila monster
pert.: arsenious
protein: ricin(e)
suma: boar tree
tobacco: henbane
tree: blind-your-eyes, milky mangrove, upas
weed: loco
wood: bumwood, manchineel, metopium, sumac
POISONOUS: attery, deadly, fatal, lethal, loco, malign, mephitic, iasmic, noxious, toxic, venomous, virulent
POKE: *attack, *drag, *pierce, *push, *spear, *stir, *urge
berry: cancer jalap
weed: american nightshade, ditch stonecrop, garget, inkberry, pocan, scoke
POLAND: polska, sarmatia
assembly: seim, sejm, seym
cake: baba
carriage: britska
checkers: quebec draughts
china: hog, pig, swine
city: beuthen, bialystok, brest, cracow, danzig, dukla, gdynia, gleiwitz, grodno, krakow, lemberg, litovsk, lodz, lublin, lyck, narev, nysa, opole, pila, posen, tarnopol, tarnow, torun, vilna, warsaw
coin: abia, dalar, ducat, fennig, grosz, halerz, korona, marka, zlot(y)
commander: anders, bor
commune: kutno, plock, radom, ruda, sopot
communist leader: gromulka

composer: chopin
dance: cracovienne, krakowiak, mazurka, polka, polonaise
dynasty: piast
housewife: pani
island: wolin
jew: galitzianer
kerchief: babushka
king: conti
lady: dziedziczka
marshes: pripet
measure: cal, cwierc, garniec, korzec, kwarterka, linja, lokiec, mila, morg, pret, sazen, stopa, vloka, wloka
nobleman: starost
president, first: pilsudski
river: bug, dniester, dwina, niemen, podra, pripet, san, seret, styr(pa), vistula
title: dziedziczka, pani, szlachta
weight: centner, funt, kamian, lut, skrupul, uncya
POLE: *beam:* caber
bird lure: stool
-cat: ferret, fitchew, marriput, musang, putorius, skunk, zoril
electric: anode, cathode, electrode, kathode
fishing: cane, gaff, pew, rod
fluke: flounder
head: tadpole
horse: wheeler
memorial: totem, xat
nautical: mast, sprit
rope dancer's: poy
-star: cynosure, focus, polaris
-to-pole: axal, axial
vault: jump, leap
vehicle: cope, neap, thill
walking: cane, stilt
POLICE: *badge:* buzzer, shield
club: billy, espantoon, nightstick, truncheon
force: carabinieri, cheka, cid, constabulary, fbi, fuzz, gendarmes, gestapo, interpol, mounties, mps,

* **Asterisk means to look up this word to find more answer words.**

mvd, nkvd, ogpu, polizia, posse, surete

hqrs.: bargello, barracks, marshalcy, station, tana

man: bailiff, bargello, beagle, beetle-crusher, blue-bottle, bluecoat, bobby, bulky, bull, burkundaz, carabiniere, catchpole, constable, cop, deputy, detective, dick, flatfoot, fuzz, gendarme, g-man, gumshoe, heat, inspector, john, kotwal, law, marshal, officer, peeler, pig, roundsman, sheriff, shrieve, tipstaff, trap, watch, zarp

pick-up: black maria

station: booby hatch, tana

POLICY: administration, contract, course, line, *plan, platform, principles, procedure, program

aggressive: big stick, blood and iron

maker: boss, chief, *head

statement: white paper

POLISH: eclat, *shine, urbanity

off: *accomplish, *end, *kill

POLITE: *correct, *fair, *gentle

POLITIC: *astute, *smart, *wise

POLL: count, *head, list, vote

POLLUX: *dioscuri

POLO: *mount:* horse, pony

part: chucker, chukker

POLONIUS: *kin:* laertes, ophelia

POLTERGEIST: *demon, *spirit

POLTROON: *coward, *mean

POLYBUS: *wife:* alcandre

POLYHYMNIA: *son:* triptolemus

POLYNESIA: *malay

POME: apple, azarole, pear

POMMEL: *beat, *hit, saddle

bag: cantina

POMP: *glory, *show, *state

POMPEII: *heroine:* ione

POMPOUS: *big, *fat, *vain

POND: *dogwood:* buttonbush

duck: mallard

fish: aquarium, pisoina

flower: alligator bonnet, cambricleaf, lily, lis

frog: ranarium

hen: coot

oyster: claire

pine: limber, loblolly, ponderosa

scum: alga

snail: coret

weed: batter dock, butterbur

PONDER: *study, *think, *wonder

PONDEROUS: *big, *dull, *fat, *great, *heavy, *important

PONTIFICAL: *pompous

PONTUS: *wife:* gaea

young: ceto, eurybia, nereus, phorcys, thaumas

PONY: dram, horse, tattoo, trot

POOK: *dwarf, *pile, *spirit

POOL: *pile, tank, *trust

ball: cue, eight, ringer, spot

POON: dilo, domba, keena, telugu

POOR: *bad, bankrupt, barren, broke, bum, deficient, dejected, destitute, down, emaciated, feeble, flimsy, hard up, humble, impecunious, impoverished, indigent, inferior, infirm, *low, meager, *mean, needy, out-of-pocket, paltry, pinched, *plain, proletarian, *rabble, *sad, seedy, *short, *sick, *simple, *sorry, *thin, unfortunate, unhappy, unsound, *weak, *wrong

fist: *error, failure

house: *asylum

joe: bird, heron

john: cod, fish, hake

man's pepper: stonecrop

man's soap: hardhack

man's weatherglass: pimpernel

marksman: bolo

patron saint: anthony

soldier: friarbird

POP: *blast, dad, drink, *report

-adam: cake, cookie, wafer

-dock: foxglove

POPE: bullfinch, *church: man*

---

* Asterisk means to look up this word to find more answer words.

cap: camauro, mitre
cape: fannel, fano(n), mozetta, mozzetta, orale, phano
chamberlain: camerlengo
church: lateran
court: curia, datary, see
crown: tiara, triregnum
deputy: cardinal
document: bull
envoy: ablegate, legate, nuntius
epistle: decretal
exile: babylonian captivity
home: regia
name: adrian, agapstus, alexander, benedict, boniface, eugenius, gregory, hadrian, john, leo, peter, pius, simon, urban, zachary
palace: lateran, vatican
pert.: papal
publication: acta sanctae sedis
residence, 1309–77: avignon
seal: bulla
tribunal: rota
POPINJAY: *fop, macaroni, parrot
POPLAR: abele, alamo, aspen, bahan, balsam, cottonwood, garab, liar, tulip
POPPAEA: *husband:* nero
POPPY: argemone, bocconia
-cock: *nonsense, rot, stuff
corn: ponceau
drug: heroin, morphine, opium
field: canker
genus: celandine, papaver
mallow: callirrhoe
red: granate
seed: maw, mohn
POPULAR: accepted, all the rage, being done, celebrated, current, democratic, easy, epidemic, familiar, fashionable, *general, *good, in, lay, liked, *low, modern, pleasant, pleasing, plebeian, prevalent, proletarian, *smart, *special, traditional, up-to-date, *usual, well-known

POPULATION: *count:* census
study: larithmics
POQUELIN: moliere
PORCELAIN: *clay:* kaolin(e)
furnace: hovel
kind: belleek, celadon, china, derby, dresden, gombroon, haviland, limoges, meissen, ming, murra, sevres, spode, wedgewood
mould: ramekin
unglazed: biscuit, bisque
PORCH: *west:* galilee
PORCUPINE: erithizon, urson
anteater: echidna
coat: quill, spine
disease: ichthyosis
fish: balloon, burr, diodon
genus: hystrix
grass: stipa
PORE: cell, *opening, *study
plant: lenticel
without: eporose
PORGY: bream, jolthead, margate, menhaden, pinfish, scup, tai
PORK: bacon, flitch, ham, pig
barrel: booty, graft, *spoil
chop: griskin
fish: catalineta, sisi
rice, with: tonkatsu
sausage: banger
strip: bacon, lardoon
PORPOISE: dolphin, inia, pelloc, seahog
PORRIDGE: atole, brochan, brose, burgoo, grout, gruel, kasheh, *mixture, pobs, polenta, pottage, samp, skillagalee
container: bicker
PORTAL, PORTCULLIS: *opening
PORTEND: *mean, *predict
PORTENT: omen, *sign, *token
PORTER: akabo, ale, beer, bellboy, berman, cargador, carrier, chokidar, concierge, coolie, darwan, durwaun, gatekeeper, guard, hamal, janitor, khamal,

* Asterisk means to look up this word to find more answer words.

ostiary, redcap, *servant, *slave, transport, tyler, usher

PORTIA: *alias:* balthazar
lover: bassanio
maid: nerissa
tree: bendy

PORTICO: pteron, stoa, veranda
inclosed: peridrome
long: verandah, xystus
wing: pteron

PORTION: *bit, *part, *piece, *quantity, quota, *share, some

PORTLY: *big, *fat, *great

PORTMANTEAU WORD: blend word

PORTRAIT: *image, *picture
pert.: iconic
sitting: seance

PORTRAY: *act, *draw, *form

PORTUGUESE: *africa:* angola
boat: moleta
brandy: aguardiente
cape: roca
city: braga(nca), coimbra, evora, guarda, lisbon, lusitania, oporto, ovar
coin: angolar, centavo, conto, coroa, crown, crusado, dobra, equipaga, escudo, macuta, moidore, pataco, testao
colony: angola, damao, diu, goa, guinea, macao, mozambique, principe, timor
crown jewel: braganza diamond
dance: fado
district: evora, loanda, tete
explorer: alvares, cabral, cao, da gama, diaz, magellan, real
festival: chamarita
folksong: fado
grape crushers: pisadores
guitar: machete
island: angola, azores, madeira
jews: sephardim
legislature: cortes
measure: alma, almud, alquier, bota, braca, covado, estadio, fanga, ferrado, geira, legoa, linha, meio, milha, moio, palmo, pipa, pollegada, quarto, selamin, tonelada, vara
native: castice, iberian
peak: serra d'estrella
poet: camoens, ramos
province: alemtejo, algarve, azores, beira, estremadura, evora, madeira, minho, tete
river: douro, duero, guadiana, minho, mondego, sado, tagus
ruler: niniz, salazar
title: dom, dona, donna, fidalgo, senhor(ita)
vessel: caravel
village: aldeament, aldeia
weight: arratel, arroba, escropulo, grao, libra, marco, oitava, onca, once
wine: carcavelhos, carcavellos

POSE: *affect, *air, *model, *place, *set, *show, *symbol

POSEIDON: asphalius, enisichthon, genethios, neptune
consort: aethra, alcyone, alope, amphitrite, amymone, anippe, arne, calyce, canace, celaeno, chione, corcyra, europa, evadne, gaea, harpale, medusa, melia, mestra, molione, phimedeia, pirene, salacia, salamis, theophane, thoosa, tyro
offspring: aeolus, aethusa, agenor, albion, *aloadae, aloeus, amphimarus, amycus, antaeus, anthas, arion, benthesicyme, boeotus, busiris, caucon, cenchrias, cercyon, charybdis, cycnus, despoena, eumolpus, eurypylus, hallirrhothius, hippothous, lycus, nauplius, neleus, pelias, polyphemus, scylla, sinis, triton, zetes
parent: cronos, rhea
sceptre: triton
servant: proteus
victim: polybutes

* Asterisk means to look up this word to find more answer words.

POSER: *problem, *puzzle
POSITION: *air, *lie, *opening,
*place, *set, *stand, *work
change: *move
defensive: bridgehead, *fort
paper: white paper
POSITIVE: *absolute, *actual,
*firm, *pure, real, sure, *true
POSSE: *force, *group
POSSESS: *get, have, hold, *secure, seduce, *seize, *take
POSSESSED: *eccentric, *insane
POSSESSION: *money, *property
POST: *bet, *part, *place, *record, *send, *support, *tie
boy: courier, yamshik
POSTAL: abbreviation: apo, pob,
ppi, rte
POSTERN: gate, *opening, side
POSTPONE: *arrest, *slow
POSTULATE: *ask, *state
POSTURE: *form, *image, *stand
POSY: bouquet, legend, motto
POT: *drug, *quantity, *vessel
boy: cupbearer, ganymode
clay: buckpot, chytra, crock,
cruse, olla
handle: bool
hat: bowler, derby
herb: chard, kale, mint, wort
herb, pert.: olitory
hole: tinaja
latch: feast, *gift
lead: graphite
liquor: brewis
pie: fricasse, stew
rustler: cook
walloper: scullion, *servant
POTABLE: *drink
POTATO: ima, oca, papa, yam
beetle: hardback
bread: boxty
bud: eye
disease: blackleg, brown ring,
curl, dartrose, pox
flour: flow
soil: otto

starch: farina
state: idaho, maine
sweet: oca, patata, yam
tule: wapatoo
POTENCY: *force, *might
POTENT: *big, *great, *strong
POTENTATE: *king, *lord,
*magnate, *ruler, *title
POTENTIAL: *open, possible
POTHER: *ado, *puzzle, *stir,
*trouble, tumult, uproar, worry
POTION: *drink, *drug, *medicine
POTPOURRI: *hash, *mixture
POTSHERD: *bit, *piece, *share
POTTER: blade: pallet
field: blood acre, cemetery
wheel: disk, jigger, kick, lathe,
palet, throw
POTTERY: bark tree: cayenne,
rose, sassafras
clay: alumina, argil, kaolin
decorated: belleek, sigillate
decoration: barbotine, broderie,
canalatura
dish: ramekin
enameled: majolica
firing box: saggar(d), sagger
fragment: shard, sherd
glass-like: vitreous
kind: aretine, awaji, basalt, belleek, bizen, blanc, boccaro, buc-
chero(nero), celadon, chun,
crouch, delft, faience, feldspar,
jasper, keramos, kuan, leeds,
majolica, sigillate, ting, tung,
uda, ware, yueh
mineral: feldspar
neolithic: bankeramik
pert.: ceramic
terra cotta: albert ware
tree: caraipa, caraipe, caraipi
unglazed: bizen, buccaro
POUCE: 1/12th: ligne
POUCH: *bag, *pack, sporran
bone: marsupial
girdle: gipser
-shaped: bursiform, saccate

* Asterisk means to look up this word to find more answer words.

POULE: *prostitute, *wanton

POULTRY: breed: ancona, dorking, leghorn, plymouth rock, rhode island red
 dealer: eggler
 disease: gapes, pip, pox, roup
 yard: barton, hennery

POUNCE: *attack, jump, *seize

POUND: *beat, *hit, *jail, *whip

POUR: *fall, *issue, run, *storm

POURBOIRE: *fee, *gift, tip

POVERTY: *need, rags

POWDER: aloes: picra
 antiseptic: aristol, boron
 astringent: boral
 beater: sinterer
 case: bandoleer, bandolier
 holder: arsenal, horn, magazine
 make: bray, calcine, grind, pulverize
 perfumed: abir
 pert.: floury, seme, semee
 skin: boral, rachel
 smokeless: amberite, cordite, filite, poudre

POWER: *ability, arms, atoms, *authority, baraka, beef, boss, brahma, bulk, capacity, clout, *control, country, effect, efficacy, efficiency, electricity, empire, energy, faculty, *force, gas, genius, *gift, grip, hold, jet, jurisdiction, *king(dom), main, mana, *move, nation, od(yl), omnipotence, operate, potency, prerogative, *press, puissance, *push, regime, reign, *right, *rule(r), *run, *skill, soup, sovereignty, *spirit, *state, steam, *strength, sway, talent, *use, vigor, virtue, warrant, *work
 attorney: agency, blank check, carte blanche, commission
 comb.: dyna, maga
 divine: afflatus
 -house: antaeus, atlas, briareus, colossus, *cyclopes, *giant, goliath, hercules, polyphemus, samson, tarzan
 lack: atony
 natural: ody, odyl, odyle
 personification: aditya, asura, danava
 ratio: bel
 structure: *establishment
 supernatural: alchera, alcheringa, arado, *magic, mana, ngai, orenda, wakan

POWERFUL: *big, *great, *strong

POWWOW: *church: man, *meeting

PRACTICE: *conduct, *try, *use

PRAIRIE: camas(s), grass, *plain
 anemone: pasqueflower
 antelope: pronghorn
 apple: breadroot
 berry: trompillo
 breaker: plow, wave
 chicken: grouse
 crabapple: bechtel's crab
 crocus: pasqueflower
 dog: barking squirrel, marmot, wishton-wish
 dog weed: marigold
 herb: carolina anemone, boebera, dyssodia
 mud: gumbo
 pigeon: plover, sandpiper
 plant: butterfly weed, gaura
 potato: breadroot
 rose: baltimore belle
 schooner: ark, wagon
 state: illinois
 tree clump: motte
 wake-robin: brown bess
 weed: cinquefoil
 wolf: coyote

PRAISE: *acclaim, apple polish, bhajan, *bless, blow up, blurb, boast of, boost, brag on, build up, carol, cheer, doxologize, crack up, cry up, eloge, elogy, emblazon, encomium, eulogy, exalt, fawn, flatter, *glory, grati-

* Asterisk means to look up this word to find more answer words.

tude, *honor, hymn, kudos, macarism, magnify, meed, paean, panegyric, plug, puff, *reward, salaam, tribute, *worship
song: anthem, bhajan, paean
the lord: hallelujah

PRANK: *caper, *joke, *trick
PRATE: *gossip, *nonsense, *talk
PRATFALL: *defeat, *error
PRATTLE: *argot, *prate
PRAY: *ask, *bless, *praise
PRAYER: ave, credo, kyrie
bead: ave, rosary
book: breviary, missal, ordo, portas(s), porthouse, ritual
call: adan, azan, bell, chime, ezan, oremus
chancery: relator
comb.: ora
consecration: epanaphora
desk: prie-dieu
dismissal: apolysis
evening: vesper
form: chant, litany
group: comprecation
last: complin(e)
liturgical: amidah
morning: aubade, matin
nine-day: novena
place: church, idgah
shawl: orale, tallith
short: benediction, grace
stick: baho(o), paho, pajo
tower: minaret

PREACHER: *church: man
PRECARIOUS: delicate, risky
PRECEDE: *head, *lead, usher
PRECEDENCE: *lead, *order
pref.: ante
PRECEPT: *act, *adage, *doctrine, *idea, *law, *order, *rule
PRECIOUS: *good, *great, perfect
PRECIPITATE: *force, *speed
PRECIS: *brief, *outline
lavinia: buckeye
PRECISE: *absolute, *actual, *particular, *right, *strict

PRECLUDE: *bar, prevent, *stop
PREDICAMENT: *mess, *mix
PREDICT: augur, auspicate, bode, call, divine, dope, forecast, omen, portend, presage, prognosticate, prophesy, soothsay, warn, *weird
PREDICTOR: *prophet, sage, seer
PREDILECTION: bias, choice
PREEMINENT: *big, *supreme
PREEMPT: *appropriate, establish
PREEN: *dress, *ornament
PREFABRICATE: *form, *make
PREFACE: herald, *open, *start
PREFER: *desire, pick, *will
PREJUDICE: bent, bias, bigotry
PRELIMINARY: *head, *opening
PREMIER: *acme, *best, *head, *principal, *ruler, *supreme
PREMISE: *foundation, *position
PREMIUM: *extra, *fee, *gift, *prize, *reward, *special
PREPARE: *accommodate, *adapt, *adjust, appoint, arm, arrange, author, boun, brew, busk, calculate, clear, compound, condition, cook, cultivate, decoct, *dress, edit, gird, instruct, insure, lay by, *make, *open, pave, *plan, prime, process, provide, *ready, *repair, *set(tle), *supply, *train, treat, write
PREPOSITION: about, after, all, alongside, at, but, by, des, except, for, from, in(to), of(f), on(to), out, over, tae, to, until, unto, upon, with
PREPOSTEROUS: *absurd, *nonsense, ridiculous
PRESAGE: *predict, *token
PRESBYTERIAN DIRECTORIES: book of discipline
PRESCRIBE: *act, *control, *order, *plan, *set, *urge
PRESCRIPT: *law, *order, *rule
PRESENCE: *air, being, *spirit

* Asterisk means to look up this word to find more answer words.

PRESENT: *acquaint, *actual, adduce, ad sum, allege, at hand, attendant, backsheesh, being, benefaction, *bring, confer, contemporary, current, direct, *display, donation, douceur, dramatize, dust off, exhibit, existent, expound, extant, favor, feature, *gift, *give, here, immediate, instant, introduce, in view, *issue, lagniappe, largesse, latest, nonce, now, on hand, *open, premier, *produce, put, *raise, *reward, say, *show, stage, star, submit, summarize, *supply, *tell, tender, that is, today, trot out, verthandi, *yield

PRESERVE: brine, can, corn, cure, dry, freeze, jam, jelly, park, pot, put up, *save, smoke

PRESIDE: *administer, *control

PRESIDENT: *head, *ruler

PRESS: *advance, assert, attach, *attack, bear, brize, business, calendar, charge, compulsion, constrain, cram, crush, dun, embrace, enroll, entreat, flatten, *force, fourth estate, goad, *group, harass, hurry, hustle, importune, insist, iron, mangle, newspapers, oblige, plea(d), *push, roll, smash, *smooth, *speed, *spur, stamp, *strain, *stress, throng, thrust, *urge
release: advance, blurb, handout

PRESSING: *important, urgent

PRESSURE: distress, duress, influence, pinch, *press, *urge
comb.: atmo, bar(o)
decrease: bernoulli effect
equal: isobaric
gauge: algometer, barograph, bourdon tube, manoscope
perception: baresthesia
unit: atmo, barad, barie, barye, mesobar

PRESTIDIGITATION: *magic, *spell

PRESTIGE: *honor, *power

PRESUME: assume, judge, *think

PRESUMPTUOUS: *arrogant

PRETEND: *act, *deceive, *pose

PRETENDER: *impostor, *quack
religious: tartuffe

PRETENSE: *act, *cover, *deception, *show, *study

PRETERMIT: *miss, *pass

PRETEXT: *escape, *pretense

PRETTY: attractive, *beautiful, betcheri, bonita, budgeree, canny, dainty, *fair, *fine, *good, jolie, moderately, petite, *pure, *sharp, wonderful

PREVAIL: *rule, *succeed, *win

PREVALENT: *general, *popular

PREVARICATE: *deceive, *lie

PREVENT: *arrest, *save, *stop

PREVIOUS: before, *over, past

PREY: *prize, *spoil, victim

PRIAM: counselor: antenor
daughter: cassandra, creusa, polyxena
father: laomedon
grandfather: ilus, tithonus
herdsman: agelaus
son: antiphus, aretus, deiphobus, hector, helenus, paris, polydorus, troilus
wife: arisbe, hecuba

PRICE: *bargain, *fee, *value

PRICK(LE): *pain, *pierce, *urge
song: descant
grass: burdock

PRIDE: *glory, *group, *show

PRIEST: *church: man, *ecclesiastic
army: chaplain, padre
fish: blackrock cod, sebastodes
garment: *vestment: religious
group: clergy, magi, salii
pert.: clerical, sacerdotal

PRIG: *sharp, *steal, *thief

PRIM: formal, neat, *smart

PRIMA DONNA: *lead, singer

PRIMARY: *great, *principal

* Asterisk means to look up this word to find more answer words.

PRIMATE: ape, *church: man
PRIME: *best, *principal, *stir
  comb.: arch, archi
PRIMER: book, cap, detonator
PRIMEVAL, PRIMITIVE: *old,
  *wild
  comb.: arch(eo), archi
PRIMODIUM: anlage, *start
PRIMP: *dress, *ornament
PRIMROSE: anagallis, androsace,
  auricula, bird's-eye, cowslip,
  oxlip, polyanthus, spink
PRINCE: *lord, *magnate, *ruler
  black: edward
  opera: igor
  rupert: macaroni, yankee doodle
  val's father: aguar
PRINCE OF: darkness: ahriman,
  beelzebub, *demon, *devil, satan
  destruction: tamerlane, timour
  evil spirits: sammael
  liars: ananias, pinto
  peace: jesus, messiah
  poets: ronsard
  sonnet: joachim du bellay
  spanish poetry: vega
PRINCIPAL: *author, capital,
  cardinal, central, chief, first,
  foremost, *great, *head, *high,
  *important, *lead, main, *para-
  mount, person, primary, prime,
  *ruler, staple, star, superintend-
  ent, *supreme, *top
  pref.: arch(e), archi
PRINCIPLE: *adage, *doctrine,
  *foundation, *rule, *source
  embodiment: avatar
  first: arche, base, cause, seed
  reincarnation: manas
  seven hindu: atman, buddhi,
  kama, linga sharira, manas,
  prana, sthula sharira
  theorem: *truth, yang, yin
PRINCIPLES: abcs, *policy
PRINK: caper, *dress, *ornament
PRINTING: blind: braille
  block: linoleum, wood

  blurred: macul
  color: chromolithography
  direction: cut, dele, stet
  error: erratum, pie, typo
  form: cut, die, frame, matrix
  instrument: biron, brayer, dabber,
  dauber
  mark: *mark: printing
  measure: agate, em, en, pica
  metal block: quad
  photoengraving: heliotype
  plate: anastatic, stereo(type)
  press part: frisket, platen, roller,
  rounce, stamp
  process: braille, cerotype, lithog-
  raphy, offset, photolitho
  spacer: quad, slug
  term: dedication, errata, folio,
  flyleaf, index, inscription, introduction, page, recto, reverso,
  table, title, verso
PRIOR: *monk, *previous, *priest
  pref.: ante, pre
PRISON: *jail
PRISTINE: *fresh, new, *pure
PRIVATE: *particular, *secret,
  *soldier, solitary, *special
  comb.: idio
  eye: *police: man, *spy
PRIVATION: *need, poverty
PRIVILEGE: *advantage, *power,
  *right, *title, *use
PRIZE: *acme, appreciate, award,
  bacon, *best, big game, blue ribbon, bonus, booty, capture,
  champ, cherish, cup, *esteem,
  estimate, *honor, laurels, lever,
  loot, *love, measure, medal,
  meed, palm, plum, premium,
  prime, regard, respect, *reward,
  *spoil, stake, *token, treasure,
  trophy, *value
PROBATION: parole, *test, *trial
PROBE: *analyze, *pierce, *search,
  *see, *test, *try
  surgical: acus, stylet, tent
PROBITY: *honor, *strength

* Asterisk means to look up this word to find more answer words.

PROBLEM: case, enigma, *flaw, hitch, *issue, knot, matter, nut, poser, proposition, *puzzle, question, riddle, topic, *trouble
solving: algorism, algorith
PROBOSCIS: beak, neb, nose
insect: antlia
monkey: kaha(u)
section: lore, lorum, nares
PROCA: son: amulius
PROCEDURE: *policy, *rule, *way
PROCEED: *advance, *issue, *move, progress, *start, stem
PROCEEDS: *fee, *income, *money, *produce, *yield
PROCESS: *act, *order, *system
organisms: meiosis
suff.: ance, ancy, ence, ency
PROCESSION: *group, *parade
comb.: cade
PROCLAIM: *cry, *open, *tell
PROCLAMATION: *law, *order
PROCNE: husband: tereus
PROCRASTINATE: *delay, *slow
PROCRIS: husband: cephalus
PROCTOR: *agent, *servant
PROCURE: *acquire, *get, *win
PROD: *push, *stir, *urge
PRODIGAL: *reckless, *wanton
PRODIGALITY: *plenty, *surfeit
PRODIGIOUS: *big, *great, *large
PRODIGY: miracle, *wonder
PRODUCE, PRODUCT: *accomplish, ante, apport, author, bear, beat, beget, berry, bloom, blossom, breed, carry, crop, *display, *fee, *form, furnish, goods, *grow, harvest, hatch, *income, input, *make, *open, originate, output, *prepare, *present, raise, rear, *result, *show, *start, *supply, *work, *yield
comb.: ade, ado
PRODUCTIVE: *active, *fat, *rich
PROETUS: brother: acrisius

wife: stheneboea
PROFANE: *bad, *evil, *smear
PROFESS: affect, *follow, *state
PROFESSION: *forte, *skill, *thing, *trade, *work
PROFESSIONAL: *ace, expert
PROFICIENCY: *ability, *skill
PROFILE: *form, *model, *plan
PROFIT: *fee, *good, *income, *interest, *return, *service, *take, *use, *value, *yield
PROFLIGATE: *bad, *evil, *fast, *free, *prodigal, roue, *wild
PROFOUND: *deep, *sharp, *wise
PROFUSE: *free, *liberal, lush
PROFUSION: *plenty, *quantity
PROGENY: *issue, race, seed
PROGNOSTICATE: *predict
PROGNOSTICATOR: *prophet
PROGRAM: *action, *agenda, *plan
PROGRESS: *move, *succeed, *way
PROGRESSIVE: *forward
PROHIBIT: *prevent, *stop
PROJECT: *plan, *venture
PROJECTILE: *missile, *spear
curve: parabola
PROJECTION: angle, archery, barb, block, boss, bracket, bragger, bulge, calk, cam, casting, cog, corbel, dent(il), ear, fang, fin, firing, flange, hob, jag, ledge, lee, overhang, *plan, *promontory, prong, protrusion, protuberance, rim, sawtooth, snaggle, sprocket, *spur, tendon, tooth
PROJECTOR: analemma, balopticon
PROLETARIAN: *poor, *rabble
PROLIFERATE: *grow, swarm
PROLIX: *dull, long, tedious
PROLONG: *draw, *spread, *strain
PROM(ENADE): *parade, *party
PROMETHEUS: captor: bia, hephaestus, kratos

* Asterisk means to look up this word to find more answer words.

parent: iapetus, themis
son: deucalion
PROMINENCE: **glory, *honor*
PROMINENT: **big, *great, *high*
PROMISE: affiance, agree, assumpsit, **assure,* avouch, avow, behight, betroth, bid fair, bond, **commit, *compact,* consent, **contract,* declare, earnest, **engage,* fiance, guarantee, hope, imply, insure, **mortgage, *note,* oath, offer, parole, pledge, prediction, suggest, swear, **token, *trust,* vow, warrant(y), **word*
PROMONTORY: bill, cape, cliff, headland, mount, nase, naze, ness, noup, point, **projection,* prominence, skaw, spit, tor
PROMOTE: **advance, *aid, *pass, *raise, *speed, *support*
PROMPT: **move, *quick, *urge*
PROMULGATE: **publish*
PRONE: **open,* prostrate, **ready*
PRONG: **projection,* tang, tine
buck: pronghorn, springbok
hooked: pew, pugh
-horn: antilocapra, berrendo
PRONOUN: all, any, both, each, he, hers, him, his, its, me, mine, my, none, one, ours, she, some, that, thee, their, them, these, they, thine, this, those, thou, us, we, what, which, who, ye, you
PRONOUNCE: **order, *report, *rule, *say, *state, *tell*
PRONUNCIATION: accent, twant
correct: orthoepy, phonology
incorrect: cacoepy, psellism
mark: *mark: printing
rough: bur, burr
PROOF: **argument, *reason, *test*
PROP: **foundation, *support*
PROPAGANDA: **doctrine*
PROPEL: **force, *move, *start*
PROPELLER: blade, driver, fan, fin, oar, paddle, pedal, rotor, screw, treadle, turbine, vane

PROPENSITY: **forte, *thing*
PROPER: **fit, *meet, *right*
PROPERTY: acquest, allod, alod, appurtenance(s), **asset(s),* attribute, aught, **bag(gage),* building(s), catallum, characteristic, chattel(s), dhan, equity, freehold, **goods,* havings, holding, land, **money,* ownership, peculiarity, **power,* production, **quality,* resource, **state,* trait
act to regain: replevin
bride to husband: dos, dowry
charge against: lien, **mortgage*
clear: alod(ium), alody
dead wife to husband: courtesy
destruction: arson, sabotage
part: gavelkind
personal: chattel(s)
pert.: cadastral
receiver: alienee
right: easement, lien
stolen: booty, loot, **spoil*
suit for: trover
PROPHESY: **predict*
PROPHET: andron, andrus, angel, astrologer, augur, crystal gazer, divinator, divine(r), druid, ecclesiastic, extispex, forecaster, fortuneteller, geomancer, haruspice, **leader,* mantis, oracle, palmist, predictor, psychic, python, **sage,* seer, soothsayer, sphinx, teacher, tiresias, vates, vaticinator
famous: amos, antevorta, asahiah, azur, cassandra, daniel, elias, elijah, elisha, ezra, haggai, hosea, iddo, isaiah, jehu, jeremiah, joel, john (smith), joseph, joshua, malachi, micah, mohammed, moses, nahum, nathan, nostradamus, obadiah, pythia, samuel, shemaiah, sibyl, spyne, syrus, zechariah
pert.: fatidic(al)
PROPITIATE: **accord, *adjust*

* Asterisk means to look up this word to find more answer words.

PROPITIOUS: *good, *happy
PROPONENT: *advocate, *agent
PROPORTION: *form, *part
PROPOSAL: *move, *offer, *plan
PROPOSE: *proposal, *start
PROPOSITION: *adage, *ask,
*plan, *problem, seduce, *try
antecedent: premise
assume: axiom, corollary, lemma
mathematical: theorem
PROPOUND: *advance, *state
PROSAIC: *dull, *plain, *usual
PROSCRIBE: *prevent, *prohibit
PROSCRIPT: *criminal, *hoodlum
PROSERPINA: *persephone
PROSPECT: *look, *picture,
*promise, *range, *see
PROSPECTUS: outline, *program
PROSPER: *advance, *succeed
PROSPERITY: *ease, *plenty
deity: frey, ing, salus
symbol: turquoise
PROSPERO: daughter: miranda
sprite: ariel
PROSPEROUS: *happy, *rich
PROSTITUTE: baggage, bat,
bawd, boom-boom, brasy, broad,
bucolique, callet, call girl, cat,
corrupt, courtesan, cyprian, drab,
fille de joie, fricatrice, gudget,
harlot, harridan, hooker, kurveh,
lorette, maquereau, marquise,
meretrix, messalina, mopsy,
mrs warren, nafka, paphian,
phryne, poule, pug, punk, putain,
quail, quean, sadie thompson,
scarlet (woman), slammock,
slattern, sloven, slubberdegullion, slummock, slut, *spoil,
stew, streetwalker, strumpet,
swine, tart, thais, traipse, trollop,
trull, twist, venal, *wanton, white
slave, whore
customer: kangourou
house: bordello, brothel, cha-
banais, maison de tolerance,
one-two-two, sphinx

male: berdache
PROSTRATE: *low, *mean, *sick
oneself: fawn, salaam
PROSY: *dull, *heavy, *stupid
PROTAGONIST: *advocate
PROTECT: *bless, *save, *secure
PROTECTION: *cover, shield
right: girth, mund
PROTEID: abrin, amine
PROTEIN: amino, histone phenyl-
alanine, rna
blood: fibrin, globulin
colorless: achroglobin
egg: albumin, avidin
deficiency: kwashiorkor
granular: aleuron(e)
group: globulin
milk: casein
poisonous: abrin, ricin(e)
seeds: aleurone, prolamins
source: bean, egg, lentil, meat
PROTEST: *argue, assert, asseverate, aver, *bark, call, challenge,
*complain, *cry, *declare, de-
fault, demur, deny, deprecate,
dispute, dissent, exception,
*howl, object, oppose, raise hell,
refuse, reject, remonstrate, repudiate, resist, scruple, sit in, snarl
literature: samizdat
PROTEUS: beanleaf roller, olm
consort: antia, julia, silvia
daughter: idothea, iphianassa,
lysippe
parent: oceanus, tethys
son: telegonus, tmolus
PROTOTYPE: *image, *model
PROTRACT: *continue, delay,
*run
PROTRUDE: interfere, stand out
PROTUBERANCE: *projection,
umbo
PROUD: *arrogant, *great, *vain
PROVE: *argue, ascertain, assay,
*assess, authenticate, be true,
bring off, check, confirm, convince, demonstrate, deraign, de-

termine, *establish, evince, hold
water, justify, make good, *reason, *set, *settle, *show, *succeed, *test, *try, validate, verify

PROVENCE: song: alba, canzo

PROVERB: *adage, brocard, haiku

PROVIDE: equip, feed, *give,
*prepare, *present, *store, *sup-
ply, *support, *yield

PROVIDENT: thrifty, *wise

PROVINCE: *forte, *limit,
*sphere, *state

PROVINCIAL: *narrow, *peasant

PROVISION: *provide, *supply

PROVOCATION: foment, *trial

PROVOKE: *agitate, *anger,
*move, *stir, *taunt, *upset

PROVOST: *head, *leader

PROWESS: courage, *skill

PROWL: lurk, roam, rove, seek

PROXIMAL: *near, next

PROXY: *agent, *substitute

PRUDE: prig, puritan, *spark

PRUDENT: *provident, *wise

PRUNE: *preen, *reduce, sned

PRURIENT: *bad, *dirty, *evil

PRUSSIA: *german
aristocracy: junker(s)
island: frisian, rugen, wollin
lancer: uhlan, ulan
measure: fuder, fuss, meile, morgan, oxhoft, rute, zoll

PRY: *ask, *look, *open, *spy

PRYTANIA: *hecate

PSALM: ode, poem, *praise
book: breviary, hallel, psalter
kind: cantate, hallel, introit,
lauds, miserere, venite
opening communion: introit
part: cathisma
word, key: selah
xlvi: alamoth
xx song: elieli

PSALTERIUM: manyplies, *stomach

PSEUDO: *false, sham, spurious

PSEUDOMORPHUS: epigene

PSEUDONYM: alias, sobriquet

PSIDIUM: arrayan, cattley, guava

PSYCHE: *mind, *spirit, *urge
consort: eros

PSYCHIATRIST: alienist, analyst,
nut doctor, shrinker, somatist
big: adler, binet, breuer, brill,
charcot, freud, horney, james,
janet, jung, mesmer, meyer,
rank, reik, ward, wundt

PSYCHIC: *occult, *prophet
disposition: pattern
emanation: aura
seizure: epilepsy

PSYCHOLOGICAL: mental
doctrine: behaviorism
lift: build-up, conditioning
moment: *crisis
school: gestalt
test: alpha, apperception, aptitude,
association, aussage, babcock-
levy, beta, binet, brown, cattel,
gesell, goldstein, ink-blot, iq,
oseretsky, rorschach, wechsler
theory: associationism

PSYCHOLOGIST: *psychiatrist:
big

PSYCHOTIC: *insane, *mad

PTAH: embodiment: apis
son: imhotep, nefertum
wife: sekhet, sekhmet

PTARMIGAN: bird, grouse, rype

PTERIC: alar, alate, winglike

PTEROSPERMUM: baroi, grewia,
pandanus

PTOLEMAEUS: father: abubus
son: lysimachus

PTOLEMY: daughter: cleopatra
teacher: aristobulus
wife: philadelphia
work: almagest

PTOMAINE: amylamine, poison

PUB: boozer, hotel, inn, saloon

PUBLIC: audience, *general,
*open, *state, *universal
relations: *image, *stand

PUBLICAN: catchpoll, *peasant

---

* Asterisk means to look up this word to find more answer words.

PUBLICATION: *book, *work
 make-up: format
 preliminary: prodromus
PUBLICIZE: *advertise, *ballyhoo
PUBLISH: *issue, *spread, *tell
PUCA: *dwarf, *spirit
PUCCINI: heroine: mimi
 opera: boheme, madam butterfly,
 manon, tosca, turandot
PUCE: brown, eureka, flea, uda
PUCELAGE: virginity
PUCK: *dwarf, *spirit
PUCKER: anxiety, *gather
PUDDING: burgoo, custard, duff,
 hoy, junket, mush, sago, sponge
 -pipe: canafistulo, drumstick
 sweet: blanc mange
 wife: bluefish
PUDDLE: *marsh, *mess, *stir
 jumper: helicopter
PUDGY: *big, *fat, *heavy
PUEBLO: acoma, hopi, keres,
 moqui, piro, tanoa, zuni
 assembly: estufa, kiva
PUERILE: *idle, *silly, *weak
PUERTO PRINCIPE: camaguey
PUERTO RICO: abracadabra:
 apio
 bark or beverage: mabi
 bird: rola, yeguita
 breadfruit: castana
 city: aguadilla, arecibo, baya-
 mon, caguas, dorado, mayaguez,
 ponce, san juan
 conqueror: miles
 fish: sama, sisi
 island: mona
 measure: caballeria, cuerda
 native: borinqueno, gibaro
 palm: yagua, yaray
 plant: apio
 port: aquadilla, arecibo
 tree: guaraguao, guayroto, mora,
 yagua, yaray
PUFF: *cover, expel, pouf, *praise,
 *smoke, swell, waff
 ball: basidiomycete, fist, fuzz

bird: barbacou, barbet, barbicon,
 bucconid, capitonid, dreamer,
 monasa
 cheek: bomba, windbag
PUFFER: blowfish, pike, tambor
PUG: *dwarf, *prostitute, snub
 -nosed: camus(e), simous
PUISNE: junior, subordinate
PUISSANCE: *force, *power
PUISSANT: *great, *strong
PULCHRITUDE: beauty, *grace
PULE: *complain, *cry, whine
PULL: *allure, *drag, *draw, favor, *strain, *try, wrench
 back: *retreat, *yield
 -devil: scrodgill
 down: *destroy, *draw, *receive
 in: *arrest, *appear, rein
 off: *accomplish, *succeed
 one's freight: depart, *escape
 one's leg: *deceive, *joke
 out: depart, *escape
 over: *arrest, shirt, *stop
 the strings: *control, *rule
PULLEY: block, fusee, lever
 part: arse, drum, rigger
PULLULATE: *grow, swarm
PULMONARIA: adam and eve,
 cowslip
PULP: magazine, mass, smash
 mining: slime
PULPIT: ambo, desk, *stand
 canopy: rester
PULPY: baccate, mushy, *soft
PULSATE, PULSE: *oscillate
 pert.: ictic
PULVERIZE: *destroy, *press
PUMICE: smooth, stone, talc
PUMMEL: *beat, *lie
PUMP: *ask, *increase, *raise
 constellation: antlia
 handle: sweep, swipe
 kind: air, aspirator, bicycle,
 bucket, centrifugal, chain, donkey, force, hydraulic, jet, left,
 piston, rotary, sand, shell, suction, turbine

* Asterisk means to look up this word to find more answer words.

medical: syringe
part: barrel, handle, ram
PUMPKIN: cucurbita, pepo, squash
head: *fool, *dolt, puritan
seed: butterfish, sunfish
PUN: *adage, *joke, mot, quibble
PUNCH: *clown, *force, *hit, *pierce, *spirit, *strike, tool
and judy: england and france
and judy dog: toby
etcher's: mattoir
first editor: lemon
spiced: negus
PUNCHINELLO: *clown, *fool
PUNCTILIOUS: *nice, *particular, *regular, *strict, systematic
PUNCTUAL: prompt, *sharp
PUNCTUATE: *mark, *stress
mark: *mark: printing
PUNCTURE: *opening, *pierce
PUNDIT: *authority, *church: man, *expert, *sage, scholar
PUNGENT: *acerb, *sharp, *sour
PUNIC: carthaginian, *false
PUNISH: *abuse, attend to, bastinado, *beat, birch, blister, cane, castigate, chastise, *correct, discipline, *fine, flog, frap, handicap, hang, *hit, *hurt, *kill, lash, lick, *pain, penalize, pillory, pommel, *rebuke, *scold, *settle, slate, spank, *torment, *torture, *whip
pert.: penal
PUNJAB: *india
PUNK: amadou, *bad, *mean, *poor, *prostitute, touchwood
source: agaric
tree: cajeput, melaleuca, paper bush, white tree
PUNT: boat, *drive, *hit, kick
PUNY: *little, *small, *weak
PUPIL: cadet, novice, *student
comb.: cor
PUPPET: *agent, *image, punch
head: aunt sally

PURBLIND: myopic, *stupid
PURCHASE: *bargain, *get, *grip, *hold, *property, *take
PURE: *absolute, abstract, aesthetic, agnes, authentic, blank, candid, cast, downright, faultless, fresh, *good, guiltless, *holy, innocent, intemperate, lily, lucid, mere, neat, net, *noble, pious, real, *right, sheer, *simple, taintless, *true, undefiled, unimpeachable, unsullied, utter
land: amida, amitabha, regirth
rain: aqua caelestis
thought: noesis
PURGE: *acquit, *dismiss, *kill
PURIFICATION: abdest, catharsis
consecration: *purge, wudu
feast: candlemas
PURIFY: *bless, *purge, wash
PURIM: festival of lots
chronicler: dositheus, lysimachus, ptolemaeus
PURITAN: ascetic, bluenose, canter, pilgrim, roundhead
last: adams
PURL: *border, curl, eddy, knit, rib, stitch, swirl
PURLIEU: area, environ, haunt
PURLOIN: filch, finger, *steal
PUROHIT: *church: man
PURPLE: amaranth, blatta, cassius, eveque, lavender, lilac, magenta, mauve, *power, puce, *ruler, uda, violet
coneflower: black sampson
copper: bornite, erubescite
finch: carpodacus
gallinule: blue peter, coot
grackle: blackbird, quiscalus
heart: award, medal, *order
medic: alfalfa, lucern(e)
ragwort: jacoby
seaweed: laver, sion
willow: bitter osier, blacktop
PURPORT: *mean, *purpose, *sign

* Asterisk means to look up this word to find more answer words.

PURPOSE: *aim, artha, cause, crusade, *desire, determine, *end, function, hang, *mean, *meaning, *plan, plot, *reason, relevance, resolution, resolve, sake, *talk, *think, *try, wish
pert.: teleological, telic
special: ad hoc
PURSE: *bag, *money, *pack
crab: ayuyu, birgus
snatcher: *thief
PURSUE: *purpose, *run, *search
PURSUIT: *forte, *trade, *work
PURSY: *big, *fat, *rich
PURVEY: *get, *provide, *supply
PUSH: *accelerate, *advance, *attack, bore, butt, cant, *crisis, emergency, *force, gang, *group, impulse, *move, nub, nudge, offense, ping, poke, *power, *press, prod, promote, propel, prosecute, shove, *speed, sponsor, *start, *stress, *support, *urge
cart: barrow, pram
in: crush, *enter, invade
off: *start
over: easy, facility, set-up
through: *end, finish, *force
PUSILLANIMOUS: *afraid, *poor
PUSS: baudrons, cat, face, girl
PUSTULE: achor, beal, bleb, burl
PUT: *bring, *establish, *force, *give, *make, *move, *place, *set, *state, *throw, *urge
about: agitate, tack, *turn
across: *accomplish, *succeed
aside: *save, *store
away: *eat, *kill, *save
back: *defeat, *return
before: *present, *tell
by: *refuse, *save, *store
down: ante, *rebuke, *stop
forth: *issue, *present, *start
in: *enter, *establish, *set
into shape: *prepare, *train

off: defer, delay, *remove
on: *affect, *cover, *false, *present, *produce, show, *use
on the dog: *dress, *ornament
out: *anger, *dismiss, *hurt, *issue, *mad, *trouble, *use
over: *deceive, *succeed
right, straight: *right, *tell
through: *accomplish, *succeed
together: *join, *set, *unite
up: *accommodate, *establish, *increase, *name, *store
upon: *attack, *torment
up with: *stand, *take
PUTAMEN: pit, seed, stone
PUTRID: *bad, *dirty, *rotten
PUTTEE: gaiter, legging, spat
PUTTYROOT: adam and eve
PUTZ: *fool, *peasant
PUZZLE: acrostic, *addle, amaze, anagram, astonish, baffle, charade, complicate, confuse, conundrum, crux, difficulty, disconcert, dismay, distract, embarrass, enigma, entangle, fickle, foitter, glaik, griph, intrigue, mystery, mystify, nonplus, palindrome, paradox, perplex, *problem, quandary, rebus, riddle, *trouble, *think
PWYLL: consort: rhiannon
PYCANTHEMUM: basil, mint, ocimum
PYGARG: addax, antelope, osprey
PYGMALION: love: galatea, statue
sister: dido
sister's husband: sichaeus
statue: galatea
PYGMY: *dwarf, *short, *small
island: blefuscu, france
musk deer: chevrotain
PYLON: *mark, *memorial, *tower
PYLOS: king: nestor
PYRAMID: *increase, *memorial
erector: cheops, imhotep

* Asterisk means to look up this word to find more answer words.

ruins: benares
-shaped stone: ben ben
site: cholula, el giza, gizeh
PYRAMIDAL: **big, *great, *large*
PYRAMUS: *lover:* thisbe
PYRE: bale, bier, **fire,* suttee
PYRENEES: *chamois:* izard
pass: perche, somport
peak: aneto
republic: andorra
resort: pau
PYRRHA: *consort:* deucalion
PYRRHUL: blood alp, finch, olp
PYTHAGORAS: *birthplace:* samos
daughter: camo
PYTHIAS: *friend:* damon
PYTHON: anaconda, boa, **sage*

QUACK: couch, crocus, **cry,*
duck, horse doctor, **impostor,*
medecin tant pis, medicaster,
pretender, sangrado
remedy: nostrum
QUAD: campus, court, park, type
QUADRAGESIMAL: forty, lent
QUADRATE: **adapt, *perfect*
QUADRIC: ellipsoid, hyperboloid
QUADRIGA: car, **chariot,* horses
QUADRILLE: allemande, **dance*
term: cavalier seul, lete
QUADROON: metis, **mixture*
QUAERE: **ask,* question, seek
QUAFF: **drink,* guzzle, swill
QUAGGY: boggy, muddy, **soft*
QUAGMIRE: **mess, *problem,*
swamp
QUAHOG: blunt, bullnose, clam
QUAIL: blench, colin, lophortyx,
lowa, massena, **prostitute, *re-
treat,* tinamou, turnix
group: bevy, covey, flock
hawk: bush hawk, nesierax
young: cheeper, squealer
QUAINT: **eccentric, *pretty*
QUAKE: **agitate, *quiver*

QUAKER: bird, broadbrim, fox,
friend, gun, moth, penn, sect
city: philadelphia
gray: acier
ladies: bluet, meadowsweet
state: pennsylvania
QUALIFICATION: **limit, *skill*
QUALIFIED: **able, *fit, *ready*
QUALIFY: **adapt, *limit, *name,
*pass, *prepare, *temper, *train*
QUALITY: **art,* atmosphere, attribute, brand, **caliber,* capacity,
*class, difference, excellence,
*form, grade, guna, **kind,
mark, mold, **part, *particular,
*position, *power, *property,
rank, rate, **skill, *stand(ard),
*state, *strain,* tamas, timbre,
trait, virtue
suff.: acity, acy, ance, ancy, ence,
ency
QUALM: doubt, fear, **pain*
QUANDARY: **crisis, *mess,
*pass, *problem, *puzzle, *upset*
QUANTITY: aggregate, **all,*
amount, any, armful, aught,
*bag, ballast, barrel, basket,
batch, bellyful, **bit,* body, box,
bulk, bunch, bundle, cargo, case,
crate, cup, deal, dose, extent,
feck, flask, **flood,* fortune, galaxy, gobs, **group,* handful, heap,
host, kettle, kitty, lac, lakh, legion, load(s), lot(s), magnitude,
mass, measure, mess, mise,
mountain, much, myriads, **pack,*
pile, pitcher, plate, **plenty,*
pocket(ful), pot(ful), profusion,
quantum, raft, rate, roomful,
scad(s), size, slew, some, spate,
*store, sum, **surfeit,* ton, total,
volume, wad(s), weight, whole,
yaffle
directionless: scalar
fixed: constant
full: complement
irrational: surd

QUANTUM: *amount, *part, *quantity, *share, *unit
QUARANTINE: ban, *limit
 station: lazaret
QUARREL: altercation, *argue, bolt, brack, breach, breeze, brique, broil, chisel, disagree, disturbance, *fight, imbroglio, misunderstanding, scene, tiff, tumult, wrangle
QUARRY: game, *kill, mine, prey
QUART: four: gallon
 eight: peck
 half: pint
 metric: liter, litre
 one-eighth: gill
 two: flagon, magnum
QUARTER: *district, *part
 note: crocket
QUARTZ: agate, amethyst, carnelian, chalcedony, citrine, crystal, flint, jasper, onyx, prase, rubasse, sard, topaz
 and albite: adinole
 conglomerate: banket
 crystal: cairngorm, cairngorum
 diorite: banatite
 hypersthene: birkremite
 monzonite: adamelite
 porphyry: beresite
 syenite: akerite
 tourmaline: carvoeira
QUASH: *abate, *destroy, *stop
QUAT: boil, pimple, *quit
QUATCH: *deceive, *move, *stir
QUAVER: fear, *quiver, shake
QUEACHY: *small, *soft, *weak
QUEAN: *prostitute
QUEASY: nauseated, *sick
QUEBEC: cape: gaspe
 carriage: caleche
 draughts: polish checkers
 island: anticosti
 patron saint: anne
QUEEN: anne's lace: carrot
 anne's melon: dudaim
 charlotte indian: haida

 city: cincinnati
 conch: cameo, cassis, helmet
 elizabeth's alias: orlana
 -like: regal, reginal, royal
 pawn: fers
QUEEN'S: arm: musket
 camel: camelot
 delight: perennial, queenroot
 flower: bloodwood, myrtle
QUEER: *eccentric, *mad, *spoil
QUELL, QUENCH: *end, *quiet
QUERULOUS: *acerb, *angry
QUERY, QUEST(ION): *ask, *test, *try
 rhetorical: eperotesis
QUESTIONABLE: *open, vague
QUIBBLE: *cheat, *lie, *scold
QUICK: *active, *acute, alert, alive, animated, apprehensive, apt, birdlike, brisk, burning, deft, docile, expert, *fast, fiery, *gay, immediate, impulsive, instant, intelligent, intense, lively, moving, passionate, peppy, prompt, rapid, *ready, rushing, sensitive, *sharp, *short, *smart, speedy, sprightly, sudden, swift, tosto, vital
QUICKSAND: *danger, *trap
QUIDDLE: *bit, *quiver
QUIDNUNC: *gossip
QUIESCENT, QUIET: *abate, appease, asleep, composure, dormant, *ease, easy, *gentle, halcyon, *happy, hushed, inactive, inert, latent, leisure(ly), lown, lull, motionless, mum, *order, pacific, passive, placid, rapt, relieve, repose, *rest, retired, secluded, serene, *settle, silent, *simple, *slow, *smooth, soothe, static, still, *stop, *tame, tranquil(ize)
QUIETUS: *death, *end, *rest
QUILL: feather, pen, shaft
 back: buffalo fish, carp
QUILLAI, QUILLAJA: soapbark
QUILT: caddow, *cover, sew
 down: duvet, eider

---

* **Asterisk means to look up this word to find more answer words.**

QUIMBOISEUR: *fetish, *magician

QUINCE: bael, bel, cydonia, tree

QUININE: bitterbark, cinchona, hop tree, horseradish tree, kina, loja, loxa, quina
 substitute: bebeerine

QUINOA: pigweed, seeds

QUINTESSENCE: *acme, *best

QUIP: *joke, *taunt, wit

QUIRE: twenty: ream

QUIRK: *quip, *trick, *turn

QUIRT: romal, *whip

QUIT: *abandon, abstain, *avoid, bow out, cease, depart, desist, discontinue, evacuate, exit, fold, forsake, *free, give up, leave, relieve, relinquish, *remove, repay, resign, retire, *retreat, *settle, shirk, *stop, surrender, *yield
 claim: *release

QUITE: really, truly, wholly

QUITTANCE: *discharge, *return

QUIVER: *active, arrows, bicker, case, cocker, dindle, flichter, flicker, flutter, frisson, nimble, palpitate, quail, quake, quaver, shake, sheath, shudder, thirl, thrill, tirl, tremble, tremor, trill, vibrate

QUIXOTIC: *eccentric, *mad

QUIZ: *ask, *gossip, *test, *try

QUOD: court, *jail

QUOIT: cromlech, disc, jukshei
 mark: mot, tee
 pin: hob

QUONDAM: erst, former, past

QUORUM: *group, *meeting

QUOTA: *part, ratio, *share

QUOTATION: bid, price, rate
 essay, made into: chria
 mark: guillemet

QUOTE: *adage, *copy, *name, *note, *repeat, *report, *say

QUOTIDIAN: *plain, *usual

QUOTIENT: *result

RA: aten, chepera, harmachis, horus, iokaris, khepera, shu, sun, tem, tum
 bull form: bacis
 child: athor, maat, mat, mu, selket, selquet, shu
 parent: geb, keb, neith, nut
 symbol: ben ben
 wife: eus-os, iusaas, mout, mut, rat, reddedet, uert-hekeu

RAAD: catfish

RAAMAH: son: dedan, sheba

RABATO: collar, ruff

RABBI: amora, *church: man, gaon, hakam, *lord, sabora, teacher
 assistant: cantor
 group: amoraim
 school: yeshiva, yeshiboth
 wife: rebbetzin

RABBIT: adapis, beljeek, bunny, capon, coney, cottontail, *coward, hare, lagomorph, lapin, leveret, rex, tapeti
 berry: beef-suet, buffalo bush
 brush: broom sage
 ear: aerial, cactus, toadflax
 eared: lagotis, oarlop
 fever: tularemia
 fish: chimaera
 flower: foxglove, toadflax
 foot: charm, *fetish, talisman
 fur: arctic seal, beaverette, coney, cony, lapin, rack, scut
 home: burrow, cage, clapper, hutch, warren
 -like animal: marmot, perameles
 meat: archangel
 mouth: harelip, snapdragon
 root: sarsaparilla
 tail: fud, scut
 trap: tipe
 wood: buffalo nut, elk nut
 young: bunny, rack, gazabo

RABBLE: canaille, *dregs, herd, hoi polloi, masses, multitude, proletariat, *refuse, ruck, scum,

---

Asterisk means to look up this word to find more answer words.

sordes, trash, vermin
-rouse: *agitate, *stir
-rouser: demagogue
RABELAISIAN: *dirty, *profane
RABID: *eager, *mad, *violent
RABIES: hydrophobia, lyssa
RACCOON: arctoid, mapach(e)
-like animal: coati, panda
RACE: *contest, *group, *run,
*speed, *strain, *waterway
apex period: hemera
board: gangplank
boat: gig, regatta, shell
classifications: adriatic, alpine,
black, brown, caucasian, malayan, mediterranean, mongolian,
negro, prehistoric, teutonic,
white, xanthochroi, yellow
colors: silks
comb.: gend, geno
consciousness: ethnicity
course: career, circus, dragstrip,
oval, ring, track
course, famed: aqueduct, ascot,
bowie, downs, epsom, gold
meadows, hialeah, hollywood
park, indianapolis, jamaica,
laurel, nurburgring, pimlico,
santa anita, saratoga, tropic
expert: dopester, tipster, tout
extermination: genocide
gait: gallop, pace, *run, trot
gods: aesir, olympians, vanir
group: clan, family, tribe
horse: bangtail, mudder, pacer,
plater, trotter
human: breed, ilk, stirps
marker: meta, pylon, tape
official: starter, timer
part: heat, lap
pert.: ethnic
relay: medley
science: athletics, ethnology
track: *race: course
undivided: holethnos
way: arroyo, canal, channel
RACER: blacksnake, jehu, speeder

RACHEL: father: laban
husband: jacob
sister: leah
son: benjamin, joseph
RACHIS: backbone, chine, spine
RACK: *agony, *pain, *strain,
*torment, *torture, *try
RACKET: *noise, scheme, *trick
RACKETEER: *criminal, *hoodlum
RACKLE: *noise, *reckless
RACY: *fresh, *rich, *strong
RADAMES: lover: aida
RADAR: loran, microwave, shoran
assembly: afc, altimeter, amplifier,
atr, cascade, detector, magnetron, mixer, modulator, oscilla-
tor, pulser, receiver, screen,
tracker, tr box, tr switch, triga-
tron
beacon: racon, ramark
countermeasure: chaff, dueppel,
jamming, spoofing, tinfoil
defection: clutter, refraction
direction finder: compass, goni-
ometer, huff-duff, sniffer, super-
duper
kind: agca, asv, cca, dew line,
dme, dvop, gca, gci, ground, iff,
law, mad, mew, mti, navaglobe,
oboe, par, rawin, sarah, scr,
search, surface, surveillance,
taxi, trw, volscan
pulse: echo, high-frequency, trigger
receive: home on, identify, lock
on, map, paint, pick up, pin-
point, scan, spot, sweet, trigger,
tune in
sound: blip
RADIANCE: *glory, *light
RADIANT: *bright, *happy
energy: black light
RADIATE: *light, *shine, *spread
RADIATION: detector: geiger
ratio: absorptance
unit: rad

* Asterisk means to look up this word to find more answer words.

RADICAL: basic, red, root, ultra
RADIO: air, broadcast, wireless
aerial: antenna
frequency: audio, band
-guided bomb: azon
interference: beep, static
man: announcer, broadcaster, disc jockey, ham, sparks
program: broadcast
signal check: monitor
station group: network
tube: grid
RADIUM: *discoverer:* curie
emanation: niton, radon
source: carnotite, uranite
RADIUS: orbit, *range, sweep
RAFFISH: *bad, *low, *mean
RAFT: barge, *plenty, *quantity
breasted: ratite
duck: bluebill, redhead, scaup
log: brail
RAG: *bit, *dress, *taunt
man: clothier, vagabond
picker: chiffonier, hobo, tramp
weed: ambrosia, helenium, iva
-wort: cow parsnip, jacoby, scabious
RAGA: nirvana, *paradise
RAGABASH: *rabble
RAGE: *anger, *cry, *desire, *passion, *storm, *style
the: dernier cri
RAGGED: *low, *mean, *poor
lady: guara, love-in-a-mist
sailor: bluebottle, cornflower
RAGING: *angry, *mad, *violent
RAGOUT: *hash, mince, salmi
RAGUEL: *child:* sarah, raphael
wife: edna
RAH: bravo, cheer, ole
RAHAB: *husband:* salmon
son: boaz, booz
RAID: *attack, *fight, *seize
RAIL: *abuse, *limit, *scold
bird: bilcock, crake, sora, wek
head: vanguard
pert.: ralline

RAILROAD: *route, *speed, *way
bedroom: berth, drawing room, lower, pullman, roomette, upper
branch: feeder, spur, stub
car: *vehicle:* railroad
center: depot, gare, round house, station, terminal
man: bakehead, brakeman, brakie, conductor, engineer, fireman, guard, motorman, porter, trainman, yardman
passenger line: amtrak, railpax
passenger ticket: eurail pass
signal: flare, fusee, semaphore, trimmer
switch: frog
term: crosstie, crow, gauge, pedestal, sleeper, tie, timber
RAIMENT: *dress, garb, togs
RAIN: *fall, *issue, *storm
bird: plover
bow: arc, asgard, iris, omen
bow bridge: bifrost
bow chaser: idealist, visionary
bow darter: blue johnny
bow-like: iridal, iridescent
bow measurer: spectrometer
check: postponement, stub
cloud: nimbus
coat: *overcoat
evening: serein
fine: drizzle, misle, mist, mizzle, serein
forest: selva
fowl: channelbill, cuckoo, woodpecker
gauge: hyetograph, ombrometer, pluvioscope, udometer
glass: barometer
god: agne, esus, frey, indra, ing, jupiter pluvius, parjanya
goddess: tefnut
icy: hail, sleet, snow
leader: downspout
-loving: ombrophilous
measure: inch
or shine: certainly, earnestly

* **Asterisk means to look up this word to find more answer words.**

pert.: hyetal, iridal, pluvial
serpent: naga
spout: cloudburst, rone
storm: brash, deluge, downpour, drencher, flood, gullywasher, monsoon, pelter, plash, root searcher, scut, shower, soaker, spate, spout, thundersquall
tree: algarroba, carob, genisaro, mesquite, saman, zaman(g), zamia
worm: earthworm, nematode
RAISE: *advance,* arouse, awaken, bonus, boss, breed, *build,* bump, cantle, conjure, construct, cultivate, elevate, enhance, enrol, erect, exalt, excite, farm, *gather,* glorify, *grow,* heave, heighten, hike, hoist, *increase,* jack, leaven, lift, lighten, muster, *prepare,* *present,* *produce,* promote, rear, recognition, relieve, *remove,* reward, rise, rouse, *start,* *stir,* *tower,* *train*
cain: *anger,* *complain,* *cry*
hell: *anger,* *cry,* *play*
RAISIN: lexia, pasa, zibeb
RAJMAHAL: bowstring, jiti, vine
RAKAN: *one of 16:* binzuru
RAKE: bomb, *gather,* roue, tool
-off: dividend, *part,* *share*
RALLY: *advance,* *attack,* *banter,* concentrate, convocation, deride, drag, encourage, *gather,* improve, *joke,* *meet,* *meeting,* mobilize, mock, *noise,* raillery, recover, recuperate, revive, ridicule, rouse, *stir,* strengthen, *taunt,* *unite*
RAM: aries, *force,* *hit,* pun
cat: male, tom
god: ammon, khnum
horn: shofar, shophar
-like: arietine, arietinous
son: amminadab, eker, jamin
RAMA(CHANDRA): *consort:* sita

half brother: bharata
RAMAGE: *wild*
hawk: brancher
RAMANANDI: *church: man*
RAMASS: *gather,* *meet,* *unite*
RAMBLE: *range,* *walk*
RAMBLING: circuitous, *free*
RAMBUNCTIOUS: *wild*
RAME: *cry,* limb
RAMEE: *pen name:* ouida
RAMEKIN: *hash,* *mixture*
RAMESES: *queen:* nefertari
RAMIE: flax, hemp, phloem, rhea
RAMP: *cheat,* *passage,* *steal*
RAMPAGE: *anger,* *cry,* *storm*
RAMPANT: *brutal,* *wanton*
RAMPART: *fort,* mole, redan
detached: ravelin
earthen: bray
ground around: escarp
-like: defilade, wall
part: agger, spur
RAMSON: bear's-garlic
RAMWAT: *church: man*
RAN: *husband:* aegir, hler
RANCH: estancia, hacienda
worker: *cow: boy*
RANCID: *acerb,* *sour,* *strong*
RAND: *edge,* *limit*
RANDY: *bad,* *dirty,* *wild*
RANGE: array, ball park, carry, chain, *class,* classify, *control,* cordillera, diapason, direction, *distance,* environment, expanse, explore, *extent,* field, forage, gamut, gaut, ghat, graze, hike, ken, *kind,* latitude, line, orbit, outlook, piece, prospect, prowl, radius, ramble, *rank,* *reach,* register, *ridge,* roam, rove, scale, scene, scope, series, sort, *sphere,* *stove,* stray, sweep, view, vista, *walk,* *way*
finder: mekometer, trekometer
RANK: *absolute,* abundant, altitude, *aristocracy,* *bad,* berth, character, coarse, dank, degree,

dense, estate, estimate, *evil,
fetid, file, glaring, *glory, grade,
gross, indecent, lush, luxuriant,
musty, nasty, *order, perquisite,
*power, prestige, privilege,
*pure, *rancid, *range, rate,
rating, *rich, *rotten, size, *sour,
*stand, station, *strong, terrible,
*thick, *wanton, *wild, *wrong
and file: *rabble
military: *army: officer
RANKLE: *hurt, *pain
RANSACK: *ruin, *steal
RANSOM: *acquit, *save
RANT: *anger, *cry, *rebuke,
*scold, *storm, *talk
RANTING: *insane, *mad
RANTIPOLE: *imp, *wild
RAP: *bit, *blow, *hit, *insult,
*scold, *strike, *taunt
RAPE: *abuse, *attack, *seize
seed: colsa, colza
RAPHAEL: angel, azarias
son: raguel
RAPID: *fast, *quick, steep
RAPIDS: chute, riff, shoot, soo
RAPIER: blade, *sword, verdun
-blade heel: ricasso
RAPTURE: *joy, *paradise, *spell
RARE: *fine, *good, *special
RASCAL: dodger, *imp, *thief
RASH: *reckless, *wild
RAT: *apostate, traitor
hare: pika
kind: hamster, metad, mole, mus,
spalax, tosher, zemni
poison: antu, arsenic, ratsbane
tail: braid
RATE: *analyze, *assess, *rank,
*rebuke, *scold, *speed, *value
RATIFY: *accept, *bless, *pass
RATING: *class, *range, *rank
RATIO: *part, *rank, *share
RATION: *limit, *part, *share
RATIONAL: *fair, *right, *wise
RATTLE: *abash, *addle, *noise,
*nonsense, *toy, *upset

-boned: lean
-brain: *clown, *fool
bush: baptisia, false indigo
mouse: bat
root: bugbane
snake: cascavel, crotulus, diamondback, massasauga, side-
winder, sistrurus
snake bite: rue
snake and rattle: button
snake fern: sporangia
snake herb: baneberry
snake pilot: copperhead
snake plantain: networt
snakeroot: bird bell
top: bugbane
trap: gewgaws, knickknacks,
mouth, ramshackle, rickety
RAVAGE: *abuse, *eat, *ruin,
*spoil, *steal, waste, wreck
RAVE: *anger, *cry, *rant
RAVEN: alala, crow, *eat
RAVINE: *opening, *waterway
RAVING: *insane, *mad
RAVISH: *ravage
RAW: cold, damp, nude, rude
-boned: gaunt, lean, scrag
-hide: *beat, *whip
RAY: alpha, anode, batfish, beam,
beta, cathode, cheer, diameter,
dorn, emanation, gamma, gleam,
gleed, glimmer, *light, manta,
obispo, sephen, shaft, shine,
sight, skate, streak, stripe, vision
comb.: actin(o)
pert.: actinic, actinoid, radial
RAYON: acetate, celanese, faille,
moire, ninon, pongee, taffeta,
tulle, viscose
RAZE: *destroy, *ruin
RAZEE: *abridge, *reduce
RAZZ: *banter, *torment
REACH: *accomplish, advene, affect, attain, bribe, carry, catch,
come, *cover, deliver, extend,
*get, grasp, *hit, influence,
length, lie, *make, overtake,

---

* Asterisk means to look up this word to find more answer words.

plain, possess, *promontory*, put forth, *range*, *run*, span, *sphere*, *spread*, stretch, *strike*, touch, *tower*

REACTOR: *agent*, bricks, furnace

READ: *study*, *understand*
ability: literacy
inability: alexia

READY: *active*, amenable, apt, available, bain, bound, *eager*, equipped, facile, forward, handy, inclined, likely, loaded, mature, *near*, *open*, *plan*, *prepare*, *quick*, ripe, *set*, supplied, *train*, willing

REAL: *pure*, *solid*, *true*
being: pert.: ontal
estate: *asset*, land, *property*
estate register: cadastre
mccoy: genuine, kosher, *true*

REALIZE: *acquire*, *get*, *know*, *sense*, *think*, *understand*

REALM: *property*, *range*, *sphere*, *state*

REAM: *draw*, lots, *quantity*

REAP: *acquire*, *gather*, *get*

REAR: *raise*, *stern*, *train*
end: derriere, duff, rump
to the: abaft, aft, astern
wheel assembly: bogie

REASON: *account*, *aim*, alibi, *analyze*, *argue*, *assess*, cause, conclude, consider, discuss, generalize, grounds, hypothesize, logic, *mind*, particularize, ponder, proof, *prove*, *purpose*, ratiocinate, rationalize, sanity, *sense*, solution, syllogize, theorize, *think*, *understand*
higher: nous
lack: amentia, mania
pert.: noetic

REBATE: *return*

REBECCA: *brother:* laban
father: bethuel
son: esau, jacob

REBEL: defy, *protest*, resist

REBOUND: echo, kick, spring

REBUKE: *admonish*, assail, *attack*, bawl out, berate, call down, chew out, *correct*, *criticize*, cuss out, jack up, jump on, lambaste, lecture, lesson, nag, object, objurgate, *punish*, rag, rake, rap, rate, reprehend, reprimand, reproach, reprove, riddle, *scold*, sermon, sit on, *skin*, slap, *take*, *taunt*, *tell*, trim

RECALCITRANT: *hard*, *obstinate*, *sullen*

RECALL: remember, summon, *think*

RECANT: back down, *yield*

RECAPITULATE: *repeat*

RECEDE: *decline*, *retreat*

RECEIPT: *answer*, *remedy*, *take*

RECEIVE: *accept*, *get*, *take*

RECEIVER: *comb.:* ceptor

RECENT: *fresh*, past, young
comb.: cene, ceno, neo

RECEPTACLE: acerra, angium, apron, ark, ashcan, autoclave, *bag*, banga, basket, billy(can), bladder, boat, boot, box, brasier, bucket, burse, cage, can(ister), capcase, carryall, casserole, catchall, cellar, chest, compote, *container*, crock, dish, ewer, font, gallipot, hopper, magazine, *package*, pail, patera, piggin, pipkin, pitcher, porringer, receiver, recipient, robbin, roll, saucer, sebilia, stoup, suttle, tray, trencher, urn, utensil, vas(e), vault, *vessel*
suff.: angium

RECEPTION: *affair*, *party*

RECESS: interval, *retreat*

RECHAB: *son:* jonadab, malchiah

RECHERCHE: *fine*, *fresh*

RECIPROCAL: *comb.:* allelo

---

* Asterisk means to look up this word to find more answer words.

RECIPROCATE: *accord, *return, revenge, *share

RECITE: *repeat, *state, *tell

RECKLESS: audacious, banzai, bayardly, blindfold, bodacious, breakneck, careless, daring, desperate, devil-may-care, *eager, folle, harum-scarum, hasty, headlong, heedless, hotspur, hurried, indifferent, *mad, neglectful, perdu, precipitate, rash, slap-bang, *wanton, *wild

RECKON: *consider, *think

RECLAIM: *save, *train

RECLINE: *lie, *rest

RECLUSE: *ascetic, *monk

RECOGNITION: gemutlich, place in the sun, satori, shibui

RECOGNIZE: *mark, *note, *see

RECOLLECT: remember, *think

RECOMMEND: *advise, *urge

RECOMPENSE: *income, *reward

RECONCILE: *adapt, *adjust

RECONDITE: *secret

RECONNOITER: *look, *spy

RECORD: *account, *agenda, annals, annotate, archives, *book, cashbook, *diary, disc, document, *enter, hansard, high point, history, inscribe, legend, *mark, matriculate, *memorial, *monument, *note, platter, *report, scroll, tab, tape, trace, transcript, write

RECOUNT: *report, *state, *tell

RECOURSE: *asylum, *use

RECOVER: *rally, rescue, *upset

RECREANT: *apostate, *coward

RECREMENT: *dregs, *refuse

RECRUIT: *add, *draft, *gather, *rally, *supply, *train

RECTIFY: *correct, *remedy

RECTITUDE: *honor, probity

RECUPERATE: *rally, revive

RECUR: *repeat, *return

RECURRENT: *common, *usual

RED: cardinal, radical, ruddy

admiral: atalanta butterfly

alga: ahnfeltia, ceramium

arsenic: realgar

astrachan: apple

azo dye: bordeaux

-backed mouse: bank vole

-backed sandpiper: dunlin

bay: evergreen magnolia

beard: barbarossa

bell: columbine

-bellied snipe: dowitcher

belly: char, grouper, terrapin

bird: cardinal, tanager

blindness: protanopia

-breast: robin

bud: judas tree

bug: bete rouge, bicho, chigger

campion: billy button, burdock, daisy, geranium, scabious

cap: bonnet rouge, carrier, extremist, goldfinch, policeman, porter, spectre, tarboosh

cattle: afrikander

cedar: arbor vitae, flindosa, juniper, sabine, savin, thuja

cell: bilirubin, erythrocyte

cent: *bit, copper, *trifle

chalk: ruddle

cherry: cerasin

circle: guze

clay: laterite

coat: bloody-back, britisher

cobalt: erythrite

coloring: anchusin, carthame

copper: cuprite

coral: blood

corpuscle: erythrocyte, hematid

corpuscle deficiency: anemia

cross founder: barton

cross knight: george

cross knight's wife: una

crystalline: brazilein

currant: rissel

deer: elaphine, hart, hind, roe, spay, stag

dog: banker and broker, high card pool, slippery sam

Asterisk means to look up this word to find more answer words.

dogwood: bloody rod, bloody twig
dress clothes: arming
drum fish: bull redfish
dye: aal, al, alkanet, anatto, annatto, arnatto, brazil, chay, choy, eosin, puccoon
dyewood: barwood, camwood
eureka: puce
eye: copperhead, fish, rudd, sunfish, vireo, whiskey
-faced: blowzed, flushed, ruddy
fever: erysipelas
flag: provocation, warning
garden flower: canna
glowing: rutilant
green blindness: daltonism
grouse: muirfowl, ptarmigan
gum: eucalyptus, strophulus
-handed: flagrante delicto
hau tree: hauula
head: carrot-top, finch, pochard, woodpecker
-headed lizard: bluetailed skink, eumeces, scorpion
hematite: acuatito
heraldry: gules
herring: artifice, capon
honeysuckle: sulla
horse: bay, roan
-hot: *ardent, *eager, *ready
iron: almandine, almandite
lead: corcoite
letter day: holiday
light district: tenderloin
man: indian
mineral: garnet
mouth: fish, grunt
oak: quercitron, she-oak
ocher: abraum, keel, kiel, raddle, ruddle, tiver
paint: chica, lake, roset
pepper: chile, chili, chilli
perch: rosefish
phalarope: bowhead
pigs: duroc
pine: rimu
planet: mars

plum: burbank
pogry: besugo, fish
powder: abir, alkannin
rag: tongue
river republican: riel
roncador: black croaker
root: bloodwort, indian paint, potentilla, puccoon, sanguinaria, tormentil, turmeric
roundel: guze
sandalwood: adenanthera, algum, almug, barbados pride, bead tree, bear tree, china tree, flower fence, necklace tree, peacock flower
sea: erythrean
sea gulf: aqaba
sea island: perim
sea peninsula: sinai
sea stingray: sephen
shank: clee
shirt: anarchist, camicia garibaldian, reserve, revolutionary, rossa, substitute
-skin: indian, savage
skin preparation: rubefacient
snapper: cachucho, etelis oculatus, huachinango
squirrel: chickaree
stone: ruby, sard
swine: duroc
tape: bureaucracy, delay, fabianism, routine, rut
tapist: official
top: agrostis, bonnet grass
trillium: bloody butchers, male orchid, nosebleed
valerian: cat-bed, centranthys
venetian: siena
viper: copperhead
willow: cornel, osier
wing: blackbird, francolin, thrush
wood: sandalwood, sequoia
-yellow: alabaster, alesan, aloma, ascot, beaver, bisque, caramel, chestnut, coconut, corn, doubloon, gypsy, kerman shah,

* Asterisk means to look up this word to find more answer words.

mauve, ocher, peachblow, sandstone, tangier, titian

REDACT: *amend, edit

REDAN: *fort

REDDEN: *fire, *light

REDE: *adage, *advise, *aid, *plan, *predict, *reason, *remedy, *story, *tell

REDEEM: *free, *rectify, *save, *settle, *substitute

REDOLENCE: perfume, *scent

REDOUBTABLE: *obstinate, *strong

REDOUND: *issue, *result, *return, *yield

REDRESS: *amend, *remedy

REDUCE: *abase, *abate, *abbreviate, abridge, *analyze, appall, assuage, *break, bring down, buff, bust, compress, curtail, decrease, deduct, *defeat, demote, depreciate, depress, deprive, *destroy, diet, dilute, dim, fletcherize, impair, impoverish, lessen, mark down, minimize, moderate, pare, pull, rend, *settle, shorten, shrink, slash, slenderize, slim, *slow, take in, *temper, *thin

REDUCTIO AD ABSURDUM: apagoge, logic, proof, *result

REDUNDANT: *extra, replete

REED: arundinaria, culm, *missile, pirn, rix, sley, thatch, tube
bird: bobolink, warbler
buck: antelope, bohor, koba, nagor, reitbok, waterbuck
bunting: black bonnet
carriers: cannophori
comb.: calam, calami, calamo
grass: carrizo
instrument: bagpipe, harmonium
pen: calamus
pert.: arundinaceous
salty: adarce

REEF: atoll, bar, cay, key, spit

REEFER: *cover, *drug, smoke

REEK: *smell, *smoke, steam

REEL: *dance, *turn, *walk

REEM: unicorn, urus

REFER: *direct, *send, *turn

REFERENCE: *book, *record
mark: *mark: printing

REFINE: *ready, *shine, *strain

REFINED: *fine, *nice, *polite

REFLECT: *copy, *study, *think

REFLECTION: *image, *smear
measurer: albedograph
pert.: catadioptric

REFLEX MEASURER: anacamptometer
movement: babinski

REFORM: *rectify

REFORMATORY: *jail

REFRACTION: *pert.:* anaclastic

REFRACTORY: *recalcitrant

REFRAIN: *pass, *song, *stop

REFRESH: cheer, quicken, *rally

REFUGE: asylum, *cover, *retreat

REFUND: *return

REFURBISH: *repair

REFUSE: *abandon, abnegate, addments, alluvium, ashes, bagasse, balk, bavin, bones, brockle, carbon, chaff, cinders, coal, coom, cot, culm, deadwood, debris, *decline, deny, depletion, deposit, drain, *dregs, detritus, diluvium, effluvium, embers, *end, feces, filings, garbage, heeltaps, hogwash, hold out, junk, leavings, leftovers, loess, marcrescence, naysay, negate, *nonsense, odds and ends, oddments, offscum, orts, overage, parings, pob, raff, rags, raspings, reject, relics, remains, renounce, *repel, residue, resign, *rest, revoke, rinsings, rubbish, rubble, *ruins, scobs, scoria, *scorn, scourings, scrap, settlings, shavings, shoddy, sinter, smut, *spoil, sprue, stand pat, straw, stubble, stump, surplus, sweepings, swill, tares, thumbs down, veto, waste

* Asterisk means to look up this word to find more answer words.

pile: basurale, cesspit, dump

REFUTE: **defeat, *refuse, *upset*

REGAL: **great, *noble, *splendid*

REGALE: **eat, *please, *tell*

REGALIA: **dress, *ornament,* paraphernalia, **symbol*

REGARD: **admire, *adore, *honor, *look, *love, *mind, *note, *prize, *see, *tell, *think*

REGARDING: about, concerning

REGATTA: **contest, *race*

REGENERATE: **holy, *redeem*

REGENT: **magnate, *ruler, *title*
bird: bird of paradise
diamond: pitt
of the sun: uriel

REGIME(N): **authority, *control, *remedy, *rule, *system*

REGION: **district, *part,* sphere
comb.: nesia
infernal: **hell*
pert.: areal, local, provincial

REGISTER: **book, *range, *record*

REGRET: **complain, *remorse*

REGRETFUL: **bad, *sorry*

REGULAR: analytic, besetting, **complete,* constant, conventional, established, fixed, frequent, habitual, methodic, natural, normal, on schedule, orderly, ordinary, periodic, persistent, **plain,* punctilious, recurrent, **right, *set, *smooth, *soldier,* systematic, thorough, typical, uniform, **usual,* well-trodden

REGULATE: **adjust, *control,* manage, **order, *remedy, *rule, *run, *temper,* time

REGULATION: **rule, *usual*

REHEARSE: **repeat, *tell, *train*

REHOBOAM: *son:* abia, abijah, attai, jeush, shelomith, shemariah, zaham, ziza
wife: abihail, maacah, mahalath

REIGN: influence, **regimen*
pert.: regnal, regnant, royal

of terror: anarchy, despotism
of st. swithin: rain

REIMKANNAR: **prophet, *sage*

REIN: **control, *slow*

REINFORCE: **increase, *support*

REINSTATE: **establish, *set*

REITERATE: **repeat*

REJECT: **dismiss, *refuse*

REJOICE: **glory, *laugh, *please*

RELATE: **account, *describe, *report, *state, *tell, *unite*

RELATED, RELATIVE: about, agnate, akin, apposite, approximate, aunt, brer, brethren, brother, bub, bud, buddy, cognate, comparable, consanguine, cousin, daughter, eme, enate, enatic, father, frater, germane, in-law, kid, kin(dred), mother, nephew, niece, nunks, parent, pertinent, praedial, relevant, sib(ling), sis(ter), son, uncle
comb.: ative, istic
favoritism to: nepotism
female line: bandhu
group: clan, family, tribe

RELAX: **abate, *amuse, *ease, *slow, *stop, *yield*

RELAXATION: **joy, *rest*

RELAY: **agent, *rest, *supply*
hounds: avantlay
post: dauk
race: medley
system: angaria

RELEASE: **acquit,* assoil, **break,* catch, catharsis, death, deliver, **discard, *dismiss, *dispense,* disperse, **escape, *free,* handout, **issue,* leave go, **let,* permit, publicity, relax, relent, relieve, **remove,* reprieve, rescue, **rest,* rid, statement, **story, *tell, *yield*

RELEGATE: **banish, *remove*

RELENT: **relax, *yield*

RELEVANT: **relative, *right*

RELIABLE: **fast, *firm, *solid, *straight,* sure, **true,* upright

---

* Asterisk means to look up this word to find more answer words.

RELIANCE: *credit, *hope, *spirit, *support, *trust

RELIC: *monument, *ruin, *token
cabinet: apse, reliquary
vendor: calmierer

RELIEF: *outline, *release, *remedy, *spell, *support
ornament: adorno, cameo, fret

RELIEVE: *remedy, *spell, supply

RELIGIEUX: *church: man, *monk

RELIGION: *doctrine, *system

RELIGIOUS: *good, *holy

RELINQUISH: *abandon

RELIQUARY: arca, chest, *tomb

RELISH: *joy, *please, zest

RELUCTANCE: unit: oerstad, rel

RELUCTANT: *afraid, *obstinate

RELY: *rest, *stand, *trust

REMAIN: *continue, *rest, *stand

REMAINDER, REMAINS: *dregs, *end, *refuse, *rest

REMAND: commit, *return

REMARK: *note, *see, *state
light: *banter

REMARKABLE: *big, *great

REMEDY: *adjust, aid, *amend, analeptic, anesthetic, antacid, antitoxin, arcanum, *balm, balsam, boot, bot(e), *correct, counteractant, diaphoretic, elixir, emend, enema, fix, help, laxative, maturative, *medicine, *money, *narcotic, nostrum, palliative, panacea, patch, physic, pill, placebo, recipe, rectify, relieve, *repair, restore, *right, sedative, *service, tonic, treat, unction
comb.: ant, anti

REMEMBER: *reward, *think

REMEMBRANCE: *gift, *memorial, *monument, *reward

REMIGRATION: *return

REMIND: *advise, *urge

REMISE: *free, *return

REMISS: *gentle, *late, *slow

REMIT: *free, *return, *send

REMNANT: *dregs, *end, *part, *piece, *refuse, *rest

REMONSTRATE: *protest

REMORA: clog, curb, delay, draf, fish, pega(dor), sucker

REMORSE: anguish, apology, attrition, ayenbite, breast beating, compassion, compunction, contrition, distress, grief, *pain, *passion, pity, qualm, regret, repentance, rue, ruth, *sorrow

REMOTE: *cool, distant, far
most: ultima thule
pert.: forane

REMOVE: ablate, abolish, amputate, aspirate, avoid, bail out, bark, blot, carry, change, class, delete, depart, depose, disbar, *discard, *dismiss, displace, divest, doff, eloign, eloin, erase, exterminate, extinguish, extirpate, gut, *kill, make off with, *part, purloin, *release, shunt, space, *steal, *strip, *take, *throw, transfer

REMUNERATION: *fee, *income

REMUS: brother: romulus
parent: mars, rheasylvia

REND: *open, *split, *tear

RENDER: *accomplish, *give, *make, *repeat, *return, *tell, *try, *yield

RENDEZVOUS: *affair, *meeting, *place, refuge, resort, tryst

RENEGADE: *agnostic, traitor

RENEGE: *decline, *err, *refuse

RENEW: *rally, refresh, *repair

RENIER: son: oliver

RENIG: *renege, welch, welsh

RENITENT: *obstinate

RENOUNCE: *abandon, *decline, *quit, *refuse, *stop, *yield

RENOVATE: *renew, *repair

RENOWN: *glory, *honor, *note

RENT: breach, *break, cenus, cleft, *engage, *fee, hole, *let, *return, rip, rupture, shabby, slit, *split, *tear

---

* Asterisk means to look up this word to find more answer words.

REPAIR: careen, darn, doctor, fix, mend, overhaul, *piece, *prepare, *ready, *remedy, restore, *service, sew, *work

REPARATION: *remedy, *reward

REPARTEE: *answer, quip, wit

REPAST: feast, food, meal, treat
light: collation
pert.: prandial

REPAY: *answer, *return

REPEAL: *abolish, nullify, void

REPEAT: *again, *answer, cite, *copy, ding, ditto, duplicate, harp, *imitate, insist, iterate, memorize, quote, rame, reaffirm, recite, redo, rehash, rehearse, reiterate, reprise, reproduce, resume, review, run over, say over, sum(marize), segno, *tell

REPEL: *beat, *defeat, *stop

REPENT: *complain, regret

REPENTANCE: *remorse, *shame

REPERCUSSION: impact, *shock

REPERTOIRE, REPERTORY: *store

REPETITION: *again, *copy
word: anaphora, cataphasia

REPINE: *complain, *repent

REPLACE: *change, *substitute

REPLENISH: *complete, *provide

REPLETE: *big, *fat, *plenty

REPLEVIN, REPLEVY: attach, detinet, redeem, *seize

REPLICA: *copy, *image, twice

REPLY: *answer, *repeat, rsvp

REPORT: *account, *advise, announce, *answer, bandy, bang, break, brief, broadcast, bruit, bulletin, buzz, cahier, canard, card, charge, commentary, criticism, *cry, declare, delineate, *describe, dilate, explosion, *glory, *gossip, hansard, hearsay, inform, minutes, pop, proceedings, pronounce, *record, relate, returns, review, rumor, say, sound, speak, *spread, *state(ment), *story, tale, *talk, *tell, verdict, voice

REPOSE: *ease, *lie, *place, *quiet, *rest, *trust

REPOSITORY: box, lode, treasury

REPREHEND: *rebuke, *scold

REPREHENSIBLE: *criminal

REPRESENT: *act, *pass, *picture, *play, serve, *show, *stand

REPRESENTATION: *act, *image, *picture, *show, *symbol
fair: epitome

REPRESENTATIVE: *agent

REPRESS: *control, *slow, *stop

REPRIEVE: delay, grace, parole

REPRIMAND: *punish, *rebuke

REPROACH: *abuse, *rebuke, *shame

REPROBATE: *criminal, *devil

REPRODUCE: breed, *repeat
asexually: clone

REPRODUCTION: *copy, *picture, (photo)stat

REPROOF: *rebuke, snub

REPROVE: *abuse, *rebuke

REPTILE: alligator, croc, frog, lizard, newt, snake, toad, worm
age: mesozoic
edible: turtle
extinct: diplodocus, pterosaur
jurassic: baptonodon
pert.: ophidian, saurian
scale: scute

REPTILIAN: *bad, *evil, knavish

REPUBLIC: *state
author: plato
imaginary: oceania
letters: literature
monasteries: athos
world's smallest: nauru

REPUDIATE: *refuse, *repel

REPUESTO: codillio, *defeat

REPUGNANCE: disgust, *hate

REPUGNANT: *bad, *evil, *ugly

REPULSE: *beat, *refuse, *repel

REPULSIVE: *bad, *evil, *ugly

REPUTABLE: *fine, *good

---

* Asterisk means to look up this word to find more answer words.

REPUTATION, REPUTE: *glory,
*image, *name, *note, *report
REQUEST: *ask, *desire, *order
REQUIN: maneater, shark
REQUIRE: *ask, *force, *need
REQUIRED, REQUISITE: de
rigueur, *fine, *good
REQUITE: *pay, *punish, *reward
RESCIND: cancel, *repeal, veto
RESCRIPT: *answer, *order
RESCUE: *free, *release, *save
RESEARCH: *study, *test
rocket: aerobee
RESEDA: green, mignonette
RESEMBLANCE: *accord, *im-
age, *picture
RESENT: *anger, *complain,
*fight, *hate
RESERVE: *engage, *save, *set
RESERVED: *cool, *shy
RESERVOIR: *store, *supply
RESIDE *abide, *live, *stop
RESIDUE: *dregs, *refuse, *rest
RESIGN: *abandon, *quit, *yield
RESILIENCE: *force, give,
*power
RESIN: alk, amber(gris), amyrin,
anime, arar, aroiera, asphalt,
balsam, benjamin, benzoin, bitumen, brea, butea, cachibou, camphor, colophony, conima, copaiba, copaline, dammar, elemi,
eserin, euphorbium, exudate,
frankincense, galipot, garnet,
guacin, gum, gutta percha, hera-
bol, incense, jalap, japan, kauri,
kava, kawa, kino, labdanum,
lacquer, mastic, megilp, myrrh,
pitch, sagapenum, sandarac,
shellac, sonora, storax, tar, varnish
RESIST: *defeat, *fight, *refuse
RESISTANCE: unit: begohm, ohm
RESISTOR: current: rheostat
RESOLUTE: *bold, *fast, *firm,
*hard, *obstinate, *true
RESOLUTION: *power, *plan,

*purpose, *spirit, *will
RESOLVE: *settle, *think, *will
RESONANT: mellow, *rich, vi-
brant
RESORT: *meeting, *retreat, *use
RESOURCE: *asset, *money,
*power, *supply, *value
RESPECT: *honor, *prize, *value
act of: bow, devoir, salaam
RESPECTABLE: *good, *honest
RESPECTING: *about, anent
RESPECTIVE: *separate, several
RESPIRATION: anapnea, breath
RESPIRE: breathe, inhale, *live
RESPITE: *break, *rest, *stop
RESPLENDENT: *bright
RESPOND, RESPONSE: *accept,
*accord, *answer, rsvp, *sense
unit: reflex
RESPONSIBILITY: onus, *trust
RESPONSIVE: elastic, obedient
REST: abide, anchor, base, be still,
bivouac, break, cease, couch,
death, depend, *ease, excess, gaffle, holiday, *idle, inactivity, lean,
lie, linger, lodging, loll, lounge,
pause, perch, *place, *quiet, recline, *refuse, relax, rely, repose,
respite, seat, *set, *settle, shelter,
siesta, silence, sleep, *slow, slum-
ber, sprawl, *stand, stillness,
*stop, *support, *surfeit, take it
easy, tranquility, vacation
harrow: cammock, weed
musket: croc, gaffle
reading: caesura
RESTAURANT: automat, bean-
ery, bistro, brasserie, buffet,
cabaret, cafe, chophouse,
deli(catessen), diner, eatery,
estaminet, grill, inn, lunch room,
night club, onearm, pub, piz-
zeria, *tavern, wineshop
RESTITUTION: *return
RESTIVE: *afraid, *obstinate
RESTORE: *remedy, *return,
*save

* Asterisk means to look up this word to find more answer words.

RESTRAIN: *arrest, *stop, *tie
RESTRAINT: *force, *law, *order
RESTRICT: *arrest, *limit, *stop
RESULT: accrue, *act(ion), conclusion, *decision, *effect, *end, fare, *follow, *issue, pan out, *product, *prove, score, sum, total, *turn, *work, *yield
suff.: ade, ado
RESUME: *abstract, *return
RESURRECTION: anastasimon, anodos, ascension, revival
RESUSCITATE: *rally, revive
RET: rot, soak, sop, steep
RETABLE: altar, predella, shelf
RETAIL: hawk, *trade, vend
RETAILER: *agent, broker, dealer
RETAIN: hold, *save, stet
RETAINER: *income, *servant
RETALIATE: requite, *punish
RETARD: *arrest, *slow, *stop
RETARDATION: down's syndrome, mongolism
RETARDED: *simple, *stupid
RETCH: gag, heave, spew, vomit
RETE: network, plexus, web
RETICENT: *cool, *quiet
RETICLE: *bag, etui, *pack
RETINACULUM: frenum, funicle
RETINUE: *staff, *train
RETIRE: *dismiss, *quit, *settle
RETIRED: emeritus, gone, *quiet
RETIRING: *gentle, *quiet, *shy
RETORT: alembic, *answer, rise
RETRACT: *abandon, *draw, pull
RETREAT: abri, adytum, ala, alcove, anacleticum, anchorage, ancona, apse, apsidiole, arbor, *asylum, back up, blench, blink, bower, bugout, burrow, castle, cave, cop out, corner, crawfish, crawl, cringe, crypt, den, depart(ure), dodge, draw back, duck, *escape, fall back, flinch, give ground, go back, hang back, haven, hermitage, hideaway, hideout, isolation, ivory tower,

jib, lair, mew, move back, nest, niche, nook, port, privacy, pull back, quail, *quit, recede, recess, respite, *rest, *return, *run, sanctum, seclusion, shelter, shrink, *shy, solitude, spa, *stop, *studio, swerve, *turn (tail), wince, withdraw, *yield
RETRENCH: *reduce, *save
RETRIBUTION: *return, *reward
goddess: ara, ate
law: karma
RETRIEVE: find, *rally, *remedy, *repair, restore, revive, *save
RETROGRADE: *decline, *retreat
RETURN: *answer, backtrack, *bring (back), compensate, *fee, *give (back), homecoming, *income, indemnity, interchange, make amends, pay, put back, reaction, reappear, recommit, recompense, recur, reddition, reelect, reentry, refund, regress, remand, remit, render, rendition, repay, reply, requite, respond, restore, retort, *retreat, revert, *reward, *send (back), setback, *take, vote, wind, *yield
home date: deros
REUBEN: son: carmi, enoch, hanoch, hezron, pallu
REUEL: son: mizzah, nahath, shammah, zerah
REUMAH: offspring: gaham, maachah, tebah, thahash
REVEAL: *advise, *display, *open, *present, *show, *tell
REVEILLE: bugle, dian, levet
REVEL: *joy, *play, *riot, *tear
REVELATION: apocalypse, *opening
REVELRY: cry: evoe
REVENANT: *demon, *spirit
REVENGE: *retaliate, *return
goddess: nemesis
REVENUE: *produce, *return
source: amani, apanage, capital

* Asterisk means to look up this word to find more answer words.

REVERBERATE: *repeat
REVERE(NCE): *admire, *bless,
  *honor, *love, *prize, *worship
REVEREND: *church: man
REVERENT: awful, *devout
REVERIE: dream, vision, *wonder
REVERSAL: comb.: all(o)
REVERSE: *catastrophe, *defeat,
  *opposite, *repeal, *upset
  pref.: ant(i)
REVERSION: atavish, *return
  cells: anaplasia, anaplasis
  to primitive: cataplasia
REVERT: *return, *turn
R E V I E W : *advise, *analyze,
  *comment, *criticize, *repeat
REVILE: *abuse, *rally, *rebuke
REVISE: *adapt, *amend, edit
REVIVAL: renaissance, service
REVIVE: *rally, *restore
REVOKE: *repeal, rescind
REVOLT, REVOLUTION: *agi-
  tate, *break, *riot, *turn, *upset
REVOLUTIONS: rate, revs, rpm
REVOLVE: *agitate, *think, *turn
REVOLVER: *gun, pistol, rod
R E W A R D : *accolade, *badge,
  *bonus, bounty, cup, *fee, guer-
  don, *honor, *income, oscar,
  *praise, *present, *prize, rec-
  ognize, recompense, *return,
  *token, utu, *yield
RHAMNUS: bearberry, bog birch,
  buckthorn, cascara, chittam
  wood, coffeeberry, dogwood
RHAPHONTIC: knapweed, pieplant, rhubarb
RHAPSODY: *paradise, song
RHEA: avustruz, bird, emeu,
  nandu, *ops, ostrich, satellite
RHEASILVIA: son: remus, romulus
RHESUS: macaque, monkey
RHETORIC: diction, eloquence
  digression: ecbole
  diminution: litotes
  plus grammar and logic: trivia

RHETORICAL: florid, ornate
RHIANNON: consort: pwyll
RHINAL: narial, nasal
RHINO: money, rhinoceros
RHINOCEROS: abada, abath,
  baluchitherium, borele, cerato-
  rhine, diceros, keitloa, nasicorn,
  reem, topan, umhofo
  beetle: uang
  bird: beefeater
  cousin: tapir
  hide: insensitivity
RHIPIDION: flabellum
RHIPSALIS: cassytha, woevine
RHIZOID: rootcell
RHIZOME: asarum, corm, root
RHODA: rose
  son: actis
RHODE ISLAND: bent: black
  couch grass, slender foxtail
  flower: violet
  founder: roger williams
  greening: apple
  insurrectionist: dorr
  tree: red maple
RHODES: festival: chelidonia
RHODESIA: city: bulawayo,
  ndola
  people: balokwakwa, bembas, ila
RHODEUS: bitterling, fish
RHODODENDRON: azalea, big-
  leaf laurel, bouquet de flore,
  caractacus, cardinal, minerva,
  rosebay, shrub, snow
  root: briarroot, brierroot
RHOMB: circle, diamond, lozenge
RHONCHUS: rale, snoring
RHUBARB: *argument, *error,
  *fight, pieplant, yawweed
  pert.: rheic
RHUS: cedar, ivy, sumac, vine
RHYME: assonance, *order, poem
RHYTHM: *meter, music, poetry
RIALTO: bridge, exchange, mart
RIANT: *bright, *happy
RIB: *banter, *joke, *support
  pert.: costal, costate

* Asterisk means to look up this word to find more answer words.

RIBALD: *dirty, *low, vulgar
RIBBON: *braid, *ornament
  binding: lisere
  bush: centipede plant
  comb.: tene
  fish: bandfish, cutlass, dealfish, guapena, oarfish
  grass: bride's-laces, dodder
  gum: eucalypt(us)
  inscribed: banderol(e)
  -like: cestood, taeniate
  tree: akaroa, houhere, lacebark
  worm: nemertine
  wort: cat's-cradle, plantain
RIBES: cassis, currant
RICE: arroz, bigas, boro, canin, chit, darac, macan, padi, paga
  beer: apong
  bird: bobolink, bunting, gallinule, sparrow
  crop: aghanee
  disease: blast
  dish: risotto, pilaf, pilau
  drink: bubud, pangasi, sake
  field: paddy, padi
  -fish dish: riasi goring
  glucose: ame
  grass: barit, broomroot
  husk: palay, shood, shud
  inferior: aga, chits
  land of: denjong, sikkim
  milk: gruel, porridge, pudding
  polishings: darac
  rail: sora
  refuse: shoo, shud(e)
  uncooked: bigas
  weevil: calandra
  wild: reed
RICH: *able, abundant, affluent, ample, canch, colorful, comfortable, copious, costly, dear, expensive, fancy, *fat, fecund, fertile, flush, *funny, generous, *great, *hearty, in, independent, loaded, lush, luxurious, melodious, moneyed, nourishing, oofy, optime, opulent, ornate, pecuni-ous, plentiful, plush, powerful, productive, prosperous, resonant, savory, *set, spicy, sumptuous, superb, tinny, valuable, wealthy
RICHARD: humpty dumpty
  horse: roan barbary, white surrey
RICHELIEU: *successor:* mazarin
RICHES: bundle, *fortune, wealth
  demon of: mammon
  discovery or region: el dorado
  worship of: plutomania
RICHTHOFEN: *squad:* jagdstaffel
RICK: *noise, *quantity, stack
RICKETY: *crazy, *weak
RICOCHET: bounce, carom
RID: *destroy, *free, *remove
RIDDLE: *pierce, *problem, *puzzle, shoot, sift
RIDE: *rally, *run, *speed
RIDGE: arete, arris, asar, back, balk, bar, bargh, bilo, brow, bulge, bult, butt(e), carina, catoctin, chine, comb, crest, crown, cuesta, elevation, eskar, fret, gyri, hause, hill, hogback, kame, loma, mountain, oesar, parma, peak, piend, plume, prominence, rand, *range, raphe, rib, rideau, ruga, serac, spur, *top, tor, yardang, zastrugi
  furrow-splitting: porcate
  growth: apodema, apodeme
  mark: wale, whelk
  oak: blackjack
  pert.: carina
  runner: frontiersman
  shell: pilae, varices
  stubble: mane
RIDICULE: *rally, *taunt
  god: momus
  object: laughingstock
RIDICULOUS: *absurd, *funny
RIDING: chevachie, equitation
  habit: jodhpurs, levis, pants
  school: academy, manege
  shoe: solleret
  whip: crop, quirt

* Asterisk means to look up this word to find more answer words.

RIFE: *plenty, *universal
RIFF: berber, diaphragm
RIFFRAFF: *dregs, mob, *rabble
RIFLE: *gun, *steal, strip
 accessory: bayonet, ramrod
 ball: minie
 breech loader: snider
 kind: enfield, garand, mauser, remington, springfield, winchester
 magazine: mauser
 man: bersagliere, jager, marksman, shot, sniper, yager
 pin: tige
 range: change
RIFT: *break, *opening, *tear
RIG: *dress, *prepare, unicorn
RIGA: balsam
 island: oesel, saare
 native: latvian, lett
RIGGING: gear, ropes, spar
RIGHT: according to hoyle, *accurate, adroit, *amend, *appropriate, appurtenance, *authority, avenge, balanced, clockwise, conservative, conventional, *correct, decent, decorous, demand, deserved, dexter, dextral, droit, emend, entitlement, equity, even, exact, expedient, fitting, gee, *good, *great, *interest, just, kosher, lawful, legal, legitimate, licit, merited, ok, okay, okeh, orthodox, pat, *perfect, perquisite, pertinent, *power, precise, pretension, privilege, proper, reactionary, recto, redress, relevant, *remedy, *service, *settle, sound, square, starboard, *straight, *strict, suitable, tory, *true, truth, *use, warrant, yes
 angle: vertical
 angle, 100th: grad
 angled: orthogonal, perpendicular, rectangular
RIGID: *firm, *hard, *set, *solid
RIGMAROLE: *nonsense

RIGOLETTO ROLE: ceprano, gilda, marullo
RIGOR: asperity, cold, *violence
RILE: *agitate, *anger, *dirty
RIM: *edge, *limit, orle
 horseshoe: web
 shield: orle
 wheel: felloe, felly, tire
RIMA: breadfruit, *opening
RIME: crack, freeze, ice, poem
 giant: ymer, ymir
 book: edda
RIMMON: son: baanah, rechab
RINALDO: steed: bajardo, bayard
RIND: *cover, *shell, *skin
 comb.: lepo
RING: circle, *group, *set
 bracelet: bangle
 carrier: best man, go-between
 color: areola, areole
 comb.: cycl, gyro
 dance: carol
 finger: annulary, jink
 game: quoit(s)
 gauge: moot
 gem setting: bezel, chaton
 hooped: gemel, gimmal
 in: arrive, *start, *substitute
 lamp flame: cric
 -leader: instigator, sparkplug
 -let: curl, lock, tress
 little: annulet, circlet
 moon: agatharchides, bode, bond
 nautical: grommet
 -necked duck: blackie, bunty
 nitrogen, pert.: azycyclic
 off: *end, silence
 ornament: bee, bracelet, leglet
 out: depart, go, leave
 ouzel: amsel, thrush
 packing: lute
 part: arc, chaton
 pert.: annular, armillary, circinate, circular
 plover: sandy
 reins: terret, territ
 seal: signet

* Asterisk means to look up this word to find more answer words.

sun: bishop's ring

-tail: bassarisk, cacomistle, cacomixle, lemur, raccoon

wedding: band

worm: annelid, barber's-itch, millipede, serpigo, tinea

worm bush: acapulco, cassia

RINGER: *sharp, *substitute

RINSE: absterge, clean, wash

RIO: coffee, *waterway

de Janeiro native: carioca

de Janeiro slums: favelas

RIOT: *agitate, broil, clem, commotion, debauche, disorder, dissipation, disturb(ance), eruption, *fight, *hit, hubbub, mutiny, *noise, pogrom, raid, revelry, revolt, row, shindig, spree, *tear, turbulence, upheaval, *upset

RIOTOUS: profligate, *wild

RIP: *open, *part, *split, *tear

RIPA: beach, coast, shore

RIPE: *fit, *ready, *rifle

RIPEN: *grow, *perfect, *prepare

RIPOSTE: *answer, quip, reply

RIPPING: fine, *great, *splendid

iron: ravehook

RIPPLE: eagre, splash, wave

RISE: ascend, *raise, *source, *start, *succeed, *tower

RISIBLE: *absurd, *funny, merry

RISK: invest, *venture

RISQUE: obscene, racy, spicy

RIT: *pierce, *split, *tear

RITE: abdest, accolade, *action, *affair, agape, augury, baptism, bora, ceremony, cult, custom, exequy, *form, funeral, hako, initiation, litany, liturgy, *magic, novena, obsequy, ordinance, orgy, pax, prayer, procedure, ritual, sacra(ment), *service, *spell, *way, *worship

evil-preventing: apotropaism

last: extreme unction

meat-inspection: bedikah

personified: brihaspati

RITTER: cavalier, knight

RIVAL: enemy, *fight, *oppose

comb.: ant(i)

RIVE(N): *split, *tear

RIVER: *plenty, *waterway

arm: estuary, tributary

bank: levee, bank, ripa, ripe

bed: bottom, channel, wadi

bed, dry: arroyo, canada

birch: betula, nigra, blue birch

boat: ark, barge, baulea(h), cabin boat, flatboat, house boat, rowboat, shallop

bottom: *river: bed

branch: billabong, tributary

changed into: acis, alpheius

channel: alveus, *river: bed

dam: weir

deity: achelous, alpheus, asopus, axius, belisama, cayster, eridanus, inachus, selinus, simois

dog: hellbender

dragon: croc(odile)

father of: mississippi

forgetfulness: lethe

gauge: nilometer

-head: *source

horse: giant, hippo(potamus)

inlet: bayou, slough, slew

king of: amazon

kubla khan: alph

lake formed by: oxbow

land: carse, flat(s)

living in: amphibian, rheophile

lochinvar's: esk(e)

log run: sluiceway

mouth: beal, boca, delta, estuary, lade

obstruction: gorce, snag

passage: bridge, ford, estuary

pert.: amnic, fluminous, fluvial, potamic, riparian, riverine

pool: cathole

sacred: ganga, ganges

side: bank, shore

small: brook, creek, rivulet, stream(let), tchai

* Asterisk means to look up this word to find more answer words.

sorrow: acheron
thief: ackman
valley: strath
weed: podostemace
winding: ess
woe: acheron
RIVET: *bolt, fasten, fix, *tie
RIVIERE: necklace
RIVOSE: channel, winding
RIXATRIX: *scold, virago
RIZPAH: *kin:* aiah, saul
RIZZOM: *bit, *part, straw
ROACH: azurine, brush, bug, coiffure, cut, fish, hill, rock, roll, soil, stone
ROAD: agger, alley, approach, artery, autobahn, avenue, beallach, belt, boulevard, career, cash, causeway, concourse, *course, court, dike, drag, drang, drive(way), drun, embankment, estrada, expressway, freeway, highway, iter, lane, main drag, main street, parkway, *pass, path, pike, place, *route, slab, speedway, street, tao, tarmac, thoroughfare, thruway, trail, turnpike, vennel, via, *way
agent: footpad, *thief
bend: hairpin, ess
block: barrier
book: atlas, gazetteer, itinerary, map
cul-de-sac: impasse
edge: berm, shoulder
goose: brant
gypsy: drun
hog: egotist, motorist
house: inn, saloon, tavern
maker: bulldozer, caterpillar, grader, harl, paver
man: drummer, salesman
military: agger
monkey: blue jay
paving: asphalt, tar(mac)
runner: cock, cuckoo, paisano
surface: bricks, concrete, gravel, macadam, pavement, sand, stones, tar
test: experiment, *try
weed: plantain
ROADSTER: auto, car, horse, runabout, vehicle
ROAM: *err, *range, *run, *walk
ROAN: bay, horse, sheepskin
antelope: bastard gemsbok
ROANOKE: *money
bell: cowslip
ROAR: *cry, *laugh, *noise, scream, shout, *storm, thunder
ROARING: boisterous, *great
ROAST: *attack, *cook, *rebuke
prepare: truss
stick: skewer, spit
ROB: *spoil, *steal, *strip
roy: canoe
ROBALO: centropomus, serranida
ROBBER: *hoodlum, pirate, *thief
fly: asilid, brachycera
frog: barking frog, texas frog
ROBBERY: heist, larceny, theft
ROBE: *cover, *dress, purple
ankle-length: smyrna, talar
baggy: bakkhu
bishop's: chimer
camelhair: aba
light: camis, camus
woman's: cymar, kimono, simar
ROBIN: bird, chewink, *clown, miro, *peasant, thrush
goodfellow: *dwarf, *spirit
ROBIN HOOD: *outlaw, *thief
admirer: richard coeur de lion
betrayer: prioress of kirklees
chaplain: friar tuck
foe: sheriff of nottingham
follower: friar tuck, john, tinker, will scarlet, will stutely
friend: allan-a-dale
love: marian
milieu: sherwood forest
right-hand man: little john
victim: guy of gisbourne

* Asterisk means to look up this word to find more answer words.

ROBINSON CRUSOE: *author:* defoe
 boy: xury
 companion: friday
ROBOT: android, automaton, golem
 blitz: bombardment
 bomb: v-bomb, vone, vtwe
 play: rur
ROBUST: hard, *solid, *strong
ROC: bird, simurg(h)
ROCCA: *fort, *jail
ROCK: *oscillate, *ridge, *stone, *trap, *yield
 aggregate: auge
 arrangement: bedding
 -away: carriage
 badger: cony
 basin: bullan
 bass: red eye
 beds, pert.: stratal
 bell: columbine, flower
 bird: murre, sandpiper
 boring tool: trepan
 bottom: base, cheapest, lowest
 bound: rugged
 brake: bird's-foot fern
 broken: attle, sand
 cavity: geode, voog, vugg, vugh
 clay: ganister, slate
 comb.: ite, peto, petro, yte
 composite: capel
 concretions: oolite
 -covered area: brule(e)
 crab: cancer
 cresses: aralies
 crystal: bohemian ruby, rose quartz, silica
 debris: attle, detritus, talus
 decay: clay, geest, gossan, laterite, saprolite
 dove: guillemot, rock pigeon
 eel: gunnel
 exploding: bulling
 falcon: merlin
 fever: brucellosis
 fine-grained: clay, sand, trap

fish: bass, bocaccio, killifish, perch, priestfish, rasher, reina, rena, sebastode, tambor
fissile: shale
flint-like: chert, quartz
fragmental: breccia, psephite
garden: alpine garden
geranium: alumroot
glacial: erratic, moraine
goat: ibex
grains: mica, sand
granitoid: diorite, dunite, gneiss, quartz
grouse: ptarmigan
gunnel: butterfish, cephalop, ephipus, kelpfish, poronotus
hard: chatoyant, chert, flint, granite, quartz, whin
hind: cabra mora, grouper
hopper: penguin
igneous: agglomerate, basalt, bill, boss, chrysolite, dacite, diabase, diorite, domite, extaxite, felsite, flint, granite, ijolite, ijussite, latite, peridot, porphyry, quartz, sial, sima, taachite, trap, trass, tufa
igneous, pert.: athrogenic
jasmine: androsace
jutting: arete, *ridge, tor
kangaroo: wallaby
laminated: gneiss, mica, shale, shaul, slate
ledge: sipe
-like: *hard, *solid
liquid, melted: aa, lava, magma
mass: aiguille, batholite, batholith, mountain, peak
melon: cantaloupe, muskmelon
melting process: anatexis
mica-bearing: dolomite
mythical: scylla
nodule: geode
oak: chestnut, chinquapin
organic: bioherm, biolite
pert.: petrean, petric, saxatile
phonolitic: apachite

* **Asterisk means to look up this word to find more answer words.**

pinnacle: needle, scar
plant: lichen, moss
point: crag, *ridge*, *top*, tor
porous: tufa, tuff
rose: cistus, hibertia
salt: amole, emol
schistose: epidosite
science: petrology
siliceous: sial
snake: krait, phthon, python
splitting: mica, schist
starling: ouzel
stratum: anticline, lenticle, syncline
tar: petroleum
tripe: lichen
trout: bodieron, boregat, greenling, hexagrammose
volcanic: lava, *rock: igneous*
warbler: cataract bird
weed: alga, black wrack, fucus, fungus, lichen, moss
whiting: fish, odax
wren: bird, turco
ROCKET: *astronaut*, *missile*, signal, *space*
bomb: bumblebomb, buzzbomb, doodlebug, robomb, robot bomb, vergeltungswaffe
combustion end: burnout
drag reducer: boattail
flight: bouquet
*fuel: *rocket: propellant*
glider: sailplane
kind: aam, asm, ata, atgr, atom, aum, bazooka, demolition, flare, gapa, gtar, gtgr, harpoon, hvar, icbm, irbm, loon, ram, retro, sam, smoke, snake, solid-fuel, ssm, stsr, supersonic, xaam, xasm
landing: reentry, splashdown
launcher: bazooka, calliope, firing table, hedgehog, mark 10, meilewagon, projector
launching: airburst, blast-off, brennschluss, flight, guided control, programming, propulsion, shoot, shot

names, american: able, abm, aerobee, aerojet, agena, asm, asp, asroc, astor, atlas, bold orion, bomarc, bullpup, cajun, centaur, corporal, corvus, crossbow, dart, davy crockett, deacon, delta, dingdong, dove, falcon, firebee, fobs, galosh, genie, golem, hawk, holy moses, honest john, hound dog, icbm, irbm, juno, jupiter, komet, lacrosse, lark, little john, lobber, loki, looh, mace, matador, mauler, minnie mouse, minuteman, mirv, nativ, navaho, nike, pershing, petrel, pofo, polaris, quail, ram, rascal, redeye, redstone, regulus, sabmis, safeguard, saturn, scout, sentinel, sergeant, shillelagh, side winder, skybolt, slam, snark, spaerobee, sparrow, spartan, sprint, talog, tartar, terrier, thor, tiny tim, titan, ulm, viking, wagtain, zuni
names, russian: belyayev, bikovsky, blackie, breezie, feoktistov, gagarin, galosh, komarov, kubasov, laika, leonov, nikolayev, popovitch, shatalov, shohin, soyuz, sputnik, talinn, terechkova, titov, yegorov
personnel hqrs.: blockhouse
pioneer: goddard, von braun
propellant: ballistite, bromine, pentafluoride
propulsion: backflash, blast, charge, exhaust, jet blast, reaction, retrorocket, thrust
upper stage: agena
vapor loss: boil-off
world war II: buzzbomb, v-bomb
ROCKY: *hard*, *obstinate*, *sick*, *solid*, unsteady, *weak*
ford: cantaloupe, muskmelon
ROCKY MOUNTAIN: *fern:* athyrium
fever: rickettsia
fir: alpine fir, balsam spruce

* Asterisk means to look up this word to find more answer words.

goat: antelope, mazame
herb: anemone, aster, saxifrage, bronze bell, stenanthella
park: estes, yellowstone
plant: goldenrod, solidago
range: absaroka, big belt, big horn, bitterroot, sangre de cristo, teton, uinta, wasatch
raspberry: boulder raspberry
sedge: alpine sedge, carex
sheep: bighorn
tree: alpine hemlock, tsuga
ROCOA: annato, annatto
ROCOCCO: *bizarre, *extreme
ROD: *beat, *gun, *staff, *stick
bundle: fasces
divining: dowsing, rhabdomancy
hundred square: acre
lead: came
-like: rhabdo, rigid, virgate
man: *hoodlum
movable: piston
official: scepter, sceptre
pert.: baculine
-shaped: bacillary, baculiform
16½ feet: perch, pole
square: perch
whip: ferule, gad, plet
RODENT: agouti, beaver, biting, capibara, cavy, cony, coypu, degu, dormouse, gopher, guinea pig, gundie, hamster, hutis, jerboa, kangaroo, lerot, mouse, mus(krat), porcupine, squirrel
pert.: rosorial
RODEO: roundup, *show
horse: buckjumper
RODGE: gadwall
RODOMONTADE: bombast, *brag
ROE: caviar, eggs, spurgeon
-buck: chevreuil, girl
-buck group: bevy
deer: capreolus
-stone: oolite
ROENTGEN RAYS: x-rays
ROGATION: *law, prayer, rosewort

ROGUE: *criminal, *demon
pert.: picaresque, *sly, wanton
ROI SOLEIL: louis xiv
ROIL: *agitate, *anger, *stir
ROISIN DUBH: *ireland
ROISTER: *brag, *play, swagger
ROLAND: author: turoldus
avenger: thierry
beloved: belle aude
foe: ferragus, gan(o), ganelon
friend: oliver
horse: veillantif
stepfather: ganelon
sword: durandel
ROLE: *bit, *part, *piece
ROLL: list, *move, *oscillate, *press, *record, *turn
back: *defeat, *retreat
onion-flavored: bialy
up: *accumulate, *gather
ROLLER: caster, pin, wave, wheel
coaster: daidarasaurus
ROLLICK: *brag, frolic, *play
ROLLS ROYCE: silver cloud
ROLY-POLY: *fat, *heavy
ROMAINE: cos, lettuce, plant
ROMAN: antiqua, brave, distinguished, frugal, honest, italian, latin, noble, papal, severe, simple, stern
amphitheatre: colosseum
amphitheatre seat: sella
apartment: decus
apostle: neri, paul, scholar
arch abutment: alette
arena: amphitheatre flavium
army troops: alares
army unit: century, cohort, curia, legion, maniple
assembly: centuriata, comitia, curiata, forum, tributa
attendant: aleiptes, aliptes
augur: auspex
author: accius, caesar, cato, catullus, cicero, cinna, gaius, horace, juvenal, livy, lucan, nepos, ovid, plautus, pliny, propertius, sallust,

---

* Asterisk means to look up this word to find more answer words.

seneca, silius, suetonius, tacitus, terence, tibullus, varro, vergil, virgil

awning: velarium

baggage cart: carrus

banner: labarum

barracks: canaba, cannaba

basilica: lateran

baths: balneae, thermae

battle array: acies

biographer: *roman: author

bishop: pope

book cover: diptych

booth: taberna

bowl: patina

box: capsa

boxing glove: ceston, cestus

boy: camillus, puer

bronze: aes

brooch: fibula

building: aedes, insula

calendar: ephemeris, kalends

camp: castrum

cap: pileus

cape: byrrus, sagum

captain: centurion

carriage: *roman: chariot

cart: birota

cathedral: lateran, vatican

catholic: calotin

cavalry: turm(a)

chariot: biga, essed(a)

chest: cist

childbirth guardian: carmenta, postverta, prorsa

children goddess: adeona

church: basilica, lateran

circus bit: carcer, meta, spina

cistern: impluvium

citadel: arx

citizen: aerarian, casca

clan: gens, gentes

class, lowest: aerian

cohort insigne: dragon

coin: aes, as(ses), aureus, decussis, denarius, dinder, semis, sesterce, sextans, solidus, victoriatus

collar: rabat

colosseum signal: jugula, mitte

comedy: exode

command post: praetorium

concert hall: odeum

conqueror: alaric, gaiseric

conspirator: catiline

consul: cinna, marius, scipio

contract: nexum

couch: accubitum

court: atria, curia, tribunal

cup: acetabulum

custom: ritus

dagger: sica

dance: carioca, samba

date: calends, ides, nones

dead, abode: orcus

dead, spirits: lemures, manes

dictator: caesar, sulla

dictionarist: ambrogio calepino

dining room: oecus

dish: lanx, patera, patina

divination: sors

diviner: augur, auspex

division: century, curia

doctor: aesculapius, archiater

earth goddess: ceres, terra

earthwork: agger

emperor: aemilianus, alexander severus, antoninus pius, augustus, aurelian, balbinus, caligula, caracalla, carinus, carus, claudius, commodus, constans, constantine, constantius, decius, didius, diocletian, domitian, elagabalus, eugenius, florianus, galba, galerius gallienus, gallus, geta, glycerius, gordian, gratian, hadrian, honorius, hostilianus, jovian, julianus, julius, libius, licinius, lucius verus, macrinus, magnentius, magnus maximus, majorian, marcus aurelius, maxentius, maximian, maximinus, nepos, nero, nerva, numerianus, olybrius, otho, pertinax, petronius, philip the arab, probus,

* **Asterisk means to look up this word to find more answer words.**

pupienus, romulus augustus, septimius severus, theodosius, tiberius, titus, trajan, valens, valentinian, valerian, vespasian, vitellius, volusanius

emperor, eastern: arcadius, justinian, leo, marcian, theodosius

emperor's physician: archiater

empress: athenais, eudocia, theodora

enemy: alaric, attila, carthage, hannibal, huns

epicure: apicius

family: annibaldi, cenci, frangipani, orsini, savelli

farmer: agricola, colonus

fate: ananke, decuma, morta, nona, parca(e)

faunus priest: lupercus

festival: agonium, ambarvalia, feria, fordicidia, lemuralia

fighter: gladiator

flask: alabastrum

fortress: castrum

founder: remus, romulus

galley: bireme, trireme, unirem

gambling cube: talus, tessera

game: ludi, munus sine missione, prolusio(nes), venatio(nes)

garland: corona

garment: abolla, alicula, paenula, palla, paludament, planeta, sagum, stola, toga, trabea, tunic

general: agricola, agrippa, antony, belisarius, caesar, marius, scipio, sulla

geographer: mela

ghost: lemure, mane, retiarius

giant: caca

girdle: balteus, cestus

gladiator types: andabatae, dimachaeri, essedarii, laquerii, mymillon, retiarii, samnite, secutores, velites

goal post: meta

god: adranus, aesculapius, amor, auster, bonus eventus, boreas, comus, cronus, deus, dis(pater), eurus, faun(us), janus, jove, jupiter, lares, lemures, mamers, mars, mercury, morpheus, mors, neptune, orcus, penates, phoebus, pluto, quirinus, sylvanus, vatican, vulcan

goddess: abeona, abundantia, adeona, adrastea, aestas, angerona, anna perenna, annona, astraea, aurora, bellona, bona dea, caca, cardea, ceres, decuma, diana, discordia, epona, felicitas, fides, flora, fortuna, juno, libitina, lua, lucina, luna, maia, nona, nox, nyx, ops, parca, pax, pronuba, proserpina, rumina, salacia, salus, selena, spes, suada, terra, urania, venus, vesta

governor: legatus, proconsul, procurator

guards: usipetes

hail: ave

harvest festival: opalia

hat: galea, petasos, petasus

healer: fabiola, marcella, paul

helmet: galea

hero: horatius

highway: appian, iter, via

hill: aventine, caelian, capitoline, esquiline, palatine, quirinal, saturnian, viminal

historian: procopius, tacitus

horn: buccina

incense jar: acerra

javelin: aclys, pile, pilum

king: ancus martius, nemi, numa pompilius, romulus, servius, tarquinius superbus, tullius, tullus hostilius

king's advisor: egeria

last: aetius

law: cern, fas, lex

legion, part: *roman: army unit

legion insigne: eagle, spqr

legionnaire: manipular

list: albe

---

* Asterisk means to look up this word to find more answer words.

litter: lectica
magistrate: aedile, archon, censor, consul, edile, lictor, praetor, pretor, tribune
market: emporium, forum
meal: cena, cibus, farina, prandium
measure: acetabulum, actus, amphora, asses, bes, centuria, clima, congius, cotyle, cubit, culeus, cyanthus, decempeda, deunx, digitus, dodrans, dolium, duella, gradus, hemina, heredium, juger, leuga, libra, ligula, millarium, modius, palmipes, palmus, passus, pertica, pes, pollex, quadrant, quartarius, rasta, saltus, scrupulus, semis, sexis, sextans, sextarius, sextula, sicilium, solidus, stadion, stadium, triens, uncia, urn(a), versus
military insigne: phalera
military machine: tenebra
military sandal: caliga
military unit: *roman: army unit
money chest: brasier, brazier
month: aprilis, augustus, december, februarius, januarius, junius, maius, martius, november, october, quintilis, sextilis
naturalist: pliny
nymph: egeria
official: *roman: magistrate
orator: cato, cicero
ornament: bulla, patera
palace: chigi, lateran
palladium: ancile
patriot: cato, cincinnatus
pavement: asarotum
peace: irene, pax
peak: arx, tarpeian rock
people: etruscans, laeti, patricians, plebeians, sabines
pert.: classical
philosopher: cato, seneca
plain: campagna
platter: lanx, patera

pledge: vas
poet: *roman: author
port: ostia
post: meta
priest: epulo, flamen, lupercus
priest, pert.: arval
priestess: vestal
procurator: felix, pilate
rite: orgy, sacra
river: po, tevere, tiber
road: agger, iter, itinera
room: ala, atrium, fumarium, tablinium
sabine gate-opener: tarpeia
scroll: stemma
seat: sella
senate and people: spqr
senate emblem: laticlave
serf: colona, servus
shield: ancile, clypeus, parma, pelta, scutum, testudo
show place: circus
shrine: sacrarium
slave: androcles
soldier: cataphract, hastatus
standard: labarum, vexillum
standard-bearer: vexillary
street: corso, platea, via
sword: ensis, falx, gladius
symbol: fasces
tablet: album
tax: annona
tax gatherer: publican
temple: cella, naos, pantheon
tenement: insula
tent: praetorium
theatre: odeum
ticket: tessera
treasurer: quaestor
treasury: aerarium
underworld: orcus
vessel: alabastrum, amphora, capanna, lanx, murrine, patera
veteran: emeritus
vintner: ausonius
virgin warrior: camilla
war flags: labara

* Asterisk means to look up this word to find more answer words.

weight: *roman: measure*
writer: macer
writing tablet: diptych
ROMANCE: *affair, court, *love,
 *story, *tell, woo
language: catalan, french, italian,
 latin, portuguese, provencal, rumanian, spanish
ROMANOV: *last:* anastasia
ROMANY: gipsy, gypsy, nomad
ROMEO AND JULIET: *role:*
 capulet, mab, montague, paris,
 tybalt
ROMP: *play, sport, tomboy
ROMULUS: *remus
ROOF: *cover, *home, *top
 comb.: stego
 kind: chopper, cricket, cupola,
 dak, flat, gable, gambrel, hip,
 jerkinhead, mansard, nave, pyramidal, sark, spire
 material: copper, gravel, pantile,
 shake, shingle, slate, terne,
 thatch, tile
 part: cleat, comb, eave, epi, fillet,
 joist, purlin, ridge, strut, truss,
 vallew
ROOK: castle, raven, *steal
ROOM: *place, *play, *range
 comb.: atrio
ROOMY: *big, *large, *plenty
ROORBACK: *gossip, *lie
ROOT: *set(tle), *spur, *start
 -cap: calyptra, calyptrogen
 comb.: radicic, rhiz(a), rhizo
 edible: beet, carrot, cassava, eddo,
 ginger, oca, orris, parsnip, potato, radish, roi, rue, rutabaga,
 sassafras, tania, taro, turnip, yam
 fragrant: orris
 medicinal: jalap, poke, senega
 pert.: radical
 pungent: ginger, taproot, taro
ROOTER: *enthusiast, fan
ROPE: cigar, lassoo, riata, *tie
 fiber: abaca, caroa, coir, cotton,
 feru, flax, hemp, imbe, istle, ixtle,

jute, manila, rhea, sisal
 loop: becket, bight, noose
 ship's: bobstay, bowline, brail,
 bridle, buntline, colt, fast, fox,
 gasket, halyard, hawser, lanyard, lift, line, marline, painter,
 parrel, ratlin(e), sennit, sheet,
 shroud, snotter, span, stay, tack,
 tye, vang, wapp
ROSE: *apple:* pomarosa
 climbing: baltimore belle
 comb.: rhodo
 disease: brown canker
 fish: bergylt, bream, cunner
 fruit: cat hip, hip
 gal: bedegar, bedeguar
 honey: rhodomel
 kind: althaea, crocus, saffron
 madder: casino pink
 oil: atar, attar, ottar, otto
 parakeet: rosella
 pogonia: snakemouth
 quartz: bohemian ruby
 sharon: aaron's-beard, althaea,
 hollyhock, marshmallow
 state: iowa, new york
 temple: cereamium, red algae
 window: catherine wheel
ROSSOM: *creation:* robot
ROSTER: *agenda, list, *schedule
ROT: *refuse, *spoil, waste
ROTATE: *beat, *circle, *turn
ROTTEN: ampery, *bad, can-
 kered, carrion, decayed, decomposed, *dirty, *evil, gangrenous,
 peccant, punk, putrescent, putrid, *rank, soiled, spoiled, ulcer-
 ated, *wrong
 comb.: sapr, sapro
 -stone: tripoli
ROTTER: *cad, *fellow, *hoodlum
ROTUND: *big, *fat, *large
ROUGH: *abuse, *hard, *violent
 -neck: *boor, *cad, *peasant
ROULETTE: *term:* bas, carre,
 dernier, enplein, impair, manque,

---

* Asterisk means to look up this word to find more answer words.

milieu, noir, pair, passe, rouge, tourneur

ROUND: *circle, *range, *sphere
clam: bullnose, quahog
lot: board lot, hundred shares
out: *complete, fulfill
table: *king arthur knights
the bend: *insane, *mad
-up: *gather, *meeting, *show
-up, last: death
worm: ascaris, nematode

ROUNDED: comb.: gyro

ROUSE: *start, *stir

ROUT: *beat, *defeat, *rabble

ROUTE: beat, circuit, itinerary, journey, *pass(age), *road, round, *run, *send, tack, trip, *walk, *waterway, *way
direct: beeline

ROUTINE: *bit, *rule, *run, *use

ROVE: *part, *range, wander
beetles: brachelytra

ROW: *fight, file, oar, *way

ROWDY: *hoodlum, *rough(neck)

ROYAL: *good, *noble, *splendid
pert.: aulic

ROYALTY: *fee, *income, nobility

RUB: *crisis, *shine, *smooth
out: *end, *kill, obliterate

RUBBER: caoutchouc, caucho, ceara, ebonite, elastic, eraser, ficus, galosh, guayule, gum, latex, masseur, para, shoe
crude: burucha
tree: castillo, seringa, ule

RUBBISH: *nonsense, *refuse

RUBE: boor, *clown, *peasant

RUBRIC: *head, *law, red, *title
book: ordines, ordo

RUCK(LE): *group, pile, *rabble

RUCTION: *fight, *noise, uproar

RUDDER: bushing: pintle
control: helm, tiller
edge: bearding
fish: black pilot, chopa
gudgeon: brace

part: yoke
post: stern

RUDE: *brutal, *rough, *wild

RUDIMENT: *source, *start

RUFFIAN: *clown, *hoodlum

RUFFLE: *provoke, swagger
neck: jabot, ruche

RUG: carpet, *cover, *wrap

RUGBY: term: fives, heeling, knockon, mark, maul, noside, pitch, scrum, tackle, touch

RUGGED: *rude, *sour, *strong

RUIN: ballywack, bane, blight, *break, bust, butch, calamity, *catastrophe, collapse, decay, *defeat, *destroy, doom, *fail, *fall, fate, havoc, *hurt, injury, loss, *memorial, rend, perdition, seduce, *spoil, subvert, tumble, wrack, wreck

RULE: *adage, belief, *control, convention, criterion, *decide, *doctrine, domineer, *form, formula, habit, *law, *lead, measure, *model, norm, *order, *power, practice, procedure, routine, *run, *system, *way
pert.: rutic
suff.: archy

RULER: aga, alder, ameer, archon, *authority, bey, cacique, caliph, chancellor, chief, dalai lama, *despot, dey, doge, emir, emperor, eparch, fuhrer, gerent, grand vizier, hierarch, hospodor, induna, kaid, king, *magnate, mikado, monarch, nawab, negus, nizam, padishah, pendragon, pharaoh, premiere, president, prime minister, prince, regent, queen, sachem, satrap, shah, sheik(h), sherif, shogun, sultan, *title, tsar
three, one of: triarch, triumvae
two, one of: duarch
wife: czarina, empress, ranee

RUM: *bad, *eccentric, *good, *great, liquor, *poor

* Asterisk means to look up this word to find more answer words.

RUMANIAN: *city:* aiud, arad, bacau, brasso, bucharest, clw, deva, galat, iasi, jassy, lasi, ploesti, sighet, torda, turnu
coin: as, ban, leu, ley, triens, uncia
composer: enesco
conservative: boyar
folk song: doina
hero: dracula
king: carol, dracul, michael
king's consort: magda, marie
mountain: negoi
oppressor: phanariot
river: aluta, arges, jiu
title: domn

RUMEN: belly, gullet, paunch

RUMOR: *gossip, *noise, *report, scuttlebutt, *story, *talk
personified: fama

RUN: *accelerate, *average, bleed, bolt, bound, branch, brash, break, brook, burst, canter, career, *control, course, dash, direct, dog trot, elope, endure, *escape, *get, go, guide, hie, hotfoot, hurry, journey, *lead, length, lope, nominate, operate, *order, pilot, point, propel, race, reach, *route, scamper, score, scour, scurry, *speed, sprint, spurt, *start, step, *tear, trip, voyage, *waterway, *work
away: *escape, overwhelming
down: *fail, find, *sick
in: *arrest, *fight, *quarrel
into: cost, *meet
out: *end, *issue, weary
over, through: *pierce, *repeat
-way: *road, *strip, trail

RUNT: *dwarf, *small, wrig

RUPTURE: *break, *split, *tear

RUSE: artifice, *trick, wile

RUSH: *attack, *press, *run
basket: frail
light: candle
load: barth, gavel
nut: chufa

toad: natterjack

RUSSELL'S: *viper:* katuka

RUSSIAN: barbarian, byzantine, muscovite, *siberian, soviet
anarchist: bakunin
antelope: saiga
apple: astrachan
aristocrat: boyar, kneeze
assembly: duma, rada, zemstvo
auto: zis
barrow: kurgan
basso: kipnis
boat: ballatoon
braid: soutache
cabinet member: commissar
calf: cappagh, caroubier
cap: aska
carriage: araba, arba, drosky, kibitka, tarantas(s), telega, troika
cathedral: sobor
caviar: ikary, ikra
chess man: alekhine, botvinnik
citadel: kremlin
clover: orel
coal area: donbas, donets
coin: abassi, altin(inck), auksinas, bisti, chervonets, deneshka, denga, grivna, grosh, imperial, kopeck, ley, piatak, poltina, poluska, ruble, shaur
commune: kokhos, kolhoz, mir
composer: arensky, borodin, cui, glinka, moussorgsky, prokofiev, rimsky-korsakov, stravinsky, tschaikovsky
coop: amtorg, arcos, artel, centrosoyus
cossack: tartar, tatar
council: duma, rada, soviet
country house: dacha
dance: cosaque, gopak, hopak, kolo, kozachok, trepak, ziganka
decree: ukase
delicacy: caviar(e)
desert: steppe, tundra
devil: chort

* **Asterisk means to look up this word to find more answer words.**

district: karelia, steppe
dog: alan, borzoi, owtchah, psovie, samoyed(e), wolfhound
dress: sarafan
drink: kvass, quas(s), slivovitz, vodka
drinking cup: bratina
edict: ukase
endearment term: kiska, kroshka
exclamation: nichevo, nitchevo
farm: sovkhos(e), sovkhoz
farmer: kulak
fiddle: gudok
fighters: migs, sukhois
fish: beluga, sterlet, sturgeon
flax: bobbin
fleet: escadra
folksong: bylina
food: black bread, borsch, caviar, pelmeni, pirozhki, sturgeon, za-kuski
forest: taiga, tundra, urman
founder: ivan
fox: corsac, karagan
general: bagramyan, buddyonny, chuikov, de tolly, golikov, mos-kalenko, rokossovsky, suvorov, timoshenko, tukhashchevski, vasilevsky, vatunin, voronov, voroshilov, yepishev, yeremenko, zhukov
government group: comintern, duma, kommandatura, politburo, presidium, rada, soviet, tsik
grandmother: babushka
guild: *russian: coop
gulf: azov, mezen
hemp: konopel, rine
hero: igor, ivan, lenin, nevski, stalin
hippie: bichi
hood: bashlik, bashlyk
horse: tarpan
house: barabara, dacha, isba
image: icon, ikon(o)
imperial order: ukase
instrument: balalaika, gusle

kerchief: analav
lagoon: liman
lake: aral, azov, baikal, balkash, byelo, elton, ilmen, lacha, neva, onega, seg, topo, vigo, vozhe
landlord: khozyain
leader: brezhnev, grishin, gro-myko, khrushchev, kosygin, kulakov, kunayev, kuznetzov, lenin, malenkov, malik, mazurov, molotov, podgorny, poliansky, shcherbakov, shcherbitsky, she-lepin, sobolov, stalin, suslov, tsarapkin, vishinsky, voronov, zorin
leather: bulgar, jufti, yuft
liberation: osvobozhdeniye
measure: arshin, botchka, bou-tylka, charka, chetvert, chkalik, duim(e), fass, foute, fut, gar-netz, korec, kroushka, ligne, liniya, loof, osmina, pajak, pa-letz, polugarnetz, pood, quar, sagene, stekar, stoff, stoof, tchast, tsarkl, vedro, verchok, verst
missile: *rocket: names, russia
monk: rasputin, starets
mountains: alai, altai, ural
name: akim, igor, ivan, olga, peter, sonya
naval academy: frunze
negative: nyet
news agency: tass
newspaper: izvestia, pravda
novelist: *russian: writer
people: byelorussian, cossack, ersar, lett, muscovite, slav
peninsula: crimea, gydanskiy, kamchatka, karelia, kola, yamal
plain: steppe(s), tundra
poet: *russian: writer
police: cheka, kgb, nkvd, ogpu
police chief: beria, shelepin
port: anapa, archangel, eisk, kronshtadt, odessa, okha, sevas-topol, vladivostok
prince: knais, knez, knyaz

* Asterisk means to look up this word to find more answer words.

prison: sremska mitrovica
propaganda: agitprop
radical: bolshevik
rickets: rachitis
rodent: miniver, zokor
ruler: ivan, peter, rollo
saint: olga
sect: bezpopovets
shelter: etape, isba
sleigh: piatnitza
slop pail: parasha
soup: borsch, bortsch, shchee
space leader: tsiolkovsky
symbol: bear, hammer and sickle
synod: sobor
tavern: caback, kabak
tax: obrok
tea urn: samovar
teacher: starets
tent: kibitka
thank you: spaseba
title: beriya, boyar(d),
  czar(evitch), czarina, tsar(evitch),
  tsaritza
travel service: intourist
vessel: bratina, samovar
village: mir
violinist: elman
whip: knout, plet(e)
worker: dvornik, stakhanovite
writer: aleksandr, annenski,
  asegev, bagritski, balmont, bely,
  blok, bunin, chekhov, dostoev-
  sky, gorki, jehuda, pasternak,
  sergyeevich, sholokhov, solzhe-
  nitsyn, tolstoi, voznesensky, yev-
  tushenko
 youth group: comsomol, kom-
  somol
RUST: **eat,* inertia, verdigris
RUSTEM: *kin:* rudabah, sohrab,
  zal
RUSTIC: **agricultural,* **boor,*
  *peasant, **plain,* swain, yokel
RUSTLE: **flow,* **steal,* **stir*
RUTH: *son:* obed
 mother-in-law: naomi

 spouse: boaz, booz, mahlon
RUTHLESS: **brutal,* merciless
RUTILATE: glitter, glow, **shine*
RUY DIAZ DE BIVAR: cid
RYE: gentleman, whiskey
 beard: awn
 fungus: ergot, rust
RYOT: **peasant,* **servant,* **slave*
RYTINA: hydrodamalis

SABER: scimitar, **sword*
SABLE: *antelope:* black buck
 fish: beshow, black cod, candlefish, cod, eulachon
SABOTAGE: **destroy,* **end*
SAC: *comb.:* asco
 fungus: blood cup, peziza
SACCARAPPA: westbrook, maine
SACCHARINE: **sweet*
 derivative: agavose, maltwort
SACHEM: boss, **magnate,* **ruler*
SACK: **destroy,* **dismiss,* **steal*
 -but: trombone
 -cloth and ashes: penance
 fiber: burlap, gunny, jute
 palm-leaf: bayon
SACRAMENT: baptism, com-
  munion, confirmation, covenant,
  eucharist, extreme unction, mass,
  matrimony, penance, **rite,*
  *service, **symbol*
SACRARIUM: **memorial,* shrine
SACRED: awesome, awful, cher-
  ished, dedicated, **holy,* ineffable,
  *perfect, **pure,* religious, re-
  vered, sacrosanct, sainted, un-
  utterable, venerable
 beetle: ateuchus, scarab
 comb.: hagio, hiero
SACRIFICE: **give,* **rite,* **yield*
 god: agni
 men of: fedayeen
 offering: hiera, sphagion
 thousand: chilicomb
SACRILEGIOUS: **bad,* **evil*

---

* Asterisk means to look up this word to find more answer words.

SACRISTY: *pert.:* vestral
SACROSANCT: *sacred*
SAD: *bad*, desolate, despondent, dire, disconsolate, dismal, distressing, doleful, dolorous, *dull*, *evil*, *heavy*, longfaced, *low*, lugubrious, painful, paltry, rare, scanty, somber, *sorry*, terrible, triste, unhappy, unlucky, wan
  comb.: tragi
SADDLE: *back:* hill, *ridge*
  bag: alforja, jagg, pannier
  boot: gambado
  corn crusher: quern
  horse: bidet, palfrey, remuda
  light: pilch, pillion
  pad: apishamore, blanket, corona, shabrack, tilpah
  part: arson, bolster, cantle, cinch, croup, crutch, girth, horn, latigo, lorimer, pad, pommel, stirrup, strap, sudadero, tore
SADDLER: cozier, lorimer
SAFE: *firm*, *secure*, *sure*
  conduct: escort, *pass*
  cracker: *hoodlum*, *thief*
  -guard: *pass*, *save*, shield
SAFETY: *asylum*, *retreat*
  pin: clasp, fibula
SAFFRON: crocus, kusum, thistle
SAG: *bend*, *settle*, *yield*
SAGA: edda, poem, *story*, tale
SAGACIOUS: *sage*, *smart*, *wise*
SAGE: *abstruse*, *acute*, argute, authority, canny, discerning, farsighted, gnostic, herb, intellect, keen, knowing, learned, longhead, master, mentor, oracle, owlish, profound, *prophet*, pundit, sane, sapient, savant, *sharp*, shrewd, *smart*, solomon, solon, *wise*, witan, witty
  brush: absinthe, artemesia
  brush state: nevada
  cheese: cheddar
  chelsea, of: thomas carlyle
  cock: grouse

  concord: ralph waldo emerson
  drama: oater, western
  ferney: voltaire
  genus: salvia
  greek: *greek:* sage
  hen: grouse, nevadan
  monticello: thomas jefferson
  pylos: nestor
  seven: *greek:* sages, seven
SAGO: palm, starch, tree
SAHARA: *part:* erg, hamada, samen
  people: arab, nomad, tuareg
  wind: leste
SAIGON: *airbase:* bienhoa
SAIL: coast, glide, travel
  boat: *boat:* sail
  cloth: canvas, duck
  fish: aguja, bannerfish, bill gar, boohoo, istiophorus, needlefish, saury, spearfish
  kind: balloon, crossjack, fore, jib, lateen, lug, main, mizzen, royal, sky, spanker, spinnaker, square, stay, studding, topgallant, try
  part: bunt, clew, earring, leach, luff, sheet, yardarm
  yard: spar, rae
SAILOR: *navy:* man, tar(pot)
SAILOR'S: *amusement:* scrimshaw
  blessing: oath
  call: ahoy, aye
  chapel: bethel
  choice: pigfish, pinfish, porgy
  furlough: leave
  goddess: brizo
  group: crew, hands
  jacket: reefer
  potion: grog
  protector: mother carey
  quarters: fo'c's'le
  saint: brendan, elmo
  song: barcarole, chantey
SAINT: *andrew's cross:* saltire
  anthony's cross: ankh, tace, tau
  barnabas' prayer: ave maria
  basil monk: caloyer

* Asterisk means to look up this word to find more answer words.

catalog: diptych
catherine's home: siena
comb.: hagi
elmo's fire: castor, corposant
francis's birthplace: assisi
george's saved: sabra
george's sword: ascalon, askelon
john's bread: algaroba, carob
john's wort: amber, androseme, ascyrum, broom brush, cammock
kitts capital: basse-terre
louis blues composer: handy
martin's bird: harrier
paul's architect: wren
peter's wreath: francoa ramosa
philip's birthplace: neri
relic chapel: feretory
vitus dance: chorea
worship: hagiolatry, hierolatry
SAKE: **end, *interest, *purpose*
SALACIOUS: **bad, *dirty, *evil*
SALADIN: ayubite, ayyubid
SALAMANDER: axolotl, hellbender, newt, olm, **spirit,* urodela
SALARY: **fee, *income,* pay
SALE: **bargain, *trade,* turnover
SALEP: eulopia, orchid
SALESMAN: **agent,* hawk, peddler
SALES TAX: alcabala
SALICYLIC ACID: aspirin
SALIENT: **important, *open*
SALISBURY: *steak:* hamburger
SALISHAN: bella coola
SALLOW: pale, saugh, willow
SALLY: **attack, *issue, *start*
in our alley composer: carey
lunn: teacake
SALMAGUNDI: **hash, *mixture*
SALMON: ayu, barramunda, blue back, botcher, brandling, burnet, gib, gilling, keta, lox, lungfish, masu, nerka, quinnat, saumont, weakfish
color: anatto, annatto, arnatto
female: baggit, hen

son: boaz
young: alevin, botcher, grilse, parr, smolt
SALOME: *husband:* zebedee
mother: herodias
sons: james, john
stepfather: herod antipas
victim: john the baptist
SALON: **affair, *party,* room
SALOON: alehouse, bar, beer garden, bistro, blind pig, brasserie, buvette, cabaret, cantina, cocktail lounge, dive, dramshop, gin mill, groggery, honky-tonk, jerry shop, joint, mughouse, parlor, pothouse, pub, rathskeller, rumshop, speakeasy, taproom, tavern
SALT: cure, **money,* nacl, **save,* **sense,* tar, taste, **top,* wit
bush: acacia, bluebush, wattle
comb.: hali, halo, sali
container: cellar, sea, shaker
grass: alkali
knowledge of: halology
-like: halid(e), haloid, saline
-making solution: bittern
marsh: lick, salina
names of, suff.: ate
of the earth: **acme, *best*
of wisdom: alembroth
-peter: anatron, natron, nitre
relish: achar
rock: halite, pig
tax: gabelle
tree: atle(e), tamarisk
water: brack, brine, sea
works pond: sump
wort: barilla, glasswort, kali
SALTY: **funny, *sharp,* spicy
SALUBRIOUS, SALUTARY: **healthy*
SALUTE: **hello, *title, *toast*
SALVAGE: **fee, *redeem, *save*
SALVATION: bodai, **rescue*
army founder: general booth
attaining by self: autosoteric
pert.: soterial, soterical

---

* Asterisk means to look up this word to find more answer words.

SALVE: *money, *quiet, *remedy
SALVO: fusillade, salute, volley
SAMARIA: aholah, aholibah
SAMARITAN: god: tartak
 people: assyrian, israelite
SAMBO: *hash, *mixture
SAME: *equal, even, similar
 comb.: aut, equi, homo, iso, tauto
SAMOAN: *malayan, polynesian
 bird: iao, lulu, lupe, manuao
 cloth: para, tapa
 council: aumaga, fono
 dance: siva
 fish: ataata, sesele
 island: manua, savaii, tutuila,
  upolu
 maiden: taupo
 mollusk: asi
 mudworm: ipo
 spirit: atua
 warrior: toa
SAMPLE: *part, *piece, *test
SAMSON: nimrod, orion
 betrayer: delilah
 city: zorah
 father: manoah
 spring: enhakkore
SAMUEL: ancestor: zuph
 child: abiah, joel
 home: ramah
 parent: elkanah, hannah
 teacher: eli
 victim: agag, agog
SAMURAI CODE: bushido
 straying: ronin
SANCHO PANZA: home: bara-
  taria
 master: don quixote
 mule: dapple
 wife: teresa
SANCTIFY: *anoint, *bless
SANCTIMONIOUS: *false, *holy
SANCTION: *allow, *let, *support
SANCTUARY, SANCTUM: *re-
  treat
 inner: penetralia
SAND: gravel, *smooth, *spirit

and clay: loam
application: arenation
-bag: *attack, *deceive, *hit
-bagger: bandit, *thief
-bank or bar: beach, hurst, reef,
  shoal, spit
bath treatment: ammotherapy
-blast: clean, depaint, grind
boil: blowout
-box: assacu, hura, regma, tree
-bur: beaked nightshade, weed
cherry: butter plum, prunus
cock: redshank
comb.: amm(o)
drift: esker
dune: areg, barchan, barkan,
  dene, medano, towan
eel: grig, hornel, launce
fine: ammochryse
fish: beaked salmon
flea: amphipod, chigger, chigoe
flounder: fluke, windowpane
george, heroine: helen, lelia
gravel: dobbin, gard
grouse: attagen, ganga
hill: *sand: dune
hog: digger
hole: bunker
lob: lugworm
-loving: ammophilus
martin: bank swallow
mineral: iserine
paper: finish, grind, *shine
particles: grains, silt
partridge: seesee
pear: pyrus
pert.: *sandy
-piper: bird, brownie, chorook,
  dunlin, fiddler, haybird, knot,
  krieker, peetweet, pume, redshank, reeve, ruff, stib, stint, tattler, terek, tiltup
pit: bunker, point
rat: gopher
shark: blue dog, dogfish
smelt: atherine, silversides
snake: eryx

* Asterisk means to look up this word to find more answer words.

spurry: tissa
-stone: arkose, articulite, blue vitriol, chestnut, grit, itacolumite, kermanshah, medina, red yellow, sarsen
-stone, ohio: berea grit
-stone, pert.: arenilitic
-storm: haboob, samum, simoom
sucker: niter
tableland: karoo
trap: bunker, mound, obstacle
verbena: abronia
widgeon: gadwall
worts: arenaria
SANDAL: alpargata, buskin, caliga, charuk, clog, espadrille, flipflop, go ahead, moccasin, romeo, rullion, *shoe,* slipper, talaria, zori
-wood: algum, almug, bucida, camwood, chandana, maire
SANDARAC: *powder:* pounce
resin: tears
sanskrit: sindura
tree: alerce, arar, callitris, morocco, realgar
SANDWICH: club, hero, hoagie, interpose, submarine, torpedo
hero: poor boy
islands: hawaii, kanaka
islands finder: captain cook
SANDY: arenaceous, arenose, eremic, gritty, plucky, tocky
SANE: *good, *right, *wise
SANGAR: *fort
SANGFROID: *composure, *cool
SANGUINE: bloody, optimistic
SANHEDRIN: assembly, court
chief: nasi
SANITY: *reason, *sense
SANKHYA PHILOSOPHY: akasa, guna
elements: ether, sky, space
SANSKRIT: *india references
SANTA CLAUS: kris(s) kringle
reindeer: blitzen, comet, cupid, dancer, dasher, donder, prancer, vixen

SANTON: *church: man
SAP: *blood, drain, elan vitale, empty, enervate, entrenchment, escavate, essence, fluid, *fool, juice, lymph, mine, *ruin, sapor, seve, sparkle, substance, trench, undermine, vitality, weaken
-wood: alburnum, blea
SAPID: savory, tasty, zestful
SAPIENT: *sage, *smart, *wise
SAPODILLA: achras, balata, chico
SAPPHIRA: *husband:* ananias
SAPPHO: *consort:* bilitis, phaon
home: lesbos
SAPPY: juicy, moist, *silly
SARACEN: arab, *mohammedan
comfrey: ragwort
corn: buckwheat
knight: rogero, ruggiero
leader: saladin
SARAH: *husband:* abraham, abram
maid: hagar
son: isaac
SARAWAK: *rajah:* sir james brooke
tribe: bakatan
SARCASM: *attack, *banter
SARCASTIC: *acerb, *sharp
SARCOPHAGUS: *roof:* tegurium
SARDINIA: *coin:* carline
port: alghero, bosa, cagliari
structure: noraghe, nuraghi
wind: bentu de soli
SARDONIC: *sarcastic
SARGON: *capital:* akkad
SARMENTUM: branch, *part
SARPEDON: *companion:* atymnius
SASH: band, belt, obi, *strip
weight: mouse
SASSAFRAS: ague, cayenne, saloop
SATAN: *demon, *devil
SATANGS: *100:* baht
SATANIC: *bad, *evil, vicious
SATCHEL: *bag, etui, *pack(age)

SATE: glut, gorge, *surfeit
SATELLITE: *moon, *rocket
 man-made: alouette, anna, ariel, cosmos, courier, echo, explorer, faith, lunik, mars, mercury-atlas, midas, oso, project-score, ranger, relay, samos, syncom, telstar, tiros, transit, vanguard, vela-hotel, vostok
SATIATE: cloy, *sate, *surfeit
SATIN: damask, etoile, *fabric: silk, pekin
 bower bird: bird of paradise
 bush: podalyria sericea
 -leaf: caimitillo, tree
 -pod: honesty
 sparrow: flycatcher
 weave fabric: camlet(een)
SATIRE: humor, irony, pasquinade
SATISFACTION: *ease, *plenty
SATISFACTORY: *fine, *good
SATISFY: *acquit, *answer, *meet
SATRAP: *despot, *ruler, *sachem
SATURATE: *penetrate, *surfeit
SATURN: cronus, iapetus, planet
 moon: dione, enceladus, hyperion, japetus, mimas, rhea, tethys, titan
 rings: ansa, moonlets
 spirit: casziel
 temple treasury: aerarium
 wife: ops
SATURNALIA: orgy, *party
SATURNINE: *dull, *heavy, *sullen
SATYAGRAHA: gandhism, non-violence
SATYR: butterfly, *demon, faun
 parent: hermes, iphthima
SAUCE: insolence, *money, sass
 kind: alec, anchovy, bechamel, bercy, bordelaise, catchup, chawdron, espagnole, gansel, garum, genevoise, hollandaise, ketchup, lear, mayonnaise, mustard, nicoise, remoulade, soubise, tartar, tobasco

SAUCER: flying: ufo
 -shaped: acetabuliform
SAUCY: *fresh, *sharp, *smart
SAUL: consort: ahinoam, rizpah
 daughter: merab, michal
 death place: gilboa
 descendant: azan
 father: hillel, kish
 general: abner
 grandfather: abiel, ner
 herdsman: doeg
 sight-restorer: ananias
 son: abinadab, eshbaal, ishui, jonathan, malchishua
 uncle: ner
 victim: achimelech, ahimelech
SAUNTER: lag, *range, *walk
SAUREL: pompano, scad, xurel
SAURY: gar, sailfish, spearfish
SAUSAGE: andouille, balloon, baloney, bologna, bratwurst, cervelat, drisheen, frankfurter, liverwurst, rollejee, salami, sassinger, saveloy, wiener
 casing: bung
 comb.: allant(o)
 poison: allantiasis, botulism
 -shaped: allantoid, botuliform
SAVAGE: *brutal, *violent, *wild
 comb.: agrio
SAVANNA: *plain
SAVANT: *sage
SAVE: *accumulate, bar, but, deliver, economize, exclude, *free, have, hold, husband, keep, preserve, prevent, protect, recover, rescue, reserve, retrench, salvage, scrape, scrimp, skimp, spare, stint, stockpile, *store, tin
SAVINE: cedar, juniper, tree
SAVOIR-FAIRE: *address, *skill
SAVOR: *scent, tang, taste, zest
SAVORY: *good, piquant, *rich
SAVVY: *sense, *skill
SAW: *adage, *gossip, tool
 -belly: alewife
 -bones: doctor, surgeon

* Asterisk means to look up this word to find more answer words.

-buck: ten dollars, tenspot
circular: burr, buzzsaw, edger
comb.: serri
crosscut: briar
cutoff: butt saw
cylindrical: crown
-dust: coom, *dregs, scobs
-fish: batoides, ray, sier
groove: kerf
horse: buck, mack, trestle
part: redan, serra, tine, tooth
surgical: trepan, trephine
SAXIFRAGE: astilbe, badan, bauera, breakstone, burnet, pearl wort, plant, seseli
SAXON: sassenach
chief: horsa
coin: sceat
king: alfred, harold, horsa, ina, ine, otto
lady: godiva, rowena
serf: esne
swineherd: gurth
SAY: *repeat, *state, *talk
SAYING: *adage
SCAB: *agnostic, mange, *rascal
SCABBARD: para, pilcher, sheath
-fish: hiku, para
trimming: chape
SCABBY: *bad, *low, *mean
SCABIOUS: bundweed, knapweed
SCAD: cigar fish, saurel, skate
SCADS: *plenty, *quantity
SCAFFOLD: *cage, gallows, giffet
SCALAWAG: *imp, *rogue
SCALD: *excite, poet
SCALE: climb, *part, *piece, *range, *reduce, slough, soar
beetle: tiger
comb.: lepo
fern: ceterach
fish: ganoid
insect: bark louse, coccid
moss: hepatica
note: *note: music
SCALLOP: crena, notch, pink
SCALY: laminar, *low, *mean

SCAMANDAR: son: teucer
SCAMP: *scalawag, *thief
SCAMPER: *escape, *run, *speed
SCAN: *look, *pass, *see, touch
SCANDAL: *affair, *shame
-monger: gossip, meddler, tattle
SCANDALOUS: *bad, *evil, *low
SCANDINAVIAN: dane, finn, geat, lapp, *norse, swede, viking
gods: *aesir, *norse references
SCANSORES: toucans, trogons
SCANT: *limit, *little, *small
comb.: oligo
SCAPEGOAT: azazel, *substitute
SCAPEGRACE: *scalawag
SCAR: *hurt, *mark, *wild
-like: cicatricial, uloid
tissue: uloid
SCARAB: beetle, *fetish
SCARAMOUCH: *clown, *fool
SCARE: *alarm, awe, boof, bree, *crisis, intimidate, *start(le)
-crow: *bugaboo, *ogre, terror
SCARF: bandanna, sash, *tie
bird: cormorant, shag
-skin: cuticle, epidermis
SCARLETT O'HARA: home: tara
husband: rhett butler
SCARP: *bit, *fort, *part, slope
SCARY: eerie, spooky, *weird
SCAT: scoot, scram, vamoose
SCATHE: *attack, *blast, *hurt
SCATHING: *acerb, *severe
SCATTER: *defeat, *dispense, *separate, *sparkle, *spread
-brain: *clown, *fool
SCATULA: *box, *package
SCAUP: blackhead, cannonball
SCENARIO: outline, *play, script
SCENE: *display, *place, *show
SCENT: *air, aroma, bouquet, breath, clew, clue, emanation, essence, fetor, flair, flavor, fragrance, get wind of, hint, hypnone, incense, inhale, inkling, intimation, nidor, nose, odor, perfume, redolence, savor, *sign, smell, sniff, spoor, stench, trail

* Asterisk means to look up this word to find more answer words.

SCEPTRE: mace, *staff, *symbol
SCHEDULE: *action, *agenda, *book, *order, *plan, program, *set, *sign, *time
SCHEME: *plan, *plot, *system
SCHISM: *breach, sect, *split
SCHIST: mica, slate, *stone
SCHIZO: split personality
SCHIZOPHRENIC: *insane
SCHLEMIEL: *fool, loser
SCHMALTZ: corn, *fat, *luck
SCHOLAR: bhat, *sage, *student
SCHOOL: *order, *style, *train
 book: primer, reader, speller
 grounds: campus, quad
 group: nea, pta
 master: ahund, pedagog, pedant
 pert.: academic, pedantic
SCHOONER: *drinking: vessel
 builder: andrew robinson
SCIENCE: art, knowledge, *skill
 dismal: economics
 god: thoth, toth
 group: think-tank
 suff.: ancy, aphy, echny, emy, ery, etry, graphy, ics, ion, ography, ology, omy, onomy, opy, phy, try, ure
SCIENTIFIC: *accurate, *deep
SCIENTIFIC TERM: suff.: alis, anum, anus, aris
SCIENTIST: *authority, *sage
SCIMITAR: saber, *sword
 -shaped: acinaciform
SCINTILLA: *bit, *spark, whit
SCINTILLATE: *shine, *spark(le)
SCION: heir, *imp, son, twig
SCOBS: *dregs, powder, *refuse
SCOFF: *laugh, *scold, *taunt
SCOLD: *abuse, barge, *beat, bullyrag, cample, cant, carp, catamaran, censor, censure, chide, *criticize, faultfinder, frondeur, nag, rail, *rally, rant, *rebuke, shrew, *skin, *talk, *taunt, termagant, virago, vixen
SCONCE: *fine, *fort, *head, hel-met, screen, *top, *trick
SCOOP: *beat, *dig, *dip, *story
SCOPE: *aim, *play, *range, span
SCORCH: burn, *hurt, *ruin, *run
SCORE: *account, *hit, *mark, *reason, run, *strike, *success
SCORIA: *dregs, *refuse, *stone
SCORN: arrogance, bismer, *contempt, contumely, flout, geck, mock, repudiate, scoff, scout, sneer, sneeze at, sniff at, snub, spurn, *taunt
SCORPION: arachnid, catapult, lizard, onager, scourge
 fish: lapon, rosefish
 heart: antares
 stinger: telson
 water: nepa, nepid
SCOT: bluebonnet, caledonian, gael, highlander, jock, pict
SCOTCH: *fee, *hurt, *mark, *stop, thrifty, thwart, whisky
 accent: birr, bur(r)
 addition: eik, eke
 arrange: ettle
 ask: spere
 attendant: gillie, gilly
 attorney: aralie, clusia
 author: *scotch: writer
 awl: elsen
 bank: brae
 beg: sorn
 bird: grouse, hern, kae, muir, snabby, swinepipe, throstle
 bism: gulf
 blessing: *rebuke, scolding
 boat: coracle, scaffy, sexern, skaffie, zulu
 bonfire: tandle
 bound: loup, mear, stend
 brain: harn
 brandy: athole
 bread: bannock, briar, saps, tammie
 brook: sike
 bull: stot
 bushel: fou

cake: bap, farl(e), scone
camp follower: gudget
candidate slate: leet
cap: balmoral, bluebonnet, glengarry, tam (o'shanter), tassel, toorie
cape: wrath
carriage: shandrydan
cascade: force, lin(n)
cattle: angus, ayrshire
celebration: kirn
chack: bite, snack
chair: regal
chalk: cauk
channel: minch
cheese: dunlop
chest: kist
chief: thegn
child: bairn, dalt, gaitt, gett, scuddy, smatchet
church: kirk, kurk
city: aberdeen, alloa, banff, dundee, edinburgh, glasgow, grunock, inverness, kilmarnock, leith, paisley, perth, st andrews, troon
cloak: cleading, plaid
clothe: clead
coin: atchison, baubee, bodle, bonnet, demy, groat, plack
congress: mod
counsel: rede, reed
court: lyon
court officer: macer
cup: tass
curlew: whaup
curlies: kale
dagger: dirk, skean
daisy: gowan
dance: bob, ecossaise, highland fling, reel, strathspey, walloch
dining room: spence
dirge: coronach
dish: choffer, scaff
dog: scottie, sealyham
drapery: pand
drinking bout: screed

duck: bufflehead
dwarf: droich, urf
elm: wych
excuse: sunyie
explorer: rae
extra: orra
fairy: fain, nis
family: ilk
farmer: cotter, crofter
fashion: scotice
festival: mod, uphelya
fiddle: itch
fingering: wool, yarn
fireplace: ingle
firth: clyde, cromarty, forth, kyle, linnhe, loch, lorn, moray, tay
fish: codfish, glashan, sile, sillock, spalding
fish term: drave, yaire, yare
flag: blue saltire
flower: bluebell, harebell
fog: haar
fort: dune, roundabout
game: shinny, shinty
garment: arisard, *cap, fecket, kilt, maud, tartan, toosh
ghost: taisch
girl: cummer, kimmer, lass(ie), quean, towdie, winklot
goldsmith: ged
grandchild: oe, oy, oye
grandfather: gudesire
granite: gowan
gutter: siver
hands: paddling
hawk: allan
heater: choffer
heir: teind
highlander: cateran, gael
hill: brae, snab, strone
icicle: shoggle
infantry: black watch, ladies from hell
inlet: gio
intellect: the admirable crichton
-irish: erse
island: aran, arran, bute, *hebrides, orkney, shetland

* **Asterisk means to look up this word to find more answer words.**

kale: borecole
keen: snell
killing pay: cro
kilt: filibeg
king: carados, robert bruce
kiss: smoorich
knife: whittle
labor, day's: darg
lake: awe, dee, fyne, gair, gare, lin(n), loch, lough, maree, ness, nevis, oich, ryan, sloy
land: carse(s)
landholder: laird, thane, thegn
land tax: cess
land tenure: feu
language: celtic, erse, lalland
leader, elected: abbot of unreason, lord of misrule
liberator: robert bruce
liquor: athole, scour, whittier
lord: laird, thane, thegn
marauder: cateran
marriage portion: dos, dote
measure: auchlet, boll, chalder, choppin, cop, crane, fall, firlot, lippie, lippy, mile, mutchkin, noggin, particate, peck, pint, rood, rope, shaftment, stimpart
mist: drow, ure
money: arles, cro, siller
mount: ben nevis, grampians
mud rake: claut
music: pibroch
musician: piper
music instrument: bagpipe(s)
name prefix: mac, mc
national symbol: thistle
negative: dinna, nae
oak: eik
odd: orra
outlaw: cateran, dhu, rob roy
ox: nowt
pantry: spence
parish: scone
patron saint: andrew
philosopher: bain, caird, hume
pillory: joug(s)

plaid: maud, tartan
poet: *scotch: writer
polaris base: holy loch
pole: caber
porridge: brose
pouch: sporan, sporran
preposition: tae
pudding: haggis
quarter day: beltane
queen: mary
resort: oban
ridge: run
river: afton, annam, ayr, clyde, dee, deveron, don, doon, esk, find, norn, north, spey, teviot, tweed
rope: soam, wanty
sausage: whitehass, whitehawse
scientist: boyd-orr, dewar, ure, watt
scythe handle: snead
seaport: alloa, banff, campbeltown, dundee, largs, leth, leven, oban
sect: berean, buchanite, glas
shawl: maud
shivering: oorie, ourie
soldier: lady from hell
song: strowd
student: bejan, nejant
sword: claymore
tenure: feu, sorehon, sorren
tern: tarret
terrier: cairn
thong: whang
tinker: caird
tithe: teind
title: bailie, laird, reeve, thane, thegn
tobacco: elder
tool: whittle
topaz: cairngorm, tassel
tower: toorock
town hall: tolbooth, tollbooth
tree: camperdown elm, riga
tweed: bannockburn
uncle: eme

* Asterisk means to look up this word to find more answer words.

unit: ane, yin
vessel: cappie, quaich, quaigh, tass
village: bank-bar, rew
warrior: kemp
waterfall: force, lin(n)
water sprite: kelpie, kelpy
weapon: claymore, skean(dhy)
wedding race: broose
weighing machine: trone
weight: boll, bushel, trone
whimbrel: whaup
whine: yirn
whirlpool: swelchie, swilkie
whiskey: athole, glenlivat, glenlivit, usquebauch
whitefish: vendace
wind: the hawk
window: winnock
writer: arbuthnot, barrie, beattie, boswell, buchan, burns, campbell, carlyle, edina, hogg, hume, moir, skene

SCOTER: boatbill, coot, fulica
SCOTLAND: albain(n), albyn, caledonia, ecosse, scotia
SCOTT: *character:* amy, anne, athelstan(e), balmawhapple, black dwarf, bois-guilbert, bradwardine, dhu, ellen, ivanhoe, lochinvar, marmion, norna, rob roy, talisman
SCOUNDREL: *cad, *cheat, *impostor, rogue, *thief
SCOUR: *polish, *range, *run
SCOURGE: *beat, *punish, *whip *of god:* attila
SCOURINGS: *dregs, *refuse
SCOUT: *agent, *look, *rally, ridicule, *scorn, *spy, *taunt
SCOWL: glare, pout, stare
SCRAGGY: *dwarf, *thin
SCRAM: *escape, *get, *quit
SCRAMBLE: *contest, *hurry, *mixture, *push, *spread, *try
SCRAP: *bit, *contest, *end, *fight, *part, *piece, *refuse
SCRAPE: *gather, *hurt, *mess, *order, rub, *save, scratch

SCRAPINGS: *bit, *dregs, *refuse
SCRATCH: *hurt, *mark, *money, rasp, *scrape, *tear, write
SCRAWNY: *poor, *spare, *thin
SCREAM, SCREECH: *cry, wail
SCREED: *bit, *diatribe, *piece
SCREEN: *cover, *hide, *pass, *setting, shield, sift, veil
SCREW: *fee, *open, *turn, wind *ball:* *eccentric, *insane, *mad *pine:* breadfruit, pandanus
SCRIMMAGE: *contest, *fight
SCRIP: *memo, *money, *token
SCRIPT: *book, scenario
SCRIPTURE: adigranth, agama, alcoran, aranyaka, arcana caelestia, atharva-veda, avesta, bhagavad-gita, bhagavata purana, bible, *book, brahmana, cabala, canon, edda, gemara, granth, haggada, halakah, holy writ, koran, masora(h), midrash, mishna(h), purana, rig-veda, sama-veda, shastra, smriti, sruti, talmud, tantra, torah, upanishad, veda
SCRIVE: cut, score, write
SCROFULA: figwort, frostweed, king's-evil, tuberculosis
SCROFULOUS: *bad, *dirty, *evil
SCROLL: *design, *schedule
SCROUGE: crowd, *press, squeeze
SCROUNGE: *search, *steal
SCRUB: *low, *mean, *polish, sub *growth:* bito, brule(e)
SCRUFF: *dregs, *refuse, scum
SCRUM: *party
SCRUNCH: *bite, *eat, gnaw
SCRUPLE: *pause, *principle *half:* obole *three:* dram
SCRUPULOUS: *precise, *true
SCRUTINIZE: *search, *study
SCUD: *run, *speed, *wind
SCUFF: *abrade, *hit, *hurt, *rabble, *riffraff, *scratch

* Asterisk means to look up this word to find more answer words.

SCUFFLE: *contest, *fight, *walk
SCULL: basket, boat, oar
SCULLION: *peasant, *servant
SCULPIN: bighead, bullhead
SCULPTURE: *form, *image, *model
  figure: acrolith
  ornament: bucrane
  paneling: boiserie
  pert.: glyphic, glyptic
  slab: metope
  term: alto relievo, bas-relief
  unit: bust, statue
SCUM: *dregs, *raffle, *refuse
  fish: choke, *hurt, suffocate
SCUPPER: drain, massacre
SCURRILITY: *abuse, billingsgate
SCURRILOUS: *bad, *dirty, *evil
SCURRY: *run, scuttle, *speed
SCURVY: *low, *mean, *sorry
SCUTAGE: fine, penalty, tax
SCUTTLE: *destroy, *run, *speed
SCUTTLEBUTT: *gossip, rumor
SCUTUM: plate, shield
SCYLLA: father: nisus
  lover: minos
  partner: charybdis
SCYTHE: angle, sickle, sye, tool
  handle: snath, snead, thole
  sweep: swath
SCYTHIAN: deity: onga
  lamb: barometz
  people: alan, arimaspian, saka
SEA: anemone: actinia, adamsia, anthozoan, opelet, polyp
  animal: coral, rosmarine
  arm: bay(ou), belt, bight, cove, estuary, fiord, firth, fjord, frith, gulf, gut, inlet, lagoon, loch, lough, mouth, narrow(s), roadstead, sinus, sound, strait(s)
  bass: cabrilla, sandfish
  bat: devilfish
  bath: bain de mer
  bird: albatross, cahow, erne, gull, kestrel, puffin, sula

blite: good king henry, goosefoot, strawberry blite
bottom: bed, deep, depths, jube
bream: baleen, braise
bridge: aphrodite, venus
catfish: ariida
comb.: hali, mari, mer, oceano
cow: dugong, manatee, rytina
cucumber: pedata, trepang
current: rip, tide, undertow
demon: wate
dog: gob, *sailor, tar
duck: coot, eider, scooter
eagle: erne, tern, osprey
ear: abalone, haliotis, snail
eel: conger, lamprey
float: algae, flotsam, jetsam
foam: meerschaum, sepiolite
food: abalone, aquaculture, clam, crab, fish, lobster, oyster, roe, scallop, shrimp
gate: beach, channel
girdles: cuvy
god: aegeus, aegir, chaos, dylan, fontus, hea, hler, ler, neptune, nereus, njord, njorth, nun, oceanus, palaemon, phorcys, poseidon, proteus, triton, varuna
goddess: amphitrite, doris, erue, eurynome, ino, leucothea, nana, nina, ran(a), salacia, siren, thetis
goods sunk at: lagan, ligan
goose: dolphin, phalarope
green: celadon
gull: annet, cob(b), gore, kittiwake, mew
gypsy: bajau, malay, semal laut
high: bounding main
hog: porpoise
holly root: eryngo
horse: hippopotamus, walrus, whitecap
inlet: *sea: arm
island cotton: bolton count, bourbon
king: ler, pirate, viking

* Asterisk means to look up this word to find more answer words.

lavender: american thrift, behn
lemon: doris
lettuce: alga, laver, ulva
life of: halibios
lion-like: otarine
maid: mermaid, nymph, siren
mammal: seal, whale
man: *navy: man
manlike: bristol fashion
mark: beacon, dan, lighthouse, meith, pharos, searchlight
mew: bird, *sea: gull
mile: knot, naut
milkwort: black saltwort
monster: cetus, hydra, kraken
needle: garfish
nettle: acaleph, blubber, jellyfish, medusa
nymph: galatea, *water: nymph
old man of: proteus
onion: squill
organism: nekton, plankton
otter's cabbage: *sea: weed
pen: anthozoan
pert.: aequoreal, bathymetric, dipsy, haliographic, hydrographic, marine, maritime, nautical, oceanic, pelagic, thalassic, vast
plant: *sea: weed
poacher: alligator fish
raven: cormorant, sculpin, squaretail
road: ala moana
robber: buccaneer, corsair, jaeger, pirate, privateer
robin: big-headed gurnard
rocket: beach-sap, cakile
route: lane
salt producer: halogen
shell: clam, conch, snail
shore, pert.: littoral, orarian
sickness: naupathia, nausea
slug: doto, nudibranch
snail: welk, whelk, wilk
snake: kerril
soldier: marine

spider: basket fish
spray: spindrift, spoondrift
squirt: ascidian, salpa, tunicate
star of: isis
starwort: blue camomile
student: thalassographer
swallow: petrel, tern
urchin: arbacia, cassidulina, centrechinoid, diadematoid, echinite, echinoderm
jaws: aristotle's-lantern
wall: boulder head, bulwark, buttress, mole
-ward: asea, makai
weed: agalloch, agar, alaria, alga, alimon, badderlocks, barilla, blind eel, carrageen, cuvy, delisk, desmid, dulse, enalid, fucoid, hempweed, kelp, kobu, laver, limu, nori, oreweed, ory, sargasso, sion, ulva, varec(h), vraic, wrack
worm: annelid, lurg, sao
wrack, dried: alva marina
SEAL: *end, otary, *secure, *settle, *sign, stamp, wafer
jewel: breloque
live: arctocephalus, bedlamer, makluk, otary, phoca, ross's, seecatch, sterrinck, ursuk
pelt: sculp
pert.: phocine
young: beater, bluesides, flipperling, holluschick, hopper, pup, quitter, saddler
SEAM: joint, *mark, raphe, unite
pert.: sutural, suturic
SEANCE: *meeting, spiritualism
SEAR: *arid, *fire, parch, singe
SEARCH: *ask, beat the bushes, burrow, cast, delve, *dig, dowse, examine, explore, ferret, fish, forage, frisk, grope, hunt, investigate, *look, mouse, nose, poke, probe, pry, pursue, quest, ransack, root, rummage, scan, scout, scrutinize, *see(k), sift, smell, survey, watch

* Asterisk means to look up this word to find more answer words.

SEASON: *perfect, *time, *train
  goddess: *horae
SEAT: *establish, *place, *set
SEAWAN: beads, *money
SEB: child: isis, osiris
  consort: nut
  father: shu
SECEDE: *quit, withdraw, *yield
SECLUDE: *hide, *remove, retire,
  screen, *separate
SECLUSION: *retreat, solitude
SECOND: *abet, *after, *period,
  *support, sustain, *time, trice
  comb.: deuter(o)
  best or class: *bad, *poor
  guess: kibbitz, kibitz
  lieutenant: shavetail
  self: alter ego, *friend
  sight: esp, instinct, intuition
  -story man: *hoodlum, *thief
SECRET: *abstruse, blind, cabal,
  cabinet, clandestine, classified,
  close, concealed, confidence,
  covert, furtive, hidden, hushed,
  hush-hush, key, mysterious,
  mystic, *obscure, private, recondite, remote, retired, secluded,
  shrouded, *shy, *sinister, surreptitious
SECRETE: bury, *hide, mask, sink
SECRETION: juice, larp, *sap
SECT: *group, *order, *party
SECTION, SECTOR: *part,
  *piece, *plot, *share, *unit
SECULAR: laic, lay, profane
SECURE: *acquire, airtight, *anchor, *arrest, *assure, *bind,
  bolt, bombproof, brace, button,
  buy, capture, clinch, confident,
  defend, elicit, *fast(en), fetch,
  *firm, fix, foolproof, *gather,
  *get, guarantee, *hold, lash,
  leakproof, make fast, moor, nail,
  pin, preserve, proof, protect, reliable, rivet, rope, safe, *seize,
  *solid, sound(proof), stable,
  *sure, *tie, tight, *win

SECURITY: *promise, *trust
SEDATE: *quiet, serious, still
SEDATIVE: *anesthetic, *remedy
SEDIMENT: *dregs, *refuse
SEDITION: *noise, *riot, treason
SEDUCE: *abuse, *force, *ruin
SEDULOUS: *active, *quick
SEE: behold, bet, call, catch, contemplate, detect, diocese, discern,
  discover, distinguish, envisage,
  envision, espy, *eye, gape, glare,
  glint, ken, know, *look, *meet,
  notice, perceive, recognize, spot,
  *spy, take in, *understand, vide,
  visit, visualize, witness
  -saw: crossruff, *oscillate
SEED: *plant, *source, *start
  apple: pip
  aromatic: anise, nutmeg
  beetle: bean beetle
  cake: wig
  cover: aril(lode), bran, burr, hull,
    husk, peel, shell, shuck, tegimina,
    tegumen, testa
  edible: bean, corn, lentil, nut, oat,
    pea, pinole, rice, sesame, wheat
  having small: acinaceous
  leaf: cotyledon
  mankind: adapa
  pert.: angi(o), arillate, arillary
  plant: endogen
  poisonous: calabar, physostigma
  remove: gin, picul, pit
  tanning: bomah nut
  vessel: boll, bur(r), capsule, car-
    pel, cod, follicle, hip, hull, leg-
    ume, pericarp, pod, shell, silique,
    theca
SEEDY: *old, shabby, *sick
SEEK: *ask, *look, *search, *try
SEEKING: zetetic
SEEL: blind, pitch, roll, *seal
SEEM: *act, *appear, *think
SEEMING: like, *look, *show
SEEMLY: *fair, *meet, *right
SEEP: *drip, ooze, percolate
SEER: oracle, *prophet, *sage

* Asterisk means to look up this word to find more answer words.

SEETHE: *agitate, *anger, *stir
SEGMENT: *bit, *part, *piece
SEGREGATE: divide, *part, sift
SEINE: fare, fish, net, *trap
SEIR: son: anah, dishon, ezar, lotan, shobal, timna, zibeon
SEIZE: *acquire, *affect, *arrest, attach, *bag, beard, *bite, clasp, claw, clench, clutch, collar, confiscate, deprive of, distrain, embargo, embrace, grab, grapple, grasp, grip, hent, *hold, hook, hug, impound, lay hold of, nab, nail, net, prey, procure, ravish, rob, snap at, snatch, *steal, *strike, *take, *trap, usurp, whip up, wrest, yoke
SEKHET: husband: ptah
SELECT: *best, *good, *separate, *supreme, *take, *try
SELECTION: pert.: apolegamic
SELENE: *moon: goddess
child: erse, nemea, pandia
father: helios, hyperion, zeus
lover: endymion, pan, zeus
mother: euryphaessa, theia
SELEUCUS: son: demetrius
SELF: atman, ego, entity
comb.: aut(o)
defense: boxing, judo, jujitsu
pert.: personal
SELL: *bargain, *trade, *trick
SELVAGE: *edge, list, rope, wire
SEMBLANCE: *air, *copy, *image, *look, *picture, *show
SEMELE: father: cadmus
nurse: beroe
sister: ino
SEMELIA: son: ananias, nathan
SEMINOLE: chief: osceola
SEMIRAMIS: consort: ninus
SEMITE: arab, aramaean, assyrian, babylonian, caucasian, *hebrew, jew, moabite, phoenician
god: anath, baal(ath), hadad, moloch, shamash, steraph
goddess: allat, ashtoreth, astarte, atargatis

language: amharic, amorite, arabic, aramic, geez, gheez, ghese, harari, tigre
weight: gerah, mina, shekel
SEMNAE: *furies
SEN: 1/10th: rin
SEND: *address, *affect, air mail, cast, commit, consign, delight, *dismiss, dispatch, drive, eject, expedite, export, fling, forward, freight, *give, *issue, mail, *move, *pass, post, propel, remand, remit, *throw, transmit
-off: parting, *start
up: *arrest, commit, imprison
SENESCENT, SENILE: *old, *weak
SENNACHERIB: general: rabshakeh
kingdom: assyria
sire: shalmaneser
son: adrammelech, esarhaddon, sharezer
SENSATION: *hit, *riot, *success
SENSE: *acumen, appreciate, apprehend, comprehend, ear, esp, experience, feel(ing), flair, *gather, *get, hearing, intuition, knowledge, *meaning, *mind, *perceive, *sapience, sight, smell, sound, taste, touch, *understand, wisdom, wit
SENSIBLE: *sage, *solid, *wise
SENSITIVE: *acute, *ardent, responsive, *sharp, tender
SENSUAL: *brutal, *wanton
SENTENCE: *adage, *decide, rap
analyze: parse
part: adjective, adverb, clause, noun, object, phrase, predicate, subject, verb, word
structure violation: anacoluthon
SENTENTIOUS: *short, *wise
SENTIMENT: *adage, *passion
SENTINEL: guard, patrol, watch
pert.: perdue
SEPAL: calyx, leaf, petal

* Asterisk means to look up this word to find more answer words.

SEPARATE: abscise, alienate, *alone*, *analyze*, assort, *break*, bust up, calve, canton, classify, demobilize, different, *dismiss*, distinct, distinguish, divorce, eliminate, fork, isolate, lone, *open*, *part(icular)*, refine, *remove*, rend, repudiate, respective, retire, secern, *seclude*, segregate, select, side, sift, sort, splice, *split*, sunder, *tear*, withdraw
  comb.: ab(s), di(s), idio
SEPPUKU: hara-kari, suicide
SEPT: *fine*, *group*, *unit*
SEQUEL: aftermath, follow-up
SEQUENCE: *order*, *run*, *set*, *straight*, succession. *train*
SEQUESTER: *seclude*, withdraw
SERAGLIO: *harem*, oda, serai
SERAI: caravansary, *harem*, inn
SERAPH: *angel*, cherub, saint
SERB: *coin:* dinar
  fairy: vila, vily
  measure: ralo
  prince: cral
SERENADE: callithump, charivari, court, nocturne, *song*, woo
SERENE: *cool*, *light*, *quiet*
SERF: *servant*, *slave*, thrall
SERGEANT: *fish:* coal, cobia
SERIAL: *part*, *piece*
SERIATIM: consecutive, neat
SERIES: *sequence*, *set*, *train*
SERINUS: canary, dendroica
SERIOLA amberfish, amberjack
SERIOUS: *deep*, *great*, *heavy*, *important*, *severe*, *stern*
SERMON: discourse, speech, *talk*
SERPENT: *devil*, *monster*, *snake*
  fabulous: basilisk
  goddess: buto
  king: sesha
  myth: ahi, amphisbaena, ananta, apepi, apophis, azhi dahaka, basilisk, buto, dahak, dragon, ellops, shesha

SERPENTINE: devious, diabolic
SERPIGO: herpes, ringworm, tinea
SERRANO: squirrelfish
SERVANT: *agent*, aillt, amah, assistant, attendant, ayah, bata, batman, bildar, bonne, bouchal, butler, chef, chela, cly, coistrel, colona, coolie, dependent, domestic, drudge, employee, equerry, esne, eta, factotum, fellah, ferash, fief, flunky, follower, gillie, gyp, hamal, handmaid, helot, help, maid, man, menial, minion, myrmidon, neif(e), page, *peasant*, *porter*, retainer, seggon, serf, *slave*, subordinate, thrall, underling, valet, vassal, villein, worker
  of god: *church: man*, *monk*
SERVE: *abet*, *accommodate*, *play*, *throw*, wait on, *work*
SERVICE: *account*, *advantage*, airforce, arm(y), assist(ance), attend(ance), avail, *benefit*, business, chakari, complin(e), cordage, devoir, devotion(s), duty, employ(ment), evensong, exercises, help, labor, lauds, mass, matins, ministry, navy, nones, office, position, *remedy*, *repair*, revival, *right*, *rite*, *set*, sext, *system*, *throw*, *use*, utility, *value*, wage, *work*
  charge: fee, gratuity, tip
  dead: dirge, elege, threnody
  feudal: angaria
  military: duty, hitch, stretch
  tree: sorb
SERVILE: *abject*, obsequious
SERVING: *bit*, *cover*, *part*
SESAME: ajonjoli, beni, benne, gama, gingili, ramtil, teel, til(seed), tulema, *word*
SESSION: *meeting*, term, vestry
SET: *accustom*, *adapt*, *adjust*, assign, assure, attitude, bear, begin, *compose*, congeal, course,

direct(ion), *draw*, *establish*, *firm*, *form*, gel, *group*, *hard(en)*, heal, impose, inveterate, jell, locate, *make*, *name*, *obstinate*, *place*, *plant*, *prepare*, put, *ready*, *remedy*, *right*, schedule, seat, series, *seth*, *settle*, *solid*, *start*, *stick*, suit(e), tend, trend, trite, *usual*

apart: partition, *separate*
aside: *abolish*, *remove*, *save*
at: *attack*, *start*
at large: *free*, *release*
back: *defeat*, *return*, *slow*
before: *present*, *tell*
down: *rebuke*, *record*
forth: *display*, *open*, *ornament*, *present*, *start*
free: *release*, *save*
gun: *trap*
off, out: *ornament*, *start*
-to: *contest*, *fight*, *quarrel*
up: *establish*, *plan*, *raise*
upon: *attack*, *press*

SETH: sutekh, typhon
brother: abel, cain, horus, osiris
father: adam, geb
mother: eve, nut
son: enos, sethite
victim: osiris
wife: nephthys

SETTING: milieu, *scene*, *trap*

SETTLE: *accommodate*, *accord*, *acquit*, *adapt*, *adjust*, amortize, bench, button up, capitulate, choose, clear, close, colonize, *compose*, confirm, conform, contract, *control*, *decide*, discharge, domesticate, *establish*, *form*, *get*, hive, inhabit, judge, *kill*, liquidate, live, locate, *make*, mediate, moor, nail, nest, park, pay, perch, *place*, *plant*, *prove*, put, *quiet*, reckon, redeem, refute, remit, residence, retire, rivet, root, *rule*, sag, satisfy, *set*, sew, shelf, *sign*, sink, sit, squat, *stick*, subside

SEVEN: *pleiad(es)*, sept, zeta
arts: arithmetic, astronomy, geometry, grammar, logic, music, rhetoric
bodies: copper, gold, iron, lead, quicksilver, silver, tin
churches: ephesus, laodicea, pergamum, philadelphia, sardis, smyrna, thyatira
comb.: hebdo, helpta, sept(a)
dwarfs: bashful, doc, dopey, grumpy, happy, sleepy, sneezy
gods of luck: *happiness: gods*
group: hebdomad, heptad, pleiad, septet
hills: *rome: hills*
-league boots: talisman
principles: *principles: seven*
sisters: cactus
virtues: *virtue: cardinal*
wonders of world: artemis temple, artemisia mausoleum, babylon gardens, pharos, pyramids, rhodes colossus, zeus statue

SEVER: *break*, *split*, *tear*
SEVERAL: different, divers
SEVERE: *acerb*, *acute*, arctic, ascetic, *bad*, bitter, blue, blunt, breme, *brutal*, caustic, exacting, *extreme*, *firm*, grim, *hard*, *obstinate*, prussian, spartan, *stern*, *strict*, *strong*, *violent*

SEVILLE: *tower:* giralda
SEW: baste, hem, knit, mend, tat
up: *end*, monopolize, *settle*
SEWAN: *money*, *ornament*
SEWING MACHINE: *inventor:* elias howe, lester
part: pleater, plicator, zipperfoot
SEXTON: *church: man*
SEYBERTITE: brandisite
SEYCHELLES: aldabra, mahe
SHABBY: *mean*, *old*, *poor*
SHACK: feed, *hut*, pursue

* Asterisk means to look up this word to find more answer words.

SHACKLE: *bind, *fetter, *tie
SHAD: alewife, allice, alose, antonio, crappie, mojarra
scale: buckwheat sage
SHADDOCK: grapefruit, pumelo
SHADE, SHADOW: *bit, *cover, *hide, *image, *obscure, *spirit
comb.: scia, scio, skia, skio
SHADRACH: hananiah
friend: abednego, meshach
persecutor: nebuchadnezzar
SHADY: *bad, *black, *cool
SHAFT: *deceive, *memorial, *missile, *monument, *spear, *staff, *stick, *tower
column: fust, scape, tige
convex: entasis
feather: scape
part: brace, helve, orlo
wagon: thill, tongue
SHAG: *chase, *cheat, hair, pile, *refuse, texture, wool
SHAGGY: rough, *thick, unkempt
SHAHARAIM: son: abitub, elpaal, jeuz, jobab, malcham, mesha, mirmah, shachia, zibia
wife: baara, hodesh, mahasham
SHAITAN: *demon, *devil
SHAKE: *laugh, *oscillate
SHAKESPEARE: actor: burton, ward
alternate author: bacon
associate: burgage, richard
clown: bottom, lavache
elf: puck
forest: arden
general: canidius
home: avon
idolator: bardolater
relative: anne, edmund, hamnet, john, judith, susanna
wife: ann
SHAKO: *cap, *hat
SHAKTI: *force, *power
SHAKY: *shy, *upset, *weak
SHALE: fissile, metal, slate
SHALLOW: *idle, *light, *simple

SHALLUM: father: tikvath
son: hanameel, hilkiah, jehizkiah, jekamiah, maaseiah
wife: huldah
SHALOM: *good: bye, peace
SHAM: *act, *deception, *show
SHAMAN: *church: man, *magician
SHAMASH: consort: ai, aya
attendant: bunene
SHAME: *abase, abomination, bismer, black eye, *blot, disgrace, dishonor, disrepute, *error, guilt, humiliation, ignominy, indecency, infamy, *mark, mortification, mortify, odium, pity, reproach, scandal, scorn, *sin, stigma, *wrong
personification: aidos
SHAMEFUL: *bad, *sad, *sorry
SHAMROCK: black trefoil, clover
land: *ireland
pea: blue oxalis, herb
SHANGHAI: *drug, *kidnap, *steal
practitioner: larry marr
SHANGRI-LA: *paradise, *utopia
SHANK: gam, leg, *shaft, shin
pert.: crural
SHANNY: blenny, *shy, *silly
SHANTUNG: pongee, silk, tussah
SHANTY: *hut
-town: bidonville, hooverville
SHAPE: *form, *image, *kind, *make, *model, *plan, *state
SHAPELESS: comb.: amorpho
SHAPHAT: kin: adlai, elisha
SHARD: *bit, *part, *piece
SHARE: *allot, *allowance, ante, apportion, *bit, *bite, bond, cant, cleave, contingent, cooperate, cut, deal, dole, half, holding, impart, *interest, measure, meed, mess, modicum, *part, *piece, pittance, proportion, quantum, quota, rake-off, ration
hundred: board lot, round lot

* Asterisk means to look up this word to find more answer words.

SHARK: acanthodian, angelfish, blue dog, cetorhinus, *cheat, con, dogfish, expert, mako, *sharp, soupfin, tope
  pilot: pega(dor), remora
  thresher: alopias

SHARP: *acerb, *acute, *adept, *angry, angular, argute, *bad, *beautiful, blackleg, *bright, bunko man, caustic, *cheat, cold, *cunning, cute, cutting, *eager, edgy, *extreme, *fine, *funny, gamester, greek, *high, *hot, *impostor, jackleg, piercing, *pretty, profound, *quick, *ready, ringer, sensitive, shark, *short, skin, slacker, *sly, *smart, spieler, steep, *violent, *wise
  comb.: acet(o), acut(i), oxy
  practice: chicanery, fraud
  shooter: marksman, sniper

SHARPEN: edge, hone, *set, strop

SHATTER: *break, *destroy, *tear

SHAVE: *cheat, *reduce, *strip

SHAVELING: *church: man, *monk

SHAVING: *bit, *part, *piece

SHAVINGS: *dregs, *refuse

SHAWL: mantle, paisley, serape

SHEA: bambara, bambui, karite, mandingo, tree

SHEAF: *package, *quantity, *tie

SHEAR: *part, *reduce, *strip

SHEATH: *dress, forel, scabbard

SHEATHE: *cover, *dress, *hide

SHEBA: balkis, saba

SHEBANG: *affair, *concern

SHECHEM: *father:* hamor
  god: baalberith

SHED: drop, *hut, *throw
  skin: ecdysis
  tear: *complain, *cry

SHEDU: *demon, *devil

SHEEN: *fair, *light, *shine

SHEEP: breed: *sheep: type
  cry: baa, blat, bleat, maa

  disease: anthrax, bane, big head, black dog, blast, bradsot, braxy, coe, core, dartars, gid, heartwater, resp, rot, scab, scrapie, shab
  dog: collie, shepherd
  dung: buttons, scur
  female: ewe, gimmer, sheder
  fleece: ket, wool
  group: flock, herd, mob
  -head: jemmy, salema
  -head broth: powsowdy
  -headed: *silly, *stupid
  keeper: abel, shepherd
  laurel: calfkill
  leather: kid, roan, suede
  -like: meek, mild, ovine, *shy
  male: bellwether, buck, heder, ram, tup, wether
  mange: scab
  mark: brand, smit
  pen: bought, bught, cote, fank, fold, kraal, ree(ve)
  pet: cosset
  pox: ovina, wildfire
  second year: bident, tag, tegg
  -skin: basan, basil, bezel, bock, bond, cape, certificate, diploma, dongola, kid, leather, mountain mint, ocimum, parchment, pelt, pycanthemum, roan, skiver
  -skin cap: calpac(k)
  tick: carapato, garrapata
  type: barwal, blackhead persian, cheviot, columbia, contentin, corriedale, cotswold, dartmoor, delaine, dorset, down, exmoor, hampshire, karakul, kerry hill, leicester, lincoln, merino, oldenburg, oxford, panama, romanov, romeldale, romney, ryeland, sha, shropshire, sna, southdown, suffolk, targhee, teeswater, welsh mountain, wensleydale
  walk: slait
  weed: bog violet, butterwort
  wild: aoudad, argal(i), arui,

---

* Asterisk means to look up this word to find more answer words.

bharal, chamois, moufflon, nahoor, nayaur, ooriel, rasse, sha, sna, urial

wool substance: suint

young: bident, eanling, four tooth, gimmer, heder, hogget, lamb, shearhog, shearling, sheder, tag, tegg, twinter

SHEER: **complete, *fine, *pure, *simple, *thin, *turn*

SHEIK: **church: man, *ruler*

SHEKEL: *1/2:* bekah

1/4: reba

1/20th: gerah

60: maneh

SHELF: **edge,* layer, reef, shoal

SHELL: ammunition, balat, bark, boat, bombard, cameo, carapace, cartridge, chitin, conch, cortex, **cover,* cowry, crust, husk, lorica, nail, obus, pericarp, plate, pod, sack, scute, shard, shield, shot, shuck, **skin,* strafe, **strip*

apple: chaffinch, crossbill

cannon: black maria, coal box

-drake: duck, merganser

-fire: barrage, strafe

-fish: abalone, cigala, clam, cockle, coquillage, crab, crawfish, crayfish, crevette, crustacean, ecrevisse, hommard, limpet, lobster, mollusk, mussel, nacre, oyster, periwinkle, pipi, scallop, shrimp, squill, whelk

flower: bells of ireland, molluca balm

game: flimflammery, fraud

groove: lira, varix

marine: turbo

mechanism: spalter

money: colcol, peag(e), sewan, uhllo, ullo, wampum

shed: exfoliate, exuviate

SHELLAC: **beat, *defeat,* resin

SHELTER: **asylum, *cover, *house, *hut, *refuge, *retreat*

SHELVE: delay, **dismiss,* table

SHEM: *brother:* ham

father: noah

son: aram, arpachsad, arphaxad, asshur, eber, elam, gether, hul, lud, meshech, uz(al)

SHEMAIAH: *son:* delaiah, elihu, elzabad, jonathan, obed, othni, rephael, semachiah, urijah

SHEMIDA: *son:* ahian, aniam, likhi, shechem

SHENANIGAN: **nonsense, *trick*

SHEOL: hades, **hell,* underworld

SHEPHERD: **direct, *lead,* tend

band: pastoureau

clock: pimpernel, salsify

club: mullein, plant

crook: pedum

dog: cebalrai, collie

god: pales, pan

hercules foe: antagoras

pert.: pastoral

pipe: flageolette, larigot, musette, oat, reed

purse: blindweed, bursa, capsella, caseweed, herb

song: madrigal

staff: cane, crook, kent

SHEPHERDESS: amaryllis, bergere

nursery: little bo-peep

SHERIF: **prince, *ruler*

SHERIFF: *jurisdiction:* bailiwick

men: bailiff, catchpoll, deputy, elisor, officer, posse

SHERRY: amontillado, oloroso, scurry, solera, wine, xeres

fine old: bristol cream

flavor: nutty, rancio

SHESHA: ananta, infinity

SHETLAND: *fishing grounds:* haaf

governor: foud

hill pasture: hoga

island: unst, yell

land: odal, udal(er), udalman

measure: ure

tax: scat

viol: gue

* Asterisk means to look up this word to find more answer words.

SHIBBOLETH: *criterion, *test
SHIELD: *cover, egis, *shell
  athena's: aegis, egis
  border: bordure, orle
  boss: umbo(nal)
  comb.: aspid(o), aspis
  division: ente, paly
  fern: buckler fern
  heraldry: blazon, escutcheon
  insect's head: clypeus
  medieval: ecu
  metal: breastplate
  part: argol, bordure, boss, ente,
    impresa, orle, paly, pointe, umbo
  sacred: ancile
  -shaped: aspidate, clypeate, clypei-
    form, peltate, scutate
  small: ecu
  strap: enarme
SHIFT: *change, *dress, *move,
  *remove, *stir, *trick, waist
SHIFTY: *cunning, evasive
SHIITE: *mohammedan
  pilgrim site: kum, qum
SHILL: *cheat, dupe, foil
SHILLING: five: decus
  1/12: penny
  20: broadpiece, pound
  21: guinea
  22: florin
SHILLY-SHALLY: *oscillate
SHIMEAH: son: jonathan
SHIMEATH: son: zabad
SHIMEI: father: gera
  son: adaiah, beraiah, eliel, elienai,
    haran, haziel, jahath, jair, jakim,
    jeush, shelomith, shimrath, zabdi,
    zichri, zilthai, zina
SHIMEL: father: ela
SHIMMER: glisten, *light, *shine
SHIMON: son: amnon, ben-hanan,
  rinnah, tilon
SHIN: climb, cnemis, crus, shank,
  tibia, *walk
  pert.: cnemial, tibial
  plaster: *money, scrip
SHINAR: city: babel

  king: amraphel
SHINDIG: *party, *riot, rumpus
SHINE: beacon, beam, bedazzle,
  beek, blink, bloom, bootleg, buff,
  burn(ish), candescence, coruscate, daze, dazzle, dido, excel,
  fulgurate, furbish, glare, glaze,
  gleam, glint, glisten, glitter,
  gloss, glow, gloze, incandescence,
  *love, luster, polish, radiate, ruti-
  late, sheen, *sparkle, specie, star,
  twinkle, uproar
SHINER: chub, eye, fish, hat,
  menhaden, minnow, roach
SHINGLE: *cover, *sign, *whip
  oak: blackjack
  splitter: prower
SHINING, SHINY: *ardent,
  *bright
SHINTO: *japan references
SHIP: ancient: galleon, nef
  auxiliary: tender
  back: aft, skag, skeg, stern
  battens: scotchmen
  biscuit: hardtack, patile
  bracket: bibb
  building piece: bosom bar, boss,
    knee, sny, spale, thwart
  building wood: angelique, hard
  capacity: burden, tonnage
  cargo: gaiassa
  cook: slushy
  crew: able, bosun, bungs, cooper,
    engineer, hand, helmsman, mate,
    oiler, navigator, purser, *sailor,
    steersman, steward, stoker, yeo-
    man
  daily record: log
  drinking fountain: scuttlebutt
  group: armada, fleet, flotilla, navy,
    squadron, task force
  gutterways: scuppers
  ironclad: merrimac, monitor
  jack: shad
  jail: brig, hulk
  kitchen: caboose, galley

* Asterisk means to look up this word to find more answer words.

lifting device: camel, capstan, crane, davit

lookout: conning tower, crow's-nest

merchant: argosy, frigate, galiot, galliot, holcad

officer: boatswain, bosun, captain, commander, master, mate, navarch, skipper

ornament: aplustre

partition: bulkhead

pole: mast, spar

record: log

room: brig, cabin, caboose, fo'c's'le, forecastle, galley, salon, steerage

-shape: taut, tidy, trim

sick bay: lazareet

timber: apron, bibb, bitt, keelson, mast, spar, stemson

war: **navy: vessel*

worm: borer, teredo

wreck: flotsam, jetsam, salvage

-wreck, causing: naufrageous

SHIRK: **avoid,* goldbrick, slack

SHIRT: **blouse, *cover, *dress*

bosom: plastron

button: stud

collar style: button-down

front, false: dicky

loose: kamis

-waist: blouse

SHIVAREE: callithump, **noise*

SHIVER: **bit, *part, *piece, *quiver,* shudder, vibrate

SHIVERY: aguish, **shy,* tremorous

SHOAL: **group, *quantity, *shelf*

SHOBAL: *son:* alian, ebal, manahath, onam, shephi

SHOCK: appall, astonish, astound, baffle, bedazzle, blast, boggle, brunt, buffet, bump, canvass, catalepsy, cataplexia, cluster, collect, collision, concussion, crowd, daunt, disgust, dismay, flabbergast, **force,* gliff, gloff,

group, hair, heap, impact, jar, jolt, misfortune, mop, nociassociation, **pain,* percussion, **quantity,* scandal, **start(le), *stop,* stun, **trap,* trauma, **upset*

absorber: buffer, bungee

therapy: cst, ict

SHOCKING: **bad, *dirty, *ugly*

SHODDY: **false, *poor, *refuse*

SHOE: balmoral, beavertop, blake, blucher, boot(ee), brodequin, brogan, brogue, buskin, campagus, casing, clodhopper, clog, congress, crakow, cue, flat(tie), gaiter, galosh, gilly, mckay, mule, oxford, pampottee, patten, pump, sabot, **sandal,* schoon, sneaker, solleret, stogy, tire

aid: horn

-bill: baleanicipites, stork

cover: gaiter, prunella, spat

form: last, tree

leather: cabretta

-maker: cobbler, cordonnier, crispin, farrier, snob, sutor

part: backstay, calk, cleat, counter, geta, heel, insole, last, lift, outsole, pull, rand, shank, slipsole, strap, tongue, vamp, welt

paste: clobber

rubber: arctic, galosh, overshoe

-shaped: calceolate

tie: aglet, aiglet, lace, latchet, strap, string, whang

wooden: clog, geta, patten, sabot, secque

SHOGUN: **magnate, *ruler*

SHOO: begone, scram, vamoose

SHOOT: **attack, *hit, *pierce, *speed, *start, *stem, *stop*

comb.: blast(o)

out: **contest, *fight, *settle*

plant: bine, cion, frond, gemma, scion, sprig, stolon

sound: bang, pop, snap, zap

the breeze: **gossip, *talk*

SHOP: atelier, boutique, burse, business, buy, emporium, establishment, mart, *plant, *store, studio, taberna, *trade
-lifter: *thief
obsession: oniomania
SHORE: littoral, *support
bird: auk, avocet, calico, curlew, daption, gull, petrel, plover, ree, ruff, sandpiper, snipe
SHORT: abbreviated, abrupt, bear, bluff, blunt, brusque, cammed, capsule, compact, compendious, condensed, cranky, *crisp, cross, curt(ailed), direct, ephemeral, friable, imperfect, lacking, laconic, *little, *low, pudgy, *quick, rough, sell, *small, snappish, stubby, succinct, suddenly, sullen, summary, synoptic, terse, *ugly, uncivil, wanting
-change: skimp
comb.: brachy, brevi
SHORTAGE: *need, ullage, want
SHORTCOMING: *decline, *need
SHORTHAND: gregg, pitman
SHORTS: bermudas, hot pants, mini skirt, scants
SHOSHONE: bannock, comanche, hopi, moki, otoe, paiute, pima, piute, utah, ute
god: pokunt
SHOT: bullet, *drink, guess, *range, shell, *try, *upset
SHOULDER: *edge, shelf, *support
angle, bastion: epaule
blade: omoplate, scapula
comb.: omo
inflammation: omalgia, omitis
muscle: deltoid
ornament: epaulet(te), tab
pert.: alar, humeral, scapular
road: berm, edge, rut
strap: baldric, bandolier, bretelle, sam johnson, sash
yoke: banghy, bangy, cowl, soe

SHOUT: *cry, *laugh, roar, yell
SHOVE: *abet, *group, *push
off: embark, launch, *start
SHOW: *act(ion), adduce, affect(ation), *appear(ance), *argue, array, assign, bear, bespeak, carnival, circus, *direct, *display, divulge, evidence, explain, fair, flair, *form(ality), *image, legit, motion picture, movie, offer, *open, ostentation, parade, performance, *play, *present, pretend, pretense, promenade, *prove, raree, repertory, represent, reveal, revue, rodeo, sham, spectacle, tender, *train
-case: counter, etalage, vitrine
SHOWER: *party, *plenty, rain
SHOWY: *artificial, *theatrical
SHRED: *bit, *part, *piece, *strip, tatter, *tear, wisp
SHREW: *hag, *scold, virago
-mouse: hyrax, migale, sorex
SHREWD: *bad, *sage, *sharp, *sly, *smart, wily, *wise
SHRIEK: *cry, *laugh, scream
SHRIKE: batara, campanero
SHRILL: *high, *sharp, *thin
SHRIMP: cameron, *dwarf, prawn
comb.: caris
SHRINE: *image, *memorial
SHRINK: *decline, *reduce
SHRINKER: psychiatrist
SHRINKING: *afraid, *shy
SHRIVE: *acquit, *confess
SHRIVEL: *decline, *reduce
SHRIVELED: *poor, *thin, wede
SHROUD: *cover, *dress, *hide
SHROVE: tide: carnival, *party
-tide fee: cockpenny
tuesday: pancake day
tuesday cake: carcake
SHRUB: aromatic: aralia, batis, lavender, mint, rosemary, sage, sassafras, tea, thyme
bushy: cade, savin, tod, wahoo
cedar: savin(e)

* Asterisk means to look up this word to find more answer words.

climbing: bignonia, clematis, liana, rubus, smilax, vitis
creeping: pyxie
dwarfed: bonsai
ericaceous: bearberry
euphorbiaceous: alem
evergreen: abelmosk, akebia, azara, box, buxus, camellia, cistus, erica, fatsia, furze, heath, hedera, ilex, jasmine, juniper, laurel, mahonia, mistletoe, myrtle, oleander, oregon grape, pepino, privet, salal, savin, smilax, titi
-flower: azalea, forsythia, itea, japonica, lantana, laurel, mignonette, mistletoe, myrtle, oleander, oleaster, privet, rhodora, spiraea, spirea, syringa, tiara
fruit: salal
genus: alder, aralia, azalea, bixa, erica, genista, inga, itea, ixora, lantana, ledum, olea, rhus, sida, sumac
group: boscage, bush
oil-yielding: croton
ornamental: andromeda, hedge, honeysuckle, ibota, privet
pert.: fruticose, fruticous
poison: ivy, rhus, sumac(h)
rosaceous: spirea
rutaceous: jaborandi
sambucus: elder
silk-like fiber: anabo, ceiba
spiny: allthorn, bramble, briar, brier, caper, furze, gorse, haw(thorn), rose, ulex, whin
SHRUFF: *dregs, *rubbish
SHRUG: *oscillate, *quiver
off: *dismiss, negate, veto
SHTIK: *part, *piece, *trick
SHTOOP: *press, *push
SHTUSS: *nonsense, *refuse
SHU: *kin:* geb, hathor, nut, ra
wife: tefnut
SHUCK: *remove, *shell, *strip
SHUDDER: *quiver, shake

SHUFFLE: *dance, *stir, *trick
SHUN: *avoid, *escape, *hate, *hide, *refrain, *run, *shy
SHUNT: *avoid, *remove, *turn
SHURA: *parent:* heber, jael
SHUT: *cover, *end, *free, *stop
off: *arrest, *separate, *stop
out: *blank, *defeat, *erase
up: *end, *jail, *quiet, *stop
SHY: anerly, *avoid, backward, bashful, boggle, cagey, chary, conscious, coy, demure, diffident, evasive, jump, modest, mousy, needy, quibble, reserved, *retreat, scruple, self-conscious, shamefaced, sheepish, shrinking, skittish, *start, *throw, timid, timorous, wary, without
SHYLOCK: *coin:* ducat
daughter: jessica
friend: tubal
SHYSTER: pettifogger, *rogue
SIAM: *thai
twins: chang, eng
SIB(LING): ayllu, *relative
SIBELIUS: *valse:* triste
SIBERIAN: *russian, *tartar
city: barnaul, blagovestchensk, bratsk, chita, irkutsk, khabarovsk, krasnoyarsk, listvenichnoye, samarkand, tashkent, tomsk, vladivostok
herb: candlestick lily, globe flower, trollius
ibex: tex
language: finno-urgric, yenisei
plant: badan, caragana
race: beltir, gilyak, kirghiz, sagai, tartar, yakut, yukagir
river: amur, ili, lena, maya, onon, olenek, sobol, tobol, tom
squirrel: calabar, miniver
tent: yurt
wild cat: manul
wind: buran
SIBILANCE MARK: cedilla, legon

* Asterisk means to look up this word to find more answer words.

SIBILATE: buzz, fizz, hiss, sip, snore, swish, wheeze, whiz

SIBLING: ayllu, *relative

SIBYL: *hag, *oracle
 home: cumae

SIC: *attack, such, thus, *urge

SICCA: die, rupee, seal, stamp

SICILY: ash: manna
 bull: phalaris
 cape: boeo, faro, passaro
 city: aci, aetna, alcamo, bidis, caltanissetta, catania, gela, girgenti, hybla, marsala, messina, modica, palermo, ragusa, trapani
 composer: bellini
 evergreen: maquis
 game: cottabus
 god: adranus
 island: pantelleria
 king: eryx
 measure: caffiso, salma
 people: elymi, sicani, sicel
 resort: enna
 river: acis, belice, mazzaro, platani, salso, simeto
 saint: agatha
 society: la cosa nostra, mafia
 volcano: aetna, etna
 whirlpool: charybdis

SICK: aeger, ailing, all overish, anemic, apoplectic, *attack, *bad, bedridden, below par, chase, confined, consumptive, crapulous, desolate, diseased, disgusted, down, dyspeptic, epileptic, *evil, exasperated, fed up, feverish, flattened, in danger, indisposed, infirm, *insane, laid up, *low, *mad, nauseated, on one's back, out of sorts, prostrate, rheumatic, rocky, scurvy, seedy, shutin, spastic, suffering, surfeited, taken ill, tired, under the weather, unhealthy, unwell, *urge, valetudinaire, valetudinarian, victim, *weak, weary

SICKER: *fast, *firm, *secure

SICKLE: hook, scythe, spur

SICYON: king: epopeus

SIDDHARTHA: *buddha

SIDE: aspect, *join, lateral, *party, *piece, surface, verge
 -arm: pistol, revolver, *sword
 -board: buffet, credenza
 husband: orion
 issue: by-product, outgrowth
 -kick: *associate, *friend
 -kicker: porch
 -line: avocation, hobby
 -piece: bar, bibb, cant
 -step: *avoid, duck, *retreat
 toward the: lateral
 -track: *err, *shunt
 -winder: crotalus, reptile
 -wise: aside, athwart, *sly
 with: *join, *support

SIDES: unequal: scalene

SIDI: wife: amine

SIDLE: crabwalk, *edge, skirt

SIDON: saida

SIEGE: *attack, *spell, surround
 pert.: obsidional

SIEGFRIED: sigurd
 ancestor: odin, rerir, sigi
 daughter: swanhild
 epic: nibelungenlied
 father: sigmund
 foster father: regin(n)
 grandfather: volsung
 helper: mime
 mother: hjordis, sieglind
 slayer: hagen, hogni
 steed: grani
 sword: balmunc, balmung, gram
 tutor: regin(n)
 victim: alberich, fafnir
 wife: gudrun, kriemhild

SIERRA: fish, *range, *ridge

SIERRA NEVADA: fog: pogonip
 gold deposit: blue lead

SIESTA: *break, nap, *rest

SIEVE: colander, *search, *test
 -like: cribrate, ethmoid

SIF: kin: thor, ull(r)

* Asterisk means to look up this word to find more answer words.

SIFT: *analyze, *ask, *separate

SIGH: *complain, *cry, long, sob

SIGHT: *look, *see, *sense, view
and hearing, pert.: audio-visual
defect: anopia, anopsia
dimness: caliginosity, caligo
loss: amaurosis, blindness
pert.: ocular, visual
second: esp, fey, psychic
weakness: amblyopia

SIGIL: *image, *magic, *sign

SIGMUND: *father:* volsung
grandfather: rerir
son: siegfried, sigurd
sword: gram
wife: borghild, hjordis

SIGN: augury, ayah, *badge, beacon, bill, caract, cipher, clew,
clue, crab, cue, earmark, *endorse, *engage, execute, *form,
gesture, hire, index, indication,
indorse, ink, *instrument, *join,
*magic, *mark, *meaning, minus,
motion, murmur, *note, omen,
paraph, *picture, plus, portent,
poster, prodigy, prognosis, ratify,
*rite, rune, seal, *set, *settle,
signal, *spell, subscribe, *symbol, symptom, *token, type, underwrite, write
division: obelus
illuminated: ad, light, neon
language: dactylology
liturgical: selah, shelah
nocturnal: zodiacal
pert.: semantic, semic

SIGNAL: *alarm, *fire, *light,
*mark, *sign, *smoke, *stop
distress: mayday, sos
fire: balefire
tower: atalaya, tantayan

SIGNATURE: john hancock,
*mark

SIGNATURE, SIGNET: john
hancock, *mark, *name, seal,
*symbol

SIGNIFICANT: *important, *solid

SIGNIFY: *mean, *show, *spell

SIGNOR: *lord, *man, *title

SIGURD: *siegfried

SIGYN: *consort:* loki
daughter: hel

SIKER: *sicker

SIKHARA: sikar, *tower
finial: amalaka

SIKH, SIKKIM: *india

SILENCE: kill, *peace, *quiet
goddess: angerona

SILENE: campion, catchfly, pink

SILENT: *cool, *quiet, *sullen

SILEX: flint, quartz, silica

SILHOUETTE: *image, *outline

SILICATE: acmite, aenigmatite,
allanite, allodelphite, aloisiite,
alvite, amphibole, andalusite,
aphrosiderite, augite, augitite,
babingtonite, barylite, bazzite,
beckelite, bementite, bodenben-
derite, calamine, catapleiite,
catoptrite, celandonite, cenosite,
cerite, epidote, euclase, iolite,
katoptrite, mica, opal, severite

SILK: *brocade:* baldachin(o)
brown: muga
*cloth: *fabric:* silk
cocoon: bave
corded: crin, faille
-cotton fabric: adansonia
-cotton fiber: kapok, kumbi
-cotton tree: bentang, bombace,
bulak, cabbagewood, ceiba
*fabric: *fabric:* silk
fiber: floss
filling: bave, brin, tram
fine: crin, shela, tulle
fishline: gimp
floss: sleave
gelatin: sericin
glossy: lute-string, taffeta
grass: istle
half-mask: loup
hank: hasp
handkerchief: barcelona

---

* Asterisk means to look up this word to find more answer words.

hat: beaver, castor, catskin, tile, top hat, topper

heavy: camaca, gros

lining: sarcenet

maker: seric

moth: atlas, eria, muga, tussah

oak: grevillea

package: moche

plant: floss, ramie

purple: blatta

quilted: matelasse

raw: grege

reeling: filature

rustle: scroop

sash: benn

source: cocoon, moth, worm

-stocking: *lord, *noble, *rich

stuff: tarse

substitute or synthetic: dacron, nylon, orlon, rayon

tester: denierer, scrimeter

thin: alamode

thread: bave, brin, floss, poil, tram(e)

tied and dried: batik

tree: ceiba

twilled: alma, tobine

unravel, unspun: sleave

waste: floss, frison, knub, noil, strass

watered: moire, tabby

-weed: milkweed

wood: calabur, muntingia

-worm: ailanthus, caterpillar, cecropia, eri(a), muga, samia, sina, spinner, tusser, tussur

-worm disease: calcino, pebrine, uji

-worm eggs: graine

-worm genus: bombyx

-worm leaves: alba

-worm organ: filator

-worm, pert.: ailantine, bombic

yarn: bourette, shap

yarn size: denier

SILKEN, SILKY: byssic, *fine, *gentle, seric, sleek, slick,

*smooth, *soft, *sweet

SILL: *edge, ledge, threshold

SILLY: *absurd, *bizarre, *dull, *fool, *funny, *idle, *insane, *simple, *stupid, *vain, *weak

SILT: dirt, *dregs, mud, *refuse

SILVER: *alloy:* albata, billon, neogen, occamy

coating: argentation

comb.: argenti, argyro

compound: acanthite, aguilarite, amalgam, andorite, animikite, aramayoite, argentide, argyrite, bromyrite, canfieldite, cerargyrite, pina

dollar: cartwheel

fir: abies, amabilis, cascade

-fish: insect, tarpon, tarpun

fox fur: platina

gibbon: camper, wou-wou

gilded: vermeil

horn: cerargyrite

ingots: *silver:* ore

instrument: argentometer

lace: filigree

leaf: acacia, boree, myall, wattle tree

maple globulin: acerin

oak: flannelbush

ore: bullion, paco, sycee

pert.: argental, argenteous, argentiferous, argyric

plover: knot

polish: almagra

purchase law: bland-allison act

reducing kettle: cazo

-sides: atherine, minnow, smelt

thaw: glaze, ice, rime

thistle: acanthus

thread: cannetille

-tongued: eloquent

tree: black stavewood

-weed: jewelweed, rue, tansy

SILYBUM: mariana, thistle

SIMEON: *parent:* jacob, leah

son: jachin, jamin, jarib, jemuel,

nemuel, ohad, saul, shaul, zerah,
zohar

SIMILE: analogy, metaphor

SIMILITUDE: *copy, *image

SIMMONS, RUTH: bridey murphy

SIMON: apostle, cephas, peter
brother: andrew, lysimachus,
menelaus
son: john, judas, mattathias

SIMPLE: arcadian, *ascetic, basic,
*dull, easy, foolish, gullible,
homespun, humble, ignorant,
*light, mute, naive, natural, oaf-
ish, *open, *plain, *pure, re-
strained, sheer, *silly, singular,
*smooth, *stupid, *superficial,
*true, unadorned, *weak
comb.: apl(o), hapl(o)
simon: *clown, goose, *fool

SIMPLETON: boor, *clown, *fool

SIMULATE: *act, *adopt, *affect

SIN: acedia, *anger, backslide,
blame, covetousness, crime, debt,
degenerate, delinquency, derelic-
tion, do wrong, envy, *err, *error, *evil, *fall, felony, folly, go
astray, guilt, heresy, idolatry, im-
morality, lust, misdeed, murder,
nonfeasance, offense, omission,
outrage, pecadillo, peccancy,
pride, sloth, violate, *wrong
offspring: ishtar
original: adam, old adam
seven deadly: anger, covetousness,
envy, gluttony, lust, pride, sloth

SINCERE: *honest, *open, *plain,
*pure, *simple, *true, *warm

SINEWY: *solid, *strong, sturdy

SINFIOTLI: *poisoner:* borghild

SINFUL: *bad, *criminal, *evil

SINGLE: *ace, *alone, *unit
comb.: aplo, hapl, mono, uni
-tree: transverse

SINGULAR: *bizarre, *eccentric

SINISTER: *adverse, augural,
*bad, bodeful, car, devious, dis-

astrous, doomful, dreary, *evil,
fateful, foreboding, gloomy, left,
lowering, malevolent, portentous,
*secret, somber, threatening,
*ugly, unfortunate, vicious

SINK: *decline, *fall, *hell, *set,
*settle, *suffer
ship: scuttle

SINKER: doughnut, *missile

SINNER: *criminal, *rogue

SINUOUS: devious, snaky, *sly

SINUS: ampulla, *opening, tract
arabicus: red sea

SIOUAN: *indian: sioux

SIP: *drink, nip, savor, taste

SIR: adoni, sahib, senor

SIREN: *alarm, *hag, *witch
famed: circe, cleopatra, lorelei
master: butes
names: aglaophone, molpe, par-
thenope, peisinoe, thelxepeia
parent: achelous, melpomene
resister: odysseus, ulysses
symbol: double flute, lyre

SISAL: agave, hemp, henequin

SISERA: *enemy:* barak, jael

SISYPHUS: *child:* glaucus
grandson: bellerophon, hipponous

SIT: *abide, *lie, *rest, *set
back: retire, *retreat
down: *settle, *strike
on: *hide, *rebuke, suppress

SITA: *consort:* rama, ravana

SITE: *place, spot, stance

SITTING: *meeting
bull's victim: custer

SITUATE: *locate, *place

SITUATION: *crisis, pass, *place,
*state, *work

SIVA: ardhanari, bhairava, isvara,
mahadeva, nataraja
snake: cobra
temples: prambanan
trident: trisul(a)
wife: devi, durga, kali, parvati,
sati, shakti, uma

SIX: hexad, roku, sechs, seis

* Asterisk means to look up this word to find more answer words.

comb.: hexa, sex, sise
dice: boxcar, sice
-eyed: senocular
feet under: buried, dead
-footed: hexapod(al)
group: hexade, senary, sextet
-pence: bender, cripple, tanner
pert.: senary
-shooter: *gun, pistol, revolver
SIXES: boxcars, sisters, sixty days,
ssang-ryouk, sugoruku
SIXTH DEGREE: *pert.:* seatic
SIXTH SENSE: esp, instinct
SIZE: *group, *quantity, *range
up: *analyze, *test, *try
SIZZLE: *anger, burn, *speed
SKAG: *split, *tear, wound
SKATE: batoides, *ruin, *slide
place: arena, ice, pond, rink
relative: nautilus
SKATIKU: *100:* auksinas
SKEDADDLE: *run, *scram
SKEESICKS: *imp, *rogue
SKEGGER: fish, parr, salmon
SKEIN: coil, hank, mesh, rap, web
SKELETON: body, past, *plan
SKETCH: *picture, *plan, *plot
SKI: *contest:* biathlon
heel spring: amstutz
marker: sitzmark
part: camber, heel, shovel, sole,
tip
position: vorlage
run: schuss, slalom
term: christy, gelandesprung, in-
run, mogul, passgang, snowplow,
telemark
turn: stem
SKID: drag, scud, *slide, slip
SKILL: *ability, accomplishment,
*address, adeptness, adroitness,
agility, *aplomb, aptitude, art,
cleverness, command, competence, craft, deftness, efficiency,
expertise, finesse, *forte, handi-
ness, industry, knack, know-how,
*knowledge, mastery, profi-

ciency, prowess, quickness,
readiness, resource, savvy, smart-
ness, technique
SKILLED, SKILLFUL: *able,
*smart
SKIM: fly, rind, *slide, *speed
SKIMPY: frugal, *mean, *poor
SKIN: *abrade, balat, bark, calf,
case, *cheat, corium, *cover,
cuticle, *deceive, *defeat, epidermis, flay, fur, hair, hide, hull,
*hurt, integument, jacket, lam-
ina, leather, overcharge, pare,
peel, pelage, pelt, rawhide, *rebuke, rind, *ruin, *sharp, *shell,
*strip, *take, tegument, *trick
boat: angeyot
-burned: eschar
comb.: cuti, derm(s), dermis
decoration: tatoo, tattoo
-diver: aquanaut
-diver equipment: aqualung, com-
pressor, flipper, mask, scuba,
snorkel, spear
dryness: xerosis
eruption: anthema, blotch, bro-
mism, hives, macula, rash
excessive pigment: melanism
exudation: perspiration, sebum,
sudor, sweat
-flint: *cheat, *miser, screw
fold: plica
game: bunco, bunko, fraud
layer: blastoderm, corium, cutis,
dermis, ecderon, ectoblast, en-
doderm, epidermis, epithelium,
hypodermis, tegument
opening: pore
pert.: cutaneous, cuticular, deric,
dermoid, epidermal
piece: blype
prepare: taw
presser: sammier
protuberance: callosity, callus,
mole, wart, wen
rug of: kaross

* Asterisk means to look up this word to find more answer words.

spot: macula, petechia, tache
without: apellous
SKINK: adda, *draw*, *drink*,
  liquor, lizard, *serve*
SKINNER: *cheat*, *hoodlum*
SKIP: dap, *escape*, hop, *pass*,
  play, ricochet, spring
-*jack:* alewife, bateau, bonito, fop,
  mackerel, saurel
SKIPPER: captain, *head*, *leader*
SKIRL: *bark*, *cry*, shriek, yap
SKIRMISH: *contest*, *fight*
SKIRR: *move*, *run*, *slide*
SKIRT: *adjunct*, *dress*, *edge*
armor: tace, tasse(t)
bullet: tutu
coat: lappet, peplum
divided: culotte
feature: balayense
hoop: crinoline, farthingale, krin-
  oline, peplum
section: gore, panel
short: bengi, blackout, engi, kilt,
  kirtle, mini, skirtle
slack-type: culotte(s), harem
steel: lamboys
velvet: base
SKIT: *act*, *dance*, *joke*, *play*
SKITTERY, SKITTISH: *shy*
SKIVE: *run*, *shave*, *slide*
SKULK: *hide*, *lie*, *steal*
SKULL: cranium, *head*, *mind*
back: occiput
bone: ethmoid, frontal, inion,
  mandible, maxilla, occipital,
  parietal, sphenoid, zygoma
cap: *cap*, *ecclesiastic: cap*
cavity: foramen, fossa, sinus
dome: calvarium
-*duggery:* *deception*, *evil*
fracture: pilation
junction: bregma, pterion
part: asterion, basion, inion
pert.: cranial, inial
the: golgotha
SKUNK: *beat*, *defeat*, *rat*
animal: civet, conepate, polecat,

putois, seganku, teledu, zoril(le)
cabbage: aracae
SKY: *acme*, *paradise*, *top*
blue: azure, celeste, cerule
comb.: scio, urano
god: abu, aether, anat, anu, argus,
  caelus, coel, dyaus, jumala, jupiter, odomankoma, tiu, tiw, tyr,
  ukko, uranus, ymir, zeus, zio, ziu
goddess: frigg(a), hathor, hecate,
  hera, iole, jacaste, jocasta, niobe,
  nut
highest part: zenith
-*lark:* bird, pipit, *play*, *run*
-*light:* abatjour, window
-*line:* horizon
personification: aether
pert.: celestial
pilot: *church: man*
-*scraper:* structure, *tower*
serpent: ahi
SLAB: *memorial*, *monument*
base: dalle, floor, foundation
pert.: stelar, stelene
SLACK: *dregs*, *gentle*, *reduce*,
  refuse, *slow*, *wanton*, *weak*
SLACKER: goldbrick, *sharp*, spiv
SLACKS: *pants*
SLAG: *dregs*, *refuse*, scoria
SLAKE: *drink*, relax, relieve
SLAM: *abuse*, *defeat*, *hit*
make a: vole
SLAMMOCK: *prostitute*
SLANDER: *gossip*, *smear*
SLANG: *abuse*, *argot*, *cheat*
SLANT: *mind*, *outlook*, *stand*
SLANTED: *awry*, *eccentric*
SLAP: *hit*, *punish*, *rebuke*
-*bang*, -*dash:* *fast*, *reckless*
SLAPPING: *big*, *great*, *large*
SLAPSTICK: *act*, *joke*, *play*
SLASH: *attack*, *reduce*
SLAT: lath, *strike*, *strip*
SLATE: *criticize*, *mark*, *plan*,
  punish, *rebuke*, *stone*
clean: tabula rasa
SLATTERN: *hag*, *prostitute*

* Asterisk means to look up this word to find more answer words.

SLAUGHTER: *end, *kill
valley of: tophet
place: abattoir, aceldama, butch-ery, shambles, stockyard
SLAUNCH: incline, *slant
SLAV: bohemian, bulgar, croat, czech, lett, moravian, pole, rus-sian, sclave, serb, sider, silesian, slavonian, slovak, sorb, vend, vened, wend
SLAVE: *addict, agency, *agent, alipin, alltud, ame damnee, ardu, blackbird, bondman, captive, ceorl, chattel, churl, cumhal, dasir, gallerian, ilot, *instrument, lascar, maroon, odalisque, *serv-ant, thane, theow, *thing, toil(er), *work
block: catasta
chief: bug jargal
dealer: biche, mango
driver: coach, despot, martinet, simon legree, tyrant
female: baubo, bondmaid, broad wife, iambe, neif(e), odalisk
free: emancipate
quarters: barracoon, crawl
states: alabama, arkansas, caro-linas, florida, georgia, kentucky, louisiana, maryland, mississippi, missouri, tennessee, texas, vir-ginia
the tempest: caliban
SLAVER: *flatter, *nonsense
SLAY: *delight, *destroy, *kill
SLEAVE: *part, *separate
SLEAZY: *poor, *thin, *weak
SLED: luge, pung, *slide
SLEEK: *sly, *smart, *smooth
SLEEP: doze, nap, *quiet, *rest
comb.: hypn(o), sopor
deep: coma, sopor, stupor
god: morpheus, soma, somnus
inducer: narcotic, opiate, sand-man, sedative, soporific
light: catnap, doze, forty winks, nap, shut-eye, siesta

personified: hypnos, sandman
pert.: somnial, soporific
place: bag, barracks, bed, berth, billet, bunk, cot, couch, cubicle, dormitory, pallet, pullman, quarters
seller: landlord
sickness: lethargy, tsetse
-walker: somnambulist
wander in: dwale
SLEEPER: *support, *tie
SLEEVE: dolman, gigot, mandrel
badge: chevron
hole: skye
SLEIGH: carriole, sled, toboggan
SLEIGHT: *skill, *sly, *trick
SLENDER: *small, *thin, *weak
SLEUTH: detective, dick, gumshoe
SLEW: *plenty, *quantity
SLICE: cut, *part, *piece
SLICK: *polish, *shrewd, *smooth
SLICKER: *cheat, moth, raincoat
SLIDE: avalanche, chute, coast, *copy, *decline, *fall, glide, glissade, glissando, glitch, in-cline, *ornament, *retreat, *run, skate, skid, skim, skip, sled, slew, slip, slither, slue, sluther, *speed
fastener: zipper
medial: cursor
SLIGHT: *little, *pass, *small
SLIM: *slight, *thin, *weak
SLIME: dirt, mire, ooze, slush
SLIMSY: *slight, *thin, *weak
SLING: catapult, *throw, womera
SLINK: creep, *slide, *steal
SLIP: *err(or), *flaw, *give, shoot, *sin, *slide, solecism
SLIPPER: mule, *sandal, *shoe
plant: bird cactus
-shaped: calceiform, calceolate
SLIPPERY: cunning, *sly, *smooth
SLIPSLOP: *nonsense, *refuse
SLIT: *open, *opening, *split
SLITHER: *refuse, *slide
SLOB: cad, *clown, *wanton
SLOBBER: drool, *slaver, spit

* Asterisk means to look up this word to find more answer words.

SLOE: gin, haw, plum, prune
SLOG: *hit, strike, *walk, *work
SLOGAN: *adage, *cry, shibboleth
SLOP: *dregs, *mess, *nonsense
 pail: parasha
SLOPE: *depart, grade, *slant
SLOSH: mud, slime, sprinkle
SLOT: *opening, track, trail
SLOTH: ai, apathy, inertia, unau
 bear: aswail, bhalu, melursus
 monkey: *loris
SLOUCH: *clown, pace, *peasant
SLOUGH: *dregs, *shed, swamp
 grass: bull grass, spartina
SLOVEN: *slouch, *wanton
SLOVENLY: *dirty, *fat, *poor
SLOW: adagio, *arrest, back pedal,
 brake, check, *cool, crawling,
 creeping, decelerate, *decline,
 delay, deliberate, detain, drag,
 draw rein, *dull, *ease, foil,
 *gentle, gradual, hinder, *hold,
 impede, keep back, languorous,
 largo, *late, lento, lingering, lose
 ground, modify, *quiet, *reduce,
 reef, rein, *rest, *stop, *stupid
 comb.: brady
 loris: bashful billy, kokam
SLUBBER: *dirty, *obscure
SLUBBERDEGULLION: *pros-
 titute
SLUDGE: *dregs, mire, *refuse
SLUE: *slide, *turn, twist
SLUG: *beat, *drag, *drink, *hit
SLUGGISH: bovine, *dull, *slow
SLUICE: *dregs, *waterway
SLUM: barrio, favela, ghetto
SLUMMOCK: *prostitute
SLUMP: *decline, *fall, *slow
SLUR: *insult, *smear, stigma
SLUT: *prostitute, *wanton
SLY: *acute, artful, bootleg, cagey,
 canny, clever, crafty, cunning,
 cute, deceitful, deceptive, feline,
 foxy, hugger-mugger, insidious,
 mischievous, *secret, shrewd,
 skillful, slee, sloan, *smart,

sneaky, stealthy, subtle, under-
 hand, wary, wily, *wise
SMACK: boat, *hit, kiss, *noise,
 savor, *strike, suddenly, tang
SMAIK: *peasant, rogue, scamp
SMALL: back, bantam, base,
 beady, brief, cursory, dapper,
 grubby, inconsequential, incon-
 siderable, infinitesimal, insignifi-
 cant, *light, lil, lilliputian,
 limited, *little, *low, meager,
 *mean, minute, moderate, mod-
 est, negligible, picayune, *short,
 *superficial, *thin, tot, trivial
 amount: *bit, *trifle
 comb.: lepto, micro, mio, obligo,
 steno, tapin(o)
 fry: child, youth
 hours: dawn, morning
 talk: chat, *gossip, *nonsense
 -time: bush, petty, two-bit
SMALLAGE: celery, march, parsley
SMALLPOX: alastrim, variola
SMARAGD: beryl, emerald, jewel
SMART: *able, *active, *acute,
 alamode, braw, *bright, chic,
 chichi, classy, dapper, dashing,
 dextrous, dressy, elite, *fire,
 *funny, *hurt, impudent, inso-
 lent, in the mode, jaunty, modish, natty, neat, nifty, nobby,
 *pain, pert, *popular, posh,
 *quick, *ready, recherche, *sage,
 *sharp, sleek, shrewd, *smooth,
 smug, spiffy, sporty, spruce,
 swanky, swell, tingle, tony, trig,
 trim, vogueish, *wise
 aleck: cheeker, hussy, malapert,
 minx, wise guy
SMASH: *break, *destroy, *fall,
 *hit, *ruin, *success, wreck
SMEAR: *abuse, asperse, befoul,
 begrime, besmirch, bleed, brand,
 call names, canard, defame, *defeat, defile, denigrate, *dirty, disparage, *flaw, gaum, *hit, libel,

*lie, malign, muckrake, mudsling, *obscure, *paint, pollute, roorback, *shame, slander, slur, smirch, smudge, *spoil, spot, spread, stigmatize, stop, sully, tarnish, vilify, whisper
dab: fish, marysole
SMELL: *breathe, detect, fume, fust, *scent, trace, whiff
comb.: bromo, osmo, ozo
loss: anosmia, anosphresia
pert.: olfactory
SMELLING SALTS: hartshorn
SMELT: atherinops, *fool, fuse, hypomesus, iuanga, osmerida, retropinna, sand launce, silversides, sparling, tomcod
by-product: *dregs, *refuse
cousin: candlefish
SMILAX: bamboo brier, bindweed, briarroot, bull grip, carolina chinaroot, carrion flower
SMILE: greet, *laugh, smirk
SMIRCH: *smear, soil, stain
SMIRK: simper, smile, snort
SMITE: *beat, *hit, *strike
SMITHEREEN: *bit, *part, *piece
SMOCK *dress, robe, shift, tunic
SMOG: *disease:* emphysema
makeup: ozone, pan, peroxyacl nitrate
SMOKE: aerosol, *anger, baconize, cheroot, cigar(ette), cloud, cure, drunk, dry, floc, fumous, funk, haze, lunt, mist, obfuscate, *puff, reek, *scent, signal, *smell, smog, smook, smother, smudge, stain, trivia, vapor
comb.: atmo, atmido
indian: kinnikinnick
signals: bush telegraph
tree: chittamwood, cotinus, fustet, venetian sumac, zante
SMOKER: auto, car, *party, stag
SMOLDER: *anger, simmer, *smoke
SMOLT: *bright, calm, salmon

SMOOTH: bland, brant, brent, composed, *cool, *cunning, dab, *dress, dub, equable, equalize, *fine, *gentle, glossy, grade, harrow, *kind, lay, legato, lene, mow, oily, palliate, pave, placate, placid, *plain, *plaster, *prepare, *press, *quiet, *regular, sand, satiny, shave, silky, slick, suave, *sweet, unbroken, unctuous, uniform, unruffled, urbane, velvety
comb.: lei(o), lio, lisso
dogfish: carcharias, sand shark
winterberry: canhoop, ilex
SMOTHER: choke, *kill, suppress
SMUDGE: *smear, *smoke, stain
SMUG: *correct, *smart, *vain
SMUT: blight, dirt, filth
fungus: anther smut
grass: black medic, black seed
SMUTCH: *smear, soil, stain
SMUZZ: *ado, *stir
SMYRNA: izmir
fig: eleme, elemi
SNACK: *bit, *eat, *part, *piece
SNAFFLE: bradoon, harness, *steal
SNAFU: chaos, *eccentric, *spoil
SNAG: danger, *part, *tear, *unit
SNAIL: abalone, achatina, alectrion, amphibola, ampullaria, ancylus, auricula, bittium, cerion, coret, ear shell, gastropod, haliotis, laggard, mitra, mollusk, nerita, nudibranch, periwinkle
flower: caracol(e)
-like: *late, *slow
shell: cochlea
SNAKE: coil, pull, *turn, *wind
-bird: anhinga, wryneck
-bite remedy: cedron, guaco
comb.: angui, herpet(o), ophi, ophid(io), ophio, serpenti
dancer: hopi, moqui, taos
doctor: dragonfly, hellgrammite

-haired woman: euryale, gorgon, medusa, stheno
killer: mongoose, roadrunner
mouth: orchid
pert.: anguine, colubrine, herpetic, ophioid, reptilian
-root: asarum, blolly, bugbane, sanicle, seneca, senega, stevia
-skin: exuvia
-weed: bistort
-worm: carphiohiops, carphophis
SNAP: *bit, *break, *cheat, instant, *noise, pep, picture, *report, sharp, *strike, *throw
dragon: antirrhinum, bulldog, bunny mouth, calf's-snout
SNAPE: bream, caji, caxi, cosaque, pargo, sesi
SNAPPISH: *angry, *edgy, *short
SNAPPY: *fast, *quick, *short
SNARE: *ambush, *steal, *trap
SNARL: *bark, bowwow, *confuse, *fight, gnar(r), *protest, sough, yap, yarr, yelp, yirr
SNATCH: *abduct, *bit, *part, *piece, *seize, *steal, *take
SNEAK: *ambush, *hide, *rogue, slink, *spy, *steal, *thief
SNEE: dagger, dirk, knife
SNEER: gibe, mock, scorn, *taunt
SNEEZE: *dismiss, scorn, snuff
pert.: errhine, sternutatory
-weed: helenium, ragweed
word: gesundheit
-wort: achillea, ball-of-snow, ptarmica, ptarmite
SNELL: *acute, *eager, *extreme, *hard, *quick, *severe, *sharp
SNIB: *rebuke, *snub, *trap
SNICKER: knife, *laugh, *sneer
SNIDE: *bad, *low, *mean, *sly
SNIFF: *scent, *smell, trace
SNIFTER: *drink
SNIGGER: ridicule, *snicker
SNIGGLE: *laugh, *trap
SNIP: *bit(e), *part, *piece
SNIPE: *attack, *fool, *shoot

cry: scape
eel: thread
fish: aulostomi, flutemouth
flock: whisp
SNITCH: *betray, *steal, *tell
SNIVEL: *complain, *cry
SNOB: brahmin, prig, sycophant
SNOBBISH: *arrogant, *proud
SNOD: *smooth, *snug, trim
SNOOD: hairnet, *snell, *tle
SNOOK: barracuda, gar, robalo, *scent, *search, snuffle
SNOOP: *look, *search, *spy
SNOOSE: rappee, snuff
SNORE: rale, rhonchus, sibilate
SNORT: *cry, *drink, *laugh
SNOW: cocaine, crystal, dessert, heroin, narcotic, sleet, winter
-bird: grouse, junco, ptarmigan
-drop: amaryllis, violet
-field: firn, neve
-flake: bunting, crystal, finch
flower: azalea, bouquet de flore, cardinal, minerva, rhododendron
flurry: skirl
granular: corn
house: iglo(o), iglu
leopard: ounce
-man, abominable: yeti
partridge: lerwa
pert.: nival, niveous
ridge: sastrugi, zastrugi
-shoe: bearpaw, pac, patten, ski
shoe component: babiche
-slide: avalanche, glissade
-storm: burga
vehicle: cariole, luge, pung, sled, sleigh, toboggan
wedding: rice
SNUB: avoid, *scold, *snib, *stop
-nosed: deformed, simous
SNUFF: bergamot, *scent, *smell
-box: mull, puffball
-box bean: cacoon, liana, mackay
pinch: shmeck tabac
-taking: dipping
SNUFFY: *bad, *dirty, horrid

* Asterisk means to look up this word to find more answer words.

SNUG: *cuddle, *neat, *safe
SO: ergo, hence, then, therefore,
  *true, very
  long: *good: by, shalom
  -so: *fair, medium, *small
SOAK: *absorb, *hit, *strike
SOAP: bribe, *money, *praise
  -bark: quillai, quillaja, tree
  -berry: akee, blighia, titoki
  -box: platform, stump
  -fish: jabon
  frame bar: sess
  liniment: opodeldoc
  plant: agave, amole, soapwort
  -stone: alberene, steatite, talc
  -suds: foam, froth, lather
  vine: go go
  -weed: amole, yucca
  -wort: boston pink, bouncing bess,
    bruisewort, daisy
  -wort gentian: calathian violet
SOAR: fly, *rise, sail, wing
  through space: astronavigate
SOB: *cry, *scoundrel, wail
SOBER: *cool, *gentle, *heavy,
  *poor, *quiet, *severe, *wise
SOBK: *demon, *devil
SOBRIQUET: *name, *title
SOCIAL: *affable, *affair, *party,
  *public, tribal
  climber: parvenu, snob, upstart
  lion: big shot, *magnate
  register: *society
SOCIALIST: bolshevik, communist, manchesterist
  famous: cabet, debs, engels, fa-
    bian, fourier, jaures, marx, owen,
    proudhon, saint simon, shaw,
    sun yat sen
SOCIETY: aristocracy, beau
  monde, bluebloods, blue book,
  bon ton, colony, commonwealth,
  confederacy, congregation, court,
  drawing room, elite, establishment, ethnos, fashion, fellow-
  ship, ffvs, four hundred, gentry,
  *group, haut monde, high life,

lodge, mankind, mayfair, *order,
  *party, population, power struc-
  ture, salon, smart set, tong,
  union, upper crust, vanity fair,
  verein
  aversion: anthropophobia, mis-
    anthropy
  entrance: debut
  island: bora bora, tahiti
  secret: black hand, camorra,
    egbo, fraternity, kkk, la cosa
    nostra, la mano nera, mafia,
    masons, ogboni, poro, sorority,
    syndicate, tong
SOCIOLOGY: demotics
SOCK: *hit, *sandal, *strike
SOCKDOLAGER: *answer, *end
SOCKET: *opening, space, *spear
  kind: alveolus, birn, orbit
SOCRATES: escape plotter: crito
  follower: ceres, plato
  intimate: alcibiades
  wife: xanthippe, xantippe
  work: apologia, meno, phaedo
SOD: clod, land, peat, turf
SODA: alkali, barilla, beverage,
  bicarb(onate), pop, saleratus
SODALITY: *group, *society
SODIUM: niter, salt, soda, trona
  compound: acmite, aegerite, al-
    bite, anatron, antiformin, barilla,
    beryllonite, blankit(e), blodite,
    borax, brazilianite, mendozite,
    natron, sal soda, soda, trona
SODOM KING: bera
SOFA: bergere, boist, boudeuse,
  causeuse, davenport, *divan,
  dosados, lounge, ottoman, squab
SOFT: comfortable, dulcet, easy,
  effeminate, *fine, foolish, *gentle, gullible, indulgent, *light,
  limp, *low, mellow, muddy,
  pulpy, queachy, *smooth, sub-
  dued, *sweet, waxy, *weak
  chess: blubber grass, bromus
  -soap: blarney, flattery, oil
SOFTEN: *move, *temper, *yield

* Asterisk means to look up this word to find more answer words.

SOFTY: coward, *fool, sissy
SOGGY: *dull, *heavy, wet
SOHRAB: *father:* rustem
SOIGNE: neat, *sleek, tidy
SOIL: *dirty, *smear, *spoil
  comb.: agro, geo
  kind: adobe, argil, clay, clunch,
  dust, groot, gumbo, humus, kaolin, lair, loam, loess, malm, marl,
  mold, sand
SOIREE: *affair, *party, social
SOJOURN: *live, *stop, tarry
SOKAGAKKAI: *term:* gohonzon,
  mantra, nam myoho renge kyo,
  society, value creation
SOLACE: *abate, *please, relief
SOLAR: *sun
SOLDAN: *slayer:* sir cawline
SOLDER: *adhere, *join, *unite
SOLDIER: amazon, antesignanus,
  anzac, askar, atkins, aussie, base
  wallah, batman, billjim, boche,
  bolo, bonach, brave, brigand,
  buckskin, buff coat, byffy coat,
  cadet, cannon fodder, carabineer,
  carmagnole, cateran, chasseur,
  commando, cossack, cuirassier,
  doughboy, dragoon, fantassin,
  fighter, fritz, fugleman, gendarme, gi joe, goldbrick, grena-
  dier, grognard, guffy, halberdier,
  hero, hessian, hoplite, impi,
  jaeger, janissary, janizary, jerry,
  jock, johnny, kern(e), kraut,
  lancer, lascar, legionnaire, malin-
  gerer, man, marine, militiaman,
  miquelet, musketeer, nizam, palikar, peon, pikeman, poilu, private, ranger, redcoat, regular,
  rifle, rok, sammy, samurai, sannup, sapper, sepoy, serviceman,
  shirk, spahee, spani, spearman,
  storm trooper, swad, toa, tol-
  patch, tommy (atkins), trooper,
  uhlan, velites, vet, veteran, warrior, yank, zouave

female: amazon, aslauga, idisi,
  valkyrie
*group: *army: unit,* infantry
hired: buccellarius, gladiator, hessian, janizary
new: bezonian, cadet, chicken,
  plebe, recruit, rookie
SOLE: fish, mere, only, *unique
  pert.: plantar
SOLECISM: *error, gaffe, *slip
SOLEMN: *important, *severe
SOLENODON: agouta, almique
SOLICIT: *ask, *seek, *urge
SOLICITOUS: *ardent, *ready
SOLICITUDE: *desire, *interest
SOLID: basic, *big, body, bulky,
  cake, cement(al), conglomerate,
  durable, enduring, entire, *fat,
  *firm, *great, *hard, *heavy,
  lump, mass(ive), real, reliable,
  rugged, sensible, set, stable,
  steady, *strong, sturdy, substantial, *thick, *true, unanimous,
  valid, whole
  comb.: prism, stereo
SOLIDAGO: goldenrod
SOLIDIFY: cake, candy, *set
SOLILOQUY: apostrophe, aside
SOLITARY: alone, only, *unique
  comb.: eremo
SOLO: aria, *piece, pilot, self
  accompaniment: obbligato
SOLOMON: jedidiah, king, *sage
  ally: hiram
  calendar officer: azariah
  chamberlain: ahishar
  enemy: hadar, jeroboam, rezon
  general: ahijah, benaiah
  gold source: ophir
  governor: ahimaaz, ahinadab,
  azariah, baana(h), ben abinadab,
  ben beber, ben dekar, ben hesed,
  ben hur, geber, jehoshaphat,
  shimei
  island: bougainville, buka, gizo,
  savo
  island gulf: huon, kula

* Asterisk means to look up this word to find more answer words.

island harbor: kieta
island volcano: balbi
king's friend: zabud
levy superintendent: adoniram
lily: black calla
parent: bathsheba, david
pillar: boaz, jachin
priest: abiathar, zadok
prince: azariah
scribe: ahiah, elihoreph
secretary of state: jehoshaphat
son: rehoboam, roboam
song: canticle, canzon(et)
SOLUTION: *answer, *issue, key, *reason, *result
kind: brine, eusol, iodine, phenol, sirup, syrup
strength: proof, titer, titre
SOLVE: *answer, *break, *get, *make, *set, *settle, *work
SOMA: aruna, bhang, haoma, hiranya, pavamana, rhubarb
SOMALILAND: *coin:* besa
desert: aror
measure: caba, chela, cubito, darat, parsalah, tabla, top
town: berbera, mogadishu
SOMBER: *heavy, *sad, *solemn
SOME: any, *part, *quantity
-body: celebrity, *magnate, vip
-what: aliquid, rather
SOMERSAULT: flip, leap, reverse
SOMITE: cephalomere, metamere
SOMMELIER: butler, cellarman
SON: ben, boy, cadet, dauphin, fils, fitz, mac, scion, youth
comb.: ap, bar, mac, mc
-in-law: athum, aydem, gener, odam
of god: jesus, redeemer, saviour
pert.: filial
-ship: filiety
SONAR: asdic
SONATA: *part:* adagio, allegro, coda, largo, minuet, minuetto, presto, rondo, scherzo, trio
SONG: air, alba, anthem, aria,

arietta, aubade, ballad, barcarole, bit, brindisi, cabaletta, calypso, cancion, canticle, canzonet, carol, cavatina, chanson, chant(ey), croon, derry, discant, ditty, epistrophe, epode, fala, lay, lied, lyric, matin, noel, paean, *poem, polyphony, psalm, rondeau, ronda, roundelay, serenade, *strain, stroud, trifle, troll, uta, volkslied
-bird: bulbul, canary, cuckoo, lark, linnet, mavis, mocker, nightingale, oriole, philomel, redstart, ringdove, robin, thrush, warbler
comb.: melo
girl: adeline, clementine, sal, susanna(h)
pert.: ariose, cantabile, lyric, melic, melodious
SONNET: *bit:* coda, octet, seste
prince: joachim
SONOROUS: loud, resonant, *rich
SOONER: before, ere, first
SOOT: *dregs, *refuse, *smut
brown: bistre, manganese
part: aizle, isel, izle
pert.: fuliginous
sawdust: coom(b)
SOOTH: *present, *soft, *sweet
SOOTHE: *compose, *quiet, *temper
SOOTHER: *drug, *salve, sedative
SOOTHSAYER: *prophet, *sage
SOOTY: *black, *dirty
SOP: *absorb, *fool, *gift
SOPHISTICATED: *smart, *wise
SOPHISTRY: *deception, *error
SOPHY: *ruler, *sage, *skill
SOPOR: *sleep, *soother
SOPRANO: canto, treble, voice
famous: alda, bori, callas, freni, lind, nilsson, patti, pons, raisa, steber, stevens
SORA: bird, crake, rail
SORATA: *peak:* ancohuma

---

* Asterisk means to look up this word to find more answer words.

SORBUS: quince, rowan
SORCERER: *magician, *sage
SORCERESS: circe, *hag, *witch
SORCERY: *magic, *rite, *spell
SORDID: *bad, *dirty, *low, *mean, *poor, *sad
SORDOR: *dregs, *refuse
SORE: *angry, *hurt, *mad
-head: birdpox, crank, grouch
kind: abscess, aposteme, blain, bleg, boil, bubo, bulla, bunion, canker, carbuncle, chancre, chilblain, eschar, fester, fistula, furuncle, kibe, papule, pet, pimple, polyp, pustule, scab, sty, wale, welt, wheal, whelk
SORGHUM: batad, broomcorn, cane, cush, dari, dhurra, durr, feterita, hegari, imphee, kafir, kaoliang, millet, milo, molasses, sorgo, syrup, wheat
SORITES: *group, *quantity
SORREL: alezan, alleluia, averrhoa, oca, oka, oxalis, roselle
SORROW: *ache, *afflict(ion), agonize, attrition, bail, bewail, bitterness, care, *cry, despair, disillusionment, dole, *hurt, mourn, *pain, *remorse, sadness, *trial, *trouble, woe
SORRY: apologetic, *bad, conscience-stricken, contrite, dickey, drear, *hurt, *low, *mean, melancholy, pitiful, *poor, regretful, *sad, shameful, straitened, wretched
SORT: *class, *group, *kind
SORTIE: *attack, foray, raid
SORTILEGE: *magic, *rite
SOS: *alarm, mayday, signal
SO-SO: *bad, *poor, *sad
SOSSLE: *mess, *refuse, slime
SOT: drunk, *fool, *obstinate
SOUARI: butternut, caryocar
SOUGH: *complain, *cry, *snarl
SOUL: alma, ame, anima, atman, atta, buddhi, jivitma, *mind, pneuma, prana, principle, satyagraha, *spirit, substance
supreme: brahma
SOUND: *firm, *noise, *perfect, *right, *solid, *strong, *wise
comb.: audio
pert.: acoustic, audio, auditory, sonic, tonal, vocal
SOUNDLESS: abyssal, *quiet
SOUP: bisque, borscht, bouillabaise, broth, consomme, gazpacho, gumbo, minestrone, mulligatawny, okra, oomph, potage, *power, puree, shchi, stchi, vichyssoise
-bone: arm
dish: bowl, cup, tureen
-fin shark: tope
-spoon: ladle
up: *increase, *speed
SOUPCON: *bit, *trifle
SOUR: *acerb, acetose, *acetic, acor, bitter, bleeze, crab(bed), embittered, *ferment, glum, green, grim, gruff, grumpy, *hard, morose, pickled, rancid, *sad, *sharp, *spoil, *sullen, tart
-dook: buttermilk
-dough: prospector, settler
-gourd: bobab, tree
-sop: annona, anona, guanabana
SOURCE: *anlage, base, bonanza, *bud, *cadre, calorie, cause, center, derivation, edition, egg, fons, font, fountain, germ, gold mine, grass roots, *head(spring), inception, knop, lode, mainspring, mine, nucleus, *opening, origin, parent, provenance, quarry, rise, riverhead, root, seed, sperm, spring, *start, stem, stirps, stock, vein, well(head)
SOUSE: *drink, *immerse, *orgy
SOUTANE: *vestment: religious
SOUTH: auster, dixie, sud, sur
comb.: austro

* Asterisk means to look up this word to find more answer words.

SOUTH AFRICAN: *african,* boer

animal: das, nenta, suricate

antelope: *african: antelope

armadillo: para

arrow poison: echugin

assembly: raad

aunt: tanta

brandy: cape smoke

breastwork: scherm

bushman: qung

caterpillar: risper

cattle enclosure: kraal

cliff: klip

club: knobkerrie

coin: cent, florin, pond, rand

condiment: balachong, blatjang

conference: indaba, raad

corn: mealie, mealy

criminal: amalaita

dialect: kitchen kaffir, taal

diamond: jager, schlenter

dish: bobooti, bobotee

dutch: afrikaans, boer, taal

dutch mistress: noi

fastener: oxreim

fish: bamboo, box salpa, sparid

flower: lachenalia, phygelius

garment: caross, kaross

gold field: rand

greenhorn: ikona

gun: roer, rohr

half-acre: erven

herb: bear's-paw, bengal lily, bermuda buttercup, bolboxalis, cabbagewort, cape fennel, foeniculum, othonna

hill: bult, kop(je), spitzkop

hippopotamus: zeekoe

hog: boschvark

hornbill: bromvogel, bucorvus

laborer: togt

maize: mealie

myth: anansi, annancy, spider

pass: nek

plain: veld(t)

plant: aloe, aponogeton, avond- bloem, cape bulb, hesperantha, ixia, kleinia, lachenalia, sparaxis

plot: erf

polecat: musang

policeman: zarp

province: transvaal

rodent: ratel

shrike: bacbakiri, telephonus

shrub: anchor plant, aspalanthus, barosma, bowstring hemp, bush tea, cape bladder senna, cyclopia, lyperia, narras, phygelius, podalyria, protea

simpleton: ikona

snake: aboma, boomslang, dendraspis, dispholidus, egg eater, elaps, mamba

spirit: tikolosh

starling: spreeuw, sprew

stream: aar

sumac: karree

swamp: vlei, vley

tableland: karoo

thong: riem(pie)

tick: tampan

tortoise: hicatee, matama

tract: zuurveldt

trader: swahili

tree: acacia giraffe, akebergia, assagai, bark cloth, beach apple, brachystegia, bufflehorn, burchelia, callitris, cape ash, eleaodendron, essenhout, euclea, gamdeboo, karroo bush, krugiodendron, olea laurifolia, tenio

valley: vaal

village: kraal, stad(t)

vine: honeysuckle, tecomaria

warrior: impi

waxbill: astrild, estrilda

weapon: assagai, assegai

weaverbird: taha

whip: sjambok

wood sorrel: bermuda buttercup

SOUTH AMERICAN: latin

animal: afara, agouara, alpaca, anteater, armadillo, coati, coypu,

guanaco, jaguar, kinkajou, llama,
nutria, paca, quica, sarigue, sloth,
tamarin, tapir, vicuna
ant: sauba, sauva
anteater: tamandu
arbor: ramada
armadillo: apar, peba, pichiciago,
poyou, tatouay
arrow poison: curara, curare
balsam: copaiba, tolu
bat: vampire
bean: tonka
beef: tasajo
beverage: mate
bird: agami, ara(cari), arara, aura,
baker, barber, barbet, barking
bird, becard, bellbird, boatbill,
cacicus, chaja, condor, curassow,
flamingo, guacharo, heron, jacamar, jacana, jacu, mitu, myna,
oilbird, puffbird, rara, screamer,
seriema, sylph, taha, terutero,
tinamou, tityra, toucan, trumpeter, turco, warrior
biscuit: panal
blanket: serape
boat: cayuco
butterfly: borboleta
cactus: airampo, borzi
catamaran: jaganda
catfish: aspredo, dorad
cattle: niata
clock: poncho
cold region: puna
cowboy: gaucho, llanero, planero
dance: areito, beguine, bolero,
cha-cha, mambo, samba
deer: brocket, cariacu, coassus,
guemal, guemul, mazama, pita,
pudu, vanada
desert: hornada
dog: agouara
dove: talpacoti
dye: lana
eel: carapo
farm: chacra, estancia, hacienda,
ranchero, rancho

fish: acapima, acara, aimara,
arapaima, bloodfin, caribe, cor-
bina, paco, pacu, paru, piranha,
piraya, scalare
flower: angel's-trumpet
fly: pium
fog: camanchaca, garua
fruit: pina
gaiter: chaparajo, chivarro
game: jai alai, pelota
game bird: guan, tinamou
garment: serape
grass: ichu
griddlecake: arepa
gruel: atole
guinea pig: cavy
hare: tapeti
hawk: caracara, carancho, carrion buzzard, chimango
herb: bead plant, biacuru, limo-
nium, pijicapu, romerillo
herdsman: llanero
hummingbird: sylph
indian: antesi, antisian, arawak,
auca, aymara, bororoan, cain-
gang, camacan, carib(ee), cayapo, chavante, corabecan, coroado, covarecan, curavecan,
curuminacan, ges, goyana, gua-
toan, inca, jivaro, ona, otuquian,
pampero, patagonian, puqina,
tama, tapa, tapuyan, timbira,
trio, voto
indian hut: toldo
island: aruba, elobey
jungle killer: motilone
jungle plant: cohoba
knife: facao, machete, navaja
lapwing: terutero
legislature: asamblea
liberator: bolivar
limestone: tosca
liquor: chicha
lizard: coati, teju
measure: manzana, vara
medicine man: peai, piay
mineral: urso

mite: acarus, mucuxim
monkey: acari, alouatte, araba, barrigudo, beelzebub, dourou-couli, grison, marmoset, ora-bassu, ouakari, pinche, saguin, sai, saimiri, sajou, saki, samiri, sapajou, tamarin, te(tee), teetee, titi
mountains: andes, sorata
opossum: quica, sarigue
ostrich: rhea
owl: utum
palm: acrocomia, assai, babassu, bacaba, bussu, coquito, datil, ita, jara, nikau, tooru, troly, troolie, tucum, ubussu, urucuri
plague: desenvolvimento
plain: llano, pampa(s), vega
plains dweller: llanero
plant: aji, albuca, angelon, cras-sula, gum, hymenaea, ipecac, tillandsia, yucuchu
porridge: atole
rabbit: tapeti
rancher: estanciero
rodent: agouti, capybara, chin-chilla, coypu, degu, hydro-choerus, moca, paca, viscacha, vizcacha
root: oca
rubber tree: para, ule
ruminant: alpaca, llama
scarf: manta, tapalo
shrub: anchiete, anchor plant, bird of paradise bush, ceibo, coca, colletia, erythrina, kapok, pepino, poinciana
snake: aboma, anaconda, bom, bushmaster, coralito, lora
sorrel: oca
stock: ona
strait: magellan
tableland: paramo(s), puna
tanager: habia, lindo, yeni
tick: carapato
tiger: chati
tortoise: matamata

toucan: aracari, toco
tree: albarco, algarroba, ana-cardium, angelique, angico, apa, araucaria, arboloco, aroeira, aspidosperma, astronium, ba-cury, balaustre, balsa, bebeeru, bertholletia, bethabara, bibiru, bignonia, breadfruit, cacao, can-dlewood, canela, cannonball, caoba, caracoli, caranna, cari-niana, carol, cebil, ceratonia, cesalpinia, fotui, gama, jaca-randa, jume, locust pod, papaya, para, pekea, quayabi, sapotizeiro, sapucai, simaba, st john's-bread, umbra, umbrella tree, vera, ya-chan
tribe: campa, motilones, oca
trumpeter: agami
tuber: oca
turtle: matamata
vine: abobra, cacur, cucumis, passiflora, punya
volcano: cotopaxi, omate
walnut: conacaste
wasteland: patagonia
weapon: bola(s)
wildcat: eyra
wind: pampero, puna, puno
wood: cesalpinia
zone: amphigaea
SOUTH CAROLINA: *bird:* wren
flower: yellow jessamine
fort: sumter
native: weasel
nickname: palmetto state
political group: woolhats
river: edisto, peedee, saluda
tree: palmetto
SOUTH DAKOTA: *bird:* pheasant
flower: pasqueflower
nickname: coyote state
tree: black hills spruce
SOUTH POLE: *bird:* penguin, skua
continent: antarctica

* **Asterisk means to look up this word to find more answer words.**

SOUTH SEAS: *malay references
island: atoll, bali, bismarck archipelago, fiji, otaheite, pitcairn,
samoa, society, sulu, tahiti,
timor, tonga
SOUTH VIETNAM: *army:* arvn
capital: saigon
general: do cao tri
SOUTHEAST: *wind:* cape doctor
wind god: eurus
SOUTHERN: austral, meridional
buckthorn: bumelia lycioides
cypress: swamp tree
lights: aurora polaris
right whale: blackfish
states: confederacy, dixie
wood: abrotanum, appleringie,
artemisia, boy's-love, wormwood
SOUTHWEST: *wind:* afer, affer,
auster, notus, squam
SOUVENIR: bibelot, curio, *token
SOVEREIGN: *free, *head, *lord,
*magnate, *ruler, *supreme
SOVEREIGNTY: *authority,
*power, *rule, *state
absolute: autarchy, tyranny
joint: condominium
SOVIET: *group, *russian
SOW: pig, *plant, *scatter
-back: *cap, drumlin, *ridge
-bane: red goosefoot
-belly: bacon, saltpork
-bread: wild cyclamen
-bug: louse, slater
fennel: brimstonewort
-gelder: *rogue, *scoundrel
-grass: swine's-cress
thistle: sonchus, weed
-tit: wood strawberry
wild: javelina
wild oats: dissipate, *play
young: elt, gilt
SOY: bean, silk, soja, soya
enzyme: urase
tablet: torfu
SPA: baths, resort, springs
SPACE: *astronaut, *distance,
*kind, *open(ing), *part, *piece,
*range, *rank, *remove, *rocket,
*separate, *set, *spread, *time
agency: nasa
-craft: *rocket
high point: apocynthion
laboratory: mol
landing: splashdown
man: *astronaut, cosmonaut
open, comb.: agor(a)
scientist: draper, goddard, hou-
bolt, von braun
SPACIOUS: *broad, *open, wide
SPADASSIN: bravo, duelist
SPADE: card, delve, didle, dig,
excavate, graft, grub, ladle, loy,
pick, pry, scavel, shovel, slane,
spud, *try
ace: spadill(a), spadille
deuce: little casino
queen: basta, black lady, calamity jane, maria, slippery anne
suit: espadas, grun, lanzas, laub,
lilies, pique, schippen
SPADO: *sword
SPAIN: espagna, iberia, *spanish
castles in: dreams
SPALACID: mole, rat, rodent
SPALL: *bit, *break, *fall, gallet,
*reduce, splinter
SPALPEEN: boy, *rascal, *rogue
SPAN: *distance, *range, *spread
SPANG: *ornament, *straight
SPANGLE: *ornament, *shine
SPANISH: *abbey:* abadia
abbey lands: abadengo
admiral: cervera topete
adventurer: almogaver
apron: delantale
article: el, la(s), los, una
author: alarcon, barea, celo, cervantes
band: cobla
bathtub: banera, bano
bay: bahia, biscay
bayonet: plant, yucca
beach: playa

* Asterisk means to look up this word to find more answer words.

bean: haba
belle: maja
blanket: manta, serape
boat: aviso, balandra, barca
bonnet: gorra
booth: tienda
boy: muchacho, nino
brandy: aguardiente
brush: cepillo
bull: toro
bullring: coso
calico: percal, zaraza
cape: trafalgar
cart: carretta
castle: alcazar
cathedral city: seville
cavalryman: ginete
cedar: acajou, cedrela odorata
cellist: casals
champion: el cid
channel: cano
chest: caja
chief: adalid, cid, jefe
church: iglesia
city: albacete, algeciras, alicante, almeden, almeria, avaro, avila, badajoz, badalona, barcelona, baza, bilbao, burgos, cabra, cadiz, cartagena, carthagena, cordova, elche, gijon, granada, irun, jerez, leon, loja, madrid, malaga, mula, murcia, olot, ronda, salamanca, santander, saragossa, siero, toledo, valencia, valladolid, xeres
coat: capa, chaleco, chaqueta, chupa, manta, zamarra, zamarro
coin: alfonso, cendavo, centen, centimo, cuartillo, cuartino, decima, dobla, duro, peseta, piaster, pistole, real, vellon
commander: adalid, caid, cid
commune: alcoy, ausa, elda, gradu, jaen, lena, lorca, naron, oliva, osuna, reus, rute, sueca, telda, tineo, ubeda, utrera, vich, yecla

composer: albeniz
conqueror: cid, conquistador, cortez, pizzaro
constable: alguacil, alguazil
contract: asiento, assiento
council: consejo, junta
count: conde
dance: baile, bolero, bouree, carioca, fandango, gitana, jaleo, jota, polo, saraband, sardana, seguidilla, tango, zapateado
deity: dios(sa)
dish: cigala, gambas, gazpacho, langosta, olla, paella, posole, serrano, zarzuela
diva: bori
division: blue devils
dramatist: alvarez, benavente, calderon, vega
dress: traje
dumpling: tamale
duty, impost: indulto
earth: tierra
elm: black sage, ramona
epic: cid
exclamation: bravo, carajo, caramba, mano, ole
execution: garotte, garrotte
explorer: balboa, cabeza de vaca, colon, coronado, cortez, mendoza, pizzaro
fabric: crea, tiraz
farm: hacienda
fascist: falangist
fashion designer: castillo
feast day: fiesta
fireplace: fogon
fish: cero, ronco, sierra
fleet: armada, flota
fly: cantharis
food shop: cantina
friend: amigo
frigate: zabra
game: jai alai, monte, ombre, pedro, pelota, seisillo, solo, tomate, tresillo, truco, tute
general: alba, alva

* Asterisk means to look up this word to find more answer words.

gentleman: caballero, cavalier, don, grandee, senor
gold: oro
governess: aya, duenna
government obligation: cedula
governor: idelantado
grass: esparto, spart
grass rope: soga
griddlecake: arepa
gruel: atole
gypsy: gitano, zincalo
habeas corpus: amparo
half-breed: ladino
hall: sala
hangman's rope: mecate
hat: boina, sombrero
head covering: mantilla
herdsman: ranchero
hero: cid
heroine: ibarruri, la pasionaria
hill: cerro, colina, morro
holiday: fiesta
horse: caballo, jennet
hotel: posada, vento
house: casa, casita
impost: indulto
-indian: guero, mestizo, tribueno
inquisition stake: brasero
instrument: atabal, bandurria, castanet, vihuela, zambomba
island: balearic, canary, ibiza, mallorca, minorca
jacinth: bell-flowered squill
jar: bucaro, olla, tinaja
jew: anusim, marrano, sephardim
judge: alcalde, entrada, juez
kettle: cazo, olla
kettledrum: atabal
king, first: geryon
kingdom: aragon, castile, leon
knife: cuchillo, machete, navaja
knight: caballero
lace: encaje
lady: dama, dona, senora
lake: albufera, lago
landmark: coto, linde, marca, mojon, senal

land tenure: caballeria
language: castilian
legal affair: acto
legion: blue devils
legislature: cortes
letter carrier: correo
licorice juice: black sugar
lighthouse: faro
linen: crea, gaea, hilo, lienzo
lowland: marisma
magic: brujeria
mahogany: caoba
man: don, hombre, senor
manager: gerente
mantle: capa
mattress: colchon
mayor: alcade, alcalde
measure: aranzada, aroba, azumbre, braza, caballeria, cafiz, cahiz, cantara, celemin, codo, copa, cordel, cuarta, cuarteron, cuartillo, dedo, estadel, estado, fanega(da), league, legua, linea, medio, milla, moyo, palmo, paso, pie, pulgada, racion, sesma, vara, yugada
monk: padre
mountain: asturian, cantabrian, gredos, guadarrama, guara, la maladetta, mulahacem, pic de netou, pyrenees, sierra de toledo, sierra morena
mounts, relay: remuda
muffler: embozo
muleteer: arriero
music: chacona, malaguena
noble: don, grandee, hidalgo
numbers (1 to 9): uno, dos, tres, cuatro, cinco, seis, siete, ocho, nueve
nun: avila, monja
ocher: almagra, tangier
officer: alcalde, alguazil
operetta: zarzuela
oyster: ostra, pinna
painter: cano, dali, goya, gris,

miro, picasso, ribera, sert,
velasquez, zuloaga
palace: escorial
pancake: arepa
pear: avocado
peasant: paisano
peninsula: iberia
people: gente
pepper: chili, pimento
pickpocket: ratero
poet: alarcon, becquer, encina
point: aurillac lace
police: policia, rurale
priest: cura, padre
queen: ena, isabella, maria luisa,
regina, reina
raisin: pasa
rapier: bilbo, espadin, estoque
relay: remuda
rice: arroz
rider: herisson
river: duero, douro, ebro, guadal-
quivir, guadiana, minho, rio,
segre, tagus
road: camino
saint: dominic, eulalie, teresa
seaport: adra, algeciras, alicante,
almeria, badalona, barcelona,
bilbao, cadiz, cartagena, malaga,
mataro, palos, vigo
sect: alombrados, illuminati
sentinel: vedet(te), videt(te)
shawl: manta, serape
sherry: amontillado, amoroso,
xeres
shirt: camisa
shoes: sabatos, zapatos
shop: tienda
sorcerer: brujo
sword: bilbo, espada
tax: alcabala
title: dom, don(a), hidalgo,
senor(a), senorita
tomorrow: manana
tower: atalaya, mirador, torre
trefoil: alfalfa, lucerne
trench: surcar, tajo

vehicle: tartana
vessel: albarello, balandra, buque,
caravel, galleon, nave, zabra
victory cry: ole
village: aldea
violinist: tartini
watercourse: arroyo, atarjea
weight: adarme, arienzo, arroba,
barril, caracter, castellano, dinero, dracma, escrupulo, frail,
grano, libra, marco, ochava,
onza, punto, quarto, quilate,
quintal, roba, tomin, tonelada
wineshop: bodega, venta
writer: alarcon, aleman, azorin,
barea, baroja, celo, cervantes,
ibanez, miguel
SPANK: *punish, *strike, *whip
SPANKING: *fine, *great, *strong
SPAR: *argue, *fight, *quarrel
SPARE: *free, *give, *save, thin
SPARK: aizle, arc, beau, *bit,
blade, cavalier, coxcomb, dandy,
date, diamond, dude, escort, es-
quire, *fellow, fop, funk, gallant, grain, *interest, izle, knight,
*love(r), nob, *pet, scintillate,
*sparkle, squire, *start, swain,
*sweetheart, swell, toff
SPARKLE: brilliance, coruscate,
*fire, flash, flicker, *joke, scat-
ter, *shine, signal, splendor,
*spirit, spray, strew
SPARKLING: *bright, *funny
SPARSE: few, meager, rare, *thin
SPARTAN: *severe, stoic, *strict
army division: mora
commander: lochage
festival: carnea, carneia
governor: harmost
king: agis, arius, leonidas, menelaus, nabis
lawgiver: lycurgus
magistrate: ephor
parchment: scytale
poet: alcman
prince: alopecus, astrabacus

* Asterisk means to look up this word to find more answer words.

queen: helen, leda
slave: helot, ilot
SPASM: *attack, paroxysm, stroke
SPAT: *fight, *quarrel, *strike
SPATE: flood, *plenty, *quantity
SPATTER: *dirty, *smear, *spoil
SPAWN: *source, *start, *yield
SPEAK: *gossip, *talk, *tell
 comb.: lalo
 inability to: aglossia, alalia,
  anepia, aphasia, mutism
SPEAKER: *head, *lead(er)
SPEAR: bayonet, bident, blade,
  bourdon, catch, fram, gaff, *get,
  gidya, gig, glaive, harpoon, impale, javelin, jireed, leaf, leister,
  *missile, *part, *piece, *pierce,
  *poke, reef, rod, shoot, shut,
  spar, sprout, *staff, stalk, stem,
  *stop, *strike, trident, weapon
 fish: billfish, gaff, gar, gig, sailfish,
  saury, tren, trident
 -head: *advance, *attack
 -like: hastate, lanciform
 -wort: belladonna
SPECIAL: *actual, commodity,
  concrete, dear, distinctive,
  *event, *extraordinary, *great,
  intimate, khas(s), limited, local,
  noteworthy, *particular, peculiar,
  *pet, *popular, rare, sale, spank-
  ing, standout, stylish, *unique
SPECIALTY: *forte, *skill
SPECIE: *money, *piece
SPECIES: *class, *image, *kind
SPECIFIC: *remedy, *special
SPECIFY: *allot, *establish,
  *limit, *name, *state, *tell
SPECIMEN: *copy, *form
SPECIOUS: apparent, colored,
  empty, eristic, *fair, *false,
  *good, hollow, *idle, illusory,
  ostensible, plausible, probable,
  seeming, *weak
SPECK(LE): *bit, *blot, *mark
SPECTACLE: *display, *show
SPECTER: *demon, *spirit

SPECTRUM: blue, colors, green,
  orange, purple, red, yellow
SPECULATE: *play, *study,
  *think, *venture
SPEECH: *gossip, *talk, *words
 goddess: vac(h)
 loss: alalia, anarthria, anaudia,
  aphasia, aphemia, aphrasia,
  dumbness, muteness
 loss, comb.: phasia
 provincial: argot
SPEED: *accelerate, amphetamine, barrel, bat, boom, bowl,
  breeze, brush, bundle, burn,
  cannonball, careen, celerity, clip,
  cover ground, cut along, dig, dispatch, *drug, exigency, fastness,
  fleet, flight, fly, further, hasten,
  hie, highball, make tracks, *narcotic, open up, pace, pour, powder, *press, progress, *push, railroad, rapidity, rate, ride, *run,
  rush, scorch, sizzle, skim, *slide,
  spank, sweep, *tear, tempo, trip,
  velocity, whisk, zip, zoom
 demon: driver, jehu
SPEEDY: *fast, *quick
SPELL: *abet, abracadabra, alternate, bewitch, bout, brief, cantrip, charm, *curse, *distance,
  drought, entrancement, *evil,
  fascination, glamor, *glory, hex,
  hoodoo, incantation, jinx, jonah,
  jynx, *magic, *mean, period,
  pinch-hit, pishogue, rapture, relate, relieve, seizure, siege, speak,
  *story, *substitute, sway, *talk,
  *tell, *trick, *turn, wanga,
  *weird, *word, write
SPEND: *give, *pass, *run, *use
SPERM WHALE: cachalot, ca-
  todont
SPHACELATE: *bad, *rotten
SPHERE: ambit, *arena, ball,
  bead, beat, blob, brahmanda,
  bulb(il), business, circle, cite,
  compass, department, *district,

---

* Asterisk means to look up this word to find more answer words.

domain, dominion, earth, geoid, globe, globule, hiranyagarbha, jurisdiction, knob, knot, lode-star, milieu, pellet, planet, polar star, *range, *reach, star, terella, theater, universe, *walk, world

SPHINX: *prophet, *puzzle

SPICY: *good, *rich, *sharp

SPIDER: arachnid, mite, skillet
big, the: john knox
bug: emesa
cell: astrocyte
comb.: arachn(o)
crab: maia(n), maja
fluid: aranein
foot hair: scopula
genus: agalena, aranea, attidae, drassidae, epeira
leaping: saltigrade
-like: arachnid, araneiform, araneose, araneous
monkey: ateles, belzebuth, coaita, quata
myth: anansi, anrancy
nest: nidus, web
orchids: brassavola, brassia
organ: calamistrum, spinneret
part: chelicera, pedipalpus
-web: attercop, nullenspiel
-wort: blue-eyed mary, collinsia, innocence, navelwort

SPIEL: *cry, pitch, *talk

SPIKE: barb, ear, *pierce, rig
bill: bird, godwit
hole: spile
lavender: aspic, mint
-let: palea
-nard: aralia, balm, ointment
-nard, pert.: araliaceous
-rush: aglet-head

SPILE: pin, rod, *rule, *stop

SPILL: *escape, *fall, *tell
blood: *kill, *war
-over: *refuse, *run, slop

SPIN: ride, *tell, *turn

SPINACH: epinard, orache, savoy

SPINDLE: axis, hasp, newel, rod

SPINE: acanthus, backbone, needle, *ridge, *spirit
comb.: acantho, acromio
cord: alba, medulla, myelion
disease: myelitis, polio
end: acromion
-less: anacanthous, irresolute
pert.: balas, cervical, dorsal, lumbar, rachidian, sacral
points: cakra, chakra
shrub: ulex
tail: duck

SPINNING: *machine:* distaff, jenny, mule, throstle
mite: spider
term: bobbin, flyer, spindle, traveler, wharve, whorl
wheel: charka, charkha

SPINSTERHOOD: *sign:* thimble

SPIRACLE: *opening, *spirit

SPIRAL: *comb.:* gyro, helic, helix
shell: caracol(e)

SPIRE: *acme, leaf, *top, *tower
cap: calotte
ornament: epi(s), finial

SPIRIT: angel, apparition, ariel, banshee, bravery, breast, breath, cognac, courage, *demon, *devil, *disposition, *dwarf, ego, elan, elixir, enterprise, enthusiasm, esprit de corps, essence, *fire, *force, ghost, grit, guts, haunt, heart, inner man, *interest, liquor, liveliness, *love, mettle, *mind, morale, nerve, *passion, phantasm, phenomenon, piquancy, poignancy, poltergeist, *power, psyche, punch, pungency, sand, shade, shadow, significance, *soul, *spark, specter, spook, spunk, *strength, sylph, *take, *temper, verve, vim, zeal
absolute: purusha
lamp: etna
leaf: manyroot

SPIRITUAL: *good, *holy, *pure, *sacred, spectral

---

* Asterisk means to look up this word to find more answer words.

meaning: anagoge, anagogics
meeting: seance
SPIT: emit, **image,* **light,* **pierce,*
saliva, **sword*
-*fire:* **crank,* **imposter*
SPITAL: den, refuge, resort
SPITE: **hate,* **hurt,* offend
SPLASH: **blot,* **mark,* **wet*
SPLAY: **adorn,* **spread,* **turn*
SPLEEN: **ardor,* **anger,* **fire*
SPLENDID: aureate, awful, bra-
vissimo, **bright,* deluxe, elaborate, extravagant, **fine,* gorgeous, **great,* **high,* **important,*
imposing, impressive, lustrous,
luxurious, **noble,* olympian, ostentatious, palatial, plush, radiant, real, rosy, silk stocking,
star(k), substantial, **supreme,*
swell, **unique*
SPLENETIC: irascible, peevish
SPLICE: **join,* **repair,* **unite*
SPLINT: fasten, **split,* strip
wood: alburnum, sapwood
SPLINTER: **bit,* **break,* **part*
SPLIT: **allot,* apportion, **betray,*
bifid, bipartite, bisect, breach,
*break, buck, cleft, **flaw,* halve,
*laugh, **open,* **opening,* **part,*
*piece, rip, rit, rive(n), schism,
*separate, **share,* **tear*
fruit: schizocarp
personality: schizophrenia
SPLITTING: **fast,* **funny,* **se-*
vere, **violent*
SPLOTCH: **blot,* **mark,* **spoil*
SPLURGE: **display,* **show,* **try*
SPLUTTER: **noise,* **nonsense*
SPOIL: addle, bitch, blad, blast,
booty, **break,* **bruise,* bugger,
confound, cripple, **decay,* **de-*
cline, **destroy,* disorganize, disrupt, foul up, gee up, graft, gum
up, hash up, haul, **hurt,* injure,
jimmy, languish, loot, louse up,
mar, **mess,* pamper, pelf, **pet,*
pillage, plunder, pork, **prize,*

queer, rob, rot, **ruin,* seduce,
*seize, snafu, **sour,* **take,*
thwart, undermine, undo, **upset,*
*violate, waste, wear
SPOLIATE, SPOLIATION: **spoil*
SPONGE: cadge, swab, zimocca
calcerous: leucon
cloth: ratine
comb.: act, aene
gourd: loof(a), loofah, luffa
opening: apopyle, osculum, pore
pert.: poriferal, porous, **soft*
spicule: actine, cymba, desma,
oxea, rhab, toxa, toxon
water: badiaga, spongilla
wood: sola
SPONSOR: angel, patron, **support*
SPONTANEOUS: **free,* **wild*
SPOOF: **deceive,* **fool,* **joke,*
*nonsense, swindle, **trick*
SPOOK: **demon,* **dwarf,* **spirit*
SPOON: ladle, **love,* **student*
bill: ajaja, paddlefish, scaup
drift: foam, spray, spindrift
-*shaped:* cochlear
SPOONY: **dull,* **fool,* **stupid*
SPOOR: **scent,* track, trail
SPORADIC: apart, **separate*
SPORE: carpel, germ, seed
case: ascus, theca
cluster: sorus
fruit: aecium, telium
-*like structure:* cyst
sac: ascus, capsule
SPORT: **contest,* **display,* **game,*
*joke, **play,* wear
area: **play:* place
event: game, meet, race
SPOT: **bit,* **dirty,* **mark,* **note,*
*place, **see,* **spy*
SPOTTED: calico, dappled, freck-
led, guttate, pied, pinto
SPOUSE: husband, mate, wife
SPOUT: **gossip,* pour, **talk*
SPRAIN: **hurt,* **strain,* **throw*
SPRAWL: **fall,* **rest,* **spread*

* Asterisk means to look up this word to find more answer words.

SPRAY: atomize, *issue, *part, *spread, sprinkle, surf, twig

SPREAD: advertisement, *allot, *annoint, bedding, *broadcast, bruit, burnish, circulate, *cover, delate, *dispense, *display, disperse, dissolve, divergence, expanse, explode, fan, *feast, flabelliform, flare, flue, *gossip, *grow, *home, *increase, *issue, layout, mantle, margin, norate, *open, outstretched, overrun, *place, prolong, publish, radiate, ramify, ranch, *range, *reach, rhipidate, scatter, *show, *smear, *size, splay, sprawl, spray, strew, *talk, *tell, unfold, unfurl, widen

bread: apple butter, butter, jam, jelly, margarine, oleo

-eagle: exaggerate, *fall, *win

SPREE: bout, drunk, *orgy, *tear

SPRIG: *part, *piece, *stem

SPRIGHTLY: *funny, *smart

SPRING: *issue, *run, *source

-back: bounce, *give, *yield

-board: alcalde, batule

harbinger: crocus, robin

nymph: aganippe, argyra, calypso, cassotis, castalia, crenae, cyane, hago, pegae, pirene

pert.: vernal

SPRINGE: gin, noose, *trap

SPRINKLE: hose, *splash, *wet

SPRINKLING: *bit, seme, *spread

SPRINT *missile, *run, *trap

SPRITE: *demon, *devil, *spirit

SPROCKET: cam, tooth, wheel

SPROIL: *action, *force

SPROUT: *grow, scion, shoot

comb.: blast(ic), blasto

SPRUCE: *dress, leather, *smart

partridge: canada grouse

tree: epinette, larch, picea

SPRY: *active, *fast, *quick

SPUNK: *anger, *spirit, *temper

SPUR: *abet, branch, calcar, excite, foment, gaff, goad, herd, incentive, incite, motive, *part, point, *press, prick, projection, provoke, *range, *ridge, rowel, stimulate, *tower, *urge

comb.: calcari

having: spicate

having two: bicalcarate

SPURGE: acalypha, adelia, alchornea, euphorbia, milkweed

SPURIOUS: *bad, *eccentric, *false, mock, pseudo, quasi

SPURN: *refuse, *scorn

SPURT: jet, *run, *speed, *start

SPUTNIK: dog: laika

SPY: *agent, beagle, drop, emissary, fifth columnist, informer, inside, intelligence, keek, *look, reconnaisance, reconnoiter, scout, secret agent, *see, snoop(er), spotter, stool pigeon, tout, undercover man, worm

famous: abel, andre, arnold, caleb, cavell, mata hari, powers, sorge

SPYRI: heroine: heidi

SQUAB: *fat, *short, *shy, thick

young: piper

SQUABBLE: *contest, *fight

SQUALID: *dirty, *mean, *poor

SQUALL: *cry, *noise, *storm

SQUAMA: alula, calypter, tegula

SQUANDER: *scatter, *spend

SQUARE: block, court, *equal, *fair, *honest, *place, *settle

-head: *fool, german, swede

SQUARELY: *right, *straight

SQUASH: *hide, *hit, *press

bug: anasa

SQUAT: *lie, *settle, *thick

SQUATTER: *squander, settler

SQUAW: coween, mahala, wife

-fish: boxhead, chappaul, chub

-root: beechdrops, cohosh, ginseng, orobancha

SQUAWK: *complain, *protest

SQUEAK: *blab, *cry, *escape

* Asterisk means to look up this word to find more answer words.

SQUEAL: *blab, *complain, *cry, *protest, *quarrel, *tell

SQUEAMISH: *anxious, *shy

SQUEEZE: *escape, *press, *push
in: *enter

SQUELCH: *blow, *fall, *hit, *quiet, *rebuke, silence, *stop

SQUIB: *piece, *spread, *throw

SQUID: calamary, cuttlefish, loligo, mollusk, octopus

SQUIGGLE: *quiver, *turn, twist

SQUINT: *look, *see, strabismus

SQUIRE: armiger, *noble, *spark

SQUIRM: *squiggle

SQUIRREL: ardilla, assapan, chickaree, chippy, gopher, sciurus, sisel, suslik, tamias
cage: routine, rut
-fish: marian, serrano
nest: dray, drey
pelt: calabar, calaber, vair
pert.: sciuroid

SQUIRT: *spurt, whippersnapper

SRI: *holy, laksmi, reverend

S-SHAPED: agee, sigmate, sigmoid

STAB: *attack, *hurt, *kill, *pain, *pierce, *spear, *try
in back: *betray, *smear

STABILIZE: *establish, *firm, *set, *settle, *support

STABLE: *firm, *group, *secure, *solid, *staff, *stall
-boy: mafu
-man: avener, groom, hostler
range or royal: mews

STACCATO: *abrupt, *sharp

STACK: flue, *group, heap, kitty, *pack, *set, shock
up with: correspond, *equal
-yard: haggard, stackgarth

STADDLE: *staff, *support

STADIUM: *play: place

STAFF: advisors, *agency, aides, alpenstock, ankus, associates, baculus, ballow, baston, bat(on), bodyguard, caduceus, cane, committee, *company, court, crook, crosier, cross, crutch, cudgel, entourage, escort, fasces, following, *force, gavel, *group, hands, henchmen, lathee, lituus, mace, man, men, mullein, paterissa, personnel, piton, retinue, rod, scepter, servants, *set, shaft, *spear, squad, stable, stave, *stick, suite, *support, *symbol, thyrsus, *train, wand
tree: catha, celestra(ce), kat, sapindale

STAG: *animal: male, *party
bush: black haw, honeysuckle
hercules: arcadian, ceryneian
horn: antler, bezantler, rial
hornless: pollard

STAGE: *period, *phase, *present
coach: diligence, *vehicle
dance: black bottom, tap
direction: all, aside, enter, exeunt, exit, loquitur, manet, omnes, senet, sennet, solus
doorman: johnnie
equipment: boards, coulisse, dock, flat, flipper, float, foot, oleo
extra: supe, super(numerary)
-hand: callboy, chips, flunky, flyman, gaffer, grip, juicer, machinist, pitman, scenist
part: boards, cloth, coulisse, curtain, dock, drop, flat, flies, flipper, float, foot, grid(iron), loft, oleo, paradus, platform, prop, rag, role, scenery, skenai, skene, tab, teaser, ring
pert.: scenical, theatrical

STAGGER: lurch, *oscillate, reel

STAGNANT: *dirty, *dull, *rotten

STAID: *cool, grave, *serious

STAIN: *dirty, *smear, *spoil

STAINLESS: *perfect, *pure

STAIR: degree, stage, step, sty
-case: caracol(e), escalator, ladder, perron
part: newel, riser, rung, tread
spindle: speel

* Asterisk means to look up this word to find more answer words.

STAKE: *bet, *interest, *mark, *money, *prize, *promise, *share, *staff, *stick, *support, *venture
-out: *ambush, *trap
pert.: palar
STALAG: *jail, prison
STALE: *bad, *old, *usual, worn
-mate: *crisis, *tie
STALK: *follow, pedicel, *staff, *stem, stride, *walk
having: petiolate
STALL: booth, *die, *end, *jail, *hut, *idle, *stand, *stop
STALWART: *bold, *firm, *strong
STAMEN: comb.: andra, andry
having: aplostemonous
lack: anandrarious, anandrous
part: anther, microsporangia
suppression: cenantry
STAMINA: *force, *power, *spirit
STAMMER: balbutiate, haw, hem
STAMP: *fix, *form, *mark, *name, *seal, *sign, *strike, *symbol, *token, *walk
background: burele
border: tressoure, tressure
collector: philatelist
fencing: appel
group: block
madness: timbromania
out: *end, *kill, *remove
paper: pelure
sheet part: pane
space: spandrel
STAMPEDE: *panic, *riot, *run
STANCH: *firm, *good, *honest, *stop, stem, tried, *true
STAND: abide, afford, appear, arise, attitude, bear, be present, block, booth, brook, cabaret, caster, cease, continue, dais, easel, endure, erect, etagere, exist, face, halt, last, lectern, maintain, *place, position, pulpit, rack, remain, resist, *rest, stall, stick, stomach, *stop, *suffer, *support, sustain, swallow, table,

*take, tolerate, treat, tripod, trivet, undergo, zarf
-in: substitute
inability to: abasia, astasia
-off: draw, *push, *tie
-out: *acme, *supreme, *top
pat: *solid
STANDARD: *acme, *adage, *flag, *image, *mark, *mean, *model, *rule, *sign, *symbol, *title, *usual, *value
pert.: vexillary
STANDISH: wife: rose
STANG: *pain, *staff, *spear
STANHOPE: buggy, chesterfield
STANZA: act, alloeostropha, apartment, baston, cinquain, couplet, decalet, distich, division, dizaine, envoi, huitan, octave, quatrain, sestet, stave, strophe, triolet, tristich, verse
STAPLE: *bit, commodity, mart, *principal, *supply, *support
STAR: *actor, *badge, *lead, *ornament, *principal, *shine
apple: balata, bully tree, caimito, mailkara, sapodilla
bright: beta, canopus, cor, nova(e), sirius
comb.: astero, astro, sidero
course: arc, orbit
covered with: seme
evening: hesper(us), moon
facet: pane
first magnitude: alpha, cygni, cygnus
fish: asteroid, bipinnaria, brachiolaria, echinoderm
five points: mullet
gazer: catfish, kathetostoma
grass: callitriche, starwort
group: asterism, cluster, constellation, galaxy, milky way, nebula, spiral
heraldry: estoile
STAR IN: andromeda (chained

---

lady): almak, alpherat(z), delta, mirac(h)

aquarius (*water bearer*): al bali, ancha, sadachbia, sadalmelik, sadalsund, skat

aquila (*eagle*): alshain, altair, deneb, difda, tarazed

argo: aspidiske, canopus, markeb, miaplacidis, milky way, naos

argo, divisions: carina (keel), malus (mast), puppis (stern), pyxis (mariner's compass or nautical box), vela (sails)

aries (*ram*): botein, el nath, hamal, mesartim, sheratan

auriga (*charioteer*): capella, el nath, kids, menkalinan

big dipper (*charles's wain*): *star in: ursa major

bootes (*herdsman*): alkalurops, arcturus, bear driver, canes venatici, guard keeper, izar, mirak, muphrid, nekkar, seginus, watcher

cancer (*crab*): acubens, altarf, asellus, praesepe, tegmine

canis major (*big dog*): adhara, aludra, dog star, furud, murzim, sirius, wezen

canis minor (*little dog*): gomeisa, procyon

canis venatico: asterion, chara, cor caroli

capricorn (*goat*): algedi, dabih, deneb, nashira

carina (*keel*): canopus

cassiopeia: caph, ruchbah, schiedar

centaurus: agena, rigil

cepheus: alderamin, alfirk, er rai

cetus (*whale*): baten kaitos, deneb, dheneb, menkar, mira

columba (*dove, noah's dove*): phaet(o), wezn

corona (*crown*): alphecca, gemma, nusakan

corvus (*crow*): al chiba, algorab, gienah

crater (*cup, goblet*): alkes

cygnus (*swan*): albireo, arided, azelfafage, deneb, gienah, northern cross, sadr

delphinus (*dolphin*): deneb, rotanev, sualocin

draco (*dragon*): adib, al rakis, al safi, altais, el asich, etamin, giansar, grumium, jugo, nodus secundus, rastaban, thuban

equuleus (*horse*): kitalpha

eridanus (*river*): acamar, achenar, ancha(t), angetenar, azha, beid, cursa, keid, theemim, zaurak

gemini (*twins*): alhena, apollo, castor, hercules, mebsuta, mekbuda, pollux, propus, wasat

hercules: cujam, kornephorus, rasalgethi

leo (*lion*): adhafera, aldhafara, algieba, denebola, duhr, rasalas, regulus, zosma

leporis (*rabbit*): arneb, nihal

libra (*balance*): kiffa, zuben el genubi, zubeneschamali

lyra (*lyre*): aladfar, shelyak, sulafat, vega, wega

ophiuchus (*serpent bearer*): cebalrai, marfic, rasalhague, sabik, yed

orion (*hunter*): alnilam, alnitak, alnitham, bellatrix, betelgeuse, betelgeux, meissa, mintaka, rigel, saiph

pegasus (*winged horse*): algenib, atik, baham, biham, enif, enri, homam, markab, matar, menkib, salm, scheat

perseus: algenib, algol (medusa head), alpherat(z), atik, attik, demon star

phoenix: nair al zaurak

pisces (*fish*): al rischa, difda, fomalhaut

pleiades: alcyone, asterope, atlas,

---

* Asterisk means to look up this word to find more answer words.

celaeno, electra, maia, merope, pleione, sterope, taurus, taygeta

sagittarius (archer): alnasi, arkab, ascella, kaus, media, nunki, rukbat

scorpius (scorpion): acrab, al niyat, antares, dschubba, graffias, lesath, shaula

serpens: alya, unuk al hay

taurus (bull): alcyone, aldebaran, asterope, atlas, celaeno, electra, el nath, hyades, maia, merope, pleiad(es), pleione, sterope, taygeta

ursa major: alcor, alioth, alkaid, alkphrah, alula, benet-masch, big dipper, dubhe, el kophrah, megrez, merak, mirak, mizar, phacd, phad, phecda, talitha, tania

ursa minor: cynosure, kochab, pherkad, polaris, yildun

virgo (virgin): almuredin, azimech, porrima, spica, syrma, vindemiatrix, zaniah, zavijava

STAR: *morning:* daystar, jupiter, lucifer, mars, mercury, phosphor, saturn, venus

new: nova, nuvo

north: loadstar, lodestar, polaris, polestar

observing instrument: armil, astrolabe, telescope

pert.: antalgol, astral, luminous, planetoid, pointed, sidereal, stellar, stellate

red: antares, mars

-shaped spicule: actine, aster

shooting: comet, leonid, meteor

strewn: seme

thistle: caltrap, caltrop

variable: caltrap, mira, nova

worship: idolatry, sabaism

-wort: aster, astrofel(l)

STARCH: amyl(oid), arrowroot, arum, backbone, carbohydrate, cassava, farina, formality, glycogen, manioc, *strength

comb.: amyl(o)

STARCHY: *precise, rigid, *thick

STARE: *look, ogle, *see, *wonder

STARK: *complete, *firm, *great, *hard, *obstinate, *pure, *set, *severe, *strong, utterly, very

STARLING: huia, myna, starnel

group: murmuration

lizard: agama, hardim

START(LE): *advance, *advantage, *alarm, *attack, *begin, birth, *bud, bundle off, dart, debut, displace, disturb, dodge, *enter, *establish, *fit, *form, *found(ation), frighten, generate, get off, go forth, handicap, *head, ignite, *issue, jar, jerk, jolt, jump, launch, *lead, leap, lever, loosen, mobilize, *move, offset, onset, *open(ing), outset, pitch in, *produce, provoke, *push, *rally, *run, sally forth, *scare, *send, *set, *shock, *shy, *source, spring, *strike, *stir, *take, *turn, *upset, *venture

STARVE: *desire, *die, *need

STASH: *end, *save, *store

STAT: *copy, dupe, print

STATE: affirm, allege, archduchy, assert, asseverate, aver, avow, body politic, canton, case, chieftaincy, *class, colony, commonwealth, condition, *crisis, domain, dominion, duchy, dukedom, earldom, establishment, estate, enounce, enunciate, estado, etat, expound, government, grand duchy, kingdom, land, lot, mandate, mode, mood, palatinate, *pass, posit, *power, preach, principality, pronounce, property, propound, protectorate, province, public, realm, recite, republic, satellite, seneschalty, settlement, situation, *style, *talk, *tell, *temper

---

* Asterisk means to look up this word to find more answer words.

comb.: acy, age, ance, ancy, ence, ency
pert.: civil, federal, political
STATELY: *splendid, *straight
STATEMENT: bill, *comment, memo, *note, *record, *report
STATIC: *noise, *quiet
STATION: *establish, *place, *position, *range, *set, *stand
break: commercial
identification: call letters
STATISTICS BOUNDARY: percentile
STATUE: figure, *image, *picture
base: plinth
living: galatea
projection: socle
primitive: xoanon
STATUS: *rank, *state, *walk
STATUTE: *law, *order, *rule
STAUNCH: *stanch
STAVE: *beat, *hit, *staff, *stick, *stop, *support, verse
bible: bands, beauty
STAY: *arrest, *live, *rest, *stop, *support, visit, wait
STEAD: *advantage, *place, *service, *support, *use
STEADFAST, STEADY: *cool, *firm, *regular, *secure, *solid, *strong, *true
STEAL: abduct, *appropriate, borrow, capture, chor, cly, cop, crib, embezzle, extort, filch, *get, glom, gyp, hook, kidnap, lift, loot, lurk, mooch, nick, nip, nim, palm, peculate, pilfer, pillage, pinch, pirate, plunder, poach, prig, purloin, ramp, ratten, rustle, scrounge, *seize, shanghai, snaffle, snare, snatch, sneak, snitch, swipe, *take, theft, thieve, trespass
STEALTHY: *secret, *sly
STEAM: *force, *power, *smoke
-boat inventor: fulton
comb.: atmo

engine inventor: watt
jet: soffione, stufa
organ: calliope
treatment: atmocausis
STEEL: bessemer, damascus, metal, *prepare, *sword, toledo
cap: cerveliere
-head: trout
-yard: balance, bismar
STEEP: *abrupt, *heavy, *high, *sharp, soap, sop, stiff
STEEPLE: minaret, spire, *tower
STEER: *advise, *control, *lead
STEEVE: *pack, *store, stow
STELE: *memorial, *monument
STELLER: *jay*: blue-fronted
sea cow: rytina
STEM: *arrest, *issue, *part, *source, *spear, *staff, *stop
comb.: caul(o)
kind: bine, caudex, corm, culm, funicle, gynophore, haulm, pedicel, petiole, stalk, stipe, tendril, tigella, tuber
part: caulome, ocrea, pith
pert.: cauline, stipular
sheath: ocrea
-winder: champion, *success
without: acaulescent
STEMMA: ancestry, pedigree
STENCH: *scent, smell
STENDAHL: marie henri de beyle
STEP: *act, *dance, *rank, *walk
-by-step: deliberate, gradatim
-mother, pert.: novercal
outdoor: perron, stile
STEPPE: *plain
storm: buran
STERILE: arid, dead, dry, *vain
STERILIZATION: antisepsis, salpingectomy, vasectomy
STERLING: *great, *supreme
STERN: abaft, *acerb, *adamant, aft, *ascetic, back, baft, *brutal, counter, exact, *firm, forbidding, *hard, heel, *obstinate, poop, rear, rigorous, rudderpost, rump,

*severe, steadfast, steer, stout, *straight, *strict, *strong, *sullen, tail

throwing: atlatl, boomerang

STERNE CHARACTER: cop trim, doctor slop, shandy, toby, trim, tristram

STERNUM: comb.: ento

STEVEDORE: cargador, carrier, lader, loader, longshoreman

STEVENSON: abode: samoa, shramsburg, upolu

character: hyde, jekyll

grave: apia

STEW: *anger, *hash, *mixture, *problem, *puzzle, *think

kind: bouillabaisse, bredi, brunswick, caldera, capilotade, chowder, couscous, curry, fricassee, goulash, haricot, mulligan, olla, ragout

STEWARD: *agent, bhandari, butler, khansamah, maitre d'

STHENIC: *active, *strong

STICK: *adhere, bastinado, battel, billet, bind, bludgeon, brand, buff, caman, cammock, *cheat, cleave, cling, cohere, confine, endure, fagot, fix, *fool, gad, hold, *hurt, *kill, lubber, mundle, overcharge, *pierce, *place, pogo, *puzzle, *set(tle), *skin, *stab(ilize), *staff, *stop, tie, wand, *whip

STICKLE: *argue, *bargain, *puzzle, *separate, *stop

STICKLER: purist, tapist, umpire

STIFF: formal, *stern, vagabond

STIFLE: *hide, *kill, *stop

STIGMA: *shame, *smear

STIGMATIZE: *dirty, *mark

STILETTO: dagger, *sword

STILL: calm, dumb, *quiet, yet

cap: alembic

-room: larder

STILT: *staff, *stick

bug: berytidae

STILTED: *stern, *stiff

STIMULANT: *drink, *drug

STIMULATE: *agitate, *fire, *interest, *move, *stir, *urge

STING: *cheat, *hurt, *pain, *pierce, *smart, *stir, *urge

STINGO: beer, *force, *power

STINGY: *hard, *mean, *sharp

STINK: *smell

bird: anna, hoactzin, hortzin

-weed: cassia, coffee senna

STINKER: asafetida, cigar, fitchew, foumart, garlic, leek, onion, polecat, reprobate, skunk, zoril

STINT: duty, *limit, *quantity, scrimp, starve, *stop, *work

STIPE: caudex, petiole, *stem

STIPEND: *fee, *income, screw

STIPULATE: *bargain, *name

STIPULATION: *compact, term

STIR: activity, *ado, *affect, *agitate, *alarm, *amuse, awaken, beat, blow, bubble, buzz, carouse, *fire, goad, inflame, instigate, *interest, *jail, *live, motion, *move, *noise, *push, *rally, rile, roil, roust, rustle, seethe, *start(le), *trouble, *upset

STIRPS: family, race, stock

STIRRUP: strap, *support

part: chapelet, tapadera

STITCH: *ache, *bit, *pain, *part, *piece, *sew, suture

-bird: ihi

-wort: allbone, alsine

STOA: portico, verandah

STOCK: *issue, *share, *save, source, *store, *supply, *usual

dove: wild pigeon

exchange: bolsa, bourse, curb

exchange term: arbitrage, bear, bull, buyer, seat, trader

-fish: cod, haddock, hake, ling, salpa, torsk

jobbing: agiotage

-man: cowboy, gaucho, vaquero

* Asterisk means to look up this word to find more answer words.

-pile: *accumulate, *save
work: carbona
STOCKADE: *fort, *jail, rampart
STOCKING: bas, buskin, caliga,
hose, hosiery, hushion, lisle,
scogger, shinner, sock, spatter-
dash, traheen
part: boot, coin
run: ladder
STOCKY: *fat, *heavy, *solid
STODGY: *dull, *fat, *thick
STOIC: *ascetic, *hard, *stern
founder: zeno
STOKE: *fire, *stick
STOLE: armil, fur, scarf, wrap
deacon's: orarion
STOLID: *dull, *heavy, *stupid
STOMA: mouth, *opening
STOMACH: abdomen, *abide, al-
vus, *appetite, belly, bingey,
bouk, breadbasket, capacity,
craw, crop, *desire, gebbies, giz-
zard, gut, maw, paunch, pleon,
pouch, resent, *spirit, *stand,
*strength, *suffer, *temper, tripe,
venter, viscera, vitals
ache: colic, nausea, tormina
comb.: gastro, ventro
first: belly, rumen
fourth: abomasum, roddikin
pert.: abdominal, celiac, gastric,
gutty, visceral
second: bonnet, reticulum
third: manyplies, omasum, psalterium
without: aneuterous
STONE: abacus, achate, adamant,
agate, ashlar, *attack, bauta,
boss, boulder, brash, breccia,
brick(bat), calculus, cenotaph,
cephas, chaton, cobble, crag,
craig, diamond, domino, egg,
ezel, face, flag, flint, gem, geode,
granite, gravel, herma, intoxicate, jewel, *kill, lapidate, lapis,
lith, marble, *memorial, mineral,
monolith, *monument, pave-

ment, pebble, pellet, *rock references, rubble, sarsen, schist,
scoria, sculpture, seed, slate,
stean, stele, talus, trap, *throw
age: neolithic, paleolithic
comb.: lapio, lith(o)
crop: bird's-bread, orpin
curlew: bankera, burhinus, bustard, thick-knee
dress: dab, nidge, nig, scabble,
spall
engraving: cameo, intaglio
famous: blarney, braganza, cullinan, dresden, excelsior, florentine, great mogul, green, hope,
jonker, jubilee, kohinoor, kohi-
nur, mogul, nassak, orloff, pitt,
plymouth rock, polar star, regent, rosetta, sancy, scone, star
of africa, star of the south, tif-
fany, vargas
fireback: cathud
fragments: brash, chips, sand
fruit: drupe, endocarp, paip, pip,
putamen, pyrene, seed
nodule: auge, geode
pert.: lapidary, lithoid
quarry: latomy
-roller: black sucker, hogsucker
sacred: baetulus, baetyl(us)
-seed: gromwell
thrower: onager, slingshot, tre-
bucket
-wall: *hard, *obstinate
-ware: ceramics, pottery
-ware bottle: bellarmine
woman turned to: niobe
-work: bossage, masonry
-worker: mason, slater
-wort: alga, candelabra plant
STONED: *drunk
STONY: *hard, *solid, *stern
STOOGE: *agent, *servant, *slave
STOOL: *apostate, *betray, *blab
foot: cricket, hassock, ottoman,
taboret
STOOP: *fall, porch, *yield

* Asterisk means to look up this word to find more answer words.

STOP: *anchor, *arrest, bar, *bind, block(ade), bode, caesura, calk, call, camp, catch, cease, cessation, chink, choke, chuck, clog, congest, conk, constipate, cork, *cover, curd, cut off, dam, daunt, deadlock, depot, destination, don't, drop, *end, flag, foil, gag, hinder, hold, impasse, jam, *kill, knock off, muffle, nip, nix, obstruct, *pack, *place, plug, *puzzle, *quit, renounce, *rest, *retreat, *settle, shut, signal, *slow, spile, stanch, *stand, staunch, stay, *stick, stuff, stump, stymie, surcease, *throw, *tie, *turn
last: death, destination, *end

STORE: *accrue, *accumulate, *bank, belief, bhandar, bin, budget, cache, canteen, cask, catalogue, coffer, commissary, confectioners, coop, ensile, etape, faith, florist, fund, *gather, grindery, grocery, *group, haberdashery, hoard, hutch, larder, list, market, *pack(age), *plenty, *quantity, repertory, reposit, reservoir, resources, saddlery, salt away, *save, *shop, stack, stash, stationers, stow, supermarket, *supply, sutlery, tattersall's, treasury, trove
-house: armory, barn, bike, camalig, camarin, depot, dock, dump, entrepot, godown, granary, lanary, magazine, promptuary, silo, staple, vault
-room: armariolum, armarium, attic, bodega, buttery, cave, cellar, gola, larder, pantry

STORK: adjutant, argala, crane, heron, ibis, jabiru, marabou
bill: erodium, plant
pert.: pelargic

STORM: *ado, *agitate, *anger, assault, *attack, baguio, bayamo, besiege, blizzard, borasco, bourasque, bravado, bura(n), burga, carry on, *catastrophe, commotion, cyclone, disturbance, eruption, explode, flood, fume, fury, gale, hurricane, khamsin, monsoon, *noise, orage, outbreak, outburst, pour, rage, rain, rampage, samiel, shaitan, siege, simoon, snow, squall, *tear, tebbad, tempest, tornado, *trouble, *tumult, typhoon, *violence
cock: petrel, woodpecker
end: st elmo's fire
god: adad, adda, addu, aloadae, hadad, otus, rudra, teshup, zu
goddess: harpy
trooper: brown shirt, fascist, sturmabteilung

STORMY: *angry, *bad, *wild
cape spirit: adamastor
petrel: allamonti, assilag

STORY: *account, *adage, analogy, article, chronicle, conte, description, *epic, episode, fib, fiction, floor, *gossip, history, jeremiad, *joke, layer, legend, *lie, lore, mystery, narrative, novel, paper, parable, piece, plot, *poem, *report, *song, tale, tradition, version, yarn
-teller: aesop, author, bard, fibber, liar, narrator, raconteur, spinner, writer
comb.: anteri

STOUND: *ache, *attack, *pain

STOUR: *great, *hard, *move, *severe, *stir, *storm, *strong

STOUT: ale, *bold, *fat, *firm, *heavy, *obstinate, *solid, *strong, *thick, tough

STOVE: calefaction, chauffer, etna, kiln, latrobe, *range
-pipe hat: caroline

STOW: *hide, *pack, *store

STOWE: character: eva, simon legree, tom, topsy

STRADDLE: hedge, *rest, *walk

STRAFE: *attack, *punish
STRAGGLE: ramble, rove, stray
STRAIGHT: *accurate, beeline, brant, continuous, *direct, down the alley, erect, *fair, fixed, *good, *great, *honest, horizontal, lineal, neat, *open, rectilinear, reliable, reputable, *right, sequence, *stern, *strict, thorough, *true, unbowed, unerring, unqualified, upright, vertical
 comb.: euthy, lineo, rect
STRAIN: bend, bloodline, brace, *breed, clean, colate, descent, effort, endeavor, exaggerate, exert, family, filter, haul, heft, *hurt, line, melody, overdo, pedigree, percolate, *press, prolong, pull, *push, race, refine, sieve, sift, *song, stock, *stress, stretch, sye, tax, tension, tone, *try, tune, weaken, *work, wrench
STRAIT: *crisis, *pass, sound
STRAMASH: *fight, *quarrel
STRAND: bank, beach, sand
 wolf: brown hyena
STRANGE: *bizarre, *eccentric
STRANGERS: comb.: xeno
STRANGLE: choke, *kill, *stop
STRAP: *beat, *punish, *whip
 fern: hart's-tongue
 kind: band, belt, enarme, fillet, halter, latigo, rein
 pert.: ligular, lorate
STRAPPING: *strong
STRASS: glass, paste
STRATEGY: *plan, *plot, *trick
STRATUM: bed, couche, layer
 pert.: erian, stratal, terrane
STRAW: bhoosa, *bit, ome, *part, *piece, *sign, stalk, *stem
 -berry: balloon berry, brandywine, fragaria, fraise
 -berry bush: wahoo
 -berry finch: amadavat
 -berry fruit: etaerio
 -berry shrub: allspice, bubby

 -berry tree: apple of cain, arbutus, cane apple, spindle
 bid: auction
 drinking: bombilla
 gown: bangkok
 -worm: cadbait, cadew, caddice
STRAY: *decline, *err, *range, *run, *sin, *vague, *walk
STREAK: *mark, *stripe, vein
STREAM: rain, *run, *waterway
 bed: arroyo, coulee, donga
 comb.: amni
 -lined: modern, *straight
 -liner: express, train
STREET: *road, *route, *way
 arab: gamin, vagabond, waif
 -car: jigger, tram, trolley
 peddler: camelot
 show: raree
 -walker: *prostitute, *wanton
STRELITZA: bird of paradise
STRENGTH: assets, beef, brawn, capacity, endurance, *force, fortitude, guts, hardihood, inner man, means, muscle, potency, *power, resolution, robustness, ruggedness, sinew, *spirit, stamina, sthenia, substance, thew, uwezo, vigor, vis, vitality
STRENGTHEN: *increase, *support
STRENUOUS: *active, *eager
STREPTOCARPUS: cape primrose
STRESS: accent, *afflict, brunt, cadence, constraint, crux, emphasis, erossure, *force, *hurt, *meter, *pain, *plague, *press, *push, *strain, thrust, urgency
 pert.: ictic
 ratio: bulk modulus
STRETCH: *distance, *range, *reach, *run, *spread, *strain
 inning: seventh
STRETCHER: angareb, *lie, litter
 -bearer: bran-cardier
STREW: *disperse, *spread

* Asterisk means to look up this word to find more answer words.

STRIA: *ridge, streak, strip(e)

STRICKEN: *upset

STRICT: *ascetic, compressed, conscientious, exigent, *firm, *hard, literal, meticulous, narrow, *obstinate, orthodox, *perfect, precise, procrustean, *pure, puritanic, *right, rugged, scrupulous, *severe, *stern, *straight, strait laced, tense, thin-lipped, tight, undeviating, unsparing

STRIDE: *distance, step, *walk

STRIDENT: harsh, rough, shrill

STRIDOR: *noise

STRIDULATE: chirk, creak, crick

STRIFE: *contest, *fight, *riot

STRIGOSE: hispid, *sharp

STRIKE: *afflict, *attack, baff, bandy, bang, bant, bash, bean, belt, bill, blackjack, bolt, boycott, butt, clap, clip, clobber, coerce, crack, *force, gowff, hammer, *hit, *hurt, jab, *kill, lash, *meet, *move, pat, pelt, picket, plug, poke, pommel, *punish, putt, quickie, revolt, slowdown, smack, *smear, soak, *succeed, *throw, tieup, *upset, walkout, whack, wham, *whip

balance: agree, *settle

-breaker: blackleg, fink, goon, rat, scab

colors: *quit, *yield

out: *fail, *fall, fan, eliminate, erase, *start, *try

STRIKING: *extra, *important

STRING: *group, *spread, *tie

STRINGENT: *severe, *sharp, *stern, *strict

STRINGY: capillary, fibrous, filamentary, ligular, thready

STRIP: *spoil, *steal, *tear

blubber: flense

kind: belt, came, cleat, cove, fillet, inwale, lath, latigo, reeve, reglet, rib, riem, slat, spline, thong, tirr, welt

-teaser: ecdysiast

STRIPE: chevron, *class, kidney, *kind, *mark, *ridge, *symbol

STRIPED: bandy, bayadere, lineate, vittate

STRIVE: *fight, *strain, *try

STRIX: barn owl, syrnium, tyto

STROKE: *act, *hurt, *mark, *shock, *success, *walk, *work

kind: serif, virgule, wedge

STROLL: *range, *walk

STROLLER: actor, peddler, pram

STRONG: *able, *acerb, *active, *adamant, andrew, *ardent, *athletic, *big, boisterous, brisk, *brutal, buckra, buirdly, doughty, *eager, energetic, *extreme, *firm, flagrant, fullbodied, gamy, *great, hale, *hard(y), hearty, hefty, herculean, husky, *important, intense, large, lusty, maduro, manly, mighty, muscular, nervy, *obstinate, overpowering, potent, puissant, *rank, robust, *severe, *sharp, sinewy, *solid, stalwart, *stern, sthenic, stiff, stout, *straight, strapping, *strict, vigorous, *violent, virile, wight, wiry, yauld, zealous

-arm: *force, *hoodlum, *power

box: safe, treasury, vault

-hold: *fort, *tower

man: *power: house

point: *fort, *forte, talent

STRONGYLURA: agujon, needlefish

STROP: hone, sharpen, whet

STRUCTURE: *build, *make

pert.: tectonic

STRUGGLE: *contest, *fight, *pain, *try, *work

a deux: duel

STRUM: plunk, twang, twank

STRUMPET: *prostitute, *wanton

STRUT: brag, *support, *walk

STRUTTING: swashbuckling

---

* Asterisk means to look up this word to find more answer words.

STRYMON: *son:* rhesus
wife: calliope, euterpe, terpsichore
STUB: butt, coupon, *end, *fool
STUBBORN: *hard, *obstinate
STUBBY: *fat, *heavy, *little,
  *short, *small, *thick
STUCK-UP: *arrogant, *vain
STUD: *adorn, aglet, ashlar, boss,
  breeder, bulge, bull, haras, knob,
  male, man, nail, *ornament,
  poker, post, prop, *spread,
  sprinkle, *support
STUDENT: aggie, auditor, bursar,
  bursch(e), cadet, catechumen,
  coed, commoner, disciple, esco-
  lier, eleve, fuchs, glene, intern(e),
  learner, monitor, neophyte, novice, plebe, prefect, pupil, scholar,
  scholastic, schoolman, tosher,
  trainee, tyro
account: battel
college: freshman, graduate, junior, senior, soph, sophomore,
  undergraduate
group: academe, academy, class,
  college, seminar, university
residence: dorm(itory), fraternity,
  hostel, house
teacher: don, monitor, tutor
STUDIED: deliberate, intent
STUDIO: abozzo, atelier, bottega,
  den, gallery, lab, library, office,
  *retreat, room, shop, spot, study
STUDY: *account, *analysis, *analyze, application, article, bone,
  brainwork, canvas, carol, check,
  con(sider), contemplate, cram,
  deliberate, devise, dig, discuss,
  document, endeavor, examine,
  exercise, *eye, grind, go over,
  headwork, *image, inspect, investigate, learn, lesson, library,
  *look, meditate, mug, muse,
  peruse, *picture, *piece, *plan,
  plunge into, ponder, pore, precis,
  read, reflect(ion), research, science, see, sketch, *studio, sub-

ject, *test, *think, trace, treatise,
  understand, weigh, *work
pert.: academic
STUFF: *bit, cram, eat, fill, *fool,
  *nonsense, *pack, *refuse, stop,
  *store, *surfeit
hard: *drug, narcotic
STUFFING: dressing, viscera
STUFFY: *angry, *dull, *thick
STUGGY: *short, *strong, *thick
STULM: *opening
STULTILOQUY: *gossip, *talk
STUMBLE: *err, *fall, *sin
inclined to: pecky
STUMP: *part, *piece, *puzzle,
  *speak, *stop, stub, *walk
STUN: daunt, paralyze, surprise
STUNNING: *beautiful, *great
STUNT: *act, *angry, *dwarf,
  *joke, *limit, *trick, *stop
STUPA: *memorial, *monument
STUPEFY: *drug, *dull, *stun
STUPENDOUS: *big, *great
STUPID: anserine, anserous, asi-
  nine, bayardly, beef-headed,
  bete, blank, blind, blockish,
  booby, brainless, calvish, chump-
  ish, clod, crass, dense, doltish,
  *dull, dumb, fat headed, gross,
  hebetate, ignorant, inane, inept,
  insensate, lumpish, *obstinate,
  opaque, senseless, *simple, *slow,
  sluggish, sottish, stolid, *thick,
  thoughtless, torpid, vacant, void
person: boor, *clown, *fool
STUPIDITY: betise, bopkes,
  chachma, folly, khaukhma
STUPOR: coma, lethargy, trance
pert.: carotic
STURDY: *firm, *hard, *strong
STURGEON: acipenser, beluga,
  caviar, elops, fish, sterlet
STURT: *stir, *startle, *trouble
STY: *hut, pen, pimple, slum
STYGIAN: hellish, infernal
STYLE: *air, architecture, art,
  calendar, call, caprice, craze,

*cry, dernier cri, diction, fad, fancy, *form, ism, *kind, *make, mode, movement, *name, pen, phrase, pzazz, rage, school, *system, technique, *thing, *title, tone, variety, vogue, *way

STYLET: awl, dagger, probe
STYLISH: *fresh, *sharp, *smart
STYLITE: *ascetic, *monk
STYLUS: pointel, scriber, spicule
STYMIE: check, foil, *stop
STYX: *hell, nymph
  child: bia, kratos, nike, zelos
  consort: pallas
  ferryman: charon
  locale: hades
  parent: oceanus, tethys
  pert.: stygian
  tributary: aornis
SUAVE: *smooth, urbane
SUBCONSCIOUS: id, psyche
SUBDIVISION: *class, *part
SUBDUE: *defeat, *tame
SUBJECT: *defeat, *open, *servant, *slave, *study, *take, theme, *thing, topic
SUBJOIN: *add, attach, *unite
SUBJUGATE: *break, *defeat
SUBLIMATION: abreaction, catharsis, suppression
SUBLIME: *great, *high, *noble, superior, *supreme, *top
SUBLIMINAL: *subconscious
SUBMARINE: pigboat, u-boat
  part: periscope, snorkel, sonar
  projectile: *missile, torpedo
SUBMERGE: *hide, immerse
SUBMISS: *low, *mean, *poor
SUBMISSION: curtsy, kneel, offer
SUBMIT: *mind, *present, *yield
SUBORDINATE: *servant, *slave
SUBSCRIBE: *accept, *support
SUBSEQUENT: *after, later
SUBSERVIENT: menial, *subject
SUBSIDE: *abate, *decline, *fall
SUBSIDIARY: *subordinate
SUBSIDIZE: *abet, *aid, *give

SUBSIDY: *aid, *gift, *income
SUBSIST: endure, *live
SUBSISTENCE: entity, *support
SUBSTANCE: *agent, *form, *foundation, texture, *thing
SUBSTANTIAL: *big, *firm, *great, *heavy, *important, *solid, *strong, *true, wealthy
SUBSTANTIATE: *prove, *test
SUBSTANTIVE: *substantial
SUBSTITUTE: *act, *agent, apology, *artificial, beetmister, bench(warmer), change, commute, compound, deputy, double, dub, dummy, enallage, *equal, equivalent, ersatz, exchange, *extra, fill in, fudge, ghost, in lieu, instead, locum tenens, makeshift, means, nominate, pinch hitter, provisional, redeem, relief, replace, represent, ringer, secondary, *spell, stand-in, succedaneum, succenturiate, super(numerary), supersede, supplant, surrogate, synthetic, switch, temporary, tentative, *token, understudy, vicar(ious), vice(regent)
  comb.: ette
SUBTERFUGE: *escape, *lie, *plan, tergiversation, *trick
SUBTERRANEAN: catachthonic, *hell, plutonic, *secret, sunk
SUBTLE: crafty, cunning, *fine, rare, *sly, *smart, wily, *wise
SUBTLETY: finesse, guile
SUBURB: environs, *place, slurb
SUBVENTION: *subsidy
SUBVERSIVE: collaborator, fellow traveler, fifth column, fraternizer, saboteur, *spy, trojan horse, underground
SUBVERT: *betray, *deceive, *destroy, *ruin, *spy, *upset
SUBWAY: bmt, cave, irt, metro, railroad, tube, underground
  entrance: kiosk

* Asterisk means to look up this word to find more answer words.

SUCCEED: *accomplish, advance, attain, bring off, catch on, click, coin money, come after, connect, do all right, *enter, fadge, fare, *follow, *get (ahead), go far, graduate, grow rich, happen, hit it, killing, *make (good), manage, prevail, progress, prosper, prove (out), pull off, put over, ring the bell, rise, *strike, supplant, *take, thrive, *win, *work

SUCCESS: eureka, *fortune, *hit, *riot, smash, victory, *win
symbol: citation, commendation, emerald, *palm, *prize, scalp

SUCCESSFUL: *happy, lucky

SUCCESSION: posterity, *strain
indicating: ordinal
male, pert.: salic

SUCCESSIVE: *after, consecutive

SUCCESSOR: heir, *substitute

SUCCINCT: *direct, laconic, pithy, *short, *straight

SUCCOR: *abet, *serve, *support

SUCCUBUS: asparas, *demon

SUCCULENT: juicy, lush, vital

SUCCUMB: *die, *fail, *fall, *stand, *yield

SUCH: *kind, like, similar

SUCK: *absorb, *drink

SUCKER: bothrium, catostomida, *clown, customer, *fool, *thief

SUCKLE: feed, nurse, *raise

SUCTION: inhalation, snuffle

SUDAN: animal: dama, oterop
beer: dolo
city: atbara, khartoum
lake: chad, tsad
language: efik, ewe, ibo, kru, mandingo, mole, nubian, tshi, vak, vei, yoruba
mountains: nuba
movement: anya, nya, scorpion
negro: egba, hausas, junje
people: bagara, balante, beri, dor, fula(h), golo, hamite, hausa, mossi, peul, sere, taureg, tibbu
stockade: zareeba, zeriba
stretcher: angareeb, angarep

SUDARIUM: handkerchief, veronica

SUDDEN: *abrupt, *quick, *short

SUDDENLY: amain, presto, subito

SUDS: beer, *dregs, *refuse

SUE: *appeal, *ask, pray, *urge

SUET: *fat, lard, tallow

SUEZ: builder: de lesseps
part: bitter lakes, port said

SUFFER: *ache, admit, agonize, *allow, bide, bleed, clem, come to grief, countenance, *cry, dree, experience, feel, get it, groan, have, *hurt, let, *pain, sink, smart, *stand, submit, *support, *take, thole, undergo

SUFFERING: *affliction, *bad, calvary, *pain, *sick
comb.: patho
reliever: samaritan

SUFFICE: *answer, *meet, *reach

SUFFICIENCY: *ability, *plenty

SUFFICIENT: *adequate, *fit, *meet, *quantity, *plenty

SUFFIX: *add, *adjunct

SUFFOCATE: choke, *kill, *stop

SUFFRAGE: *aid, *right, vote

SUFFUSE: *cover, fill, *spread

SUFI: *ascetic, *mohammedan
concept: fana
disciple: murid
saint: abdal
stages: ahwal

SUGAR: acrose, aldose, allose, bios, cassonade, bribe, cane, dextrose, glucose, maple, melada, *money, muscovado, panela, piloncillo, *sweet
addition: chaptalization
apple: biriba, sweetsop
boiling kettle: flambeau
candy: alphenic, caramel
cane disease: iliau, serch
cane refuse: bagasse, mare

cleaning: elution
comb.: ose, osid
extract: betain(e), lycine, oxy-
   neurine
liquid: sirup, syrup
lump: cube, loaf
measure: saccharimeter
muscle: inosite
percentage: brix scale
pills: placebo therapy
-plum: bonbon, **sweetmeat*
raw: brown, cassonade, gur
refining device: elutor, granu-
   lator, tiger
sack: bayon
source: beet, cane, corn, fruit,
   grape, maple, milk, sap
substitute: honey, saccharin
syrup: molasses, treacle
water: ambrosia, nectar
works: usine
SUGGEST: **mean*, **promise*
SUGGESTION: **image*, **meaning*
SUGGESTIVE: racy, risque
SUICIDE: banzai, felo-de-se, hari-
   kari, seppuku, suttee
fighter: kamikaze
SUIT: **accommodate*, **action*,
   *adapt, **dress*, **please*, **trial*
-case: **bag*, etui, gladstone
SUITABLE: **adequate*, **fair*,
   *good, **meet*, **ready*, **right*
SUITE: **abode*, **group*, **staff*
SUITOR: **love*, **spark*, swain
SUKARNO: *dream:* nasakom
SUKU: **bantu*
SULAWESI: celebes
SULCUS: fissure of rolando
SULFA: miracle drug
SULK: **complain*, **pet*, scowl
SULKY: carriage, **sullen*, **weak*
SULLAGE: **dregs*, mud, **refuse*
SULLEN: bearish, black, boorish,
   churlish, cranky, cross, **dull*,
   grouty, **heavy*, moody, moping,
   mopy, **obstinate*, peevish, petu-
   lant, pouty, rusty, saturnine,

*short, silent, solitary, somber,
*sour, **stern*, surly, testy, **ugly*
SULLY: **dirty*, **smear*, **spoil*
SULPHATE: alum, alunogen,
   baryta, beaverite, bianchite,
   blende, botryogen, brimstone,
   hepar, ilesite, matte
SULPHIDE: alaskaite, galena
SULPHUR: quebrinth
alloy: niello
bacteria: beggiatoa
-bottom: blue whale
containing: thionic
water: barege
weed: brimstone-wort
SULPHURIC ACID: vitriol
SULTAN: caliph, murad, padishah, **ruler*, selim
decree: irade
residence: serai
SULTRY: **hot*, humid, **wet*
SULU: *island:* jolo, siassi
SUM: **add*, **money*, **quantity*
SUMAC: anacardium, anam,
   balinghasay, dogwood, rhus
SUMATRA: *animal:* balu, banxring, napu, orang, tanu, tupaia
camphor: borneol
city: achin, bonkulin, indrapoor,
   jambi, medan, padang, palem-
   bang
fiber: caloee
gutta: siak
island: nias, sunda
kingdom: achin, atjeh
lake: toba
measure: etto, jankal, paal, pakha,
   sukat, tub, tung
people: batak, batta(k), lampong,
   malayan, rejang
raft: rakit
river: indragiri, jambi, musi,
   rokan
silk: ikat
squirrel: shrew, tana, tanu
volcano: merapi
weight: candil
wind: bohorok

---

* Asterisk means to look up this word to find more answer words.

SUMER: *city:* eridu
deity: abu, anu(nnaki), enlil
SUMMARIZE: **present, *repeat*
SUMMARY: abstract, brief, digest, epitome, precis, resume, review, **short*, total
SUMMER: *goddess:* aestas
haze: calina
herring: blackbelly, sockeye salmon
pert.: canicular, estival
SUMMIT: **acme, *ridge, *top*
pert.: apical
SUMMON: bid, call, cite, page
SUMMONS: command, signal
SUMP: bog, marsh, pool, well
SUN: bask, orb, relax, tan
apartment: solarium
asphyxia: sunstroke
bath: apricate, aprication
-beam: banana
bear: bruang
bettle: amara
bittern: caurale, helias
-bow: iris
-burn: actino, dermatitis, heliosis, tan
clock: sundial
comb.: helio, soli
dial part: gnomon, substyle
disk: aten, aton
disk center: cazimi
-dog: halo, parhelion, rainbow
equatorial: equinox
excess over lunar: epact
exploding: nova, novae
-fish: black-ears, blue bream, bluegill, blue joe, bream, lepomis, mola, pondfish
fleck: lucule
-flower: aster, balsamroot, heliotrope, marigold, rockrose
-flower maid: clytie
-flower state: kansas
-god: aditya, agni, amaterasu, amen(-ra), apollo, asvins, atmu, atum, baal, babbar, balder,

belenus, beli, chepera, dyaus, endymion, frey, hadad, helios, hiruko, horus, ing, inti, janus, khepera, khepri, lleu, llew, ment(u), mithras, nergal, nigihaya-hi, ninib, osiris, paiva, phaethon, phoebus, ra, reharakhti, rhe, savitar, shamash, shu, sokaris, sol, surya, tem, titan, tum, utu(g), varuna
goddess: ai, al-lat
greatest distance from: apsis
lamp: argand
-light: yang
light around: corona, halo
measurer: pyrheliometer
mock: parhelion
pain: hemicrania
path: ecliptic, orbit
pert.: heliac, solar
planet representation: orrery
-ray measurer: actinometer
-rise: dawn, daybreak, morning
-rise goddess: aurora
-rise song: aubade
-set: dusk, evening, twilight
-set, pert.: acrondic, crepuscular
-set god: endymion, tem, zeus
shade: awning, parasol, visor
-shine state: florida, new mexico, south dakota
-spot: facula, freckle, lucule, macula, penumbra, umbra
spurge: cat's-grass, cat's-hair, cat's-milk
standing still: solstice
-stroke: calenture, ictus, insolation, siriasis
worshipper: heliolater, idolator, parsee, parsi
year excess: epact
SUNAPEE: saibling, trout
SUNDA ISLAND: bali, borneo, celebes, java, lambok, raoul, sumatra, timor
SUNDAY: sabbath
low: quasimodo
pert.: dominical

---

* Asterisk means to look up this word to find more answer words.

SUNDER: *break, *part
SUNNA: ambary, hemp, sana
SUNNY: *bright, *happy, *warm
SUP: *absorb, *eat, *drink
SUPAWN: mush, porridge
SUPER: *actor, *extra, *supreme
SUPERABUNDANCE: *plenty
SUPERANNUATE: *age, *dismiss
SUPERANNUATED: anile, *old
SUPERB *splendid, *supreme
SUPERCHERIE: *deception
SUPERCILIOUS: *arrogant
SUPEREROGATORY: *plenty
SUPERFICIAL: apparent, *artificial, bird's-eye, casual, cursory, dilettante, *dull, empiric, empty, external, *false, flimsy, formal, half-baked, hasty, hollow, immature, left-handed, *light, sciolistic, *simple, *small, sophomoric, spurious, *thin, *vain, *weak
SUPERFLUOUS: *extra, *plenty
SUPERHUMAN: lemurian, yaktavian
SUPERINTEND: *administer, *control, *direct, *lead, *run
SUPERIOR: *best, *fine, *great, *head, *leader, *supreme
SUPERLATIVE: *acme, *supreme
SUPERNAL: *divine, *high
SUPERNATURAL: *great, *magic
SUPERNUMERARY: *substitute
SUPERSEDE: *succeed, supplant
SUPERSTITION: *fetish, *magic
pert.: goetic
SUPERVISE: *superintend
SUPERVISOR: *head, *leader
SUPINE apathetic, *dull, *idle
SUPPLANT: *dismiss, *substitute
SUPPLE *active, *fast, *quick
SUPPLEMENT: *add, *adjunct
SUPPLICATE: *ask, pray, sue
SUPPLY: *accommodate, advance, *asset, backlog, *bank, cater, *dispense, dose, equip, estovers, feed, fill, food, gear, *give, grist, *issue, means, *money, ordnance, *package, *plenty, prescribe, provisions, *quantity, relay, relief, relieve, *spread, staple, *store, *support, underwrite, well, *yield
SUPPORT: *abet, advance, *advocate, afford, approval, arch, arm, *asset, assist, atlas, back, bail, baluster, barrow, base, bolster, brace, bracket, bridge, bulwark, buoy, buttress, cheer, cherish, comfort, confirm, consent, corroborate, cradle, cushion, defend, dependence, encourage, further, harquebus, keep, leg, limb, livelihood, living, mainstay, manna, nourish, nurture, patronize, pedestal, pier, pillow, preserve, prop, protect, provide, reinforce, reliance, *rest, rib, sanction, second, shore, shoulder, *staff, *stand, stay, strut, sustain, trivet, uphold, *urge
SUPPORTER: *enthusiast
SUPPOSE: *gather, guess, *think
SUPPOSING: although, in case
SUPPOSITION: surmise, theory
SUPPOSITITIOUS: *artificial
SUPPRESS: ban, cancel, check, *kill, quash, smother, *stop
SUPPURATE: fester, *run, weep
SUPREME: *absolute, *ace, *acme, *big, *best, capital, cardinal, *fine, glorious, *good, *great, *high, immense, imperial, *important, incomparable, last, magnificent, marvelous, meritorious, out of this world, peak, peerless, preeminent, prime, pure gold, *special, *splendid, stately, sterling, sublime, superior, superlative, *top, terrific, transcendent, ultimate, wonderful
SURCEASE: *end, *rest, *stop
SURCINGLE: band, girdle, saddle
SURCOAT: cyclas, jupon

* Asterisk means to look up this word to find more answer words.

SURE: *actual, authentic, certain, *fast, *firm, positive, real, safe, *secure, stable, *strong, *true

SURETY: bail, bond, fact, pledge, security, sponsor

SURF: foam, ocean, sea, spray
-fish: alfiona, rhacochilus
noise: rote, surge
scoter: blossom-bill, box coot
shiner: sparada

SURFACE: apparent, face, meros, pave, shallow, *top, veneer
flat: area, orlo, *plane
patches on: sorediate
pert.: acrotic, obverse
toward: ectad

SURFEIT: acrasia, choke, *cloy, congest, cram, crowd, drench, dull, excess, *extra, feed, nimiety, overload, pack, pall, *plenty, plus, *quantity, sate, satiety, satisfy, saturate, soak, stuff, *supply, surplus

SURFER: patchhead

SURGE: flow, gush, jet, pour, rise, soar, swell, tide, wave

SURGEON: *medical, *medicine
anesthetic: *drug, *narcotic
-fish: acanthurus, barber, tang
instrument: abaptiston, ablator, acus, aspirator, bedpan, bilabe, bistoury, cannula, canula, cardiograph, catheter, catlin(g), crutch, cystoscope, drain, ecraseur, fleam, forceps, goosebill, gorget, hemostat, hypodermic, lance(t), levator, ligator, microscope, needle, otoscope, pincette, pipette, plessor, probe, rongeur, scala, scalpel, speculum, splint, stiletto, stylet, swab, syringe, tampon, tent, terebellum, tourniquet, trepan, trephine, trocar, tweezers, vectis, vulsellum, xyster
puncture: centesis
stitch: suture
thread: seton

SURINAM: city: paramaribo
coin: bit
hut: benab
measure: ketting
toad: pipa(l)
tree: lana, quassia
tribe: boni, djuka

SURLY: *sour, *sullen

SURMISE: *gather, *think

SURMOUNT, SURPASS: *beat, *defeat, *top, *win

SURPLICE: cotta, ephod, pelisse

SURPLUS: *plenty, *surfeit

SURPRISE: *alarm, *ambush

SURREALISM: founder: dali
style: abstract expressionism

SURRENDER: *quit, *yield

SURREPTITIOUS: *secret, *sly

SURROGATE: *substitute

SURROUND: *ambush, besiege, encircle, loop

SURROUNDING: *range, *sphere

SURTOUT: coat, garment, hood

SURVEILLANCE: reconnaissance

SURVEY: *look, *plan, *plot, *range, *see, *study, view

SURVEYING: geodesy
man: arpenteur, chainman, lineman, poleman, rodman
term: target
tool: alidad(e), aligner, caliper, level, odolite, perambulator, rod, spad, stadia, stratameter, theodolite, transit, vernier

SURVIVAL: endurance, relic
science: ecology

SURVIVE: last, remain, *stand

SUSA: eunuch: gabatha, tharra
inhabitant: elamite

SUSANNA: father: hilkiah
husband: joakim

SUSANOWO: kin: amaterasu

SUSCEPTIBLE: allergic, *open, *sensitive, tending

SUSPECT: *gather, *think

SUSPEND: *dismiss, hang, *stop

---

* Asterisk means to look up this word to find more answer words.

SUSPENDERS: belt, braces, gallows, galluses, garter, gibbet, hook, knob, nail, peg, pothook, ring, spar, strap
SUSPENSE: *alarm, *anxiety
SUSPENSION: *break, *rest, *stop
SUSPICION: *bit, hint, touch
SUSPICIOUS: leery, skeptical
SUSTAIN: foster, *support
SUSU: congo, dolphin, fish
SUTLER: supplier, vivandiere
SUTLERY: *shop, *store
SUTTEE: *suicide
SUTTUNG: kin: bangi, gunnlod
SUTURE: arthrosis, pterion, raphe, *seam, *sew, stitch
SUZERAIN: *lord, *magnate
SVELT: *smooth, *thin
SWAB: boor, clean, *clown, *fool, mop, *peasant, wash
SWACK: *drink, *hit, *supple
SWADDLE: *bind, *dress, *wrap
SWAG: *money, *spoil, strut
SWAGE: dolly, jumper, *upset
SWAGGER: brag, swell, *walk
 stick: *staff
SWAGGERING: swashbuckling, thrasonical
SWAIN: *love, *peasant, *spark
SWALE: fen, marsh, moor, swing
SWALLOW: *absorb, *destroy, *drink, *eat, *end, take
 inability: aglutition, aphagia
 -tail: papilio polyxenes
 -tailed flag: burgee
SWAMP: *defeat, *marsh references, slough, terai, vlei
 fox: marion
 hen: coot
 honeysuckle: azalea
 tree: alder
SWAN: bird, cob, cygnet, elk(e), olor, pen, *surprise, *swear
 eternity: hansa
 group: bank, wedge
 river: avon

 river daisy: brachycome
SWANHILD: father: siegfried
SWANK: *display, *swagger
SWANKY: posh, *rich, *smart
SWAP: *bargain, *trade
SWARD: grass, lawn, sod, turf
SWARM: *pack, *press, *quantity
SWART(HY): *black, *dark
SWASH: *move, *noise, *strike
SWASHBUCKLER: *rogue, *soldier
SWASTIKA: *fetish, flyfot, gammadion, *symbol
SWAT: *blow, *hit, *strike
SWATHE: *bind, *dress, *wrap
SWAY: *affect, *power, *rule
SWEAL: burn, melt, singe, waste
SWEAR: *abuse, *promise
SWEAT: ferment, *think, *work
 foul: bromhidrosis, osmidrosis
SWEATER: bolero, bulky, cardigan, jersey, knittie, pullover, slip-on, slipover, topper, turtle neck, windbreaker
SWEDISH: sverige
 artist: zorn
 astronomer: angstrom, censius
 battle: lund
 botanist: bromel, fresia
 bread: knackerbrod
 cheese: fontina, jarlberg
 chemist: berzelius
 city: boras, edane, eskilstuna, falkoping, falun, gavle, goteborg, gottenburg, halsingborg, jonkoping, lund, malmo, norrkoping, nykoping, orebro, stockholm, uppsala
 clover: alsike
 coin: carolin, krone, ore
 dance: polska
 division: amt, gotaland, lan, laen, norrland, skane, swealand
 dynasty: vasa
 explorer: hedin
 farm: thorp, torp
 guard, royal: brabant

* **Asterisk means to look up this word to find more answer words.**

gulf: bothnia
island: gotaland, oeland
king: bernadotte, eric, oscar, wasa
lake: asnen, hielmar, malar, mala-
ren, siljan, ster, varern, vatter(n),
wennen, wetter
legislature: andra, diet, forsta,
kammaren, riksdag
liquor control: bratt system
match: taendstikker
measure: alar, aln, am, carat,
famn, fjarding, foder, fot,
jumfru, kanna, kappe, kappland,
kollast, koltunna, last, linje, mil,
nymil, oxhuvud, ref, spann,
stang, stop, tum, tunna, tunn-
land
milk: tatmjolk
money: skilling
mountain: sarjek
nightingale: jenny lind
philosopher: ihre
port: malmo, pitea, umea, visby
river: gota, kalix, klar, lainio,
ljungan, ljusne, lulea, pitea,
ranea, tornea, umea, windel
sculptor: milles
soprano: lind, nilsson
statesman: branting, essen
tribe: geatas
weight: ass, carat, centner, last,
lispund, lod, nylast, ort, skalpund, skeppund, sten
writer: arnoldson, bellman, berg-
man, carlen, lagerlof
SWEEP: *range, *reach, *slide,
*speed, *spread, *win, wipe
-*stakes:* *bet, lottery, race
SWEEPING: *general, thorough
SWEET: agreeable, ambrosial,
candied, darling, delightful, dessert, douce, dulcet, *fine, fresh,
*gentle, *good, honeyed, *kind,
lovely, millifluent, melodious,
nice, olent, pastry, pleasant,
saccharine, *smooth, *soft, sug-
ary, syrupy, tender

abyssum: alison
bay: beaverwood, brewster, hackberry
-*bread:* bur(r), ris de veau, rusk,
thymus
-*briar:* bedeguar, eglantine, hip
cassava: aipi(m)
cherry: belladonna, black choke,
burbank
cicely: anise, myrrh
clover: bokhara, melilot
coltsfoot: bitter bur
fennel: azorian
fish: ayu, plecoglossus
flag: acorus, araca, beewort, calamus, carminative, tonic
gale: baybush, bogbean, buck
bean, burton myrtle, gagl, myrica
gum: alligator tree, amber, bilsted, liquid ambar
-*heart:* adorer, agrah, amaryllis,
amorosa, bird, bully, captive,
catch, cheri(e), chick, conquest,
courtesan, doll, doudou, doxy,
enamorato, *fellow, flame, gill,
girl, honey, inamorata, ipo, jill,
jo(e), judy, lady love, lass,
leman, *love, mistress, moll, pet,
sis, *spark, steady, *top, valentine, *wanton, winner
-*meat:* balushai, cake, candy, caramel, caraway, cates, confection,
confetti, dessert, dragee, hard-
bake, marchpane, marzipan, preserve, sugarplum
pinesap: carolina beechdrops
potato: batata, camote, manroot,
ocarina, patat, yam
pudding: bakewell
-*sop:* annona, annonce, ata, ates,
atta, fruit, tree
-*sour:* agrodolce
spire: itea
-*talk:* flatter, honeyfogle
tooth: appetite
violet: blaver

* Asterisk means to look up this word to find answer words.

william: blue phlox, bunch pink
wood: cascarilla
SWELL: *good, *great, *grow, *increase, *noble, *smart, *spark, *splendid, *surge
fish: bellows fish, blowfish, pike, puffer, snipe, trumpet
-head: braggart
-mob: pickpocket, *thief
SWELLING: *big, *fat, *tumor
pert.: edematous, nodal
SWELTER: burn, haste, sweat
SWELTERING: *hot, humid
SWERVE: *change, *retreat, *shift, tack, *turn, veer
SWEVEN: dream, sleep, vision
SWIETENIA: caoba, mahogany
SWIFT: *fast, hepialus, *quick
animal: yahoo
lady friend: stella
pen name: bickerstaff, cadenus, drapier
tom, friend: rover
SWIG: *drink
SWILL: *dregs, *drink, *refuse
SWIM: float, natate, *style
nude: skinny-dip
stroke: back, breast, crawl
SWIMMER: cloelia, diver, duck, fish, frogman, leander, mermaid
SWIMMING: aquatics, dizzy, naiant, natant, vertigo
SWINDLE: *cheat, *deceive, *sew, *skin, *take, *trick
SWINDLER: *criminal, *hoodlum, *impostor, *sharp, *thief
famous: brinkle, goat gland, chadwick, coster, insull, kreuger, law, lustig, musica, ponzi, reavis, yellow kid
victim: esau, sucker
SWINE: aper, barrow, boar, *hog, peccary, *pig, porker, *rogue, sow, suid, *wanton
breed: berkshire, cheshire, duroc, essex, hampshire, hereford, jersey, landrace, mangalitza, poland china, razorback, tamworth, yorkshire
cress: brass buttons, buckhorn plantain, carara, coronopus
feeding: pannage
fever: bullnose, rouget
herd: eumaeus, stockman
herd, pert.: sybotic
SWING: *action, *change, *meter, *oscillate, *quiver, *range, *speed, *turn
music: hep, jazz, jive, rag
musician: hepcat
SWINGE: *beat, impetus, *whip
SWINGING: *great
SWINISH: boarish, *brutal, porcine, sensual, suilline
SWINK: drudgery, *slave, *work
SWIPE: *drink, *hit, *steal, *strike, wipe
SWIRL: boil, eddy, *turn, whirl
SWISH: hiss, *rustle, *smart, sound, *strike, *whip
SWITCH: *beat, *change, *hit, *part, *shift, *substitute, toggle, *trade, *turn, *whip
-board: exchange, panel, pbx
grass: black bent, foxtail
-hitting: ambidextrous
SWITZERLAND: colin tampon, helvetia, ladin, suisse, schweiz
alps man: brison
archer: william tell
army: landwehr
ax: piolet
bay: uri
botanist: candolle
breeze: bornan, rebat
canton: aargau, aarau, altdorf, appenzell, basel, basle, bern(e), fribourg, geneve, genf, glaris, glarus, graubunden, grisons, lucerne, luzern, neuchatel, neuenberg, nidwald, nyon, obwald, sankt gallen, schaffhausen, schwytz, solothurn, st gall, tessin, thurgau, ticino, unterwalden, uri,

---

* Asterisk means to look up this word to find more answer words.

valais, vaud, waadt, wallis, zug, zurich
canton officer: amman
card game: jass
castle: chillon
cheese: emmentaler, gruyere, sapsago, schweizer (-kase)
chemist: abderhalden
coin: angster, baetzner, batz, blaffert, centime, duplone, franc, hallar, rappe(n)
commune: aarau, chur, davos, sion, thun, uster, vevey
composer: bloch
conductor: ansermet
flower: edelweiss
food: benerplatte
hat: alpine
herdsman: senn
hero: william tell
historian: burckhardt
house: chalet, riegelhaus
instrument: alphorn
lake: beilersee, biel, bienne, brienz, constance, geneva, leman, lugano, lungern, morat, neuchatel, sarnen, sarnersee, thon, thunersee, viervald, zub, zurich
language: french, german, italian, ladin, romansch, roumansh, switzerdeutsch
legislature: grosserat
magistrate: amman, avoyer
mathematician: euler
measure: aune, elle, fuss, holzlafter, imi, immi, juchart, klafter, lieue, ligne, linie, maase, moule, muid, perche, pouce, quarteron, saum, schuh, setier, strich, viertel
mountain: adula, alp, blanc, burgenstock, cenis, dom, eiger, genis, jungfrau, jura, matterhorn, pilatus, rigi, rosa, sentis, st gothard, todi
mountain pass: bernina, gemmi, simplon, usteri
nickel: batz

painter: klee
pert.: alpen, alpine
physicist: bloch
pine: arolla, cembra
psychiatrist: bleuler
river: aar(e), doubs, inn, reuss, rhine, saxane, thur
scientist: argand, bernouilli, haller
sled: luge(r)
song: yodel
theologian: barth, brunner
weight: centner, pfund, quintal, zugthierlast
wind: bise, bize, bruscha
writer: amiel, anet, usteri, wyss

SWIVEL: hinge, *swing*, *turn*
chain: buckle
SWIZ: *swindle*
SWIZZLE: *drink*
SWOB: *swab*
SWOLLEN: *big*, *fat*, *great*, pompous, round, tumid, turgid
SWOON: drop, faint, stupor
SWOOP: pounce, *seize*, souse
SWORD: acinates, andrew, bancal, barong, bilbo, blade, bolo, bowie, brackmard, brandiron, catan, cattan, chiv, claymore, cutlass, damascus, degen, diego, dusack, epee, espadon, estoc, estoque, falchion, falx, ferrara, floret, foil, glaive, khanda, kris, kukri, macana, machete, parang, pata, rapier, saber, schiavone, schlager, scimitar, slasher, spatha, toledo, verdun, yataghan
famous: almace, askelon, balmung, colada, curteen, excalibur, gram, khaled
-fish: aus, broadbill, dorado, espadon, xiphias gladius
-fish feature: serra
lily: gladiolus
-man: dueler, fighter, epeeist
pert.: ensate, ensiform, gladiate, xypho
short: anlace, balas, baselard,

* **Asterisk means to look up this word to find more answer words.**

basilard, bayonet, bodkin, creese,
cris, dirk, katar, khangar, miseri-
corde, obelisk, pointel, poniard,
skean, snee, snickersnee, stiletto,
stylet
SWORN: devoted, inveterate
to secrecy: tiled
SWUEAK: sennight, week
SYBARITE: epicure, voluptuary
SYBIL: *sibyl*
SYCAMORE: buttonwood, plane
tree
lady: athyr, hathor
SYCOPHANT: courtier, flatterer,
leech, parasite, stooge, toady
SYE: *fall,* scythe, *strain*
SYLLABLE: arsis, mora, *part,*
penult, sonant, term, ultima
lacking: apocope, catalectic
lengthening: estasis
*music: *note:* music
omission: apocepe
pert.: dactylic
shortening: apocope, elision, systole
SYLLABUS: abstract, *analysis,*
epitome, precis, synopsis
SYLLOGISM: barbara, dilemma,
enthymeme, epicheirema, figure,
lemma, sorites
SYLPH: *dwarf,* *spirit*
SYLVAN: *god:* faun, pan, satyr
SYLVIA: becca fico, blackcap,
figpecker, garden warbler
SYMBOL: abbreviation, apotro-
paion, attribute, *badge,* button,
character, charm, contribution,
creed, crest, *cross,* diagram, expression, *fetish,* *flag,* *form,*
hiero, *image,* *mark,* *memorial,* *monument,* motif, *name,*
number, orant, *ornament,* palm,
regalia, representation, *sign,*
similitude, *staff,* *stick,* swastika, tablet, talisman, *token,* totem, trademark, *word*
SYMEON: *son:* john, levi
SYMMETRICAL: *equal,* *regular*

SYMMETRY: balance, harmony
SYMPATHETIC: *gentle,* *good,*
kind, kosher, *soft,* *warm*
SYMPATHY: *passion,* response
lack: dyspathy
SYMPHONY: music, *symmetry*
SYMPTOM: *alarm,* *symbol*
SYNAGOGUE: church, congregation
founder: ezra
great, the: anshe keneseth hagge-
dolah
official: baal kore, parnas
platform: almemar, alminbar,
bema, bimah
pointer: yad
sephardic: anoga
singer: cantor, chazan, chazzan
SYNAXIS: *meeting,* *rite*
SYNCHRONIZE: *form,* *organize*
SYNCOPATE: *swing*
SYNCOPE: faint, swoon
SYNDICATE: *trust,* *underworld*
SYNOD: council, *meeting*
SYNOPSIS: prospectus, *syllabus*
SYNTAX: *order,* *system*
analyze: parse
error: solecism
SYNTHESIS: *abstract,* *synopsis*
SYNTHETIC: *substitute*
SYRACUSE: *founder:* archias
ruler: agathocles, diocles, dion-
(ysus), gelon, hermocrates,
hiero(nymus), timoleon, thrasy-
bulus
SYRIAN: amorite, shemite
animal: addax, daman, dubb
bishop: abba
buried city: dura
church plan: triconch
city: aleppo, alexandretta, antioch, balbec, beirut, beyrout,
calneh, calno, damascus, derra,
emesa, homs, seleucia
commandos: as-saiqa
deity: allat, baal, el, gad, hadad,
mammon, resheph, rimmon

* Asterisk means to look up this word to find more answer words.

fanatic: baathist
flower: juniper, retem
goat: angora
governor: quirinius, sisinnes
grass: johnson
gypsy: aptal
hymn writer: narsai
king: benhadad, hazael, rezin
lake: merom, tiberias
mallow: okra
metal cloth: acca
money: piaster, pound, talent
mountain: carmel, libanus
part: amurru, golan, hauran
party: ba'ath
peasant: fellah
people: ansarie, druse
plant: cumin
river: jordan, orontes
script: peshito, serta
sect: druse
silk: acca
tetrarchy: abilene
tribe: ansairieh, ansarie, ansariyah, aptal
weight: artal, artel, cola, ratel, rotl, talent
wind: simoon
SYRINGA: lilac, mock orange, olive, philadelphus, shrub
SYRT: bog, quicksand
SYRUP: clairce, dhebbus, glucose, honey, karo, maple, orgeat, sorghum, treacle
SYSTEM: aggregation, arrangement, bureaucracy, code, *doctrine, *group, hypothesis, mode, *order, party, philosophy, *plan, regimen, regularity, *rite, rote, *rule, *service, universe, *way
SYSTEMATIC: *regular
SYSTEMATICS: taxonomy

TAAL: afrikaans, lake, volcano
TAB: bill, strap, strip, tongue

TABARD: cape, coat, *cover
inn host: baillie, bailly
TABASHEER: bamboo sugar
TABBY: *dress, *gossip, puss
cloth: moire, moreen
moth: agloosa
TABEBUIA: amapa, cedar, gum
TABERNACLE: *abode, church
feast: succoth
TABETIC: *low, *mean, *poor
TABETIC, TABID: *mean, *poor
TABITHA: dorcas, gazelle
TABLE: *analysis, chart, delay, list, *place, roll, *stand
calculating: abacus, fare, list
centerpiece: epergne
communion: altar, credenza
companion: metter, tapis
cover: baize, cloth, tapis
game: pool
lamp: bouillotte
land: altiplanicie, balaghat, bench, karoo, mere, mesa, pamir, paramo(s), *plain, plateau, puna
linen: napery, napkins
mountain: amba, mensa
philosopher: deiphosophist
three-legged: tripod, trivet
top: bouchon
workman: bench, siege
writing: desk, escritoire
TABLEAU: *picture, register
TABLET: *memorial, *monument, *ornament, pad, sheet, slab
stone: stela(e), stele(s)
symbol: pax
three-leaved: triptych
two-leaved: diptych
writing: pad, slate
TABOO, TABU: ban, bar, *stop
opposed to: noa
TABULATE: *record, *schedule
TACAMAHAC: balsam, calaba
TACHLIS: heart, nub, point
TACHYPTERELLUS: apple curculio

* Asterisk means to look up this word to find more answer words.

TACIT: implicit, silent
TACITURN: brief, laconic, terse
TACK: *beat, brad, *join, *route, *secure, *turn, *unite
TACKLE: *attack, *seize, *try
  anchor: cat(fall)
  block: burton
TACKY: crude, dowdy, *thick
TACT: *address, poise, stroke
TACTICS: *plan, *system
TADPOLE: bullhead, polliwog
TAEL: part: li, mace
TAFFY: candy, *welsh: people
TAG: *bit, *end, *join, *title
TAGALOG: *philippine
TAGETES: *marigold
TAGRAG: *rabble, vagabond
TAGTAI: satellite, sycophant
TAHITI: apple: ambarella, hevi
  canoe: pahi
  capital: papeete
  centipede: veri
  curlew: kioea
  dialect: beche-de-mer
  garment: maro, pareu
  god: oro, taaroa
  minstrel society: areoi, arioi
  mulberry: aute
  old name: otaheite
  plant: awapuhi, taro
  woman: wahini
TAHOE: trout: pogy
TAI: *thai
TAIL: appendage, detective, *end, *escape, *follow, *stern
  comb.: caud(o), cerc(o)
  kind: bob, bun(t), cauda, empennage, fud, plume, scut, stern, streamer, strunt, twist, wreath
  pert.: caudal, cercal
  train: caboose
  without: acaudal, anurous
TAILOR: busheler, carzee, draper, *fit, *form, *make, snip, snyder, stitch, tailleur
  goose: flatiron, sadiron
  itinerant: cardooer

lapboard: panel
pert.: sartorial
TAINT: blemish, *smear, *spoil
TAINTED: *bad, *high, *rank
TAJ MAHAL: site: agra, eastasica
TAKE: *accept, *acquire, *adopt, appropriate, *arrest, borrow, cadge, captivate, charm, *cheat, check, choose, collar, conduct, contact, cop, *deceive, deduce, dispossess, *gather, graft, gravy, haul, hog, *income, infer, occupy, photo(graph), pocket, pork, possess, purse, receive, *seize, *skin, *spoil, *stand, *steal, swag, swallow, swindle, *trap, *trick, usurp, *yield
aback: dismay, *start(le)
advantage: *deceive, move, *use
another's place: *substitute
apart: *destroy, *end, *ruin
a powder: *escape, flee, *run
away: *remove, *seize, *steal
back: *retreat, *return
by storm: *attack, *seize
charge: *lead, *rule, *run
down: *note, *rebuke, *record
exception: demur, qualify, veto
five: *rest
for granted: *accept, *think
in: *gather, *get, hear, *see
into custody: *arrest
it easy: relax, *rest
it out on: *punish, *rebuke
leave: depart, *separate
off: *copy, *escape, *start
on: *accept, *fight, *succeed, *use, worry
one's measure: *look, *try
orders: obey, *yield
out: date, escort, *remove
over: arrogate, *seize
pains: be careful, *try
part: compete, *join, share
root: *grow, *settle
shape: crystallize, *form
the cake: *succeed, *win

* Asterisk means to look up this word to find more answer words.

the count: *fail, *fall, lose
the pledge: *abstain, *quit
the veil: *quit, retire
time: delay, fabianize
to: *desire, *train, *try
to task: *punish, *rebuke
unawares: *ambush, *seize, *start(le), surprise
up: *adopt, *consider, *gather, *rebuke, *settle, *start, *try

TAKER: *comb.:* ceptor
TAKIN: budorcas, gazelle
TAKT: *beat, *meter
TALAPOIN: *church: man, guenon, *monk, monkey, poonghee
TALC: agalite, conte, powder, soapstone, steatite
TALE: *gossip, *lie, *story
TALENT: *ability, *gift, *power, *skill, *turn
1/60th: mina
TALIERA: palm, tara, tree
TALINUM: fame-flower
TALISMAN: *fetish, *magic, *staff, *stick, *symbol
TALK: *address, amphigouri, *argot, *argue, *argument, *blab, blather, bleeze, bukh, bull, cackle, caquet(erie), chin, clack, click, colloquy, conference, confess, converse, crack, descant, dialect, dialogue, diction, filibuster, gaff, *gossip, guff, gush, harangue, harp, hot air, jaw, jeremiad, *joke, language, lingo, *noise, *nonsense, orate, parlance, parley, *rally, rave, *rebuke, *report, *scold, shoot the breeze, speech, spiel, spout, *state, tattle, *tell, *word, yak, yap
comb.: logue
TALL: *big, *great, *high, long
TALLOW: *fat, *smear, suet
comb.: sebi
tree: candlenut, cera

TALLY: *account, *copy, *equal, point, run, score, square, suit
TALMUD: commentaries, debates
academy: yeshiboth, yeshivah
liturgy: abodah
material: aggadah, aggadoth
part: gemara, mishnah
student: bahur
title: abba
treatise: berakah
TALON: claw, fang, foot, hallux, hand, nail, spur, zipper
TALOS: *slayer:* daedalus
TALUK: estate, tract
TALUS: ankle, incline
TAM: balmoral, beret, cap, hat
TAMAR: *child:* pharez
consort: er, judah, onan
TAMARA: *domain:* imeritia
TAMARACK: hackmatack, larch, lodgepole pine, mummey brown
TAMARIND: amli, sampaloc
TAMARISK: atle, jhow, salt tree
TAMASHA: *display, *show
TAMBOUR(INE): cup, daira, drum, *ornament, tabor, timbrel
vibrance: travale
TAME: *break, bust, civilize, *defeat, docile, domesticate, *dull, *gentle, harmless, inert, insipid, prune, servile, *stop, *train
TAMERLANE: *grandson:* ulugebek
TAMIL: dravidian, *indian
capital: madras
caste: vellala
yercum: mudar
TAMMANY: *man:* bucktail, politico
officer: wiskinkie, wiskinky
TAMMUZ: *love:* ishtar
sister: belili
TAMP: drive, pound, *press, ram
TAMPER: *fix, meddle, *plot
TAMPICO: *fiber:* istle
TAMPION, TAMPO(O)N: *cover, plug, *stick
nasal: rhinobyon

* Asterisk means to look up this word to find more answer words.

TAMUS: baneberry, bindweed, black byrony

TAN: *beat, *hit, *strike, *whip
back: napa, ross
color: adust, beige, brown, buff, dun, ecru, tawny
liquor: owse

TANAGER: cashew, habia, lindo, redbird, spindalis, yeni

TANCEL: *abuse, *beat, *whip

TANDAN: catfish

TANG: bite, flavor, *smell, zest
fish: pike, surgeonfish
plant: rockweed, seaweed

TANGANYIKA: leader: karume, nyerere, sayid
island: tanzania, zanzibar
party: afro-shrazi
peak: kibo, meru
people: arusha, goma, swahili, wabunga, wagogo, wagoma
title: sayid
weight: farsalah

TANGIBLE: *actual, real, tactile

TANGIER: measure: kula, mudd

TANGLE: *fight, *puzzle, *trap
-berry: blue huckleberry
foot: aster, deerweed, *drink
-legs: liquor
thread: snarl

TANGO: bingo, *dance

TANIA: aroid, blue eddoes

TANITH: caelestis

TANK: basin, cistern, cuvette, *drink, pachucha, *pack(age), piscina, pond, pool, *stomach
armored: panzer
part: tread, turret
weapon: bazooka

TANKARD: facer, goblet, hanap
leather: bombard

TANKED: *drunk

TANKER: freighter, oiler, vessel

TANNER: barker, bateman
chemical: bomah, borax
extract: amaltas, arjan, arjum, bate, cutch

gum: angico, kino
plant: alder, sumac(h)
substance: splate
tree: amla, amli

TANOAN: isleta, pueblo

TANSY: bitter buttons, cammock, ragwort, tanacetum

TANTADLIN: dainty, dumpling

TANTALIZE: *plague, *torment

TANTALUS: father: zeus
young: broteas, niobe, pelops

TANTAMOUNT: *equal

TANTARA: *noise, fanfare

TANTIVY: *fast, gallop, *speed

TANTRA: agama

TANTRUM: *anger, *fit, *temper

TANZANIA: *tanganyika

TAO: cosmic order, truth
head: chang tao-ling, celestial teacher, heavenly preceptor
philosopher: chuang chou, chuang tzu

TAP: *dance, drain, *open, *pierce, *strike, tavern, touch
cinder: bulldog, slag
dance: buck and wing
room: bar, buvette, *saloon

TAPE: band, bind, *record, *tie
grass: celery grass
needle: bodkin
worm: appetite, cestoda, entozoan, flatworm, platyhelminth, strobila, taenia
embryo: oncosphere
larva: bladderworm, coenurus, cysticercus, hydatid, measle
medicine: brayera
part: bothridium, bothrium
provide: arrase

TAPER: candle, lessen, sharpen

TAPERING: conical, fusiform
comb.: spiri

TAPES: carpet shell, clam, venerida

TAPESTRY: arras, aubusson, audenarde, bayeux, beauvais,

bruges, dosser, dossiere, fabric, gobelin, *picture, tapis
beetle: carpet bug
moth: trichophaga tapetzella
screen: ceiling
TAPIO: *daughter:* tuulikki
son: nyyrikki
wife: mielikki
TAPIOCA: casava, cassave, manihot, manioc, salep
TAPIR: anta, anteater, buffalo, bush cow, danta, saladang
TAPIS: band, sash, *tapestry
TAPNET: basket, frail
TAPPET: cam, lever
TAPUYA: apinage, auca, botocudo, caingang, camacan, caraho, cayapo, chavante, coroado, gesan, goyana, juya, timbra
TAR: alchitran, brea, maltha, pavement, pitch, *sailor
and feather: *torture
bush: black brush
TARANAKI: *volcano:* egmont
TARBOOSH: cap, fez, turban
TARDY: *late, *slow
TAREG: discount, *dregs, weed
TARGET: bull's-eye, *desire, *end, goal, *limit, *mark, *objective, *ornament, quintain
distance from: mark shot
rifle: bull gun
TARIFF: list, rate, *system
TARNISH: *dull, *smear, *spoil
TARO: aroid, bleeding heart, caladium, cocgo, coco, dasheen, eddoe, gabe, koko, poi, tania
TARPON: elops, milkfish, sabalo, savanilla, silverfish
related: chiro
TARRAGON: biting dragon
TARRAROM: *ado, hullabaloo
TARRY: *abide, dally, idle, wait
TARSHISH: galle
TARSIGER: bush robin, ianthisa
TARSUS: ankle, hock, pala, shank
governor: cleon

insect: manus
saint: paul, saul
TART: *acerb, pie, *severe, *sharp, *sour, *wanton
candy: acid drop
TARTAN: plaid, sett, sheet
plaid: bracken
TARTAR: argal, argol, calculus, crank, kalmuck, toba, turk
drink: kumiss
dynasty: kin, wei
group: chambul, horde, uhlans
horseman: cossack
militiaman: uhlan, ulan
noble: murza
republic capital: kazan
royalty: agib, khan(ate)
scales: beeswing
tent: balagan
tribe: alani, huns, shor(tzy)
TARTARUS: hades, *hell
daughter: echnidna
jailer: campe
prisoner: danaid, ixion, sisyphus, titans, tityus
wife: gaea
TARTARY: *lamb:* barometz, boramez, lycopodium
wild horse: tarpan
TARTUFFE: *false, hypocrite
maid: dorine
TASK: chore, stint, tax, *work
take to: *rebuke, *scold
undoable: aladdin's window
TASMANIA: *animal:* anteater, echidna, phalanger, tapoa, thylacine, tiger, wolf, wombat
bird: pardalote
cape: grim
lake: westmoreland
peak: barrow, ben lomond, brown, drome, grey, humboldt, nevis, wellington
river: arthur, derwent, huon, jordan, tamar
town: hobart, launceston
TASS: bowl, cup, draft, heap

---

* Asterisk means to look up this word to find more answer words.

TASSEL: *adorn, brush, cordelle, *ornament, tag, thrum, zizith

TASTE: elegance, gusto, lick, palate, polish, *sense, *smell
absence: ageusia, ageustia
bud: papilla, tongue
delighting: friand
perversion: malacia

TASTELESS: *dull, *low, *mean

TAT: *absolute, crochet, embroider, tangle, touch

TATAR: *tartar

TATOU, TATU: armadillo, peking

TATTER: *bit, *part, *tear

TATTLE: *gossip, *talk, *tell

TATTLER: *editor:* steele
publisher: bickerstaff

TATTOOING: moko, pounch

TAU: cross, *fetish, *symbol

TAUNT: *aggravate, *banter, barrack, charge, check, come back, cut, dare, dig, flaunt, fleer, fling, gibe, *insult, jab, jape, jeer, jibe, *joke, mock, needle, nettle, niggle, poohpooh, provoke, quirk, rail, *rally, *rebuke, reply, reproach, revile, scoff, *scold, scout, scurrility, slam, slate, sneer, tease, tempt, *torment, upbraid, vex

TAUREG: awellimiden

TAUROMACHY: bullfight, *contest

TAURUS: bull, pleiades

TAUT: *firm, *severe, *strict

TAUTOG: blackfish, chub

TAVERN: alehouse, bar, bierstube, brauhaus, brewery, buvette, cantina, hotel, inn, khan, spa, tambo, *tap: room

TAW: alley, *beat, marble, tan

TAWDRY: garish, gaudy, loud

TAWNY: dusky, olive, swart
owl: billy wix

TAX: assess, burden, capitation, cast, charge, contribution, cost, duty, exaction, *fee, *fine, geld, hidage, importune, impose, levy, load, onus, ratal, revenue, scat, scot, *settle, stent, *strain, task, tenth, tithe, toll, tribute, *try
gatherer: catchpole, catchpoll
kind: abkari, advalorem, annale, annates, auxilium, avania, boscage, burghal, capital gain, carucage, cess, chaukidari, cro, customs, estate, excise, export, finta, gabelle, gift, head, import, income, inheritance, license, likin, liquor, mise, nuisance, octroi, patente, pavage, poll, prisage, property, sales, scat, screwing, severance, single, soc, surtax, tailage, taille, tariff, tithe, use, vinage, war profit, withholding
protest: boston tea party

TAXI: cab, *move, *start

TEA: beverage, *party, supper
bowl: chawan, pot, samovar, track, urn
box: caddy, calin, canister
-cake: scone
constituent: caffeine, theine
extract: adenine
-house site: naha, okinawa
-kettle: suke, sukie, suky
kind: assam, bohea, black, bouillon, cambric, cha(a), chia(s), congo(u), emesa, go-widdie, gunpowder, hyson, mate, ledum, oolong, oopak, padra, pekoe, ptisan, tcha, thea, tisane, tsia, yerba
-pot cover: cosy, cozy
rose: bon silene, bride
table: ambulante, teapoy, tepoy
tree: manuka, ti

TEACH: *direct, *lead, *train
edward: blackbeard, pirate

TEACHER: abecedarian, alim, coja, docent, doctor, don, guide, hoja, instructor, khoja, maestro, master, mentor, mollah, mullah, munshi, pedagog(ue), pedant, preacher, professor, scribe, tutor

TEAK: angili, cocoa, puriri, saj, teca, tectona, tree

TEAL: crick, duck, fowl, garganey

TEAM: *group, *join, set, *staff

TEAMSTER: bearer, carrier, carter, drayman, driver, skinner
command: gee, haw

TEAR: *agitate, bacchanal, bead, *break, *destroy, *drunk, explode, fine, *flaw, hurry, *hurt, jag, jamboree, lachryma, laniate, *move, *open, orgy, *pain, *part, *party, *passion, *pierce, *remove, rend, rent, revel, rip, rive, *run, *separate, shatter, slit, snag, *speed, *split, spree, tatter, toot, *torment, trip, waste, weep, wrench
off: *start, *take
pert.: lachrymal, lachrymose
pit: larmier
up: arache, assart, pluck, *take

TEASE: *abuse, *banter, ride, *taunt, *torment, *trouble

TEASEL: boneset, comb, thistle

TEBBAD: sandstorm, *storm

TEBELDI: baobab

TECHNICAL: fussy, professional
expert: boffin
name, comb.: onym
terminology: cant

TECHNIQUE: *art, *form, *skill, *style, *system, *way

TECOMA: angelin, fiddlewood, peroba, roble, trumper creeper

TED: *spread, *turn, waste

TEDIOUS: dreary, *dull, *slow

TEE: bullhead, cock, mound

TEEHEE: *laugh, snicker, titter

TEEL: sesame

TEEM: pour, swarm, throng

TEEN: *hurt, *pain

TEETER: *change, *oscillate

TEETH: *tooth

TEETING: titlark

TEETOTAL: *abstain, *complete

TEETOTALER: nephalist, rechabite

TEEWHAAP: lapwing

TEFNUT: *consort:* shu

TEGEA: *king:* aleus

TEGUA: *sandal, *shoe

TEGUEXIN: lizard, teju

TEGULA: alula, appendage, tile

TEGUMENT: *cover, *skin, testa

TEGURIUM: *hut, *memorial

TEICHER: bleed, ooze

TEIIDAE: ameiva, lizards, teju

TEIND: *tax, tithe

TEIRESIAS: *daughter:* manto

TEJU: lizard, teguexin, teiidae

TEKOA: *herdsman:* amos

TEL AVIV: *newspaper:* haaretz

TELA: membrane, tissue, web

TELAMON: atlantes, caryatid
brother: peleus
father: acheus, aeacus
friend: hercules
son: ajax, teucer

TELEGRAM: answer, cable, flash, message, radio, wire(less)

TELEGRAPH: *inventor:* morse
part: anvil, baud, key, siphon, spacer, tapper
underwater: cable

TELEKINETIC: psychic(al)

TELEMACHUS: *sire:* odysseus

TELEPATHY: esp, intuition

TELEPHONE: buzz, call, dial
exchange: central, pbx
inventor: bell

TELEPHONUS: bacbakiri

TELEPHUS: *mother:* auge

TELESCOPE: collapse, fold, lens

TELEVISION: box, tube, tv, video
cable: coaxial
interference: snow
network: abc, cbs, nbc
program: telecast
reception: ghost, grid, *image, *noise, *picture, rain, snow
recording: kinescope

---

* Asterisk means to look up this word to find more answer words.

technician: audio monitor, cameraman, sound man

term: adder, catv, encoder, evr, kinescope, mixer, orthicon, pickup, relay, scan, scophy, screen, signal, telecast, televise, uhf, vhf, video, vidicon

TELL: *advise, *affect, *blab, *broadcast, calculate, carp, communicate, count, dictate, disclose, discourse, explain, express, fictionize, figure, *gossip, impart, impress, influence, *issue, know, mention, narrate, novelize, own, *present, recognize, recount, regard, relate, render, *repeat, *report, request, romance, *spread, *state, storify, *talk, utter

home: altdorf, uri

off: *rebuke, *scold

TELLER: banker, cambist, potdar

TELLING: *important, valid

TELLURIDE: altaite, hessite

TELLUS: *festival:* fordicidia

TELSON: pleon, segment, somite

TEMERITY: *power, *spirit

TEMON: helm, rudder

TEMPER: *abate, *accommodate, *adapt, *adjust, *anger, *anneal, attune, bait, bate, blend, condition, *control, curb, dander, delay, *direct, *disposition, govern, harden, heal, heat, humor, ire, irish, manage, mean, mingle, mix, moisten, mollify, monkey, *pet, *reduce, relax, *remedy, restrain, season, soften, soothe, *spell, *spirit, *state, steady, *tie, *time, tone, toughen, tune, *violence

TEMPERAMENT: crasis, *temper

TEMPERANCE: restraint, sobriety

TEMPERATE: *cool, *gentle

TEMPEST: *storm, *tumult, *wind

character: alonso, antonio, ariel, caliban, ceres, iris, juno, miranda, prospero

TEMPESTUOUS: gusty, *violent

TEMPLAR: mason

battle cry: beauseant

TEMPLATE, TEMPLET: *form

TEMPLE: church, *memorial

kind: cella, covil, deul, dewel, duomo, fane, girja, huaca, jinsha, kiack, masjid, mosque, pagoda, synagogue, taa

pert.: hieron, marai

vestibule: antarala

TEMPO: *meter, *speed, *time

pert.: agogic

rapid: presto

slow: grave

TEMPORAL: civil, laic, worldly

TEMPORARILY: interim, nonce

TEMPORARY: *substitute

TEMPORIZE: delay, *yield

TEMPT(ATION): *allure, *draw

TEN: decade, dix, iota, sawbuck

TENACE: fourchette, high cards

TENACIOUS: *fast, *firm, *thick

TENACITY: nerve, pluck, *spirit

TENAIL(LE): *fort

TENANT: laet, leud, saer, vassal

TEND: *head, *lead, *move, *supply, *turn, wait, *work

TENDENCY: bent, *set, trend

TENDER: *gentle, *gift, *kind, *money, *soft, *warm, *weak

-*foot:* cheechako, tyro

TENDING: *comb.:* acious, ative, centric, telic

TENDON: muscle, sinew, thew

bone: sesamoid

TENDRIL: capreol, filament, *part, shoot, *stem, stipule

having: capreolate

TENEBRIFIC, TENEBROUS: *sad

TENERIFE: *volcano:* teide

TENNESSEE: *bird:* mockingbird

flower: iris, passionflower

governor: sevier

nickname: big bend state, old franklin, volunteer state

tree: tulip poplar

---

* Asterisk means to look up this word to find more answer words.

TENNIS: *cup:* davis
score: ace, deuce, love
stroke: backhand, chop, cut, lob(b), serve, set, smash
term: advantage, alley, court, cut, drive, fault, game, let, match, placement, racket, rally, receive, run on, stroke, toss, volley
TENNYSON: *character:* arden, elain(e), enid, enoch, hallam, king arthur, maud
TENON: coak, cog, mortise
TENOR: course, drift, feck, gist, mood, nature, trend
TENREC: centedid, hedgehog
TENSE: *firm, *hard, up tight
verb: aorist, conditional, future, past, pluperfect, present, preterite
TENSION: fatigue, *strain
TENT: aul, big top, camp, canopy, canvas, *cover, dressing, *hut, ibitka, kedar, lodge, marquee, paul, pavilion, pawl, probe, shelter, tepee, tilt, *top, tupek, wigwam, witu, yurt(a)
dweller: arab, bedouin, camper, gypsy, nomad, scenite, yuruk
TENTACLE: antenna, brachium, feeler, hair, palp, tendril
having: actinal
without: acerous
TENTERHOOK: agog, *strain
TENTH: *part:* deci, tithe
TENUOUS: *fine, *thin, *weak
TENURE: burgage, period, term
land: socage
TEPEE: *hut, *tent
TERAH: *father:* nahor
son: abraham, haran
TERAPH: idol, *image
TERBIUM europium, gadolinum
TEREBRINTH: teil, turpentine
TEREDO: borer, shipworm
TEREUS: *consort:* procne
son: itis, itylus, itys
TERGAL: dorsal, posterial

TERGIVERSATE: *lie, *oscillate
TERM: *limit, *name, *state, *time, *title, *trick, *word
TERMAGANT: *hag, *scold
TERMINAL: *end, *limit, station
negative: cathode, kathode
positive: anode
TERMINALIA: anagep, anaguep, araca, arjan, arjun, bahera, broadleaf, griselina, kalumpit, myrobalan, puka
TERMINATE: *end, *result, *stop
TERMITE: anai, ant, calotermitid
larva: bushman rice
TERN: anous, darr, fowl, kip, noddy, noio, pirr, spurre
TERNARY: triad, trinity, triple
TERRACE: bank, dais, patio, parterre, *plain, tier, *way
TERRAIN: *district, *sphere
TERRAPIN: chelonia, coodle, emyd, potter, tortoise, turtle
TERRESTRIAL: earthy, mortal
TERRIBLE: *bad, *evil, *great, *rank, *sad, *ugly, wretched
comb.: dino
TERRIER: airedale, bedlington, boston, bull, cairn, dandie, dog, fox, irish, scottish, sealyham, skye, welsh
TERRIFIC: *extreme, *good, *great, *supreme, *terrible
TERRIFIED: *afraid, scared, *shy
TERRITORY: *area, *district, land, realm, *state
TERROR: *demon, *devil, fear
TERRORIST: apache, goon, thug
TERRORIZE: menace, threaten
TERSE: *abrupt, *short
TERTULIA: club, *party
TESSELLATED: *mosaic, tile
TESSERA: password, *token
T E S T : *analysis, *analyze, approve, assay, *assess, criterion, crucible, cupel, dry run, evaluate, experience, experiment, inquire, norm, oral, ordeal, per-

---

* Asterisk means to look up this word to find more answer words.

formance, probation, proof, prove, question, quiz, *study, taste, tempt, *trial, *try, *will
tube: buret, burette
tube, within: vitro
TESTA: arillode, *cover, shell
TESTAMENT: covenant, scripture
TESTIFY: *affirm, *blab, *state
TESTIMONIAL: *honor, *memorial, *monument, *symbol
TESTIMONY: evidence, *word
TESTUDO: *cover, lyre, screen
TESTY, TETCHY: *short, *sullen
TETANUS: lockjaw
TETE-A-TETE: seat, sofa, *talk
TETHER: *limit, *range, *tie
TETHYS: *oceanus references
TETRAGON: rhombus, square
TETRIC: *acerb, *sullen
TETTER: eczema, fret, herpes, lichen, psoriasis
-wort: bloodroot, indian paint, potentilla, puccoon, redroot, sanguinaria, tomentil
TEUCRIUM: betony, germander
TEUTONIC: *german, goth, yekke
deity: *aesir
law: salic
TEWEL: bore, funnel, heater, hole, louvre, tuyere, vent
TEXAS: *bird:* mockingbird
bronco: mustang
citadel: alamo
cowboy jacket: chaqueta
fever: blackwater
flower: bluebonnet
hat: stetson
itch: cattle mange or scab
nickname: lone star state
pioneer: austin, houston
river: neches, neuces, pecos, red, rio grande
shrub: anagua, anaqua, baretta
state motto: friendship
state police: ranger
tree: pecan
university: rice, smu, tcu

TEXT: body, content, *copy, script, subject, theme, topic
book: abecedarium, algebra, anatomy, arithmetic, battledore, biology, cocker, geography, grammar, history, logic, manual, mcguffey's, primer, reader, speller
TEXTILE: cloth, fabric, fiber
dealer: mercer
plant refuse: hurds
ring device: poteye
screw pine: ara, pandan
worker: reeder, reedman
TEXTURE: grain, wale, web, woof
TEZ: *sharp, *violent
THACKERAY: *character:* amelia, amory, becky sharp, blanche, lady clavering, pendennis
THAI: kuy, shan, siam, tai
barge: balloen, balloon
cab: samlaw, samlo(r)
canal: klong
city: ayuthia, bangkok, chiengmai, kiangmai, lopburi, puket, singora, songkla, sukhothai
coin: at(t), baht, bia, bullet money, catty, fuang, pynung, salung, satang, tical
demon: nat
dress: panung
fabric: siamoise
fruit: mango, papaya, pumelo
game: saka, tau tem
island: phuket
isthmus: kra
king: rama
language: ahom, lao, tai
measure: anukabiet, can, chai meu, chang awn, cohi, kabiet, kam meu, kanahn, ken, keup, kwien, laang, leeng, ngan, niou, niu, nmu, rai, roeneng, sat, sen, sesti, sok, tanan, tang, vouah, wa, yot(e)
people: lao, lawa, siamese, tai

* Asterisk means to look up this word to find more answer words.

river: chaophraya, chi, mekong, menam, meping, mun, nan, ping
temple: vat, wat
weight: baht, catty, chang, coyan, fuang, grani, haph, kati, klam, klom, pai, pay, picul, salung, sompay, tamlung
THAIS: *prostitute, *wanton
composer: massenet
THALIA: bloom, brace
sister: *grace
slayer: erato
THALASSA, THALATTA: eureka
THALLOPHYTE: ascolichene
THAMAR: *son:* ben hur
THAMES: isis
boat: bawley
estuary: nore
town: eton, london
tributary: tyburn
THANA: *jail, prison
THANATOS: death
mother: nyx
THANE: *servant, warrior
THANK: *bless, *praise
THANKS: cumshaw, grace, gramercy, mahalo, much obliged
THAPE: gooseberry
THARF: *heavy, *stiff
THARM: catgut, *stomach
THAT: because, lest, what, which
is: e.g., id est, i.e., namely, present
THATCH: face, neti, nipa
THAUMAS: *daughter:* arce, *harpies, iris
wife: electra
THAUMATURGICS: *magic, *rite
THAW: melt, relent, soften
THC: cannabis, hemp
part: olivetol, resorcinol
THEATER: arena, auditorium, cinema, circus, coliseum, colosseum, drama, hippodrome, movie, music hall, odeon, odeum, opera, playhouse, stage

award: oscar, tony
company: troupe
curtain: drop, teaser
district: broadway, great white way, rialto
group: anta, ascap, habima
lead: hero(ine), star
low class: gaff
notice: pan, rave
part: baignoire, balcony, box, circle, footlights, foyer, gallery, loge, orchestra, parquet, parterre, proscenium, scena, skene, stage, vraia
pert.: broadway, histrionic
sign: sro
THEATRICAL: *artificial, campy, emotional, histrionic, pompous, showy, stagy, vivid
THEBAINE: paramorphine
THEBES: *acropolis:* cadmea
bard: pindar
deity: ament, amon, amun, mentu, mut, neith
enemy: alcmaeon, *thebes: seven
founder: cadmus
king: amphion, cadmus, creon, eteocles, laius, lycus, oedipus, pentheus
queen: aedon, dirce, jocasta, niobe
seven against: adrastus, amphiaraus, capaneus, hippomedon, parthenopaeus, polynices, tydeus
soothsayer: tiresias
THECA: anther, capsule, case
THEFT: burglary, job, larceny
THEIA: *husband:* hyperion
child: eos
THEME: *piece, *study, *text
THEMIS: euboulos, soteira
child: astraea, irene, prometheus
THEN: alors, anon, hence, next
THEOLOGIAN: *church: man
famous: aquinas, arius, barth, buber, fosdick, luther, merton, murray, schweitzer
unity study: irenics

* Asterisk means to look up this word to find more answer words.

THEORBO: lute
THEOREM: *adage, *rule, *text
THEORETICAL: *abstract, ideal
 power: odyl(e)
THEORY: *analysis, *doctrine,
 ism, *plan, *scheme
 atomic: bohr
 proving: apagoge
 psychologic: associationism
THEOW: *servant, *slave
THERAPY: *medicine, *remedy
THERE: *able, *ready, voila
THEREFORE: argal, ergo, hence
THERMAL: *hot, *warm
 balance: calenture
 comb.: eury
 unit: bot, btu, calorie
THERMOMETER: black-bulb,
 calorimeter, celsius, centigrade,
 dry-bulb, fahrenheit, pyrometer,
 pyrostat, reaumur, register, resistance, thermostat
THERSITICAL: *dirty, profane
THESAURUS: dictionary, lexicon
THESEUS: consort: antiope, ariadne, helen, hippolyte, perigune,
 phaedra
 father: aegeus, poseidon
 friend: peirithous
 mother: aethra
 son: acamas, hippolytus
 victim: cercyon, minotaur, pal-
 lantids, periphetes, phaea,
 polypemon, procrustes, sciron,
 sinis
THESIS: *meter, *text, *theme
 opposite: arsis
THESPESIA: bago, banago, bendy
THESPIAN: *actor
THESPROTIAN: queen: callidice
T H E S S A L Y : king: admetus,
 aeolus, erysichthon
 peak: ida, osa, ossa, pelion,
 psiloriti
 valley: tempe
 witch: aganice
THESTOR: son: alcmaon

THETIS: husband: peleus
 son: achilles
 wooer: poseidon, zeus
THEURGY: *magic, miracle, *rite
THEW: *force, *form, muscle,
 *power, *press, *quality
THICK: abundant, beamy, *big,
 blobber, broad, brosy, bull
 necked, bushy, chummy,
 *clumsy, condensed, corpulent,
 crass, crowded, *dull, excessive,
 familiar, fat, *firm, friendly,
 greasy, guttural, *hard, hazy,
 *heavy, hoarse, husky, impene-
 trable, inarticulate, intimate,
 laticostate, luxuriant, middle, numerous, overgrown, plump, roily,
 shaggy, *solid, squat, sticky,
 stodgy, *stupid, turbid, viscid
 -head: bluetongue
THICKEN: *dry, *increase
THICKET: boscage, brake, bush,
 ceja, chaparral, coppet, covert,
 *group, heath, hedge, jungle,
 motte, spinney, wood
THICKNESS: layer, mass, stratum
THIEF: abductor, ackman, angler,
 arrant, bramble, brigand, budge,
 burglar, cannon, chor, cloyer,
 *criminal, cutpurse, depredator,
 drawlatch, embezzler, filcher,
 footpad, freebooter, ganef, ga-
 nof, ghoul, gilt, gozlen, grifter,
 highwayman, *hoodlum, hooker,
 klepto(maniac), ladron(e), lar-
 cener, lifter, looter, miscreant,
 nevison, nimmer, peculator, pickpocket, piker, pilferer, pirate,
 plagiarist, poacher, prig(ger),
 prowler, purloiner, rascal, robber, rogue, rustler, sansi, scamp,
 schlep, scoundrel, shoplifter,
 sneaker, snoop, stealer, sucker,
 swiper, waster, whyo
 famous: autolycus, bill sikes,
 claude duval, dick turpin, fagin,
 jack sheppard, jesse james, jona-

* Asterisk means to look up this word to find more answer words.

than wild, macheath, mercury,
robert macaire, robin hood

THIEVES: *god:* mercury
latin: *argot, slang
leader: ali

THIGH: coxa, femur, gammon,
ham
comb.: mer(o)
pert.: crural, femoral

THILL: fill, plank, shaft

THIMBLE: bushing, cap, ferrule
-*rigger:* *cheat, *impostor

THIN: attenuate, bony, cadaverous, extenuated, *fine, gaunt,
gracile, insipid, lank, lean, *light,
*little, narrow, papery, rare, *re-
duce, scraggy, sheer, shrill, slender, slim, *small, spare, *superficial, svelt, transparent, *weak
comb.: sero
man's dog: asta
man's wife: nora

THING: *act, *affair, assembly,
*bag, being, *bit, cause, deed,
entity, existence, *forte, hang-up,
idea, incident, *instrument, *machine, matter, notion, noun, object, *particular, point, possession, property, reason, *slave,
*style, *tool
accomplished: acta, deed
assumed: postulate, premise
complete: entity, unity
contrary to logic: alogism
cursed: anathema
disgusting: chaloshes
done: act, acta, action
extra: bonus, bounty, lagniappe
following: sequel
found: discovery, trove
law: chose, res
opposite: antipode
out of place: anachronism
out of time: atavism
reasoned: noumenon
sensed: phenomenon
small: *bit

suff.: ance, ancy, ence, ency
unimportant: bagatelle, bauchle,
bean, *bit, nihil, nonentity,
nought, pinhead, plack, resnihili,
resnullius, stiver

THINGAMAJIG: gadget, gismo

THINGS: gear, goods, property
to be done: agenda

THINGUMBOB: doohickey, doo-
hinkus

THINK: *accept, *account, *analyze, *assess, believe, brood, calculate, cerebrate, cogitate, conceive, concentrate, conjecture,
daresay, deem, expect, *gather,
gloat, guess, hold, ideate, imagine, *mind, mull, opine, *plan,
presume, *purpose, *puzzle,
*reason, recall, reckon, regard,
ruminate, seem, sleep on, speculate, stew over, *study, suppose,
surmise, *understand, *wonder,
view, ween, weigh, wis

THIRD: fersion, tertian, tierce
comb.: trit

THIRL: *pierce, *thin, *tie

THIRST: appetite, *desire
absence: adipsia
excessive: anadipsia
producing: dipsetic
quenching: adipsous

THIRSTY: arid, avid, *eager

THIRTEEN: baker's dozen
fear: triakaidekaphobia

35 CUBIC FEET: ton

39.37 U.S. INCHES: meter

THIS: ce, esta, haec, hoc, yis

THISBE: *consort:* pyramus

THISTLE: achillea, anacyclus,
anaphalis, antennaria, anthemis,
aplopappus, arctotis, arnica, artemisia, aster, baccharis, baeria,
bedeguar, bellis, bidens, boebera,
borrichia, buphthalmum, cartha-
mus, dyssodia, *thorn
-*down:* egret, fluff, pappus
eater: cardophagus, donkey
sage: annual sage, chia

---

* Asterisk means to look up this word to find more answer words.

THITHER: distant, far, yonder
THIXLE: ad(z), hatchet
THJAZI: *consort:* njorth
 daughter: skathi
 home: thrymheim
THOCANUS: *son:* hezekias
THOLE: *allow, oarlock, *suffer
THOMAS: didymus, the twin
 opera: hamlet, mignon
T H O N G : amentum, babiche, knout, lash, lasso, *whip
 -*shaped:* lorate
THOR: donar
 consort: grid, sif
 hammer: mjollnir, mjolnir
 home: thrudvang
 palace: bilskirnir
 parent: jord, odin
 son: magni, modi, ull(r)
 talisman: girdle, glove, hammer
 victim: thrym
THORAX: alitrunk, chest, pereion
THORN: adam's-needle, *bane, bramble, briar, burr, cactus, needle, prickle, spike, spine, *thistle, *trouble, *urge
 -*back:* dorn, ray, roker, skate
 -*bearing:* spinate
 comb.: acanthus, spini
 -*less:* anacanthous, inerm
 tree: retama
THORNY: *sharp, vexatious
THOROUGH: *perfect, *pure
THOROUGHBRED: *noble
THOROUGHFARE: *road, *way
T H O T H : aah-te-huti, djehuti, zehuti
 father: geb, ra
 master: horus, osiris
 son: hornub
 wife: maat, nehmauit, seshata
THOUGH: however, nevertheless
T H O U G H T : *design, *image, *mind, *model, *picture, *reason
 comb.: ideo
 control: brainwashing
 force: phrenism

law doctrine: noetics
transference: telepathy
THOUGHTFUL: *gentle, *kind
THOUGHTLESS: *dull, *stupid
THOUSAND: chiliad, grand, mil
 comb.: kilo, mill(e), milli
 million: billion
 ten: myriad(s)
 years: chiliad, millennium
THOUSANDTH: millesimal
THRACE: *city:* cestos
 goddess: bendis
 hero: orpheus
 king: acesius
 musician: orpheus, philammon
 people: bessi, bisaltae, edoni, satrae
 river: aegospotami
THRALL: *servant, *slave
THRASAEUS: *son:* appollonius
THRASH: *defeat, *hit, *whip
THREAD: babiche, bave, filament, line, lisle, *meaning, purl, stamen, tenor, tram, twine
 ball: clew, clue
 -*bare:* *mean, *poor, stale
 bits: lint, ravelings
 cell: cnida
 comb.: byss, mit(o), nem(a)
 -*fin:* barbu(do), berycoid
 -*fish:* catfish, cobbler, cutlass, herring, shad
 group: beer, cop
 network: capillitium
 pert.: fibroid, filate, filose, linear, nemaline, *thin
 surgical: seton
THREADS: *cross:* reticle
 crossed: warp, weft, woof
 refuse: bur, burr
 separate: sleaves
THREAP, THREEP, THREIP, THREPE: *affirm, *argue, *beat, *press, *quarrel, *scold, *urge
THREAT: *press, *push, *trouble
 futile: brutum fulmen

THREATEN: harass, menace, warn

THREATENING: *big, *sinister

THREE: crowd, drei, tern, trey
-branched: triskele, triskelion
comb.: ter, tri(s)
-dimensional: caliper, cubic, *solid, spatial, stereo, *thick
group: cock eyes, gleek, leash, tern, tierce, triad, triangle, trio, triumvirate, troika
-hour period: tandem
pert.: ternal, ternary, thrice, tierce, trebal, trinac, trine, triple, triply
-sided: trihedral, triquetrous

THRENODY: coronach, dirge

THRESH: *beat, *best, *thrash

THRESHER: beater, combine, flail

THRESHOLD: *opening, *start

THRIFT: economy, *work

THRIFTY: frugal, miserly, spare

THRILL: *quiver, *start, *stir

THRILLING: electric, vibrating

THRIVE: *grow, *prove, *succeed

THROAT: esophagus, fauces, gorge
comb.: lemo
covering: barb
infection: angina, croup, cynanche, quinsy, squinancy
lozenge: pastil(le), troche
part: glottis, gula
pert.: esophagal, gular, guttural, jugular
skin: dewlap
sore: housty
swelling: frog

THROB, THROE: *ache, *pain

THRONE: apse, asana, chair, gaddi, gadhi, musnud, *power
room: aiwan

THRONG: *group, *quantity

THROTTLE: choke, *kill, *stop

THROUGH: across, during, final
comb.: di(a)

THROW: bowl, blow, buck, bung, cant, catapult, *change, chuck, chunk, cop, crank, curve, dart, dash, *defeat, deal, *discard, *dismiss, *fire, flick, fling, flip, *force, fork, heave, hurl, jerk, kest, lateral, let fly, lob, *pass, peg, pelt, pitch, *produce, project, prostrate, put, *remove, retard, screwball, *serve, *shy, sling, snap, sprain, *spread, spring, *start, stone, *stop, *strike, stroke, thrust, thwart, tilt, toss, *upset, wrap, wrench
a fit: *anger, *rage, *storm
back: *defeat, *refuse, *return
in the towel: *quit, *yield
in with: *join, *unite
one's weight: *rule, *urge
out: *discard, *dismiss
up the sponge: *quit, *yield

THRUM: *part, *repeat, tassel

THRUSH: aptha, mavis, missel, omao, ouzel, robin, shama, sprue, throstle, veery

THRUST: *attack, *force, *pass, *pierce, *power, *press, *push, *run, *spirit, *spread, *strain, *throw, *urge
back: *defeat, repulse
out: *discard, *dismiss, remove

THUD: *beat, *hit, klop, *press, *push, *strike

THUG: *criminal, *hoodlum, thief

THUJA: arbor vitae, cedar

THULE: denmark

THUMB: digit, *mark, *part, peachwort, phalanx, pollex
pert.: thenar
print feature: whorl

THUMP: *beat, *defeat, drum, *hit, *punish, *strike, *whip

THUMPING: *big, *great, tattoo

THUNDER: *fire, *noise, *storm
-bolt, comb.: cerauno
comb.: bront(o)
cyclops: arges, brontes
-fish: catfish, loach, raad

---

* Asterisk means to look up this word to find more answer words.

god: donar, jupiter, indra, lei-
 kung, taranis, thor, zeus
-head: cloud, omen, warning
maker: bronteon, bronteum
sons of: boanerges
-stone: belemnite
-storm: bayamo, borasco
THUNGE: **thump*
THUNNIS: bluefin tuna
THURIFER: **church: man*
THUS: ergo, hence, sic
THWACK: **beat, *strike, *thrash*
THWART: **defeat, *frustrate,*
 *ruin, *spoil, *stop, *upset
THYESTES: *brother:* atreus
 father: pelops
 son: aegisthus
THYLACINE: tiger, wolf, yabbi
THYRSUS: **staff, *stick*
TIAMAT: *consort:* apsu, kingu
TIARA: coronet, crown, miter
TIBER: *ancient name:* tivoli
TIBERIAS: galilee
TIBET: sitsang
 animal: chiru, dgoba, goa, panda,
 shou, shue, sus, yak
 ass: kiang
 banner: tanka
 beer: chang
 brigand: khamba
 cabinet: kashag
 cap: chuba
 chamberlain: phala
 chief: pombo
 city: lhasa, lassa, noh
 coin: tanga
 dialect: bhutanese, bhutani
 ecclesiastic: dalai lama
 food: tsamba
 garment: chuba
 goat fleece: pashm
 god: chenrezi
 hay: komal
 heaven: honorable field
 kingdom: nepal
 language: bodskad
 leader: chime youngdong

mammal: ounce
monastery: benchen
monk: dalai lama
palace: potala
people: bhotia, bhotiya, tangut
pony: tanghan, tangum
region: jyekundo
religion: bon(bo)
river: indus, tsangpo
ruminant: serow, takin
sheep: bharal, nahoor, nayaur,
 oorial, sha(bo), urial
thanks: thujichenja
traitor: ngabo phakpala
tribe: khamba
wildcat: manul
TIBIA: flute, shinbone
 part: armilla
 pert.: cnemial
TIBURON: little village, shark
 island indian: seri
TIC: nystagmus, vellication
TICK: acarid, achenes, arachnid,
 argas, **cover,* insect, **mark*
 bird: beefeater
 fever: blue disease, cyanosis
 seed: dodder, knotweed, spurry
 trefoil: beggarweed, desmodium
TICKET: ballot, **note, *pass,*
 *plan, *schedule, slate, **token*
 free: annie oakley, **pass*
 part: stub
 season: abonne(ment)
 sell illegally: scalp
TICKLE: **please, *stir, *thrill*
TIDAL: *creek:* estero
 wave: aigre, bore, eagre, ebb,
 neap, surge, tsunami
TIDBIT: beatille, **bit,* item
TIDE: agger, current, neap, surf
 pert.: cnemial, neap
TIDINGS: **gossip,* news, **report*
TIDY: **fair, *fix, *good, *great,*
 *meet, spruce, trim
 -tips: aster, flower
TIE: **allegiance, *anchor,* beam,
 *bind, brace, break even, bridge,

---

* Asterisk means to look up this word to find more answer words.

cadge, cast, constrain, constrict, cord, couple, dead heat, *draw, duty, *equal, *fetter, influence, *join, knot, lace, lash, ligate, link, marry, moor, obligation, *pack, photo finish, pledge, post, relation, restrain, restrict, *secure, shackle, sheaf, sleeper, stalemate, standoff, *stop, tache, tape, teck, temper, tether, trammel, *trap, trice, union, *unite, yerk, yoke

kind: ascot, black, bow, cravat, four-in-hand, paisley, shoestring, white

the can to: *discard, *dismiss

up: promotion, *strike

T'IEN SHAN: heavenly mountains

TIER: apron, bank, *rank, row

TIERCE: cask, parry, *three

TIERRA DEL FUEGIAN: agni, ona

TIFF: *fight, *pet, *quarrel

TIFFIN: lunch, repast, tea

TIGER: bully, cat, chati, cub, feline, jaguar, leopard, rake, sher, shir, thylacine

finch: amadavat

-fish: carcharhinus, carcharias

milk: liquor

mouth: foxglove, snapdragon

wood: bush tamarind, machaerium

TIGHE, VIRGINIA: bridey murphy

TIGHT: *firm, *hard, *ready, *secure, *severe, *smart, *solid

-fisted: cheap, stingy

spot: jam, mess, pinch

TIGHTEN: compress, *tie

TIGHTWAD: miser, piker, screw

TIKOR: bombay arrowroot

TIKVATH: *son:* jahaziah, shallum

TIL: *mark, plant, sesame

TILE: carreau, favus, imbre, kashi, pantile, *quarrel, slab

fish: blanquillo, caulolatilus

game: dominoes

glazed: azulejo

pert.: slaty, tegular

TILER: kiln, *servant, *thief

TILIA: basswood

TILL: cultivate, drawer, *dress, *get, plow, *train, while

TILLER: farmer, helm, lever

TILT: *argue, *contest, *fight, list, *speed, *throw, *upset

hammer: oliver

TIMAEUS: *son:* bartimaeus

TIMALIA: babbling thrush

TIMARAU: buffalo

TIMBER: beam, cahuy, camber, forest, lumber, spars, wood

bend: camber, rafter, sny

cut: bunk, fallage, lumber

defect: conk, doze, lag, shan

end: tenon

estimator: biltmore stick, cruiser, scaler

foundation: batten, sill

heartwood: duramen

hemlock: alaska pine, tsuga

part: board, joist, purlin(e), rafter, rib, sill, spale

rotten: doat, dote, doty

truck: wynn

wolf: arctic wolf, lobo

TIMBRE: *drum, *meter, *quality, *symbol, *token

pert.: tonal

TIMBREL: drum, sistrum, tabor

TIME: *accent, aeon, age, clock, *control, date, day, duration, eld, eon, epoch, era, eve, fuss, hour, leisure, *limit, measure, *meter, minute, moment, month, occasion, *opening, period, schedule, season, second, spell, tempo, tense, term, tid, *turn, watch, week, year, yore

allowed: usance

being: nonce

bill: certificate

blossom: blutezeit

---

* Asterisk means to look up this word to find more answer words.

break: hiatus
card: chronicle
clock: bundy, recorder
fast: daylight saving, dst, lent
gone by: ago, past, syne, yore
happy: *orgy, *party, *tear
-honored: traditional
long: century, coon's age, forever, millennium
money: loan
music: adagio, presto
out: lull, respite, *rest
pert.: eral, horal, temporal
piece: clock, dial, watch
TIMELY: happy, lucky, prompt
TIMID: nervous, *shy, *weak
TIMNA: *child:* amalek
TIMON: cynic, helm, rudder
character: caphis, flavius, lucius, titus
TIMOR: *capital:* dili
coin: avo, pataca
island: leti, roti
TIMOROUS: *timid
TIMOTHY: *grandmother:* lois
mother: eunice, lois
TIMPANO: kettledrum
TIN: *cover, inferior, *money, *pack(age), *save, stannum
alloy: pewter, tinstone
can island: niuafoo
foil: tain
horn: petty, piker
pert.: stannic, stranic
plate: terne
type: daguerreotype
TINAMOU: tataupa, ynambu, yutu
TINCT: color, imbue, *mixture
TINDER: amadou, fuel, punk
TINE: *destroy, *pain, *trouble
TINGE: color, *smear, *tinct
TINGLE: girl, *smart, *stir, *support, *thrill
TINKER: caird, mackerel, *repair
TINNY: brittle, *rich, *thin
TINSEL: fake, sham, shoddy

TINT: color, hue, shade, stain
TINY: *fine, *little, *small
TIP: *end, *gift, *give, *top
cart: butt
having sharp: aristate
off: *alarm, *tell
over: *upset
staff: bailiff, *police: man
toe: *eager, *quiet
top: *best, *great
TIPPET: almuce, amice, cape, liripoop, palatine, patagium, scarf, snell, victorine
TIPPLE: *drink, lose, *upset
TIPPLER: alcoholic, carouser, drinker, pigeon, soak, toper
TIPSY: *drunk, *happy, *high
TIRADE: *abuse, *diatribe, *talk
TIRE: cloy, fag, fatigue, pall, recap, weary
part: carcass, casing, rim, shoe, tread, tube
TIRESOME: *dull, tedious, trite
TIRL: *oscillate, *turn
TIRR, TIRVE: strip, uncover
TIRZAH: *brother:* hur
TISSUE: fabric, fiber, phloem
animal: bone, fat, gelatine, gum, keratin, seur, suet
comb.: histo
connective: fascia
decay: caries, cataplasia
hardening: sclerosis
human: albedo, *animal, diploe, ligament, tendon
hyphal: trama
layer: stratum
nerve: ganglion
pert.: histoid, telar
reproduction: anagenesis
skeletal: cartilage
substance: sarcine
torn: avulsed
transplantation: anaplerosis
vegetable: bast, endarch, lignin, meristem, xylem
wasting away: phthisis

* Asterisk means to look up this word to find more answer words.

TIT: bird, *draw*, girl, horse

TITAN: astraeus, bana, coeus, crius, cronus, *demon*, *devil*, epimetheus, *giant*, hyperion, iapetus, *monster*, oceanus, pallas, *powerhouse*, prometheus, saturn, sesha
female: dione, eurynome, leto, maia, mnemosyne, phoebe, rhea, tethys, theia, themis
parent: gaea, uranus
war with gods: gigantomachy

TITANATE: isarate, rutile

TITANIA: *husband:* oberon

TITANIC: *big*, *great*, *large*

TITANITE lederite, sphene

TITANIUM: *ore:* ilmenite
alloy: anastase, blomstrandine, brookite, octahedrite

TITHE: canon, cess, tiend, toll

TITHONOUS: *consort:* eos
child: laomedon, memnon

TITHYMALUS: caper spurge

TITI: buckwheat, callithrix, hapale, marmoset, monkey

TITILLATE: *amuse*, *interest*

TITIVATE: *dress*, *ornament*

TITLE: address, *army: officer*, asset, book, caption, *church: man*, claim, deed, designation, equity, *flag*, *head*, *honor*, identification, *image*, inscription, legend, letterhead, *lord*, *magnate*, *mark*, masthead, movie, *name*, officer, official, play, potentate, property, *rank*, *right*, *ruler*
pert.: nominal, titular

TITMOUSE: bird, blackcap, blue button, chickadee, fuffit, goosander, heckimal, jackdaw, mag, mumruffin, nun, oxeye, parida, parus, puffer, sparus, titmall, tomnoup, tomtit, verdin, yaup

TITO: broz
foe: chetnik, mihailovic

TITRATE: *analyze*

TITTER: giggle, *laugh*, tehee

TITTLE: *bit*, *gossip*, *mark*

TITTUP: caper, frisk, prance

TITUREL: *son:* amfortas

TITUS: *daughter:* lavinia
queen: tamora

TITYRA: becard, bird

TIU, TIWAZ: ear

TIVOLI: tiber

TIZZY: dither, *pet*, snit

TLASCALAN: *god:* camaxtli

TLINGIT: auk, indian, tonga(s)

TMEMA: *part*, *piece*

TMESIS: diacope, metastasis

TNT: dynamite, trinitrotoluol

TO: *be:* am, einai, esse(re), etre, is, sein, was
boot: also, and, over
do: ado, flurry, fuss, *stir*
the end: a outrance, utterly
the limit: *perfect*, *pure*
wit: scilicet, videlicet
your health: *toasts*

TOAD: aglossa, agua, alytes, anura, bufo, crapaud, hyla, natterjack, paddock, peeper, pipa, quilkin, rana, salimentia, spadefoot, tade
eater: sycophant
extract: bufagin, bufotalin
fish: sapo, sarpo
flax: bread-and-butter, bride weed, butter-and-eggs, green brier, meadowsweet, ramsted
group: knot
stone: bufonite
stool: canker, mushroom

TOADY: serve, sycophant, *ugly*

TOAST: *burn*, *fire*, *warm*

TOASTS: a votre sante, bottoms up, brindare, brindisi, cento anni, cheers, health, kampai, propine, prosit, prosperity, salud, skal, skoal, vive, waes hael, wahz-hile, wassail

TOBACCO: broadleaf, latakia, perique, uppowoc, vuelta
ash: dottel, dottle
caked: cavendish

* Asterisk means to look up this word to find more answer words.

camphor: nicotine, nicotinin

chewing: cud, fid, fudgeon, hard, plug, quid, rockhound candy, scrap, spit and run

cigarette: bull, rag

coarse: caporal, shag

disease: blackfire, black shank, calico, walloon

dryer: oast

flavoring: petune

hard-spun: pigtail

inferior: bug dust, shag

ingredient: nicotine

juice: ambeer, ambier

leaf heart: ratoon

leaf moistener: caser, kase

low-grade: boots, bug dust, crumbs, shag

package: sack of dust

paste: goracco

pipe: chibouk, dust, fillins, goat hair, tumblins

pipe bowl: calabash

pouch: doss

receptacle: hooka(h), humidor, narghile, pipe

roll: carotte, cigar, nailrod, pudding, segar, stogie

ropes: bogie

sailor's: cornucopia, fair maid, faithful lover

smoke hater: misocapnist

symbol: blackamoor, highlander, turk, wooden indian

twist: pricke

TOBOGGAN: *decline,* sled, *slide*

TOBIAS: *father:* tobit

foot swallower: fish

friend: azarias, raphael

son: hyrcanus

wife: sarah

TOBIT: *kin:* ahikar, tobias

obsession: interment

wife: anna

TOBY: cigar, jug, *road,* *way*

TOCHER: dower, *part,* *piece*

TOCSIN: *alarm,* bell, signal

TOD: fox, mat, *pack,* shrub

TODAY: here, now, present

pert.: diurnal, hodiernal

TODDLE: dance, *walk*

TODE: boat, haul, sled

TOE: *comb.:* dactyl, digiti

clip: beak

great: halux

little: minimus

without: adactylous

TOFF: *fellow,* *spark*

TOFFISH: *smart,* stylish

TOG(A): *dress,* *symbol,* *token*

TOGETHER: *comb.:* com, con

TOGGLE: bolt, cotter, pin, rod

TOGO: *city:* ho, lome

TOGUE: namaycush

TOIL: *slave,* *trap,* *try,* *work*

TOILET: biffy, cloaca, *dress*

case: *bag,* etui, etwee

goods: notions

water: bay rum, eau de cologne

TOILS: grip, net, snare, *trap*

TOKEN: *accolade,* amoret, antique, *badge,* *certificate,* chip, counter, coupon, curio, dib, emblem, evidence, fare, feature, *fetish,* *flag,* forbysen, *form,* garland, *gift,* handsel, *honor,* *image,* keepsake, *mark,* medal, memento, *memorial,* memory, *monument,* *name,* omen, *ornament,* ostent, pawn, presage, *promise,* reminder, script, *sign,* slug, souvenir, *substitute,* *symbol,* tessella, tessera, ticket, trophy, virtu

taker: irt

TOKO: flogging, shop, store

TOKOLOSHE: *spirit*

TOKYO: edo, yeddo, yedo

districts: akasaka, asakusa, ginza, roppongi, shinjuku, shinsekai, ueno, yoshiwara

TOLA: *son:* jahmai, jeriel, jibsam, rephaiah, samuel, uzzi

TOLBOOTH: hall, *jail,* market

---

* Asterisk means to look up this word to find more answer words.

TOLCUS: *king:* pelias
TOLDO: **hut, *tent*
TOLERABLE: **fair, *pretty,* so-so
TOLERANCE: forbearance, patience
TOLERANT: broad, liberal
TOLERATE: **stand, *suffer*
TOLL: **fee,* price, rate, tax
TOLLY: **staff, *tower*
TOLTEC: *ruins:* tula
TOLU: balsam
TOLUENE: methylbenzene, tnt
TOLYPEUTES: apar(a), armadillo
TOM: *cat:* gib
  o'bedlam: lunatic, madman
  of lincoln: bell
  pepper: liar
  sawyer friend: huckleberry finn
  thumb: **dwarf*
  -tom: gong, **meter*
  tulliver's river: floss
TOMAHAWK: **attack, *strike*
TOMATO: love apple
  disease: black dot, buckeye, dartrose, rhizoctonia
  sauce: catsup, ketchup
  soup: gazpacho
TOMB: grave, **memorial*
  guardian: anubis
  recess: arcosolium
TOMBAUGH: *discovery:* pluto
TOMBOY: hoyden, **wanton*
TOME: atlas, book, volume
TOMFOOLERY, TOMMYROT: **nonsense*
TOMORROW: domani, manana
TONE: **meter, *note, *quality, *spirit, *style, *strain,* tenor, **way*
  chord: concento
  color: timbre
  combination: chord
  down: mute, soft pedal, soften
  lack: asonia, atony, atonic
  musical: siren(e), syren
  painting: harmonization
  quality: resonance, timbre

  rapid: tremolo
  series: octave, scale
  sharp: skirl, tang
  single: monotone
  singsong: sough, sugh
  succession: melos
  thin: sfogato
  third: mediant
  variation: nuance
  vibrant: twang
TONG: **group, *society*
TONGA: ono, tofua, vavau
TONGS: tenail(le), tueiron
TONGUE: **argot,* glossus, **gossip, *talk,* taste, voice
  bird: wryneck
  bone: hyoid
  comb.: glosso
  disease: agrom
  -fish: sole
  -lash: **rebuke, *scold*
  -like process: ligula
  mother: vernacular
  oxcart: cope
  part: blade, corona, raphe
  pert.: apical, glossal, lingual
  pivoted: pawl
  projection: papilla
  serpent: fang
  -tie: ankyloglossia
  -tied: mute, **quiet,* silent
  wagon: neap, pole
  without: aglossia
  worm: acorn worm, balanoglossid
TONIC: elixir, nostrum, **remedy*
  kind: absinthum, aloe, barberry, bayberry, berberis, bitters, boneset, chirata, chiretta, dope, gentian, gilo, goldenseal, mahonia, nervine, quassia, quinine, roborant, soda, tansy, wormwood
TONSIL: *comb.:* amygdal(o)
TONSILLITIS: antiaditis
TONY: **smart*
TOO: also, and, else, then, very
  bad: alas, averah

* Asterisk means to look up this word to find more answer words.

much: nimiety, satiety, trop
much, comb.: ard, art
TOOL: **instrument*
aptitude for: chrestic
boring: auger, awl, bit, burr, corkscrew, drill, gimlet, reamer, trephine, wimble
-box: chest, etui, etwee, kit
edged: adz(e), ax(e), belduque, bill, bistoury, blade, chisel, cleaver, colter, gouge, hack, hatchet, hoe, knife, lance(t), machete, mattock, panga, pick, plowshare, razor, saw, scalpel, scissors, scoop, scythe, share, shears, sickle, slotter, snips, tomahawk, wedge
mechanics: awl, bar, bevel, bodkin, bradawl, buffer, calipers, crowbar, dibble, edger, emery wheel, file, flail, forceps, fork, grapnel, hawk, header, jackscrew, lathe, level, monkey, pincers, planer, pliers, puncheon, ram, screwdriver, shaper, spatula, square, stapler, tackle, tamp, tapper, tongs, tweezers, vise
prehistoric: eolith, paleolith
theft: ratten
TOOM: empty, leisure, **thin*
TOON: blue pine, cedar, lim
TOOT: **drink, *fool, *spread, *spy, *tear,* tutu
TOOTH: appetite, cog, cuspid, denture, fang, grinder, incisor, molar, **projection,* scrivello, snag, tang, tusk
-ache: dentagra, odontalgia
-billed pigeon: dodlet
body: dentine
canine: cuspid, laniary, tush
comb.: odonto
decay: caries, cavity, saprodontia
drawer: dentist
enamel: amelification
facing: cusp, enamel
false: denture, plate

fungus: bear's-head, hydnum
grinding: bruxism
grinding surface: mensa
layer: cementum
long: fang, tush, tusk
molar: wang
paste: prophylactic
projecting: buck, snag
pulp: nerve
relic: buddha's tooth
replacement: bridge
saw: serra
sockets: alveoli
sprocket wheel: gub
wheel: cam, cog, gear, tine
TOOTHLESS: agomphious, edentate
TOP: **absolute, *ace,* acmatic, **acme, *best,* bonnet, cap(ote), ceil(ing), clearstory, climax, coif, consummate, **cover,* cream, **crown,* culminate, **defeat, *dome,* endome, epi, **equal,* exceed, **extreme,* finial, foremost, **good, *great, *hat, *head, *high,* hood, **important, *lead,* maximum, meridian, pick, pinnacle, **ridge,* roof, salt, **society,* summit, **supreme,* surface, surmount, surpass, **tent,* tip, topple, toy, tuft, tumble, **unique,* upmost, **upset,* zenith
kick: sergeant
-knot: onkos, panache, plume
-notcher: **ace, *wonder*
pert.: cacuminal, capital
TOPE: **drink,* junk, **memorial,* shark, shrine, **tower,* wren
TOPHET: **hell*
TOPI: antelope, cap, hat
TOPIC: **issue, *reason, *remedy,* subject, text, theme, thesis
TOPPLE: **defeat, *fall, *upset*
TOPSY-TURVY: askew, awry
TOR: crag, peak, pinnacle, **top*
TORAH: pentateuch, revelation
founder: moses

TORCH: cresset, fish, flambeau
frame: cresset
man: linkman
-wood: boswellia, canarium
TOREADOR, TORERO: bull-fighter, matador, escamillo
TORMENT: *afflict(ion)*, *aggravate*, bait, bale, burden, convulse, crucify, discomfort, excruciate, grate, harry, *hell*, horror, lacerate, macerate, martyrize, nightmare, ordeal, *pain*, *passion*, persecute, *plague*, *press*, provoke, *punish*, *scold*, scourge, spasm, *tear*, tease, *torture*, *trial*, *trouble*, try
TORMENTER: baiter, strigil
TORMENTIL: bloodwort, indian paint, potentilla, puccoon, red root, tetterwort, turmeric
TORNADO: *storm*, *wind*
junction: trinidad
TORO: bull, cavalla, cowfish
TORPEDO: *attack*, batoides, *criminal*, *destroy*, *end*, *hoodlum*, mine, numbfish, petard, *ruin*, shoot, sink
boat: catamaran, submarine
fish: ray
inventor: whitehead
TORPID: *dull*, *slow*, *stupid*
TORPOR: acedia, apathy, coma, languor, lethargy, sleep, sloth
TORQUE: chain, collar, *strain*
TORRENT: cascade, spate, stream
TORRID: *ardent*, *eager*, *hot*
TORRUBIA: blolly
TORTOISE: chelonia, emyd, galapago, terrapin, turtle
beetle: cassida, chrysomelida
land: mungofa
pert.: chelonian
shell: bekko, carapace
tablets: ke pouk hpai
TORTUOUS: anfractuous, cranky, labyrinthine, sinuous, spiral
TORTURE: boot, brainwashing,

break, cruelty, draw and quarter, flay, impale, *kill*, picket, strappado, *torment*
instrument: alfet, banca cava, barnacle, boot(ikin), bull of brass, iron heel, oregon boot, rack, scarpines, screw, wheel
TORUS: baston, boltel, molding
TOSH: neat, *nonsense*, tidy
TOSK: *albanian*
TOSS: *oscillate*, *raise*, *throw*
pot: *dipsomaniac*
up: *equal*, *tie*
TOT: *bit*, calculate, *drink*
TOTAL: *all*, *plenty*, *universal*
TOTEM: *fetish*, *symbol*, *tower*
TOTTER: *oscillate*, *quiver*
TOUCAN: aracari, guarani
TOUCH: *affect*, *bit*, *interest*, *meet*, *move*, *rebuke*, *steal*
comb.: aphia, tac
loss: anaphia
pert.: haptic, tactile, tactual
-stone: criterion, standard
wood: amadou, punk, tinder
wood, pert.: agaric
TOUCHED: *insane*, *mad*
TOUCHY: *short*, *sullen*
TOUGH: *brutal*, *firm*, *hard*, *obstinate*, *severe*, *strong*
TOUR: *beat*, *spell*, *travel*
TOURACO: bird, lory, parrot
TOURELLE: *tower*, turret
TOURMALINE: achroite, aprizite, borosilicate, chrysoberyl
TOURNAMENT: *contest*, *meet*
TOURNURE: bustle, pad
pit: ome
TOUSLE: *drag*, pull, *tear*
TOUT: *praise*, *spy*, *thief*
ensemble: altogether, nudity
TOW: *drag*, *draw*, pull, tug
cloth: canvas
flax: codilla, hards, hurds
rope: tew
-row: *fight*, *quarrel*
TOWAI: beat, kamahi, tree

TOWARD: against, anent, near
comb.: ad, ob, oc
TOWEL: clean, cloth, dry, wipe
fabric: huck, linen, terry
hot: oshibori
TOWER: arise, ascend, aspire, babel, belfry, campanile, colossus, derrick, *dome, dominate, elevate, exalt, fleche, *fort, gazebo, gopura, *grow, *jail, mansion, martello, *memorial, mirador, mole, *monument, overlook, pagoda, pinnacle, pylon, *raise, reach, shaft, shikara, sikar(a), sikhara, skyscraper, soar, spire, steeple, surmount, surpass, tope, tor, totem pole, tourelle, turret, vimana, ziggurat, zikurat
famous: babel, eiffel, london, minar, pisa
TOWERING: *big, *great, *high, *tall, *violent
TOWHEE: bunting, chewink, joree
TOWN: *comb.:* muni, tre
hall: cabildo, court
pert.: civic, oppidan, urban
suff.: by, ton
talk: *gossip
TOWNSMAN: burgher, citizen, gillie, oppidan, urbanite
TOXEMIA: pyemia, septicemia
TOXIN: poison, venom, virus
TOXOPHILITE: amor, cupid, eros
TOY: *bit, doll, *fool, *interest, kazoo, *play, sport
TOYON: christmasberry, holly
TRABUCO: blunderbuss, cigar
TRACE, TRACK: *bit, *copy, *draw, *follow, *mark, *record, *sign, *smell, *step, *token, *walk, *way
TRACKER: guide, puggi, *tower
TRACT(ATE): area, *piece, *plot, space, stretch, *study, zone
TRACTION: *power, utility
TRACTOR: amphibian, bulldozer,

cat(erpillar), duck, dukw, grader, halftrack, tank
TRADE: action, art, bandy, *bargain, career, change, *commerce, course, craft, deal, *forte, job, manner, method, occupation, patronize, practice, profession, purchase, pursuit, sale, sell, speculate, swap, traffic, truck, *work
god: vanir
in: cauponate
last: compliment
-mark: brand, *name, *symbol
TRADER: *agent, broker, monger
caste: balija, bania(n)
TRADING POST: agora, canteen, *fort, mart, pit, px, station
TRADITION: *doctrine, legend, mores, myth, practice, usage
TRADUCE: *abuse, *smear
TRAFFIC: *trade
light: blinker, signal
sacred things: simony
TRAGACANTH: bassorin, gum, tree
substitute: badam,
TRAGEDY: buskin, cothurnus
muse: melpomene
personification: ate
TRAGIC: *bad, *black, *sad
TRAGOPAN: bird, fowl, pheasant
TRAIL: *road, *trace, *way
-blazer: pioneer
TRAIN: *accustom, aim, *break (in), caravan, coach, develop, *direct, discipline, *dress, dry nurse, exercise, fit, *force, *form, foster, groom, *group, guide, housebreak, improve, *lead, nurture, perfect, practice, *prepare, procession, qualify, *raise, *ready, rehearse, *set, *staff, *tame, teach, trail, *try
captain: conductor
hawk: afaite
man: *railroad: man
railroad: cannonball express,

choo-choo, electric, express, flier, freight, interurban, limited, local, rattler, shuttle, special, streamliner

underground: *subway

TRAINER: driller, gymnasiarch, lanista, paedotribe, stockman

airplane: jeep, link, penguin

TRAIPSE: *walk, *wanton

TRAIT: *mark, *quality

TRAITOR: *apostate, betrayer, brutus, double-dealer, ganelon, informer, iscariot, judas, quisling, renegade, runagate

TRAJAN: *arch site:* benevento

TRAJECTORY: *route, *way

TRAM: beam, car, limb, shaft

TRAMMEL: *bind, *fetter, *tie

TRAMP: bimbo, bum, hobo, nomad, vagabond, *walk, *wanton

TRAMPLE: *defeat, *destroy, *hurt, step (on)

TRANCE: dream, rapture, stupor

TRANQUIL: *mild, *quiet, *smooth

TRANQUILLITY: *peace, *rest

TRANQUILIZER: *drug, *narcotic, pill

pert.: bromal

TRANSACT: conduct, perform

TRANSACTION: *action, *affair

TRANSCEND: *raise, *top

TRANSCENDENT: *great, *supreme

TRANSCRIPT: *copy, *record

TRANSFER: cede, deed, *move, *pass, *remove, *succeed

design: decal

TRANSFIGURE: exalt, glorify

TRANSFINITE CARDINAL: aleph

TRANSFIX: *pierce, *spear

TRANSFORM: *change, *turn

TRANSFORMER: alembic, changer

TRANSGRESS: *err, *sin, *wrong

TRANSIENT: fugitive, migratory

TRANSIT: *change, travel

TRANSITION: *change, *pass (age)

TRANSITORY: brief, caducous

TRANSLATE: decode, read, render

TRANSLUCENT: *bright, *light

TRANSMISSION: conduct, segue

TRANSMIT: bear, post, *send

TRANSPARENT: clear, *thin

TRANSPIRE: happen, occur

TRANSPORT: *joy, *move, *pack, *please, *send, *take

TRANSPOSITION: anagram, *change

sounds: spoonerism

TRANSUBSTANTIATION: *believer:* capernaite

denier: berengarian

TRANSVAAL: *capital:* pretoria

district: rand

legislature: raad

policeman: zarp

TRANSVERSE: *argue, *cross, *quarrel, *route, *turn, *way

baffle: bridgewall

bar: arch, axle

pin: toggle

rail: bearer

TRAP: *ambush, *bag, bait, benet, *bind, birdlime, blind(set), bow net, brake, buggy, cage, caparison, capture, carriage, cobweb, confound, corner, creel, deadfall, *deceive, detect, dionaea, dragnet, drop, enmesh, ensnare, entangle, fishhook, fly fyke, *get, gin, involve, inveigle, jig, lariat, lasso, luggage, lure, mesh, mouth, net, noose, *opening, pit(fall), *police: man, portal, rock(s), seine, *seize, separate, set gun, *shock, snare, sniggle, springe, *start(le), steps, stratagem, surprise, *take, tan-

gle, *tie*, toil(s), tree, *trick*,
web, weel, weir
-*shooting*: skeet
TRAPPING: *dress*, *ornament*
TRASH: *dregs*, *refuse*, waste
TRASHY: *low*, *mean*, *poor*
TRAUMA: *hurt*, *shock*
TRAVAIL: *pain*, *torment*, *work*
TRAVEL: *move*, *pass*, *run*
  allowance: batta
  pert.: viatic
TRAVELER: *agent*, pilgrim
  company: caravan, safari
  deity: isis, mercury
  's-joy: bindwith, clematis
  salesman: brinjary, drummer
  show: carnival
TRAVERSE: *pass*, *range*, *walk*
TRAVESTY: comedy, satire
  pert.: parodic
TRAWL: pull, *trap*, troll
TREACHEROUS: *bad*, *false*
TREACLE: molasses, *remedy*
TREAD: *mark*, *press*, *walk*
TREASON: betrayal, sedition
TREASURE: esteem, *money*,
  prize, *store*, *value*
  state: montana
TREASURY: bursary, funds, safe
  agent: t-man
TREAT: *argue*, *dress*, *prepare*,
  remedy, *set*, *stand*, *use*
  comb.: ize
TREATISE: *piece*, *story*, *study*
  introduction: isagoge
TREATY: armistice, *compact*
TREBLE: shrill, soprano, triple
TRECULA: breadfruit, mulberry
TREE: *aromatic*: aloes, cedar, jasmine, sassafras
  bear: raccoon
  bignoniacious: catalpa
  blinding sap: alipata
  clump: motte, tump
  coniferous: alder, cedar, fir,
  gnetales, larch, pine, spruce,
  thuja, tsuga, yew

covering: bark
cretaceous: betulite
cyrillaceous: titi
dead: rampick, rampike
deciduous: broadleaf tree
derivative: pinic
devil: dita
devil's cotton: abroma
disease: black sap, bottom rot,
  butt rot, melaxuma
drupe-bearing: bito
dwarf: arbuscle, bush, shrub
dye: anatto, annatto, arnatto, hur-
  singhar, mora, tua, tui
evergreen: abroma, balsam, be-
  berry, carob(e), cedar, coigue,
  fir, holly, holm, juniper, larch,
  madrona, matsu, ocote, olive,
  pine, savin(e), tarata(h), tawa,
  yew
expert: dendrologist
exudation: chicle, gum, lac, latex,
  resin, rosin, sap, tar, xylan
fabaceous: agati, *locust: tree*
family: stemma
fern: pulu
fiber: bentang, bulak, simal, terap
flowering: agati, catalpa, cleaster,
  elder, mimosa, oleaster, redbud,
  titis, tulip
fodder: mahoe, tagasaste
food: akee
forgetfulness: lotus
frog: hyla
fruit: annona, araca, avocado,
  bakupari, banana, bel, biriba,
  capulin, custard apple, echo, fig,
  gab, gaub, genip(ap), gingko,
  icho, lemon, lime, litchi, mahis,
  medlar, papaw, pawpaw, sapota,
  tamarind, tangelo, tangerine
goddess: pomona
group: boscage, bosk, camp, coppice, copse, forest, glade, grove,
  orchard, tope, wood(s)
gum: alveary, amapa, babul,
  balata, banildad, bansalague,

---

bumbo, eucalyptus, gamboge, icica, nyssa, owenia, sapota, sapotilha, sapotilla, sloe, tuart, tupelo, xylan, zapote

hardwood: aalii, aranga, ash, bethabara, cocobolo, ebony, elm, flooded gum, gee, gidgea, gidya, heartwood, hickory, kaneelhart, lana, loblolly pine, mabee, macaasin, mahogany, maple, narra, ngaio, oak, poon, quebracho, slash pine, teak, tindalo, walnut, zante

jobber: *woodpecker

knot: burl, gnur, knag, node

leguminous: angelique, bean, carob, catalpa, dicorynia, hyacinth, laburnum, zebrawood

life: arbor vitae

measurer: caliper, calliper

medicinal: sumac(h), wahahe

meliaceous: cedar

mimosace: acacia, gama, siris

moraceous: upas

moss: lichen, usnea

moth: egger

myrtaceous: eugenia

nail: nog, peg, pin, spike

nut: akhrot, almendron, chicha

oil: bel, ben(ne), candlenut, eboe, mahua, mahwa, poon, tung

oleaceous: ash, olive

part: bark, bole, branch, knot, leaf, root, trunk, twig

pert.: arboreal, sylvan

pinaceous: araucaria, arbor vitae, kauri, sequoia, thuja

pod-bearing: catalpa

poisonous: bunk, hemlock, sassy, upas

pruner: averruncator

runner: nuthatch

rutaceous: aegle, bael, bel, bengal quince, lime

science: silvics

shade: ash, catalpa, elm, linden, maple, oak, poplar, sycamore, teil

softwood: ambay, balsa, cork

sprout: sapling, sprig

sterculiaceous: cacao, cocoa

thorny: acacia, barriguda, bel, bito, brea, chichicaste

tissue: cambium

toad: hyla

tropical: anubing, ates, balsa, bauhinia, cedron, clusia, cola, colima, cycas, dagame, dali, inga, nepal, papaw, pawpaw, sapota

trunk: bole, caber, caudex

turned into: daphne, heliads

worship: dendrolatry

TREFOIL: bedstraw, clover, medic

TREK: *draw, *pull, *trip

TRELLIS: arbor, espalier, lattice, pergola

TREMATODE: bilharzia, cercaria, fluke, schistosome, worm

TREMBLE: *oscillate, *quiver

TREMELLOSE: *thick, viscid

TREMENDOUS: *big, *great

TREMOLITE: amphibole, grammatite

TREMOR: *thrill, *tremble

TREMULOUS: *shy, *upset, *weak

TRENCH: *fort, *waterway

angle: boyau, zig(zag)

rear wall: parados

TRENCHANT: *acerb, *sharp

TRENCHER: plate, sycophant

-man: eater, glutton

TREND: *run, *set, *tenor

TREPAN: *cheat, *trap, *trick

TREPANG: balate, beche-de-mer, holothurian sea cucumber

TREPIDATION: *alarm, *tremor

TRESPASS: *enter, *err, *venture

TRESS: braid, curl, lock, plait

TRESTLE: *stand, *support

TREWS: breeches, trousers

---

* **Asterisk means to look up this word to find more answer words.**

TRIAL: *affliction*, anguish, assize, attempt, audience, *bore*, bout, case, *contest*, cross, devilment, discomfort, evidence, examination, experiment, hardship, harm, harrass(ment), *headache*, *hell*, inquest, inquiry, inquisition, investigation, lawsuit, molestation, nuisance, *pain*, *plague*, suit, *test*, *torment*, tribulation, *trouble*, *try*, worry
pert.: empiric

TRIANGLE: affair, delta, trigon
decoration: pediment
flag: burgee
insert: gore, gusset
side: leg
type: equilateral, obtuse, scalene

TRIBE: clan, *group*, *kind*, race
chief: dato, datu
customs study: agriology
symbol: totem

TRIBULATION: *trial*

TRIBULUS: burnut, caltrap

TRIBUNAL: bar, bench, court

TRIBUNE: dais, magistrate

TRIBUTARY: fork, *ruler*, *state*

TRIBUTE: *gift*, homage, *praise*
feudal: brennage

TRICE: jiffy, pull, *tie*

TRICK: *beguile*, begunk, blind, bob, boy, brogue, caper, catch, characteristic, *cheat*, child, chouse, cog, cully, *deceive*, *deception*, defraud, device, diablerie, dido, dodge, dupe, feat, feint, fetch, *fetish*, finesse, fob, *fool*, fox, fraud, gaff, gawd, gimmick, gleek, gum, gyp, habit, hand, have, illusion, imposture, intrigue, *joke*, knack, legerdemain, levee, *magic*, maneuver, mannerism, palter, *pass*, period, phase, prat, prestidigitation, pretext, sell, shab, shift, shtickl, shuffle, *skin*, skite, sleight of hand, *spell*, stratagem, stunt, subterfuge, swindle, *take*, term, thwart, *trap*, trepan, *trifle*, *turn*, wile
out: *dress*, *ornament*

TRICKLE: drip, flow, ooze, seep

TRICKSTER: *impostor*, *sharp*

TRICKY: *sly*, *smart*, wily

TRIDENT: fork, gig, *spear*

TRIESTE: *measure:* orna, orne

TRIFLE: ambsace, bagatelle, bauble, bean, betise, *bit*, boondoggle, breath, bubble, button, cent, child's play, continental, coquet, curse, dabble, damn, dawdle, doodle, drop, equivocate, faddle, farce, farthing, feather, fico, fidget, fleabite, flirt, *fool*, fribble, gewgaw, gimcrack, hair, hoot, idle, *joke*, kickshaw, knickknack, mock, molehill, monkey, niggle, nonentity, *nonsense*, nothing, *ornament*, peanut, picayune, piddle, pin, pistareen, *play*, potter, prune, putter, rap, shucks, song, stiver, *trick*, *trimming*, *wanton*

TRIFLING: inane, *little*, *small*

TRIG: *firm*, *run*, *smart*, *stop*, *strong*, *support*

TRIGGER: cause, ignite, *start*
fish: bessy cerka, black oldwife, durgon
man: *criminal*, *hoodlum*

TRIGLYPHS: *space:* metope

TRIGO: grain, wheat

TRIGON: harp, lyre, triangle

TRIGONELLA: amyris, balsam, baumier, bird's-bill, blue melilot, calomba, ocimum

TRIGONOMETRY: *function:* cos(ine), secant, tangent

TRILL: *meter*, *quiver*, sing
result: uvular, velar

TRILLION: *comb.:* treg(a)

TRILLIUM: bathflower, benjamin birthroot, bloody nose, castilleja, nose bleed, orchid

---

* Asterisk means to look up this word to find more answer words.

TRILOBITE: agnostus, arthropod, asaphus, calymene, crab
shield: caphalon
TRIM: **defeat, *dress, *fine, *ornament, *punish, *rebuke, *smart, *trick, *trig, *whip*
TRIMMING: beading, bertha, braiding, cape, collar, **deception,* falbala, flots, frieze, fringe, furbelow, gard, garniture, gimp, jabot, lace, **ornament,* passementerie
TRIMURTI: brahma, shiva, vishnu
TRINE: hang, march, triad
TRINIDAD: *gulf:* paria
music: calypso
tree: cyp, mora
TRINIL: *race:* ape-man
TRINITY: **ornament, *trimurti*
college drink: audit ale
TRINKET: **bit, *trifle*
TRIP: dance, **err, *fall,* journey, kick, **play, *run, *sin, *stop,* tour, **trap*
hammer: bellyhelve
TRIPE: **nonsense, *refuse*
TRIPLE: **increase,* three-bagger
tail: berrugate, black grunt
worship poet: anacreon
worships: love, muses, wine
TRIPOD: brandreth, cat, easel, **spider, *stand,* trivet
decorative: athenienne
TRIPOLI: rottenstone
coin: piastre
measure: dra(a)
ruler: dey
TRIPTYCH: **image, *picture*
wing: volet
TRISMUS: lockjaw, tetanus
TRISTAN, TRISTRAM: *beloved:* isaude, isault, iseult, isolde, isolt(a), isoude, isulte, yseut
villain: melot
TRISTE: **dull, *sad*
TRITE: **dull, *old, *set, *usual*
TRITICUM: amelcorn, speltz

TRITON: eft, newt, salamander
father: poseidon
mother: amphitrite
TRITURATE: grind, rub, pulverize
TRIUMPH: **defeat, *success, *win*
TRIUMVIRATE: *first:* caesar, crassus, pompey
second: antony, lepidus, octavius
TRIVET: **stand, *support*
TRIVIA: **bit, *dregs, *refuse*
TRIVIAL: **poor, *small, *vain*
TROCHE: lozenge, pastil, pill
TROCHEE: choreus, **meter*
TROCHILUS: goldcrest, humming bird, warbler
TROILUS: *kin:* hector, paris
enemy: ajax
father: priam
wife: cressida
TROJAN: dardanian, ilian
ally: amphius, antiphus, aruns, asteropasus, asterope
commander: antenor
founder: ilus, tros
hero: aeneas, agenor, alcon, amopaon, antimachus, antiphates, dardan, eneas, hector, palamedes, paris
horse: **ambush, *trap*
horse builder: epeus
horse designer: sinon
king: paris, priam
mountain: ida
prince: aeneas, anchises
region: troad, troas
slave: sinon
soothsayer: helenus
war cause: helen
TROLL: **demon, *gnome, *run,* sing, **turn, *wanton*
TROLLEY: barrow, car, tram
TROLLOP: **prostitute, *wanton*
TROMBONE: sackbut, sambuke
TRONA: mineral, nitrum, urao
TROOP: army, **group, *party*

* Asterisk means to look up this word to find more answer words.

TROPHY: *honor, *memorial, *prize, *reward, *spoil, *token

TROPIC: *limit, solar, zone

TROPICAL: animal: agama, agouti, alco, coati, eyra, iguana

ant: army, driver, legionary

bird: ani, bananaquit, boatswain, booby, cacicus, coereba, jacamar, jaeger, jalap, manakin, motmot, tody

clay: laterite

disease: aden ulcer, ainhum, buba(s), dengue fever, dhobie itch, sprue, yaws

dog: alco

fern: adiantopsis, alsophila, basket, bird's-foot, blechnum, cheilanthes, male, nephrolepsis, pellaea, rock brake, sword

fish: anableps, astropecten, barracuda, coachman, chromid, danid, gerres, inia, paco, robalo, salema, sargo(n), scarida, squetee, toro

fruit: banana, date, guava, inga, mango, papaw, papaya, pineapple, plantain, tamarind

fungus: balanophorace

grass: alang, bamboo, bambusa

herb: achimenes, ageratum, altea, amaranth, amaryllis, aristolochia, bacopa, barbados lily, billygoat weed, blood berry, boerhavia, bouvardia, bramia, caapeba, cajanus, catjang, celosia, coxcomb, evea, laportea, pareira, pigeon pea, piperaca, pothomorphe, rivina, sida, tacca, urena

moth: anaphe

plant: abelmosk, abutilon, agave, alacad, algalia, aloe, alonsoa, altea, ananas, angraecum, aphelandra, arrowroot, arum, bacchar, billbergia, bleo, bomarea, bromelia, browallia, cacanthus, cacoon, caladium, calalu, canna(s), cowhage, dal, dasheen,

fuchsia, gardenia, geonoma, hamelia, hibiscus, lantana, liana, mallow, mangrove, musa, palm, pepino, redwithe, sida, taro, udo, yucca, zamia

shrub: aali, abelia, abrus, abutilon, adelia, anapanapa, ardisia, asis, avicennia, bauhinia, bay-bay, bignonia, bouvardia, broomwood, bursara, flueggea, frangipani, henna, inga, ipecac, lantana, olacad, sida

tree: abura, acacia, acapu, achiote, achras, agba, akee, alchornea, amaranth, amate, anacardium, andira, anime, annatto, arenga, arjan, artar, asak, assai, attalea, axe master, bactris, bacury, bago, bakula, balanites, balsa, banago, baobab, barbas, bendy, billy webb, bindoree, bongo, bustic, cacao, calabur, callindra, candelabrum, capulin, carica, cashew, cauchillo, cazaba, cecropia, chupon, cocoa, colima, dagame, dalbergia, dali, eboe, espave, etua, frangipani, guachipilin, guacimo, huamuchli, icica, mabi, machineel, mangrove, mast, mulberry, nitta, njave, palm, papaw, papaya, pawpaw, quebracho, sapodilla, seron, silkwood, sweetsop, tamarind

vine: allamanda, bejuco, cassabanana, ceriman, cucurbita, curuba, ipomoea

TROS: son: assaracus, ilus

TROT: child, dance, *run, *walk

TROTH: belief, *promise

TROUBLE: *ache, *ado, adversity, *afflict(ion), *agitate, *anger, caddle, chagrin, concern, difficulty, dilemma, disadvantage, *disease, disturb, exertion, failure, *headache, *hell, hornet's nest, *hurt, ill(s), irk, meddle, molest, *noise, onus, *pain, *plague, pother, *press, *problem, put out, *puzzle, *scold, *sore, *sorrow, *stir, *torment, *trial, *violence

maker: *gossip, *hoodlum, *imp

TROUGH: basin, channel, trug

TROUNCE: *beat, *punish, *scold

TROUSERS: *pants

TROUT: alekey, aurora, char, finnac, fish, gilaroo, grilse, kelt, longe, malma, namaycush, oquassa, peal, saibling, sewen, sewin, speckled, squeteague, steelhead, sug, togue, waha

pert.: truttaceous

tahoe: pogy

TROW: *think, *trust

TROY: iliac, ilian, ilion, ilium, teucrian, troad, *trojan

TRUANT: hobo, *idle, tramp

TRUCE: *compact, *peace

TRUCIAL STATES: qashran

TRUCK: lorry, *move, *nonsense, *refuse, *trade, *trivia, van

small: barney, pickup

TRUCKLE: bend, cringe, *yield

TRUCULENT: *brutal, *mean

TRUDGE: pace, plod, *walk

TRUE: *accurate, *actual, aline, authentic, bona fide, certain, constant, *correct, exact, factual, faithful, *firm, *good, *honest, just, level, literal, loyal, official, *perfect, precise, proper, *regular, *right, scrupulous, steady, *straight, very

comb.: aletho

TRUFFLE: earthnut, fungus

TRULL: *prostitute, *wanton

TRULY: indeed, really, verily

TRUMP: *beat, *best, *top

cards: atout, atutti, basta, brick, deckhead, dis, dix, masterpiece, matador, menel, nell, pedro, playboy, polt, ponto, punto, triunfo, turn-up

TRUMPERY: *deception, *dregs, *nonsense, *refuse

TRUMPET: bugle, clarion, horn

blare: fanfare, sennet, tantara

creeper: bignonia, catalpa, indian bean, plant, tecoma

fish: bellows, snipe, swell

-like: buccinal

lily: bermuda, easter lily

signal: chamade

-wood: cecropia peltata

TRUMPETER: agami, bird, herald, pigeon, swan, trout, yakamik

perch: mabo, mado, fish

TRUNCHEON: *beat, *stick

TRUNDLE: roll, *truck, wheel

TRUNK: *bag, nose, *pack, torso

-fish: boxfish, chapin

-line: mainline, railroad

TRUSS: *pac, *support, *tie

TRUST: assurance, belief, believe, care, carry, cartel, charge, coalition, combine, confide(nce), corner, credence, credit, custody, duty, enterprise, equity, faith, fiduciary, fee, fie, keeping, loyalty, monopoly, pool, *promise, rely, repose, *rest, security, syndicate, trow, truth, zaibatsu

deed: mortgage

fund: wakf, waqf, wukf

-worthy: kosher, *secure, *sure

TRUSTEE: *agent, treasurer

TRUTH: *doctrine, *good, *right

comb.: aleth(o)

drug: pentothal

goddess: alethia, ma(at), una

self-evident: *adage

serum: psychotherapy

study: alethiology

TRUTHFUL: *fair, *honest

TRY: *aim, annoy, audition, beset, bid, choose, court martial, crack, hansel, hear, investigate, irritate, judge, *prove, rack, render, sample, screen, select, *separate, shot, stab, *start, *strain, strive, struggle, tax, *test, *torment, *trial, *use, *work

TRYING: *hard, *severe

TRYST: *affair, *meeting

TSAR: *despot, *ruler

TSETSE: glossina, kivu, nagana
disease: encephalitis

TSINE: banteng, wild ox

TSUGA: alaska pine, hemlock

TSWANA: bechuana, fish

TUB: bucket, pot, *vessel

TUBA: euphonium, helicon
mouthpiece: bocal

TUBAL: *ancestor:* japheth, noah

TUBALCAIN: *father:* lamech

TUBE: ampoule, canal, cannon, duct, matrass, pipe, television
pert.: capillary

TUBER: beet, bulb, eddo, jalap, oca, potato, root, salep, taro, truffle, uva, yam

TUBERCLE: *projection

TUBERCULOSIS: angleberry, asbolin, consumption, marasmus, phthisis, scrofula

TUCHIN: *house:* yamen

TUCK: *cover, *draw, *gather, *press, *scold, *sword

TUCKER: *bore, food, meal, tire

TUCKAHOE: arum, plant, poria

TUFA: limestone, toph, trass

TUFT: *bit, beard, plume, wisp
pert.: comal

TUG: *contest, *draw, *strain

TULE: bulrush, cattail, scirpus
potato or root: wapatoo

TULIP: *cheek:* lalla rookh
orchid: cattleya
tree: aspen, canoewood, poplar

TULLE: kata, mesh, net

TUMBLE: collapse, *fail, *fall
-down: dilapidated, ramshackle
-weed: amaranth, bugseed

TUMBLER: acrobat, dove, lever

TUMBREL: dumpcart, wagon

TUMERIC: *turmeric

TUMID: bombastic, plethoric

TUMMEL: disorder, *noise

TUMMY: *stomach

TUMOR: acanthoma, adenoma, ambury, amper, angioma, atheroma, beal, blastoma, cancer, cat's-hair, cavernoma, cementoma, cyst, edema, glioma, keloid, lipoma, moro, neoplasm, osteoma, phyma, pian, pustule, sarcoma, swelling, wen, yaw
comb.: cele, coele, oma
operation: ancotomy

TUMULT: *ferment, *fight, *noise, *riot, *storm, *temper
place: bear garden

TUMULUS: barrow, dune, mound

TUN: *drink, *stomach, vat
half a: pipe
shell fossil: dolite

TUNA: albacore, bluefish, maguro

TUNDRA: *plain

TUNE: *adapt, *play, *strain
to lower pitch: anesis

TUNER: pitch pipe

TUNGSTEN: scheelite, wolfram

TUNGSTITE: ocher, ochre

TUNIC: action, blouse, camise, chiton, *cover, gipon, jama, palla, shirt, smock, stole

TUNICATE: ascidian, bulb, salpa

TUNIS: *cape:* bon, ras addar
city: bizerte, ferryville, gabes, gafsa, grombalia, mateur, nabeul, sfax, sousse, susa, tebourba, zaghouan
gulf: gabes, hammamet
island: djerba
measure: cafiz, mettar, millerole, saah, sah, whiba
president: bourguiba
river: medjerda
ruler: bey, dey
weight: artal, kantar, ratel, rotl, saa, uckia

TUNNEL: adit, *opening, tube
famous: arlberg, baltimore, bitterroot, cascade, cenis, connaught,

cumberland, detroit, gallitzin, gothard, gunnison, holland, hoosac, lincoln, lotschberg, mont d'or, montcenis, mt roberts, otira, severn, simplon, spiral, st clair, st gotthard, trans-andine, wasserfluh

TUNNY: amia, botarga(o), *tuna
TUP: butt, cuckold, mallet, ram
TUPAIA: banxring
TUPEK: *hut
TUPELO: gum, nyssa, pepperidge
TUPI: anta, bororoan, mura
  devil: anhanga
  snakebird: anhinga
TUR: aurochs, goat, ibex, pea
TURANIA: *people:* akkad
TURBAN: cap, fez, hat, mandil, pata, patta, seerband, turf
  flower: tulip
TURBID: *dirty, feculent, murky
TURBOT: bannock fluke, bret, brill, flatfish
TURBULENCE: *temper, *tumult
TURBULENT: *mad, *violent, *wild
TURDUS: amsel, blackbird
TURF: dirt, fuel, grass, track
  hut: barabara, barbora
  modern: astro
  pert.: cespititious, cespitose
TURGENT, TURGID: swollen
TURK: aga, horse, kizilbash, mongoloid, osmanli, ottoman, sard, tartar, tatar
TURKESTAN: *lake:* hara, shor
  moslem: salar
  mountain: alai
  native: kirghiz, sart, usbeg
  river: ili, kulja
TURKEY: alderman, anatolia, bomb, dud, failure, flop, porte
  beard: basket grass
  breed: bourbon red
  buzzard: aura, catharta, gallinazo, vulture
  comb.: bubbly-jock, cock

  draw: lottery
  male: tom
  oak: adriatic, blackjack, cerris
  red: madder
  sound: gobble (gobble)
  wild: bustard, tom
  young: curassow, poult
TURKISH: *agent:* kehaya
  ambassador: elchee
  army corps: alai, ordu
  army officer: *turkish: official
  barn: ambar
  bath: hamman
  boat: caique, mahone
  brandy: rakee, raki
  cabinet: divan
  caliph: ali
  camp: palanka
  cap: calpac(k), fez
  cape: baba
  capital: angora, ankara
  caravansary: imaret
  carpet: smyrna
  castle of cotton: pamukkale
  cavalryman: spahee, spahi
  chief: *turkish: official
  christian: raia
  city: adana, adrianople, afyon, afyonkarahisar, aidin, akhisar, angora, ankara, antakiya, antalya, antioch, bergama, boghazkoy, broussa, brusa, constantinople, corum, diyarbekir, edessa, edirne, elaziz, erzurum, eskisehir, homs, istanbul, izmir, kayseri, konya, marash, samsun, scutari, sert, sestos, siirt, sivas, skutari, smyrna, stamboul, tire, tokat, uskudar
  coin: akcha, akcheh, altilik, altun, beshlik, chequin, chiquin, iklik, lira, mahbub, onlik, othmany, para, pataque, piaster, pound, purse, rebia, yuzluk, zecchino
  college: ulema
  commander: *turkish: official
  council: divan, diwan

* Asterisk means to look up this word to find more answer words.

court: porte
court man: bostangi, bostanji
decree: firman, hatti-humayum, hatti-sherif, irade
division: adana, caza, eyalet, vilayet, villayet
dollar: piaster
dress: charshaf, jelick
drink: airan, boza, mastic, rakee, raki
dynasty: seljuk
empire: ottoman
fabric: agaric, chekmak, cottonee, terry
fig: eleme, elemi
flag: alem, horsetail, toug
float: kalak
founder: kemal ataturk, osman
free land: mulk
garment: dolman, caftan
government: porte
governor: *turkish: official
gulf: cos, izmir
harem: seraglio, serai
harem ladies: kadein
hat: calpac(k), fez
hill: dagh
hot springs: pamukkale
house: selamlik
infidel: giaour
inn: cafenet, imaret, serai
invader: ghuz, uighur
javelin: jereed, jerid
judge: cadi(lesker), kadi
man-of-war: caravel(le)
measure: alma, almud, arshine, djerib, draa, fortin, halebi, hatt, khat, kile(h), nocktat, nul, oka, parmack, pik, zirai
military camp: ordu
military rank: bimbashi, binbashi, chaoush, chiaus
monk: dervish
mountain: ala, ararat, dagh
mountain range: alai
music instrument: canoon, canum, kanum, kussier, zither

musket: tophaike
oak: cerris
official: aali, aga, agha, ali, ameer, amir, atabeg, atabek, bashaw, begler-beg, bey, binbashi, cadi, dey, emeer, emir, kahaya, kaimakam, kemal, mir, mudir, mufti, mutasarrif, osmanli, pacha, pasha, selim, seraskier, sirdar, subashi, subbassa, wali
palace: serai
parade: alai
patent: berat
pavilion: kiosk
peasant: raya
people: afshar, aissor, aushar, avshar, azerbaijani, kurd, ogor, tartar, tatar
pipe: chibouk
policeman: zaptiah, zaptieh
president: inonu, kemal ataturk
province: eyalet, vilayet
regiment: alai, arni
religious war: crescentade
reservist: redif
river: aras, araxes, mesta, sarus, seihun, seyhan
royal grant: firman
rug: konia
ruler: bey, calif, caliph, chambul, dey, khan, mudir, president, sultan
saber: obolus, yataghan
sailor: galiongee, galionji
seaport: adalia, alanya, antalya, bodrum, enos, fethiye, foca, iskenderun, istanbul, izmir, kusadasi, marmaris, mersin, pergamum, smyrna, troy
ship: caramoussal, saic
slave: eunuch, mameluke
soldier: arnaout, arnaut, bashibazouk, janizary, nizami
standard: alem, toug
statue: tanzimat
storage place: ambar
storm: samiel, simoon

* Asterisk means to look up this word to find more answer words.

subject: raia, rayah
sultan: abdul, ahmed, ali, aziz, hamid, ilderim, mejid, saladin, selim
summerhouse: kiosk, yali
swindler: osman the peasant
sword: *saber
tambourine: daira, daire
tax: avania, caphar, vergi
title: baba, effendi, mufti
tobacco: chibouque, latakia
treasurer: deftedar
veil: maharmah, yashmak
weight: artal, artel, batman, cequi, cheke, dirhem, drachma, dram, kantar, kerat, kileh, maund, miskal, obolu, oka, quintal, ratel, rotl, yusdrum
wheat: bulgur
wine: doluca, kavak lidere

TURKMEN: *carpet:* afghan, bokhara, tekke, yomud
city: ashkhabad, poltoratsk
tribe: ersar, viddhal

TURMERIC: ango, azafrank, bloodroot, curcuma, huldee, olena, potentilla, puccoon, rea, redroot, saffron, sanguinaria, tetter, tormentil

TURMOIL: *tumult

TURN: act, bear, beat, bend, bent, bias, burnish, cant, circuit, *crisis, cramp, crook, deal, deflect, detour, deviate, direction, *disposition, distort, evert, favor, *ferment, *form, guise, gyrate, hinge, journey, metamorphose, *oscillate, pirouette, pivot, *place, reverse, revert, revolve, rotate, shunt, slew, slue, *spoil, *start, swerve, swivel, tack, talent, *time, *trick, veer, *venture, *walk, whirl, *wind, zigzag
back: *defeat, *return, *stop
coat: *apostate, *traitor
comb.: tropo
down: *refuse, veto

extra: bis, bisque
left: haw, port, wynd, wyne
on: *attack, *drug, *move, *start
one's back upon: *discard, *quit
out: *dismiss, *prove, *result
over: deliver, *error, *upset
pike: *road, *route
right: gee, starboard
stone: calico, plover, redleg
-table: lazy susan
the corner: *rally, recover
to: *open, *start

TURNIP: baga, brassica, rutabaga
-like: napiform
wild: breadroot, navew, rape

TURPENTINE: camphine, gallipot, resin, rosin, tarata, terebinth

TURPIN: *sword:* almace

TURRET: *fort, *tower

TURTLE: arrau, emyd, jurara, matamata, terrapin, tortoise
group: bale
part: calipee, carapace

TUSCANY: *city:* arezzo, firenze, florence, greve, livorno, perugia, pisa, sienna

TUSSLE: *contest, *fight

TUT: *rebuke, *scold

TUTELARY: *gods:* *demon, genii, lares, penates

TV: *television

TWADDLE, TWATTLE: *nonsense

TWELFTH: *as:* uncia

TWELVE DOZEN: gross

TWENTY: icosa(n), score

TWIDDLE: bit, *nonsense, *trifle

TWIG: *part, *see, shoot
bundle: barsom, fagot

TWILIGHT: crepuscule, *obscure
goddess: helen, phaedra
gods: gotterdammerung, ragnarok
gods, edda: voluspa
gods, field: vigrid

TWIN: couple, *gemini, similar

TWINE: anamite, coil, hemp, wind

TWINGE: *ache, *pain

* Asterisk means to look up this word to find more answer words.

TWINK: nictate, *punish, wink
TWINKLE: flash, *shine, *spark
TWIRL: *move, querl, *turn
TWIST: *coil, grind, spin, *tor-
  ment, *torture, *turn
 comb.: spiri
TWIT: *joke, *rebuke, *scold
TWITCH: *pain, *start, *tie
TWIZZLE: *twirl
TWO: brace, pair, span, twins
 -bit: bush, small time
 -branched: bifurcate
 comb.: amph(i), bi(n)
 -faced: *false
 pert.: amphibian, ancipital, bifari-
  ous, binary, didymous, double,
  dual, duplicate, twice
TYCHE: fortune
TYCOON: *lord, *magnate, *ruler
TYDEUS: enemy: amphiaraus,
  melanippus
 half brother: meleager
 son: diomedes
TYE: child, dog, *peasant
TYEE: chief
TYNDAREUS: consort: leda
 stepchild: helen
TYPE: *form, *group, *kind,
  *mark, *model, *sign, *symbol
 comb.: arch, branch
 part: beard, body, counter, face,
  feet, groove, kern, neck, nick,
  serif, shank, stem
 style: agate, aldine, bembo, bodoni, bradley, brevier, bulmer,
  caslon, century, cloister, cochin,
  elite, elziver, futura, gothic,
  goudy, granjon, hess, ionic, italic,
  minion, pearl, pica, roman,
  ronde, runic, script, times, vogue
 term: font, galley, quad, quat
TYPEWRITER: part: carriage,
  platen, shift, spacer, tabulator
TYPHOID FEVER: tabardillo
TYPICAL: *general, *usual
TYPIFICATION: *symbol

TYR: dyaus, saxnot, thincsus,
  things, tiu, tiw, ziu
TYRANT: *despot, *ruler, *title
TYRE: destroyers: moslems
 king: hiram, huram
 princess: dido
 town: es, sour, sur, zor
TYRIAN: purpuraceous
TYRO: amateur, neophyte, rookie
 consort: cretheus, enipeus, poseidon
 mother-in-law: sidero
 parent: acidice, salmoneus
 son: neleus, pelias
TZIGANE: gypsy

UANG: beetle, insect
UBEROUS: abundant, copious
UBIQUITOUS: everywhere
UELE: ababua, abarambo, amadi
UGANDA: capital: entebbe
 cattle: ankoli
 people: bahima, bunyoro, huma,
  kopi, wahima
UGLY: awful, *bad, disagreeable,
  displeasing, *evil, frightful, grew-
  some, gruesome, hideous, horrible, ill-tempered, inartistic, in-
  elegant, irascible, loathsome,
  ominous, *plain, repulsive, *rotten, *short, *sinister, *sullen, terrible, toady, vicious, vile
UGRIAN: avar
UKASE: decree, edict, *order
UKKO: wife: akka, maan-eno
UKRAINE: city: artemovsk, berdi-
  chev, cernauti, kiev
 dance: gopak
 legislature: podolia, rada
 money: grivna, schagiv
 music instrument: bandura
 port: odessa
ULCER: abscess, angioma, aposteme, canker, egilops, fossette,
  kyle, lesion, noma

* Asterisk means to look up this word to find more answer words.

ULCEROUS: *bad, *rotten
ULIANOV: lenin
ULL: father: sif
ULLA: son: arah, haniel, rezia
ULMO: hardwood, muermo
ULNA: bone, cubitus
end: ancon
ULTIMA: ratio: force
thule: iceland
ULTIMATE: *acme, *best, *end
atom: monad
fate: ananke
ULTRA: *best, *extreme, *top
-ultra: fashionable, modern
ULULATE: *cry, howl, roar, wail
ULYSSES: *odysseus
UMBO: boss, knob, spike, stud
UMBRAGE: offense, *temper
UMBRELLA: brolly, chatta, gamp
bird: cephalopterus
finial: tee
grass: millet
palm: canterbury palm
tree: ginseng, magnolia, catalpa
UMBRETTE: bird, hammerkop
UNADORNED: *plain, *simple
UNADULTERATED: *pure
UNANIMOUS: *absolute, *solid
UNARMED: comb.: anopl(o)
UNASSUMING: *open, *plain,
*shy
UNAU: animal, sloth
UNBELIEVER: *apostate, heretic
UNBENDING: *obstinate,
*straight
UNBROKEN: *all, *regular,
*smooth, *straight
UNBURDEN: *ease, *free
UNCANNY: *eccentric, *weird
UNCAS: beloved: cora
father: chingachgook
transportation: canoe
UNCERTAIN: *obscure, *vague
UNCIVIL: *bad, *rough, *short
UNCIVILIZED: *brutal, *wild
UNCLE: eam, eme, nunka, oom,
tio

pert.: avuncular
remus author: harris
remus rabbit: brear, brer
UNCLEAN: *bad, *dirty, vile
UNCO: *great, strange, *weird
UNCOMMON: *eccentric, *fresh,
*particular, *special, *unique
UNCOMPROMISING: *firm, *se-
vere, *solid, *stern, *strict
UNCONCERNED: *cool, *dull,
*free, *open, *quiet, serene
UNCONDITIONAL: *absolute
UNCONVENTIONAL: *eccen-
tric, *free, *wild
UNCOUTH: *uncivil, *mean
one: *clown, *fool, *peasant
UNCOVER: *open, *remove
UNCTION: anele, oil, *passion
UNCTUOUS: *false, *smooth
UNCULTURED: *uncivil(ized)
UNDAUNTED: *bold, *strong
UNDER: below, less, *short
-brush: abature, thicket
comb.: hyp(o), sub
cover: *secret, *spy
garment: balmoral, bloomers,
bra(ssiere), bustle, corset,
drawers, lingerie, panties, petticoat, shorts, slip, smock, undies
-go: *pass, *stand, *suffer
-ground: *secret, subway, *train
-ground army: haganah
-ground explosion: camouflet
-ground newspaper: free press
-ground reservoir: cenote
-hand: *secret, *sly, *trick
-line: *mark, stress
-mine: *reduce, *spoil, weaken
UNDERSTAND: absorb, *accept,
appreciate, dig(est), fathom, follow, *get, grasp, infer, interpret,
read, realize, *reason, sabe,
savvy, *see, *sense, solve, *think
UNDERSTANDING: *compact,
*knowledge, *sense
lack: betise
pert.: psychic

* Asterisk means to look up this word to find more answer words.

UNDERSTATEMENT: litotes
UNDERTAKE: *accept, *attack, *enter, *promise, *start, *try
UNDERTAKER: cerer, mortician
UNDERTAKING: *act, *venture
UNDERTOW: riptide, vortex
UNDERWORLD: black hand, crime, gangdom, *hell, la cosa nostra, mafia, mob, rackets, syndicate
  god: anubis, bran, cerberus, charon, cog, *demon, *devil, dis(pater), enmeshara, erebus, gwyn(n), hades, kaneloa, manes, minos, ningishzia, orcus, osiris, pluto, pwyll, python, rhadamanthus, rot, satan, serapis, thanatos, thantos, titan, tuoni, yama
  goddess: allatu, ament, belili, cora, dana, danu, demeter, despoina, don, frigg, fury, gaea, hecate, hel, kore, laruna, persephassa, persephone, pher, proserpina, prytania, trivia, tuonetar
  pert.: chthonian
  river: *hades: river
UNDERWRITE: *back, *support
UNDINE: *dwarf, *spirit
UNDO: *betray, *defeat, *destroy, *free, *open, remove, *ruin, *spoil, *upset, *wrong
UNDUE: *bad, *extreme, *wrong
UNDULATE: *oscillate, *quiver
UNEARTHLY: *eccentric, *weird
UNEASY: awkward, difficult
UNEQUAL: comb.: anis(o)
UNEQUIVOCAL: *open, *plain
UNERRING: *straight, *true
UNEVEN: *eccentric, *rank
  comb.: anis, aniso
UNEXCEPTIONAL: *general, *regular, *usual
UNEXPECTED: *sudden
UNFADING: immarcescible
  flower: amaranth
UNFAIR: *evil, *hard, *wrong
UNFAITHFUL: *bad, *evil, *false

UNFAMILIAR: *fresh, *weird
UNFASHIONABLE: *bad, *old
UNFASTEN: *free, *open
UNFAVORABLE: *low, *mean, *poor
UNFEELING: *brutal, *dull, *hard, *stern, *tough
UNFIT: *bad, *sick, *wrong
UNFOLD: *air, *open, *spread
UNFORTUNATE: *bad, *poor, *sad
UNFRIENDLY: *cool, hostile
UNFURL: *open, *spread
UNGAINLY: *clumsy, *ugly
UNGENEROUS: *hard, *mean
UNGODLY: *bad, *evil, *wrong
UNGRACEFUL: *clumsy, *thick
UNGUENT: balm, ointment, salve
UNGULA: claw, hoof, nail
UNGULATE: animal(-like)
UNHANDY: *clumsy
UNHAPPY: *sorry, *unfortunate
UNHEARD-OF: *fresh, *weird
UNHOLY: *bad, *evil, *wrong
UNHORSE: *free, *throw
UNICORN: monoceros, reem
  -fish: filefish, lija, narwhale
UNIFORM: *equal, *plain, *regular, *smooth, *symbol
UNIMPORTANT: *paltry, *small
UNINTELLIGENT: *stupid
UNINTERESTING: *dry, *dull
UNINTERRUPTED: *direct
UNION: *accord, afl, amalgam, anastomosis, anschluss, apposition, artel, ascap, cio, coherence, concurrence, fusion, gremio, *group, guild, hanse, hui, ila, ilgwu, ita, liaison, linkage, local, marriage, *meeting, merger, organized labor, raphe, seam, *society, trade guild, *trust, twu, uaw, unicum, *unity
  comb.: apsis
  jack: *flag
  member: blue shirt, hard-hat
  official: business agent

UNIQUE: alone, *bizarre*, choice, *eccentric*, exceptional, *fresh*, *great*, *important*, lone, matchless, notable, one, only, *particular*, single, *special*, *splendid*, *top*, uncommon, *unusual*

UNISON: equivalent, *union*

UNIT: *ace*, *bit*, branch, *group*, one, *part*, *union*, whole
hypothetical: id(ic), od, pangen(e)

UNITE: *add*, *adhere*, adjoin, ally, amalgamate, *associate*, band, braze, club, cohere, combine, consolidate, converge, federate, fuse, graft, hasp, integrate, *join*, meld, mix, *pair*, *piece*, rabet, *rally*, seam, sew, solder, *tie*, wed, weld, yoke

UNITED NATIONS: *agencies:* fao, icao, ilo, imco, iro, ito, itu, unesco, unrra, upu, who, wmo
economic: ecafe, ece, ecla, unicef

UNITED PROVINCES: friesland, gelderland, groningen, holland, overijssel, utrecht, zeeland

UNITED STATES: (*also AMERICAN*) america, columbia, uncle sam
art critic: berenson
artist: abbey, avery, baziotes, beal, bellows, benton, berman, bingham, bouche, burchfield, cadmus, cassatt, catlin, copley, eakins, flagg, homer, hopper, johns, marin, moses, peale, pyle, ryder, sargent, sloan, stuart, wyeth
astronomer: aitken
astrophysicist: abbot
author: adams, ade, agee, aiken, akins, albee, alcott, algren, anderson, arendt, asch, auslander, austin, bacheller, bagley, bailey, balch, bangs, barlow, barrett, barry, barth, bates, baum, beebe, beecher, beer, behrman, belasco, bellamy, bellow, bemelmans, bemis, benchley, benedict, benet, bierce, bishop, blackmur, boden-

heim, bogan, bowen, boyle, bradbury, bradford, bradstreet, bragdon, bromfield, brooks, brown, brush, bryant, buck, bullfinch, burgess, burnett, burroughs, cabell, caldwell, canby, cary, cenedella, clemens, cobb, cooper, crothers, crouse, dana, davis, day, dreiser, emerson, faulkner, ferber, field, grey, harte, hawthorne, hayward, hemingway, hersey, holmes, hurst, inge, irving, james, jewett, jones, kantor, kilmer, lanier, lardner, lewis, longfellow, lowell, mabie, mailer, malamud, michener, millay, miller, moore, morley, nash, nye, odets, o'hara, ohenry, o'neill, parkman, poe, porter, pyle, quinn, reese, rice, riley, roe, rogers, salinger, saroyan, sinclair, snyder, stein, stewart, stowe, tarkington, thoreau, thurber, towne, tripp, twain, uris, vaughan, wallace, ward, whitman, whittier, williams, wolf, wylie
carriage: buckboard, buggy, carryall, concord bunny, dearborn, shay, surrey, trap
cartoonist: arno, block, briggs, capp, fisher, gould, mauldin, nast
chemist: acheson, baekeland, bishop, flory, mark, pauling, rumford, seaborg, urey
choreographer: balanchine
coin: bit, cent, dime, dollar, eagle, nickel, penny, quarter, rosa, trime
composer: antheil, arlen, barber, basie, bergoma, berlin, bernstein, blitzstein, bond, bowles, brubeck, cadman, cage, copland, damrosch, foote, foss, foster, gershwin, grothe, kern, macdowell, nevin, porter, rogers, sousa, taylor
dance: ace of diamonds, big ap-

ple, breakdown, bunnyhug, cake-walk, charleston, fox trot, frug, hoedown, lindy hop, monkey, square, twist, two-step, virginia reel

dramatist: *united states: author*

editor: bentley, blackwell, bok, botkin, dana, greeley, hearst, ochs, sulzberg, white

educator: angell, babbitt, bloomfield, butler, dewey, eliot, hutchins, james, kerr, mann, o'shea, sproul, wilbur

emblem: eagle

engineer: bush, eads

explorer: andrews, boone, byrd, clark, lewis, logan, long, pike, perry

financier: biddle, gates, hill, morgan, rockefeller

first child: virginia dare

flagmaker: betsy ross

fur trader: astor, harmon

historian: beard, becker, breasted, elson, morison

humorist: *united states: author*

indian: *indian references*

inventor: bell, berliner, bryant, edison, fiske, fitch, fulton, hoe, howe, ives, morse, whitney

jurist: brandeis, burger, chase, frankfurter, hand, holmes, jay, marshall, reed, stone, story, taney, warren

missile: *rocket: name*

mountain: cumbre, elbert, helena, hood, katahdin, massive, mckinley, pikes, rainier, shasta, whitney

naturalist: agassiz, akeley, audubon, baird, beebe, muir, seton, thoreau

orator: bryan

outlaw: billy the kid, bonney, capone, chessman, clyde, dillinger, jesse james, manson, speck, strangler, sutton, zodiac

philanthropist: barton, brookings, carnegie, ford, lenox, riis, rockefeller

physician: blackwell, mayo, minot, reed, rush

physicist: *united states: scientist*

pioneer: appleseed, boone, bowie, calamity jane, carson, clark, cody, crockett, lewis

poet: *united states: author*

president: great white father

range: adirondack, appalachian, black, cascade, green, sangre de cristo, rockies, sierra nevada, teton, uinta, wasatch

scientist: bardeen, bethe, brattain, bridgman, compton, einstein, hooton, millikan, nichols, parran, teller, tesla, urey, von braun, waksman

sculptor: barnard, baskin, bertola, borglum, calder

speaker: cannon, carlisle, rayburn, thomas

suffragist: anthony, catt

traitor: benedict arnold

UNITY: identity, *union

UNIVAC: computer, machine

UNIVERSAL: *absolute, *all, catholic, continual, cosmic, cosmopolitan, *doctrine, eclectic, ecumenical, *general, global, infinite, pandemic, *philosophy, public, *regular, rife, total, unlimited, *usual, very, whole

UNIVERSE: earth, olam, *sphere, *system, world

  comb.: cosmo

  pert.: cosmic

UNIVERSITY: *college references*

UNJUST: *false, *wrong

UNKEMPT: *dirty, dowdy, *fat

UNKIND: *brutal, *hard, *severe, *stern, *strict

UNKNOWN: anonymous, incognito, *obscure, *weird

  comb.: adelo

---

* **Asterisk means to look up this word to find more answer words.**

UNLESS: except, nisi, *save
UNLIMITED: *free, *open, *unique, *universal
UNLOAD: *discard, *remove, sell
UNLOCK: *analyze, *open
UNLUCKY: *unfortunate
UNMASK: *display, *open, *show
UNMATCHED: azygous, *unique
UNMENTIONABLE: *under: garment
UNMISTAKABLE: *open, *plain
UNMITIGATED: *absolute
UNMOVED: cool, *firm
UNNATURAL: *eccentric, *weird
UNORTHODOX: heretical
UNPLEASANT: *bad, *rotten, *sour
UNPREPOSSESSING: *evil, *ugly
UNPRODUCTIVE: *arid, barren
UNPROFITABLE: barren, futile
UNPROTECTED. naked, *open
UNQUALIFIED: *perfect, *pure
UNRAVEL: *open, *undo
UNREAL: *false, *weird
UNREASONABLE: *absurd, *insane, *mad
UNREFINED: *broad, *brutal, raw
UNREGENERATE: *bad, *evil, wrong
UNRELENTING: *firm, *hard, *obstinate, *severe, *stern
UNREST: *ado, *alarm
UNRESTRAINED: *free, *wild
UNROLL: *display, *open, *show
UNRUFFLED: cool, *quiet, *smooth
UNRULY: *violent, *wanton, *wild
UNSEAT: *remove, *throw
UNSEEMLY: *bad, *wrong
UNSETTLE: *stir, *upset
UNSETTLED: fickle, *insane, *mad
UNSHEATHE: *draw, *remove
UNSOPHISTICATED: *fresh,

*open, *pure, *shy, simple
UNSOUND: *bad, *evil, *false, *insane, *rotten, *sick, *weak
UNSPOKEN: *quiet, *secret
UNSTABLE: astatic, ephemeral
UNSTEADY: capricious, rocky
UNSUBSTANTIAL: *light, *thin
UNSUITABLE: *bad, inapt, *wrong
UNSULLIED: *fresh, *pure
UNTAMED: *brutal, *wild
UNTIDY: *unkempt
UNTIE: *free, *release
UNTOLD: *infinite, *secret
UNTOUCHED: *fresh, *pure
UNTOWARD: *clumsy, *obstinate
UNTRUTH: *error, *lie, *wrong
UNUSUAL: *eccentric, *fresh, *great, *unique, *weird
comb.: anom(o)
UNWELCOME: de trop, non grata
UNWHOLESOME: *bad, *dirty, *evil, *rotten, *wrong
UNWIELDY: *clumsy, *fat, *great
UNYIELDING: *firm, *hard, *obstinate, *set, *stern
UP: *increase, over, *raise
comb.: an, ana, ano
in arms: *ready
to: *able, *ready
UPANISHAD: isha
UPAS: antiar, dita
UPBEAT: arsis
UPBRAID: *abuse, *rebuke, *scold
UPEND: *defeat, *throw, *upset
UPHEAVAL: *catastrophe, *storm
UPHOLD: *abet, *support
UPHOLSTERY: material: damask, lampas, mohair, rep, tabaret, tournay, valance
UPOLU: capital: apia
UPON: above, atop, near, over
comb.: epi, supra, sur

* Asterisk means to look up this word to find more answer words.

UPPBAD: bevaring
UPPER: *comb.:* ano
UPPERMOST: *supreme
UPPISH: proud, snooty
UPRIGHT: *fair, *honest, *true
UPRISING: *ado, *noise, *riot
UPROAR: *fight, *noise, *riot,
*stir, *trouble, turbulence
UPSET: *agitate, *alarm, *anger,
anxious, bouleverse, bowl over,
capsize, cave in, confuse, coup,
crush, dash, *defeat, demoralize,
discomfit, disconcert, distress,
disturb, embarrass, fall, frantic,
nervous, overpower, overthrow,
overturn, overwhelm, over-
wrought, passionate, perturb, re-
fute, reverse, revolution, *riot,
*shock, shot, *spoil, *start(le),
*stir, *strike, subvert, *throw,
*top(ple), vanquish
UPSHOT: *issue, *limit, *result
UPSILON: -shaped: hyoid
UPSTAGE: *shy, snobbish
UPSTART: parvenue, snob, sprout
UPSY-DAISY: alley-oop, excelsior
UP TIGHT: nervous, tense
UPTURN: *increase
UPWARD: *comb.:* an, ana, ano
URAEUS: asp, *ornament, *symbol
URALITE: amphibole
URANIA: *lover:* amphimarus
son: linus
URANIUM: carnotite, ianthinite
URANORNIS: bird of paradise
URANUS: *consort:* gaea
mother: gaea, gaia
offspring: aegaeon, aphrodite,
briareus, *cyclopes, *furies,
*hecatoncheires, meliae, pontus,
*titans
satellite: ariel, miranda, oberon,
titania, umbriel
slayer: cronus
URAO: minteral, trona
URBAN: civic, metropolitan

URBANE: civil, polite, suave
URCHIN: brat, gamin, *imp
URDE: cleche, pointed
URE: custom, exercise, *use
UREA: carbamide
UREDO: hives, urticaria
URFA: edessa
URGE: *abet, *advise, allege, animate, ankus, assuade, augment,
bear upon, blandish, broad, busk,
call upon, coax, compel, crowd,
demand, *desire, ding, drive, enjoin, entreat, ert, exasperate,
fillip, flog, *force, gad, hag, hie,
high pressure, lash, lure, needle,
oxgoad, persuade, plod, ply,
pray, *press, prosecute, *push,
recommend, root, rowel, solicit,
*spur, sting, *stir, sue, *support,
*thorn, twist arm, verve, *whip,
work on, yen
URGENCY: *need, *stress
URGENT: *critical, *important
URI: *son:* bezaleel, marmathi
URIAH: *son:* meremoth
wife: bathsheba
URIAL: oorial, sha, sheep
URISK: brownie
URN: amphora, capanna, vessel
-shaped: urceolate
URODELA: amphibia, eft, newt,
salamander
URSINE: arctoid, bear-like
baboon: chacma
howler: araguato
URSULINE: *founder:* angela me-
rici
URTH: norn, past, wyrd
URTICARIA: hives, rash, uredo
URUGUAY: *city:* durazno, florida, maldonado, melo, minas,
montevideo, paysandu, rivera,
rocha, salto
coin: centesimo, peso
estuary: plata
lake: merin, mirim
measure: cuadra, suerte, vara

* Asterisk means to look up this word to find more answer words.

river: cebollary, malo, negro, tacaurembo, ulimar
soldier: jose artigas
weight: quintal
URUS: aurochs, ox, tur
USAGE: **form*, **system*, **way*
USE: **accustom*, adhibition, administer, administration, **advantage*, appliance, apply, bear, bestow, borrow, **cheat*, consume, consumption, custom, disposal, **disposition*, dupe, employ, enjoy, equity, exercise, exert, exhaust, expend, exploit, **form*, frequent, handle, hire, **interest*, manage, maneuver, **need*, occupy, operate, **play*, ply, practice, privilege, profit, put out, recourse, **right*, **service*, spend, stead, take advantage, treat, **try*, ure, utility, **value*, wear, wield, **work*, **wrong*
USEFUL: **good*, practical
USELESS: **idle*, otiose, **vain*
USHA: *father:* bana
USHER: herald, **lead*, **show*
house of lords: black rod
USNEA: fungus, lichen, moss
USNECH: *son:* naoise
USQUEBAUGH: cordial, whiskey
USSR: **russia*
USUAL: analogical, **average*, consuetudinary, conventional, customary, everyday, household, orthodox, **popular*, realistic, **regular*, **set*, stale, standard, stereotyped, stock, unexceptional, **universal*, vernacular, wonted
USUCAPTION: monopoly, **trust*
USURER: moneychanger, shark
USURP: **seize*, **take*
USURPER: **despot*, tyrant
USURY: overcharge, premium
UTAH: *bird:* seagull
flower: sego lily
lake: salt, sevier, swan

mormon name: deseret
mountain: peale, uinta, wasatch
nickname: beehive state
river: colorado, grand, green, jordan, sevier
town: american fork, beaver, brigham city, delta, eureka, heber, kanab, lehi, ogden, orem, provo, richfield, tooele
tree: blue spruce
UTENSIL: **instrument*, **thing*
UTILITY: **service*, **use*, **value*
UTILIZE: **use*, **work*
UTMOST: **end*, **extreme*, **limit*
UTOPIA: agapemone, annfwn, annwn, atlantis, cloudland, cockaigne, dixie, dreamland, erewhon, estotilandia, fairy land, goshen, happy valley, icaria, land of milk and honey, land of prester john, land of the leal, laputa, lemuria, lotus land, millennium, nauvoo, new jerusalem, oceana, **paradise*, **persian: utopia*, shangri-la
author: more
harrington's: oceana
UTOPIAN: edenic, quixotic
UTRAQUIST: calixtin(e), hussite
UTRICLE: **bag*, **opening*, sac
UTRICULARIA: bladdersnout
UTTER: **air*, **complete*, **extreme*, **great*, **issue*, **perfect*, **state*
UTURUNCU: werewolf
UTZ: goat, **scold*, **torment*
UVA: arrow-cane, fruit, grape
grass: cana brava
UVULA: cion, scion
UVULARIA: bellflower, campanula
UZ: *brother:* aran
UZAI: *son:* palal
UZZI: *son:* arna, zerahiah
UZZIAH: *captain:* hananiah
parent: amaziah, jecoliah
scribe: jeiel

---

* Asterisk means to look up this word to find more answer words.

son: athaiah, jehonathan, jotham
wife: jerushah
UZZIEL: *son:* amminadab, micah,
jesiah

VACANCY: *opening, space, void
VACANT: *free, *idle, *open
VACATE: *move, *quit, *yield
VACATION: holiday, *rest
working: busman's holiday
VACCINE: antisepsis, *remedy
inventor: jenner, sabin, salk
VACCINIUM: bilberry, blue-
berry, huckleberry, whortleberry
VACHELLIA: cassie, huisache
VACILLATE: *oscillate, *quiver
VACUOUS: *dull, *stupid
VACUUM: *opening, void
tube: audion, diode, tetrode
VADIUM: mortgage, *promise
VAGABOND: bum, hobo, tramp,
waif
VAGANS: quintus
VAGARY: caper, prank, *trick
VAGRANT: blackguard, *vagabond
VAGUE: blear(y), blind, broad,
confused, dreamy, equivocal,
faint, feeble, forlorn, futile,
fuzzy, general, hazy, ill defined,
inarticulate, indecisive, indeterminate, inexact, intangible, lax,
*light, loose, lost, misty, muddy,
nebulous, nonspecific, *obscure,
pale, shadowy, sketchy, stray,
uncertain, unclear, *weak
VAIN: *arrogant, baseless, boot-
less, conceited, chimeric, *dull,
foolish, gorgeous, hopeless,
*idle, ignorant, ineffectual, in-
valid, proud, silly, smug, snooty,
stuck-up, *superficial, unimportant, upstage, useless, vapid,
*weak
VAINGLORY: *boasting, *show

VAISHNAVA: *vishnu
VAISYA: *caste:* aroras
VAKEEL, VAKIL: attorney
VAL: *father:* aguar
VALANCE: curtain, palmette
VALE: *good: bye, *waterway
VALEDICTION: *address, *good:
bye
VALENCE: adicity, *power,
*value
VALENTINE: *gift, *love, *token
VALENTINITE: antimony bloom
VALERIAN: allheal, heliotrope,
nard, panacea, *remedy, setwall
VALET: butler, man, *servant
VALETUDINAIRE: patient, *sick
VALI: *parent:* odin, rind
VALIANT: *bold, *great, *strong
VALID: *good, *solid, *strong,
substantial, sufficient, *true
VALIDATE: *establish, *set
VALIDITY: *force, *strength
VALISE: *bag, portmanteau
VALJEAN: *discoverer:* javert
friend: marius
protege: cosette
VALKYRIE: brynhild, freyja, kara
VALLETTA: *people:* maltese
VALLEY: *opening, *waterway
VALLOTA: amaryllis
VALOR: *power, *strength, *value
VALOROUS: *valiant, *valid
VALPARAISO: flaming coast
VALUABLE: dear, *good, *great
VALUE: *account, *adjudge, *ad-
mire, *advance, *advantage, ap-
praise, apprize, *assess, *asset,
assizes, average, benefit, carat,
excellence, face, feck, *fee,
mean(ing), moment, *money,
net, opinion, par, pennyworth,
*prize, rate, resource, respect,
sterling, utility, weigh(t), worth
creation society: sokagakkai
relative: ad valorem
VALVE: cock, cusp, gate, piston
medium line: raphe
VAMOOSE: *run, scat, scram

* Asterisk means to look up this word to find more answer words.

VAMP(IRE): *demon, *monster
up: *repair
VAN: *advance, *head, truck
VANADATE: carnotite, uranium
VANDAL: hun, iconoclast
VANDELLIA: candiru, catfish
VANDYKE: beard, notch, picture
VANE: blade, feather, *flag
VANESSA: angle wing, polygonia
VAN GOGH: *city:* arles
VANILLA: amlong, coumarin
wild: deer's-tongue
VANISH: *end, *pass, recede
VANITY: conceit, ego, *vain
case: *bag, etui, etwee
fair: *society
fair role: amelia, becky sharp
symbol: margery daw
VANQUISH: *defeat, *throw
VAPID: *dull, inane, *stupid
VAPOR: ether, fog, gas, *smoke
comb.: atmid(o), atm(o)
pocket: cavitation
VAPORY: ethereal, *vain
VAPORS: *remedy:* atmiatry
VAQUERO: *cow: boy
VARANGIANS: ros, rus, russ
VARIABLE: fickle, protean
VARIANCE: argument, difference
text: lection
VARIATION: change, *turn
from: normal: acatastasia
recorder: auxograph
vowel: ablaut, apophony
VARIEGATE: diversify, *oscillate
VARIEGATED: calico, motley
VARIETY: *kind, *mixture, *style
VARIOLA: smallpox, virus
VARIOUS: diverse, manifold
comb.: vari, vario
VARLET: *scoundrel, *servant
VARMINT: animal, *sharp,
*smart
VARNISH: *ornament, *paint
part: copal, dammar, elemi, lac,
mastic, resin, rosin
tree: anacardium

type: japan, megilp, lacquer
VARUNA: amburaja, jadapati,
jalapati
consort: aditi, urvasi
son: agastya
VARY: *oscillate, *quarrel, *range,
shift, vacillate
VAS: duct, *promise, vessel
VASCULAR: arterial, marsupial
pert.: haemal, hemic
VASE: amphora, askos, casolette
VASHTI: *esther
VASSAL: *man, *servant, *slave
military: arriereban
pert.: enfeoff, feudal
VAST: *big, *great, *large
VAT: gyle, kier, tun, vessel
VA-T'EN: begone, scram, vamoose
VATICAN: *chapel:* sistine
ism: curialism
statue group: laocoon
VAULT: crypt, jump, safe, tomb
recess: apse
roof: camera
VAUNT: boast, brag, crow
VAURIEN: wretch
VAYU: *child:* hanuman
VE: *brother:* odin
VEADAR: adar sheni
VECTOR: course, *force, rotor
opposite: scalar
VEDIC: *india references
VEER: deviate, *shy, *turn, yaw
VEGA: *plain
constellation: lyra
VEGETABLE: entree, food, legume
carbonized: lignite
dealer: costermonger, green grocer, huckster
decayed: duff, humus
disease: black rot
dish: chiffonade, salad, zimmis
esculent: legume
existence: inertia, stagnation
extract: amaroid
exudation: lac, resin, sap

* Asterisk means to look up this word to find more answer words.

ferment: yeast

fuel: peat

green: sabzi

kind: artichoke, asparagus, bean, beet, bell pepper, brassica, broccoli, brussels sprout, cabbage, carrot, cauliflower, celery, chard, chicory, chili pepper, chive, collard, coriander, corn, cress, cucumber, eggplant, endive, fennel, finocchio, frijole, garbanzo, garlic, green, gumbo, hominy, horse radish, kale, leek, lentil, lettuce, maize, mushroom, okra, onion, parsley, parsnip, pea, pepper, pimento, pimiento, pomato, potato, potherb, pumpkin, radish, romaine, rutabaga, salsify, scallion, shallot, soya, spinach, squash, succory, tomato, truffle, turnip, yam, zucchini

mold: humus

oil: *oil: vegetable

oyster: salsify

pear: chayote

pepsin: caroid

pod: hull, pease

poison: abrin

rubbish: wrack

stunted: scrub

sugar-yielding: beet

tinder: amadou

tracing paper: ecu

VEGETATE: *grow, hibernate

VEGETATION: *afloat:* sadd, sudd

god: adonis, amaethon, anodos, attis, atys, bacchus, dagan, dionysus, esus, faunus, nebo, pan, tammuz, triptolemus

goddess: annona, ceres, cora, cotys, demeter, despoina, flora, gaea, isis, kore, ops, persephone, proserpina, tellus mater

VEHEMENCE: *fire, *force, heat, *passion, rage, *violence, zeal

VEHEMENT: *eager, *hot, *violent

VEHICLE: car, carriage, coach, *instrument, *machine, sedan

animal-man operated: araba, bandy, barouche, barrow, berlin, bicycle, bike, bounder, brake, branchard, break, brett, brougham, buckboard, bus, byke, cab, cabriolet, calash, caleche, calesa, caravan, cariole, caroche, carromata, cart, chaise, charet, chariot(ee), clarence, coach, concord, conestoga, croydon, curricle, cycle, dandy, dearborn, democrat, dennet, diligence, dilly, dogcart, dolly, dosados, drag, dray, droschky, droshky, drosky, duke, ekka, equipage, essed(a), fiacre, fourgon, four-in-hand, germantown, gharry, gig, goat, gocart, gondola, growler, gurry, hack, hackery, hackney, handcart, hansom, hearse, herdic, hurly, jerry, jingle, jinker, jinricksha, jinrikisha, jutka, kibitka, kosong, landau, limber, luge, mail, morfrey, morphrey, ordinary, phaeton, plow, pram, pushcart, putt, quadrigg, rath(a), reckla, rig, ricksha(w), rockaway, runabout, rut, sado(o), safety, scooter, shay, shoful, sociable, spider, stagecoach, stanhope, stretcher, sulky, surrey, tallyho, tandem, tarantas(s), tartana, team, telega, tilbury, tonga, trap, tricycle, troika, truckle, tumbler, tumbrel, turnout, unicorn, velocipede, vettura, victoria, vis-a-vis, voiture, volante, wheelchair

automobiles: ambulance, auto, berlin, black maria, cab, cabriolet, camion, charabanc, coupe(let), drag, dumpcart, flivver, hack, hearse, jaloppy, jalopy, jeep, jigger, jitney, landau, limousine, lorry, motorcar, motor-

* Asterisk means to look up this word to find more answer words.

cycle, omnibus, roadster, runabout, scooter, sedan, sidecar,
suburban, tank, taxi(cab), torpedo, tourer, tractor, trailer,
tram, trolley, voiture, wynn
baby-child: bicycle, buggy, gocart, pram, scooter, stroller, tricycle, velocipede, walker
four-in-hand: tallyho
four-wheel: buckboard, buggy,
coupe, landau, limousine, phaeton, rockaway, surrey, victoria
hauling: dray, lorry, sled, tractor,
trailer, truck, van
one-horse: buggy, cariole, dennet,
fly, gig, shay, sulky
part: axle, battery, bonnet, box,
brake, bumper, cam, carburetor,
chassis, clutch, cylinder, engine,
exhaust, fan, flywheel, gear(shift),
handlebar, hood, ignition, intake,
magneto, mudguard, muffler, oil
gauge, pedal, pillar, piston, plug,
radiator, reins, rim, rumble, saddle, shaft, shoe, spark plug,
spoke, spring, sprocket, thill,
throttle, tire, tongue, tonneau,
wheel, wiper
portable: cacolet, dandy, dooley,
howdah, juan, kago, kuruma, litter, muncheel, norimon, palanquin, sedan, stretcher, telega,
tomjon
public: bus, cab, charabanc,
hansom, jinricksha, jinrikisha,
omnibus, rickshaw, taxi, tram,
train
railroad: boxcar, brake-van,
buggy, caboose, caravan, chair
car, club car, coach, coal car,
day coach, diesel, diner, dinghy,
dolly, dummy, engine, flatcar,
giraffe, gondola, hog, hopper,
jopper, kinkey, locomotive,
mail car, mogul, parlor, piggy-
back, pullman, rattler, reefer,
refrigerator, sleeper, smoker,

speeder, tank, tender, trap car,
waggon, wagon(lit)
runnered: *vehicle: wheelless
three-horse: troika
two-wheel: bicycle, caleche, care-
tella, carromata, cart, chaise,
chariot, cisium, dennet, essed,
gig, hansom, jinricksha, jinrikisha, shay, stanhope, sulky,
tonga, vinaigrette
wheelless: bob(sleigh), coaster,
cutter, go-devil, hurdle, jampan,
jumper, palki, pulk, pulka, pung,
ship, skate, ski, sled(ge), sleigh,
toboggan, train, travois(e)
VEIL: *cover, *hide, *wrap
VEIN: *mood, *source, tone
arrangement: neuration
comb.: veno
enlarged: varix
fluid: blood, ichor
inflammation: phlebitis
mining: bonanza, lode, roke
pert.: veinal, venous
stone: gangue, matrix, mine
without: avenous
VELD(T): *plain
VELLEITY: *desire, hope, wish
VELOCITY: *speed
unit: farad, kin, strob
VELVET: bagheera, panne, profit
bur: cat's-tongue, verbena
grass: calfkill
leaf: pareira
scoter: basque
VENAL: corrupt, *mean, sordid
VEND: market, sell, *trade
VENDETTA: *fight, *quarrel
VENEER: *cover, *polish
VENERABLE: *old, *sage, *wise
VENERATE: *love, *prize, *value
VENERATION: *awe, *honor,
*love
religious: dulia, latria
VENERIDA: carpet shell, clam
VENETIAN: *venice

* Asterisk means to look up this word to find more answer words.

VENEZUELAN: *city:* aroa, asuncion, atures, barcelona, barines, barquisimeto, caracas, coro, cumana, guanare, maracay, maturin, ocumare, san carlos, san cristobal, san felipe, san fernando, san juan, tacupita, trujillo

coin: bolivar, centimo, fuerte, medio, morocota, venezolano

fiber: erizo

god: tsuma

grassy plain: llano

hero: bolivar

indian: carib, guarauno, motilone, pume, timote(x)

lake: maracaibo, tacarigua

measure: estadel, fanega, milla

mountain: andes, concha, cuneva, icutu, imutaca, pacaraima, parima, roraima, sierra nevada de merida

orchid: butterfly, oncidium

plain: llano

poet: andres bello

port: carupano, ciudad bolivar, la guayra, maracaibo, puerto cabello

revolutionist: miranda

river: apure, arausa, caroni, caura, orinoco, pao, ventuar

snake: lora

tree: balata

VENGEANCE: reprisal, revenge

god: alastor, erinys

goddess: ara, ate, nemesis

symbol: bloody shirt

VENIAL: *small*, trivial

VENICE: *beach resort:* lido

boat: bucentaur, gondola

bridge: bridge of sighs, rialto

canal: grand rii, rio

church: frari

coin: bagattino, betso, bezzo, croisat, ducat, gazzetta, grosso, osella, sequin

court: quaranty

district: rialto

island: burano, rialto

magistrate: doge, podesta

medal: oscella, osela, oselle

merchant of: antonio

of north: stockholm

painter: bellini, giorgione, tintoretto, titian, veronese

river: brenta

song: barcarole, barcarolle

traveler: conti, marco polo

VENISON: pemican, pemmican

VENNEL: alley, gutter, sewer

VENOM: atter, poison, spite, toxin

VENT: *escape*, *opening*, *state*

VENTILATE: *air*, expose, review

VENTRAL: abdominal, haemad

VENTRILOQUISM: hariolate

VENTRILOQUIST: engastrimyth, gastriloquist

VENTURE: adventure, *ante*, assume, *bet*, chance, contingency, courage, danger, dare, *enter*(*prise*), essay, feeler, fling, flyer, fortune, gamble, gest(e), hap(pen), hazard, invest(ment), jeopardy, lark, luck, peril, presumption, project, quest, speculate, stake, *start*, *test*, trespass, *trial*, *try*, *turn*, undertake, undertaking, wage(r)

VENUE: *hit*, *place*, *set*

VENUS: anadyomene, aphrodite, astarte, cytherea, vesper

island: melos

's-flytrap: dionaea, plant

's girdle: cestus

's-hair: maidenhair, spleenwort

son: amor, cupid, eros

sweetheart: adonis

VERACIOUS: *accurate*, *true*

VERACITY: *honor*, *truth*

VERANDA: lanai, loggia, porch

VERB: *comb.:* ate, esce, ire, ise

table: paradigm

VERBASCUM: adam's-flannel, herb, mullein, weed

---

* Asterisk means to look up this word to find more answer words.

VERBENA: aloysia, ashthroat, cat's-tongue, lantana, plant, tectona, vervain

VERDANT: *fresh*, green, raw

VERDI: *opera:* aida, ernani, oberto, othello, rigoletto, traviata
role: amneris, radames

VERDICT: *order*, *rule*, *word*

VERDURE: greenness, *smell*

VERECUND: bashful, *shy*

VEREIN: *group*, *order*, *society*

VEREUK: *cheat*, *skin*, *take*

VERGE: *edge*, *limit*, *range*

VERGIL: *virgil*

VERIFY: *correct*, *establish*, *prove*, *test*, *try*

VERISIMILITUDE: *truth*

VERITABLE: *honest*, real, *true*

VERITY: *thing*, *truth*

VERMIN: bugs, fleas, flies, lice, mice, *rabble*, rats

VERMONT: *bird:* hermit thrush
flower: red clover
motto: freedom and unity
mountains: green, taconic
nickname: green mountain state
tree: sugar maple

VERNACULAR: *argot*, *usual*

VERNAL: *fresh*, *gentle*, *warm*

VERNE: *lunar craft:* columbiad

VERONICA: bird's-eye, bluebell, brooklime, cat's-tail, charm, cloth, handkerchief, speedwell, sudarium, veil

VERSAILLES: *palace:* grand trianon

VERSATE: *oscillate*, *turn*

VERSE: *meter*, *stanza*
end: acroteleutic, doxology

VERSED: *able*, *adept*, *wise*

VERSION: *account*, *form*, *report*, *story*

VERTEX: *ace*, *acme*, *top*

VERTICAL: *straight*

VERTIGO: megrims, staggers

VERTUMNUS: *beloved:* pomona

VERVE: *passion*, *spirit*

VERY: much, real, *true*, well
comb.: cat(a), cath, eri, kat(a)

VESICLE: bleb, bursa, cyst, sac

VESPER: evening, hymn, star

VESSEL: *boat*, *bottle*, *ship*
comb.: angio
container: aftaba, aiguirre, alcarraza, alembic, aludel, ama, bocal, boss, bowl, cadus, canteen, capillary, cask, cell, cog, *container*, creamer, decanter, diota, dixy, doni, dubber, etna, firkin, font, funnel, lota(h), olla, olpe, *pack(age)*, pan, patera, pot, *receptacle*, rier, stein, *tank*, utensil, via
drinking: *drinking: vessel*
engine-driven: aviso, coaster, collier, droger, lighter, powerboat, speedboat, steamer
famous: aotea, argo, arizona, bismarck, bonhomme, bounty, clermont, endeavor, half moon, hartford, horouta, matatua, merrimac, missouri, monitor, nina, olympia, pinta, titanic
pert.: vasal
sailing: argosy, baggala, baghla, baidar, balinger, ballahoo, barge, bark, barque(ntine), batel, bugeye, bully, caique, cangia, caravel, casco, catboat, dahabeah, dandy, dogger, dromon, felucca, galiot, galleon, ketch, koff, lugger, mackinaw, patamar, piragua, polacca, praham, prahu, pram, proa, pulwar, razee, saic, sampan, scaffy, schooner, settee, sharp, sloop, smack, snow, tartan, tongkang, tosher, trabacolo, xebec, yacht, yawl, zabra, zulu
warship: *navy: vessel*

VEST: *dress*, *give*, jacket
-pocket: *little*, *small*

VESTA: asteroid, lighter, taper

VESTAL: *pure*, spinster, virgin

VESTIBULE: hall, *pass(age)*

* **Asterisk means to look up this word to find more answer words.**

VESTIGE: *mark, *sign, *token
VESTMENT: *cover, *dress, robe
 religious: abnet, alba, almuce, amice, amphibalus, apron, bands, berretta, biretta, black gown, buskins, calotte, cap(pa), capuche, capuchin, casaque, cassock, chasuble, chimer(e), cincture, cingulum, cloak, cloth, cope, cotta, crucifix, cuculla, dalmatic, dowl, ephod, fannel, fano(n), frock, geneva, gown, gremial, hood, lappet, lawn sleeves, maniple, mantelletta, mantellone, miter, mozzetta, orale, orarion, pallium, pontificalia, rabat, robe, rochet, saccos, sandals, scapular(y), scarf, shovel hat, simar, skullcap, soutaine, stole, subcingulum, surplice, tiara, tippet, tonsure, triple crown, tunic(le), vagas, vakass, zimarra, zucchetto
VESTRY: chapel, sacristy
VETCH: akra, arvejon, astragal, ers, faba, fitch, sativa, tare
VETO: deny, *end, *kill, *stop
VEX: *anger, *puzzle, *scold
VIAL: *receptacle, *vessel
VIAUD: pen name: loti
VIBRATE: *oscillate, *quiver
VICAR: *church: man, *substitute
VICE: *crime, *evil, *force, *sin, *substitute, *wrong
VICEROY: butterfly, *magnate
VICIOUS: *bad, *brutal, *evil
VICTIM: butt, dupe, prey
VICTOR: crown: garland, laurel
 fish: aku
 hugo group: cenacle
VICTORY: conquest, success, *win
 celebrating: epinician
 costly: pyrrhic
 cry: aboo, abu
 deity: nike, odin
 sign: bidigitation, vee

 trophy: scalp
VIDELICET: scilicet, viz
VIE: *fight, *try
VIENNA: wien
 landmark: ring
 palace: schonbrunn
 park: prater
VIETNAM: annam, cochin-china, *indochina, tonkin
 alligator: cayman
 army: arvn, cosvn, viet cong
 bull: zebu
 capitals: hanoi, saigon
 delta: mekong
 holiday: tet
 hut: hootch
 massacre: my lai, quang ngai, song my
 people: anamese, bodo, hos, khas, meos, mru, tai, yaos
 people, nickname: dinks, gooks, slants, slopes
VIEW: *look, *picture, *see
VIGILANT: *eager, *sharp
VIGOR: *force, *power, *spirit
VIGOROUS: *fresh, *strong
VIKING: *norse references
VILE: *bad, *brutal, *evil, *low, *mean, *poor, *sad, *wild
VILLAGE: burg, castle, dorp, kraal, oppidum, pueblo, town
 comb.: burg, by
VILLAIN, VILLEIN: *peasant, rascal, rogue, *servant, *slave
VIM: *fire, *spirit, *vigor
VINCA: myrtle, periwinkle
VINDICATE: *acquit, *support
VINE: grape, ivy, liana, soma
 comb.: ampel(o), viti
 parasite: aphid, aphis
 part: cirrus, tendril
 support: risel, trellis
VINEGAR: acetate, alegar, eisell
 bottle: cruet
 comb.: aceto
 dregs: mother
 pert.: acetic

preserve in: brine, marinate, pickle

weed: ambrosia, camphor, blue curls, ragweed

VINEGARY: **acerb,* **sharp*

VINEYARD: *protector:* priapus

VIOL: rebat, rebec, sarinda

bass: double, string, violon(e)

VIOLA: alto, gamba, pomposa

VIOLATE: **abuse,* **wrong*

VIOLENCE: agitation, ardor, bensail, bensall, bensell, bensil, blitz, blood and thunder, bloodshed, bluster, coercion, cruelty, ferocity, **force,* hubris, inclemency, mob law, **noise,* outrage, **passion,* severity, **storm,* the sword, **trouble,* uproar, war, whirlwind

VIOLENT: abnormal, **ardent,* **bad,* bloodthirsty, bloody, boisterous, **brutal,* drastic, **drunk,* **evil,* extravagant, **extreme,* forceful, forcible, **great,* **hot,* **insane,* loud, **mad,* manic, piercing, raging, rammish, **reckless,* rigorous, rough, **severe,* **sharp,* **short,* splitting, stormy, **strong,* unbalanced, unnatural, vehement, vivid, **wild*

contact: anstoss

VIOLET: anchiete, mauve, purple

dye: archil

perfume: irone, orris

ray: beam

root: iridin, orris

-tip: butterfly

VIOLIN: amati, cremona, fiddle, ruana, strad

forerunner: rebab, rebec

player: aner, bull, elman, menuhin, nero, ole, zimbalist

VIP: big shot, **lord,* **magnate*

VIRAGO: **hag,* **scold,* **witch*

VIRGIL: *birthplace:* mantua

family name: maro

friend: maecenas

plant: baccar, bacchar

poem: aeneid, eneid, epic

role: aeneas, amata, camilla, corydon, damon, dido, eneas

VIRGIN: **fresh,* green, **pure*

island: st croix, tortola

island coin: bit, daler, franc

island discoverer: columbus

mary follower: marigold

mary mourning: pieta

mother: anna, anne

warrior in "aeneid": camilla

VIRGINIA: diemenia, potamophis

bird: cardinal

cowslip: american lungwort

creeper: ampelopsis, ivy, joy, woodbine

flower: dogwood

goat's-rue: catgut

grass: lyme, terrell

motto: sic semper tyrannis

mountain: cedar

nickname: old dominion

quail: bobwhite

pine: loblolly

poke: hellebore

rail: bull

river: dan, james, potomac, rapidan, rappahannock

snakeroot: birthwort, sangrel

swamp: dismal

VIRGINITY: celibacy, pucellage

VIRGULARIAN: searod

VIRILE: masculine, **strong*

VIRTU: **ornament,* **token*

pieces: bijouterie, bric-a-brac

VIRTUE: **honor,* **power,* purity

cardinal: charity, faith, fortitude, hope, justice, prudence, temperance

goddess: fides

paragon: saint

VIRTUOUS: **good,* **honest,* **pure*

VIRULENCE: **anger,* **hate*

VIRULENT: **acerb,* **sour,* **violent*

VIRUS: bug, dna, flu, rna, toxin

* **Asterisk means to look up this word to find more answer words.**

VISCERA: guts, entrails, vitals

VISCID, VISCUOUS: *thick

VISHNU: *avatar:* balarama, bhagavat, buddha, kalki, karma, krishna, jagganath, juggernaut, matsaya(vatara), narasimha, narsinh, parshuram, rama(chandra), vaman(avatara), varah(avatara)

bearer: garuda

biography: bhagavata purana

bow: saran

brother: balarama

curser: durvasas

grandson: aniruddha

incarnation: *vishnu: avatar

paradise: goloka

parent: devaki

priest: gosain, gusain

race: yadava

saint: alvar

serpent: naga, sesha, vasuki

soul of universe: vasu

stick: mount mandara

3 strides: air, earth, heaven

wife: bhumi devi, lakshmi, sri

worshipper: bhagavata, bhakta

VISIBLE: macroscopic, *open

VISIGOTH: *king:* alaric

VISION: *eye references, *image, *picture, *wonder

VISIONARY: chimeric, utopian

VISIT: *join, *meet, *see

VISTA: *range, *view, *vision

VITAL: *active, *live, *quick

VITAMIN: *a:* carotene, carotin

b: cobalamin, cyanocobalamin, flavin, folic acid, niacin, oryzanin, pyridoxine, riboflavin, thiamine

c: ascorbic acid

d: calciferol, cholecalciferol, ergocalciferol, ergosterol, lumisterol

e: d-alpha tocopherol, wheat germ

g: riboflavin

h: biotin

k: phylloquinone, phytonadione

m: folacin, folic acid, pga

p and x: citrin

VITIATE: *hurt, *spoil, weaken

VITRIOLIC: *acerb, *sharp, *sour

VITUPERATE: *abuse, *rally, *rebuke, *scold, vilify

VIVACITY: *fire, *force, *spirit

VIVID: *fresh, *rich, *sharp

VIXEN: fox, *scold, *witch

VIZIER: *lord, *magnate, *ruler

VOGUE: *image, *style, *way

VOICE: *state, *talk, *tell

box: larynx

fault: lisp, stammer, stutter

flourish: roulade

loss: anaudia, aphonia, aphrasia, aphthongia

natural: di petto

part: glottis

pert.: phonetic

range: alto, baritone, bass, contralto, falsetto, mezzo, soprano, sotto voce, tenor, treble

sound: blahlaut, *symbol, *word

stop: affricate

stress: arsis, ictus

VOID: *end, *free, *idle, *remove, vacate, vain, veto

VOLAND: *brother:* egil

VOLATILE: capricious, *light

VOLCANO: antisana, apo, askja, asosan, burning mountain, cotopaxi, etna, fuji, krakatau, mauna loa, pelee, popocatepetl, rainier, stromboli, vesuvius

cinder: scoria

extinct: alagez, aragats, asosan, shasta

glass: australite, obsidian, perlite, pumice

hill: puy

lava: lapilli, latite, pumice

matter: aa, lava, moya, pumice

mouth: crater, fumarole, maar

mud: moya, salse

rock: andesite, dacite, feldspar,

---

* Asterisk means to look up this word to find more answer words.

perlite, rhyolite, tephrite, terras, trass, tufa
steam: stufa
threatening: solfataric
VOLE: campagnol, microtis
VOLGA: rha
VOLITION: choice, option, will
VOLLEY: barrage, fire, salvo
VOLPONE: *character:* mosca
VOLSTEAD ACT: prohibition
VOLSUNG: *hero:* siegfried, sigurd
king: atli
oak: barnstock, branstock
VOLT: ampere, ohm, repolon, watt
VOLTAIRE: arouet
work: candide, nanine, zadig
VOLUBLE: fickle, glib, wordy
VOLUME: book, **quantity*, tome
VOLUND: *brother:* egil(1)
VOLUNTEER: enlist, enrol(1), **enter*, offer, proffer, **stand*
state: tennessee
VOLUTE: **turn*, whorl
VOMIT: cast, emetic, erupt, spew
VOODOO: **fetish*, **magic*
charm: doll, juju, mojo, obi
god: loa, zombi
marauder: bourhousse
wizard: quimboiseur
VORACIOUS: **eager*, edacious
VORSTELLUNG: **image*
VORTEX: eddy, gyre, maelstrom
VOTARY: **enthusiast*, fan, ite
VOTE: decide, name, poll, **will*
group: bloc, body politic
receptacle: box, situla
right: franchise
VOTYAK: *water spirit:* vu-kutis, vu-nuna, vu-murt, vu-vozo
VOUCH: affirm, back, **support*
VOUCHSAFE: assure, **give*, **yield*
VOW: assert, **promise*, swear
VOWEL: *contraction:* crasis, diphthong
gradation: ablaut, apophony
group: digram, digraph

line over: macron, tilde
omission: aphesis, elision
point: tsere
short: breve
sign: dieresis
sound: dental, labial, palatal
sound, pert.: vocalic
VOYAGE: **pass(age)*, **run*, trip
VULCAN: **hephaestus*
VULGAR: **bad*, **brutal*, **general*, **low*, **mean*, ordinary, profane
VULNERABLE: exposed, liable
point: achilles heel
VULPINE: artful, crafty, cunning
VULTURE: buteo, buzzard, condor, griffon, harpy, urubu, zopilote
bearded: hammergeier

WAAG: grivet, monkey
WABAYO: ouabaio
WABBLE: change, **oscillate*
WACHNA: cod(fish)
WACKER: quaker
WACKY: **eccentric*, **mad*
WAD: **pack*, **part*, **quantity*
-set: mortgage
WADDY: **attack*, **staff*, **stick*
WADE: **demon*, **pass*, **walk*
WADI: oasis, **waterway*
WAFER: cake, obley, ubblie
ash: agrimony, ague bark
box: pyx
WAFF: **bad*, **low*, **smell*
WAFFLE: cake, **err*, **error*
WAFT: blow, carry, **smell*
WAG: **gossip*, **move*, **oscillate*
WAGE: **fee*, **fight*, **money*, **use*
WAGER: ante, **prize*, **venture*
WAGNER: *opera:* gotterdammerung, lohengrin, meistersinger, parsifal, rheingold, rienzi, tannhauser, tristan and isolde
role: amfortas, elsa, erda
wife: cosima

---

* Asterisk means to look up this word to find more answer words.

WAGON: carriage, *vehicle
body: buck
-load: burden, cargo, fother
maker: wainwright
part: blade, clevis, neap, pole,
  rave, thill, tongue
WAH: measure, panda
WAHOO: basswood, burning-bush,
  cascara buckthorn, *nonsense,
  peto, tilia, umbrella tree
WAIF: gamin, stray, vagabond
WAIL: *cry, lament, ululate
WAIN: cart, *vehicle, wagon
charles: constellation, dipper
WAINSCOT: base, line, *part
WAIST: basque, body, girth
-band: belt, cestus, obi, sash
-coat: benjy, jerkin, vest, weskit
decoration: jabot
WAIT: *ambush, *rest, *stop
on: escort, help, serve
WAITER: salver, *servant, *spy
WAIVE: *quit, *stop, *yield
WAKE: funeral, *stir, track
island: otori
-robin: arum, calf's-foot, cuckoopint, orchid, trillium
WALE: choose, *mark, *whip
WALES: cambria, cymru, *welsh
WALK: airing, alameda, allee,
  alure, amble, ambulate, ankle,
  arcade, arena, balteus, behavior,
  circuit, clump, conduct, consti-
  tutional, daddle, dogtrot, echelon, esplanade, foot, gad, gait,
  gallery, haunt, hike, hobble,
  hoof, jaunt, jog, leg, limp, loiter,
  lumber, mall, march, mince,
  mope, mosey, *move, pace, pad,
  parade, pasear, *pass(age), path,
  patrol, peg, perambulate, pere-
  grinate, plod, prance, promenade, ramble, ramp, *range, reel,
  *road, roam, roll, round, route,
  saunter, scuffle, shuffle, slog,
  *sphere, stalk, stamp, status,
  straddle, stray, stretch, stride,

stroll, strut, stump, toddle, totter,
  track, trail, traipse, tramp, tread,
  *turn, wade, wag, wander, *way
inability to: abasia
-on: bit part, role
-out: strike
over: *defeat, victory, *win
WALL: barrier, *fort, fence
arena: spina
bracket: corbel
defensive: bailey, ballium
-eyed pike: blowfish, dore, pick-
  erel, puffer, swellfish
flower: bloody warrior, keiri
handwriting: mene, tekel, upharsin
hanging: *picture, *tapestry
part: bahut, copping, cornice,
  gable, panel, pier, plinth, template, templet, wainscot
pert.: mural, parietal
WALLABA: apa, arawak, eperua
WALLABY: brush kangaroo
WALLAH: *agent, *servant
WALLET: alforja, *bag, bouge
WALLOP: *hit, *strike, *whip
WALLOW: grovel, pitch, roll
WALLY: *fine, *splendid, *strong
WALNUT: *husk:* bolster
skin: hull, shell, zest
tree, changed into: carya
WALRUS: bruta, edentata, morse
herd: pinnipedia, pod
WALTZ: boston, valse, vienna
WAMARA: brown ebony, coffee-
  wood
WAMBLE: change, *oscillate
W A M P U M : cowrie, *money,
  peage, roanoke, seawan, sewan
WAN: ashen, *sad, *weak
WAND: *staff, *stick, *symbol
WANDER: *err, *range, *walk
WANDERER: nomad, *vagabond
WANDEROO: macaque
WANE: *decline, fade, recede
WANGA: *fetish, *magic, *spell
WANGLE: *plot, *trick, wag

WANT: *fail, *need, *short

WANTON: animal, *arrogant, aspasia, *bad, bona roba, cadgy, carnal, chippy, chowlah, cocotte, concubine, concupiscent, dally, delilah, demimond(aine), demi-rep, dissipate, doxey, doxy, drab, easy, extravagant, fallen, fla-grant, floozy, frail, *free, frisky, frolic(some), grisette, hetaera, hussy, immoral, impish, incon-stant, jade, jezebel, lais, lascivi-ous, lavish, lecherous, lewd, *liberal, libertine, *light, loose, lorette, lubricious, lustful, mere-tricious, messalina, mopsy, para-mour, phryne, pickup, piece, *play, prodigal, *prostitute, pru-rient, pushover, rampant, *rank, *reckless, sensual, slack, slut, sport, strumpet, tart, thais, trifle, trull, vulgar, wench, *wild

WAP: *fight, *storm, *strike

WAPITI: deer, elk, stag

WAR: *contest, *fight, *hell
cry: aboo, abu, alala, aux armes, banzai, beauseant, tora, warison, whoop
engine or machine: *engine: war
god: anhur(-shu), ares, assur, asur, coel, dagda, enyalius, indra, ira, irra, koel, mamers, mars, ment, mont, montmenthu, nergal, odin, ophois, quirinus, sutekh, thor, tiu, tyr, woden
goddess: alea, anahita, anath, anunit, athena, bella, bellona, belona, enyo, ishtar, minerva, neith, sekhmet, vacuna
-mouth: black sunfish
pert.: belligerent, military

WARBLE: carol, trill, yodel
fly: botfly, cattle grub

WARD: area, guard, heir, *jail, *part, precinct, repel, watch

WARDEN: alcayde, castellan, cus-todian, goalie, keeper

WARDER: *staff, *stick

WARDROBE: armoire, trousseau

WARE: china, *ready, *wise
-house: depot, etape, storage

WARM: alive, amorous, *angry, *ardent, balmy, bask, beek, char-ismatic, clement, comfortable, enthusiastic, excite, *fire, genial, glowing, grateful, haimisher, *hot, humid, *mad, mild, muggy, *near, sincere, summery, sunny, sympathetic, temperate, tender, tepid, thermal, toasty, tropic

WARMTH: *anger, *passion

WARN: *advise, *alarm, *tell

WARNING: jiggers, *mark, *sign
formal: *alarm, caveat, sos
sound: alarum, siren, tocsin
system: antenna, bmews, dew

WARP: *end, *hurt, *spoil, *turn

WARRAGAL: dingo, myall, *wild

WARRANT: *pass, *promise, *right

WARRIOR: *soldier

WART: acrochordon, *bit, ecphyma, sycoma, tumor, ver-ruca
-cress: carara, coronopus

WARWICK: *horse:* black saladin

WARY: *quick, *shy, *wise

WASH: clean, lave, purge, tye

WASHINGTON: *city:* aberdeen, anacortes, bellingham, bremer-ton, everett, olympia, pasco, se-attle, spokane, tacoma, walla walla, yakima
flower: western rhododendron
nickname: evergreen state
portraitist: stuart
river: columbia, quinault, sno-homish, snoqualmie, yakima
sound: puget, rosario
state bird: willow goldfinch
tree: cherry, fanleaf, hemlock
volcano: rainier

WASP: hornet, jiga, vespid, whamp
genus: bembex, sphex

* Asterisk means to look up this word to find more answer words.

nest: bike, bink
pert.: vespal, vespine
WASSAIL: **drink, *tear*
WASTE: **destroy, *dregs, *eat,*
 *refuse, *ruin, *spoil, *use
allowance: tret
WASTED: **low, *poor, *weak*
WASTREL: prodigal, **vagabond*
WATCH: **look, *mark, *spy*
 -man: argus, cerberus, chokidar,
 guard, heimdallr, mina, scout,
 sentinel, sentry, sereno, super,
 vedette, warden
 part: face, hand, stem
 word: **adage, *cry,* slogan
WATCHFUL: **afraid, *ready*
WATER: *ash:* agrimony, fraxinus
 bag: chagul
 betony: bishop's-weed, broom-
 wort
 bird: auk, bidcock, coot, dipper,
 diver, gallinule, gull, loon, osprey, ousel, pelican, thrush
 boatman: backswimmer, corixa
 body: bahr, bay, gulf, lagoon,
 lake, ocean, pond, pool, sea
 buffalo: bubalus, carabao, ox
 carrier: aquarius, bheestie
 cavy: capybara
 centipede: hellgrammite
 chestnut: caltrap, caltrop, ling
 chicken: gallinule
 chickweed: blinks
 chinquapin: bonnet
 clock: clepsydra
 cock: kora
 -color: aquarelle, painting
 comb.: aqueo, aqui, aquo
 cooler: icer, olla, refrigerant
 -craft: **boat, *ship, *vessel*
 -cress: brassica, perro, roripa
 crow: coot, snakebird
 crowfoot: buttercup, herb
 cure: hydrotherapy
 deer: chevrotain
 deficiency: anhydremia
 dipper: calabash

dock: bloodwort
element: hydrogen, oxygen
elephant: hippopotamus
-fall: cascade, cataract, linn
father: mississippi
fennel: belder root, oenanth
gauge: bathometer, fluviograph,
 hydrometer, marigraph, nilometer, udometer
germander: mint
glass: clepsydra, goblet, tumbler
god: ahti, ahto, **sea: god*
goddess: anahita, anaitis, **sea:*
 goddess
grampus: hellgrammite
hawthorn: aponogeton, pondweed
hemlock: brook tongue, cicuta
hickory: bitter pecan
hog: bush pig, capybara
hole: alberca, **oasis,* pool
leaf: brook flower
lift: **water: wheel*
lily: bobbin, calla, candock, lotus,
 nelumbo, nenuphar, nuphar,
 nymphaea, wocas, wokas
living in: amphibian, aquatic,
 lenitic, lotic
-mark: flood mark, plimsoll line
measurement: acre-foot
melon: anguria, citrul, cucumis,
 gourd, sandia
meter: venturi
mill: clow
mineral: pullna, selter(s), seltzer,
 shasta, vichy
mint: ammi, bishop's-weed, brook
 mint, goutweed, wood betony
moccasin: snake, viper
mold: aphanomyce
neck: strait
nymph: ariel, asparas, crena,
 galatea, hydriad, kelpie, kelpy,
 limnad, naiad, nereid, nix, nixie,
 oceanid, pegae, rusalki, sprite,
 undine
on the brain: hydrocephalus
ousel: bird, dipper, thrush

* Asterisk means to look up this word to find more answer words.

parsnip: sium
pepper: biting knotweed
pert.: aquatic, hydatoid, marine
pig: capybara, gourami
pipe: hooka(h), nargile
plant: alga, lotus, sudd, trapa
plug: faucet, fireplug, hydrant, spigot, tap
pocket: tinaja
rail: bidcock, rallus
rat: arvicola, muskrat, thief, vole
receptacle: basin, bucket, pail
reservoir: cenote, dam, lake
sapphire: iolite
-shed: crest, ridge
sheet: nappe
shield: brasenia
skin: matara
snake: hydrus, moccasin
sound: plash, splash
speedwell: brook pimpernel
spirit, sprite: *water: nymph
-spout: *storm, *waterway
spouting: waikiki
starwort: callitriche, grass
substance: baregin, glairin
surface: ryme
vessel: aam, aftaba, banga, basin, bottle, bucket, canakin, cannikin, canteen, carafe, cowl, croft, cruse, ewer, flash, goglet, jug, lota(h), olla, pail, pitcher, stamnos, tinaja
-way: acequia, aguador, aqueduct, arroyo, bahr, basin, bayou, bed, billabong, bogue, bourn(e), brook, burn, canada, canal, canyon, channel, chute, cleft, conduit, cove, creek, dhoon, dike, ditch, donga, drain, dyke, flume, foss(e), furrow, gap, geo, gio, glen, gorge, groove, gulch, gully, gutter, hondo, khor, kill, lade, levee, linn, millstream, moat, nullah, *oasis, *opening, pipe, race, ravine, relais, ria, rill, rio, river, rivulet, run, runlet, run-

nel, sike, sluice, spruit, stream, trench, vale, valley, wadi, wady, yora, zanja
weed: duckweed, pondweed
wheel: danaide, kiyeh, noria, pump, ram, sakieh, sakiyeh, shadoo(f), taboot, tympanum
wort: elatine
WATERED: moire, wet
WATERING: *place:* aguada, baden, bar, baths, battis, *oasis, pool, pump, resort, *saloon, spa, spring, well
pot shell: aspergilla, brechite
WATERLESS: *comb.:* anydr(o)
WATERY: *thin, *weak, wet
WATTLE: acacia, barbel, blue bush, caruncle, dewlap, gill, saltbush, *stick, *whip
-tree: acacia, boree, callicoma, cooba(h), myall, silverleaf
honeyeater: iao, manuao
WAUGH: faint, insipid, *weak
WAVE: *display, *oscillate
comb.: ondo
WAVER: change, *oscillate, *turn
WAX: *fat, *increase, *polish
-bill: amadavat, astrild, avadavat, estrilda
candle: bougie
comb.: cer(a)
gourd: ash pumpkin
moth: galleria, pyralid
myrtle: arrayan, candleberry
myrtle bark: bayberry
palm: carnauba, copernica
pert.: ceral, cerate
-wing: bohemian chatterer
WAXY: *mad, *soft, yielding
WAY: ambage, bypath, calle, cut, *disposition, *distance, *doctrine, entrance, fashion, *form, habit, *instrument, manner, modus operandi, *order, *pass, passage, *plan, process, progress, railroad, *range, *rite, *road, *rule, scheme, *sphere, *style,

---

* Asterisk means to look up this word to find more answer words.

*system, terrace, track, *turn, *usage, *waterway, wise, wont

WAYWARD: *obstinate, *wanton

WEAK: adynamic, amyous, anemic, anile, asthenic, bauch, brittle, compliant, debile, debilitated, decrepit, dissolute, droopy, *dull, effete, exhausted, faded, feckless, fickle, flabby, flaccid, frail, gone, imbecile, impotent, infirm, languorous, lax, *light, limber, *low, marrowless, pale, peccable, pithless, powerless, puny, sapless, *simple, slack, *soft, *thin, unsound, *vague, *vain, wan, watery, wayward, worn

comb.: asthen(o)

fish: acoupa, cynoscion, squeteague, totuava

WEAKEN: *decline, *dull, *fail, *reduce, *sap, *thin, undermine

WEAKLING: chicken, coward, sissy

WEAL: *mark, *ridge, *state

WEALTH: *money, *plenty, *store, *supply, treasure, *value

comb.: pluto

god: bhaga, plutus, tsai-shen

goddess: shree, shri, sri

WEALTHY: *full, *rich, *solid

WEAPON: *gun, *spear, *sword

WEAR: carry, *decline, *display, *dress, *show, *spoil, *use

WEARISOME: *dull, *stupid

WEARY: *plague, *sad, *weak

willie: idler, laggard, tramp

WEASEL: ermine, ferret, ratel

cat: linsang

words: *nonsense

WEATHER: elements, *force, *wear

gauge: barometer, sonde

map line: isobar

-proof: *secure

WEAVE: *join, *make, *unite

WEAVER: bird: baya, bittern, boonk, botaurus, bottle bump,

maya, munia, taha

bobbin: pirn

reed: sley

WEAVING: goddess: ergane

product: textile

term: beam, beer, bobbin, caaming, cop, evener, lappet, lathe, lay, lease, lisse, loom, neck, plexure, ravel, shuttle, sley, uni, woof

WEB: filament, net, *plot, tela, *trap, *trick, vexillum

-footed animal: beaver, hydromys

-footed bird: albatross, avocet, duck, goose, loon, platypus

-maker: spider, spineret

pert.: palmate, retiary, telary

WED: *join, *tie, *unite

WEDDING: anniversary: bronze, candy, china, copper, coral, cotton, crystal, diamond, emerald, flower, fruit, golden, iron, ivory, lace, leather, linen, paper, pearl, pottery, sapphire, silk, silver, steel, tin, willow, wooden, wool

canopy: chuppa, huppa

gift: dot, dow(e)ry, mahr

symbol: band, rice, ring

WEDGE: angle, bar, cam, chock, coign, cotter, cuneus, fix, froe, gib, glut, gore, gusset, jam, key, quoin, shim, sprag

pert.: cuneal, cuneate, cuneiform, sphenoid

WEE: *little, *small, tiny

WEED: cigar, cultivate, *dress, darnel, herb, plantain, tare

WEEDS: clothes, *dregs, *refuse

WEEDING: machine: aberuncator

WEEK: hebdomad, ouk, sennet, sennight, swueak

-day: feria

feast: pentecost, shabuoth

intervals: octan, septan

two: fortnight

WEEP: *cry, lament, mourn, sob

WEEPING: *philosopher:* heraclitus
  spruce: brewer's spruce, picea
  statue: niobe
  willow: babylonian willow
WEEVER: catfish, trachinus draco
WEEVIL: anthonomus, beetle, boll, calandra, curculio, lota
WEFT: film, texture, warp, woof
WEIGH: *support, *think, *value
  anchor: launch, *open, *start
WEIGHT: *quantity, *power, *value
  allowance: bug, tare, tret
  comb.: baro
  equal: isobaric
  perception: barognosis
  pert.: baric
WEIGHTY: *big, *heavy, *large, *severe, solemn, *solid, valid
WEIR: bank, burrock, dam, *trap
WEIRD(O): awful, *bizarre, deathly, *eccentric, eerie, eery, eldritch, *fate, *fetish, foretell, macabre, *magic, *predict, spectral, *spell, spookish, spooky, uncanny, unco, unearthly, *wild
WELCOME: *good, greet, hail
WELD: *join, solder, *unite
WELFARE: charity, prosperity
WELKIN: air, heaven, sky
WELL: *fair, *good, healthy
  -*armed:* *ready
  -*being:* health, success
  born, bred: *gentle, *noble
  -*built:* *solid, *strong
  comb.: agath(o), bene, eu
  curb: puteal
  -*done:* bien, bravo, bully, euge, *good, ole, overcooked
  -*fixed:* *rich, wealthy
  -*groomed:* chic, *sharp, *smart
  -*head:* *source, *spring
  -*heeled:* *rich, loaded
  known: famous, notorious
  lining: stean, steen
  -*nigh:* almost, nearly

-*off:* *fat, *rich, *set
-*qualified:* *able, capable
-*to-do:* *fat, *rich, *set
-*versed:* *sharp, *smart
WELLINGTON: *charger:* copenhagen
WELSH: cambrian, cymric, shirk
  bard: aneurin, merlin, ovate, taliessin
  cheese: caerphilly
  city: aberdare, amlweh, bangor, caerleon, caernarvon, cardiff, hereford, holyhead, kidderminster, pembroke, rhondda, swansea
  dog: cardigan, corgi
  drake: gadwale, gadwell
  fine: saraad
  floral emblem: leek
  god(dess): *celt: god(dess)
  island: anglesey, caldy
  lake: bala
  law: galanas
  marriage fee: amober
  measure: cantref, cover, crannoc, lestrad, listred
  musical assembly: eisteddfod
  musical instrument: pibcorn
  name pref.: caer
  onion: cibol
  people: brython, cambrian, celt, cymry, kymry, silures, taffies
  person: taffy
  prince, legend: idris, madoc
  servant: aillt
  tribe: awabakal
  utopia: annfwn, annwn
  zone: olenus
WELT: *edge, *limit, *ridge, strip, *trouble, *whip
WELTER: *oscillate, *upset
WEN: cyst, talpa, *tumor
WENCH: damsel, girl, *wanton
WEND: *pass, slav, *turn, *walk
WENT: *road, *way, yode
WENZEL: jack, knave

* Asterisk means to look up this word to find more answer words.

WEREWOLF: loup-garou, lycan-thrope, uturuncu
WERGILD: blood money, cro, eric
WESKIT: benjy, vest, waistcoat
WESSEX: *king:* inex, ini
WEST AFRICAN: ashantee
baboon: drill, wood
fiber: bolo bolo
monkey: mona, patas, potto
plant: esere
reedbuck: nagor
sheep: zenu
tree: abura, akee, almique, bu-binga, bumbo, daniella, dide-lotia, manilkara, mitragyna, odum
WEST INDIES: *aroid:* tania
bark tonic: canella
bayberry: ausu, auzu
bird: ani, arar, mucaro, tody
boat: catamaran, droger
cactus: barbados gooseberry, blade apple, bull sucker, opuntia, pereskia
carriage: kittereen
charm: obeah, obi
coal island: caicos
coin: anchor money, daler
drum: bamboula, bongo, gumby
evergreen: calaba
fish: atinga, bacalao, bang, banner pompano, bessy cerka, boga, burfish, carbonero, cero, cling-fish, elephotoxon, marian, paru, pegador, pelon, peto, picudilla, pintado, robalo, ronco, scirenga, sesi, tang, testar, trachinotus, triggerfish
flatfish: acedia
flea: chigoe, chigre
food fish: blackfin snapper
fruit: genipap, papaya, pawpaw
gastropod: bleeding tooth
gaulin: egret, heron
gherkin: bur cucumber, cucumis
grunt: lobotes, tripletail
herb: ass's-foot, coltsfoot

idol: zeme, zemi
indian: carib
insect: fourmi-fou
island: anguilla, antilles, aruba, bahamas, barbados, barbuda, cuba, dominica, grenada, guade-loupe, haiti, hispanola, jamaica, nevis, puerto rico, tobago, trini-dad
king: cacique
liquor: mobbie, mobby, rum, taf-fia, tafia
lizard: ameiva, anoli, arbalo
locust: algaroba, algarroba
magic: obeah, obi
magician: quimboiseur
mistletoe: gadbush
music: calypso
myrtle: ausu, bayberry
orchid: purple lips
palm: grigri, grugru, yagua, yuray
people: carib, creole, ebo(e), gul-lah, taino
pert.: antillean, caribbean
plant: redwithe
plum: jobo
raiders: brethren of the coast
region: malabar
remora: pega
rodent: agouti, hutia, jutia
sardine: bang
scrapper: caji
shark: gata
sheephead: salema
shrub: anil, annatto, basket hoop, bay lavender, cassava, croton, ebo(e), inga, joewood
snake: fer-de-lance
sugar works: usine
sweetheart: doudou
taro: tania
tortoise: hicatee, hiccatee
tree: acana, acapu, aceituna, al-macigo, almique, aloe, angelin, aralie, ausu(bo), balata, balsa, bayberry, bay rum, black cinna-mon, black fig, bonace, bustic,

***** Asterisk means to look up this word to find more answer words.**

cabbage, candlewood, cera, china tree, cockspur, cocullo, cocuswood, cocuyo, drumwood, genip, gomart, gumbo limbo, gwazuma, incense cedar, libidi, loblolly, mastic tree, papaw, papaya, pawpaw, ramoon, ribbonwood, sapodilla, sapote, wild clove, yucca

treewood: galba

vine: basketwood, byrony

volcano: pelee

WEST POINT: *island:* lona

mascot: mule

student: cadet, plebe, yearling

WEST QUEEN: athyr, hathor

WEST SAXON: *earl:* godwin

WEST VIRGINIA: *bird:* cardinal

flower: bog rhododendron

nickname: mountain state

tree: sugar maple

WESTERN: fiction, hesperian, horse opera, oater, occidental

bluebird: mexicana occidentalis

range horse: broom tail

wheat grass: andropogon, blue joint, dwarf palmetto

WET: *crazy, damp, dank, dewy, drench, *drink(er), *drunk, foggy, humid, *immerse, *insane, lax, *mad, mire, moist(ure), off, perspire, rain(y), ret, saturate, soak, sopping, splash, sprinkle, sweat, tipsy, uvid, wat, *wrong

-back: bracero, peon, worker

bird: chaffinch

blanket: bore, drip, killjoy

WETHER: eunuch, ram, sheep, wool

WHACK: *beat, *hit, *part, *piece, *share, *try, *whip

WHACKING: *big, *great, *large

WHACKY: *insane, *weird, *wild

WHALE: abramus, balaena, baleen, basilosaurus, *beat, beluga, besugo, black bream, blower, bottlehead, bowhead, bream,

cachalot, cet(e), excel, finback, grampus, graso, humpback, huse, kremy, leviathan, lick, mammal, marsoon, orca, otary, poggy, ripsack, rorqual, scrag, sperm, spouter, *strike, *whip, whopper, zalophus, ziphian

-back: steamship

-bird: gull, petrel, phalarope, turnstone

-bone: baleen, *severe, stiff

carcass: krang, kreng

comb.: cet(o)

cry: fall

fat: blubber

food: brit, herring, sprat

group: gam, pod

-head: shoebill

nostril: blowhole

oil: sperm(aceti)

oil cask: cardel, rier

pert.: cetacean, cetic

secretion: ambergris

shark: mhor

-ship visit: gam

skin: muktuk, sculp

sperm: cachalot

strip blubber from: flense

sucker: remora

tail part: fluke

young: calf, shorthead, stunt

WHALING: *big, *great, *large

WHANG: *piece, *strike, *throw

WHANGEE: bamboo, *stick

WHARF: dock, jetty, pier, quay

fish: cunner

WHATNOT: etagere, *thing

WHEAL: *mark, *ridge, suppurate

WHEAT: durra, emmer, spelt, suji

beard: awn

bird: lark

coat: bran

cracked: groat, semolina

crushed: bulgur, burgul

disease: aecia, black chaff, bunt, colbrand, ergot, fungus, rust, stinking smut

---

* Asterisk means to look up this word to find more answer words.

duck: baldpate, widgeon
ear: bill, bird, chack, chat, chick-
   ell, gorsehatch
middlings: semolina
WHEEDLE: cajole, coax, entice
WHEEL: bike, circle, *turn,* vip
   comb.: troch(o)
   ore: bouronite, sulphide
   part: arbor, axle, cam, cog, felloe,
      felly, hob, hub, nave, rim, rowel,
      shoe, spoke, sprag, sprocket,
      strake
   pert.: rotate, rotiform
WHEELER DEALER: *big: shot*
WHEEZE: *joke,* *trick*
WHELK: pimple, pustule, snail
WHELP: boy, cub, dog, pup, rogue
WHERENESS: ubiety
WHET: incite, sharpen, *stir*
   -stone: bur(r), novaculite
WHEWL: *cry,* howl, whine
WHEY: fluid, serum
WHICKER: bleat, neigh, whinny
WHIFF: *bit,* *smell,* waft, wind
WHIFFLE: *oscillate,* *turn*
WHILE: albeit, interim, *pass*
WHILOM: erst, once, past
WHIM: *bit,* idea, *trifle*
   having: vagatonic
WHIMPER: *complain,* *cry*
WHIMSICAL: *funny,* *eccentric*
WHIMSY: *whim*
WHIN: furze, gorse, whun
WHINE: *complain,* *cry,* yammer
WHINNOCK: *complain,* *cry*
WHINNY: bray, neigh
WHIP: *agitate,* azote, black
   snake, cast, cat-o'-nine-tails, chi-
   cote, churn, cream, crop, *de-
   feat,* dick, emulsify, expediter,
   flagellate, flail, foam, froth,
   goad, hasten, *hit,* *hurt,* knout,
   koorbash, kurbash, pound, *punish,* quirt, scourge, sjambok,
   stick, *stir,* *strike,* swinge,
   switch, *torment,* *urge,* wale,
   wallop, whale, whisk

WHIR: *whirr*
WHIRL: *try,* *turn,* *walk*
   wind: cyclone, *storm,* tornado
WHIRR: *move,* *speed,* *turn*
WHISK: *speed,* *whip*
   broom: ringe
WHISKEY: bourbon, hooch, liquor, poteen, rotgut, usquebauch
WHISPER: *gossip,* *report,* *talk*
WHIST: game, *quiet,* silence
   hand: tenace, yarborough
   term: grand, misere, slam, solo
WHISTLE: *duck:* goldeneye
   pig: ground hog, woodchuck
   stop: campaign, village
WHIT: *bit,* *small: amount*
WHITE: *fair,* *good,* *happy,*
   honest, ivory, *pure,* truth
   ant: anai, anay, termite
   antimony: vanentinite
   cap: crest, wave
   cell: leukocyte
   clay: bolus alba, kaolin
   cockatoo: abacay, calangay
   comb.: alb(o), leuc(o)
   crow: vulture
   curema: blueback mullet
   elephant land: burma, ceylon, in-
      dia, siam, thailand
   ermine: lasset, miniver
   -eye: blight bird, zosterops
   fish: atinga, bloater, bowback,
      buffaloback, cisco, coreponus,
      lavaret, menhaden, pilan, pollan,
      vendace
   flag: surrender, truce, *yield*
   friar: alsatian, carmelite
   gentian: feverroot
   goods: bedding, linen, sheets
   grouse: ptarmigan
   horse nettle: trompillo
   house designer: hoban
   indian hemp: milkweed
   iron pyrites: marcasite
   jade: alabaster
   latifolia: bladder campion
   lead: blanc d'argent, ceruse

* Asterisk means to look up this word to find more answer words.

lettuce: cancer-weed
man: buckra, cachila, paragon
mapau: carpodetus, escalloniace
marble: carrara, dolomite
mica: muscovite
monk: cistercian
mule: gin, moonshine, whiskey
plague: consumption, phthisis, tuberculosis
plantain: pussy's toes
pyrite: marcasite
sanicle: snakeroot
shell: pupu kea
-side: goldeneye
slave: *prostitute, *wanton
snipe: avocet, sanderling
spruce: cat pine, epinette
stuff: *drug, morphine
sturgeon: beluga, hausen, whale
-thorn: mayflower
-throat: babillard
tree: cajeput, paperbush, punk
walnut: shagbark, sycamore
-wash: acquit, blanch, calcimine, *defeat, *hide
water lily: bobbin, cuckoopint
weed: daisy
-wing: chaffinch, sail, scoter
-wood: canary wood, canella
zebu: brahmany bull
WHITEN: bleach, etiolate
WHITLOW: *criminal, hangnail
grass: draba
-wort: anychia
WHITTLE: *reduce, *remove
WHOA: holla, pruh, *stop
WHOLE: *all, *perfect, *well
comb.: al, all, tot(i), toto
WHOOP: *cry, *praise, *urge
WHOOPING: *cough:* pertussis
WHOP: *hit, *strike, *throw
WHOPPER: *lie, *story
WHOPPING: *big, *great, *large
WHORE: *prostitute, *wanton
WHORL: coil, spiral, *turn
WHYO: *criminal, hoodlum, *thief
WICKED: *bad, *evil, *wrong

WICKIUP, WIKIUP: *hut, shelter
WIDGEON: baldpate, bluebill, duck, *fool, marica, smew, whim
WIDOW: almona, dowager, suttee
share: *gift, mite, terce
veil: bandore
WIELD: *power, *rule, *use
WIG: *rally, *scold, toupee
WIGWAM: *hut, tent, tepee
WILD: abandoned, absurd, agrestal, amuck, *ardent, barbarous, blatant, breachy, *brutal, cerrero, desolate, different, dissolute, distraught, dramatic, *drunk, *eager, *eccentric, excited, *extreme, fanciful, ferocious, *great, licentious, *mad, meshugge, native, natural, prodigal, profligate, rampageous, ree, tumultuous, turbulent, uncivilized, unruly, *violent, visionary, waste, *weird
alder: goutweed
arum: cuckoopint
banana: papaw, pawpaw
box: indigo, inkberry, randia
carrot: bird's-nest, hilltrot
chervil: ass parsley, hemlock
cinnamon: barbasco, canella
coffee: feverroot
comb.: agrio
crocus: pasqueflower
hog: babiroussa, peccary
honeybee: angelito, dingar
irishman: tumatakura
jalap: mayapple
kale: charlock, radish
lettuce: butterweed
man: maniac, yahoo, yanigan
masterwort: goutweed
musk: alfilaria
mustard: charlock
olive tree: oleaster
pink: carolina catchfly
plantain: balisier
pumpkin: calabazilla
radish: cadlock

* Asterisk means to look up this word to find more answer words.

rye: canada lyme grass
sage: clary
succory: chicory
sweet pea: catgut, goat's-rue
thyme: brotherwort, pennyroyal
valerian: avens, bennet, burnet
WILDE: *pen name:* melmoth
WILE: **deception, *plot, *trick*
WILL: **appetite,* behest, bequest, command, conation, **decide, *decision,* design, **desire,* determination, **disposition,* fancy, intention, opt, **order, *passion,* pleasure, **power,* prefer, **purpose,* testament, velleity, volition, vote, wish
  appendix: codicil
  beneficiary: devisee
  comb.: bulia
  loss: abulia
  maker: devisor
WILLFUL: **mad, *obstinate*
WILLIAM: *tell canton:* uri
  final home: caen
  half brother: odo
  the conqueror's daughter: adela
WILLING: **eager, *ready*
WILLOW: bahan, edder, itea, iva, osier, salix, sallow, **trap*
  basket: prickle
  catkin: ament, rag, spike
  hat: salacot
  plaited: wicker
  twig: sallow, withe
  warbler: bank jug
  wren: chiffchaff
WILLY-NILLY: bon gre, cyclone, mal gre, tornado, wagtail
WILSON'S: *thrush:* bird, veery
  snipe: cache-cache
  warbler: blackcap
WILY: **astute, *smart, *sly*
WIN: **accomplish, *acquire, *allure,* attain, beat, best, captivate, capture, carry, charm, conciliate, **defeat,* drub, earn, entice, **get,* influence, prevail, **secure, *suc-*

ceed, **take,* vanquish, victory
WIND: afflatus, **air,* blast, blow, breeze, coil, contort, corkscrew, crinkle, crook, curl, current, draft, draught, escallop, exhalation, flaw, flurry, gust, inhalation, meander, scallop, **scent,* screw, scud, serpentine, sim, sinuate, squall, **storm,* twine, twirl, twist, vine, whorl, worm, **wrap*
  comb.: anemo
  -fall: blessing, bonanza, boon, buckshee, **gift,* godsend, jackpot, luck
  famous: afer, afghanet, barat, belat, bentu de soli, bise, bohorok, bora, boreas, brick fielder, briza, brubu, bruscha, buran, burga, buster, cape doctor, caurus, chinook, etesian, eurus, favonius, foehn, gregale, harmattan, kabibonokka, kamsin, khamsin, kona, leste, levant, mistral, mudjekeewis, notus, pampero, ponente, puna(leste), puno, samiel, santa ana, santana, sarsar, shawondasee, simoom, siroc(co), solano, sures, tedbad, tramontane, vayu, vendaval, wabun, zephyr
  father: astraeus
  flow: flurry
  flower: anemone, gentian
  god: adad, adda, adou, aeolus, afer, argestes, astraeus, boreas, caecias, caurus, erus, eurus, favonius, kaare, kabibonokka, mudjekeewis, njord, notus, shawondasee, vayu, wabun, zephyrus
  -hover: kestrel
  pert.: aeolian, eolian
  -pipe, comb.: bronchi, tracheo
  shake: anemosis
  tree: bitterwood
WINDOW: eye, fenestra, **light, *opening,* oriel, transom
  part: came, casing, frame, lead-

ing, ledge, mouse, mullion, muntin, pane, sash, sill, transom
pert.: fenestral
worker: glazier
WINDROW: furrow, swathe, trench
WINE: ambrosia, ichor, nectar
aroma: seve
-berry: bilberry, gooseberry, makomako, raspberry
bottle: *bottle: sizes, small,* boxbeutel, carafe, fiasco
broker: courtier
bucket: cooler, icer
cask: boss, butt, leaguer, pipe, tun
collection: cellar
comb.: oen(o)
component: stum
concoction: negus
cruet: burette
cup: ama, amula, chalice, goblet
delicacy: seve
deposit: argol, griffe, tartar
disease: casse
dregs: marc, salin, vinasse
drink: clary, mulse, negus, punch
dry: brut, sack, sec
eucharist: krama
evaporation: ullage
expert: oenologist
film: beeswing
glass, extra: backhander
god: bacchus, dionysus, soma
golden: bual, sercial
honey and: mulse, oenomel
hot: negus
leather bag: askos, olpe
list: card, carte
lover: bacchant, oenophilist
maker: abkary, vigneron
new: must
of the country: vins de pays
palm: beno
pert.: vinic, vinous
region-named: generic
retailer: vintner

science: oenology
season: vintage
server: sommelier
-shop: bar, bistro, bodega, bush, cafe, estaminet, saloon
spiced: hippocras, sangaree
spirit: brandy, cognac
WING: ala, alette, annex, arm, *part, *piece, *speed, vane
cover: elytron
pert.: ala, alar, alary, alate, pteric, pteroid, pterotic
WINGED: aliferous, aligerous, *fast, pennate, pinnate
deity: amor, cupid, eros, hermes, mercury, nike
WINK: *look, nictate, signal
WINKING: blepharospasm
WINNOW: *analyze, *separate
WINSOME: blithe, gay, merry
WINTER: brume, hibernate
's-bark: canelo
-berry: black alder, canhoop, cassioberry, ilex
bloom: azalea
cherry: alkekengi
cress: bermuda, cassa bully
festival: brumalia
flounder: blackback
green: canada tea, pipsissewa, pyrola
melon: casaba
pear: seckel, warden
pert.: *wintry
squash: cushaw
WINTRY: arctic, boreal, brumal, cold, hibernal, hiemal, hyemal
WIPE: *beat, *deceive, *defeat, *destroy, *end, *kill, *ruin, *strike, swab, *trick
WIRE: cable, cord, line, litz, *note, *thief, *tie, *trap
brush: card
bundle: cable
cover: sull
cutters: pliers, secateur
foil: lametta

* Asterisk means to look up this word to find more answer words.

measure: mil, stone
platinum-looped: oese
service: ap, ins, reuters, upi
system: network, reticle
worm: agriotis, beetle, millepede,
    myriapod
WIRY: **hard, *quick, *strong*
WISCONSIN: *bird:* robin
    flower: pansy, wood violet
    nickname: badger state
    specialty: dairies
    tree: sugar maple
WISDOM: **knowledge, *sense*
    embodiment: achamoth
    god: ea(r), ganesa, ganesha, mi-
    mir, nabu, nebo, odin, sabu, sin,
    tat, thoth, toth
    goddess: athene, minerva, pallas,
    prudence, themis
    symbol: dragon
    tooth: molar
WISE: aware, circumspect, cogni-
    zant, deep, discreet, erudite, ex-
    pedient, explain, hep, inform(ed),
    judicious, omniscient, prudent,
    rational, sagacious, **sage*, sensi-
    ble, **sharp, *sly, *smart*, sound,
    *tell, wary, **way*
    -acre: fool
    -crack: **joke, *story*
    man: **greek: sages, *magi,* sage
WISH: **appetite, *need, *will*
    -bone: **fetish,* furculum
    -wash: **nonsense,* swill
WISHY-WASHY: **sick, *thin,*
    *weak
WISP: **bit, *small: amount*
WISTERIA: fuji, purple, violet
WIT: humor, **mind, *sense*
WITCH: acrasia, alp, babajaga,
    beldam(e), bruja, canidia, car-
    line, circe, **demon,* duessa,
    fright, grimalkin, **hag,* hecate,
    hellcat, hex, lamia, lilith, mara,
    medusa, ogress, shamaness, she-
    wolf, sibyl, siren, sorceress,
    termagant, tigress, weird sisters

city: endor, salem
craft: **fetish, *magic, *spell*
doctor: boolya, brujo, goofer,
    koradji, shaman, sorcerer
-hazel: hamamelis, hornbeam
male: **demon, *devil,* warlock
WITH: along, plus, through
    comb.: col, com, cyn, pro, syn
    -draw: **avoid, *remove, *quit,*
    surrender, **yield*
    -draw agent, comb.: agog(ue)
    -hold: **hide, *refuse, *stop*
    -in, comb.: end(o), ento, eso
    it: alive, groovy, stylish
    -out: empty, less, minus, void
    -out, comb.: ac, an, ect(o), se
    -stand: defy, endure, resist
WITHER: age, **fail,* shrink, wilt
WITLESS: **insane, *mad, *stupid*
WITNESS: **certificate, *see*
WITT: *planetoid:* eros
WITTICISM: gag, **joke,* quip
WITTY: **bright, *funny, *sharp*
WIZARD: **demon, *magician,*
    *sage, shaman, thaumaturgee
    voodoo: quimboiseur
WIZARDRY: **magic*
WOBBLE: **oscillate, *quiver*
WOE: **evil, *pain, *torture*
    -begone: **sad, *sorry*
    river: acheron
    -vine: cassytha, rhipsalis
WOLF: canine, libertine, lobo
    bane: aconite, monkshood
    -berry: buckbush, coralberry
    -fish: anarchichas, catfish
    -hound: alan, borzoi
    pert.: lupine, thooid
    sheep's clothing: **impostor*
WOLSEY: *birthplace:* ipswich
    death forseer: mother shipton
    son: thomas winter
WOLVERINE: carcajou, gulo
WOMAN: *adviser:* egeria
    apartment: boudoir, harem, oda,
    seraglio, thalamus, zenana
    beautiful: aphrodite, belle,

charmer, doll, filly, houri, man-
trap, musidora, peri, siren, sylph,
venus, zenobia
celibate: agapeta, vestal
deserted: agunah
extravagant: araminta
famous: anne royal, aspasia, caroline norton, cleopatra, delia bacon, delphine delamare, lady
emma hamilton, lady jane ellen-
borough, lais, marie duplessis,
pauline borghese, phryne, queen
maria luisa, valeria messalina
first: embla, eve, izanami
frenzied: maenad, menad
general: hays, hoisington
goddess: hera, juno, mut, sati
group: altrusa, amvs, circle, dar,
ebell, lib, pilot, quota, sister-
hood, soroptimist, sorority,
waac, wac, wave, wren, wsp
hater: misogynist
ill-tempered: *scold, *witch
kept: concubine, demimondaine,
inamorata, mistress, paramour
-kind: calico, distaff
lawyer: portia
lib leader: ellmann, friedan,
greer, lupscomb, millet, quigley,
steinem, vivrost
loose: *prostitute, *wanton
old: crone, *hag, *witch
personified: eimer, emer
pert.: female, feminine, gynecic,
gynaecic, mulebral
suffrage leader: anthony, catt,
mott, stanton, stone
warrior: amazon, camilla, joan
d'arc, valkyrie
WOMBAT: badger, marsupial
WONDER: *ace, admiration,
amazement, astonishment, awe,
dismay, doubt, dream, fantasy,
gape, *magic, marvel, meditate,
phenomenon, ponder, prodigy,
reverie, *sign, speculate, stare,
*study, suspect, *think, *top

berry: black nightshade, morel
land: *paradise, *utopia
land girl: alice
state: arkansas
WONDERFUL: *fine, *good,
*great, *splendid, *supreme,
*unique
WOO: *address, court, *spark
WOOD: forest, lumber, *tree
alcohol: methanol, methyl
ball: knot, knur
bane: aconite, monkshood
betony: beefsteak plant, bishops-
wort, water mint
billet: sprag
bine: cigar, creeper, honeysuckle,
jasmine, peridot
blemish: catface
block or brick: dook, nog
bowl: kitty, mazer
-chat: bird, shrike
-chopper, poor: ali baba
-chuck: marmot, moonack
-cock: becasse, bogsucker, peewee, pewee, rubicola, snipe
-cock group: fall
comb.: hylo, ligni, xylo
dark: ebony, teak
dye: brasilein
*god: *forest: deity
grass: bushy blue stem
grating: babracot
grove: nemora
-hen: weka(s)
hoopee: irrisor
hyacinth: bluebell, squill
-kern: *criminal, thief
light: balsa, cork, edder, osier,
willow
-louse: slater
lustrous: latine
nettle: albany hemp
nymph: arethusa, dryad, grayling
part or piece: batten, billet,
board, deal, dingbat, dowel, fid,
lath, nog, *peg, reglet, rig, shim,

* **Asterisk means to look up this word to find more answer words.**

slat, spile, splint, sprag, stave, tenon

-*pecker:* carpintero, chab, flicker, hickwall, iynx, ivory bill, picule, sapsucker, tapper, wryneck, yaffle, yunx

-*pecker-like bird:* jacamar

-*pecker, pert.:* picine

peg: bung, fid, skeg, spile, stopper, thole

pert.: arboreal, nemoral, treed

pore: lenticel

pussy: polecat, skunk

rot: doat

sacred: asherah

shoe: clog, geta, patten, sabot, secque

steward: woodreeve

striped: fleck, roe

thrush: bellbird, campanero

-*work:* boiserie, bratticing

-*worm:* termite

WOODEN: **dull, *firm, *hard, *solid, *stupid,* tense, vacant

WOODLAND: *deity: *forest: deity*

WOOL: *blemish:* mote

clean: garnett

cloth: *fabric: wool

cloth strainer: tamis, tammy

comb.: lani

deposit in: suint

detached lock: frib

dryer: fugal

fabric: *fabric: wool

fat: anaspalin, lanolin(e), suet, suint

fiber: nep, noil

implement: carder, comb, distaff, shears, spindle, teaser

inferior: brokes, cleamer, head

measure: butt, fadge, heer

pert.: fleecy, lanate, peronate

piece: cleamer, frib, tate

pulled: slipe

quality: blood

reclaimed: mungo, shoddy

refuse: backing, cot, fud

roll: carding, slub

sheep's leg: gare

sheets: batt(ing)

skirtings: broke

spun: yarn

twill: caddice, caddis

unravel: card, tease, tosy, tum

watered: moreen

yarn: abb, eis

WOOZY: **drunk,* muddled

WORD: **account, *adage, *advice, *gossip, *honor, *name, *order, *promise, *report, *talk*

blindness: alexia

book: cyclopedia, dictionary, lexicon, libretto, speller, thesaurus, vocabulary

combination: asyntactic

contraction: haplology

corresponding: analogue

cutting: apocope

deafness: aphasia

deletion: apocope

derived from another: paronym

division: syllable, tmesis

figurative use: metonym, trope

for word: literal, verbatim

formation: acronym, acrostic, analogue, antonym, heteronym, homonym, metonym, poecilonym, spoonerism, synonym

game: anagrams, categories, charades, coffeepot, ghosts, hangman, murder, observation, salvo, scrabble, testimony

history: etymology

imitative: echoic, onomatopoeia

improper use: solecism

initials, from: acronym

inventor: coiner, neologist

last: amen, selah, thirty

magic: abracadabra, eureka, presto, sesame

meaning: semantics

mishearing: otosis

misuse: catachresis, heterophemy, malapropism

---

* Asterisk means to look up this word to find more answer words.

mystical: anagoge
new: neologism, neoterism
omission: apocope, syncope
opposite meaning: antonym
order: morpheme
order inversion: anastrope
puzzle: acrostic, anagram, charade, crossword, rebus
repetition: anaphora, ploce
root: etym(on), radical
same backward and forward: palindrome
scrambled: anagram
separation: diacope, tmesis
sign: logogram
square: palindrome
substitute: metonym, trope
transposition: anagram
unifying: copula
vowel omission: aphesis
WORDS: *fight, *quarrel, *talk
WORK: *accomplish, *act, *action, arbeit, assignment, bother, bubble, business, calling, career, chore, drudge, duty, employment, ergon, fag, *ferment, *form, *fort, *forte, function, grind, grub, industry, *interest, job, labor, manipulate, manuscript, *memorial, moil, *monument, *move, operation, opus, pains, *plan(t), *produce, profession, *run, *slave, solve, stint, *strain, task, *trade, *use
comb.: erg(o)
house: *jail
out: *plan, *result
shop: atelier, mill, *plant
unit: calorie, erg(on), joule, kilerg, man-hour, megajoule
WORKER: hand, *servant, *slave
group: *force, *staff, union(ist)
migratory: arkie, boomer, bracero, gastarbeiter, hobo, oakie, wetback
WORLD: earth, globe, *sphere
serpent: ananta

soul: anima mundi
tree: yggdrasil
-wide: ecumenic, omnipresent, pandemic, planetary, universal
WORM: ess, fluke, inch, leech, loa, maggot, naid, nematode, reprobate, reptile, termite, *turn, wind, wriggle, writhe
pert.: helminthoid, vermian
-weed: pinkroot
-wood: absinthe, liquor, moxa
WORRY: *plague, *torment
WORSHIP: *admire, *adoration, awe, discipline, exalt, homage, *honor, *love, *praise, *prize, puja, revere(nce), ritual, serve, title, venerate
object: *fetish, idol
pert.: liturgic
place: altar, bethel, church, mosque, synagogue, temple
WORST: *bad, *defeat, terrible
WORTH: *account, *use, *value
WORTHLESS: *bad, *dregs, *evil, *idle, *insane, *low, *mean, paltry, *poor, *rotten, vile
WORTHY: *good, *honest, *noble
WOUND: *hurt, *pain, *pierce, puncture, stab, *tear
-wort: allheal
WOW: *amuse, *hit, success
WRACK: *dregs, kelp, *refuse, *ruin, seaweed, wreck
WRAITH: *demon, ghost, *spirit
WRANGLE: *argue, *contest, *fight, *quarrel, spar, spat
WRAP: barracan, bitt, boa, bob, cade, camlet, cape, cere, *cover, *dress, embrace, encompass, fold, furl, *hide, lap, overcoat, *pack(age), roll, shawl, sheath, shroud, surround, swaddle, swathe, veil, *wind
WRASSE: ballan, bluehead, cunner
WRATH: *anger, *passion, *storm
WREATH: garland, *token, *wrap

* Asterisk means to look up this word to find more answer words.

WRECK: *break, *hurt, *ruin
WRENCH: *hurt, *pain, *strain
WREST: *gather, *seize, *take
WRESTLE: *contest, *fight, *try
WRESTLING: place: palestra, ring
 ceremonial: sumo
 term: backheel, chancer, chip, click, fall, grapevine, half nelson, hank, hipe, hitch, hype, lock, mare, nelson, pin, scissors
WRETCH: loser, outcast, pariah
WRETCHED: *mean, paltry, *sad
WRIGGLE: *oscillate, *turn
WRING: *hurt, *press, *torture
WRINKLE: groove, *ridge, rumple
 covered with: alutaceous
 free from: erugate
WRIST: bone: capitatum, carpus, os magnum, ulna
 comb.: carpo
 guard: bracer
 mark: rasceta
 ornament: band, bracelet
 pert.: carpal
WRIT: *certificate, *order
WRITE: compose, *record
 inability: agraphia
WRITHE: *suffer, *turn
WRITING: *piece, *story, *study
 ancient: boustrophedon
 character: *sign, *word
 comb.: graph(o)
 demotic: hieroglyphics
 sacred: bible, koran, psalms, scripture, talmud, testament
WRONG: *abuse, agley, amiss, awry, *bad, *cheat, *crime, *err(or), *evil, *false, foul, haywire, *hurt, immoral, imposition, improper, inaccurate, inapt, incorrect, indecorous, iniquitous, injure, injustice, misdeed, mistaken, oppress, outrage, *poor, *rank, *rotten, *shame, *sin, tort, transgress(ion), undue, uneven, unfit, unjust, untrue, vice, villainy, wicked, wry
 comb.: mis
WROTH, WROUGHT UP: *mad, *upset
WRY: *obstinate, *turn, *wrong
 -mouth: blenny, ghostfish
 -neck: jynx, loxia, snakebird, torticollis, weet
WYCLIFFE: man: hussite, lollard
WYOMING: bird: meadowlark
 flower: indian paintbrush
 mountain: gannett, moran, teton
 nickname: equality state
 tree: cottonwood
WYSTAN: auden, poet

XANADU: prince: khan
 river: alph
XANTHINE: bloody
XANTHIPPE: *scold
 husband: socrates
XANTHIUM: arctium, burdock, canada thistle, cocklebur
XANTHOSOMA: blue eddoes, calalu, spoonflower
XENAGOGUE: guide
XENICUS: bush wren
XENIUM: *gift, *present
XENOPHON: attic muse
 teacher: isocrates
XEROPHYLLUM: bear grass, yucca
XIPHIAS: broadbill, swordfish
X-RAY: irradiate, *picture
 hardness measure: benoist scale
 inventor: roentgen
 picture: cathograph, radiograph
 principle: bragg's law
 science: roentgenology
X-SHAPED: chiasmal, cruciate
XUREL: saurel, scad
XUTHUS: consort: creusa
 son: achaeus, dorus
XYLEM: hadrome
XYLOID: ligneous, woody

* Asterisk means to look up this word to find more answer words.

XYLOPHONE: gambang, game-lang, gigelira, marimba, saron, sticcado, vibraharp

XYSTUS: porch, stoa, *walk

YABBI: dasyure, thylacine, wolf

YABBY: crayfish

YACHT: boat, race, sail, ship
pennant: burgee
term: aloft, astern, backwind, cheater, cover, guy, halyard, jib, lanyard, leeward, quarter, sheets, spinnaker, spitfire, staysail, tack, to weather

YAFFLE: bird, woodpecker

YAHOO: *clown, *peasant, savage

YAK: sarlak, *talk, zobo

YAKAMIK: trumpeter

YAKKA: labor, *work

YAKSHA: *demon, *dwarf, *spirit
offering: bali

YALE: bulldog, eli

YALTA: *palace:* livadia
sea: black, marmora

YAM: boniata, buckra, hoy, ig-name, inamia, kaawi, kama, po-tato, tugni, ube, ubi

YAMMER: *complain, *cry

YANG: *cry, honk
-kin: dulcimer
opposite: yin

YANK: blow, hoick, jerk, pull

YANKEE: american, northerner
bump: pothole
doodle: prince rupert

YAP: *complain, *cry, *eager, *hoodlum, *mark, *noise, *quick, *ready, *scold, *talk, yell, yelp
money: fei, stone

YARD: area, *staff, *stick
5½: rod
600: heer
16th: nail
220: furlong

YARM: *cry, wail, yell

YARN: boucle, crewel, *joke, *lie, *story, thread, tow
combing: noil
count: typp
quantity: clew, clue, cop, hank, hasp, spangle, skein
snarl: twit
waste: thrum
winder: pirner

YARR: growl, snarl, spurrey

YARROW: achillea, ahartalav, allheal, cammock, milfoil

YATAGHAN: balas, saber, *sword

YAULD: *active, *sharp, *strong

YAUP: *cry, shout, yarn, yelp

YAUPON: cassena, holly, ilex

YAW: *oscillate, *turn

YAWL: *cry, drane, vessel

YAWN: chasm, *opening, oscitate

YAWP: *complain, *cry

YAWS: frambesia, pian

YAYA: copa, lancewood

YCLEPT: called, named, styled

YEAR: *book:* almanac, annual
part: month, quarter, raith, sea-son, semester, trimester
solar excess: epact
1,000: chiliad, millennium

YEARLING: colt, hornotine, teg

YEARLY: annual, etesian

YEARN: *ache, *desire, *pain

YEAST: barm, *ferment, koji

YEGG: criminal, *hoodlum, *thief

YELL: *complain, *cry, *protest

YELLOW: acacia, amber, cowardly
alder: sagerose
alloy: aich, brass
avens: bennet, burnet, hemlock
beard: fer-de-lance
-bird: goldfinch
buckthorn: bog birch, rhamnus
bugle: eve, iva
butter: blake
canary: meline
clintonia: blueberry
comb.: luteo, xanth(o)

* Asterisk means to look up this word to find more answer words.

copper: chalcopyrite

copperas: copiapite

daisy: coneflower, rudbeckia

fever: black vomit, bulam

fever carrier: aedes, mosquito

fish: ide, orf(e)

flag: quarantine, warning

gentian: bitterwort, dandelion

hammer: finch, flicker, skite, woodpecker, yeldring, yite

hammer state: alabama

iris: sedge

jacket: hornet, nembutal

kings: orpiment

mustard: charlock

ocher: sil

parilla: canada moonseed

pert.: xanthic

quintonia: blue bead

river: hwangho

star: sneezeweed

starwort: elecampane

timber: aniba, bois de rose

wagtail: barleybird, nightingale

water lily: beaver root, bobbins, brandy-bottle, cuckoopint, numphar

YELLOWS: jeterus

YELP: *complain, *cry, *protest

YEMEN: *city:* dahhi, damar, mocha, mukha, sana

native: arab, yemeni

ruler: imam

YEN: *desire, *urge

YEOMAN: beefeater, *servant

YERK: *pierce, *strike, *throw

YET: again, and, before, still

YIDDISH: *hebrew references

YIELD: accede, *accept, acknowledge, acquisition, afford, aftermath, agree, appease, assent, avale, back down, be pliant, bend, bow, bring, buckle, capitulate, cede, cess, collapse, concede, contract, cost, crumple, defer, *fall, *fee, forfeit, fruit, furnish, *give, impart, *income,

lose, obey, output, *present, *produce, *product, *quit, relinquish, render, sag, soften, stoop, submit, succumb, *supply, *throw, vintage, waive

YIELDING: buxom, pliant, *soft

YIP(E), YIRM, YIRN, YIRR: *yelp

YMIR: *cow feeding:* audhum(b)la

slayer: odin, vili, woden

YODEL: call, carol, sing

YOGA: asceticism, bhakti, hatha, jnana, karma, mysticism

angas, three: dharana, dhyana, samadhi

posture: asana

practices: anga

trance: *posture, rapture

YOGI: *ascetic, *church:* man, jnani, mystic, swami

YOKE: *join, *tie, *union

comb.: zygo

-fellow: comrade, mate, partner, spouse, wife

part: bow, riem(pie), skey

YOKEL: *clown, *fool, *peasant

YOKELESS: alecithal

YOLD: shlemiel, *yokel

YORE: ago, before, erst, past

YOUNG: *fresh, new, offspring

god of: apollo, attis, attys

goddess of: hebe

YOW(L): *yelp

YTTRIUM: dysprosium, erbium, holmium, lutetium, thulium

YUCA: cassava, manioc

YUCATAN: *city:* merida, uxmal

drink: balche

tree: yaxche

YUCCA: adam's-needle, amole, bear grass, dasylirion, sotol

fiber: isote, izote

YUGOSLAV: croat, serb, slovene

city: agram, belgrade, beograd, bitolj, bosna, dubrovnik, llubljana, monastir, morava, mostar, nis(h), pirot, prilep, sarajevo,

---

* Asterisk means to look up this word to find more answer words.

sava, senta, skopje, subotica, trogir, varsac, zadar, zagreb
coin: dinar, para
commune: pec, stip, veles
drink: rakia, slivovitz
island: arbe
measure: akov, dan oranja, donum, khvat, lanaz, motyka, palaze, ralico, rif, stopa
river: danube, drava, drina, morava, sava, vardar
ruler: broz, peter, tito
secret service: udba
weight: dramm, oka, satlijk, tovar, wagon
YUM-YUM: consort: nankipoo
friend: nankipoo

ZABAD: son: ephlal
ZABBAI: son: baruch
ZAC: goat, ibex, zebuder
ZACATE: forage, grass, hay
ZACCHAEUS: innocent, *pure
ZACCUR: son: hanan, michaiah
ZADOK: daughter: jerushah
son: achim, ahimaaz, meshullam, salemus, shallum
ZAFTIG: buxom, juicy, plump
ZAIBATSU: monopoly, *trust
ZAL: relative, rustam
ZAMBAL: *malay(an)
ZAMBALES: *philippines
ZAMBIA: northern rhodesia
capital: lusaka
national park: luanga valley
ZAMINDAR: bhaiyachari, pattidari
ZANNI, ZANY: *clown, *fool
ZANZIBAR: *tanganyika
ZAP: *hit, shoot, *strike
ZARAEAS: son: eliaonias, mareroth
ZARATHUSTRA: *zoroaster
ZARF: cupholder, *stand
ZARZUELA: *hash, *mixture

ZATI: macaque, monkey
ZATTU: son: aziza, eliashib, elioenai, jeremoth, mattaniah
ZEAL: *desire, *fire, *force, *interest, *passion, *spirit
ZEALOT: *enthusiast, simon
ZEALOUS: *ardent, *eager, *warm
ZEBEDEE: consort: salome
son: boanerges, james, john
ZEBOIIM: king: shemeber
ZEBRA: dauw, quagga
swallow tail: ajax butterfly
tailed lizard: callisaurus
wood: araroba, marblewood, myrtle, naked wood
ZEBU: brahmany bull, yak, zobo
ZECHARIAH: child: abijah, jahaziel, john, joiarib, uzziah
wife: elizabeth
ZEDEKIAH: eunuch: ebedmelech
parent: hamutal, hasadiah, josiah
son: mahseiah
ZEME, ZEMI: *fetish, *spirit
ZEN: founder: bodhidharma
master: roshi
ZENANA: harem, seraglio
ZENITH: *acme, apogee, *top
ZENO: follower: stoic
ZEPHYR: aura, breeze, wind
consort: chloris, podarge
son: balius, carpus, xanthus
ZERO: blank, love, nihil, zilch
ZERUAH: son: jeroboam
ZERUBABBEL: son: abuid, berechiah, hananiah, hasadiah, hashubah, jushab-hesed, meshullam, ohel, rhesa
ZERUIAH: son: abishai, asahel
ZEST: gusto, kick, *spirit, *zip
ZESTFUL: *ardent, *eager, gay
ZEUS: aegiochus, agoraeus, alastor, ammon, anchesmius, aphesius, cappotas, carius, ephestios, gamelios, jove, jupiter, milichios, philios, soter, stator, teleios, zan
consort: aegina, aegle, alcmene, anaxithea, antiope, callisto,

* Asterisk means to look up this word to find more answer words.

carme, cassiopeia, danae, demeter, dione, elara, europa, eurynome, hera, hesione, io, juno, latona, leda, leto, maia, mera, metis, mnemosyne, neaera, niobe, phthia, protogenia, selene, semele, thalia, themis, thymbris

daughter: aphrodite, artemis, athene, britomartis, dictynna, dike, eunomia, *fates, *graces, kore, *muses, nemea, pandia, persephassa, persephone, proserpin, proserpina, venus

father: cronus, kronos

festival: bouphonia, dipolia

host: baucis, philemon

messenger: hermes, iris

mother: ops, rhea

nurse: amalthaea, cynosura

oracle: dodona

son: aecus, amphion, apollo, arcas, argos, argus, atymnius, dardanus, dionysus, *dioscuri, epaphus, hephaestus, hercules, hermes, lacedaemon, locri, minos, olenus, opuns, orchomenus, palici, pan, pirithous, sarpedon, tantalus, tityus, vulcan, zethus

ZIARA(T): *memorial, shrine

ZIBEON: *son:* aiah, anah

ZIGZAG: *oscillate, *turn

ZILLAH: *husband:* lemech
 son: naamah, tubal-cain

ZILPAH: *husband:* jacob
 son: asher, gad

ZINC: adamite, blende, gallium
 alloy: blackjack, blue powder, calamine, gostarite, paktong, tutenag

ZING: *force, *spirit

ZION: *heaven, israelites
 clergyman: volivo
 organization: avukah, ito

ZIP: *force, *speed, *spirit

ZIPPORAH: *father:* jethro
 husband: moses
 son: eliezer, gershom

ZIZANY: cockle, darnel, tares

ZOBEIDE: *sister:* amina

ZODIAC: *sign, 1st to 12th:* aries, taurus, gemini, cancer, leo, virgo, libra, scorpio, sagittarius, capricorn, aquarius, pisces

ZOMBI: *clown, *fool,

ZONE: area, *district, *range

ZOO: menagerie, vivarium

ZOOM: climb, soar, *speed

ZOOMBAR: *lens:* big bertha

ZOPHAH: *son:* beera, beri harnepher, hod, imra, ithan shamma, shilshah, shual, suah

ZOROASTER: *convert:* vishtaspa
 demon: ahriman, angra mainyu
 follower: gheber, mazdaist, parsee, parsi
 god: ahura-mazda, ormazd
 revelation: vohu-mano
 sacred book: avesta, gathas, venidad, vispered, yasht, yasna, zend-avesta
 tempter: angra mainyu

ZOSTER: belt, girdle

ZOSTEROPS: blightbird

ZUISIN: bird, duck, widgeon

ZULU: *army:* impi
 capital: eshowe
 head man: induna
 king: cetewayo
 marauder: viti
 meeting: indaba
 people: bantu, kaffir
 salutation: bayete
 spear: assagai, assegai

ZUNI: *land:* cibola

ZYLOPHONE: marimba

ZYTHUM: beer

* Asterisk means to look up this word to find more answer words.